SACR

S0-AUI-515

SACRAMENTO, CA

12/2010

ADVANCE PRAISE FOR *FREEDOM BOU*

"*Freedom Bound* is a truly magisterial work by o
ing in the field of legal history. It is about no less a topic than the origins of modern
America – and, in particular, about the law that framed its genesis and its early
development. In this exceptionally erudite study, Christopher Tomlins succeeds
in achieving an unusual 'thickness' of description, notable alike for its breadth
and depth, its subtlety and its comprehensiveness. Even more, he brings an acute
analytic eye to a story of enormous complexity, making this a must-read for anyone
with a serious interest in either modern American history or law and society."

– John Comaroff, University of Chicago and American Bar Foundation

"Beautifully written, deeply researched, and elegantly argued, *Freedom Bound* is
legal history that changes the way we understand U.S. history. Tomlins master-
fully retells the story of America's founding by following the developing relationships among labor, law, and civic identity. While focused on early America, *Freedom
Bound* speaks broadly to questions about freedom and equality that continue to
define the nation's history into the twenty-first century."

– Laura F. Edwards, Duke University

"An ambitious effort to remake the landscape of the history of the origins of
American culture, Tomlins' learned and masterful volume may well turn out to
be the most important work published in American history over the past quarter century. Transcending the conventional disciplinary categories – England and
America, colonial and national – that contribute to the myopia of so many scholars, he leads his reader through a complex, sober, penetrating, and highly persuasive analysis of the fundamental and interactive role of labor, law, and civic
imperatives in shaping American society from the late sixteenth century to the
American Civil War. Challenging many existing orthodoxies, including the depiction of the American Revolution as a sharp break with the colonial past, it deserves
the careful attention of any serious student of not only the American past, but of
the establishment of settler, colonial, and national regimes all over the globe."

– Jack P. Greene, The Johns Hopkins University

"Take time to savor this magisterial book, the fruit of decades of research and
reflection. Christopher Tomlins brilliantly revises our understanding of the ideas
and practices that shaped the lives of working people, households, and politics,
in an account that stretches from England's Atlantic empire to the eve of the U.S.
Civil War. Be warned: many familiar generalizations lie shattered."

– Linda K. Kerber, University of Iowa

"Christopher Tomlins has written a passionate, provocative, brilliant book about
how law enabled English colonizers to justify taking what was not theirs and then
to keep and work what they had taken. With wide-ranging erudition, he uncovers
the legalities that shaped what the English expected to find; what they saw; how
they interpreted what they found; how they justified what they did; and what social,
political, and legal structures they erected in America. *Freedom Bound* is, by any
standard, a magisterial work of stunning originality."

– Bruce H. Mann, Harvard Law School

"This sweeping and superb magnum opus is a fascinating account of intricate patchworks of disparate legal systems and codes that ranges all across British North America. Law was anything but a national singularity; rather, it encompassed plural discourses and institutions. The constantly evolving relationship between various freedoms and unfreedoms gives the work a powerful and poignant story line."

– Philip Morgan, The Johns Hopkins University

"From the beginnings of colonization of the American mainland to the American Civil War, few historians have the knowledge or stamina to rewrite the narrative of American history on such a broad scale. Christopher Tomlins does and has: *Freedom Bound* is the story of how, from its first imaginings, freedom was bound, limited to white males, secured by the land Native Americans had claimed and populated and by the productive and reproductive labor of wives and slaves. Colonial America is not a time apart; rather it is, in Tomlins' retelling, the formative era of modern America. This is a demanding book – demanding in length, in the range of methodologies it so expertly employs, but most of all in its conclusions. Majestic. Unrelenting. Haunting. Unanswerable."

– Barbara Young Welke, University of Minnesota

"Tomlins shows how the vast expanse of land available to British colonizers in North America created the conditions for unfreedom. Scarce labor – free and bound – had to be policed. As a technology of power, law was core to the project of creating the blueprints for the plural forms of colonial governance that provided flexibility in disciplining labor. *Freedom Bound* takes us from British workshops to the marchlands of North America, from America's initial European settlement to its struggle, after independence, as an expansive republic with the legacy of slavery. More importantly, with deftness, intellectual ambition, and remarkable erudition, it forces us to reconsider how new worlds harbor both potential utopias and dystopias. One word best describes this book: magisterial."

– Steven Wilf, University of Connecticut

FREEDOM BOUND

Freedom Bound is about the origins of modern America – a history of colonizing, work, and civic identity from the beginnings of English presence on the mainland until the Civil War. It is a history of migrants and migrations, of colonizers and colonized, of households and servitude and slavery, and of the freedom all craved and some found. Above all, it is a history of the law that framed the entire process. *Freedom Bound* tells how colonies were planted in occupied territories, how they were populated with migrants – free and unfree – to do the work of colonizing, and how the newcomers secured possession. It tells of the new civic lives that seemed possible in new commonwealths, and of the constraints that kept many from enjoying them. It follows the story long past the end of the eighteenth century until the American Civil War, when – just for a moment – it seemed that freedom might finally be unbound.

Christopher Tomlins is Chancellor's Professor of Law at the University of California, Irvine. Since 1992 he has been a member of the research faculty of the American Bar Foundation in Chicago. Tomlins began his career at La Trobe University in Melbourne; he has also taught at the Marshall-Wythe Law School, College of William & Mary in Virginia; at Northwestern University Law School; and at Tel Aviv and Haifa Universities in Israel. His interests and research are cast very broadly – from sixteenth-century England to twentieth-century America and from the legal culture of work and labor to the interrelations of law and literature. He has written or edited six books, including, most recently, the multivolume *Cambridge History of Law in America*, co-edited with Michael Grossberg. His publications have been awarded the Surrency Prize of the American Society for Legal History, the Littleton-Griswold Prize of the American Historical Association, and the Hurst Prize of the Law and Society Association. Tomlins currently edits two Cambridge University Press book series: Cambridge Historical Studies in American Law and Society and Cambridge New Histories of American Law (with Michael Grossberg).

FREEDOM BOUND

Freedom Bound is about the origins of modern America – a history of colonizing, work, and civic identity from the beginnings of English presence on the mainland until the Civil War. It is a history of migrants and migrations, of colonizers and colonized, of households and servitude and slavery, and of the freedom all craved and some found. Above all, it is a history of the law that framed the entire process. *Freedom Bound* tells how colonies were planted in occupied territories, how they were populated with migrants – free and unfree – to do the work of colonizing, and how the newcomers secured possession. It tells of the new civic lives that seemed possible in new commonwealths, and of the constraints that kept many from enjoying them. It follows the story long past the end of the eighteenth century until the American Civil War, when – just for a moment – it seemed that freedom might finally be unbound.

Christopher Tomlins is Chancellor's Professor of Law at the University of California, Irvine. Since 1992 he has been a member of the research faculty of the American Bar Foundation in Chicago. Tomlins began his career at La Trobe University in Melbourne; he has also taught at the Marshall-Wythe Law School, College of William & Mary in Virginia; at Northwestern University Law School; and at Tel Aviv and Haifa Universities in Israel. His interests and research are cast very broadly – from sixteenth-century England to twentieth-century America and from the legal culture of work and labor to the interrelations of law and literature. He has written or edited six books, including, most recently, the multivolume *Cambridge History of Law in America*, co-edited with Michael Grossberg. His publications have been awarded the Surrency Prize of the American Society for Legal History, the Littleton-Griswold Prize of the American Historical Association, and the Hurst Prize of the Law and Society Association. Tomlins currently edits two Cambridge University Press book series: Cambridge Historical Studies in American Law and Society and Cambridge New Histories of American Law (with Michael Grossberg).

Freedom Bound

LAW, LABOR, AND CIVIC IDENTITY
IN COLONIZING ENGLISH AMERICA, 1580–1865

Christopher Tomlins

CAMBRIDGE
UNIVERSITY PRESS

CAMBRIDGE UNIVERSITY PRESS
Cambridge, New York, Melbourne, Madrid, Cape Town, Singapore,
São Paulo, Delhi, Dubai, Tokyo, Mexico City

Cambridge University Press
32 Avenue of the Americas, New York, NY 10013-2473, USA

www.cambridge.org
Information on this title: www.cambridge.org/9780521137775

© Christopher Tomlins 2010

This publication is in copyright. Subject to statutory exception
and to the provisions of relevant collective licensing agreements,
no reproduction of any part may take place without the written
permission of Cambridge University Press.

First published 2010

Printed in the United States of America

A catalog record for this publication is available from the British Library.

Library of Congress Cataloging in Publication data
Tomlins, Christopher L., 1951–
Freedom bound : law, labor, and civic identity in colonizing English America,
1580–1865 / Christopher Tomlins.
p. cm.
Includes index.
ISBN 978-0-521-76139-0 (hardback) 978-0-521-13777-5 (pbk.)
1. Labor–United States–History. 2. United States–Colonization.
3. Labor laws and legislation–United States–History.
4. United States–History–Colonial period, ca. 1600–1775.
5. United States–History–Revolution, 1775–1783. 6. United States–
History–1783–1865. 7. United States–Economic conditions–To 1865.
8. United States–Social conditions–To 1865. 9. National characteristics,
American. I. Title.
HD8068.T66 2010
331.0973'0903–dc22   2010019216

ISBN 978-0-521-76139-0 Hardback
ISBN 978-0-521-13777-5 Paperback

Cambridge University Press has no responsibility for the persistence or
accuracy of URLs for external or third-party Internet Web sites referred to in
this publication and does not guarantee that any content on such Web sites is,
or will remain, accurate or appropriate.

For Francis Barker (1952–1999)
Fierce mourning; fierce hope.

See, I have this day set thee over the nations and over the kingdoms,
to root out, and to pull down, and to destroy,
and to throw down, to build, and to plant.

Jeremiah 1:10

We are guests who enter through a door
underneath a suspended sign
that sways in the breeze,
a door behind which
eternity and rapture await us.

Walter Benjamin, "The Image of Proust"

Ban' ban' Ca-caliban,
Has a new master, get a new man.
Freedom, high-day; high-day freedom; freedom high-day, freedom.

William Shakespeare, *The Tempest*, 2.2.179–82

Contents

Tables and Figures   *page* xi
Acknowledgments   xiii

Prologue   Beginning: "As much freedome in reason as may be ..."   1

Part I   Manning, Planting, Keeping

1   Manning: "Setteynge many on Worke"   21

2   Planting: "Directed and Conducted Thither"   67

3   Keeping (i): Discourses of Intrusion   93

4   Keeping (ii): English Desires, Designs   133

Part II   Poly-Olbion; or The Inside Narrative

5   Packing: New Inhabitants   193

6   Unpacking: Received Wisdoms of Law and Work   231

7   Changing: Localities, Legalities   296

Part III   "What, then, is the American, this new man?"

8   Modernizing: Polity, Economy, Patriarchy   335

9   Enslaving: *Facies Hippocratica*   401

10 Ending: "Strange Order of Things!"   509

Appendices to Chapter 1   571
Index   599

Tables and Figures

Chapter 1

1.1 European Migration, Servant Migration, and
Population Estimates, Maryland and Virginia, 1600–1700   *page* 37

1.2 European Servant Migration and Persistence
in Population, Maryland and Virginia, 1600–1700   38

1.3 Indentured Servants in the Chesapeake Labor
Force, 1640–1700   40

1.4 Slaves and Servants in Population, Chesapeake Colonies   41

1.5 Slaves and Servants in the Chesapeake Labor
Force, 1640–1700   41

1.6 Immigration to the Delaware Valley, 1680–1780   43

1.7 Servant Immigration to the Delaware Valley, 1680–1780   44

1.8 Delaware Valley Servant Population, and Pennsylvania
European Population Based on Immigration
Estimates, 1680–1780   45

1.9 Servants in Philadelphia Population and Workforce   46

1.10 Slaves in Philadelphia Population and Workforce   48

1.11 Slaves and Servants in Philadelphia Population   49

1.12 Slaves and Servants in Philadelphia Population
and Workforce   50

Appendices to Chapter 1

A1 Eighteenth-Century Migration to the Thirteen Mainland
Colonies, by European Ethnic Group   576

A2 Eighteenth-Century Migration to the Thirteen Mainland
Colonies, by European Ethnic Group and Status   581

A3 European Servant Migration and Persistence in Population,
Maryland and Virginia, 1600–1700: Alternate Estimates   586

A4 Servant Persistence in the Maryland Population, 1640–1760   588

A5 Servant Incidence in the Virginia Population, York
County, 1660–1700   589

A6 Servant Incidence in the Philadelphia Population and
Workforce, 1720–1775 (Adapted from Salinger Estimates)   590

A7 Slave Incidence in the Philadelphia Population and
Workforce, 1720–1775 (Adapted from Salinger Estimates)   590

A8 Servants and Slaves in the Philadelphia Population
    (Adapted from Salinger Estimates)   591
A9 Servants and Slaves in the Philadelphia Population
    and Workforce (Adapted from Salinger Estimates)   592

Figure – Appendices to Chapter 1

A1 Computation of Attrition Rates, Seventeenth-Century
    Chesapeake   585

Acknowledgments

My first and enduring acknowledgment must be of the extraordinary richness of scholarship in the field of early American history. The work for this book has taken me the better part of fifteen years. Had I imagined at the outset it would take me so long to reach a point at which I felt I could stop, I doubt I would have started.

For all the years I worked on this book I was fortunate to be a member of the research faculty of a unique institution, the American Bar Foundation. Throughout, I enjoyed not only the Foundation's material support but also the friendship of an immensely accomplished and distinguished group of colleagues. Such is the collective collegiality of the American Bar Foundation that it seems almost invidious to single out particular individuals from among my colleagues. Nonetheless, I should especially like to thank John Comaroff, Carol Heimer, Bonnie Honig, Beth Mertz, and Laura Beth Nielsen, not just for stimulating conversations in and out of seminars but also for simple acts of kindness and encouragement at moments of difficulty. I should also like to thank former ABF Director Bryant G. Garth, his successor, Robert L. Nelson, and the Foundation's Board of Directors for their consistent support of the work involved.

Others at the Foundation, Lila Stromer and Crina Archer in particular, helped me by undertaking their part of different tasks in which we were both involved with such dazzling efficiency that I could spend more time on this work than might otherwise have been possible. Relatively early on, I benefited from the talented and vigorous assistance of Tamara Kay, Brian Roraff, and Andrew Cohen, all of whom have long since made important careers for themselves elsewhere. Since then I have practiced relentless self-sufficiency. My fellow historians at the Foundation – Bill Novak, Dylan Penningroth, and Victoria Woeste – were, all things considered, remarkably tolerant of my reclusive habits.

Beyond the American Bar Foundation I have had the support and understanding of some wonderful people. Ann Tomlins has somehow found more room in her life for my preoccupations than I have any right to expect, and I thank her and love her for it. Our daughters, Jasmin and Meredith, have grown to adulthood alongside this book, but I have tried to make sure they did not have to live with it – they have their own lives to live. Michael Grossberg and Bruce Mann have been as good friends as anyone could want. So has Kunal Parker, whose many conversations have introduced me to much that I would otherwise have left unread. Laura Edwards, Bruce Mann, Barbara Welke, and Steven Wilf all read the manuscript in its entirety and have helped me make it much better than it was when they first saw it. I owe a major debt to Laura and to Barbara in particular for the time they spent discussing aspects of the book with me. Ron Levi and Mariana Valverde, Paul Craven and Doug Hay, Marianne Constable and Hilary Soderland all read, listened to, commented on, or criticized one or another aspect of the manuscript. I have tried to follow their advice – their reactions have always been telling, their company always a delight. Farley Grubb genially shared resources from his immense archive of migration and indentured servitude, David Barry Gaspar and April Lee Hatfield courteously answered my questions about aspects of their published research, Andrew Fitzmaurice offered acute, laconic observations on my conception of English colonizing, Linda Kerber spurred me on by wondering pointedly what I was up to. My dear friend Fredrika Teute took time from her own unforgiving schedule to read an early draft of the prologue and made suggestions whose reverberations reach far into the substance of the book. Over the many years of thought and research, countless scholars have generously read and discussed scores of papers offered to seminars and conferences all over the United States and far beyond – from Toronto to Vancouver to Sydney to Tel Aviv to Glasgow. All have helped me to arrive at what appears here. Among the many others who have also helped me at one time or another, in one way or another, I should like to mention two in particular – Laurie Rofini of the Chester County Archives for her enthusiastic interest and passion for ice hockey, and Cary Carson of Colonial Williamsburg for his sheer bonhomie.

At Cambridge University Press, Frank Smith, a friend now for more than twenty years, patiently listened to my halting attempts to explain what the book was about, and trusted me to translate them into serviceable prose. In that task I have been greatly assisted by Karen Verde's copyediting. Jeanie Lee, Shelby Peak, and Bindu Vinod have carefully kept track of the many tasks required to prepare the manuscript for production. Errors of fact or interpretation that remain despite all our best efforts are, of course, my responsibility.

I began writing the first complete draft of the manuscript of this book during the spring of 2008, whilst a member of a research working group on the history of legal transplants at the Institute for Advanced Studies of Hebrew University in Jerusalem. The group was organized by two gifted Israeli legal historians, Ron Harris and Assaf Likhovski, and included Morty Horwitz, Amalia Kessler, Pnina Lahav, Steven Wilf, and Yoram Shachar. A more congenial group of colleagues and friends one could not hope to find, nor a setting more marked by empire after empire that could remind one more starkly of the long and layered world history of the conjunctions that I try to address here – of migrations, forced and unforced; of colonizing and displacement; of time; of work; and of the work of law.

There, late one Saturday afternoon, I decided that if I ever finished this book I would dedicate it to the memory of a friend from long ago, whose own work has had a pronounced impact on me. I wish he were alive still, to tell me what he thought of mine.

Many elements of this manuscript have appeared in earlier drafts as published articles, or chapters or essays in edited collections. Research for Chapter 1 first appeared as "Reconsidering Indentured Servitude: European Migration and Labor Force in the Early American Case," *Labor History*, 42, 1 (February 2001), 5–43, republished in part by permission of Taylor & Francis Ltd, and in revised and updated form as "Indentured Servitude in Perspective: European Migration to the North American Mainland and the Composition of the Early American Labor Force, 1600–1775," in Catherine Matson, editor, *The Economy of Early America: New Directions* (University Park, Pa., 2005), 146–82, republished in part by permission of Pennsylvania State University Press. Chapter 1 is a further and final revision and the most complete statement of that work. Significant elements of Chapter 1 and Chapter 2 were included in "Law, Population, Labor," in Michael Grossberg and Christopher Tomlins, editors, *The Cambridge History of Law in America* (Cambridge and New York, 2008), 211–52, republished in part by permission of Cambridge University Press. A summary version of Chapters 3 and 4 will appear as "The Legalities of English Colonizing: Discourses of European Intrusion upon the Americas, c. 1490–1830," in Shaunnagh Dorsett and Ian Hunter, editors, *Law and Politics in British Colonial Thought: Transpositions of Empire* (London and New York: Palgrave-MacMillan, 2010). A partial and preliminary version of Chapter 4 first appeared as "The Legal Cartography of Colonization, the Legal Polyphony of Settlement: English Intrusions on the American Mainland in the Seventeenth Century," *Law and Social Inquiry*, 26, 2 (Spring 2001), 315–72 [reprinted in *Analyzing Law's Reach: Empirical Research on Law and Society* (Chicago, 541–97], and in even more truncated form as "Law's Empire: Chartering English Colonies on the American Mainland in the Seventeenth Century," in Diane Kirkby and Catharine Coleborne, editors, *Law, History, Colonialism: The Reach of Empire* (Manchester, 2001), 26–45, republished in part by permission of Manchester University Press. A summary version of Chapters 5 through 7 appeared as "Early British America, 1585–1830," in Paul Craven and Douglas Hay, editors, *Masters, Servants, and Magistrates in Britain and the Empire, 1562–1955* (Chapel Hill, 2004), 117–52, republished in part by permission of University of North Carolina Press. Elements of Chapter 8 were first sketched in "Subordination, Authority, Law: Subjects in Labor History," *International Labor and Working Class History*, 47 (Spring 1995), 56–90, and "Why Wait for Industrialism? Work, Legal Culture and the Example of Early America – An Historiographical Argument," *Labor History*, 40, 1 (January 1999), 5–34, republished in part by permission of Taylor & Francis Ltd. A summary version of Chapter 9 appears as "Transplants and Timing: Passages in the Creation of an

Anglo-American Law of Slavery," *Theoretical Inquiries in Law*, 10, 2 (2009), 389–421. Chapter 10 (and also the introduction to Chapter 9) is informed by "Law's Wilderness: The Discourse of English Colonizing, the Violence of Intrusion, and the Failures of American History," in John Smolenski et al., editors, *New World Orders: Violence, Sanction and Authority in the Early Modern Americas, 1500–1825* (Philadelphia, 2005), 21–46, republished in part by permission of University of Pennsylvania Press; a somewhat more extended version was published as "In a Wilderness of Tigers: The Discourse of English Colonizing and the Refusals of American History," *Theoretical Inquiries in Law*, 4, 2 (2003), 505–43. Chapter 10 is also informed by my work on Walter Benjamin, on display in "To Improve the State and Condition of Man: The Power to Police and the History of American Governance," *Buffalo Law Review*, 53, 4 (Fall 2005), 1215–71; "The Threepenny Constitution (and the Question of Justice)," *Alabama Law Review*, 58 (2007), 979–1008; "The Strait Gate: The Past, History and Legal Scholarship," *Law, Culture and the Humanities*, 5, 1 (February 2009), 11–42; "Revolutionary Justice in Brecht, Conrad and Blake," *Law and Literature*, 21, 2 (Summer 2009), 185–213; and "Toward a Materialist Jurisprudence," in Daniel W. Hamilton and Alfred L. Brophy, editors, *Transformations in American Legal History, II: Law, Ideology, and Methods – Essays In Honor of Morton J. Horwitz, Volume II* (Cambridge, Mass., 2010). Throughout, the book bears the mark of thoughts first expressed in "The Many Legalities of Colonization: A Manifesto of Destiny for Early American Legal History," in Christopher L. Tomlins and Bruce H. Mann, editors, *The Many Legalities of Early America* (Chapel Hill, 2001), 1–20, and "Constellations of Class in North America and the Atlantic World," in Simon Middleton and Billy G. Smith, editors, *Class Matters: Early North America and the Atlantic World* (Philadelphia, 2008), 213–33.

Excerpts from *Illuminations* by Walter Benjamin, copyright © 1955 by Suhrkamp Verlag, Frankfurt a.M., English translation by Harry Zohn copyright © 1968 and renewed 1996 by Houghton Mifflin Harcourt Publishing Company, reprinted by permission of Houghton Mifflin Harcourt Publishing company (epigraphs in the frontispiece and to Chapter 10). The epigraph to Chapter 7 from Julius Goebel's "King's Law and Local Custom in Seventeenth Century New England," *Columbia Law Review*, 31, 3 (March 1931), 418, is reprinted by permission of the Columbia Law Review Association, Inc. The epigraph to Chapter 8 from Carole Pateman's *The Sexual Contract* (Stanford: Stanford University Press), 87, is reprinted by permission of Carole Pateman.

Irvine, California
February 2010

FREEDOM BOUND

PROLOGUE

Beginning: "As much freedome in reason as may be ..."

> This is the ware wherein consists my wealth;
> And thus methinks should men of judgment frame
> Their means of traffic from the vulgar trade,
> And as their wealth increaseth, so enclose
> Infinite riches in a little room.
>
> Richard Marlowe, *The Jew of Malta* (c. 1589)

In the year 1616, with England's first attempts at colonizing the American mainland mired in uncertain infancy, the Elizabethan-Jacobean adventurer Captain John Smith presented to the "Right Honourable and worthy Lords, Knights, and Gentlemen, of his Majesties Councell, for all Plantations and discoveries" and as well to "the Right Worshipfull Adventurers for the Countrey of New England, in the Cities of London, Bristow, Exceter, Plimouth ... and in all other Cities and Ports, in the Kingdome of England" what he was pleased to call a "rude discourse," entitled *A Description of New England: Or the Observations, and discoueries, of Captain Iohn Smith (Admirall of that Country) in the North of America, in the year of our Lord 1614*. His purpose was to put beyond doubt "the present benefit this Countrey affoords."[1]

By 1616, Smith had already proven himself an adept chronicler of early English colonizing. His *True Relation of such occurrences and accidents of noate, as hath hapned in Virginia, since the first planting of that Collony*, published in 1608, had set down the original narrative of the first chaotic months of the Jamestown expedition.[2] In 1612, he had embellished greatly upon the *True Relation* in his more extensive *A Map of Virginia* and his *Proceedings of the English Colonie in Virginia*.[3] Later works would gather all Smith's North American narratives into a *Generall Historie* (1624), and add an account of his early life and adventures as a soldier of fortune in Europe, Asia, and

---

[1] John Smith, *A Description of New England*, in Philip L. Barbour, editor, *The Complete Works of Captain John Smith* (Chapel Hill, 1986), I, 305–70, at 305, 310, 311. This book's study of English colonizing is confined geographically to the North American mainland.

[2] John Smith, *A True Relation*, in Barbour, ed., *Complete Works*, I, 23–117.

[3] John Smith, *A Map of Virginia. With a Description of the Countrey, the Commodities, People, Government and Religion. Written by Captaine Smith, sometimes Governour of the Countrey*, and *The Proceedings of the English Colonie in Virginia since their first beginning from England in the yeare of our Lord 1606*, both in Barbour, ed., *Complete Works*, I, 131–90, 199–289.

North Africa – *The True Travels, Adventures and Observations of Captain Iohn Smith* (1630).[4]

The *Description of New England*, however, was different in its essentials from Smith's travel narratives and histories; less a work of reportage and self-justification than of advocacy. As its dedications indicate, the *Description* addressed the political and commercial elites of the nascent English imperial state, to whom Smith spoke as a man of action; rough and "ignorant" to be sure, and likely (for his accounts of the first Virginia colony had not been without their critics) to be "diversly traduced by variable judgements of the Times opinionists," but possessing many years' first-hand experience of fighting and planting and oceanic travel – more than enough, in fact, to convince himself, and hopefully his interlocutors, that in this second Virginia colony, which Smith now dubbed New England, would be found the "sure foundation" upon which the struggling English colonizing enterprise begun thirty years before might finally begin to prosper.[5]

Smith did not try to make his case with the persuasion of great riches easily won – the gold, precious stones, and rare spices that Crown patentees had coveted since the resumption of English North Atlantic voyaging in the 1570s. "Had I returned rich, I could not have erred," he remarked, a shade wistfully. All New England had to offer was "a mean and a base commoditie" – fish. Still, fish were "well worth the labour," and Smith entreated his readers "to adventure their purses as I, purse, life, and all I have" in their pursuit. For fish were but the beginning. "Now having onely such fish as came to my net, I must be taxed," he wrote, with good humor. "But because I speake so much of fishing, if any take mee for such a devote fisher, as I dreame of nought else, they mistake mee. I know a ring of golde from a graine of barley, aswell as a goldesmith: and nothing is there to bee had which fishing doth hinder, but furder us to obtaine."[6] Here was a place fit for fishing in the first instance and more thereafter; a place to plant and possess, to "obtaine."[7]

What made John Smith so passionate in his advocacy? What benefit did he dream of, besides fish? Smith's alpha and omega was always the New

---

[4] John Smith, *The Generall Historie of Virginia, New England, and the Summer Isles*, in Barbour, ed., *Complete Works*, II, 33–488; John Smith, *The True Travels*, in Barbour, ed., *Complete Works*, III, 137–251.

[5] *Description of New England*, 310. Smith's reference here is Isaiah 28:16 (Authorized [King James] Version; hereinafter AV). "Therefore thus saith the Lord GOD, Behold, I lay in Zion for a foundation a stone, a tried stone, a precious corner stone, a sure foundation: he that believeth shall not make haste." For verse 16 in context, see the third epigraph to Chapter 9.

[6] *Description of New England*, 311–12, 330.

[7] Note that the etymology of "obtaine" in early modern English usage includes "To come into the possession of" and specifically "to gain (territory, a kingdom, etc.) by conquest, to conquer." See OED at http://dictionary.oed.com/ (accessed 22 August 2009). For a more comprehensive survey of this usage focused on the late sixteenth and early seventeenth centuries, see the Lexicons of Early Modern English database at http://leme. library.utoronto.ca/ (accessed 22 August 2009).

World's sheer material abundance; it bred in him a fierce belief in the possibility of widespread prosperity. "And here in Florida, Virginia, New-England, and Cannada, is more land than all the people in Christendome can manure, and yet more to spare than all the natives of those Countries can use and culturate."[8] The observation itself was hardly novel: discovery of the northern mainland's abundance of land was not original to Smith (any more than his fish would have been news in Bristol). What's more, the Jamestown experience had already borne witness to the difficulty of turning apparent abundance into actual wealth. In 1616, Jamestown remained a place of intrigue, conflict, oppression, privation, death.

But the present benefit that Smith saw in colonizing New England was not simply a matter of material opportunity. His "sure foundation" had social, political, and legal ramifications.

Over the years, as he returned again and again to reflect on Jamestown's extremities, Smith found their origin less in the physical difficulties of settling a strange land than in the impracticalities and pretensions of the colony's promoters.[9] The lives of Virginia's planters had been made the playthings of "some few here in London who were never there, that consumed all in Arguments, Projects, and their owne conceits, every yeere trying new conclusions, altering every thing yearely as they altered opinions." The Londoners had written "tedious Letters, directions and instructions" for the development and production of commodities, full of "strange absurdities and impossibilities." They had created "many great and stately officers and offices … as doth belong to a great Kingdome," along with "privileges for Cities, Charters for Corporations, Universities, Free-schooles, and Glebe-land," all to be put in place "before there were either people, students, or schollers to build or use them, or provision or victuall to feed them were then there." And they had sent to the colony "Masters, Gentlemen, Gentlewomen, and children" whose "idle charge" was "very troublesome, and the effects dangerous." One hundred good laborers would have been worth more "than a thousand such Gallants as were sent me, that could doe nothing but complaine, curse, and despaire."[10]

A withering contempt for "drones [that] steales their labour," whether they were ignorant company officers in London or idle gallants in the first colony, steered Smith's plans for New England.[11] The "lamentable experience" of Jamestown had taught that although America's "commodities,

[8] John Smith, *Advertisements For the unexperienced Planters of New-England, or any where. Or The Path-way to experience to erect a Plantation*, in Barbour, ed., *Complete Works*, III, 259–307, at 276. Compare these sentiments from his last published work (1631), with the *True Relation*, his first, at 81: "most excellent fertill ground, so sweete, so pleasant, so beautifull, and so strong a prospect, for an invincible strong Citty, with so many commodities, that I know as yet I have not seene."

[9] The first words of Isaiah 28, to which verse 16's "sure foundation" is counterpoint, proclaim, "Woe to the crown of pride, to the drunkards of Ephraim."

[10] Smith, *Advertisements for the unexperienced*, 270, 272.

[11] Smith, *Description of New England*, 311.

pleasures, and conditions" were the equal or more of any to be found throughout the known world, they would have to be physically wrestled out of the landscape. America's commodities could be won only by "industrious people" willing to pledge "long labour and diligence."[12]

Because planting was hard work, its fruits should properly fall to those who did the work. "A servant that will labour, within foure or five yeares may live as well there as his master did here." But Smith contemplated more than an enhanced material well-being within an unaltered social and political structure. Hard work should earn the laborer all the advantages of a free proprietor. "Let every man so it bee by order allotted him, plant freely without limitation so much as hee can, bee it by the halfes or otherwayes. And at the end of five or six yeares, or when you make a division, for every acre he hath planted, let him have twenty, thirty, forty, or an hundred; or as you finde hee hath extraordinarily deserved, by it selfe to him and his heires for ever." In its determined counterpoint to Jamestown, Smith's *Description* imagined a New England of unprecedented freedom from others' coercive hierarchies. "No hard Landlords to racke us with high rents, or extorted fines to consume us; no tedious pleas in law to consume us with their many years disputations for Justice. No multitudes to occasion such impediments to good orders, as in popular states. So freely hath God and his Majesty bestowed those blessings on them that will attempt to obtaine them, as here every man may be master and owner of his owne labour and land; or the greatest part in a small time."[13]

Freedom was good policy. Free English proprietors in American colonies would "increase our shipping and sailers, and so employ and encourage a great part of our idlers and others that want imployments fitting their qualities at home, where they shame to doe that they would doe abroad." Could these "but once taste the sweet fruites of their owne labours, doubtlesse many thousands would be advised by good discipline, to take more pleasure in honest industrie, then in their humours of dissolute idlenesse."[14] Who could "desire more content, that hath small meanes; or but only his merit to advance his fortune, then to tread, and plant that ground hee hath purchased by the hazard of his life?" Though at the outset "hee have nothing but his hands," nevertheless "he may set up this trade; and by industrie quickly grow rich." Industriousness and free proprietorship went hand in hand in the creation of wealth. "Let all men have as much freedome in reason as may be, and true dealing" was Smith's ultimate retort to the miseries of Jamestown. "For it is the greatest comfort you can give them, where the very name of servitude will breed much ill bloud, and become odious to God and man."[15]

---

[12] Ibid., 310, 333.

[13] Smith, *Advertisements for the unexperienced*, 287; *Description of New England*, 332.

[14] Smith, *Description of New England*, 338.

[15] Ibid., 332, 343; *Advertisements for the unexperienced*, 287.

John Smith's dream of what migrating Englishmen might make of themselves in America has been represented as a foundational statement of colonial New England's economic culture.[16] It was that, and much more besides. Smith had a shrewd grasp of the process of English colonizing, of its desires and difficulties, its greed and grandiosity, its will to destroy and to create. His writings display a canny realization of the absolute centrality of work and labor to success in colonizing. And, though he had no means of knowing how things would unfold, he clearly understood that colonizing's effect on the social and civic identities of all those it touched might well be transformative. This book takes as its subject all three aspects of John Smith's dream.

The intimacies of colonizing, work, and civic identity, and their transformative interrelationships, are pronounced. Their common connective tissue, I argue here, the bridge from one to the next, is law.

Richard Hakluyt the elder – a lawyer – sets our scene when, a quarter century before Jamestown was settled, he situated the problematic of colonizing at the intersection of three related processes: "manning" new territories (recruiting migrant populations); "planting" them (transporting population and mixing it with land and other resources); and "keeping" them – claiming sovereignty (*imperium*), securing occupancy, and realizing jurisdiction (*dominium*, or in other words possession or rule).[17] To address and manage the problematic, colonizers required means to "frame" their enterprise; that is, to define its terms and mobilize human and material resources to give those terms effect. Law would be their means. As a technology, a means of doing and making do, law could furnish the institutional capacities to establish migration and settlement overseas as legitimate, organized processes. As a discourse, a means of knowing and making known, law would supply the arguments that enabled colonizers to justify – to themselves, to their rivals, to those they displaced – taking what they could keep and keeping what they had taken. And as a modality of rule, the expression of sovereignty, law was integral to the creation and implementation of governance – the concrete realization of jurisdiction,

---

[16] See in particular Stephen Innes, "Fulfilling John Smith's Vision: Work and Labor in Early America," in Stephen Innes, editor, *Work and Labor in Early America* (Chapel Hill, 1988), 3–47; Stephen Innes, *Creating the Commonwealth: The Economic Culture of Puritan New England* (New York, 1995), 64–5, 74–83.

[17] Richard Hakluyt (the elder), *Pamphlet for the Virginia Enterprise* (1585), in E.G.R. Taylor, editor, *The Original Writings and Correspondence of the Two Richard Hakluyts* (London: for the Hakluyt Society, 1935), II, 333–4. "People" stated Robert Johnson in *Nova Britannia* (London, 1609), sig. Dr, were "especially required … to make the plantation." See also Abbot Emerson Smith, *Colonists in Bondage: White Servitude and Convict Labor in America 1607–1776* (Chapel Hill, 1947), 4 (According to the Council of Foreign Plantations, c. 1664, "people were the foundation for the improvement of all Plantations 'and … increased principally by sending of Servants'"); David Galenson, "The Settlement and Growth of the Colonies: Population, Labor and Economic Development," in Stanley L. Engerman and Robert E. Gallman, editors, *The Cambridge Economic History of the United States* (Cambridge and New York, 1996), I, 153.

which is to say the recreation of existing territories as well-ordered "new commonwealths" and the installation of both once and future inhabitants in transformed identities (the indigenous alienated, the newcomers domesticated).[18] All this was what obtaining entailed.

In none of these aspects was the "law" of colonizing the common-law monolith "time out of minde of man" beloved of its protectors and inheritors. Given the growing turmoil in the high politics of the English constitution, common-law immemoriality and supremacy might be ever more heatedly claimed; nevertheless, the law of colonizing was a construct from many sources.[19] The Roman law "received" by later medieval Europe was the *ius commune* of the sixteenth century, the point of legal reference for England's continental rivals in the colonizing exploits on the edge of which the English hovered.[20] English discourses of keeping created claims to sovereign possession by drawing on ideologies of right and habitation embedded in that law – in *ius gentium* (nations) and *naturale* (nature), in expositions of just war and conquest – no less than the vernacular arcana of common-law tenures, and English ideologies of waste and improvement.[21] Actual English designs for transatlantic jurisdictions drew on a plethora of organizational models – crown-licensed adventures and conquests,

---

[18] On English colonizing as the creation of new commonwealths, see Andrew Fitzmaurice, *Humanism and America: An Intellectual History of English Colonisation, 1500–1625* (Cambridge, 2003), 1–19.

[19] See Sir Edward Coke, "To the Reader," preface to *Le Tierce Part des Reportes del Eduuard Coke Lattourrney General le Roigne* (London, 1610), sig. c₄r.; Peter S. Du Ponceau, *Dissertation on the Nature and Extent of the Jurisdiction of the Courts of the United States* (Philadelphia, 1824), ix, 91–2. John Pocock writes that "by Coke's time the increasing activity of a nearly sovereign monarchy had made it seem to most common lawyers that if a right was to be rooted in custom and rendered independent of the sovereign's interference it must be shown to be immemorial in the full sense of 'traceable to no original act of foundation'. The idea of the immemorial therefore took on an absolute colouring, which is one of the key facts in Stuart historico-political thought." J.G.A. Pocock, *The Ancient Constitution and the Feudal Law: A Study of English Historical Thought in the Seventeenth Century* (New York, 1967), 37. On Coke, see Daniel J. Hulsebosch, *Constituting Empire: New York and the Transformation of Constitutionalism in the Atlantic World* (Chapel Hill, 2005), 22–32. Though his understanding of common-law diffusion is sophisticated (see Chapter 2, Section III), Hulsebosch nevertheless accepts that "English common law" was "imperial fundamental law" (28–41). On the diversity of legal rationales for English Tudor-Stuart expansion, see Brian C. Lockey, *Law and Empire in English Renaissance Literature* (Cambridge and New York, 2006), 1–13, and in particular 160–86. On the place of civil lawyers close to the Crown and its enterprises, see Brian P. Levack, *The Civil Lawyers in England, 1603–1641: A Political Study* (Oxford, 1973).

[20] The English, of course, had undertaken their own reception of the same Roman law through Bracton. See *Bracton: De Legibus et Consuetudinibus Angliæ (Bracton on the Laws and Customs of England)* attributed to Henry de Bratton c. 1210–1268, Samuel E. Thorne, trans. (Cambridge, Mass., 1968–77).

[21] Ken MacMillan, *Sovereignty and Possession in the English New World* (Cambridge, 2006); Jess Edwards, "Between 'Plain Wilderness' and 'Goodly Cornfields': Representing Land Use in Early Virginia," in Robert Appelbaum and John Wood Sweet, editors, *Envisioning an English Empire: Jamestown and the Making of the North Atlantic World* (Philadelphia, 2005), 222–35. See generally Chapters 3 and 4.

chartered corporate enterprises seeking commodities and "trafficke," direct crown rule, delegated seigneurial privilege. And on the ground, where the business at hand went forward – that is, the actual performance of work, the hard graft of creating commodities, constructing colonies, building empire – law proved not only protean but plural in the extreme, refracting New World circumstance through the multiple regional cultures of early-modern England from which migrants came, creating distinctive legal cultures of work and labor that, for some, would sustain degrees of civic freedom unknown in England.

New civic lives are always a possibility when you create new commonwealths. Colonizing meant the kind of quotidien piecemeal transformations that can add up to profound change: transformations realized in the daily acts of taking possession, and in the manner of working the fields once possession was secured; transformations in the status of those who worked; transformations in the way rule was exercised over them, and by them.[22] These were transformations of which, by the end of the seventeenth century, even the metropolis had become aware.[23] By then, for some at least, Captain John Smith's dream was coming true.

Free ...? Bound ...?

To most historians of colonial labor, Smith's anticipation that the migrating everyman might quickly become his own master will appear at best naïve, if not downright misleading, as a depiction of the reality of England's American colonizing. Historians assume that most of the work in the early colonies was done by servants immured by indenture in wretched lives of bondage.[24] Indeed, servitude, not freedom, has long been identified as the foundational reality of the life awaiting the vast majority of transatlantic migrants, voluntary and involuntary, on the mainland. The classic statement is Abbot Emerson Smith's: "Labor was one of the few European importations which even the earliest colonists would sacrifice much to procure, and the system of indentured servitude was the most convenient system next to slavery by which labor became a commodity to be bought and sold."[25] Over the course of the seventeenth and eighteenth centuries, the proportion of Europeans arriving in the mainland colonies bound to service, hence "unfree," has been estimated to range at different

[22] John Wood Sweet, "Introduction: Sea Changes," in Appelbaum and Sweet, eds., *Envisioning an English Empire*, 17–18; Michael Zuckerman, "Identity in British America: Unease in Eden," in Nicholas Canny and Anthony Pagden, editors, *Colonial Identity in the Atlantic World, 1500–1800* (Princeton, N.J., 1987), 115–57.

[23] Peter C. Herman, "'We All Smoke Here': Behn's *The Widow Ranter* and the Invention of American Identity," in Appelbaum and Sweet, eds., *Envisioning an English Empire*, 254–74.

[24] Sweet, "Sea Changes," 19–20. See generally Jacqueline Jones, *American Work: Four Centuries of Black and White Labor* (New York, 1998), 31–2, 62–4.

[25] Smith, *Colonists in Bondage*, 4.

moments from 50 to 90 percent, comprising overall at least two-thirds of all migrants across the two centuries.[26] From the late seventeenth century these numbers were supplemented by rapidly rising rates of importation, and subsequent natural increase, of enslaved Africans, who would become the cardinal exemplification of coerced labor in the eighteenth-century colonies. Although it has been recognized that work in early America took a profusion of forms – wage work, independent production, and household production as well as servitude and slavery – it has been argued that all performers of labor were alike in one transcendent essential: all were subject in their different ways to generic forms of criminalized discipline. Coerced unfreedom, that is, was the default characteristic of *all* early American work relations.[27]

Migrant indentured servitude *was* an important component in mainland English America's original work regimes; over the course of the seventeenth and eighteenth centuries, a majority of European migrants to mainland America *did* arrive as indentured servants. But too ready an acceptance of indentured servitude's ubiquity has allowed it to narrow our field of vision. First, migrant indentured servitude was a temporary not a permanent condition. Indentured servants ceased to be servants when their indentures expired. Second, the aggregate numbers that have convinced historians (two-thirds of all migrants across two centuries) are misleading: once disaggregated by time and place, migrant servitude becomes a far less ubiquitous phenomenon than aggregates imply. Third, lack of servant persistence in population on the one hand and rising rates of natural increase in the white Creole (native-born) population on the other left migrant indentured labor of diminished significance in total working population well before the end of the seventeenth century. Fourth, in most areas of settlement "most of the labor available ... was family labor," and the household was the institutional locus of production.[28] Once all this is taken into account, one may question whether migrant servitude should be granted the distinctive influence on early American labor systems that it has heretofore been accorded.[29]

The claim that the legal culture of work in general was a default culture of generic unfreedom must also be reexamined. Alongside the statutory

---

[26] McCusker and Menard, *The Economy of British America*, 242, 238–57.

[27] On servitude as the normal state of migrant labor, see Smith, *Colonists in Bondage*, 3, 4; on legal unfreedom as the default status of all labor, see Robert Steinfeld, *The Invention of Free Labor: The Employment Relation in English and American Law and Culture, 1350–1870* (Chapel Hill, 1991), 3–5; Farley Grubb, "Does Bound Labour Have to be Coerced Labour? The Case of Colonial Immigrant Servitude versus Craft Apprenticeship and Life-Cycle Servitude-in-Husbandry," *Itinerario*, 21, 1 (1997), 29; Karen Orren, *Belated Feudalism: Labor, the Law, and Liberal Development in the United States* (Cambridge and New York, 1991), 4.

[28] McCusker and Menard, *The Economy of British America*, 246.

[29] My analysis of indentured servitude is developed in detail in Chapter 1. The significance of the household as a site of legal relations, both as to work and to politics, is considered in Chapter 8.

regimes defining indentured servitude and later slavery, one encounters law that recognized other, voluntary, work relations. Legalized coercion was not ubiquitous, rendering all labor "unfree." Work's legal culture was not uniform but highly differentiated.[30]

Reconceptualization of free and unfree labor in early America can be assisted by the vigorous discussion of free and unfree labor in general that has been ongoing since the mid-1980s, an outgrowth of efforts by scholars of development studies to reexamine the assumptions of varieties of modernization theory, and also of varieties of revisionist Marxist analysis concentrating on the "transition to capitalism" question. Modernization theory accepted labor unfreedom as an historical reality but maintained that the spread of capitalism had been accompanied by the decline of labor unfreedom in all its forms and the rise of free workforces: emancipation from unfreedom hence was a progressive effect of capitalist development. Orthodox Marxist theory, meanwhile, took the existence of unfree labor, particularly in rural economies, as crucial evidence for the persistence of pre-capitalist or non-capitalist modes of production, and its disappearance as a sign of the transformation of the mode of production. Both bodies of theory, then, privileged free labor and associated it with capitalism and progress, though each arrived at quite distinct conclusions as to the historical lesson the emergence of free labor taught. Liberal modernizers saw free labor as an *individual* condition of self-proprietorship whose achievement vindicated capitalism's emancipatory promise. Marxists located substantive freedom in *collective* action, its ultimate vindication the collective decision to transcend the formal freedoms of capitalist relations (formal self-proprietorship, legal personality) and undertake the further transition to a fully socialized mode of production. Both, however, drew clear distinctions between unfreedom and freedom and associated those differences with distinct modes of production. And, fundamentally, both associated the linear succession of modes of production with history, history with progress, and progress with the widening of freedom.[31]

Critics have collapsed the classic distinction between unfree and free labor. They have done so, roughly, in two distinct ways; either by noting the persistence of objective conditions of unfreedom in the capitalist mode, or by finding a persistent ambiguity in the conditions and definition of both unfreedom and freedom, whenever and wherever historically situated. The former critique finds a capitalist mode of production quite compatible with unfreedom and hence relaxes the causal "relations of production" assumptions shared by both liberal modernizer and orthodox Marxist. But it maintains a clear distinction between unfreedom and freedom.[32]

---

[30] This argument is developed at length in Chapters 5, 6, and 7.

[31] For a critique of this approach as exemplified by the work of E. P. Thompson, see Chapter 8, introduction and section I.

[32] Tom Brass, "Free and Unfree Labour: The Debate Continues," in Tom Brass and Marcel van der Linden, editors, *Free and Unfree Labour: The Debate Continues* (Bern, 1997), 18–24.

The latter finds few bright lines in history, either in qualitative distinctions between modes of production, or between the forms of social relation associated with them. Jan Lucassen, for one, points out that historically, unfree dependent labor (slavery, indentured servitude) has existed quite easily alongside free dependent labor (that is, "free to current legal standards") and free independent labor (small farming, cottage industry), and that their coexistence is generally marked by considerable shifting back and forth from category to category, all within the same general mode of production.[33]

In a distinct approach, Robert Steinfeld and Stanley Engerman have argued that not only are the boundaries between categories permeable but that the categories themselves tend to collapse into each other. Historians are accustomed to classify different forms of labor as free (waged) or unfree (apprenticeship, indentured servitude, contract labor, peonage, serfdom, slavery), but "'types' of labor, like 'wage labor' and 'contract labor' [or peonage or indeed slavery] never did possess a set of fixed, natural characteristics, but were defined by a range of characteristics ... depending upon the precise characteristics they possessed in any particular place, such types might be considered either 'free' or 'unfree'." The observation leads Steinfeld and Engerman to conclude that the "different 'types' of labor were, in certain respects, not nearly as discrete and discontinuous as the standard picture implies. At the boundaries the 'types' of labor frequently blur and merge."[34] Steinfeld in particular has tended to interpret this fluidity as significant in one direction only, arguing that ubiquitous legalized coercion blurs all forms of differentiation, draining freedom into unfreedom.[35] But their conclusion has attracted strong criticism. Tom Brass, for example, holds that Steinfeld and Engerman's "difference-dissolving claim that no distinction exists between free and slave labour in terms of a requirement to work overlooks abundant evidence to the contrary."[36]

---

[33] Jan Lucassen, "Free and Unfree Labour before the Twentieth Century: A Brief Overview," in Brass and van der Linden, eds., *Free and Unfree Labour*, 45–56.

[34] Robert J. Steinfeld and Stanley L. Engerman, "Labor – Free or Coerced? A Historical Reassessment of Differences and Similarities," in Brass and van der Linden, eds., *Free and Unfree Labour*, 107–8. And see 113–15, 120–2, 125. Unfortunately, Steinfeld and Engerman do not address independent labor – a major failing from the point of view of this study, given independent labor's considerable importance in the mainland colonies (see Chapters 5, 6, and 7). See, however, Stanley L. Engerman, "Introduction," and Leon Fink, "From Autonomy to Abundance: Changing Beliefs about the Free Labor System in Nineteenth-Century America," both in Stanley L. Engerman, editor, *Terms of Labor: Slavery, Serfdom and Free Labor* (Stanford, Calif., 1999), 9–11 and 116–36; Stanley L. Engerman, "Servants to Slaves to Servants: Contract Labour and European Expansion," in P. C. Emmer, editor, *Colonialism and Migration: Indentured Labor before and after Slavery* (Dordrecht, 1986), 263–94.

[35] Steinfeld, *Invention of Free Labor*. For a refinement of *Invention*'s account, see Robert J. Steinfeld, "Changing Legal Conceptions of Free Labor," in Engerman, ed., *Terms of Labor*, 137–67. Engerman's position is elaborated in his Introduction to *Terms of Labor*, 1–23.

[36] Brass, "Free and Unfree Labour," 21, and generally, 12–13, 20–2.

The English mainland colonies lend themselves to the general project of examining anew the categories of free and unfree labor. The particularization and, to a degree, permeability of categories described by revisionists accommodates colonial experience better than any classic polar distinction between free and unfree. Lucassen's suggested typology of coexisting particularized and dynamic categories – free and unfree, dependent and independent[37] – is particularly helpful and suggestive, for Mainland English America's working population was highly segmented. Not only was it internally differentiated by migrant status (the "classic" unfree/free distinction), but status was crosscut by age, gender, and racial difference. In addition, the working population varied markedly in composition *and* legal character from region to region.

To investigate work and labor in early America, then, to understand what was free and what was not, and when and why, and how the whole intricate structure was maintained, one must pull apart a putatively familiar phenomenon. For the most part the variegated legal culture of work and labor that empirical research exposes does not correspond to consistent conceptual polarities of free and unfree. As we pursue the exercise, however, we will find that certain broad distinctions resist reconstruction. First, hired and indentured labor were everywhere distinct legal categories. Second, sustained legal-cultural demarcations imprinted age and gender upon the performance of work. Third, though the tendency to link the colonial institution of indentured servitude to that of slavery as variations on the same phenomenon of legalized bondage produces valuable insights into both, to analogize the restraints applied for periods of years to comparatively small numbers of white people to the permanent and absolute subjection of multitudes of Africans is of limited utility. As David Eltis puts it, though a "coercive element in labour loomed large on both sides of the Atlantic in the seventeenth century ... chattel slavery was always perceived as different."[38]

From the Law of Work to the Work of Law

My account of the mainland's starkly segmented, highly differentiated, regionally distinct working populations, and its implications for the relationship between colonizing processes and legal cultures of freedom and unfreedom, is presented here in successively wider contexts. Following the example of the elder Richard Hakluyt, I choose to begin with the concrete, with "manning" – the actual numbers of people, over time, conducted across the ocean and inducted into the various locales and categories of

---

[37] Lucassen, "Free and Unfree Labour before the Twentieth Century."

[38] David Eltis, "Labour and Coercion in the English Atlantic World from the Seventeenth to the Early Twentieth Century," *Slavery and Abolition*, 14, 1 (April 1993), 212. See also David Eltis, "Slavery and Freedom in the Early Modern World," in Engerman, ed., *Terms of Labor*, 26–49. The lasting difference and consuming importance of chattel slavery are emphasized in Chapters 9 and 10.

the mainland's working population. Manning was the condition of success in planting and keeping, the sine qua non for the establishment of colonizers' new commonwealths and, it follows, whatever new civic identities that might emerge as a result. And so I begin in Chapter 1 by establishing the relative proportions of unfree and free, dependent and independent, at different times and places on the North American mainland. To inform that account, I develop a spatial demography of the colonies' working populations by disaggregating migration into the distinct regional patterns that characterized the movement of migrants and their diverse cultural traditions across the ocean. In Chapter 1, and in more detail in Chapter 5, I develop the argument that the social and legal plurality of the mainland's working population was to an important extent a creature of plurality at its points of English origin.

In Chapter 2, I investigate a second context for "manning" by examining the institutional mechanisms that enabled migrants to depart one side of the Atlantic and plant themselves on the other. Migration necessarily means mobility, but what did mobility mean in the free/unfree air of early modern Anglo-America? What were its conditions and effects? What was the law of "loco-motion" for transatlantic migrants?

In Chapters 3 and 4, I consider an altogether larger setting for mobility, that of the phenomenon of colonizing itself. Europeans did not simply "settle" (or "people") the North American mainland. Theirs was a wilful, forceful intrusion upon existing indigenous civilizations that devastated the mainland's established ways of living. The legal culture of work and labor that is the primary object of attention here developed within expansive European enclaves planted by colonizers whose business it was to forestall competitors and "keep" new territories within their control. As John Smith has told us, labor was essential to colonizing because labor constructed the means of keeping – labor transformed the face of the land. For those who labored, law would determine who kept what, and within the enclaves enough was kept by Smith's men of small means to make their new commonwealths' promise of enhanced civic capacity a reality.[39] But the business of keeping required far more work of law than a law of work. Keeping required the elaboration of discourses of intrusion – of claiming and dispossession and justification (Chapter 3). Specifically English discourses (Chapter 4) initially emphasized the legalities of appropriation by conquest, but came to give particular emphasis to the legality of appropriation by construction. Land put to use (in English ways) was land rescued from degeneracy, old ties destroyed, land improved, hence land won. Here the legal culture of work and labor takes on an entirely new significance as the English, in an immense paroxysm of institutional formation, created entirely new economies, new states, new societies beneath which they buried those they had encountered upon landfall. Here the interests of men

[39] This matter is pursued primarily in Chapters 7 and 8.

of small means and large could coincide. Cleared land was land kept, by smallholder and metropolitan patentee alike.

Work was the means by which empire would be created and kept, but so was law. "Heaven and earth never agreed better to frame a place for mans habitation being of *our* constitutions, were it fully manured and inhabited by industrious people."[40] Smith had been baffled by the "strange absurdities and impossibilities" to which metropolitan planners had insisted labor be devoted. Their obsession with creating "stately officers, and offices ... as doth belong to a great Kingdome" in a primitive settlement, with granting "privileges for Cities, Charters for Corporations, Universities, Free-schooles, and Glebe-land" where none existed, had earned his derision. But "where none existed" was actually the point; the strange absurdities upon which metropolitan planners insisted were the first in the blizzard of signs that remade the mainland in English ways, signifiers of the burial that would follow.[41] And indeed, for all his contempt, in his double-edged invocation of people of "*our* constitutions" as the beneficiaries of human and providential frames for new habitations in the new world, Smith seemed to catch a glimpse of the planners' intent.

The narrative of colonizing intertwines with the legal culture of work and labor that developed in the English colonies (the subject of Chapters 5, 6, and 7) in a second fashion, for it is a narrative not only of European impositions of new commonwealths upon the ruins of old civilizations but also of European impositions upon themselves. Promoters designed new commonwealths to secure their hold on new territories, but also to secure their hold on the migrating masses on whom promoters depended to do the actual manuring – that is, to implement promoters' plans. When the designs of colonizers failed to comport with the ambitions of migrants, conflicts erupted between them. I have already remarked upon the first example: John Smith's vision for New England was born in his conflict with the metropolitan promoters of Jamestown over their preference to debate elaborate plans for building all the appurtenances of a "great Kingdome" rather than concentrate their energies on maintaining the first planters' ragtag encampment. From this clash arose Smith's ambition to see "as much freedome in reason as may be" realized in a second Virginia colony. So also, we shall see, elsewhere. In the braided history of colonizing and work and law, one encounters real material foundations for what becomes the American historical tradition's familiar narrative of departures and exceptions – of new world from old, of America from Europe, of modernity from ancien régime.

---

[40] Smith, *Map of Virginia*, 144 (emphasis added). See also Innes, "Fulfilling John Smith's Vision," 14–15.

[41] Smith, *Advertisements for the unexperienced*, 272. As Michael Ryan puts it, the assimilation of new worlds "involved their domestication." Michael T. Ryan, "Assimilating New Worlds in the Sixteenth and Seventeenth Centuries," *Comparative Studies in Society and History*, 23, 4 (October 1981), 523.

In that same braided history, however, one encounters other key, and lasting, and indubitably modern, characteristics of the legal cultures of the mainland colonies, notably their common expression, albeit varying in intensity, of a pronounced institutionalization of segmentation in personal and civic (legal and political) identity.

Quite recently, another Smith – Rogers – has underlined the persistent influence on American conceptions of identity of "an array of fixed, ascriptive hierarchies" grounded in the nation's origins. "Men thought themselves naturally suited to rule over women, within both the family and the polity. White northern Europeans thought themselves superior, culturally and probably biologically, to Africans, Native American Indians, and all other races and civilizations." British Americans thought their Protestantism made them "morally and politically, as well as theologically, superior to Catholics, Jews, Muslims and others." These hierarchies, Smith argues, had been generated "by ideological and institutional traditions of political identity" that "provide elaborate, principled arguments for giving legal expression to people's ascribed place in various hereditary, inegalitarian cultural and biological orders, valorized as natural, divinely approved, and just."[42] In the legal history of colonizing, work, and civic identity, we will find fecund soil for Smith's ascriptive hierarchies, for their valorization, and for their lasting expression: notably in the "masculine systems" of œconomy and polity (Chapter 8) and the *facies Hippocratica* – the "all but death" – of slavery (Chapter 9). We will perceive how hierarchies of gender

---

[42] Rogers Smith, *Civic Ideals: Conflicting Visions of Citizenship in U.S. History* (New Haven, 1997), 17–18. Smith's synthesis is indebted to a long generation of scholarship in African-American history, women's history, and the history of race that has reshaped the history of the founding era and the early republic, and which in so doing necessarily also reshapes the questions one asks of what went before. A small but crucial fraction of that scholarship whose influence is evident in these pages is Jeanne M. Boydston, *Home and Work: Housework, Wages, and the Ideology of Labor in the Early Republic* (New York, 1990); Nancy F. Cott, *The Bonds of Womanhood: "Women's Sphere" in New England, 1780–1835* (New Haven, 1977); Barbara Jeanne Fields, "Slavery, Race and Ideology in the United States of America," *New Left Review*, I/181 (May–June 1990), 95–118; Leslie M. Harris, *In the Shadow of Slavery: African Americans in New York City, 1626–1863* (Chicago, 2003); Joan M. Jensen, *Loosening the Bonds: Mid-Atlantic Farm Women, 1750–1850* (New Haven, 1986); Linda K. Kerber, *Women of the Republic: Intellect and Ideology in Revolutionary America* (Chapel Hill, 1980); Linda K. Kerber, *No Constitutional Right to be Ladies: Women and the Obligations of Citizenship* (New York, 1998); Joanne Pope Melish, *Disowning Slavery: Gradual Emancipation and "Race" in New England, 1780–1860* (Ithaca, N.Y., 1998); Gary B. Nash and Jean R. Soderlund, *Freedom by Degrees: Emancipation in Pennsylvania and its Aftermath* (New York, 1991); Nell Irvin Painter, *Sojourner Truth, A Life, A Symbol* (New York, 1996); David R. Roediger, *The Wages of Whiteness: Race and the Making of the American Working Class* (New York, 1991); Alexander Saxton, *The Rise and Fall of the White Republic: Class Politics and Mass Culture in Nineteenth-Century America* (New York, 1990); Laurel Thatcher Ulrich, *Good Wives: Image and Reality in the Lives of Women in Northern New England, 1650–1750* (New York, 1982); Shane White, *Somewhat More Independent: The End of Slavery in New York City, 1770–1810* (Athens, Ga., 1991). See also, generally, Barbara Young Welke, *Law and the Borders of Belonging in the Long Nineteenth-Century United States* (Cambridge and New York, 2010).

and race were tied to the relative egalitarianism prevailing among white men, a conjunction in which each performed as the other's condition of civic existence.[43]

Awakening from John Smith's Dream

Here, as in much of what follows, I have used the words "labor" and "work" more or less as synonyms. And indeed, as Hannah Arendt remarked more than half a century ago, "there is hardly anything in either the pre-modern tradition of political thought or in the large body of modern labor theories" to warrant drawing a distinction between them. Yet in *The Human Condition*, her account of the conditions and possibilities of *vita activa* (the free disposition of one's self), Arendt nevertheless did distinguish between labor, by which she meant humanity's necessitous bond to the essentialities of life itself, that is subsistence and reproduction (*animal laborans*), and work, the activity of fabricating "the sheer unending variety of things" by which we enter actively into engagement with and transform the received material world that surrounds us (*homo faber*). In the act of drawing her distinction, Arendt produced – in effect dialectically – a third essential species of human activity, which she called "action." Action encompasses all that might occur relationally among human beings without the intermediation of the material. It corresponds, therefore, to the uncontained, unrestrained, expression of the plurality of human life. In that correspondence, Arendt discerned the necessary condition, inclusion, of all genuine politics.[44]

Arendt's distinctions help us to make sense of John Smith's Anglo-American dream, in that for Smith, the promise of the New World's abundance lay precisely in the prospect that there, those of small means might overcome their bondage to necessity through the exercise of their own transformative capacities, from which might arise a new-made world of their own, and also new relational "action" – a politics of law *that included them* – to sustain it. In what follows we shall see that Smith had reason to dream, but that posterity would nevertheless eventually awaken to a

---

[43] As David Eltis writes, "freedom as it developed in Europe meant in part the freedom to exploit others." Eltis, "Slavery and Freedom in the Early Modern World," 49. See also David Eltis, "Europeans and the Rise and Fall of African Slavery in the Americas: An Interpretation," *American Historical Review*, 98, 5 (December 1993), 1399–1423.

[44] Hannah Arendt, *The Human Condition* (Chicago, 1958), 7–9, 79–80, 96, 136, 175, and generally 79–175. In the term "inclusion" I mean to summarize what Bonnie Honig describes variously as resistance to closure, recognition of remainders, and a politics of "augmentation." On Arendt and politics, see Bonnie Honig, *Political Theory and the Displacement of Politics* (Ithaca, N.Y., 1993), 10, 2–17, 76–125. In observing that "the language of the Romans ... used the words 'to live' and 'to be among men' (*inter homines esse*) or 'to die' and 'to cease to be among men (*inter homines esse desinere*) as synonyms," (7–8), Arendt reminds us that those who were not "among men" – their plurality contained, excluded from the realm of action – were thereby rendered (politically and socially) dead. Arendt, *The Human Condition*, 7–8.

distinct experience of modernity in which it became clear that the dream of freedom had been made possible for some only by the profound liabilities – the containment (both figurative and literal, both relative and absolute) – they had imposed on others.[45] In Chapters 8 and 9 I traverse the meaning and terms of containment: looming labor disciplines, patriarchy, slavery. Chapter 10 ends the book with an account of the mid-nineteenth century's climactic demand for containment's continuation, articulated in *Dred Scott v. Sandford* (1857), and the disintegration of the republic of 1787 that followed Lincoln's answering refusal.

Lincoln's refusal to countenance the terms on offer in *Dred Scott*, I argue, meant an end to the particular constellation of law and labor and civic identity examined here.[46] Refusal entailed a final reckoning with slavery, the elemental evil (absolute containment) to which the mainland colonies had yoked themselves two hundred years before. This was not a reckoning that could be brokered by law: in *Dred Scott* the law at the heart of this book stood revealed as co-conspirator in the constellation of un/freedom upon which the New World's new commonwealths, and the slaveholders' successor republic, had been built.[47] And so instead the reckoning was brokered by war. The war would be followed by a new constellation of un/freedom, of course; every age has its own.[48] But that new constellation lies beyond the scope of this book.

Though this long account has many levels and byways, it is bound together by three recurring threads. First, both the freedoms and the unfreedoms that are its concern were very real. I have tried hard to convey their reality. Second, freedom and unfreedom come together, conditions of each other's existence, like life and death. Third, like the constellations of un/freedom it nurtures, the law is always with us.

[45] For the concept of containment employed here, see William James Booth, *Households: On the Moral Architecture of the Economy* (Ithaca N.Y., 1993), particularly at 89–91. For further discussion of *Households*, see Chapter 8.

[46] As this indicates (and as the book's title makes clear), my sense of the appropriate chronological bounds for "early America," at least for my purposes here, stretches from the late sixteenth century to the Civil War. For a telling discussion of the merits of extending colonial-era perspectives well into the nineteenth century – "a colonization, as it were, of American national history" – see Jack P. Greene, "Colonial History and National History: Reflections on a Continuing Problem," *William and Mary Quarterly*, 3rd Ser., 64, 2 (April 2007), 249, and generally, 235–50.

[47] Mark A. Graber, *Dred Scott and the Problem of Constitutional Evil* (Cambridge and New York, 2006). See also, generally, Norman W. Spaulding, "Constitution as Countermonument: Federalism, Reconstruction, and the Problem of Collective Memory," *Columbia Law Review*, 103 (2003), 1992–2051.

[48] On which, in the American case, see Eric Foner, *The Story of American Freedom* (New York, 1999); Welke, *Law and the Borders of Belonging*; Steven Mintz and John Stauffer, editors, *The Problem of Evil: Slavery, Freedom and the Ambiguities of American Reform* (Boston, 2007); Christopher Tomlins, "Afterword: Constellations of Class in Early North America and the Atlantic World," in Simon Middleton and Billy G. Smith, editors, *Class Matters: Early North America and the Atlantic World* (Philadelphia, 2008), 213–33.

Threads are thin and sometimes in a medley they may disappear for a while, to resurface elsewhere in the weft. I do my best to keep track for the reader, for threads are crucial.[49] Follow them, and one may enjoy rare moments of encounter with the true object of study, the living-on; moments in which a historian realizes that the work of history, and its responsibility, is remembrance.

[49] I borrow both the metaphor and, I hope, something of its inspiration from Walter Benjamin, "Eduard Fuchs, Collector and Historian," in Howard Eiland and Michael W. Jennings, editors, *Walter Benjamin, Selected Writings* (Cambridge, Mass., 2002), III, 269 (first published in the *Zeitschrift für Sozialforschung*, fall 1937).

PART I

Manning, Planting, Keeping

Thou hast a lap full of seed,
And this is a fine country.
Why dost thou not cast thy seed,
And live in it merrily?

Shall I cast it on the sand
And turn it into fruitful land?
For on no other ground
Can I sow my seed,
Without tearing up
Some stinking weed.

William Blake, *Poems from the
Rossetti Manuscript*, I (c. 1793)

1

Manning: "Setteynge many on Worke"

This enterprice will mynister matter for all sortes and states of men to worke upon: namely all severall kinds of artificers, husbandmen, seamen, marchauntes, souldiers, capitaines, phisitions, lawyers, devines, Cosmographers, hidrographers, Astronomers, historiographers, yea olde folkes, lame persons, women, and younge children by many meanes wch hereby shall still be mynistred unto them, shalbe kepte from idlenes, and be made able by their own honest and easie labour to finde themselves wthoute surchardginge others.

Richard Hakluyt (the younger), "Discourse of
Western Planting" (1584)

Immense resources were mobilized in the service of English ambition to take possession of the North American mainland. None was more important than people. Richard Hakluyt the elder – lawyer of the Middle Temple, Member of Parliament, confidant of statesmen, and propagandist for colonizing – said it first and best. To "keepe" the country, it had to be "planted" – occupied and rendered productive. But planting required people. It was an imperative, hence, that the country be "man[ned]."[1]

The elder Hakluyt gave the existing inhabitants but a sidelong glance. The ultimate objective being lasting territorial possession rather than mere gain through a bilateral commerce, he held the indigenous population largely irrelevant to the colonizer's purposes – "of small consideration" other than as an obstacle to be negotiated.[2] Manning meant migration, the introduction of alien populations into North America as new inhabitants clearly within the colonizer's jurisdiction, to be marshaled to serve the colonizer's ends: first, as a manageable labor force to produce commodities for European buyers; second, and more generally, as a physical presence, human facts on the ground to establish occupancy. Approximately 800,000 people (60 percent European, 40 percent African) crossed the Atlantic during the two centuries that followed the first intrusions of the 1580s – nearly 200,000 during the seventeenth century, more than 600,000 during the eighteenth. Manning made the colonizer's claim to dominion materially manifest.

---

[1] Richard Hakluyt (the elder), *Pamphlet for the Virginia Enterprise* (1585), in E.G.R. Taylor, ed., *The Original Writings and Correspondence of the Two Richard Hakluyts* (London: for the Hakluyt Society, 1935), II, 333.
[2] Ibid.

"Colonization," John McCusker and Russell Menard write in their classic, *The Economy of British America, 1607–1789,* "can be understood as the movement of labor, management, and capital from the metropolis to the colony in order to exploit the [colony's] untapped resources."[3] Over its full course this book will engage with English mainland colonizing on a wider plane than this. Yet the statement captures an absolute truth. In the history of the English mainland colonies, population and the means to manage its movement, distribution, and behavior had unsurpassed importance. When one writes of colonizing, much demands one's attention, but, bluntly, manning was the essential condition of keeping. So that is the place to begin.

I. Population and Migration: the Currents of Mainland Demography

In the late sixteenth century, at the beginning of sustained English colonizing attempts, the portion of the North American landmass that would eventually comprise the thirteen English mainland colonies – a belt some two hundred miles deep (somewhat deeper in the Ohio Valley) stretching along the Atlantic seaboard from present-day Maine to Georgia – was home to approximately 500,000 indigenous inhabitants, organized in a plethora of extended family groups, clans, and regional ethnic federations, and engaged in subsistence economies dependent in differing degrees and combinations upon hunting, gathering, and cultivation. Although not sedentary, indigenous societies practiced a purposeful mobility, with a settlement pattern of periodic intraregional migration among different forest or forest-edge areas. Within this long coastal strip, indigenous population had already been in decline for a century as a result of European contact. In the Southeast, indigenous population fell by some 23 percent over the course of the sixteenth century. In the Northeast, where fewer intrusions occurred, decline over the same period was less marked, with population falling by less than 5 percent. The arrival of the English in force during the seventeenth century would change the equation. Overall, rates of indigenous population decline accelerated catastrophically, accompanied by a relative shift in emphasis to the Northeast as the locale of greatest loss. By the end of the seventeenth century the indigenous population of English America had fallen by half. Eighty percent of the decline occurred in the Northeast, where population decreased from 346,000 in 1600 to 150,000 in 1700.[4]

---

[3] John J. McCusker and Russell R. Menard, *The Economy of British America, 1607–1989* (Chapel Hill, 1989), 21. See also, generally, Marilyn C. Baseler, *"Asylum for Mankind": America, 1607–1800* (Ithaca, N.Y., 1998).

[4] See Peter C. Mancall, "Native Americans and Europeans in English America, 1500–1700," in Nicholas Canny, editor, *The Origins of Empire: British Overseas Enterprise to the Close of the Seventeenth Century,* volume 1 of *The Oxford History of the British Empire,* ed. William R. Louis (Oxford, 1998), 331 (table 15.1), 328–50. See also Neal Salisbury, "The History of Native Americans from Before the Arrival of the Europeans and Africans

Massachusetts Bay

Signs of catastrophe were thick on the ground from early on. European disease wrought such devastation on coastal groups in the Massachusetts Bay region that travelers would liken the bones and skulls of the unburied dead to "a new found Golgatha."[5] To the English, this indigenous Golgatha was a wonder worked by providence on their behalf. In 1620, the New England patent invoked the "wonderfull Plague" that God had visited upon "the Sauages and brutish People there, heeretofore inhabiting, in a Manner to the utter Destruction, Deuastacion, and Depopulacion of that whole Territorye" as a bounty releasing "those large and goodly Territoryes, deserted as it were by their naturall Inhabitants" into the hands of "such of our Subjects and People as heeretofore have and hereafter shall ... be directed and conducted thither." For as Oxford's Regius Professor of Civil Law, Alberico Gentili, had written more than thirty years earlier, "'God did not create the world to be empty'. And therefore the seizure of vacant places is regarded as a law of nature."[6]

English migration to Massachusetts Bay began seriously in the early 1630s, bringing some 21,000 people into the region during the decade. A combination of early mortality and reverse migration winnowed this founding group to a resident regional population of approximately 13,500 by 1640, but although migration tapered off sharply thereafter, high rates of natural increase meant that by the 1670s New England's settler population had exceeded 60,000. By the 1770s, it would be well in excess of 600,000.[7]

until the American Civil War," in Stanley L. Engerman and Robert E. Gallman, editors, *The Cambridge Economic History of the United States. Volume 1: The Colonial Era* (Cambridge, 1996), 1–52; Bruce G. Trigger and William R. Swagerty, "Entertaining Strangers: North America in the Sixteenth Century," and Neal Salisbury, "Native People and European Settlers in Eastern North America, 1600–1783," both in Bruce G. Trigger and Wilcomb E. Washburn, editors, *The Cambridge History of the Native Peoples of the Americas*, volume 1, *North America*, Part 1 (Cambridge and New York, 1996), 325–98 and 399–460.

5 Thomas Morton, *New English Canaan: or, New Canaan* (Amsterdam, 1637), 23.

6 The Charter of New England (1620), in Francis Newton Thorpe, *The Federal and State Constitutions, Colonial Charters, and other Organic Laws of the States, Territories and Colonies Now or Heretofore Forming The United States of America* (Washington, D.C.: Government Printing Office, 1909), III, 1828–9. Alberico Gentili, *De Iure Belli Libri Tres*, John C. Rolfe, trans. (Oxford, 1933), 80. In his "Reasons to be considered for iustifieinge the vndertakeres of the intended Plantation of New England" (1629), John Winthrop noted inter alia that "God hath consumed the Natiues with a great Plauge in those partes, soe as there be few Inhabitantes lefte." *Winthrop Papers* (Massachusetts Historical Society, 1931), II (1623–30), 141. The observation had originated in the Reverend John White's "General Observations" to the same end (id. at 113). In his *The Planters Plea. Or the Grovnds of Plantation Examined and Usuall Objections Answered* (London, 1630), at 31, White added, "it will be more advantagious to this worke to beginne with a place not so populous: For as the resistance will be lesse, so by them having once received the Gospell, it may be more easily and successfully spread to the places better peopled." Both Gentili and the law of vacant places are discussed in detail in Chapters 3 and 4.

7 McCusker and Menard, *The Economy of British America*, 103 (table 5.1). See also *Historical Statistics of the United States, Earliest Times to the Present: Millennial Edition* (Cambridge and

Continuous population increase meant constant pressure on available resources, particularly land. Complaints of overcrowding in settled areas were heard by the mid-1630s, only a few years after migration began. Crowding generated dispersal and, inevitably, conflict with the region's surviving indigenous societies. By the end of the 1670s, New England's settlers had fought two major wars – with the Pequots in 1637 and the Algonquians in the mid-1670s. Both wars were savage. Both culminated in the devastation of indigenous societies by massacre, mass execution, and the enslavement and deportation of survivors. Both removed restraints on settler expansion. Both invoked – indeed depended for their sense of legitimacy upon – a legal discourse of "just war." In his *De Iure Belli* (1588), Gentili had observed that those who violated canons of human society established by nature – kinship, love, kindliness, and a bond of fellowship – were brutes, upon whom war might justly be made, their lands appropriated, their persons enslaved. So also, in the first edition of his better-known *De Jure Belli ac Pacis* (1625), Hugo Grotius held that war might justly be undertaken against, among others, "those who kill Strangers that come to dwell amongst them," for this was against Nature, and "War is lawful against those who offend against Nature."[8] On the mainland, resistance to European encroachments – their crops, their fences, their animals, their constant movement – became an offense against nature.

The Chesapeake

Continuous settlement in the Chesapeake region had begun earlier, in 1607, under the auspices of the Virginia Company, but for fifteen years the colony's survival as a populated settlement was in doubt. Migrants arrived in an irregular trickle, the region was far less healthy for Europeans than New England, and it was populated by well-established indigenous groups with whom within two years of their arrival the intruders became engaged in intermittent conflict. Mutual antagonisms peaked in March 1622, three years into a period of much more systematic influx supported by the Company that had brought some 3,570 migrants into the colony. Amid expansion of settlement and grazing, an attack on Jamestown killed 347 colonists and nearly wiped out the colony altogether. In far more deadly retaliation, the English engaged in a wholesale "expulsion of the Salvages" from the vicinity, "and so winne all that large extent of ground to our selves," gaining "the free range of the countrey" and permanently securing their position. "For it is infinitely better to have no heathen among us, who at best were but as thornes in our sides, then to be at peace and league with them."[9] As in New England,

New York, 2006), vol. 5, table Eg1–8 (Total population, Maine, New Hampshire, Vermont, Plymouth, Massachusetts, Rhode Island, Connecticut) (hereafter cited as *HSUS*).

[8] Gentili, *De Iure Belli*, 122; Hugo Grotius *De Jure Belli ac Pacis Libri Tres* (1625 edition) quoted in Richard Tuck, *The Rights of War and Peace: Political Thought and the International Order from Grotius to Kant* (Oxford, 1999), 103.

[9] "Letter of Sir Francis Wyatt, Governor of Virginia, 1621–1626," *William and Mary Quarterly*, 2nd Ser., 6, 2 (April 1926), 118.

the pattern of a growing settler population that pressed on finite resources leading to brutal warfare and coerced removal of indigenous groups would repeat intermittently throughout the following half century.[10]

By that time the Chesapeake's white population had reached some 50,000. Immigration to the Virginia colony had picked up substantially after its security was assured, and particularly after the successful establishment of tobacco cultivation. From the mid-1620s through the end of the century, between 100,000 and 110,000 English migrants entered the Chesapeake region. Actual population grew more slowly than immigration rates suggest, to a total of some 70,000 whites at the end of the century. From the beginnings of settlement, the Chesapeake region's demography always owed far more to a disastrous (for Europeans) disease environment than to indigenous antagonism. The first twelve years of settlement, for example, had produced a Virginia colony population of some 1,194 persons.[11] Notwithstanding the 3,570 new migrants who arrived in the next three years, population at the time of the Jamestown massacre was no more than 1,240. While more than 300 people were killed in the massacre, in other words, more than 3000 had died during the three years preceding from "seasoning" (initial adverse reaction to an alien disease environment) and other causes. The Chesapeake's white population would not become self-sustaining until late in the seventeenth century. From the late 1670s onward over the next century, however, it expanded at a more or less constant rate, from 50,000 to nearly half a million, a performance in which immigration was of ever decreasing significance.[12]

The second half of the seventeenth century saw a third component forcibly added to the Chesapeake population, enslaved Africans. Africans, both enslaved and free, had been present in the Chesapeake virtually as long as the English, but their numbers did not begin to increase significantly until the 1660s. In 1670, this black population totaled about 3,200 (more than 6.5 percent of the total non-indigenous population); a decade later blacks comprised 4,600 (7.5 percent).[13] That decade had seen the first significant importation of African slaves into the Chesapeake – probably about 1,000 and perhaps double that number (given the rate of population increase, the latter figure would be more in line with mortality rates in the entering

---

[10] Anthony S. Parent, Jr., *Foul Means: The Formation of a Slave Society in Virginia* (Chapel Hill, 2003), 11–24. For details of intervening conflicts, see also Chapter 4, n.66.

[11] William Thorndale, "The Virginia Census of 1619," *Magazine of Virginia Genealogy*, 33 (Summer 1995), 160.

[12] McCusker and Menard, *The Economy of British America*, 136 (table 6.4). See also *HSUS*, vol. 5, table Eg33–34 (Maryland and Virginia, white population). Edmund Morgan, *American Slavery, American Freedom: The Ordeal of Colonial Virginia* (New York, 1975), 98.

[13] Calculated from *HSUS*, vol. 5, tables Eg13–14, Eg33–34, Eg52–53 (Maryland and Virginia total population, white population, black population). See also Gregory E. O'Malley, "Beyond the Middle Passage: Slave Migration from the Caribbean to North America, 1619–1807," *William and Mary Quarterly*, 3rd Ser., 66, 1 (January 2009), 138, 141 (table 1). Thorndale, "The Virginia Census of 1619," 155, reports 32 blacks present in the Virginia colony in March 1619/20.

cohort of European migrants).[14] Importation continued at an average of some 3,500 per decade through the end of the century. Imports to Virginia alone increased to over 7,000 per decade through 1720, then doubled to an average of 13,500 per decade over the next thirty years. Arrivals began tailing off in the 1750s and 1760s to 9,500 per decade, and in the 1770s to fewer than 4,000.[15] The black population, meanwhile, increased for most of the century at rates higher than could be accounted for by slave importation. The proportion of new arrivals in overall population declined more or less continuously, paralleling the phenomenon in the white population of rates of natural increase rising as the pool of survivors of earlier migrant generations grew larger. In 1700, the Chesapeake's black population was approaching 20,000 (more than 20 percent of total population). In 1720 it was nearly 40,000 (over 25 percent). By 1750 it was 150,000 (40 percent), a proportion that remained relatively constant thereafter.[16]

The Lower South

In the Lower South (the Carolinas and later Georgia), continuous white settlement began in 1670, growing to 13,500 by the end of the century and to nearly 300,000 by 1780. Initially building an economy based on trade with the region's indigenous inhabitants for hides and Indian slaves for West Indies plantations, by the 1700s white settlers were also pressing on available land supplies. Trade and land disputes culminated in the devastating Yamasee War of 1715–16. Staple crop cultivation, notably rice, stimulated demand for labor, which meant the importation of African slaves: South Carolina showed little of the Chesapeake's extensive initial reliance on indentured servitude. In South Carolina, slaves arrived with the first settlers from Barbados. Systematic importation began in the 1690s in numbers that essentially doubled each decade, rising to more than 20,000 in the 1730s. Slave importation fell off almost completely in the 1740s in reaction to the Stono revolt of 1739, but arrivals surged again in the 1750s and peaked at nearly 22,000 in the 1760s. Over the period from 1750 through 1790, slave arrivals averaged 17,000 per decade, compared with fewer than 6,000 per decade to Virginia.[17]

---

[14] Russell R. Menard, "From Servants to Slaves: The Transformation of the Chesapeake Labor System," *Southern Studies*, 16, 4 (Winter 1977), 366–7.

[15] Philip D. Morgan, *Slave Counterpoint: Black Culture in the Eighteenth-Century Chesapeake and Lowcountry* (Chapel Hill, 1998), 58–62 (incl. tables 9 and 10). See also Ira Berlin, *Many Thousands Gone: The First Two Centuries of Slavery in North America* (Cambridge, Mass., 1998), 110.

[16] Calculated from *HSUS*, vol. 5, tables Eg–14, Eg33–34, Eg52–53 (Maryland and Virginia total population, white population, black population). See also Morgan *Slave Counterpoint*, 61 (table 10). Some variation exists between black population numbers reported for the first decade of the eighteenth century by John J. McCusker in *Historical Statistics* and by Morgan. Variation can also be found later in the series. The trends are the same; the variation comes down to assessment of precisely how rapidly the population is growing at particular intervals.

[17] Morgan, *Slave Counterpoint*, 58–62 (incl. tables 9 and 10); O'Malley, "Beyond the Middle Passage," 140, 142 (table 2), 143.

The Lower South's reliance on slave importation for labor meant that for most of the century the region's white population formed a smaller proportion of total population than in the Chesapeake. Blacks comprised 20 percent of the region's introduced population in 1700, 37 percent by 1720, and peaked at 47 percent in 1740. Black incidence in total population then slowly declined over the second half of the century to 41 percent in 1780. Unlike the Chesapeake, natural increase did not contribute significantly to black population growth until after the 1740s. Throughout the first half of the century, slave importation accounted for virtually all growth in South Carolina's black population.[18]

The Mid-Atlantic

Of all the regions of mainland settlement, the mid-Atlantic colonies – Pennsylvania, the Jerseys, New York – hosted the most diverse population. Indigenous groups and confederations – Algonquians on the coast, Iroquois to the north and west – were strong and plentiful. European settlement was begun in the 1630s by the Dutch in the Hudson and Delaware Valleys, and also included Swedish-founded settlements in the Delaware Valley and some English settlements on Long Island. The Dutch created an extensive trading network centered on Albany, and New Amsterdam became an important hub for coastal and oceanic trade.[19] By 1660, the European population stood between 4,000 and 5,000, mostly concentrated in the Dutch settlements and supplemented by about 600 Africans. A more rapid influx began in the 1670s, after the English took control of New Amsterdam and New Netherland, and after the creation of English proprietary colonies on both sides of the Delaware River. In the fifty years after 1680, the regional population grew from 14,000 to approaching 140,000. By 1780 it had reached nearly 680,000. Much of the initial late seventeenth-century growth came from Northern English, Welsh, and Scottish migrants moving to Pennsylvania and the Jerseys. The eighteenth century saw considerable diminution of the English component relative to the development of substantial migrant flows from Ulster, Southern Ireland and in particular from the Rhine lands of Middle and Southern Germany, along with continued migration from Scotland. All these flows had become noteworthy by the 1730s and developed even more rapidly thereafter, creating the same expansionist pressures on indigenous populations as elsewhere, although accompanied by less violence, at least until mid-century. Feeding into the mid-Atlantic settlements principally through New York and Philadelphia, many migrants extended their mobility westward to the Susquehanna River and thence on toward the Ohio Valley, where they met others heading west

---

[18] Calculated from *HSUS*, vol. 5, tables Eg15–17, Eg35–37, Eg54–56 (North Carolina, South Carolina, Georgia, total population, white population, black population). On natural increase, see Morgan, *Slave Counterpoint*, 80–6.

[19] See, generally, Donna Merwick, *Possessing Albany, 1610–1710: The Dutch and English Experiences* (Cambridge and New York, 1990); Simon Middleton, *From Privileges to Rights: Work and Politics in Colonial New York City* (Philadelphia, 2006), 19–20, 49.

from the Chesapeake. As in New England, however, population growth in the mid-Atlantic region was far more a creature of natural increase than of migration. The region's black population, meanwhile, grew from 1,500 to 40,000 in the century following 1680, generally averaging 6–8 percent of the region's total introduced population. Slavery was not as widespread in the mid-Atlantic as in the southern colonies, but during the fifty years after 1680, significant slave populations were present in urban areas such as Philadelphia and New York; during the fifty years following, mid-Atlantic slavery became more dispersed between urban and rural areas.[20]

Over the two centuries after 1580, then, the English mainland colonies were "manned" by some 800,000 migrants. About 490,000 (+/- 20,000) of them were British and other Europeans (of whom about 11 percent were convicts or prisoners of war); about 310,000 (+/- 2,000) of them were enslaved Africans, the vast majority arriving during the century after 1670.[21] Over the same period the introduced population had grown from zero to 2.7 million – 79 percent white, 21 percent black – and had spread in tentacular fashion up and down western river valleys far beyond the narrow

---

[20] Calculated from *HSUS*, vol. 5, tables Eg9–Eg11, Eg29–31, Eg48–Eg50 (New York, New Jersey, and Pennsylvania total population, white population, black population). For details of European origins, see Appendix I to this chapter. For westward expansion during the eighteenth century, see Eric Hinderaker, *Elusive Empires: Constructing Colonialism in the Ohio Valley, 1673–1800* (Cambridge and New York, 1997); David Hackett Fischer, *Albion's Seed: Four British Folkways in America* (New York, 1989), 605–39.

[21] For British and other European migration, see Appendix I to this chapter. For African migration, see Philip D. Curtin, *The Atlantic Slave Trade: A Census* (Madison, 1969), 136–46; Aaron Fogleman, "Migration to the Thirteen British North American Colonies," *Journal of Interdisciplinary History*, 22, 4 (Spring 1992), 697–8, 700; Aaron S. Fogleman, "From Slaves, Convicts and Servants to Free Passengers: The Transformation of Immigration in the Era of the American Revolution," *Journal of American History*, 85, 1 (June 1998), 44, 69–70, 73; O'Malley, "Beyond the Middle Passage," 166. For a summary of overall migration, offering distinct but compatible numbers (520,000 European, 263,000 African), see James Horn and Philip D. Morgan, "Settlers and Slaves: European and African Migration to Early Modern British America," in Elizabeth Macke and Carole Shammas, editors, *The Creation of the British Atlantic World* (Baltimore, 2005), 19–44.

Gregory O'Malley has estimated the number of enslaved Africans brought to the mainland for the period 1619–1810 at 452,766, including imports to the non-English mainland colonies. Excluding the non-English mainland colonies adjusts O'Malley's overall total to 422,839. Aaron Fogleman's estimate for the same period, 426,200, is very similar. Applying Curtin's estimate of 92,000 slaves imported to the former English colonies during the period 1780–1810 would result in a figure for the period prior to Independence of 331,000–334,000, but Curtin's estimate is generally considered too low; Fogleman's estimate for the same period is 114,600. More recently, James McMillin has proposed a revised estimate for the same period of 170,000 slaves imported to all mainland colonies and 138,000 to the former English colonies. See James A. McMillin, *The Final Victims: Foreign Slave Trade to North America, 1783–1810* (Columbia, S.C., 2004), 48. Appraisal of McMillin's estimate indicates it should be treated as too high (see David Eltis, "Book Review," *Journal of Social History*, 40, 1 (Autumn 2006), 237–39). The midpoint of the range between Curtin and McMillin (115,000) coincides more or less exactly with Fogleman's estimate. Subtracting this figure from O'Malley's estimated 422,839 for 1619–1810 establishes 307,839 for the colonial period. Fogleman's estimate for the colonial period is 311,600.

coastal strip to which the colonizing population of the seventeenth century had largely confined its settlements. Meanwhile, the indigenous population of the same regions had fallen from roughly 500,000 to substantially less than half that number. Established patterns of social and political organization, land use, and economic behavior had been disrupted by repeated demographic disasters, by wars, and by the lure of procuring for European trading and slaving networks. Indigenous social structure, cohesion, and group identity had all been devastated. American Indians found themselves pushed and pulled together in new-created polyglot communities, makeshift worlds of fragments of what had been.[22]

Ironically, these makeshift indigenous worlds of fragments had something of a parallel in the swarming polythetic populations introduced by the colonizers. Properly to become the resource that Hakluyt had foreseen, however, migrant populations had to be organized and disciplined, for this too was part of what "manning" meant.

II. Indentured Servitude

The recruitment and deployment of European labor for and in mainland English America has long been identified with the phenomenon of indentured servitude. Some years ago, David Galenson designated the practice "an important early solution to the labor problem in many parts of English America" that was "widely adopted," becoming "a central institution in the economy and society of many parts of colonial British America." In the Southern colonies, Jacqueline Jones has argued, indentured servitude furnished "the bulk of labor until slavery began to predominate." J. H. Elliott is the most recent subscriber to the convention, finding in 2004 that "indentured service was ... the dominant form of labor" during the half century that preceded Virginia's transition to slavery.[23]

Observations like these identify European labor in early English America as continuously and predominantly unfree. Indeed, scholars have

[22] See James H. Merrell, "Shamokin, 'the very seat of the Prince of darkness': Unsettling the Early American Frontier," in Andrew R. L. Cayton and Fredrika J. Teute, editors, *Contact Points: American Frontiers from the Mohawk Valley to the Mississippi, 1750–1830* (Chapel Hill, 1998), 16–59; Daniel K. Richter, "Native Peoples of North America and the Eighteenth Century British Empire," in P. J. Marshall, editor, *The Eighteenth Century*, volume 2 of *The Oxford History of the British Empire*, ed. William R. Louis (Oxford, 1998), 359.

[23] David W. Galenson, "The Settlement and Growth of the Colonies: Population, Labor and Economic Development," in Stanley L. Engerman and Robert E. Gallman, editors, *The Cambridge Economic History of the United States* (New York, 1996), I, 158, and "The Rise and Fall of Indentured Servitude in the Americas: An Economic Analysis," *Journal of Economic History*, 44, 1 (March 1984), 1; Jacqueline Jones, *American Work: Four Centuries of Black and White Labor* (New York, 1998), 31; J. H. Elliott, "The Iberian Atlantic and Virginia," in Peter H. Mancall, editor, *The Atlantic World and Virginia, 1550–1624* (Chapel Hill, 2007), 556. Elliott's statement is something of a throwaway, invoking an assumed consensus. Aaron Fogleman's is the most recent general statement: "For the first two centuries of the history of British North America, one word best characterizes the status of the vast majority of immigrants – servitude." Aaron S. Fogleman, "From Slaves,

concluded that only in the Revolutionary era does one begin to encounter in the English colonies anything other than an overwhelmingly unfree workforce. Not incidentally, the imputed transition to a largely free work-force during the early republic has been treated as a powerful signifier of post-revolutionary America's departure from the patterns of the old regime, a departure that renders African slavery, in effect, an anomalous pre-modern remainder, destined as such itself eventually – inevitably – to disappear. The supposition of a radical transformation in the legal condi-tions of work for white labor creates an essential foundation for the expan-sive discourse of progress that has animated modern American history and simultaneously distances modern America from its colonial origins.[24]

But the available evidence mostly supports other conclusions. An exami-nation of migration to the three regions of mainland North America that received the vast majority of English and other European migrants during the seventeenth and eighteenth centuries – New England, the Chesapeake, and the Delaware Valley – fundamentally alters our understanding of just how prevalent migrant indentured servitude was during the colonial era.[25] Estimates of servant incidence in population that allow for mortality, con-tract length, and overall population growth indicate that the incidence of migrant servitude in the early American population and labor force was substantially lower than scholars have supposed. Though unquestionably an important source of early colonial-era labor power, migrant indentured servitude was nevertheless considerably less significant in establishing a foundational character for the performance of work in the colonial era than has been assumed. Participation in the performance of work was widespread in the population as a whole – virtually everyone worked in

Convicts and Servants to Free Passengers: The Transformation of Immigration in the Era of the American Revolution," *Journal of American History*, 85, 1 (June 1998), 43. See also Mary S. Bilder, "The Struggle over Immigration: Indentured Servants, Slaves, and Articles of Commerce," *Missouri Law Review*, 61 (1996). Fogleman's linkage of servitude to immigration accurately reflects social reality, for the evidence that servitude as such had significant incidence as a condition of working life among the non-African native-born is quite sparse. Bound labor certainly existed among white Creoles in the form of apprenticeship, pauper servitude, debt servitude, compensatory servitude by those convicted of crimes, but apart from apprenticeship, formal binding was incidental in Creole work relations. See, for example, Farley W. Grubb, "Immigration and Servitude in the Colony and Commonwealth of Pennsylvania: A Quantitative and Economic Analysis" (Ph.D. dissertation, University of Chicago, 1984), 163–5. Socially, culturally, and legally, indentured servitude was identified overwhelmingly with immigration.

[24] For Fogleman, the American Revolution is a transformative event in the history of free-dom in North America. "Slaves, Convicts and Servants," 45, 65–6. David Montgomery likewise sees the half-century after the Revolution as one of decisive repudiation of "tra-ditional" society's hierarchies, affirming "the durable legacy of egalitarian practice" left by the Revolution. See his *Citizen Worker: The Experience of Workers in the United States with Democracy and the Free Market during the Nineteenth Century* (New York and Cambridge, 1993), 5, 13–51. See also Robert J. Steinfeld, *The Invention of Free Labor: The Employment Relation in English and American Law and Culture, 1350–1870* (Chapel Hill, 1991), 122–46.

[25] Migration to the British Caribbean does not feature in this analysis.

some capacity – and the institutional structure of performance far more diverse. Correspondingly, the companion assumption that the American political economy followed a clear trajectory from ubiquitous "unfreedom" toward a late eighteenth and nineteenth-century "free" waged workforce norm (market-driven allocation of individual capacities to labor through unregulated wage contracts) also becomes suspect, or at the very least vastly more complicated than prevailing analyses have supposed.[26]

In the remainder of this chapter I investigate the migration and population history of the major regions and periods of intake. My purpose is to call into question the significance of the aggregates upon which scholars have relied to set scenes and characterize political, legal, and economic cultures. Numbers are a good place to begin, if only because they help shake us free of certain misunderstandings. In their wake one must reexamine assumptions, set different scenes. But of themselves, numbers possess limited explanatory capacity, and so after this chapter I will leave numbers behind for a while and attempt instead to bring to the fore the ideas, the institutions, the structures, the processes, and the cultures that, I hope, will help us understand better what the numbers can and cannot tell us. I will return to numbers in Chapter 9 when I undertake a close examination of slavery in early America. I have intentionally separated that discussion from the analysis presented in this chapter, which concentrates largely on the European-origin population.[27] Still, both (like everything in between) are parts of one large whole. Overall, the goal of this book is to show in detail how manning knits together with English "planting" and "keeping" of the mainland, and, no less, how the plurality of new commonwealths built on the ruins of old civilizations served as the breeding ground for the American identities, free and bound, that would prevail not only through the end of the eighteenth century, but far beyond.

IIA. Numbers

The legal-transactional basis of early American indentured servitude was a written agreement committing one party to make a series of payments benefiting the other – settlement of transport debt, provision of subsistence, and a one-time payment in kind or, less usually, cash at the conclusion of

[26] I canvass the broad issue in Christopher Tomlins, "Why Wait for Industrialism? Work, Legal Culture and the Example of Early America – An Historiographical Argument," and "Not Just Another Brick in the Wall: A Response to Rock, Nelson, and Montgomery," *Labor History*, 40, 1 (1999), 5–34, 45–52. Chris Tilly and Charles Tilly have emphasized the crucial importance of recognizing how a range of differentiated relational settings supply meanings for work as social action. Free labor markets embody an unusual, historically specific organization of work. Even under contemporary capitalism, a majority of work-performance "in terms of labor-time expended" occurs outside the labor market as the latter is conventionally understood. Chris Tilly and Charles Tilly, *Work Under Capitalism* (Boulder, Colo., 1998), 22, 23–32.

[27] I advert to slavery in this chapter where appropriate, but reserve the most detailed discussion for Chapter 9.

the term of service – in exchange for which the beneficiary agreed to be completely at the disposal of the payor, or the payor's assigns, for performance of work, during the term stipulated.[28] All aspects of the transaction were secured by law.[29]

Immigrant Europeans working under indenture can be found in all regions of mainland North America during the seventeenth and eighteenth centuries (and well into the nineteenth century too).[30] As a decisive contributor to labor supply, however, indentured servitude is primarily associated with two periods of substantial migration into two mainland regions: the Chesapeake (Virginia and Maryland) between 1630 and the early 1700s, and the Delaware Valley (primarily Pennsylvania and the Jerseys, but with continuing inflow also to Maryland) between the late 1670s and the early

---

[28] An indenture is a form of deed; that is, a formal writing documenting an agreement ("signed, sealed and delivered"). Clauses of agreement contained in a deed are called covenants. During the seventeenth century, commercial migrant servitude was founded on deeds of indenture committing migrants to labor for a negotiated period on terms agreed with a shipper prior to embarkation in exchange for transportation. The shipper would recover transportation costs and margin by selling the servant's indenture on arrival. Costs of migrants who neither paid their own passage nor negotiated indentures prior to departure would be recovered on arrival from planters to whom the servants in question were bound on standard terms and conditions of service ("the custom of the country") prescribed in local legislation and processed through local courts. Court-processed servitude largely involved children (on which see Section IIB in this chapter).

During the eighteenth century, a variation on seventeenth-century practice developed in the Delaware Valley labor market, in which the migrant did not commit to a future service agreement prior to embarkation but instead indemnified the shipper by agreeing to enter a service contract on terms sufficient to liquidate the transportation debt within a specified period after arrival should other means to satisfy the debt (such as advances or gifts from family, friends, or former neighbors) fail to materialize. This so-called redemptioner system, which might also be viewed as a variation on debt servitude, dates from the 1720s and was dominant in the migrant servant trade by the 1750s. See David W. Galenson, *White Servitude in Colonial America: An Economic Analysis* (Cambridge and New York, 1981), 3–4; Farley Grubb, "The Auction of Redemptioner Servants, Philadelphia, 1771–1804: An Economic Analysis," *Journal of Economic History*, 48, 3 (September 1988), 583–603; Aaron S. Fogleman, *Hopeful Journeys: German Immigration, Settlement, and Political Culture in Colonial America, 1717–1775* (Philadelphia, 1996), 77–8; Georg Fertig, "Eighteenth-Century Transatlantic Migration and Early German Anti-Migration Ideology," in Jan Lucassen and Leo Lucassen, editors, *Migration, Migration History, History: Old Paradigms and New Perspectives* (Berne, 1997), 271–90. A further innovation appearing in the 1770s was the "indenture of redemption," which comprised an assignable pre-negotiated agreement to serve that could be voided by the migrant if better terms or unexpected resources were available on arrival. See Farley Grubb, "Labor, Markets and Opportunity: Indentured Servitude in Early America, a Rejoinder to Salinger," *Labor History*, 39, 2 (1998), 237 n.14.

[29] On the efficacy of legal oversight, see Christine Daniels, "'Liberty to Complaine': Servant Petitions in Colonial Anglo-America," in Christopher L. Tomlins and Bruce H. Mann, editors, *The Many Legalities of Early America* (Chapel Hill, 2001), 219–49.

[30] Farley Grubb, "The Disappearance of Organized Markets for European Immigrant Servants in the United States: Five Popular Explanations Reexamined," *Social Science History*, 18, 1 (Spring 1994), 1–30, at 1. See also Steinfeld, *Invention of Free Labor*, 164–5.

1770s.[31] Migrant indentured servitude was far less significant in other regions of European settlement. In New England, servants were of modest incidence (15–20 percent) in a migration that was itself largely confined to one convulsive spasm between 1630 and 1640.[32] Migration into the Appalachian backcountry was more sustained, but "remarkably few"

[31] Very few of the mid-Atlantic region's migrant servants wound up in New York. See Middleton, *From Privileges to Rights*, 133, and Chapter 9, section V.

[32] All available sources agree that servant incidence in the New England migrant stream was much lower than in seventeenth-century migrant streams to other mainland regions. Nor did servants persist in the landed population in significant numbers beyond the first decade. There is little evidence of an organized trade in servants to New England (there is some scattered evidence in the early eighteenth century of unsuccessful efforts to encourage one – see *Province Laws* ch. 11 (26 February 1708/9), *An Act to Encourage the Importation of White Servants* reiterated and revised in ch. 3 (23 August 1712), *An Act Prohibiting the Importation or Bringing into this Province Any Indian Servants or Slaves*). Migrant servants entering after 1640 appear to have been recruited directly through family and community networks by heads of household returning temporarily to England for that purpose.
Estimates of the numbers of servants in the New England migrant stream have reported incidences varying from 1 in 3 to 1 in 6 of all male migrants. Overall, sources suggest roughly 60% of all migrants were males and (again roughly) that male servants outnumbered female by 3 to 1 (Fischer, *Albion's Seed*, 16, 27, 28; Richard Archer, "New England Mosaic: A Demographic Analysis for the Seventeenth Century," *William and Mary Quarterly*, 3rd Ser., 47, 4 (October 1990), 477–502, at 480, 486–7; Roger Thompson, *Mobility and Migration: East Anglian Founders of New England, 1629–1640* (Amherst, Mass., 1994), 122–3). This suggests that servants constituted no fewer than 12.5% and no more than 25% of the Great Migration. Estimates have tended to cluster at the lower end of this range. See Richard S. Dunn, "Servants and Slaves: The Recruitment and Employment of Labor," in Jack P. Greene and J. R. Pole, editors, *Colonial British America: Essays in the New History of the Early Modern Era* (Baltimore, 1984), 160 (15% of 1630s migrants); Daniel Vickers, *Farmers and Fishermen: Two Centuries of Work in Essex County, Massachusetts, 1630–1850* (Chapel Hill, 1994), 37 ("almost 17 percent"); Fogleman, "Slaves, Convicts, and Servants," 46 ("about 16 percent"). In *Coming Over: Migration and Communication Between England and New England in the Seventeenth Century* (Cambridge and New York, 1987, 52–3, 66), David Cressy identifies a somewhat higher 21% of migrants as servants based on analysis of eleven passenger lists from ships embarking migrants at a variety of English ports in 1635, 1637, and 1638. In *Migration and the Origins of the English Atlantic World* (Cambridge, Mass., 1999, 27–30, 52), Alison Games argues for a much higher 33.8%. Games's estimate, however, is not empirically acceptable as an overall proportion, being based on a single year (1635) and biased upward by her exclusive concentration on London departures. Both Thompson and Archer report a very low incidence of servants among those migrating from greater East Anglia, who embarked from North Sea and Channel ports. Thompson positively identifies only 5% of migrant East Anglians as servants (although he speculates that up to 12% might have been servants). See, generally, Thompson, *Mobility and Migration*, 26, 114–25; Archer, "New England Mosaic," 486–7.
In the matter of persistence, Cressy proposes that servants formed about 25% of New England's landed population (*Coming Over*, 53). Games suggests that the nearly 34% incidence of servants among all migrants leaving London in 1635 translates directly into a similar incidence of servants in the landed population (*Origins*, 72, 74). It is not plausible, however, to maintain that servants persisted in population at migrant ratios after the flow of migration slowed virtually to nothing after 1640. Even were one to accept Games's 34% rate as accurate and that it persisted throughout the 1630s, assuming a total migration during this period of 21,000 with peaks in 1634–5 and 1637–8, allowing moderate mortality (25 per 1000) after initial "seasoning" (75 per 1000) and an average term of 5

migrants entered the region as indentured servants and the institution did not develop any lasting presence.[33]

Historians have offered widely varying accounts of the total numbers of Europeans migrating to America during the seventeenth and eighteenth centuries and of the likely incidence of servants in those migrant populations. In the mid-1980s, Richard S. Dunn estimated that roughly 350,000 servants entered all of British America (mainland and island) between 1580 and 1775, constituting "about half" of all white migrants.[34] Ten years later, Philip Morgan suggested a figure of 500,000 servants in a total European migration of 750,000, or two-thirds of all migrants, was more appropriate.[35] Such disparities in aggregate outcomes produced by experienced scholars indicate the degree to which global migration and population portraits remain

years' service, it is still highly unlikely that there were more than 2,500 migrant servants in New England at the end of 1640 (that is, no more than 18.5% of the white population at that time, rather than 34%). Allowing Cressy's 21% rate to persist throughout the decade with all other conditions held constant, the servant population would be closer to 1,500, or about 11% of white population at the end of 1640. Using the estimates that cluster at 15–17% incidence of servants in overall migration would drop the servant population at the end of 1640 to approximately 8.5%. Given the absence of further significant migration thereafter, one can expect servant numbers to have decreased rapidly. Vickers, for example, offers 5% of population as an absolute upper bound for servants in the later seventeenth century and sets his lower bound at under 2%. On the scarcity of servants after 1640, see Vickers, *Farmers and Fishermen*, 55–8.

On mortality, see Games, *Origins*, 86; Fischer, *Albion's Seed*, 112. Games cites impressionistic contemporary evidence that suggests an early mortality rate among landed migrants of up to 100/1,000, but levels this high are not supported in any other source. In my estimates I have chosen an early rate of 75/1,000. This is applied to each year's entry cohort of servants, followed by reversion to the "normal" regional mortality rate of 25/1000 reported by Fischer. But see also Robert P. Thomas and Terry L. Anderson, "White Population, Labor Force and Extensive Growth of the New England Economy in the Seventeenth Century," *Journal of Economic History*, 33, 3 (September 1973), 647 (reporting a mortality rate of 22/1,000). I am not aware of any available per annum influx breakdown, so I have assumed an annual "base" of 1,000 per annum throughout the period 1630–40, with peaks of 2,000 in 1630, 3,000 in 1634, 5,000 in 1635, 2,000 in 1637, and 3,000 in 1638. For a rough guide to this influx distribution, see Thompson, *Mobility and Migration*, 22–3. On contract term, Lawrence W. Towner reports a New England average of 3–5 years, with variation. I have adopted the top of the average range. See Lawrence W. Towner, *A Good Master Well Served: Masters and Servants in Colonial Massachusetts, 1620–1750* (New York, 1998) 39. (Obviously, both my initial mortality assumption and my contract length assumption bias the persistence of servants in population upward.) New England population at the end of the 1630s (13,700) is taken from McCusker and Menard, *The Economy of British America*, 103. For a distribution by settlement that produces a very slight variation on this total – 13,679 – see *HSUS*, vol. 5, table Eg2–8 (New England, total population). Given a migration of 21,000 over the previous decade into a relatively benign disease environment, this figure reflects significant return and onward migration, on which see Games, *Origins*, 193–206; Cressy, *Coming Over*, 191–212.

[33] Fischer, *Albion's Seed*, 614.

[34] Dunn, "Servants and Slaves," 159. Dunn estimated 315,000 came from the British Isles and Ireland, including 50,000 convicts, and 35,000 from Germany.

[35] Philip D. Morgan, "Bound Labor," in Jacob E. Cooke et al., editors, *Encyclopedia of the North American Colonies* (New York, 1993), 2, 18.

unavoidably tentative and dependent on approximations.[36] Nevertheless, as specialists have refined their methods, a somewhat narrower range of numbers has begun to emerge. For the mainland alone, through 1780, prevailing estimates indicate a total European migration between 472,000 and 513,000. Of these, approximately 54,500 were convicts or prisoners of war, the vast majority of whom (50,000–52,200) entered North America during the eighteenth century.[37] Of the 417,500–458,500 "voluntary" migrants, the analysis presented here indicates some 48–50 percent were committed to an initial period of servitude by indenture or similar arrangement. This status was more common during the seventeenth century, when it applied to some 60–65 percent of voluntary migrants, than the eighteenth, when it applied on average to 40–42 percent.[38]

THE CHESAPEAKE. In the Chesapeake case, the sole contemporary measure of servant incidence in settler population is a 1625 Virginia census that counted servants somewhat in excess of 40 percent of total population.[39] For other moments in early Chesapeake history, incidence can be calculated from overall immigration and population estimates. Russell R. Menard's decadal series for immigration to the Chesapeake, together with compatible population estimates, permits development of decadal servant migrant estimates that chart shifts in the proportion of servants in total population over time.[40] Among early American historians the default assumption has been that throughout the colonial period, between half and two-thirds of all European migrants to mainland North America were indentured servants, with fluctuations up to and even beyond 80 percent not unimaginable for particular places at particular moments. In light of the overall results already mentioned (48–50 percent), "half to two-thirds" throughout

[36] Sampling studies drawing on particular historical records, in contrast, can provide dependable information on the internal characteristics of a given population, but do not easily extrapolate to distinct populations in different periods and regions, and therefore cannot answer global questions.

[37] On involuntary European migration (transported convicts and other prisoners), see A. Roger Ekirch, *Bound for America: The Transportation of British Convicts to the Colonies, 1718–1775* (Oxford, 1987), 26–7, 70–132; Fogleman, "Slaves, Convicts, and Servants," 44. Ekirch suggests 50,000 convicts transported during the eighteenth century, Fogleman 2,300 during the seventeenth century, and 52,200 during the eighteenth.

[38] The global figures summarized in the text have emerged from an analytic synthesis of a substantial number of sources. Full details of sources and methods of analysis appear in the appendices to this chapter.

[39] Dunn, "Servants and Slaves," 159. Two eighteenth-century Maryland censuses are treated in Table A4 in the appendices to this chapter.

[40] Russell R. Menard, "British Migration to the Chesapeake Colonies in the Seventeenth Century," in Lois Green Carr et al., editors, *Colonial Chesapeake Society* (Chapel Hill, 1988), 104–5 (tables 2 and 3); McCusker and Menard, *Economy of British America*, 136 (table 6.4). *HSUS*, vol. 5, tables Eg13–14, Eg33–34 (Maryland and Virginia, total population, white population). See also Henry Gemery, "Markets for Migrants: English Indentured Servitude and Emigration in the Seventeenth and Eighteenth Centuries," in P. C. Emmer, editor, *Colonialism and Migration: Indentured Labor before and after Slavery* (Dordrecht, 1986), 33–54, at 40.

the colonial period is clearly too broad a range with too high an upper bound, certainly as a percentage of voluntary migrants. The lower third of the range is feasible (through 55 percent) but only if all convict migrants are included.[41] In the seventeenth-century Chesapeake, however, the incidence of servants in total migration did indeed approach 80 percent. In the estimates given in Table 1.1, therefore, I have assumed that a consistent 80 percent of all Chesapeake migrants were indentured servants.[42]

Over the course of the century, these figures indicate, more than 85,000 servants migrated into the Chesapeake. But how many were in the region at any given moment, and what was their incidence in population? Answers require production of an annual average from the estimated number of landed migrants for each decade, allowing for term of service and for attrition – both initial seasoning and general mortality.[43] As Table 1.2 indicates, the outcome is a more or less continuous decline in the incidence of indentured servitude in population, from near majority at the beginnings of sustained migration in the late 1620s, to slightly over 5 percent by the end of the century.

[41] Ekirch concludes that although a majority of transported convicts were probably indentured to labor on arrival, certainly not all were. *Bound for America*, 119–20. Hence even the lower end of the default range is a little shaky. See also Farley Grubb, "The Transatlantic Market for British Convict Labor," *Journal of Economic History*, 60, 1 (March 2000), 94–122. It is worth noting that the higher the proportion of transported convicts involved in indentured servitude, the more comprehensible (whether justified or not) contemporary descriptions of the character of servants in general become, and the more comprehensible also the severity of disciplinary penal and criminal sanctions embodied in local legislation governing servitude. "Honest hired servants are treated as mildly in America every where as in England: But the Villains you transport and sell to us must be ruled with a Rod of Iron." Benjamin Franklin, "A Conversation on Slavery," (30 January 1770), in Leonard W. Labaree et al., editors, *The Papers of Benjamin Franklin* (New Haven, 1959–), XVII, 42.

[42] Data for Table 1.1 are derived from sources detailed in n.40, this chapter. Menard suggests that "at least 70 percent" of Chesapeake migrants were indentured servants. "British Migration to the Chesapeake Colonies," 105–6. Other estimates of seventeenth-century migration to the Chesapeake range from 100–150,000, and place the incidence of servants in the range 70–85%. See Appendix I to this chapter; also Lois Green Carr, "Emigration and the Standard of Living: The Seventeenth Century Chesapeake," *Journal of Economic History*, 52, 2 (June 1992), 271–91, at 272. For computations based on the range of alternative estimates, see Appendix III, Table A3.

[43] On term of service see James Horn, *Adapting to a New World: English Society in the Seventeenth-Century Chesapeake* (Chapel Hill, 1994), 66 ("four to five years"); Galenson, *White Servitude*, 102 (average adult term of four years); Gloria L. Main, *Tobacco Colony: Life in Early Maryland, 1650–1720* (Princeton, 1982), 98–9 (customarily five years); David Eltis, "Seventeenth Century Migration and the Slave Trade: The English Case in Comparative Perspective," in Lucassen and Lucassen, eds., *Migration, Migration History, History*, 102 (mean term 4.5 years). For attrition (seasoning and mortality) estimates see Appendix II. The average length of contracts concluded prior to embarkation appears to be 4.5 years. Because the servant population contained significant numbers of minor children migrating without indentures and serving on arrival by "custom of the country" (see Appendix IV on servants' ages), this average length should be revised upward. The use of a 5-year period of service in Table 1.2 assumes 80% of total estimated servant migrants had concluded indentures prior to embarkation with terms averaging 4.5 years, and 20% were serving by custom of country with terms averaging 7 years.

TABLE 1.1. *European Migration, Servant Migration, and Population Estimates, Maryland and Virginia, 1600–1700 (in thousands)*

Decade Ending	Maryland			Virginia			Total	
	All Migrants	Servant Migrants	White Population	All Migrants	Servant Migrants	White Population	Servant Migrants (@ 80%)	Total White Population
1610						0.35		0.35
1620[a]				3.0	2.40	2.18	2.40	2.18
1630[a]				4.0	3.20	2.45	3.20	2.45
1640	0.7	0.56	0.56	8.2	6.56	10.29	7.12	10.85
1650	1.8	1.44	4.20	6.0	4.80	18.33	6.24	22.53
1660	4.6	3.68	7.67	11.6	9.28	26.07	12.96	33.74
1670	12.2	9.76	12.04	6.5	5.20	33.31	14.96	45.35
1680	12.4	9.92	16.29	8.1	6.48	40.60	16.40	56.89
1690[b]			21.86			43.70	10.64	65.56
1700[b]			26.38			42.17	11.12	68.55

[a] Approximation

[b] For 1690 and 1700, Menard does not report separable Maryland and Virginia figures but lump totals of 13,300 (1690) and 13,900 (1700). These totals provide my "total servant migrants" estimates for 1690 and 1700.

TABLE 1.2. *European Servant Migration and Persistence in Population, Maryland and Virginia, 1600–1700 (in thousands)*

Decade Ending	Number of Servants Migrating[b]	Landed Servant Population[c]	Servant Population after Attrition	White Population at End of Decade	% Servant
1610				·35	**
1620[a]	2.40	1.20	0.81	2.18	37.2
1630[a]	3.20	1.60	1.08	2.45	44.1
1640	7.12	3.56	2.39	10.85	22.0
1650	6.24	3.12	2.09	22.53	9.3
1660	12.96	6.48	4.35	33.74	12.9
1670	14.96	7.48	5.03	45.35	11.1
1680	16.40	8.20	5.51	56.89	9.7
1690	10.64	5.32	3.58	65.56	5.5
1700	11.12	5.56	3.74	68.55	5.5

[a] Approximation
[b] From Table 1.1
[c] Column 1 adjusted to show notional servant population for any one year within the decade allowing for persistence through an average contract length of 5 years (N migrating ÷ 10)(x 5).

The declining incidence of migrant servants in the white population over the course of the seventeenth century is less surprising than the implication that at no time after the 1620s did migrant indentured servants furnish more than a quarter of the settled European population, that by mid-century they comprised significantly less than 15 percent of population, and by the end of the century, about 5 percent. Alternative estimates considering the effect of longer terms of service and inflated numbers of migrants indicate it is highly unlikely migrant servants could have comprised more than 20 percent of population at mid-century or more than 7 percent by the end.[44] This outcome, particularly the rapid decrease under way by mid-century despite strong migration rates, is explained by the development of a local reproducing population, and eventually of absolute population growth through natural increase.[45]

[44] Appendix III (Supplementary Estimates), Table A3. Table A3's alternate estimates of the incidence of migrant servants in population (a) vary the length of terms of service and (b) consider the effect of substantially larger numbers of migrants.
    Migrant indentured servants persist as a significant component of population somewhat longer in seventeenth-century Maryland than in Virginia, and remain more numerous in the eighteenth century. See Table 1.8 at b, and Appendix III (Supplementary Estimates), Table A4.
[45] "Most counties in Virginia and Maryland managed to achieve rapid natural growth by the 1690s." Daniel Blake Smith, "Mortality and Family in the Colonial Chesapeake," *Journal of Interdisciplinary History*, 8, 3 (Winter, 1978), 409. And see Lorena Walsh and Russell R. Menard, "Death in the Chesapeake: Two Life Tables for Men in Early Colonial Maryland," *Maryland Historical Magazine*, 69, 2 (Summer 1974), 211–27.

Further adjustments to population figures allow the development of an estimate of migrant servant incidence in labor force, using the proportions proposed in 1978 by Terry Anderson and Robert Thomas.[46] The estimates, shown in Table 1.3, indicate that in 1640 indentured servants comprised less than one-third of the labor force; in 1670, less than one-fifth; and by 1700, about 12 percent.

The actual incidence of servants in the working population was probably rather lower than these estimates indicate. Anderson and Thomas's calculations of labor force participation employ a concept of labor force "as found in modern developed countries."[47] In such environments, work is

[46] Terry L. Anderson and Robert P. Thomas, "The Growth of Population and Labor Force in the 17th-Century Chesapeake," *Explorations in Economic History*, 15, 3 (1978), 300 (table 4), 304 (table 7).

[47] Ibid., 304. Anderson and Thomas hypothesize that the proportion of population in labor force is equivalent to all adult males plus 10% of adult females. Restating this hypothesis in terms of an actual population of men, women, and children, they estimate that the components of labor force at any given moment will be all single males under sixty plus a proportion (declining over time from 44% to 31%) of "reproducibles" (that is, paired males and females, and children). Compare the estimates of workforce for the eighteenth century offered by Carole Shammas on the basis of differential participation rates of a population disaggregated by age and race (whites aged 16+, 90%; whites 10–15, 45%; blacks 10+, 85%). Shammas also offers lower bound estimates based on uniform white adult participation rates of 85% and blacks 10+ of 80%.

Percentage Estimates of Population in Workforce (1700–1790) by Region (lower-upper bound)

Year	New England	Mid-Atlantic	South	Total
1700	50.4–52.9	55.1–58.0	58.5–61.7	54.8–57.7
1755	50.9–53.4	51.8–54.4	51.8–54.7	51.5–54.2
1774	52.2–54.9	51.8–54.5	50.5–53.3	51.3–53.4
1790	52.2–54.9	50.9–53.5	50.8–53.5	51.3–53.9

Source: Carole Shammas, "Defining and Measuring Output and the Workforce in Early America" (unpublished paper, prepared for the conference on "The Economy of Early British America: The Domestic Sector," Huntington Library, October 1995). Shammas's results show average workforce participation rates declining over the eighteenth century from approximately 56% to approximately 52.5% for the mainland as a whole, but with pronounced regional variation. Shammas hypothesizes that seventeenth-century rates were substantially higher than those she develops for the eighteenth century, which suggests that the Anderson and Thomas figures understate seventeenth-century Chesapeake participation rates, especially for the second half of the century. There is also reasonable seventeenth-century evidence from both New England and the Chesapeake, and from the late seventeenth-century Delaware Valley, that migrant and settler children were considered fully capable of productive work by age ten, and thus that the participation rate of children fifteen and under is likely considerably higher during the first century of settlement than the levels suggested by Anderson and Thomas and, indirectly, by Shammas. See Appendix IV, "Servants' Ages." Shammas does note that participation rates of children under sixteen tended to increase relative to those of the adult component of population during the eighteenth century. This reflects the increasingly youthful character of the population of the major regions of settlement outside New England.

TABLE 1.3. *Indentured Servants in the Chesapeake Labor Force, 1640–1700 (in thousands)*

Decade Ending	White Population	% Population in Labor Force (A&T est.)	White Labor Force	White Servant Population	Servants as % of Labor Force
1640	10.850	75.62	8.200	2.390	29.1
1650	22.530	71.38	16.082	2.090	13.0
1660	33.740	66.46	22.424	4.350	19.4
1670	45.350	57.74	26.185	5.030	19.2
1680	56.890	58.13	33.070	5.510	16.7
1690	65.560	51.45	33.730	3.580	10.6
1700	68.550	45.68	31.314	3.740	11.9

seen "as a discrete activity in a distinct 'economic' realm."[48] Work in early America, however, was not thus compartmentalized.[49] Virtually everyone worked. Applying modern definitions of "labor force" to the seventeenth century will understate general population participation rates, and hence overstate the importance of those whose participation is known for sure, notably migrant servants.[50]

Finally, by adding in the Chesapeake's slave population one can produce a rough measure of the overall size of the explicitly bound component of the regional population. As Table 1.4 indicates, migrant servants accounted for a majority of the Chesapeake's unfree population until the 1680s, at which point the combined population of servants and slaves had been a stable 16–17 percent of total population for thirty years. Thereafter, while servant numbers continued to dwindle, rising slave imports and natural increase saw rapid growth in the black population.

Expressing the combined count of servants and slaves as a proportion of "labor force" (setting aside the latter's conceptual problems), Table 1.5 shows that the incidence of bound labor sits fairly consistently in the range of one-quarter to one-third of the Chesapeake labor force for most of the

[48] Patrick Joyce, "The Historical Meanings of Work: An Introduction," in Patrick Joyce, editor, *The Historical Meanings of Work* (Cambridge and New York, 1987), 2.

[49] McCusker and Menard argue that "the conventional definition of the labor force as 'all persons producing marketable goods and services' seems inappropriate to economies in which people's productive energies were focused in large part on subsistence rather than on the market." *The Economy of British America*, 236. Alice Hanson Jones suggests the colonial labor force "be defined to include most adult men and women, most youths from 16 to 21 and considerable numbers of younger children." Given the lack of specific information on participation rates, Jones suggests total adult population as a rough proxy for colonial labor force. See Alice Hanson Jones, *Wealth of a Nation to Be: The American Colonies on the Eve of the Revolution* (New York, 1980), 56.

[50] Simply put, the higher the labor force participation rate in the general population, the lower the proportionate contribution of indentured migrants to labor force.

TABLE 1.4. *Slaves and Servants in Population, Chesapeake Colonies (in thousands)*

Decade Ending	Black Population[a]	Servant Population[b]	Sum of Columns 1 and 2	Total Population	% Slave and Servant
1610				0.35	**
1620	0.020	0.81	0.83	2.20	37.7
1630	0.050	1.08	1.13	2.50	45.2
1640	0.170	2.39	2.56	11.025	23.2
1650	0.705	2.09	2.795	23.235	12.0
1660	1.708	4.35	6.058	35.446	17.1
1670	3.190	5.03	8.22	48.535	16.9
1680	4.611	5.51	10.121	61.500	16.5
1690	11.507	3.58	15.087	77.070	19.6
1700	19.617	3.74	23.357	88.164	26.5
1710	27.295		27.295	117.254	23.3
1720	39.058		39.058	153.890	25.4
1730	53.820		53.82	211.713	25.4
1740	84.031		84.031	296.533	28.3
1750	150.550		150.550	377.754	39.8
1760	189.574		189.574	501.993	37.8
1770	251.423		251.423	649.615	38.7
1780	303.582		303.582	785.963	38.6

[a] *Historical Statistics of the United States*, tables Eg52–53
[b] From Table 1.2, column 4

TABLE 1.5. *Slaves and Servants in the Chesapeake Labor Force, 1640–1700 (in thousands)*

Decade Ending	White Labor Force	Black Labor Force[a]	Total Labor Force	Slave/Servant Population	%
1640	8.200	0.170	8.370	2.56	30.6
1650	16.082	0.705	16.787	2.795	16.6
1660	22.424	1.708	24.132	6.058	25.1
1670	26.185	3.190	29.375	8.22	28.0
1680	33.070	4.611	37.681	10.121	26.9
1690	33.730	11.507	45.237	15.087	33.3
1700	31.314	19.617	50.931	23.357	45.9

[a] This column assumes that the entire black population should be included in black labor force.

seventeenth century, the rise in the African-American population in the
last quarter of the century substituting for the declining numbers of servants during that period.[51] At the end of the century we see the beginning
of a rapid increase in bound labor's incidence in total labor force as the
Chesapeake turns decisively to slavery.

All these figures are, by their nature, approximations. Their utility lies
in their refinement of the simple magnitudes, such as total numbers of servant immigrants over the entire colonial period, that scholars have tended
to rely on to substantiate indentured servitude's importance. The results
are not one-sided: for much of the seventeenth century migrant indentured
servitude was clearly a significant enough presence in the Chesapeake to
influence the social and legal relations of Europeans at work. On the other
hand, even before mid-century substantially more work was being performed outside indentured relations than within.

Migrant servitude was not "crowded out" by resort to slavery. The declining
demographic importance of migrant indentured servitude instead reflects
the general expansion of regional population, increasingly Creole (native-
born) in origin, among whom unfree migrant servants formed a decreasing
minority. When the final commitment to slavery came, decisively, at the end
of the century, it was as a solution to increasing unfree labor scarcity. It created a bound labor force of a size never before seen in the colony.[52]

THE DELAWARE VALLEY. During the eighteenth century the principal
site of indentured labor importation was the Delaware Valley. Table 1.6

[51] On substitution, see Farley Grubb and Tony Stitt, "The Liverpool Emigrant Servant Trade
and the Transition to Slave Labor in the Chesapeake, 1697–1707: Market Adjustments
to War," *Explorations in Economic History*, 31, 3 (July 1994), 376–405; Gloria L. Main,
"Maryland in the Chesapeake Economy, 1670–1720," in Aubrey C. Land et al., editors,
Law, Society and Politics in Early Maryland (Baltimore, 1974), 134–52; Menard, "From
Servants to Slaves," 355–90; Eltis, "Seventeenth Century Migration and the Slave Trade";
David Eltis, "Labor and Coercion in the English Atlantic World from the Seventeenth to
the Early Twentieth Century," *Slavery And Abolition*, 14, 1 (April 1993), 207–26.

[52] That bound labor force is also likely to have become relatively more "adult" in character
over time than its seventeenth-century predecessor. So far as arrivals are concerned, Philip
Morgan reports in *Slave Counterpoint* that "most slave shipments" to southern mainland
destinations "were overwhelmingly adult" (70). The definition of adult, however, includes
adolescents, whom, Morgan notes (at 71), Chesapeake planters preferred (as they had in
securing European labor the previous century) to mature men and women. For good measure, Morgan also notes that the proportion of children in shipments to the Chesapeake
reached 20%. In "Children in European Systems of Slavery: An Introduction," *Slavery &
Abolition*, 27, 2 (August 2006), 163–82, Gwyn Campbell, Suzanne Miers, and Joseph C.
Miller likewise emphasize both the relative domination of adult males in the transatlantic
slave trade, the preference for young adult males, and the rising proportion of children
carried during the course of the eighteenth century. Taking into account rates of natural
increase in the resident Chesapeake slave population, however, the absence of exit (unlike
the adolescent servant population of the seventeenth century) necessarily meant native-
born slaves would remain enslaved from infancy to death, and hence that the "adult"
component of the bound population would tend to grow over time.

TABLE 1.6. *Immigration to the Delaware Valley, 1680–1780 (in round numbers)*

Decade Ending	British	German	Southern Irish	Northern Irish	Total Arrivals	Arrivals in Philadelphia
1680	1500				1500	
1690	11000	77			11077	
1700	3000	76			3076	
1710	2500				2500	
1720	5000	646			5646	
1730		2956	723	296	3975	3000
1740		13006	3362	2476	18844	17000
1750		20850	4047	5284	30181	24000
1760		30374	3547	8191	42112	36000
1770	4215	8058	3737	12141	28151	21000
1780	2830	4926	1741	7150	16647	13000

Sources: For the British column, 1670–1720, Fischer, *Albion's Seed*, 421 n.5; 1760–76, Bernard Bailyn, *Voyagers to the West: A Passage in the Peopling of America on the Eve of the Revolution* (New York, 1986), 206–7, 230–1; for the German and Irish columns, Marianne Wokeck, *Trade in Strangers: The Beginnings of Mass Migration to North America* (University Park, Penn., 1999), 45–6, 172–3; for Philadelphia arrivals, see Susan Klepp, "Demography in Early Philadelphia, 1690–1860," *Proceedings of the American Philosophical Society*, 133, 2 (1989), 85–111, at 111. See also Appendix I.

presents estimates of immigration to the Delaware ports of Newcastle and Philadelphia.[53]

Table 1.6 shows the initial English and Welsh migration of the late seventeenth and early eighteenth centuries, followed by an overwhelmingly German and Irish migration in full swing by the late 1720s, and finally the resumption of British (predominantly English, some Scottish) migration after 1760. As in the Chesapeake estimates, these general migration figures become the basis for estimates of the numbers of migrants arriving as servants, as shown in Table 1.7.[54]

Having established a count of total servant imports, one can proceed to a measure of the servant population and of its incidence in general population. Table 1.8 suggests that at no time after the initial migration of the

[53] My estimates in Table 1.6 assume that the totals Bailyn reports for the period 1773–76 represent constant flows for the previous ten years as well. In addition, Wokeck's estimates of Irish migration includes residuals to account for vessels whose ports of embarkation could not be determined. I have allocated these to the Northern and Southern columns according to the annual ratio of identified Northern and Southern migrants.

[54] In contrast to the seventeenth-century Chesapeake, where the estimates presented assumed a uniform 80% of European migrants entered as servants, the better-developed secondary literature on Philadelphia's intake allows somewhat less rough-and-ready estimates. See discussion in Appendix I.

TABLE 1.7. *Servant Immigration to the Delaware Valley, 1680–1780 (in round numbers)*

Decade Ending	British @ 35%[a] @ 66%[b]	German @ 35%[c] @ 58%[d]	Southern Irish @ 66%	Northern Irish @ 25%	Total Servant Imports
1680	525				525
1690	3850				3850
1700	1050				1050
1710	875				875
1720	1750	226			1976
1730		1034	477	74	1585
1740		4552	2219	619	7390
1750		7297	2671	1321	11289
1760		10630	2341	2048	15019
1770	2781	4673	2466	3035	12955
1780	1868	2857	1149	1787	7661

[a] 1670–1720
[b] 1760–1776
[c] 1720–1760
[d] 1760–1776

1670s and 1680s did servant incidence in population exceed 5 percent. For the century, incidence averaged 2.6 percent, fluctuating in a range of 1–4 percent.[55]

Estimates specific to the city of Philadelphia may be gleaned from the work of Sharon Salinger.[56] Salinger has calculated figures for a servant workforce that, when combined with her figures for population and workforce for the city as a whole in Table 1.9, indicate that servant numbers did not exceed 7.5 percent of the city's population, nor 15 percent of its

[55] Table 1.8 assumes that migrant servants entering the mid-Atlantic region served an average five-year term. This is a distinctly upper bound. Most scholars agree that contract lengths dropped well below four years as the century progressed. See, for example, Grubb, "Labor, Markets, and Opportunity," 239; Fertig, "Eighteenth Century Transatlantic Migration," 282; Wokeck, *Trade in Strangers*, 162. Table 1.8 also applies an attrition rate of 14.3%, calculated to reflect an early mortality rate (seasoning) among new migrants reported to be about 1.7 times higher than the general Philadelphia-region mortality rate of 47/1,000 (i.e., recent migrants died off at a rate approaching double the Creole rate). This calculation reflects an overall survival rate over a four-year contract term of almost 80% (i.e., where N^1 is the size of the entry cohort, the % of survivors (N^2) is calculated as $[(N^1-8\%)(-4.7\%)(-4.7\%)(-4.7\%)] = N^2$, which is 79.6%.) For further details, see the explanation of the similar Chesapeake calculation in Appendix II. On death rates in the Philadelphia region during the eighteenth century, see Klepp, "Demography in Early Philadelphia," 94, 96, 103–5, table 2.

[56] Sharon Salinger, *"To Serve Well and Faithfully": Labor and Indentured Servants in Pennsylvania, 1682–1800* (Cambridge and New York, 1987), 172–84, tables A.1–A.3.

TABLE 1.8. *Delaware Valley Servant Population, and Pennsylvania European Population Based on Immigration Estimates, 1680–1780 (in round numbers)*

Decade Ending	Servant Imports	Landed Servant Population[a]	Servant Population after Attrition	Pennsylvania White Population[b]	% Servant
1680	525	263	225	655	34.4
1690	3850	1925	1650	11180	14.8
1700	1050	525	450	17520	2.6
1710	875	438	375	22875	1.6
1720	1976	988	847	28962	2.9
1730	1585	793	680	50466	1.3
1740	7390	3695	3166	83582	3.8
1750	11289	5646	4838	116794	4.1
1760	15019	7510	6436	179294	3.6
1770	12955	6478	5552	234296	2.4
1780	7661	3831	3283	319450	1.0

[a] Column 1 adjusted to show notional servant population for any one year within the decade allowing for persistence through average contract length (N migrating $\div$10 x 5).
[b] *Historical Statistics of the United States*, vol. 5, table Eg31 (Pennsylvania white population). Numbers of migrant servants entering the Delaware Valley did not remain in Pennsylvania but went on to New Jersey, Delaware, and a few to New York. Using Pennsylvania population figures to produce an estimate of servant incidence in population therefore overstates incidence. Numbers of servants imported through Delaware Valley ports also traveled south to Maryland, and beyond. On the other hand, Maryland remained a site of servant importation during the eighteenth century, numbers of whom may have entered the Delaware Valley region, perhaps offsetting those who left. On Maryland as a destination, see John Wareing, *Emigrants to America: Indentured Servants Recruited in London, 1718–1733* (Baltimore, 1985), 27. [30% of 1,544 registered servant departures 1718–33 named Maryland as destination. Of the remainder, 47% named Jamaica and other W.I. destinations, 14% Pennsylvania, 7.5% Virginia.]

workforce, and that for most of the eighteenth century, servant incidence was substantially lower.[57]

Salinger's figures for city population are substantially lower than other more recent estimates.[58] To the extent that Salinger understates city population (and hence by extension "work force"), her figures will overstate the significance of servitude in both measures. Incorporating the updated city

[57] In producing my figures, I have summed Salinger's columns 7 and 9 to achieve a total Philadelphia workforce estimate. Where there are data gaps in Salinger's table, I have estimated workforce on the basis of the proportion of population in workforce in adjoining periods for which data are available.

The concept "workforce" used here poses the same conceptual difficulties as "labor force" discussed earlier in the Chesapeake context. Salinger's data indicate that "total workforce" varies from 40–54 percent of population over the period in question (1729–75). See n.47, this chapter, and compare.

[58] Compare, for example, Klepp, "Demography in Early Philadelphia," 103–5, table 2.

TABLE 1.9. *Servants in Philadelphia Population and Workforce (in round numbers)*

Decade Ending	Servant Population[a]	Philadelphia Population[b]	% Servants in Population	Philadelphia Workforce[c]	% Servants in Workforce
1730	285	5808	4.9	3177	9.0
1740	575	8017	7.2	4249	13.5
1750	635	10720	5.9	4996	12.7
1760	903	13413	6.7	6266	14.4
1770	238	15718	1.5	6438	3.7
(1775)	457	18692	2.4	7526	6.1

[a] Decadal averages derived from Salinger, *"To Serve Well and Faithfully"*, table A3, column 3 ("Servant Immigration – Total") and 4 ("Servant Work Force"). The substantial decline in average servant population in the 1760s is explained by the virtually complete cessation of passenger landings between the mid-1750s and mid-1760s reported by Salinger.
[b] Decadal averages derived from data in ibid., table A3, column 8 ("Philadelphia Population").
[c] Decadal averages derived from data in ibid., table A3, columns 7 ("Total Unfree Work Force") and 9 ("Philadelphia Work Force").

population figures while holding constant the proportion of population in workforce suggested by Salinger's estimates indicates that servants did not exceed 6 percent of city population or 11 percent of workforce.[59]

Salinger's figures also indicate that over the same period (1720–75) Philadelphia absorbed some 17 percent of all Delaware Valley servant imports (9,500 of 56,000). Presuming servant labor was indeed concentrated in Philadelphia at much higher levels than elsewhere, the remainder would have been dispersed so widely through the rural population that the servant population of non-urban areas could not remotely have approached the levels observable in the city.[60]

[59] See Appendix III, Table A6. Expressing population on a decade-by-decade basis will smooth out exceptional periods when servant numbers rise above (or fall below) secular trends. In the early 1750s, for example Salinger's data indicate that servant numbers exceeded 10% of city population whether one uses her own or Klepp's city population estimates. On the other hand, Salinger's data may overstate the number of servants actually retained in the city by Philadelphia masters. See Farley Grubb, "Book Review," *Journal of Economic History*, 48, 3 (1988), 774.
[60] Salinger, *"To Serve Well and Faithfully"*, 172–7 (tables A.1 and A.2). The "Town Book" for Goshen, Chester County, 1718–1870 (iv. Chester County Historical Society) lists 60 servants "Imported into this Province and purchased by the Inhabitants of this Township" covering the period 1736–72. The 28 purchasers comprised only one-third of Goshen's farmers. Moreover, 11 of the 28 only ever bought one servant; 10 only ever bought two. One family alone accounted for nearly 30% of all purchases; 3 families accounted for 50%. Migrant servants would thus be encountered routinely only in a small minority of households. See also Barry Levy, *Quakers and the American Family: British Settlement in the Delaware Valley* (New York, 1988), 240.

Overall, estimates of the incidence of servants in general population for Philadelphia and for Pennsylvania indicate that, even more than in the seventeenth-century Chesapeake, the influence of migrant indentured servitude in defining the social and legal relations of work in the eighteenth-century Delaware Valley was substantially overshadowed by the rapid growth of the region's white Creole population. Certainly the institution was of importance in shaping the performance of work. Just as certainly, the great bulk of work was performed within a much wider range of productive relations.

As in the Chesapeake, an analysis of migrant indentured servitude is incomplete without reference to slavery.[61] Mary Schweitzer has argued that slavery "simply was not common" in Pennsylvania, "particularly in the countryside."[62] Salinger's figures indicate that in Philadelphia, on the other hand, slavery had a presence of some significance both in population and "work force" (Table 1.10).

In Pennsylvania, unlike the Chesapeake, slaves did not substitute for servants. "Rather, servants and slaves were used interchangeably throughout the history of the colony, and when unfree labor disappeared it was replaced by free labor."[63] That replacement appears to have been under way from quite early in the eighteenth century. We have seen that, considered as a percentage of Pennsylvania population, imported servants did not exceed 5 percent during the century and were concentrated in Philadelphia. Together, servants and slaves reached about 22 percent of Philadelphia's population in the 1730s, but from that point onward the trend for all bound labor was downward (Table 1.11). Slaves, like servants, were concentrated in Philadelphia although the concentration weakened in the second half of the century as slaves became relatively more numerous in rural areas.[64] Within Philadelphia, they were almost always more numerous than migrant servants.

Workforce estimates (Table 1.12) tell the same story. Slaves peaked at a little more than 20 percent of the Philadelphia workforce in the 1730s, falling thereafter to a range of 13–18 percent in the next three decades, and 10 percent in the 1770s. Although the number of slaves in the city continued to increase, the rate did not keep pace with the general expansion of the population. Together, slaves and servants constituted on average 30 percent of Philadelphia's workforce through 1760, but declined quite rapidly from those levels in the fifteen years before the Revolution.[65]

---

[61] Discussion of slavery here is preliminary only. As indicated above, a full consideration of the overall demographics and law of slavery has been reserved for Chapter 9.

[62] Mary Schweitzer, *Custom and Contract: Household, Government and the Economy in Colonial Pennsylvania* (New York, 1987), 45.

[63] Salinger, *"To Serve Well and Faithfully"*, 17.

[64] See Chapter 9, Section V.

[65] Derived from data in Salinger, *"To Serve Well and Faithfully"*, table A3, column 6 ("Slave Work Force"). Where data are unavailable, I have assumed that the slave workforce constituted 70% of the total slave population. This figure is consistent with those that Salinger reports through 1757. It is not wildly inconsistent with Shammas's lower/upper bounds of slave workforce at 80–85% of the population aged 10+. To narrow the gap would require information on the number of children below age ten in the Philadelphia black population 1720–75.

TABLE 1.10. *Slaves in Philadelphia Population and Workforce[a] (in round numbers)*

Decade Ending	Slave Population	Philadelphia Population	% Slaves in Population	Slave Workforce	Philadelphia Workforce	% Slaves in Workforce
1730	880	5808	15.2	616	3177	19.4
1740	1209	8017	15.1	882	4249	20.8
1750	1131	10720	10.6	792	4996	15.8
1760	1136	13413	8.5	795	6266	12.7
1770	1682	15718	10.7	1139	6438	17.7
(1775)	1394	18692	7.5	655	7526	8.7

[a] Decadal averages derived from data in Salinger, "*To Serve Well and Faithfully*," table A3, column 5 ("Slave Population").

TABLE 1.11. Slaves and Servants in Philadelphia Population (in round numbers)

Decade Ending	Servant Population	Slave Population	Servant: Slave Ratio	Philadelphia Population	% Servants in Philadelphia Population	% Slaves in Philadelphia Population
1730	285	880	1:3	5808	4.9	15.2
1740	575	1209	1:2	8017	7.2	15.1
1750	635	1131	1:2	10720	5.9	10.6
1760	903	1136	1:1	13413	6.7	8.5
1770	238	1682	1:7	15718	1.5	10.7
(1775)	457	1394	1:3	18692	2.4	7.5

TABLE 1.12: *Slaves and Servants in Philadelphia Population and Workforce (in round numbers)*

Decade Ending	Combined Slave/Servant Population	Philadelphia Population	% Slaves and Servants in Philadelphia Population	Slave/Servant Workforce[a]	Philadelphia Workforce	% Slaves and Servants in Workforce
1730	1165	5808	20.0	901	3177	28.4
1740	1784	8017	22.3	1457	4249	34.3
1750	1766	10720	16.5	1427	4996	28.6
1760	2039	13413	15.2	1698	6266	27.1
1770	1920	15718	12.2	1377	6438	21.4
(1775)	1851	18692	9.9	1112	7526	14.8

[a] The sum of "servant population" column, Table 1.9 and "slave workforce" column, Table 1.10

These measures of incidence also use the Philadelphia population estimates that more recent work suggests should in fact be substantially higher.
Results that incorporate more recent population figures suggest that at
the 1730s peak, servants and slaves accounted for less than 20 percent of
Philadelphia's population, and that their combined incidence in population
thereafter fell at a fairly consistent rate to approximately 6 percent in the
1770s. The same trends appear in workforce estimates. Slaves constituted
about 16.5 percent of the city's workforce in the 1730s, falling thereafter to
9–12 percent in the next three decades, and 5 percent in the 1770s. Although
for most of the eighteenth century the actual number of slaves in the city
grew, the rate of growth did not keep pace with the general expansion of
the population. Together, slaves and servants peaked at roughly a quarter of
Philadelphia's workforce in the 1730s and remained around 20 percent until
the 1760s, declining thereafter to less than 10 percent in the 1770s.[66]

IIB. Flows

According to Bernard Bailyn's examination of the dimensions and structure of migration from Britain to North America in the years immediately
prior to the American Revolution, what took place at that time was a "dual
emigration."[67] First, substantial numbers of young unmarried males, traveling alone, migrated from south, central, and western England. Labeled,
somewhat misleadingly, a "metropolitan" migration, this movement
included few women or families and a high incidence of indentured servants.[68] Simultaneously, a distinct "provincial" migration took place from
northern and western ports, involving migrants from Yorkshire, the north
of England, and Scotland. This stream included substantial numbers of
women and children, a high incidence of family groups, and a low incidence of indentured servants. Collectively, metropolitan migrants' principal resource was their labor power. The ideal-typical metropolitan migrant
was "an isolated male artisan in his early twenties, a bondsman for several years of unlimited servitude."[69] The ideal-typical provincial migrant,
in contrast, was a family member. Collectively, provincial migrants represented "the transfer of farming families, whose heads were men of some
small substance, or at least to some extent economically autonomous."[70]
Different people from different places, Bailyn's "metropolitan" and "provincial" migrants had different destinations. Metropolitan migrants went
to Pennsylvania, Virginia and, overwhelmingly, Maryland, where labor was

---

[66] See Appendix III, Tables A6–A8.
[67] Bernard Bailyn, *Voyagers to the West: A Passage in the Peopling of America on the Eve of the
Revolution* (New York, 1986), 126–203.
[68] The accuracy of the label "metropolitan" is questionable because Bailyn uses "metropolis" to refer specifically to London. But migrants leaving from London were in no sense
exclusively from London. They came from all over the country. See n.92, this chapter.
[69] Ibid., 203, 188–9.
[70] Ibid., 203.

in demand. Provincial migrants went to North Carolina, New York, and Nova Scotia, where they hoped to find relief from the hardships (but not destitution) that they had left behind. Not a "general milling and thronging of people," Bailyn's migration was patterned and purposeful: "a work force to the central colonies; a social movement of substantial families to New York, North Carolina, and Nova Scotia."[71]

Though the product of intensive analysis of one short paroxysm of trans-Atlantic movement, Bailyn's conclusions describe tendencies readily detectable in 150 years of prior migrations. First came a seventeenth-century sequence, in which an almost exclusively English migration transferred a total of some 132,000 people to New England (virtually all 1630–40) and the Chesapeake (1625–1700), with about 15,000 to the Delaware Valley after 1675 and a smaller number of others to the Lower South. Second came an eighteenth-century sequence, in which a more varied European migration transferred an additional 307,000–350,000 people to a variety of destinations along the Atlantic seaboard from Georgia to New York, most of whom went to the Delaware Valley and Maryland.

Each sequence exhibits the distinctive "dual" pattern that Bailyn describes. The initial phase of seventeenth-century migration, involving some 35,000 people between 1625 and 1640, was a dual movement of families and of single young males headed for different destinations. Families were in the majority among those going to New England. Migration to the Chesapeake in contrast was completely dominated by unattached youthful males. After migration to New England tapered off dramatically in the early 1640s, seventeenth-century migration temporarily lost its dual quality, becoming until the late 1670s almost exclusively a movement to the Chesapeake of some 50,000 people, largely single, young, and male.[72] After 1675, migration reverted to the earlier dual pattern as continuing Chesapeake migration was supplemented by a flow of families from the northwest Midlands into the Delaware Valley. All told, some 15,000 migrants moved into the Delaware Valley between 1675 and 1700 (23,000 between 1675 and 1715). Both families and single male servants participated.[73]

For the eighteenth century, studies of migrants entering the port of Philadelphia after 1725 contrast the family-oriented migration originating in Germany and Ulster (by far the largest groups of migrants) with the continuing youthful, single, and male character of flows from Britain

---

[71] Ibid., 228, and generally 204–28. See also Nicholas Canny, "English Migration into and across the Atlantic during the Seventeenth and Eighteenth Centuries," in Nicholas Canny, editor, *Europeans on the Move: Studies on European Migration, 1500–1800* (Oxford, 1994), 52.

[72] See, generally, Horn, *Adapting*, 30–8; Games, *Origins*, 27, 47.

[73] Fischer suggests that somewhere between 40% and 60% of the Delaware Valley's initial migrants migrated in family groups. *Albion's Seed*, 434. In *Quakers and Politics: Pennsylvania, 1681–1726* (Princeton, 1968), 50, Gary Nash suggests that approximately 66% of early Delaware Valley migrants (and a bare majority of adult male migrants – 51%) arrived free of indenture.

(considerably diminished for most of the period from 1720 until 1760) and Southern Ireland. The incidence of families in German migration declined over the course of the eighteenth century, relative to migration of younger single persons. David Hackett Fischer argues, however, that during the same period, migration from "North Britain" (North West England, the border counties, Scotland, and Ulster) into the Appalachian Back country was consistently one of families.[74]

The dual migration model usefully refines assessments of migrant population structure. Bailyn's division of that population into "family" (relatively intact households) and "labor force" streams, however, wrongly implies that colonial work relations assigned exclusive, or at least predominant, participation in labor to single, youthful male migrants restrained in conditions of bonded servitude. We have seen that such persons did not represent anywhere near the sum of the colonies' labor force, nor even its largest collectively identifiable component.[75] Given the clear evidence of extensive engagement of women and children in agricultural and proto-industrial work in seventeenth- and eighteenth-century Europe, given the ubiquity of household relations of production and family reproduction throughout the mainland colonies, to include only youthful males in one's description of an eighteenth-century migratory labor force is highly misleading. "Labor force" and "family" or "household" all represent forms of work relations rather than distinct spheres of work and not-work.[76]

---

74 On the character of German and Irish migration, see Wokeck, *Trade in Strangers*; Marianne Wokeck, "German and Irish Immigration to Colonial Philadelphia," *Proceedings of the American Philosophical Society*, 133, 2 (1989), 128–43; and Marianne Wokeck, "The Flow and the Composition of German Immigration to Philadelphia, 1727–1775," *Pennsylvania Magazine of History and Biography*, 105, 3 (July 1981), 249–78. On trends in German family migration, see Wokeck, "Flow and Composition," 266–73, and Grubb, "Immigration and Servitude," 104–5. Both Wokeck and Grubb date the relative decline in family migration to the resumption of emigration flows following the interruption of the Seven Years War (1755–62). Even then, however, Grubb finds that "German immigrants had over four times the proportion of dependent movers" as English. "Immigration and Servitude," 105. On migration into Appalachia, Fischer reports that at its 1770s peak, 61% of northern English emigrants traveled in family groups, 73% of Scottish, and 91% of Ulster emigrants. *Albion's Seed*, 610. See also Bailyn, *Voyagers to the West*, 134–47. See generally the discussion in Appendix I.

75 That distinction belongs, of course, to enslaved Africans.

76 Maxine Berg, "Women's Work, Mechanisation and the Early Phases of Industrialisation in England," in Joyce, ed., *The Historical Meanings of Work*, 64–98; David Levine, "Production, Reproduction, and the Proletarian Family in England, 1500–1851," in David Levine, editor, *Proletarianization and Family History* (Orlando, Fla., 1984), 87–127; R. E. Pahl, *Divisions of Labour* (Oxford, 1984), 17–62; K.D.M. Snell, *Annals of the Labouring Poor: Social Change and Agrarian England, 1660–1900* (Cambridge, 1985), 270–373; Steven Mintz and Susan Kellogg, *Domestic Revolutions: A Social History of American Family Life* (New York, 1988), 49–50; Laurel Thatcher Ulrich, *Good Wives: Image and Reality in the Lives of Women in Northern New England, 1650–1750* (New York, 1982), 13–50, and "Martha Ballard and her Girls: Women's Work in Eighteenth-Century Maine," in Stephen Innes, editor, *Work and Labor in Early America* (Chapel Hill, 1988), 70–105; Christopher Clark, "Social Structure and Manufacturing before the Factory: Rural New England, 1750–1850," in Thomas

With this firmly in mind, let us now consider in detail the characteristics of the populations that seventeenth- and eighteenth-century migrations delivered to the various recipient regions.

NEW ENGLAND. From 1630 through 1640, some 21,000 people migrated from different parts of England to Massachusetts Bay. After 1640, migration tailed off sharply to an average of at most a few hundred per decade.[77] Commonly identified as a religiously motivated Christian exodus,[78] the migration drew a plurality (38 percent) of its participants from the puritan stronghold of East Anglia (Norfolk, Suffolk, and Essex) and from Kent. These people traveled in cohesive household groups with few unattached single males.[79] A further 17 percent of the migrants came from London and the remaining Home Counties, and 16 percent from the southwest. The rest were a scattering from virtually every other region of England.[80] The proportion of youthful unattached males was much higher among migrants from outside East Anglia than from within. In all, approximately 60 percent of all migrants were under age twenty-four; about half of

Max Safley and Leonard N. Rosenband, editors, *The Workplace before the Factory: Artisans and Proletarians, 1500–1800* (Ithaca, N.Y., 1993), 11–36, particularly 19–23; Eric Nellis, "The Working Lives of the Rural Middle Class in Provincial Massachusetts," *Labor History*, 36, 4 (Fall 1995), 505–29; Gloria L. Main, "Gender, Work, and Wages in Colonial New England," *William and Mary Quarterly*, 3rd Ser., 51, 1 (January 1994), 39–66; Joan M. Jensen, *Loosening the Bonds: Mid-Atlantic Farm Women, 1750–1850* (New Haven, 1986), 36–113; Allan Kulikoff, *The Agrarian Origins of American Capitalism* (Charlottesville, 1992), 24–33; Jeanne M. Boydston, *Home and Work: Housework, Wages, and the Ideology of Labor in the Early Republic* (New York, 1990), 1–29; Schweitzer, *Custom and Contract*, 34–5; Vickers, *Farmers and Fishermen*, 60–77.

To recognize the household as a site of working (productive and reproductive) relations does not entail an embrace of the simple model of "capitalist transformation" in which capitalism brings about the modern idea of work with its gendered division of labor by separating work from home, market from community, public from private. It is clear, as Berg writes, that "workplace organisation, techniques of production and their community [and household] context" have always incorporated forms of gender and age division that impact upon the meaning of work, rendering the "organic" pre-industrial "household economy" a myth (64, 89). On this, see also Tilly and Tilly, *Work Under Capitalism*. See also Chapter 8. But the observation does not affect the point being made here – that the household (however organized) is a site of work. Hence, to include only youthful males in one's description of an eighteenth-century migratory workforce is incorrect.

[77] Thomas and Anderson, "White Population, Labor Force and Extensive Growth of the New England Economy," 641–2.
[78] Fischer, *Albion's Seed*, 18.
[79] Thompson, *Mobility and Migration*, 14; Archer, "New England Mosaic," 483. Compare Fischer, *Albion's Seed*, 16–17, 31–6. See also Fischer, "*Albion* and the Critics: Further Evidence and Reflection," part of "*Albion's Seed: Four British Folkways in America* – A Symposium," *William and Mary Quarterly*, 3rd Ser., 48, 2 (April 1991), 260–308, at 264–74.
[80] Archer, "New England Mosaic," 483. Because she concentrates on selected groups of migrants during one year (those taking passage on ships departing London during 1635) Alison Games cannot help us much in constructing an overall demographic profile of the region's population. However, her discoveries are in general reasonably consistent with those reported here. See Games, *Origins of the English Atlantic World*, 42–71.

these (or roughly one-third of the original settler population) were single unattached males.[81] Although few can be identified explicitly as servants, it has been suggested that up to 34 percent of the emigrant population might have been destined for service in New England. Even this extreme upper bound estimate of incidence produces a servant population falling well below 20 percent of total population by the end of the Great Migration.[82] Thereafter, the migrant servant population would have dwindled very rapidly indeed, exacerbating major labor shortages.[83]

As elsewhere in areas of mainland settlement, the surplus of single males among the original settlers meant delayed marriage for men and early marriage for women. Given the region's healthy diets and high fertility rates, early marriage for women meant a much higher actual rate of childbearing than in England. Unlike other mainland regions, the healthy environment and relatively even distribution of wealth promoted family stability and personal longevity. As sex ratios stabilized with the maturing of the first Creole generation, male age at marriage began to drop.[84] These

[81] Archer, "New England Mosaic," 479, 481. See also Cressy, *Coming Over*, 52–63. Fischer faults Archer for inaccurate age and sex ratios, preferring those of Virginia DeJohn Anderson ("*Albion* and the Critics," 268). The difference in age ratios is slight, in sex ratios more substantial although not wildly so. Archer argues that 60–67% of the migrants were males ("New England Mosaic," 480, 482), Anderson slightly under 57%. See her *New England's Generation: The Great Migration and the Formation of Society and Culture in the Seventeenth Century* (New York and Cambridge, 1991), 222, 223. Games (*Origins*, 47) finds New England migrants leaving via London in 1635 to have been 61% male. Games (25, 47, 51, 72–4) generally stresses the youthfulness and maleness of migrants in general and of servants in particular, while also noting the relatively less youthful/male pattern of New England migrants (leavened by family migration) as compared to the Chesapeake.

Both Thompson and Archer report a very low ratio of servants in total migrants among those migrating from Greater East Anglia. Of those East Anglians that could be determined to be servants, Thompson shows most were adolescents or younger: 66% of servants of identifiable age were under 20 (75% of the males and 60% of the females). The youngest was 7. Thompson also shows that these servants were by-and-large "living in the households of their masters and mistresses," came from the same local area as the host household, and migrated as part of the household. This East Anglian "servant parochialism" contrasts with the substantially greater numbers and much greater mobility of the non–East Anglian young males in the migration, who were largely unattached. See, generally, Thompson, *Mobility and Migration*, 114, 124; Archer, "New England Mosaic," 486–8.

[82] See discussion in n.32, this chapter. As we have seen, Games is the only scholar to propose an incidence of servants in total migration as high as 34%, the preponderance of opinion being in the area of 16–17%. At an incidence of 16.5% but holding all other assumptions stable, the servant population by the end of 1640 would have been slightly less than 1,200, or 9%.

[83] References to the scarcity of labor in New England are common in local records and become more pronounced during the 1640s. See, for example, Vickers, *Farmers and Fishermen*, 45–64; Thompson, *Mobility and Migration*, 230; Stephen Innes, *Creating the Commonwealth: The Economic Culture of Puritan New England* (New York, 1995), 101–5.

[84] Archer, "New England Mosaic," 486, 488–92, 494–5. See also Robert V. Wells, "The Population of England's Colonies in America: Old English or New Americans," *Population Studies*, 46, 1 (March 1992), 90–100; Daniel Scott Smith, "American Family and Demographic Patterns and the Northwest European Model," *Continuity and Change*,

conditions enhanced the demographic trends already in place: for the
remainder of the colonial period, "New Englanders had low infant mortality, large families, and long lives." Hence, "the population grew without
the need for new colonists or an imported labor force."[85] Already by the
early 1650s, the emergence of self-sustaining population growth and stable
families had established local natural increase as the principal source of
new labor and family-centered households as the principal institutional
structure through which work would be organized and workers procured.
Near-universal participation in marriage and family-formation confirmed
the pattern.

Labor supply and labor control hence followed an explicitly generational
and intrafamilial dynamic. Age was the crucial line demarcating the legal
difference between master and servant.[86] In itself, this was no different
from other areas of colonial settlement, nor indeed from Britain:[87] in all
areas of British mainland settlement, servitude and youth were closely associated (at least among Europeans). In New England, however, the availability of local sources – one's own children, local adolescents[88] – meant there
was no need for continuous renewal of the region's labor supply through
regular influxes of youthful migrant servants, and hence little impact of
the particular condition of migrant servitude on the legal relations of
work. This would give work and its legal culture a distinctive character
compared to the seventeenth-century Chesapeake.[89]

8, 3 (1993), 395–6; Jim Potter, "Demographic Development and Family Structure," in
Pole and Green eds., *Colonial British America*, 139–42.

[85] Archer, "New England Mosaic," 499.

[86] Vickers, *Farmers and Fishermen*, 52–77; Christopher L. Tomlins, *Law, Labor, and Ideology in
the Early American Republic* (New York and Cambridge, 1993), 244–7.

[87] On the close identity of youth and servitude in Britain, see Paul Griffiths, *Youth and
Authority: Formative Experiences in England, 1560–1640* (Oxford, 1996), particularly
290–350; Ann Kussmaul, *Servants in Husbandry in Early Modern England* (New York and
Cambridge, 1981); M. F. Roberts, "Wages and Wage-Earners in England: The Evidence of
the Wage Assessments, 1563–1725" (unpublished D.Phil. thesis, Oxford University, 1981),
133–63. See also D. C. Coleman, "Labour in the English Economy of the Seventeenth
Century," *Economic History Review*, 2nd Ser., 8, 3 (April, 1956), 284–7; Keith Thomas, "Age
and Authority in Early Modern England," *Proceedings of the British Academy*, 62 (1976),
205–48.

[88] Vickers, *Farmers and Fishermen*, 52–77. See also Main, "Gender, Work and Wages," 56–7.
See generally *Diary of Joshua Hempstead of New London, Connecticut, 1711 to 1758* (New
London County Historical Society, 1901).

[89] See Chapters 6 and 7. During the 1620s, as David Cressy shows, New England's original projectors had conceived of the colony as an extractive plantation; "no place for
a man with a wife and small children" but "a company-controlled settlement" like the
Chesapeake, "manned by indentured workmen." Even when family settlement began to
be mooted, the model remained one of labor supply replenished by constant migration.
Cressy quotes John White, *The Planters Plea. Or the Grovnds of Plantations Examined, and
Vsuall Objections Answered* (London, 1630), 59: "youths and girls ... must be continually
drawn over to supply the rooms of men-servants and maid-servants, which will marry
away daily and leave their masters destitute." (White's statement carries the clear implication that men- and maid-servants could not be restrained from marrying, nor retained

THE CHESAPEAKE. Organized emigration to the Chesapeake began in 1607 and continued spasmodically through the early 1620s, then strengthened substantially in the decades after 1630. Migration had peaked by the early 1670s, but continued strong until flows were disrupted by European warfare between 1688 and 1713.[90] Chesapeake migrants came from roughly the same general areas as the majority of those to New England: at first mostly from the southeast (London, the Home Counties, Kent, and Essex); later from southwest England, South Wales, and the West Midlands, through Bristol, and the north, through Liverpool.[91] London served both as a regional center and as a magnet that drew eventual trans-Atlantic emigrants from all over the country.[92] Bristol's hinterland was more concentrated. The very substantial East Anglian influence that imprinted a lasting familial character on migration to New England was, however, absent from the Chesapeake migration. Family migration to the Chesapeake was largely restricted to the small minority of wealthy migrants.[93]

in service after marriage.) After 1630, however, "the emphasis shifted firmly in favour of a residential and agricultural settlement, peopled by free migrants and their families." See Cressy, *Coming Over*, 42, 44–45 and generally 54–68. I have already noted the low incidence of bound labor in migration to New England. Nor did it have any significant incidence in the resident settler population (Vickers, *Farmers and Fishermen*, 56–7, notes 51 and 52). Winifred Rothenberg speculates that "an agricultural labor force, unconstrained and free to move, may well be a New England innovation." *From Market-Places to a Market Economy: The Transformation of Rural Massachusetts, 1750–1850* (Chicago, 1992), 181. Seventeenth-century evidence suggests that the institutional conditions of that innovation were established early in New England's history.

90 On the earliest decades see, generally, Morgan, *American Slavery, American Freedom*, 71–130; Virginia Bernhard, "'Men, Women and Children' at Jamestown: Population and Gender in Early Virginia, 1607–1610," *Journal of Southern History*, 58, 4 (November 1992), 599–618. On later migration, see Menard, "British Migration to the Chesapeake Colonies," in Carr et al., eds., *Colonial Chesapeake Society*. Horn argues that the peak period of British migration was 1630–60, while Menard's figures suggest the peak period was somewhat later, 1650–80. There is no disagreement, however, that substantial in-migration was a constant feature of the Chesapeake throughout the period 1630–80, and the overlap would suggest that the decades either side of mid-century constituted a period of particularly substantial movement. Horn, *Adapting to a New World*, 24–5. On the abridgment of European migration at the end of the seventeenth century, see Menard, "From Servants to Slaves," 355–90; Grubb and Stitt, "Liverpool Emigrant Servant Trade," 376–405.

91 Horn, *Adapting*, 39–48.

92 On migration to London and eventual transatlantic migration from London, see James P. Horn, "Servant Emigration to the Chesapeake in the Seventeenth Century," in Thad W. Tate and David L. Ammerman, editors, *The Chesapeake in the Seventeenth Century: Essays on Anglo-American Society* (Chapel Hill, 1979), 51–95, at 70–4; Games, *Origins*, 13–41. On the pull of London and migration patterns in general in sixteenth- and seventeenth-century England, see Peter Clark and David Souden, "Introduction," in Peter Clark and David Souden editors, *Migration and Society in Early Modern England* (Totowa, N.J., 1987), 11–48.

93 Fischer, *Albion's Seed*, 212–46; Horn, *Adapting*, 19–77; Horn, "Servant Emigration to the Chesapeake," 51–95. Horn and Fischer debate the interpretation of regional migration patterns in James Horn, "Cavalier Culture? The Social Development of Colonial Virginia," and Fischer, "*Albion* and the Critics," both in "*Albion's Seed* – A Symposium," 238–45 and 277–89.

Chesapeake migrants, like New England's, were strikingly young. Unlike New England, however, single males were absolutely predominant; the male:female sex ratio among indentured migrants was 6:1 in the 1630s, dropping to 3:1–2:1 during the second half of the century. Males also predominated among the 15–25 percent of migrants who paid their own way (at a ratio, roughly, of 2.5:1). Self-supporting migrants tended to be single, like the indentured, but somewhat older: 75 percent were below age thirty-five but they clustered in the 20–34 age range. Indentured migrants were considerably more youthful – 30 percent under nineteen (increasing to 50 percent by the end of the century) and 80 percent under twenty-four.[94] In fact, the servant population was substantially more youthful than even these figures indicate. Scholars have calculated migrant age ranges from the records of terms of service agreed before departure. But not a few who would become servants in the Chesapeake arrived without pre-negotiated indentures, destined to serve according to terms and conditions specified in local statute law. The characteristics of servants in this group can be learned only from the records of the local Chesapeake courts responsible for determining the new arrivals' ages and terms of service. Although no comprehensive survey of those records has been undertaken with this specific issue in mind, piecemeal research has established that servants retained according to local statute were consistently younger than those negotiating indentures in England. Accordingly, one may conclude that throughout the seventeenth century, male servant migrants clustered in the lower rather than the upper half of the "typical" 15–24 age range. On this evidence, male servant migrants on the whole are more appropriately considered boys and youths than young adults.[95]

The Chesapeake colonies attracted few formed families. Nor did the region prove particularly conducive to local family formation. Disease

---

[94] On sex ratios, see Horn, *Adapting*, 36–7; Games, *Origins*, 47. On age at embarkation, see Horn, *Adapting*, 35–6. Thomas, "Age and Authority," 216, states that of 5,000 1635 migrants leaving for American plantations, well over half were below age 24. Among them were unattached children of age 10–11. Games (*Origins*, 25) finds 70% of this group below 24. Horn (*Adapting*, 36) supplies the following breakdown of youthful indentured migrants by age and sex at several points throughout the century, based on embarkation registrations:

	1635 London Servants		1682–86 London Servants		1697–1707 Liverpool Servants	
Age	Males % (N=1740)	Females % (N=271)	Males % (N=414)	Females % (N=159)	Males % (N=518)	Females % (N=284)
0–15	3.8	3.0	6.5	1.9	23.0	4.2
15–19	27.4	30.0	21.0	25.8	32.0	30.6
20–24	39.9	48.1	51.0	57.2	26.8	46.5

[95] See Appendix IV (Servants' Ages).

routinely claimed a significant proportion of the entering population; those who survived enjoyed much shorter life expectancy than northern colonists. The extreme surplus of single males among migrants delayed marriage for men, and although it encouraged early marriage for women the legalities of indentured servitude greatly inhibited entry into marriage for that portion of the reproducing population encompassed by the institution, whether men or women, thus further hindering the extent of family formation. Late marriage and foreshortened life expectancy for parents limited the size of families. Poorer general health and greater inequalities in resource distribution than in New England dampened fertility. All told, the Chesapeake population was not self-sustaining until late in the seventeenth century.[96]

Nevertheless, local reproduction took place from the outset. Although not sufficient to replace population lost through death and out-migration until the 1670s, accelerating local reproduction meant that reliance on immigration to maintain and increase population declined continuously, at least in relative terms.[97] Until the last quarter of the century, migrant servants completing their terms had greater opportunity to acquire or at least rent land and enter into independent production than they could expect in England.[98] Families were formed, children were born, and a Creole population developed that married earlier and lived longer than its migrant parents, "acquiring time to have more children." Creoles' longer life spans meant children could grow to maturity less impeded by early parental death.[99] The social effects are obvious. Immigration

---

[96] Horn, *Adapting*, 136–9; Carr, "Emigration and the Standard of Living," 271–87; Russell R. Menard, "Immigrants and their Increase: The Process of Population Growth in Early Colonial Maryland," in Land et al., eds., *Law, Society and Politics in Early Maryland*, 88–110.

[97] Anderson and Thomas, "The Growth of Population and Labor Force," 295–305, esp. 303; Carr, "Emigration and the Standard of Living," 273.

[98] Carr, "Emigration and the Standard of Living," 282–6. Horn (*Adapting*, 151–9, 292) argues for a rather more constrained range of opportunity, particularly in Virginia and particularly after 1670. Games (*Origins of the English Atlantic World*, 105) agrees. Yet even on the tougher terms they set, migrants – if they could survive early mortality – do not seem to have disadvantaged themselves by their migration. Acquisition of land, though not easy, was easier than in England. Poverty, though in evidence, was not the poverty of malnutrition or underemployment – "most able-bodied workers [could] feed and clothe themselves adequately" (*Adapting*, 156) – rather, it was a poverty marked by inability to improve one's lot *beyond* subsistence. Without exaggerating opportunity's extent, particularly during the last quarter of the century when increasing out-migration testified to the Chesapeake region's growing concentrations of land-holding and general economic difficulties, Horn acknowledges the comparative advantage of migration: "the region provided opportunities for poor immigrants who survived the disease environment and the rigors of servitude to earn a modest livelihood and perhaps move a few rungs up the social ladder" (*Adapting*, 159). Or again later, "there was the possibility, if they lived long enough, of forming their own households on their own land, which was more than England offered them." Given a choice, "it is unlikely that many would have chosen to return home" (*Adapting*, 292).

[99] Carr, "Emigration and the Standard of Living," 273. See, generally, Lois Green Carr and Lorena S. Walsh, "The Standard of Living in the Colonial Chesapeake," *William and Mary Quarterly*, 3rd Ser., 45, 1 (January 1988), 135–59.

meant a constant supply of new youthful labor, but increasingly migrant servants became one part of, rather than the main component in, local population.[100]

The distribution of servants in the third quarter of the century reinforces an image of a society not starkly divided between a small free and a large bound population. Most plantations were small, worked by families or male partners; many had no bound laborers at all. Most servants were scattered among small plantations, not concentrated on large units. Most plantation masters relied on a mixture of servants, family members, and hired hands.[101] Indeed, to the extent that youthful migrant servants substituted for scarcities in local family labor, one can conclude that immigrant servitude in the Chesapeake sustained a local society that shared certain structural characteristics with New England. In both regions, settlers set up production in household units; in both, they relied upon the young to supply most of the dependent labor. The relational form that youthful dependency took differed, but not the fact of it.

As the century progressed, however, Chesapeake settlers increasingly divided the land differently than those of New England. A sustained increase in the average size of plantations began after mid-century, as a minority of established planters began adding considerable new investments in land and migrant labor to their existing holdings. Concentration of landholding squeezed poorer planters and comprehensively undermined opportunities for migrants completing terms of service to acquire land. The effects of both developments – the drive to expand production and to improve the rate of return from land, and the deterioration of opportunity for migrant servants who had done their time – were accentuated by poor tobacco prices, which placed a premium on ready access to capital and credit networks as well as on returns to scale.[102] By the 1690s, the result was heightened stratification within Creole society and rates of out-migration among

---

[100] Horn argues that by the 1660s the population was divided into two roughly equal segments. One segment was "dependents" – that is "servants, slaves, and recently freed men and women." The other was the free Creole population, mostly (about 40%) "small and middling planters, including tenant farmers, who used their own family labor to work their holding or who possessed a few servants," the rest (about 10%) "wealthy planters, merchants, gentry, and a small group of artisans (*Adapting*, 160). My own estimates (assuming that 5 years is a reasonable demarcation of "recently freed") suggest that by the 1660s the "dependent" segment of the population was rather closer to one-third than one-half, and that this segment was itself divided 60–40 between bound workers and the recently freed.

[101] Lois Green Carr and Lorena S. Walsh, "Economic Diversification and Labor Organization in the Chesapeake, 1650–1820," in Innes, ed., *Work and Labor in Early America*, 153, 149–57. Horn, *Adapting*, 281–3.

[102] Russell R. Menard, "From Servant to Freeholder: Status Mobility and Property Accumulation in Seventeenth Century Maryland," *William and Mary Quarterly*, 3rd Ser., 30, 1 (January 1973), 37–64, at 57–9, 60; Lorena S. Walsh, "Servitude and Opportunity in Charles County, Maryland," in Land et al., eds., *Law, Society and Politics in Early Maryland*, 127. On accelerating land engrossment and declining opportunity for smallholders and former servants after 1660, see Parent, *Foul Means*, 25–40.

former servants reaching "epidemic" proportions.[103] Meanwhile, European warfare's interruption of shipping after 1688 disrupted what was already a dwindling supply of youthful migrant labor. Wealthy planters' demand for labor after mid-century had been responsible for the initial (post-1660) movement toward serious slave importation. The circumstances of the 1690s turned Chesapeake planters at large to greatly expanded reliance on slavery.[104] Servant immigrants continued to enter the region, particularly Maryland, but their presence in the labor force was completely overshadowed by the importation (and natural increase) of enslaved Africans. Henceforth, slavery would determine the dynamics of work relations in the Chesapeake, not only between whites and blacks, but also among whites.[105]

THE MID-ATLANTIC COLONIES. Seventeenth-century British emigrants to New England and the Chesapeake came largely from southern and western England. As movement from these areas slowed toward the end of the century, emigration from the Midlands and the north of England increased – at first from the North Midlands (Cheshire, Nottinghamshire, Derbyshire) and the Pennine counties (Lancashire and Yorkshire), but increasingly supplemented by movement from the border counties (Cumberland and Westmoreland), Scotland, and Ulster. Some movement from these areas had already occurred through the staging areas of London and Bristol, but by 1680 Liverpool had become a rival and much more convenient point of embarkation.[106]

Some of these "North British" emigrants continued to land in the Chesapeake.[107] Beginning in the 1680s, however, substantial numbers headed for the Delaware Valley, a region already thinly settled by a scattering of European migrants.[108] After 1713 this movement widened to encompass the first non-British mass immigration, that of ethnic Germans from the southern Rhineland (southwest Germany and Switzerland).[109]

---

[103] Lois Green Carr and Russell R. Menard, "Immigration and Opportunity: The Freedman in Early Colonial Maryland," in Tate and Ammerman, eds., *The Chesapeake in the Seventeenth Century*, 236, 230–40.

[104] Menard, "From Servants to Slaves," 373–4, 385–8; Grubb and Stitt, "Liverpool Emigrant Servant Trade," 380–83; Allan Kulikoff, *Tobacco and Slaves: The Development of Southern Cultures in the Chesapeake, 1680–1800* (Chapel Hill, 1986), 37–40; Parent, *Foul Means*, 55–79.

[105] The classic account of this dynamic is Edmund Morgan's. See his *American Slavery, American Freedom*, 295–387.

[106] See Horn, *Adapting*, 43, 39–41.

[107] Grubb and Stitt, "Liverpool Emigrant Servant Trade," 385–7.

[108] Fischer, *Albion's Seed*, 420–4, 445–51. One should assume that after 1688, wartime interruptions also caused lengthy pauses in the flow of North British emigrants into the Delaware Valley.

[109] By mid-century, Germans were the largest single ethnic group in the Pennsylvania region, at some 42% of population. Settlers of English and Welsh origin accounted for approximately 28%, as did Ulster and Southern Irish. See Fischer, *Albion's Seed*, 431 n.7. On German migration, see generally A. G. Roeber, *Palatines, Liberty and Property: German Lutherans in Colonial British America* (Baltimore, 1993), 27–205, 243–82; Grubb, "Immigration and Servitude," 1–12; Wokeck, *Trade in Strangers*; Fogleman, *Hopeful Journeys*.

In several respects the first phase of migration into the Delaware Valley (1675–1715) resembled the Great Migration to New England a half-century before. Approximately the same number of people was involved. Each movement had a strong ideological and institutional core inspired by dissenting religion, Quakerism in the Delaware Valley case. Each had a strong regional core, the trans-Pennine north and North Midlands in the Delaware Valley case.[110] Finally, each had a pronounced "family" character: approximately 50 percent of the Delaware Valley migrants arriving during the first half of the 1680s traveled in family groups.[111]

The familial imprint on the early Delaware Valley migrant stream attests to the likelihood of an emigrant population somewhat younger than the contemporaneous English population, and thus suggests an age profile similar to other seventeenth-century English migrations to North America. The earliest emigrants also included numbers of servants.[112] Higher than in the earlier migration to New England, the incidence of servants in the Delaware migration did not approach the levels witnessed in the Chesapeake.[113] Socially, however, they were similar. First, migrants traveling apart from family groups were much more likely to be male than female. Second, they were also much more likely to be adolescents than adults. Local court records indicate that, as in the Chesapeake migration, a substantial proportion of imported servants were boys in early- to mid-adolescence.[114] Servants traveling with family groups in intact households were also likely (as in the East Anglian migration to Massachusetts) to be children.[115] Overall, service and youth were as closely related in the early Delaware Valley as elsewhere on the North American mainland.

[110] The Delaware Valley's ethnic Germans also shared a core regional point of origin, as Fogleman makes clear in *Hopeful Journeys*, 15–65.

[111] Fischer, *Albion's Seed*, 434.

[112] Ibid., 437.

[113] Gary Nash suggests that approximately 34% of all early settlers were indentured, and 49% of adult males, but that persistence in population had fallen to no more than 10% by the end of the seventeenth century. *Quakers and Politics*, 50, 279. David Galenson concludes that although Pennsylvania began appearing as a recorded destination for indentured servants in the 1680s, it did not become a major importer of servants until the eighteenth century. *White Servitude*, 85.

[114] In the eight years following October 1683, 83 persons were recorded as appearing before the Chester County Court of Quarter Sessions to have terms of service set in "custom of country" hearings. Of these, three were adults and the remaining eighty minors. The mean age of the minors (as judged) was 13 years 2 months. Sixty-seven were boys (mean age 13) and 13 were girls (mean age 13½), a ratio of 5:1. See Chester County, Pennsylvania, *Docket and Proceedings of the County Court*, v.1–2 (1681–97), transcribed as *Records of the Courts of Chester County, Pennsylvania*, 2 v.

[115] According to Gary Nash, "many of the servants were actually nephews, nieces, cousins, and children of friends of emigrating Englishmen, who paid their passage in return for their labor once in America." Gary Nash, *The Urban Crucible: Social Change, Political Consciousness, and the Origins of the American Revolution* (Cambridge, Mass., 1979), 15. Barry Levy similarly observes that the servants who accompanied Quaker settlers were "often the children of neighbors in England." See his *Quakers and the American Family*, 138. Levy suggests that Quaker migrants confronted by the laborious

After 1713, migrants from the Palatinate and from Ulster became prominent in the Delaware Valley migrant stream. Migrants' characteristics, however, remained relatively constant. Both the German and the Ulster (although not the Southern Irish) migrants came largely in family groups with considerable numbers of dependent children. Given that almost 44 percent of adult male migrants and 37.5 percent of females were in the sixteen to twent-five age bracket, and that they were accompanied by large numbers of dependent children, one may be certain that at least 60 percent of ethnic-German migrants were below age twenty-five and that at least 47 percent were below the age of twenty.[116] Among the Germans, the numbers of independent single males migrating rose over time, hence the composition of the German migration became relatively less family-oriented. But there was little change in its age distribution.[117]

Migrant numbers rose as the century progressed, but migration was a secondary factor in sustaining Delaware Valley population growth. Virtually from the beginning of English settlement, local population growth rates consistently exceeded those of New England and the Chesapeake.[118] Fertility rates across the region were high, reflecting the youthfulness of the population, early marriage ages for women, and the comparatively healthy environment. Early birth rates were retarded by male-female gender imbalance, which capped family-formation, and by servitude's imposition of a delay of entry into marriage, mostly affecting men. Nevertheless, by the early eighteenth century the region's population was growing primarily by natural increase.[119] The young family orientation of the German migrant stream furthered the process.[120] By the 1720s, even Philadelphia – described as

demands of colonizing the Delaware Valley supplemented the labor of their own children and accompanying child servants by also taking unaccompanied "strangers" into their households as laborers. But as we have just seen (in n.114) – and as was the case throughout the seventeenth-century mainland colonies – these "strangers" were as likely as not to be children too.

116 During the period 1730–8, for example, 10,670 Germans were recorded as taking passage for Philadelphia. Of these, 3,997 were men over 16 and the remainder, women and children. The latter group breaks down at approximately 1.176 children per woman, suggesting that there were 3,607 children and 3,066 women. Given that 44% of the men, 37.6% of the women, and all of the children were 25 or younger, one can conclude that 61% of the migrant stream was below that age. Given that 19% of the men, 20.3% of the women, and all the children were 20 or younger, one can conclude that 47% of the migrant stream was below that age. Estimates calculated from figures supplied in Wokeck, "Flow and Composition," 260, adjusted for age and social composition by the estimates presented in Farley Grubb, "German Immigration to Pennsylvania, 1709 to 1820," *Journal of Interdisciplinary History*, 20, 3 (Winter 1990), 421, 427.

117 Grubb, "German Immigration to Pennsylvania," 427.

118 Russell R. Menard, "Was There a 'Middle Colonies Demographic Regime'?" *Proceedings of the American Philosophical Society*, 133, 2 (1989), 215–18, at 216.

119 Susan E. Klepp, "Fragmented Knowledge: Questions in Regional Demographic History," *Proceedings of the American Philosophical Society*, 133, 2 (1989), 223–33.

120 Grubb, "German Immigration," 435–6.

a "demographic disaster" during its early years – was moving toward self-sustaining growth.[121]

Immigration continued to supply bound labor. Overall, about 40 percent of all voluntary migrants entering the Delaware Valley after 1720 underwent a period of servitude.[122] Yet the rapid growth of the Creole population underscores that, as elsewhere, immigrants were only one of a number of sources of labor for the region. Bound immigrant labor substituted for shortages of family labor in the households – rural and urban – that, as elsewhere, were the key units of production. We have seen that over time, the servant population became concentrated in Philadelphia and other regional urban centers, but initially servants were as likely to be found in rural and agricultural pursuits as in urban. More to the point, however, in no area did their percentage incidence in population exceed single digits.[123]

Conclusion

The purpose of this opening chapter has been to confront and reconsider a commonly held perception of the composition of the early American working population. Specifically, I have demonstrated that migrant indentured servitude was not as significant either in supplying labor en masse or in determining the structure and culture of early American work relations as historians have argued.[124] Although an important source of labor power for many of the mainland colonies of English North America in their crucial initial phases of establishment and early growth, migrant servitude became substantially less crucial as settler populations moved toward self-sustained growth and as local reproduction became a significant source of labor power. The ideal-typical migrant servant was not a

---

[121] Klepp, "Demography in Early Philadelphia," 92, 91–96. As Klepp shows, Philadelphia did not enjoy a sustained positive rate of natural increase until mid-century, when death rates began to fall consistently. By the 1720s, however, birth rates had risen to the point where they at least offset high death rates.

[122] Between 1720 and 1770, the incidence of servants in overall migration appears to vary narrowly around 40% between 1720 and 1750 and around 46% between 1760 and 1775, with an intervening fall to about 36% in the 1750s. These figures reflect the varying incidence of servitude among different ethnic migrant groups. For a detailed breakdown, see Tables 1.6 and 1.7, and Appendix I.

[123] See Tables 1.8 and 1.9. See also Farley Grubb, "Immigrant Servant Labor: Their Occupational and Geographic Distribution in the Late Eighteenth-Century Mid-Atlantic Economy," *Social Science History*, 9, 3 (Summer 1985), 249–75, at 251–5.

[124] For similar conclusions see Abbot Emerson Smith, *Colonists in Bondage: White Servitude and Convict Labor in America, 1607–1776* (Chapel Hill, 1947), 336 (by the 1670s, servants constituted about 10% of the mainland white population and declining in incidence); Farley Grubb, "The End of European Immigrant Servitude in the United States: An Economic Analysis of Market Collapse, 1772–1835," *Journal of Economic History*, 54, 4 (1994), 796 n.5 (servants, under 10% of the mainland colonial population by 1700); Alice Hanson Jones, *American Colonial Wealth: Documents and Methods*, 2nd ed. (New York, 1978), 3, 1787, table 4.21 (servants, 2.3% of the population by 1770s).

gang-laborer in waiting but a youth who substituted for scarcities in family labor in a mode of production largely organized through households.

This simple amendment has important consequences. First, one is freed to appreciate the variety of performances of work and labor – material production and reproduction – in early America. Rather than a colonial-era European workforce predominantly unfree and debased, continuously refreshed in that character by successive waves of bound migrants, gradually giving way in the late eighteenth century to the "free labor" of modern imagination, one encounters a working population segmented by age, gender, and race, and working according to highly differentiated legal regimes. I shall establish later in this book that legal relations of work clearly approximating "free" labor existed among white Creole males well over a century before the Revolution, just as legal relations reproducing forms of unfree or legally coerced labor for civically "free" persons clearly existed long after.[125] Given the prevailing segmentation of the working population before and after the Revolutionary era, the contention that the era itself marked a decisive point of transition from unfreedom to freedom as the prototypical condition of working life, a transformation in civic identity of historic proportions that "alter[ed] the outlook for 'freedom' for most Americans,"[126] is unsustainable. In light of the composition and conditions of the colonial-era working population and continuities in those conditions with its antebellum successor, trends outlined by scholars in support of that contention turn out rather less momentously transformative, and certainly less linear, than they have supposed. If one were to identify a transformational moment in the history of material production and reproduction in Mainland English America, it would necessarily be the massive and decisive and widespread turn to African slavery that began in the later seventeenth century and continued for nearly two centuries.

To make the point simply, I have presented the numbers here as if they could "speak for themselves," that is, more or less on their own, bereft of context. But to broaden the portrait of migration, servitude, and labor force composition detailed here, it is necessary to move beyond the numbers per se. Numbers do not create their own meanings. Manning (or "peopling") is not an autonomous self-directing process that occurs independently of environments, ideas, or institutions. Early American history has tended to treat the arrival and "settlement" of European migrants on the North American mainland as if it were a naturally occurring event. It was not. The elder Hakluyt, we have seen, succinctly identified manning

---

[125] See principally Chapters 6, 7, and 8. Christopher Tomlins, "Early British America, 1585–1830," in Paul Craven and Douglas Hay, editors, *Masters, Servants, and Magistrates in Britain and the Empire, 1562–1955* (Chapel Hill, 2004); Tomlins, *Law, Labor and Ideology,* 223–92. See also Robert J. Steinfeld, *Coercion, Contract and Free Labor in the Nineteenth Century* (New York and Cambridge, 2001); Amy Dru Stanley, *From Bondage to Contract: Wage Labor, Marriage, and the Market in the Age of Slave Emancipation* (New York and Cambridge, 1998).

[126] Fogleman, "Slaves, Convicts, and Servants,"45, 65–6.

as a deliberate act integral to colonization – to "planting" and "keeping."
Manning injected alien populations into the North American landmass to
produce commodities but also to occupy territory and create tangible signs
of possession. To assess more fully the significance of manning, I will next
consider how these serial migrations were managed. Then I will consider
the larger meaning of the process to which manning contributed so much –
the process of colonizing itself, and of keeping what was colonized.

2

Planting: "Directed and Conducted Thither"

"It is not a kingdom without subjects and government."

Bates' Case (Exchequer 1606), Judgment of Baron Clark

To examine the demographic history of early America is to discover certain abiding continuities. The first is the simple ubiquity of *movements* of population – whether indigenous, European, or African, whether transoceanic or intraregional, vast or small, voluntary or coerced – and an accompanying consciousness of movement.[1] Second comes the equally ubiquitous phenomenon, among the introduced populations, of rapid *growth*. During the first two centuries, the non-indigenous peoples of the mainland English colonies grew from none to 2.7 million. Though rates of population growth varied across regions and periods, natural increase quickly outpaced increase attributable to immigration. From these facts of life one can identify a third continuity in the demographic history of English America, that from its inception its foundational reality was one of relentless *expansion*. Migration and natural increase transformed the first tattered enclaves of foreign strangers into teeming Creole populations, whose expansive mobility and incessant demand for productive land pressed unremittingly on indigenous inhabitants decimated by disease and warfare. According to the Shawnee people of the mid-eighteenth century Ohio Valley, the newcomers were "like Piggons." Suffer but a pair to reside, "thayd Draw to them whole Troopes" and take all the land from its inhabitants.[2]

The Shawnee experience was but one of many indigenous encounters with the physical, spatial expression of the "manning, planting and keeping" outlined by the elder Richard Hakluyt two centuries earlier. Collectively those encounters expose one of the deep connections between law and political economy upon which the process of colonizing depended for its dynamic; namely, the facilitation of transfer, the displacement of one population by another, through the agency of legal ideas and instrumentalities. Intermingled discourses – of sovereign jurisdiction over transoceanic territory and of the right to occupy and rule that territory so far

---

[1] Particularly evidenced in widespread statutory restraint of illicit mobility (runaway servants and slaves). See Chapters 6 and 9.

[2] In Eric Hinderaker, *Elusive Empires: Constructing Colonialism in the Ohio Valley, 1673–1800* (New York and Cambridge, 1997), 136.

as it should please the Crown to do so (the majestic claim of *imperium* and *dominium*); of civility in encounter with barbarity and of the justice of the wars that resulted; of rights of conquest, of occupation of vacant spaces, of title earned by use and improvement – all molded English possession and inhabitation of the mainland. Their deployment rendered law a principal technology for the colonizing project's realization.[3] Documents such as Crown letters patents (charters), agreements and treaties, imported practices such as tenures and deeds (the impedimenta of English land law, whether of the "feudal type,"[4] or its modern contractual successors) together imposed a dense structure of both jurisdictional and substantive claims upon the North American landmass and its indigenous populations. Confronted by a later resort to such instrumentalities, the Tswana-speaking peoples of Southern Africa would aptly call law "the English mode of warfare."[5]

Both as intellectual project and as actual event, colonizing began not on the frontier, where "contact" was made, but in the metropolis.[6] It was there that English propensities for demographic mobility, for adventure, for conquest, were transformed into the potent actuality of transoceanic expedition. As projectors undertook the work of imagining England's intrusions upon mainland North America, further, metropolitan law would furnish the ideational structures of rule, jurisdiction, and ownership that began the reorganization of mainland terrain into English "colonies."

---

[3] These matters are discussed at length in Chapters 3 and 4. For earlier thoughts, see Christopher Tomlins, "The Legal Cartography of Colonization, the Legal Polyphony of Settlement: English Intrusions on the American Mainland in the Seventeenth Century," *Law and Social Inquiry*, 26, 2 (Spring 2001), 315–72; and "Law's Wilderness: The Discourse of English Colonizing, the Violence of Intrusion, and the Failures of American History," in John Smolenski et al., editors, *New World Orders: Violence, Sanction and Authority in the Early Modern Americas, 1500–1825* (Philadelphia, 2005), 21–46. See also Ken MacMillan, *Sovereignty and Possession in the English New World: The Legal Foundations of Empire, 1576–1640* (Cambridge and New York, 2006).

[4] James Willard Hurst, *Law and the Conditions of Freedom in the Nineteenth-Century United States* (Madison, Wis., 1956), 12.

[5] John Comaroff, "Colonialism, Culture and the Law: A Foreword," *Law & Social Inquiry*, 26, 2 (Spring 2001), 306. The indigenous experience in British America was not discernibly distinct. "Delawares, Iroquois, Shawnees, and others discovered that while they considered a treaty sustenance for a relationship between peoples, colonists thought of it primarily as an engine of empire." James H. Merrell, *Into the American Woods: Negotiators on the Pennsylvania Frontier* (New York, 1999), 281.

[6] Patricia Seed has done much to remind historians of the complexity of the enactments of possession through which European colonizers proclaimed rule on their arrival in the New World: "planting crosses, standards, banners, and coats of arms – marching in processions, picking up dirt, measuring the stars, drawing maps, speaking certain words, or remaining silent." Patricia Seed, *Ceremonies of Possession in Europe's Conquest of the New World, 1492–1640* (Cambridge, 1995), 2. But a point is missing, namely that at least in the English case the most important initiating ceremonies of all were those that took place in Europe, for it was there that the "territories" in question were created, named, claimed, and divided, rights recognized, usages planned and outlined, and disputes settled. Ceremonies of possession in the New World were ceremonies of culmination, not initiation.

Chapters 3 and 4 will examine the law of intrusion and reorganization in some detail. But law did more than facilitate and justify the displacement of indigenous occupants. Law supplied the institutional means by which not just new commonwealths (colonies) but new populations to inhabit them were organized. Law established the conditions of migrants' departure and of transit. Upon their arrival, law had already sketched out the terms on which they were "planted" – turned into settlers and producers.

The history of law in its relationship to the colonizing of mainland America has not much dwelled on its macrostructural capacities.[7] The focus of investigation (whether affirmative or critical) into law's place in the process of English transfer has remained the venerable trope that settlers carried with them "as birth-right and inheritance" so much of English law as was applicable to their new circumstances.[8] In this usage, bits of English law are tucked away in the migrant's cultural baggage. The bits are unpacked on the far side of the ocean like the odds and ends of an incomplete tool set, the account itself one strand of a self-absorbed history of settlers setting up shop in an empty landscape. The trope of legal transplantation has proven resilient for the very good reason that, carefully stated as a plural and fragmentary rather than a holistic and unitary phenomenon, it conveys important information about the legal-cultural resources of ordinary migrants, and their deployment.[9] Part II of this book will examine in some detail the legal cultures packed in England and unpacked on the mainland. But law was more than a means by which settlers might implement customary "English ways" that would render their new localities a little less strange. Law was the conceptual structure, the organizational discourse, by which their moves were enabled, the bridge that bore them across the ocean and planted them on the other side. First, law established the context for migrants' liberty to be mobile by prescribing its extent; that is, the extent of their freedom to depart one place and move and set

---

[7] But see Anthony Pagden, *Lords of all the World: Ideologies of Empire in Spain, Britain and France, c. 1500–1800* (New Haven, 1995); David Armitage, *The Ideological Origins of the British Empire* (Cambridge, 2000); MacMillan, *Sovereignty and Possession*; and particularly Lauren Benton, *A Search for Sovereignty: Law and Geography in European Empires, 1400–1900* (Cambridge and New York, 2010). See also Mary Sarah Bilder, *The Transatlantic Constitution: Colonial Legal Culture and the Empire* (Cambridge, Mass., 2004); Daniel J. Hulsebosch, *Constituting Empire, New York and the Transformation of Constitutionalism in the Atlantic World, 1664–1830* (Chapel Hill, 2005).

[8] *United States v. Worrall*, 28 F. Cas. 774, 779 (1798). Scholars who would not consider themselves historians of law have tended not to consider law as a technology susceptible to historical analysis, but rather as a "transhistorical constant." See Joyce E. Chaplin, *Subject Matter: Technology, the Body, and Science on the Anglo-American Frontier, 1500–1676* (Cambridge, Mass., 2001), 58.

[9] For examples of varied and sophisticated expositions, see George Lee Haskins, *Law and Authority in Early Massachusetts: A Study in Tradition and Design* (Hamden, Conn., 1968); David Thomas Konig, *Law and Society in Puritan Massachusetts: Essex County, 1629–1692* (Chapel Hill, 1979); David Grayson Allen, *In English Ways: The Movement of Societies and the Transferral of English Local Law and Custom to Massachusetts Bay in the Seventeenth Century* (Chapel Hill, 1981).

down elsewhere. Second, in chartering colonies, law created the new complex jurisdictional and governmental structures into which migrants were fed. Third, within those structures law established the actual conditions and effects of mobility and settlement, influencing who might go where, and who might own what (and whom) and on what terms. That is, law organized mobile migrating masses into discrete socioeconomic segments with very distinct legal-relational profiles: freemen; households (masters and servants, husbands and wives, parents and children); landowners and the landless; the settled and the wanderers; vagrants and runaways; slaves. This great labor of organization was perhaps the most important substantive contribution law made to the English Atlantic empire, at least so far as creation of a macrostructural context for a colonizing process driven by the deployment of labor to produce agricultural commodities was concerned, for this was nothing less than the organization of population to undertake the work necessary, as the elder Hakluyt had realized, to render land permanently occupied and productive beyond subsistence. Finally, throughout the first two centuries of Atlantic expansion, law composed discourses of status that defined the legal and political standing of populations in relation to jurisdictional claims on the territories they occupied; discourses, that is, of subjecthood, citizenship, and sojourn, in relation to constituted authority, both local and imperial.

In Chapters 3 and 4 I describe the structures and discourses of rule, possession, and ownership that created the new western edge of the Atlantic empire. There we will plumb the juridical discourses that naturalized European expansion into the New World, and simultaneously denatured, pushed aside (out, as it were, from among men[10]), those upon whom Europeans intruded. Then in Parts II and III I examine law's labors of construction. Here, however, I propose to linger for a moment on the bridge of migration to observe how law shaped the transoceanic movement of Europeans westward. Here the relationship between law and migration is less conceptual – the creation of an ideal jurisdictional emptiness meet to be filled with sovereign possession and ownership – than instrumental – the means to direct and conduct thither those who would fill that emptiness and the varied statuses they were handed in the process. The migrating population was a vital resource for colonizers. It could not be left to its own devices. Nor was it, either in the terms and forms of its mobilization, nor in its activities once planted.

I. Loco-motion

Basic to migration is the law's place in defining the very phenomenon, capacity for mobility, that is the essential condition of "peopling" itself. What William Blackstone described as "the right which the king has, whenever he sees proper, of confining his subjects to stay within the realm, or

---

[10] See Prologue, n.44.

of recalling them when beyond the seas," underscored the development, traces of which can be found in early-modern England, of an understanding of population – both in general and as particular kinds of subjects – as a resource of the Crown, to be rendered mobile or immobile *propter communem utilitatem*, that is, according to the best interests of the state.[11] In the English case, this understanding was embodied specifically in the prerogative writ *Ne exeat Regnum*,[12] which gave expression both to subjects' duties of ligeance and to the key signifier of sovereignty, the Crown's capacious authority over territory.[13] Blackstone made much of the centrality of "the power of loco-motion, of changing situation, or removing one's person to whatsoever place one's own inclination may direct" to the Englishman's personal liberty within the kingdom, second only to personal security in the great catalogue of ancient and absolute rights of persons secured by English law.[14] But it was, Blackstone noted, a right that could be abridged: "The king indeed, by his royal prerogative, may issue out his writ *ne exeat regnum,* and prohibit any of his subjects from going into foreign parts without licence" whenever "necessary for the public service, and safeguard of the commonwealth."[15] Blackstone's brief history of locomotion's legalities was annotated with examples of restraints stretching over six hundred years to the twelfth century. "Some persons there antiently were, that, by reason of their stations, were under a perpetual prohibition of going abroad without licence obtained." Those specifically forbidden

---

[11] William Blackstone, *Commentaries on the Laws of England* (Chicago, 1979) I, 255–56; John Beames, *A Brief View of the Writ Ne Exeat Regno: With Practical Remarks upon it as an Equitable Process* (London, 1812), 5–6; Kenneth Diplock, "Passports and Protection in International Law," *Transactions of the Grotius Society,* 32 (1946), 44. As the younger Richard Hakluyt wrote in 1584, population was "the honoʳ and strengthe of a Prince." Richard Hakluyt (the younger), "Discourse of Western Planting," in E.G.R. Taylor, editor, *The Original Writings and Correspondence of the Two Richard Hakluyts* (London: for the Hakluyt Society, 1935), II, 211–326, at 238. See, generally, David Harris Sacks, "Discourses of Western Planting: Richard Hakluyt and the Making of the Atlantic World," in Peter C. Mancall, editor, *The Atlantic World and Virginia, 1550–1624* (Chapel Hill, 2007), 410–53.

[12] "The writ of *ne exeat regnum* comprehends a prohibition to him to whom it is directed, that he shall not go beyond the seas; and this may be directed at the king's pleasure to any man who is his subject." *Bates' Case* (Exchequer 1606), judgment of Baron Clark, in Thomas Bayly Howell and Thomas John Howell, compilers, *Complete Collection of State Trials and Proceedings for High Treason and Other Crimes and Misdemeanors,* in 34 volumes (London, 1809–26), II, 371–534, at 386.

[13] See generally Beames, *A Brief View*; Leonard B. Boudin, "The Constitutional Right to Travel," *Columbia Law Review,* 56, 1 (January 1956), 47–8.

[14] Blackstone, *Commentaries,* I, 130–1.

[15] Ibid., 133. See also 261 ("the established law is, that the king may prohibit any of his subjects from leaving the realm"). Should the subject ignore the prohibition "he shall be punished for disobeying the king's command" (256). Diplock, "Passports and Protection," 44, argues that English subjects had anciently enjoyed no common-law right of departure and were prohibited from departing the realm without leave of the Crown, but that by Blackstone's time the onus of restraint was reversed, so that the Crown was required to forbid departure explicitly by writ rather than license exceptions to a norm of no departure, as formerly.

departure without license included all ecclesiastics (by the Constitutions of Clarendon of 1164); all peers "on account of their being counsellors of the Crown"; all knights, "who were bound to defend the kingdom"; and in addition archers and artificers "lest they should instruct foreigners to rival us in their several trades and manufactures."[16] By the reign of Edward I, according to Fleta (c. 1290), *any* person desiring to depart the realm "would act wrongly or unadvisedly, (*inconsultè*), unless he had previously obtained the King's License."[17]

In 1381, in an attempt to control flows of bullion out of the kingdom, an Act of Richard II prohibited carriage of "Money, Vessel, Plate, and Jewels" beyond the realm, except by "the Prelates, Lords and others of the same Realm, to whom sometimes it behoveth necessarily to make Payments beyond the Sea," as also by certain merchants to make good on exchanges undertaken in England. It confirmed the prohibition on unlicensed departure of "all Manner of People," save only "the Lords and other Great Men of the realm and true and notable Merchants" already mentioned, and also "the King's Soldiers," on pain of forfeit to the King "as much as he hath in goods."[18] The Act of 1381 was eventually repealed in 1606 by the statute generally abrogating "all memory of Hostilitie" between England and Scotland adopted in the wake of James VI of Scotland's accession to the English throne,[19] but the requirement that Crown permission be obtained before departing the realm evidently remained unaffected.[20] According to Beames:

> In all the successive alterations which the Rule appears to have sustained by the Constitutions of Clarendon – the pages of Fleta and Britton, and the Statute of Richard the Second, one cannot but perceive, that the Prerogative was clearly the gainer. If its convenience alone was on all occasions suffered to dictate the alteration, so its power was virtually admitted, in being allowed to qualify the Rule at its pleasure, and to shape it in a manner the best adapted to answer its own purposes. The result of the different fluctuations, which the Rule itself sustained, seems to have been the settled notion or proposition, which we find so repeatedly reiterated from one Law-writer to another, namely, that *no person whatever*, let his rank or station be what it might, if he

---

[16] Blackstone, *Commentaries*, I, 256.

[17] Beames, *A Brief View*, 4.

[18] 5 R. II. Stat. 1. c.2 (1381), in *The Statutes of the Realm*, II (London, 1816), 17–18.

[19] 4 Jac. I c.1 (1606), "An Act for the utter abolicion of all memory of Hostilitie and the Dependances thereof beweene England and Scotland, and for the repressinge of occasions of Discord and Disorders in tyme to come," in *The Statutes of the Realm*, IV (London, 1819), 1134.

[20] Failure to comply could result in loss of the liberties of a subject, notably of inheritance (though not as a sanction so much as a necessary consequence). Thus, in *Hyde v. Hill*, Cro. Eliz. 4, 78 English Reports 270 (1582), it was held "if baron and feme English go beyond sea without licence, or tarry there after the time limited by the licence, and have issue, that the issue is an alien, and not inheritable." Though the parents remained subjects and were accountable as such, their breach of license meant their child had been born beyond the envelope of the Crown's protection and was thus an alien.

were a subject, possessed the right of quitting the Realm, without the King's License previously obtained.[21]

Beames's observation is born out in all the letters patent and charters granted trans-Atlantic projectors by the Crown after 1606. The original (1606) Virginia patent specifically licensed the departure of "Sir Thomas Gates, Sir George Somers, Richard Hackluit, Edward-Maria Wingfield, Thomas Hanham, Ralegh Gilbert, William Parker, and George Popham" and all who should willingly accompany them for America, "to travel thitherward, and to abide and inhabit there, in every the said Colonies and Plantations." The grant was permissive and expansive, extending its license to depart prospectively to "all and every time and times hereafter," but it was not a formality, carrying the proviso "that none of the said Persons be such, as shall hereafter be specially restrained by Us, our Heirs or Successors."[22] In the second (1609) Charter of Virginia the Crown again invoked its right to license departure by granting explicitly, as in the first, "that it shall be lawful and free" for promoters of the colony and those they might take with them to depart and inhabit "the said Plantation," allowing the same permissions and provisos as in 1606.[23] License was granted on the same terms in the third (1611) Virginia Charter.[24] In the Charter of 1620 creating the Council of New England, the Crown expressly granted the New England Council lawful authority "att all and every time and times hereafter, out of our Realmes or Dominions whatsoever, to take, load, carry, and transport in, and into their Voyages, and for, and towards the said Plantation in New England, all such and so many of our loveing Subjects, or any other Strangers that will become our loveing Subjects, and live under our Allegiance, as shall

---

[21] Beames, *A Brief View*, 7–8 (emphasis added). MacMillan, *Sovereignty and Possession*, 74, states "It was standard protocol at the time for gentlemen to request permission to leave the kingdom and to report back to the monarch upon return."

[22] The First Charter of Virginia (1606), in Francis Newton Thorpe, *The Federal and State Constitutions, Colonial Charters, and other Organic Laws of the States, Territories and Colonies Now or Heretofore Forming The United States of America* (Washington, D.C.: Government Printing Office, 1909), VII, 3786. Compare Elizabeth I's 1578 letters patent to Sir Humphrey Gilbert for voyages of discovery and conquest to Newfoundland, which granted him and all who might accompany him license to "goe and travell thither, to inhabite or remaine there ... the statutes or actes of Parliament made against Fugitives, or against such as shall depart, remaine or continue out of our Realme of England without licence, or any other acte, statute, lawe or matter whatsoever to the contrary in any wise notwithstanding." Sir Walter Raleigh's 1584 letters patent contained precisely the same language. See Letters Patent to Sir Humfrey Gylberte (June 11, 1578) and Charter to Sir Walter Raleigh (1584), both in Thorpe, *Federal and State Constitutions*, I, 49, 53.

[23] The Second Charter of Virginia (1609), in Thorpe, *Federal and State Constitutions*, VII, 3799. See also "A Proclamation Touching Passengers," (August 23, 1606) in Clarence S. Brigham, editor, *British Royal Proclamations Relating to America, 1603–1763* (New York, 1968), 3–4 (regulating the departure of "Women and persons under the age of twenty and one yeeres").

[24] The Third Charter of Virginia (1611–12), in Thorpe, *Federal and State Constitutions*, VII, 3807.

willingly accompany them ... provided, that none of the said Persons be such as shall be hereafter by special Name restrained by Us, our Heire, or Successors."[25] The Maryland Charter of 1632 granted "Power, License and Liberty, to all the Liege-Men and Subjects, present and future, of Us, our Heirs and Successors, except such to whom it shall be expressly forbidden, to transport themselves and their Families to the said Province."[26] Virtually identical language appears in the Carolina charters of 1663 and 1665 and the Pennsylvania Charter of 1681.[27]

The Georgia Charter of 1732 contained the same expansive grant of license "at all times hereafter, to transport and convey" the Crown's subjects and appended no qualifying restriction.[28] The English Solicitor General had previously affirmed the Crown's authority to prohibit subjects' departures in 1718, however, when restrictions were imposed on the migration of skilled workers. Additional regulations on the migration of artisans were enacted in 1750 and 1765.[29] The prerogative capacity to restrain departures was defended by Blackstone, for though "at present every body has, or at least assumes, the liberty of going abroad when he pleases. Yet undoubtedly if the king ... thinks proper to prohibit him from so doing" it would be

---

[25] The Charter of New England (1620), in Thorpe, *Federal and State Constitutions*, III, 1834–5. And see also The Charter of Massachusetts Bay (1629) in Thorpe, *Federal and State Constitutions*, III, 1854–5.

[26] The Charter of Maryland (1632), in Thorpe, *Federal and State Constitutions*, III, 1681. See also The London and Bristol Company Charter (1610) and the Grant of the Province of Avalon to Sir George Calvert (1623) both in Keith Matthews, comp., *Collection and Commentary on the Constitutional Laws of Seventeenth Century Newfoundland* (Maritime History Group, Memorial University of Newfoundland, 1975), 25, 49–50. See also The Grant of the Province of Maine (1639) by Charles I to Sir Ferdinando Gorges, which reads in part, "that these Presents shalbee a sufficient Lycense and Warrant for any person or persons that shalbee by him or them sent and ymployed thither to goe beyond the Seas and in that manner soe as the persons soe to bee shipped sent or transported as aforesaid bee not such as are or for the tyme being shalbee prohibited by Proclamacon of us our heirs or successors or by any order or orders of the Lords or others Commissioners for Forraigne Plantacons for the tyme being." In Thorpe, *Federal and State Constitutions*, III, 1634. Similar provisions are included in Charles II's 1664 and 1674 grants of Maine to the Duke of York, in Thorpe, *Federal and State Constitutions*, III, 1639, 1643. For contemporaneous restraints on unlicensed departure, see "A Proclamation against the disorderly Transporting His Majesty's Subjects to the Plantations within the Parts of America" (April 30, 1637), in Brigham, ed., *British Royal Proclamations*, 80–2. See also Marilyn C. Baseler, *"Asylum for Mankind": America, 1607–1800* (Ithaca, N.Y., 1998), 30–1.

[27] The Charter of Carolina (1663) and (1665), in Thorpe, *Federal and State Constitutions*, V, 2746–7; 2765. The Charter of Pennsylvania (1681), in Thorpe, *Federal and State Constitutions*, V, 3039.

[28] The Charter of Georgia (1732), in Thorpe, *Federal and State Constitutions*, II, 773.

[29] See, e.g., "An Act to prevent the Inconveniencies arising from seducing Artificers in the Manufactures of Great Britain into foreign Parts" 5 Geo 1 c 27 (1718), and "An Act for the effectual punishing of Persons convicted of seducing Artificers in the Manufactures of Great Britain or Ireland, out of the Dominions of the Crown of Great Britain [and for other purposes]" 23 Geo II c 13 (1750), both in Blackstone, *Commentaries*, IV, 160; Bernard Bailyn, *Voyagers to the West: A Passage in the Peopling of America on the Eve of the Revolution* (New York, 1986), 54–5.

"a high contempt of the king's prerogative" to disobey.[30] The significance of Blackstone's reaffirmation of Crown authority deepens when one considers that it came at a time of rising clamor over "depopulation" of the British Isles by unprecedented levels of transoceanic migration following the cessation of Anglo-French hostilities in Europe and North America in 1763. Debates of the 1760s and early 1770s explicitly recognized population as a resource of the nation-state – its increase to be measured, its movements tracked, its capacities mobilized in the service of the nation's social and economic betterment. The calls for wholesale restrictions on migration to which the debates gave rise were spurred by competition between English and American interests to control this resource; both sides recognized that increase of population, economic vitality, and territorial expansion were intimately related, that population was the ultimate foundation for national power.[31] As Benjamin Franklin wrote in December 1773, artfully speaking the parts both of an Englishman opposed to restriction and of an American lauding the country's development (and thus tempting the migrant), "New farms are daily every where forming in those immense Forests, new Towns and Villages rising; hence a growing Demand for our Merchandise, to the greater Employment of our Manufacturers and the enriching of our Merchants. By this natural Increase of People, the Strength of the Empire is increased; Men are multiplied out of whom new Armies may be formed ... for the manning of our Fleets in time of War." The increase of colonial populations, whether by unrestricted migration or natural growth, would render the colonies "more secure ... they are attached to your Nation by natural Alliance and Affection, and thus they afford an additional Strength more certainly to be depended on, than any that can be acquired by a Conquering Power."[32]

Two hundred years earlier, debates over English population had been just as prominent, but had pointed in quite the opposite direction; not to the loss of an essential resource but to population's excess and accompanying disorder.[33] Legal debates over departures from the realm had focused less on the Crown's prerogative authority to restrain than its authority to banish. The point particularly agitated, that is, was not freedom to depart but elite desires for protection from forcible expulsion. Even though the polarity of debate swung back and forth over the centuries, however, the

---

[30] Blackstone, *Commentaries*, I, 256.

[31] Bailyn, *Voyagers to the West*, 29–66. On English population debates during the seventeenth and eighteenth centuries, see Daniel Statt, *Foreigners and Englishmen: The Controversy over Immigration and Population, 1660–1760* (Newark, N.J., 1995). For a brilliant assessment of the significance of population in pan-European discourses of governance at this time, see Michel Foucault, *Security, Territory, Population: Lectures at the Collège de France, 1977–78*, Michel Senellart ed., Graham Burchell trans. (Basingstoke, Hants, and New York, 2007).

[32] Leonard W. Labaree et al., editors, *The Papers of Benjamin Franklin* (New Haven, 1959–), XX, 522–8, at 526–7.

[33] A. L. Beier, *Masterless Men: The Vagrancy Problem in England, 1560–1640* (London and New York, 1985), 14–48; Bailyn, *Voyagers to the West*, 51–2.

point at the center of the contest – that movements of population could never occur autonomously of sovereign authority – remained consistent.

Nor was this simply a question of movements beyond the Crown's realm, or to new domains claimed beyond the ocean. Large segments of early modern English law addressed quite precisely the police of population within the realm. From poor relief and the control of vagrancy, through the disciplining of labor and mobilization of the idle, to the very enjoyment of civic capacity, the English state attempted to set the terms of social and economic organization under which people lived, worked, and moved. "The result was the creation of a substantial corpus of social and economic legislation, the bulk of it passed in the years 1563–1624."[34] The Elizabethan poor laws were central: beginning with the act of 1572, climaxing in those of 1597 and 1601, legislation established compulsory poor rates for the relief of the impotent, directed the unemployed to work, and severely penalized vagrancy. The latter doubled as a police of the young. Half of all vagrants apprehended were under the age of sixteen, two-thirds younger than twenty-one. In 1597, "vagrant" was defined as any able-bodied wanderer over the age of seven, reduced from the age of fourteen in 1572.[35] Each of these strands of state policy hinted at an understanding of population as a resource to be managed for the benefit of the commonwealth (as did the taking of censuses) though overshadowed by a more elemental anxiety that "masterless" masses posed a threat to social order that could not be controlled through the agency of available social and economic institutions, to which a statutory regime of criminally disciplinable subordinations was the first and main retort.[36]

Propagandists of colonization stepped into this debate, arguing that overseas settlement would remove the threat by "draw[ing] off the excess population and put[ting] to some productive use the swarms of sturdy vagrants who roamed the countryside and infested the city slums."[37] The refrain in the works of the Hakluyts was constant. "Yea, if we woulde beholde with the eye of pitie how al our prisons are pestered and filled with able men to serve their Countrie," wrote the younger Hakluyt in 1582, "wee would hasten and further every man to his power the deducting of some Colonies of our superfluous people into those temperate and fertile parts of America."[38] In his "Discourse of Western Planting," presented to Queen Elizabeth I in 1584, the revival of decayed English trades and the employment of the idle were second only to the advancement of Christianity in the

---

[34] Steve Hindle, *The State and Social Change in Early Modern England, 1550–1640* (New York, 2002), 58–9.

[35] Ibid., 51, 168. See "An Acte for punishment of Rogues Vagabondes and Sturdy Beggars" 39 Eliz. c 4 (1597), clause xv; "An Acte for the Punishment of Vagabondes, and for Releif of the Poore & Impotent" 14 Eliz. c 5 (1572), clause ii.

[36] Hindle, *State and Social Change*, 26, 37–65, 146–75.

[37] Bailyn, *Voyagers to the West*, 52.

[38] Richard Hakluyt (the younger), Preface to *Divers Voyages*, in Taylor, ed., *Original Writings and Correspondence*, I, 175–81, at 175–6.

colonial project. "[W]ee for all the Statutes that hitherto can be devised … cannot deliver our common wealthe from multitudes of loyterers and idle vagabondes."[39] Hakluyt the elder likewise emphasized how, through settlement overseas, "the poore and Idle persons w[ch] now are either burdensome or hurtefull to this Realme at home" might be made "profytable members," particularly the young, with whom "the Realme shall abound too too much."[40]

By the time continuous English settlement was established in Virginia, active Crown engagement in projects to penetrate the "rude parts" of the British archipelago – the Anglo-Scottish Borders, the Scottish Highlands and Hebrides, Ireland – had already brought the establishment of plantations and, particularly in the case of the Munster and Ulster plantations, significant resettlements of population.[41] In embracing the North American colonizing project, the early modern English state added further to its capacities to manage domestic population by encouraging the mobilization of its "excess" for more productive use elsewhere. In the American case, the management of population was elaborated initially in the charters (letters patents) that created colonies, which established how authority was to be exercised over population. Charters licensed departures. They also established jurisdictions to manage arrivals. Migration became a process of moving people from one jurisdiction to another.

Colonial jurisdictions were embodied generally in the creation of structures of governance and relations of authority, and specifically in provisions establishing explicit powers over the movements of people, as in the first Virginia Charter, for example, which granted its licensees authority to expel "all and every such Person or Persons, as without the[ir] especial License … shall attempt to inhabit"[42] within the precincts of the territory assigned in the charter, and as in the third Virginia Charter of 1611, which added a clause granting the London-based Virginia Council broad authority to police migrants' departures to and returns from Virginia, including authority "to remand and send back" offenders against "such Laws and Ordinances … in Use there, for the well-ordering and good Government of

---

[39] Richard Hakluyt (the younger), "Discourse of Western Planting," in Taylor, ed., *Original Writings and Correspondence*, II, 211–326, at 234.

[40] Richard Hakluyt (the elder), "Pamphlet for the Virginia Enterprise" (n.d.), in Taylor, ed., *Original Writings and Correspondence*, II, 339–43, at 340; *Pamphlet for the Virginia Enterprise* (1585), in Taylor, ed., *Original Writings and Correspondence*, II, 327–38, at 330. And see Mark Netzloff, *England's Internal Colonies: Class, Capital and the Literature of Early Modern English Colonialism* (New York, 2003), 95–104.

[41] Jane H. Ohlmeyer, "'Civilizinge of those Rude Partes': Colonization within Britain and Ireland, 1580s–1640s," in Nicholas Canny, ed., *The Origins of Empire: British Overseas Enterprise to the Close of the Seventeenth Century*, volume I of *The Oxford History of the British Empire*, William Roger Louis, general editor (Oxford, 1998), 124–47. See also Michael MacCarthy-Morrogh, *The Munster Plantation: English Migration to Southern Ireland, 1583–1641* (Oxford, 1986).

[42] The First Charter of Virginia (1606), in Thorpe, *The Federal and State Constitutions*, VII, 3787.

the said Colony." The same clause appeared in the New England Charter.[43]
When it came to realizing the Crown's grant of authority "to take, load,
carry, and transport" migrants,[44] however, the practicalities were managed by resort to a distinct body of law, the legal incidents of servitude. In
English law here lay the most fertile cache of capacity for policing populations on the move.

II.   Servitude as Regulatory Capacity

The examination in Chapter 1 of the incidence of migrant servitude in
population in English mainland colonies during the colonial period cau-
tioned against inflating indentured servitude's importance as a determinative characterization of the colonies' working populations. But that
examination did not question that servitude was a significant phenomenon in the process of *migration* or in the police of indentured migrants
on their arrival. As we saw, about half of all European migrants to the
mainland colonies arrived committed to a period of servitude – more commonly in the seventeenth century (60–65 percent) than the eighteenth
(40–42 percent) – with substantially larger proportions (up to 80 percent)
among migrants to particular regions, such as the Chesapeake. In other
words, there is no doubt that indentured servitude was the single most
important institutional mechanism available for controlling the process
of assembling migrants, financing their passage, and distributing them on
arrival. Once migration got fully under way in the 1630s, therefore, it is no
surprise that "most of the laws dealing with … the voluntary transoceanic
movement of people were laws relating to indentured servants."[45] Transfers
of population were crucial to the success of English colonizing in North
America because controllable labor was the key to permanent occupation.
It is unremarkable that labor law – servitude – should become the means to
the organization of those population transfers because the law of servitude
was the early modern era's most efficient means to the control of mobility.
In its turn, servitude became the line of demarcation upon which civic status, its relativities (for men and women, adults and children, masters and
servants), and its absence (for enslaved Africans) were erected.

Historically, few areas of English governmental activity have proven
more constitutive of state capacities to oversee population than the regulation of work and labor. It is precisely in the ambition to control the performance and mobility of labor that one finds the historical point of origin
of what Margaret Somers has called England's "national legal sphere," the
Ordinance (1349) and Statute (1351) of Labourers, conceived in reaction

43 The Third Charter of Virginia (1611–12), in Thorpe, *Federal and State Constitutions*, VII,
   3809; The Charter of New England (1620), in Thorpe, *Federal and State Constitutions*,
   III, 1839.
44 The Charter of New England (1620), in Thorpe, *Federal and State Constitutions*, III, 1834.
45 Mary Sarah Bilder, "The Struggle over Immigration: Indentured Servants, Slaves, and
   Articles of Commerce," *Missouri Law Review*, 61 (Fall 1996), 751.

to the trauma of the Black Death.[46] So too, the Statute of Artificers two centuries later, which in certain respects attempted to give labor regulation national-level expression. Its stated intent, to reduce the several laws on the books "into one sole Lawe and Statute" that "beyng duly executed, shouyld banishe Idlenes," lends some support to the traditional perception of the statute as the domestic key to a systematic mercantilist policy of labor regulation and restraint.[47]

Appearances can deceive, as detailed examination of the statute will indicate.[48] In many respects, the Statute of Artificers was less a transformation than an elaborate accommodation of existing legal-economic jurisdictional structures, corporate and regional. But where no embedded interests held sway, the statute could be forceful. Thus, its regulation of apprenticeship in husbandry was highly prescriptive, undertaken in the name of an objective, "the better advauncement of Husbandrye and Tillage," that underlined perceptions of available population as a resource deployable in the general interest. In pursuit of that objective, the statute required that all "fit to be made Apprentice" (persons aged 10–18 without other calling) enter the service of qualified householders until at least age twenty-one, "the said reteynour and taking of an Apprentice to be made and done by Indenture."[49]

Apprenticeship in husbandry targeted the same broad stratum of the population – rural youth – as the more familiar institution of service in husbandry. But farm service and farm apprenticeship were very different institutions. Servants in husbandry were effectively self-activating. Beginning in early adolescence, they served by the year for board and wages, contracting annually on their own behalf with successive masters until reaching the age of their majority, or until they married.[50] The institution was brought under the umbrella of the Statute of Artificers, which provided for the general enforcement of yearly hirings by justices of the peace or officers of municipal corporations, but the statute had no substantive impact on its form. By contrast, apprenticeship in husbandry was intended specifically for surplus children, orphaned or of impoverished families, unable to find positions as yearly servants. They were required to remain in the service of a single master for the length of whatever term of service was secured by their indenture – anything from three to eleven years – in a relationship supervised by local authorities.[51]

---

[46] Margaret Somers, "Citizenship and the Place of the Public Sphere: Law, Community, and Political Culture in the Transition to Democracy," *American Sociological Review*, 58, 5 (October 1993), 596.

[47] An Act towching dyvers Orders for Artificers, Laborers, Servantes of Husbandrye and Apprentises [the Statute of Artificers], 5 Eliz. c 4 (1563) clause i. Richard B. Morris, *Government and Labor in Early America* (Boston, 1981), 1–4.

[48] See Chapter 6, section I.

[49] 5 Eliz. c 4 (1563) clause xviii.

[50] Ann Kussmaul, *Servants in Husbandry in Early Modern England* (Cambridge, 1981), 3–10, 31.

[51] 5 Eliz. c 4 (1563) clause v, xxviii.

Because English farm servants appear demographically similar to migrant servants (male, mobile, and youthful) migrant indentured servitude has been taken by scholars to be an adaptation of contractual farm service to the economics of transoceanic labor transfer. The Atlantic crossing was simply one more in a series of journeys; "instead of moving from one village to another to enter service, after 1607 English youths frequently moved to another continent." The indenture was a variation on contract; "a credit mechanism by which the servant, unable to borrow elsewhere the money necessary for the passage fare, borrowed against the future returns from his labor. The indenture was thus a promise to repay the loan, and the security on the loan was the servant himself. The length of the term depended on the amount of time necessary for repayment."[52] No doubt numbers of migrant servants were recruited in this fashion, particularly those in late adolescence who had gained experience negotiating contracts as English farm servants and who managed to exert a degree of influence on the terms of indentures agreed before embarkation. Nevertheless, indentured servitude was not a credit-driven adaptation of yearly farm service. Apprenticeship in husbandry had already made indentured servitude well known in England as a means to manage idle or surplus youth. It provided the necessary statutory definitions, and the model of criminal compulsion enforcing a multiyear indenture besides. Both were easily restated in transoceanic terms.

Building the structure of transatlantic migration on indentured servitude thus meant building migration on an English legal foundation designed specifically to ensure that the youngest and poorest layers of the rural population, beginning at age ten, or even younger in the case of orphans, were mobilized for work.[53] Legal design was fulfilled in social outcome. The transoceanic migrant population recruited to service in the colonies, overwhelmingly young and heavily male, reproduced much of the demographic character of the population that apprenticeship in husbandry was intended to cover. Indigent children feature prominently in the early (1618–19) attempts of the Virginia Company to promote systematic migration.[54] The association of children with migrant indentured servitude remained a prominent characteristic of the entire seventeenth century.

Although forcible dispatch of destitute children by English local authorities featured quite prominently in the Virginia Company's recruitment efforts, the mechanism by which the mobilization of population was managed in the transatlantic case was less one of direct state compulsion than

---

[52] David W. Galenson, *White Servitude in Colonial America: An Economic Analysis* (Cambridge, 1981), 8, 9; see generally 5–10.

[53] See Christine Daniels, "Liberty to Complain: Servant Petitions in Maryland, 1652–1797," in Christopher L. Tomlins and Bruce H. Mann, *The Many Legalities of Early America* (Chapel Hill, 2001), 219–49, at 221–2.

[54] Abbot Emerson Smith, *Colonists in Bondage: White Servitude and Convict Labor in America, 1607–1776* (Chapel Hill, for the Institute of Early American History and Culture, 1947), 12, 148–9.

of mercantile investment backed by legal enforcement. By specifying a saleable quantum of service (a multiyear period) over and above the capacity to perform labor, the indenture commodified the migrant laborer as an article of commerce. Migrant servants were exported to the colonies in the course of transoceanic trade. This status – article of commerce – was confirmed in statutes enacted by colonial legislatures to regulate trade. "In regions with a substantial trade in indentured servants," Mary Bilder has pointed out, "statutes often referred to the indentured servants as commodities or discussed their regulation alongside the regulation of other commodities."[55] Virginia statutes of the 1630s and 1640s, for example, "stated that the master of the ship must present a list of persons brought on the ship 'for the prevention of forestallinge the markett and ingrossinge of comodities.'"[56] Migrant indentured servants, moreover, remained within the stream of commerce. Unlike annual servants in England, servants in the colonies could be bought and sold throughout their period of service.[57]

The most elaborated role played by colonial statutes, however, was the policing of migrant labor as a segment of population; that is, specifying terms and conditions of service, disciplining behavior, restraining mobility, enforcing subordination, and generally creating migrant labor as a factor of production. Such police statutes can be found in all colonies, their appearance prompted by the beginnings of substantial migration in the 1630s.

We shall see that, in the mainland colonies, the statutory police of migrant servitude established a crucial line of legal status both in the performance of work and general mobility among Europeans – a line of demarcation between enforceable and unenforceable obligation, between freedom and restraint. The indenture signified when, and when not, the assertion of capacity to control another was legally allowable, of what labor was not "free" and mobile, and what was. It existed in an environment crosscut by numerous other and intersecting lines of social demarcation – of age and gender, of race – to which the police of labor was intimately related. The legal structure of labor was a hierarchy, one in which the freedoms of adult white Creole males stood out against, and were buttressed by, enforceable obligations of service visited more weightily upon others: the young, migrants, and of course, especially, slaves. At the same time, among Europeans, the legal hierarchy was life-cyclical, and as such temporary. It was African enslavement that would establish the cardinal measure of servility, designating a segment of the early American population a permanent

---

[55] Bilder, "Struggle over Immigration," 764.

[56] Act XXVIII (February 1631/2), in William Waller Hening, *The Statutes at Large: Being a Collection of All the Laws of Virginia from the First Session of the Legislature in the Year 1619* (New York, 1823), I, 166; Bilder, "Struggle over Immigration," 764.

[57] Galenson, *White Servitude*, 8–9. Like annual servants in England, English apprentices in husbandry were not legally assignable from one master to another. However, in their case a *practice* of assignment was not at all uncommon. See, e.g., Thomas G. Barnes, *Somerset, 1625–1640: A County's Government During the "Personal Rule"* (Cambridge, Mass., 1961), 186–7.

underclass of workers. It is in slavery, in early America, that one encounters "master and servant" as an expansive and permanent polarity of freedom and its absence.[58]

III.   Natural Subjects and Free Denizens – Calvin's Case

As well as outlining powers to manage migration and govern population, Crown charters also established the overall legal statuses into which migrants and their descendants would fit. Migrants and their children were to be "subjects" of the English Crown.[59] As such they were to "have and enjoy all Liberties, Franchises, and Immunities, within any of our other Dominions, to all Intents and Purposes, as if they had been abiding and born, within this our Realm of *England,* or any other of our said Dominions" (the first Virginia Charter); they were to be "Free Denizens and natural Subjects" with those same liberties and privileges (the second Virginia charter, the New England Charter).[60] Precisely what these terms meant was clarified in *Calvin's Case* (1608), which, in the course of

---

[58] These matters are explored in detail in Chapters 6 through 9.

[59] This was established from the outset. Thus, in the Letters Patents issued to Sir Humphrey Gilbert in 1578 authorizing his voyages of discovery and conquest to Newfoundland, one finds the following clause: "And for uniting in more perfect league and amitie of such countreys, landes and territories so to bee possessed and inhabited as aforesayde, with our Realmes of England and Ireland, and for the better encouragement of men to this enterprise: wee doe by these presents graunt, and declare, that all such countreys so hereafter to bee possessed and inhabited as aforesayd, from thencefoorth shall bee of the allegiance of us, our heires, and successours. And wee doe graunt to the sayd sir Humfrey, his heires and assignes, and to all and every of them, and to all and every other person and persons, being of our allegiance, whose names shall be noted or entred in some of our courts of Record, within this our Realme of England, and that with the assent of the said sir Humfrey, his heires or assignes, shall nowe in this journey for discoverie, or in the second journey for conquest hereafter, travel to such lands, countries and territories as aforesaid, and to their and every of their heires: that they and every or any of them being either borne within our sayd Realmes of England or Ireland, or within any other place within our allegiance, and which hereafter shall be inhabiting within any the lands, countreys and territories, with such licence as aforesayd, shall and may have, and enjoy all the priveleges of free denizens and persons native of England, and within our allegiance: any law, custome, or usage to the contrary notwithstanding." The same clause appears in the Letters Patents granted Sir Walter Raleigh in 1584. See Letters Patent to Sir Humfrey Gylberte (June 11, 1578) and Charter to Sir Walter Raleigh (1584) both in Thorpe, *Federal and State Constitutions,* I, 50–1, 55.

[60] The First Charter of Virginia (1606), in Thorpe, *The Federal and State Constitutions,* VII, 3788; The Second Charter of Virginia (1609), in Thorpe, *The Federal and State Constitutions,* VII, 3800; The Charter of New England (1620), in Thorpe, *Federal and State Constitutions,* III, 1839. Note that the transition to proprietary organization of colonial projects (discussed in detail in Chapter 4) induced changes in the expression of subject status. Thus, in the Grant of the Province of Avalon to Sir George Calvert (1623), in Matthews, comp., *Constitutional Laws of Seventeenth Century Newfoundland,* at 50–1, the Crown provided "that the said Province shall be of our allegiance. And that all, and singular the subjects and liege people of us our Heires and Successors transported or to be transported into the said Province and their Children there already borne or hereafter to be borne Be and

mediating the jurisdictional consequences for English law of James VI of Scotland's accession (1603) to his inherited English throne as James I, also, indirectly, addressed certain of the implications of departure overseas for the status of subjects-turned-migrants, and more generally the actual compass of "as if" – that is, of English law (liberties, franchises, immunities) outside the realm of England.[61]

Calvin's Case arose as a contrived dispute, heard by a special court consisting of the Lord Chancellor and the judges of all the king's common-law courts, intended to resolve the particular question whether subjects of the Scottish Crown of James VI could claim the liberties and immunities enjoyed by subjects of the English Crown of James I after the latter's accession. By resolving that question, *Calvin's Case* would also resolve the more general question of the consequences for English law of the addition of the realm of England to the realm of Scotland.

Resisting a union of kingdoms in any form beyond the purely dynastic union signified by James's accession, the English parliament had rejected the proposition, jointly advanced by English and Scottish high commissioners, that all natural subjects of each kingdom should be recognized as natural subjects of and in the other. English parliamentarians' immediate concern was jurisdiction over the movements of population – they imagined that mutual recognition would result in an unstoppable influx of indigent Scots, exacerbating the problem of English population excess. But they also opposed recognition of the king's Scottish subjects in principle, so as to avoid a "mutual naturalizing of *all* nations that hereafter fall into the subjection of the king, although they be very remote," an outcome that would "disorder the settled government of every of the particulars."[62] Scots per se were to remain aliens, subjects with the rights and privileges of their own kingdom but without the rights and privileges of subjects in England.

Calvin's Case mapped the precise borders of English refusal by considering the status of a particular subset of Scottish subjects, the so-called *postnati*; that is, those born after James's English coronation. With the Scottish king now ruling an additional English domain, the case tested the question whether the *postnati* were exceptional, with the rights of subjects in each one of the king's domains. The vehicle was an examination

shall be Denizens and Leiges of us." In The Charter of Maryland (1632), in Thorpe, *Federal and State Constitutions*, III, at 1681, the same clause underwent further modification, providing "that all and singular the Subjects and Liege-Men of Us, our Heirs and Successors, transplanted, or hereafter to be transplanted into the Province aforesaid, and the Children of them, and of others their Descendants, whether already born there, or hereafter to be born, be and shall be Natives and Liege-Men of Us."

61 *Calvin's Case* 7 Coke Report 1a, 77 English Reports 377 (1608). For summaries, see W. S. Holdsworth, *A History of English Law* (London, 1926), IX, 72–86; James H. Kettner, *The Development of American Citizenship, 1608–1870* (Chapel Hill, for the Institute of Early American History and Culture, 1978), 13–28.

62 Sir Edwin Sandys, M.P., quoted in Daniel J. Hulsebosch, "The Ancient Constitution and the Expanding Empire: Sir Edward Coke's British Jurisprudence," *Law and History Review*, 21, 3 (Fall 2003), 448 (emphasis added). See also Hulsebosch, *Constituting Empire*, 20–8.

of the right of the infant Robert Calvin (born 1606 in Scotland of Scottish parents) to sue in English courts to protect his title to land inherited in England, of which, if judged an alien, he might be disseised.

Land holding in England, with rights of inheritance and transmission, and access to the king's courts to sue in their defense, was a privilege of those who were born English subjects. The privilege might be extended to aliens by the Crown through a formal grant of letters patent of denization, though only prospectively and without heritability.[63] In *Calvin's Case* it was agreed that the vast majority of Scots who were *antenati* – born prior to James's accession to the English Crown – could not be considered born English subjects, and thus could not hold English land or bring real actions in English courts. The *antenati* were aliens, subjects of James's Scottish kingdom alone. At best they could become denizens in England. As a *post-natus*, however, Robert Calvin's status was held quite distinct. Sir Edward Coke, then Chief Justice of Common Pleas, published his opinion in the case, which as a result has become authoritative.[64] Calvin, it was agreed, had been born within James's domain of parents who owed James obedience (and enjoyed his protection). Hence, Calvin was born into relations of ligeance. At the time of Calvin's birth, James's royal domains had already grown to encompass England in addition to Scotland. No political union or unification of Crowns had occurred: considered as polities, Scotland and England remained as distinct after James's coronation as before, simply sharing a king.[65] But ligeance was a personal bond prevailing between the natural person of the king and the natural subject wherever he or she might reside in the king's domains, and hence transcended whatever political and legal distinctions might exist among and between those domains. Ligeance meant that the king's subject enjoyed the king's protection wherever the king ruled at the moment that the relation of ligeance was formed. As a natural subject of the king, Calvin was hence entitled to enjoy rights and seek remedies obtainable from the king's *English* courts within their sphere of jurisdiction and according to the laws of that place, just as he was from *Scottish* courts within their sphere of jurisdiction, or indeed from courts anywhere within the king's domains as they were constituted at the time of his birth.[66]

---

[63] "If the plaintiff's father be made a denizen, and purchase lands in England to him and his heirs, and die seised, this land shall never descend to the plaintiff, for that the King by his letters patent may make a denizen, but cannot naturalize him to all purposes, as an Act of Parliament may do; neither can letters patent make any inheritable in this case, that by the common law cannot inherit." 77 E.R. 385.

[64] On the contemporary influence of other opinions delivered in the case, see MacMillan, *Sovereignty and Possession*, 33–4.

[65] The king himself was of a distinct opinion, telling the English Parliament following his coronation, "I am the Husband and all the whole Isle is my lawfull Wife; I am the Head and it is my Body; I am the Shepherd, and it is my flocke." King James VI and I, *Political Writings*, Johann P. Sommerville, editor (Cambridge, 1994), 136.

[66] See Hulsebosch, "The Ancient Constitution and the Expanding Empire," 454–8. Several years before his English coronation James had written that a king on his coronation

Calvin's Case has long been read for its implications for English over-seas expansion. Certainly, by articulating a "theory of allegiance and sub-jectship" at the very moment the first material expressions of expansion were coming into being, the case clarifies the contemporary meanings that attended the terms "subjects" or "natural subjects" or "liege-men" and "free Denizens" of the English Crown used in the Crown's charters.[67] But as Daniel Hulsebosch has pointed out, both colonists and, later, his-torians would invoke Coke's opinion as evidence for a further claim "that the English common law and related liberties migrated to British North American colonies with British settlers," arguing that the decision in *Calvin's Case* established that subjects of the English monarchy anywhere within the royal dominions had access to the benefits of English law. Indeed, dicta in *Calvin's Case* did have implications for overseas expansion, albeit indirect, but there was little in them to suggest the grand extensibil-ity of English law that later propagandists would claim.[68]

Necessarily, given the circumstances of the case and its substance, Coke's opinion in *Calvin's Case* addressed the legal-jurisdictional consequences attending the addition of new territories to existing sovereign domains. Coke's argument probed the particular question of addition by sovereign accession, adopting for this purpose the position already widely accepted in European law that acquisition of territory came about in one of two ways, either by conquest or by inheritance. Inter alia, this confirmed the acceptance of the conquered/inherited distinction into English law, ren-dering it presumptively available as a point of legal reference for English acquisitions. But this was hardly the point of the case or the reason for the opinion: in *Calvin's Case*, the territory being acquired was the realm of England. Coke's analysis answered to the necessity to establish what conse-quences for English law followed from the accession of an alien sovereign to the English throne.[69]

In cases of conquest, Coke argued, if the conquered territory were Infidel, little restrained the conqueror: existing laws might be abrogated ipso facto and the conquering king might govern at his pleasure "by himself and such Judges as he shall appoint," restrained only by natural equity until such time as certain laws were established.[70] If the territory conquered were Christian, the conquering king was subject to somewhat greater restraint. He might alter its laws, but until such changes were made,

became "a naturall Father to all his Lieges." *The True Lawe of free Monarchies: or, The Reciprock and Mutuall Dutie Betwixt a free King and his naturall Subjectes* (Edinburgh: printed by Robert Waldegrave, 1598), sig. B₅v.

67 Kettner, *Development of American Citizenship*, 7. "Denizens" make their appearance for the first time in the first revision of the Virginia Charter (1609).

68 Hulsebosch, "The Ancient Constitution and the Expanding Empire," 440. See also Bilder, *The Transatlantic Constitution*, 37, who argues, "Although the case tantalizingly hinted at a theory of the legal relationship between England and future colonies ... Coke's opinion merely opened a space for argument."

69 Hulsebosch, *Constituting Empire*, 25; Bilder, *Transatlantic Constitution*, 37.

70 77 E.R. 398.

the territory's existing and established laws would remain in effect. And, Coke observed, English practice in Ireland had established additional vernacular restraints on the exercise of monarchical prerogative. In the wake of Henry II's conquest of Ireland, King John "had given unto them, being under his obedience and subjection, the laws of England for the government of that country." Once granted, English laws thus given could not be altered by the King "without Parliament."[71] Coke was also satisfied that in the interim – that is, the period after Henry II's conquest but before King John's grant, when Ireland had still been under the governance of its established and separate laws – the English Parliament had gained as a result of the conquest the capacity to assert a specific and particular (not general) jurisdiction over Irish circumstance, for "the title thereof being by conquest, the same by judgment of law might by express words be bound by Act of the Parliament of England."[72] Thus, the English Parliament might presume it had authority to legislate (though only "by express words") for territory that conquest had added to the king's realms.

Monarchs like James I, who acceded to a throne by inheritance and not conquest, acted under greater restraint yet. Such a monarch, said Coke, could not alter an inherited kingdom's laws except by consent of its parliament, for upon the laws of the kingdom inherited hung the very validity of the inheritance itself. James was so bound in each of his several kingdoms – in his original inherited kingdom of Scotland to the laws of Scotland and the Scottish Parliament; in his newly inherited kingdoms of England and Wales, and of Ireland, by the laws and parliaments of those kingdoms. James I thus had no authority to alter the laws of England to encompass his Scottish subjects without the English Parliament's consent – which, obviously, he did not have. Aliens remained aliens. But though England and Scotland might be "several and distinct kingdoms ... governed by several judicial and municipal laws" and possessed of "several distinct and separate Parliaments," the *postnati* were not aliens, for as in the case of Ireland after the conquest, though "the realm of England, and that of Ireland were governed by several laws, any that was born in Ireland was no alien to the realm of England."[73]

Because Scotland was equally a kingdom of inheritance rather than conquest, James could not "give" English laws to his Scottish subjects, as King John eventually had to conquered Ireland, without Scottish parliamentary consent. Supposing the Scottish Parliament did so consent, what might be the effect of having English laws adopted in Scotland? A wholesale naturalization of the *antenati*? A backdoor unification? It would appear not. Under King John, "the laws of England became the proper laws of Ireland,"

[71] Ibid. "Parliament" here means the Irish Parliament. See Barbara A. Black, "The Constitution of Empire: The Case for the Colonists," *University of Pennsylvania Law Review*, 124 (1975–6), 1175–91.

[72] 77 E.R. 398. See also Kettner, *Development of American Citizenship*, 24–7.

[73] 77 E.R. 394, 398.

yet Ireland had not thereby become part of the realm of England but had remained, as it had been after Henry II's conquest, "a distinct dominion." For, Coke argued, "they have Parliaments holden there whereat they have made divers particular laws," and "they retain unto this day divers of their ancient customs." Ireland, that is, had once been given English laws; yet the laws had diverged by subsequent action of Irish Parliaments and the application of local custom, such that, domestically, Ireland remained "governed by laws and customs, separate and diverse from the laws of England."[74] How much more would this be the case in Scotland, where under James parliaments would continue to act and distinct local custom prevail. How much more again, one might add, in other dominions, where it was recognized that the laws to prevail were required only to be "not repugnant or contrary, but (so far as conveniently may be) agreeable to the Laws, Statutes, Customs, and Rights of this Our Kingdom of England."[75]

English laws might extend to such other places if extension were explicitly specified "by express words." So, for example, it had been resolved "by all the Judges of England" that by a statute of Henry VIII an Irishman who committed high treason in Ireland might be indicted, arraigned, and tried for the same in England, the words of the statute being "That all treasons, &c. committed by any person out of the realm of England shall be from henceforth enquired of, &c."[76] Here in effect was a specific instance of

---

[74] Ibid., 404.

[75] The Charter of Maryland (1632), in Thorpe, *Federal and State Constitutions*, III, at 1680. On "repugnancy" see Bilder, *Transatlantic Constitution*, 2–3, 40. Bilder (at 40) notes that the phrase expressed both "the desire for uniformity with the laws of England and acknowledged the reality of diversity" flowing from transoceanic circumstance. But one must also note that "the laws, statutes, customs and rights" of England with which uniformity was presumptively desirable were themselves characterized by an immense diversity. As Haskins, *Law and Authority*, 5, puts it: "the 'laws of England' ... included more than the statutes of parliament, more than the law of the king's courts which we call the common law. In the days before the common law had achieved its later ascendancy, the laws of England included the customs of the merchants, the local and divergent customs of towns and manors, as well as the laws enforced by the ecclesiastical tribunals and by numerous other courts and commissions of specialized jurisdiction" – and, as we shall see in Chapter 5, even more besides, both in origin, and in interpretation, application, and administration of what was supposedly uniform. On town and manor custom, see, for examples, Warren O. Ault, *The Self-Directing Activities of Village Communities in Medieval England* (Boston, 1952).

[76] 77 E.R. 404–5. Coke's report cited the statute incorrectly as the 23 H.8 c.33. The statute to which he referred was "An Acte concerninge the triall of Treasons cõmytted out of the Kinges Majesties Domynions" 35 H.8 c.2 (1543) in *The Statutes of the Realm*, III (London, 1817), 958. The relevant passage reads in full: Forasmuche as some doubtes and questions have bene moved, that cten kindes of Treasons, mysprisions and concealmentes of treasons, done ppetrated or cõmytted out of the Kinges Majesties Realme of England and other his Graces Dnions, cannot ne maye by the cõmon Lawes of this Realme be enquired of herd and defmyned within this his saide Realme of Englande; For a playne remedye ordre and declaracõn therein to be had and made, Be it enacted by auctoritie of this pˡsent parliament, that all manner of offences being alredye made or declared, or hereafter to be made or declared by any the Lawes and Statutes of this Realme, to be Treasons, mysprisions of Treasons, or concelementes of Treasons, and done ppetrated or

extraterritorial ("out of this land"[77]) extension by an act of the English Parliament of English common law courts' jurisdiction to the English Crown's other dominions. So also, English courts might claim final authority over the extraterritorial application of English laws, for "by judgment of law a writ of error did lie in the King's Bench in England of an erroneous Judgment in the King's Bench of Ireland."[78] But this hardly meant that "English law" went wherever the English went. Indeed, in *Calvin's Case*, Coke's point was rather the opposite. Each of the King's dominions was distinct – Scotland with its distinct "judicial or municipal" laws and a distinct parliament; Ireland, apparently, with no less, notwithstanding King Henry's conquest and King John's gift. Inhabitants of the King's distinct dominions with the necessary standing (that is, natural-born subjects, whether post-conquest Irish or *postnati* Scottish) might avail themselves of English law, in England. So might they be in equal measure reached by English law, in England.[79] But the message of the case was that English common-law remedies were jurisdictionally confined to the realm of England. Except as specifically provided by the English Parliament, as in 35 H. 8 c.2 (and even then only by courts within that realm acting "*as if*" the matter before them had taken place within the realm), English common-law courts were not available "to redress matters that occurred in imperial territories outside of England."[80]

Though the counter-contention that English subjects settling new lands carried with them the laws of England by dint of birthright would not be formulated for well over a century,[81] *Calvin's Case* did not entirely deny it foundation. Coke certainly implied that the king's subjects had a right to some form of parliamentary governance wherever in the king's dominions they might be. Coke also insisted, explicitly, that "in the case of a conquest of Christian kingdom," the king's subjects, whether they had served in the wars of conquest or not, whether *antenati* or *postnati*, were all "capable of lands in the kingdom or country conquered, and may maintain any real

---

cŏmytted or hereafter to be done ppetrate or cŏmitted by anye pson or psons out of this Realme of Englande, shalbe from hensforth inquired of herd and determyned before the Kinges Justices of his Benche for plees to be holden before himselfe, by good and laufull men of the same Shire where the saide Benche shall sytt and be kepte, or els before suche Cŏmissioners and in such Shire of the Realme as shalbe assigned by the Kinges Majesties Cŏmission, and by good and laufull men of the same Shire; in like manner and forme to all ententes and purposes as if suche treasons mysprisions of treasons or concelementes of treasons had been done, ppetrated and cŏmytted within the same Shire where they shalbe so inquired of harde and defmyned as is aforesaid." For the later significance of 35 H.8 c.2 in American history, see John Phillip Reid, *Constitutional History of the American Revolution*, volume 3, *The Authority to Legislate* (Madison, Wis., 1986), 281–6.

[77] 77 E.R. 405.
[78] Ibid., 398.
[79] Ibid., 408.
[80] MacMillan, *Sovereignty and Possession*, 34. Hulsebosch, *Constituting Empire*, 26.
[81] Hulsebosch, "The Ancient Constitution and the Expanding Empire," 474. But see *Blankard v. Galdy* 91 English Reports 356, 2 Salk. 1 (1693).

action, and have the like privileges and benefits there, as they may have in England."[82] That is, subjects were to carry with them into conquered kingdoms the same capacities to hold lands and vindicate their claims as they had in England. But Coke did not specify what jurisdictional or institutional form either parliamentary governance or the vindication of landed property rights might take – whether by the creation of councils or assemblies or courts or by other means. Rather, *Calvin's Case* consistently supported the argument that wherever they were within the king's domains, his subjects might have resort to the parliamentary and juridical institutions with jurisdiction in that place – "*the like privileges and benefits there, as they may have in England.*"[83] Hence, natural subjects in Virginia had access to and were ruled by the law as it stood in Virginia, administered according to the jurisdictional design, substantive provisions, and institutional structures outlined in the Virginia charters granted by the English Crown. This was not "English law" but law "as near as conveniently may ... be agreeable" to English law. So also in New England under the New England Charter: local law was simply to be "not contrary" to English laws; so also in the Massachusetts Bay Company charter: "not contrarie or repugnant" to English law.[84] *Calvin's Case* underlined that English law as such was available to all natural subjects and free denizens, wherever within the king's dominions they might be born or domiciled, only in England. Guaranteed the status of natural subjects, migrants and their offspring would enjoy those rights on their return. When domiciled overseas and answerable to a local jurisdiction, however, subjects did not gain access to English law per se, but to such law that had been formulated according to the limits specified, and through the jurisdictional structures described, in the charters granting permission to proceed with settlements.

Conclusion

Through the device of the charter or royal letter patent, English law granted migrants permission to depart, created apparatuses of governance to receive and rule them on arrival, and assured them status as legal persons (subjects, denizens) within the king's dominions. Together, English statutes and those prevailing in English North American colonies wrought from the law of servitude an institutional framework for the actual conveyance of the majority of migrants from one place to the other; a relational bubble, as it were, within which they might be "directed and conducted thither"[85] and by which they might be distributed – planted – on arrival.

---

[82] 77 E.R. 398.

[83] Ibid. (emphasis added).

[84] The Second Charter of Virginia (1609), The Charter of New England (1620), and The Charter of Massachusetts Bay (1629), all in Thorpe, *Federal and State Constitutions*, VII, 3801, III, 1832, and III, 1853, respectively.

[85] The Charter of New England (1620), in Thorpe, *The Federal and State Constitutions*, III, 1829.

And if the terms of that framework as specified in colonial statutes might depart from the terms suggested in English statutes, English law had early established a formal relationship between the laws prevailing in England and those prevailing in distinct locales within the Crown's *imperium* and *dominium* that spoke to the disparity, the terms of which were clarified by Sir Edward Coke in *Calvin's Case*: English law was for England; the laws of Virginia were for Virginia.[86] At the same time, by relaxing the relationship between status and place of origin and assigning it instead to birth, Coke's discourse of ligeance allowed natural subjecthood to become fully portable. Francis Bacon asserted a doctrine of "original submission" that was "natural and more ancient than law," that kings had originally governed by "natural equity," that subjection to the prince was "the work of the law of nature."[87] The English state was thus enabled to maintain subjects in a state of continuing jurisdictional accountability to the Crown wherever they might go. Each was a person (subject) that could be policed anywhere within the Crown's dominions overseas, distinct though they might be, no less than in the realm of England, through structures of governance established for that purpose peculiar to each locale.[88]

"I apprehend," Benjamin Franklin wrote in 1773, "that every Briton who is made unhappy at home, has a Right to remove from any Part of his King's Dominions into those of any other Prince where he can be happier. If this should be denied me, at least it will be allowed that he has a Right to remove into any other Part of the same Dominions."[89] If the claim to a "right" to migrate had been controverted or qualified by Crown pronouncement at one time or another, Britons had nevertheless chosen

---

[86] It is worth noting, for example, that in the course of argument in *Blankard v. Galdy* (1693), the application of the Statute of Artificers to Jamaica was comprehensively denied. 87 English Reports 360, 4 Mod. 222.

[87] Francis Bacon in *Calvin's Case* as cited in Keechang Kim, *Aliens in Medieval Law: The Origins of Modern Citizenship* (Cambridge, 2000), 179–80.

[88] Kim notes (ibid., 180–1), "the focal issue of *Calvin's case* [is] whether allegiance was a bond of subjection institutionalised by the law of the kingdom or archetypal submission grounded upon the law of nature." He elaborates (179), "Those who were against Calvin's claim argued that … 'allegiance [was] tied to laws'… that the bond of allegiance between the king and his subjects was a bond of law," and that "'every nation hath a precinct wherein the laws have operation'." Thus allegiance was subject to law; subjection to the Crown had no independent effect outside the precinct of the nation. The *postnati*, not being subject to English law, could not have its benefits. "However, a new generation of lawyers such as Francis Bacon looked upon this argument as unsuitable for 'a warlike and magnanimous nation fit for empire'. They needed a conclusion that 'the king's power, command and protection extendeth out of England'. Sir Edward Coke wanted the same conclusion. He hoped that the king's 'subjects in all places may be protected from violence, and that justice may equally be administered to all his subjects'. In fact, they were advocating James I's imperial claim that all the peoples under his subjection – in and out of England – should be united in one political and legal unit. In order to achieve such a union, it was necessary to have the notion of allegiance liberated from the confines of the kingdom and its law."

[89] *Papers of Benjamin Franklin*, volume XX, 527.

to remove themselves across the Atlantic, or had been removed, with relatively little obstruction. Nevertheless, European population mobility took place within structures that imposed limits upon choice, that "directed and conducted" the process of removal. And for others involved in the processes of colonizing, whether as involuntary hosts to new European arrivals or as involuntary migrants dispatched to the colonies to work for life and for lives without end, the law bubble that contained them and determined their fate allowed them no choice at all.

Calvin's Case underlines how one of the most important characteristics of that law bubble was that at least initially its foundations were constructed from materials that expressed not English common law at all, but sovereign prerogative. Crown charters made reference to English "laws, statutes, customs and rights" as an index of appropriate action on the part of projectors of colonies, but the charters themselves expressed an antecedent sovereign claim that owed little to common law. As Sir Mathew Hale pointed out in the 1650s, "The course was that the king issued a commission to seize such and such continents, between such and such degrees of latitude and longitude, in the name of the king, and to set up his standard in token of his possession. Thus the continents of Virginia and New England ... Greenland, and the northern plantations ... The Caribbea islands ... and so for divers others." Such acquisitions, Hale continued, were "in right of the crown of England and are parcel of the dominions though not of the realm of England."[90]

Hale here draws attention to the fundamental jurisdictional distinction between processes of sovereign acquisition and domestic English law. His point was twofold. First, acquisition was undertaken as an exercise in and an expression of the sovereign's absolute prerogative powers. Second, the law of the realm of England – as *Calvin's Case* had acknowledged – had no particular jurisdictional ascendancy or place in the law of distinct dominions, except insofar as the monarch's commissions (that is, the Crown's letters patents and charters) might allow, whether as particular rule or as general point of reference. As Lord Chancellor Ellesmere had put it in *Calvin's Case*, echoing Bacon, "diversitie of Lawes and Customs makes no breach of that unitie of obedience ... which all liege subjects owe to their liege King."[91] Hence, Hale continued, "upon the acquest the English laws are not settled there, or at least are only temporary till a settlement made. And therefore we see that there is in all these plantations administration of justice and laws much differing from the English laws." Planters carried with them essential liberties "incident to their persons," but such other laws prevailing in the Crown's distinct dominions "are settled according to

---

[90] Sir Mathew Hale, *The Prerogatives of the King*, D.E.C. Yale, editor (London 1976), 43; MacMillan, *Sovereignty and Possession*, 36–7.

[91] In Louis A. Knafla, *Law and Politics in Jacobean England: The Tracts of Lord Chancellor Ellesmere* (Cambridge and New York, 1977), 237. "It is the king, and not the common law, to whom the people owe their allegiance." MacMillan, *Sovereignty and Possession*, 34.

the king's pleasure, who is lord and proprietor of them, till he shall dispose of them by patent."[92]

Hale's observations focus on English colonizing, yet at the same time help to underline that the English law that "directed and conducted" population across oceans can tell us relatively little about the processes by which the English joined with other Europeans in "acquiring" the transoceanic territories into which population was poured. In Hale's terminology, European sovereigns commissioned the seizure of continents. But upon what legal basis did Europeans in general intrude upon the New World? What course, in particular, did the English follow? In underlining the utility of the law of nature, *Calvin's Case* has already revealed part of the answer. To investigate the matter more fully, I turn now to the third panel of the elder Hakluyt's triptych – from manning, and planting, to "keeping."

[92] Hale, *The Prerogatives of the King*, 44; MacMillan, *Sovereignty and Possession*, 37.

3

Keeping (i): Discourses of Intrusion

As the light accompanieth the Sunne and the heate the fire, so lasting riches do wait upon them that are jealous for the advancement of the Kingdom of Christ, and the enlargement of his glorious Gospell.

Richard Hakluyt (the younger), *Preface* to
Divers Voyages Touching the Discoverie of America (1582)

The Sun arises in the East,
Cloth'd in robes of blood and gold;
Swords and spears and wrath increas'd
All around his bosom roll'd,
Crown'd with warlike fires and raging desires.

William Blake, *Poems from the*
Rossetti Manuscript, I (c. 1793)

European colonizers began refining their plans for the New World virtually from the moment of Columbian landfall. Conventionally the English are absent from this story, latecomers by better than ninety years. English Atlantic voyaging goes largely unnoticed before the 1580s, when "the horizons of English leaders, merchants, intellectuals, and adventurers began to broaden" and attempts to create mainland outposts commenced in earnest.[1] Continuous landed settlement dates only from 1607; English presence is not secured for the better part of two decades.

But the New World had early attracted English no less than Iberian attention. Henry VII had offered Columbus English patronage for his first voyage westward in 1492. In 1496 and again in 1498, Henry issued letters patent to John Cabot and his sons "*super Terra Incognita Investiganda*" – to search out "whatsoeuer isles, countreys, regions or prouinces of the heathen and infidels whatsoeuer they be, and in what part of the world soeuer they be, which before this time haue bene vnknowen to all Christians."[2]

---

[1] John Wood Sweet, "Introduction: Sea Changes," in Robert Appelbaum and John Wood Sweet, *Envisioning an English Empire: Jamestown and the Making of the North Atlantic World* (Philadelphia, 2005), 12.

[2] Letters Patent to John Cabot, in Francis Newton Thorpe, *The Federal and State Constitutions, Colonial Charters, and other Organic Laws of the States, Territories and Colonies Now or Heretofore Forming The United States of America* (Washington, D.C.: Government Printing Office, 1909), I, 45–7, at 46.

Cabot's voyages made landfall on the far northern mainland, brought back news of abundant offshore fisheries (perhaps not news at all in the backstreets of Bristol[3]), and established claims to Newfoundland and Labrador, all virtually at the same moment that the renewed voyaging of Columbus and Amerigo Vespucci had focused Iberian attention on the south – the Caribbean, the Gulf of Mexico, and the southern continent. English fishing fleets were seasonal visitors to the inner coastal cod fisheries and shores of Newfoundland throughout the sixteenth century. Nor did the English confine their attention to the North Atlantic: English Caribbean voyages were recorded from 1527 and became relatively commonplace after midcentury as merchants began outfitting commercial expeditions. But English knowledge of navigation to and from the Caribbean was limited,[4] and when Martin Frobisher resumed English voyaging under Crown patronage in 1576 it was once more to the far north – Labrador, Baffin Island, Greenland.

The renewal of Crown interest in the North Atlantic was prompted in good part by the work of scholars and propagandists of empire, notably the Tudor mathematician, astrologer, and geographer John Dee (1527–1608), and the equally remarkable cousins both named Richard Hakluyt, the elder (1532–91) and the younger (1552–1616). Dee traveled widely in Western Europe during the mid-sixteenth century and was an advisor to Elizabeth I throughout her reign. The elder Hakluyt never crossed the coast. He owned land in Herefordshire but resided for most of his life in London, where he was a lawyer of the Middle Temple, a member of parliament, a confidant of adventurers, merchants, and ministers of state. The younger grew up a scholar of Westminster School in London and of Christ Church in Oxford, became a professor of theology and moral philosophy, a student of cosmography and navigation, an ordained prebendary of Holy Trinity, Bristol, and a canon of Westminster. He was also a diplomat, an advisor to the Crown, and a Virginia patentee. He once got as far as Paris.[5]

---

[3] Andrew Fitzmaurice, *Humanism and America: An Intellectual History of English Colonisation, 1500–1625* (Cambridge, 2003), 25.

[4] Philip D. Morgan, "Virginia's Other Prototype: The Caribbean," in Peter C. Mancall, editor, *The Atlantic World and Virginia: 1550–1624* (Chapel Hill, 2007), 349, 357. Morgan writes that "Between 1550 and 1624, the English launched at least three hundred separate voyages to the region" (349).

[5] On Dee, see Ken MacMillan, *Sovereignty and Possession in the English New World* (Cambridge, 2006), 50–78. On the Hakluyts, see E.G.R. Taylor, "Introduction: the Two Richard Hakluyts," in *The Original Writings and Correspondence of the Two Richard Hakluyts* (London: for the Hakluyt Society, 1935), I, 1–7, 27–30, 33–4, 39, 46, 61. On the younger Hakluyt, see Peter C. Mancall, *Hakluyt's Promise: An Elizabethan's Obsession for an English America* (New Haven, 2007); David Harris Sacks, "Discourses of Western Planting: Richard Hakluyt and the Making of the Atlantic World," in Mancall, ed., *The Atlantic World and Virginia*, 410–53. See also A. G. Bradley, "Introduction," in Edward Arber, editor, *Travels and Works of Captain John Smith* (Edinburgh, 1910), I, ii: "If Raleigh was the most active promoter of the colonising spirit which was gradually taking fast hold of England, the great geographer Hakluyt … was no whit behind him as a stimulating force, and was

Together, these were the seminal theorists of Elizabethan England's grab for the brave new world of transoceanic acquisition. None brought first-hand experience to their theorizing. Each, rather, sought to employ and redirect the experience of others, deriving from their own learned knowledge the enlightenment that would interpret and organize that experience.[6] Thus, they used their time to mobilize discourses of Christianity and commerce, and of geography and law, for the plotting of transoceanic expansion.

Dee's *General and Rare Memorials Pertayning to the Perfect Arte of Navigation* written in 1576 encouraged Crown investment in Frobisher's first voyage. His subsequent treatise on the *Limits of the British Empire* presented to Elizabeth I in 1577–8 sustained Crown interest in Frobisher's voyaging and instructions to claim Meta Incognita (the Arctic regions above 50°N latitude), and resulted in the grant of letters patent to Sir Humphrey Gilbert licensing voyages of discovery and conquest to colonize Newfoundland and other "remote, heathen and barbarous lands, countreys and territories not actually possessed of any Christian prince or people."[7] Dee's arguments combined a geographer's analysis of Spanish claims in the Central and South Atlantic with conjectural historical accounts of a millennium of British oceanic voyaging, culminating in Cabot's expeditions, to advance legal claims of British *imperium* and *dominium* that encompassed virtually the entirety of the Northern Atlantic littoral – islands and coastlines from the Orkneys and Shetlands to Greenland (the Arctic), Baffin Island, and Estotiland (Labrador and Newfoundland) to Drogio (the Canadian Maritimes), and to the American mainland from Norumbega (New England) all the way south to Florida, which Dee acknowledged as the northerly frontier of Spain's American empire.[8] Six years later, many

---

much in his confidence. Hakluyt's influence was immense." In his otherwise inspired *American Slavery, American Freedom: The Ordeal of Colonial Virginia* (New York, 1975), at 14–15, Edmund Morgan chooses, oddly and mistakenly, to disparage the Hakluyts. Both were "undistinguished ... Neither stood close to the centers of power."

[6] In *European Encounters with the New World: From Renaissance to Romanticism* (New Haven, 1993), 51–4, Anthony Pagden stresses the crucial importance of what he calls "the autoptic imagination" in the European reception of America. By this he means "the appeal to the authority of the eye-witness." But he also stresses the authority of the epistemological canon that determined what could be said about what was seen, and indeed thereby determined what was seen. Neither Dee nor the Hakluyts were eye-witnesses. Each, rather, labored within, and advanced the assimilative authority of, the interpretive canon. See also Pagden, 10. For particular emphasis on the eye-witness relative to the metropolitan *imaginaire*, see Karen Ordahl Kupperman, *Indians & English: Facing Off in Early America* (Ithaca, N.Y. and London, 2000), x; See also her *Settling with the Indians: The Meeting of English and Indian Cultures* (Totowa, N.J., 1980).

[7] MacMillan, *Sovereignty and Possession*, 51–3; Letters Patent to Sir Humfrey Gylberte (June 11, 1578) in Thorpe, *Federal and State Constitutions*, I, 49–52. Gilbert's voyage did not come about until 1583.

[8] MacMillan, *Sovereignty and Possession*, 54–66. For pioneering research on the legal basis of English claims to North Atlantic territories, see John T. Juricek, "English Territorial Claims in North America under Elizabeth and the Early Stuarts," *Terrae Incognitae*, 7 (1975), 7–22.

of Dee's arguments reappeared in the younger Richard Hakluyt's better-known "Discourse of Western Planting," which claimed that the English Crown could assert title "more lawfull and righte then the Spaniardes or any other christian Princes" to at least as much of America "wch is from Florida beyonde the Circle articke."[9] Hakluyt's "Discourse" was presented to Elizabeth I in support of Sir Walter Raleigh's petition for Crown letters patent licensing further expeditions of discovery and conquest to the North American mainland, for which his elder cousin prepared instructions and advice. Raleigh's letters patent reproduced the wide grants of authority and possession earlier made to Gilbert.[10]

Late sixteenth-century metropolitan discourses upon the geography, history, and legalities of North Atlantic empire offered the Tudor monarchy the New World as a territorial site onto which it might project English

---

[9] Richard Hakluyt (the younger), "Discourse of Western Planting," in Taylor, ed., *Original Writings and Correspondence*, II, 211–326, at 290. Or, as he had put it in the Preface to his previous collection, *Divers Voyages*, to "those landes, which of equitie and right appertain unto us, as by the discourses that followe shall appere most plainely." Richard Hakluyt (the younger), Preface to *Divers Voyages*, in Taylor, ed., *Original Writings and Correspondence*, I, 175.

As the writings of Dee and the Hakluyts indicate, English claims of the Elizabethan era extended from the far north southward, stopping short of the point of Spain's northward extension and thus avoiding challenges to Spanish *dominium* in what Morgan calls "the complex region of islands and adjoining mainlands that made up the circum-Caribbean area." Morgan, "Virginia's Other Prototype," 346. Morgan emphasizes the importance of English *experience*–acquisition of knowledge – in the circum-Caribbean to the subsequent settlement of the Chesapeake, but that experience established no territorial claims in the region, which the Spanish would not in any case have tolerated. Under the 1494 Treaty of Tordesillas with Portugal (see n.29, this chapter), Spain claimed the entire mainland coastal region from the Gulf of Mexico to Newfoundland, calling it "La Florida." But the Spanish knew little of the Atlantic seaboard north of the Florida peninsula and made no attempt to settle there until French voyaging after mid-century appeared to threaten Spanish *dominium* in the circum-Caribbean. Spain established a peninsula settlement at Santa Elena in 1559 (present-day Parris Island in Port Royal Sound just north of Hilton Head, S.C.), and in 1565 destroyed the three-year-old French peninsula colony at Fort Caroline (east of present-day Jacksonville). Spain then established St. Augustine, about 40 miles to the south of where Fort Caroline had been, which would become its northernmost permanent settlement on the Atlantic seaboard. In the last quarter of the century, English voyaging in the North Atlantic focused English territorial designs on the Northern mainland, manifested in Elizabethan letters patents and again confirmed by the Crown following the accession of James I. See generally J. H. Elliott, "The Iberian Atlantic and Virginia," in Mancall, ed., *The Atlantic World and Virginia*, 541–57.

[10] Namely "free libertie and licence from time to time, and at all times for euer hereafter, to discouer, search, finde out, and view such remote, heathen and barbarous lands, countries, and territories, not actually possessed of any Christian Prince, nor inhabited by Christian People, as to him, his heires and assignes, and to euery or any of them shall seeme good, and the same to haue, holde, occupie and enjoy to him, his heires and assignes for euer, with all prerogatiues, commodities, jurisdictions, royalties, priuileges, franchises, and preheminences, thereto or thereabouts both by sea and land, whatsoeuer we by our letters patents may graunt, and as we or any of our noble progenitors haue heretofore graunted to any person or persons, bodies politique or corporate." Charter to Sir Walter Raleigh (1584) in Thorpe, *Federal and State Constitutions*, I, 53.

sovereign desire. Some sixty years before, Sir Thomas More's equally remarkable discourse upon "the beste state of a publique weale, and of the new yle, called *Utopia*" (1516), had also adopted the New World into the English *imaginaire*, somewhat distinctly, as an intellectual site upon which to project an ideal civic order.[11] More presented his island common-wealth (the name might be understood as *Outopeía* – Οὐτοπεία – meaning "no-place land," or alternatively *Eutopeía* – Εὐτοπεία – "good-place land") in the form of an account by a fictional Portuguese traveler and philosopher, Raphael Hythloday, who had voyaged with Amerigo Vespucci to the coast of South America where lay "townes and Cities and weale publiques [commonwealths], full of people, governed by good and holesome lawes."[12] Utopia was the most remarkable of them all, a city-state, or more accurately a state of cities, fifty-four in all, "agreyng all together in one tonge, in lyke maners, institucions, and lawes." Its origins lay in a deliberate foundational act undertaken by an invading king, Utopus, who upon obtaining victory over the land's inhabitants – "rude and wilde people" – had "caused xv. myles space of uplandyshe grounde, where the sea had no passage, to be cut and dygged up. And so brought the sea rounde about the lande." Created anew in an immense frenzy of labor as an island state, Utopia had been brought to an "excellente perfection in al good fassions," its citizenry characterized by "humanitye, and civile gentilnes, wherin they nowe goe beyond al the people of the world."[13]

Works like John Dee's *Limits* and More's *Utopia* stand as archetypes of two strands of metropolitan discourse upon the New World, the one a discourse of *imperium* and *dominium* that proposed to define the terms upon which English sovereignty might be claimed and realized over transatlantic territories in competition with other European claimants, the other a discourse of improvement that used the New World as a palimpsest for the creation of perfected societies unattainable – unattained, at any rate – in Europe. Though distinct both in effect and intent, the two discourses bled into each other in the works of late sixteenth-century promoters of English colonizing such as the Hakluyts and Sir George Peckham, notably at the several points that promoters drew upon the repertoire of contemporary legalities to establish the legitimacy and justice of the outcomes they advertised. These distinct discourses of sovereign possession and idealized creation, in other words, provided a common foundation for validation of the activities they described and promoted. As the pace of English colonizing gathered, their arguments merged more and more completely.

To identify things American as constructs of English legal culture is hardly novel: it has long been common for historians to argue that received English legalities furnished a template for law in early America. Much of

---

[11] George Sampson, editor, *The Utopia of Sir Thomas More, Ralph Robinson's Translation* (London, 1910), xxvii; Fitzmaurice, *Humanism and America*, 190.

[12] Sampson, ed., *Utopia*, 24–5, 27; Thomas More, *Utopia*, George M. Logan and Robert M. Adams, editors (Cambridge, 2002), xi.

[13] Sampson, ed., *Utopia*, 83.

American history, indeed, assumes that English legal culture was a founding source of liberties more perfectly realized by a revolutionary America.[14]
This tends, however, to be an exercise in the measurement of the parameters of legal exchange – a matter of determining the extent of peripheral
reproduction of doctrines or theories current in metropolitan common-
law texts, courtrooms, or constitutional discourse. Such an exercise has
its own importance and is not to be belittled; later in this book I pursue
my own variation on the theme. First, though, it is necessary to explore
the template furnished by the law that authorized colonizing adventures
per se. One must address the law of colonizing before one considers the
laws of the colonies that resulted, for it was the former, not the latter, that
first projected specific legal and institutional structures onto transatlantic
landscapes to create a colonized English America.

The law of colonizing as it applied to English Atlantic expansion is the
subject of the next two chapters. It is to be found in the first instance in
sixteenth-century intra-European debates that addressed the legalities of
post-Columbian intrusion. Drawing heavily on the Roman law of nature and
nations – *ius naturale* and *gentium* – recovered in the eleventh and twelfth
centuries, European sovereigns created intellectual means to acknowledge
and negotiate each others' assertions of claims to *imperium* and *dominium*
over transatlantic territories, and to justify claims to possess vis-à-vis each
other and (more occasionally) incumbent indigenous possessors. It is to
be found in the second instance in the numerous letters patent and charters[15] granted by the Crown over the course of the late sixteenth century
and the seventeenth century to license the manifold schemes of western
planting presented by mercantile and gentry adventurers in order to realize through their agency the actuality of its transatlantic sovereign claims.
The elaborated legality of chartering secured Crown approval for complex
arrays of activities that necessarily implicated the exercise of the Crown's
sovereign authority within its established jurisdictions both in England

---

[14] See, for example, Peter Hoffer, *Law and People in Colonial America* (Baltimore, 1992); John
Phillip Reid, *The Concept of Liberty in the Age of the American Revolution* (Chicago, 1988).

[15] Mary Sarah Bilder points out, "Historians tend to use *charter* as a generic term to refer
to the Crown's grants for mainland settlements. In fact, most of these documents were
letters patent and referred to themselves as such." Bilder describes the technical and
traditional differences between letters patent and charters as follows: *Letters patent* "were
grants under seal by which the Crown gave privileges and authority but did not necessarily constitute any particular political entity. *Patent* referred to the open or public
nature of the grant." A *charter* was more formal, "a grant of privileges in perpetuity."
Bilder observes that the first Crown grants to projectors of colonies in North America
that deserve the technical designation *charter* were the proprietary grants that began in
the early 1620s. See Mary Sarah Bilder, "English Settlement and Local Governance," in
Michael Grossberg and Christopher Tomlins, editors, *The Cambridge History of Law in
America* (Cambridge and New York, 2008), I, 65–6. One should note that the Crown can
be found using both terms to describe the same document. See, e.g., the Grant of the
Province of Avalon to Sir George Calvert (1623), in Keith Matthews, comp., *Collection
and Commentary on the Constitutional Laws of Seventeenth Century Newfoundland* (Maritime
History Group, Memorial University of Newfoundland, 1975), 40, 63.

and overseas: licenses, permissions, subsidies, waivers, guarantees, tenures, grants, and prohibitions. Simultaneously chartering gave projectors means to propose and to plan enterprises whose practical dimensions could not be known with any certainty. Here discourses of sovereignty and improvement merge: chartering expressed both sovereign prerogative *and* the designs that projectors created – for which they sought sovereign imprimatur – in concepts and language that allowed pursuit of concrete territorial claims formulated, necessarily, in abstract, because they were distant and largely unknown except in the most general outline. Finally, the legalities of chartering furnished projectors an opportunity to declare in considerable detail their conceptions of the appropriate, the familiar, the envisioned order of things and people that the work of colonizing would create, and to foreshadow the effect of imposing those conceptions onto social and physical circumstance thousands of miles away.[16] As such, both as a language of claiming and, in the English case, as a language of improving, the law of colonizing was the perfected expression of the language of keeping.

I. The Legalities of Colonizing

At the very outset of New World voyaging, Robert Williams has proposed, law – Europe's "most respected and cherished instrument of civilization" – simultaneously provided Europeans with their "most vital and effective instrument of empire."[17] It did so, Williams thinks, in two ways. First, Catholic Christian doctrine identified the evangelization of all humanity as the divine mandate of the Roman church, rendering all, whether Christian, infidel, or heathen, ultimately subject to papal jurisdiction. The evangelical impulse was founded on original claims of universal temporal and spiritual dominion for Roman Christianity advanced within Europe and its vicinity for half a millennium: "*De facto* there might exist other kings in the world, just as *de facto* there existed other belief systems besides Christianity. But *de iure*, there could be only one emperor and only one religion."[18] It was sharpened during the fifteenth century by voyages of oceanic exploration that confirmed the existence of "certain islands and mainlands" occupied by non-Christians "remote and unknown and not hitherto discovered."[19]

Second, Eurocentric assertions of the universality of natural law appeared to equip Europeans both with an expansive jurisdictional mandate and

---

[16] For an elaboration of these ideas, see Christopher Tomlins, "The Legal Cartography of Colonization, the Legal Polyphony of Settlement: English Intrusions on the American Mainland in the Seventeenth Century," *Law & Social Inquiry*, 26, 2 (Spring 2001), 315–47.

[17] Robert A. Williams, Jr., *The American Indian in Western Legal Thought: The Discourses of Conquest* (New York, 1990), 6.

[18] Anthony Pagden, *Lords of all the World: Ideologies of Empire in Spain, Britain and France, c. 1500–1800* (New Haven, 1995), 27.

[19] The papal bull *Inter caetera* (Alexander VI) dated 4 May 1493, in Frances Gardiner Davenport, editor, *European Treaties Bearing on the History of the United States and its Dependencies to 1648* (Washington, D.C., 1967 [1917]), 75–8, at 76. See also *Inter caetera*

presumptive legitimacy for measures taken to realize it. Although late medieval Christian natural law teaching allowed that both as men and as nations non-Christians no less than Christians enjoyed reason and hence possessed rights – to hold property, to exercise governance over their own territories – the same natural law teaching also held that both as men and as nations non-Christians no less than Christians were subject to correction for violations of natural law, or for resistance to the Christian evangelizing that was the ultimate means to salvation from unnatural temporal and spiritual life.[20] For the law of nature was explained as "participation in the eternal law [God's law] by rational creatures."[21] Though the particular laws of particular men [positive law] might implement natural law in distinct ways, natural law itself was true everywhere. Its first principles "underpinned man's relationship with the world about him and governed every practice within human society."[22] Natural law was expressed as such by the law of nations (*ius gentium*), that body of law enacted, as it were, by a universal consensus of humanity – by "the whole world, which is in a sense a commonwealth" – which might thus properly countermand those laws and practices of men that departed natural law.[23]

Initially, stress lay upon the papacy's mandate to evangelize.[24] Iberian expansion beyond the Mediterranean into the cis-Atlantic identified the

(Alexander VI) dated 3 May 1493, and *Eximiae devotionis* (Alexander VI) dated May 3, both in the same, 56–63, 64–70.

[20] See generally Richard Tuck, *The Rights of War and Peace: Political Thought and the International Order from Grotius to Kant* (Oxford, 1999), 58–61, 68–75.

[21] Anthony Pagden, "Introduction," in Anthony Pagden and Jeremy Lawrance, editors, *Francisco de Vitoria: Political Writings* (Cambridge and New York, 1991), xiv. At greater length: "Since all things subject to Divine providence are ruled and measured by the eternal law … it is evident that all things partake somewhat of the eternal law, in so far as, namely, from its being imprinted on them, they derive their respective inclinations to their proper acts and ends. Now among all others, the rational creature is subject to Divine providence in the most excellent way, in so far as it partakes of a share of providence, by being provident both for itself and for others. Wherefore it has a share of the Eternal Reason, whereby it has a natural inclination to its proper act and end: and this participation of the eternal law in the rational creature is called the natural law." *The Summa Theologica of St. Thomas Aquinas*, Literally translated by Fathers of the English Dominican Province, Second and Revised edition (np, 1920), *Prima Secundæ Partis*, 91, 2, *answer*, available at http://www.newadvent.org/summa/ (accessed 22 August 2009).

[22] Pagden, "Introduction," xv.

[23] Ibid. Francisco de Vitoria, *On Civil Power* [*De Potestate Civili*] (1528), in Pagden and Lawrance, eds., *Francisco de Vitoria: Political Writings*, 40. Again, at greater length: "the law of nations (*ius gentium*) does not have the force merely of pacts or agreements between men, but has the validity of a positive enactment (*lex*). The whole world, which is in a sense a commonwealth, has the power to enact laws which are just and convenient to all men; and these make up the law of nations. From this it follows that those who break the law of nations, whether in peace or in war, are committing mortal crimes, at any rate in the case of the graver transgressions such as violating the immunity of ambassadors. No kingdom may choose to ignore this law of nations, because it has the sanction of the whole world."

[24] Williams, *The American Indian*, 72.

evangelization of all humanity as its purpose and the divine mandate of the Roman church as sufficient authority. To this was joined a further and crucial papal role of mediation and demarcation between rival expansionist European powers. The whole, but particularly the latter, was expressed at length in the papal bull *Romanus pontifex* (1455), issued in several iterations in response to Portuguese and Castilian competition for ascendancy over new lands and islands discovered in the course of fifteenth-century voyaging along the Atlantic coasts of Africa in the wake of the Portuguese conquest (1415) of Ceuta, on the North African side of the Straits of Gibraltar. "Contemplating with a father's mind all the several climes of the world and the characteristics of all the nations dwelling in them and seeking and desiring the salvation of all," and believing universal salvation could be quickened by the bestowal of "suitable favors and special graces on those Catholic kings and princes, who ... restrain the savage excesses of the Saracens and of other infidels, enemies of the Christian name, but also for the defense and increase of the faith vanquish them and their kingdoms and habitations, though situated in the remotest parts unknown to us, and subject them to their own temporal dominion," Pope Nicholas V confirmed that by previous "letters of ours" Portugal (in the persons of the *infante* [prince] Henry the Navigator and King Alfonso V) enjoyed

> free and ample faculty ... to invade, search out, capture, vanquish, and subdue all Saracens and pagans whatsoever, and other enemies of Christ wheresoever placed, and the kingdoms, dukedoms, principalities, dominions, possessions, and all movable and immovable goods whatsoever held and possessed by them and to reduce their persons to perpetual slavery, and to apply and appropriate to himself and his successors the kingdoms, dukedoms, counties, principalities, dominions, possessions, and goods, and to convert them to his and their use and profit

and as well an exclusive, just and lawful right to possess by right of conquest all such "islands, lands, harbors, and seas" theretofore acquired or to be acquired.[25] Further, "in order to confer a more effectual right and assurance," Pope Nicholas extended Portuguese exclusivity to encompass "the provinces, islands, harbors, places, and seas whatsoever, how many soever, and of what sort soever they shall be, that have already been acquired and that shall hereafter come to be acquired, and the right of conquest also" stretching from the capes of Não [Chaunar] and Bojador "as far as through all Guinea, and beyond."[26]

---

[25] The papal bull *Romanus pontifex* (Nicholas V) dated 8 January 1455, in Davenport, ed., *European Treaties*, 20–6, at 20–1, 23. See also *Dum diversas* (Nicholas V) dated 18 June 1452, for the original grant of essentially unlimited authority to Alfonso V to enslave all Saracens, pagans, and unbelievers wherever encountered.

[26] *Romanus pontifex*, 23–4. Islands particularly in contention at this point were the Canaries, but *Romanus pontifex* also contained references to the Indies, which Portugal sought. The Portuguese claim was granted in the bull *Inter caetera* (Calixtus III) dated 13 March 1456. Castilian refusal to accept Portuguese ascendancy in the Canaries and Guinea led to conflict and eventually to the Treaty of Alcáçovas (4 September 1479) between Portugal

Romanus pontifex having "forever give[n], grant[ed], and appropriate[d]" the African Atlantic mainland and islands to Portugal, in *Inter caetera* (1493) the Spanish-born Pope Alexander VI granted Ferdinand of Aragon and Isabella of Castile and Leon the territorial fruits of Columbus's first trans-oceanic voyage – "certain very remote islands and even mainlands that hitherto had not been discovered by others; wherein dwell very many peoples living in peace ... going unclothed, and not eating flesh" – which "as becomes Catholic kings and princes ... you have purposed with the favor of divine clemency to bring under your sway the said mainlands and islands with their residents and inhabitants and to bring them to the Catholic faith." Because previous bulls had described no western perimeter to Portuguese exclusivity, *Inter caetera* composed a line of demarcation between Spanish and Portuguese Atlantic claims. Ferdinand and Isabella obtained gift, grant, and assignment "together with all their dominions, cities, camps, places, and villages, and all rights, jurisdictions, and appurtenances, [of] all islands and mainlands found and to be found, discovered and to be discovered towards the west and south" of a line drawn from pole to pole "distant one hundred leagues towards the west and south from any of the islands commonly known as the Azores and Cape Verde," excepting any such lands "in the actual possession of any Christian king or prince" as of Christmas 1492.[27] Four months later, amid continued Spanish-Portuguese friction, Alexander VI issued a further bull, *Dudum siquidem*, which appeared to permit Spanish infringement upon the Portuguese "sphere."[28] The resulting Treaty of Tordesillas (1494) adjusted the line of Atlantic demarcation westward and confirmed Portuguese claims to the east. The Treaty of Tordesillas was acknowledged by the Papacy in the bull *Ea quae* (1506).[29]

Unlike *Romanus pontifex*, Alexander VI's *Inter caetera* included no explicit acknowledgment of Spanish right to possess new-discovered islands and mainlands by conquest.[30] Columbus's voyage, Alexander noted, had been

and the Spanish Crowns of Castile and Aragon, which confirmed Castile as possessor of the Canary Islands and Portugal of Guinea, while granting all further insular acquisitions made by Christian powers off the African coast, or on the mainland (and eastward to the Indies) to Portugal. The treaty was recognized by the papacy in the bull *Aeterni regis* (Sixtus IV) dated 21 June 1481, which otherwise confirmed the earlier *Romanus pontifex* and *Inter caetera*. For the Treaty of Alcáçovas, see Davenport, ed., *European Treaties*, 33–48. For *Aeterni regis*, see 49–55.

[27] *Inter caetera* (Alexander VI), in Davenport, ed. *European Treaties*, 75–8, at 76, 77. Alexander VI issued two bulls both entitled *Inter caetera*, dated respectively the 3rd and 4th of May 1493. The bull of May 4th repeated in more emphatic detail the grant originally made in the bull of May 3rd and added the line of demarcation between Spanish and Portuguese "spheres." For the bull of May 3rd, see Davenport, *European Treaties*, 67–70.

[28] The papal bull *Dudum siquidem* (Alexander VI) dated 26 September 1493 (extending the Apostolic Grant and Donation of the Indies to Spain), in Davenport, ed., *European Treaties*, 79–83.

[29] For the Treaty of Tordesillas, see Davenport, ed., *European Treaties*, 84–100; for the papal bull *Ea quae* (Julius II) dated 24 January 1506, see the same, 107–11.

[30] Note, however, that "all and singular the graces and privileges, exemptions, liberties, faculties, immunities, letters, and indults [permissions]" granted the kings of Portugal

mounted in fulfillment of Ferdinand and Isabella's long-intended purpose "to seek out and discover certain islands and mainlands remote and unknown and not hitherto discovered by others, to the end that you might bring to the worship of our Redeemer and the profession of the Catholic faith their residents and inhabitants." It appeared, moreover, that "these very peoples living in the said islands and countries believe in one God, the Creator in heaven, and seem sufficiently disposed to embrace the Catholic faith and be trained in good morals." In the hope that, "were they instructed, the name of the Savior, our Lord Jesus Christ, would easily be introduced into the said countries and islands," *Inter caetera* created a delegated guardianship that gave, granted, and assigned title to the discovering Christian prince, who was commanded in turn to appoint "worthy, God-fearing, learned, skilled, and experienced men, in order to instruct the aforesaid inhabitants and residents in the Catholic faith and train them in good morals."[31]

in *Romanus pontifex* were extended to the Spanish monarchs without further elaboration by the bull *Eximiae devotionis* (Alexander VI), dated 3 May 1493.

[31] *Inter caetera* (Alexander VI), 76, 77. Ferdinand became "perpetual administrator by apostolic authority." See Lewis Hanke, *The Spanish Struggle for Justice in the Conquest of America* (Philadelphia, 1949), 26.

We should note that Ferdinand and Isabella's original grant of "privileges and prerogatives" to Christopher Columbus commissioned a voyage not of discovery and evangelization but of discovery and conquest. Columbus had been sent "by our command, with some of our vessels and men, to discover *and subdue* some Islands and Continent in the ocean." His commission expressed the hope that "by God's assistance, some of the said Islands and Continent in the ocean will be discovered *and conquered*." See "Privileges and Prerogatives Granted by their Catholic Majesties to Christopher Columbus–1492," in Thorpe, *Federal and State Constitutions*, I, 39–40 (emphasis added). The commission expressed prevailing Catholic doctrine (as displayed, for example, in *Romanus pontifex*) "that permitted military conquest of non-Christian societies *not* well disposed to accept Christianity." *Inter caetera* responded to the initial absence of indigenous hostility by declaring a distinct basis – papal authority (as *dominium mundi*) to appoint Christian princes to act as guardians of peaceful non-Christian peoples and bring them to Christianity – for Spanish sway over their territories. See Williams, *The American Indian*, 80 (emphasis in original).

Actual colonizing practice, of course, married religious and moral instruction to the Crown's material interests in ensuring returns on its colonizing venture, as made evident in orders issued by King Ferdinand to the first royal governor of Hispaniola, Nicolás de Ovando, in 1503: "Because of the excessive liberty the Indians have been permitted, they flee from Christians and do not work. Therefore they are to be compelled to work, so that the kingdom and the Spaniards may be enriched, and the Indians Christianized." Ferdinand's instructions had added that the Indians were "to be paid a daily wage and well treated as free persons, for such they are, and not as slaves" – a reproach to practices put in place by Columbus on his return to Hispaniola in late 1493, which relied on violent repression and enslavement to extract labor. Under Columbus, indigenous labor had been requisitioned under the so-called *repartimiento* or labor allocation system. After Columbus's replacement by Ovando, the terms of Indian compulsion were refined by the institution of the *encomienda* [trust] system, under which Indians were assigned in groups to Spanish soldier-settlers who were made formally responsible for indigenous instruction and well-being as well as enjoying returns from indigenous labor. See Hanke, *Spanish Struggle*, 20; Williams *The American Indian*, 82, 83–4. Both *repartimiento* and *encomienda* were modeled on established Iberian Peninsula institutions. The New

Inter caetera's delegated guardianship was not without its advantages to the Spanish Crown. The emblematic instrument of Spanish *dominium* in the Americas, the *Requerimiento* (1512), incorporated the bull's assertions of universal papal jurisdiction and donation as legal justification for wars of enslavement launched to suppress indigenous resistance to Crown authority, whether apostolic (Christian evangelizing and moral instruction) or temporal ("full and free power, authority, and jurisdiction of every kind").[32] Denunciation of the treatment of indigenous populations by such as Antonio de Montesinos and Bartolomé de Las Casas – authors of the foundational texts of the *Leyenda Negra* – would nevertheless provoke profound reflection upon the expression and basis of Spanish New World rule.[33] Reflection did not lead to outright repudiation, however, but rather to a critical reexamination that has since been interpreted as a successful attempt to disentangle Spanish expansion from specific reliance on papal jurisdiction for justification and represent it instead as legitimate conquest the justice of which could be found in natural law. Whether that interpretation of the intent of Spanish reexamination is justified we shall shortly see. Intended or not, one effect of discarding the specific authority of *Inter caetera* as the legal basis of Spanish rule was to render the natural-law language of "legitimate conquest" generally available to any Christian nation desirous of advancing and realizing New World claims.

The principal intellectual architect of *relection* (re-reading) of Spanish New World rule was the University of Salamanca theologian and canon lawyer, Francisco de Vitoria, who lectured on the matter early in 1539.[34] Vitoria was a leading exponent of Thomistic theology, the infusion of later-medieval Christianity with Aristotelian philosophy. St. Thomas Aquinas had hypothesized "law" as encompassing four essential categories: eternal universal (divine) law; natural law (*ius naturale*) known to all social and reasoning creatures; human laws promulgated in obedience to general principles of nature and reason, or *ius gentium*; and the positive laws of particular kingdoms, commonwealths, states, or communities that should – but might not – be at one with natural law. From this Thomistic division, Vitoria drew four conclusions.

World *encomienda* regime was refined in the *Leyes de Burgos* (1512), which ordered Indians resettled in agricultural villages "next to the estates of the Spaniards who have them in *encomienda*" and their former inhabitations burned "since the Indians will have no further use for them: this is so that they will have no reason to return whence they have been brought" (par. I). The *Leyes* ordered *encomenderos* to construct churches, made elaborate provision for catechizing, confession, and baptism, defined the *encomienda*'s regime of work and discipline and the *encomendero*'s responsibilities for subsistence and payment. For an English translation of the *Leyes*, see http://faculty.smu.edu/bakewell/bakewell/texts/burgoslaws.html (accessed 22 August 2009).

[32] *Inter caetera* (Alexander VI), 77; Sharon Korman, *The Right of Conquest: the Acquisition of Territory by Force in International Law and Practice* (Oxford, 1996), 49–50; Hanke, *Spanish Struggle*, 33.

[33] Hanke, *Spanish Struggle*, 17–22. J. H. Elliott, *Empires of the Atlantic World: Britain and Spain in America, 1492–1830* (New Haven, 2006), 66–8.

[34] Pagden and Lawrance, eds., *Francisco de Vitoria: Political Writings*, 231.

First, far from exercising a supreme divinely instituted mandate over the affairs of the world, the papacy had no particular authority or determinative capacity in matters temporal but only spiritual, from which it followed that the donative capacities assumed by Alexander VI in *Inter caetera* had no foundation. Papal authority was confined to the church. Civil power in the world was exercised by civil sovereigns.[35] Second, all temporal rule throughout the world was informed by the law of nature and nations. Third, the Indians of the New World were social and reasoning creatures and hence both knew and were subject to the law of nature and nations, whence derived both rights and protections, and also obligations. As free people, not natural slaves, and the owners of the territories they inhabited, the Indians could no more be dispossessed by Christian discovery or by any human law enacted without consent or cause than by papal fiat. But, fourth, as social and reasoning creatures bound by natural law and the law of nations, they owed certain duties to those who traveled to their lands and remained peaceably among them – duties of "natural society and fellowship," of unhindered commerce, and of unhindered access to all such as was common to both natives and strangers.[36] As pagans, moreover, the Indians were bound to receive Christians, who had "a right to preach and declare the Gospel in barbarian lands." Indian refusals of any of their obligations constituted breaches of the law of nations, giving just cause for war.

> If, after the Spaniards have used all diligence, both in deed and in word, to show that nothing will come from them to interfere with the peace and well-being of the aborigines, the latter nevertheless persist in their hostility and do their best to destroy the Spaniards, then they can make war on the Indians, no longer as on innocent folk, but as against foresworn enemies, and may enforce against them all the rights of war, despoiling them of their goods, reducing them to captivity, deposing their former lords and setting up new ones, yet withal with observance of proportion as regards the nature of the circumstances and of the wrongs done to them.[37]

Wrong – violation of the law of nations – was the condition precedent. But once a substantial wrong had been done the Spaniards by the Indians, grounds existed for the Spaniards to wage war and exercise all rights of war, up to and including seizure of "the provinces and sovereignty of the natives"; that is, a right of territorial conquest and enslavement. For it

---

[35] Francisco de Vitoria, *On the Indians Lately Discovered* [*De Indis: Relectio Prior*] in Francisci de Victoria, *De Indis et De Iure Belli Relectiones*, ed. Ernest Nys, trans. John Pawley Bate (Washington, D.C., 1917), 135–8. And see Pagden, "Introduction," xxii–iii.

[36] Vitoria, *On the Indians Lately Discovered*, 151–3. One should note that such obligations – to allow passage, grant access, and so forth – are obligations of those exercising jurisdiction, i.e., of "native princes," of "the sovereign of the Indians" (152). In *On Civil Power*, 17–18, Vitoria states there can be no doubt that legitimate sovereigns and magistrates exist among pagans, "so neither Christian sovereigns nor the Church may deprive non-Christians of their kingship or power on the grounds of their unbelief, unless they have committed some other injustice."

[37] Vitoria, *On the Indians Lately Discovered*, 155, 156.

was, said Vitoria, citing Justinian, "a universal rule of the law of nations that whatever is captured in war becomes the property of the conqueror," extending even to people themselves.[38] Just war doctrine, Vitoria allegedly found, granted the Spanish New World empire a renewed legal legitimacy. All that he had held impossible and without justification under the authority of *Inter caetera* seemed to have become conceivable and justifiable by the authority of *ius gentium*.[39]

Accounts of Spanish New World rule circulating in English in the second half of the sixteenth century furnished narrative support for Vitorianesque arguments from the law of nature and nations and began the work of translating those arguments into the language of English ambition. In 1553, for example, Richard Eden published *A Treatise of the Newe India*, an English translation of extracts from Amerigo Vespucci's narrative of his south Atlantic voyaging a half century earlier, rich in claims of Indian violations of the law of nature – cannibalism, irreligion, want of elementary civility. Two years later Eden followed up with *The Decades of the New Worlde or West India*, in which he presented abridged translations of the accounts of Spanish conquest written by Pietro Martire (Peter Martyr) and Gonzalo Fernández de Oviedo that repeated claims of Indian cannibalism and savagery.[40] All of Eden's works emphasized the opportunities for English evangelizing, commerce, and conquest to the north of the Spanish possessions.

---

[38] Ibid., 155, 156.

[39] Thus, Sharon Korman holds that "In *De Indis* Vitoria set out to determine what, in terms of the law of nations, might constitute a legitimate defence of the Spanish acquisition of the New World by conquest, and not to argue that the acquisition of empire by conquest was ipso facto invalid." Korman, *The Right of Conquest*, 54. This was the interpretation offered by Hugo Grotius at the outset of *Mare Liberum* (1609) when he wrote, "Victoria holds that the Spaniards could have shown just reasons for making war upon the Aztecs and the Indians in America, more plausible reasons certainly than were alleged, if they really were prevented from traveling or sojourning among those peoples, and were denied the right to share in those things which by the Law of Nations or by Custom are common to all, and finally if they were debarred from trade." Hugo Grotius, *The Freedom of the Seas, or the Right Which Belongs to the Dutch to take part in the East Indian Trade* [Hugonis Grotii, *Mare Liberum, Sive De Iure Quod Batavis Competit Ad Indicana Commercia Dissertatio*], Ralph Van Deman Magoffin, trans. (New York, 1916), 9. See also the views of Grotius's pupil, Samuel Pufendorf, *De Jure Naturae et Gentium Libri Octo, Volume Two – The Translation of the Edition of 1688*, C. H. Oldfather and W. A. Oldfather, trans. (Oxford 1934), 364–6, 370, attributing to Vitoria an account of "the adequate grounds on which the Spaniards felt themselves entitled to subdue the Indians" (364).

[40] See Edward Arber, editor, *The First Three English Books on America [?1511]–1555 a.d. Being chiefly Translations, Compilations, &c., by Richard Eden, From the Writings, Maps, &c., of Pietro Martire, of Anghiera (1455–1526) Sebastian Münster, the Cosmographer (1489–1552) Sebastian Cabot, of Bristol (1474–1557) With Extracts, &c., from the Works of other Spanish, Italian, and German Writers of the Time* (Birmingham, U.K., 1885). A similar, brief account of the people "of suche partes of America, as are by trauaile founde out" was published by William Cunningham in his *The Cosmographical Glasse: Conteinyng the Pleasant Principles of Cosmographie, Geographie, Hydrographie, or Nauigation* (London, 1559), ff. 200–1: "The people bothe men, & women are naked, neither suffer they any heare to growe on their bodies, no not on their browes, the head except ... They haue warre with th'inhabitauntes of the country next them, which haue an other language. But it is not for richesse, for inlarging

Later proponents of English Atlantic empire took advantage of Vitoria's case against the authority of *Inter caetera* to undermine or limit the legitimacy of the papal gift and thereby establish openings for English sovereign claims vis-à-vis other European princes. In their works in support of English ventures, scholars like John Dee and the younger Richard Hakluyt put considerable intellectual effort into refuting Spanish claims of exclusivity in the Western hemisphere derived from *Inter caetera*. Dee argued that the bull was promulgated to mediate intra-Iberian disputes and stressed the limits rather than the extent of the donation, specifically its emphasis on granting Spain lands to the west *and south* of the proclaimed longitudinal demarcation line beginning at the latitude of the Azores. In Dee's analysis, the bull simply did not extend to the Northern Atlantic, where both Spanish geographical ignorance and a long conjectural history of English voyaging combined to prove superior title in the English Crown. Unlike Vitoria, Dee did not labor to deny papal temporal *imperium*, hence authority to grant transoceanic lands, per se. His preferred goal was to establish the irrelevance of papal temporal *imperium* to the North Atlantic while simultaneously assembling positive evidence of ancient English *imperium* there as a basis for commensurate temporal capacity in the English Crown to make grants by letters patent in realization of that historical *imperium*.[41]

The younger Hakluyt's "Discourse of Western Planting" drew similar attention to *Inter caetera*'s language of west and south. Hakluyt contended in addition that the extent of actual Spanish ascendancy even within the bounds of the papacy's notional gift was largely confined to the Gulf of Mexico and its islands and coastlines, without presence on any part of the North Atlantic mainland "excepte the Towne of St. Helen and one or twoo small fortes in fflorida."[42] Unlike Dee, however, Hakluyt added that the bull could not in any case establish the basis for any Spanish claim to territories beyond those the Spanish had actually discovered and occupied, for "God never gave unto the Popes any suche aucthoritie ... to give away kingdoms of heathen princes."[43] Here Hakluyt's arguments closely followed Vitoria. Just as Christ had neither enjoyed nor sought temporal kingdom, so the pope (Christ's vicar) could possess only spiritual authority, without

---

their segniory, or election of a king: but for to reuenge the deaths of their prædicessors. There is no lawe or order obserued of wedlocke, for it is lawful to haue so many wemen as they affect, & to put them away with out any daunger. They be filthy at meate, & in all secrete actes of nature, comparable to brute beastes. Their bread is rotes, & theyr meate mans fleshe, for all theyr enemies, which they ouercome, they with great bankettyng deuoure ... they vse no kinde of Marchandise, and as for golde, Pearle, stone, & that we haue in great prise: they haue in no estimation." Another English account of Caribbean cannibalism appeared in 1578 in *A Briefe Description of the Portes, Creekes, Bayes, and Hauens, of the Weast India*, John Frampton's translation of a text of Martin Fernández de Enciso. See Morgan, "Virginia's Other Prototype," 346; Williams, *The American Indian*, 126–7.

[41] MacMillan, *Sovereignty and Possession*, 49–78.

[42] Richard Hakluyt (the younger), "Discourse of Western Planting," 250; and see 297–313. "St. Helen" is the settlement of Santa Elena referred to in n.9 of this chapter.

[43] Ibid., 307. For the younger Hakluyt's full critique of *Inter Caetera* see 297–313.

jurisdiction to judge among temporal princes. The pope might properly desire to promote Christian evangelization, "But none of the prophetts made Bulls or donations in their palaces under their handes and seales and dates, to bestowe many kingdoms wch they never sawe nor knewe, nor what nor how large they were, or to say the truth whether they were extant in *rerum natura*, as the Pope hath done in gevinge all the west Indies to the kinges of Spaine."[44] To do so was, as Vitoria had concluded, to make war on innocents (which, Hakluyt stressed, the Indians were – though "idolaters" and withal "wretched" – being "goodd and of a gentle and amyable nature, wch willingly will obey, yea be contented to serve those that shall with gentlenes and humanitie goo aboute to allure them, as yt is necessarie for those that be sente thither hereafter so to doo"[45]). The pope "shoulde firste have don as the prophetts dyd, that is he shoulde firste have gon himselfe and preached the worde of God to those Idolatrous kinges and their people, and then if they would not by any meanes have repented, he mighte have pronounced the severe and heavie judgemente of God ... that one kingdome is translated from another for the sinnes of the Inhabitantes of the same, and that God in his justice woulde surely bringe some nation or other upon them to take vengaunce of their synnes and wickednes." Here was an argument not at all unlike that which Vitoria had made from the law of nature and nations.[46] But, Hakluyt then added, so to pronounce

---

[44] Ibid., 300.

[45] Ibid., 214, 216, 223. Vitoria too had questioned the adequacy and sincerity with which Christianity had been preached by the Spanish. "It is not sufficiently clear to me that the Christian faith has yet been so put before the aborigines and announced to them that they are bound to believe it or commit fresh sin." Rather than "persuasive demonstration," the Indians had met with "scandals and cruel crimes and acts of impiety." Christianity had not been preached to them "with such sufficient propriety and piety that they are bound to acquiesce in it." Nor "although the Christian faith may have been announced to the Indians with adequate demonstration and they have refused to receive it" was this "a reason which justifies making war on them and depriving them of their property." Those (unbelievers) "who have never received the faith, like Gentiles and Jews, are in no wise to be compelled to do so." War was "no argument for the truth of the Christian faith. Therefore the Indians can not be induced by war to believe, but rather to feign belief and reception of the Christian faith, which is monstrous and a sacrilege." Refusal to receive Christianity, Vitoria concluded, was not adequate and lawful reason "for the seizure of the lands of the aborigines." Vitoria, *On the Indians Lately Discovered*, 144–5.

[46] Richard Hakluyt (the younger), "Discourse of Western Planting," 300. Vitoria had argued that although the Indians could not be compelled to convert, the Spanish had a right by the law of nature and nations to preach and propagate Christianity. "They can teach the truth to those willing to hear them, especially as regards matters pertaining to salvation and happiness, much more than as regards matters pertaining to any human subject of instruction ... because the natives would otherwise be outside the pale of salvation, if Christians were not allowed to go to them carrying the Gospel message," and "because brotherly correction is required by the law of nature, just as brotherly love is. Since, then, the Indians are all not only in sin, but outside the pale of salvation ... it concerns Christians to correct and direct them." Having previously established that "if the Indians allow the Spaniards freely and without hindrance to preach the Gospel, then whether they do or do not receive the faith, this furnishes no lawful ground for making war on

was not in any case a jurisdiction confined in exercise to the papacy. "[T]hus moche not onely Popes but also any other godly and zealous Bisshoppe or mynister may doo beinge called thereunto by God extraordinarily, or havinge the ordinarye warrante of his worde."[47] Here was less a rejection than an assimilation of papal capacity fully in conformity with the spirit of the English Reformation. Henry VIII had created a formally unified English protestant church and state that denied any dependence on other temporal or spiritual authority. The Henrician Reformation had not destroyed the ecclesial authority enjoyed by the papacy but had rather appropriated it to the English Crown as an act of national state ascendancy, claiming for the monarchy the jurisdiction over church formerly vested in the papacy as well as state.

For John Dee, and for both Hakluyts, younger and elder, Christian evangelism was the point of departure and general underpinning for English planting. Dee held it a fundamental requirement of Roman law that all Christian princes, whether Protestant or Catholic, engage in the evangelization of barbarians. To fail to evangelize was to transgress the law of nations.[48] So also, the first of Richard Hakluyt the younger's nineteen principal arguments for western planting was that it be "greately for thinlargement of the gospel of Christe," emphasizing at the same time that the gospel in question was that "whereunto the Princes of the refourmed relligion are chefely bounde" amongst whom "her ma^{tie} ys principall."[49] Of thirty-one "Inducements to the Liking of the Voyage intended towards Virginia" developed by the elder Hakluyt in 1585 to advise Raleigh, printed in pamphlet form in 1602, the first two were "The glory of God by planting of religion among those infidels," and "The increase of the force of the Christians."[50]

them," Vitoria announced the corollary that if the Indians, whether princes or populace, prevented the preaching of the Gospel, or threatened converts, the Spaniards "may then accept or even make war, until they succeed in obtaining facilities and safety for preaching the Gospel" and protecting the faithful. Ultimately, "if there is no other way to carry on the work of religion, this furnishes the Spaniards with another justification for seizing the lands and territory of the natives and for setting up new lords there." Vitoria, *On the Indians Lately Discovered*, 156–7.

[47] Richard Hakluyt (the younger), "Discourse of Western Planting," 300–1.

[48] MacMillan, *Sovereignty and Possession*, 62–3.

[49] Richard Hakluyt (the younger), "Discourse of Western Planting," 211. Unlike the Thomist theologians of Salamanca who followed Aquinas in emphasizing that all rights (*iura*) whether of subjects or rulership were natural, "the consequence of God's law, not of God's grace," protestant theologians of the Reformation (principally Luther) and their forebears, John Wyclif (c. 1325–1384) and Jan Huss (c. 1369–1415), argued that the authority of rulers (and the rights of subjects) flowed directly from God's grace, hence that only a godly ruler was legitimate and only a godly subject had rights. When it came to the rights of non-Christians, whether princes or peoples, Protestant doctrines of grace carried with them the obvious threat of legitimate displacement: pagan rulers could not be godly rulers; pagan peoples could not be saved by rights founded in natural law. Pagden, "Introduction," xvi. Vitoria discusses the conflict between doctrines of grace and law at some length in *On the Indians Lately Discovered*, 121–5.

[50] Richard Hakluyt (the elder), *Pamphlet for the Virginia Enterprise* (1585), in Taylor, *Original Writings and Correspondence*, at 327.

When it came to establishing a design for English colonizing as a practice, however, propagation of the gospel appeared more beneficiary than immediate focus.[51] Before the younger Hakluyt's exposition of the initial proposition of the "Discourse" was a quarter complete, it had passed from the end of evangelism to the means. "It remayneth to be throughly weyed and considered by what meanes and by whome this most godly and Christian work may be perfourmed, of inlarginge the glorious gospell of Christe, and reducinge of infinite multitudes of these simple people that are in errour into the right and perfecte waye of their salvacion." Preachers should be sent if souls were to be saved, but "the meanes to sende suche as shall labour effectually in this busines ys by plantinge one or twoo Colonies of our nation upon that fyrme, where they may remaine in safetie." From that point on, *planting* grabbed center stage in Hakluyt's "Discourse," its deployment and prospects for success (developed in the remainder of his first proposition, and those that followed) his abiding concern: revival of trades, production of commodities, employment of the idle, and withal a general accretion in "the strengthe of our Realme."[52]

The younger Hakluyt's deliberative trajectory was followed, more tersely, by his cousin. Debating "The ends of this voyage [to Virginia]," the elder Hakluyt's 1585 "Inducements" considered that they were "To plant Christian religion. To trafficke. To conquer. Or, to doe all three." He continued, virtually in the form of a syllogism:

> To plant Christian religion without conquest, will bee hard.
> Trafficke easily followeth conquest: conquest is not easie.
> Trafficke without conquest seemeth possible, and not uneasie.
> What is to be done, is the question.[53]

The elder Hakluyt's reasoning appeared to favor a simple "trafficke," that is, commerce or "vent": the opening of markets with others, a mutual bartering of commodities. Here was an expression of that natural right of Europeans acknowledged by Vitoria as "natural society and fellowship" with the Indians – to travel and abide peacefully, to have access to all that was in common ("running water and the sea are common to all, so are rivers and harbors ... Therefore it is not lawful to keep any one from them"), to communicate, to trade ("provided they do no hurt to citizens").[54] But the practicalities of the matter were not so simple. Trade depended on an impulse to exchange, but "If the people be content to live naked, and to content themselves with few things of meere necessity, then trafficke is not." If, on the other hand, the people "be clothed, and desire to live in

---

[51] Simply one element in an enterprise that "blurred any real distinction between military glory, God's work and profit." Pagden, *Lords of all the World*, 35. For a close analysis of the relationship between evangelization and colonizing in the younger Hakluyt's "Discourse," see Sacks, "Discourses of Western Planting," 410–53.

[52] Richard Hakluyt (the younger), "Discourse of Western Planting," 214, 215, 270, 313–19.

[53] Richard Hakluyt (the elder), *Pamphlet for the Virginia Enterprise*, (1585), at 332.

[54] Vitoria, *On the Indians Lately Discovered*, 151–2.

the abundance of all such things as Europe doth, and have at home all the same in plentie, yet we can not have trafficke with them, by meane they want not any thing that we can yeeld them." Or admit a third variation (also the likeliest) – "that they have desire to [our] commodities" but "neither Golde, Silver, Copper, Iron, nor sufficient quantitie of other present commoditie to mainteine the yeerely trade." On any of these premises the chances of a successful "trafficke" with the people of the mainland appeared much reduced, offering few real possibilities. And from this point on, "trafficke" in the elder Hakluyt's "Inducements" took on something of the appearance of evangelism in his cousin's "Discourse," an honorable and virtuous pursuit but dependent for its achievement upon a prerequisite – planting – attention to which completely alters the end originally articulated.[55]

The necessities of planting altered the elder Hakluyt's nominal goal ("trafficke") by introducing a qualitative shift in its expression.[56] The "Inducements" constantly invoke commerce, but the meaning of commerce shifts from the bilateral exchanges of commodities between peoples across trading frontiers with which Hakluyt began, to the colonizer's appropriation of local resources, principally land and raw materials, and organization of production for export. That is, Hakluyt's "trafficke" becomes a commerce in commodities produced by the colonizers (planters) themselves. The indigenous population ceases to be significant, either as consumer or producer. It becomes an irrelevance, fades from view:

> The soile and climate first is to be considered, and you are with Argus eies to see what commoditie by industrie of man you are able to make it to yeeld, that England doth want or doth desire ... admit the soile were in our disposition (as yet it is not) in what time may this be brought about?
>
> ...
>
> how the naturall people of the countrey may be made skilfull to plant Vines, and to know the use, or to set Olive trees, and to know the making of Oile, and withall to use both the trades, that is a matter of small consideration: but to conquer a countrey or province in climate & soile of Italie, Spaine, or the Islands from whence we receive our Wines & Oiles, and to man it, to plant it, and to keepe it ... were a matter of great importance.[57]

---

[55] Richard Hakluyt (the elder), *Pamphlet for the Virginia Enterprise* (1585), at 332–3.

[56] It is worth noting that by far the larger part of the elder Hakluyt's writings on trade and commerce addressed the opening of English commerce with northeastern Europe and the eastern Mediterranean, forms of commerce which in no sense involved the creation of plantations and the migration of peoples. See, for example, his *Notes on Dyestuffs* (1579), *Instructions for the North-east Passage* (1580), *Notes on the Levant Trade* (1582), and *Notes for a Factor at Constantinople* (1582), all in Taylor, ed., *Original Writings and Correspondence*, I, 137–8, 147–58, 182–3, 184–95.

[57] Richard Hakluyt (the elder), *Pamphlet for the Virginia Enterprise* (1585), at 333–4. Later in this book we shall encounter Daniel Defoe, whose travel writings and political economy (always intimately related) identify Defoe as an eighteenth-century successor to both Hakluyts as a propagandist of empire. For the present it is enough to note Defoe's authorial debt to the Elizabethans, as Martin Green does in his *Dreams of Adventure, Deeds of*

Evangelizing and commerce, the first articulated justifications for transoceanic English expansion, thus faded in practical significance as the
earliest theorists and designers of expansion turned in the 1580s to the
measures necessary for their realization. Evangelism is of effect only insofar as it rests upon, and justifies, the occupation of territory from which
evangelization of "the naturalls" may at some unspecified future moment
safely begin.[58] Commerce, ostensibly and in principle a mutually civilizing, mutually beneficial "trafficke" between peoples, in practice becomes
an activity in the success of which one can be confident only to the extent
that it is actually segregated from the indigenous population. Instead of an
agency of mutuality, commerce is transformed, becomes an expression of
wholly intra-English relationships – between *colon* occupants of new territories and their metropolitan sponsors. Nor, even in these desiccated forms,
is either Christianity or commerce independently self-realizing: both
require planting, yet neither furnishes the instrumentalities or technologies that are conditions of planting's success. Rather, both serve planting, and planting's ultimate expression, keeping, for as Vitoria's critique
of Spanish colonizing acknowledges, in both spheres indigenous refusals
might be seized upon as breaches of the law of nature and nations to justify wars of conquest. The elder Hakluyt was well aware of this. Although

Empire (London, 1980), 71, but also to employ him briefly to demonstrate how the transformed "trafficke" of Hakluyt's "Inducements" anticipates the mercantilist political economy of the first British Empire, as expressed in Defoe's political economy some 150 years
later. As J. A. Downie puts it, an "insistence on imperialism runs through Defoe's writings
on economics, and finds a place in his narratives." Writing of *Robinson Crusoe*, Downie
continues, "Crusoe is *not* the prototype colonist because he never has the opportunity to
trade with the home country, and this is of central importance to Defoe's economic vision.
His mercantile view led him to accept as axiomatic the need for a favourable balance of
trade, and the more hands through which goods passed the better, providing those hands
were British." Hakluyt's "trafficke," that is, was what would become Defoe's imperial political economy – the commercial system of the navigation acts, of British colonies trading
the products of British hands with Britain, of "naturall people of the countrey" shifted to
the margins, out of sight, "of small consideration." See J. A. Downie, "Defoe, Imperialism
and the Travel Books Reconsidered," in Roger D. Lund, *Critical Essays on Daniel Defoe*
(New York, 1997), 87–8. On this transition, see Alison Games, *The Web of Empire: English
Cosmopolitans in an Age of Expansion, 1560–1660* (New York, 2008), 117–46.

[58] Richard Hakluyt (the younger), "Discourse of Western Planting," 216. In earlier writings, the younger Hakluyt had been critical of Martin Frobisher's northwestern voyaging
(1576–8) for his "preposterous desire of seeking rather gaine then God's glorie." See
his Preface to *Divers Voyages*, 178. Frobisher's expedition to mine what he thought was
gold off Baffin Island had resulted in his return to England with several hundred tons
of worthless quartz. See Morgan, *American Slavery, American Freedom*, 19. But Hakluyt's
"Preface" made clear the strong positive relationship he perceived between laudable
wealth-producing activity (planting rather than extraction) and godliness. "Godliness is
great riches ... if we first seeke the kingdome of God, al other thinges will be given unto
us ... as the light accompanieth the Sunne and the heate the fire, so lasting riches do
wait upon them that are jealous for the advancement of the Kingdom of Christ, and the
enlargement of his glorious Gospell" (178). On the tensions in sixteenth-century humanism between colonizing as wealth-seeking and as an instantiation of virtue and *vita activa*,
see Fitzmaurice, *Humanism and America*, 1–3.

his "Inducements" express considerable caution about the difficulties of conquest, recommend that "the people of those parties" be drawn "by all courtesie into love with our nation," and advise that "a gentle course without crueltie and tyrannie" will best plant Christianity and best preserve "our seating most void of blood, most profitable in trade of merchandise, most firme and stable, and least subiect to remoove by practise of enemies," he does not doubt that the English can also take legal advantage of resistance.[59] The point is made most cogently in an undated, likely preliminary, draft of the "Inducements":

> Yf we fynde any kinges readye to defende their Tirratoryes by warre and the Countrye populous desieringe to expell us that seeke but juste and lawfull Traffique, then ... [we may] be revenged of any wronge offered by them and consequentlie maye yf we will conquere, fortefye and plante in soyles moste sweete, most pleasaunte, moste fertill and strounge. And in the ende to bring them all in subjection or scyvillitie.[60]

Planting in the name of Christianity and commerce might thus easily become keeping. Hakluyt's advice was virtually a formal briefing on how *ius gentium* renders indigenous resistance to "juste and lawfull Traffique" a "wronge" that can be lawfully revenged by conquest.[61]

II. Terra Nullius?

Having traced the clear presence of discourses of Christianity and commerce in the most important Elizabethan colonizing tracts, it is of some interest to note that the Crown's letters patent to Sir Humphrey Gilbert and Sir Walter Raleigh licensing the voyaging of the 1580s, which the writings of Dee and the Hakluyts supported and informed, did not in fact begin from either an evangelizing or a commercial premise at all. Virtually identical in phrasing, by the "especial grace, certaine science, and meere motion" of the Crown

---

[59] Richard Hakluyt (the elder), *Pamphlet for the Virginia Enterprise* (1585), at 334.

[60] Richard Hakluyt (the elder), "Pamphlet for the Virginia Enterprise" (n.d.), in Taylor, ed., *Original Writings and Correspondence*, II, 339–43, at 342. Hakluyt's pamphlet of the same title dated 1585 (The "Inducements") contains similar phrasing but breaks up the passages in such a way as to obscure founding the justice of conquest upon indigenous obligations to allow English "trafficke" under the law of nature and nations. See his *Pamphlet for the Virginia Enterprise* (1585), at 329–30.

[61] See also Sir George Peckham, *A True Reporte, Of the late discoueries, and possession, taken in the right of the Crowne of Englande, of the New-found Landes: By that valiant and worthye Gentleman, Sir Humfrey Gilbert Knight. Wherein is also breefely sette down, her highnesse lawful Tytle thereunto, and the great and manifolde Commodities that is likely to grow thereby to the whole Realme in generall, and to the Aduenturers in particular. Together with the easiness and shortness of the Voyage* (London, 1583), chapter 2, sig c₂v, which "sheweth that it is lawfull and necessarye to trade and traficke with the Sauages. And to plant in their Countries"; William Strachey, *The Historie of Travaile into Virginia Britannia: Expressing the Cosmographie and Comodities of the Country, Togither with the Manners and Customes of the People*, R. H. Major, ed. (written 1609–12; published London 1849), 16–17, 19–20 [elaborating the right to trade and to plant under the law of nations, and the right to retaliate against aggression].

each gave effect to voyages of discovery and conquest "to discouer, search, finde out, and view such remote, heathen and barbarous lands, countries, and territories, not actually possessed of any Christian Prince, nor inhabited by Christian People." Ken MacMillan has argued that the letters patent were addressed principally to the English Crown's European competitors in transoceanic voyaging. They served as an expression of the Crown's extended claim of *imperium* (sovereignty) and of its prerogative authority to realize actual *dominium* (possession, rule) within its *imperium* by distributing lands not previously distributed or actually possessed to its licensees "to haue, holde, occupie and enjoy." Purposely imitating the language of *Inter caetera* in their foundation of authority upon the monarch's "especial grace, certaine science, and meere motion" – phrasing that appears repeatedly in letters patent and charters licensing colonizing schemes throughout the following century – the letters stated the Crown's purpose as the acquisition of dominion through agents acting for it within its claimed *imperium*. To complete the acquisition the letters enjoined the licensee to take actual possession – "to inhabite or remaine there, to build and fortifie."[62]

In these initial letters, as in subsequent seventeenth-century letters patent (charters) licensing schemes of colonizing the English were, MacMillan contends, deliberately crafting their claims to *imperium* and *dominium* according to the language and concepts of Roman law. They had two reasons to do so. First, medieval reception of Roman law had furnished Europe's *ius commune*; English common law was merely a local vernacular legal language. To employ the conceptual discourse of Roman law to craft English claims was to improve the chances that the broader European community of transoceanic competitors would recognize, or at least acquiesce, in English activities.[63] This was undoubtedly the most important consideration. But second, MacMillan argues that common law "possessed no doctrines for the acquisition of sovereignty over territory because the doctrine of tenures held that no land subject to the common law could be outside a state of sovereignty." The *acquisition* of sovereignty over new found lands could therefore occur only through resort to a legal system that did offer the necessary doctrinal capacities. Roman law furnished useful precedents "for the acquisition of territorial sovereignty and possession of *terra nullius*."[64]

Roman law certainly offered language attractive to those who coveted new found lands, but it is questionable whether Roman law actually did offer doctrinal grounds on which acquisition of sovereignty could be defended absent a crucial (and closely related) ally, the law of war.[65] Vitoria, after

---

[62] Charter to Sir Walter Raleigh (1584), 53. MacMillan, *Sovereignty and Possession*, 1–48.

[63] MacMillan, *Sovereignty and Possession*, 13–15.

[64] Ibid., 33, 106. This argument is also embraced by Elliott in *Empires of the Atlantic World*, 12, 30–2.

[65] As we shall shortly see, with only one rare and highly particular exception, Roman law no more hypothesized the possibility of land existing outside a state of sovereignty than English common law. Claims that Roman law exhibits a "doctrine" of *terra nullius* distract attention from the far more potent resources represented in the law of war.

all, had found no basis for Spanish "sway" over the Indians in claims of either temporal or papal *imperium* or of papal donation. What Vitoria *had* allowed was that the Spanish could claim just cause to seize provinces and sovereignty by wars of conquest if those wars were founded upon the failure of the Indians to abide by the duties and obligations of natural society and fellowship under the law of nature and nations.[66] In the course of *De Indis*, Vitoria had twice taken note of Roman law's so-called occupant's title, "inasmuch as things that belong to nobody are acquired by the first occupant according to the law of nations," but on the first occasion he dismissed its relevance to Spanish territorial claims, and on the second acknowledged it only within the limits of its own express, distinctly nonterritorial, meaning. Nowhere, that is, did Vitoria grant first occupancy any credibility as a basis for *territorial* acquisition.[67]

---

[66] Vitoria, *On the Indians Lately Discovered*, 151–3.

[67] Vitoria's first comment on occupant's title came in his discussion of the validity of title by right of discovery, by virtue of which "Columbus the Genoan first set sail." This, he said, "seems to be an adequate title because those regions which are deserted become, by the law of nations and the natural law, the property of the first occupant [citing Justinian's *Institutes*, II, 1, xii *ferae bestiae*]. Therefore, as the Spaniards were the first to discover and occupy the provinces in question, they are in lawful possession thereof, just as if they had discovered some lonely and thitherto uninhabited region." But the regions in question were not deserted, having lawful possessors and true owners in situ. That is, the barbarians themselves already enjoyed sovereignty and dominion "both from the public and from the private standpoint." The rule of the law of nations was "what belongs to nobody is granted to the first occupant, as is expressly laid down in … the *Institutes*. And so, as the object in question was not without an owner, it does not fall under the title which we are discussing." Occupant's title gave no more support to a seizure of the territories of the aborigines "than if it had been they who discovered us." Ibid., 139.
  Given that the title asserted had no relevance to the facts of the matter, Vitoria found it unnecessary at this point to consider in any detail the validity of the analogy from the *Institutes*' statement of occupant's title (which deals with rules for the appropriation of animate objects, that is *ferae bestiae* [wild beasts], and inanimate objects found in public places) to uninhabited land. He alluded to the possibility, deferring discussion, that occupant's title "when conjoined with another, can produce some effect here," but when one comes to that deferred discussion (at 153), one finds that it too has nothing whatever to do with the occupation of lands but addresses rather the effect on Spanish claims of what the *Institutes* actually indicate are the full extent *and limits* of occupant's title when conjoined with Spanish claims based on the natural right of communication and participation. "If there are among the Indians any things which are treated as common both to citizens and to strangers, the Indians may not prevent the Spaniards from a communication and a participation in them. If, for example, other foreigners are allowed to dig for gold in the land of the community or in rivers, or to fish for pearls in the sea or in a river, the natives can not prevent the Spaniards from doing this, but they have the same right to do it as others have, so long as the citizens and indigenous population are not hurt thereby." And "Inasmuch as things that belong to nobody are acquired by the first occupant according to the law of nations [again citing *Institutes*, II, 1, xii] it follows that if there be in the earth gold or in the sea pearls or in a river anything else which is not appropriated by the law of nations those will vest in the first occupant, just as the fish in the sea do." Ibid., 153.
  Anthony Pagden and Jeremy Lawrance contend that there is a contradiction between Vitoria's denial of occupant's title in the first instance and recognition of it in the second.

The English Crown's letters patent accorded occupant's title a somewhat enhanced significance. First, by directing its agents specifically to territories "not actually possessed of any Christian Prince, nor inhabited by Christian People," the Crown indicated that it would limit its claims to those territories within its notional North Atlantic *imperium* over which it might actually realize *dominium* by its own occupation without disturbing prior Christian occupants, which is to say other European claimants in actual possession. Second, and more interesting, by remaining studiously silent about non-Christian occupants notwithstanding clear knowledge of their existence and physical presence *in situ*, the Crown appeared to claim that only Christian possession counted as first possession. Lands without Christian possessors were simply vacant.[68]

But was there, in fact, any consistent conception of first occupant's title in Roman law that could be applied to New World territories in such fashion? Vitoria, it seems clear, thought not. What of other scholars? Second, did contemporary expositors of the meaning of sovereign possession indeed fail to acknowledge non-Christians?

In his treatise on the law of war, *De Iure Belli* (first published in parts in 1588–9), the Italian humanist and Oxford University Regius professor of civil law, Alberico Gentili, held without qualification that seizure and occupation of vacant places was recognized to be "a law of nature." For "'God did not create the world to be empty'." So exiles might take possession of the places they came to dwell "which were then without inhabitants."[69] Gentili elaborated, citing Justinian's *Digest*. "The ruling of

---

See Pagden and Lawrance, annotated comments on *Relection of the Very Revered Father Friar Francisco de Vitoria ... a.d. 1539 [De Indis]* in *Francesco de Vitoria: Political Writings*, 264 n.63, and 280 n.77. But there is no contradiction. In the first instance, prior barbarian dominion renders claims to occupant's title irrelevant; empirical circumstance renders it unnecessary even to consider the matter. In the second, Vitoria simply adduces what effect occupant's title *can* have in empirical circumstances to which it does apply – things recognized by the indigenous themselves as things held in common or in the public domain – that is, in circumstances that are precisely within the terms of what the *Institutes* (and, at greater length, the *Digest*) have to say about the application of occupants' title.

[68] In the Gilbert and Raleigh patents there was no explicit intimation that the territories in question were unpossessed and uninhabited, simply that they were not possessed by *Christian* princes or inhabited by *Christian* peoples. Evidence of Crown knowledge that the lands in question were possessed by princes and inhabited by peoples is manifest in the documents and memorials prepared in support of the issuance of the patents, which were peppered with references to inhabitants – heathen people, barbarians, people, idolators, savages and so forth – and in the letters patents themselves, which referred to "heathen and barbarous lands." See, e.g., MacMillan, *Sovereignty and Possession*, 62–3, 72–3; the younger Hakluyt's "Discourse of Western Planting," 214, 216, 217, 223. For a contrary view, see Patricia Seed, *American Pentimento: The Invention of Indians and the Pursuit of Riches* (Minneapolis, 2001), 29.

[69] Alberico Gentili, *De Iure Belli Libri Tres, Volume Two – The Translation of the Edition of 1612*, John C. Rolfe, trans. (Oxford 1933), 80 [citing *Digest* 41.1.3]. See *The Digest of Justinian*, Latin text edited by Theodore Mommsen with the aid of Paul Krueger, English translation edited by Alan Watson, in 4 vols. (Philadelphia, 1985), IV, Book 41 at 1.3. Amongst exiles ("those who ... are driven from their own country or are compelled to leave it

our jurists with regard to unoccupied land is, that those who take it have a right to it, since it is the property of no one."[70] Such statements are often taken as invocations of a concept of *terra nullius* as if it were a doctrine alive and known in Roman law and as such available to European colonizers. But the passage Gentili cited actually says nothing of the sort:[71] no such concept as *terra nullius* existed, either in ancient or in early-modern Roman law – as, indeed, Gentili's next comment acknowledged: for though unoccupied and uncultivated, "such lands belong to the sovereign of that territory."[72] Granted, "because of that law of nature which abhors a vacuum, they will fall to the lot of those who take them. So be it, but let the sovereign retain jurisdiction over them."[73] Gentili in fact took considerable exception to Spanish claims that it was "beyond dispute ... lawful to take possession of those lands which were not previously known to us"; as if, he observed, "to be known to none of *us* were the same thing as to be possessed by no one."[74]

through some emergency and to seek another home") Gentili included those (as in More's *Utopia*) whom "the excessive growth of their population has sent forth, in order to relieve their own cities," 79.

Gentili's treatise was first written during the 1580s as a series of three commentaries on the law of war published seriatim in London in 1588 and 1589, and also as a continuous work (*De Jure Belli Commentationes Tres*; London, 1589). The commentaries were revised and rewritten and published as a treatise, *De Iure Belli Libri Tres* in 1598 (in Hanau, Prussia). A Protestant, Gentili was educated at Perugia. He arrived a refugee in London in August 1580, by way of Tübigen and Heidelberg. After moving to Oxford in November 1580, he was appointed Professor of Roman Law at St. John's College; he was appointed Regius Professor of Civil Law in 1587. Gentili's work on the concept of just war and on the law of nations and nature was highly influential in England. See Gesina H. J. Van Der Molen, *Alberico Gentili and the Development of International Law* (Leyden, 1968), 35–54; K. R. Simmonds, "Some English Precursors of Hugo Grotius," *Transactions of the Grotius Society*, 43 (1957), 147–57.

70 Gentili, *De Iure Belli*, 80.

71 The passage Gentili cites to support his elaboration [*Digest*, 41.2.1.1] comments on theories of the origins of ownership and outlines a precise category of things that might be considered still subject to possessor's title: "The younger Nerva says that the ownership of things originated in natural possession and that a relic thereof survives in the attitude to those things which are taken on land, sea, or in the air; for such things forthwith become the property of those who first take possession of them. In like manner, things captured in war, islands arising in the sea, and gems, stones, and pearls found on the seashore become the property of him who first takes possession of them." The remainder of the passage discusses how possession can be acquired – whether in person, through agents and so forth.

72 Gentili, *De Iure Belli*, 81.

73 Ibid., 81. And note the original language of the entire passage discussed here: "Deus non ad inanitatem creavit terram. & ergo iuris naturæ censetur occupatio vacuorum. Sic in prisco factum mundo. Sic Bataui ... vacua cultoribus loca, quæ nunc tenent, occuparunt. Sic alii fecerunt, & facient. Sic de terris *incultis*, ut quærantur occupanti quasi nullius, nostri docent. & principis territorii et si sint, quod alii volunt, cedent tamen occupanti propter ius naturæ, quæ nihil vult vacuum. Sic: & maneat iurisdictio principis." Alberico Gentili, *De Iure Belli Libri Tres, Volume One – The Photographic Reproduction of the Edition of 1612* (Oxford 1933), 131 (emphasis added).

74 Ibid., 89 [emphasis added].

Roman law certainly allowed, as Vitoria had noted, that under the law of nations a thing (*res*) that "presently belongs to no one" might become "by natural reason the property of the first taker." But the principle's points of reference are, with one exception, invariably animate: "all animals taken on land, sea, or in the air, that is, wild beasts, birds and fish." These, further, are things that may "escape from our custody and return to their natural state of freedom." When they do, "they cease to be ours and are again open to the first taker."[75] To its pronounced emphasis on beasts, birds, and fish (also swarms of bees, which "are wild until ... housed by us in our hives," but which, upon leaving, cannot be claimed as property once out of sight),[76] the *Digest* added categories of inanimate objects open to appropriation – acquisition of ownership – by a first taker. First came "gems, stones, and pearls found on the seashore," for seashores were public "not in the sense that they belong to the community as such but that they are initially provided by nature and have hitherto become no one's property."[77] Second came "things captured in war" – although strictly speaking only free men could be appropriated (enslaved) by a "first taker" in war; and, like wild animals, "those who escape the power of the enemy regain their original freedom." Of other things captured in war, the *Digest* held that under the law of nations "property taken from the enemy is forthwith the property of the taker." But this was a forcible transfer or conversion of what was already property, hardly a first taking.[78]

The *Digest* makes but one reference to *land* in the category of things open to appropriation by a "first taker," namely "an island arising in the sea." This it denominates "a rare occurrence."[79] The reference is not to new-*discovered* lands appearing on the horizon but to the physical consequences of geological events, volcanic or tectonic, the literal appearance of new land. The circumstances that rendered this new land open to appropriation by a first taker were very special. Because the island arose in the sea, which is "by natural law common to all,"[80] it was analogous to a pearl on the seashore, also common to all. Neither island nor pearl exists in any relationship to a prior structure of ownership. The point is underlined emphatically by all other discussion of new and vacant land in the *Digest*, which deals minutely with the ownership of putatively "new" islands that arise in rivers ("a frequent occurrence") by the action of alluvion, or by natural changes in water courses. No new riverine land was open to appropriation by a first taker; ownership was predetermined by the existing structure of ownership of adjacent or proximate land. Underlining this, the term

---

[75] *Digest*, IV, 41.1.3.

[76] Ibid., 41.1.5.2–4.

[77] Ibid., 41.2.1.1, 41.1.14. Note the same in Vitoria, *On the Indians Lately Discovered*, 152.

[78] Ibid., 41.2.1.1, 41.1.7, 41.1.5.7. Note that the *Digest*'s discussion of possession of things had long been well known to English law because it is reproduced more or less intact by Bracton. See *Bracton: De Legibus et Consuetudinibus Angliæ (Bracton on the Laws and Customs of England)* attributed to Henry de Bratton c. 1210–1268, Samuel E. Thorne, trans. (Cambridge, Mass. 1968–77), II, 39–47.

[79] Ibid., 41.1.7.3

[80] *The Institutes of Justinian*, trans. J. B. Moyle (Oxford, 1913) 2.1.1.

for "land" used in the Digest in such cases is not *terra* at all, but *fundus* or estate: that is, land already the property of someone.[81]

Ownership and possession, whether of land or things, were of course quite distinct concepts. Possession might be claimed mentally, as by an owner, but it could not be asserted against other claimants except by physical control.

[81] For example, *Digest* 41.1.7.1–6, 41.1.29, 41.1.30.1–4. On the intellectual history of *terra nullius*, see Andrew Fitzmaurice, "The Genealogy of *Terra Nullius*," *Australian Historical Studies*, 38 (2007), 1–15. See also Andrew Fitzmaurice, "Moral Uncertainty in the Dispossession of Native Americans," in Mancall, ed., *The Atlantic World and Virginia*, 383–409, at 387–8, n. 6. Fitzmaurice identifies *terra nullius* as an early twentieth-century latinate formulation (or, less flattering, tag) invented in the wake of the more specific term *territorium nullius* (no sovereign's land) which had itself been coined in the late nineteenth century by international lawyers. The impulse behind the invention of *territorium nullius* was European and American desire to establish rules for the partition of territories deemed suitable for colonization, notably Africa. Though a modern invention, Fitzmaurice argues that *terra nullius* and its cognates were produced by "the history of dispossession and the larger history of European expansion." See "Genealogy of *Terra Nullius*," 2. On the origins and usage of *territorium nullius* in international law, see M. F. Lindley, *The Acquisition and Government of Backward Territory in International Law: Being a Treatise on the Law and Practice Relating to Colonial Expansion* (London, 1926; repr. New York, 1969), 1–40.

Examination of the relationship of discovery to claims of occupant's title in land appears in the work of Hugo Grotius. See *Mare Liberum*, 13 (citing *Digest* 41.1.3), 21; Hugo Grotius, *De Jure Belli ac Pacis Libri Tres*, Francis W. Kelsey trans. (Oxford and London, 1925), II.2.4 (191–2). I discuss Grotius in Chapter 4. Here it suffices to say that *Mare Liberum* largely reproduces Vitoria's arguments (as described earlier, in n.67), whereas *De Juri Belli ac Pacis* clearly extends occupant's title to uncultivated land. Apparent references by Grotius to a territorial application of *res nullius* in *Mare Liberum* are the work of the translator – the words are not used as such in the original Latin. The first contemporary definition of "res nullius" as a category in English appears to occur in Thomas Wood, *A New Institute of the Imperial or Civil Law. With Notes, Shewing in some Principal Cases amongst other Observations, how the Canon law, the Laws of England, and the Laws and Customs of other Nations differ from it. In Four Books.* (London, 1704), 67 (*res nullius* references "things which are not the Goods of any Person or Number of Men" and including "Derelicts, wild Beasts, Birds, Fishes and Pearl found in the Sea, or Treasure found in the Ground"). As a doctrinal category *res nullius* may have acquired its capacious Anglophone meaning in the later nineteenth century through Henry Sumner Maine, *Ancient Law: Its Connection with the Early History of Society, and its Relation to Modern Ideas* (5th ed., London, 1874; first published 1861), 244–53. Discussing "the practice of occupancy" (*occupatio*), that is the "taking possession of that which at the moment is the property of no man," Maine described the practice as extending to "The objects which the Roman lawyers called *res nullius* – things which have not or never had an owner," namely "wild animals, fishes, wild fowl, jewels disinterred for the first time, and lands newly discovered or never before cultivated" (245). Maine insisted, further, that "The Roman principle of Occupancy, and the rules into which the jurisconsults expanded it, are the source of all modern International Law on the subject of Capture in War and of the acquisition of sovereign rights in newly discovered countries" (246). Lindley comments simply "Maine goes too far" (10), that in Roman law, occupancy had no application in matters involving sovereignty and inhabited lands even if newly discovered. For a recent examination of the issue, see Lauren Benton and Benjamin Straumann, "Acquiring Empire by Law: From Roman Doctrine to Early Modern European Practice," *Law and History Review*, 28, 1 (February 2010), 1–38.

Somewhat in contrast to this intellectual history, Patricia Seed has credited the invention of *terra nullius* to William Blackstone in 1765, citing his *Commentaries on the Laws of England*. See Seed, *American Pentimento*, 155–6. A search of the *Commentaries* fails to disclose any reference to *terra nullius* as such. Blackstone (echoing Gentili and Grotius)

"Possession is so styled ... from 'seat,' [*sedibus*] as it were 'position,' because there is a natural holding, which the Greeks call κατοχή[82] by the person who stands on a thing."[83] Standing on a thing did not create title, except by long and undisputed standing (prescription), but it did signify exclusivity of possession as long as the possessor retained actual standing, no matter who the "lawful" owner might be. "For it is no more possible that the same possession should be in two persons than that you should be held to stand on the same spot on which I stand or sit in the place where I sit."[84] Some of the commentators collected in the *Digest* thought that possession might be lost by simple loss of will or intent to possess – that is, voluntary abandonment or dereliction; others addressed loss of possession by dint of another's physical intercession. Involuntary loss of possession through the intercession of another required more than the other's physical presence. "Should you be in possession by will alone, you continue to possess the land, even though someone else be physically present on it." Loss implied the necessity of some form of physical usurpation, ranging from uncontested entry of another all the way to forceful ejection. Thus "If someone should inform the owner that his house has been occupied by brigands and, in terror, the owner does not return there, he has certainly lost possession of the house. But if the slave or tenant, through whom I was physically in possession, should die or go away, I retain possession solely by intent" until actually usurped by a competing possessor. "For it is settled that we remain in possession until either we voluntarily abandon it or we are ejected by force."[85] Possession, then, was an active condition of control, or mental intention to control; ownership, per se, an assertion of legal title. Title could not be vacated by another's intervening physical possession; but ownership de jure could not secure possession in fact from a determined interloper.

III. Indigenous Sovereigns?

Gentili touched on the distinction between possession and ownership in identifying unoccupied land as both vacant for possession and "belong[ing] to the sovereign of that territory." A large question arises, however, from

does refer to "lands claimed by right of occupancy only, by finding them desart and uncultivated and peopling them from the mother country," and to a natural right to migrate to "desart uninhabited countries." William Blackstone, *Commentaries on the Laws of England* (Chicago, 1979) I, 104; II, 7. Here, however, Blackstone arguably does no more than reiterate Gentili's passages on exiles' right to occupy vacant places, subject to the jurisdiction of the sovereign owner, an interpretation reinforced by Blackstone's explicit reference to the English North American colonies not as *terra* (or *res*) *nullius* but as "conquered or ceded countries." *Commentaries*, I, 105.

[82] Meaning, variously, occupancy, occupation, possession, tenancy, tenure.

[83] *Digest*, 41.2.1. It should be noted that "seate" is the term Hakluyt the elder chose for the initial position to be established by a colonizer. See Richard Hakluyt (the elder), "Notes on Colonisation" (1578), in Taylor, ed., *Original Writings and Correspondence*, 116–22, at 116.

[84] *Digest*, 41.2.3.5.

[85] Ibid., 41.2.3.7–9.

his further observation that with *belonging* went *jurisdiction* over occupants intruding upon vacant lands ("let the sovereign retain jurisdiction over them").[86] Here Gentili was discussing the accommodation of exiles driven by circumstance from their own country into the lands of another. They were obliged, he argued, to recognize and submit to the jurisdiction of the sovereign of the lands they occupied. Though it was understandable that exiles might resist if refused hospitality and met instead with hostility, "the newcomers ought to do what is most just and submit to the rule of him who is lord of the land."[87] Mere entry and occupation of territory did nothing to disturb a sovereign's right to rule over persons who entered the sovereign's territories. The sovereign's "slight loss" (of vacant land) would be compensated by "an increase in the number of the citizens" populating his territories.[88]

Did, then, English colonizers occupying vacant New World lands subject themselves to the jurisdiction of the sovereign of *that* territory? Who was sovereign in the North American case?

So far as the English Crown was concerned the answer was – itself. The whole point of the legal, geographical, and historical scholarship of Dee and the Hakluyts had been to establish historical-legal foundations for the English Crown to assert mental *imperium* over the Northern Atlantic. The Crown's letters patent formally notified Christian (European) princes actually possessing lands within that mental *imperium* that it would not assert any claim of sovereignty over their possessions. They announced that the Crown had elected to concentrate instead on discovering and occupying lands within its *imperium* not already actually possessed by others. Hence, *imperium* and *dominium* as between Europeans was addressed.

Aside from Christian Europeans already *in situ*, the obvious competitors with the English Crown for the title of sovereign in North America were indigenous (non-Christian) princes. And indeed, by licensing its agents in voyages of conquest as well as discovery the English Crown appeared to concede the possibility that it was not clearly sovereign, that it contemplated gaining possession by force, by seizing territory from indigenous princes, just as the Spanish had done.[89]

---

[86] Gentili, *De Iure Belli*, 81.

[87] Ibid. Exiles who entered the lands of others and were not received with hospitality and were forced to engage in wars in search of places to live did so by unavoidable necessity, hence justly. Yet their wars remained just only for so long as they remained commensurate with necessity. "Care must be taken lest those wanderers grow discontented with the humble means which of course they can acquire for themselves without war, and presently seek still better localities. For that would be an unjust and barbarous action" (80).

[88] Ibid., 81. Recall the younger Hakluyt's observation in the "Discourse of Western Planting," at 238, that population was "the honor and strengthe of a Prince."

[89] Both the Letters Patent to Sir Humfrey Gylberte and to Sir Walter Raleigh (1584) licensed voyages of discovery and conquest. Discovery meant finding out in detail what existed within the English Crown's claimed North Atlantic *imperium*. Conquest meant the overthrow of those non-Christian possessors and inhabitants found to be enjoying or claiming sovereignty within that *imperium*. See, generally, Korman, *Right of Conquest*, 42–7. Noteworthy in this connection is Gentili's defense of the lawfulness of despoiling

We have seen that sovereignty was an essential concept in the intra-European system of state relations governed by *ius gentium* from early in the sixteenth century – well prior, that is, to the "foundational" Westphalian system. Had it not been, states would have had no reason to play the elaborate intra-European Roman law game of *imperium* and *dominium*.[90] To what extent, however, did European colonizers pay heed to the "sovereignty" of transoceanic indigenous princes? Anthony Anghie has argued at some length that they did not, in any meaningful sense. According to Anghie, the transoceanic contacts of the Columbian era induced changes in the European conception of sovereignty designed precisely to rule out the possibility that indigenous peoples exercised a sovereignty that Europeans were bound to respect, while simultaneously refining how Europeans might assert sovereignty over them: "in the first place, the Indian is excluded from the sphere of sovereignty; in the second place, it is the Indian who acts as the object against which the powers of sovereignty may be exercised in the most extreme ways." That is, "through its application to the Indian ... new aspects, powers and techniques of sovereignty can be discovered," for "few limits are imposed on sovereignty when it is applied to the Indian."[91] Anghie's case relies on a lengthy analysis of Vitoria's 1539 *Relectiones – De Indis* and *De Iure Belli*. Vitoria, he concedes, identified certain characteristics of indigenous societies that appeared to count as manifestations of sovereignty, but denied Indians "the most characteristic and unique powers of the sovereign," namely the power "to wage a just war." Sovereign is he, Vitoria declares in effect, "who declares war and exercises all the rights of war."[92] But only just wars are lawful under *ius gentium*. Because the Indians are pagans they cannot wage just wars, they can only be the objects of just wars. Moreover, according to European conceptions of sovereignty, because the Indians are pagans, wars may be prosecuted against them in peculiarly unhinged fashion.[93] In Anghie's analysis, Vitoria's *Relectiones* are indeed the key that refashions the legality of the Spanish New World Empire.

Anghie's statement of Vitoria's understanding of Indian sovereignty is in certain respects debatable, for Vitoria's approach to Indian sovereignty in the *Relectiones* is rather more accommodating than Anghie allows. What is a state, he asks in the second *Relectio*, and what a sovereign prince? "A state is properly called a perfect community." A perfect community, or state, is one complete in itself, sufficient unto itself, "not a part of another community, but has its own laws and its own council and its own magistrates." Such was the Kingdom of Castile and Aragon, the Republic of Venice, and the like. A

---

the conquered of their adornments. Subjugation – loss of sovereignty – is signified precisely by the conqueror's *removal* of existing symbols of sovereignty and substitution of his own. *De Iure Belli*, 310–14.

[90] This point is thoroughly established by MacMillan in *Sovereignty and Possession*.

[91] Anthony Anghie, *Imperialism, Sovereignty and the Making of International Law* (Cambridge, 2004), 27–8, and generally 13–31.

[92] Ibid., 25, 26, 28, and generally 24–8.

[93] Ibid., 26–7.

sovereign prince is he who wields the authority of such a state.[94] In the first *Relectio* Vitoria had already allowed that Indian affairs did in fact manifest statehood. "There is a certain method in their affairs, for they have polities which are orderly arranged and they have definite marriage and magistrates, overlords, laws and workshops, and a system of exchange ... they also have a kind of religion." For these and other reasons, Vitoria concluded that before the intrusions of the Spanish, the Indians had indeed been sovereign. They "had true dominion in both public and private matters, just like Christians," throughout their territories.[95] And indeed, both the logic of the *Relectiones* and particular facts adduced by Vitoria suggest that from Vitoria's point of view, even after the intrusions of the Spanish the Indians continued to demonstrate that in important respects they retained sovereignty.[96]

The purpose of Vitoria's first *Relectio* was to establish on what basis *if any* Spanish ascendancy over the aborigines of the New World might be maintained. Vitoria successively rejected claims founded upon imperial (Holy Roman) suzerainty, papal donation, Spanish discovery, Indian refusal of Christian religion, their mortal sinfulness, their alleged acquiescence, and divine will. He allowed only that Indians' violation of their duties and obligations under the laws of nature and nations could constitute a basis upon which "Indians and their lands could have come or might come into the

94 Francisco de Vitoria, *On the Indians or on the Law of War Made by the Spaniards on the Barbarians* (Second Relectio) [*De Indis Relectio Posterior, sive De Iure Belli Hispanorum in Barbaros*], in *Francisci de Victoria, De Indis et De Iure Belli Relectiones*, Ernest Nys, ed., John Pawley Bate, trans. (Washington, D.C., 1917), 169.

95 Vitoria, *On the Indians Lately Discovered*, 127–8. "It would be harsh to deny to those who have never done any wrong, what we grant to Saracens and Jews, who are the persistent enemies of Christianity. We do not deny that these latter peoples are true owners of their property, if they have not seized lands elsewhere belonging to Christians." 128.

96 Vitoria's consideration of the lawful titles whereby, under the law of nature and nations, the Indians could fall under Spanish sway (ibid., 151–9), assumes throughout the existence of sovereign indigenous lawgiving entities and considers the consequences arising were they to fail in the performance of their obligations whether toward strangers or subjects under the law of nature and nations. For example, "If there are among the Indians any things which are treated as common both to citizens and to strangers, the Indians may not prevent the Spaniards from a communication and participation in them. If, for example, other foreigners are allowed to dig for gold in the land of the community or in rivers, or to fish for pearls in the sea or in a river, the natives can not prevent the Spaniards from doing this, but they have the same right to do it as others have ... [The Spaniards] may make use of the laws and advantages enjoyed by all foreigners" (153). Or if "those who bear rule among the aborigines of America" rule tyrannically or adopt tyrannical laws that "work wrong to innocent folk there" then the Spaniards might intervene to defend the innocent "and it is especially the business of princes to do so" (159). The best example of Vitoria's acknowledgment of indigenous sovereignty, however, is his reference to the Tlaxcaltec-Spanish alliance: "the cause of allies and friends is a just cause of war, a State [that is, the Tlaxcaltec] being quite properly able, as against foreign wrongdoers, to summon foreigners [the Spanish] to punish its enemies [the Aztecs]," 160. The point is not that Vitoria compiles an inventory of the circumstances under which the Spanish can claim lawful title of conquest, but rather, that in Vitoria's analysis the Indians *retain* all the powers of sovereignty *until and unless* they give the Spanish just cause for wars to take sovereignty from them.

possession and lordship of Spain."[97] In the second *Relectio*, Vitoria inquires more closely into the Spanish "seizure and occupation of those lands of the barbarians whom we style Indians" to determine to what extent it comported with the law of war.[98] In fact, his inquiry touches but lightly on the particulars of Spanish action: those have already been addressed in the first *Relectio*.[99] The object of the second *Relectio* is to discuss more fully the law of war to which he adverted in the first, particularly the crucial concept of just cause. The discussion is structured by four inquiries: whether Christians may make war at all; whence derives authority to declare or

[97] Ibid., 160. Note that nowhere in *De Indis* does Vitoria allow that the Indians have actually given the Spanish just cause.

[98] "Inasmuch as the seizure and occupation of those lands of the barbarians whom we style Indians can best, it seems, be defended under the law of war, I propose to supplement the foregoing discussion of the titles, some just and some unjust, which the Spaniards may allege for their hold on the lands in question, by a short discussion of the law of war, so as to give more completeness to that *relectio*." Vitoria, *On the Indians or on the Law of War*, 165.

[99] Accompanied by intimations of doubt: "I fear measures were adopted in excess of what is allowed by human and divine law ... what in itself is lawful [may] be made in the circumstances wrong." Ibid., 158.

Vitoria was less restrained in private correspondence. Writing to Miguel de Arcos in 1534 of news of massacres, assassinations, and despoliation in Peru, he confided, "No business shocks me or embarrasses me more than the corrupt profits and affairs of the Indies. Their very mention freezes the blood in my veins." Acknowledging with admirable candor that his usual course when confronted by defenders of Spanish conquest and seizure of property was "*to run away from them,*" Vitoria nevertheless held that "*if utterly forced* to give a categorical reply" on the question whether the perpetrators of conquest could claim just cause, his answer was that they could allege no title to justify their depredations other than could be found in the law of war. In the remainder of his letter he rehearsed the themes of inquiry to which he would give full attention five years later in *On the Indians or on the Law of War*.

"I do not understand the justice of the war. *I do not dispute* the emperor's right to conquer the Indies, which I *presuppose* he may, most strictly; but as far as I understand from eyewitnesses ... [none of the Indians] had ever done the slightest injury to the Christians, nor given them the least grounds for making war on them." Defenders of the conquest would respond that this was of no significance – soldiers must follow orders. "*I accept this response* in the case of those who did not know that there was no other cause for this war than sheer robbery – which was all or most of them." But "other more recent conquests have, I think, been even more vile" and "I cannot let the matter rest at this."

Vitoria was ready to grant, if only for the sake of argument, "that all the battles and conquests were good and holy," but even if the Spaniards' war were just, the Indians were "*truly ignorant*" of its justice, "convinced that the Spaniards are tyrannical oppressors waging unjust war on them." So that "Even if the emperor has just titles to conquer them, the Indians do not and cannot know this. *They are most certainly innocents in this war.*" And supposing the war indeed were just in its cause, the Spaniards had nevertheless violated all the commandments of just war: "*hostilities may not proceed* beyond subduing them and compelling them to accept the emperor as prince *with the infliction on them of as little damage and loss as possible.*" But instead the Indians had been despoiled, robbed, and left "destitute *of everything regarding their temporal goods.*" Vitoria knew "of no justification for robbing and plundering the unfortunate victims of defeat of all they possess and even what they do not possess."

Francisco de Vitoria to Miguel de Arcos (8 November 1534), in Pagden and Lawrance, eds., *Francisco de Vitoria: Political Writings*, 331–3 (emphases in original).

wage war; what furnishes just cause for war; and, to what measures may an enemy be subjected in a just war.

To the first, Vitoria answers that Christians may indeed make war, whether purely defensive wars to resist aggressors or wars initiated to avenge wrongs done to them.[100] Defensive war, he insists, might be waged by *anyone*, "even a private person," as a matter of "blameless self-defense" in response to an immediate threat, whether to person or property, from which there was no opportunity to escape.[101] Authority to declare – that is, initiate – and wage war, however, belonged to states and their princes (the leaders of states) alone. The personal right to self-defense enjoyed by all ceases the moment the immediate threat has passed, but a state enjoyed a continuing authority not only to defend itself but also to prosecute wars to avenge wrongs done to itself and its subjects. This was essential, else the state could not "adequately protect the public weal."[102]

Was Spanish seizure and occupation of Indian lands just under the law of war? Wars could only be just under the law of war as vengeance for a wrong actually received.[103] Nor could this be merely a slight wrong.[104] Nor could mere *belief* that a cause was just actually render a war just absent an actual wrong received, for then many wars would be just on both sides and all belligerents would be innocents. "Even Turks and Saracens might wage just wars against Christians."[105] Claims of just cause must therefore be earnestly debated and determined by "wise and upright men."[106] Those without authority to debate might be guided by the decisions of the wise;

---

[100] In the second case, quoting St. Augustine, "as where punishment has to be meted out to a city or state because it has itself neglected to exact punishment for an offense committed by its citizens or subjects or to return what has been wrongfully taken away." Vitoria, *On the Indians or on the Law of War*, 167.

[101] Ibid., 167–8.

[102] Ibid., 168.

[103] Ibid., 170. This is, in fact, the only moment in the course of the second *Relectio* that Vitoria specifically addresses Spanish wars against the Indians. Vitoria restates the points made in the first *Relectio* – that neither difference of religion (Indian refusal to accept Christianity), or extension of Empire, or personal glory, or gain to the prince can justify resort to war, but only "a wrong received."

[104] Ibid., 171.

[105] Ibid., 173. Anghie argues Vitoria held as a fundamental proposition that unbelievers were inherently incapable of waging just wars. *Imperialism*, 26. But this is not so. "The Indians themselves sometimes wage lawful wars with one another and the side which has suffered a wrong has the right to make war." See *On the Indians Lately Discovered*, 160. Vitoria's proposition might better be stated as rejection of the possibility that unbelievers could ever have a just cause of war *against Christians*. But even this seems an overstatement in light of the first *Relectio*, in which at one point Vitoria clearly considers that, under certain circumstances it was quite possible to grant that the Indians, though unbelievers, might wage just war against the Spanish: "to keep certain people out of the city or province as being enemies, or to expel them when already there, are acts of war. Inasmuch, then, as the Indians are not making a just war on the Spaniards (*it being assumed that the Spaniards are doing no harm*), it is not lawful for them to keep the Spaniards away from their territory" (151, emphasis added). See also later discussion, on the justness of "invincible ignorance."

[106] Vitoria, "On the Indians or on the Law of War," 174.

yet still they might be called to account, for "the proofs and tokens of the injustice of [a] war may be such that ignorance would be no excuse." Were it otherwise, "unbelievers would be excused when they follow their chieftains to war against Christians and it would be unlawful to kill them, it being certain that they deem themselves to have a just cause of war."[107] Yet if the side in error were convinced by "invincible ignorance" that its cause was just, then its war indeed *was* just "in the sense of being excused from sin by reason of good faith, because invincible ignorance is a complete excuse." Invincible ignorance was most likely among subjects who followed in good faith; hence subjects on both sides "may be doing what is lawful when they fight." However, princes who waged war in good faith that their cause was just might also be deemed free from fault and therefore exempt from the punishments or exactions justly levied against the guilty.[108]

What of the conduct of wars? War might be justly prosecuted to the extent necessary to "the defense and preservation of the State," and the restoration of conditions of "peace and security."[109] Hence "everything is lawful which the defense of the common weal requires" – the recapture and redress of losses, destruction of an enemy's capacity to threaten, and punishment for wrongs done, particularly those done to the honor and authority of the state itself. Innocents might not be deliberately slaughtered or punished, for a just war is one to avenge a wrong done and the innocent (by definition) do no wrong. And though innocents might die in a just war or be killed knowingly for the greater good of its prosecution, yet "it is in no wise right."[110] Nor should the innocent be despoiled, unless required by the conduct of the war. "When a war is at that pass that the indiscriminate spoliation of all enemy-subjects alike and the seizure of all their goods are justifiable, then it is also justifiable to carry all enemy-subjects off into captivity, whether they be guilty or guiltless." Here Vitoria drew a pointed distinction between wars against pagans and wars among Christians:

> inasmuch as war with pagans is of this type, seeing that it is perpetual and that they can never make amends for the wrongs and damages they have wrought, it is indubitably lawful to carry off both the women and the children of the Saracens into captivity and slavery. But inasmuch as, by the law of nations, it is a received rule of Christendom that Christians do not become slaves in right of war, this enslaving is not lawful in a war between Christians; but if it is necessary having regard to the end and aim of war, it would be lawful to carry away even innocent captives, such as children and women, not indeed into slavery, but so that we may receive a money-ransom for them.[111]

[107] Ibid., 174. "The soldiers who crucified Christ, ignorantly following Pilate's order, would be excused. Also, the Jewish mob would be excused which was led by the elders to shout 'Away with Him, crucify Him'."

[108] Ibid., 177. See also Vitoria's initial consideration of invincible ignorance in his 1534 letter to Miguel de Arcos, in n.99.

[109] Ibid., 171, 172. Vitoria adds, "tranquility and peace are reckoned among the desirable things of mankind and so the utmost material prosperity does not produce a state of happiness if there be no security there," 172.

[110] Ibid., 180.

[111] Ibid., 181.

Might one slaughter the guilty? "In the actual heat of battle ... *all* who resist may be killed indiscriminately."[112] After victory and the elimination of danger the guilty might still be killed, for the justice of the war lay in avenging their wrong and in preventing the enemy from wronging again in the future. But the purpose of war is peace; therefore the punishment (killing) of the guilty must be proportionate to the wrong done. Nor did the guilty include those who followed their prince in good faith, for they were without fault. And so, after they had been defeated they might not be killed.[113] If peace and security could not be had except by destroying all enemies – "and this is especially the case against unbelievers, from whom it is useless ever to hope for a just peace on any terms" – then all who could bear arms ("provided they have already been in fault") might be destroyed. But not, says Vitoria, in a war with Christians, for such would be to the ruin of Christianity.[114] So also cities might be sacked, property seized, territory occupied, but all in proportion to the necessities of prosecuting the war and ensuring its appropriate outcome. So also princes of the enemy might lawfully be deposed and new ones appointed, or their provinces kept, if sufficient and lawful cause were to be found either in the degree and nature of the enemy's offense or for the achievement of lasting security and peace. But "it will not always suffice to justify the overthrow of the enemy's sovereignty and the deposition of lawful and natural princes." Such would be "utterly savage and inhumane."[115]

Considered summarily, Vitoria's discussion of the law of war establishes the following: First, anyone, including Indians, might justly wage defensive war in resistance to immediate aggression. Second, a wrong having been done them, Indian princes might wage just wars against other Indians, or indeed against anyone other than Christians. Third, because Vitoria held in doubt the possibility that any non-Christian – Turk or Saracen, pagan or Jew – might ever have a just cause of war against Christians, he held that as a rule the Indians might not wage just war against the Spanish. Yet Vitoria also seemed ready to concede that, were the Spanish to have done them an initial harm, Indians might have a just cause of war against the Spanish.[116] Moreover, even without just cause, invincible ignorance would excuse them from fault in waging an unjust war, or engaging in a war that they were justified in believing was just. Fourth, the Spanish might wage just war against the Indians, as they might against Turks and Saracens, but only provided a prior (and serious) wrong had first been done them. Absent a wrong, Spanish warfare would be unjust and resistance to it no wrong. Fifth, to remain just, war in a just cause had to be prosecuted in a manner proportionate to the wrong suffered, and only to the extent required to restore peace and security. Sixth, all war, no matter whom the protagonists,

---

[112] Ibid., 182 (emphasis added).
[113] Ibid., 182–3.
[114] Ibid., 183.
[115] Ibid., 186.
[116] See n.105, this chapter.

was governed by an injunction against the intentional slaughter of the innocent, who had done no wrong. Beyond this single injunction, proportionality knew no absolute limitation except in wars among Christians to which certain additional prudential injunctions applied, notably rules against enslavement of captives and indiscriminate slaughter of the guilty.[117]

Clearly, Vitoria thought Indians inferior to Christians in their capacity to exercise sovereignty.[118] But Vitoria did not deny Indian sovereignty. Indeed, he held that Indian sovereignty could justly be infringed only when the Indians had provided prior cause by violating the law of nature and nations – the same condition that governed the justice of wars among Christians. And for such violation Vitoria found no evidence. Though Spanish conquest might be justifiable, therefore, Spanish conquest was not justified.

Appearing half a century after Vitoria's *Relectiones*, Alberico Gentili's *De Iure Belli* seems at first a better fit for Anghie's analysis.[119] Gentili addressed Spanish conquest in the New World only incidentally, an episode to be drawn on as needed in a much more comprehensive historical and legal exegesis on the law of war. But in one crucial respect Gentili represented the status of New World people as quite exceptional, justifying exceptional methods against them in precisely the fashion Anghie suggests.

Gentili's theory of war was distinct from Vitoria's, taking as its point of departure the proposition that the meaning of "war" as such was "a *just* and *public* contest of arms" between two equal parties (*hostes*).[120] Thus defined, war was necessarily both "legitimate" and "regular."[121] Neither "a broil, a fight" nor "the violence of private individuals" could count as war. "War" could only be "waged by sovereigns."[122] The proposition invoked a foundational assumption of the law of nations. Nature had established among

---

[117] Compare this summary of the second *Relectio* with the themes Vitoria sketched in his letter to de Arcos, in n.99, this chapter.

[118] At the end of *De Indis*, Vitoria discusses the contention that "the aborigines in question" were "unfit to found or administer a lawful State up to the standard required by human and civil claims" because "wanting in intelligence," and whether "It might, therefore, be maintained that in their own interests the sovereigns of Spain might undertake the administration of their country, providing them with prefects and governors for their towns, and might even give them new lords, so long as this was clearly for their benefit." Vitoria would not affirm that such could be "at all" a lawful basis for Spanish sway over the Indians, but added, "nor do I entirely condemn it." Vitoria, "On the Indians Lately Discovered," 160–1.

[119] The best fit of all is probably the less-noticed work of Pierino Belli, published in 1563, *De Re Militari et Bello Tractatus*, which states that "With good right ... the Spaniards enslaved those Indians of the West, who live far away from our world, and were unknown to the Greeks and Romans, but who were discovered in our times through perilous and bold navigation." See *De Re Militari et Bello Tractatus*, Herbert C. Nutting, trans. (Oxford 1936), 85.

[120] Gentili, *De Iure Belli*, 12 (emphasis added). Gentili defined *hostis* as "a person with whom war is waged and who is the equal of his opponent," 12.

[121] Ibid., 13–14.

[122] Ibid., 12, 15. The absence from *De Iure Belli* of Vitoria's distinction between defensive and aggressive war identifies war with organized states. For Gentili, war always connotes a "public" act.

men "kinship, love, kindliness, and a bond of fellowship." From human kinship nature had fashioned the world as one body. "She has implanted in us love for one another and made us inclined to union." This "association of the human race" was the prerequisite for the law of nations and also of relations among sovereign nations – relations of war as well as of peace.[123] For mankind as a whole belonged to a *societas gentium*, "a community of states," independent but also interdependent. Relations among sovereign nations in the society of nations were analogous to relations among individuals within a single nation-state: "the rule which governs a private citizen in his own state ought to govern a public citizen, that is to say a sovereign or a sovereign people, in this public and universal state formed by the world."[124]

The breadth of Gentili's conception of *societas gentium* is striking. Human *societas* encompassed all – not merely Christians but infidels and barbarians too: for "it is a hard task, but not impossible, to induce mortals to observe justice, a gift which the favor of Providence has to such an extent bestowed upon the sense of all men, that even those who know nothing of the laws yet recognize the principle of truth."[125] *Societas gentium* encompassed all states, so long as they were identifiable as politically organized nations (sovereigns or sovereign peoples).[126] All identifiable as such might wage war. And because in Gentili's usage war *meant* "regular" and "just," all had an equal and unambiguous claim to wage just wars. States were not differentiated one from the next by the kinds of wars they waged.

As striking, however, were those on the outside, those whom *societas gentium*, and hence the law of nations and the law of war, excluded: pirates, brigands, rebellious slaves, brutes.[127] Pirates were the epitome of the excluded, "the common enemies of all mankind."[128] A state of war could not exist with pirates for pirates had no existence within *societas gentium*: not only had they cast themselves out of mankind's *societas* by their misconduct, they were in any case literally stateless. An enemy [*hostis*] was he "who has a state, a senate, a treasury, united and harmonious citizens, and some basis for a treaty of peace, should matters so shape themselves."[129] Pirates had none of these. They lacked sovereignty. Even if they followed the customs of war in practice "yet they do not wage war," for they were not lawful enemies with the equality and rights "and the privileges of regular warfare" that the words (*iusti hostes*) implied.[130] Neither were brigands or rebellious slaves, nor indeed any who had acted contrary to justice, who transgressed the law. "Such men are no more deserving of consideration in establishing a code of

[123] Ibid., 67.
[124] Ibid., 68; and see 1, 124. Coleman Phillipson, "Introduction," in Gentili, *De Iure Belli*, 20a, 22a–23a.
[125] Ibid., 6. And see 53–7.
[126] Ibid., 397–403. Phillipson, "Introduction," in Gentili, *De Iure Belli*, 25a–26a.
[127] Ibid., 7, 22–26.
[128] Ibid., 22.
[129] Ibid., 25.
[130] Ibid., 25.

laws than wild beasts ... 'Such savagery in human form and bestial cruelty should be banished from what we may call the body of human society'."[131]

Hence wars for the common interest, against such common enemies, were just, for "if war is made against the wicked it is not disgraceful to make war." Here follows Gentili's remarkable observation directly on the Spanish conquest:

> Therefore I approve the more decidedly of the opinion of those who say that the cause of the Spaniards is just when they make war upon the Indians, who practiced abominable lewdness even with beasts, and who ate human flesh, slaying men for that purpose. For such sins are contrary to human nature, and the same is true of other sins, recognized as such by all except haply by brutes and brutish men. And against such men ... war is made as against brutes."[132]

It is important to understand that Gentili, like Vitoria, expressed considerable doubt about the sufficiency of the other grounds commonly advanced to justify Spanish conquest; that is, the Indians' obligation under the law of nature and nations to obstruct neither Christian proselytizing nor commerce. Gentili shared Vitoria's opinion that wars undertaken to extend a religion were unjust,[133] nor did anything he wrote suggest he accepted Vitoria's distinct observation that obstruction of Christian proselytizers might constitute a violation of the law of nature and nations, hence a "wrong" sufficient to justify wars to seize territories and enslave inhabitants. Rather, discussing commerce, he noted simply that obstruction was to be expected, for "it is a common characteristic of all uncivilized peoples to drive away strangers."[134] Nor were the Indians obliged to allow strangers to go wherever they desired.[135] Gentili allowed that "commerce is in accordance with the law of nations," and hence that Indian prohibitions upon commerce would justify the Spanish in making war upon them. But to suffice as a cause of war, an interruption of commerce had to prevent all trade, not simply restrain this or that aspect. Natives of a territory had a right to determine what forms of trade would and would not be allowed, and strangers had "no right to argue about these matters, since they have no licence to alter the customs and institutions

---

[131] Ibid., 7. And again, at 41, "such men, being the common foes of all mankind, as pirates are, ought to be assailed in war and forced to adopt the usages of humanity. For of a truth those seem to be dangerous to all men, who, wearing the human form, live the life of the most brutal of beasts," even those who "have a kind of religion." See also Belli, *De Re Militari*, 83: "people whose hand is against every man should expect a like return from all men, and it should be permissible for any one to attack them."

[132] Ibid., 122. See also 41. See also Hugo Grotius, *De Jure Belli ac Pacis*, II.20.40 (505–6): "wars are justly waged against those who act with impiety toward their parents ... who feed on human flesh ... who practise piracy." Against such barbarians, "wild beasts rather than men," war "was sanctioned by nature." See generally Daniel Heller-Roazen, *The Enemy of All: Piracy and the Law of Nations* (New York, 2009), 103–11.

[133] Ibid., 38–41.

[134] Ibid., 89.

[135] Ibid., 87–8, 89–90.

of foreign peoples." Nor in any case had Spanish allegations of Indian "wrongs" been advanced in good faith. "The Spaniards were aiming there, not at commerce, but at dominion."[136] In all these respects, then, Gentili, too, likened the Indians to sovereign nations. To the extent he approved the Spanish cause, it appears, Gentili's basis was the Indians' apparent inhumanity, their alleged brutishness.

Conclusion

Whether or not Crown licensing of English voyages of "conquest" as well as "discovery" in its earliest letters patent was an implicit admission in fact of the sovereignty of indigenous non-Christians over those "lands not actually possessed of any Christian Prince, nor inhabited by Christian People" that early-modern expositors of Roman law admitted in theory, colonizers' advisors certainly acknowledged both the presence and authority of local sovereigns – indigenous princes and peoples – in the territories that colonizers designed to occupy, and addressed the necessity, indeed the advantages, of reaching strategic accommodations with them en route to gaining dominion over them. The elder Hakluyt warned Gilbert that "we might not be suffered by the savages to enjoy any whole countrey or any more than the scope of a Citie." He advised alliances to overcome resistance. If Gilbert chose his "seate" wisely he might "enter into amitie with the enemies of [his] next neighbours," and in the same way gradually "force the next neighbours to amitie," and by and by "become of all the provinces round about the only governour."[137] Hakluyt offered the same advice to Raleigh seven years later. "If our nation do not make any conquest there, but only use trafficke and change of commodities, yet by meane the countrey is not very mightie, but divided into pety kingdoms, they shall not dare to offer us any great annoy." For "where there may be many petie kings or lords planted on the rivers sides, and by all likelihood mainteine the frontiers of their severall territories by warres, we may by the aide of this river ioine with this king heere or with that king there ... and in the end bring them all in subiection and to civilitie."[138] Such advice would to an important degree be followed in actual behavior on the ground, particularly after the beginnings of continuous English presence in the Chesapeake in 1607 where, as a purely practical matter, the survival of the original settlement depended in good part on recognizing and exploiting local rivalries by creating and attempting to co-opt allies.[139]

---

[136] Ibid., 89, 90.

[137] Richard Hakluyt (the elder), "Notes on Colonisation" (1578), 119, 120–1.

[138] Richard Hakluyt (the elder), *Pamphlet for the Virginia Enterprise* (1585), at 328, 329–30.

[139] See James Horn, "The Conquest of Eden: Possession and Dominion in Early Virginia," in Appelbaum and Sweet, *Envisioning an English Empire*, 42; "Imperfect Understandings: Rumor, Knowledge and Uncertainty in Early Virginia," in Mancall, ed., *The Atlantic World and Virginia*, 513–40; and generally, *A Land as God Made It: Jamestown and the Birth of America* (New York, 2005).

Yet the first decades of actual English attempts also saw the discourse of intrusion undergo something of a transformation. Throughout, the articulation of English claims qua European rivals remained consonant with intra-European dispositions of transoceanic acquisitions inflected by Roman law. But as an activity on the ground – a set of techniques for achieving goals, the goals themselves, and their rationalization – colonizing acquired a distinct English idiom, in which, increasingly, attention focused on the possession of territory *to the exclusion* of its inhabitants.[140] It is not entirely fortuitous that Vitoria's first *Relectio* addressed "the *Indians Lately Discovered*" whereas a half century later Sir George Peckham's 1583 *Discourse on the Western Discoueries* would wax lyrical on "New-found *Landes*."[141] With all its attendant cruelties, justifications, critiques, and regrets, Spanish colonizing was a narrative of the conquest of *peoples* living in civil societies. The narrative of English colonizing is one that progressively banishes existing inhabitants to the margins of its consciousness by denying their civic capacity, their sociability. In the English narrative the indigenous become brutes, in whose place the colonizer first desires, then actively imagines, an empty landscape to populate anew.[142]

[140] As Anthony Pagden indicates, only the Spanish created an American empire "based upon people, defeated subjects who could be transformed into a pliant labour force." Increasingly, the working principle of English seventeenth-century colonizing became to exclude the indigenous population from their colonies, or "exterminate" them. Pagden, *Lords of all the World*, 65, 73. See also Patricia Seed, *Ceremonies of Possession in Europe's Conquest of the New World, 1492–1640* (Cambridge and New York, 1995), 187, who comments that "the English had comparatively little interest in preserving indigenous peoples; their presence constituted a barrier to English occupation." In similar vein, Jack P. Greene writes that in the English imagination, "Amerindians, like the land and other resources of America, were essentially passive objects who had no integrity or selfhood of their own and whose own priorities and objectives ordinarily demanded no consideration and had to be taken into account only when they represented an obstacle to English designs." Jack P. Greene, *The Intellectual Construction of America: Exceptionalism and Identity from 1492 to 1800* (Chapel Hill, 1993), 44.

[141] Peckham, *True Reporte*. Anthony Pagden notes that Francis Bacon wrote at approximately the same time, "I like a plantation in a pure soil; that is where people are not displanted to the end, to plant in others; for else it is rather an extirpation than a plantation." Bacon thought it acceptable to plant "where savages are," Pagden continues, but only as long as the savages did not "plant" themselves. See Francis Bacon, "Of Plantations," in Basil Montagu, editor, *The Works of Francis Bacon* (Philadelphia, 1852), I, 41; Pagden, *Lords of all the World*, 79. The thrust of my argument here and in the first part of the next chapter is that developments in English colonizing discourse that Andrew Fitzmaurice has contended await the years after 1609 are well in evidence a quarter-century earlier. See Fitzmaurice, "Moral Uncertainty," 400–3, 409.

[142] The elder Hakluyt's references to "many petie kings or lords planted on the rivers sides" in the region to be penetrated by Raleigh's 1585 expedition, at least allowed the indigenous occupants a recognizable form of social and civic organization, hence a certain rough equivalence with the English. Richard Hakluyt (the elder), *Pamphlet for the Virginia Enterprise* (1585), at 329. But as we have seen, he thought them of small account, and other Englishmen were already well advanced in their denials of Indian civility. On the later construction of the North Atlantic seaboard's indigenous economy of mobility as "absence," for example, see Jean M. O'Brien, *Dispossession By Degrees: Indian Land and Identity in Natick, Massachusetts, 1650–1790* (New York and Cambridge, 1977), 1–30.

4

Keeping (ii): English Desires, Designs

Plutarch said long ago that the civilizing of barbarians had been made the pretext for aggression, which is to say that a greedy longing for the property of another often hides itself behind such a pretext.

Hugo Grotius, *Mare Liberum* (1608)

Drive your cart and your plow over the bones of the dead.

William Blake, *Proverbs of Hell* (1790–93)

Thus far I have concentrated on early-modern narratives of the legalities of colonizing that held the conquest and subjugation of barbarian indigenous peoples justifiable by their antagonistic responses to the intrusions of strangers, from which the occupation and possession of the territories they inhabited followed as a necessary consequence of the wars appropriately waged against them. These narratives were pan-European in expression, and rooted in a half millennium of warfare in and around the Mediterranean basin. Considered idiomatically, they and their critics dominated sixteenth-century colonizing discourse. In this chapter, I will describe the emergence of a new narrative trajectory that appeared in the late sixteenth century and came to predominate in the seventeenth. Rather than pan-European in expression, this narrative was in important respects a peculiarity of the English. It elevated land over people as the primary object of the colonizer's attention. It rearranged both the legalities and the institutional mechanisms of colonizing accordingly.

Though new and distinct, the English narrative of colonizing overlapped with its predecessor, with which it had much in common. Its traces can be found in early sixteenth-century humanism; its roots lay in the law of nature and nations, to which it annexed vernacular English inflections. And its shift of emphasis was necessarily relative rather than absolute; for, inconveniently, indigenous inhabitants in reality remained obstinately present in the imagined empty landscape of English desire, and so had to be acknowledged in one fashion or another.[1] Yet for all those remainders,

[1] Something of the restless jockeying between people and land in the English *imaginaire* is conveyed in Jess Edwards' description of John Smith's chorography (or, as Edwards prefers, "verbal geography") of Virginia as "vacillat[ing], as his cartography might be said to do, between generalizing declarations of the land's emptiness and availability for colonial exploitation, and detailed observations of its current native use ... Lacking

what is surely a remarkable and distinguishing characteristic of the English colonizing project's impact on the North American mainland is the thoroughness of its reinvention (legal, political, material, jurisdictional) of the terrain upon which projectors seated their colonies – its fierce concentration upon the appropriation of territory, its mental and physical conversion of that territory to distinct usages and spatial disciplines, its establishment of going agricultural concerns, and, underlying all, the substantial and protracted task of replacing an existing and intractable population, in which it had little interest, with new populations introduced to occupy the land, build plantations and farms, work their fields, and generally undertake the immense labor of constructing the civic extrastructure of European inhabitation.

In turning to consider the specificities of English colonizing narratives, this chapter completes Part I's account of the relationships pertaining between the three elements in the elder Hakluyt's succinct statement of English priorities – manning, planting, keeping. In Part II I will move on to an examination of the "inside" of English colonizing – its people, its processes and promises, its labors, laborers, and laws. In Part III I will turn to colonizing's liabilities, both as regards its people and their posterity.

I. Roots

Two hints of the new English narrative, specific to the New World, are detectable in Alberico Gentili's *De Iure Belli*. First, as previously noted, Gentili was disposed to exclude the New World's indigenous inhabitants from human society, to label them brutes and as such render them entirely marginal, people who, though they took human form, "should be reckoned in the

the significant details of English cultivation, the 'plainness' of this well-framed space seems indeed to suggest the inviting emptiness of cartographic geometry. Yet Smith also maps ... the perfectly industrious practices of Indian agriculture." Jess Edwards, "Between 'Plain Wilderness' and 'Goodly Cornfields': Representing Land Use in Early Virginia," in Robert Appelbaum and John Wood Sweet, editors, *Envisioning an English Empire: Jamestown and the Making of the North Atlantic World* (Philadelphia, 2005), 217.

The contrasting depiction of regional interiors in Smith's maps of the Chesapeake (1612) and New England (1614) is graphically illustrative of Smith's cartographic vacillation; Smith's New England interior is as empty of Indians as his Chesapeake is full of them. Interestingly, it is the first map's inclusion of indigenous village sites that has been found "remarkable," not the second's exclusion of them. David B. Quinn, "Maps of the Age of European Exploration," in David Buisseret, editor, *From Sea Charts to Satellite Images: Interpreting North American History through Maps* (Chicago, 1990), 44. The Chesapeake map depicts the English planted, tentatively, at Jamestown amid others – "this king heere, or ... that king there," as the elder Hakluyt had put it in his *Pamphlet for the Virginia Enterprise* (1585), in E.G.R. Taylor, editor, *The Original Writings and Correspondence of the Two Richard Hakluyts* (London: for the Hakluyt Society, 1935), 330. The New England map, in contrast, affirms indigenous absence and the anglicization of space. Reproductions of the maps can be found in Edward Arber, editor, *Travels and Works of Captain John Smith, President of Virginia and Admiral of New England, 1580–1631*, introduction by A. G. Bradley (Edinburgh, 1910), II, 384, 694.

number of beasts," who "'show the savage cruelty of a beast'." War against brutes is "honourable," as in the interest of all men. It is not restrained by law.[2] Second, Gentili elsewhere muses on the New World itself as "unoccupied," virtually without people, and uncultivated, likened to "the wilderness of primeval times."[3]

Both ideas also appear, somewhat more prominently, in Sir George Peckham's near-contemporary *True Reporte* (also known as his *Discourse on the Western Discoueries*) published in 1583: on the one hand a vast expanse of potentially fruitful land, on the other a scattering of inhabitants who were, virtually, brutes.[4] Peckham quite evidently was very familiar with Vitoria's

[2] Alberico Gentili, *De Iure Belli Libri Tres, Volume Two – The Translation of the Edition of 1612,* John C. Rolfe, trans. (Oxford, 1933), 7, 122. See also 41.

[3] Ibid., 81. Andrew Fitzmaurice argues that Gentili here writes "in clear reference to the Roman and natural law *ferae bestiae,*" that is, the right of the first taker. See his "Moral Uncertainty in the Dispossession of Native Americans," in Peter C. Mancall, editor, *The Atlantic World and Virginia, 1550–1624* (Chapel Hill, 2007), 400. But this is disputable, at least as an exclusive attribution, for Gentili's point of reference here is as much the *Digest*'s discussion of the appropriation of land from a prior owner, or land derelicted and abandoned, as *ferae bestiae* (which, we have seen, the *Digest* never applied to land at all except in one unique instance). See *The Digest of Justinian*, Latin text edited by Theodore Mommsen with the aid of Paul Krueger, English translation edited by Alan Watson, in 4 vols. (Philadelphia, 1985), IV, Book 41 at 1.3 and 41.2.1, discussed previously in Chapter 3, section II.

[4] Sir George Peckham, *A True Reporte, Of the late discoueries, and possession, taken in the right of the Crowne of Englande, of the New-found Landes: By that valiant and worthye Gentleman, Sir Humfrey Gilbert Knight* (London, 1583).
Peckham's brief, crude ethnography of some indigenous inhabitants of the North Atlantic seaboard was contemporary with the vastly more sophisticated and scholarly work of José de Acosta, principally his *De Procuranda Indorum Salute* (written 1577, first printed 1588, and his *Historia Natural y Moral de las Indias* (first printed 1590). The two works were closely related – editions of *De Procuranda* appearing in the early 1590s included the first two books of the *Historia*. For a full account of Acosta's work, see Anthony Pagden, *The Fall of Natural Man: The American Indian and the Origins of Comparative Ethnology* (Cambridge and New York, 1982), 146–97.
In *De Procuranda*, Acosta developed a comparative ethnology that categorized all the world's "barbarians," from the Chinese to the Caribs, in three distinct types according to the degree of their observable civilization. Acosta's third and lowest category was that of "savages who are close to beasts and in whom there is hardly any human feeling" (Pagden, *Fall*, 164). (Acosta thought such savages brute-like rather than brutes by nature.) Fitzmaurice has argued that Acosta's work was of immense influence in dispelling the "moral uncertainty" felt by the projectors of the Virginia Company in the matter of the justice of dispossessing the indigenous inhabitants of the Chesapeake. "Clearly, these people [the third class of the world's barbarians], who for Acosta included the Natives of the northern parts of America, could not be dispossessed because they did not possess. They had no *meum* and *tuum*, no mine and yours. In contrast to the second class of barbarians, they had failed to create dominion through the exploitation of the laws of nature. From 1609, writers redescribed Virginia in these terms." Fitzmaurice, "Moral Uncertainty in the Dispossession of Native Americans," 403. The evidence that Fitzmaurice adduces for Acosta's influence is persuasive, yet one may wonder whether 1609 was quite the pivot-point that Fitzmaurice describes. First, we have seen that writers on English colonizing (Peckham, the elder Hakluyt) had long contemplated the dispossession of savages, displaying little in the way of moral uncertainty. Second, Acosta's

1539 *Relectiones* and attended carefully to the lawfulness of English intrusions under the law of nations, whether "trade and traficke," or evangelization, or planting, "wythout which, Christian Religion can take no roote,
be the Preachers neuer so carefull and diligent."⁵ He sought no removal
of the indigenous. But his preoccupation was the land they occupied
and possession of it in "such competent quantity ... as euery way shall
be corespondent to the Christians expectation, & contentation."⁶ Land
could be had, thought Peckham, "by the good likeing and willing assent
of the Sauages," who "considering the great aboŭdance that they haue
of Lande, and howe small account they make thereof" could not in any

Historia, published in English as *The Naturall and Morall Historie of the East and West Indies*
(1604), though clearly informed by his ethnology, described the Indians that were its
subject almost entirely in the terms of its first and second categories of barbarians. In one
chapter of three pages (in a book of 600), Acosta alludes briefly to "men very barbarous
and savage," who lived in caves and bushes in "the roughest partes of the mountaines
beastlike, without any pollicie, and they went all naked." These were "the antient and
first Inhabitants." They "did neyther till nor sowe the land, they left the best and most
fertile of the country vnpeopled" and lived only by hunting "wilde beasts, hares, connies,
weezles, mowles, wilde cattes, and birdes; yea vncleane beasts, as snakes, lizards, locusts
and wormes, whereon they fed, with some hearbs and rootes." They had no superiors nor
gods; they lived without "any manner of ceremonies or religion." Most had been displaced
or marginalized by more advanced peoples (*Navatalcas*) skilled in cultivation – indeed,
Acosta's short description of the ancient inhabitants was intended simply as an introduction to a progressive history of successively more advanced Mexican civilizations – but he
noted that remnants of the ancients remained: "Some will say, that those in New *Spaine*,
which they call *Ottomies*, were of this sort, being commonly poore Indians, inhabiting a
rough and barren land." If the *Ottomies* were any guide the near-bestial savagery of the
ancients was to be doubted, for "they are in good numbers, and live together with some
order, and such as do know them, find them no lesse apt and capable of matters of christian religion, than others which are held to be more rich and better governed" (497–8).
    Acosta's brief reference in the *Historia* to the displacement of brutish first inhabitants
who did not cultivate by more advanced peoples who did certainly grew out of the sophisticated classification presented in *De Procuranda*. It would undoubtedly have helped
dispel English "moral uncertainty" and Fitzmaurice shows it was used to good effect
by Virginia Company adherents ("Moral Uncertainty," 403–4). Still, this was a story the
English had begun telling themselves in the early 1580s. And when it comes to the question who had to be persuaded, the Crown had already displayed its own convictions, and
no moral uncertainty at all, two years before the Virginia Company was even chartered.
In 1604, James VI had described the Indians of the Americas as entirely "barbarous and
beastly" in manner, "wilde, godlesse, and slauish ... slaues to the *Spaniards*, refuse to the
world" who "denie God and adore the Deuill." See his *A Counterblaste to Tobacco* (London
1604), sigs. B₂v, B₂r.
⁵ Peckham, *A True Reporte*, sig. C₂r.
⁶ Ibid., sig. C₄v. What such "competent quantity" might be is suggested in the draft "Articles
of Assuraunce, betweene the Principall assignes of Sir Humfrey Gilbert Knight" and
those who would adventure with them "in the voyage for the Westerne Discoueries"
annexed to Peckham's *True Reporte*, which promised "for ever" 2,000 acres of land to each
adventurer for each £12.10/- adventured, up to 16,000 acres for £100, "to bee peopled
and manured at his pleasure, holding the same in socage tenner by Fealtie onely, with
aucthoritie to keepe Court Leete, and Court Barron vppon the same, at his pleasure,
with as great roialties in as large & ample maner as any Associate there, or other Subiect
in this Realme now enioyeth any landes in *England*." Sig. I₂v.

case justly object. And if they did object, Christians being thus "vniustly repulsed" could lawfully take it from them, for that Christians "doo seeke to attaine and maintaine the right for which they doo come."[7] Indigenous resistance to occupation of vacant land did not feature in Vitoria's discussion of wrongs that justified war, but Peckham made much of it.[8] Indeed, throughout Peckham's *True Reporte* the "Sauages" appear in marked counterpoint to their abundant bountiful land, balanced precariously on the edge of humanity – sometimes "miserable and wretched" creatures, "sillie soules" who were "fearfull by nature"; sometimes "Pagans, so long liuing in ignoraunce and Idolatry," their senses "grosse," their nature "Barbarous," their neighbors "Canniballs" themselves "horrible Idolat[ors]" given to the "wicked custome of most vnnaturall sacrificing of humaine creatures."[9] In either case, whether miserable or horrible, in Peckham's imagination the inhabitants appear almost parasitical, a burden upon the land from whom the land itself sought relief. In a striking anthropomorphic image that occurs early in the text, the body of the land itself reaches out to the English, summoning their assistance so that it might achieve its destiny. It "dooth (as it were with arme aduaunced) ... stretche out it selfe towardes England onelie. In manner praying our ayde and helpe as it is not onelie set foorth in Mercators generall Mappe, but it is also founde to bee true by the discouery of our nation."[10] The land aches with desire to realize its life's

---

[7] Ibid., sigs. C_2r, C_4v.

[8] Thus, Peckham concluded (sigs. C_4v-r):

> But if after these good and fayre meanes vsed, the Sauages neuertheles will not be heerewithall satisfied, but barbarously wyll goe about to practise violence either in repelling the Christians from theyr Portes and safe Landinges or in withstanding them afterwardes to enioye the rights for which both painfully & lawfully they haue aduentured themselues thether.
>
> Then in such a case I holde it no breache of equitye for the Christians to defende themselues, to pursue reuenge with force, and to doo whatsoeuer is necessary for the attayning of theyr safety: For it is allowable by all Lawes in such distresses, to resist violence with violence. And for theyr more securitie to increase their strength by building of fortes, for auoyding the extremities of iniurious dealing.
>
> Wherein if also they shall not be suffered in reasonable quietnes to continue, there is no barre (as I iudge but that in stoute assemblies, the Christians may issue out, and by strong hande pursue theyr enemies, subdue them, take possession of theyr Townes, Citties, or Villages, (and in auoyding murtherous tyranny) to vse the Lawe of Armes, as in like case among all nations at thys day is vsed: and most especially to the ende they may with securitye holde theyr lawfull possession ... And in so doing, doubtles the Christians shall no whitt at all transgresse the bondes of equitie or ciuility, for as much as in former ages (yea, before the incarnatiŏ of Christ) the like hath beene doon by sundry Kings and Princes, Gouerners of the children of *Israell* : cheefely in respect to beginne theyr Planting ... as also since the natiuity of Christ, myghty and puissaunt Emperours and Kinges haue performed the like, I say to plant, possess, and subdue.

[9] Ibid., sigs. B_4r, B_4v, C_3r, C_4v, C_4r.

[10] Ibid., sig. B_4r.

purpose, to be fruitful. For "I doo verily think that God did create lande, to the end that it shold by Culture and husbandrie, yeeld things necessary for mans lyfe." To enable the land to achieve its reason for being, the English would take possession of it from the burdensome ignorance of its current inhabitants, who themselves

> being brought from brutish ignoraunce, to ciuility and knowledge, and made them to vnderstand how the tenth part of their land may be so manured and emploied, as it may yeeld more commodities to the necessary vse of mans life, then the whole now dooth: What iust cause of complaint may they haue?[11]

Transformed, freed from their parasitic ways, and rendered fit for their new circumstances (and diminished acreage) by "knowledge how to tyl and dresse their grounds," the inhabitants

> shalbe reduced frŏ vnseemly customes, to honest maners, from disordred riotous rowtes and companies, to a wel gouerned common wealth & with all shalbe taught mecanicall occupations, artes, and lyberal Sciences.[12]

Both in sentiment and in figure of speech, Peckham's *True Reporte* stood in line of descent from Sir Thomas More's humanist epic *Utopia*, which it pressed into direct contact with Vitoria's and Gentili's subsequent observations on the legalities of colonizing. All three were brought together in the service of founding new commonwealths in the New World. Recall that *Utopia* was precisely an account of a perfected society begun in the conquest of lands inhabited by "rude and wilde people."[13] Whenever, subsequently, pressure of population demanded expansion beyond its original bounds, Utopia reproduced itself, amoeba-like. Taking citizens from each of their island's fifty-four cities, the Utopians would cross the sea and "build up a town under their owne lawes in the next land where the inhabitauntes have much waste and unoccupied ground." They would invite those inhabitants to join with them in reproducing Utopia by making common cause under Utopian laws. "But if the inhabitauntes of that lande wyl not dwell with them to be ordered by their lawes, then they dryve them out of those boundes which they have limited, and apointed out for them selves. And if they resiste and rebel, then they make warre agaynst them. For they counte this the most juste cause of warre, when anye people holdethe a piece of grounde voyde and vacant [*inane ac uacuum*] to no good nor profitable use, kepyng other from the use and possession of it, whiche notwithstanding by the lawe of nature ought thereof to be nouryshed and relieved."[14] New conquests sired new commonwealths.

---

[11] Ibid., sig. F₃r. For analysis of similarly anthropomorphic figurations of Virginia, as "nubile nymph who longed for the English embrace," see John Gilles, "Shakespeare's Virginia Masque," *ELH (English Literary History)*, 53, 4 (Winter, 1986), 677–8.

[12] Peckham, *A True Reporte*, sig. F₃r.

[13] George Sampson, editor, *The Utopia of Sir Thomas More, Ralph Robinson's Translation* (London, 1910), 83.

[14] Ibid., 102–3.

Andrew Fitzmaurice has established that sixteenth-century humanism is of considerable importance to comprehending the intellectual history of Tudor-Stuart colonizing. As he puts it, "the humanist imagination dominated colonizing projects." He has argued in particular that *Utopia*, "the greatest work of early sixteenth-century English humanism," stood as "a model for future humanist projects for the foundation of real commonwealths in the New World."[15] It is not surprising, then, that one encounters in More's brief description of Utopian colonizing virtually all the matters for debate – the movement of populations, the occupation of vacant land, claims to rightful possession vindicated by the law of nature and nations – that increasingly animated Tudor-Stuart colonizers.

Still, *Utopia*'s disquisition upon the legalities of conquest and expulsion of aboriginal inhabitants is exceedingly brief. More's main subject was Peckham's other concern, the civic design – the new commonwealth – that would obliterate all trace of the rude and the wild. True to humanism as a language "of the city," More's Utopia was a state of cities, each more or less equal in population, proportion, and design.[16] Each city owned and governed the country surrounding, denominated a "shiere," into which the entire land area of the island was equally parceled. Each built "houses or fermes" throughout its shire, "wel appointed and furnished with all sortes and instruments and tooles belongynge to husbandrye." Each purposefully circulated its citizens back and forth between city and country, so that cultivation was both marked as the responsibility of all and simultaneously known to all as the material base for city life.[17] In both city and shire the interior order of individual households was patriarchal, each household "under the rule and order of the good man, and the good wyf of the house."[18] But households themselves were meticulously organized into groups of thirty, each group overseen by an elected "Philarche" or "head baylyffe" (magistrate), and management of their composition lay with the city.[19]

[15] Andrew Fitzmaurice, *Humanism and America: An Intellectual History of English Colonisation, 1500–1625* (Cambridge, 2003), 1, 28. Jeffrey Knapp likewise observes that More's was "perhaps the first Tudor attempt to elaborate a theory of colonization," and that the theory itself, "which turns the accusation that a land is 'idle and waste' into a justification for colonizing it, came in fact to be repeated time and again in the American propaganda of Renaissance England." Jeffrey Knapp, *An Empire Nowhere: England, America and Literature from Utopia to The Tempest* (Berkeley and Los Angeles, 1992), 21.

[16] Fitzmaurice, *Humanism and America*, 8, 19; Sampson, ed., *The Utopia of Sir Thomas More*, 83–4.

[17] Sampson, ed., *The Utopia of Sir Thomas More*, 84. Indeed, each also treated the citizens of their foreign towns as a reserve to draw upon should the island's population chance to fall "that it cannot be fylled up agayne ... for they had rather suffer theire forreyne townes to decaye and peryshe, than any cytie of theire owne Ilande to be diminished" (103).

[18] Ibid., 84.

[19] Ibid., 91, 101–2. Each city consisted of 6,000 families. Families might include an indeterminate number of children younger than fourteen, but no family might contain fewer than ten or more than sixteen persons aged fourteen and above. Families outside these limits would be adjusted by redistribution.

Outside the individual household, much of Utopian life was lived publicly and collectively. With no idle rich or vagrant poor to support, labor consumed but a moderate proportion of the day, six hours in twenty-four, the remainder devoted to rest and refinement. Peckham's words in 1583 closely reproduced how More had imagined Utopia's idealized civic life: "a wel gouerned common wealth" where all pursued "mecanicall occupations, artes, and lyberal Sciences."[20]

More's model new commonwealth typified what Engin Isin has termed "eutopolis," the ideal of the city (*civitas*[21]) as a perfected social and jurisdictional order that organized population in carefully ordered harmony, and a political order that singled out an ideal inhabitant, the free man, segregated from the remainder ("vagrants, poor, vagabonds, beggars") by civic capacities, the whole comprising "a technology of citizenship."[22] English projectors and propagandists of colonizing active in the later sixteenth and early seventeenth centuries treated civic humanism's eutopolitan ideal virtually as a blueprint for the creation of ordered settlement.[23] Nowhere is the association of eutopolis and colonizing more pithily expressed than in the writings of the elder Richard Hakluyt, where the city stands – as it did for More – as the perfected representation of civic association and civilization. For Hakluyt, planting the city in the transatlantic wilderness was an essential condition for success in colonizing. It meant the creation of actual "cities" – physical emplacements of Englishness, of brick and stone, houses and roofs and walls – but also of all those other "thinges without which no Citie may bee made nor people in civill sorte be kept together" – legalities, revenues, arms, authority, relations of power and acquiescence, governance.[24] From Ulster to the Virginia colony and New England, and on to Carolina and Pennsylvania and even Georgia, the creation of cities and townships featured prominently in colonizers' designs for ordered, concentrated settlement, in their strategies for planning inhabitation, securing territory, and governing both. The projectors of plantations in Ulster emphasized the creation of market towns within each county; for as Edmund Spenser wrote in 1596, "nothing doth sooner cause civility in any country than many market towns, by reason that people repairing often thither for

---

[20] Ibid., 93–109; Peckham, *A True Reporte*, chapter 6.

[21] On the place of the *civitas* in the discourse of European expansion, see Anthony Pagden, *Lords of all the World: Ideologies of Empire in Spain, Britain and France, c. 1500–1800* (New Haven, 1995), 18–28; David Armitage, *The Ideological Origins of the British Empire* (Cambridge, 2000), 73–4. On the *civitas* in Utopia, see Thomas More, *Utopia*, George M. Logan and Robert M. Adams, editors (Cambridge, 2002), 43 n.6.

[22] Engin Isin, *Being Political: Genealogies of Citizenship* (Minneapolis, 2002), 160. The suffocating orderliness of Utopian good governance is underlined to great effect in Stephen Greenblatt, *Renaissance Self-Fashioning: From More to Shakespeare* (Chicago, 1980), 39–54.

[23] See generally Robert Home, *Of Planting and Planning: The Making of British Colonial Cities* (London, 1997), 8–35.

[24] Richard Hakluyt (the elder), "Notes on Colonisation" (1578), in Taylor, ed., *Original Writings and Correspondence*, 117. See also, generally, Phil Withington, *The Politics of Commonwealth: Citizens and Freemen in Early Modern England* (Cambridge and New York, 2005).

their needs will daily see and learn civil manners."²⁵ The first permanent English settlement on the mainland (in the Chesapeake) was quite deliberately named James *Cittie*.²⁶ Among other early settlements were three named as "cities" – Henrico, Charles, and Bermuda. In 1619, James Cittie, Charles Cittie, Henrico Cittie, and Elizabeth Cittie were incorporated by the Virginia Company, each with an extensive tract of land that in 1634 would be denominated a shire. Projectors of the Virginia colony's "particular plantations" also planned settlement based on the establishment of towns surrounded by plantation tracts, such as Wolstenholme Towne in Martin's Hundred.²⁷ In Massachusetts Bay, famously, John Winthrop's *Arbella* sermon on "Christian Charity" denominated the Massachusetts Bay colonizing project an exemplary eutopolis, "a city upon a hill."²⁸ Townships, not dispersed settlement, were the key to the organization of the region's population.

Cities embodied the promise and actuality of "well-ordering and good Government," of governance and jurisdiction.²⁹ The proprietary colonies of the Restoration offered their own elaborations on the ideal. In his design for Carolina, for example, Anthony Ashley Cooper (later first earl of Shaftesbury) developed a eutopolitan "Grand Modell" for orderly planting in townships to avoid "stragling and distant Habitations," for "if men be not overruled theire Rashnesse and Folly will expose the Plantation to

---

²⁵ Home, *Of Planting and Planning*, 9.

²⁶ In the second paragraph of his *A True Relation of such occurrences and accidents of noate, as hath hapned in Virginia, since the first planting of that Collony*, John Smith describes how choice was made "for our scituation, a verie fit place for the erecting of a great cittie" immediately upon landfall. See Philip L. Barbour, editor, *The Complete Works of Captain John Smith* (Chapel Hill, 1986), I, 29. Earlier, in his second attempt to settle Roanoke Island, Sir Walter Raleigh had erected "the governor and assistants of the City of Raleigh in Virginia" as a "Bodye pollitique and Corporate" to exercise authority in the colony. See Mary Bilder, "English Settlement and Local Governance," in Michael Grossberg and Christopher Tomlins, editors, *The Cambridge History of Law in America* (Cambridge and New York, 2008), I, 69.

²⁷ Emily Rose, "The Politics of Pathos: Richard Frethorne's Letters Home," in Appelbaum and Sweet, *Envisioning an English Empire*, 99. On the early "city" settlements, see Martha W. McCartney, "An Early Virginia Census Reprised," *Quarterly Bulletin – Archeological Society of Virginia*, 54 (1999), 180–6.

²⁸ "For wee must consider that wee shall be as a citty upon a hill. The eies of all people are uppon us." John Winthrop, A Modell of Christian Charity (1630), *Collections of the Massachusetts Historical Society*, ser. 3 (Boston, 1838), VII, 31–48. Note also John Cotton's description, in a sermon preached early in April 1630 at Southampton immediately prior to the *Arbella*'s departure, "to plant a Colony, that is, a company that agree together to remove out of their own Country, and settle a Citty or common-wealth elsewhere." John Cotton, *God's Promise to his Plantations*, a sermon delivered at Southampton in 1630 (London, 1634), 9.

²⁹ As we shall see, this phrase, and variations upon it, is a crucial commonplace of English American colonizing. See, for example, The Third Charter of Virginia (1611–12), in Francis Newton Thorpe, *The Federal and State Constitutions, Colonial Charters, and other Organic Laws of the States, Territories and Colonies Now or Heretofore Forming The United States of America* (Washington, D.C., 1909), VII, 3809; The Charter of New England (1620), in Thorpe, *Federal and State Constitutions*, III, 1839.

Ruin."[30] Orderly planting, planned in advance of settlement, gave spatial embodiment to the dense legal-political order outlined in the *Fundamental Constitutions.* Carolina's settlement plan required inhabitants to build houses together on quarter-acre town lots, the whole surrounded by a ring of ten-acre garden lots with eighty-acre country lots for cultivation beyond. The intent was to "balance the interests of the proprietors with those of freeholders" and with the "colonial hereditary aristocracy" created by the *Fundamental Constitutions.* William Penn created a similar design for early Pennsylvania, planning a central city, contiguous concentrated settlement patterns, and an elaborated political order all well in advance of actual settlement.[31]

Common to each of these cases was both explicit civic design – a spatial embodiment of political-legal jurisdiction – and an explicit purpose: an intended institutional order, created in advance of settlement, to receive and organize a migrating population. Collectively, repeatedly, they brought about a century-long shift in the focus of English colonizing, from its initial reliance upon the discourses of discovery and conquest of unknown lands and transformation of barbarous heathen peoples that framed European expansion in the sixteenth century, to a seventeenth-century discourse of *settlement* and *improvement* – the creation of new English commonwealths to be inhabited by one's own migrants.

In the service of settlement, the English became focused on the terms on which land might be occupied. Fitzmaurice contends that throughout the first century of English colonizing, promoters of colonies drew upon available arguments and justifications willy-nilly, with the result that "arguments were not only incoherent between authors and across time, but often the same author would resort to a range of mutually contradictory arguments."[32] He cites the familiar justifications – evangelical Christian purpose, rights of commerce, just war and conquest, the occupation of vacant lands – and certainly all are on display in English promotional tracts. Still, sixteenth-century legal argumentation had worked its way through most of these to produce relatively precise statements of when they did and did not apply. Thus, wars of religion were unjustifiable, but aggressive reception of peaceful Christian "ambassadours" might justify war to suppress the aggressors; the same as to commerce; vacant lands might be occupied but respect was due the sovereignty of its owners; brutes beyond the pale of common humanity might be dispossessed, deported, enslaved, even exterminated.

As English colonizing expeditions multiplied, English argumentation tended to focus relatively less on the spread of Christianity and commerce, concentrating instead on land for the keeping; that is, the legalities of

---

[30] Home, *Of Planting and Planning,* 9, 18. See also Barbara Arneil, *John Locke and America: The Defence of English Colonialism* (Oxford, 1996), 123–4.

[31] Home, *Of Planting and Planning,* 10, 19–20.

[32] Fitzmaurice, *Humanism and America,* 137.

taking and retaining possession.[33] Here one encounters arguments that mobilized and greatly embroidered upon Gentili's hints that Indians might be thought "brutes" and the New World a primeval wilderness, arguments that might produce in actuality what More's humanist fantasy had long before employed as its justification for Utopian colonizing: "grounde voyde and vacaunt" put "to no good nor profitable *use*."[34]

We have seen that, contrary to much opinion, the legal fate of "grounde voyde and vacaunt" was not governed by any "doctrine" of *terra nullius* in Roman law opening unoccupied land to appropriation by a first taker. There was none such. Certainly Roman law recognized "vacant" land, by which it meant land empty of habitation and cultivation that might be appropriated for habitation by exiles. But all land in Roman law, even when vacant in this fashion, was owned by some sovereign and subject to that sovereign's jurisdiction.[35] English arguments turned instead on a novel combination of claims. First, unlike the Indians encountered by the Spanish, the Indians of the northern mainland exhibited in the English *imaginaire* none of the appurtenances or capacities of sovereignty. They lived, wrote William Symonds, "in a waste country ... like Deere in heards"; they had not "the first modestie that was in Adam, that knew he was naked." They were outside *societas gentium*, "brutish sauages," according to Robert Gray, which "participate rather of the nature of beasts then men."[36] Whether

---

[33] Peckham's *True Reporte*, we have seen, juggles all these themes, with land for the keeping increasingly to the fore. By characterizing the Indians as brutes, Peckham was able to use the natural-law arguments of Vitoria's *Relectiones* against their intended indigenous beneficiaries, turning Vitoria's critique of Spanish actions into justification for English takings. The elder Hakluyt's 1585 *Pamphlet for the Virginia Enterprise* also stresses land for the keeping.

[34] Sampson, ed., *The Utopia of Sir Thomas More*, 102.

[35] "The Roman view" says Richard Tuck, "was that any land had a ruler, and that the ruler could determine what happened to it." Richard Tuck, *The Rights of War and Peace: Political Thought and the International Order from Grotius to Kant* (Oxford, 1999), 48. I have pointed out and explored the single ("rare") exception ("islands arising in the sea"). See Chapter 3, section II. Gentili, we have seen, adopts the more aggressive humanist interpretation of the rights of intruding exiles and the responsibilities of use earlier articulated by More, but still acknowledges the sovereign ruler's prevailing jurisdictional rights. Gentili, *De Iure Belli*, 79–81. If we look forward, for a moment, to Blackstone, we will find that Blackstone's references to lands "claimed by right of occupancy only, by finding them desart and uncultivated and peopling them from the mother country," and to a natural right to migrate to "desart uninhabited countries" depart in no particular from Gentili's exposition of exiles' rights. Further, Blackstone's description of English North American colonies as "conquered or ceded countries" clearly acknowledges a pre-existing indigenous sovereign right. William Blackstone, *Commentaries on the Laws of England* (Chicago, 1979), I, 104, 105; II, 7.

[36] William Symonds, *Virginia. A Sermon Preached At White-Chappel, In The Presence of many, Honourable and Worshipfull, the Adventurers and Planters for Virginia* 25 April 1609 (London, 1609), 15; Robert Gray, *A Good Speed to Virginia* (London, 1609), sig. B₂v. William Strachey thought them "grosse and barbarous," comparable to "brute beasts," descended from "the vagabond race of Cham." William Strachey, *The Historie of Travaile into Virginia Britannia: Expressing the Cosmographie and Comodities of the Country, Togither with the Manners and Customes of the People*, R. H. Major ed. (written 1609–12; published London 1849), 47.

beasts or brutes or both, they had no state and hence exercised no sovereign jurisdiction or sovereign ownership over the lands they inhabited.

Second, what determined whether land was vacant was less ownership or even habitation than *use*. This, Richard Tuck has emphasized, was a crucial humanist innovation in natural-law thinking.[37] It was first articulated, briefly, by More. It was reiterated more vigorously by Peckham and by Gentili. It began to undergo real development in the early seventeenth century as the circle of English humanists grouped around the Virginia Company and, more or less simultaneously, Hugo Grotius, took up the idea. William Strachey conjured a vast "circuit" (area within a circumference, tract) of American land lying "vayne and idle" around islands of indifferent, indolent savages. "Nature" required its use. How could it possibly be unlawful, then, for the English "to fortefie, and strengthen our selves (as nature requires)" by setting down in those "wast, and vast, unhabited growndes ... of which not one foote of a thousand, doe they either use, or knowe howe to turne to any benefitt"?[38] The slippage from simple inhabitation to productive use was highly expedient. It is in evidence in John Donne's famous sermon (1622) before the Virginia Company. What was the difference, Donne asked, between "A Land never inhabited, by any, or utterly derelicted and immemorially abandoned by the former Inhabitants" – that is, land that the law of nature and nations declared vacant and hence available for occupation – and land that, as indubitably, *was* inhabited but whose inhabitants "doe not in some measure fill the Land, so as the Land may bring foorth her increase for the use of men." Donne's answer? No difference at all. Inhabited land could still be vacant land. "For as a man does not become proprietary of the Sea, because he hath two or three Boats, fishing in it, so neither does a man become Lord of a maine Continent, because he hath two or three Cottages in the Skirts thereof."[39] The measure of rightful possession was efficient use.

> That rule which passes through all *Municipal Lawes* in particular States, *Interest reipublicæ ut quis re sua bene utatur, The State must take order, that every man improove that which he hath, for the best advantage of that State*, passes also through the Law of *Nations*, which is to all the world, as the *Municipall* Law is to a particular State, *Interest mundo, The whole world, all Mankinde must take*

[37] Tuck, *The Rights of War and Peace*, 49–50.

[38] William Strachey, "A Præmonition to the Reader," in his *Historie of Travaile into Virginia Britannia*, 19. As we have seen, Peckham had written in very similar terms more than twenty years earlier.

[39] *A Sermon Preached to the Honourable Company of the Virginian Plantation. 13° November 1622. By Iohn Donne, Deane of St. Pauls, London* (London, 1622), 11, available at http://www.lib.byu.edu/dlib/donne/ (accessed 22 August 2009). Donne's reference to proprietorship of the sea, of course, invokes Hugo Grotius, *The Freedom of the Seas, or the Right Which Belongs to the Dutch to take part in the East Indian Trade* [Hugonis Grotii, *Mare Liberum, Sive De Iure Quod Batavis Competit Ad Indicana Commercia Dissertatio* (1608)], Ralph Van Deman Magoffin, trans. (New York, 1916), but also Gentili, who observed twenty years before Grotius, that the sea "is by nature open to all men and its use is common to all, like that of the air. It cannot therefore be shut off by any one." Gentili, *De Iure Belli*, 90.

care that all places be emprov'd, as farre as may be, to the best advantage of Mankinde in generall.[40]

Here, Donne takes Gentili's observation that "the rule which governs a private citizen in his own state ought to govern a public citizen, that is to say a sovereign or a sovereign people, in this public and universal state formed by the world"[41] and transforms it from a rule of unmediated mutual regard of human beings for other human beings to a rule of mutual (civil) responsibility to *manure* the world.[42] Gentili's rule cast out of *societas gentium* those whose behavior proved them brutes, contrary to human nature; Donne's cast out those who did not improve their land. Robert Gray had already shown how to restate the one as the other: "Although the Lord hath giuen the earth to the children of men, yet this earth which is mans fee-simple by deede of gift frŏ God, is the greater part of it possessed & wrongfully vsurped by wild beasts, and vnreasonable creatures, or by brutish sauages, which by reason of their godles ignorance, & blasphemous idolatrie, are worse than those beasts which are of most wilde & sauage nature. As Ahab therfore sometimes said to his seruants, 1. King 22. 13. Know ye not that Ramoth Gilead was ours, and we stay & take it not out of the hands of the King of Aram? So may man say to himselfe: The earth was mine, God gaue it me, and my posteritie."[43] Brutes were they who did not cultivate. From here it was but a short step to the complete displacement of habitation from the determination of vacancy and its replacement by "cultivation," as in Grotius's seemingly casual addition in *De Jure Belli ac Pacis*, as if the matter were long settled, of uncultivated land to the *Digest*'s class of things open to first takers.[44] "Of such sort are many places hitherto uncultivated [*loca multa inculta adhuc*], islands in the sea, wild animals, fish, and birds."[45] By the 1620s, if not before, cultivation was what defined possession, and the "rare occurrence" of the *Digest* had become "many places" – a veritable avalanche of opportunity.[46] The empty

---

[40] *A Sermon Preached to the Honourable Company of the Virginian Plantation*, 11 (emphasis in original). On the provenance of Donne's sermon, see Stanley Johnson, "John Donne and the Virginia Company," *ELH* (*English Literary History*), 14, 2 (June 1947), 127–38.

[41] Gentili, *De Iure Belli*, 68.

[42] In contemporary usage, to *manure* meant, narrowly, to spread dung or muck, but also, more broadly, to till, plough, cultivate. See *Lexicons of Early Modern English*, Ian Lancashire, ed., at http://leme.library.utoronto.ca/ (accessed 22 August 2009).

[43] Gray, *A Good Speed to Virginia*, sig. B₂v.

[44] Hugo Grotius, *De Jure Belli ac Pacis Libri Tres*, Francis W. Kelsey, trans. (Oxford and London, 1925), II.2.4 (192). Grotius's sole authority for the addition was Bembo's inclusion in his *History of Venice* (1551), of the following account of Christopher Columbus's activities on his return to Hispaniola in November 1493: "Columbus set about building a town at a suitable spot and putting the land under cultivation, in view of the fertility of the soil and the size of the island." [*Columbus revertisset, propter soli bonitatem, magnitudinemque insulae, oppidum opportune loco, condere ac terram colere coepit.*] Pietro Bembo, *History of Venice*, Robert W. Ulery, ed. and trans. (Cambridge, Mass., 2007–8), vol. II, book VI, 92–3.

[45] Ibid., 192.

[46] Grotius had actually laid the basis for this conversion in *Mare Liberum*, in the course of his demonstration that the Portuguese had no right by title of discovery to sovereignty over

landscape of the English *imaginaire* was open for business, its inhabitants conjured out of sight.[47]

Matters indeed went further even than "cultivation." Grotius's addition of uncultivated land to the *Digest*'s list appears casual only because it took for granted his new theory of property rights, apparent also in the writings

the East Indies (Ceylon, Java, the Moluccas), and hence could not exclude other trading nations. In *Mare Liberum*, 11–14, Grotius had argued in the manner of Vitoria, first, that the islands known as the East Indies had their own kings, governments, laws, and legal systems, and that the Portuguese traded there by leave rather than by right – they "do not go there as sovereigns but as foreigners." Though sovereignty per se was in any case insufficient, inasmuch as it was *possession* that was the essential condition of significance – "for having a thing is quite different from having the right to acquire it" – it was nonetheless clear that the existence of sovereigns *in situ* rendered the Portuguese claim to sovereignty by discovery unsustainable.

Nor, second, could their claim of discovery grant the Portuguese possession, for they had taken no "real" possession. The Grammarians gave the expressions "to find" (to discover) and "to occupy" (to take possession) the same signification. However, "natural reason itself, the precise words of the law, and the interpretation of the more learned men [citing *Institutes* 2.1.13] all show clearly that the act of discovery is sufficient to give a clear title of sovereignty only when it is accompanied by actual possession. And this only applies of course to movables or to such immovables as are actually inclosed within fixed bounds and guarded [citing *Digest* 41.2.3]." The Portuguese could maintain no such claim because they had established no bounds and garrisons.

Nor, in addition, could discovery as such give legal rights over things "unless before the alleged discovery they were *res nullius*" [citing *Digest* 41.1.3]. [Note that here and later in the chapter, as explained in Chapter 3 n.81, the insertion of *res nullius* as if Grotius were invoking it as a doctrinal category is in fact the work of the translator. The original wording is "*Praeterea inventio nihil iuris tribuit, nisi in ea quae ante inventionem nullius fuerant*" (13).] He continued, "Now these Indians of the East, on the arrival of the Portuguese, although some of them were idolators, and some Mohammedans ... had none the less perfect public and private ownership of their goods and possessions, from which they could not be dispossessed without just cause." Grotius cited Vitoria's *On Civil Power [De Potestate Civili]* (1528) [1.9, that is §9] to confirm that Christians could not deprive infidels of their civil power and sovereignty simply on the ground that they were infidels, embracing the Thomistic position that sovereignty was derived from natural or human law, not religious belief [grace]. After considering other possible bases for the Portuguese attempt to exclude, he concluded: "Wherefore, since both possession and a title of possession are lacking [in the Portuguese], and since the property and the sovereignty of the East Indies ought not to be considered as if they had previously been *res nullius*, and since, as they belong to the East Indians, they could not have been acquired legally by other persons, it follows that the East Indian nations in question are not the chattels of the Portuguese, but are free men and *sui juris*" (21).

The corollary that appeared in *De Jure Belli ac Pacis*, however, was that anything that *could* be considered *nullius* [i.e., characterized by the absence of ascertainable prior possession or manifestation of sovereignty *in situ*, and properly an object of possession] could be claimed by discovery, and that the class of things that could be so considered extended well beyond the class of things so described in the *Digest – ferae bestiae* and the movables annexed thereto – to immovables in general, including, obviously, many places hitherto uncultivated, were they in some fashion taken into "real" possession by means such as (but not limited to) "determination of boundaries" (25–6), as Columbus had done on his return to Hispaniola. Grotius comes close to drawing this conclusion explicitly in *Mare Liberum* in considering the case of land that falls to no owner as "undefined ... undetermined by boundaries" (27).

[47] It was, wrote Robert Cushman, "a sufficient reason to proue our going thither to liue, lawfull" that "their land is spatious and void & there are few and doe but run ouer the grasse,

of the English humanists, which carries us far into the seventeenth century, toward Locke. Gray's word, *interest*, is crucial in understanding the transformation. As Richard Tuck explains, the essence of Grotius's theory of property was "the claim that we have rights to those things – and only those things – in which we have a *personal* interest."[48] Grotius uses the idea, as Tuck remarks, to differentiate between sea and land. *Mare Liberum* was premised on the idea that one could have private property "only in things which one can either personally consume or personally transform," which included fish caught in the sea but not the sea itself. "The fisherman needs to protect his catch from rivals, but he does not need to protect the sea itself, for there is (Grotius argued) always enough for other fishermen in it." Crucially, Grotius added the further step that "if something cannot become private property, it cannot come under the control of a state either: 'Ownership [*Occupatio*] ... both public and private, arises in the same way'."[49] Grotius, that is, both assimilated states and individuals and reversed their priority: "If an individual could not own something, he could not give his rights in it to a state; and since 'every right comes to the state from private individuals', a state could not have political control over unownable territory."[50] This sufficed to undermine the contention that although the sea could not be owned, states might still claim jurisdiction over it. But both ideas were also put to work for American land.[51] First, as a

as doe also the Foxes and wilde beasts: they are not industrious, neither haue art, science, skill or facultie to vse either the land or the commodities of it, but all spoiles, rots, and is marred for want of manuring, gathering, ordering, &c. As the ancient Patriarkes therefore remoued from straiter places into more roomthy, where the Land lay idle and waste, and none vsed it, though there dwelt inhabitants by them, as *Gen.* 13.6.11.12. and 34.21. and 41.20. so is it lawfull now to take a land which none vseth, and make vse of it." Robert Cushman, "Reason & Considerations Touching the Lawfulnesse of remouing out of *England* into the parts of *America*," in William Bradford et al., *A Relation or Iournall of the Beginning and Proceedings of the English Plantation Setled at Plimoth in New England, by Certaine English Aduenturers Both Merchants and Others* (London, 1622), 68.

[48] Tuck, *Rights of War and Peace*, 90 (emphasis added). "When property or ownership was invented, the law of property established to imitate nature. For as that use began in connection with bodily needs, from which as we have said property first arose, so by a similar connection it was decided that things were the property of individuals." Grotius, *Mare Liberum*, 25.

[49] Ibid., 90–1. See Grotius, *Mare Liberum*, 26–8.

[50] Tuck, *Rights of War and Peace*, 92. And see Grotius, *Mare Liberum*, 34–5.

[51] Note the tendency among English theorists of colonizing to treat the American mainland as if it were an (inexhaustible) ocean of land. We have seen Donne's resort to the metaphor (n.39, this chapter). See also Gray, *A Good Speed to Virginia*, sig. C₄r. The most elaborated statement would await John Locke's *Two Treatises of Government: In the Former, the False Principles and Foundation of Sir Robert Filmer, and His Followers, are Detected and Overthrown. The Latter is an Essay Concerning the True Original, Extent, and End of Civil-Government* (London, 1698), 184–202 [§§25–51 "Of Property"], and particularly 189–90, 191–2: "appropriation of any parcel of Land, by improving it" could prejudice no other "since there was still enough, and as good left; and more than the yet unprovided could use. So that in effect, there was never the less left for others because of his inclosure for himself. For he that leaves as much as another can make use of, does as good as take nothing at all. No Body could think himself injur'd by the drinking of another Man, though he took a good Draught, who had a whole River of the same Water left him to quench his thirst. And the case of Land and Water, where there is enough of both, is perfectly

general principle, "if the sea could not be owned by the men who hunted over it, neither presumably could the land."[52] Second, that which had not been made private property by an individual's personal transformative act could not be claimed as, independently, within the jurisdiction or control of a state, or a sovereign, or – in the American case – their equivalents (if such they were allowed to be), such as a clan, a tribe, a regional collective. Mere inhabitation did not vest a property right in individual inhabitants, nor in the collective of inhabitants, but only acts of deliberate transformation – cultivation. As Robert Gray put it, "Some affirme, and it is likely to be true, that these Sauages haue no particular proprietie in any part or parcell of that Countrey, but only a generall residencie there." Nor would collective cultivation suffice to create property rights in the collective ("things were the property of individuals"[53]). Only individual transformative acts counted. Hence Gray could conclude, because "there is not *meum* or *tuum* amongest them" – that is, no observable practice of individuated property right – "if the whole lande should bee taken away from *them* there is not a man that can complaine of any particular wrong done unto *him*."[54] The absence of a system of exchange *in the manner of the English* signified the land's essential emptiness.

For all their determined marginalization of the indigenous as brutes that did not use the land or, therefore, possess the land, English writers – Symonds, Strachey, Gray, Donne, Crashaw – disclaimed any intent simply to take all the land. "There is no intendment to take away from them by force that rightfull inheritaunce which they haue in that Countrey."[55] This begged, of course, the immense question just traversed, namely what in English eyes differentiated "rightful inheritance" (owned land) from vacant land open to occupation. The English answer should by now be familiar to us: individual property right, grounded on improvement. "Admitteth it as a Principle in Nature, That in a vacant Soyle, hee that taketh possession of it, and bestoweth culture and husbandry upon it, his Right it is."[56] Land appropriated peaceably and improved, which "hath continued in our

---

the same." Suppose a man were "straitned for want of room to plant in" where the world seemed full, "let him plant in some in-land, vacant places of America, we shall find that the Possessions he could make himself, upon the measures we have given, would not be very large, nor, even to this day, prejudice the rest of Mankind."

[52] Tuck, *Rights of War and Peace*, 104.

[53] Ibid., 25.

[54] Gray, *A Good Speed to Virginia*, sig. c₄r. (emphasis added).

[55] Ibid. See also Cushman, "Reason & Considerations," 68–9.

[56] Cotton, *God's Promise to His Plantation*, 5, and see generally 4–5. Cotton uses the biblical example (Genesis 21: 25, 30) of a well dug by Abraham unjustly seized by servants of Abimelech in whose lands Abraham sojourned, "for his right whereto he pleaded not his immediate calling from God (for that would have seemed frivolous amongst the Heathen) but his own industry and culture in digging the well. Nor doth the King reject his plea, with what had he to doe to digge wells in their soyle," but instead admits Abraham's right as a principle in nature. (John Winthrop had used the same example in his "General Observations for the Plantation of New England," discussed in n.58, this chapter, which is clearly a source for Cotton's sermon.)

peaceable possession ever since without any interruption or Claim," was rightfully possessed by the English. "Being thus taken and possessed as *vacuum domicilium*," John Winthrop stated, "gives us a sufficient title against all men."[57] Only such land of which the Indians themselves had likewise gained actual possession by use, Winthrop allowed, was land not open to English occupation; if the English wanted that land they must purchase it. But even then, Indian right was inferior: Indians had only a natural right of ownership, never the civil right that their creation of commonwealths had earned the English.[58] Winthrop's answer was also John Cotton's,

[57] John Winthrop, quoted by David Grayson Allen, "Vacuum Domicilium: The Social and Cultural Landscape of Seventeenth-Century New England," in Jonathan L. Fairbanks and Robert F. Trent, eds., *New England Begins: The Seventeenth Century* (Boston, 1982), 1. Winthrop uses the term *vacuum domicilium* quite frequently. See Richard S. Dunn and Laetitia Yeandle, editors, *The Journal of John Winthrop, 1630–1649* (Cambridge, Mass., 1996), 122 [July 1634 – "besides The Kings grant, they had taken vp that place as vacuum domicilium, & so had continued without interuption or claim of any of the natiues for diverse years"], 283 [March 1639 – "we claimed Winicowett as within our patent, or as vacuum domicilium, and had taken possession thereof by building an house there above two years since"], 527 [August 1644 – "the king giving us land which was none of his, but we were forced to purchase it of the natives, or subdue it as vacuum domicilium, we are not bound to hold that of him which was not his"]. Note that Winthrop tends to distinguish between land within the boundaries of "the Kings grant" or "our patent," which is English as of sovereign right, and land which is not, but is nonetheless vacant and therefore meet for appropriation by occupation and/or subjugation, and improvement.

[58] Both matters (of natural and civil right in land) are illustrated in the dispute over Winicowett (see n.57, this chapter), briefly recorded in Winthrop's journal. John Wheelwright, the banished brother-in-law of Anne Hutchinson, had purchased land from local Indians to found the town of Exeter, New Hampshire. In a letter to Wheelwright of March 1638/9, Winthrop rejects Wheelwright's claim to title in the land by purchase, and goes on to discuss the implications of Wheelwright's claim for the distinctions on which the colony's land policy was grounded. According to Winthrop the land in question was within the colony's patent and the colony had taken possession by building a house on it, "and so it hath continued in our peaceable possession ever since without any interruption or Claim of any Indian or other, which being thus taken and possessed as vacuum domicilium gives vs a sufficient title against all men." Wheelwright's title by purchase was hence invalid, first because of the patent, second because of the prior possession, third because the Indians from which he had purchased the land had no more claim to it than any other Indians in the locality, fourth because as a matter of course "the Indians heere can [not] have any title to more lands then they can improve, which we have stood vpon from the first, though to take away occasion of offence ... we have been content to give them some consideration in that kind." Men might gain an "interest" in land in two ways – by natural right, that is, by right to take and make use of land where another had not before taken possession by prior use "as our fishermans stages and his possession determineth his interest"; and by civil right, founded on the development of "Civil Societies" and their arts and trades, by which men gain the capacity to improve and thereby acquire an interest in far more land than any one man might acquire by his individual use, and with it as well the legal capacity to pass their interest to their posterity and so accumulate land in their possession. The "Civill bodye can, and will withhold" [i.e., enable men to accumulate more land than they could use] but not the Indians who had no "artes, Cattle or other menes" to subdue and improve any more land than they actually planted. Because they had no civil society, "These natives have no other but a naturall right, and that is only to so much land as they have means to subdue and improve." *Winthrop Papers* (Massachusetts Historical Society, 1944), IV (1638–44),

revealed in his response to Roger Williams' charge that English planters could have no title because the country belonged to the Indians. English planters had dispossessed no one, said Cotton. They had "plant[ed] themselves in a *vacuum Domicilium,* or if they sit downe upon the Possession of

101–2. See also James K. Hosmer, editor, *Winthrop's Journal: "History of New England," 1630–1649* (New York, 1908), I, 294. The Massachusetts General Court had embraced Winthrop's reasoning in 1633; A. Leon Higginbotham, Jr., *In the Matter of Color: Race and the American Legal Process, the Colonial Period* (New York, 1978), 69. See generally William Cronon, *Changes in the Land: Indians, Colonists, and the Ecology of New England* (New York, 1983), 54–81.

Winthrop's distinction between natural and civil rights of property in his description of the basis of English title shows the influence of Grotius's property theory on display in *Mare Liberum* and *De Juri Belli ac Pacis* (note for example his reference to the foundation of civil society, hence state jurisdiction, in the accumulation of individual property rights by improvement) and to a degree anticipates Locke (both in the source of property in appropriation out of nature for use, and in the multiplier effect of civil jurisdiction upon accumulation manifest most clearly in Locke's theory of money). His letter to Wheelwright also recalls the succession of intimately related rehearsals of arguments for and against undertaking the New England expedition developed ten years earlier in 1629, notably the "General Observations for the Plantation of New England" (in several versions), and the "Reasons to be considered for iustifieinge the vndertakeres of the intended Plantation in New England," all in *Winthrop Papers* (Massachusetts Historical Society, 1931), II (1623–30), 111–24, 138–45. (Winthrop's arguments also show the influence of contemporary English enclosure debates and practices, on which see Chapter 5. Winthrop was himself from an old-enclosed region.)

The "General Observations" ("Higginson Copy") assert (118) "The whole earth is the Lord's garden and hee hath given it to the sons of Adam to bee tilled and improved by them, why then should we stand starving here for places of habitation (many men spending as much labor and cost to recover or keepe sometymes an acre or two of lands, as would procure him many hundreds acres, as good or better in another place) and in the meane tyme suffer whole countryes as profitable for the use of man, to lye waste without any improvement?" To the objection "what warrant have we to take that land, which is and hath been of long tyme possessed of others the sons of Adam?" the "General Observations" continue as follows (120):

> That which is common to all is proper to none. This savage people ruleth over many lands without title or property; for they inclose no ground, neither have they cattell to maintayne it, but remove their dwellings as they have occasion, or as they can prevail against their neighbours. And why may not christians have liberty to go and dwell amongst them in their waste lands and woods (leaving them such places as they have manured for their corne) as lawfully as Abraham did among the Sodomites? For God hath given to the sons of men a twofould right to the earth; there is a naturall right and a civil right. The first right was naturall when men held the earth in common, every man sowing and feeding where he pleased; Then, as men and cattell increased, they appropriated some parcells of ground by enclosing and peculiar manurance, and this in tyme got them a civil right. Such was the right which Ephron the Hittite had to the field of Machpelah, wherein Abraham could not bury a dead corpse without leave, though for the out parts of the countrey which lay common, he dwelt upon them and tooke the fruite of them at his pleasure. This appears also in Jacob and his sons, who fedd their flocks as bouldly in the Canaanites land, for he is said to be lord of the country; and at Dotham and all other places men accounted nothing their owne, but that which they had appropriated by their own industry.

the Natives, to receive the same from them by a reasonable Purchase, or free Assignment."[59]

By a reasonable purchase. The English idea of what constituted reasonable exchange was, inevitably, self-serving (as Cotton's preference for free assignment suggests). It was also always larded with menaces.[60] Once

The "Reasons to be considered" proceed similarly, but somewhat more ambitiously. First, to the assertion that God had given the earth to humanity Winthrop added God's injunction (Genesis 1:28) to "increace and multiplie, and replenish the earth and subdue it," in knowledge of which men should not "suffer a whole Continent as fruitfull and convenient for the vse of man to lie waste without any improuement" (139). Second, to the question of the settlers' warrant to land possessed by others, Winthrop answered with greater specificity, "That which lies common, and hath neuer been replenished or subdued is free to any that possesse and improue it" (140). Repeating that God had granted "a double right" to the earth – that is a natural right and a civil right – Winthrop now made it clear that because the natives "inclose noe Land, neither haue any setled habytation, nor any tame Cattle to improue the Land by" they could never enjoy more than "a Naturall Right to those Countries. soe as if we leaue them sufficient for their vse, we may lawfully take the rest" (141). That is, the English possessed a natural right to share in that which was common to all. In addition they had a (superior) civil right of individual ownership of that appropriated from the common store by laborious improvement.

59 "John Cotton's Answer to Roger Williams," *Proceedings of the Massachusetts Historical Society, 1871–1873* (Boston, 1873), 352. See, generally, Stuart Banner, *How the Indians Lost their Land: Law and Power on the Frontier* (Cambridge, Mass., 2005), 31–5, 45.

Paul Corcoran has argued that "vacuum domicilium" was an idiosyncratic Latinate formulation possibly invented by Winthrop himself and used occasionally by "pilgrim preachers" in the 1630s "to dignify, with supposed legal terms of art, the Massachusetts [Bay] Company's charter to settle and govern in dangerous and always fractious circumstances." See Paul Corcoran, "John Locke and the Possession of Land: Native Title vs. the 'Principle' of *Vacuum Domicilium*," 9–10 (Australasian Political Studies Association Annual Conference, 2007; available at http://arts.monash.edu.au/psi/news-and-events/apsa/refereed-papers/#political_theory, accessed 22 August 2009). Corcoran is correct to cast doubt on scholarly invocations of "*vacuum domicilium*" as if it were a received Roman law doctrine of ancient lineage, any more than *terra nullius*. That said, unlike *terra nullius* the idea does have a clear genealogy in the early modern law of nations. Take for example the familiar passage from the *Digest* 41.1.3, granting property rights to the first taker. "Quod enim nullius est, id ratione naturali occupanti conceditur" ["What presently belongs to no one becomes by natural reason the property of the first taker."] We have already seen this and related passages from the *Digest* variously cited and discussed by Vitoria, Gentili, and Grotius, among others. Gentili's discussion comes particularly close to furnishing both the reasoning and the vocabulary for Winthrop's terms of art (see Chapter 3, section II), for Gentili paid particular attention to the rights of exiles to vacant places, a matter of considerable relevance to the Puritan migration as indicated by Winthrop in the "General Observations" and the "Reasons to be Considered," and by Cotton in *God's Promise to His Plantation*. See also *An Answer to Some Cases of Conscience Respecting the Country. By Solomon Stoddard, A.M. Pastor in Northampton* (Boston, 1722), 12–14. See generally Avihu Zakai, *Exile and Kingdom: History and Apocalypse in the Puritan Migration to America* (Cambridge and New York, 1992).

60 Writers such as William Strachey and Robert Gray vowed that although indigenous rights of possession were, in English terms, debatable, the English would not seize land by force. Strachey held that the savages should keep "what they clense and manure" and that the English would "prepare and break up newe growndes" for themselves, and further that "every foote of land which we shall take unto our use, we will bargaine and buy of them, for copper, hatchetts, and such like commodityes," seeking quiet possession by consent.

"manning" was fully under way, by the 1620s in the Chesapeake, the 1630s in New England, the pressure of the introduced population and its uses on indigenous inhabitants and theirs became persistent and relentless. "Just warres" were fought where and when necessary.[61] Nor did their objectives change much over time. As William Crashaw had described English desires and expectations early on, "*land and roome* for vs to plant in, their countrey being not replenished by many degrees: in so much as a great part of it lieth wild & inhabited of none but the beasts of the fielde ... as the present state of *England* stands, we want roome, and are likely enough to want more ... *Timber, Masts, Crystall* (if not better stones) *Wine, Copper, Iron, Pitch, Tar, Sassafras, Sopeashes* (for all these and more, we are sure the Countrey yeeldes in great abundance) and who knows not we want these, and are beholden to some for them, with whom it were better for vs if we had lesse to doe."[62] What was articulated as an essentially modest wish to share in nature's abundance – to seek and obtain a sufficiency of "roome" for people and plantations – thus bred an impatience to realize English

This was to make a virtue of necessity, for the Virginia colony was weak and vulnerable throughout the period of which Strachey wrote. Nevertheless, he added in familiar natural-law language (endorsing Peckham) that if resisted – "inhumanely repulsed" – Christians might "seeke to attayne and mayntaine the right for which they come ... for what soever God, by the ministration of nature, hath created on earth, was, at the beginning, common among men; may yt not then be lawfull nowe to attempt the possession of such lands as are voide of Christian inhabitants, for Christ's sake." See his "A Præmonition to the Reader," in *The Historie of Travaile into Virginia Britannia*, 19, 20. Gray, too, claimed that the Indians were "willing to entertaine vs, and haue offered to yeelde into our handes on reasonable conditions, more lande than we shall be able this long time to plant and manure ... as much of their Countrey yielded vnto vs, by lawfull grannt from them, as we can or will desire, so that wee goe to liue peaceablie among them, and not to supplant them ... except succession and election, there cannot bee a more lawfull entrance to a kingdome than this of ours." But then he added the usual threat: "all Politicians doe with one consent, holde and maintaine, that a Christian king may lawfullie make warre upon barbarous and Sauage people, and such as liue under no lawfull or warrantable gouernment, and may make a conquest of them." Gray, *A Good Speed to Virginia*, sig. C$_4$r.

[61] See generally Jill Lepore, *The Name of War: King Philip's War and the Origins of American Identity* (New York, 1998); Nathaniel Philbrick, *Mayflower* (New York, 2006), 148–57, 177–9, 198–358. See also Daniel K. Richter, *Facing East from Indian Country: A Native History of Early America* (Cambridge, Mass., 2001), 69–109. On warfare in early Virginia and its significance for other English settlements, and on the Pequot War of 1636–7, see Alden T. Vaughan, *Roots of American Racism: Essays on the Colonial Experience* (Oxford and New York, 1995), 105–27, 177–99. In 1645, John Winthrop's brother-in-law Emanuel Downing – taking advantage of fears consequent upon the renewal of settler-Indian warfare in Virginia the previous year – petitioned him to engage in "juste warre" with the Pequots once more, so that captives might be acquired to exchange in Barbados for slaves. In Lorenzo J. Greene, *The Negro in Colonial New England, 1620–1776* (New York, 1968 [1942]), 60.

[62] William Crashaw, *A Sermon Preached in London before the right honorable the Lord LaWarre, Lord Gouernour and Captaine Generall of Virginea, and others of his Maiesties Counsell for that Kingdome, and the rest of the Aduenturers in that plantation.* February 21, 1609 (London, 1610), sigs. D$_4$v-r.

ascendancy, to actualize the chartered claim of *dominium*: jurisdiction, uncontested control. "These things they haue," wrote Crashaw; "these they may spare, these we neede, these we will take."[63] The English would decide what could be spared; the English would take of it what they wanted; the English would fight if obstructed.

And, Crashaw added, the English would determine the return to the natives, into the bargain. "We will giue them such things as they greatly desire, and doe hold a sufficient recompence," but more than that "we will giue them ... such things as they want and neede." What might such things be? "Civilitie for their bodies [and] Christianity for their soules."[64] Later exchanges involved more material goods, but the English remained the price-setters, always the reward that accompanies the jurisdictional (and martial) high ground. Yet, Stuart Banner has argued, Indian property rights were not denied; Indian lands were purchased, not seized. Nor were they purchased only when properly identified in English eyes as cultivated. Though the matter was always contested, the strict division of theory was relaxed in practice; no distinction was drawn in purchasing between what was properly "owned" and what was within an indigenous group's territory but vacant.[65]

Purchase was expedient, particularly in the earliest years of English settlement when colonists clung rather desperately to their beachheads, for war was always costly.[66] But purchase was not a concession of sovereignty;

[63] Ibid., sig. D₄r. And see Vaughan, *Roots of American Racism*, 117–18, 192.

[64] Crashaw, *A Sermon Preached in London*, sig. D₄r.

[65] Banner, *How the Indians Lost their Land*, 49–84. See also Eric Kades, "History and Interpretation of the Great Case of *Johnson v. M'Intosh*, *Law and History Review*, 19, 1 (Spring 2001), 72–4; Eric Kades, "The Dark Side of Efficiency: *Johnson v. M'Intosh* and the Expropriation of American Indian Lands," *University of Pennsylvania Law Review*, 148, 4 (April 2000), 1076–7. Following Yasuhide Kawashima, *Puritan Justice and the Indian: White Man's Law in Massachusetts, 1630–1763* (Middletown, Conn., 1986), Kades argues that throughout the history of continental expansion, more Indian land was purchased than seized (1077). But as Jean M. O'Brien points out in *Dispossession By Degrees: Indian Land and Identity in Natick, Massachusetts, 1650–1790* (New York and Cambridge, 1997), 19–26, and as Kades also argues in outlining his theory of "efficient expropriation" (1078–80, 1104–9), authority to define the rights conveyed by purchase, and who were the legitimate parties to land transactions, was entirely within the jurisdictional realm of the colonizer. See also Seed, *American Pentimento*, 19–21; Nan Goodman, "American Indian Languages and the Law of Property in Colonial America," *Law, Culture and the Humanities*, 5, 1 (2009), 77–99. Recall what John Winthrop told Wheelwright: "we deny that the Indians heere can have any title to more lands than they can improve, which we have stood vpon from the first, though to take away occasion of offence ... we have been content to give them *some consideration* in that kind." John Winthrop to John Wheelwright, March 1638/9, in *Winthrop Papers*, IV, 101–02 (emphasis added).

[66] Seizure of land by force, nevertheless, was far more frequent than Banner implies. Note, for example, the moment of candor in which the Virginia Assembly in 1662 acknowledges that "the mutuall discontents, complaints, jealousies and ffeares" that had attended the relations between English and Indians over the previous half century had proceeded "cheifly from the violent intrusions of diverse English made into their lands forcing the Indians by way of revenge to kill the cattle and hogs of the English, and by that meanes injuries being done on both sides, reports and rumours are spread of the hostile

the English were at some pains to deny the possibility that "their" Indians had sovereigns or even elementary civility. Gray likened them to forest creatures, "wild beasts" that "range and wander up and downe the Countrey, without any law or government, being led only by their owne lusts and sensualitie."[67] William Bradford's remarkable history of Plymouth Plantation places the pilgrims at landfall among savages who forfeit any claim to elementary human fellowship by refusing them assistance. "Being thus passed ye vast ocean … they had now no freinds to wellcome them, nor inns to entertaine or refresh their weatherbeaten bodys, no houses or much less townes to repaire too, to seeke for succoure. It is recorded in scripture as a mercie to ye apostle and his shipwraked company, y^t the barbarians shewed them no smale kindnes in refreshing them, but these savage barbarians, when they mette with them (as after will appeare) were readier to fill their sids full of arrows then otherwise." Surrounding the newcomers was "a hidious and desolate wildernes, full of wild beasts and willd men"; the whole country untamed, "full of woods & thickets, represented a wild and savage heiw," standing far distant "from all ye civill parts of ye world."[68] A better description of what lay beyond *societas gentium* could not be imagined.

But suppose their Indians *did* have sovereigns and "government" (and in fact on the ground the English were early on inclined to hedge their

intentions of each to other, tending infinitely to the disturbance of the peace of his majesty's country." *Concerning Indians*, Act CXXXVIII, in William Waller Hening, *The Statutes at Large; Being a Collection of all the Laws of Virginia, from the First Session of the Legislature, in the Year 1619* (New York, 1823), II, 138, available at http://www.vagenweb.org/hening/ (accessed 22 August 2009). During the half century in question the Assembly had been preparing for war, engaged in war, or maintaining the colony in a posture of "watchful waiting" for most of the twenty years following the Jamestown Massacre, again during the mid-1640s, and again during the mid-1650s. See, for example, Act III of October 1629 (authorizing marches upon the Indians); Act VIII of March 1629/30 (effectual prosecution of war); Act LXI of February 1631/2 and XXVII of September 1632 (Indians "irrecosileable enimies"); Assembly Order of August 1633 (appointing county lords lieutenant "the same as in England, and in a more especial manner to take care of the war against Indians"); Remonstrance of April 1642 (calling for "settling of peace and friendship with Indians"); Act IV of October 1644, VIII and IX of February 1644/5, and XIII of March 1645/6 (resumption of "marches against our salvage enemies" particularly on the south side of the James River and the western end of the York Peninsula); Act XVIII of March 1645/6 (Indians "dispersed and driven from their towns and habitations"); Act I of October 1646 (peace treaty with Necotowance securing the entire York Peninsula for English settlement "nor any Indians [to] repaire to or make abode vpon the said tract of land, vpon paine of death"); Assembly Order of November 1654 ("Concerning the March against the Rappahannock Indians); and Act I of March 1655/6 ("Wheareas wee have bin often putt into great dangers by the invasions of our neighbouring and bordering Indians which humanely have bin only caused by these two particulars our extreame pressures on them and theire wanting of something to hazard & loose beside their lives") all in Hening, *Statutes at Large*, I, 140–1, 153, 176, 193, 224, 237, 285, 292–4, 315, 317–19, 323–6, 389–90, 393–6.

[67] Gray, *A Good Speed to Virginia*, sig. c₄r.

[68] *Bradford's History "Of Plimoth Plantation." From the Original Manuscript* (Boston, 1898), 94–6.

bets, as in Christopher Newport's clumsy attempt to vassalize the Powhatan chieftain Wahunsonacock[69]), what meaning did it carry? If in the seventeenth century's new property regime "every right comes to the state from private individuals," the absence of *"meum* and *tuum"* amongst these particular individuals suggested they had precious few rights to convey. Even if the existence of indigenous sovereigns and governments were acknowledged, in other words, what rights did they actually possess? What did they actually govern?[70]

For Grotius, as for Gentili, this devolved to a question not about rights over property but about jurisdiction over territory and people. Local sovereigns might be tolerated for their exercise of jurisdiction over those on the territory they claimed as "theirs," but if they obstructed the entry of others, or free passage, or the occupation of uncultivated land, they "will have violated a principle of the law of nature and may be punished by war waged against them."[71] The law of nature and nations had been harmonized with, even transformed into an expression of, the new property regime. The objective of war to vindicate natural law might be limited to the insistence that local sovereigns allow access and occupation and the conversion of waste to property by individuated cultivation. Or, more aggressively, it might be to overthrow that local sovereignty and establish a new "stable and effective right to command anyone who entered into a certain area of land," that is a new "jurisdiction over territory," which would complement rather than obstruct the new property regime by punishing those who stood in its way.[72] For, as Grotius wrote, to a degree echoing Vitoria, but also departing from him,[73] "kings and those who possess rights equal to those kings"

---

[69] Described by John Smith in his *The Proceedings of the English Colonie in Virginia since their first beginning from England in the yeare of our Lord 1606* (1612), in Barbour, ed., *Complete Works,* I, 236–7. The colony's 1646 peace treaty with the Pamunkey chieftain Necotowance (son of Opechancanough) required that Necotowance "acknowledge to hold his kingdome from the King's Ma'tie of England, and that his successors be appointed or confirmed by the King's Governours from time to time." Hening, *Statutes at Large,* I, 323.

[70] See, generally, Tuck, *Rights of War and Peace,* 89–108.

[71] Ibid., 106. Grotius, *De Jure Belli ac Pacis,* II.2.11–23 (196–205).

[72] Tuck, *Rights of War and Peace,* 106–8.

[73] "Princes have authority not only over their own subjects, but also over foreigners, so far as to prevent them from committing wrongs, and this is by the law of nations and the authority of the whole world" and natural law too, for "society could not hold together unless there was somewhere a power and authority to deter wrongdoers and prevent them from injuring the good and innocent." Francisco de Vitoria, *On the Indians or on the Law of War Made by the Spaniards on the Barbarians* (Second Relectio), in *Francisci de Victoria, De Indis et De Iure Belli Relectiones,* Ernest Nys ed., John Pawley Bate trans. (Washington, 1917), 172. Grotius discusses the extent of his differences with Vitoria on the matter in *De Jure Belli ac Pacis,* II.20.40.3–4 (505–6). See also Tuck, *Rights of War and Peace,* 103. Perhaps the most pointed difference lies in Grotius's statement (at 506), which recalls Gentili on the Spanish conquest, that princely authority encompassed the punishment of beasts, and that "the most just war is against savage beasts, the next against men who are like beasts."

have the right of demanding punishments not only on account of injuries committed against themselves or their subjects, but also on account of injuries which do not directly affect them but excessively violate the law of nature or of nations in regard to any persons whatsoever. For liberty to serve the interests of human society through punishments ... now after the organization of states and courts of law is in the hands of the highest authorities, not, properly speaking, in so far as they rule over others but in so far as they are themselves subject to no one. For subjection has taken this right away from others

...

And for this cause Hercules was famed by the ancients because he freed from Antaeus, Busiris, Diomedes and like tyrants the lands which, as Seneca says, he traversed, not from a desire to acquire but to protect, becoming ... the bestower of the greatest benefits upon men through his punishment of the unjust ... elevated among the gods because of his espousal of the common interest of the human race.[74]

II.   Labors of Hercules

Such epic humanist heroism – restoration of existential justice, bestowal of benefit – elevated English expeditions. But their activities also exhibited their own vernacular edge. As Sir Edward Coke reflected upon the matter in 1608, even the more cultured barbarians, infidels, were "perpetual enemies" against whom Christians were pitted in "perpetual hostility"; and for that reason, "if a Christian King should conquer a kingdom of an infidel, and bring them under his subjection, there ipso facto the laws of the infidel are abrogated, for that they be not only against Christianity, but against the law of God *and of nature.*" And "until certain laws be established amongst them, the King by himself, and such Judges as he shall appoint, shall judge them and their causes."[75] How much more certainly, then, might the English justify their encroachments, their gift of well ordering, upon lesser barbarians.

Herculean labors created new jurisdictions in distant places. English colonizers counted themselves engaged in just such a process; if need be they had their own documentation to prove it. "Many cases may be put, when not onely *Commerce,* and *Trade,* but *Plantations* in lands, not formerly our owne, may be lawfull," John Donne advised departing Virginia adventurers in 1622. "And for that *Accepistis potestatem,* you have your *Commission,* your *Patents,* your *Charters,* your *Seales* from *him,* upon whose acts, any private

---

[74] Grotius, *De Jure Belli ac Pacis,* II.20.40.1–2 (504–5).

[75] *Calvin's Case* 7 Coke Report 1a, 77 English Reports 377 (1608), at 397–8 (emphasis added). Brian Lockey comments, "Coke's formulation shares more with those medieval writers who saw non-Christian polities as illegitimate by the very fact that they were not Christian, than it does with sixteenth-century Neo-scholastics or humanists, who affirmed that non-Christians and Christians alike could have legitimate dominion over territory." *Law and Empire in English Renaissance Literature* (New York and Cambridge, 2006), 9. As we have just seen, however, it is not difficult to find the same inflection on the law of nature in Gentili and Grotius.

Subject, in Civill matters, may safely rely."[76] Like Peckham, as they proceeded land increasingly filled their horizon. But so did governance. The
letters patent authorizing the first English mainland colonies – Gilbert's,
Raleigh's – had vested in the recipient and his heirs "full and meere power
and authoritie to correct, punish, pardon, governe and rule by their, and
every or any of their good discretions and policies ... all such our subjects
and others" who "shall at any time hereafter inhabite any such lands, countreys or territories ... according to such statutes, lawes and ordinances"
as they might devise "for the better governement of the said people."[77]
The first Virginia charter (1606) promised the introduction of "settled
and quiet government"; The New England charter (1620) conjectured a
recent history of chaos and emptiness – "utter Destruction, Deuastacion,
and Depopulacion of that whole Territorye" – as the basis for its mandate
of "better Plantacion, ruling and governing," of "well ordering and good
Government."[78] William Bradford's Plymouth colonists, surrounded by
brutes, created a new jurisdiction from amongst themselves, filling the
civic void on arrival with those "whose names are underwriten," who did
"covenant & combine our selves togeather into a civill body politick, for our
better ordering & preservation & furtherance of ye ends aforesaid"; by virtue whereof they empowered themselves "to enacte, constitute, and frame
such just and equall lawes, ordinances, acts, constitutions, & offices, from
time to time, as shall be thought most meete and convenient for ye generall
good of ye Colonie."[79]

Rather than proffer detailed plans, the earliest letters patent delegated
the implantation of new jurisdictional authority upon the territories they
granted to Crown assignees invested with law-making authority. They were
sufficient nevertheless to establish a model for English colonizing as a
process that throughout the following century would use law to project
elaborately detailed English designs onto the mainland that appropriated
American territory to an English epistemology: English politics and economics, English representations, English purposes.

Future English charters – of which there were many[80] – were far more
complex documents than the first letters patent, but they performed in

---

[76] *A Sermon Preached to the Honourable Company of the Virginian Plantation*, 11.

[77] "Letters Patent to Sir Humfrey Gilberte" and "Charter to Sir Walter Raleigh," both in
Thorpe, *The Federal and State Constitutions*, I, 49–52, 53–7, at 51, 55, providing only that
such laws be "as neere as conveniently may, agreeable to the forme of the lawes and pol-
licy of England."

[78] In Thorpe, *Federal and State Constitutions*, VII, 3784, III, 1828–9, 1839. See also the Avalon
charter and the charters of Maryland, Carolina, and Pennsylvania ("good and happy
government"), Rhode Island ("peaceable and orderly Government"), and Delaware
("Well-being and good Government"), all in Thorpe, *Federal and State Constitutions* III,
1679, V, 2745, V, 3037, VI, 3217, I, 558, except for the Avalon charter, for which see Keith
Matthews, comp., *Collection and Commentary on the Constitutional Laws of Seventeenth Century
Newfoundland* (Maritime History Group, Memorial University of Newfoundland, 1975), 45.

[79] *Bradford's History "Of Plimoth Plantation,"* 110.

[80] Between 1606 (the first Virginia charter) and 1681 (Pennsylvania), some twenty-eight
major territorial charters and grants were promulgated, dealing with the establishment,

essence the same role, mobilizing legal discourses both instrumentally and imaginatively to imprint *England* on America. All mapped both territory and the institutional and cultural forms in which authority would be applied to (and within) that territory. For much of the century the mapping of territory was largely chorographic. Possession was claimed by description of boundaries and interior character. In James I's 1623 grant of the province of Avalon (Southeastern Newfoundland) to Sir George Calvert, for example, the charter walked the reader around the boundary of the grant by means of a topographic narrative:

> All that entyre porcon of Land scituate within our Country of Newfoundland aforesaid, beginning southerly from the middle part of a certaine Neck of Land or Promontorie scituate between the two Harbours of Fermose, and Aquaforte and from thence following the Shoare towards the North unto the middle part or half way over a little Harbour called in that reguard Petit Port or Petit Harbour which boundeth upon the South part of the Plantacon of St. John's includeing the one half of a certaine fresh River that falleth into the said Port of Petit Harbour, and soe tending all along the south Border of the said Colony of St John's extendeth itself to a certaine little Bay commonly called Salmon Cove lyeing on the South syde of the Bay of Conception includeing the one half of the River that falleth into the said Cove as also ye one half of ye sd. Cove itselfe, from whence passing along the Shoare of the said Bay towards the South and reaching into the Bottome thereof where it meets with the Lands of John Guy Citizen of Bristoll named Sea Forrest is bounded with a certain River or Brooke which there falleth into the sea and from the Mouth of the said Brooke ascended into the farthest Spring or Head thereof from thence passeth towards the South for Six Miles together along the Borders of ye said John Guy his plantation and there crossing over westward in a right line reacheth into the Bay of Placentia and the space of one League within the said Bay from the Shoare thereof. Hence turning again towards the South passeth along the Harbour of Placentia with the like Distance from the Shoare and descending into New Falkland towards the north and west part thereof stretcheth itself in a right line Eastward continueing the whole southerly length upon the Bounds of the said New Falkland, into the middle part or point of the Promontory or Neck of Land aforementioned between the said Ports of Formose and Aquafort at which place is described and finished the perambulacon of the whole Precinct.[81]

reestablishment, or confirmation of English (and one Scottish) settlements on the North American mainland. This listing comprises: the first, second, and third charters of Virginia (1606, 1609, 1612); the London & Bristol Company charter for Newfoundland (1610); the New England Council charter (1620); the three Alexander charters for Nova Scotia (1621, 1625, 1628); the Maine grants (1622, 1639, 1664, 1674); the Avalon charter for Newfoundland (1623); the Heath patent for Carolina (1629); the Plymouth charter (1629); the Massachusetts Bay Company charter (1629); the New Hampshire grants (1629, 1635); the Maryland charter (1632); the Kirke charter for Newfoundland (1637); the Connecticut charter (1662); the Rhode Island charter (1663); the Carolina charters (1663, 1665); the New Jersey grants (1664, 1674, 1682); the Pennsylvania charter (1681).

[81] In Matthews, comp., *Collection and Commentary*, 40–2. At the risk of stating the obvious, it is worth noting that the description possesses the place for the English because (with a few concessions to French proper names) it is an entirely anglicized description. Colin

Although all Crown charters necessarily described locales for colonization and settlement, language as precise as this was not always present.[82] Nor, when it was, did it translate into actual precision on the ground. Topography often did not conform to the landscape described. Grants were often inconsistent with other grants, conflicting and overlapping, a sign of intense competition for territory. Years ago, Charles M. Andrews wondered whether "any of the Crown lawyers or chancery officials ever consulted the old patents in making out a new one, or ever studied the geography of the regions they so easily gave away."[83] This could be interpreted as ignorance, or alternatively as a sign of the relative unimportance of geographic and topographic accuracy in achieving control of territory, compared with the densely woven fabric of law.

Carefully expressing the claim that territory was legitimately appropriated by use, all the charters are catalogs of intense creative activity that emphasize systematic transformative action on the land. The New England charter of 1620, for example, endowed "Adventurers, intending to erect and establish ffishery, Trade and Plantacion."[84] Charters in general underscored possession of fisheries, harbors, and soils, to which they added emphasis on cultural signs of occupation and specificities of use – the division of lands, the erection of churches, fortifications, towns and markets, manors and manorial institutions. The Carolina charter (1663) granted "full power, liberty and license to erect, raise and build ... so many forts, fortresses, castles, cities, buroughs, towns, villages" and to "constitute, erect and appoint such and so many markets, marts and fairs" as well as "so many mannors" as might seem appropriate; "and in every of the said mannors to have and to hold a court baron, with all things whatsoever which to a court baron do belong, and to have and to hold views of 'frankpledge'

Calloway notes how "New towns were given European names to replace their ancient Indian names, and the pattern of settlement rapidly obscured the Indian past and presence. In seventeenth-century New England, for example, Agawam became Ipswich; Shawmut became Boston; Naumeag, at the mouth of the Pequot River, became New London; and the river itself became the Thames." See his *New Worlds for All: Indians, Europeans, and the Remaking of Early America* (Baltimore, 1997), 11–12. J. B. Harley made the same point. One hundred and fifty years after the first English intrusions on the American mainland, the mid-eighteenth century's maps of the interior showed "how successfully a European colonial society had reproduced itself in the New World." Their depictions of place-names, settlements, roads, and local administrative boundaries were a constant reminder of "the structures and consequences," the "European geography," and the European economy that English colonization had created. It was "as if the Europeans had always lived there." J. B. Harley, "Power and Legitimation in the English Geographical Atlases of the Eighteenth Century," in John A. Wolter and Ronald E. Grim, editors, *Images of the World: The Atlas Through History* (Washington, D.C., 1997), 189.

[82] The charters evince some tendency to become more precise over time, although the nature of their precision also becomes more abstract (see, for example, the Pennsylvania charter's description of territorial extent later in this section).

[83] Charles M. Andrews, *The Colonial Period of American History*, 2nd. ed. (New Haven, 1964), I, 323.

[84] "Charter of New England," in Thorpe, *Federal and State Constitutions*, III, 1828.

and 'court leet,' for the conservation of the peace and better government of those parts."[85]

As interesting as the actual territorial grants and the constructive activity to which aspiring possessors committed themselves, where there is considerable continuity in English discourse, are the structures of authority through which claimants proposed to pursue control of and organize activity in their territories (that is, build states), where continuities are less apparent. These structures should not be thought of as merely *responses* to the immediate exigencies of colonizing; in most cases they were elaborate and detailed *plans*. Nor, although always expressed in vernacular language, were the plans in question necessarily reproductions of structures actually prevailing in contemporary England. Often, in fact, they were, like *Utopia*, idealized projections of forms of socio-legal order that colonizers desired to create.[86] We shall later see that they were also projections that often proved impossible of achievement, or that were challenged in practice.

Virginia, Massachusetts

The first comprehensive expression of Crown chartering as a means to establishment of a legalized strategy of colonial planning came in the first charter of Virginia, granted in 1606 by James I, which began continuous English presence on the American mainland.

James I's letters patent for Virginia licensed two schemes of "habitation and plantation" that would "deduce" (lead forth) colonies "of sundry of our People into that part of *America* commonly called VIRGINIA," territory "not now actually possessed by any Christian Prince or People." One scheme was pioneered by a company comprising "certain Knights, Gentlemen, Merchants, and other Adventurers" of the city of London, the other by similar inhabitants of the cities of Bristol, Exeter, and Plymouth. The first was to be located anywhere on the American Atlantic coast between 34° and 41° of northern latitude, the second anywhere between 38° and 45°. Each was to have "all the Lands, Woods, Soil, Grounds, Havens, Ports, Rivers, Mines, Minerals, Marshes, Waters, Fishings, Commodities, and Hereditaments"

---

[85] Charter of Carolina – 1663," in Thorpe, *Federal and State Constitutions*, V, 2750–1.

[86] It is noticeable, for example, that the charters' property discourse, whether landed or mineral, is more absolutist in its contemplation of possession than contemporary English discourse. That is, the charters appear to replicate the new theories of property rights that we have already seen in Grotius and in the writings of contemporary English humanists. There is little indication that any of the complex of "multiple overlapping claims by many individuals and casual or regular uses by many others" that characterized English land rights discourse into the eighteenth century had any play in American colonizing, except perhaps in water rights. Given that the trend in English law was toward the discovery of land as property, and property as exclusive this is perhaps not surprising, but it does suggest how the charters could accommodate political and/or economic expectation, or fancy, unleashed from domestic restraint. On changes in the concept of property, see David J. Seipp, "The Concept of Property in the Early Common Law," *Law and History Review*, 12, 1 (Spring 1994), 29–91, at 87 and 88–91.

lying within "the Space of fifty miles of *English* statute measure" inland and along the coast, and a hundred miles out to sea. Neither was to be established within a hundred miles of the other. Each colony's patentees were granted "all the lands, Tenements, and Hereditaments" within its precincts, to be held of the Crown, "as of our Manor at *East-Greenwich*, in the County of *Kent*, in free and common Soccage only, and not in Capite,"[87] whereon they might "inhabit ... build and fortify" at their discretion, reserving to the Crown "the fifth Part" of any gold or silver dug, and the fifteenth part of copper. Both colonies were granted particular privileges (for example, the right to unencumbered flows of people and armaments, the right to levy customs and excise duties) that confirmed them in actual command of their own territorial expanse. Each was to have its own council appointed by its parent company, to "govern and order all Matters and Causes, which shall arise, grow, or happen, to or within the same ... according to such Laws, Ordinances, and Instructions, as shall be, in that behalf, given and signed with Our Hand or Sign Manual, and pass under the Privy Seal of our Realm of *England*." Each was to be subject to a ruling Council of Virginia established in England for the "superior Managing and Direction" of their affairs, and for the government of the entire Virginia tract; that is, everything between 34° and 45° of northern latitude, including any further schemes of colonizing licensed within that territory.[88] This structure created a clear hierarchy of control: local company authority specific to company projects subordinated to general Crown authority asserted over

---

[87] Socage was "a tenure of land by certain and determinate service" and was a feudalized tenure. Socage tenures carried with them an obligation on the part of the tenant to pay certain charges, both recurrent (aids) and one-time (relief), as a condition of holding the land in question. Villeinage was a base socage tenure, free socage an "honorable" one. Land held in socage may be contrasted to land held by knight service, which required of the holder military services in addition to exposure to a wider range of payments (primarily wardship – a payment to be made by a minor heir on reaching majority) in addition to aids and relief. Land held "in capite" was held directly of the Crown (*ut de corona*) and the holder was considered a tenant-in-chief, or vassal, whose tenancy was burdened by potentially heavy obligations to the Crown (notably primer seisin, the profits of the first year), but who in turn enjoyed substantial privileges and authority in relations with lesser landlords whose land was held of the tenant-in-chief. Land held "as of" a royal manor (*ut de manore*) meant royal land held not directly of the Crown, and hence subject to the certain and determinate services of a manorial relationship rather than the uncertain services (because military in origin) of a chivalrous one. Land held "as of" a manor in free and common socage not in capite was thus a combination of conditions that added up to "much the easiest tenure," particularly when the tenant was a corporation, for corporations were exempt from paying relief. See John B. Saunders, editor, *Mozley & Whiteley's Law Dictionary*, 9th ed. (London, 1977), 185, 318; Viola Florence Barnes, "Land Tenure in English Colonial Charters of the Seventeenth Century," in *Essays in Colonial History Presented to Charles McLean Andrews by his Students* (New Haven, 1931), 4–7. During the mid-seventeenth century, by resolutions of the recalled Long Parliament (1640) and of the Civil War Parliament (1645), and by acts of the Commonwealth and Restoration Parliaments (1656, 1660), all feudal tenures were converted to socage tenure, which became the basis of all forms of modern landed property in English law.

[88] "The First Charter of Virginia," in Thorpe, *Federal and State Constitutions*, VII, 3783–9.

the entire Virginia territory and "the several colonies" which then were or, presumably, might later be established "within the aforesaid Precincts of four and thirty and five and forty Degrees abovementioned."[89]

Using the charter to plan and distribute political, legal, and economic resources (powers and institutions of government, relief from customs duties, the right to charge their own duties) and to define both the extent and means of disposition of physical resources (land, minerals) was a practical exercise in the creation of jurisdiction. The Crown also used the charter to confirm additional crucial jurisdictional arrangements to govern the disposition of other vital resources, notably population, affirming its own supervening jurisdictional authority over its subjects by explicitly permitting their departure for purposes of colonizing. It also extended a common civic status to the inhabitants of the Virginia settlements, and simultaneously situated the settlements within a web of like polities – "our Realm of *England*, or any other of our said Dominions" – amongst which population was (in civic personality and circulation) fungible. In this respect the charter expresses a fundamental distinction between representation of the prospective population – "as if" within England, hence culturally "settled" though physically distant – and the actual indigenous population, "Infidels and Savages" who lived "in Darkness and miserable Ignorance of the true Knowledge and Worship of God." They were to be beneficiaries of English processes but not participants, spectators on the margins briefly invoked to establish that their want of civic personality rendered them unsettled and without government, therefore without sovereign jurisdiction over the lands they inhabited, unfit to occupy what they, in fact, occupied. Only the creation of English colonies (not, one should note, propagation of Christianity per se) might bring them "to a settled and quiet Government."[90]

The Virginia charter at once licensed colonization, expressed the process's epistemology, and furnished a medium in which to plan and articulate that expression. The essential configurations of colonizing – physical (location), economic (the distribution of land and other resources, the control of flows of population), political (the structure of government) and civic (the allocation of jurisdiction, the legal character of colonial personhood, the basis upon which all other listed privileges might be claimed) – were all granted points of English reference that, instrumentally, allowed

---

[89] Ibid., 3785–6. The hierarchy was complicated because the royal council was actually appointed from among the members of the two companies, while the actions of the company councils were mediated by the Crown (The councils were to "govern ... according to such Laws, Ordinances and Instructions, as shall be, in that behalf, given and signed with Our Hand ... and pass under the Privy Seal of our Realm of England" [3785]). There was no "compliance with English laws" clause in the first Virginia charter, but the charter did contain a "liberties of the subject" clause. All this suggests some difficulty in determining how to create simultaneously structures appropriate for managing a company and governing a territory.

[90] Ibid., 3788, 3784.

the process to take place; and they were given a language (law) that not only provided the medium in which colonization could take place, but also rendered the colonizing process transactionally continuous with a myriad other enabling processes (moving, borrowing, buying, selling, protecting, punishing; that is, the processes of civil and criminal law), and in which its legitimacy (and as important its limits and boundaries) could be signified to other European audiences. The whole comprised an authoritative representation of a vast and remote tract of territory ("Florida to the Circle Articke"[91]) in familiar English designs that both underscored English possession and at the same time rendered existing inhabitants and their practices virtually invisible.[92]

Between 1607 and 1609, the London and Plymouth companies each established a settlement, at Jamestown ("James Cittie") on the James River, and at Sagadahoc in Maine. Only the Jamestown settlement survived, and that only barely. Its difficulties prompted the London adventurers to seek major refinements in the arrangements established in 1606, formally separating from the Plymouth adventurers and reconstituting themselves as a separate joint-stock company controlled by a new London-based council. The new charter (1609) abolished the royal council created in 1606, substantially enlarged the London company's original grant of territory, vested an enlarged authority to govern the colony in the company's ruling council situated in London, and empowered the latter to replace the Jamestown settlement's local council with an appointed governor, whose authority was to be equivalent to that of a county lord lieutenant.[93] Two years later, additional refinements incorporated in a third charter (1611–12) broadened participation in company affairs beyond its ruling council to the generality of its members by establishing a structure of greater and lesser company courts. The former (the "Great and General Courts of the Council and Company of Adventurers for Virginia") were at-large assemblies to be called quarterly "for the handling, ordering and disposing of Matters and Affairs of greater Weight and Importance" such as might involve "the

---

[91] In his *Historie of Travaile into Virginia Britannia*, at 23, William Strachey defined "Virginia Britannia" as "a countrye in America" lying "betweene the degrees of 30 and 44 of the north latitude" (that is from St. Augustine in Florida to Muscongus Bay in present-day Maine).

[92] The indigenous population had no English existence because they had no recognizable civic presence. They of course had their own existence and were recognized as such, but that existence was as savages. Moreover, one can watch the import accorded that physical presence decline in the documentary trail of early English colonization. In the earliest of the elder Hakluyt's observations, for example, the indigenous exist as objects of statecraft whose reduction must be plotted – kings to be made allies, suborned, or conquered. By the time of his cousin's "Instructions for the Virginia Colony" (1606), in *Original Writings and Correspondence*, II, 492–9, they have lost the descriptive appurtenances of sovereign statehood ("kings") and have become merely "native people" or "country people" or "naturals," of whom one should be cautious but who were possessed of no political significance.

[93] The Second Charter of Virginia (1609), in Thorpe, *Federal and State Constitutions*, VII, 3790–3802, at 3796–8, 3801. The second charter included a "compliance" proviso.

Weal Publick and general Good of the said Company and Plantation" –
manner of government, disposition of land, the establishment of particular forms of trade. The latter, consisting of five members of the council
(always including the treasurer or his deputy) and fifteen of the generality,
was to be called into session as needed "for the handling and ordering,
and dispatching of all such casual and particular Occurrences, and accidental Matters, of less Consequence and Weight ... concerning the said
Plantation." The third Virginia charter also delegated substantial judicial
authority over delinquent colonists returning to England to the company
council in London.[94]

The initial structures of authority projected by participants in the
Virginia enterprise, then, underwent a transition from Crown licensing of
unincorporated adventuring within a Crown domain, to a form of partnership between the Crown and incorporated investors, to enhanced company
capacity to manage the colony within the framework of royal prerogative.
For the next decade, the latter provided the ascendant legal-organizational
model for English planting overseas. The year after the "Treasurer and
Company of Adventurers and Planters of the City of London, for the first
Colony in Virginia" was established in 1609, for example, James I issued letters patent to the "Treasurer and the Companye of Adventurers and plant-
ers of the Cittye of london and Bristoll" for a "Collonye or plantacon in
Newfoundland" on a near-identical basis.[95] The Somers Island (Bermuda)
Company followed in 1615.[96]

In the 1620s matters began to change. The first outburst of English colonizing had been carried on a wave of heroic ambition, strategic occupation

---

[94] "The Third Charter of Virginia" (1612), in Thorpe, *Federal and State Constitutions*, VII,
3802–10, 3805.

[95] The colony was to be situated in Southeastern Newfoundland, where for fifty years and
more English subjects had repaired to fish, intending by plantation and inhabitation to
secure the fishing trade and "to make some comendable benifitt for the vse of mankynde
by the landes and p[ro]ffittes thereof which hetherto from the beginnyng (as it seems
manifest) hath remayned vnprofittable ... We being well assured that the same lande or
Countrie ... remayneth soe destytute and soe desolate of inhabitance that scarce any one
savage p[er]son hath in manye yeares byn scene in the most partes thereof And well knowing that the same lying ... vacant is as well for the reasons aforesaide as for manye other
reasons verie comodious for us and our domynions. And that by the law of nature and
natons wee maye of our Royall authoritie possease our selves and make graunt thereof
without doeing wrong to any other Prince or State considering they cannot instyle p[re]
tend any Sovaignetye or right therevnto in respecte that the same remayneth soe vacant
and not actually possessed and inhabited by any Christian or any other whomsoever And
therefore thinking it a matter and accon well beseemyng a Christian king to make true
vse of that which God from the beginning created for mankynd And thereby intending
not onlye to worke and p[ro]cure the benifitt and good of manye of our Subjectes but
principally to increase the knowledg of the omnipotent God and the p[ro]pagacon of our
Christian faith." In Matthews, comp., *Collection and Commentary*, 17–18.

[96] On the founding of the Somers Island (Bermuda) company, see Andrews, *Colonial Period*,
I, 215–17. Other trading companies chartered for colonizing activity were the Guiana
Company (1626), the Massachusetts Bay Company (1629), and the Providence Island
Company (1630).

with an eye to European competitors, and the prospect of wealth, whether through the discovery of mineral riches or the production of a wide variety of exotic commodities.[97] But none of the ventures was adequately capitalized, largely because established merchant investors had no particular interest in underwriting the uncertainties of New World plantation rather than simply continue to "trafficke" with established sources of supply. Gentry investment was forthcoming, but not at all sufficient to the need.[98] The companies' only material asset, land, could not be realized without security of possession, nor mobilized for investment without a demonstration of return from successful cultivation. But as a practical matter possession remained insecure well into the 1620s, nor would cultivation of any kind occur without population, nor population without continuous investment to transport and subsidize it until it became economically self-sustaining. Therein lies the sustained significance of the elder Hakluyt's incantation: manning, planting, and keeping were interdependent processes. Each required long-term investment. Without investors, joint-stock plantation was a perilous undertaking. Within a decade of its formation the London and Bristol Company had failed. The Virginia Company's inability to secure its colony led to the assumption of direct Crown rule in 1625. Only the Bermuda Company proved resilient in the long term. With the exception of the New England and Massachusetts Bay Companies

[97] On the moral economy of Tudor and Jacobean colonizing, see Fitzmaurice, *Humanism and America*, 20–101; Andrew Fitzmaurice, "The Commercial Ideology of Colonization in Jacobean England: Robert Johnson, Giovanni Botero, and the Pursuit of Greatness," *William and Mary Quarterly*, 3rd Ser., 64, 4 (October 2007), 791–820. Expectations for the production of commodities from New World plantations ran high – particularly as replacements for costly imports from Europe and the Orient, as is perhaps best signified by the following list of commodities and activities anticipated by the elder Richard Hakluyt (taken from his "Pamphlet for the Virginia Enterprise" (n.d.), in Taylor, ed., *Original Writings and Correspondence*, II, 339–43, at 340–1): "mynes of goulde, sylver, copper ... dregginge of Pearle ... plantinge of sugar canes ... silke wormes for sylke and dressinge of the same ... gatheringe of Cotten ... Tyllinge of the Soyle there for grayne ... plantinge of Vynes for wyne ... Ollives for oyle ... Trees for orrenges, leomandes, Almondes, fygge and other fruictes ... sowing oade and madder for [dyers] ... Hempe and flaxe for Clothes Cordage ... dressinge of raw hydes of dyvers kindes of Beastes ... makinge of Salte ... killing the whale, wherpole, seale, and porpose etc. for Trayne oyle ... ffyshinge saltinge and dryinge Lynge Codd Salmon ... makinge of Ropes and other Cordages ... makinge and gatheringe Honye, waxe, Pitche, Tarre, Rosen, and Turpentyne ... hewinge and shapinge of Stone as marble, gete, Christall, freestone ... felling of Timber, hewinge and sawinge the same ... makinge of Caske owers and all other manner of staves ... buildinge of Churches Townes fortes ... powdringe and barellinge of fyshe and fowles ... drying sortinge and packinge of feathers ... Soe as by reason of the varyable Climates in the saide Countryes and excellent Soyle wth the industrye aforesaide we may retorne from thence all the Commodyties wch we nowe receave from Barbarye, Spayne, Portugale, Italy, Danske, Norway and Muscovia better cheape than nowe we have them and not inrytche our doubtfull frendes and infydelles as nowe by our ordynary trade we doe."

[98] Robert Brenner, *Merchants and Revolution: Commercial Change, Political Conflict, and London's Overseas Traders, 1550–1653* (Princeton, 1993), 92–112. For a distinct interpretation, see Fitzmaurice, *Humanism and America*, 61.

established at the end of the decade, the commercial joint stock company would not be seen again in American mainland colonizing.

The First Proprietaries

Where corporations had furnished the institutional model for colonial "states" during the initial phase of settlements, thereafter the model became proprietorial lordship. Were one to use *Utopia* as a point of reference, one might say that in the process of planting new English commonwealths, attention shifted from the civics of the city to those of the shire. Expectations for the development of a commerce in sophisticated commodities that could sustain a diversity of callings, moderate labor, and lives of "mutual conversation" were replaced by an agricultural economy ("that harde and sharpe kynde of lyfe"[99]) built on cruder staples and the command of extensive territories.[100]

The proprietary model meant new approaches to the exercise of jurisdiction. In the corporate phase, the Crown had become used to granting extensive powers to intermediaries to facilitate their exercise of territorial control on its behalf. We have seen that the Crown's exercise of direct jurisdiction over territory within which particular colonies would be created – the royal council of Virginia (1606) – was not sustained beyond the reorganization of the Virginia Company in 1609. When the Virginia Company eventually collapsed, the royal council was recreated and government of the colony taken over directly by the Crown. But this move was not reproduced elsewhere.[101] Rather, the reverse: English colonizing became an exercise in the delegation of extensive sovereign capacity to landed proprietors.[102]

The initial expression of the proprietary model came in qualified form in 1620, with James I's patent creating the "Councill established at Plymouth, in the County of Devon for the planting, ruling, ordering, and

---

[99] Sampson, ed., *The Utopia of Sir Thomas More*, 85.

[100] Ken MacMillan, *Sovereignty and Possession in the English New World* (Cambridge, 2006), 97.

[101] No other royal colony was created before the Restoration, and only Rhode Island at that point; Not until the late seventeenth century does the move in that direction become pronounced. Nor, incidentally, is it clear what, if any, practical legal-institutional distinction Virginia experienced locally as a result of becoming a royal colony. See Jack P. Greene, *Peripheries and Center: Constitutional Development in the Extended Polities of the British Empire and the United States, 1607–1788* (New York, 1990), 12.

[102] The Crown's letters patent to Sir Humphrey Gilbert and Sir Walter Raleigh had granted their bearers title to lands by homage and allegiance, a feudal tenure creating a relationship of vassalage in which land was held directly of the Crown by the vassal as tenant-in-chief. (This was also the basis of Henry VII's letters patent to John Cabot and his sons, designated "our vassals, and lieutenants.") See Thorpe, *Federal and State Constitutions*, I, 46–57. Both Gilbert and Raleigh had power to dispose of land in fee simple (which is "the most absolute interest which a subject can possess in land," *Mozley & Whiteley's Law Dictionary*, 135). Thereafter, until 1623 all charter grants were in free and common socage *ut de manore* to companies, which might in turn subdivide them on the same terms.

governing of New-England, in America" (Council for New England). The charter recreated the jurisdiction granted to the Bristol and Plymouth adventurers in the original Virginia Charter of 1606, but transferred it to an incorporated board of proprietors "composed of some of the most distinguished of the king's officials and courtiers," to which was "give[n], grant[ed] and confirm[ed] … and unto their Successors for ever, all the aforesaid Lands and Grounds, Continent, Precinct, Place, Places and Territoryes" from 40° to 48° northern latitude, from sea to sea, together with "the Firme Lands, Soyles, Grounds, Havens, Ports, Rivers, Waters, Fishings, Mines, and Mineralls, as well Royall Mines of Gold and Silver, as other Mine and Mineralls, precious Stones, Quarries, and all, and singular other Commodities, Jurisdictions, Royalties, Priveliges, Franchises, and Preheminences" all to be held in free and common socage as of the King's manor of East Greenwich. The council was granted complete freedom to dispose of the territory under its command – making sub-grants, creating particular colonies or plantations, appointing their governors, appointing an overall "principall Governor" with the powers (as in the Virginia Company case) of a lord-lieutenant of an English county. All were to have authority "to correct, punish, pardon, governe, and rule" such of the King's subjects as should inhabit New England, according to such "Laws, Orders, Ordinances, Directions, and Instructions" established by the council, as near as might conveniently be agreeable to the "Laws, Statutes, Government and Policie" of England.[103]

The substance of authority granted the council, though considerable, was not novel. In many respects the Council for New England's patent recapitulated that of the Virginia Company. What was novel was the proprietary form.[104] First advanced in the Council's original patent, this was refined in a succession of territorial charters granted between 1621 and 1640 that, collectively, re-presented most of the North Atlantic mainland in the image of a marchland.[105] While on their face the proprietary grants

[103] "Charter of New England," in Thorpe, *Federal and State Constitutions*, III, 1827–40. Andrews, *Colonial Period*, I, 323.

[104] Charles M. Andrews comments that the Council, "though proprietary in fact was corporate in law," and that its intent was to surrender its original charter and negotiate a new one that would strip off its corporate skin and make it "an absolute proprietorship" in law through the regrant of lands *in capite*, which might then be subinfeudated. *Colonial Period*, I, 405. It is worth noting that the Council's principal legal advisor was Sir Henry Spelman, the first English historian of feudal tenures and, in effect, the inventor of the history of English feudalism. On Spelman, see Susan Reynolds, *Fiefs and Vassals: The Medieval Evidence Reinterpreted* (Oxford, 1994), 7, 323, 355. We should also note that, according to Reynolds, so-called feudal or vassalage tenures in fact conveyed property that was no less free and heritable than any other. In other words, the seigneurial charters granted to American mainland proprietors were in part an idealization of "feudal" relationships that had never existed as such, in part a means for the beneficiaries to gain secure legal possession (and autonomous governance) over very large expanses of overseas territory.

[105] For sixteenth-century parallels, see Steven G. Ellis, *Tudor Frontiers and Noble Power: The Making of the British State* (Oxford, 1995).

had all the appearance of an ever-widening scramble for control of over-seas territory among English landed elites, in chartered expression they expressed an idealized legal culture founded on delegated territorial lord-ship. Where the company charters had sought to develop forms of institu-tional authority appropriate to colonizing by extrapolating from corporate undertakings, the proprietorial charters extrapolated from the very differ-ent referent of landed magistracy.[106]

The first of the "pure" proprietorships was James I's 1621 grant, in his capacity as James VI of Scotland, of "the Lordship and Barony of New Scotland in America" to Sir William Alexander of Menstrie. New Scotland comprised a tract of land stretching from Cape Sable, near 43°N, north-west to St. Mary's Bay, then across the bay to the St. Croix river and its westernmost source, then northward "by an imaginary straight line which is conceived to extend through the land" to the first tributary of "the great river of Canada" encountered, thence east to the coast at Gaspé, southeast to Cape Breton at 45°N and finally back southward to Cape Sable.[107] The land was to be divisible at Alexander's pleasure, and he was to have "full power, privilege, and jurisdiction of free royalty, chapelry and chancery for ever: with the gift and right of patronage of churches, chapels and benefices ... power of setting up states, free towns, free ports, villages, and barony towns," of establishing markets and fairs, holding courts of justice and admiralty and generally exercising all the privileges of a Baron of the Kingdom of Scotland.[108] He and his heirs were to be the King's hereditary

[106] Rowland Berthoff and John M. Murrin, "Feudalism, Communalism, and the Yeoman Freeholder: The American Revolution Considered as a Social Accident," in Stephen G. Kurtz and James H. Hutson, editors, *Essays on the American Revolution* (Chapel Hill, 1973), 264. See also Vicki Hsueh, *Hybrid Constitutions: Challenging Legacies of Law, Privilege, and Culture in Colonial America* (Durham, N.C., 2010).

[107] "Charter in favor of Sir William Alexander" (1621), in *Sir William Alexander and American Colonization* (Boston, 1873), 129–30.

[108] Ibid., 131. Alexander's charter contained one of the more elaborated inventories of pos-session to be found anywhere among the mainland grants. He was "To hold and to pos-sess, the whole and undivided, the said region and lordship of New Scotland, with all the bounds of the same within the seas above mentioned, all minerals of gold and silver, cop-per, steel, tin, lead, brass, and iron, and any other mines, pearls, precious stones, quar-ries, woods, thickets, mosses, marshes, lakes, waters, fisheries, as well in fresh water as salt, as well of royal fishes as of others, states, free towns, free ports, towns, baronial villages, seaports, roadsteads, machines, mills, offices, and jurisdictions, and all other things gen-erally and specially mentioned above; with all other privileges, liberties, immunities, and accidents, and other things above mentioned, to the aforesaid Sir William Alexander, his heirs and assigns, from us and our successors, in free covenant, inheritance, lord-ship, barony, and royalty, for ever, through all their just bounds and limits, as they lie in length and breadth, in houses, buildings, erected and to be erected, bogs, plains, and moors; marshes, roads, paths, waters, swamps, rivers, meadows, and pastures; mines, malt-houses and their refuse, hawkings, huntings, fisheries, peat-mosses, turf-bogs, coal, coal-pits, coneys, warrens, doves, dove-cotes, workshops, maltkilns, breweries and broom; woods, groves, and thickets; wood, timber, quarries of stone and lime; with courts, fines, pleas, heriots, outlaws, rabbles of women, with free entrance and exit, and with fork, foss, sok, sac, theme, infangthieff, outfangthieff, wrak, wair, veth, vert, vennesonn, pit, and gallows; and with all other and singly, the liberties, commodities, profits, easements, and

lieutenants-general, with full powers of government and the establishment and alteration of "laws, rules, forms, and ceremonies" (provided they be as consistent as possible with those of Scotland), powers of martial law, and powers also to confer "favors, privileges, gifts and honors." The latter, reconfirmed in 1625 by Charles I's "Novodamus" charter, became the basis for the creation of an order of Knights Baronet of New Scotland, to which between 1625 and 1638 approximately one hundred appointments were made, with grants of land.[109]

The New Scotland charter is notable for the idealized feudalism of its institutions, but also for its articulation of an ideology of territorial appropriation with somewhat different emphases than had commonly prevailed a half century before. The general purpose of which the patent was an instance was, as before, "planting new colonies in foreign and uncultivated regions" without inhabitants, or inhabited by infidels "whose conversion to the Christian faith most highly concerns the glory of God."[110] But in fact the charter's discussion of the establishment of Christianity emphasized less evangelization of the indigenous, than cultivation of "peace and quiet" in relations with them so that "*our* beloved subjects" might worship undisturbed.[111] Overall, its emphasis lay on colonizing as an act of *self*-renewal undertaken by a substantial population in motion:

> We, thinking how populous and crowded this land now is by Divine favor, and how expedient it is that it should be carefully exercised in some honorable and useful discipline, lest it deteriorate through sloth and inaction, have judged it important that many should be led forth into new territory, which they may fill with colonies.[112]

Sentiments first articulated by the Hakluyts had by the 1620s become commonplace. Increasingly, Crown charters made reference to colonies not only as sources of commodities but as permanent destinations for large numbers of people. Sir Robert Heath's 1629 Carolina patent, for example, talks of "the multitude of people thronging thither." Cecilius Calvert wanted to plant "a numerous Colony of the English Nation" in Maryland, his father "a very great and ample" one in Newfoundland. Proprietorship should not be understood as a rejection of commodification. The purpose of occupancy was to render territory into tillable land, and sloth into activity, through cultivation. Still, the emphasis in these charters turned as much on the creation of structures to manage and order the occupation

their rightful pertinents of all kinds, whether mentioned or not, above or below ground, far and near, belonging, or that can belong, to the aforesaid region and lordship, in any manner, for the future, freely, quietly, fully, wholly, honorably, well, and in peace, without any revocation, contradiction, impediment, or obstacle whatever." Ibid., 144–5.

[109] Ibid., 132–3. For the Novodamus Charter, see *Sir William Alexander and American Colonization*, 217–31. The Roll of the Knights Baronets of New Scotland appears at 233–7.

[110] "Charter in favor of Sir William Alexander," 127–8.

[111] Ibid., 136–7.

[112] Ibid., 128.

of territory by substantial resident populations as on the extraction of resources.[113]

The New Scotland charter was followed in short order by the Avalon charter, issued in 1623 by King James to Sir George Calvert (this time in his English jurisdiction). The Avalon charter granted Calvert a substantial part of Newfoundland (still known as the Avalon Peninsula) with authority similar in form to that granted Alexander – patronage of churches, creation of titles of nobility, the making and enforcement of laws, the enjoyment of martial law powers, the appointment of magistrates and officers, the pardoning of any and all offenses, the incorporation of towns and boroughs. Certain restraints on that authority stand out, as in earlier company patents. Calvert's law-making powers were subject to the assent of the province's freeholders (whom, however, he was to assemble "in such sort, and forme as to him shall seeme best"); persons transported to the province, or borne there, were confirmed denizens and possessed of English "Liberties, Franchises and priviledges."[114]

Two novel features make the Avalon patent particularly noteworthy. First, Calvert's proprietary powers were premised on a grant of land "in Capite," that is, directly of the king, and "by Knights service," that is, by a tenure that promised defined military services to the Crown in return for the tenancy, rather than in free and common socage as in earlier English patents.[115] Second, Calvert was granted "Rights Jurisdictions, priviledges, prerogatives, royalties, Liberties, Immunities, and Franchises" equivalent to those enjoyed by the Bishop of Durham, one of several "palatine" jurisdictions within the Crown's domain and the only one, by the seventeenth century, whose lordship had not been assumed by the monarch. Land held "in capite" established its holders in a direct relationship with the monarch, as seigneurial tenants-in-chief: as such they enjoyed rights to create

---

[113] See Thorpe, *Federal and State Constitutions*, I, 72, III, 1677; Matthews, comp., *Collection and Commentary*, 39. Obviously an anticipation of migration was always on display in the charters. As we have seen, among the propagandists of English expansion the discovery of outlets overseas where surplus population could be "set on work" bulked large in the advocacy of colonizing. The younger Hakluyt wrote in 1582 that "the Bees, when they grow to be too many in their own hive at home, are wont to be led out by their Captaines to swarme abroad." See his Preface to *Divers Voyages*, in Taylor, ed., *Original Writings and Correspondence*, I, 176. More prosaically (as was his wont), his elder cousin recommended that "If this realme shall abound too much with youth" it could benefit from seeking their employment overseas, and that in general there was much opportunity to set the poor and idle ("waste people") to work. See his *Pamphlet for the Virginia Enterprise* (1585), in *Original Writings and Correspondence*, II, 330, 331. But although much discussed, substantial movements of population did not begin until the 1620s and, particularly, the 1630s. Only as colonizing came to emphasize command of territory over traffic in commodities did migration become a more explicit (and leading) component of what it entailed. With that came growing emphasis on managing migrant populations through law.

[114] "A Grant of the Province of Avalon," in Matthews, comp., *Collection and Commentary*, 39–63.

[115] Calvert discharged his obligations by payment of a white horse on each entry of his territory made by the king. Ibid., 44.

subtenures to govern the lands they disbursed to others that created lines of allegiance terminating in themselves rather than in the Crown. The exercise of a palatine jurisdiction, meanwhile, vested in proprietors an essentially vice-regal authority over a defined territory.[116]

Within England, the earldoms of Chester, Lancaster, and Richmond, and the bishopric of Durham – all marchland (border) territories – were palatinates. In Ireland, Anglo-Norman earldoms, such as that of Desmond in Munster, also enjoyed palatine authority. All lived in tension with the Crown. Long before the sixteenth century the earldoms of Chester, Lancaster, and Richmond had been resumed by the Crown itself. In 1536 the Bishops of Durham lost their judicial supremacy. In 1583, the Earl of Desmond lost his head, and his palatinate – dissolved – became the basis of the Munster plantation.[117] Thus, the palatine powers granted such American patentees as Calvert invoked a seigneurial capacity that over the previous century had been significantly weakened in Britain. Nevertheless, the idea itself expressed the ambition shared by Crown and proprietors alike to control England's American territorial claims through the assertion of jurisdiction over and occupancy of the land itself, and to do so through particular institutions and powers – those designed for remote and contested regions – that allowed local authorities to exercise effective regional sovereignty. In the American patents, furthermore, palatine powers were granted in language not restricted by recent history: in Newfoundland, Sir George Calvert was to "have exercise use and enjoy the same as any Bishop of Durham, within the Bishopprick or County Palatine of Durham, in our Kingdome of England hath at any time heretofore had, held, used, or enjoyes, or of Right ought or might have had, held, used or enjoyed."[118] This clause set the pattern.[119]

The proprietorial idea re-created mainland colonizing both in process and purpose by imposing upon it a new discourse of authority and jurisdictional relationships. From the early 1620s, English charters made palatine authority and institutions key features of the evolving design of North American colonization. Sir Robert Heath's patent as "true lord and proprietor" for the enormous province of Carolina, "in our lands in the parts of America betwixt one & thirty & 36 degrees of northerne latitude," granted lands on the same basis, "in Cheife by knights service," as Calvert's Avalon patent, and contained the same genus of empowering clauses: to have, exercise and enjoy "Rights, Jurisdictions, priviledges, prerogatives Royaltyes libertyes immunityes with Royall rights and franchises

---

[116] See generally Barnes, "Tenure in English Charters."

[117] Kenneth Emsley and C. M. Fraser, *The Courts of the County Palatine of Durham* (Durham, 1984), 1; Michael MacCarthy-Morrogh, *The Munster Plantation: English Migration to Southern Ireland, 1583–1641* (Oxford, 1986), 1–2.

[118] "A Grant of the Province of Avalon," 43.

[119] On the general significance of palatine powers in their relationship to English colonial charters, see Tim Thornton, "The Palatinate of Durham and the Maryland Charter," *American Journal of Legal History*, 45, 3 (July 2001), 235–55.

... in like manner as any Bishop of Durham within the Bp^ricke or County palatine of Durham in our kingdome of England ever heretofore had held used or enjoyed or of right ought or could have hold use or enjoy"; to make and enact "what lawes soever may concerne the publicke state" or private profit of the province, with the "counsell assent & approbation of the Freeholders of the same Province or the Major part of them," called together in such manner and form as the proprietor shall think best; to appoint, constitute and ordaine "Judges & Justices Magestrates & officers" for all causes; to have power, himself or by deputies, to punish by loss of life and limb; to have power "of remitting, releasing, pardoning & abolishing"; provided only that the laws made and enforced shall be consonant to reason and "(as conveniently as may be done) consonant to the lawes, statutes, customes & rights of our Realme of England." Heath also had the same right of resort to martial law, the same right to create honors, the same right to erect villages and incorporate them into boroughs "and Borowes into Cittyes."[120]

Cecilius Calvert's Maryland patent (1632) was no different in the detail of the authority it granted, in the jurisdictional foundations it established, or in the sheer density of jurisdiction that it implied. Elaborating on the terms of the Avalon patent obtained by his father, Sir George Calvert (who had been made Baron of Baltimore in 1625 but had died early in 1632 before his petition for the Maryland patent was answered), the Crown's patent for Maryland granted the Calverts some 12 million acres of what had formerly been territory within the jurisdiction of the now-defunct Virginia Company. The charter reproduced Avalon's wide palatine jurisdiction and other perquisites, but was chiefly remarkable for its combination of palatine vice-regality with virtually unrestricted land tenures. First, the proprietor was awarded land in free and common socage, held as of the Castle of Windsor, rather than in capite. Second, he was accorded "full and absolute License, Power, and Authority" at his pleasure "to assign, alien, grant, demise, or enfeoff so many, such, and proportionate Parts and Parcels of the Premises, to any Person or Persons willing to purchase the same ... in Fee-simple, or Fee-tail, or for Term of Life, Lives or Years" to be held of him rather than of the Crown, the statute *Quia Emptores Terrarum* specifically notwithstanding.[121] The charter also permitted "the same Baron of Baltimore ... to erect any Parcels of Land within the Province aforesaid, into Manors, and in every of those Manors, to have and to hold a Court-Baron, and all Things which to a Court Baron do belong ... for the Conservation of the Peace and better Government of those Parts, by themselves and their Stewards, or by the Lords ... of other of those Manors when they shall be

[120] "Sir Robert Heath's Patent" (1629) in Thorpe, *Federal and State Constitutions*, I, 69–76.
[121] *Quia Emptores Terrarum* (1290) had permitted the sale of land without penalty. Essentially this meant that subinfeudation could be replaced by substitution. Subinfeudation meant that a new grantee of land held land of the grantor, thus adding an additional tenant to the tenurial chain. Substitution meant that a new grantee displaced the grantor, so that no new tenant was added to the chain.

constituted." In effect the Calvert family had gained a more absolute lordship over Maryland than any granted to that date anywhere.[122]

The Maryland patent was the most extreme example of proprietorial ascendancy, but it was by no means untypical. The Montgomery patent of 1628 had granted territory in the West Indies to the Earl of Pembroke in much the same form as in Maryland; The "Syon" petition of 1629 sought creation of a palatinate in the northern part of the Virginia Company grant (that is, in the land that Calvert would seek three years later) held as of Dublin Castle. The Plowden petition of 1632 sought creation of another palatinate, to be called New Albion, in the Delaware River valley, also to be held of the Crown as king of Ireland. In 1637, Sir David Kirke and others successfully applied for a patent to Newfoundland that vacated the former (and unfulfilled) Avalon grant and replaced it with a jurisdiction that named them "true and absolute Lords and Proprietors" in Newfoundland.[123]

Meanwhile, the Council for New England had begun dividing its territory, with the creation of another "New Albion" (this between the Kennebec and Penobscot Rivers) in 1622 and the grant of the province of Maine (between the Merrimack and the Sagadahoc Rivers) to Ferdinando Gorges and John Mason (also 1622). Mason also gained the "Marianna" grant stretching roughly from Cape Ann to the Merrimack, and in 1629 would be granted the New Hampshire patent. Numbers of additional smaller grants were made as well as patents issued for particular plantations, notably that to the Leyden Separatists for what had already become Plymouth Plantation. Throughout the early 1620s, the Council sought amendments to its charter that would transform it into a palatine authority, abrogate *Quia Emptores*, and allow subinfeudation, but without success. It returned to the task in 1632 in the wake of the Maryland patent. Finally, in 1639 Gorges obtained a patent from Charles I, reconfirming the 1622 Maine grant with a new authority to establish manors and subinfeudate, and granting him a palatine jurisdiction, albeit "subject to the power and reglement of the Lords and other Commissioners here for forraigne Plantacons" (also known as the Laud Commission) which had been established by the Crown in 1634.[124]

---

[122] "Charter of Maryland" (1632), in Thorpe, *Federal and State Constitutions*, III, 1677–86. See also Andrews, *Colonial Period*, II, 282–3. Robert Mitchell writes that the Calvert ideal was "a semifeudal society based on manorial land tenure, a traditional landed gentry and aristocracy, a strong family nexus [and] nucleated village settlement." Robert D. Mitchell, "The Colonial Origins of Anglo-America," in Robert D. Mitchell and Paul A. Groves, editors, *North America: The Historical Geography of a Changing Continent* (Totowa, N.J., 1987), 109.

[123] "Grant of Newfoundland to the Marquess Hamilton" (1637), in Matthews, comp., *Collection and Commentary*, 82–116; Barnes, "Tenure in English Charters," 24–7; Andrews, *Colonial Period*, II, 222–3.

[124] See "Grant of New Hampshire" (1629, 1635) and "Grant of the Province of Maine" (1622, 1639), in Thorpe, *Federal and State Constitutions*, IV, 2433–44, III, 1621–37; Andrews, *Colonial Period*, I, 279–82. On the Laud Commission, see Charles M. Andrews, *British*

By the end of the 1630s, therefore, the conceptual representation of colonization revealed in English patents had altered quite sharply from a primary goal emphasizing appropriation for commerce to one emphasizing appropriation for permanent occupation. One may see this, crudely, as a move from adventure to lordship, from "commodity" to "propriety,"[125] a transformation in colonization's civic form. Assuredly, commodity and occupancy do not stand for conceptually separate ideologies of colonizing: each was a condition for the success of the other. Each nevertheless implied distinct institutional outcomes, distinct ideals of social and state formation. To the extent that each received the same "subjects" (migrants) with the same "liberties, franchises and priviledges," those subjects were inserted into different legal, political, and economic environments.

The charters were representations of intent. Elevated plans were implemented rudely; much of what was foreshadowed simply did not occur. Some of what did occur was more hybrid than expression of one or other trajectory. Take for example the successful puritan colonization of Massachusetts Bay. In 1627 the Council for New England, at that time barely active as a collective proprietorship and dominated by its president, Robert Rich, Earl of Warwick, transferred territory between the Merrimack and Charles Rivers to the New England Company, a voluntary unincorporated joint-stock company and effective successor to a fishing plantation venture, the Dorchester Company. The New England Company then obtained a charter of incorporation as the Massachusetts Bay Company, in large part to protect its title from conflicting claims. Counter to the trend of the 1620s toward broad and increasingly absolutist proprietorships, the Massachusetts Bay Company was incorporated as a trading company, governed by a governor, deputy-governor, and eighteen assistants chosen out of the company freemen, with provision for a monthly court and a quarterly general court (requiring a quorum of seven, including the Governor or Deputy in each case) to handle the company's business and, in general court, to "make Lawes and Ordiñces for the Good and Welfare of the saide Company, and for the Government and ordering of the saide Landes and Plantačon, and the People inhabiting and to inhabite the same ... soe as such Lawes and Ordinances be not contrarie or repugnant to the Lawes and Statuts of this our Realme of England," as also for the election of officers and the "setling of the Formes and Ceremonies of Governm^t and Magistracy, fitt and necessary for the said Plantačon, and the Inhabitants there ... according to the Course of other Corporacons."[126] In form, the charter was modeled on the Virginia Company charter, but gave more attention to the structure of

---

Committees, Commissions, and Councils of Trade and Plantations, 1622–1675 (Baltimore, 1908), 16–17.

[125] For the play of these themes in later American history, see Gregory S. Alexander, *Commodity & Propriety: Competing Visions of Property in American Legal Thought, 1776–1970* (Chicago, 1997).

[126] "The Charter of Massachusetts Bay" (1629), in Thorpe, *Federal and State Constitutions*, III, 1846–60.

company governance and made explicit provision for a role in government for the generality of the company. The charter acknowledged the evangelizing purpose expressed by all previous European colonizers; to spread "the Christian Fayth" was the plantation's "principall Ende." But like Sir William Alexander's New Scotland, emphasis was more on the creation of a religious settlement for migrants who thought of themselves as exiles than on converting heathen. To the extent the puritan migration was to spread Christianity, it was to do so by example rather than by proselytizing. Migrant inhabitants were to govern themselves "religiously, peaceablie, and civilly," such that their "good Life and orderlie Conversacon" might "wynn and incite the Natives of Country" to Christianity. Winthrop's "city upon a hill," his exemplary commonwealth, had two audiences.[127]

Once established, however, the Massachusetts Bay Company behaved in a fashion not dissimilar to its proprietary contemporaries. That is, though unable to secure a degree of formal autonomy equivalent to their palatine jurisdictions, it sought by practical means (principally by absconding with its own charter) to insulate its pursuit of planting from metropolitan oversight or mediation. Unlike earlier expressions of the company model, moreover, that pursuit was, in practice, both densely institutional and, if not anti-commercial, at least studiedly ambivalent. Obviously not a lordly proprietary either in jurisdiction or in practice, Massachusetts Bay nevertheless designed its commonwealth to govern the occupation of territory by a migrating population.

Given their emphasis on the command of territorial expanse, what had the early proprietorial patents to say of their lands' indigenous populations? As English colonizing gained momentum, local populations, always slighted, were increasingly subject to conceptual and physical displacement. This is particularly noticeable in the patents drawn up in the years after the Jamestown massacre of March 1622, in which indigenous populations suddenly begin to appear not as inhabitants of the territories in question, with whom some form of mutual accommodation might be reached, but as deadly alien enemies threatening them from beyond. The original Virginia patent had glanced only briefly at "such People" but it had not displaced them, suggesting rather that they would be beneficiaries of English colonizing. The New Scotland charter had shifted the emphasis, noting the presence of "native inhabitants" who were "savage aborigines" and "barbarians" as a threat to be controlled, through treaties of alliance where possible or force – "whereby they may be reduced to order" – if necessary.[128] The New England charter had declared native inhabitants savage, brutish, and – most important – *absent* from the territories in question, which had therefore "as it were" fallen to possession and organization by "our Subjects and People."[129]

[127] Ibid., 1857.
[128] "Charter in favor of Sir William Alexander" (1621), 137.
[129] "Charter of New England," in Thorpe, *Federal and State Constitutions*, III, 1828–9.

The Avalon patent, the first to grant palatine authority, was also the first granted after the Jamestown massacre. It was as well the first English patent that, conceptually, expelled indigenous populations from the territory it covered and authorized uninhibited warfare against them. The patent recognized that the lands granted, "not yet husbanded or planted," were "in some parts ... Inhabited, by certaine Barbarous people." It proceeded then to separate the existing inhabitants from the land they occupied by renaming them barbarian invaders against whose "Incursions ... as of other Enimies, Pirats and Robbers" the proprietor was empowered "to make warre ... even without the Limmits of the said Province and by God's assistance to vanquish and take them and being taken to putt them to death by the Lawe of warr, or to save them" – that is, enslave them – as the proprietor or "his heires and assignes" might think fit.[130] One will recall here Gentili's identification of pirates and brigands as the epitome of all those "common enemies of mankind" beyond *societas gentium*, and observe how the Avalon patent first transforms indigenous inhabitants into barbarous savages and enemies, aggressive invaders of the places where they actually lived (naming their habitations as incursions) and then, seamlessly, pairs them with pirates and robbers as the legitimate objects of unlimited aggressive warfare and pursuit unto death.[131] Precisely the same steps were taken in Sir

[130] "A Grant of the Province of Avalon," in Matthews, comp., *Collection and Commentary*, 53–4. Neither this clause nor anything like it appears in any previous charter. It would appear in all subsequent palatine charters in "standardized" form, with minor modifications to fit the circumstances of the particular grant. Here is the wording, taken from the "Grant of the Province of Maine" (1639), in Thorpe, *Federal and State Constitutions*, III, 1630:

> And because in a Country soe farr distant and seated amongst soe many barbarous nations the Intrusions or Invasions aswell of the barbarous people as of Pirates and other enemies maye be justly feared Wee Doe therefore for us our heires and successors give and graunte unto the said Sir Fardinando Gorges his heires and assignes full power and authoritie that hee the said Sir Fardinando Gorges his heires and assignes aswell by him and themselves as by his and theire Deputyes Captaynes or other Officers for the tyme being shall or lawfullye maye muster leavie rayse armes and ymploye all person and persons whatsoever inhabiteing or resideing within the said Province or Premisses for the resisting or withstanding of such Enymies or Pyrates both att Lande and att Sea and such Enimies or Pyrates (if occasion shall require) to pursue and prosecute out of the lymitts of the said Province or Premisses and then (if itt shall soe please God) to vanquishe apprehende and take and being taken either according to the Lawe of armes to kill or to keepe and preserve them att their pleasure.

[131] Gentili, *De Iure Belli*, 15, 22. The significance of the Jamestown massacre (on which see Vaughan, *Roots of American Racism*, 105–27; James Horn, *A Land as God Made It: Jamestown and the Birth of America* (New York, 2005), 249–78) is plain. Christopher Brooke's *Poem on the Late Massacre in Virginia* (London, 1622) – written by a lawyer, who likened himself in the poem's opening stanzas to the scribe Ezra, "Pen-man, in the sacred law" – called upon his countrymen "to consider what those Creatures are, /(I cannot call them men) no Character /Of God in them: Soules drown'd in flesh and blood; /Rooted in Euill, and oppos'd in Good; /Errors of Nature, of inhumane Birth, /The very dregs, garbage, and spawne of Earth," and drew the conclusion "If these (I say) be but consider'd well, / (Father'd by Sathan, and the sonnes of hell, /What feare or pittie were it, or what sin, /

Robert Heath's patent for the Carolina territory, in Calvert's Maryland patent, and in Ferdinando Gorges' Maine patent. In each, English migrants were named the territory's true "inhabitants" and indigenous populations became "barbarous nations" amongst whom the colonies of the English had been set down, displaced to the edges of the conceptually emptied spaces in which the colonies were "seated," constantly threatening invasion, looming perpetual enemies to be killed or enslaved as the proprietor, empowered by the Crown and the law of war, should determine.[132]

(The rather since with vs they thus begin) /To quite their Slaughter, leauing not a Creature /That may restore such shame of Men, and Nature." The horticulturalist John Bonoeil called for "iust warring" with the "native Sauages," and whom he termed successively "against all my Lawes … most unnaturall, and so none of mine" and "naturally borne slaves" who should be enslaved. John Bonoeil, *His Maiesties Gracious Letter to the Earle of South-Hampton, Treasurer, and to the Councell and Company of Virginia heere: Commanding the Present Setting Vp of Silke Works, and Planting of Vines in Virginia* (London, 1622), 85–6. In *Virginias Verger* (1625), Samuel Purchas denied them the name of "Inhabitants" and expelled them from *societas gentium*, placing them outside the law of nature and nations among the common enemies of mankind, exposed "to the chastisement of that common Law of mankind; and … to the seueritie of the Law of Nations … not worthy of the name of a Nation, being wilde and Sauage: yet as Slaues, bordering rebells, excommunicates and out-lawes, are lyable to the punishments of Law, and not to the priuiledges; So is it with these *Barbarians*, Borderers and Outlawes of Humanity." Purchas represented the indigenous as incestuous rapists who had despoiled their own country, "Virginia … violently rauished by her owne ruder Natiues," and so forfeited any right to its bounties. Their "disloyall treason" had "confiscated whatsoeuer remainders of right the vnnaturall Naturalls had, and made both them and their Countery wholly English." See *Purchas His Pilgrimes* (London, 1625), IV, 1811, 1813; Peter Hulme, "The Spontaneous Hand of Nature: Savagery, Colonialism and the Enlightenment," in Peter Hulme and Ludmilla Jordanova, editors, *The Enlightenment and its Shadows* (London, 1990), 23–4. The idiom of "treason" is particularly interesting; though the English had clearly desired that indigenous sovereigns become vassals of the English monarchy, they had no basis whatsoever to believe they had been successful. On indigenous vassalage, see Nicholas Canny, "England's New World and the Old, 1480s-1630s," in Nicholas Canny, ed., *The Origins of Empire: British Overseas Enterprise to the Close of the Seventeenth Century*, volume I of *The Oxford History of the British Empire*, William Roger Louis, general editor (Oxford, 1998), 156–8.

[132] See Thorpe, *Federal and State Constitutions*, I, 73, III, 1630, 1682. All this was predicted, as it were, by Edward Waterhouse in his pamphlet, *A Declaration of the State of the Colony and Affaires in Virginia: With a Relation of the Barbarous Massacre in the time of peace and League, treacherously executed by the Natiue Infidels vpon the English, the 22 of March last*, written at the behest of the Virginia Company and published in 1622, just a few months after the event. Waterhouse wrote (at 22–6) that the massacre "must needs bee for the good of the Plantation," adducing it a great untying of restraints and a birth of opportunities: because such betrayal of trust and innocence "neuer rests vnpunished"; because "our hands which before were tied with gentlenesse and faire vsage, are now set at liberty by the treacherous violence of the Sauages;" because "we … may now by right of Warre, and law of Nations, inuade the Country, and destroy them who sought to destroy vs: whereby wee shall enioy their cultiuated places"; because "those commodities which the Indians enioyed as much or rather more then we, shall now also be entirely possessed by vs"; because "the way of conquering them is much more easie then of ciuilizing them"; because "the *Indians*, who before were vsed as friends, may now most iustly be compelled to seruitude and drudgery, and supply the roome of men that labour, whereby euen the meanest of the Plantation may imploy themselues more entirely in their Arts and

The Restoration Proprietaries

Processes of territorial occupation and jurisdictional expansion stalled during civil conflict in England between 1640 and 1660,[133] but resumed after the Restoration. The Restoration grants were notable both for the size of the territories involved, their overwhelmingly proprietorial character, and, in two cases, for the density and sophistication of the interior organization (the civic establishment) they envisaged.

Much post-Restoration chartering activity abrogated earlier patents, but left intact earlier jurisdictional ideologies. The Carolina charter of 1663, for example, took the immense territory formerly granted Sir Robert Heath in 1629 (whose patent was formally dissolved) and vested dominion in eight lords proprietor, whose terms of possession and authority were made as absolute as those granted Heath and Calvert thirty years before. The proprietors' law-making powers were subject to the "advice, assent and approbation of the freemen of the said province," but the forms of assemblage and advising were left to the proprietors to determine, who in any case had power to govern also by ordinance. More generally, the charter conveyed the now-familiar density of powers, rules, jurisdictions, and privileges through which territory became defined and population managed: erection of "forts, fortresses, castle, cities, buroughs, towns, villages and other fortifications whatsoever," appointment of "governors, deputy governors, magistrates, sherriffs and other officers, civil and military," creation of corporations, appointment of "markets, marts and fairs," erection of mannors ("so many ... as to them shall seem meet and convenient") with courts baron "with all things whatsoever which to a court baron do belong."[134] In 1665, the proprietors' domain was further enlarged, along with authority "to erect, constitute, and make" such "counties, baronnies, and colonies" throughout the area as they might see fit. As in the earlier seventeenth-century proprietorial patents, English migrants were cast as the territory's inhabitants; indigenous inhabitants were recast as its invaders.[135]

Organization of the whole was attempted in 1669 through promulgation of the *Fundamental Constitutions of Carolina*. Drafted by the young John Locke in his capacity as secretary to Anthony Lord Ashley,[136] the

Occupations, which are more generous"; and because "this will for euer hereafter make vs more cautelous and circumspect, as neuer to bee deceiued more by any other treacheries." And so, wrote Waterhouse, "vpon this Anvile shall wee now beate out to our selues an armour of proofe, which shall for euer after defend vs from barbarous Incursions." See also Chapter 10, section V. See generally Daniel Heller-Roazen, *The Enemy of All: Pirates and the Law of Nations* (New York, 2009).

[133] The Commonwealth had ambitions to integrate overseas empire and metropolis, but to the extent that it sponsored colonial expansion its attention was drawn first to the Caribbean, specifically to Jamaica, where its entire "Western design" stalled in the second half of the 1650s. See Andrews, *Colonial Period*, III, 1–34.

[134] "Charter of Carolina" (1663), in Thorpe, *Federal and State Constitutions*, V, 2743–53.

[135] Ibid., 2761–71, at 2763, 2769–70.

[136] On which see David Armitage, "John Locke, Carolina, and the Two Treatises of Government," *Political Theory*, 32, 5 (October, 2004), 602–27. See also Chapter 8.

Constitutions stand as the most elaborated statement of English proprietorial colonization's mapping of governmental and social authority onto an expanse of mainland territory. In 120 clauses the *Constitutions* created layer upon interwoven layer of office, honor, privilege, obligation, definition, boundary, rule, and regulation: a medley of institutions and cultural signs, cascading down upon virtually every aspect of public and private life. Minutely feudal in appearance, the whole structure of legal, political, and social institutions was actually built directly upon extensive and unencumbered distributions of landed property designed to underwrite a polity as utopically republican as it was feudal.[137]

The *Constitutions* named some forty different forms of office, low and high, anticipating and entailing (as the province became organized) the appointment of hundreds of officeholders. Beginning with the eight proprietors, the *Constitutions* created the eldest as palatine and the remainder as high officers (admiral, chamberlain, chancellor, constable, chief justice, high steward, treasurer). They also created a bi-level hereditary nobility (landgraves and caziques). The province was divided into counties, each of 480,000 acres (twelve, initially, were anticipated), each with one landgrave and two caziques. Each proprietor was to have a 12,000-acre seigneury in each county, in all comprising one-fifth of its extent; the remaining acreage of each county was to be divided between eight 12,000-acre baronies distributed among the hereditary nobility of landgraves (four baronies each) and caziques (two baronies each), the total comprising a further fifth of county extent, and four 72,000-acre precincts. Each precinct was to be divided into six 12,000-acre colonies and then subdivided into manorial lordships (3,000–12,000 acres) and smaller freeholds. Alienation of proprietorial and noble land was to be limited after the turn of the century and primogeniture was to apply in all cases. The estates of landgraves, caziques, and lords of manors would be worked by leet-men bound to the estate in exchange for land. Courts leet and baron "for trying of all causes" were to be established throughout the manors, baronies, and seigneuries with differential rights of appeal to county and precinct courts staffed respectively by a sheriff and four justices (county) and a steward and four justices (precinct).

The *Constitutions* established eight supreme courts. The first of the eight was the palatine's court (on which sat all the proprietors), the remainder were courts of the province's seven high officers. Each of the seven enjoyed

---

[137] "The Fundamental Constitutions of Carolina" (1669), in Thorpe, *Federal and State Constitutions*, V, 2772–86. See also Vicki Hsueh, "Unsettling Colonies: Locke, 'Atlantis' and New World Knowledges," *History of Political Thought*, 29, 2 (Summer 2008), 299–308, and in particular *Hybrid Constitutions*, 60–69. On the strategic importance of office holding to civic participation in early-modern England, see Mark Goldie, "The Unacknowledged Republic: Officeholding in Early Modern England," in Tim Harris, editor, *The Politics of The Excluded, c. 1500–1850* (Basingstoke, Hants., and New York, 2001), 153–94. See, generally, J.G.A. Pocock, *The Machiavellian Moment: Florentine Political Thought and the Atlantic Republican Tradition* (Princeton, 1975), 423–61.

a jurisdiction appropriate to its principal's office; the relevant high officer presided, assisted by six councilors and supported by a college of twelve assistants. The councilors of the seven courts all themselves held particular offices (vice-chancellors, justices, marshals, consuls, under-treasurers, comptrollers, vice-chamberlains), as did the assistants (recorders, masters, lieutenants-general, proconsuls, auditors, surveyors, provosts). Each court was equipped with intricate jurisdictional rules. There was to be a grand council of the proprietors and councilors, a deliberative parliament of the four estates (proprietors, landgraves, caziques, and freeholders – the latter elected, one to a precinct, the remainder sitting of right) in which all business was initiated by the grand council and a majority of any one estate could negate any proposition. The *Constitutions* also prescribed town officers (mayors, twelve aldermen, twenty-four common councilors), county officers (constables), precinct officers (registrars), and colony officers (registrars). They provided for hierarchical registration of the births, deaths, marriages, and ages of all inhabitants; marriage regulations; church establishment and construction; freedom of worship; and an absolute endorsement of slavery (but freedom of worship for the enslaved).[138]

The Duke of York's proprietorship, far to the north, was almost entirely innocent of such elaboration.[139] His charter was brief, and not, in its express terms, innovative. It, also, was built on abrogation of previous patents along with reconstitution of their modalities of rule. Dating from 1664, the Duke's grant made him proprietor of the Maine territory, of everything from the Connecticut River to the Delaware and north to Albany, of Long Island and other former Dutch possessions, and later the west bank of the Delaware. Essentially his proprietorship brought together several previously distinct jurisdictions within the territory formerly claimed by the Council of New England – from 40° to 48°N and "from Sea to Sea." It excepted Massachusetts and Connecticut but absorbed the competing claims of the Dutch in the Hudson and Delaware valleys. Its terms differed from the contemporary Carolina proprietorship in that they included no palatine grant, which under the circumstances was perhaps unnecessary. Instead they reconstituted in the person of the Duke the jurisdiction originally vested in the Council of New England. Like the Council, the Duke held lands in free and common socage and exercised absolute authority

---

[138] The slavery clauses are discussed in Chapter 9, section III. Estimating the number of officeholders and titleholders anticipated by the *Fundamental Constitutions* on the basis of the declared initial intention to create 12 counties, allowing for the establishment of two towns per county and the creation of manors of varying sizes across one quarter of available land in each county (a rough total of, say, 10 manors), one arrives at a total approaching 2,000 offices and titles.

[139] Though less complex in conception, New York's execution of land distribution would demonstrate great commonality with the other restoration proprietorships (and post-Restoration Virginia) in making a very substantial commitment to large estates in general and to manorial conceptions of landed elite organization in particular. See, generally, Sung Bok Kim, *Landlord and Tenant in Colonial New York: Manorial Society, 1664–1775* (Chapel Hill, 1978).

unimpeded by provision for any freeholder assembly. Like the Council, he "could control all appointments, make all laws and ordinances – provided they were in conformity with those of England – and determine all judicial matters, capital and criminal, civil and marine."[140] Like the Council, he had control of the region's trade, its borders, its defense, its internal order (including martial law powers), and the further distribution of its lands. Finally, the Duke was guaranteed ascendancy over all rival claims to exercise rule within the territory's extent.[141]

William Penn's charter for Pennsylvania (1681) was the last of the great seventeenth-century proprietorial grants. Although the smallest of the Restoration proprietaries,[142] the grant was substantial. As important, its definition hinted at the intrusion of new, abstract, scientific conceptions of territorial marking on the chorographic perambulations that had theretofore supplied the metes and bounds within which the American charters had built their layers of legal authority. Spatially, Pennsylvania would be

> "all that Tract or Parte of Land in America, with all the Islands therein conteyned, as the same is bounded on the East by Delaware River, from twelve miles distance Northwards of New Castle Towne unto the three and fortieth degree of Northerne Latitude, if the said River doeth extend soe farre Northward, then by the said River soe farr as it doth extend; and from the head of the said River, the Easterne Bounds are to be determined by a Meridian Line, to bee drawne from the head of the said River, unto the said three and fortieth Degree. The said Lands to extend westwards five degrees in longitude, to bee computed from the said Easterne Bounds; and the said Lands to bee bounded on the North by the beginning of the three and

[140] "Grant of the Province of Maine" (1664), in Thorpe, *Federal and State Constitutions*, III, 1637–40; Andrews, *Colonial Period*, III, 70–1, 97–100. The charter reserved to the king authority to hear appeals.

[141] "These our letters patents or the enrollment thereof shall be good and effectuall in the law to all intents and purposes whatsoever notwithstanding the not reciting or menconing of the premises or any part thereof or the meets or bounds thereof or of any former or other presents patents or grants heretofore made or granted of the premises or of any part thereof by us or any of our progenitors unto any other person or persons whatsoever bodyes politique or corporate or any act law or other restraint incertainty or imperfection whatsoever to the contrary in any wise notwithstanding." Thorpe, *Federal and State Constitutions*, 1640. Andrews suggests that the particular target of this clause was the colony of Connecticut, which in 1662 had received a royal charter of incorporation as "Governor and Company of the English Colony of Connecticut in New England in America" recognizing the colony as comprising all that part of New England from the Massachusetts border in the north to the sea (Long Island Sound) in the south and from the Narragansett River in the east to the end of the Massachusetts line (the south sea) on the west. See "Charter of Connecticut" (1662), in Thorpe, *Federal and State Constitutions*, I, 529–36; Andrews, *Colonial Period*, III, 97. The Duke's grant cut Connecticut's western extent off at the Connecticut River, which was the western boundary contemplated originally by the Council of New England in 1632, but never formalized.

[142] I am not taking account here of the Jerseys, which were obtained by indenture from the Duke of York. The Duke divested territory to John Lord Berkeley and Sir George Carteret, who claimed to have been granted their own proprietary province of New Caesaria, or New Jersey.

fortieth degree of Northern Latitude, and on the South by a Circle drawn
at twelve miles distance from New Castle Northward and Westward unto
the beginning of the fortieth degree of Northern Latitude, and then by a
streight Line Westward to the Limitt of Longitude above-mentioned.

One may take these scientistic impositions on local topography (merid-
ians, straight lines, arcs, latitudes and longitudes) as a sign of high English
self-confidence, of complete mastery in the imposition of precise European
form on American space that clearly contrasts with earlier attempts to
identify bounded spaces through proclamations of autoptic intimacy with
local physical details. Then again, charters had never extended their concern for the specificities of locales much beyond chorographic marking
and the appropriation of resources. Local political institutions, the local
economy, local culture, local peoples, had always vanished beneath a welter of English impositions. Pennsylvania was no exception. All the significant points of social, economic, political, and cultural reference in Penn's
charter projected English appropriation, English jurisdiction, English
ambition – *Englishness* – onto an inert mainland. Penn himself was made
a "true and absolute" proprietor, holding his land in free and common
socage, as of the Castle of Windsor, the whole described as a "Province
and Seigniorie" of the name "Pensilvania." He was granted "free and absolute" power to divide the country into "Townes, Hundreds and Counties,"
to "erect and incorporate Townes into Borroughs, and Borroughs into
Citties, and to make and constitute ffaires and Marketts." He was to be
free to "assigne, alien, Grant, demise, or enfeoffe" without restriction, *Quia
Emptores Terrarum* notwithstanding. He was to be free to "erect any parcells
of Land ... into Mannors" and in every one such to have and hold Court-
Baron, and "View of ffrank-pledge." He was to have

> free and undisturbed use and continuance in, and passage into and out of all
> and singuler Ports, Harbors, Bays, Waters, Rivers, Isles, and Inletts, belong-
> ing unto, or leading to and from the Countrey or Islands aforesaid, And all
> the Soyle, lands, fields, woods, underwoods, mountaines, hills, fenns, Isles,
> Lakes, Rivers, waters, Rivuletts, Bays, and Inletts, scituate or being within, or
> belonging unto the Limitts and Bounds aforesaid, togeather with the fish-
> ing of all sortes of fish, whales, Sturgeons, and all Royall and other Fishes, in
> the Sea, Bayes, Inletts, waters, or Rivers within the premisses, and the Fish
> therein taken; And also all Veines, Mines and Quarries, as well discovered as
> not discovered, of Gold, Silver, Gemms, and Pretious Stones, and all other
> whatsoever, be it Stones, Mettals, or of any other thing or matter whatsoever,
> found or to bee found within the Countrey, Isles or Limitts aforesaid.[143]

And though the Pennsylvania charter revived earlier designs to "reduce
the savage Natives by gentle and just manners to the Love of Civil Societie
and Christian Religion," it also granted the proprietor that same extraordinary authority, in evidence since 1622, to make war against "incursions

---

[143] "Charter for the Province of Pennsylvania" (1681), in Thorpe, *Federal and State Constitutions*,
V, 3035–44.

as well of the Savages themselves, as of other enemies, pirates and robbers," to pursue them beyond the limits of the province, to "vanquish and take them, and being taken to put them to death by the Law of Warre, or to save them, at theire pleasure."[144]

Considered within its *English* context, however, Penn's charter signified a diminution of capacity, the closing of an era that relied upon extensive delegation of colonizing responsibilities and governing authority. Though proprietorial, Pennsylvania was not palatine. Penn's charter powers were not as extensive as those of the Carolina proprietors, nor of the Calverts before them. Like them he could make laws, with the approbation of the province's freemen, and appoint "Judges and Justices, Magistrates and Officers ... for what Causes soever." But his power to "remitt, release, pardon, and abolish ... crimes and offences" was subject to restriction; the Privy Council had oversight of provincial laws; and as in the Duke of York's case the King retained the right to hear appeals.[145] Proprietorial discretion in the disposition of land was constrained by restrictions on subinfeudation. Proprietorial discretion in the control of trade was constrained by the requirement of strict adherence to the acts of navigation. Proprietorial control of the economy was limited by royal claims of a right (with parliamentary consent) to impose taxes. By the 1680s, in fact, what Penn's charter revealed in its English context was that the proprietorial design for English colonizing was fast being eclipsed by the expanding English state. English colonizing was re-presented once more, this time explicitly as an enterprise of the state and an expression of nation. "The members of the Board of Trade at Whitehall ... desired to get rid of the proprietary system altogether and to obtain for the proprietary colonies a more efficient order of [royal] government, to the greater peace and contentment of the colonists and the advantage of the mother country."[146]

Conclusion

"More vividly perhaps than any other developments during the first century," Jack Greene has argued, "the number and range of [colonizing] experiments illustrates the extent to which America had been identified among Europeans as a site for the realization of dreams and hopes that could not be achieved in the Old World." By experiments, Greene here refers to English designs for the establishment of commercial plantations, territorial lordships, and exilic sanctuaries, through the agency of which the North American mainland was manned, planted, and kept. "Of course," he continues, "all of these efforts were failures" and their failure was "almost immediate." Intricate designs yielded to cruder material realities – resource allocations, demography, and economy. New World settlers

---

[144] Ibid., 3036, 3042.
[145] Ibid., 3037–8.
[146] Andrews, *Colonial Period*, III, 225; Greene, *Peripheries and Center*, 13–17.

substituted as "their principal collective social goal the creation of some sort of recognizable version of the metropolitan society."[147]

One can allude to the "failure" of English colonization designs only if one has first assumed a position on the inside of English expansion. Viewed from the outside, "failure" seems less appropriate. The first objective of colonial chartering was to secure English *imperium* and *dominium* on the North American mainland from European competitors. That objective was clearly achieved. The second objective was to employ the discourses and methods of law and (where appropriate or unavoidable) war to displace indigenous sovereigns and impress Englishness, in detail, in their place. That objective, too, was clearly achieved.[148] The third objective was to establish particular economies and institutional structures – "weale publiques" (states) – for the colonies themselves. Here Greene's conclusion is more justifiable: colonial establishments and institutions departed their particular chartered designs. Still, an irrelevance that was "almost immediate"? The circumstances of their founding remained a primary point of ideological orientation for most of the English settlements far into the eighteenth century.[149] The discourse of territorial appropriation, occupation, and improvement, ubiquitous in the charters, was embraced everywhere. Seen for what they were, means to express and implement colonizing and expansion and displacement (manning and planting and keeping), the founding designs for English mainland colonies do not seem unimportant to the mainland's subsequent history – or, indeed, to its settler populations' construction of that history.[150]

---

[147] Jack P. Greene, *The Intellectual Construction of America: Exceptionalism and Identity from 1492 to 1800* (Chapel Hill, 1993), 58, 66.

[148] See, for example, Nathan Fiske, *Remarkable Providences to be Gratefully Recollected, Religiously Improved, and Carefully Transmitted to Posterity. A sermon preached at Brookfield on the last day of the year 1775* (Boston, 1776), an extract from which appears as the epigraph to Part III of this book. In Fiske's sermon, the anthropomorphic landscape rejoices in its fruitfulness, the realization of a destiny through English intervention first mooted in Sir George Peckham's *True Reporte* some two centuries before.

[149] See, for example, Bernard Bailyn, *The Ideological Origins of the American Revolution* (Cambridge, Mass., 1967), 190–98; Jack P. Greene, *The Quest for Power: The Lower Houses of Assembly in the Southern Royal Colonies, 1689–1776* (Chapel Hill, 1963), 14; John Phillip Reid, *The Constitutional History of the American Revolution*, volume 3, *The Authority to Legislate* (Madison, Wis., 1986), 172–91. On the persisting importance of the ideologies of founding in New England, see, e.g., Kenneth A. Lockridge, *A New England Town, the First Hundred Years: Dedham, Massachusetts, 1636–1736* (New York, 1970); Richard L. Bushman, *From Puritan to Yankee; Character and the Social Order in Connecticut, 1690–1765* (Cambridge, Mass., 1967). For the sustained influence of the politics and expressions of proprietorial design in the political development of colonies like Maryland and Pennsylvania, see Alan Tully, *Forming American Politics: Ideals, Interests and Institutions in Colonial New York and Pennsylvania* (Baltimore, 1994).

[150] See Michael Kammen, "The Meaning of Colonization in American Revolutionary Thought," *Journal of the History of Ideas*, 31, 3 (1970), 337–58. It is also worth considering whether the charters should be type-cast as "experimental." Important elements of the colonization process were clearly utopian and the necessities of crystallizing their utopianism in the form of a colonial charter required the deployment of institutional configurations in novel "experimental" ways. Yet the institutions themselves were usually not

For much of the last half century, the legal history of the colonized mainland has been written from the ground up, as if its only significant referent were the quotidien social behavior of its settler populations. But it is important to recognize that English settlement did not occur in vacant legal-conceptual space, any more than it did in vacant physical space. The Crown's charters were license and blueprint, declarations of intent and maps of desire. Collectively they established a "legal cartography" of English colonizing. They were both means to the projection of power and a record of the developing concepts of colonizing embraced by English projectors to be read over time.[151]

unfamiliar, nor even their configurations unprecedented. The company charters were not out of place in a long line of trading company charters; the proprietorial and quasi-proprietorial charters had resonance with English palatinates and Irish plantation charters, nor was their manorialism at all odd in sixteenth/seventeenth-century England. One might ask what non-experimental designs would look like.

[151] In "Deconstructing the Map," *Cartographica*, 26 (1989), at 13, the late J. B. Harley argues that to "catalogue the world is to appropriate it." We have already seen how the English charters catalog the mainland prospectively. Harley underlines how maps perform a similar function. Analyzing a map of the Dutch province of Gelderland produced in 1542 for the Emperor Charles V, depicting its "Towns, villages, monasteries, castles, with all the fine and excellent rivers, measured and plotted according to the true art of Geography," Harley and Kees Zandvliet comment, "it is the classification of objects worthy of recording in the landscape that is critical ... Why 'Towns, villages, monasteries, castles?' This is not the landscape 'as it really was,' but a redescription of the countryside that had been scrutinized and controlled to produce an image fit for an emperor concerned with the subordination of space. Each of the items is a class of political motif. Each symbolizes a layer of political power. The map as a whole represents a social hierarchy, a selective discourse ... in support of Spanish dominion and its universal religion in the Low Countries." J. B. Harley and Kees Zandvliet, "Art, Science and Power in Sixteenth-Century Dutch Cartography," *Cartographica*, 29 (1992), 15–16.

As this suggests, law and cartography are indeed very much alike in this essential representational regard. Both furnish "technical processes" that represent "acts of control" over the image of the world. Harley, "Deconstructing the Map," 13. In a very basic way, maps, like law, give their creators, and their creators' sponsors, "the means to construct, no less than project, an image of power and possession abroad." Benjamin Schmidt, "Mapping an Empire: Cartographic and Colonial Rivalry in Seventeenth-Century Dutch and English North America," *William and Mary Quarterly*, 3rd Ser., 54, 3 (July 1997), 551. See also J. B. Harley, "Maps, Knowledge, and Power," in Denis Cosgrove, editor, *The Iconography of Landscape: Essays on the Symbolic Representation, Design, and Use of Past Environments* (Cambridge and New York, 1988), 277–311. The elder Richard Hakluyt's desire for "a large world map" that could be manipulated to conform to both the present resources and the future ambitions of its intended audience, the rising English commercial and professional bourgeoisie, underlines his awareness of the point. See Richard Hakluyt, lawyer, of London, to Abraham Ortelius, Cosmographer, of Flanders (n.d., circa 1567), in Taylor, ed., *Original Writings and Correspondence*, 81.

What distinguishes law from cartography in early English colonizing is that law is the dominant medium for detailed planning. Later, cartography would come into its own. Harley associates cartography's accession to authority over the world's image with the Enlightenment's faith in the realism of science. "The map has attempted to purge itself of ambiguity and alternative possibility. Accuracy and austerity of design are now the new talismans of authority culminating in our own age with computer mapping. We can trace this process very clearly in the history of Enlightenment mapping in Europe. The topography

In light of what I have so far established in this book, what can one say at this point of law as a constituent element in colonizing? Recent historical and anthropological examinations of colonization, John and Jean Comaroff tell us, have commonly insisted upon "the centrality of law in the colonization of the non-European world," emphasizing its role "in the making of new Eurocentric hegemonies [and] in the creation of colonial subjects," providing "tools of domination and disempowerment; blunt instruments wielded by states, ruling classes, reigning regimes." The Comaroffs question this line of analysis. Colonizing's legalities were less an instrumental facilitation of a "linear, coherent, coercive process" than an imaginative resource not entirely under the colonizer's control. Clearly, law could have instrumental effects in discrete circumstances, but considered as a general phenomenon law's effectivity was "inherently ambivalent, contradictory."[152]

Examination of the charters that authorized English intrusions onto the American mainland, and the discourses of intrusion in which they were embedded, both relativizes and reinforces the Comaroffs' critical claim for a lack of linearity, an inherent contradictoriness, in the relationship between law and colonization. The claim is relativized because, considered as a genus of legal activity, chartering was quite linear and not at all self-contradictory. Its goal was unambiguous – to advance the creation of English colonies. And it was successful. In the nineteenth- and twentieth-century British Empire (notably in India and Africa), indigenous colonial subjects were able to discover means to appropriate the colonizer's legalities; to employ, however inadequately, his ideology of rights in

as shown in maps, increasingly detailed and planimetrically accurate, has become a metaphor for a utilitarian philosophy and its will to power." Harley, "Deconstructing the Map," 10. See also Matthew H. Edney, *Mapping an Empire: The Geographical Construction of British India, 1765–1843* (Chicago, 1997). Yet for most of the seventeenth century, colonial survey was neither consistent in its methods nor definitive in its results, nor mapping at all a routine practice for recording claims. Sarah Hughes, *Surveyors and Statesmen: Land Measuring in Colonial Virginia* (Richmond, 1979), 1–3,8–9, 28–54. In the North American case the "great period" of English map making was not that of seventeenth-century intrusion but of eighteenth-century consolidation. See J. B. Harley, "Introduction," and David B. Quinn, "Maps of the Age of European Exploration," both in David Buisseret, editor, *From Sea Charts to Satellite Images: Interpreting North American History through Maps* (Chicago, 1990), 11, 46; Harley, "Power and Legitimation," 181–91; Schmidt, "Mapping an Empire," 562–64; William P. Cumming, *British Maps of Colonial America* (Chicago, 1974). But see also MacMillan, *Sovereignty and Possession*, who argues that early modern British cartography was more sophisticated than has been thought: "the best geographical knowledge conveyed through English-drawn maps of newfound lands remained in manuscript, so that the crown and the trading companies solely could benefit from this valuable intelligence. Printed maps of newfound lands were usually optimistic, speculative and unrepresentative, and could be used as propaganda without compromising secret intelligence" (150, and generally 148–77).

[152] John L. Comaroff and Jean Comaroff, *Of Revelation and Revolution (II): The Dialectics of Modernity on a South African Frontier* (Chicago, 1997), 365, 367; John L. Comaroff, "Foreword," in Mindie Lazarus-Black and Susan F. Hirsch, editors, *Contested States: Law, Hegemony and Resistance* (New York and London, 1994), ix, x.

their struggles against his mights.[153] The English North Atlantic Empire of the seventeenth and eighteenth centuries offers rather less evidence of this phenomenon.[154] Seventeenth-century English colonizing was insular and largely (until quite late in the century) monocultural, an expansion of enclaves founded on social, cultural, and economic separation between the colonizers (the "settled," the civically endowed, the true inhabitants) and the non-European world that they had entered (unsettled, "savage," threatening), a world of limited overlaps, particularly after "the Naturalls" had proven themselves beyond all doubt treacherous and brutal "common enemies of mankind."[155] Applied to the Atlantic empire, in short, the Comaroffs' arguments against the reduction of law to a technology of European rule carry only moderate weight.

Once past that foundational characterization of law as an activity expressing and projecting Englishness and English rule onto the mainland, law's singular linearity becomes less evident, its plurality more easily appreciated. First, much of the substance of the law mobilized was not

[153] See, for example, Sally Engle Merry, *Colonizing Hawai'i: The Cultural Power of Law* (Princeton, 2000), 8, 264; Peter Fitzpatrick, "Passions out of Place: Law, Incommensurability, and Resistance," in Eve Darian-Smith and Peter Fitzpatrick, editors, *Laws of the Postcolonial* (Ann Arbor, 1999), 53–4. But see also Jeannine Purdy, "Postcolonialism: The Emperor's New Clothes?" in Darian-Smith and Fitzpatrick, eds., *Laws of the Postcolonial*. Fitzpatrick argues that occidental consciousness of their "incommensurability" with the colonized became intellectually problematic only in the wake of the Enlightenment. Early modern European colonizers "had used their incommensurability with the populations of the Americas to reason that the supposed absence of property relations enabled them to occupy the land. Indeed, incommensurability was to become not just a prime justification for Europe's colonial extraversion hut also a foundation for the identity of the European as exemplary of modernity" (40). But Purdy goes a lot further, denying that the post-Enlightenment liberal problematic actually resulted in any real difference between early-modern and liberal-modern imperialisms, or between colony and postcolony. "Dressing law in the borrowed garb of postcolonialism has made us blind to the ways in which law continues to function as it always has in the colonial context ... 'to speak the language of pure force'" (222).

[154] This is not to say attempts were not made. See, for example, Katherine Hermes, "'Justice Will Be Done Us': Algonquian Demands for Reciprocity in the Courts of European Settlers," in Christopher L. Tomlins and Bruce H. Mann, editors, *The Many Legalities of Early America* (Chapel Hill, 2001), 123–49. But see also Ann M. Plane, "Customary Laws of Marriage: Legal Pluralism, Colonialism, and Narragansett Indian Identity in Eighteenth-Century Rhode Island," in Tomlins and Mann, *Many Legalities*, 181–213, which demonstrates the vulnerability of indigenous usages to English legalities.

[155] See nn.130–32, this chapter, and accompanying text. One can observe the completeness of the conceptual displacement of the indigenous achieved over the previous century in the Georgia Charter of 1732. The objective of colonizing is "to settle ... our provinces in America"; to cultivate their lands "at present waste and desolate"; and to defend them from "Indian enemies ... neighboring savages" who lie permanently in wait on the other side of the "unsettled" frontier for opportunities to "la[y] waste with fire and sword and great numbers of English inhabitants, miserably massacre[ ]." See "Charter of Georgia" (1732), in Thorpe, *Federal and State Constitutions*, 765. In Georgia, as Lisa Ford has made clear, physical displacement would prove a messier process. See her *Settler Sovereignty: Jurisdiction and Indigenous People in America and Australia, 1788–1836* (Cambridge, Mass., 2010).

English at all; Roman law, not common law, gave the activity of colonizing much of its juridical cosmography. Second, the English developed several distinct legal models for colonies, each with different implications for the structure of the colonizing enterprise itself and for the social and political orders envisaged as appropriate for the project. Third, certain of the chartered representations of Englishness were simultaneously innovative variations on prevailing English practices – as, for example, in provisions for possession of land, which were in general substantially less qualified and more absolute (at the point of implementation) than in English usage. No one model of "Englishness" was conveyed within the colonizing impulse. One encounters instead a plurality of representations of Englishness, and plural modalities of rule.

By the 1680s, an attempt to create a singular metropolitan representation of mainland colonizing was in the offing, one facet of the expansion of the metropolitan state that would become (both in Britain itself and, eventually, in North America) so marked a feature of the eighteenth century.[156] The attempt was constrained by the diversity of state forms, both residual and established, embraced by planting's projectors over the course of the seventeenth century. But that diversity of institutional design was overlain by another and greater source of plurality, the multiple migrations that had actually provided the colonies' occupants. Overwhelmingly "English" though they might have been, the migrants of the first century were far from a single "people" with a shared cultural purpose (conscious or not) to create one sort of Englishness in America. Rather, the migrants that cemented English colonial occupancy of the mainland arrived possessed of quite distinct repertoires of habits, customs, ideologies, and social practices. Manifested in law, these diverse social and cultural birthmarks imprinted not one but several varieties of Englishness on the American landscape. Their pluralism was at odds with the worlds of the metropolis and of colonizing's magnate projectors alike.

That pluralism is the theme of the next stage of this narrative. For if the almost immediate irrelevance of foundational designs for English colonization seems worth reconsideration, so does the companion assertion that what settlers substituted was an approximation or general amalgam of metropolitan culture. Cultural variety, not uniformity, is the distinguishing characteristic of the English inhabitation of America.

Hypothesizing some years ago that the original settler cultures of the North American mainland tended to establish and reproduce not an approximation or amalgamation of metropolitan culture but serial regionally specific English cultures based on regional migrations, David Hackett Fischer assembled a wide array of local English practices and institutions into more systematic regional variations, then demonstrated their persisting influence in the shape of reconstituted American regionalisms.[157] It is

---

[156] See generally John Brewer, *The Sinews of Power: War, Money, and the English State, 1688–1783* (New York, 1989); Greene, *Peripheries and Center*, 13–18, 49–54. And see also Chapter 8.

[157] David Hackett Fischer, *Albion's Seed: Four British Folkways in America* (New York, 1989).

debatable whether the migrations Fischer describes were quite as solidary in all cases as he claims, but it is indisputable that each of the mainland's recipient regions became home to influential pluralities who were, in their origins, distinctive and who brought many elements of that distinctiveness to bear in the ways that they "inhabited" their new environment.

The legal field is not the least of those in which systematic regional variation within England may be observed. Migration and resettlement, that is, resulted in the reestablishment in English America of distinct regional *legal* cultures with origins in differing metropolitan locales, bred up there by distinct institutional trajectories, histories, and local practices. Alongside the structures of authoritative socio-legal order planned by projectors, in other words, existed others that were implicit in the massed migrations of actual settlers. By counterposing the two, one can acknowledge the reality in many cases of settlers' inchoate disagreements with and departures from projectors' designs. We have seen that as a discourse of authority-in-general, law had a crucial role to play in the processes by which English colonizers manned, planted, and kept the American mainland. Law played an equally considerable role as a discourse of authority-in-detail (as a modality of home rule, so to speak), this time subject to the rather more considerable refractions of widespread cultural and institutional variation imported by migrants. Well-documented tensions that arose between settler legal cultures and chartered authority came about, one may conjecture, as a result of cultural dissociations between the two stemming from processes of migration that confronted people from one English region with authority structures designed on the basis of practice in another. Endemic proprietor-settler conflicts in Pennsylvania, for example, can be understood in such terms.

During the later seventeenth century, and as the seventeenth became the eighteenth, English colonizing on the North American mainland became more and more a self-colonization; no longer, that is, primarily a visitation of power upon strangers[158] but rather a labor of transformation wrought by the English upon their own kind.[159] This labor of self-transformation – the

---

[158] The stranger is the "other" of early-modern law of nations, "For strangers are those who never at any time have been associated in friendship or by any treaty, being unknown either through war or peace, such as were those far away nations to the Portuguese and Spaniards, separated by the long voyage across the Ocean." Belli, *De Re Militari*, 286.

[159] We have seen that the creation of disciplined labor forces in overseas colonies through transportation or migration of surplus populations is a theme of English colonization argumentation from the younger Richard Hakluyt onward. See, for example, his "Discourse of Western Planting," Cap.4 ("That this enterprize will be for the manifolde ymployment of nombers of idle men") in Taylor, ed., *Original Writings and Correspondence*, at 233–9. English historians examining the nineteenth century have noted, meanwhile, how colonization's aspect as the transformation of peoples extended simultaneously to the "internal" colonization (geographic and social) of the British Isles. On this see, for example, Michael Brogden, "An Act to Colonize the Internal Lands of the Island: Empire and the Origins of the Professional Police," *International Journal of the Sociology of Law*, 15, 2 (May 1987); Robert D. Storch, "The Policeman as Domestic Missionary: Urban Discipline and Popular Culture in Northern England, 1850–1880," *Journal of Social History*, 9, 4

"anglicization" of colonial subjects who were, in the sense of shared origins, already overwhelmingly English – meant processes of institution- and state-formation that attempted to cut across existing cultural affinities, rearrange hierarchies of rule, and seek uniformities of practice where previously there had existed severalty and custom. In the mainland colonies, as in Britain (for Britain was undergoing a thorough "anglicization" of its own), law proved an important medium for the realization of social transformation. But also, through its rights-claims and its persistent regionalisms, colonial law provided some kinds of inhabitants with alternatives, particularly as the century wore on and the process of change took on increasingly imperial overtones that exposed these inhabitants of English colonies, by now overwhelmingly Creole in origin, not, after all, as English at all (no matter how hard they might protest) but themselves as "others" to be addressed and transformed by the metropolis.[160]

(June 1976). As we shall see in Chapter 8, this dialectic between metropolitan and colonial social transformation had become explicit by the early eighteenth century in the political economy of Daniel Defoe. It would later be greatly extended by theorists like Patrick Colquhoun. See, for example, his *A Treatise on the Police of the Metropolis* (London, 1796), and *Treatise on the Wealth, Power, and Resources of the British Empire* (London, 1814). For an application of this argument to the late sixteenth and early seventeenth centuries, see Mark Netzloff, *England's Internal Colonies: Class, Capital and the Literature of Early Modern English Colonialism* (New York, 2003).

[160] Greene, *Peripheries and Center*, 59–76, 88–92, 96, 144–9; John Phillip Reid, *Constitutional History of the American Revolution*, 4 vols. (Madison, Wis., 1986–93); Daniel J. Hulsebosch, *Constituting Empire: New York and the Transformation of Constitutionalism in the Atlantic World, 1664–1830* (Chapel Hill, 2005), 71–144; Christopher L. Tomlins, *Law, Labor, and Ideology in the Early American Republic* (Cambridge and New York, 1993), 47–55.

PART II

Poly-Olbion; or The Inside Narrative

It is a great worke, and requires more skillfull artificers
to lay the foundation of a new building,
than to uphold and repayre one that is already built.
If great things be attempted by weake instruments,
The effects will be answerable.

> John Winthrop, "General considerations for the
> plantation in New England" (1629)

5

Packing: New Inhabitants

Of *Albions* glorious Ile the Wonders whilst I write,
The sundry varying soyles, the pleasures infinite ...
What helpe shall I invoke to ayde my Muse the while?

Michael Drayton, Poly-Olbion (1612)

I am Lord *Frampull,*
The cause of all this trouble; I am he
Haue measur'd all the Shires of *England* ouer:
Wales, and her mountains, seene those wilder nations,
Of people in the *Peake,* and *Lancashire;*
Their Pipers, Fidlers, Rushers, Puppet-masters,
Iuglers, and Gipseys, all the sorts of Canters
And Colonies of beggars, Tumblers, Ape-carriers,
For to these sauages I was addicted,
To search their natures, and make odde discoueries!

Ben Jonson, The New Inne (1629)

Of all the late sixteenth century's monuments to the prospect of English colonizing, none more effusively reinvented the world as Albion's oyster than the younger Richard Hakluyt's triumphal record of voyaging, *The Principall Nauigations, Voiages, and Discoveries.*[1] Froude would call it "the Prose Epic of the modern English nation."[2]

But if Hakluyt's efforts wrote a nation in prose, it was prose that manufactured *nation* from the outside. Within, discourses of Christianity, geography, economy, and law better describe a "poly-Olbion."[3] English Christianity meant not one reformed church but conflicting faiths, a

---

[1] *The Principall Navigations, Voiages and Discoveries of the English nation, made by Sea or ouer Land, to the most remote and farthest distant Quarters of the earth at any time within the compasse of these 1500 Yeeres: Deuided into three seuerall parts, according to the positions of the Regions wherunto they were directed.* By Richard Hakluyt Master of Artes, and student sometime of Christ-church in Oxford (London, 1589).

[2] J. A. Froude, *Short Studies on Great Subjects* (London, 1867), 296.

[3] Richard Helgerson writes of the work of this name, published by Michael Drayton in 1612, that it epitomizes a representational movement from monarchy to land, from nation singularly embodied in the Crown to nation plurally embodied in country. See Richard Helgerson, *Forms of Nationhood: The Elizabethan Writing of England* (Chicago, 1992), 117–24, and generally 107–47.

multiplying division of sectarian offshoots and, withal, bitter political-religious conflict. Spatially, both geographers in action and geography in fact provided compelling evidence of England's deep and lasting regional variety. Organizationally, economy described an expanding but highly differentiated sphere of activity experiencing fundamental alterations in its structure: wrenching disruption and reconstitution of regional economies, wrenching social changes accompanying them. Whether in its competing abstractions or its concrete expressions, finally, law was anything but a national singularity. Rather, law described both plural discourses and institutions and, within them, a congeries of local particularities that in their application exhibited sufficient regional and social variation to demonstrate the existence not of one English legal culture but many.[4]

The inside narrative of English colonizing is much the same as the inside narrative of England itself. Poly-Olbion, not Albion, was what went overseas to inhabit the colonies that the younger Hakluyt and his peers promoted.[5] We have already encountered something of that plurality. As an enterprise of elite invention, colonizing projects had not embraced any uniform institutional template during the first century of English expansion but had appeared in successive designs – individual Crown licensees, corporate, proprietorial – whose relative successes, failures, and residues would deposit a diversity of institutional forms on the mainland. All had established Englishness, but had done so according to no single pattern. In other words, even as an elite enterprise, colonization had created institutional and cultural severalty.

As an enterprise that was always (but increasingly) one of migration and settlement, dependent upon the importation of population en masse to establish boundaries, cement occupancy, and in all essentials to perform the actual work – "to throw down, to build and to plant"[6] – colonizing

---

[4] See generally, ibid., 65–147, 249–94. See also: On religious diversity, Stephen Foster, *The Long Argument: English Puritanism and the Shaping of New England Culture, 1570–1700* (Chapel Hill, 1991), 1–137; On commercial change and general socio-economic transformation, Robert Brenner, *Merchants and Revolution: Commercial Change, Political Conflict, and London's Overseas Traders, 1550–1653* (Princeton, 1993), 3–184; David Underdown, *Revel, Riot and Rebellion: Popular Politics and Culture in England, 1603–1660* (Oxford, 1985), 1–43; and generally Keith Wrightson, *English Society, 1580–1680* (New Brunswick, N.J., 1982); Margaret Spufford, *Contrasting Communities: English Villagers in the Sixteenth and Seventeenth Centuries* (Cambridge, 1974); Buchanan Sharp, *In Contempt of All Authority: Rural Artisans and Riot in the West of England, 1586–1660* (Berkeley, 1980); On law's pluralities, E. P. Thompson, *Customs in Common* (New York, 1991), 97–184; John Brewer and John Styles, editors, *An Ungovernable People: The English and their Law in the Seventeenth and Eighteenth Centuries* (New Brunswick, N.J., 1980); Andy Wood, "Custom, Identity and Resistance: English Free Miners and their Law, c.1550–1800," in Paul Griffiths, Adam Fox, and Steve Hindle, editors, *The Experience of Authority in Early Modern England* (New York, 1996), 249–85; A. J. Fletcher and J. Stevenson, "Introduction," in Anthony Fletcher and John Stevenson, editors, *Order and Disorder in Early Modern England* (Cambridge, 1985), 1–40.

[5] See generally David Hackett Fischer, *Albion's Seed: Four British Folkways in America* (New York, 1989).

[6] See the first epigraph to this book, taken from Jeremiah 1:10.

imported all the additional polyphony of the migrants' English locales. To the origins of those "of small meanes" who went overseas to create new commonwealths, I now turn.

I. Places of Origin

Late sixteenth- and seventeenth-century England, into which the bulk of the North American mainland's first 200,000 migrants were born, was a land undergoing substantial alteration. Population growth meant rising food prices, periodic dearths and basic alterations in the balance and location of arable (tillage) and pastoral (grazing) agriculture. Small-holding husbandmen and landless laborers pushed out of arable regions by rising rents and manorial fines, and by engrossment and enclosure, crowded into areas of more extensive commons and wastes, fens (wetlands), and woods or forest, where squatting and subsistence farming remained viable. Rising popular mobility and dearth crises prompted substantial alteration in the structure of political-legal relations encompassing central and local authority.[7] Such fundamental levels of social and material change help explain the heightened popular propensity to migrate. The indubitably regional pattern of migration, however, makes national-level generalizations about the process suspect.

English population history during the first half of the second millennium follows a pattern in which periods of secular growth are ended by outbreaks of catastrophic disease. In the three centuries following the Norman Conquest (1066), population more than tripled, from approximately 1 million in the mid-eleventh century to more than 3.5 million by the mid-fourteenth century. Particularly rapid growth occurred in the seventy-five years beginning with the last quarter of the thirteenth century, interspersed with shocks of increasing mortality from famine and disease. These culminated in the Black Death plague outbreak of 1348–51, which killed between one-third and one-half of the population. By the end of the fourteenth century, population had fallen to 2.1 million; it would remain at approximately this level for the next hundred years. Slow growth resumed early in the sixteenth century and accelerated after 1530, though interrupted, as before, by disease shocks (notably the influenza outbreak of the late 1550s and serial plague outbreaks during the seventeenth century) and by famine and dearth. The outcome overall was an effective doubling or more of population between the 1520s and the 1650s, from some 2.3 million to more than 5.5 million, but rapid population growth was confined to particular periods,

---

[7] See generally Spufford, *Contrasting Communities*; Sharp, *In Contempt of All Authority*; and Buchanan Sharp, "Popular Protest in Seventeenth Century England," in Barry Reay, editor, *Popular Culture in Seventeenth Century England* (New York, 1985), 271–308; Wrightson, *English Society*; Fletcher and Stevenson, eds., *Order and Disorder in Early Modern England*; Ann Kussmaul, *A General View of the Rural Economy of England, 1538–1840* (Cambridge and New York, 1990); Steve Hindle, *The State and Social Change in Early Modern England, c.1550–1640* (New York, 2002).

notably the decades between 1560 and 1590.[8] After the 1650s population declined somewhat, dropping by upwards of 500,000 (approximately 10 percent) between 1670 and 1686, slowly stabilizing thereafter to a little over 5 million in 1700. The population peak of the 1650s would not be reached again until 1721. It was not exceeded until sustained strong growth set in during the remainder of the eighteenth century.[9]

Population increase and cycles of disease and famine were intimately related. In the fourteenth century, rapid population growth meant rising demand for agricultural produce. With few innovations under way in agricultural technique, demand could only be met by the expansion of cultivation to marginal lands, resulting in lower overall yields and higher prices, hence reduced diet and weakened resistance to disease. Again, in the later sixteenth and first half of the seventeenth centuries, population increase meant a combination of downward pressure on wages coupled with upward pressure on agricultural prices. Between 1590 and 1640, periodic harvest failure combined with population increase and rising prices to induce significant periods of dearth.[10] Famine and catastrophic disease were, however, absent: ironically, the comparatively greater health of the population overall, as compared with the fourteenth century, allowed population increase to coexist with widespread suffering and deprivation.[11]

---

[8] It was toward the end of this period that rising concern over a lack of employment and excessive mobility among people of working age became manifest in the tracts of colonizers. See, for example, Richard Hakluyt (the elder), "Pamphlet for the Virginia Enterprise" (n.d.) in E.G.R. Taylor, editor, *The Original Writings and Correspondence of the Two Richard Hakluyts* (London, 1935), II, 339–43, at 339, 340, 343: "By inhabytinge of Countreyes wth Englishe people dyvers Comodyties will ensue ... the poore and Idle persons w[ch] nowe are ether burdensome or hurtefull to this Realme at home maye hereby become profitable members by ymployinge them ether at home ... [or] in those Countryes ... the wounderfull increase of our people here in Englande and a great number of them voyde of any good trade or ymployement to gete their lyvinge maye be a sufficient cause to move not onlye the marchaunts and Clothiers but alsoe all other sortes and degrees of our nacion to seeke newe dyscovereyes of peopled regions for vente of our Idle people, otherwyse in shourte tyme many mischeifs maye ensue."

[9] The figures given in this paragraph draw upon the following: Richard Lachmann, *From Manor to Market: Structural Change in England, 1536–1640* (Madison, Wis., 1987), 47; Pauline Gregg, *Black Death to Industrial Revolution: A Social and Economic History of England* (London, 1976), 200; R. M. Smith, "Geographical Aspects of Population Change in England, 1500–1730," in R. A. Dodgshon and R. A. Butlin, editors, *An Historical Geography of England and Wales*, 2nd ed. (London and San Diego, 1990), 151–79, at 153–4; Keith Wrightson and David Levine, *Poverty and Piety in an English Village: Terling, 1525–1700* (Oxford, 1995), 3–4; Kussmaul, *General View*, 174; Hindle, *State and Social Change*, 39–40. See generally E. A. Wrigley and R. S. Schofield, *The Population History of England, 1541–1871* (London, 1981). Population decline in the later seventeenth century correlates with tightening English labor markets, relatively freer access to resources for subsistence, and dwindling migration.

[10] Namely, 1596–8, and 1622–3. Both crises, particularly the second, were far more acute in their effects in the north-west of England than the south and south-east. See Smith, "Geographical Aspects of Population Change," 158.

[11] Ibid., 161–4. D. C. Coleman, "Labour in the English Economy of the Seventeenth Century," *Economic History Review*, 2nd Ser., 8, 3 (1956), 283–4.

The same half century (1590–1640) was also a period of significant population redistribution. After the Black Death, conditions of acute labor shortage and suddenly plentiful land saw arable cultivation retreat from the marginal lands to which it had been extended since 1300. These areas reverted to waste, or to less-laborious pastoral agriculture, with results beneficial to the much-diminished surviving population. "The use of the land with the highest yields and the greater emphasis upon less labor-intensive pastoral farming resulted in a decline of food prices, and especially those of meat."[12] These tendencies were accompanied by structural change in the organization of agriculture that reflected competition among landlords to attract now-scarce tenants, the consolidation of vacant smallholdings into enlarged farms, the commutation of manorial labor services into rents, and the development of new forms of manorial land title (notably copyhold) to replace villeinage. All had the effect of significantly increasing the mobility of the surviving rural population.[13] After population growth resumed, and particularly as the rate of growth accelerated during the latter part of the sixteenth century, mobility continued to increase, but this time as a response to constricted rather than increased opportunity. Impoverished northerners headed south from crowded pastoral areas where incessant subdivision of smallholdings was exhausting local capacity to continue absorbing generational increases in population. As the fielden (tillage-land) parishes typical of lowland England likewise found their capacity to absorb their own growing population and its demand for new agricultural holdings increasingly constrained, their surplus was similarly forced to migrate into regions with substantial commons and wastes, woodpasture and fens and forest regions, all of which offered means to practice subsistence farming and to engage in rural industrial by-employments. Towns provided another destination, both regional centers such as York, Leicester, Salisbury, Worcester, Exeter, Norwich, and Bristol, and in particular London, whose population increased from some fifty thousand at the beginning of the sixteenth century to some four hundred thousand by the middle of the seventeenth.[14]

The broad implications of population redistribution in the later sixteenth and seventeenth centuries – the migration-inducing pressures of population growth in the northwest uplands, the exhaustion of opportunity in fielden parishes, migration to pastoral, fens, and forest – can only

---

[12] Lachmann, *From Manor to Market*, 52.

[13] Ibid., 52–8, 61–5.

[14] Wrightson, *English Society*, 125–8; Ralph A. Houlbrooke, *The English Family, 1450–1700* (New York, 1984), 28. See generally Peter Clark, "The Migrant in Kentish Towns," in Peter Clark and Paul Slack, editors, *Crisis and Order in English Towns, 1500–1700: Essays in Urban History* (London, 1972), 117–63; Paul Slack, "Vagrants and Vagrancy in England, 1598–1664," in Peter Clark and David Souden, editors, *Migration and Society in Early Modern England* (Totowa, N.J., 1988), 49–76; Peter Clark, "Migration in England during the Late Seventeenth and Early Eighteenth Centuries," in Clark and Souden, eds., *Migration and Society*, 213–52, at 214–15.

be understood fully in light of the distinctive structure and evolution of the English rural economy. The classic model is that developed by Joan Thirsk. It begins on a decisively ecological note:

> Beneath the man-made landscape, and underlying all the institutions of society which differentiated neighbouring communities and united widely separated ones, nature had laid a foundation which men were forced to accept ... To the inhabitants of the north and west of England belonged a land dominated by mountains and moors, where soils are poor and thin, the valleys and plains few and far between, where the whole countryside lies athwart the path of rain-carrying winds, affording a cool, wet climate. Except in certain favoured districts, the sixteenth-century farmer, like his forbears and successors, had to accept this as grass-growing country, and to specialize in animal production. The south and east of England, in contrast, was blessed with a different kind of country and climate. It is an undulating lowland, with smaller hills, gentler slopes, a richer deeper soil, and a drier climate. It can grow corn as well as grass, and so allows the farmer a wider choice of alternatives in his farming. This was the country of mixed farming in the sixteenth century.[15]

English farming types were thus split geographically in two. Population growth's accentuated demand for food and land exaggerated the split, for it encouraged farmers in each region to increase production by concentrating on their comparative advantage.[16] Indeed, Thirsk's emphasis on geography as the prime determinant of agrarian practice may actually understate the influence of comparative advantage in transforming agriculture. More recent analysis of the structure of farming regions suggests that the essentially static "classic" model is actually more a representation of changes occurring during the course of the seventeenth century than the diktat of nature. At the beginning of the century, significant arable farming was being pursued in regions that fall well within the bounds of the "pastoral" belt, notably throughout the southwestern and western counties of Somerset, Dorset, Gloucestershire, Hereford, and Worcestershire. In the late sixteenth century, Hereford and its adjoining counties (Worcestershire and Gloucestershire) were known "as 'the barns for the corn'" in that part of the country.[17] Over the succeeding century, however, a "dramatic" inversion of the distribution of farming practice took place in the west, "a wholesale shift from arable employment to employment in [stock] rearing." Through 1640, the west appears "nearly homogenous" in its emphasis on arable agriculture. It is the century thereafter (1640–1740) that sees the west acquire its distinctive and familiar pastoral profile.[18]

[15] Joan Thirsk, "The Farming Regions of England," in Joan Thirsk, editor, *The Agrarian History of England and Wales: Volume IV, 1500–1640* (Cambridge, 1967), 2. For a critique of this formulation and of the social and cultural history that it has spawned, see Neil Davie, "Chalk and Cheese? 'Fielden' and 'Forest' Communities in Early Modern England," *Journal of Historical Sociology*, 4, 1 (March 1991), 1–31.

[16] Kussmaul, *General View*, 67, 110–12. See generally 103–25.

[17] Thirsk, "Farming Regions," 100.

[18] Kussmaul, *General View*, 88. See generally 76–102.

The west provides the starkest example of the phenomenon of rural transition, but, albeit to a lesser extent, the same transition is detectable elsewhere. In East Anglia and the southeast, farming was regionally sub-divided between arable and pastoral concentrations, the former largely (though not exclusively) to be found in coastal areas of downlands and wolds (gently rolling hills), mainly in the form of sheep-corn husbandry,[19] the latter in interior woodpasture areas. Though now associated with ara-ble agriculture, the importance of pastoral activity in early seventeenth-century East Anglian agriculture is clear:

> At its southern end, Essex and parts of Suffolk produced cereals, meat and dairy products for the ever-growing London market. A central sweep of these counties and of south Norfolk – the wood-pasture region – was largely enclosed, with independent farmers virtually emancipated from medieval manorial conventions. The lighter soils of north and east Norfolk, east and west Suffolk and east Cambridgeshire were devoted to sheep-cereal hus-bandry with a considerable amount of open-field farming. There were still many areas of marsh and fenland: southeast Essex; parts of the Suffolk, Norfolk, and Lincolnshire coasts; and a great swathe running from central Lincolnshire down to northwest Norfolk and north Cambridgeshire. Cattle were fattened on these coastal marshlands and parts of the fens during the drier months. In eastern Lincolnshire these vast watery flatlands were inter-rupted by the rise of the Wolds, uplands producing fine wools.[20]

Over the course of the seventeenth century, as the west moved toward a distinctively pastoral profile, so East Anglia and the south-east moved fur-ther away from it.[21] By the end of the century, Norfolk, Suffolk, and Essex were displaying a more distinctively arable profile. Pastoral activity did not entirely disappear from the region, but overall the outcome confirms perceptions that a "spatial rearrangement of economic activity over the English countryside" occurred during the second half of the seventeenth century, raising productivity of both land and labor, stimulating an impor-tant degree of market integration, and generally bringing about a more sharply differentiated rural England, both economically and socially.[22]

[19] Sheep were folded on arable land to graze on the stubble and to manure the soil.

[20] This description of "Greater East Anglian" agriculture in the early seventeenth century is taken from Roger Thompson, *Mobility and Migration: East Anglian Founders of New England, 1629–1640* (Amherst, Mass., 1994), 17.

[21] Kussmaul, *General View*, 88–9. In "Wages and Wage-Earners in England: The Evidence of the Wage Assessments, 1563–1725" (unpublished D.Phil. thesis, Oxford University, 1981), 114–17, 234–65, Michael F. Roberts accumulates considerable empirical evidence to demonstrate the increasing attention that magistrates in the south-east paid over the course of the seventeenth century to wages and employment structures particular to harvest labor.

[22] Kussmaul, *General View*, 170, 100–1. By the mid- to late eighteenth century, as Eric Hobsbawm and George Rudé emphasized some years ago, the devotion of the south and east of England to an arable cereals agriculture of engrossed and enclosed farms and hired labor was complete. See Eric Hobsbawm and George Rudé, *Captain Swing: A Social History of the Great English Agricultural Uprising of 1830* (New York, 1975), 23–37. See also K.D.M. Snell, *Annals of the Laboring Poor: Social Change and Agrarian England, 1660–1900* (Cambridge, 1985).

Population increase and the internal and external migrations that it stimulated cannot be separated from these structural trends in agrarian practice. First, agrarian transition itself was a response to population growth – a shift from a relatively unspecialized rural economy, in which most regions attempted to grow at least enough grain to meet local demand, to an increasingly specialized rural economy, in which farmers sought opportunity by pursuing the comparative regional advantages made possible by the development of denser market and communications networks, particularly those feeding the ever-increasing maw of London.[23] Second, transition generated upheaval. The countrywide realignment of arable and pastoral activity "disrupted locally sustained tendencies towards balance between local supplies of, and demand for, agricultural labour." East Anglia, slowly becoming more arable as the century progressed, "experienced labour shortages." Regions abandoning grain production for stock rearing, as in the southwest, "found themselves with labour surpluses."[24] Third, transition was generally accompanied by additional population-uprooting phenomena: enclosure of common or open fields, and of commons and wastes. These processes eroded the local economic position of smallholders and of the landless poor, who relied upon common right to guarantee their subsistence.[25]

The population effects of enclosure became pronounced during the seventeenth century. Enclosure per se was in no sense an innovation: major stretches of East Anglia (particularly Suffolk and Essex), and of the counties to the north and south of London (Hertfordshire, Surrey, Kent, Sussex), were already fully or substantially enclosed at the end of the sixteenth century, as were parts of Hampshire and Dorset on the south coast, much of Somerset, Devon, and Cornwall in the southwest, and significant areas of the Welsh border counties and the northwest, like Hereford, Shropshire, Cheshire, and Lancashire.[26] Enclosed land amounted to some 47 percent of total English acreage in 1600, much of it enclosed by agreement.[27] As

---

[23] Wrightson and Levine, *Poverty and Piety*, 4.

[24] Kussmaul, *General View*, 146.

[25] Ibid., 96–7. On the place of common right in the rural economy, see J. M. Neeson, *Commoners: Common Right, Enclosure and Social Change in England, 1700–1820* (Cambridge, 1993); Thompson, *Customs in Common*, 97–184; Snell, *Annals of the Labouring Poor*, 138–227.

[26] E.C.K. Gonner, *Common Land and Inclosure* (London, 1912), appendix map D; Joan Thirsk, "Enclosing and Engrossing," in Thirsk, ed., *Agrarian History, IV*, 200–55, particularly 203; J. R. Wordie, "The Chronology of English Enclosure, 1500–1914," *The Economic History Review*, 2nd Ser., 36, 4 (November 1983), 483–505. For a critique of Wordie's chronology, see Hindle, *State and Social Control*, 44–5.

[27] Wordie, "Chronology of English Enclosure," 489–91. Enclosure by agreement should not be taken to signify enclosure without controversy. As Thirsk shows in "Enclosing and Engrossing," 203–4, in districts with large areas of old-enclosed land or where husbandry systems were not particularly threatened by land shortages, as in much of the north and northwest, the west and the southeast, enclosure "stirred few passions." Elsewhere, however, for example in the east Midlands, enclosure was highly controversial. Agreement between the manorial lord and the most substantial rights holders would squeeze out

no more than 2 percent of that acreage had been enclosed during the sixteenth century, it is clear that nearly half of England had been enclosed for at least a century and probably longer, at a time of little or no overall population growth. Related population effects had been absorbed, albeit with difficulty.[28] Certainly that was true of the old-enclosed woodpasture regions of East Anglia, and of the mixed and pastoral farming districts of Essex, Kent, and Devon. As for the highlands of the west and north, that land "was either completely enclosed by the beginning of the sixteenth century, or, if ... worth enclosing at this time, could and often did undergo painless enclosure."[29] When English population began to grow again during the sixteenth century, however, old-enclosed parishes became a spur to population mobility because they restricted local capacities to absorb growth by denying newly formed couples shares of now-enclosed open fields or access to commons and wastes[30] – although this caused fewer problems in those locales (such as the northwest) where partible inheritance remained viable and lower upland fertility meant less pressure to enclose commons. But it was the new enclosure of the late sixteenth and seventeenth centuries that had the more direct consequences. After about 1575 the rate of enclosure began to increase substantially, affecting some 25 percent of previously unenclosed arable and commons by the end of the seventeenth century against the sixteenth century's 2 percent. Much of it was piecemeal, taking place "piece by piece, the common land disappearing gradually, often over a long period of time." But much was general, occurring primarily in the east Midlands, England's fielden core, in the classic common-field country of Warwickshire, Leicestershire, and Northamptonshire.[31] And it was depopulating. "Seventeenth century enclosures in this region ... *were* associated with the laying down of permanent grass." That is, arable uses changed to pasture.[32] Enclosed parishes became fully "closed" to new entrants and to

small holders. "The most inflammable situations seem to have arisen in lowland villages possessing attenuated common pastures, large areas of common field, and an increasing population which leaned heavily on its common grazing land for the feeding of its animals. In such villages no one could enclose without risk of hurting others. Even when the individual encloser surrendered a proportion of his share in the common grazing to compensate for the close he had made in the arable fields, the remaining commoners might derive less benefit from their commons than before, because the enclosure divided the land into scattered bits and pieces, and forced men to keep moving their stock from one small piece of grazing to another." And when both common fields and waste were being enclosed simultaneously, "the farming routine of the community was liable to be severely disrupted by the sudden reduction in its total resources of common pasture." This was, however, much more a seventeenth- than a sixteenth-century problem.

[28] Roger B. Manning, *Village Revolts: Social Protest and Popular Disturbances in England, 1509–1640* (Oxford, 1988), 33.

[29] Thirsk, Farming Regions of England," 6.

[30] Kussmaul, *General View*, 97.

[31] J. Yelling, "Agriculture, 1500–1730," in Dodgshon and Butlin, *Historical Geography*, 184; Hindle, *State and Social Control*, 45–6; Manning, *Village Revolts*, 33.

[32] Kussmaul, *General View*, 97 (emphasis in original). For Parliamentary attempts in the 1580s and 1590s to forestall conversion of arable land to pasturage, see David Dean,

their own increase, stagnant and static, "small populations and no available positions for resident laborers." The remainder found themselves "confined to 'open' villages, preventing their encroachment upon enclosed estates."[33]

Population increase and rising food prices were also accompanied by engrossment – the tendency for wealthier farmers to increase the size of their holdings by absorbing the less viable farms of their poorer neighbors. Cambridgeshire illustrates the process. By the mid-seventeenth century, "very considerable economic division" had come about between "yeomen" and those described as "husbandmen" or "labourers." The phenomenon was particularly a feature of Cambridgeshire's arable farming regions. Poor harvests hurt the smallholder with only a limited marketable surplus and few common rights. His situation was not assisted by the practice of settling fragments of land on younger sons, which further eroded the economic viability of the formally impartible main farm. Both processes led to the immiseration of the smallholder and the transfer of land to the engrossing farmer. By the middle of the seventeenth century the small landholder had effectively disappeared from arable areas, demoted to landless cottager, or departing migrant. "The economic forces pressing such people off the land into the increasing ranks of wage-labourers were stronger than the constant endeavors made by the community to provide land for as many of its sons as possible."[34] The contrast with Cambridgeshire's pastoral and fens regions was pointed. There, "the existence of the fens and their grazing rights" meant that younger sons "could remain and still make a living from their fragments of land, without weakening the main holding."[35]

The comparatively greater viability (at least in the short term) of the Cambridgeshire smallholder or landless cottager in pastoral, forest, or fens parishes retaining extensive commons was replicated across the country at large. In many cases, these were also areas characterized by resources supportive of rural industry – mining, charcoal burning, iron smelting, cloth weaving – which acted as further encouragements to the retention of population and in-migration from elsewhere. Enclosure and engrossment in fielden England thus promoted mobility and the redistribution of surplus population away from arable areas, while the existence of both agricultural and industrial opportunity in woodpasture and fens-forest regions sustained their resident populations and attracted migrants.[36]

Law-Making and Society in Late Elizabethan England: The Parliament of England, 1584–1601 (Cambridge, 1996), 161–5, 167–8.

[33] Lachmann, *From Manor to Market*, 137; Yelling, "Agriculture," 188.

[34] Spufford, *Contrasting Communities*, 37, 87. See generally 46–119. The modern connotations of the "country cottage" inhibit the word's capacity to convey the squalor of the dwellings of the landless rural poor. "Cottage" meant a rude, flimsy structure, hastily erected on surviving wastes and commons, best thought of as a cabin or hut. Spufford draws our attention to a surviving example, "constructed of poles literally tied together with string" (49, n.19).

[35] Ibid., 165. See generally 121–67.

[36] Wrightson and Levine, *Poverty and Piety*, 4–7; Kussmaul, *General View*, 137–45; Peter Clark and David Souden, "Introduction," in Clark and Souden, ed., *Migration and Society*, 29–32.

The seventeenth century's "spatial rearrangement of economic activity over the English countryside" does much in general terms to explain the contours and timing of English emigration to the American mainland. Although, considered as a total movement, migrants to the American mainland came from all over England, particular regions at particular times can be identified as points of concentrated exodus: London, the southeast, and the southwest from the 1630s through the 1670s; East Anglia in the 1630s; the North Midlands and north in the 1670s and 1680s.[37]

London acted as a catchment area for migrants from all over the home counties (those counties bordering the city) and the East Midlands as well as from farther afield – the country population crowding the roads unable to find work in the enclosing and engrossing rural economy. Largely young, male, and unmarried, their movement was a constant of the century, one that gathered strength, particularly at mid-century, as the spatial rearrangement of the rural economy proceeded.[38] Those from the mobile rural population who went to New England went as servants and were no different, except in number, from those who went to the Chesapeake.[39] East Anglian migrants, on the other hand, were different. Both pastoral and arable farmers traveled in solidaristic kin and family groups that included young servants. These were whole households on the move.[40] Their exodus, however, lasted but a short time. East Anglians had essentially ceased migrating by the early 1640s. Their motivation was complex, as much religious as economic. Both reasons were somewhat attenuated by the 1640s, the religious by the outbreak of the English Civil War, the economic by the replacement of the 1620s' dislocations of the rural/rural-industrial economy with rising demand for agricultural labor. As their pastoral and rural-industrial emphases underwent relative atrophy, "regions becoming more arable, like East Anglia ... experienced labour shortages," and higher wages.[41] As secular population increase first stalled and then reversed after mid-century, a general growth in competition for labor resulted in expanded opportunities within their home regions for youthful farm servants, and greater opportunity for adult landless laborers to marry, establish a household, and subsist. In general, farmers' resort to service in

---

[37] For details, see Chapter 1.

[38] Clark and Souden, "Introduction," 31–2. See also David Souden, "'East, West – Home's Best'? Regional Patterns in Migration in Early Modern England," in Clark and Souden, eds., *Migration and Society*, 292–332; A. L. Beier, *Masterless Men: The Vagrancy Problem in England, 1540–1640* (London, 1985), 14–48.

[39] Richard Archer, "New England Mosaic: A Demographic Analysis for the Seventeenth Century," *William and Mary Quarterly*, 3rd Ser., 47, 4 (October 1990), 479–88; David Cressy, *Coming Over: Migration and Communication Between England and New England in the Seventeenth Century* (Cambridge and New York, 1987), 40, 42–5, 52–63.

[40] Thompson, Mobility and Migration, 114–25.

[41] Kussmaul, *General View*, 146. On East Anglia's "exceptionalism" in English internal migration history, see Beier, *Masterless Men*, 36. See also John Patten, "Patterns of Migration and Movement of Labour to Three Pre-Industrial East Anglian Towns," in Clark and Souden, eds., *Migration and Society*, 77–106.

husbandry, in decline since the second half of the sixteenth century, bottomed in the 1650s and then rebounded sharply from the l66os onward as farmers resumed annual contracting to try to guarantee themselves labor in conditions of shortage.[42] At the same time as their numbers in employment expanded absolutely, however, youthful servants began to decline as a proportion of the total farm labor force relative to day labor, suggesting that the expansion of opportunity in arable England was oriented less to youthful service than adult day labor.[43] This helps us account for the perpetuation of transatlantic youthful migration well into the late seventeenth century despite the reversal of population expansion and hence growing labor shortages. Indeed, it helps account for the character of that migration, which became younger and poorer over time as youth from the margin became a higher and higher proportion of recorded migration.[44]

The spatial rearrangement of English agriculture also played a role in the substantial southwestern migration to New England, as it did in the later migration from the same region to the Chesapeake.[45] "Regions turning from the production of grain to rearing, like the west, would have found themselves with labor surpluses, driving down local wages."[46] Surpluses were partially absorbed by rural industry, or by the expanding pastoral/ dairying economy, but out-migration was also strong, to areas (pastoral and forest) with unenclosed commons, to towns and cities, and thence, in increasingly substantial numbers, from both across the Atlantic.[47]

II. Manorialism

The broad brush of agriculture's spatial arrangement and rearrangement can be applied to more than explanation of regions of departure. The farming regions of England differed not only in their dispersion along a

---

[42] Ann Kussmaul, *Servants in Husbandry in Early Modern England* (Cambridge, 1981), 97–119.

[43] Ibid., 11–18. Wage assessment evidence gives substance to the proposition that the arable labor force became more retentive of day labor than of youthful servants. See Roberts, "Wages and Wage-Earners in England," 234–65.

[44] Russell R. Menard, "British Migration to the Chesapeake Colonies in the Seventeenth Century," in Lois Green Carr et al., editors, *Colonial Chesapeake Society* (Chapel Hill, 1988), 128.

[45] Anthony Salerno, "The Social Background of Seventeenth Century Emigration to America," *Journal of British Studies*, 19, 1 (Autumn 1979), 32–8.

[46] Kussmaul, *General View*, 146.

[47] Clark and Souden, "Introduction," 36–7. See also, generally, Clark, "Migration in England," 213–52. In *The Enforcement of English Apprenticeship: A Study in Applied Mercantilism, 1563–1642* (Cambridge, Mass., 1956), Margaret Gay Davies shows that the incidence of private prosecutions for non-observance of the Apprenticeship provisions of the Statute of Artificers was high in the western counties of Devon, Somerset, Wiltshire, Worcestershire, and Warwickshire, and that prosecutions targeted the "lonely hamlets and cottages" of the western areas' rural districts rather than "established clothing villages" (80, 110). These observations suggest that a rapid expansion of textile production was occurring in the west as rural industry absorbed surplus labor, and that the

continuum of prevalent agricultural systems but also in the social organization and political-legal culture that structured those systems. Depending on their point of origin, then, migrants carried with them distinctly differentiated political, social, and legal practices. Once again, Joan Thirsk supplies the point of departure. Her analysis suggests that what is most at issue is the relative significance across different locales and farming regions of manorialism as an institutional phenomenon in the organization of English agriculture and as a jurisdictional focus for the practice of law and governance:

> The social framework of community life in upland and lowland England was as distinct as the farming arrangements. Common fields were associated with nucleated villages in the lowlands, and with nucleated villages or, at least, small hamlets in the highlands. Nucleated villages were usually associated with a highly organized manorial community, except in those cases where an absentee landlord by his neglect allowed his estate to be carelessly administered, or where, through the sale of a manor and the parcelling of its demesnes, the whole manorial structure fell asunder ... [T]his course of events was far less usual in the lowlands ... than in the highlands.

> In the pastoral districts of England, the more typical unit of settlement was either the hamlet or the single farmstead having little working association with its neighbours except sometimes in the use of common grazing grounds. Manorial control was more difficult to exercise since the centres of settlement were many, and farming matters demanding communal regulation were so few as to afford little occasion for bringing the community together.[48]

Manors were "bundles of economic claims and legal prerogatives." Manors varied considerably in size and value, but their significance as a "basic unit" of landed power and governance in early-modern English agricultural society is not in doubt; William Hunt counts 1,100 of them in Essex alone.[49] Until the Henrician dissolution of the monasteries (1536), manors were distributed among the Crown, clergy, and lay landlords, roughly in the proportion of 10 percent Crown, 30 percent clergy, and 60 percent lay landlords (25 percent of whom were magnates – men of particular wealth and eminence). These groups shared offices and state capacities in roughly the same proportion, which meant that the Crown appointed relatively few salaried office holders, "preclud[ing] a centralized bureaucracy for tax assessment and collection or for judicial administration." In the judicial realm, for example, the sixteenth-century monarchy appointed but twelve judges to serve on the central courts of King's Bench and Common Pleas and to ride circuit to the county assizes. The Crown also appointed much larger numbers of justices of the peace in the localities, but "was limited

absorption was particularly marked outside traditional centers where collective oversight of work practices had already established a local "police" of apprenticeship.
48 Thirsk, "Farming Regions," 8.
49 William Hunt, *The Puritan Moment: The Coming of Revolution in an English County* (Cambridge, Mass., 1983), 14–15.

in practice to choosing JPs from among manor lords of each county." The Crown, then, enjoyed "minimal ability" to influence or control manorial resources or governance beyond those manors it held itself.[50]

The dissolution of the monasteries and the English reformation rendered the clergy far more dependent on the Crown, but at the same time the Crown dissipated the proceeds from monastic land sales in warfare and in patronage designed to secure the allegiance (and dependence) of the country's great magnates. Hence, the tripartite national elite structure became dual. One arm, made up of the Crown "and a court composed of dependent churchmen, magnates, merchants, and lawyers," had control of national-level institutions – "military affairs, international trade, Parliament, the English church, and the king's courts." The other consisted of "locally-based landlords," that is, the gentry. With the magnates isolated at court by Crown patronage, the gentry – by now owning most of the manors in England – came to "dominate[ ] county government … and control[ ] access to land on the local level." Still lacking a national tax-collecting and judicial bureaucracy, the Crown remained dependent "upon officials appointed from the ranks of local landlords."[51] Concentration of manorial holdings and county office in gentry hands created "tight" gentry elites in numbers of counties. Those elites then used their strategic authority at the county level to enhance further their authority in the localities. "Manorial resources and the authority to allocate those resources were concentrated in the hands of an elite organized at an intermediate level, as county-based gentry gained control over land in conflicts with peasants, clergy and Crown."[52]

This pattern of authority showed considerable variation. East Anglian counties were not given to strong manorial institutions, exhibiting instead a significant degree of manorial fragmentation and weak lordship. Most Cambridgeshire communities, for example, were "multi-manorial" with "a multiplicity of lords, many, or all, of whom were non-resident." Where manorialism was strong in East Anglia, it correlated with arable areas: single manors tended to be congruent with single communities, lords were resident, communities deferential, and manor courts the primary source of local jurisdiction. In contrast, pastoral areas exhibited weak manorialism: there manorial jurisdiction was fragmented or non-existent: communities were "accustomed to self-government" and self-direction.[53]

The same pattern was evident elsewhere. In southern (fielden) Warwickshire, for example, "the nucleated village was the typical community; society was close-knit, traditional and highly manorialised." Most of Warwickshire's greater gentry lived in the county's fielden region, where

---

[50] Lachmann, *From Manor to Market*, 68, 69, 71.
[51] Ibid., 96–7, 99.
[52] Ibid., 128.
[53] Spufford, *Contrasting Communities*, 122, 300, and see generally 58–167; Thirsk, "Farming Regions," 40–9.

they "occupied the pinnacle of a tightly knit, hierarchical society." In northern Warwickshire – known as Arden – in contrast, "the pattern of settlement ... remained that of a forest, slowly cleared and settled by individuals or families rather than by communities." Manorial jurisdiction in the Arden region was weak and fragmented, with significant lapse of manorial rights and non-resident lordship. Arden arable land was old-enclosed; the predominant agricultural practice was dairying. Land holding and wealth were more broadly dispersed than in fielden Warwickshire and society was "more open, mobile."[54] The same correlation holds in the southwest. In Wiltshire, Dorset, and Somerset, "the arable village was nucleated, tightly-packed around church and manor-house (often with a resident squire), the whole structure firmly bound by neighborhood and custom, and by powerful mechanisms of social control."[55] In East Devon's sheep-corn and arable country, too, villages were "tightly nucleated."[56] In the region's pastoral, dairying, and woodlands districts, in contrast, "there was a very different pattern of settlement. Parishes tended to be larger, the inhabitants scattered in small hamlets or isolated farms." Local culture was "likely to be more individualistic, less circumscribed by ancient custom."[57]

Somerset and Devon have both been identified as examples of gentry-ruled counties.[58] The region also shows the pronounced influence of manorial institutions, particularly in the Vale of Taunton, where "the great Manor of Taunton" was the focus for an extensive manorial jurisdiction. Elsewhere in the southwest, an even more extensive and active hierarchy of manorial institutions was to be found in Gloucestershire, where "the wide area of the Vale of Berkeley ... had been ruled over, time out of mind, by a series of mutually-related Courts of the Lord of Berkeley Castle."[59] Strong manorial institutions were not, of course, confined to the Southwest, but their importance there is noteworthy.[60]

Manorialism set the conditions of a community's relative openness to mobility. Manorial institutions' control of local land use and commoning, for example, established the practical restrictions that inhibited

---

[54] Ann Hughes, *Politics, Society and Civil War in Warwickshire, 1620–1660* (Cambridge, 1987), 4–5.

[55] Underdown, *Revel, Riot and Rebellion*, 5.

[56] Mark Stoyle, *Loyalty and Locality: Popular Allegiance in Devon During the English Civil War* (Exeter, U.K., 1994), 9.

[57] Underdown, *Revel, Riot and Rebellion*, 5. See also Stoyle, *Loyalty and Locality*, 7–13, 22–3.

[58] Underdown, *Revel, Riot and Rebellion*, 20 (Somerset); Stoyle, *Loyalty and Locality*, 18–20 (Devon).

[59] Sidney and Beatrice Webb, *English Local Government from the Revolution to the Municipal Corporations Act: The Manor and the Borough* (London, 1924), I, 40, 34; and see generally 34–44.

[60] Ibid., 44. On the sustained importance of manor courts and other local courts in Tudor and Stuart England, see Christopher Harrison, "Manor Courts and the Governance of Tudor England," and Craig Muldrew, "Rural Credit, Market Areas and Legal Institutions in the Countryside in England, 1550–1700," both in Christopher Brooks and Michael Lobban, editors, *Communities and Courts in Britain, 1150–1900* (London, 1997), at 49–51, and generally 43–60 (Harrison) and 166–77 (Muldrew).

migration into arable areas, and pushed those rendered landless by enclosure, engrossment, impartible inheritance, and population increase to depart; their weakness or practical absence in most pastoral and fens-forest areas permitted the crowding in of that mobile population that was so marked a feature of the seventeenth century. Manorialism also set the conditions of a community's political-legal organization and culture. In the vales of Yorkshire and Lincolnshire, as in the East Midlands, as in arable Cambridgeshire, as in the arable southwest, "the main centre of settlement was the village, and the lands of the township were frequently coterminous with the lands of the manor. Communal cultivation of the fields was regulated in the manorial court, and in one-manor villages the squire and his steward had undivided authority over the community." Such indeed were the characteristics thought appropriate for the governance of all of rural England. But the extent of their practice was rather more limited. Contemporaries distinguished "'the people bred amongst woods,'" where manorialism was weak, as undesirables, by nature "'more stubborn and uncivil than in the champion [fielden] countries,'" where manorialism was strong. They were "'mean people [who] live lawless, nobody to govern them, they care for nobody, having no dependence on anybody'."[61]

Such observations suggest an ideal typology of local cultures that distinguishes among them according to agricultural type and political-legal structure:

> In the nucleated villages characteristic of [fielden areas], forms of society were often deeply rooted, social classes were relatively stable and distinct, manorial customs fairly rigid, political habits comparatively orderly, and the labourer's outlook deeply imbued with the prevalent preconceptions of church and manor-house ...

> In the isolated hamlets characteristic of forest settlements, by contrast, the roots of society were often relatively shallow, the population was largely composed of a single social class, the customs of the manor were sometimes vague or difficult to enforce, the instincts of the poor were anything but law-abiding, and the authority of church and manor-house seemed remote. In these areas, labouring society frequently consisted, on one hand, of a core of indigenous peasants with sizeable holdings and a relatively high standard of living; and on the other, of an ever-growing number of very poor squatters and wanderers, often evicted from lately-enclosed fielden villages.[62]

There is no lack of evidence of systematic social and regional difference in English conceptions of legal and political order, and more generally of authority. That evidence has been framed, however, according to a distinct typology that, though rich in illustration, approaches legal variation primarily in terms of center and periphery, contrasting "central" authority with "peripheral" localism. Keith Wrightson, for example, points

---

[61] Thirsk, "Farming Regions," 33, 111.
[62] Alan Everitt, "Farm Labourers," in Thirsk, ed., *Agrarian History of England and Wales, IV, 1500–1640*, 462–3.

to both the intensification of the "infrastructural reach" of the state in seventeenth-century England, *and* the substantive refraction of its effects by an endemic "variability in contexts and options" exhibited across the country's nine thousand parishes. In localism's endemic variability, Wrightson finds no suggestion of systematic differentiation but only fragmentation: "a lack" below the gentry "of alternative conceptions of the social order"; communities swaddled "in relationships of communality and deference" and in "the localism which gave those ties force and meaning."[63] Writing of the eighteenth century, E. P. Thompson similarly situates "the customs, or habitual usages of the country," particularly the *lex loci* or "local customs of the manor," at the interface between local practice and state law. Unlike Wrightson, Thompson detects in locality a capacity to stiffen "resistance" to the center and to laws increasingly written at a distance from plebeian communities. Nevertheless, Thompson agrees with Wrightson in stressing local legality's infinite variety, its lack of pattern: it was "a lived environment comprised of practices, inherited expectations, rules which both determined limits to usages and disclosed possibilities, norms and sanctions both of law and neighborhood pressures." Its composition differed "from parish to parish according to innumerable variables."[64]

More recent research has qualified Thompson's emphases. Andy Wood's studies of customary free mining law confirm that the "localised and specific" nature of its jurisdiction "sharpened [miners'] sense of collective identity and proved to be an enabling force in the miners' resistance to their rulers' wishes." Among the lead miners of the Derbyshire peak district, it was the lead field itself that "contained and defined the miners' political culture."[65] Wood's evidence suggests, however, that free mining jurisdictions did not operate in fragmented isolation. For one thing, free mining law influenced miners in adjoining localities, and indeed percolated across regions as miners migrated from one area to another.[66] For another, all the strongholds of free mining law exhibited similar social character and legal-institutional practices. Wherever free mining claims had gained "a firm legal basis and a strong hold on male plebeian culture" – among the tin miners of the Devon and Cornwall Stannaries, coal and iron in the Forest of Dean (western Gloucestershire), coal in Kingswood (north of Bristol), lead in the Somerset Mendips and the Peak District of Derbyshire – it bred

---

[63] Wrightson, "Politics of the Parish," 26, 31; Wrightson, *English Society*, 65, and see also 40–1, 64–5, 222–8.

[64] Thompson, *Customs in Common*, 4, 97, 102. See also Keith Wrightson, Two Concepts of Order: Justices, Constables and Jurymen in Seventeenth-Century England," in Brewer and Styles, eds., *An Ungovernable People*, 21–46.

[65] Wood, "Custom, Identity and Resistance," 250–1. Andy Wood, *The Politics of Social Conflict: The Peak Country, 1520–1770* (Cambridge, 1999), 262–3.

[66] Wood, *The Politics of Social Conflict*, 262, 324, 218–48; Wood, "Custom, Identity and Resistance," 249–85. As such, migrating free miners excited antagonism from local gentry, whose manorial command of local mineral resources and local social authority was threatened by free mining law's institutional and cultural intrusions.

"senses of rights and liberties" rooted in its distinctive practices and in the "collective political engagement against social superiors" that protection of those practices necessitated.[67] The west country Stannaries, institutionally the most highly developed example of free mining law in action (a distinct court system, a distinct representative body to legislate for the industry, exemption from county and national taxation, the right to muster their own militias), have been described as "virtually a self-governing state within the state." In Devon, "county authorities had no jurisdiction over the Stannaries … the tinners emphasized their independence from local society by referring to all other men as 'foreigners'."[68] In the Peak District, mining law was administered through barmote courts distinct from the prevailing institutional patterns of local governance, allowing the district's miners to enjoy "unusual freedoms" that distinguished them "as an identifiable collectivity" within the region. "Free mining liberated the miners from the discipline of an agrarian manorialism while barmote law institutionalized and legitimated their collective independence."[69] The Forest of Dean's Mine Law courts exercised a similar distinct jurisdiction, allowing the region's coal miners to enjoy a degree of independence not unlike that of the Peak's lead miners. In the Mendips, local manorial lords enjoyed somewhat greater influence over the region's Minery Courts than was the case in administration of mining law elsewhere, but the courts nevertheless pursued a distinct and autonomous industrial jurisdiction over all matters arising "'as well between the lord of the soile and workmen as between workmen and workmen.'"[70]

If local legalities thus exhibited patterns that belie endemic "difference" – of which free mining jurisdictions stand as perhaps the clearest but by no means the only example – the imagined uniformities of the center displayed in fact and practice no lesser capacity for distinct contingencies. Historians have underscored the rootedness of customary legalities in the specificities of place in part to contrast it with the generality of common law, "an almost mystical intellectual system which was a central part of the ideology of the political nation,"[71] and indeed, such a contrast was a constant of seventeenth-century legal culture. But the very necessities of its assertion also signify uniformity's limits. Certainly England was dense in institutions that exhibited the common law as national custom.[72] Measured

---

[67] Wood, *Politics of Social Conflict*, 144.

[68] Stoyle, *Loyalty and Locality*, 17.

[69] Wood, *Politics of Social Conflict*, 143.

[70] Wood, "Custom, Identity and Resistance," 261. In "Wages and Wage-Earners in England," 123, Michael Roberts notes that Somerset magistrates excluded wages in the Mendip coal and lead mines from assessment, which suggests they lacked jurisdiction over the industry.

[71] James Sharpe, "The People and the Law," in Reay, ed., *Popular Culture in Seventeenth-Century England*, 244.

[72] See, for example, Alan Macfarlane, *The Justice and the Mare's Ale: Law and Disorder in Seventeenth-Century England* (Oxford, 1981), 196–9; Sharpe, "The People and the Law," 244–70.

by the availability of legal process, by litigation rates, or by the expansion in the numbers of lawyers, "law, whether it was serving to socialise, to punish, to harass, to protect private property and private interests, or to maintain the political and economic status quo, was of central importance in the way in which people went about their everyday lives."[73] This notwithstanding, there was nothing unitary about English law as a cultural field.[74] Critics labeled it "dispersed and uncertain," unsystematic and unimproved, hence worrisomely uncivilized, "barbaric." Sir Edward Coke's nationalizing project of "writing English law" was the product of "persistent awareness" of systematized rivals "against which English law had to defend and define itself." I have already noted the importance at the center itself of systems of law rival to common law, as in civil or Roman law. There, too, existed other potent claims to determinative national authority rival to those of common-law advocates and judges: executive ascendancy, Crown prerogative (in domestic affairs as well as external), sheer monarchic will. Like so many contemporary English nationalisms, Coke's passion for national-legal consolidation "had a double-face … turn[ing] inward to find out and eliminate those practices and those institutions that failed to reflect back its own unitary image" as well as outward "to declare its defining difference" as system and ideology from competing systems and ideologies.[75]

Institutions like free mining law declare some of the clearer manifestations of English law's inner polyphony, its diverse institutions and practices. A finer-grained polyphony in English legal culture was also recorded in the same chorographic perambulations that detailed the diversity of the country's regions and topography. In their accounts of the distribution of authority, English chorographers depicted no routines of transcendent central influence, royal or otherwise, but instead "words and images, caught in a complex and mutually self-constituting exchange between individual authors, the communities to which they belong, and the land they represent." Chorographic accounts displayed authority "not centered but dispersed."[76] Place had geographical but also legal-institutional particularity, in common law no less than *lex loci*. Take, for example, the work of the Kent Justice of the Peace William Lambarde, who in the 1570s and '80s wrote about the county in both the chorographic idiom – his *Perambulation*

---

73 Sharpe, "The People and the Law," 264–5.
74 As Wilfrid Prest puts it, "It is straining language to speak of an early modern English legal *system*. There was little thought out or coherent about that fragmented chaos of overlapping (and frequently conflicting) jurisdictions – national, regional and local courts, ecclesiastical and secular courts, courts occasional and permanent, courts dispensing English common law, Roman civil law, canon law and a bewildering variety of local customary law, courts of considerable antiquity and courts newly erected or asserted, courts swamped with business and courts moribund for lack of suitors." Wilfrid R. Prest, "Lawyers," in Wilfrid R. Prest, editor, *The Professions in Early Modern England* (London, 1987), 64–5 (emphasis in original). See also George Lee Haskins, *Law and Authority in Early Massachusetts: A Study in Tradition and Design* (New York, 1960), 163–4.
75 Helgerson, *Forms of Nationhood*, 71.
76 Ibid., 124.

of Kent (1576) was the first of the histories of English counties – and the legal,
discoursing on the peculiarities of Kentish gavelkind in his *Perambulation*,
and more generally using Kentish materials as the basis for his equally
classic *Eirenarcha* (on the office of the justice of the peace) and other volumes on the duties of officers of local government.[77] Justices in general
"established conventions and customs to meet local needs." The exemplary
hostility of justices in the localities toward the Caroline *Book of Orders* of
1630–1, in which the Privy Council attempted to require identical forms
of enforcement of social legislation to be practiced in every county, has
been described as resistance to "Charles's semi-conscious assault on local
autonomy and his insistence on obedience to the letter of the statute law."[78]
But such hostility, or at least studied indifference, was not novel.[79]

While assuredly an essential element of the "great tradition" of supra-
local elite culture and rule, then, law was no great tradition monopoly –
except, perhaps, in its ritual presentations.[80] Law, first, was "part of *popular*
culture, at least for those plebeian strata above the labouring poor ... something which people used and participated in." Even among the labouring
poor, "popular consciousness was capable of forming and articulating its
own opinions on the nature of the rule of law."[81] More important, though

---

[77] William Lambarde, *Eirenarcha: or of The Office of the Iustices of Peace* (London, 1581); William
Lambarde, *The Duties of Constables, Borsholders, Tythingmen, and such other lowe Ministers of
the Peace* (1582). See Conyers Read, editor, *William Lambarde and Local Government: His
"Ephemeris" and Twenty-Nine Charges to Juries and Commissions* (Ithaca, N.Y., 1962). Read
argues that Lambarde's *Eirenarcha* was wholly based on Lambarde's experience as a justice in Kent, and that his focus in that office was wholly local (7–8, 60). But see also David
S. Shields, "The Genius of Ancient Britain," in Peter C. Mancall, editor, *The Atlantic World
and Virginia, 1550–1624* (Chapel Hill, 2007), 500, who argues that in *Eirenarcha*, no less
than in his collection of pre-Norman Saxon laws, *Archaionomia* (1568), or his *Archeion: Or
a Discourse upon the High Courts of Justice in England* (1591), Lambarde's intent was to use
local traces to elaborate the ancient Anglo-Saxon origins of English institutions and
liberties. On Lambarde as chorographer, see Helgerson, *Forms of Nationhood*, 136–8.

[78] John Morrill, *Revolt in the Provinces: The People of England and the Tragedies of War, 1630–1648*
(London, 1999), 35. See also Henrik Langelüddecke, "Law and Order in Seventeenth-
Century England: The Organization of Local Administration during the Personal Rule
of Charles I," *Law and History Review*, 15, 1 (Spring 1997), 49–76. As Lawrence Stone
put it in *The Causes of the English Revolution, 1529–1642* (London, 1972), 106: "When an
Englishman in the early seventeenth century said 'my country' he meant 'my county'.
What we see in the half century before the civil war is the growth of an emotional sense
of loyalty to the local community, and also of institutional arrangements to give that
sentiment force. The county evolved as a coherent political and social community, with
reference to – and potentially in rivalry with – both other counties and the central executive and its local agents."

[79] Davies, *The Enforcement of English Apprenticeship*, 220–8, 230–9.

[80] The most evocative account of the latter remains Douglas Hay's exploration of the cultural significance of eighteenth-century criminal law. See his "Property, Authority and
the Criminal Law," in Douglas Hay et al., *Albion's Fatal Tree: Crime and Society in Eighteenth-
Century England* (New York, 1975), 17–63. Hay's wider argument also underscores how, by
the early eighteenth century, law *was* becoming a "great tradition" monopoly.

[81] Sharpe, "The People and the Law," 262 (emphasis added), 261.

the discursive singularity "law" implied unity in origin and meaning, a received ideology that cemented consensus, the existence of differentiated social opinions about law coupled with the clear spatial variation of local legalities can also be taken to indicate the existence of quite distinct conceptions of what "law" actually was. Hence, not only were distinct "conceptions of legality, order and authority ... articulated by different social groups," but those distinct conceptions actually reflected real differences.[82]

Analysis of difference beyond the simple polarity of central state versus local custom is made possible by further deployment of the pastoral-arable (Thirsk-Everitt) thesis. The thesis serves as foundation for the proposition that localities in England manifested not limitless variety but rather a more systematic variation within the bounds of a political geography substantially influenced by regional location.

English historians have enjoyed some success in invoking the idea of systematic variation in agrarian culture to explain quite specific aspects of seventeenth-century political behavior. Take for example David Underdown's analysis of local and regional variation in patterns of popular allegiance during the English Civil War. Refining histories of allegiance that emphasized unrefracted "provincial" or "county" identities existing in tension and rivalry with the "central" state,[83] Underdown has proposed that contrasts in allegiance were rooted in "the earlier emergence of two quite different constellations of social, political and cultural forces" that gave birth to polar viewpoints on contemporary society, one "relatively stable and reciprocally paternalistic and deferential" predictive of popular engagement in pro-royalist politics, the other "more unstable, less harmonious, more individualistic" and predictive of pro-parliamentarian politics. Those constellations varied according to regional and subregional geography, the former principally embedded in arable areas, the latter in woodpasture, rural-industrial regions.[84]

Underdown's argument has tempted the label of "ecological determinism,"[85] and indeed it suffers from a number of problems. First, though premised on an initial recognition of socioeconomic change during the first half of the seventeenth century, the argument is quite static: it is an account of the effects of exogenous change according to its reception within ecologically distinct areas, those characterized by pastoral land use and those by arable. But we know that such areas were themselves undergoing endogenous transformation, the frontiers of farming regions altering substantially across the course of the century.[86] What Underdown describes

---

[82] Wood, "Custom, Identity and Resistance," 250.

[83] For example Stone, *Causes of the English Revolution*, 106; Morrill, *Revolt in the Provinces*, 24–74.

[84] Underdown, *Revel, Riot and Rebellion*, 40–1.

[85] Wrightson and Levine, *Poverty and Piety*, 215. See also John Morrill, "The Ecology of Allegiance in the English Revolution," *Journal of British Studies*, 26, 4 (October 1987), 451–67. For a more sympathetic critique, see Stoyle, *Loyalty and Locality*, 3–6, 245–6.

[86] Kussmaul, *General View*, 76–102.

may have been less the consequence of change refracted by stable ecological identifications than change in the regions themselves, both in their
organization and in their prevailing ecology. Second, the Civil War was
in itself a major supervening political event, as such likely to provoke allegiance patterns that transcended as much as reproduced the influence of
local cultural variation. Exemplary variation may be better displayed in
matters where, comparatively, rather less is at stake.[87]

A more recent approach to regional variation developed by Margaret
Somers reemphasizes the Thirsk-Everitt model's acknowledgment of institutional, and not simply ecological, variation. Somers' historical sociology of
English law proposes the existence of distinct modes of legal consciousness
arising from "types" of legal culture associated with ecologically distinct
regions. The population of pastoral and rural-industrial regions tended to
manifest a plebeian consciousness of citizenship rights and obligations as
"freeborn Englishmen" entitled to participate in law-making processes. The
population of arable regions tended to manifest a consciousness of right-
lessness and deference. "Whereas the working population in the pastoral
regions looked to the law to guarantee their rights, the working peoples of
the arable regions feared the law as a form of social control." Somers attributes variation to "regional differences in public spheres," that is, in modes
and ideologies of governance. "In the pastoral regions, the public sphere
encompassed *local village* governance, which encouraged *popular* participation; in the arable regions, governance was *countywide* and wealthy land-
lord-elites *monopolized* participation."[88] The strength of manorial lordship
typical of arable regions created private spheres of power and "a hierarchical chain of relationships." The bulk of the rural population – husbandmen and laboring poor – lived and worked "under the direct political and
residential supervision of their yeoman-farmer employers and gentry landlords." Lacking autonomy, they were "unable to take advantage of public
participatory rights and, despite the legal freedom granted by public law,
were subordinated anew through the legal process." In pastoral communities, in contrast, the characteristic weakness or absence of manorialism
and hence of powerful provincial elites translated into a greater degree of
local autonomy. Communities were more solidaristic, family cohesion was
higher, officeholders closer to the people. These institutional conditions

---

[87] John Morrill, for example, stresses the supervening sufficiency of religious division as
an explanation of allegiance patterns in the English Civil War. See his "The Ecology of
Allegiance," 462–7. Mark Stoyle, too, affirms that conclusion. See his *Loyalty and Locality*,
254–5.

[88] Margaret R. Somers, "Citizenship and the Place of the Public Sphere: Law, Community
and Political Culture in the Transition to Democracy," *American Sociological Review*, 58,
5 (October 1993), 594 (emphases in original). See also Margaret R. Somers, "Rights,
Relationality and Membership: Rethinking the Making and Meaning of Citizenship,"
Law & Social Inquiry, 19, 1 (1994), 97–9; Mark Goldie, "The Unacknowledged
Republic: Officeholding in Early Modern England," in Tim Harris, editor, *The Politics of
The Excluded, c. 1500–1850* (Basingstoke, Hants., and New York, 2001), 153–94.

created a stronger basis for association and participation, for a viable local civic sphere.[89]

III. Destinations

Both conceptually, and in some important and concrete particulars, these hypotheses are relevant to our understanding of the legal cultures that English migrants established on the early North American mainland. The migrant streams that fed New England in the 1620s and 1630s and the Delaware Valley after 1675, for example, had clear "pastoral" resonances through their roots in, respectively, East Anglia and the Pennine North. The legal cultures established in the regions of settlement were manifestly influenced by the regions of departure. Migration to the Chesapeake had more substantial elite connection to the arable-manorial South and Southwest, and many Chesapeake migrants were culled from the displaced population of formerly arable regions. These characteristics are sufficient to mark Chesapeake legal culture as, potentially, quite distinct from that of New England and the Delaware Valley.

The significance of English regional variation to the study of American settlement is not a new discovery,[90] but its potential was not fully revealed until the publication of David Hackett Fischer's *Albion's Seed*, which offered an intriguing argument for the long-term persistence in mainland America of four distinct regional cultures, each founded on a distinctive migration of people and folkways from a particular region of the British Isles. "Britain," Fischer tells us, is not a homogenous cultural entity: "British" migrants had far less in common as a group than they did as members of four distinct groups, each journeying from a specifiable region of origin to a distinct location on the North American mainland, each carrying specifiable folkways, each planting those folkways on arrival as seeds that would sprout as American ways of living.[91]

Critics have called Fischer's account "procrustean," implying that the distinctive results he claims rely upon a pulling and reshaping of cultural circumstances at both ends of the migrations he describes. They dismiss Fischer's representation of the geography of pertinent British regions – "East Anglia," "Wessex," "North Britain" – as idiosyncratic, even

---

[89] Somers, "Citizenship and the Place of the Public Sphere," 601; Somers, "Rights, Relationality and Membership," 97. See also Wrightson, *English Society*, 171–3; Thirsk, "Farming Regions," 109–12; and in general Joan Thirsk, *The Rural Economy of England: Selected Essays* (London, 1984).

[90] See, for example, T. H. Breen, "Persistent Localism: English Social Change and the Shaping of New England Institutions," *William and Mary Quarterly*, 3rd Ser., 32, 1 (January 1975), 3–28. George Lee Haskins remarked in 1960 that "English life and culture in the seventeenth century presented no single pattern. Farming practices, architectural styles, town and rural government, even speech, often differed from county to county." *Law and Authority*, 163.

[91] Fischer, *Albion's Seed*, 6–7.

arbitrary; adjusted to fit post hoc conceptual needs rather than conform-
ing to accepted understandings. They hold his analysis of regional folkways imprecise, lumping generalities indiscriminately with specificities in
a fashion that clouds rather than clarifies the extent of difference or sameness among the regional cultures whose movements are under examination. His classifications and descriptions of habit, belief, and behavior owe
far too much to the habits of a prominent few, far too little to the mass of
undeniably humble migrants.[92]

Criticism notwithstanding, *Albion's Seed* has also been praised as "the
most sustained and compelling case yet made for the importance of metropolitan cultural inheritances in the formation of colonial American
regional cultures" and for its disaggregation of a spuriously homogenous
"metropolitan culture" into heterogenous regional parts. In particular,
Fischer has been credited for underlining the instrumental role of core
groups (in his terms "elites") in cultural transmission and persistence.
"Small groups dominate every cultural system," Fischer writes, "by controlling institutions and processes, so that they become the 'governors'
in both a political and a mechanical sense." Such cultural ascendancy is
in no sense unchallengeable: "Every culture might be seen as a system of
bargaining, in which elites maintain their hegemony by concessions to
other groups." But bargaining does not disrupt elite ascendancy. Elites are
active; they shape processes and contexts. Companion groups are reactive;
they experience processes and contexts. Migrations are inevitably plural,
but "those who were most strategically situated among the first arrivals in
every region exerted a defining influence in the 'crystallization' of colonial
American cultures."[93]

Fischer's emphasis on elites parries much of the critique of his analysis's
insufficiencies and idiosyncrasies. To the critics, what is problematic about

---

[92] Virginia Anderson attacks Fischer's "procrustean" ways. See "Forum: *Albion's Seed: Four
British Folkways in America* – A Symposium," *William and Mary Quarterly*, 3rd Ser., 48, 2
(April 1991), 223–59, at 235. Fischer's response to critics appears in "*Albion* and the
Critics: Further Evidence and Reflection," in "Forum: *Albion's Seed*," 260–308, at 264–74.
The critics are a little cavalier in their denunciations of Fischer's regional designa-
tions. Take "Wessex" for example. Fischer sees Wessex encompassing the counties of
Wiltshire, Dorset, Somerset, Gloucestershire, Devon, Hampshire, Berkshire, West
Sussex, West Surrey, Oxfordshire, and Buckinghamshire. In *Wessex to AD 1000* (London,
1993), 1, Barry Cunliffe describes "Wessex" as congruent with the present-day counties
of Wiltshire, Dorset, Somerset, (Southern) Gloucestershire, Hampshire, and Berkshire.
Although thus truncating somewhat Fischer's eastern and northeastern quadrant,
Cunliffe also notes that Wessex "is not a natural geographical entity," that its physical
geography stretches eastward as far as the Weald (the borders of Surry and Sussex) and
north to the Thames Valley (southern Oxfordshire), and that its precise boundaries are
indefinite enough as to comprise "Central Southern England."

[93] Fischer, *Albion's Seed*, 896. The "crystallization" statement is Jack Greene's. See
"Forum: Albion's Seed," 230. For additional commentary on Fischer's model, see
David Eltis, Philip Morgan, and David Richardson, "Agency and Diaspora in Atlantic
History: Reassessing the African Contribution to Rice Cultivation in the Americas,"
American Historical Review, 112, 5 (December 2007), 1329–31.

the regional migrations that Fischer describes is that they are rather less distinctive than he allows, and indeed quickly become minorities within the regions they settle. The "East Anglian" migration to New England was in fact a plurality, the size of which depends on the elasticity of one's definition of the extent of East Anglia. Outside its East Anglian core, the Great Migration to New England drew on wide swathes of southern and western England, where it overlapped with the contemporary movement of emigrants to the Chesapeake. Fischer identifies Chesapeake migrants primarily with the English southwest, but Chesapeake migrants came from a broader range of English regions, with the important qualification that very few originated in East Anglia.[94] The first migration to the Delaware Valley differed from earlier seventeenth-century movements in coming predominantly from the North of England, but it also contained substantial Welsh and Southern contingents. More important, within fifty years of the first Quaker migration, German and Irish migrants were appearing in the Delaware Valley in substantial numbers. By the mid-eighteenth century, more than half of Pennsylvania's population was of German, not British (and far less "North" British) origin.[95]

To see the mass of migrants moving into any one of these mainland regions as the means of carrying a sustained distinctive set of regionally homogenous cultural habits thus seems to belie the empirical reality of culturally plural movements. One may, however, explain the persistence of certain dominant cultural patterns in those regions, notwithstanding the plurality of backgrounds to migrant movements, by concentrating on Fischer's "elites," the cohesive core groups that occupied positions of social and cultural significance.

It is important not to get carried away with the term "elite." One must, for example, distinguish settler core groups from the elite negotiators and beneficiaries of the Crown patents that gave mainland colonizing its macro-level authority structures. Although there were exceptions, most of those who sought Crown patents were absentees from the actual process of settlement. That is, none of the British migrant streams reproduced anything like the full social hierarchy of contemporary Britain. Nor did the German or Irish migrations represent anything approaching a full cross-section of the social hierarchy pertaining to those points of origin. Migrant "elites" were generally unremarkable in their social origins, their status a product of their standing relative to the overwhelming modesty of each migration's social composition. The social range of the East Anglian core of the Puritan migration to New England, for example, has been described as predominantly that of the "middling strata" of English society, the topmost being county gentry like John Winthrop – people reasonably prominent

---

94 "Forum: Albion's Seed,"232–3, 239–43; Archer, "New England Mosaic," 483; Fischer, *Albion's Seed*, 31–6, 236–41.

95 Fischer, *Albion's Seed*, 438–45. On the regional composition of British migrations to the Delaware Valley, as well as to New England and the Chesapeake, see Chapter 1.

on a local or regional scale in Britain, but nationally insignificant – while the mass were yeomen, husbandmen, merchants and traders, artisans and craftsmen, and their households. Those who were from outside the East Anglian core are also likely to have been drawn predominantly from the low end of the social order – overwhelmingly single, youthful, and mobile servant labor. They were thus doubly removed from positions of social influence; by their humble status and by their regional origin.[96] They were in no sense destitute; the social distance between New England's migrant elites and its bottom sills was relatively modest. Nevertheless, the social distance was sufficient to allow one to identify a core group role in the transmission of key aspects of social and cultural ordering.[97]

In the Chesapeake a different, more hierarchical, pattern prevailed. British migration to Maryland and Virginia included a much larger number of young people of humble social standing than in the New England case, fewer middling commoners, and also a more pronouncedly established, even aristocratic, upper caste. The imprint of the latter did not last undiluted. "Efforts to promote a rigidly-stratified society" failed in both Chesapeake colonies. The composition of the local elites that eventually emerged reflected the presence of minor gentry and merchant-traders who did not differ significantly in social standing from the leaders of the Puritan migration to New England. Nevertheless, the migration's upper-caste core shared tighter regional origins in the English southwest than did the mass, and embraced political, social, and cultural values that more

[96] Those of New England's migrating servants who originated within the East Anglian core region traveled largely as members of a pre-established local social structure – one of established households migrating from the same locale as that in which the servants had their origins. Those originating in other regions of England had traveled greater distances and migrated unattached. Within the servant migration to New England, one thus observes two patterns well known from studies of servitude in England – the localized "putting-out" of children into neighboring families, and the longer-distance migrations of "masterless" adolescents and young adults forced into greater mobility by the inability of their localities to absorb them. On the contrast between East Anglian and other servants, see Thompson, *Mobility and Migration*, 114–25, 225. On the crisis of adolescent absorption in the first half of the seventeenth century, see Kussmaul, *Servants in Husbandry*, 97–103. Servant migration to the Chesapeake was almost wholly of the second sort. Servant migration to the Delaware Valley, in contrast, was originally very similar to New England's.

[97] This is suggested in the formation of the *Mayflower* compact, which, as Christopher Hill has noted, was drawn up by 'the people' (forty-one male adults) to form themselves into a 'body politic,' but which excluded youthful servants and 'strangers received at London' who had given vent to 'mutinous speeches as if there were now no authority over them.' Servants traveling within household groups could be construed as having virtual representation among the people through the person of their head of household. "Strangers" (servants and others who were unattached to households) could not be so construed and were deliberately excluded. See Christopher Hill, *Liberty against the Law: Some Seventeenth-Century Controversies* (London, 1996), 146, 247. One might observe that in the moment of their migration, these East Anglian Puritans encountered precisely that (the threat of social disorder embodied in unruly "masterless" adolescents) which they deemed emblematic of England's wickedness.

closely resembled the archetypes of English county elites than the self-consciously dissenting core group of the Puritan migration.[98]

Like New England's migration, the original movement to the Delaware Valley was one of self-conscious dissenters. Also like New England's migration, the movement had a strongly defined regional core, a pronounced familial character, and a flattened social structure. Indeed, of the three migration streams on which I have concentrated, that to the Delaware Valley, at least in its earliest years, was, socially, the most homogenous. "Pennsylvania's immigrants tended to be men and women of humble origin, who came from the lower middling ranks of English society." Few called themselves yeomen, almost none gentlemen. They were husbandmen, craftsmen, small traders, and merchants. The region's elites reflected this initial absence of social differentiation. "A remarkably large proportion were of humble rank – country artisans, petty traders, tenant farmers, servants and laborers."[99] Unlike the Chesapeake colonies, these were not people with pre-established social authority or resources to mobilize. More like New England, the Delaware Valley's local elites were drawn from a core group of early arrivals sharing a particular ideocultural tradition and common regional background.[100] At the same time, unlike New England, it was a core group whose social environment underwent quite rapid change. By 1720, Delaware Valley inhabitants were dividing and subdividing along national, linguistic, and denominational, as well as socioeconomic, lines.[101] What was particularly important about the region, which by the mid-eighteenth century was the most heterogeneous of the three areas of settlement, however, is that its humble elite of early Quaker arrivals "established the rules of engagement among different ethnic groups." It was the values of the first settlers that "remained embedded in the institutional structure of this region even as they became a minority of the population."[102]

In the Delaware Valley, then, as elsewhere on the mainland, those who were to become colonial "elites" were elites in part by default, selected by the process of migration itself, by who did not come as well as by who did. To the extent that elites represented a transported block of knowledge, relationships, and ascendancies, these were local and regional knowledges,

---

[98] James P. Horn, *Adapting to a New World: English Society in the Seventeenth-Century Chesapeake* (Chapel Hill, 1994), 28, 147–8, 379–80, 427–9; Warren Billings, "The Transfer of English Law to Virginia, 1606–1650," in K. R. Andrews et al., eds., *The Westward Enterprise: English Activities in Ireland, the Atlantic and America, 1480–1650* (Liverpool, 1978), 219–20. Fischer, *Albion's Seed,* 207–25.

[99] Fischer, *Albion's Seed,* 434, 436, 464–5. See also James T. Lemon, *The Best Poor Man's Country: A Geographical Study of Early Southeastern Pennsylvania* (Baltimore, 1972), 1–41; Barry Levy, *Quakers and the American Family: British Settlement in the Delaware Valley* (New York, 1988), 25–52.

[100] Fischer, *Albion's Seed,* 419–55.

[101] For details of German immigration into the Delaware Valley, and its impact, see Aaron Spencer Fogleman, *Hopeful Journeys: German Immigration, Settlement, and Political Culture in Colonial America, 1717–1775* (Philadelphia, 1996).

[102] Fischer, "Albion and the Critics," 289.

relationships, and ascendancies, not national. This served community leaders well; the survival of their local cohesions were real assets in colonial regions in which, by dint of migration from a diversity of points of origin, many in the colonial population were strangers to each other, thrown together anew. It also meant that the institutions, ideas, customs, and folkways upon which they relied to establish their rules of engagement with each other were expressions of, or refracted through, disparate local cultures.

Of all the means to the establishment of such "rules of engagement," not only for the Delaware Valley, but also for New England and the Chesapeake, few had more import than law.[103] We have seen that processes of European colonial expansion had always been framed in a discourse of legalities, both as justification and general legitimation, and in the more specific matter of designing *dominium* and establishing jurisdiction – procedures for the occupation of territory, the marginalization of its inhabitants, and the organization and government of new settler populations. Particularly at the second level, effectivity was built on the assumption that European inhabitants possessed legal consciousness, placing considerable stress on legal institutions and offices as manifestations of public authority.[104] More generally, in the "order ways" of each region of settlement, authority was manifested as a legal phenomenon. Considered ideologically, as an essential value in itself, as "the rule of law," law was not the only nor necessarily even the most important mode of authorizing behavior. Considered as a means to implement cultural authority, however, law and legal institutions had considerable potency.[105]

Colonizing no more exhibited a common national legal culture in migration than any other facet of Albion's social seeding.[106] Still, English regional diversity lends itself to a degree of typologizing in this matter that,

---

[103] See generally David Thomas Konig, *Law and Society in Puritan Massachusetts: Essex County, 1629–1692* (Chapel Hill, 1979); Cornelia Hughes Dayton, *Women Before the Bar: Gender, Law, and Society in Connecticut, 1639–1789* (Chapel Hill, 1995); William M. Offutt, Jr., *Of "Good Laws" and "Good Men": Law and Society in the Delaware Valley, 1680–1710* (Urbana, Ill., 1995).

[104] See Chapters 3 and 4; James Muldoon, "Discovery, Grant, Charter, Conquest or Purchase: John Adams on the Legal Basis for English Possession of North America," in Christopher L. Tomlins and Bruce H. Mann, editors, *The Many Legalities of Early America* (Chapel Hill, 2001); Haskins, *Law and Authority*, 1–8; A. G. Roeber, *Faithful Magistrates and Republican Lawyers: Creators of Virginia Legal Culture, 1680–1810* (Chapel Hill, 1981); Offutt, *Of "Good Laws" and "Good Men,"* particularly 22–4; Konig, *Law and Society in Puritan Massachusetts,* particularly xii–xiii.

[105] In *Law, Labor and Ideology in the Early American Republic* (Cambridge and New York, 1993), xiii–xiv, I developed the concept of law as "a modality of rule" to underline the social and cultural particularities inherent in *legal* modes of authorizing. See also Peter Goodrich, *Languages of Law: From Logics of Memory to Nomadic Masks* (London, 1990), vii–viii, 1–52.

[106] The classic statement of the issue is of course Julius Goebel's. See his "King's Law and Local Custom in Seventeenth Century New England," *Columbia Law Review,* 31, 3 (1931), 416–48. Haskins writes, "under the first Stuarts ... the pattern of English law, like that of so much else in that age, was one of great diversity." *Law and Authority,* 164.

in turn, suggests useful generalization. David Grayson Allen's excavation of the English roots of five early Massachusetts towns warns that "regional and subregional variations in England produced a complicated social fabric." While each of the two broad zones of the Thirsk-Everitt model "had its own agricultural practices, social structure, and local customs," within them "regional specialization in agriculture and certain distinctive features of community life were increasing in the sixteenth and seventeenth centuries," accentuating subregional variation.[107] Yet both at the general conceptual level and in some important particulars, the relevance of the Thirsk-Everitt model and the historical sociology of law built on it remain readily apparent to our understanding of the legal cultures of the early North American mainland.

New England

New England's local institutions in the seventeenth century gave particular emphasis to the town community as the unit of collective proprietorship, settlement, land distribution, and local governance.[108] Initially varying according to "regional differences in the mother country," local institutions quickly developed in the direction of common individual freehold, partible inheritance, and pastoral agriculture. Their practices also illustrated "the peculiar ease" with which participatory local government evolved in the region. In Rowley, Massachusetts, settlers from Rowley in Yorkshire replicated the manorial society that they had left – a stable, static, agrarian community, dominated by open-field farming, cloth-making, and a "tightly defined" social structure. Rowley settlers were slow to divide the town's land; when they did so, their distributions relative to neighboring communities were made in small parcels that – reflecting the community's stratification – were quite unequal in extent. Rowley's legal culture reflected its manorial roots, with dense local bylaws passed by common consent regulating common agricultural practice and widespread office holding to oversee enforcement. But this was not quite an exact replication. Although Rowley settlers had brought manorial habit with them, they had not brought the manor itself, with its lord and his manorial rights, with its courts leet (to try petty offenses) and baron (to enact bylaws) presided over by manor lord or steward. These institutions were discarded in Massachusetts, resulting in a structure of participatory decision making founded on town meeting and town officers. In Massachusetts, Rowley's manorialism was a decapitated version of the original.[109]

---

[107] David Grayson Allen, *In English Ways: The Movement of Societies and the Transferal of English Local Law and Custom to Massachusetts Bay in the Seventeenth Century* (Chapel Hill, 1981), 14, 18. See also Davie, "Chalk and Cheese?" 2–25.

[108] G. B. Warden, "Law Reform in England and New England, 1620–1660," *William and Mary Quarterly*, 3rd Ser., 35, 4 (October 1978), 674.

[109] Allen, *In English Ways*, xv, 21, 210, and generally 19–54.

Hingham is likewise informative. Geographically, Hingham was central Norfolk, abutting both woodpasture and arable. Its inhabitants' lives followed a pattern of "vulnerable subsistence," dependent upon dairying, corn-livestock rearing, and cloth-making. With manorialism in this area in desuetude, open-field agriculture was in decline with scattered enclosures amid woods. Hingham, Massachusetts reproduced a non-manorial structure, centered on an explicit notion of corporate "townsmanship," collective responsibility, relative social and economic equality, and an explicit web of connection between community office holding and family.[110]

Allen's studies of Newbury, Ipswich, and Watertown all demonstrate similar local variation. What is particularly important about them collectively, however, is their common illustration of the striking ease with which, as distinct from contemporary England, local government "by consent" could evolve in Massachusetts. Allen sees this as a matter of distinction, not difference. "People in Stuart England were not incapable of directing their own lives. The most illuminating example is Hingham, where in both the English parish and the New England town the approval of the town meeting was an essential element of government." Self-government, in short, developed naturally in lordless environments, whether these were in old England or new. The principal distinction "new" England offered was greater possibility, given the absence of extremes of riches and poverty, given near complete local control insulated from outside authority, "for working out the long-term implications of government by consent."[111] In New England, however, this distinction in opportunity was conditioned by an institutional distinction. New England's lordlessness was complete.

The Chesapeake

If early Massachusetts' local legal culture emphasized the town, that of the Chesapeake focused, by the 1630s, on the county.[112] Counties and county courts existed in both Virginia and Massachusetts, established in Virginia in 1634 and in Massachusetts in 1643. In Massachusetts, the county courts and county officers developed roles of considerable institutional importance alongside the self-governing towns.[113] In the Chesapeake, in contrast,

[110] Ibid., 57, 70, and generally 55–81.

[111] Ibid., 210–11, 212, and generally 205–22. See also William Cronon, *Changes in the Land: Indians, Colonists, and the Ecology of New England* (New York, 1983), 70–81; Sumner Chilton Powell, *Puritan Village: The Formation of a New England Town* (Middletown, Conn., 1964), 140–1; Breen, "Persistent Localism," 18–28. On the significance of New England's unique civic order, see Stephen Innes, *Creating the Commonwealth: The Economic Culture of Puritan New England* (New York, 1995), 9.

[112] See generally Lois Green Carr, "The Foundations of Social Order: Local Government in Colonial Maryland," and Robert Wheeler, "The County Court in Colonial Virginia," both in Bruce C. Daniels, editor, *Town and County: Essays on the Structure of Local Government in the American Colonies* (Middletown, Conn., 1978), 72–110, 111–33.

[113] For contrasting assessments of the relative strengths of county and town institutions in Massachusetts, see David Thomas Konig, "English Legal Change and the Origins of

formal legal culture and local government centered not on the original "citties" – except insofar as they were redefined as counties[114] – but almost exclusively on the county court. One finds in the Chesapeake little of the density of local communal organization visible in Massachusetts. The only institution with governmental responsibilities affecting individual settler households apart from the county and its officers was the parish vestry, which itself was intimately interwoven with the structure of county-level governmental power.[115]

In part the dominance of the county in the Chesapeake is attributable to settlement patterns that departed the projectors' original plans. "Settlement in the tidewater appeared scattered, 'solitary and unsociable'... 'dispersedly and scatteringly seated upon the sides of Rivers' ... 'thinly inhabited'." Towns and villages did not develop. "There was nothing in Virginia or Maryland that replicated English urban experience."[116] Under this surface, however, one finds, as in New England, hints of influence from the region's English cultural backgrounds. Pointing to the importance of migration from the south and west of England in shaping Chesapeake folkways, for example, Fischer stresses characteristics of the region – manorialism, sheep-corn husbandry, rigid social hierarchy, gentry domination, a substantial landless population of cottagers and farm laborers – that Somers associates with the "arable" model of legal culture. As Somers points out, county-level government is the primary institutional expression of the "arable" model. And Fischer concurs. "The ordering institutions of Virginia were as hierarchical as the idea of order itself. The most important order-keepers were not town constables who had been elected by the people, as in New England, but county sheriffs who had been appointed in the name of the Crown." Alongside the sheriff sat the county court composed of the county's justices of the peace, offices "controlled by the county gentry who regarded [them] as a species of property which they passed on to one another."[117]

One must be careful of too facile an identification of a historically specific legal culture with an over-schematic ideal type. A recurring theme in discussions of migration is its presumed capacity to create new cultural mixes from previously nonexistent proximities. While the dominance of county-level government in the Chesapeake does signify and reinforce the influence of the colonial gentry, James Horn asserts, one cannot associate that dominance with a particular inherited regional legal culture. "Certain regions supplied more emigrants than others, of course, and in the first

Local Government in Northern Massachusetts," in Daniels, ed., *Town and County*, 29–37; Allen, *In English Ways*, 205–22.

[114] The colony's four original "cities" – James Cittie (the first), Charles Cittie, Henrico Cittie, and Elizabeth Cittie – all became counties ("shires") in 1634.

[115] William H. Seiler, "The Anglican Church: A Basic Institution of Local Government in Colonial Virginia," in Daniels, ed., *Town and County*, 134–59.

[116] Horn, *Adapting to a New World*, 234–5.

[117] Fischer, *Albion's Seed*, 398, 406. See also Horn, *Adapting to a New World*, 195–6.

half of the century many areas of the tidewater may have had a decidedly southern or southeastern flavor. Nevertheless, provincial cultures did not have the same impact in the Chesapeake as they apparently did in parts of New England." The diversity of sources for Chesapeake emigration meant a jumbling there of multiple local influences. That diversity meant that no one "identifiable English provincial culture established itself in, or exerted extensive influence on, Virginia and Maryland society." Yet Horn's conclusion is not that diversity turned Chesapeake society into a staggeringly variegated culture, but rather that it became a "simplified" one. "The rich particularity of the past could not be replicated in America; what emerged were compromises and approximations."[118]

Certainly, judging by records from the port of Bristol, many of the Chesapeake's indentured migrants came not from identifiable downland areas but from the increasingly populous pastoral parishes, forests, and wastes of western Gloucestershire and Wiltshire and northern Somerset. The cultural significance of this is not obvious, however, for many in these parishes were themselves newcomers displaced from the region's arable areas by engrossment of small holdings, conversions to pastoral husbandry, and, especially in the case of the young, by a cyclical weakening in demand for farm service. Thus, Chesapeake migrants leaving through Bristol, like many of those drawn to London, may well have been displaced arable populations.[119] Nevertheless, it is conceivable that one dynamic of migration to the Chesapeake was to place a culturally pastoral population of migrants within the framework of institutions built by core group elites upon quite distinct foundations.

Under these circumstances the real issue – at least where formal authoritative institutions, sinews of power, are concerned – becomes one of cultural ascendancy: who is to say what institutional forms will rule? On the face of it this was a question more likely to be resolved by elite minorities, "the well-born and the wealthy," than by the mass of plebeian, largely youthful, emigrants. And did the "simplified" institutions that those minorities chose, gentry-dominated county courts and parish vestries, really represent a pattern of governance and legal culture "broadly familiar" to the generality of emigrants and "reminiscent of a variety of jurisdictions," or can their roots be specified more precisely? Judging by what those core minorities created, at least in its legal culture the Chesapeake was less a cultural compromise or composite than an imitation of downland arable

---

[118] Horn, *Adapting to a New World*, 14, 148.

[119] Ibid., 69–76; Salerno, "Social Background," 31–52. In his "Inducements," the elder Hakluyt refers specifically to the existence in America of "great waste Woods" where "many of our waste people may be imployed." Waste having quite a specific meaning in sixteenth- and seventeenth-century England (unenclosed, open to casual settlement), it is unlikely that Hakluyt here wished to refer simply to "surplus" people. See his *Pamphlet for the Virginia Enterprise* (1585), in Taylor, ed., *Original Writings and Correspondence*, II, 331. See also Dean, *Law-Making and Society*, 167. On demand for farm servants, see Kussmaul, *Service in Husbandry*, 97–100. On the movement away from arable husbandry in the seventeenth-century southwest, see Kussmaul, *General View*, 1–13.

England. Just as New England tipped toward one pole of a cultural continuum, the Chesapeake tipped toward the other.[120]

The Delaware Valley

The character of early migration to the third primary area of British settlement, the Delaware Valley, was more homogenous than the Chesapeake's. It furnishes strong evidence for the influence of a distinctively "pastoral" legal culture among the first settlers. This is not to say that cultural confrontation lacks the explanatory potential in the Delaware Valley that one may accord it in the Chesapeake; the Pennsylvania patent clearly envisioned a manorial society of well-disciplined agricultural communities.[121] The pattern of land distribution that characterized the colony exhibits a distinctively manorial twist, helping to explain some of the basic and enduring frictions animating the colony's politics in the eighteenth century, for the existence of those frictions owed much to the culturally distinctive origins of the mass of the first settlers. Most came from the Pennine North and North West England, areas as pastoral as one could hope to find; weak in manorial institutions, lacking powerful oligarchic local elites, their social relations characterized by family and household cohesion, the inhabitants possessed of "'a reputation for independence,' and a custom of equality among themselves."[122] What those settlers created in early Pennsylvania was very different from what the proprietor had planned – not disciplined agrarianism at all but "a transplantation of upland, provincial, British society." It was a transplantation "profoundly modified by radical religion" (that is, Quakerism). But rather than introduce qualitative changes to a familiar social order, the settlers' Quakerism in fact organized and accentuated key aspects of the experience of living in upland plebeian pastoral society. Religious ideology reinforced the distinct culture of its settler-adherents, tightening their key social experiences into an explicit ideology of social authority.[123]

Of the many aspects of local culture transplanted by settlers, most important was the family. Typically, the Northern and Northwestern districts from which the Delaware Valley's first settlers came were characterized

---

[120] Horn, *Adapting to a New World*, 148, 428–9. Though descriptively rich, analytically *Adapting* always tends to fall between two stools. By emphasizing endemic local variety Horn denies the possibility of systematic translocal variation between regions; by emphasizing cultural transference as a process of "simplification" that reveals lowest common denominator familiarity, he assumes that an essentialist core of sameness – "Englishness" – prevails at the stripped-down heart of all local cultures. On this point see also Fischer, "Albion and the Critics," 286.

[121] Lemon, *The Best Poor Man's Country*, 50–7, and generally 42–70. See also Edward T. Price, *Dividing the Land: Early American Beginnings of our Private Property Mosaic* (Chicago, 1995), 264–7.

[122] Fischer, *Albion's Seed*, 448.

[123] Ibid., 448; Levy, *Quakers and the American Family*, 6.

by low population densities and a subsistence economy dominated by dispersed smallholder farming, mostly on long tenancies but with a minority of freeholders. The region's economy offered its inhabitants few opportunities to achieve household independence, whether through accumulation of sufficient land to support multiple children or through alternative means for self-support (such as trade apprenticeships). Younger children could not hope for land, and "even the commonest trades of southeastern English villages were often absent" in Wales and the Northwest. Families were faced with the constant migration away of the majority of their children. To compensate and "provide family continuity and personal dignity in the face of scarcity and individual household poverty," northwestern households developed practices of pooling resources "among a number of different people and households." These practices became "the sinews of northwestern society." Barry Levy argues that in the pastoral northwest Quakerism developed "as a radical, charismatic version" of the inhabitants' social practices, one that stressed child-rearing, familialism and, in particular, reliance on "informal human relations" over formal institutions. Even as Quakers separated from non-Quaker society first in England and subsequently by migration to Pennsylvania, Quaker ideology continued to place kinship and an extended sense of family at the center of what was now a separate Quaker social practice.[124]

Quakerism itself arising on the back of practices designed to compensate for the harsh social and environmental conditions of the Pennine and northwestern uplands, Quaker migration proceeded out of a desire to transcend local limitations altogether and to realize regional social values – austerity, equality, simplicity, hard work, family continuity, and cohesion – in a less hostile environment. "The problem was not the high standards of Quaker family life and discipline per se," but the barriers posed by a poor economy and religious persecution to the fulfillment of those exacting standards. Migration to the Delaware Valley offered access to the resources that would make Quaker familialism workable. "The northwestern British Quakers had known poverty and had consequently lost their children. In Pennsylvania, the Quakers prudently chose to stock their communities with wealthy households which could retain their children."[125]

So strong was Quaker familialism in the Delaware Valley, so pronounced the emphasis on private space in social practice, that quite apart from the dissonance between the legal forms of proprietary government and the legal culture of the migrating population, formal public institutions of any sort initially played only a secondary role in the settlers' social and cultural practices. This was particularly clear in religious practices, where no religious establishment was created, toleration was widespread, and the calendar of "meetings" the only interposition on an otherwise spontaneous communalism. But it was also clear in Quaker political economy and legal

[124] Levy, *Quakers and the American Family*, 32, 37, 84–5, 100, 102.
[125] Ibid., 88, 128.

culture. In economic and political development, as in social and religious practices, radical domesticity – "pluralism, disciplined privatism, child-centeredness, and wealth" – was the chosen vehicle. Radical domesticity lent Quaker legal culture a certain anti-authoritarian, or at least an abstentionist, character. Disputes between Quakers were generally composed within meetings rather than taken "to law."

Communal institutions outside the household, however, were not absent. Layers of local government and legal process existed from the outset of settlement, operating through both township and county, which divided responsibilities for local administration: road building and maintenance, poor relief, licensing, livestock regulation. Justices of the Peace appointed by the Governor were strategic figures at both levels: at county level, collectively, they presided over quarter sessions and, until replaced by locally elected county commissioners, over all county administration; at township level, individually, they arbitrated or settled minor disputes. Other county-level figures, such as the sheriff and the coroner, were equally strategic. Officers "were not controlled by a small clique of county gentry as in Virginia, nor elected by the consensus of a local community as were the constables of New England." Rather, they were appointed centrally from among a limited field of nominees (two) who were chosen in county-wide elections.[126] In the context of Quaker ideology, the role of these public officials was one of social ordering through mediation within the locality as much as the projection of public disciplinary power into the locality – mediation initially between Quakers and "the world"; subsequently, as Delaware Valley society diversified, mediation among the plurality of groups that migrated into the region. As Quakers became outnumbered, legal institutions – participatory in procedural emphasis, local in focus – became key to sustaining Quaker influence.[127]

Conclusion

Legal cultures established in areas of North American mainland settlement and sustained by locally ascendant core groups (Fischer's elites) reproduced legal cultural patterns current in migrants' original English locales. English migration to mainland America was responsive to, and cannot be understood apart from, the country's sixteenth- and seventeenth-century demographic history. In turn, that history can only be understood fully in the context of the distinctive structure and evolution of the English rural economy as developed by Joan Thirsk and Alan Everitt, and brilliantly refined by Ann Kussmaul. Though crude in some respects, the distinction between *arable* and *pastoral* legal cultures offers us a means to gain

[126] Fischer, *Albion's Seed*, 585. In practice the biggest vote-getter was chosen. Formal authority thus flowed from the center. Practical authority, however, flowed from the locality.

[127] Offutt, *Of "Good Laws" & "Good Men,"* 11. See also Alfred L. Brophy, "'For the Preservation of the King's Peace and Justice': Community and English Law in Sussex County, Pennsylvania, 1682–1696," *American Journal of Legal History*, 40, 2 (April 1996), 167–212.

conceptual purchase on the incidence of systematic difference in the nature, ideology, and institutional organization of legal and social authority in the areas of mainland settlement under examination. It provides a *via media* between infinite English variety and a North American approximation of lowest metropolitan common denominators – denominators to which no migrant would, in any case, have had access, but only the scholar, after the event and as a device.

In analysis of the impact of systematic local variation on English legal culture, one aspect stands out as of particular importance. Initial variation may be attributed to a variety of interrelated factors breeding differences in local social practice: geography, for example, or environment; demographic variations, or local political or religious tradition, or regional chauvinism. Sustained legal cultural variation, however, is interactive. When the "center" attempts initiatives, particularly a center without a bureaucracy, local variation means a spectrum of contexts exist within which the center's presumptively uniform legal initiatives are subject to reaction and reinterpretation in the course of implementation. Central initiatives end up manifested in quite distinct fashions, thereby reinforcing the variation. Different regions, that is, "generated different patterns of justice and rights" when receiving and responding to the same central governmental initiatives. This "local contextualizing of legal processes" reinforced and accentuated legal-cultural variation.[128]

In no area of governmental activity was the local contextualizing of legal process more important, its impact on apparently uniform institutional processes more profound, than in the regulation of work and labor. As I shall suggest in the next chapter, accounts of early-modern English legal cultures of work and labor that give proper attention to variation across locality and region have the same considerable relevance to the history of English colonizing as accounts of English cultural variation in general.

To this point their promise has not been much investigated. In Richard Morris's *Government and Labor in Early America*, still authoritative, the regulation of labor in the mainland colonies appears as a wisdom received from

---

[128] Somers, "Rights, Relationality and Membership," 98. The most complete representation of the variety of factors at work in England's geography of initial socio-cultural difference can be found in Mark Stoyle's study of Civil War era popular allegiance in Devon, *Loyalty and Locality*. (Among many innovations, Stoyle's study is notable for its discussion of regional racial and ethnic division between, for example, Anglo-Saxon England and Celtic Cornwall. See 149–51, and more generally 239–41, 250, 255.)

For theoretical reflections on analogous contemporary processes, see Gunther Teubner, "Legal Irritants: Good Faith in British Law or how Unifying Law ends up in New Divergences," *Modern Law Review*, 61, 1 (1998), 11–32. Engaging with the extensive literature on the phenomenon of legal transplantation, Teubner argues that the metaphor is inadequate. "Transplant" offers only two outcomes – integration or repulsion. "Irritant" offers a more plausible scenario of constant friction. Applied to the case at hand, central initiatives irritate the local, producing reactions that vary according to distinct regional-cultural patterns. Applied to the migration of people and institutions, we have already seen that migrants irritate the host; distinct migrant groups and cultures also irritate each other.

a single metropolitan source: a regime of law, rooted "to a large degree" in old world strategies of social and economic regulation driven by a coherent mercantilist ideology.[129] Just as England's overseas trade flows and relations with colonies were to be controlled and directed, through subsidy and protection, in the interests of metropolitan wealth accumulation, so in the case of work and labor, domestic policy was "to assure profit to the English entrepreneur by guaranteeing him an adequate labor supply at a subsistence wage."[130] Implicit in each of mercantilism's components, then, was a conception of a national program implemented by central authority. The domestic "keystone" was the Tudor state's Statute of Artificers (1563). Its regulatory program was "largely taken over" in early America.[131]

Morris wrote of early America from a position of hindsight, firmly located on the far side of what he took to be the great historical divide separating the first two centuries of English colonizing from the "laissez-faire capitalism" and the "freeing the individual from [external] restraints" that would follow American independence. He did not write as a scholar unsympathetic to labor regulation; indeed, his objective was in large part to recover an American pedigree for regulatory activity that would grant "the Revolution in the government's relations with business and labor, inaugurated in 1933" historical precedent. Hence his stress on labor regulation as an integral element of mercantilism, and on mercantilism as a self-conscious and centralizing program.[132]

But it is difficult to sustain a representation of the Statute of Artificers as the domestic key to a systematic proactive Tudor economic policy. It was not central government but a diversity of local needs and initiatives that set the terms and conditions of work in early modern England. That diversity was reproduced in the statute, not only in its administration but in its very formulation. The statute, that is, was more descriptive than proactive.[133]

Second, as I have just suggested, rather than furnish a vehicle for the transportation of centralizing mercantilist institutions across the Atlantic, patterns of migration to and settlement on the American mainland imported legal-cultural diversity into the colonies, a diversity that mainland

---

[129] Richard B. Morris, *Government and Labor in Early America* (Boston, 1981 [1st edition New York, 1946]). Marcus Rediker attests to *Government and Labor*'s eminence in his 1988 survey, "Good Hands, Stout Heart and Fast Feet: The History and Culture of Working People in Early America," in Geoff Eley and William Hunt, editors, *Reviving the English Revolution: Reflections and Elaborations on the Work of Christopher Hill* (London, 1988), 242–3. See also Graham Russell Hodges, "In Retrospect: Richard B. Morris and *Government and Labor in Early America*," *Reviews in American History*, 25, 2 (1997), 360–8.

[130] Morris, *Government and Labor*, 2.

[131] Ibid., 4.

[132] Ibid., 1, 53.

[133] We might note that in 1956, D. C. Coleman observed, "One of the first things we need to do if we want to learn more about the English economy of the seventeenth century, and within it the position of labour, is to start by jettisoning that misleading and cumbersome portmanteau, that unnecessary piece of historical baggage – the idea of 'mercantilism'." See Coleman, "Labour in the English Economy of the Seventeenth Century," 295.

conditions did little to diminish. In comparison with central-local government communications in Britain, transatlantic links between colonies and
metropolis were significantly attenuated. Nor on the American side was
there any particular reason to coordinate policy among colonies, so considerably did labor supply and working conditions differ from region to
region.[134]

With little to counteract provincial tendencies to atomization, and
plenty to accentuate it, the result was not reproduction of a schema of work
and labor regulation "largely taken over" from Britain, as Morris had it,
but rather the development of a variety of systems of work and labor regulation, some of which differed quite radically from the deceptively familiar
British model. Colonizers' Herculean labors built Englishness in mainland
America, but the way they went about it displayed all the plurality that one
might expect from a poly-Olbion, and more besides.

---

[134] See generally Richard J. Ross, "Legal Communications and Imperial Governance: British
North America and Spanish America Compared," in Michael Grossberg and Christopher
Tomlins, editors, *The Cambridge History of Law in America* (Cambridge and New York,
2008), I, 104–43. Ross finds that "a significant measure of local control and diversity"
characterized mainland legal systems (143), and that diversity persisted despite increasing metropolitan pressures for integration during the eighteenth century in good part
due to the lack of incentive to communicate legal information on the colonial side, and
the relative absence of standardized legal models to impose on the metropolitan side.

6

Unpacking: Received Wisdoms of Law and Work

> From such as would our rights invade
> Or would intrude into our trade
> Or break the law Queen Betty made
> *Libera nos Domine*
>
> Seventeenth-century English
> wool combers' song

More than sixty years after its publication in 1946, Richard B. Morris's *Government and Labor in Early America* continues to set the tone for much of the scholarship addressing the legalities of work and labor on the colonized mainland through the end of the eighteenth century. "The world of labor that the Revolutionary generation inhabited," Robert Steinfeld argues in *The Invention of Free Labor*, "was a world derived from English labor practices of an earlier era. The English colonists who settled the North American mainland in the seventeenth century brought with them many basic legal features of a labor system that had been in place for centuries." Characterized by "pervasive ... legal intervention in the lives of ordinary laboring people," it was a system grounded on medieval and early modern statutes – the medieval statutes of labourers and in particular the Tudor Statute of Artificers – "enforced throughout the realm." Those same statutes served as a template for "American" legal rules that reproduced all the essentials of that English system in the colonies.[1] Steinfeld, in fact, has extended Morris's writ into territory that Morris himself declined to enter. Where, for example, Morris found embedded in the statutes a purpose not only to guarantee the employer adequate labor at subsistence wages but also "to safeguard the worker against unrestrained exploitation," Steinfeld finds only the former, an "oppressive regime of legal regulation" that constituted coerced restraint as labor's normal legal form by criminalizing all forms of contract breach. Individual freedom of movement is Steinfeld's definitive measure of civic autonomy in Anglo-American legal culture. So measured, he concludes, "free labor"

---

[1] Robert J. Steinfeld, *The Invention of Free Labor: The Employment Relation in English and American Law and Culture, 1350–1870* (Chapel Hill, 1991), 8, 13. See also Karen Orren, *Belated Feudalism: Labor, the Law and Liberal Development in the United States* (New York, 1991), 12.

is a definitively modern phenomenon, a creation of the early republic's proto-capitalist economy.[2]

In this chapter, which continues Part II's inside narrative of the legalities of colonizing, I examine whether accounts that posit the transplantation of an essentially unitary array of legal regulations to govern the foundational colonizing activities of work and labor must be reconsidered once one takes note of the endemic variation that characterized both conception and execution of the relevant legalities across locality and region. First, I trace the history of English labor statutes prior to the Statute of Artificers; then I consider the formation of that statute and its administration in England. Upon inspection, it becomes apparent that representations of a singular and long-established English labor "system" – rooted in the fourteenth century, epitomized by the Statute of Artificers, uniformly enforced, uniformly oppressive – do not comport with early-modern reality. Variety, not "uniform national rules"[3] and uniform oppression, is the mark of early-modern England's legal culture of work. Equally important, to define civic "freedom" only as the absence of legislative incursions on individual autonomy is (as Morris himself seemed to realize) stunted. The variability of English regional legal cultures meant that statutory initiatives were implemented in a diversity of jurisdictional contexts. That diversity created opportunities for the collective construction of civic rights, or at least expectations of rights, out of putatively regulatory measures.[4] Neither in England nor, by the same token, in colonial English America,

---

[2] Ibid., 8–9. Richard B. Morris, *Government and Labor in Early America* (Boston, 1981 [1st edition New York, 1946]), 2. Steinfeld's emphasis on individual autonomy as the measure of freedom is reiterated in Markus Dubber's stark contrast between states of autonomy and heteronomy in his *The Police Power: Patriarchy and the Foundations of American Government* (New York, 2005).

[3] Steinfeld, *Invention of Free Labor*, 22.

[4] Margaret Somers stresses the capacity of working people, depending on their jurisdictional location, to find civic opportunity in state regulatory initiatives. See, for example, her "Rights, Relationality and Membership: Rethinking the Making and Meaning of Citizenship," *Law & Social Inquiry*, 19, 1 (Winter 1994), 83–108. As Somers and others have shown, it is an error to associate "rights" solely with individual claims acknowledged in public law. Rights develop as much in associative practices, gaining initial expression in the "action" of specific forms of jurisdiction – guilds, corporations, or communities – and only subsequently emerging as public claims in response to a "public" intervention in the specific arena of associational activity. Thus, for example, the Statute of Artificers was treated by significant segments of the English working population as an implementation of widely articulated rights-claims grounded in guild-corporate practices. See R. A. Leeson, *Travelling Brothers: The Six Centuries' Road from Craft Fellowship to Trade Unionism* (London, 1979), 59–79; Jonathan A. Bush, "'Take This Job and Shove it': The Rise of Free Labor," *Michigan Law Review*, 91, 6 (May 1993), 1392. For recent commentary on corporate expressions of communitarian right in early America, see Simon Middleton, "The New York City Revolt, 1689–1691: A Class Struggle in Early America?" in Simon Middleton and Billy G. Smith, editors, *Class Matters: Early North America and the Atlantic World* (Philadelphia, 2008), 88–98. See also Christopher Tomlins, "Constellations of Class in Early North America and the Atlantic World," in idem, 213–33.

should a purely negative liberty – "individualism" – be assumed a doctrine "glorified" among laborers.[5]

Second, this chapter begins, and the next will continue, an examination of the "reception" of England's plural legal cultures of work on the American mainland. Here, as in other aspects of colonial legal culture, one finds law transplanted piecemeal in a fashion that reproduces cultural variation in migrants' regions of origin, a quite rapid development of further distinct variations that respond to conditions prevailing in regions of reception, a generally more limited ambit for regulatory action grounded in political division, and with it, for some among the new inhabitants, a much earlier growth of "freedom" in Steinfeld's sense of absence of incursion upon autonomy than *The Invention of Free Labor* is willing to allow. For those who enjoyed it, that freedom was serious and real. As developed here and discussed further in Part III, however, freedom cannot be thought of as an absolute state but one subject to fundamental limit conditions, or liabilities, obedient to three legal-cultural demarcations: age, gender, and race.

I. England

The Ordinance and Statute of Laborers

Ambitions to regulate work and labor provided key impetus for the first attempts to create an English national state equipped with governmental capacities.[6] The plague-induced Ordinance (1349) and Statute (1351) of Labourers stand as the primary statutory embodiment of efforts to establish a "more cohesive government" that appeared during the second half of Edward III's reign, its purpose to preserve as much as possible of the existing structure of society in the face of demographic catastrophe. Between 1348 and 1350, the Black Death killed between one-third and one-half of the country's population. In the wake of the epidemic, as never before, "the king's government became responsible for the running of the whole society." Coercing the lower orders "to work effectively and well" became government's major task and objective. To do so it turned to include "the upper orders in the exercise of governance" far more comprehensively than before the plague. Simultaneously, it expanded "the concerns of centralized governance to the lower levels of society." It aggressively employed law as a means to that end.[7]

---

[5] Samuel McKee, Jr., *Labor in Colonial New York* (New York, 1935), 179. And see J. E. Crowley, *This Sheba, Self: The Conceptualization of Economic Life in Eighteenth Century America* (Baltimore, 1974).

[6] Margaret Somers, "Citizenship and the Place of the Public Sphere: Law, Community, and Political Culture in the Transition to Democracy," *American Sociological Review*, 58, 5 (October 1993), 596.

[7] Robert C. Palmer, *English Law in the Age of the Black Death, 1348–1381: A Transformation of Governance and Law* (Chapel Hill, 1993), 1, 5, 139, 294. On the transformative socio-legal effects of the Black Death, particularly in the realm of labor regulation, see 1–6, 14–27, 59–61, 139–44.

Before 1348, English common law did not regulate agricultural or artisan labor. Such regulation as took place was piecemeal and local, and dealt with labor in terms of incidents of service arising from personal status and custom.[8] The Ordinance and Statute of Labourers added central regulation to local, imposing compulsion to work at accustomed wages on a wide range of agricultural and artisanal occupations, and setting wage standards and terms of hire. "The intention was to retain the status quo as it had been prior to the Black Death by reinforcing the lord's control over his tenantry, by forcing people to work and at reasonable rates, and by preventing excessive competition for the smaller labor pool."[9] But while restrictive in its effects at least in the short run, the establishment of a national sphere of regulation of labor also suggested the possibility of an enhanced freedom for those made subject to state oversight. By intervening in the status relationship between dependent labor and manorial lord and giving oversight of that relationship to state officials, the legislation created a foundation for assertions of legally secured rights as well as obligations.[10] "Villeins were being tried and convicted by the justices of labourers exactly like free men ... they were themselves bringing audacious suits in quarter sessions against their own masters" who now preferred to rely on "crown-appointed officials" to secure their relations with their tenants, free or bond. "The cataclysm of the Black Death had hastened the break-down of the old system and had accelerated changes in economic and social relations throughout the community."[11] Statutory labor regulation after the

---

[8] Ibid., 14; Chris Given-Wilson, "Service, Serfdom and English Labour Legislation," in Anne Curry and Elizabeth Matthew, editors, *Concepts and Patterns of Service in the Later Middle Ages* (Woodbridge, Surrey, 2000), 21–37. See also Elaine Clark, "Medieval Labor Law and English Local Courts," *American Journal of Legal History*, 27, 4 (October 1983), 330–53; Bush, "'Take This Job and Shove it'," 1388–9; Madonna J. Hettinger, "Defining the Servant: Legal and Extra-Legal Terms of Employment in Fifteenth Century England," in Allen J. Frantzen and Douglas Moffat, editors, *The Work of Work: Servitude, Slavery and Labor in Medieval England* (Glasgow, 1994), 206–28. Orren, *Belated Feudalism*, 38, holds that medieval and early-modern English labor statutes "codified" an already existing common law of servitude, but this is incorrect.

[9] Palmer, *English Law*, 18; Bertha Putnam, *The Enforcement of the Statutes of Labourers During the First Decade after the Black Death* (New York, 1908), 157–65; L. R. Poos, "The Social Context of Statute of Labourers Enforcement," *Law and History Review*, 1, 1 (Spring 1983), 36–7. Historians who stress the restrictive and coercive motivations of the ordinance and statute rarely note that the legislation was directed at price restraint as well as restraint on wages and labor mobility. Bertha Putnam concludes that the "increase in both wages and prices" after the plague was so enormous as to constitute "a crisis of an unprecedented character, involving real danger to the welfare of the community." Regulation "was honestly meant to include prices as well as wages whenever there had been a rise in the former also; under these circumstances it seems unreasonable to consider [regulation] as unfair oppression of the working classes." (77, 87, 220). Poos (28, 33–6) similarly discounts "class bias" explanations of the legislation and stresses instead the opportunities it offered to "lesser men."

[10] Somers, "Rights, Relationality and Membership," 83–96.

[11] Putnam, *Enforcement* 222–3, and see generally 179–214; Palmer, *English Law*, 12, 24; Hettinger, "Defining the Servant," 213–25; Given-Wilson, "English Labour Legislation."

Black Death established opportunities for widespread lordly and employer control over those who worked for them, whether villeins, covenant servants, free tenants, agricultural laborers, or artisans. But the grounds were economic, contract rather than status.[12]

The effort to regulate labor was essential to and a central aspect of the revolution in governance. The Black Death brought into existence a government "of inherent authority" that was both "newly responsible and newly intrusive." Central state power grew substantially. But that power was exercised through mechanisms that "emphasized delegation and cooperation among the upper orders." Notable in this process was the endowment of the knightly classes with state authority through the medium of justice of the peace commissions, bringing this new provincial gentry decisively into the circle of rule where it served as the means to link the localities to central authority. The new gentry "dominated the Statute of Laborers commissions from the beginning."[13]

A focus upon the causal centrality of sudden demographic catastrophe in explaining the transformation of English governance and law displaces accounts of legal change that have relied on "internal conceptual" accounts of legal evolution. Legal change after the Black Death "derived not from specifically legal thought but from governmental policy responding to drastically changed social conditions. Social needs constituted a force distinctly external to legal logic or the dictates of the writs." Legal change was not endogenous but "the imposition of government policy."[14] The argument is extremely effective, but necessarily also has important applications to and implications for subsequent developments. The sudden loss of between 30 percent and 50 percent of population engendered extreme measures to contain social dislocation and to coerce the lower orders to stand to their obligations. Such dramatic change being bred by extraordinary exogenous catastrophe rather than more gradual evolution, so, as the ripples of catastrophe subsided, one might plausibly expect some degree of relaxation. Structurally, the state created in the wake of the plague, with its national legislation, its policies of "delegation and cooperation" among elites high and low, and its new nonfeudal jurisdictional-administrative mechanisms linking center and provinces, remained intact. It meant "a lasting change to governance in England."[15] Over time, however, the expression and enforcement of rule changed. Apparently effective implementation of the Ordinance and Statute of Labourers to restrain wages in the short term was succeeded by complaints, spurred by the resumption of wage increases, that

See also P.J.P. Goldberg, "What Was a Servant?" in Curry and Matthew, eds., *Concepts and Patterns of Service*, 1–20.

[12] Palmer, *English Law*, 14–17.

[13] Ibid., 1, 6, 12, 23.

[14] Ibid., 298, 299, 300. For accounts that give greater emphasis to the endogenous, see Steinfeld, *Invention of Free Labor*; Gareth H. Jones, *"Per Quod Servitium Amisit,"* *Law Quarterly Review*, 74 (January 1958), 39–58.

[15] Palmer, *English Law*, 11, 12.

the statutes were ineffective. Amendments followed giving greater emphasis to wage assessment, and also building up the authority, and hence the discretion, of local justices.[16] Crown augmentation of local authority certainly increased overall state capacity. Reliance upon provincial and local elites to perform state activities, however, inevitably meant over time the use of Crown authority in the service of local interests – cooperative accommodation of regional and local difference in the supply of labor and the structure of the economy – leading to the supervening influence of locality on the interpretation and application of the national sphere's products, and eventually substantial local and interregional variation in the performance of state activities. In other words, the practical consequence of granting local officials (petty constables and other village-level officials below the level of peace-session officers and juries) the primary role in "enforcement processes at their most basic levels" was to create functions "of social control *within* rural communities as much as economic control imposed from *above*" with the result that "although in principle the legislation may have stood as ultimately a landlord's sanction, in practice the law could operate as an instrument by which certain groups within communities furthered their own interests."[17]

Local participation in the implementation of law and governance thus brought the accommodation of local interests, creating potent local legal-regulatory cultures. This is why the English state that emerges in the early-modern period is possessed of "universal legal rules and power" that are "plural, porous and variously embedded in public spheres rather than unitary, absolute, and wielded only from above."[18]

Locality and Legality: Writing and Administering the Statute of Artificers

These characteristics of the English state are clearly on display in the specific example of the Statute of Artificers (1563). The immediate

---

[16] On short-term success, see Putnam, *Enforcement*, 219–23. For longer-term failure, see idem, 223–4; Richard Lachmann, *From Manor to Market: Structural Change in England, 1536–1640* (Madison, Wis., 1987), 27, 58–65; Michael F. Roberts, "Wages and Wage-Earners in England: The Evidence of the Wage-Assessments, 1563–1725" (unpublished D.Phil thesis, Oxford University, 1981), 16–21. On further statutory and administrative innovation, see Given-Wilson, "English Labour Legislation," 24–37.

[17] Poos, "Social Context," 28 (emphasis added). Given-Wilson comments, "Emergencies, real or imagined, have so often proved the occasion for governments to assume more extensive and more summary powers [that] there are theories of governmental development based on precisely this premise. The trick, naturally enough, is not to allow such powers to lapse once the crisis has passed." Yet "it is surely very doubtful whether legislation of such a sweeping nature could be enforced in a society such as late medieval England, unless a sufficient number of 'ordinary people' could be persuaded that it was in their own interests to enforce them." Given-Wilson, "English Labour Legislation," 35–6.

[18] Somers, "Citizenship and the Place of the Public Sphere," 596. See also, generally, Gerald Harriss, "Political Society and the Growth of Government in Late Medieval England," *Past & Present*, 138 (February 1993), 28–57.

circumstances of the statute's passage were not dissimilar to those attending the Ordinance and Statute of Labourers, although far less lasting in their effects. Secular population increase had resumed early in the sixteenth century, resulting in price inflation in the shrunken agricultural economy. Population growth was abruptly interrupted in the late 1550s, however, by savage influenza outbreaks. The crisis meant immediate pressure on labor supply – rising competition for labor and heightened labor mobility – and the threat of harvest failure.[19] Several of the statute's most notorious measures were responses to this renewal of demographic crisis, notably its criminalization of contract breach, its creation of processes to control wages and to force vagrants (persons without employment or other means of livelihood) and others to perform agricultural work.[20] These were not novel responses: the statute had "more than two centuries of custom and legislation" on which to draw.[21] Nor, however, do they alone, or even primarily, define the statute's purpose or long-term significance.

The Statute of Artificers was represented in debate as omnibus legislation to address the shortcomings of "a greate nomber of Actes and Statutes concerning the reteyning departing wages and orders of Apprentices Servantes and Labourers" and to reduce the several laws on the books "into one sole Lawe and Statute, & in the same an uniforme Order prescrybed and lymitted concerning the Wages and other Orders for Apprentises Servauntes and Laborers." Like the post–Black Death statutes two centuries earlier, the Statute of Artificers once more gave labor regulation national-level expression. And once implemented, "the same Lawe, beyng duly executed, should banishe Idlenes advance Husbandrye and yeeld unto the hired pson both in the tyme of scarsitee and in the tyme of plentye a convenient proporčon of Wages."[22] All this lends some support to the old-established view of the statute as a centrally promulgated "industrial code" of labor regulation and restraint; systematic, proactive, and oppressive.[23]

---

[19] Crude death rates during 1556–1558 averaged 48 per thousand. Between 1556 and 1560, population fell by 6 percent. See E. A. Wrigley and R. S. Schofield, *The Population History of England, 1541–1871* (London, 1981), 234. Parliamentary bills touching on work and labor began appearing in 1559. See Stanley T. Bindoff, "The Making of the Statute of Artificers," in S. T. Bindoff et al., editors, *Elizabethan Government and Society: Essays Presented to Sir John Neale* (London, 1961), 80–3.

[20] *An Acte towching dyvers Orders for Artificers Laborers Servantes of Husbandrye and Apprentises* (1563) 5 Eliz. c.4 [popularly known as *The Statute of Artificers*, sometimes *The Statute of Apprentices*], in *The Statutes of the Realm*, IV (London, 1819), 414–22, at 415–18 (clauses 5, 6, 10, 11, 15); Roberts, "Wages and Wage-Earners in England," 198.

[21] Leeson, *Travelling Brothers*, 59. See Given-Wilson, "English Labour Legislation," 21–37.

[22] 5 Eliz. c.4, clause 1.

[23] Morris, *Government and Labor*, 3, 1–4. At the end of the nineteenth century, James Thorold Rogers identified the Statute of Artificers as the point of inception for "a conspiracy, concocted by the law ... to cheat the English workman of his wages, to tie him to the soil, to deprive him of hope, and to degrade him into irremediable poverty." See his *Six Centuries of Work and Wages: The History of English Labour* (8th ed., London, 1906), 398. Rogers' opinions were disputed by R. H. Tawney, "The Assessment of Wages in England by the Justices of the Peace," and R. Keith Kelsall, "Wage Regulation under the Statute of

But at least a half century of research has cast doubt on representation of the statute in such traditional mercantilist terms. Perceptions of the statute as a restraining device, according to Frederick Fisher, emphasize short-term phenomena: demographic crisis, wage competition, and surging labor mobility.[24] One should recognize that wage assessment processes quickly adapted from restraint to the accommodation of wages to conditions of price inflation.[25] Stanley Bindoff's analysis of the statute's making, meanwhile, shows it to have been less a systematically formulated code than an unwieldy compilation of distinct and sometimes contradictory components, serving different purposes, stitched together (literally) by a Commons committee.[26] In 1980, Donald Woodward offered general support both to Fisher's recognition of the influence of short-term economic exigencies and Bindoff's description of policy-formation as an exercise in expedient accommodation of regional difference, and supplied important additional evidence for the salience of local initiative in setting the terms and conditions of work. In the years immediately prior to the statute's passage, both national and local governments were engaged in attempts to assert control over labor markets. Each attempted control of wages, control of working conditions and the terms of hire, and control of apprenticeship. In the statute itself, local ascendancy was recognized, or at least accommodated, in each policy area.[27] Hence its inconsistencies, the result of serving distinct purposes generated in distinct provincial contexts. In the assessment of wages, for example, what was noticeable was not the uniformity of enforcement but rather the "astonishing variety in form and in types of work covered." In the case of apprenticeship, not only was enforcement overwhelmingly dependent upon the vagaries of private prosecution, with its attendant "dilution of the law's force and legalized evasion of its intent," but in those instances involving public authorities, "the enforcement of new statute law was effectively taken up ... only when it met an urgent need of the local community or was in harmony with strong public sentiment." Execution of statutory law was dependent upon the willingness of "local individuals and bodies to enlarge their traditional circle of duties and responsibilities. The cohesive strength of customary obligation, so

---

Artificers," both in Walter E. Minchinton, editor, *Wage Regulation in Pre-Industrial England* (Newton Abbott, Devon, 1972), 38–91 and 94–197.

[24] F. J. Fisher, "Influenza and Inflation in Tudor England," *Economic History Review*, 2nd Ser., 18, 1 (August 1965), 125–8.

[25] Roberts, "Wages and Wage-Earners in England," 198.

[26] Bindoff, "The Making of the Statute of Artificers," 56–94. See also G. R. Elton, *The Parliament of England, 1559–1581* (Cambridge, 1986), 262–7. Disagreeing with Bindoff, Elton argues the statute was more conciliar in its origins. Walter Minchinton, however, concludes (like Bindoff) that the Statute "was not a grand design which was the product of one mind but a less coherent affair, the patchwork creation of many hands." See Walter E. Minchinton, "Wage Regulation in Pre-Industrial England," in Minchinton, ed., *Wage Regulation*, 10–36, at 18.

[27] Donald Woodward, "The Background to the Statute of Artificers: The Genesis of Labor Policy, 1558–63," *Economic History Review*, 2nd Ser., 33, 1 (February 1980), 32–44.

essential to the functioning of voluntary local government, operated also to retard its adoption of novelties."[28] These findings have been corroborated in more recent research on the implementation of the statute's wage assessment clauses, which have been shown to exhibit persistent local and regional variation both in the forms of compilation and the substance of assessment itself.[29]

Though the Statute of Artificers fails to live up to its reputation as a mercantilist vision of centrally imposed uniformity and order backed by coercion, it was not incoherent. Rather, it brought under one umbrella the three main areas of regulation that both local and national governments had regarded as key: regulation of the contract ("reteyning departing"); regulation of wages; and regulation of apprenticeship. It did so not to centralize control over these three areas, but rather as an attempt at establishing a jurisdictional map of effective authority in their administration.

In the case of wages, the statute's first focus of attention, two centuries of parliamentary rating were abandoned "for that the wages and allouances lymytted and rated in many of the [former] Statutes, are in dyvers places to small and not answerable to this tyme, respecting thadvancement of Pryses of all thinges belonging to the said Servantes and Labourers, the said Lawes cannot conveniently w^thout the great greefe and burden of the poor Labourer and hired man, bee put in good and due execution." In its place the Statute created a "system of local regulation under the supervision of JPs."[30] This meant acknowledgment not merely of price inflation but of the existence of regional variation in labor markets, and hence in wage and price outcomes. "Without regulation on a local basis the official rates

---

[28] R. Keith Kelsall, "Wage Regulations under the Statute of Artificers," in Minchinton, ed., *Wage Regulation*, 93–197, at 103; Margaret Gay Davies, *The Enforcement of English Apprenticeship: A Study in Applied Mercantilism, 1563–1642* (Cambridge, Mass., 1956), 161, 162.

[29] Roberts, "Wages and Wage-Earners in England," 97–125. By the early 1580s, the incidence of disciplinary prosecution under the Statute was falling sharply as the effects of the influenza-induced labor shortage ebbed. See William Hunt, *The Puritan Moment: The Coming of Revolution in an English County* (Cambridge, Mass., 1983), 64–5. Wage fixing proceeded with less volatility, precisely because "the principle of locally established rates" had carried the day in the statute, and because justices typically took advantage of this discretionary power to assess wages *above* the old maxima. Woodward, "Background to the Statute of Artificers," 41; Michael Roberts, "'Waiting Upon Chance': English Hiring Fairs and their Meanings from the 14th to the 20th Century," *Journal of Historical Sociology*, 1, 2 (June 1988), 119–60, 126. Local discretion in wage revision was further underscored when disputes over wage levels arose at the turn of the century in the clothing districts. Justices were first required to ensure that assessed rates were sufficient to provide for local subsistence (1598), and later empowered if necessary to set wage *minima* (1603). See 39 Eliz c.12 (1598), 1 Jac. c.6 (1603).

[30] 5 Eliz. c. 4, clause 1. Roberts, "Wages and Wage-Earners in England," 23. Stanley Bindoff, "The Making of the Statute of Artificers," 74, observes that "to the justice of 1563 – of whom there were upwards of a hundred in the house of commons" the duty "of annually compiling and continuously enforcing a set of wage-rates for every occupation practised within their jurisdiction" would have appeared "not an old, familiar burden, but a strange new one."

might prove 'in dyverse places' impossible to maintain, the practice of wage regulation fall into disrepute, and good order among servants and labourers collapse.["]31 Placing wage assessment in local hands meant, of course, that regional differences in the way social, economic, and governmental authority was organized and distributed would play key roles in determining outcomes, accentuating variation, particularly between an emerging higher-wage south-east and south and lower-wage north-west and north.[32] At the same time, the overall tendency of localized wage assessment was less to establish maximum rates with freedom for variation downward, than to create regionalized norms ("officially-sanctioned 'customs'") toward which local paid rates gravitated. "Inflation served to strengthen the interpretation of the official rates as norms, to be neither exceeded by any significant degree, nor undercut ... this view was given encouragement by the statutory definition of textile rates as minima in 1603–4."[33]

In the case of apprenticeship, the statute created a structure of rules that elaborated upon practices (control of entry to trades, limitation of numbers, the delegitimation of untrained rivals, discipline) long since used inside the craft companies to regulate craft apprenticeship and the craft itself for their own purposes. The elaboration was careful and qualified and complex; its structure of rules was shadowed by a parallel structure of exceptions and accommodations of existing interests. "Each main part of the Statute sought to balance the interests of one group against another."[34] Thus, the statute's apprenticeship provisions did not apply at all to craft apprenticeship in the city of London, nor to the manufacture of worsted in the city of Norwich; in each case craft companies were dominant. Elsewhere, that is in any other "Citie or Towne Corporate," or, with certain qualifications, "Market Towne," the ambit of permissible craft apprenticing was declared to extend to any householder above the age of twenty-four "exercising any Arte Misterye or Manuell Occupačon," who might retain as his apprentice the son of any Freeman of that or any other city or town, "not occupieng Husbandrye nor being a labourer." Minors fit to be made apprentices but refusing to enter the service of an eligible master might be compelled to do so, on complaint to local authorities. The statutory terms of craft apprenticeship were not defined, but declared simply to be "after the Custome and Order of the Citie of London." The only aspect of the relationship actually elaborated in the statute was its duration, a minimum seven-year term not to expire before age twenty-four. No provision was made for the registration of indentures before local authorities, although justices in the counties, and the "Mayoʳ Bailiefes or Head Officer"

---

31 Roberts "Wages and Wage-Earners" 24. Roberts adds, at 66, that "It was assumed by the compilers of the Statute of Artificers and its subsequent amendments that wage regulation would proceed in each corporate town, county or division on an independent basis."

32 Ibid., 202–9.

33 Ibid., 228, 334–5. See also Woodward, "Background to the Statute of Artificers," 41.

34 Leeson, *Travelling Brothers*, 61.

of a "Citie Towne Corporate or Market Towne" were required to exercise jurisdiction over master-apprentice disputes.[35]

Where the crafts were organized, in short, they could expect to exercise substantial influence on the structure and administration of apprenticeship.[36] That influence extended to the terms of the statute itself. Vested interests in restriction of entry were recognized in the statute by explicit qualifications on the ambit of apprenticeship in certain enumerated trades outside London. In "any Citie or Towne Corporate," apprenticeship to Merchants and to master Mercers, Drapers, Goldsmiths, Ironmongers, Embroiderers, and Clothiers was restricted to their sons or to the children of freeholders worth 40/- (shillings) per annum; in market towns the freehold restriction was declared at 60/- per annum. In lower-status manual (and rural) trades, on the other hand, the statute declared the doors of apprenticeship wide open: "any psone using or exercising Tharte or Occupation of a Smithe Whelewright Plowghwright Myllwright Carpenter Roughe Mason Playsterer Sawyer Lymeburner Brickmaker Bricklayer Tyler Slater Healyer Tilemaker Lynnen weaver Turner Cowper Millers Earthen potters Wollen weaver weaving Houswiefes or Householde Clothe onely and none other, Clothe Fuller otherwise called Tucker or Walker Burner of Oore and Woade Ashes Thatcher or Shingler, wheresoever he or they shall dwell or inhabite" might retain any other person's son as apprentice, without any freehold qualification. Yet even here, qualifications were immediately elaborated, reflecting complex vested interests. Outside cities, towns corporate, or market towns (that is in "any Village Towne or Place") no woollen cloth weaver other than those residing in Cumberland, Westmoreland, Lancaster, and Wales and weaving "Fryzes Cottons or Huswyves Clothe onely," might take as an apprentice any person not his son or the child of a freeholder worth 60/- per annum. Nor might any "Clothemaker Fuller Shereman Weaver Taylo[r] or Shoomaker" retain more than two apprentices without also employing one journeyman for every additional apprentice.[37]

In contrast to its careful navigation of craft apprenticeship, the statute dealt with apprenticeship in husbandry peremptorily, with little qualification, as a quite distinct institution. With no preexisting structure of corporate control, apprenticeship in husbandry was the state's to define. It did so (as we saw in Chapter 2), in the name of a general good – "the better advauncement of Husbandrye and Tillage." In that service its object was to

---

[35] 5 Eliz. c. 4, clause 19, 21, 28. In market towns, apprenticing was restricted to inhabitants who were themselves not occupied in husbandry or were laborers but who used or exercised any "Arte Misterye or Manuell Occupačon," and who might take as apprentice the child or children of any artificer.

[36] The organized crafts were, of course, intimately involved in the exercise of municipal authority in corporate cities and towns, particularly the policing of apprenticeship. The period, however, was one of increasing friction within the crafts over the enforcement of trade regulations. On this see Leeson, *Travelling Brothers*, 59–78; Christopher L. Tomlins, *Law, Labor, and Ideology in the Early American Republic* (Cambridge and New York, 1993), 116–17. See also, generally, Davies, *Enforcement of English Apprenticeship*.

[37] 5 Eliz. c. 4, clause 20, 22, 23, 25, 26.

mobilize all "as are fit to be made Apprentices," defined as "any pson above thage of tenne yeres and under thage of eightene yeres," in the service of any householder "having and using half a Ploughe Lande at the least in Tillage" for apprenticeship in husbandry "untill his Age of one and twentye yeres at the least, or until thage of foure and twentye yeres as the pties can agree ... the seyd reteynour and taking of an Apprentice to be made and done by Indenture." As in the crafts, persons fit to be made apprentices in husbandry might be compelled to enter service on appeal to local authorities.[38]

Though its denizens came from the same elements of the rural population as service in husbandry – children and adolescents – apprenticeship in husbandry was clearly a distinct institution. Most obviously, as defined in the statute husbandry apprentices did not serve by the year, contracting with successive masters until reaching the age of their majority, or marriage, but remained in the service of a single master throughout a multiyear term secured by indenture, in a relationship supervised by local authorities.[39] The husbandry apprenticeship clauses of the statute, that is, were a clear case of "indentured servitude."[40]

Where the statute's wage regulations and contract-discipline provisions do not appear on their face age-specific, its apprenticeship provisions certainly are. It has been suggested, further, that in fact the statute as a whole was introduced "to curb 'the unadvised rashness and licentious manner of youth'." The statute's apprenticeship provisions "pressured [young people] into entering service" because "structured work (and time) offered one solution to the many problems raised by disorderly youth." The statute's

---

[38] 5 Eliz. c. 4, clause 18, 28. Stanley Bindoff points out that although the clauses dealing with husbandry apprenticeship (18 and 28) introduce and conclude the statute's apprenticeship section, they share nothing in substance with the craft apprenticeship clauses, which appear to have been inserted rather arbitrarily between them during amendment prior to the statute's passage. Bindoff argues that application of compulsory service to the enumerated crafts in clause 28 was also an amendment. Originally confined to husbandry, "in a time of labour scarcity the land was not to be allowed first claim on all surplus labour." See Bindoff, "The Making of the Statute of Artificers," 61–8, 77, 93. Ralph A. Houlbrooke, *The English Family, 1450–1700* (New York, 1984), 167, claims the husbandry apprenticeship clauses "remained very largely a dead letter," but this is not supported by the evidence of the assessments (see below); even were it so, the husbandry apprenticeship clauses remained on the books as a legal structure applicable to the organization of transatlantic indentured servitude.

[39] Apprentices in husbandry came under the jurisdiction of the justices of the relevant county; in cities, towns corporate, or market towns, craft apprentices came under the jurisdiction of the mayor, bailiffs, or head town officer, respectively. 5 Eliz. c.4, clause 28.

[40] On the many facets of distinction between apprentices and servants, and in particular between apprentices in husbandry and servants in husbandry, see Roberts, "Wages and Wage-Earners," 143–63. It is worth noting that justices' wage assessments drew qualitative distinctions between husbandry servants and apprentices, emphasizing that the latter were "a species of farm servant characterised by a longer contract and a more subordinate position." Particularly associated with childhood and adolescence, husbandry apprentices' remuneration "consisted primarily of food, drink and clothing, with a small sum of money added here and there" (157).

"reteyning" and "departing" clauses – provisions for compulsory service and the criminalization of premature departure from service – served the same purposes.[41] Even its wage assessment provisions can be seen in the same light, for analysis of wage assessment evidence reveals a clear association of youth with wage-work in the statute's administration. "The attention JPs devoted to young workers is one of the most notable features of this material."[42]

The statute's emphatic attention to youth is hardly remarkable when considered in light of the age structure of the population in the middle decades of the sixteenth century. Substantially in excess of 50 percent of the population (54% in 1551, 53% in 1561) was twenty-four years old or younger.[43] If one treats persons aged fifteen and under, or over sixty, as "dependents," population estimates suggest a "working" population that was at least one-third youthful, but this is a substantial underestimate, particularly under the demographic circumstances of recovery from the late 1550s crisis. Statutory consideration and contemporary opinion both suggest that a child was considered capable of labor from age 5–7, reaching a threshold of efficiency around age 10; life expectancy during the second half of the century averaged thirty-eight years.[44] It is reasonable to assume that in the later sixteenth century as for the seventeenth, "the labour force of the community was characterized by a relatively short span of working life at maximum productive efficiency."[45] Considering the age span from ten to forty to comprise the efficient labor force, it will be evident that a substantial majority of this group was in the 10–24 age range – that is, children, adolescents, and young adults. It was precisely this cohort with which JPs were, apparently, preoccupied in the wage assessment process. The statute's ostensible "universalization" of labor regulation notwithstanding, its target population of apprentices and wage workers was overwhelmingly youthful, an association that was only strengthened by the demographics of the subsequent period.[46]

[41] Paul Griffiths, *Youth and Authority: Formative Experiences in England, 1560–1640* (Oxford, 1966), 36, 76, and see generally 351–89.

[42] Roberts, "Wages and Wage-Earners," 133.

[43] Wrigley and Schofield, *Population History*, table A3.1.

[44] On capacity to work, see Roberts, "Wages and Wage-Earners," 137–9; Griffiths, *Youth and Authority*, 19–34; Houlbrooke, *The English Family*, 153–5. On early-modern conceptions of childhood, see Holly Brewer, *By Birth or Consent: Children, Law and the Anglo-American Revolution in Authority* (Chapel Hill, 2005). On population trends and life expectancy, see Wrigley and Schofield, *Population History*, 234 and tables 7.15, A3.1, and A3.3. Contrasting with the crisis-period of the late 1550s, when life expectancy at birth fell below 30, the initial period of the statute's effective operation, between the mid-1560s and the mid-1580s, was the best for life-expectancy in the century, averaging 39.3. Over the same period crude death rates halved from the crisis years, and substantial population growth resumed. These factors produced both an expanding and a young labor force.

[45] D. C. Coleman, "Labour in the English Economy of the Seventeenth Century," *Economic History Review*, 2nd Ser., 8, 3 (April 1956), 285.

[46] Roberts, "Wages and Wage-Earners,"138. As we have already seen, this was also the demographic segment of the English population upon which late sixteenth-century promoters

Just as important, the implementation of the statute was decisively mediated by diverse local legal cultures of work. Like the earlier Ordinance and Statute of Labourers, the Statute of Artificers was locally administered through the discretionary activities of justices of the peace and village constables. Legislation embedded local labor markets "within the rules and institutions of public law," but the actual products of the national legal sphere were given all their practical effect and meaning by local officials responding to local contexts.[47]

The previous chapter gave considerable attention to those local contexts, in particular to the hypothesis that arable and pastoral regions evidenced clearly distinguishable legal cultures in which the latter exhibited "greater solidarity and autonomy." Somers argues that these characteristics were "institutional preconditions for their greater capacity for association and participation and hence their ability to appropriate and convert regulatory laws into citizenship rights." That is to say, in pastoral communities the weakness or absence of manorialism and hence of the powerful provincial elites that manorialism sustained translated into a capacity in the local community to shape the administration and enforcement of national labor laws. In the case of the Statute of Artificers, pastoral communities appropriated its wage and apprenticeship rules as civic rights. "The regulated labor market was a right ... Freedom and independence were conditional not on freedom *from* the state, but on [popular] rights as *members* of the English polity to make claims on the national state through participatory actions in their local public spheres." Hence "collective actions directed toward enforcement of the laws regulating apprenticeship and wages were a constant feature" of these communities.[48]

So far in this chapter I have described a Statute of Artificers far less proactively "national" and "uniform" in its implications, far more accommodating of contemporary disaggregated legal practice (whether arising from regional economic difference or vested corporate interests) in managing a largely youthful labor force that was significantly segmented in craft status. Those accommodations, particularly the craft apprenticeship clauses, help explain why "Queen Betty's Law" came to be perceived as a potent reinforcement of craft corporate rights, why in turn its implications for relations between masters and men – particularly for claims of journeymen to safeguarded employment, and for the trade distinction between "fair" and "forren" (illegal) shop practices – were fought over so vociferously as the craft corporations disintegrated during the seventeenth century into

of colonizing were fixated and which would migrate at the highest rates in the seventeenth century.

[47] Somers, "Citizenship and the Place of the Public Sphere," 600. The embeddedness of the statute's administration in local cultures meant that its administration was hostage to regional variation in the most basic ways – such as the very meaning to be ascribed to its most important terms: servants, labourers, artificers. See Roberts, "Wages and Wage-Earners," 144–6.

[48] Somers, "Citizenship and the Place of the Public Sphere," 603, 607.

warring "liveries" and "yeomanries."[49] Similarly, because the statute left its administration in local hands, and because local structures of administrative authority varied profoundly in the manner in which public authority expressed itself according to regional differences, the statute's clauses could also become a basis for assertions of right in localities outside the craft-corporate communities.

II. America

Understanding the Statute of Artificers in the terms advanced so far carries us a considerable distance from the uniform and oppressive "old regime" of U.S. scholarly imagination. Examination of early American legal cultures of work and labor carries us further still. Scholars have supposed the statute's master and servant regime effectively transferred *tout court* in purpose, if not in full detail. But on the few occasions that the Statute of Artificers or specific elements of it were actually invoked in early American proceedings, courts invariably indicated in word or deed that it had not been "received." This does not mean that it was uninfluential. Colonial authorities in Virginia and Massachusetts had resort to certain of the statute's wage-fixing provisions during initial phases of high-volume migration when competition for scarce artisanal labor in construction trades drove up wages. But there is little sign of the survival of wage-fixing beyond the very short term. The statute's husbandry apprenticeship clauses became the point of origin for the institutional development of the transatlantic indentured servitude regime, but the craft apprenticeship clauses were largely stillborn. Skilled migrant labor was subject to local statutory disciplines in Virginia well into the eighteenth century, but there is much less evidence for regulation of hired Creole labor beyond the mid-seventeenth century. Performance disputes, when brought into court, were resolved through civil proceedings, not by the imposition of criminal penalties. Colonial legislatures concentrated their attention on the waves of strangers brought in as indentured servants. This meant that their labor regulations were largely a regulation of migrating adolescents.

Patchy, varied, and partial, the laws applied to Europeans laboring in early America cannot be understood as a reproduction of a uniform metropolitan model. How, then, should the legal culture of work in early America be understood? Was it *sui generis*? What, if any, was the influence of the English provincial variations that regional circumstance and actual practice had created, and how was that influence transmitted? Second, did work and its legal regulation offer the same strategic and contested potential for the creation of civic freedoms in early America as apparently it did in England? That is, to what extent did early American statutes and common law practices represent the creation of new public legal spheres offering distinct potentials for civic membership?

[49] Tomlins, *Law, Labor, and Ideology*, 116–18.

For answers, let us return to the three leading areas of mainland settlement on which I began to concentrate in Chapter 1: New England, the Chesapeake, and the Delaware Valley. In each case I will focus here on a particular colony: Massachusetts, Virginia, and Pennsylvania.

New England

Wage labor enjoyed substantially greater mobility in the economic culture of New England than in contemporary old England. Material conditions – the abundance of land relative to the working population – explain the opportunity for mobility, but local legalities were decisive in securing it. In England a common response to the comparative scarcity of labor was to impose restrictions on its opportunities to circulate, either indirectly, by attempting to dampen wage competition through assessment, or directly, by criminalizing departure. Evidence of such interventions in Massachusetts is not lacking, but it suggests interventions were at best sporadic and lacked support.

In August 1630, toward the end of the first summer of the Great Migration, the Massachusetts Court of Assistants attempted to set colony-wide wage maxima in certain construction trades: "carpenters joyners brickelayers sawers and thatchers shall not take aboue 2^s [shillings] a day, nor any man shall giue more vnder paine of x^s to taker and giuer and that sawers shall not take aboue 4^s-6^d ye hundred for boards, att 6 scoore to the hundred, if they haue their wood felled and squared for them, & not aboue 5^s-6^d if they fell and square their wood themselves." In September "noe maister carpenter mason joyner or brickelayer" was to take "aboue 16^d [pence] a day for their worke, if they haue meate and drinke, & the second sort" that is those who were under age 24 and hence not yet masters "not aboue 12^d a day." Ordinary laborers' wages were restricted to 12^d daily and "not aboue 6^d" if they also received sustenance. But at the beginning of the following spring, without explanation, the Court abandoned its attempts at restraint, leaving transactions "free & att libertie as men shall reasonably agree."[50] In October 1633, two years after the first restraining order, the Court once more proclaimed wage maxima for master tradesmen in the construction trades, for "the best sorte of labourers," and for other artificers undertaking work "by the greate." Penalties for noncompliance were now set at 5/-. The Court left "Inferior workemen of the said occupaçons" and "inferior labou^{rs}" to have their wages set locally, by "the Constable of the said place & 2 other inhabitants that hee shall chuse." The Court also ordered "that all workemen shall worke the whole day alloweing convenient tyme for foode and rest." In justification the Court cited "extorçon vsed by dyvers psons of little conscience & the greate disorder wch grewe herevpon, by vaine and idle wast of much precious tyme, & expence of those imoderate

---

[50] *Records of the Court of Assistants of the Colony of the Massachusetts Bay, 1630–1692*, II (Boston, 1904), 3, 5, 6, 12. One shilling = 12 pence.

gaynes in Wyne strong water and other supfluities." In other words, such was the demand for labor driven by the arrival of migrants that wages had increased to a point where workmen found it appropriate to substitute leisure.[51]

The Assistants accompanied their reimposition of wage restraints with the proclamation of price controls on necessities. But neither price nor wage intervention was effective. Corn price restraints were abandoned within six months; other price controls went by the board the following year. In the case of wages, restraints were proclaimed reactively rather than in anticipation of scarcities, and then quickly set aside. On both occasions that the Assistants established wage maxima, August/September 1630 and October 1633, the action came toward the end of the construction and migration seasons, when demand for labor would have been slackening and wages falling, rather than at the beginning of the season. Indeed, the 1630 restraints were lifted in March 1631, precisely when demand would have been building again. The Assistants' 1633 penalties for excessive giving of wages lasted through the following season, but were widely ignored and were lifted in September 1634 by the General Court, which replaced them with a process for arbitration of wage inequities by local townsmen empowered to set new rates. Penalties for taking excessive wages were abandoned in 1635. Only two proceedings for taking excessive wages appear in the Assistants' records during the period the penalties were in effect, one against James Rawlens for hiring his servant to another at rates in violation of the order, the other against four workmen. In each case the 5/- penalty was assessed, but in the second case the level of payment was somewhat mitigated at the Assistants' subsequent session, and shortly after the General Court abolished the penalty. In 1636, the Court ordered "prices and rates of all workmen, laborers, and servants' wages" left to the towns to assess as they saw fit. The *Lawes and Libertyes* of 1648, restated in 1660 and 1672, authorized towns to regulate "oppression in wages and prices," but town action was rare, reproducing little of the detailed regulation to be found in contemporary England. In all, Stephen Innes has estimated that wage restraint was in effect for little more than 6 percent of the period from 1630 to 1684, mostly in the first decade of migration-driven expansion. Attempts to establish detailed colony-wide restraints in the early 1670s were twice rejected by the General Court and were not repeated. As to regulation of working conditions and terms, Massachusetts settlers "innovated by simply not receiving the considerably more rigid institutions and doctrines of the mother country." In short, the absence of "direct carryovers" from English law in the realm of labor practices meant that laboring people were part of the region's civic order of formal freedom from the outset.[52]

[51] Ibid., 36–7, 39.

[52] Ibid., 39, 47, 56, 57. Stephen Innes, *Creating the Commonwealth: The Economic Culture of Puritan New England* (New York, 1995), 227. See also Tomlins, *Law, Labor, and Ideology* (New York, 1993), 241.

Innes's inquiry into early New England's economic culture, along with congruent research, establishes that no metropolitan-standard legal culture of work of the kind assumed by Richard Morris was ever imported into the Massachusetts Bay colony.[53] It is less clear to what extent quotidien practice departed from the provincial legal cultures of the region's leading English settlers, but there are grounds for supposing that here too, Massachusetts practice was innovative.[54] East Anglian gentry prominent in the colony's early resident leadership, such as the Governor, John Winthrop, were critical of the extent to which, in England, "the authoritie of the Law" imposed obligations that inhibited working people's enjoyment of civic freedom, and implied that in New England matters would be different. In this they exhibited the same unease at the intrusion of metropolitan statutes into the provinces (particularly the poor laws), the same desire to see local and regional accommodations maintained, that can be found everywhere among English provincial justices in the later 1620s. But, it has been argued, there was something more to their concern – a feeling for "the plight of men and women of small means"; ambition to create "a commonwealth in which men and women would work in order to 'entertain one another in brotherly affection'"; rejection of those who lived off the labors of others – all founded on the hard times (harvest failures and a disrupted cloth industry) of the1620s but also on the peculiar institutional and ideological configuration (weak manorialism, disciplined self-rule, localized authority close to the people, communal solidarities) associated with pastoral legal culture. "Merchants, ministers, magistrates, even the governor, were expected to perform manual labor when necessary. This was to be a society with laborers, but without a distinct laboring class."[55]

The same gentry, nevertheless, saw no contradiction between a community of self-disciplined labor pursuing a covenanted collective good and the social subordinations considered due even in relatively solidaristic East Anglian communities. When subordination proved vulnerable to mobility engendered by economic improvement, Winthrop and the rest of the colony leadership (the Governor, Deputy-Governor, and eighteen Assistants who were the chartered executive officers of the Massachusetts

---

[53] In addition to Innes, *Creating the Commonwealth*, see Tomlins, *Law, Labor, and Ideology*, 241–8; Daniel Vickers, *Farmers and Fishermen: Two Centuries of Work in Essex County, Massachusetts, 1630–1850* (Chapel Hill, 1994), 25–7.

[54] The topic taken up here is also pursued in detail in Chapter 7.

[55] Innes, *Creating the Commonwealth*, 70, 76, 77. On changes in central-local government relations and local government structure initiated by Charles I, see Henrik Langelüddecke, "Law and Order in Seventeenth-Century England: The Organization of Local Administration during the Personal Rule of Charles I," *Law and History Review*, 15, 1 (Spring 1997), 49–76. On the contemporary English economy, see Keith Wrightson, *English Society, 1580–1680* (New Brunswick, N.J., 1982), 144–6; Innes, 73–5. On state and society, see Steve Hindle, *The State and Social Change in Early Modern England, 1550–1640* (New York, 2002). On the civic humanist impulse informing such ideas, see Andrew Fitzmaurice, *Humanism and America: An Intellectual History of English Colonisation, 1500–1625* (Cambridge, 2003).

Bay Company and, as the Court of Assistants, the earliest effective government of the Colony) sought its reinstitution in law and legal institutions,[56]
specifically through wage controls and sumptuary legislation to control
'superfluous' consumption, and through the Assistants' assumption of the
role of magistrates and eventual creation of a system of quarterly courts in
the main centers of settlement (Boston, Cambridge, Salem, and Ipswich)
as "an indispensable support for the Puritan ideal of communalism."[57]

The magistracy's desires proved unsustainable. Sumptuary controls,
largely focused upon enforcing social uniformities of dress during periods
of prosperity, were attempted in the 1630s, and again, following recovery
from harder economic times, in the 1650s and'60s. The very repetition
of condemnations of popular "excesses" in the matter of garb suggests
the limited success of legislation intended to quash them.[58] Colony-wide
wage controls, we have seen, were vulnerable to strong traditions of local
administration brought by the settlers, which meant that they were quickly
devolved to the towns where, as in England, local practice and preference
dictated outcomes.[59] Wage assessment as a practice was in any case vulnerable to the material circumstances of New England's settler economy.
Winthrop acknowledged as much in 1641. "Experience" had by then proven
"that it would not avail by any law to redress the excessive rates of labourers' and workmen's wages" because controls would simply provoke those
subjected to them "either [to] remove to other places where they might
have more, or else being able to live by planting and other employments of
their own, they would not be hired at all."[60] Further observations recorded
in Winthrop's journal a few years later, including an illustrative story that
has become well-known, highlighted the consequences of these legal and
material circumstances for the magistracy's preferred social order:

> The wars in England kept servants from coming to us, so as those we had
> could not be hired, when their times were out, but upon unreasonable terms,
> and we found it very difficult to pay their wages to their content, (for money
> was very scarce). I may upon this occasion report a passage between one of
> Rowley and his servant. The master, being forced to sell a pair of his oxen to
> pay his servant his wages, told his servant he could keep him no longer, not

---

[56] This had also been the reaction in England, wherever mobility and disorder had been
stimulated by large-scale change in agricultural organization, dearth, and trade depres-
sion. See, variously, William Hunt, *The Puritan Moment: The Coming of Revolution in an
English County* (Cambridge, Mass., 1983), 24–84; Buchanan Sharp, *In Contempt of All
Authority: Rural Artisans and Riot in the West of England, 1586–1660* (Berkeley, 1980); and
particularly David Underdown, *Revel, Riot and Rebellion: Popular Politics and Culture in
England, 1603–1660* (Oxford, 1985).

[57] David Thomas Konig, *Law and Society in Puritan Massachusetts: Essex County, 1629–1692*
(Chapel Hill 1979), xiii, and see 20–9.

[58] Innes, *Creating the Commonwealth*, 101–3.

[59] Vickers, *Farmers and Fishermen*, 26–7. We have already seen that in the case of ordinary
workpeople, wage assessment was placed in the hands of local representatives (the constables and their choice of assistants) virtually from the outset.

[60] Tomlins, *Law, Labor, and Ideology*, 241; Innes, *Creating the Commonwealth*, 179–80.

knowing how to pay him the next year. The servant answered, he would serve him for more of his cattle. But how shall I do (saith the master) when all my cattle are gone? The servant replied, you shall then serve me, and so you may have your cattle again.

Winthrop saw fit to record in marginalia his vexation at the "insolence" that the exchange appeared to him to represent, but vexation may as easily have been frustration. No move to countermand the imputed insolence by statutory discipline resulted.[61]

One powerful explanation for the existence of restraints on magistrates and employers' practical capacity to invoke legal disciplines in the social relations of work lay in the constitution of New England's settler legal culture itself. The Massachusetts Charter had described a basis for civil authority in the Commonwealth that rested substantially on the discretionary rule of leaders confined only by the ambit of activity "not repugnant to the laws and statutes" of England. In England, local legal cultures considerably refracted the sweep of metropolitan legalities, but in New England matters went further still, toward the founding of local legalities on "a popularly based determination to uphold rule by fundamental law."[62] The relationship between the colony's settler inhabitants and law throughout the first generation of settlement is best represented in language that appears in the *Lawes and Libertyes* of 1648, as the product of a struggle over the "Countenance of Authoritie."[63] The phrase signifies acceptance of the legitimacy of governmental rule over the lives, liberties, and properties of inhabitants, but simultaneously conveys two fundamental principles – that rule should have a definite basis or expression rather than be discretionary and mysterious; and, hence, that it should be knowable. In other words, before authority could be "countenanced" (entertained, approbated, tolerated, recognized), authority had to have a "countenance" (appearance, demeanor, expression) that rendered authority knowable and hence provided the confirmation, measure, or accounting ("countenance") of the legitimacy of its exercise. In New England, according to the *Lawes and Libertyes*, the basis upon which authority would be countenanced was to be "expresse Law of the country ... established by a General Court & sufficiently published," failing which, it was to be "the word of God."[64] This "Countenance of Authoritie" and the civic freedoms that embodied it were the product of struggles during the colony's first two decades. Together they constituted the colony's public sphere.[65]

[61] John Winthrop, *The History of New England, from 1630 to 1649.* 2 vols., James Kendall Hosmer, ed. (New York, 1908), II, 228. In England, the "insolence" of working men would eventually provoke a far more coercive response. See Chapter 8.

[62] Innes, *Creating the Commonwealth*, 201.

[63] Daniel R. Coquillette, "Introduction: 'The Countenance of Authoritie'," in Daniel R. Coquillette et al., editors, *Law in Colonial Massachusetts, 1639–1800* (Boston, 1984), xxi.

[64] John D. Cushing, editor, *The Laws and Liberties of Massachusetts, 1641–91*, 3 vols. (Wilmington, Del., 1976), I, 7.

[65] See generally Innes, *Creating the Commonwealth*, 201, 204–16; Daniel R. Coquillette, "Radical Lawmakers in Colonial Massachusetts: The 'Countenance of Authoritie' and

Local designs to replace the Charter's bestowal of discretionary authority on the colony's executive with an explicit frame of laws were in evidence from the early 1630s. Throughout, the existence of towns as significant claimants of jurisdictional authority proved something of an irritant to the colony's leadership, while providing insurgents with an independent base of support. The first signs of friction came in 1632, when the company/ colony's freemen proposed that the Assistants be elected, annually. In 1634, they proposed that all law making should henceforth be conducted at General Court (which they had the right to attend) and that for law-making purposes freemen should be represented at General Court by deputies elected from each existing town.[66] In 1636, the colony's magistracy reasserted its own authority through a series of orders that required "any newe plantation" or new gathering of churches to be approved by a majority of magistrates, and established the quarterly court system as an expression of magistratical rule outside the sphere of the towns. But the towns were then formally constituted and recognized as legal entities of their own with powers and institutions of self-management.[67]

The previous year, that is prior to the establishment both of quarterly courts and of the towns as legal entities, the freemen's deputies had

the Lawes and Libertyes," *New England Quarterly*, 67, 2 (1994), 179–211. More generally, David D. Hall notes seventeenth-century New England exhibited a certain "fluidity of power." David D. Hall, *Worlds of Wonder, Days of Judgment: Popular Religious Belief in Early New England* (New York, 1989), 19. Karen Kupperman has recently emphasized the important contrast in Puritan experience between the successful Massachusetts Bay settlement and the rather less successful "other Puritan colony" of Providence Island. In part, the contrast illustrates how very different conceptions of governance were embraced by absentee metropolitan Puritan "grandees" who founded Providence Island on an oligarchic, county-based model intended to maintain settlers "in a relationship of total dependence," and the resident provincial gentry who allowed Massachusetts Bay to take a very different direction. The record of that different direction in Massachusetts suggests, however, that the resident gentry were reluctant collaborators in the path the colony followed, dragged in the wake of initiatives from below. As Winthrop put it in 1639, "The people had long desired a body of laws, and thought their condition very unsafe, while so much power rested in the discretion of magistrates ... Two great reasons there were, which caused most of the magistrates and some of the elders not to be very forward in this matter. One was want of sufficient experience of the nature and disposition of the people, considered with the condition of the country and other circumstances." The other was fear of transgressing the Charter. See William H. Whitmore, "Introduction," in William H. Whitmore, editor, *The Colonial Laws of Massachusetts ... Together with the Body of Liberties of 1641* (Boston, 1890), 7. On Providence Island, see Karen Kupperman, *Providence Island, 1630–1641: The Other Puritan Colony* (New York, 1993), 17, 21, and generally 1–80.

[66] Whitmore, "Introduction," 3–6. We have already noted the impact of the deputies in the reconstitution and decentralization of wage assessment. It is also worth noting how the struggle within the company/colony between its assistants and freemen has certain clear parallels to contemporary struggles within English craft corporations between liveries and yeomanries. See n.36, this chapter.

[67] Konig, *Law and Society in Puritan Massachusetts*, 26. Konig disputes the jurisdictional significance generally accorded the town in Massachusetts local government. See generally 19–29.

proposed the creation of a body of explicit laws as should be judged useful
"for the well ordering of this plantation" and, clearly, for the well ordering of its magistracy. Winthrop and the magistracy resisted through inac-
tion, but the matter was pressed again in 1636.[68] The outcome was two
documents: *Moses, his Judicialls,* presented to the General Court in 1636
by the Reverend John Cotton; and *The Liberties of the Massachusets Colonie
in New England,* more commonly known as *The Body of Liberties,* prepared
between 1636 and 1639 by Nathaniel Ward. Both were circulated through
the towns, where they became the object of intense discussion. The relationship between the two was explained some years later by Increase
Nowel: "about nine years since wee used the help of some of the Elders
of our Churches to compose a modell of the Iudiciall lawes of Moses with
such other cases as might be referred to them, with intent to make use of
them in composing our lawes, but not to have them published as the lawes
of this Jurisdiction: nor were they voted in Court. For that book intitled
The Liberties &c: published about seven years since (which conteines also
many lawes and orders both for civil & criminal causes), and is commonly
(though without ground) reported to be our Fundamentalls that we owne
as established by Authoritie of this Court, and that after three years experience & general approbation." As this suggests, *Moses his Judicialls* never had
any status as colony law per se; as for Ward's *Body of Liberties,* it was accepted
by the General Court as established authority after three years general
discussion and approval, although not as "Fundamentalls" but as a basis
for further deliberation.[69]

Cotton's and Ward's documents were in fact quite unlike each other.
Cotton's conceded all to divinely inspired agencies of rule and nothing
to their restraint ("The Lord is our Judge, the Lord is our Lawgiver, the
Lord is our King, He will save us"). Ward's, in contrast, though not secular, was classically civic, a Roman-model code that summarized the social
structure of the settlement by defining the "liberties, Immunities and privileges" enjoyable by different categories of persons – Free Men, Women,
Children, Servants, Foreigners and Strangers – in their relations with each
other. Ward's code also included protections against misuse for "Bruite
Creatures" and a clear rejection of feudalistic conceptions of property.
Each of the codes, however, suggested legal cultures with no immediate
basis in English experience. Cotton's substituted biblical authority, making no reference to English law at all. Ward's altered numbers of received
wisdoms, particularly in its layers of safeguards for household dependents
(wives, children, servants). Both, then, were "self-conscious, abstract models that proposed a total restructuring of a legal system." Neither owed anything to prevailing institutions or authority. "Nothing like this had been
seen before. This was a totally new initiative in lawmaking."[70]

---

[68] John D. Cushing, "Introduction," in Cushing, ed., *Laws and Liberties,* I, xvi.
[69] Cushing, ed., *Laws and Liberties,* I, 5–6.
[70] Coquillette, "Radical Lawmakers in Colonial Massachusetts," 188–9, 192, 202.

Deliberations climaxed in 1648 with the General Court's adoption of the *Lawes and Libertyes*. This "extraordinary book" was the culmination of fifteen years' agitation, debate, and discussion. It combined *The Body of Liberties*' statement of the fundamental liberties of persons with a detailed code of legal conduct – all "lawes of generall concernment" – much of which was "entirely different from equivalent common law rules."[71] As such, the *Lawes and Libertyes* provided inhabitants with an explicit description of the bases of legitimate rule in political and social relations, a "countenance" for, and of, authority, in both its public aspect as civic rule, and its personal aspect as keystone to the structure of social and legal relations pertaining among and between inhabitants.

Insofar as *The Body* and the later *Lawes and Libertyes* can be said to have defined the colony's legal culture of work and labor, what they sketched were relationships substantially freer of detailed statutory discipline than those developing in contemporary English law. They also gave authority a countenance that was as much protective as coercive. *The Body*, for example described liberties of servants that were exclusively concerned with the servant's welfare.[72] Taking adolescent apprenticeship as its model for "service," *The Body* enumerated protections for those fleeing the "Tiranny and crueltie" of masters, prescribed release from service and compensation for any servant subjected to ill-treatment, forbade the assignment or hire of a servant to another for any period longer than one year and without the consent of authority, and made provision for freedom dues payable on expiration of seven years' service.[73] The only disciplinary note was sounded by the qualification to the last clause, that "if any have bene unfaithfull, negligent or unprofitable in their service, notwithstanding the good usage of their maisters, they shall not be dismissed until they have made satisfaction according to the Judgement of Authoritie." The *Lawes and Libertyes* repeated these provisions verbatim, prefacing them (in order of their original passage) with the orders earlier promulgated by the Court of Assistants and the General Court that had successively prohibited servants from dealing in commodities without permission of their masters (1630), required "workmen" (paid by the day) to work a full day (1633), made provision for the return of servants who had run from their masters (1635), delegated to the towns the authority to set such rates "of all workmens Labour[ers] and servants wages" as might be deemed appropriate (1636), and allowed payment of wages for work or service in corn (1641). The *Lawes and Libertyes* also reproduced the order of 1646 enabling town constables to call upon

---

[71] Ibid., 187, 197–8.

[72] Whitmore, ed., *Colonial Laws of Massachusetts*, Tit. "Liberties of Servants" 51–3, (clause 85–88).

[73] On assignment, see "Answer to the Petičon of Mr Thomas Makepeace and William, his sonne" (2 June 1653), in Nathaniel B. Shurtleff, editor, *Records of the Governor and Company of Massachusetts Bay in New England* (Boston, 1853–4), IV, 150, where it was stated that "no aprentice or servant is in any way liable to ans^r his masters debts, or become servant to any other than his master, but by assignement, according to lawe."

artificers and handicraftsmen not otherwise employed to work in the harvest for wages, but exempted anyone attending to his own business. Failure to comply was punishable by fine. As a code of conduct for those in service, the *Lawes and Libertyes* recalled aspects of English law but with little of the detail and virtually none of the measures subjecting hireling labor to criminal discipline. Winthrop's recognition in 1641 that restraining laborers and workmen would simply result in their departure elsewhere or withdrawal from wage work, though addressed principally to the likely effects of wage restraint, had clear application to other aspects of work's legal culture.[74] Only covenanted servants – those explicitly bound by indenture or other form of written contract to furnish services on demand for a prescribed term[75] – were unambiguously subject to restraint, and the deleterious consequences of their restraint were qualified in part by the oversight of the conditions of restraint that *The Body*'s prescribed liberties required "authoritie" to exercise.

That statutory work disciplines should, by the 1640s, appear relatively circumscribed is not necessarily surprising, given the local urge to constrain the general ambit of "authoritie." But the explanation lies also in the demographic characteristics of the early New England workforce. We have seen that the migrating population for whom the orders and liberties culminating in the *Lawes and Libertyes* were prescribed consisted of East Anglian families, in which the propensity to labor was represented by the head of household and household dependents (that is, wives and children), and unattached males of diverse regional origins, predominantly single and youthful, traveling under a commitment to labor for a term of years in return for passage and subsistence. Under these circumstances, disciplinable service became identified principally with two kinds of people, outsiders and youth. As to "outsiders," as the native-born population grew, service's identification with immigration produced a sense of status differentiation between Creole and non-Creole populations. One early and substantial hint appears in the *Lawes and Liberties*, where a measure on bond-slavery originally adopted in 1641 specified three kinds of people that could be subjected lawfully to the loss of liberty that the disciplines of servitude entailed. All were in one form or another outsiders to the local

---

[74] For example, an order of 15 May 1672 noting "oppression" on the part of "worke men and labourers" by demanding "an allowance of licquors or wine euery day, ouer and aboue their wages" makes pointed mention of the workmen's refusal to work without the allowance but addresses the matter by prohibiting employers from giving wine or liquor to workmen, not by criminalizing refusals to work. See Shurtleff, ed., *Records*, IV, 510. It is also worth noting that the embezzlement order of 4 November 1646 (*Records*, II, 180) drew a distinction between "servants" who answered to their "masters" and "workmen" who answered to "such as set yᵐ on worke" in making provision for restitution.

[75] Thus the order of 13 December 1636 established that "no servant shalbee set free ... until hee have served out the time covenanted." Shurtleff, ed., *Records*, I, 186. By the law of 14 October 1668 ("Maritime Affairs"), sec. 5, 22, 23, the service of "Marriners" was ordered secured by explicit covenant, and in consequence seamen rendered criminally disciplinable as servants. Cushing, *Laws and Liberties*, I, 200–1, 204.

community: "lawfull captives, taken in just warrs," which meant Indian captives; "such strangers as willingly sell themselves, or are solde to us," that is, imported indentured servants and/or slaves; and persons "who shall be judged thereto by Authoritie," that is, persons committed to serve others by judicial execution – persons convicted of criminal offenses, or debtors delivered by court execution to serve creditors.[76]

As to the second category, "youth," migrant indentured servitude substantially meant youthful servitude. But the Creole population also reproduced venerable practices – life-cycle service, craft apprenticeship – of the English local communities from which the first settler generation had come and to which English regional legal cultures were responsive. Indeed, as migration fell away after 1640, drying up the supply of migrant "outsiders," Creole youth increasingly became practically the only source of deployable labor available to local inhabitants.[77] Because youth was outside the community of household heads (and because youth is always everywhere considered simultaneously socially vulnerable and socially dangerous, and hence meet for restraint), justifications of its subjection to "authoritie" were relatively easy to come by, as they were not for adult wage workers whose extreme scarcity preserved their mobility. In this respect, then, Massachusetts law reproduced the age-specificity of England's legal culture of work, but with even greater precision, and an even clearer age-specific division in status. Throughout the remainder of the colonial period – that is, once the anomalous demographic effects of the Great Migration were past – statutory propensities to identify disciplinable service with youth became one of the clearest characteristics of the legal culture of work in Massachusetts.[78]

The identification appeared early on. In 1642, for example, the General Court's orders for the good education of children treated the terms "child," "servant," and "apprentice" as if they were synonymous. The orders required town selectmen to ensure that "masters of families" were taking steps to ensure the education of their "children & apprentices" and to catechize their "children and servants" weekly, and that "such children and apprentices" be required to demonstrate their religious knowledge before the selectmen. The selectmen were to ensure, further,

---

[76] Cushing, *Laws and Liberties*, 10. George H. Moore, *Notes on the History of Slavery in Massachusetts* (New York, 1866), 17, argues that being originally listed under the category of "*Forreiners and strangers*" the title on bond-slavery had no relevance to indentured servitude, but only to Indian and black [heathen] slavery, and to criminals. It is debatable, however, whether strangers meant *only* heathen; certainly in seventeenth-century colloquial English usage "forreiner" could mean anyone from outside the locality, or outside the county in which the locality was situated. "Strangers" does, however, suggest restricted applicability. Massachusetts' bond-slavery title is discussed in greater detail in Chapter 9.

[77] Vickers, *Farmers & Fishermen*, 52–60, 64–76, 82.

[78] Tomlins, *Law, Labor, and Ideology*, 244–7. On service and adolescence see Griffiths, *Youth and Authority*; Ilana Krausman Ben-Amos, *Adolescence and Youth in Early Modern England* (New Haven, 1994).

that all parents & masters do breed & bring up their children & apprentices in some honest Lawfull calling, labour, or imployment, either in husbandry or some other trade, profitable for themselves and the Common-wealth, if they will not, or cannot train them up in learning to fitt them for higher imployments. And if any of the Select men after admonition by them given to such masters of families shall find them stil negligent of their duty in the particulars afore mention[n]ed, whereby children & servants become rude, stubborn & unruly, the sayd Select men with the help of two Magistrates or the next County Court for that Shire, shall take such children or apprentices from them, and place them with some masters for yeares, (boyes till they come to twenty one, & girls eighteen years of age compleat) which will more strictly look unto, & force them to submit unto government, according to the Rules of this order if by fair means & former instructions they will not be drawn unto it.

In the 1658 revision of the *Lawes and Libertyes*, digested under the heading "Children & Youth," this order was supplemented by others providing that children and servants who disobeyed their parents, masters and governors "to the disturbance of families, & discouragment of such parents & Governours" were subject to be whipped on order of a magistrate; and also ordering that anyone insinuating themselves into the company of "the young people of this Country ... whether children, servants, apprentices, schollers belonging to the Colledg, or any Latine schoole," and seducing them from their "callings, studyes, and honest occupations, & lodginge places" should make it their business to hasten "all such youths" back to "their several imployments & places of abode" or face a fine of forty shillings.[79]

Attempts to impose controls upon the mobility of youthful labor gathered pace in the later seventeenth century (suggesting the existence both of heightened concern and unsuppressed mobility). Beginning in 1668, town constables were required to take note of all young persons living "from under Family Government, viz. do not serve their Parents or Masters, as Children, Apprentices, hired Servants, or Journey men ought to do, and usually did in our Native Country, being subject to their Commands and Discipline."[80] Selectmen were to bind idle (or poor) children and youth to serve.[81] Masters of ships were subject to fine for entertaining "any man's son, being under age, or apprentice, or covenant servant" as a crewmember, without leave of his parent or master. Apprentices or servants who unlawfully absented themselves to join vessels were required on expiration of their indentures to compensate their masters for time lost, up to one year.[82]

[79] Cushing, *Laws and Liberties*, I, 86–7. For the original orders, see Shurtleff, *Records*, III, 242 (order of 14 October 1651) and 355 (order of 22 August 1654). As summarized in May 1658 (*Records*, IV, 325), the "office and power of a counstable" included taking notice "of such as shall harbor any young people, children, servants, apprentices, students or schollers, & not hasten them to their respective imployments."

[80] Cushing, *Laws and Liberties*, I, 187. See also the 1672 revision of the *Laws and Liberties*, Tit. Children and Youth, in Cushing, *Laws and Liberties*, II, 252–4.

[81] "An Act for Regulating of Townships..." *Province Laws, 1692–3*, ch.28, sec.7, 67.

[82] "An Act for Preventing of Men's Sons or Servants Absenting themselves from their Parent's or Master's Service Without Leave," *Province Laws, 1694–5*, ch.23, 192. See also "An Act

The quarterly courts had jurisdiction over all complaints arising from master-servant relationships. Restatement of the courts' jurisdiction as county institutions underlined the identification of bound servitude with youth. "Whereas there frequently happens in the several counties through this province many failures both on the part of masters and mistresses, and on the part of indented servants, in the performance of their respective covenants or duties, as expressed in their indentures or deeds of covenant whereby said servants are bound ... it shall and may be lawful for the courts of general sessions of the peace for the respective counties ... where any indented, bought, or any way legally bound, servant or apprentice have been abused or evil treated by their masters or mistresses, or that the education of *such children* in reading or writing and cyphering, according to the tenor of their indentures, has been unreasonably neglected, to take cognizance of such representation or complaint ... and the said court may order such child or children to be liberated or discharged." Correspondingly, poor children indented to masters by overseers of the poor or selectmen who absented themselves from service were required to make satisfaction "either by service or otherwise, as [to the justices of the court of sessions] shall seem meet."[83]

With three additions, this catalog of statute law with impact upon the understanding of servitude in the Massachusetts colony is complete; and the additions, in fact, confirm the identification of servitude with youth and "outsiders." The first consists of what one might loosely term "public order" or police statutes, which identify "dangerous" groups who should be singled out for oversight and control. They are "apprentices, servants, Indians and negros"; "Indian servant[s], or negro or molatto servant[s], or slave[s]"; "Indian, negro and molatto servants and slaves"; and "negro, Indian or molatto servant[s]." The second, an act of July 1701, attempted to impose judicial controls on Indian servitude, particularly on the "oppression which some of the English exercise towards the Indians, by drawing them to consent to, covenant or bind themselves or children apprentices or servants for an unreasonable term." The third, an act of February 1708/9, sought in attempts to encourage the importation of youthful white servants from Britain to avoid the growing possibility of an unwelcome dependence upon Indian and African servitude for deployable labor. The act offered a bounty of forty shillings per head for every male servant between the ages of eight and twenty-five brought into Massachusetts from Great Britain between April 1709 and April 1712 and disposed of in service.[84]

---

for the Preventing of Persons Under Age, Apprentices or Servants, Being Transported out of the Province without the Consent of their Masters, Parents or Guardians," *Province Laws, 1718–19*, ch.14, 119.

[83] "An Act in Further Addition to an Act Intitled, 'An Act in Explanation of and Supplement to an Act Referring to the Poor'." *Province Laws 1758–9*, ch.17 (emphasis added).

[84] On public order, see, for example, "An Act to Prevent Disorders in the Night," *Province Laws, 1703–04*, ch.11; "An Act to Prevent the Breaking or Damnifying of Lamps," *Province Laws, 1752–3*, ch.16; "An Act for Further Preventing ... Disorderly Assemblies," *Province Laws, 1752–3*, ch.18. On Indian servitude, see "An Act for Preventing Abuses

Bounties notwithstanding, migrant indentured servitude would have little impact on eighteenth-century Massachusetts labor markets. It had never played much of a role in furnishing the colony with labor. As in other mainland regions, deployable labor in Massachusetts was predominantly youthful; but unlike the regions that experienced significant migration, it was also almost exclusively Creole. Massachusetts farm households relied on their own children, occasionally – but rarely – supplemented by children obtained from England, usually through extended informal networks rather than the commercialized "trade" in migrant servants characteristic of other regions of settlement. Children in service to their fathers or (less often) bound out to neighbors were the dominant segment of the rural economy's deployable labor supply. "New England conceit they and their Children can doe enough."[85] Hence it is not surprising that the legal culture of work in New England was one that not only was preoccupied with controlling youth, but that it should also comprehensively muddy the distinction between *son* and *servant*.[86]

The Chesapeake

If the Massachusetts statute record indicates colonial New England's legal culture of work and labor represented no more than a faint echo of the standard metropolitan master/servant model – one, furthermore, refracted through the peculiar legalities of the pastoral regions from which its core settlers came – Virginia's record seems at first much more familiar to eyes attuned to the general outlines of English law. Indeed, particularly in the colony's early years, Virginia's legal culture of work in some respects overshot the metropolitan model by a distance no less impressive than that by which Massachusetts fell short. Historical examination, however, suggests not that the Chesapeake represented a more faithful, even exaggerated, reproduction of the English model than New England could manage, but rather that Virginia's legal culture of work and labor, like that of Massachusetts, in its own way, was in good part an expression of the legal culture dominant in those regions of England that provided the most telling influences upon Virginia's social and political development. Where early New England shows the influence of England's pastoral legal cultures, early Virginia manifests that of the arable: manorialism,

to the Indians," *Province Laws, 1700–01*, ch.9. On the importation of white servants, see "An Act to Encourage the Importation of White Servants," *Province Laws, 1708–09*, ch.11. Encouragement of the importation of adolescent labor from England had been a theme of colony discourse since the end of the Great Migration. See, for example, Innes, *Creating the Commonwealth*, 104–5.

[85] Abbot Emerson Smith, *Colonists in Bondage: White Servitude and Convict Labor in America, 1607–1776* (Chapel Hill, 1947), 29.

[86] Vickers, *Farmers and Fishermen*, 76, and see generally 64–8. As Vickers notes, unceasing dependence on intrafamilial labor tended also to muddy the line between majority and independence. *Farmers and Fishermen*, 68–77. See also Philip J. Greven, *Four Generations: Population, Land, and Family in Colonial Andover* (Ithaca, N.Y., 1970).

hierarchical social relations, strong county elites, powerful justices of the peace, powerful county courts, and a comparatively atomized population that had few centers of countervailing authority.[87]

Virginia's earliest history as a civil society was the product of three compelling influences: environment, experience, and the civic imagination of its Tudor-Stuart adventurer-promoters. The Chesapeake environment was hostile; disease, starvation, and volatile relations with the region's indigenous inhabitants were endemic throughout the half century following the first, temporary, appearance of the English at Roanoke, 100 miles to the south, in 1585. The first real English attempt at strategic disruption of Spanish claims to the mainland north of Florida, the Roanoke colony's purpose was in part to serve as a sign of English sovereign possession, in part as a shore base for privateering (in effect, a martial equivalent to the commercial fishing camps of Newfoundland and the North Atlantic coast[88]). Established in 1585, reestablished in 1587, the colony disappeared within two years, leaving little behind it but memories of privation and expectations unfulfilled.

Roanoke's organization had not been entirely *sui generis*; the colony had its parallels nearer to home than Newfoundland, in the armed plantations, or manors, that the same generation of Elizabethan adventurers had earlier established at Munster, Leinster, Ulster, and Connacht in Ireland. Far from attempts to "reconstitute English society or legal institutions in an overseas setting," these were autonomous "authoritarian settlements ... centrally planned and highly structured colonies on classical and military lines" populated by an emigrant tenantry of soldier-farmers with military obligations and subject to military discipline.[89] On the inside, however, one can also see these settlements and their Chesapeake successors as attempts to realize an ideal of social organization that seemed impossible in swarming England – the disciplined commonwealth of widespread civic duty and active participation embraced by the sixteenth century's civic humanists from More onward. Such was the society described by Sir Thomas Smith, promoter of Irish settlements, in his famous *De Republica Anglorum*, which envisaged England as a mixed commonwealth of monarch, aristocracy,

---

[87] This section concentrates on Virginia. We should note, however, that Maryland was laid out as "the most complete transplanting of a manorial system that was to be attempted anywhere in English America." David W. Galenson, "The Settlement and Growth of the Colonies: Population, Labor, and Economic Development," in Stanley L. Engerman and Robert E. Gallman, editors, *The Cambridge Economic History of the United States* (Cambridge and New York, 1996–2000), I, 143. See also Edward T. Price, *Dividing the Land: Early American Beginnings of our Private Property Mosaic* (Chicago, 1995), 98–9.

[88] On Roanoke and the Newfoundland fisheries, see David T. Konig, "'Dale's Laws' and the Non-Common Law Origins of Criminal Justice in Virginia," *American Journal of Legal History*, 26, 4 (1982), 361–2. For details of the organization of the early North Atlantic fishery, see in addition Vickers, *Farmers and Fishermen*, 85–90.

[89] Nicholas Canny, "The Permissive Frontier: The Problem of Social Control in English Settlements in Ireland and Virginia, 1550–1650," in K. R. Andrews et al., editors, *The Westward Enterprise: English Activities in Ireland, the Atlantic, and America 1480–1650* (Liverpool, 1978), 17–44, at 18.

and the multitude of others: gentry, yeomen, and at the base the wide class of day laborers, poor husbandmen, copyholders, artificers and others with "no voice nor authoritie in our common wealth" of whom little account was taken. Represented in affairs of law and government by their superiors, their fate was "only to be ruled, and not to rule other." Yet the gentry and yeomen were of civic importance, particularly in parliament, and even the "multitude" not altogether without civic capacity:

> For in cities and corporate townes for default of yeomen, enquests and Juries are impaneled of such manner of people. And in villages they be commonly made Churchwardens, alecunners, and manie times Constables, which office toucheth more the common wealth, and at the first was not imployed upon such lowe and base persons.[90]

Smith grounded his Irish plantation schemes upon the idea of martial citizenship – "every Souldiour ... Mayster and owner of his land" – that invoked the ethos of civic participation he would later develop in *De Republica Anglorum*. Reality was messier. The Irish plantations "were far from the models in civil living that had been intended," characterized by "patterns of settlement radically different from those originally envisaged," their promoters unable "to maintain control over those to whom had been entrusted the task of colonization."[91] Nor, with a few leading exceptions, were the English adventurers who returned to the American mainland in 1607 to establish their Virginia outpost experienced *coloni* soldier-farmers, but predominantly gentry cocooned in status and unprepared for work, minds turned more to gold and glory than cultivation and corn.[92] In a pattern to be repeated throughout Jamestown's early years, most of the new arrivals died wretchedly within a few months of landfall, for they "would rather starve and rot with idlenes, then be perswaded to do anything for their owne reliefe."[93]

---

[90] Sir Thomas Smith, *De Republica Anglorum: A Discourse on the Commonwealth of England* (written between 1562 and 1565; first published 1583), L. Alson, ed. (Cambridge, 1906), 46; Fitzmaurice, *Humanism and America*, 22–5. On social disorder in England, see A. L. Beier, *Masterless Men: The Vagrancy Problem in England, 1560–1640* (London, 1985). The issue is discussed in Konig, "'Dale's Laws'," 359–60.

[91] Canny, "The Permissive Frontier," 17.

[92] Edmund Morgan, *American Slavery, American Freedom: The Ordeal of Colonial Virginia* (New York, 1975), 83–6.

[93] John Smith, *A True Relation of such occurrences and accidents of noate, as hath hapned in Virginia, since the first planting of that Collony* (1608), in Philip L. Barbour, editor, *The Complete Works of Captain John Smith* (Chapel Hill, 1986), I, 35. Between them, John Smith and the Virginia Company ensured that the "lazy gentry" of Jamestown would enter the lore of early English colonizing. But as John Gilles has emphasized, one must recognize the condemnation of "intemperate" colonists as a profoundly important rhetorical strategy pervading the entire representation of the Virginia enterprise in Virginia Company documents during the critical years of 1608–10. In the *True Declaration of the Estate of the Colonie in Virginia* (1610) and its companion, *True and Sincere Declaration of the purpose and ends of the Plantation begun in Virginia* (1610), the company responded to the previous year's reports of disease and death at Jamestown and the catastrophic failure of the relief expedition led by Sir Thomas Gates and Sir George Somers, culminating in the wreck of the

The response in London to the venture's continued difficulties, whether attributable to indolence or indiscipline, was further resort to the humanist ideal of authoritarian civic commonality.[94] Enjoined by its charter to accord settlers the same "Liberties, Franchizes, and Immunities" as they would enjoy in England, the Virginia Company's leaders chose to interpret and implement their obligation through the quasi-martial model of extensively devolved executive discretion enumerated among the powers of English county lords-lieutenant and actively in use in British border regions.[95] Thus embodied in the *Lawes Divine, Morall and Martiall*, in force from 1609 until 1619, colony government became an exercise in survival that invoked "martial discipline in the civic tradition."[96] Though the *Lawes* read more extremely than, one suspects, they came to operate,[97] their existence is one more reminder of the range of resources available in English legal culture. In socially and regionally diverse emigrant populations, legal practice could follow any of a plurality of regional and ideological patterns. There was no single pattern of metropolitan legal habit to be imported from the "mother country," but rather multiple variations.

The system implemented by the *Lawes* encouraged compact, disciplined settlement. It retained all land in the ownership of the company and farmed it collectively with a gang-organized workforce of company servants. It "contained popular disturbance, although not flight to the Indians, but it met with continued opposition from army officers and freemen who sought greater autonomy."[98] Evidence of the extent of restraint on the latter is supplied by events during the governorship of Samuel Argall, who in 1618 noted that resort to martial powers had enabled him to defy claims to the privileges of freemen insisted upon by the citizens of Bermuda Hundred and "force the artificers there to follow their arts,"

Sea Venture, with news of the miraculous recovery of Gates and Somers in the Bermudas and the successful relief of Jamestown by Lord De La Warr. "What was needed," writes Gilles, "was a rhetorical strategy that would confirm the original myth of Virginia while instilling a new and more realistic mood of forbearance in inevitable hardship – along with a (less realistic) willingness to postpone profits indefinitely. Temperance was one answer to this promotional problem." In the *True Declaration* the reports of "disease, the embarrassing topics of shipwreck and starvation are parlayed into the more manageable *topos* of intemperance" and idleness. "Virginia had not ceased to be fruitful: the colonists had simply become too lazy to avail themselves of the abundance that surrounded them." See John Gilles, Shakespeare's Virginia Masque," *ELH* (*English Literary History*), 53, 4 (Winter 1986), 679, 680.

94 Canny, "The Permissive Frontier," 39; Warren M. Billings, "The Transfer of English Law to Virginia, 1606–1650," in Andrews et al., eds., *The Westward Enterprise*, 216–17.

95 Second Charter of Virginia (1609), in Francis Newton Thorpe, editor, *The Federal and State Constitutions, Colonial Charters, and other Organic Laws* (Washington, D.C., 1909), VII, 3790–3802, at 3800; Konig, "'Dale's Laws'," 357.

96 Fitzmaurice, *Humanism and America*, 85.

97 Finbarr McCarthy, "The Influence of 'Legal Habit' on English-Indian Relations in Jamestown, 1606–1612," *Continuity and Change*, 5, 1 (1990), 45–6, 51; Smith, *Colonists in Bondage*, 10–11; Morgan, *American Slavery, American Freedom*, 88–9.

98 Canny. "Permissive Frontier," 39.

whose refusal to do so had been "to the great prejudice [of the] Colony."[99]
With the successful development of tobacco as a staple crop after 1617,
however, came growing insistence among local planters that they be freed
from such coercive restraints and left to labor for themselves, and that
additional labor be imported to work for them. Thereafter, opposition to
metropolitan control of livelihood and settlement grew apace among the
free population; their numbers, though initially tiny, by this time had been
augmented by the emergence from servitude of the survivors of the first
generation of company servants.[100] The animating vision of the Company
during the "survival" phase had not been fundamentally hostile to private
opportunity. "One of the principal aims of civic government was to create
the conditions in which citizens could enjoy private lives unthreatened by
the invasive claims of arbitrary rule." But though profit was legitimate it
was "secondary to the common good." Tobacco cultivation changed the
equation.[101]

Free planters' demands for opportunities to work on their own behalf
and for recruitment of additional labor to work for them as well as for
the company became the basis of an accommodation with London.
Restrictions on settlement were eased, additional labor was recruited,
the restrictive *Lawes* abandoned, and an assembly instituted to admit
freemen to the process of formulating local law, hitherto a process
monopolized by the governor and council.[102] The result was rapid
planter dispersion and rapid immigration: between 1619 and 1622, some
3,570 people entered the colony (compared with perhaps 2,500 since
the settlement of Jamestown). The dispersion of settlement and influx
of new migrants meant heightened conflict with the region's indigenous
population, leading to the Jamestown Massacre (1622). In the short term
a major setback, the Massacre bred such savage retaliation that for some
years local Indians ceased to offer any kind of restraint on the spread of
settlement.[103]

---

[99] Konig, "'Dale's Laws'," 365.
[100] The white population in 1619/20 numbered approximately 1,200 (figure includes about
300 recent arrivals.) The established population was 928 in 222 habitable houses: 878
men (73.5%), 124 women (10.4%), and 192 children (16.1%). Also present were 15
African men and 17 African women. William Thorndale, "The Virginia Census of 1619,"
Magazine of Virginia Genealogy, 33, 3 (Summer 1995), 155–70.
[101] Fitzmaurice, *Humanism and America*, 86. On law at Jamestown and the transformative
impact of tobacco cultivation, see William E. Nelson, *The Common Law in Colonial America*,
volume 1, *The Chesapeake and New England, 1607–1660* (Oxford, 2008), 13–47.
[102] Canny, "Permissive Frontier," 40; Morgan, *American Slavery, American Freedom*, 96; Finbarr
McCarthy, "Participatory Government and Communal Property: Two Radical Concepts
in the Virginia Charter of 1606," *University of Richmond Law Review*, 29, 2 (March 1995),
327–8; James Horn, *A Land as God Made It: Jamestown and the Birth of America* (New York,
2005), 239–48.
[103] Morgan, *American Slavery, American Freedom*, 98–101. As Morgan shows, mortality rates
during this first period of frequent migration were a far greater threat to the colony's
stability.

The intensification of tobacco cultivation and the corresponding rise in demand for labor imports in the years after 1619 determined the direction of the post-survival legal culture of work and labor in Virginia. When promoters scoured for labor to rebuild and replenish the settlement during Jamestown's first decade, they found themselves forced to draw upon those very elements whose disorderliness in England they most feared and despised, those least capable of the participatory civic role that the population of a new commonwealth was supposed to perform – homeless children from the streets of London, convicts and rebels, vagrant adolescent farm servants, the displaced rural poor:

> We can be sure ... that the majority were either ignorant or misinformed concerning conditions in the New World; and it is likely that they were both poorly equipped and poorly motivated for what lay ahead of them. It soon became evident that they had no intention of making extraordinary sacrifices for the advancement of civility, and they reacted quickly against the harsh laws, the privations, and the organized labour which they were called upon to endure. Almost every description of the work force in Virginia mentioned that they were "full of mutenie and treasonable intendments."[104]

The result was a legal culture of work and labor that departed the civic ambitions of the Virginia Company's creators for something far cruder: an ad hoc contrivance that emerged piecemeal during the thirty years following the establishment of the Assembly. It was a local creation that responded to local contexts by drawing selectively on elements of English statute law that addressed agricultural cultivation. It retained something of the blunt severity of the *Lawes*, while transforming the primary objective of discipline from that of collective survival and civic order to individual planter profit. It developed in a context of institutional evolution. And extremity, particularly in rates of mortality and accompanying social instability, remained its constant companion.

The earliest steps taken by the Assembly (1619) required the recording of indentures of servants arriving in Virginia and made provision for their enforcement. Without a record, masters in Virginia anticipated they would be unable legally to hold incoming servants to service for periods longer than the annual hiring customary in English service and assumed in common law. One year's service was no recompense for the costs of transporting settlers and maintaining them while in service.[105] At the same time, the

---

[104] Canny, "The Permissive Frontier," 27.

[105] Warren M. Billings, "The Law of Servants and Slaves in Seventeenth Century Virginia," *Virginia Magazine of History and Biography*, 99, 1 (1991), 48. Economic historians have provided considerable evidence for the "efficiency" of markets in indentured labor, by which is meant the rational adjustment of contract length to costs of passage and maintenance, and variations in human capital. See generally Galenson, *White Servitude in Colonial America*; Farley Grubb, "The Market for Indentured Immigrants: Evidence on the Efficiency of Forward-Labor Contracting in Philadelphia, 1745–73," *Journal of Economic History*, 45, 4 (December 1985), 855–68. Unfortunately little of this work covers the first half of the seventeenth century.

Assembly's move to require proof of an individual's commitment to serve represented a variation on prior practice that marked imported servants as a distinct segment of the population. The first trickle of English migrant labor recruited by the Company during the decade after 1609 had been styled "adventurers" (investors) in the Company, not servants, committed to seven years of residence and labor in exchange for a cash advance for the voyage, subsistence, and a division of lands and profits on completion. Though little of the anticipated wealth eventuated, land had been granted to survivors in 1618. The concept of subsidized passage in return for commitments to labor and some form of claim to land survived but increasingly the Company acted not as an enterprise procuring settlers for its own lands but as an agent procuring manual labor for Virginia's population of free planters. Imported labor "became a distinct class in the community."[106]

Simultaneously, individuals outside the company also began recruiting and exporting labor. Toward the end of the first decade after the establishment of the Jamestown settlement, the Virginia Company had begun granting secondary patents to independent groups of proprietors that permitted them to establish independent plantations ("particular plantations") outside the company's aegis. Their patents afforded the proprietors extensive discretion, and these plantations – Bermuda Hundred, Berkeley Hundred, West Shirley Hundred, Flowerdew Hundred, Martin's Hundred – tended to function as self-contained communities analogous to England's manor-dominated "closed" parishes, or the armed Irish plantations, and "quite likely, went their own way with regard to any system of justice." Like the company, the proprietors transported settlers and granted them rights to land in exchange for labor commitments.[107]

In 1625, 487 persons were listed as servants in the colony out of a total population of 1,227. Largely children and young adults in the age range 15–24, their demographic profile prefigured what would emerge in the years of peak servant migration ahead. The Assembly did not pay attention to the details of their legal status until the 1630s, however, when the

[106] Smith, *Colonists in Bondage*, 9, 16. See also Price, *Dividing the Land*, 91–4.
[107] David W. Konig, "The Williamsburg Courthouse: A Research Report and Interpretive Guide," unpublished manuscript (Colonial Williamsburg Foundation, 1987), 78, and generally 78–82. The patent for Martin's Brandon, granted in 1616 and one of the most generous, allowed the patentee to "enjoye his landes in as lardge and ample manner, to all intentes and purposes, as any Lord of any Manours in England doth holde his grounde." In Alexander Brown, *The Genesis of the United States* (Boston, 1897), II, 943. Edward Price terms these patented estates "the first genre of large estate in British North America ... virtual subcolonies that fall in the line of descent of the later slave-worked plantations" and "virtually independent colonies under the Virginia Company ... even possessing limited political independence." Between 1619 and 1623, 44 such "particular" plantations were patented in return for patentees' promises to transport settlers. Price, *Dividing the Land*, 20, 93–4. William Thorndale's analysis of the 1619 census shows that at that time only about half of the population was within the jurisdiction of the Virginia Company, per se, the remainder divided among the secondary patentees and private plantations that had been setting up since 1616. Thorndale, "The Virginia Census of 1619," 155–70.

numbers of migrants began to mount. During the Assembly's first decade, while investment in tobacco cultivation was expanding rapidly but before the influx of migrants began appreciably to quicken, its concerns focused more on the costs of hireling labor (as in Massachusetts during the construction boom of the early Great Migration period) than with defining the condition of indentured labor, adopting measures that emphasized the role of magistrates in assessing wages and that forbade laborers and artificers to leave work unfinished "unlesse it be for not payinge of his wages."[108]

During the 1630s, these English-origin hireling statutes ceased to have effect: they do not appear in any subsequent Assembly revisals of Virginia law.[109] Simultaneously the Assembly's attention turned to indentured servitude. Piecemeal, several distinct measures established servitude in Virginia as a rigorous condition of subordination to a master.[110] Absconding was made liable to severe punishment, as was clandestine marriage, fornication and, in general, entry into any relations with another that implied an

---

[108] Act XXX (February 1631/2), adopting 1 Jac. c.6 (1603) which required Justices to conform to the wage assessment provisions of the Statute of Artificers and empowered them to set wage minima, and Act XXVIII (September 1632), adopting essentially word for word the first full section of clause x of 5 Eliz. c.4 (1563), the Statute of Artificers: "every artificer or laborer that shall be lawfully reteyned in and for the buildinge or repayringe of any church, house, shipp, milne, or every other peice of worke taken in greate, or that shall hereafter take uppon him to make or finish any such thinge or worke, shall continue and not depart from the same unlesse it be for not payinge of his wages, or hire agreed on, or otherwise by lawfull authoritie taken from the sayd worke, or lycense to depart by him, that hath the charge thereof before the finishinge of the sayd worke uppon penaltie of one mounthes imprisonment without bayle or mayneprize and the forfeiture of the sum of £5 sterlinge to the partie soe greaved, over and besides such ordinarie costs and damages as may or ought to be recovered by the common lawes for any such offence"; both in William Waller Hening, *The Statutes at Large; Being a Collection of all the Laws of Virginia, from the First Session of the Legislature, in the Year 1619* (New York, 1823), I, 167, 193, available at http://www.vagenweb.org/hening/ (accessed 22 August 2009). See also Act V of February 1632/3, I, 208, requiring tradesmen "to worke at theire trades and not suffered to plant tobacco or corne or doe any other worke in the ground" and to have "good payment made unto them for theire worke."

[109] The Assembly revised and restated the colony's laws in 1632, 1642, 1652, and 1662. On each occasion the goal was to clarify and bring order to the accumulation of statutes passed over the previous decade. In 1652 and 1662, the Assembly had the added motivation of adjusting to the effects of metropolitan political events – the Protectorate and the Restoration. See generally Billings, "Transfer of English Law," 226–7.

[110] Court records from the 1630s and early 1640s indicate that hired workers and some artisans were made subject to orders to perform agreed terms of service, or agreed tasks, in the face of a later refusal or early departure, but these orders peter out in Virginia thereafter. See Tomlins, *Law, Labor, and Ideology*, 250, notes 85 and 86. This, and the abandonment of the disciplinary statutes on artisans and hirelings, suggests that although the civic status of "free" Virginia settlers remained tenuous through the 1620s (see Konig, "Dale's Laws" 368–75), by the 1630s the steady and increasing flow of overwhelmingly male and potentially unruly juvenile laborers had concentrated the Assembly's attention on policing indentured servitude, concomitantly strengthening the distinction between unfree and free in the legal culture of work.

infringement of the immediate master's jurisdiction.[111] Protections of the servant's interests were not extensive. Nevertheless, Assembly statutes interposed law and courts between masters and servants as arbiters of disputes. To avoid "prejudice" to either party, those entering without indentures or covenants describing a term of service and without independent means of support (that is, not entering "free") were required to serve customary terms established by statute (four years if over twenty; five years if over twelve, and seven if under).[112] Servants might have recourse to justices of the peace where they had "just cause of complaint against their masters or mistrises by harsh or vnchristianlike vsage or otherways for want of diet, or convenient necessaryes" and if cause were found the complaint might be taken to county court for disposition, and "care be had that no such servant or servants be misvsed by their masters or mistrises."[113]

The county courts and justices that were to perform so important a role in enforcing and overseeing relations between masters and servants in Virginia were, I have already noted, also an outgrowth of the 1630s. Monthly courts had been created at Charles City and Elizabeth City in 1624, under the effective control of the "military commanders and manorial lords" of which Virginia's early leadership was comprised.[114] The dispersal of population beyond the "citties," patented plantations, and incorporated armed forts of the first two decades, however, meant that by the 1630s additional instruments of local government had become necessary. Consequently, in 1634 the Assembly created eight counties and placed their government in the hands of monthly county courts. The courts were staffed by justices of the peace appointed from among the most prominent planters in each locality, with the assistance of a bevy of lesser office-holders. "By mid century, the county courts had ... garnered a large measure of control over local affairs in Virginia."[115]

In the case of master-servant relations, as in other areas, what the courts administered was local statute law. The first justices, though drawn from local elites, were not the educated gentry of the English counties, but largely a raw and inexperienced "sot-weed gentry" with little of the command of

---

[111] These laws, passed individually during the 1630s, were later collated in the second major revisal of Virginia law. See Act XX-XXII (March 1642/3), in Hening, *Statutes at Large*, I, 252–5; Billings, "Transfer of English Law," 239.

[112] Act XXVI (March 1642/3), in Hening, *Statutes at Large*, I, 257. As migration to Virginia picked up, the influx of servants without indentures accelerated, rendering ineffective previous requirements that all entering servants have written indentures. Clearly, then, this legislation reflected masters' desires for reinforcement of their capacity to hold immigrant labor to multiyear terms notwithstanding the absence of previously agreed indentures. At the same time, the legislation attempted to establish standards for terms and conditions that courts could enforce.

[113] Act XXII (March 1642/3), in Hening, *Statutes at Large*, I, 255. "Unchristianlike" differentiates between the treatment of servants and slaves. See n.135, this chapter, and accompanying text, and also Chapter 9.

[114] Konig, "The Williamsburg Courthouse," 78, 82–6.

[115] Billings, Transfer of English Law," 224.

English common law that their English equivalents possessed, dependent for applicable knowledge upon the custom of the regions and localities from which they had migrated.[116] Their conception of their responsibilities, at least during the county court system's early years, tended to be crude, cursory, and self-interested, their conduct often notorious. This did not last. By the end of the century both the Assembly's enactments and their administration in the counties had undergone considerable sophistication. At least in the period prior to Bacon's Rebellion, however, both tended to be frankly exploitative in method and intent.

The rigors of Virginia's servant laws were reaffirmed in the third general revision of colony statutes undertaken shortly after Virginia's accession to the Commonwealth regime in March 1651/2, just as Virginia entered upon its period of heaviest servant migration. The following decade shows sustained attention to the subject.[117] New provisions directing county courts to determine the ages of servants imported without indenture were adopted by 1652.[118] Clandestine marriage, fornication, and absconding penalties were reaffirmed at the same time, as were prohibitions directed at the free population against trading with servants, harboring runaways, or retaining those already hired by others. As in 1642/3, servants who had served out their time were required to obtain certification of their freedom from former masters before hiring or agreeing on shares with anyone else.[119]

---

[116] Warren M. Billings, "Justices, Books, Laws, and Courts in Seventeenth-Century Virginia," *Law Library Journal*, 85, 2 (Spring 1993), 291. On early law knowledge in Virginia, see Warren M. Billings, "English Legal Literature as a Source of Law and Legal Practice in Seventeenth-Century Virginia," *Virginia Magazine of History and Biography*, 87, 4 (October 1979), 403–16; "Pleading, Procedure, and Practice: The Meaning of Due Process of Law in Seventeenth-Century Virginia," *Journal of Southern History*, 47, 4 (November 1981), 569–84. Arguing that they were mostly "innocent of formal training in English law" ("Pleading," 573), Billings emphasizes the importance of English local law and custom "with which they had greater familiarity" in shaping magistrates' activities. "Since the literature to which Virginians turned for guidance articulated the duties of local magistrates, it emphasized the significance of local traditions. That accent reminded the colonists of their own earlier acquaintance with English law and reinforced their notion that local tradition was the form of English law most applicable to the situation in Virginia" ("Transfer," 221). In fact, evidence from the Assembly suggests the lack of any general circulation even of English JP manuals in Virginia until the second half of the seventeenth century. See *An Act for Law Bookes*, Act XX (October 1666) in Hening, *Statutes at Large*, II, 246. For arguments in favor of an earlier circulation, see Billings, "English Legal Literature," 408–14.

[117] Warren M. Billings, "Some Acts not in Hening's *Statutes*,": The Acts of Assembly, April 1652, November 1652, and July 1653," *Virginia Magazine of History and Biography*, 83, 1 (1975), 23, 24, 37–9, 41, 47. See also Act XI (March 1655/6), Act XIV-XVI, Act XVIII, Act XXVI (March 1657/8), Act III (March 1658/9), Act XIII-XV (March 1659/60), all in Hening, *Statutes at Large*, I, 401, 438–40, 441–2, 445, 517–8, 538–40.

[118] Those under sixteen were to serve until age twenty-one; those over sixteen for four years. Billings, "Some Acts," 41.

[119] Act 28 of April 1652, in Billings, "Some Acts," 38; Act XV (March 1657/8), in Hening, *Statutes at Large*, I, 439; compare Act XXI (March 1642/3), in Hening, *Statutes at Large*, I, 253–4.

The county courts' oversight of the relationship was also reaffirmed. Servants' rights of resort to the courts were reenacted; so also, concern at the "audacious vnruliness of many stubborn and incorrigible servants" brought about an act to punish with two years' additional service any who laid "violent hands on his or her master or mistresse or overseer."[120]

In 1662, following the Restoration, the Assembly undertook its fourth general review of the whole corpus of colony law enacted theretofore, continuing some and repealing the rest. The results confirm both the regularization of the law of indentured labor and also that clear distinctions (of origin, age, and status) set off migrant labor from other forms.[121] Measures that had clearly long since fallen by the wayside were those passed in the 1630s dealing with wage fixing and the performance of contracts by artisan labor. Certification of freedom continued to be required of freemen entering new terms of service "by indenture custome or after contracts for wages," but the statute's penalties were directed at masters who harbored or entertained freemen employed by another, not the employee.[122] Specific performance of labor contracts by free persons was not entirely abandoned, but it was confined to cases of "person[s] comeing free into the country"; that is, migrants.[123] In the case of indentured servants, clandestine marriage, fornication, and runaway punishments were all reenacted, although the physical disfigurement of persistent runaways (branding and hair cropping) was discontinued. Default "custom of country" terms of servants imported without indenture continued to vary, those above age sixteen now required to serve five years, those below until age twenty-four. Age on entry was to be determined exclusively by the courts. Prohibitions on trading with servants were also reenacted, as was the "unruly servant" measure first passed two years earlier. For the first time, however, servants gained specific protections from mistreatment by masters through a separate enactment that condemned "the barbarous usuage of some servants by cruell masters" for bringing "scandall and infamy" on the country in general. The Act ordered "compotent dyett, clothing and lodging," warned

---

[120] Act XIII (March 1659/60), in Hening, *Statutes at Large*, I, 538.
[121] Act XCVIII – Act CV (March 1661/2), in Hening, *Statutes at Large*, II, 113–19.
[122] Act CI (March 1661/2), in Hening, *Statutes at Large*, II, 115–16. The only penalty in the statute directed at the hireling – two hours in the pillory on court day – applied to those found to have forged a freedom certificate. This represented a change from the equivalent statutes enacted in 1642/3 (Act XV), 1652 (Act 28), and 1657/8 (Act XXI), which had provided that one who hired out to a new employer while still hired to an existing employer should "Receive such Censures, and punishment as shall be thought fitt by the governor and Councell" (Act 28 of 1652, amended to "by the court" in Act XXI). In none, however, was the hireling considered a runaway.
[123] Act CI (March 1661/2). In the companion runaway statute (Act CII), the penalty for absconding from work was time added on after the servant's "time[] by custome or indenture is expired," which implies that the statute's double time penalties on running away did not apply to those hired on wage contracts. Earlier runaway statutes enacted in 1642/3, 1652 (Act 29), and 1657/8 had applied only to indentured servants. See Act XXII (March 1642/3) and Act XVI (March 1657/8), in Hening, *Statutes at Large*, I, 254–5, 440.

masters not to exceed "moderation" in correcting their servants and confirmed the availability of the courts to hear servants' complaints.[124] In 1677, masters were foreclosed from renegotiating indentures with their servants outside the presence of a justice.

The 1662 revisal was comprehensive and substantive enough a statement of indentured servant law to remain in place for the rest of the century. The Assembly took up the subject again, however, in 1705. This renewed attention came toward the end of a momentous period of transition in the sources of Virginia's labor supply that had accelerated in the years after Bacon's Rebellion (1676), from the youthful English servants that had provided the bulk of the colony's bound labor force since the 1630s, to reliance instead upon importation of enslaved Africans. The capstone was "An Act concerning Servants and Slaves," a hybrid enactment that combined restatement of 1662's comprehensive assemblage of indentured servant law with an elaborated legal framework for the racial slavery that would dominate the eighteenth century.[125]

Bacon's Rebellion had created considerable consternation among Virginia's elites. Beneath its bloody confusion lay the social instabilities inherent in importing thousands of young single males for years of hard labor while simultaneously frustrating the survivors' ambitions to acquire land by engrossing what was available, forcing the land-hungry to the most dangerous margins of settlement. Despite the anxieties, the only obvious concession made to servants' grievances in the wake of the Rebellion was the Assembly's 1677 legislation foreclosing masters from pressing servants to renegotiate their indentures.[126] Demand for servants appears to have remained reasonably stable during the late seventeenth century, at least until the supply began to be seriously disrupted by European wars.[127] Yet these were also years of relative decline in servant supply and increased resort to African slavery, underlining the interest of at least some planters in turning to a different source of labor. During the late seventeenth

---

[124] Act CIII (March 1661/2), in Hening, *Statutes at Large*, II, 117–18. Between 1660 and 1720, self-identified "servants" entered 115 petitions before the York County Court seeking redress in one or other aspect of their relationship with their masters. Of these 80 (70%) were successful and 15 (13%) were unsuccessful. In the remaining 20 cases (17%), the outcome was either ambiguous or no outcome was recorded. If the no-result cases are excluded one can record a success rate of 85%. See York County Transcripts, *Deeds Orders and Wills*, III-XVI. In Maryland, of 261 complaints filed by or on behalf of servants that have been traced in county and provincial court records, 1652–1797, 222 were completed. In those 222 completed cases, servants were successful in 185, a success rate of 83.3%. For full details, see Christine Daniels, "To Petition for Rights: Masters' Duties and Servants' Voices in Anglo-America," in Christopher L. Tomlins and Bruce H. Mann, editors, *The Many Legalities of Early America* (Chapel Hill, 2001), 219–49.

[125] Ch.XLIX (October 1705), in Hening, *Statutes at Large*, III, 447–62.

[126] Morgan, *American Slavery, American Freedom*, 276.

[127] Farley Grubb and Tony Stitt, "The Liverpool Emigrant Servant Trade and the Transition to Slave Labor in the Chesapeake, 1697–1707: Market Adjustments to War," *Explorations in Economic History*, 31, 3 (1994), 376–405. See also, Chapter 1, section IIA.

century, Assembly legislation tracked that interest, offering increasingly detailed definitions of who was to be considered a slave.

African slaves had been present in Virginia within a few years of the colony's establishment, but although they were distinguished from servants in daily life by their race, their assumed barbarity and lack of Christianity, and the permanence and perpetuity of their servitude, little in the colony's laws before the 1662 revisal identified slavery in any detail as a differentiated institution in daily life.[128] Indeed, both slaves and servants shared the distinction of originating "outside" the colony. The first reference to slaves as such in Assembly legislation appears in 1655/6, providing that Indian children held as hostages would not be treated as slaves. Other measures passed within the next decade strengthened the association of imported Africans with the condition of slavery while distinguishing others, notably Indians.[129] Bacon's Rebellion ended

---

[128] It is clear that almost as soon as they appeared in Virginia, Africans were considered legally distinct from whites. It is also clear that most were considered slaves – that is, permanently in bond to others – from the moment of their arrival, presumably because purchased and held as such. Some, however, were considered servants, and a few became freemen. From the outset, those that were enslaved were legally distinguished as heritable property from those that were not; those that might be enslaved were defined by legal elaboration of racial categories. But although both property and race were thus essential concepts in Virginians' understanding of what "slave" meant, neither furnished the substantive regulatory content of slavery in Virginia law: that content came from the police statutes that controlled the lives and bodies of slaves, and from the law of servitude elaborated over the course of the seventeenth century and adapted during the last four decades to the condition of persons serving for life, as their numbers became sufficiently large to require distinct treatment.

I elaborate at length on the law of slavery in Virginia and throughout the English colonies in Chapter 9. For a guide to aspects of race and enslavement in early Virginian law, see Thomas D. Morris, *Southern Slavery and the Law, 1619–1860* (Chapel Hill, 1996), 19–23, 37–48. On the "non-linearity" of processes of "black debasement and degradation," see T. H. Breen and Stephen Innes, *"Myne Owne Ground": Race and Freedom on Virginia's Eastern Shore, 1640–1676* (New York, 1980), 5. For skepticism, see Philip D. Morgan, *Slave Counterpoint: Black Culture in the Eighteenth Century Chesapeake and Lowcountry* (Chapel Hill, 1998), 16. Douglas Deal offers a detailed account of the history of Virginia's eastern shore that gives much greater emphasis to the strict and endemic limitations on African agency. See his *Race and Class in Colonial Virginia: Indians, Englishmen and Africans on the Eastern Shore During the Seventeenth Century* (New York, 1993). For a more general account that draws conclusions compatible with Deal's from a distinct standpoint, see Kathleen M. Brown, *Good Wives, Nasty Wenches and Anxious Patriarchs: Gender, Race and Power in Colonial Virginia* (Chapel Hill, 1996), 107–86.

[129] *English running away with negroes*, Act XXII (1660/1), required English servants running away in the company of Negroes incapable of making satisfaction by addition of time to serve the Negroes' time for them; *Concerning Indians*, Act CXXXVIII (1661/2), inter alia prohibited the sale as slaves of Indians who had been brought into the colony as servants; *Negro womens children to serve according to the condition of the mother*, Act XII (1662/3), declared perpetual bondage for the children of enslaved Negro women; *An act declaring that baptisme of slaves doth not exempt them from bondage*, Act III (1667/8), held that children born as slaves were not freed from their condition by baptism; finally, *What tyme Indians to serve*, Act XII (1670/1), held that servants, not being Christians, imported by shipping, were slaves, whereas servants, not being Christians, brought in by land were not. All in

the exemptions of Indians,[130] but the identification of slavery remained overwhelmingly with those brought by sea, that is, Africans. In 1682, the Assembly offered the first comprehensive and explicit definition of slaves as "all servants, except Turkes and Moores, whilest in amity with his majesty[,] which from and after publication of this act shall be brought or imported into this country, either by sea or land, whether Negroes, Moors, Mollattoes or Indians, who and whose parentage and native country are not christian at the time of their first purchase of such servant by some christian, although afterwards, and before such their importation and bringing into this country, they shall be converted to the christian faith; and all Indians which shall hereafter be sold by our neighbouring Indians, or any other trafiqueing with us as for slaves are hereby adjudged, deemed and taken, and shall be adjudged, deemed and taken to be slaves to all intents and purposes any law, usage, or custome to the contrary notwithstanding."[131]

We have become familiar with the intellectual relationship between European enslavement of others and centuries of papal authorization of European Christian rulers' expeditions to conquer and occupy the lands of non-Christian peoples, and also with the refined sixteenth-century justifications of enslavement available under the law of war. All informed the terms used as legal authority for enslavement in English mainland America.[132] The Virginia Assembly's references to Christianity in 1682 in distinguishing between persons subject to enslavement and persons merely bindable to servitude express not just an assertion of distinction between English and "other" identity but also an absolute civic distinction based on the legal authority invoked in the very act of colonizing itself.

In 1660, the Chesapeake's African population was substantially less than two thousand. By 1680, it had nearly tripled. In 1705, when the Virginia Assembly passed its hybrid amalgam of the law of slavery and servitude, the region's African population stood at twenty thousand, more than 80 percent of which was in Virginia. The indentured servant population, meanwhile, was in decline from its 1670s peak of more than five thousand, and by the turn of the century sat in the mid-three thousands. Like previous statutes defining who were to be slaves, the 1705 statute registered this profound long-term alteration in the composition of the bound labor force.

Hening, *Statutes at Large*, II, 26, 143, 170, 260, 283. See also Brown, *Good Wives, Nasty Wenches*, 135–6.

[130] Bacon's Laws, Act I (1676), continued in substance by order of the restored Assembly (February 1676/7) and later confirmed (1679). In Hening, *Statutes at Large*, II, 346, 404, 440.

[131] *An act to repeale a former law makeing Indians and others ffree*, Act I (1682), in Hening, *Statutes at Large*, II, 490–2. On the "triangular" relationship of Englishmen, Turks, and Moors underlying the exemption of such racial strangers from enslavement whilst "in amity with his majesty," see generally Nabil Matar, *Turks, Moors, and Englishmen in the Age of Discovery* (New York, 1999). On the origin and meaning of the phrase "to all intents and purposes" in early modern statutory construction, see Chapter 9, n.122.

[132] This argument is elaborated in detail in Chapter 9.

Unlike those previous statutes, however, the 1705 statute comprehensively reorganized the substance of the existing law of servitude around slavery.[133] Indeed, the precise timing of the statute appears to be explained by the particularly rapid increase in resort to slave imports in the face of the renewed shutdown of the servant trade after 1701.

The 1705 statute's main theme was to elaborate substantively on the series of distinctions already established in Virginia law between those servants who were slaves and those who were not as a means to accommodate a bound labor force increasingly bifurcated in character. Beginning from the position that "servant" actually meant "imported servant," the statute defined slaves as a distinct category of imported servants, namely all those who were not Christians at their time of entry into Virginia (subsequent conversion notwithstanding). Children born in Virginia were to be "bond or free, according to the condition of their mothers."[134] Powers and duties common to all relations of servitude were specified, but discriminations in treatment and the availability of redress were prominent: for example, masters were forbidden to "whip a christian white servant naked"[135] but could brutalize a slave without fear of retribution: one who might happen to kill a slave in the course of "correction" for their resistance or disobedience was to be considered "free and acquit of all punishment and accusation for the same, as if such accident had never happened."[136] Servants, but not slaves, could complain to a Justice of a master's neglect of duty, or mistreatment, or nonpayment of wages.[137] Servants were also held entitled to maintenance if sick during their term of service, to freedom dues at the end of it, and to the protection of the courts in renegotiating indentures.[138]

---

[133] *An Act Concerning Servants and Slaves*, ch. XLIX (October 1705), in Hening, *Statutes at Large*, II, 447–63.

[134] Ibid., §§4–6, 36. These provisions repeated the statutes of 1662/3 (perpetual bondage for the children of enslaved Negro women), 1667/8 (children born as slaves not freed from their condition by baptism, widened to all slaves), and 1682 (enslavement of non-Christian servants imported by sea, with exceptions for "Turks and Moors in amity with her Majesty"); §§5 and 6 allowed a qualified exception for anyone who could prove they had formerly been free inhabitants of any Christian country, whether themselves Christian or not.

[135] Ibid., §7. This prohibition had long been entrenched in local practice. See Complaint of Mary Adney against Jno Wright "for barbarous usage to her" (24 April 1683), York County, *Deeds, Orders and Wills*, VI, 493–4. Wright was ordered by the York County court to pay a fine of 1,000 pounds tobacco, and further to be detained in the custody of the sheriff until he should enter into bond in the sum of £500 that he "shall not beat, strike, whipp or any other ways evilly intreate any Christian servt or servts whatsoever" nor order any overseer so to act, and that if he should find cause that any such servant deserve correction "he is hereby ord for redress thereof to make complaint to the next majistrate."

[136] Ibid., §34. *An act about the casuall killing of slaves*, Act I (1669), had already established that the death of a slave as a result of "extremity" of correction was not to be considered a felony (that is, murder). In Hening, *Statutes at Large*, II, 270.

[137] Ibid., §§7, 8, 10. By this time, court oversight of indentured servitude was well-established (see n.124, this chapter).

[138] Ch. XLIX (October 1705), §§8, 9.

All were required to obey their masters' just and lawful commands, neither servants nor slaves were allowed to trade without permission, and procedures for the recovery and corporal punishment of runaways were specified without distinction between servants and slaves. But miscegenation penalties and established racial categorizations of enslavement prescribed fundamental race separation.

The creation for long-term use of distinct legal categories of origin (European/African, Christian/non-Christian) to manage the substantial shift under way in the composition of *imported* bound labor suggests that native-born (Creole) whites formed a distinct third category of labor, beyond the ambit of the legislation. The statute made no mention of artisans or tradesmen, and its requirements for certification of servants' freedom on completion of their terms distinguished "poor people ... [seeking] emploiment" from "servants" in a fashion consistent with prior usages distinguishing bound migrant labor from Creoles.[139] Internally, the statute was not completely consistent in its descriptions of the category "servant," including within its disciplinary reach not only "imported" persons but also those "become servants of their own accord here, or bound by any court or church-wardens." Elsewhere it referred to servants "whether by importation, indenture, or hire here," or in another clause "by importation, or by contract, or indenture made here." Conceivably all such descriptions were meant to apply only to persons whose origins were outside Virginia, or who had been designated community outsiders by legal process (criminals, bound-out paupers). As in earlier statutes, there is support for this interpretation in those sections of the statute that deal with penalties.[140] Still, the ambit of the 1705 statute was not completely clear. Amendments passed in 1726 shed some light. By then the transformation of the bound labor force to one based on racial slavery was complete, and the amendments correspondingly altered the law dealing with runaways in a fashion that suggested runaways would almost invariably be black.[141] The amendments also added three clauses punishing refusals to work and misrepresentations of ability on the part of tradesmen and workmen "on wages,"

---

[139] Ibid., §21.

[140] Ibid., §§8, 10, 14, 21. Persons "become servants of their own accord here" could have been intended to ensure coverage of those entering indentures only after arrival. It could also have been intended to cover Creole apprentices, who do not appear as a distinct legal category in Virginia until "apprenticeship" as such was incorporated in the 1748 revision of the statute. See ch.XIV §24 (October 1748), in Hening, *Statutes at Large*, V, 558. Persons bound by courts and church-wardens means paupers and criminals. The statute's penalty provisions on departure generally assume (e.g., §§12, 14, 17, 18, 21) that those to whom they apply are all serving terms defined by "indenture, custom, or former order of court" rather than contract of hire. The only references to servants by hire are in §10 confirming access to judicial determination of grievances and wages owed, and in §21 regulating forged freedom certificates.

[141] Ch. IV (May 1726) in Hening, *Statutes at Large*, IV, 168–75. In his *Office and Authority of a Justice of Peace* (Williamsburg, 1736), at 281–7, Webb reproduces the law of servant as well as slave runaways, but all his form examples assume the subject will be black."

but the clauses were confined in scope entirely to migrants imported into the colony.[142] The effect of the 1726 statute was to strengthen the association of whiteness with freedom from restraint in matters of work discipline already on display in the 1705 statute (and, Chapter 7 will show, in local seventeenth-century case law) while identifying imported labor as a partial and necessarily temporary exception.

The Assembly confirmed these trends at mid-century, in 1748, and again in 1753.[143] The 1748 statute subtly revised the provisions of the 1705 statute that applied to white labor in ways that made it unmistakably a law confined to labor imported under indenture. Servants were those who labored for others for terms set "by act of parliament, indenture, or custom."[144] Hireling labor was nowhere to be found among the statute's categories,[145] and the statements describing the substance and procedure of servants' complaints were restated in ways that indicated the statute had indentured servants exclusively in mind.[146] All these provisions were reconfirmed by reenactment in 1753.

The course of Virginia's statutory servant law shows that a specific legal form for indentured servitude emerged piecemeal as the practice itself developed as a reliable means for facilitating extensive large-scale transoceanic transfers of youthful migratory labor, and policing their activities once arrived. That form, however, owed much to the labor practices of England's arable regions. Intensive tobacco cultivation turned Virginia's initial civic order – authoritarian idealization of martial citizenship – toward a hierarchical "bastard-manorialism" that distributed imported juvenile laborers among scattered plantations where they were secured by multiyear indentures. Bastard manorialism hindered the development of a public sphere and office holding at anything below county level, cutting off master-servant relationships from anything other than perfunctory oversight. As Virginia's institutional complexity grew, and as migrant servitude furnished larger

---

[142] Hening, *Statutes at Large*, IV, 174–5 §§22–4. At this point craftsmen were about the only category of English labor still coming into Virginia under indenture. (As a general point, Nicholas Canny notes that "English migrants to the mainland colonies ... were becoming more highly skilled and specialist in the eighteenth century." See his "English migration into and across the Atlantic during the Seventeenth and Eighteenth Centuries," in Nicholas Canny, editor, *Europeans on the Move: Studies on European Migration, 1500–1800* [Oxford, 1994], 52.)

[143] *An Act Concerning Servants and Slaves*, ch.XIV (October 1748) in Hening, *Statutes at Large*, V, 547–58 (repealed by proclamation); *An Act for the Better Government of Servants and Slaves*, ch.VII (November 1753), in Hening, *Statutes at Large*, VI, 356–69.

[144] That is, convicts; migrants with indentures agreed in England; or migrants whose terms were established in Virginia law according to estimates of their age on entry. Ch.XIV (1748) §1; ch.VII (1753) §1.

[145] §13 repeated the 1705 statute's provisions on freedom certification for former imported servants.

[146] §6 of the 1748 statute (reenacted as §6 of the 1753 statute) dealing with procedures for hearing complaints of servants listed "diet, cloathing, lodging, correction, whipping, freedom, or freedom dues" as petitionable complaints, but not wages, hours, or other contractual terms of employment. As we shall see (in Chapter 7), such disputes had been dealt with for nearly a century by civil suit.

numbers of laborers, master-servant relationships took on a more closely observed and regulated character. But its early form – hierarchical, youthful, and extended – remained a constant. Institutionally, migrant servitude drew upon English husbandry apprenticeship in its enlistment of youthful workers in agricultural production for extended periods of time secured by indentures, in the sociology of its subjects, and in the severity of their legally defined subordination to their planter-masters. Although usually presumed an adaptation of English service in husbandry forced by the exigencies of transatlantic transfer, the legal form of indentured servitude in Virginia owed far more to the explicit bindings of parish orphans and pauper children into husbandry apprenticeships[147] and to the law of vagrancy and its obsession with control of the mobile, the deviant, and the unruly young.[148] But this character also set indentured servitude qualitatively apart from other forms of European labor, both migrant and Creole. The length of the term of undifferentiated labor demanded of servants in order to compensate for costs of transportation, subsistence, and freedom dues had no parallel in English law outside husbandry apprenticeship.[149] Nor were the disciplinary subordinations of indentured servant to master replicated in any other European laboring relationship in the colony. Covenants confirmed masters in the enjoyment of authority over the disposition of servant labor for extended periods, and gave them an assignable property right in the person of the servant. But it was the length of term that required an explicit covenant, setting the terms of the relationship and justifying the authority wielded by the master in pursuit of their fulfillment.[150]

On average, the total length of the period a youth spent as an indentured servant did not differ significantly from the total of serial yearly hirings entered into by the average English farm servant. Indeed, for many it may well have been shorter. For survivors, furthermore, the practical outcome was not dissimilar: freedom dues replicated the savings that adolescent farm servants supposedly accumulated to finance their transition

---

[147] That is, as we have seen, the practice of binding out indigent children without employment in annualized wage labor to multiyear terms for maintenance and upbringing. See nn.38–40, this chapter, and accompanying text; Ben-Amos, *Adolescence and Youth*, 59–60.

[148] Not simply a law of labor contracting, in the extent of its subordination of mostly juvenile migrants to the control of their planter-masters, the statute law of indentured servitude in Virginia also reflected a felt need to control dangerous adolescent youth. Hence the enormous impact of the failure of control represented by Bacon's Rebellion in 1676, and the resultant increased interest both in acquiring a replacement bound labor force and in devising forms of civic accommodation with the existing one. Brown, *Good Wives, Nasty Wenches*, 149–86.

[149] Craft apprenticeship contemplated multiyear terms, but accompanied these with training rationales beyond simple subsistence. Municipal and craft company regulation also ordained changes in the content of the apprenticeship over time, as the apprentice matured.

[150] This and other institutional differences are discussed by Farley Grubb, "Does Bound Labour Have to be Coerced Labour? The Case of Colonial Immigrant Servitude Versus Craft Apprenticeship and Life-Cycle Servitude-in-Husbandry," *Itinerario*, 21, 1 (1997), 28–51.

to an attempt at independent living, marriage, and family-formation; the actual availability of land for much of the seventeenth century made independent living a more realizable ambition in Virginia than in England. But the extent of statutory supervision was less rigorous than in the case of life-cycle service, the circle of the master's power more extensive, the function of social reproduction more thoroughly subordinated to the crude extraction of labor power to achieve return for the profit-seeking planter. Until the later seventeenth century, in dealings between the nascent overseer state and Virginia's planter-masters (if indeed it makes sense to distinguish between them), it was the latter who had the whip hand. In general, the treatment of indentured servants was substantially freer from oversight than in English law, even as the servant's multiyear commitment to a single master rather than to serial dealings with several heightened the consequences of a poor relationship.

If indentured servitude's development as a legal category distanced it from its English analogs, that development also distanced it from Creole work relations. In Virginia, explicit legal subordination to the authority of a master became a condition identified particularly with youth, as in England, but also with persons imported from elsewhere to labor for the resident population, rather than with anyone who undertook "work" at large. Far more obvious in the case of slavery's bestowal of conditions of comparative elevation upon the unenslaved,[151] one can see well before the end of the seventeenth century qualitative civic distinctions – youth/adult, migrant/Creole, bound/free – wrought into the legal culture of work as a consequence of the presence of indentured servitude.

It was slavery, nevertheless, that finally enabled Virginians to achieve a stable relationship between work and civic status. In the wake of Bacon's Rebellion, planter elites had been torn between a need to secure and a need to appease their unruly white indentured labor force. Their eventual wholesale turn to an enslaved plantation labor force allowed pursuit of labor force security and white appeasement simultaneously. "White servant men were incorporated into the social order with the promise of future status as voters, citizens, and patriarchs." Enslaved African laborers were defined as incapable of enjoying any such status. "By the early eighteenth century, Virginia's political system had achieved a stability built on the division of white and black laborers ... and an incipient Anglo-Virginian identity that rested precariously upon the fragile bonds uniting white men."[152] In eighteenth-century Virginia the legal culture of work would bestow real civic capacity, but only by simultaneously becoming a legal culture of race.

The Delaware Valley

Like the first migrants to New England and the Chesapeake earlier in the century, Delaware Valley settlers in the 1680s entered a legal environment

---

[151] The essential theme of Morgan, *American Slavery, American Freedom*.
[152] Brown, *Good Wives, Nasty Wenches*, 181, 186.

whose broad contours came predefined in the shape of crown patents – specifically in this case the Pennsylvania charter – embodying metropolitan plans. As in each of those previous instances, friction developed between the founding model of law and authority that the project's initiators proposed for the government of the mass of participants, and the participants' own preferences. As in Massachusetts, argument in Pennsylvania occurred *within* an overall ideo-religious consensus. Nevertheless, it was informed by the substance of legal-cultural difference that has helped us explore the dynamics of English settlement elsewhere. In Pennsylvania, plebeian Quaker migrants from pastoral northwest England and Wales encountered a model of government and local legal order designed by affluent, largely nonresident, Quaker grandees that invoked the stronger manorial ideals of the downland arable South. The influence of both can be seen in the laws that were written and the practices that those laws framed. The friction between them helped shape the initial course of Pennsylvania's political and legal culture and left marks that remained visible throughout the eighteenth century.

Unlike New England and the Chesapeake, at the time the Pennsylvania charter was granted, the Delaware Valley had already been a site of European settlement and ordering for some years. First penetrated by a scattering of Swedish and later Dutch *coloni*, organized somewhat in the style of martial planting that one also observes in the first English Chesapeake expeditions,[153] the area came under English control following the conquest of New Netherland and became part of the territories granted to the Duke of York. As such, its legal order was at first defined by the eponymous *Duke's Laws*, published in April 1665 at Hemsted on Long Island, upon the Duke's formal assumption of authority over the region.[154] Collected "out of the Severall Laws now in force in his Majesties American Colonyes and Plantations," the *Laws* were compiled under the direction of Richard Nicholls, first governor of New York. Initially their jurisdiction was confined to Long Island. They were not proclaimed in the Delaware Valley region until 1676.[155]

---

[153] See Edward Armstrong, "Introduction," in Edward Armstrong, editor, *Record of Upland Court* (Philadelphia, 1959), 11–21; Cheesman A. Herrick, *White Servitude in Pennsylvania: Indentured and Redemptioner Labor in the Colony and Commonwealth* (Philadelphia, 1926), 27.

[154] See William H. Loyd, *The Early Courts of Pennsylvania* (Boston, 1910), 10–22; Robert C. Ritchie, *The Duke's Province: A Study of New York Politics and Society* (Chapel Hill, 1977), 34–9. On the origins of the *Duke's Laws*, see generally George Lee Haskins, "Influences of New England Law on the Middle Colonies," *Law and History Review*, 1, 2 (Fall 1983), 238–50. For the original draft, see Gail McKnight Beckman, comp., *The Statutes at Large of Pennsylvania*, I: 1680–1700 (New York, 1976), 71–111.

[155] *Duke of York's Book of Laws (Introduced September 22, 1676)*, in Staughton George et al., editors, *Charter to William Penn, and Laws of the Province of Pennsylvania* (Harrisburg, 1879), 1–77, at 1. The *Duke's Laws* were, in effect, the Duke of York's seigneurial grant of laws to his province, somewhat in the manner described by Sir Edward Coke in *Calvin's Case*, 77 English Reports 377, 398 (1608).

The *Duke's Laws* contemplated layers of legal authority stretching from an annual Court of Assize down through tri-annual Courts of Sessions (with jurisdiction over "Ridings" rather than counties) staffed by Justices of the Peace, and Town Courts staffed by petty constables and overseers. Town officers (petty constables, overseers, and petty office-holders such as viewers of pipe staves) were to be elected by freeholders. All others – high constables, high sheriffs, justices – were appointed by the Governor in Council. Localities were also divided into parishes with church wardens responsible for presenting morals offenders at sessions. Land was to be held free of "fine and Licence," but former purchasers were required to acknowledge the claim of the proprietor (the Duke) to prior possession by purchasing new patents. In the realm of work relations, the substance of the *Duke's Laws* drew freely from Massachusetts' *Lawes and Liberties*, but in a way that accommodated more explicitly both indentured servitude and slavery.[156] The *Laws*, however, included no specific details of either practice, or any of Virginia's detailed regulation of labor importation: for example, no "custom of country" provisions to govern the assignment of unindentured servant imports were included. Nor did the *Laws* include provision for the regulation of artisan or other wage labor.[157]

The *Duke's Laws* remained in force in the Delaware region from 1676 until 1682, when William Penn obtained his proprietary charter for Pennsylvania from Charles II; they continued to inform local law more or less by default roughly until the turn of the century.[158] The reason for this continuation, notwithstanding the alteration in overall jurisdiction, was the political instability that attended the first years of the colony's existence.

William Penn's ambitions for Pennsylvania centered his proprietary project on the creation of a society of Christian harmony founded on principles of liberty of religious conscience. Penn's idealism is not in doubt, but harmony does not come free of social and political meaning. Certainly, Penn's Christian harmony did not imply either social or racial equality, or political democracy. Penn was no leveler.[159] He thought "Subordination

---

[156] George et al., eds., *Charter to William Penn*, 12 (tit. "Bond slavery"). Compare Beckman, *Statutes at Large*, 78.

[157] As in Massachusetts, the *Duke's Laws* identify servants with children, and with multiple-year terms secured by indentures. *Charter to William Penn*, 12 (tit. "Bond slavery"), 19–20 (tit. "Children and Servants"). The *Duke's Laws* also largely reproduced the *Lawes and Liberties'* title "Masters, Servants, & Labourers" but without its wage-fixing clauses (further evidence they had fallen into disuse) and otherwise limiting its jurisdiction over unindentured labor to the general statement that "All Labourers and Servants" (not "All Workmen," as in Massachusetts) should work "the whole day ... allowing [ ] convenient time for food and rest" (37–8). Migrant indentured servitude was not widely promoted in the Duke's proprietary jurisdiction; much greater emphasis was placed on slavery. The significance of the *Duke's Laws* for the promotion of slavery in New York and the mid-Atlantic settlements is discussed in Chapter 9.

[158] Joseph E. Illick, *Colonial Pennsylvania: A History* (New York, 1976), 71–2.

[159] Caroline Robbins, "William Penn, 1689–1702: Eclipse, Frustration, and Achievement," in Richard S. Dunn and Mary Maples Dunn, editors, *The World of William Penn* (Philadelphia, 1986), 81.

and Dependency" natural and inevitable in human society, preaching obedience to parents ("He that begets thee ... has a natural Right over thee"), to magistrates, to masters, and to monarchs.[160] Those in authority had an obligation to wisdom in its exercise – "Where example keeps pace with Authority, Power hardly fails to be obey'd, and Magistrates to be honour'd" – but not to share that exercise. Rather, "Let the People think they Govern and they will be Govern'd."[161] As to racial equality, Christian harmony meant that "[God] has made of *One* Blood all Nations," but not that he had "rang'd or dignified them upon the *Level*."[162]

In large part, Penn's goal of a New World social order built on "love and brotherly kindness" expressed nostalgia for an imagined English past of organic social unity, buried beneath the seventeenth century's detritus of religious conflict, social turmoil, and civil war. Penn's ideal social order was one of benevolent patriarchy; "'obedience to superiors, love to equals, and help and countenance to inferiors'."[163] It would be a repudiation of the degenerate materialism and secularism of the Restoration's metropolitan elites, a revival, then, of humanism's civic virtue, a recreation of the proper harmony of metropolis and country, city and shire.[164] "Of old time the Nobility and Gentry spent their Estates in the Country, and that kept people in it; ... Now the Great men (too much loving the Town and resorting to London) draw people thither to attend. ... The Country being thus neglected, [there is] no due Balance kept between Trade and Husbandry, City and Country."[165]

Penn's political ideas reveal a similar unease at the Restoration period's unstable social peace, and a deep desire for restorative "balancing" of society's different orders, expressed in the classic "mixed" government theories of the English constitution and its balance of magistracy, nobility, and commoners.[166] Unsurprisingly, these sentiments haunted the legal-

---

[160] See William Penn, "Some Fruits of Solitude in Reflections and Maxims," Nos. 175, 176, 195–207, 330–69, and "More Fruits of Solitude, Being the Second Part of Reflections and Maxims," Nos. 205–12, 255, all in *Remember William Penn, 1644–1944, A Tercentenary Memorial* (Harrisburg, Pa., 1945).

[161] "Some Fruits of Solitude," Nos. 336, 337.

[162] "More Fruits of Solitude," No. 255. Harmony did not forestall the introduction of slavery to early Pennsylvania; Penn was himself an owner of slaves.

[163] In David Hackett Fischer, *Albion's Seed: Four British Folkways in America* (New York, 1989), 461.

[164] Fischer, *Albion's Seed*, 461. See also Gary B. Nash, *Quakers and Politics: Pennsylvania, 1681–1726* (Princeton, 1968), 30–1; Illick, *Colonial Pennsylvania*, 16–17; Vicki Hsueh, *Hybrid Constitutions: Challenging Legacies of Law, Privilege, and Culture in Colonial America* (Durham, N.C., 2010), 86–96.

[165] In Illick, *Colonial Pennsylvania*, 16–17. Just as God had created subordination, dependency, and the ranking of humankind so, according to Penn, God exalted the Country over the City. "The *Country* Life is to be *preferr'd*; for there we see the Works of *God*; but in Cities little else but the *Works of Men*: And the one makes a better Subject for our Contemplation than the other." Moreover, "God's Works declare his *Power, Wisdom* and *Goodness*; but Man's Works, for the most part, his *Pride, Folly* and *Excess*. The one is for *use*, the other, chiefly, for *Ostentation* and *Lust*." See "Some Fruits of Solitude," Nos. 220, 222.

[166] "Some Fruits of Solitude," Nos. 329–69. Fisher, *Albion's Seed*, 461.

political structures designed to realize Pennsylvania. Take, for example, the charter provisions governing disposal of land within Penn's grant, and the series of interactions between the proprietor and the leading "adventurers and purchasers" in the project (that is, co-investors to whom he sold land) that produced Penn's *Frame of the Government* in 1682. By the time of that negotiation, Penn had already become deeply involved in selling some half-million acres of his proprietary grant to several hundred "first purchasers" to assist in the financing of the colonizing enterprise. Almost half of this land would go to forty-one particularly large landholders in 5,000- and 10,000-acre blocks.[167] As already noted, disposal of land was, according to the charter Penn had obtained, entirely at the proprietor's discretion. He might organize, assign, alienate, or grant land freely on whatever terms he chose. In particular he might "erect any parcells of Land within the p[ro]vince aforesaid, into mannors." He might "in every of the said mannors, to have and to hold a Court Baron, with all things whatsoever, which to a Court Baron do belong."[168] Persons to whom manors were granted or assigned might then grant on all or any part of the land in fee simple or other form of title "to be held of the said mannors," while further alienations were to be "held of the same Lord and his heires, of whom the alienor did then before hold, and by the like rents and services, which were before due and accustomed."[169] Penn "cherished the plan of erecting manors within the province." He gave considerable attention to provisions for his own proprietorial manors, and offered extensive manorial grants to others. In 1685, for example, one Eneas MacPherson was granted 5,000 acres in free and common socage "with powers to erect the same by these presents into the barony of Inversie" with the right "to hold court baron, view of frank pledge, and court leet by himself or stewards."[170]

---

[167] Illick, *Colonial Pennsylvania*, 16; Nash, *Quakers and Politics*, 16.

[168] "Charter for the Province of Pennsylvania" (1681), in Thorpe, *Federal and State Constitutions*, V, 3035–44, at 3042. See also William R. Shepherd, *History of Proprietary Government in Pennsylvania* [volume VI, Columbia University Studies in History, Economics and Public Law] (New York, 1896), 15–19.

[169] "Charter for the Province of Pennsylvania," 3042. Subinfeudation was hence rendered impossible. In terms of land disposition, Penn's proprietorship was absolute. All land was held as of the proprietor (not the Crown) no matter whether it had been sold on or not. "Pennsylvania then may be viewed as a seigniory, but divested of the heaviest burdens imposed by feudal law, and endowed with such powers of territorial control as distance from the realm of the lord paramount required." Shepherd, *Proprietary Government*, 16–17.

[170] Ibid., 45–6. Proprietary manors were originally conceived of as a 10% reservation of the best land available in all tracts granted by the proprietor. In all, proprietary manors either held directly by the Penns or settled on others totaled some 600,000 acres in about 80 distinct holdings. Nine of these, in the 2,000–10,000-acre range, were situated in the immediate area of first settlement, on the Delaware and Schuylkill Rivers. The largest single tracts were to the west: Springetsbury in York County (64,000 acres) and Maske in Adams County (43,000 acres). Price, *Dividing the Land*, 264–7. Proprietary manors continued to be laid out at different moments throughout the eighteenth century (see, for example, Shepherd, *Proprietary Government*, 27, 155).

Penn's plans for the settlement of the mass of the population were animated by the same desires for an organic, ordered, manor-centered society. Like the Carolina proprietors, Penn abhorred indiscriminate settlement. He planned "agricultural villages" of up to twenty families, each village set in a 5,000-acre township tract; precisely the nucleated, manor-centered settlement pattern of downland southern and central England. Fifty such townships had been laid out by 1685. Not all of these took the form of manorial grants, but the creation of manors remained integral to proprietorial perceptions of the proper forms of settlement for the migrating population well into the eighteenth century, notwithstanding that in Pennsylvania "the spirit of the people was particularly opposed to the institution."[171]

Not surprisingly, attempts to draft a plan for the government of Pennsylvania proposed at first to reproduce hierarchies of landed privilege in governing institutions. Discussion of the matter occupied Penn for several months during late 1681 and 1682. One of the earliest proposals made the centerpiece a bicameral assembly, called a senate, of "lords" and "renters." The upper house (of hereditary "lords") was to consist of the first fifty purchasers of estates of 5,000 or more acres, and their heirs. The purchasers or heirs were to retain their rights of membership in the lords (their "baronage") as long as they retained personal proprietorship of at least 2,000 acres. The upper house alone initiated all legislation. It also controlled appointments of all officers of state, and church. Unlike the lower house it sat at its own pleasure. The lower house ("renters") consisted of representatives elected by all the tenants residing within a 20,000-acre area. Its role was to come into session to approve legislation initiated by the upper house; any proposals of its own were subject to the lords' veto. This proposal created a political system that corresponded to a society in which manorialism would be predominant and citizens would be divided predominantly into two groups: a small number of large landowners

---

[171] James T. Lemon, *The Best Poor Man's Country: A Geographical Study of Early Southeastern Pennsylvania* (Baltimore, 1972), 50–7, and generally 42–70; Shepherd, *Proprietary Government*, 47, 48–53. In *Dividing the Land*, 268, Edward Price argues that the designation "manor" was purely formal – that there was "little intention to operate the holdings as manors, such a social structure probably being incompatible with Quakerism and with Penn's plan to people the colony with landholding farmers." But in England Penn never appeared to feel his Quakerism was incompatible with life and position as "a substantial squire" in Hertfordshire and Sussex, where he tended toward a level of extravagance and social expectation in his habits befitting "leading county families," habits that earned him condemnation "as a noxious hypocrite who pretended to adopt a plain and simple style 'while hee swims himselfe in wealth'." Richard S. Dunn, "Penny Wise and Pound Foolish: Penn as a Businessman," in Dunn and Dunn, eds., *World of William Penn*, 39, 41. As we shall see, the proprietor's persistent pursuit of manorialism in the face of popular opposition in Pennsylvania, and despite a lack of lasting success in creating functioning manorial institutions, rather suggests an ongoing clash in regional-cultural conceptions of appropriate social structure and agrarian organization. The South-of-England squire was serious about recreating manorialism as the proper structure for his settler-farmers. His northwestern Quaker migrants were equally serious in their opposition.

with controlling political and executive authority, and a large number of tenants.[172]

Penn himself opposed this scheme, not for its hierarchical character but for its proposal to limit the proprietor's role in government to the exercise of two votes in the upper house "and no other power in the government, or over the state," and to make the proprietor himself subject to the authority of the senate – which meant, given the effective organization of government, subordination of the proprietor to his barons, the colony's major landowners. Perhaps to mollify Penn, a revised scheme allowed the proprietor to exercise executive authority through his deputy or "governor," acting with the assistance of a council. The governor was also given presiding authority over an enlarged upper house, now called the "court or house of proprietors." Provision was made for the lower house also to be enlarged, to have a speaker, and to share voice with the upper in appointments to the governor's council.[173]

Opposition was also manifested in altogether different form, namely that of an alternative scheme of government, described in the draft of twenty-four principles known as the "Fundamental Constitutions." Credited by some as the first attempt to design a government for Pennsylvania, the draft was apparently inspired by the radical Whig theorist Algernon Sidney. Defining government as a "constitution of good laws wisely set together for the good ordering of people in society" and stressing protection of religious liberty and moral order as government's primary ends, the Fundamental Constitutions proposed a General Assembly of instructed delegates, with powers to initiate legislation, elected by the colony's freeholders from specified election districts; and a council elected by the assembly from among its own members, which would act as a second legislative house, to receive and consent to legislation from the General Assembly, and to advise and assist the governor in the execution and administration of government.[174]

The Fundamental Constitutions proved unacceptable to Penn's purchasers, who sought guarantees for the representation of their own large propertied interests, and more generally desired a strategic role for those of the colony's inhabitants "most eminent for virtue, wisdom, and substance."[175]

---

[172] Illick, *Colonial Pennsylvania*, 18; Shepherd, *Proprietary Government*, 226–7. For the most explicit elaboration of hierarchical agrarian government in the Restoration colonies, see *The Fundamental Constitutions of Carolina*, in Thorpe, ed., *Federal and State Constitutions*, V, 2772–86 (discussed in Chapter 4).

[173] Shepherd, *Proprietary Government*, 227–8. Further variations on the same theme followed (228–31).

[174] Ibid., 231–4. The "Fundamental Constitutions" are normally credited to Penn himself and represented as a radically democratic innovation. It is worth noting, however, that in the "Fundamental Constitutions" the authority of the position of governor and protection accorded the interests of the proprietor were both substantially broader than earlier proposals. For example, all bills agreed between assembly and council were to be presented to the governor for approval. No bills were to "infring[e] the rights of the proprietor either in his just share in the government or his property" (233).

[175] Ibid., 235.

What ultimately emerged as the *Frame of the Government* represented an accommodation of those concerns. As before, the basic components of government were a Governor (the proprietor or his appointee), and an Assembly and Provincial Council both elected by all freemen. But in the *Frame* the council was accorded pride of place. Council members, elected to three-year terms, were to be "persons of most note for virtue, wisdom, and ability."[176] The council itself was to have sole powers to initiate legislation, and was to assist and advise the governor in all matters of execution and administration. The Assembly was to be elected annually for an eight-day session in which it would examine the laws prepared by the governor and council and offer (or withhold) "concurrence." Finally, there was to be a commission of "conservators," twelve in all, appointed from among the principal landholders, who, with the proprietor, were to have custody of the charter, with power to declare any law or ordinance contrary to the charter and hence null and void. To the *Frame* was annexed a schedule of forty "Laws Agreed Upon In England" that, inter alia, defined a freeman as any Christian male over 21 holding 100 acres by purchase (having cultivated ten) or 50 by release from servitude (having cultivated twenty), or any "inhabitant, artificer or other resident" paying "scot and lot" (a personal tax). As this indicates, the laws contemplated that the purchasers and adventurers would fill their lands in part at least through importing indentured servants, to whom they would grant land on completion of terms.[177]

The *Frame* had not retreated all the way back to houses of "lords" and "tenants." Nevertheless, when compared to the Fundamental Constitutions, it has been called both "oligarchic" and "authoritarian." Its provenance is attributable directly to Penn's intent "to calm the fears and accommodate the desires" of his wealthiest (mostly nonresident) co-investors.[178]

It is worth examining the origins of the first purchasers. According to David Hackett Fischer's research, of 589 purchasers of Pennsylvania land in 1681–6, the vast majority were English (88 percent), with small numbers of Irish and Welsh and a scattering from further afield. Of those identifiable as English, 25 percent of first purchasers were from the North Midlands and the Pennine North, the areas from which the mass of Pennsylvania's early Quaker population came. Roughly half of these Northern first purchasers were from Cheshire alone. The remaining 75 percent were all from outside those regions. Forty percent came from London and the home counties; 30 percent came from the South and West, with the largest concentration from Bristol and its hinterland. The rest were from the South Midlands. Almost none were from East Anglia. From the same figures, Barry Levy has

---

[176] Ibid., 237, n.1. Shepherd notes that in late seventeenth-century discourse, *ability* in this context means *wealth*.

[177] Ibid., 17–18, 235. For the "Laws Agreed Upon in England," see *Charter to William Penn*, 99–103.

[178] Ronald Schultz, *The Republic of Labor: Philadelphia Artisans and the Politics of Class, 1720–1830* (New York, 1993), 16; Shepherd, *Proprietary Government*, 226–7, 231–4, 235, and see also 227–31; Nash, *Quakers and Politics*, 15–16, 33–47.

determined that most of Penn's first purchasers were rural buyers (313 of 589, or 53 percent), that most of the rural buyers came from upland pastoral England rather than from champion country, and that of these upland purchasers a plurality was from the prime areas of initial Quaker recruitment. The plurality, however, were predominantly small purchasers. The fifty-five Cheshire purchasers, for example, bought an average of just over 500 acres apiece. Twenty-three Welsh first purchasers bought more heavily, accounting for 43,130 acres, but according to Levy they were in fact agents for at least seventy-three other Welsh farmers. Thus, their purchases average out to smaller lots than the Cheshire purchasers – fewer than 450 acres per head.[179]

Penn's *Frame of the Government* appears to have been designed with the interests of the largest first purchasers firmly in mind. Of these, most were from regions outside the pastoral upland areas that fed Pennsylvania with its original resident population of predominantly poor and plebeian North West England migrants. In other words, a basic contradiction existed between the legal and political culture implicit in the Proprietor's conception of appropriate agrarian organization and that characteristic of the areas that were to furnish most of its early population. Penn's classic "arable" settlement model of nucleated manorialized agricultural villages contrasted with the "sprawling townships" of dispersed farmsteads, reminiscent of pastoral upland England, that actually appeared.[180] Disputes over proprietorial control of settlement patterns and quit rents, over squatter "invasions" of the proprietor's manors, over the very legal character of possession, were the basis for much of the political conflict that characterized early Pennsylvania.[181]

Anti-proprietary friction was in evidence in the colony from the beginning. Initially, much of it came from the area's scattered original settler population, suspicious of the implications of Quaker proprietary government. This was clearly manifest at the Assembly called to meet at Chester

---

[179] Fischer, *Albion's Seed*, 441; Barry Levy, *Quakers and the American Family: British Settlement in the Delaware Valley* (New York, 1988), 279–80.

[180] As Levy puts it, spatially (though not spiritually), the Delaware Valley Quakers created townships that "sprawl[ed] … looked uncommunal. Their settlement pattern, especially when set besides spacially [sic] tight and tidy New England towns, could seem the onset of promiscuous commercialization, privatization, and individualism." But these sprawling townships nevertheless "connected like-minded people to their institutions. The Welsh and Cheshire settlers lived on dispersed farmsteads in Pennsylvania, because the uplanders had known no other type of agriculture. They were accustomed to keeping communities over considerable space." *Quakers and the American Family*, 127–8.

[181] See generally Illick, *Colonial Pennsylvania*, 130–2; Nash, *Quakers and Politics*, 90–1; Levy, *Quakers and the American Family*, 127–8; Lemon, *Best Poor Man's Country*, 98–111; Shepherd, *Proprietary Government*, 239–54; Schulz, *Republic of Labor*, 16–19. The Penn family was active throughout much of the colonial period in attempting to enforce feudal obligations (specifically quitrents) upon grantees of land. See Mary M. Schweitzer, *Custom and Contract: Household, Government, and the Economy in Colonial Pennsylvania* (New York, 1987), 7. Nash notes Penn's "inability to appreciate that semifeudal privileges seemed anachronistic to a majority of the colonists in the Delaware Valley" (237).

(Pennsylvania) in December 1682 to ratify the *Frame of the Government* and formally adopt the annexed "Laws Agreed Upon in England," as well as an additional fifty laws more recently formulated. Both the original *Frame* and fully a fifth of the proprietor's proposed laws were rejected. Anti-proprietor sentiments continued to be in evidence the following year at a General Assembly called to amend the original *Frame*, and fed revisions that increased considerably the powers of the council vis-à-vis the proprietor while also modestly enlarging the role of the Assembly in colony government.[182] Political conflicts widened to encompass divisions within the new Quaker migrant population that stemmed from disagreements over the proprietor's land distribution policies and over the extent of his control of the colony's courts and laws. The result, particularly after the departure of Penn in 1684, was a politics of institutionalized factionalism, a "party system," in which the proprietor's original supporters split into an increasingly isolated group that remained loyal and a newly emergent local Quaker migrant elite of merchants and larger resident landowners that turned against Penn. The latter's rise to prominence – by 1688 they dominated Penn's new executive Commission of State, the Council (now akin to an upper house of legislature), proprietary and provincial offices, and the county courts – in turn provoked the emergence of a second Quaker grouping of "lesser men": small merchants and artisans from Philadelphia and small landowners from beyond the city who were opposed to the merchants and their landed allies. The chronic factionalism of these groups continued to mark the colony's politics throughout the first two decades.[183]

Quaker factionalism left a permanent impress on Pennsylvania's political culture. Successful in making the proprietary system unworkable, its other main effect during the colony's early years was to render legislative government at the colony level mostly ineffective. "There was no systematically compiled and comprehensive body of laws" for the first two decades. As a result "it was often impossible to determine either the nature or the extent of the laws relating to any given subject … no printed copies of any legislation existed to serve the needs of bench or bar."[184] Such legislation that was passed was often disallowed in England; that was the fate, for example, of most of the colony's judicature acts between 1701 and 1722. But although factionalism dominated the surfaces of political life, its effects did not penetrate very deeply. Disputes over the court system, for example, did not prevent local government from functioning effectively, at first through the agency of county courts and townships, later through locally elected county commissions. Anti-proprietorial politics was felt in continual attempts to expand the authority of local courts against proprietorial

---

[182] Nash, *Quakers and Politics*, 67–73.

[183] Fischer, *Albion's Seed*, 590–1; Shepherd, *Proprietary Government*, 254–316; Nash, *Quakers and Politics*, 89–240.

[184] John D. Cushing, "Editorial Note," in John D. Cushing, editor, *The Earliest Printed Laws of Pennsylvania, 1681–1713* (Wilmington, Del., 1978), vii–viii. Hence the continuing relevance, by default, of the *Duke's Laws*.

designs for the centralization of judicial authority. Indeed, whether the subject was proprietorial attempts to control settlement or to centralize legal institutions, what was conveyed in early Pennsylvania's response was the ethos of instinctive anti-authoritarian localism, carried over from the North West England pastoral cultures from which its early migrants had come. What is important to emphasize is that Pennsylvania's disputatious political culture had arisen from the clash between the assertion of proprietorial authority and the stubborn refusal to accept it, not from a disputatiousness endemic to Pennine pastoral regions. The goal in the Delaware Valley, as formerly in England, was household-centered social peace.[185]

Like other aspects of early Pennsylvania society, the legal culture of work and labor that Delaware Valley migrants had created by the early eighteenth century bore the influence of the largely rural society centered on dispersed family households that they had left behind in England. As such – again like other aspects of early Pennsylvania society – it varied from the model implicit in proprietorial plans.

Servitude was known in the region before Penn's charter was granted. Present in the scattered fortified outposts of the Swedes and Dutch and brought northward from Maryland by planters migrating out of the Chesapeake region, servitude had been made subject to the jurisdiction of the *Duke's Laws*. In their regulation of work and labor, we have seen, the *Duke's Laws* evidence considerable dependence upon the *Lawes and Libertyes* of Massachusetts. Adaptations wrought in the *Laws and Libertyes*, however, focused labor regulation in the Delaware Valley on covenanted servitude (indentured migrant servitude and apprenticeship) and slavery.[186]

Penn's relations with the established settler population were generally accommodating, and this no doubt extended to their labor practices. But Penn's earliest agreements with his first purchasers also provide independent indications that he endorsed the transportation of indentured labor. For example, the "Certain Conditions or Concessions" agreed in 1681 contemplated a head-right system of land grants, as in the early Chesapeake, that would reward the first purchasers for importations of servants.[187]

---

[185] Wayne L. Bockelman, "Local Government in Colonial Pennsylvania," in Bruce C. Daniels, editor, *Town and County: Essays on the Structure of Local Government in the American Colonies* (Middletown, Conn., 1978), 216–37; William M. Offutt, Jr., *Of "Good Laws" and "Good Men": Law and Society in the Delaware Valley, 1680–1710* (Urbana, Ill., 1995), 4, 8–10, 12–13.

[186] Herrick, *White Servitude*, 27–8. Original clauses providing for the public assessment of wages and proposing to bind "workmen" to their tasks were omitted. (By the time the *Duke's Laws* were compiled, as we have seen, these clauses had long been a dead letter both in Massachusetts and in Virginia.) As elsewhere, the *Duke's Laws* extends to servants the presumption that they will largely be juveniles. Thus, see the section of the Laws entitled "Children and Servants" in *Charter to William Penn*, 19–20. See also Alfred L. Brophy, "Law and Indentured Servitude in Mid-Eighteenth Century Pennsylvania," *Willamette Law Review*, 28, 1 (Winter 1991), 76–80.

[187] Fifty acres were allocated per servant imported to each master, at a quit rent of 4/- per annum, and a further 50 acres were to be allocated to the imported servant, at the end of service, at a quit rent of 2/-. In the "Certain Conditions or Concessions" (1681), *Earliest Printed Laws of Pennsylvania*, 190–3, at 191.

Additionally, taking a cue from the maturing Chesapeake of mid-century, the *Laws Agreed Upon in England* sketched the beginnings of a regulatory system to control the process of servant importation by providing for a register of all servants in the province,[188] and for regulation of terms of service and freedom dues: servants were not to be kept "longer than their time," and "such as are careful [should] be both justly and kindly used in their service, and put in fitting equipage at the expiration thereof, according to Custom."[189] Here was a vestigial "state" disciplining (however benevolently) individual planters' relations with indentured laborers.

As telling an indicator of Penn's intentions was the charter he gave the Free Society of Traders, an elaborate project reminiscent of the particular plantation schemes of Ireland and early Virginia, and fully in keeping with Penn's manorial conception of appropriate agrarian organization for the colony.[190] The terms on which the Free Society was established made it a distinct corporate entity within the province, complete with manorial jurisdiction over its 20,000 acres of land (the Society might "forever hold a Court Barron ... Courts leet & veiw of Franke pleadge" within the grant, called the manor of Franke, to "performe and execute all Such matters & things as are belonging or Incident unto or are used & accustomed to be done" in such courts, and further might enjoy general jurisdiction "wherein no other Justices or other officers of the said Province Shall Intermeddle"). The Society's goal was to import several hundred bound tradesmen and farm servants, and create a diversified agricultural and trading economy for the region.[191]

Under these various auspices, approximately one-third of the first flurry of arrivals recorded between 1682 and 1686 were servants.[192] As servant imports proceeded, the first two meetings of the provincial Assembly, at Upland (Chester) in December 1682 and at Philadelphia the following March, adopted a detailed set of disciplinary measures expanding upon the

---

[188] *Laws Agreed Upon in England*, in *Charter to William Penn*, 101 (twenty-third law). Initially, the register was to record "names, time, wages, and days of payment." At the Assembly held in Newcastle in May 1684, the Registry was amended to become explicitly a registry of all arrivals and refocused on place of birth and age at time of arrival. See ch. CLXIII (1684) in *Charter to William Penn*, 170.

[189] *Laws Agreed Upon in England*, 102 (twenty-ninth law). Reinforcing the linkage of servitude to childhood, the twenty-eighth law, immediately preceding, provided that "all children within this province of the age of twelve years, shall be taught some useful trade or skill, to the end none may be idle, but the poor may work to live, and the rich, if they become poor, may not want." The *Laws* also provided that felons be put to servitude to compensate victims (101; twenty-fourth law).

[190] For contemporary developments in New York that followed the same model, see Sung Bok Kim, *Landlord and Tenant in Colonial New York: Manorial Society, 1664–1775* (Chapel Hill, 1978), 3–43.

[191] See the "Charter for the Free Society of Traders," in Dunn and Dunn, eds., *The Papers of William Penn*, II, 246–56, at 248–9. See also Shepherd, *Proprietary Government*, 45. The Society began importing company servants in 1682, but it was to prove an ill-conceived venture.

[192] Nash, *Quakers and Politics*, 50; Herrick, *White Servitude*, 35.

regulatory role hinted at in the "laws agreed upon in England." Remaining generally within the orbit prescribed in the *Duke's Laws*, these measures declared punishment of servant insubordination to be the business of the courts; confirmed the creation of a servant registry; adopted the *Duke's Laws'* pass system; prohibited the sale of servants out of the province; made assignment of servants subject to the approval of two justices; rendered property in servants immune from attachment; forbade the concealing, entertaining or harboring of servants; forbade servants from trading the goods of their masters or mistresses without consent; provided that servants convicted of assaulting or menacing their masters or mistresses be punished "at the Discretion of two justices of the peace, so it be sutable to the nature of the offence"; and declared statutory freedom dues (one suit, ten bushels of wheat or fourteen of corn, one Axe, and two hoes). As in the Chesapeake, the Assembly established statutory terms of service for servants imported without indenture or covenant – five years for those seventeen or older, and until age twenty-two for those younger than seventeen (the county courts to adjudge ages). At its third meeting, in Philadelphia in October 1683, the Assembly added a measure that prescribed five days' additional service for each day an absconding servant was absent, together with costs of pursuit.[193] Reenacted in codified form in 1700,[194] these measures remained the core of Pennsylvania's statute law of servitude throughout the eighteenth century. Subsequent supplementary statutes added penalties for servants who married without permission and female servants who bore bastard children, and made additional provision for the binding of orphans and (much later) the regulation of apprenticeship.

Although servitude was thus established from Pennsylvania's beginnings and would continue throughout the eighteenth century, in important respects it was a very different institution than that created in the Chesapeake. Compared with Virginia's seventeenth-century statute law of indentured servitude, for example, Pennsylvania's measures from the beginning placed much more emphasis on court oversight of the master-servant relationship and left much less to the discretion of the master.[195] Provision for court supervision of punishments and assignments, for example,

---

[193] Herrick, *White Servitude*, 31, Appendix 289–91; *Charter to William Penn*, 113, 119, 151–3, 166. Herrick notes that the 5 for 1 penalty for absconding was proposed by Penn himself.

[194] "An Act for the better Regulation of Servants in this Province and Territories" (1700), in *Laws of the Province of Pennsilvania* (Philadelphia, 1714), ch.49.

[195] The divergence first appears in the *Duke's Laws*, where it underscores the preeminent influence of Massachusetts law in the *Laws'* formulation. The contrast was only reinforced by Virginia's turn to slavery in the eighteenth century, which further emphasized the authority of the master as compared to that of the regulatory state. The contrast described here expresses distinct cultures of legal authority and state mobilization that comport with Somers' important distinction between arable and pastoral legal-political culture. The arable manifests the relative ascendancy of regional hierarchical power, hence lessened opportunities for local mobilizations of countervailing state authority. The pastoral manifests no overweening regional hierarchy of power hence greater opportunities for local mobilizations of countervailing state authority.

helped realize Penn's adage that masters be careful to "mix Kindness with Authority."[196] Kindness, of course, was in the eye of the beholder. Requiring runaways to serve five additional days for each day of absence was one of the more severe responses to absconding anywhere on the mainland. It gave considerable edge to Penn's further advice, this aimed at the servant's ears, that "the Glory of a Servant is *Fidelity*," and that "if thou wilt be a *Good* Servant, thou must be *True*."[197] As important, however, is the nature of the population to whom these injunctions were addressed. None of the measures enforcing servitude ever touched hired or artisan labor. Laborers who bargained for wages and were hired for defined terms were "privileged to withdraw from their service if they so wished, though this might mean the forfeiture, wholly or in part, of the wages earned."[198] Nor were artisans hired to complete specific tasks subject to legal restraint. Unlike the early seventeenth-century Chesapeake, disciplinary incidents of English law reinforcing specific performance of labor contracts that rendered hireling labor's freedom ambiguous had no reception in Pennsylvania. Penn did make some attempt to introduce provisions for wage regulation, but to little effect. Always at a premium, hirelings enjoyed wages that compared extremely favorably with English experience.[199]

Equally important, the character of servant migration into Pennsylvania increasingly departed the pattern that had earlier prevailed in the Chesapeake. In the earliest years of settlement, the activities of the Free Society of Traders and of other first purchasers in importing multiple servants meant that the influx was not dissimilar in appearance from that in evidence in contemporaneous flows to the Chesapeake: a movement in which young unattached males bulked large.[200] This flow, however, never reproduced the levels that had been apparent in the Chesapeake and by the end of the seventeenth century had dried up completely. Some of the abatement may be attributed to interruptions in overall migration occasioned by European warfare, but there was in any case substantially less demand in the Delaware Valley for "bulk" supplies of servant labor on the Chesapeake model. The Free Society's failure to establish company plantations confirmed the mode of organization for the rural economy that the regional origins of Delaware Valley migrants would predict – dispersed

---

[196] "Some Fruits of Solitude," No. 195.

[197] Ibid., Nos. 192, 204.

[198] Herrick, *White Servitude*, 2. One might note here yet another of Penn's adages: "As it is not reasonable that Men should be compell'd to serve; so those that have Employments should not be endured to leave them humorously." In "Some Fruits of Solitude," No. 368. See also Adolph B. Benson, *Peter Kalm's Travels in North America: The English Version of 1770* (New York, 1937), I, 204. In 1767, Gottfried Achenwall observed of "those hiring themselves out for a half or full year" that "the term is voluntary on both parts." See Gottfried Achenwall, "Some Observations on North America from Oral Information by Dr. Franklin," in Leonard W. Labaree et al., editors, *The Papers of Benjamin Franklin* (New Haven, 1959–), XIII, 355.

[199] Schweitzer, *Custom and Contract*, 54; Offutt, *Of "Good Laws" and "Good Men*," 4.

[200] Nash, *Quakers and Politics*, 50–1.

contiguous farm households characteristic of upland England producing a wide variety of crops and home manufactures. That mode of organization did not stimulate the levels of demand for labor that had characterized the tobacco-planting, land-engrossing staple economy of the Chesapeake.[201]

In the Delaware Valley, servant labor was supplementary to the immediate nuclear family. Demand was dictated by the family's needs. Demand was higher than in North West England because production of the area's main commercial crop, wheat, required more intensive cultivation than the upland livestock farming that migrant pastoral farmers had left behind.[202] But most of the area's deployable English servants continued, as in their regions of origin, to be children: initially children of the first settlers' neighbors, bound in England and brought along as part of the migrating family group; later children of local Delaware Valley neighbors bound out as domestic servants and farm apprentices. A few continued to be of the "classic" unattached youthful male migrant sort, but this supply had dwindled virtually to nothing by the end of the century. As in Virginia, Valley farmers and Philadelphia artisans turned to slavery to meet labor shortages caused by the interruption of European migration during the first two decades of the eighteenth century, but never on a scale remotely comparable to the Chesapeake colonies.[203] And when European migration resumed in the 1720s, the deployable rural labor force (unlike the Chesapeake's) once more became predominantly a mixture of Creole children and migrant servants, the latter ranging from unattached youth, through the offspring of German and Irish migrant families, to occasional entire family groups of children and adults.[204] Other sources of bound labor – transported

[201] Ibid., 279; Levy, *Quakers and the American Family*, 10.

[202] Schweitzer suggests that the "preferred production unit" for wheat farming generated a demand for "five or six older teenagers and young adults." *Custom and Contract*, 47. The incidence of servitude in the Delaware Valley (see Chapter 1) suggests that insofar as the generality of farms approached this optimal situation, they met most of the labor demand from their own resources. The most important single factor in determining resort to servants was the host family's life-cycle – that is, the loss of labor capacity of mothers to pregnancy, childbirth, and infant care, the eventual availability of children, the ageing of parents. Levy, however, argues that at least in Pennsylvania's early years the demands of farm-formation were such that the English neighbors' children brought as servants, and the settlers' own children, "seemed an inadequate labor force to clear and plant the land" and that Quaker farmers therefore supplemented their children's labor with that of "strangers" – unrelated indentured servants, slaves, and later redemptioners. *Quakers and the American Family*, 138. One should note that Delaware Valley agriculture offers a degree of contrast in labor demand with New England's pastoralism, where average to poor soils meant noncommercial yields and a reliance on mixed subsistence farming based on Indian corn as a main crop, and livestock. New England's farming was relatively less labor-intensive, and its needs were met to an even greater extent (as we have seen) by sole reliance on family labor. In both areas, finally, one finds resort to (short-term) wage labor for ancillary construction tasks and harvest work.

[203] Schweitzer, *Custom and Contract*, 45–7; Illick, *Colonial Pennsylvania*, 115. Pennsylvania slavery is addressed in greater detail in Chapter 9.

[204] Farley W. Grubb, "Immigration and Servitude in the Colony and Commonwealth of Pennsylvania: A Quantitative and Economic Analysis" (Ph.D. dissertation, University of Chicago, 1984), 97–105; Schweitzer, *Custom and Contract*, 47–8.

convicts,[205] debtors, criminals required to make restitution through work – simply helped confirm that, for the European population, servitude was a status increasingly explicitly demarcated (as elsewhere) by age and origin; a condition for children and foreigners or community outsiders.[206] Absent circumstances of voluntary debt servitude or involuntary servitude to make restitution for criminal activity – socially important, but quantitatively insignificant – few instances of servitude among Creole adults in Pennsylvania can be found at any time during the colonial period.[207]

The incidence of servitude of any kind in rural Pennsylvania was in any case low. Of the inventories of first-generation settlers, 24.4 percent reported servants or slaves; among second-generation inventories the figure was 27.2 percent.[208] An examination of 572 Chester County inventories concentrated in selected periods between 1717 and 1751 shows that generally about 20 percent of estates reported bound labor (servants or slaves). The highest incidence was 23.5 percent in 1732–7.[209] Analysis of servant holdings in Goshen township, Chester County, indicates that no more than 23 percent of farmers resident in the township in 1753 (17 of 75) bought servants at any time between 1736 and 1772. Nor did the number of servants typically held by Pennsylvania farmers remotely reproduce the concentrations of bound labor to be found in the Chesapeake. In Goshen, for example, 70 percent of purchasers recorded during the thirty-six years covered by the township's servant list bought no more than one or two servants (20 purchasers of 28). Only eight bought more than two; the largest number bought by any individual was five.[210] More broadly, Schweitzer

205 On convict servitude, see generally A. Roger Ekirch, *Bound for America: The Transportation of British Convicts to the Colonies, 1718–1775* (Oxford, 1987). Benjamin Franklin called convict servants "venomous Reptiles," and stressed the influence of convict servitude on Pennsylvania's law. "The Villains you transport and sell to us must be ruled with a Rod of Iron … We do not thank you for forcing them upon us. We look upon it as an unexampled Barbarity in your Government to empty your Gaols into our Settlements." Labaree et al., eds., *Papers of Benjamin Franklin*, IV, 131–2; XVII, 42.

206 It is worth noting that the "Act for Imposing a Duty on Persons Convicted of Heinous Crimes and Imported into this Province as Servants, or otherwise" (1722), specifying the registration of names of servants imported and requiring importers to attest to their character, essentially identifies two categories of imported servant – convicts and children.

207 Farley Grubb, "Servant Auction Records and Immigration into the Delaware Valley, 1745–1831: The Proportion of Females Among Migrant Servants," *Proceedings of the American Philosophical Society*, 133, 2 (June 1989), 157, reports the incidence of "local" adult servants in records of bindings in Philadelphia at 4.4% (35 of 790) in 1745–6, and 4.7% (192 of 4113) in 1771–3. Combined, and expressed as a percentage of all contracts recorded, the percentage is 3.8%.

208 Levy, *Quakers and the American Family*, 240.

209 Schweitzer, *Custom and Contract*, 46, table 1.6.

210 "Entries of Servants Imported into this Province and purchased by the Inhabitants of this Township," in *Goshen Town Book, 1718–1870* (1v), in Archives of the Chester County Historical Society (Westchester, Pa.). In his own independent analysis of this same source, Barry Levy notes that the ten richest households in Goshen alone accounted for nearly 60% of servant purchases, and that 77% of Goshen ratepayers never bought any servants. See *Quakers and the American Family*, 240.

concludes that the 20–25 percent of householders in Pennsylvania who bought servants "seldom used more than one servant of any kind." The contrast with neighboring Maryland is marked, as Schweitzer shows that during the same period 50–75 percent of estates reported bound labor (largely slaves), with a mean holding that ranged from eight to more than ten per estate.[211] Sharon Salinger argues that "the broad economic orientation" of the farm economy made "reliance on unfree labor unnecessary."[212] Despite high levels of wages, short-term hired labor was consistently preferred by farmers seeking assistance beyond that which could be supplied by their own children or an indentured boy. And it was consistently available. By the second half of the eighteenth century, free landless wage laborers called "freemen" (grown sons of resident landholders who were not heads of their own households) or "inmates" (cottagers) had become the fastest-growing segment of the rural labor force.[213] By the early nineteenth century (we shall see in Chapter 7) it would also be, legally, the most downwardly mobile.

Philadelphia evidence shows that similar patterns characterized the colony's primary urban area. Indentured servitude in eighteenth-century Pennsylvania was predominantly an urban phenomenon. By the 1760s, servants made up no more than 3 percent of the workforce in Lancaster and Chester counties and in the rural districts of Philadelphia County. In Bedford and Northampton counties the proportion was far lower.[214] In the city workforce during the 1760s and early 1770s the incidence of servants was two to three times higher.[215] What is more to the point, however, is that

---

[211] Schweitzer, *Custom and Contract*, 47 and table 1.6 (46). James Horn's analysis of work units in Anne Arundel county shows that in Maryland a trend toward larger plantation workforces was already well under way by the mid-seventeenth century. Although throughout the second half of the century the majority of work units remained in the 1–3 laborer range, at mid-century 25% of servants and slaves worked on plantations with 10 or more laborers. By the early 1660s, this figure had grown to 40%. James P. Horn, *Adapting to a New World: English Society in the Seventeenth-Century Chesapeake* (Chapel Hill, 1994), 281.

[212] Sharon V. Salinger, *"To Serve Well and Faithfully: Labor and Indentured Servants in Pennsylvania, 1682–1800* (Cambridge and New York, 1987), 22.

[213] On freemen and inmates, see Lucy Simler, "Tenancy in Colonial Pennsylvania: The Case of Chester County," *William and Mary Quarterly*, 3rd Ser., 43, 4 (October 1986), 542–69; Paul G. E. Clemens and Lucy Simler, "Rural Labor and the Farm Household in Chester County, Pennsylvania, 1750–1820," in Stephen Innes, editor, *Work and Labor in Early America* (Chapel Hill, 1988), 106–43; Lucy Simler and Paul G. E. Clemens, "The 'Best Poor Man's Country' in 1783: The Population Structure of Rural Society in Late-Eighteenth-Century Southeastern Pennsylvania," *Proceedings of the American Philosophical Society*, 133, 2 (1989), particularly 236–40; Lucy Simler, "The Landless Worker: An Index of Economic and Social Change in Chester County, Pennsylvania, 1750–1820," *Pennsylvania Magazine of History and Biography*, 114, 2 (April 1990), 163–99. See also Levy, *Quakers and the American Family*, 248–51.

[214] Salinger, *"To Serve Well and Faithfully,"* 71, 71 n.106.

[215] According to Salinger's estimates, these levels were considerably lower than in the late 1740s and early 1750s, when the incidence of servants in the city workforce had exceeded 25% and briefly approached 30%. Ibid., 178–80, table A.3. As I argue in Chapter 1, however, those estimates are not sustainable.

the greater density notwithstanding, city holding patterns appear to have replicated those in the country. At this time, between 10 percent and 20 percent of Philadelphia households included servants; of those city inhabitants owning servants, 75 percent owned no more than one.[216]

Clearly, Pennsylvanians did not avoid the inclusion of legally unfree labor in their culture of work. Just as clearly, unfree labor was supplementary to total demand for labor rather than the basis of the provincial economy.[217] As in the Chesapeake, servitude in Pennsylvania was overwhelmingly identified with adolescence and immigration. But in statutory character it differed, providing for considerably greater oversight of master-servant relationships.[218] Moreover, as in New England and also eighteenth-century Virginia, in contrast to England, one finds wage labor left altogether free of statutory restraint, whether in terms of wages received or movement.

Conclusion

When, in 1629, John Winthrop ruminated on the "great worke" of settling Massachusetts Bay, he doubtless had in mind the spiritual mission of renewal that motivated English Puritans to migrate in large numbers to a strange and distant place where they might join together in laying the foundation of a new exemplary building.[219] But for all that Winthrop's thoughts were elevated, his metaphor was not. The new foundations he contemplated required great work in a very practical sense, as Winthrop (an eminently practical man) well knew. In this, the requirements for success in colonizing were no different in the matter of harvesting souls than the tobacco that preoccupied the English settlements farther south. In both places colonizing was, as John Smith had predicted, hard work.

There (and elsewhere too), similarity mostly ended. Legal cultures of work differed from place to place. Early American statutes suggest no adoption of any uniform metropolitan model but a highly selective adaptation of specific elements of English statute law, a process further refracted by

---

[216] Ibid., 69–70.

[217] As Levy puts it, what distinguished "the radical Quaker family system" of the Delaware Valley was "the moral use of family labor and generous equitable distributions of property." In the Chesapeake, "planters used slave rather than family labor and encouraged habits of leisure and command, not convivial industry, in their children." New England's farmers "almost exclusively relied on family labor and were also committed to using household relations to promote personal conscience and religious Grace. But generally lacking good soil and convinced of the social and religious necessity of patriarchal dominance and control, New England farmers generally paid their sons and daughters less and later than Delaware Valley farmers." *Quakers and the American Family*, 188.

[218] In addition to the legislation already cited, see "An Act for the Regulation of Apprentices within this Province" (1765), passed "for Want of some Law to regulate their Conduct and Behavior during their Apprenticeships, to prevent their absenting themselves from their said Masters or Mistresses Service, without Leave, to punish them for any disorderly or immoral Behaviour, and to make the Covenants between them mutually obligatory."

[219] See the epigraph to Part II of this book.

the distinct regional cultures from which English settlers came, and by the exigencies of variation in mainland economies and production regimes.

By targeting particular segments of the available working population rather than creating a regulatory regime for the performance of work as a whole, local statutory regulation established interstitial zones of freedom in each region of colonial settlement. At the same time, because "the law Queen Betty made" was broken into fragments and only very particular elements transplanted, the potential for labor regulation per se to become – under the right circumstances – a means to the construction of civic rights, as it had in parts of England, died. Freedom took on a very different connotation, particularly as the intensive legal regimes of slavery spread. As Samuel McKee put it so long ago, but so well, during the first two centuries of mainland settlement "free labor" came to mean "without public or private regulation" – the absence of incursion upon self-direction – but also "without special privilege as a class."[220] McKee plainly doubted that freedom as absence of regulation had lasting substantive worth; he thought its limitations revealed by "the impact of the factory system."[221] Those who did not have self-direction in the first place, of course, had no need to wait that long to learn its shortcomings.

---

[220] McKee, *Labor in Colonial New York*, 179. Effectively revisiting McKee's book after seventy years, Simon Middleton's *From Privileges to Rights: Work and Politics in Colonial New York City* (Philadelphia, 2006) has given labor in colonial New York a vastly enriched history, but has not greatly altered the trajectory that McKee sketched. Middleton's account stresses an artisanal culture present from the beginnings of Dutch settlement, shaped always by market interactions, governed initially by inherited early-modern corporate craft regulation, altered over time by a transformation of that culture of corporate privilege into one of public political right. "Tradesmen in New Amsterdam occupied a preferential position in the civic order, sustained by a bundle of identifications that marked them as freeborn subjects, burghers, and craft practitioners who claimed privileges and bore reciprocal duties to work at their occupations in the interests of the common good." By the early eighteenth century, however, the capacity of city artisans to sustain claims of "special occupational consideration and protection" had been significantly diminished. "The shift of political influence from city to province, the rise of English-style elections, the introduction of the English common law, and the professionalization of legal recourse all undermined claims regarding local practices and privileges." Artisans joined other "ordinary male property-holders" cast as "plainspeaking and virtuous political subjects whose consent legitimated provincial and imperial government," an exchange of a "late medieval political culture that secured their status and rights on the basis of their privileged place within a prescriptive local hierarchy" for a modern political culture of "free men possessed of equal rights." Crucially, in New York City this transformation of the basis of civic and municipal participation, from craft-corporate privilege to propertied "free man" was possible only because it was accompanied by the simultaneous development of a slave-labor underclass. Here, indeed, lies Middleton's cardinal revision to and supplement of McKee's fine work. New York artisans lost their corporate privileges but remained "free" (certainly freer than their English brethren) though without public regulation to replace the private (corporate) regulation they had lost. In New York, as in Virginia, that quintessentially "modern" freedom was instead underpinned by slavery. See Middleton, *From Privileges to Rights*, 9, 227, and generally 8–9, 226–8, 131–62.

[221] McKee, *Labor in Colonial New York*, 179.

The general question of freedom's substance will be pursued further in Part III. First though, it is important to be sure that early American statutes accurately convey early American practices. We have seen that, in England, one cannot read practice from legislation: local legal cultures refracted putatively homogenous laws in dissimilar ways. No examination of the legal culture of work in early America can be complete, then, without attention to local law in action.

7

Changing: Localities, Legalities

The colonist will avail himself of his cultural heritage whether this has to do with religion, with law, or with methods of farming ... Instead of comparing the English common law with the legal monuments in the colonies, our task now becomes inevitably more complex. It is necessary for us to determine what was the cultural heritage of the first settlers, and in what form this heritage first expressed itself in the new land.

Julius Goebel, "King's Law and Local Custom" (1931)

By now it should be clear that rather than planting a template of "English" law, the inside story of English colonizing is one of successive seedings of mainland North America with a plurality of legal cultures, each expressing the designs of projectors but also heavily influenced by migrants' regional English origins. In the case of the legal culture of work and labor, surveying and comparing local legal practices takes us beyond their distinctive regional origins to the question how the wide range of work practices and authority relationships routinely present in different mainland communities were accommodated and how disputes presented to their courts were adjudicated.

Examination of local legal practice confirms the hypothesis that the labor of colonizing was a highly variegated social activity, performed by highly segmented populations. When it comes to the performance of work and labor, however, historians have represented the role of colonial courts as one reflective more of uniformity than variety. The legal culture of work was primarily an exercise in the reinforcement of coercion. At bottom, all labor was legally unfree because all performances were coerced.[1] This representation is not justified. It is certainly true that the criminalization of resistance to work discipline (notably departure) was an essential feature of the mainland colonies' regimes of servitude. But servitude had its institutionalized protections as well as its disciplines, as the statutes of

[1] See Robert J. Steinfeld, *The Invention of Free Labor: The Employment Relationship in English and American Law and Culture, 1350–1870* (Chapel Hill, 1991), 3–5. Farley Grubb also argues that "the common law governing labor relations was the same in England as in her American colonies, and was the same for the many forms of voluntary bound labour as for free labour (wage labour by the day)." See Farley Grubb, "Does Bound Labour Have to be Coerced Labour? The Case of Colonial Immigrant Servitude Versus Craft Apprenticeship and Life-Cycle Servitude-in-Husbandry," *Itinerario*, 21, 1 (1997), 29.

different regions have already shown, and courts played a significant role in protecting as well as in coercing. Second, and more important, as both actual numbers (Chapter 1) and the statutes themselves (Chapter 6) indicate, mainland labor was far from uniformly unfree. That is confirmed by this chapter's study of local practices. In numerous litigated disputes arising from work relationships, one finds civil not criminal procedures uppermost, the courts' role one more of mediation than coercion.

What the manuscript records of courts tend to reveal is not a generic legal regime of work discipline applicable across a basic categorical divide between people who worked and people for whom they worked. Instead they reveal the existence of a variety of legal statuses with differentiated characters and consequences. Most determinative of legal outcomes were local statutes: as one might expect, where they could, the courts of each mainland region relied closely on the guidance of the legislated statutory regime of that particular region. Where this proved inapplicable, however, they constructed rules. Their rules did not follow what historians have taken to be concurrent English law,[2] but rather paid considerable attention to nuances of local status and work practice. I can best demonstrate this by returning once more to the three regions of settlement on which I have been concentrating – New England, the Chesapeake, the Delaware Valley – this time to focus on a particular county within each of the three colonies that featured in the last chapter.[3]

I. The Chesapeake

York County, Virginia, stretches for some 40 miles along the southern bank of the York River, from north of the Jamestown settlement downstream beyond Yorktown to the river's Chesapeake Bay mouth. Approximately 100 square miles in extent, the county occupies roughly half the land area of the peninsula between the James and York Rivers, an area of rich soils entered by English migrants in the 1620s and 1630s as increasing European immigration pushed settlement beyond the James River basin. In 1634, when the county was created, some 510 persons were recorded living in the area. At the end of the century, the population was close to 2,000. Growth during the century proceeded on a cyclical pattern of peaks roughly every twenty years interspersed with declines. Particularly after 1660, persistent high levels of migrant mortality offset a rising Creole birthrate. Land distribution among freeholders was relatively even, but the population contained significant numbers of non-landowners. The out-migration of younger sons, no doubt in reaction to the growing difficulty of acquiring

[2] James P. Horn, *Adapting to a New World: English Society in the Seventeenth-Century Chesapeake* (Chapel Hill, 1994), 337; Steinfeld, *Invention of Free Labor*, 47.

[3] For a similar study of the law of work and labor as revealed in the records of one locality, and the intricate differentiation of status they display, see Simon Middleton, *From Privileges to Rights: Work and Politics in Colonial New York City* (Philadelphia, 2006), particularly 163–88.

land within the county, and low levels of indentured servant imports relative to other tidewater counties probably hastened York planters' resort to slave labor, which certainly was under way earlier in the county than elsewhere in tidewater Virginia. Among tithables (all white males and all slaves above the age of sixteen), free heads of household outnumbered bound laborers until the late 1670s. At about the same time, slaves began to outnumber indentured servants. In the eighteenth century, population growth was steadier, and marked by the consolidation of slavery. It was also marked by the development of two of the tidewater's principal urban areas, Yorktown and Williamsburg.[4]

Records from York County's courts exist in some form for most of the period from the county's founding, although prior to 1658 they are fragmentary and nonsequential.[5] Examination of the full run of available records nevertheless indicates that work relations were frequently a subject for juridical inquiry and determination. Most common are several classes of proceedings that arose in the course of the administration of unfree relations, but there are also others that deal with work relations between free persons. In most cases, disposal was routine and the record too abbreviated to offer significant qualitative information, but occasional proceedings offer opportunities to probe into the reasons for outcomes that diverge from the expected.

Among the categories of disputes arising from unfree relations, those that have tended to excite most interest among historians are disputes confirming courts' disciplinary role, notably the punishment of instances of flight or other indiscipline among indentured servants. And indeed, these are constants in York County records. Among the earliest entries in the court's records, for February 1645/6, for example, one finds the case of William Keaton, bound by indenture in February 1641 to serve W—— Hockaday the term of five years "& sd Keaton absenting himselfe [from] his sd master uppon pretence of being free from the sd Hockaday as alsoe that the sd Keaton did runn away from his sd [master] June last to his great hinderance and damage the Ct doth therefore order that the sd Wm Keaton shall serve the sd Hockaday til the 28 Feb next accord. to indenture and for his running away and peremtory answeare [to] the Ct in refuseing the performance of there ord herein the sherr shall forthwith cause the sd Keaton to be whippt at the whipping post and to rec 30 lashes on his bare shoulders."[6] One finds here no presentation of a claim of time lost, and thus no addition of "double the tyme of service soe neglected" as provided by the Assembly three years earlier for punishment of runaways.

[4] See generally Kevin P. Kelly, "A Demographic Description of Seventeenth-Century York County, Virginia," unpublished manuscript (Colonial Williamsburg Foundation).
[5] See generally York County Transcripts, *Deeds, Orders, Wills [DOW]*, I-XIX (1633–1746/7, with gaps); *Judgments & Orders [JO]*, I (1746/7–1765, with gaps); *Order Books [OB]*, I (1765–1768); *Judgments & Orders*, II (1768–1774); *Order Books*, II (1774–1783); all located at the Department of Historical Research, Colonial Williamsburg Foundation.
[6] 25 Feb 1645/6, in *DOW*, II, 101a.

Double time, however, was employed in the case of Benjamin Hallyard, servant to Thomas Curtis, who "hath divers tymes runn away and absented himselfe to the number of 30 days whereby the Ct doth therefore order that the sd Benjamin Hallyard shall make good the sd Damage by double the tyme of his being absent in such servis as he shalbe imployed in by his master according to Act & also shall [illeg.] receive 20 stripes on his bare shoulders [at the] whipping post."[7]

The early York entries are sufficiently ambiguous to accommodate speculation that in the 1640s the criminal enforcement of service in Virginia extended beyond the multiyear transoceanic migrant indentures that were the object of the Assembly's statutes to shorter-term local covenants more nearly resembling the annual hires characteristic of English agricultural service. Take, for example, Edmund Smith who "hath in Ct confessed that he hath divers Saturdayes absented himselfe from the servis of Mr John Chew being his covenant servant. It is therefore ord with the consent of the sd Smith that he shall serve the sd Chew twenty [day]es longer than by covenant hee is bound in consideration of his neglect afforesd."[8] Here time is added to compensate for time lost by the servant's neglect. At the same time, the proceeding stands apart from those involving multiyear indentures in two notable respects. First, in adding time in compensation for time lost, the court makes no mention of the 1642 Act or its double-time provision, nor of any corporal punishment. Second, the court's decision requires that Smith consent to the addition of time, which implies that other forms of compensation – monetary, for example – might have been acceptable alternatives in this instance. John Duncombe's indenture of 30th July 1646, for example, had bound him to serve Nicholas Brooke one year, or to compensate him in tobacco "to the value thereof." When he did not perform, the court ordered "with the consents of sd Brooke & Duncombe" that Duncombe arrange security "for the paymt of one thousand lbs tob on 20th Nov next in full consideration of the sd on yrs servis."[9] In the 1640s, then, York's county court can be found enforcing covenants of service and assessing penalties (or, more accurately, compensation) for their neglect.[10] At the same time the

---

[7] 25 Sept 1646, in *DOW*, II, 169. See also 30 Nov 1647 *DOW*, II, 297: "Whereas it appeareth to the Ct by suff. proof that James Pinor servt to Capt Willm Taylor several times absented himself from his masters servis by running away by wch meanes it appeared that sd Capt Taylor was damnified by the loss of many of his catle wch were comitted to the care of sd Pinor This Ct ord that sd Pinor shall accord. to Act of Ass. make sd Taylor satisfaction by serving him one complete yr after he is free by his indenture or other covenant."

[8] 20 Oct 1646, in *DOW*, II,185.

[9] 24 Jan 1647/8, in *DOW*, II, 322.

[10] See, in addition to cases cited, 16 Dec 1647, in *DOW*, II, 321: "Whereas John Weekes did by his owne confession agree with to serve Willm Light 2 months for wch he was to receive one cotton bed a boulster and one old blanket and a pair of pott Hookes the Ct doth therefore ord that sd Weekes make good the sd servis to the sd Light and that then sd Light pay to him the sd bed boulster & blanket & pott hookes otherwise execution."

court differentiates among categories of service according to their legal effects.[11]

The same intimation of conscious differentiation among distinct forms of work relation according to their distinct legal incidents can be detected in court proceedings during the second half of the seventeenth century, when the parameters of difference become somewhat easier to observe.[12] As in the earliest records, servants absconding from service to which they were bound by a multiyear indenture were routinely brought into court by masters to be punished for their departures by the addition of double-time penalties. In these proceedings the court would ritually cite the existence of a prior obligation to serve by dint of the existence of an indenture, or prior judicial determination arising from a "custom of the country" hearing, or prior court order. This in turn became the basis for invoking statutory authority and applying the legislated double-time penalty. The court's authority to act was unquestioned; there is no indication in the record of any such proceeding of any requirement that the court obtain a servant's consent to the addition of time. A number of proceedings, however, depart quite markedly from this pattern. Collectively, they suggest the clear emergence of a qualitative difference between the treatment of indentured migrants and Creole hirelings. Thus, in May 1674, Henry Jenkins sought recovery of a debt of 400 lbs tobacco and cask owed by one Richard Crane as wages for a year's service. Crane alleged that Jenkins had absented himself "a great part of his time." Had he been an imported indentured servant, Crane could have claimed double time for Jenkins's absences. Under contemporary English law, Crane could have had him imprisoned. Certainly Crane could have withheld Jenkins's wages. Instead, the court merely discounted the debt in proportion to Jenkins's actual absences, and ordered payment for the time he had actually spent in Crane's employ. "Ord that he be paid but 200 lbs tobo. & ca. & costs als exec."[13] Similarly, Michaell Robbarts successfully recovered payment of a debt of corn and tobacco owed him by Mr. David Condon for service as an overseer, despite evidence of frequent absences offered by Condon and others. "This Robbarts in the time he lived with Mr Condon as to the mannageing of his Crop was ever very neglective in the workeing of the hands ... he was either in to sleep or also gone from the hands they not seeing of

[11] For a similar pattern of outcomes in Accomack-Northampton, see Susie M. Ames, editor, *County Court Records of Accomack-Northampton, Virginia, 1632–40* (Millwood N.Y., 1975), and *County Court Records of Accomack-Northampton, Virginia, 1640–45* (Charlottesville, 1973), both as excerpted in Christopher L. Tomlins, *Law, Labor, and Ideology in the Early American Republic* (Cambridge and New York, 1993), 250–1, notes 85–7.

[12] Ibid., 250–1.

[13] 25 May 1674, in *DOW*, V, 68. See also Robert Newton agt. Thomas Spillman and Thomas Spillman agt. Robert Newton, both 6 May 1686, in *DOW*, VII, 163–4, 177–8 [Newton brought suit for payment owed for work done. Spillman countersued for neglect and departure from work. Testimony tended to show that Newton had left Spillman's employ in a dispute over diet. Spillman's suit was dismissed for want of cause and judgment entered for Newton in the amount of 350 lbs tobacco and cask.

him sometimes in three dayes time but his Generall Custome was every day and likewise away on a Saturday not seeing him againe whilst the Tuesday following." Testimony notwithstanding, the court ordered Condon to pay.[14] When, in February 1690/1, one David Jenkins sued Captain James Archer under similar circumstances, "itt evydently appearing in ct by the oathes of severall evydences that Jenkins did voluntarily leave his cropp before compleated, contrary to the condicons & w/out any occassions of sd Archer," the suit was dismissed.[15] But there is no indication that anyone thought Jenkins could be restrained from departing, or that he could be punished for it.[16] Nor, when George Glascock refused to complete a term as laborer for William Cheseley, did Cheseley do anything more than "aske the sd Glascock what he would allow him and he would finish the crop and discharge the sd Glascock of any further trouble." The parties agreed on a payment of 100 lb tobacco, which Glascock neglected to pay. Glascock's failure to pay brought Cheseley to court, but in a civil action for recovery of the debt, not a criminal complaint against an absconding servant. Moreover, when Cheseley failed to pursue the matter, the outcome was a nonsuit of 50 lb tobacco to Glascock.[17]

What such proceedings indicate, regrettably abbreviated as they are, is the existence of clear distinctions in the extent to which legal authority was made available to discipline the performance of work. These Creole laborers and overseers were subject to a distinct legal regime in the construction of their work relations compared with migrant servants imported under indenture, one that invoked no criminal sanctions to punish departures[18] but instead placed disputes in a civil realm of compensatory adjustments that did not even treat contracts for services as entire but instead apportioned wages owed according to actual time worked.

Further evidence supporting this hypothesis may be found in an additional genus of county court proceedings involving master-servant relations, those arising from attempts to legislate prohibitions on extramarital

---

[14] 26 Jan 1684/5, in *DOW*, VII, 6, 15–16.

[15] 24 Feb 1690/1, in *DOW*, IX, 1.

[16] On freedom to depart see also the deposition of Henry Shittle, 24 March 1684/5, at *DOW*, VII, 59.

[17] 24 April 1685, *DOW*, VII, 69.

[18] In addition to cases cited, see two proceedings involving James Lucas. In the first, of 24 June 1675, *DOW*, V, 116, "Whereas Francis Barnes in behalfe of James Lucas did promise to see Mr Joseph Ring satisfied 600 of tob. & ca. being a debt contracted by the sd Lucas & hee have deserted his cropp whereby the {sd} Barnes is likely to be damadged" it was ordered not that Lucas return to his work for Barnes but rather that "the sd Lucas give the sd Barnes counter security & pay costs als exec." In the second, of 24 August 1683, *DOW*, VI, 513, Lucas had become "an indented servt to Mr Jno Deane" but had "absented himself from his service." In this case the court ordered Lucas to return to Deane "that he may serve his sd time as in sd indenture is expressed." But no extra time penalty was added. Hired servants were treated differently from indented servants, these proceedings show, and the rare indentured Creole servant was treated differently from indentured migrants.

sexual relations in the population at large, and in particular – through prosecution and exemplary punishment – fornication and bastardy among servants. The legislature's statute of March 1661/2, *Against fffornication* (Act C), was particularly explicit. Any man or woman convicted of simple fornication, whatever their status, was liable to pay a fine of 500 lb tobacco. If a servant woman were convicted of bastardy, however, then "in regard of the losse and trouble her master doth sustaine by her haveing a bastard [she] shall serve two yeares after her time by indenture is expired or pay two thousand pounds of tobacco to her master besides the ffine or punishment for committing the offence."[19] The reasoning behind the Assembly's distinction is straightforward. Like absence, pregnancy, childbirth, and care for an infant all represented intrusions upon a master's command of a servant's covenanted time, and were therefore to be compensated by the addition of time. The court's record of conviction entered against Diana Jones in 1683 is typical:

> Whereas Diana Jones servt unto Major Otho Thorpe was this day presented to Ct for fornication & bastardy it is therefore ord that she serve her sd master 2 yrs after her time by indenture or custome is expired & for the filthy sin of fornication ord that the sher take her into his custodie & give her 30 lashes on the bare back well laid on Major Samll. Weldon having in open Court obliged himself to pay 500 lbs tobo to the parish the infliction is remitted & she ord. to serve the sd Maj. Weldon half a yr for the same.[20]

In certain bastardy cases, however, persons described as servants but who were not indentured migrants were not required to serve compensatory time. If their 500 lb fornication fine were paid on their behalf by their master, or (as in Diana Jones's case) some other person, then the court would specify service as a means to repay the debt, as indeed it might specify service for any debtor without assets. But no exemplary punishment accompanied the transaction; rather, what accompanied it was an intimation of a felt necessity on the part of the justices to secure the defendant's consent to remit the debt with labor. Thus, Elizabeth Mullins "servant woman to Mrs Elish. Vaulx" and summonsed for bastardy was fined 500 lbs tobacco for fornication "and is willing to serve her sd Mrs Vaulx halfe a [year] Mrs Vaulx by her note to the Ct obligeing herselfe to pay" the fine. Vaulx testified that Mullins's child "was borne in her servitude," though Mullins was "free before I had her to Court."[21] Again, in May 1709 Rachel Wood, "English servant woman" to Mongo Ingles, was ordered to serve "one whole year after her time by indenture custom or former order is expired" for bastardy, but the order was later rescinded, for "on consideracon of the

---

[19] William Waller Hening, *The Statutes at Large; Being a Collection of all the Laws of Virginia, from the First Session of the Legislature, in the Year 1619* (New York, 1823), II, 115, available at http://www.vagenweb.org/hening/ (accessed 22 August 2009).

[20] 24 April 1683, *DOW*, VI, 492. See also case of Katherine Higgins, 26 January 1684/5, *DOW*, VII, 7; case of Mary Baker, 24 March 1690/1, *DOW*, IX, 11.

[21] 24 Jan 1680/1, *DOW*, VI, 279, 288.

law in that case … [the Court] are of oppinion that (the sd Woods time by indenture being expired) there is no service due to her master." Wood's obligation was subsequently reinstated, Ingles demonstrating to the court's satisfaction that in fact her indenture had not expired. But this outcome only reinforces the lesson that local law treated indentured servitude as a distinct category of working relationship to which particular disciplines applied.[22]

Consider finally the evidence of disputes arising from the performance or nonperformance of promises to undertake work. In 1632, we have seen, the Virginia Assembly temporarily adopted most of Clause 10 of the Statute of Artificers by requiring artificers or laborers retained "in greate" to perform "uppon penaltie of one mounthes imprisonment" and a statutory penalty of £5 payable to the party aggrieved, in addition to damages and costs.[23] There is no indication that the statute remained in effect beyond the early 1640s, but York records in the 1660s and 1670s do furnish examples of orders to perform contracts. In April 1666, the court resolved a suit between Arthur Dickeson and John Babb by ordering that the latter "perform the condition between them by fencing the old field & payment a barrell of corn p. head for all the deft employed to plant on the sd Dickeson plantation & do also accomplish all things enjoyned to by the sd condition & pay costs of suit."[24] It is not clear whether Babb had been retained by Dickeson to undertake work on his behalf or whether the improvements had been specified as a condition of Babb's leasing Dickeson's plantation. One suspects the latter. Thus, as an example of a specific performance order, the proceeding is not without ambiguity. Clearly, however, the court was ordering work to be performed. Another 1666 proceeding is clearer, the court requiring William Belvin to honor his agreement with Captain Daniel Park – to erect a house or pay 2,000 lb tobacco in forfeit – by ordering the payment.[25] And in 1671, one Thomas Price was ordered "to perform a condition between him & Mr David Newell about the plaistering of his house to begin the work within 9 days."[26] None of these proceedings specified what sanction backed the order, and none invoked any criminal penalty, but none allowed an alternative to performance unless the parties had negotiated an alternative in their original agreement.

Within a few years, however, simple performance ceased to be the sole course of action offered. In 1686, in a suit brought by Mr. Thomas Ballard, Jr., Jeremiah Wing was ordered to undertake forthwith "and finish the glaseing work he was to doe & finish some considerable time hence" or instead pay damages of forty shillings and costs.[27] More interesting than this was a

[22] 24 May 1708, *DOW*, XIII, 137; 24 May 1709, *DOW*, XIII, 216; 24 Jan 1709/10, *DOW*, XIII, 263.

[23] See Chapter 6, n.108.

[24] 24 April 1666, *DOW*, IV, 59.

[25] 12 November 1666, *DOW*, IV, 111.

[26] 10 January 1670/1, *DOW*, IV, 306.

[27] 6 May 1686, *DOW*, VII, 163.

case that had arisen a few years earlier, in August 1679. Thomas Sloper, a sawyer, had been retained by Robert Spring to work "for halfes" with a servant of Spring's in sawing boards. Spring petitioned that "sd Sloper never came to worke … accord. to agreemt." Spring did not try to compel performance, however, instead claiming damages in mitigation. Two witnesses confirmed both the bargain and Sloper's neglect. Once before a jury, however, the plaintiff's case was rejected and costs awarded the defendant.[28]

The law of artisan work relations was revisited on an altogether more complex scale in the early eighteenth century in a tangle of damage and debt suits brought to the York County court over a four-year period by Robert Hyde, a housewright, against James Morris, a carpenter, in a dispute over unfinished carpentry work. Hyde's first suit was filed early in March 1704/5 in an action on the case seeking 50/- damages. Simultaneously he began a second suit, this one in debt, claiming £40. A third suit, entered a few weeks later, claimed damages of £8. A fourth, filed in July, claimed damages of £20.[29]

All of Hyde's suits (and also two additional suits filed three years later, one by each party)[30] grew out of a dispute over unfinished carpentry work on the interior of a house in Hampton that Hyde had employed Morris to perform. The damage suits all alleged breach of agreement and neglect of work. The debt suit sought to punish Morris for his nonperformance and alleged departure from employment. It did so by invoking "the statute of Queen Eliz made in the fifth year of her reigne entitled an act containing divers orders for artificers," or in other words the Statute of Artificers (5. Eliz. c.4). "[T]he sd James contrary to his agreemt made w/the sd plt on the first day of Aug in the year of our Lord God 1703 in the Psh of Hampton in this cnty & the above recited act did depart and finally leave such carpenters work wch by the sd plt the sd deft was retained in before he had finished the same w/o lawfull cause to his the plt dam 40£ sterl."[31]

Details of the dispute are difficult to reconstruct, for they exist only in the fragments of writs, pleas, and arguments filed in Hyde's several suits, and can be recovered only to the extent these were in turn entered into the court's written record. What emerges, however, is that Hyde alleged he had retained Morris on August 1, 1703 "in order to finish the sd Hyde's inside work of his house so far as he the sd Hyde would have it done & to be payd therefore so much as it should be worth," that Morris had neglected Hyde's

---

[28] 24 August 1679, *DOW*, VI, 114, 116.

[29] See variously, 2 March 1704/5, *DOW*, XII, 295 (continued through XII, 348); 24 March 1704/5, *DOW*, XII, 322 (continued through XII, 332); 2 March 1704/5, *DOW*, XII, 295 (continued through XII, 374); 24 July 1705, *DOW*, XII, 346 (continued through XII, 448).

[30] 25 March 1708, *DOW*, XIII, 128 (continued through XIII, 198); 24 March 1708/9, DOW, XIII, 210 (continued through XIII, 221).

[31] 5 Eliz.c.4, §x, states that a laborer who should depart before completing work he had been retained to undertake should forfeit £5 to the party by whom he had been retained, "for the wch the sayd ptie may have his Action of Debt against him that shall so depte … over and besides such ordinarye Costes and Damages as may or ought to be recovered."

work, "sometimes working but half a day & sometimes one hour or two & then absenting himself for the space of two days sometimes three & sometimes a week & sometimes a month & more," and that as a result "the work that the sd Morris did keep in hand by such his neglect," which "he the sd Morris or any other good workman might have done ... in three weeks" still remained unfinished sixteen months later.

Morris's response to all of Hyde's actions for damages was not to deny that the work about which Hyde was complaining was unfinished, but rather to bring in accounts in set-off, charging Hyde for thirty-five days of carpentry work at a rate of 5/- per day. In other words, Morris alleged that he should be paid for the work he had performed, rather than punished for the work he had failed to perform. Hyde vehemently protested Morris's claim to be credited for labor on a daily rate, stating that he "never agreed w/the sd Morris to work by the day." He also protested the form in which Morris's account of days worked was presented. "[I]t appears by the sd Morris's sd acct agt the sd Hyde that he the sd Morris while he was at work for the sd Hyde never intended or pretended to work for the sd Hyde by the day in doing the sd work for if he had intended to work by the day his acct ought to have been particularly wch [it] is not that is so many days from such a day of such a month to such a day of that month or some other and the sd hours & days added so that the ct might have adjudged of the time & not to have charged the sd Hyde thirty five days at five shill p day w/ out showing by his acct for what or when or any parte thereof." The account brought in discount was "impossible & unfair, untrue & unreasonable." No account "charged in the manner ought to be allowed" in court.

The court disagreed and allowed Morris's accounts in set-off. As a result, Hyde's 50/- suit netted him 9/6d, and his £8 suit was dismissed, "the deft bringing a greater sume in discount upon oath." Hyde continued to pursue his punitive debt action and also promptly filed his £20 damage suit. But in October the York court threw out his punitive suit. Hyde's remaining damage suit remained on the docket until May 1706, when it too was dismissed, "neither party appearing."

The dismissal of Hyde's third damage suit did not end matters, for two years later Morris filed suit alleging that Hyde had never paid him for the work that had been performed. After a full hearing a jury returned a verdict for Morris for £5.5.0, which Hyde accepted but to which he immediately offered a discount of £18.16.0. The latter was owed him by Morris for a bill of exchange used by Morris in March 1706 to settle the £20 dispute between them that had subsequently been protested. Hyde's discount was not allowed and he was only able finally to recover what he was owed by filing yet another suit against Morris. This, heard in May 1709, won him a judgment for £13.11.0 – his only success in the four-year fight.

The dispute between Robert Hyde and James Morris offers an opportunity to reflect on the intersection of law with work in early Virginia. First, their altercation is at one with other cases involving accusations against artisans, overseers, and wage laborers departing or neglecting work in underscoring the absence of resort to criminal proceedings in cases involving unindentured labor. In situations where one might expect to encounter criminal sanctions – for which, in fact, statutory criminal sanctions were expressly designed in English law – one finds none. Hyde's attempt to invoke the Statute of Artificers in Virginia is the only such proceeding in 150 years of York County court records. His failure is good evidence for the irrelevance of the statute, and confirms that even the highly abbreviated form in which the Statute was adopted in 1632[32] had not survived the subsequent revisals of early Virginia law undertaken before mid-century.

Second, the outcome in this series of suits, as well as in earlier suits already cited, suggests the unpopularity in Virginia – certainly by the last quarter of the seventeenth century – of construing retainers of wage and artisan labor as "entire" contracts. Morris, after all, was able to recover for the work he had actually done, even though his thirty-five days of work were spread over sixteen months, were not accounted save as a lump sum, and had left the task he had undertaken unfinished. In general, the court's records show that as a matter of routine, disputes over the completion of artisan work (almost always in relation to the building or repair of houses) were dealt with precisely on a *quantum meruit* basis, with the net value of what had actually been accomplished determined by referees.[33] The only instances in the York records in which artisan labor was subjected to compulsion occur in instances subject to statutes that penalized indentured migrants for failing to exhibit craft skills they had professed.[34]

Together, the Virginia statutes examined in Chapter 6 and the York County court records examined here point to two related conclusions. First, insofar as large-scale reliance on servile plantation labor distinguishes the culture of work in early Virginia from that of more northerly areas of settlement, some of the roots of that distinction are to be found in the oligarchic legal cultures of arable southern England. Second, what developed out of this in Virginia was not a generic legal culture of labor unfreedom but a stratified legal culture which accommodated distinct regimes of work; significantly more oppressive than those supposed to be typical of England for some, significantly less oppressive for others. Third, the comparatively greater oppressions of indentured servitude were a condition of the existence of the comparatively greater freedoms of Creole artisan and hireling labor. By occupying the legal-cultural space of unfreedom, the largely adolescent migrants imported as plantation labor established a context – a baseline, in effect, constituted by explicit legal obligations and procedures applicable to both parties – for the relatively greater autonomy of "free" Creole labor that had no clear parallel in the arable legal cultures from

[32] See text accompanying n.23, this chapter.

[33] See, for example, the dispute between John Alford and Mr. Thomas Shelston over carpentry work done by Alford. 24 January 1667, *DOW,* IV, 163 (continued through IV, 185).

[34] See, for example, James Dixon agt Samuel Patterson, 17 May 1742, *DOW,* XIX, 99.

which Virginia's law of labor was drawn. In this way, migrant servitude performed a role in early Virginia's legal culture not dissimilar from that which Edmund Morgan has attributed to slavery in the region's later colonial years. By furnishing an "other," both materially and ideologically, it assisted forms of freedom to evolve.

II. New England

Essex County, Massachusetts, abuts Massachusetts Bay, north of Boston. English settlement of the north shore began in the late 1620s and the area's settler population grew substantially during the Great Migration: settlers established townships along the coast from Lynn in the south to Newbury in the north. Natural increase kept population growth alive and stimulated movement to the west. By 1700 the filling out of township lands had scattered the population over a rough rectangle of territory some 500 square miles in extent, bounded on its northeastern and its southeastern borders by the Atlantic, meeting at Cape Ann, and to the west by the borders of the townships of Andover and Haverhill. The county's most famous township, Salem, lies on the Atlantic coast south of Cape Ann. It has been suggested that the backdrop to Salem's notorious late seventeenth-century tensions was an economic and cultural collision between burgeoning seaborne commerce and back-country subsistence.[35] Whether true or not, the contention usefully summarizes the county's characteristic occupational traits. Faithful to its geography, in which it was a microcosm of the region, this was a county whose people were largely dependent either on farming or on the sea for their livelihoods.[36]

Whether landed or maritime, Essex county livelihoods were intensively laborious. They were also intensively social, requiring the ongoing concerted effort of several persons rather than the isolated labor of a single individual. As such, they could become intensively legal. We have already seen that Massachusetts statutes paid considerable attention to the performance of labor. Court records confirm that in early Massachusetts, "Authoritie" oversaw the day-to-day relations of work with no less attention than it applied to its supervision of other aspects of daily life. For, as Michael Walzer wrote over forty years ago, underlined more recently by both Daniel Vickers and Steven Innes, work, for Puritans, was "the primary and elemental form of social discipline, the key to order, and the foundation of all further morality."[37]

The records of Essex's county court are substantially complete for the period from the initial founding of quarterly courts in March 1635/6

---

[35] Paul S. Boyer and Stephen Nissenbaum, *Salem Possessed; the Social Origins of Witchcraft* (Cambridge, Mass., 1974).

[36] See generally Daniel Vickers, *Farmers & Fishermen: Two Centuries of Work in Essex County, Massachusetts, 1630–1850* (Chapel Hill, 1994).

[37] Michael Walzer, *The Revolution of the Saints: A Study in the Origins of Radical Politics* (Cambridge, Mass., 1965), 211.

through the late seventeenth century.[38] The eighteenth-century record is less complete, but still informative. Overall, the record is comprehensive enough to permit a survey of the relation between legal authority and the performance of work throughout the colonial period. What emerges is considerable variety. As in Virginia, local legal records describe a legal culture of work that was overtly segmented – in Essex's case largely by age. Unlike Virginia, it was a culture in which continuous labor immigration did not play a significant role. Hence, explicit status distinctions between Creole and migrant labor had less salience in determining degrees of freedom.[39] As in Virginia, hired labor was significantly freer from restraint than in contemporary England, but distinctive practices developing out of maritime wage work add a layer of legal relations wholly absent from the Virginia record. Finally, the Essex and York records appear to grow more distinctive over time. From the beginning, the social relations of work that had developed in the two counties were different, but one encounters sufficient initial similarities to suggest that settlers enjoyed at least some points of common reference. By the end of the seventeenth century, however, the distinctive characters of the two regions' migrant populations, and of the local economies and local law they had produced, had resulted in very different legal cultures of work.

As in Virginia, certain of the work relations illustrated in the Essex record clearly belong in a category of unfree labor. Notwithstanding its demographic insignificance after the first decade of settlement, indentured servitude nevertheless furnished business for the court. Mostly this took the form of masters of servants seeking court-ordered punishments of servants for insubordination and court-ordered compensation for time lost to illegal departures from service. Jonathan Adams was ordered whipped for running from his master in September 1636; so was "William Dodg's boy" (unnamed), later that year; so was Jane Wheat a few months after that. All told, in the court's first three years nine servants were ordered whipped for absconding. Indeed, whipping was the response to most servant offenses, whether absconding, insubordination, or drunkenness. Few early proceedings mention any addition of compensatory time; William Poole, servant to Colonel John Endicot (a justice of the peace) was the first runaway to be required to make up time lost.[40] Massachusetts never adopted statutory time-on penalties for runaway servants (in itself a sign of their rarity) but left the matter to the courts. Court orders providing for compensatory service were at best occasional and had a discretionary quality quite distinct from the statute-guided routines of the Chesapeake.[41]

[38] Published as *Records and Files of the Quarterly Courts of Essex County, Massachusetts*, (*RFQE*) vol. 1–8, 1636–83 (Salem, 1911–21; repr. 1988), vol. 9, 1683–6 (Salem, 1975).

[39] However, see Vickers, *Farmers & Fishermen*, 58–9 (suggesting an important correlation between "servants" and "outsiders" in Essex).

[40] See *RFQE*, I, 3 (September 1636), 4 (December 1636), 5 (June 1637), 8 (June 1638), 9 (September 1638).

[41] The first statutory mention of compensatory service came in the "Act for Preventing of Men's Sons or Servants Absenting Themselves from their Parent's or Master's Service

From the outset, Essex court records confirm the close association of service and youth that this book suggests was ubiquitous in mainland English America. William Dodge's runaway was a "boy." Richard Gell, before the court for stealing in 1640, was "an apprentice boy." Benjamin Hammon, who slandered his master in December 1640, was "yong, rash, unsetled & indiscreet."[42] As the record becomes more detailed over time, its descriptions of bound service yield increasing evidence of an explicit relationship between legitimacy of restraint in service, indentures or other written authority, and youth. In the Essex record, however, the relationship again has a discretionary quality that underlines both the exceptional nature of migrant servitude and the ambiguities imparted to the legalities of "restraint" in servitude by the region's greater reliance on long continuities in family labor.[43] Locally, "youth" meant roughly from age ten, when minors were considered able to earn their keep, until twenty-one, when they attained legal majority.[44] But legal majority in Essex did not necessarily signify independence. The ambiguities could breed controversy, particularly because Massachusetts had no statutory "custom-of-country" legislation defining "default" terms of service in the absence of indentures.

Some migrant servants tended to act as if majority conveyed a right to depart. Consider the case of Richard Coy, who in 1645 sued William Hubbard for wages owed. Coy had been brought to New England in 1638 by one Whittingham, with two elder siblings, Mathew (aged fifteen) and Mary, and several other juveniles – Haniell Bosworth, Robert Smith, John Annable. Coy, who was approximately thirteen at the time, became servant to Hubbard, but left him in 1645, claiming he was to serve only seven years and that he was owed wages for time spent in Hubbard's employ thereafter. "If hee had knowne," Hubbard allegedly had told Coy, "hee shod not akept him agaynst his will Butt if you will stay with me still i will giue you wagges as to other men." But in court Hubbard claimed Coy was to have served ten years, not seven, or until age twenty-four, not twenty-one. His brother, two years older, had served eight years, and their imported fellows all testified that Richard, like them, was to have served for ten, and Coy was ordered to return to Hubbard (although he left again, permanently, well before the ten years were up). Later litigation revealed that Hubbard's claim was based not on an indenture but on an amortization of his costs, which "cannot here be lesse worth than £15 or £16." Further, "for a boy of 13 yeares of

Without Leave" (*Province Laws*, ch. XXIII, 1695), which allowed at the discretion of the court the addition of up to one year's service in the specific case of "sons and servants" who deserted the service of parents or masters to enter on board any ship or vessel. A wider grant of discretion came in 1759 (Province Laws, ch. XVII), which permitted courts "to order satisfaction to be made" by runaways "by service or otherwise, as to them shall seem meet."

[42] *RFQE*, I, 18 (June 1640), 23 (December 1640), and see also 25 (March 1641), 27 (June 1641).

[43] One may hypothesize that the discretionary quality of the Essex record reflects the greater degree of trust accorded local courts in a more communal, solidaristic society.

[44] Vickers, *Farmers and Fishermen*, 58, 68.

age to be layd out here for 10 yeares service cannot … seem injurious to ye servant or much advantageous to ye Master all wch considered it seemeth to mee the plaintiffe hath no cause to complaine." The court agreed.[45]

Similarities abound in the case of William Downing and Phillip Welch, arrested to court in 1661 for refusing to serve their master, Samuel Symonds. Both were "Irish youthes" who in 1654 had been "stollen in Ireland, by some of ye English soldiers, in ye night out of theyr beds" and sold into servitude. Now being "aboue 21 years of age" both refused to serve longer, "7 yeares seruice being so much as ye practise of old England, & thought meet in this place." Symonds claimed that both were to serve nine years (that is until approximately age 24). He had no indenture but produced a covenant of sale to that effect. He also sought damages for time and work lost to their refusal to serve. A jury held in a special verdict that if the covenant of sale were legal the terms should stand, and this outcome was confirmed by the court. But the court allowed Symonds no compensation, the servants' refusal and departure creating no independent grounds for recovery.[46] That is, it was the covenant of sale that was Symonds' sole authority to restrain Downing and Welch. It could not be implied from their position in Symonds' employ.[47]

Daniel Vickers has recently underlined the early New England farm economy's dependence upon the labor of children. Dependence was not modeled on arable England's service-in-husbandry – its circulation of youthful labor on a system of annual hires. Nor was it modeled on plantation-style indentured servitude. We know that after 1640, unlike the Chesapeake, migrant servitude was of minimal significance in furnishing labor to Essex's settlers. New England farms generated neither the demand for continuous labor imports that came from the plantation regions, nor the revenues to pay for them. Instead, close-knit patriarchal households retained their own male children in generational subordination over an extended period of household dependency from late infancy through adulthood and beyond.[48] Where the labor of offspring was insufficient the household might add an imported servant, but servants were supplemental, and their "careers" followed the dominant household-familial pattern, coming into households young and remaining over extended periods of time, rather than forming a distinct culture of work.[49]

[45] *RFQE*, I, 87 (September 1645), 381–2 (March 1655). See also Works Progress Administration *Transcripts* (Salem, Peabody-Essex Museum), vol. 3 (hereafter *WPAT*).

[46] In fact, Downing and Welch had offered to "Stay or goe on in their worke till their case was [before] the Court and if then they were freed he Should pay them for their time if otherwise it Sho [illeg. – torn] as part of their time," but Symonds had demanded security for this arrangement, which they had refused.

[47] *RFQE*, II, 294–7, 310–11 (June 1661). See also *WPAT*, vol. 6. See also *William Deane v. Mr Jonathan Wade*, "for prosecuting him after the manner of a runaway, the plaintiff being free," *RFQE*, II, 62–3 (March 1658), *WPAT*, vol. 4.

[48] This was an expression of the classic English pastoral model: partible inheritance and the retention of children.

[49] James Coleman, for example, testified during litigation over John Cogswell's will that he had joined his master William Cogswell's household in 1652, or approximately at

The story of John Cogswell, of Ipswich, furnishes a partial case study. In 1653, widowed and with three young children to care for, Cogswell journeyed to England to seek a new wife, and to find servants. He retained five, all minors: William Thomsonn, aged about five; John Palmer and George Stimpson (each between seven and nine years old); Robert Powell (about fourteen); and Thomas Fowler (about fifteen). Thomsonn was the grandson (or nephew) of Cogswell's cousin Samuell, and Powell was the son of an acquaintance of Samuell's. Palmer had been sold to Cogswell in London for a term of twelve years, Fowler probably had relatives in New England. Stimpson's origins are unknown. (Needless to say, this pattern of personal recruitment emphasizing relationship or acquaintance is substantially different from that typical of the Chesapeake.) Whether relatives or not, none was bound above age twenty-one. Indentures for Thomsonn and Powell are both in the court record. In Thomsonn's case, Cogswell was to receive £31 to pay for his passage and maintenance until age ten, and from then to keep the child freely until age twenty-one, maintaining him in food and clothes, teaching him to read and write and to undertake the art of husbandry, "the child to be in all one obedience & subjection to him." In Powell's case the boy was to go as a servant for six years, to have his passage paid, to have "meat, drinke, & cloths in a fitting way & ten pounds in money after the expiration of his 6 years." Cogswell guaranteed him good treatment and undertook not to sell him to anyone else.

Cogswell's untimely death on the voyage home opened his estate, twenty years later, to litigation by his infant son, now come of age, against his uncle. The details of the litigation are unimportant, but the case itself provides us with an opportunity to view Cogswell's will, which made arrangements for his children in the event of his death. Cogswell indicated that each of his sons (John and Samuel) was "to be bound prentice at ten years old, to a godly honest man, where he may be well Brought up, and know how to order husbandry affaires." His daughter Elizabeth to "be bred at scoole, untill she is fourteene years old, and then to goe to Service, and earne her liveing, and not allowed anything toward there maytenance." Ten was a common age of male apprenticeship, court records show, although individuals as young as seven or as old as twenty might be found bound by apprenticeship indentures. Upon his sons attaining twenty-one, Cogswell's farm was to be divided between them.[50]

As the circumstances of John Cogswell's life and death illustrate, in Essex imported servants were strictly a supplementary, life-cyclical phenomenon. Cogswell needed servants because his household was in turmoil; a wife recently deceased and three children no more than infants. But the

---

age 9, and had remained there "15 yeares prentice and covenaunted servant." *RFQE*, VI, 68 (September 1675). In his dispute with Samuell Symonds, Philip Welch at one point offered to remain "if his master would give him as good a portion as any of his children." *RFQE*, II, 297 (June 1661).

[50] Elizabeth was to get a share of Cogswell's remaining possessions at age 21, or upon her marriage, if earlier.

servants he recruited were simply more children, the youngest little older than his own. The means he used to obtain them depended on exploiting old-country family connections, not on tapping into any commercial "servant trade." His plans for his own children bespeak his intent to mobilize their labor for household benefit (relief, at any rate of the costs of their sustenance) as soon as feasible.[51]

Migrant servitude was one exceptional form supplementary labor took in Essex; slavery was another, also numerically rare.[52] Adult Creole servitude was not unknown, but as elsewhere it became confined to the discharge of debts and as a means of restitution for criminal conviction.[53] Apprenticeship, as Cogswell's will indicates, was a more common means of mobilizing youthful labor, and by the eighteenth century had become the principal subject of Massachusetts' labor statutes and the predominant meaning of "servant."[54] Vickers has emphasized the absence of any systematic practice of putting children out to neighbors in rural Massachusetts, but insofar as households did, apprenticeship was the means they employed. Certainly it was not confined to trade education, but was used as a means to convey a child's or youth's labor to another for an extended period without mention of specific trade obligations.[55]

"Bound" labor, in Essex, thus meant the labor of children, debtors, and convicts: all could be compelled to perform at the behest of their respective masters.[56] But children, debtors, and convicts were not the sum of the Essex labor force. Farmers seeking additional assistance also had resort to adult hireling labor,[57] though more often to each other. The latter could

---

[51] *RFQE*, II, 307–8 (September 1653), VI, 68 (September 1675), 151–60 (June 1676). See also *WPAT*, vol. 23.

[52] Vickers, *Farmers and Fishermen*, 230–1.

[53] Occasionally adults would bind themselves to trade apprenticeships. Edmond Ashby, for example was 22 years old when he bound himself an apprentice hat maker to Samuel Graves. *RFQE*, II, 256 (June 1670), *WPAT*, vol. 16. See also *Perkins v. Cooke*, *RFQE*, VII, 259–61 (1679). As often, however, adult "apprenticeship" contracts were plainly another form of migrant indentured servitude. See, for example, *Petherick and Alley*, *RFQE*, IX, 62 (June 1683), *WPAT*, vol. 39.

[54] Tomlins, *Law, Labor, and Ideology*, 244–6.

[55] In August 1644, for example, Ezekiell Wathen, a boy of about eight years and a half, was committed to Thomas Abre as an apprentice until he was twenty years old, "if his master live so long" with no further ado. *RFQE*, II, 72.

[56] Courts by no means treated compulsion as a routine incident of bound labor, however. When Nathaniel Merrill refused to allow his son John to proceed in John Clements's service for five months because he doubted Clements's creditworthiness, he was found to have breached no undertaking, notwithstanding a genuine engagement and payment of an advance. "Ye said John Clements was Much Damnified for want of the said Merrills help which he had hired," his brother Abraham deposed, "for ye said John Clements was then About to build A house and was fourced to hire Another Man in his Roome." Nevertheless, neither service by the son nor damages by the father was found to be owed. *RFQE*, VIII, 265–7. See also *WPAT*, vols. 37, 38, 39.

[57] For an example of supplementary hiring, see "Articles of Agreement [for the lease of William Tyng's farm] … Betweene William Tyng of Boston in New England, merchant, of the one parte, and John Reade of Waymouth in New England Planter, of the other

comprise no more than a "swapp[ing of] chores."[58] Or it could comprise paid task work, as in the hiring of an artisan to undertake construction or repair of a house or a boat. Both forms of relation generated disputes, but these show little evidence of any resort to criminal law to underwrite employment commitments.

Hireling relations gave rise to several different kinds of dispute. Occasionally employers complained about excessive rates of pay. Only four such complaints were filed during the first forty years of court sessions in Essex, however, and only the first resulted in any material penalty – a fine.[59] The issue did not arise again. Complaints against employers for nonpayment of wages were more frequent, arising both in agricultural and in maritime employment. Better than half of the seventeenth-century suits prosecuted by hirelings to recover wages were successful. Wage recovery suits continued to appear in the eighteenth-century record, characterized by a noticeable rising incidence of resort to *quantum meruit* claims, usually presented in tandem with an *indebitatus assumpsit* count. *Quantum meruit* was little found in seventeenth-century wage recoveries, which (when spelled out) alleged a debt on the basis that the task or term agreed was complete but the sum agreed was unpaid. Whereas debt implied entirety and recovery after completion, *quantum meruit* implied valuation of what had actually been done. Unsurprisingly, in this light, eighteenth-century wage suits also give increasing prominence to *rates* of pay agreed between the parties, rather than actual lump obligations accumulated.[60]

parte"(1639), in *Note-Book Kept by Thomas Lechford, Esq., Lawyer, in Boston, Massachusetts Bay, from June 27, 1638, to July 29, 1641* (Cambridge, 1885), 94–100, at 98, para. 26: "Itm, the sayd William Tyng shall and will from time to time during the sayd term pay halfe the charges for hire and maintenance of workmen or women, when any shall be hired and employed over and above the sayd servants, as need shall require for planting, reaping, mowing and making of hay." See generally Vickers, *Farmers and Fishermen*, 53–5.

[58] Vickers, *Farmers and Fishermen*, 61. See also 55, 60–1. For a contemporary account of regional farm labor practices, see *Diary of Joshua Hempstead of New London, Connecticut ... From September, 1711, to November, 1758* (New London, 1901).

[59] See *RFQE*, I, 3 (June 1636), 49 (December 1642); II, 152 (March 1659); V, 37 (May 1672) (also *WPAT*, vol. 18). The second case resulted in a partial abatement, in the third the defendant was admonished, and in the fourth the complaint was dismissed.

[60] See, for example, *Follet v. Morrill*, Ipswich Common Pleas, NE#92 (March 1756); *Lufkin v. Ellery*, Ipswich Common Pleas, NE#55 (March 1757). It is worth noting Benjamin Wadsworth's advice early in the century that "as to *hired Servants*, their *Wages* should be duely honestly and seasonably paid them ... If we keep back the *Wages of Hirelings*, or defraud them of their due; their cries will enter into the ears of the Lord of Sabbaoth (the Lord of hosts) and great will our guilt and danger be." Wadsworth quoted Deuteronomy 24:15 ("*At his day thou shalt give him his hire ... lest he cry against thee to the Lord, and it be Sin unto thee*") and Leviticus 19:13 ("*The wages of him that is hired shall not abide with thee all night, until the Morning*") (AV). These injunctions, he continued, seemed "to refer to *Day Labourers*; but the law in proportion, may extend to Servants hired for some longer time." See Benjamin Wadsworth, *The Well-Ordered Family: Or Relative Duties* (Boston, 1712), 107–9 (emphases in original). On the forms of action in work and labor cases, see also Middleton, *From Privileges to Rights*, 163–79.

Most interesting among the complaints arising from hireling relations, however, were breach of contract, nonperformance, or departure complaints. As in Virginia, punitive strictures on hirelings are rare from early on. In 1655, for example, Richard Jacob complained against Mordecai Larkum (a married adult) for neglecting his service. The complaint was proven, but Larkum was neither required to perform nor imprisoned, but instead ordered to pay damages of 25/- in lieu (10–14 days' wages).[61] This tells us only that there were alternatives to court orders to perform. Two actions brought by Francis Urselton against John Godfrey in September 1659, in which the record is more complete, tell us more. Urselton's first suit was in case, "for not pforming of a somers work, which he promised to doe, for the plt: (for the wch he receiued pt of his pay in hand) the want of which worke pformed is to the pltfs great damage," to the amount of £20. Witnesses testified that in the spring of that year Godfrey "did ingadge himselfe to helpe the Sayd Usseltone from the 15th or 20th of Aprill last, until Micharlmase then ffollowing," that Urselton "was to giue him eight shillings ye weeke dureing the sayd time," and that on his retainer, "in Consideration of the sayd ... Service," Godfrey had received four pounds fourteen shillings, or one half of the total payable for such a period. After Godfrey abandoned his service, Urselton called witnesses to inspect his corn (about 6 acres in all), who deposed that it "was spoiled for want of tending with the hoe" and that Urselton "was Damnified for lacke of an end fence." Urselton waited for the end of the period agreed upon, then sued Godfrey to recover the whole value of his crop. The court returned a verdict for Urselton (although there is no record of the amount of damages awarded). But Urselton's second and parallel suit, which was in debt and attempted to recover a penalty of £5 to be levied on Godfrey for his departure, was nonsuited. The debt action can only be explained as an attempt (analogous to the Hyde-Morris dispute in York County) to invoke the Statute of Artificers' penalty on laborers leaving work unfinished. The nonsuit indicates the statute was considered inapplicable.[62] No other attempt to invoke it can be identified from Essex court records during the entire colonial period.

Some years later, in March 1670, Thomas Knowlton sued William Knowlton for breach of a covenant to be his journeyman, for which William had received an advance of 50/-. The court, however, merely required that William return the advance and pay 5/- damages for the breach.[63] From the other side of the hiring relation, when Thomas Rumerye sued John Norman for wages for sawing timbers, Norman defended himself by showing that he had paid in full, excepting only an amount withheld "Bee Cause Rumery Carried away the saw to saw a logg ffor Jeremiah Neal and

[61] *RFQE*, I, 404 (September 1655). For Larkum's marital status, see 416.
[62] *RFQE*, II, 175 (September 1659), 185 (November 1659); *WPAT*, vol. 5. And see n.31, this chapter.
[63] *RFQE*, II, 223 (March 1670); *WPAT*, vol. 15.

Left his work." The defendant had not pursued the plaintiff for his premature departure, nor withheld all his wages, but had simply refused to pay in full for incomplete performance. Apparently in approval of this 'practical' *quantum meruit* outcome, the court found the defendant had no cause to answer.[64]

Damages, too, were the order of the day in actions brought against artisans for failure to complete work. In June 1661, Georg Emory recovered £5 from John Norman, Sr. "for not finishing a house according to agreement." The court did not order completion but provided for further damages to become due in two months if the house remained incomplete.[65] This represented a change of tack from some years before, September 1648, when in an action brought by Henry Archer against John Fullar and Samuell Heiford the court appeared to order performance of the defendants' covenant to set up a fence without considering damages in lieu.[66] Yet the report in this case may simply register the court's acknowledgment of an arrangement already worked out by the parties in dispute. Indeed, several years earlier still (1641) the court had implied in another dispute over completion of a house, between William Fisk and Mathew Waler, that damages in lieu of completion was an acceptable remedy. And in 1662, in settling Zarubbabell Endecott's action against John Norton "for non-performance of covenant in building a house" for which he had already been paid, the verdict for the plaintiff was purely for damages, with performance simply left up to the defendant as an alternative means of compliance.[67]

Essex County's fishing and maritime economy adds further dimensions to the legal culture of work on display in the court record. Seeming to share much in common in distinction from landed agricultural labor, the respective legal cultures of fishing and maritime work were actually less similar than one might assume.

Fishing contrasted with the land-bound economy in any number of respects. Organized from the beginning as a capitalized commercialized institution, the New England fishery appeared in a succession of productive forms. It originated as a transatlantic merchant-financed enterprise using a workforce recruited in the West of England on seasonal retainers. After permanent European settlement of New England, the transatlantic fishery began to experience endemic instability as superior wage rates resulting from labor shortages on land constantly tempted crew members to abandon their retainers and pursue landed occupations. Adaptation eventually

---

[64] *RFQE*, VIII, 108–9 (June 1681), *WPAT*, vol. 35. See also *Clements v. Merrill* (March 1682).

[65] *RFQE*, II, 282–3 (June 1661), *WPAT*, vol. 6. In a counter-suit (at 283), Norman attempted to recover payment for the work that *had* been completed, but this was denied by the court. [Given the amount of damages granted (£5), one might suspect this was another attempt, this time successful, to invoke the penalty clause of the Statute of Artificers (5 Eliz c.4, x). But this would be incorrect, for the statute specified that an action for the penalty should be in debt.]

[66] *RFQE*, I, 147 (1648).

[67] *RFQE*, I, 26 (June 1641); II, 388–9 (June 1662), *WPAT*, vol. 7.

resulted in a reorganized, locally based fishery drawing upon a largely transient North Atlantic maritime workforce who labored not for wages but on their own behalf on shares. Independent "companies" of fishermen (crews of men and boys) contracted with local merchants for advances of supplies and boat hire, secured by a commitment of exclusive rights to purchase the catch on their return.

From the outset, the maritime workforce remained largely distinct in origins and culture from the landed population. Distinctions remained even after it began to put down roots in coastal communities like Gloucester and Marblehead. These communities exhibited greater poverty, poorer life expectancy, greater social turbulence, and none of the household interdependencies that characterized the rural interior. "Fishing families were generally not working units."[68] The culture of shipboard work was quite unlike the paternal authority and gendered or age-demarcated dependence of the landed household.[69] Members of a fishing company were partners working on agreed shares rather than a crew under a master's authority. The transience of the workforce and resultant instability of crew composition across successive fishing seasons always brought friction within crews, but neither the merchant-company relationship nor the company's internal relations depended structurally on legitimated compulsion. Manifestly, the system could become oppressive if creditors chose – as they commonly did – to use debt as a means to trap their clients.[70] Usually, their goal was to guarantee that the indebted supplier always return to the same merchant-creditor, thus assuring the latter of a continuing supply of fish. Where, however, the merchant himself became active as an owner and operator of boats, debt often became directly the means to obtain crews and then control their labors.

Dr. Richard Knott, who operated a fleet of shallops, appears to have been particularly adept at preying on indebted itinerant seamen, first assuming their debts and then converting that control into an obligation of the seaman to labor for him. William Jarmin, "not learned nor edicated in Reeding or writing," had come to Marblehead in the mid-1670s "and meeting with bad voyages Run himselfe into Mr. Brown his debt." Crewing for Knott, but enjoying no more success, Jarmin also fell into debt to Knott. Knott prevailed upon Jarmin to allow Knott to assume the debts owed

---

[68] Vickers, *Farmers and Fishermen*, 138.

[69] Indeed, when Samuell and Hezekiah Dutch recruited John Meager to go with them fishing for pollock and mackerel in 1665 and 1666, they assured him "wee are all three young men and can goe when wee will and com when wee will and our father shall have nothinge to dow with us." *RFQE*, III, 328 (1666), *WPAT*, vol. 11; *RFQE*, III, 350 (1666), *WPAT*, vol. 12.

[70] Developed "to deal with the problems of risk and the scarcities of capital and labor," Daniel Vickers has called this "clientage" system a "maritime equivalent" of the landed economy's patriarchal work culture. Frequently it trapped fishermen in such "massive indebtedness" that, unlike children who eventually outgrew and outlived their fathers, they remained entangled in financial dependence for life. Vickers, *Farmers and Fishermen*, 141.

Brown, but Knott then demanded payment and in lieu obtained execution of Jarmin as a debt servant for three years. Jarmin later found himself once more entangled in new debts owed to Knott, and when he tried to make arrangements to crew for others to pay them off, Knott attempted to repeat the sequence. The second time around, however, the court threw out his suit and Jarmin escaped, though likely only as far as the next helpful patron.

Job Tookey's relations with Knott two years later tell a similar tale. Tookey was another itinerant seaman (though not an illiterate one, claiming to be the son, grandson, and great-grandson of ministers and a sometime matriculant – admittedly short-lived – of Emmanuel College, Cambridge). Like Jarmin he became indebted through misfortune, in his case by reason of six months' lameness caused by a severe injury to his hand; and like Jarmin, Knott offered to pay off his debts. In exchange, Tookey was to agree to perform a seven-month fishing voyage, for 40/- per month and outfit. Early in 1682, Tookey worked a month preparing the voyage but then refused to work further for Knott, claiming that the vessel in question was short-manned and that he himself was ill with gout. Knott offered evidence that Tookey was ill with drink, not gout, and also that he had rejected an alternative voyage that Knott had offered. Tookey meanwhile claimed that Knott had agreed to pay him for his month and had also agreed to allow him to seek a voyage with another boat, but that Knott had then reneged and instead obtained a warrant ordering Tookey attached to answer his complaint "in an action of the case about nine pounds silver or ffish as silver for denying and disobeying the said Knotts commands, Contrary to an agreement which is made betweene the said Knott and said Tookey." Tookey spent the next ten weeks in gaol awaiting the county court's June 1682 session. Then, once before the court in June, Knott withdrew the action.

Knott's maneuvers illustrate the merchant-proprietor's power in the fisheries. They do not, however, indicate that this was power that derived from the legitimated authority of a master. Indeed, neither case confirms Knott's magisterial power over a "servant." Knott lost the first action and withdrew the second. What both illustrate, rather, is the formidable persuasive power inherent in debtor-creditor relations and in the coercive procedural sanctions (incarceration pending hearing was the inevitable fate of anyone with no assets to attach sufficient to cover the size of the suit) that applied in such cases.[71]

Two other cases arising from shipboard relations in the fishery in the early 1680s suggest, however, that issues of hierarchical authority were beginning to impinge directly on the fishery in ways that suggest an important transformation in its organization was under way. Before the 1680s,

---

[71] On the history of the Essex County fishery, see, generally, Vickers, *Farmers and Fishermen*, 85–203. On William Jarmin, see *RFQE*, VII, 333–6 (March 1680); on Job Tookey, see VIII, 330–8 (June 1682), *WPAT*, vol. 37.

the fishery had been a small-boat fishery employing shallops. Shallop fishery crews came together and worked on a collaborative basis. When Samuell and Hezekiah Dutch proposed to John Meager that he accompany them on a voyage for polock and mackerel in 1665 and 1666, they promised him "you shall goe with us winter and sumer and wee will goe out and cach the polock scoole then wee will hall a shore our boat and sett her for to goe doune to maneymoy and thare wee will mack our fish ... wee will goe as lovinge as three brothers and please god noe other shall goe with us ... and wee will macke but three sheares and all a licke." Meager and the Dutch brothers were to have an epic falling-out, but neither they nor, subsequently, the Essex county court conceived of the crew of their shallop as one divided into masters and man. Following their winter voyage the Dutch brothers tried to break off their arrangement with Meager because, they claimed, he had spoiled fish. But when Meager sued them for non-performance he was treated as a wronged partner, not as an incompetent hired hand.[72]

By the 1680s, however, the introduction of ketches and schooners was changing the collaborative, shallop-based fishery in structure and scale. Voyages were lengthening, crews becoming larger, work for the merchant for a proportion of the catch, or wholly on wages, was replacing the sharing of earnings, shipmasters were being appointed to oversee, coordinate, and command an increasingly complex and dangerous process.[73] Violent arguments between ketch masters and crew became common. In June 1682, for example, complaint was made against William Russell for his "abusive carriages" toward Thomas Jeggles, master of the ketch *Prosperous*. Russell had first argued with and sworn at Jeggles, then absented himself, only to return to attack Jeggles and other members of the crew with a knife, threatened them, and thrown part of the catch overboard. He was sentenced "to be severely whipped." The following year another ketch master, Peter Hinderson, complained against two members of his crew, Robert Bray and Richard Bale, for their abusive carriage and willful disobedience in refusing to do their duty in hauling up the anchor and otherwise obstructing the departure of the vessel from harbor, and assaulting him. At issue in both cases – implicitly in the first, explicitly in the second – was the ketch

---

[72] *John Meager v. Samuell Dutch, RFQE*, III, 328 (1666), *WPAT*, vol. 11. See also *Samuell Dutch v. John Meager* (plaintiff not prosecuting), *RFQE*, III, 350 (1666), *WPAT*, vol. 12.

[73] See generally Vickers, *Farmers and Fishermen*, 143–203. Richard Knott, it is worth noting, was in the forefront of this process, adding a ketch in 1681 to his fleet of shallops. Indeed, the very argument that led to Knott's dispute with Job Tookey began over Tookey's refusal to join the crew of Knott's new ketch, the *Endeavour*. When asked why he refused, he reportedly responded that the vessel was too large for the crew contemplated, that "he had worked enough already," that he "would not goe noe longer with that Master," and that he would go instead in one of Knott's shallops. Tookey, that is, contrasted the size and discipline of the ketch with the relatively greater freedom of the small-boat shallop fishery: when Knott asked him whether he would go in any of his boats [shallops], Tookey reportedly replied he was willing to go where "the men weare willing to [accept] him." *RFQE*, VIII, 331.

master's legal authority to command. The growing scale and complexity of fishery operations, these incidents suggest, was putting increasing pressure on the legal culture of "men in partnership" and its functional, cooperative expression in the performance of work.[74]

As the scale of the fishery continued to increase during the eighteenth century, clientage withered: merchants increasingly invested in larger boats and longer voyages, and the direct employment of crews. Before the end of the century, fishing clearly was characterized by capitalist employment relations – employers controlling the means of production and directly employing a property-less labor force dependent on wage labor for survival. As changes in capitalization brought larger work units and less collaborative work relations, the fishery's legal culture of work tended to move in a direction quite distinct from that suggested by Essex's household-centered farms, toward the established hierarchical work law of the Atlantic maritime industry, which routinely pitted masters against men in fights over wages and discipline and prescribed rules that reinforced norms of shipboard authority.[75]

Examining the application of maritime work and labor law in Essex in occasional seventeenth-century and more frequent eighteenth-century cases, one detects some local variations tending to moderate commanders' authority. Ironically, Dr. Richard Knott features once again as an early illustration, this time on the receiving end. In 1677, as surgeon on board the ship *John & Ann*, Knott departed the ship in Lisbon without permission and demanded his wages. According to the captain's shipping articles, the voyage was from Boston to the Isle of Madeira "and what other ports, which shall present" with payment of wages due at every third port of discharge, leaving three months' pay in hand. Lisbon was the first port of call after Madeira: wages were not due until the next port of discharge. But Knott refused to proceed further and demanded payment. The captain complained to the consul, who offered to secure him, in the normal fashion, "tell the ship was redey to sayle" but the captain eventually decided "to Clere himm, and pay him his waeges; which I did rather than to be troubled with him." Once back in Essex, the resourceful Knott brought suit against the Captain for abusing him, and won.[76] Also successful the same year was Thomas Hewson, bosun and gunner on the *John Bonadventure*. Hewson had joined the ship at Gravesend in February and signed articles for a voyage to Massachusetts Bay, thence to the Iberian Peninsula and a return to London for discharge. According to testimony of the captain, confirmed by the mate and other crew members, Hewson had gone absent at Boston and again at Marblehead, where he "uniustly left and absented ye shipp and searvice instructed on him." Hewson had refused to rejoin the ship even though warned he would not subsequently be allowed back aboard,

[74] *RFQE*, VIII, 348 (November 1683), IX, 145 (November 1683), *WPAT*, vol. 40.

[75] On which see Marcus Rediker, *Between the Devil and the Deep Blue Sea: Merchant Seamen, Pirates, and the Anglo-American Maritime World, 1700–1750* (New York, 1987).

[76] *RFQE*, VI, 328–30 (September 1677), *WPAT*, vol. 27.

and the ship had left for Salem one man short. Hewson sued for recovery of his effects (detained on board) and for wages for the six months from signing on at Gravesend until his departure at Marblehead. Notwithstanding the terms of the voyage, the court granted his suit, in effect applying a *quantum meruit* rule to an entire agreement.[77]

Less fortunate, six years later, was the crew of the *James*. In 1683 Captain Samuel Cole, of the *James* of London, entered a complaint before Justice Bartholomew Gedney against eight of the ship's eleven crew members for neglecting their service and failing to perform their agreed voyages. According to the articles, offered in evidence, the signatories had agreed a voyage from Gravesend to the Île de May, thence to New England and thence to the West Indies, "Soe Recll [receivable] ye full propotion of our wages in Every Libering Cort [port of discharge] according to ye Customs of ye Country for aible semen 25s a month onely too months pay keept in ye Mrs hands as an obligation to performe ye voye to this place againe if God permit & those persons yt doth nott performe ye voye shall loose there too months pay & suffer ye Law." Once in Salem, the eight defendants had departed en masse. Before Gedney, the defendants argued "that theire agrement was to be clear from the ship Losing 2 months wages." Gedney, however, ruled that their refusal to proceed further with their voyage was sufficient warrant to commit them for a hearing before a full bench of the county court, where they were ordered to return on board and attend to their duty, those refusing to be taken on board by the constable.[78]

The indulgence shown Thomas Hewson compared with the crew of the *James* – whose terms of voyage were certainly ambiguous enough to allow the interpretation they had offered to be taken seriously – may have reflected preference accorded a single local man returning home, as against the concerted departure of a group of absconding strangers, or perhaps reflected the court's conclusion that Hewson had been given insufficient opportunity to recant his initial refusal and rejoin his vessel. Too, the *James*'s crew members were defendants not plaintiffs, and were trying to avoid a criminal penalty for desertion, not pursuing a civil action for wages owed. Hence, the difference in outcome may have signified nothing more than the difference between a case in which local legal practice amenable to the apportionment of wages took precedence over transatlantic maritime law disciplining seamen, and one in which the opposite prevailed. At the same time, the return to duty enforced upon the crew of the *James* suggested that the more integrated Massachusetts' maritime economy became with that of the Atlantic as a whole, the less distinctive its legal culture of maritime work would become. In the fishery in contrast, and to some extent in the coasting trade, generic maritime rules remained of limited influence. Local practice continued to be influential.[79]

[77] *RFQE*, VI, 331 (September 1677), *WPAT*, vol. 27.

[78] *RFQE*, IX, 59 (June 1683), *WPAT*, vol. 39.

[79] For examples of continuity in established practices attending wage payment and contracting in the fishery and coasting trades, see *Lufkin v. Ellery*, Ipswich Common Pleas

The legal culture of work – landed and maritime – on display in the Essex court records was in important respects quite different from that of the early Chesapeake. Statutory legal disciplines structuring hierarchical work relations were substantially less in evidence, courts were left with greater discretion, the household was a more active locale of authority. In part, one can attribute these differences to the regions' contrasting economic and demographic environments, but in part, one can also credit variations in the legal cultures from which the most influential portions of the regions' original migrant populations came. Relatively free of the manorial influences of strong local and regional lordship and its hierarchical impulses, New England's legal culture initially reproduced the influence of communities of solidaristic households more oriented toward local self-government than government by strong regional elites. That culture was sustained by demographic and environmental conditions that favored strong families organized in extended households that exhibited considerable generational continuity, produced substantial numbers of children who furnished their primary labor supply, practiced partible inheritance and were, geographically, relatively stable. Just as Virginia was in important respects "arable" in its cultural heritage, so, demographically, sociologically, and legally, New England was pastoral.

In both regions, however, the existence of unfree – legally subordinated – working populations permitted the development of exceptional degrees of legal freedom in work relations for white male, and to a lesser extent female,[80] adults. In New England the subordinated populations were essentially life-cyclical; that is, they were defined principally by age. Their legal subordination was temporary. In the Chesapeake, the fact of a practice of temporary legal subordination in the form of juvenile servitude paved the way for the more permanent and extreme subordinations of race

---

(March 1757), NE#55; *Emerson v. Foster*, Ipswich Common Pleas (March 1768), NE#33; *Noyes v. Board*man, Ipswich Common Pleas (March 1768), NE#75; *Gage v. Vickre*, Ipswich Common Pleas (April 1790), NE#117. As the scale of the fishery continued to increase during the eighteenth century, its productive organization conformed more and more closely to capitalist employment relations: employers controlling the means of production and directly employing a property-less labor force dependent on wage labor for survival. On this see generally Vickers, *Farmers and Fishermen*, 143–203. Vickers infers that into the nineteenth century this transformation was *not* accompanied by any major changes in the legal culture of fishery work, but in fact the legal context of the fishery did change somewhat before then. Thus, see *An Act concerning certain fisheries of the United States and for the regulation and government of the Fishermen employed therein* 1792 c.6 (2nd Congress, 1st session), *United States Statutes at Large* 1, 229–32, which at §4 explicitly declared the applicability of maritime employment law, with all its severe hierarchies and criminal penalties, to the crews of all fishery vessels of twenty tons or more – precisely the size of vessel (ketches and schooners) that, earlier in the century, had become commonplace in the Massachusetts fishery.

80 The relativities of adult gender inequality in seventeenth- and eighteenth-century New England are well expressed in Laurel Thatcher Ulrich, *Good Wives: Image and Reality in the Lives of Women in Northern New England, 1650–1750* (New York, 1982), 8.

enslavement, with its concomitant effect of more fully underwriting the freedoms of the white.

III.   The Delaware Valley

Chester County, Pennsylvania, lies on the western bank of the Delaware River, more or less due west of the city of Philadelphia. Founded in 1682/3, the county stretches in a rough wedge some thirty miles to its northern and western borders, 500,000 acres (some 760 square miles) largely of dispersed family farms engaged in a mixed grain and livestock husbandry. To the southeast, across the river, lay West Jersey and the Delaware Bay. To the southwest was Cecil County, Maryland's northern edge.[81]

Regular influxes of transatlantic migrants, and the contiguity of the Delaware and Chesapeake Bays and the waterways that fed them, all encouraged constant population dispersal and mobility throughout the Delaware Valley region. Many migrants entering through Philadelphia stayed in Pennsylvania, but others headed north toward New York and the Hudson Valley, or south to the Chesapeake, or west into Appalachia and beyond. Indenture records show that servants landing in Philadelphia moved into the city's craft shops and the surrounding farming regions, but also went south to the Chesapeake, particularly Maryland, or to the Jerseys, and a few to New York.[82] Runaways were pursued into Pennsylvania from the Chesapeake, runaways from Pennsylvania headed in all directions. Geography, then, gave the Delaware Valley labor force more opportunity for movement than perhaps any other locale of settlement. Indeed, prosecutions of absconding apprentices and servants were sometimes joined in the Delaware Valley courts by prosecutions of absconding *masters*, abandoning failing businesses and their dependent apprentices and fleeing south or west to begin anew.[83]

---

[81] James T. Lemon, *The Best Poor Man's Country: A Geographical Study of Early Southeastern Pennsylvania* (Baltimore, 1972), 98–183.

[82] Samuel McKee argues that there were few indentured servants in New York at any time during the later seventeenth and eighteenth centuries. Most eighteenth-century migrant servants went to Pennsylvania and Maryland. He bases his argument in part on analysis of the Earl of Bellomont's 1698 census, in part on the general "infrequency of court cases which dealt with indentured servants," and in part on "remarks of government officials," like Governor Robert Hunter's recommendation (1712) that the legislature enact bounties to encourage the importation of white servants, or James De Lancey's call in 1757 for a poll tax on slaves the better to encourage a turn to white servants. McKee is undoubtedly correct in his argument, but his analysis of Bellomont's census is quite wrong in its assumption that indentured servants had to be adults. See Samuel McKee, *Labor in Colonial New York, 1664–1776* (New York, 1935), 93–4. See also Middleton, *From Privileges to Rights*, 131–62, and Chapter 9.

[83] See, for example, Chester County General and Quarter Sessions (*CCGQ*), February 1728/9 (petition of Joseph Wade); November 1742 (petition of William Grimer); Philadelphia Mayor's Court, July 1763 (petition of Ephraim Hyatt); Philadelphia County General and Quarter Sessions, March 1774 (petition of John Davis).

James T. Lemon has observed that Pennsylvania's "relatively open society" meant that people in motion encountered few hindrances.[84] To this one might add that Pennsylvania's "relatively open society" existed as such on the basis of quite sharply defined distinctions between freedom and restraint. Mobility complemented the cultural habits of English upland settlers in rendering Penn's original ambitions for orderly inhabitation under manorial supervision unworkable; the dispersed farm household became the locus of social order, not the nucleated village. Nevertheless, the proprietor's impulse to control movement remained. Pennsylvania's pass law required all persons traveling beyond their counties of residence to carry official certification of their place of residence, on pain of apprehension and return, or incarceration as a presumptive runaway. When drafted as one of the *Duke's Laws*, the pass law had been offered, like Virginia's, in response to the "frequent Complaints [that] have been made of Servants who runn away." Penn's law stretched further, potentially rendering all travelers vulnerable to challenge.[85]

In practice, control of mobility did focus on bound servants, and the county courts were instrumental in its implementation. During the period 1715–75, restraint of runaways accounted for 80 percent of all proceedings against servants initiated by masters in the Chester County court. Virtually all were found in favor of the master. The severity of the penalty – five additional days' service for each day absent – made runaway time a valuable resource, and masters recorded absences diligently, often presenting them for balancing at the end of a term of service, rather like book debt. At the same time absconding appears quite exceptional; the average number of proceedings was but three per annum. It has been estimated that 95 percent of all servants under indenture quietly completed their terms without incident. Penalties may have discouraged absconding, but on the Chester evidence the principal predictor of the incidence of runaway proceedings (as in the related matter of detentions under the pass laws) was change in the overall flow of migration into the area.[86]

Servants also petitioned the courts, though less frequently than masters and with more ambiguous results.[87] Servants petitioned primarily for

---

[84] Lemon, *Best Poor Man's Country*, 96, and generally 71–97.

[85] "Orders Made and Confirmed at the Generall Court of Assizes held in New Yorke" (October 1672), 3, in *Charter to William Penn*, 72, and compare Statutes at Large of Pennsylvania 1, 156 ("Laws made Att an Assembly Held att Philadelphia in the Province of Pennsilvania the 10th day of 1st Month March 1683"), Ch. 134 "That Unknown persons shall not presume to travel or go without the limits of the county wherein they reside, without a pass."

[86] Christopher Tomlins, "Early British America, 1585–1830," in Douglas Hay and Paul Craven, editors, *Masters, Servants and Magistrates in Britain and the Empire, 1562–1955* (Chapel Hill, 2004), 144–5 and table 3.1. See also Grubb, "Does Bound Labour Have To Be Coerced Labour?" 31; Alfred L. Brophy, "Law and Indentured Servitude in Mid-Eighteenth Century Pennsylvania," *Willamette Law Review*, 28, 1 (Winter 1991), 104, 108.

[87] Masters were plaintiffs in 63% of master-servant disputes presented to Chester County General and Quarter Sessions between 1715 and 1774, servants (including in this

enforcement of their right to freedom dues. But they also petitioned for enforcement of masters' other contractual obligations: to provide promised instruction, or to furnish appropriate food, clothing, and accommodation. Less often servants sought dissolution of indentures allegedly obtained deceptively or unfairly,[88] or simply presented courts with accounts of situations they felt were intolerable and sought relief.[89]

Servant petitioners might be thought vulnerable to intimidation, or at least to pressure to accede to disadvantageous accommodations. Fragments in the record indicate, however, that servants could be quite forthright in asserting their claims, or at least that the legal discourse of intermediaries could function as an equalizer. Thus, Margaret Moffett informed James Gill "to take notice that I intend to apply to the next Court of General Quarter Sessions ... in order to be relieved from the indenture of servitude which you have wrongfully obtained from me at which time and place you may attend if you think fit and shew cause if any you have why I should not be discharged from your service." Moses Line's notification to Robert Smith of his intent to petition for redress desired that he take notice "that I intend to ... compel you to comply with the terms of a certain indenture of servitude entered into between us."[90] Nor do the petitions themselves reveal any especial hesitancy in their authors' invocation of legal intervention, written by and large in plain language that straightforwardly catalogues grievance. Where servants were publicly obsequious it was toward the court, not the master. George Brandon, seeking dues and a formal release after seven years' service to Edward Richards, approached the court "most Humbly," praying that "your Honours will be so good as to see that

category filings by parents of minors), 37%. These proportions coincide exactly with those reported by Brophy in "Law and Indentured Servitude," 104, for the subperiod 1745–51. Masters had a vastly superior win:loss ratio, although this disproportion is almost entirely a consequence of results in runaway cases, which appear in the record as administrative determinations based mechanically on indentures proven and accounts presented. Excluding runaway cases, masters lost one case in every ten filed and their actual win:loss ratio in cases with determinable outcomes was 7:1. Servants lost roughly one case in every twelve filed, but at 4.5:1 their actual win:loss ratio was still substantially lower than that of masters because over 50% of servants' cases filed had no determinable outcome. The latter suggests frequent resort to informal accommodation, although the organization of the Chester County file papers somewhat inhibits the tracing of actions on servant petitions, so the absence of evidence of formal closure is not entirely conclusive. It is unlikely that the court was simply ignoring servant petitions because over the years the share of servant-initiated cases in total master-servant filings increased steadily. In the decade 1715–24, for example, servants' filings accounted for less than 19% of total master-servant filings. By 1765–74, servant filings were accounting for over 45% of total filings. The increase suggests that servant petitioners were encouraged by the court's reaction, not dissuaded by indifference.

[88] See, for example, *CCGQ*, May 1747 (Petition of Bartholomew McGregor).

[89] See, for example, *CCGQ* (at a Court of Private Sessions), December 1724 (Petition of Henry Hawkins).

[90] *CCGQ*, November 1731 (Petition of Margaret Moffett), February 1775 (Petition of Moses Line).

Justice is Dun me," continuing "for I have no other Fathers in this Strange Land but your honours too whome [to look] for Reliefe." But respectful language did not divert Brandon from pursuit of what was due him, and when Richards' promise to pay "in 2 or 3 weeks time" proved unreliable, Brandon returned for an order to compel performance. The same blend of supplication and consciousness of right was on display three years later when John Jacob Nies came to seek payment of his freedom dues. Though "a Foreignerr," Nies was still "one of his majesties Subjects." Though humble in his desire for "the Clemency of the English nation," he pointedly reminded the "Honourable Bench" that "by the Laws of this Province" it was "the sole Gaurdian of the Oppressed and Seeing them Righted." The court issued the order he sought.[91]

Servants thus did not yield the jural space of the county court to their masters, but instead tried when they could to invoke the court's statutory authority to supervise master-servant relationships as a means to blunt the asymmetries of power inherent in their situation. That the court may have chosen to mediate settlements in the majority of disputes meant that petitioners could be vulnerable if justices were capricious in composing settlements. Still, servant-petitioners were willing to press complaints even against members of the bench itself when they felt disserved.[92] Nor should one assume that masters were confident of the courts' favor. In 1751, for example, after losing a dispute over possession of a minor servant, David John complained bitterly to the quarterly court that "if your nobel honors letts any of your m[e]mbers serve us so we may expect to keep not a sarvant amongst us."[93]

The policing of disputes between masters and indentured servants, therefore, was no more crudely one-sided in Pennsylvania than elsewhere.[94] It is clear, nevertheless, that the courts pursued their role within the compass of a general understanding that, both socially and legally, the relationship of master and indentured servant was legitimately one of authority and subordination. The master's authority was to be overseen, but its lawful exercise protected. Emblematic of this was the courts' almost mechanical processing of runaways, which nicely exemplified the key characteristic of servitude, namely the legality of restraint.

As elsewhere, however, indenture was the condition of legitimate restraint. This is made abundantly clear in local proceedings. In May 1732, for example, Jonathan Strange sought redress against one Humphrey Reynolds, who had neglected his promise to "faithfully and truly serve him the sd Jonathan" three months in consideration of £2.1.8d advanced by the plaintiff. But Strange's action was a civil suit seeking damages for

[91] *CCGQ*, February 1747/8 (Petition of George Brandon); February 1751 (Petition of John Jacob Nies).

[92] See, for example, *CCGQ*, August 1766 (Petition of Daniel Blare).

[93] *CCGQ*, November 1751 (Petition of David John).

[94] See Chapter 6, n.124, on servant petitions in Maryland and Virginia.

Reynolds' failure to perform, not an invocation of the criminal penalties so routinely applied to indentured runaways. And, unlike the summary disposal of those runaways, Strange's suit (like most civil suits in Chester, and elsewhere) simply languished on the docket (in this case for three years) before being composed, privately, by the parties themselves.[95]

As elsewhere, in short, "servants" were a distinctive legal subset of the Delaware Valley's working population, distinguished by an indenture and rendered subject to a singular legal regime. The tenor of that distinctiveness emerges in Joanna Long's 1763 petition for relief from the ill-treatment accorded her by her master, Richard Hall, of Springfield. About four months before, Long told the court, she had gone to work for Hall "as a hireling" and had "tarried with him a considerable time on wages." With "fair speeches and specious promises," Hall and his wife prevailed upon Long to bind herself to them for a term of two years. Her situation then changed quite abruptly. "Ever since your petitioner signed the said Indenture, she hath been very ill used by them," and the previous week had been "beat and abused ... in a barbarous manner," causing her to abscond. Long's complaint was referred to two justices for a hearing, and settled, though the settlement was not recorded. But clearly, by binding herself she had brought about a drastic change in her social and legal circumstances. In the same way, it was the *absence* of an indenture that allowed Martha Liggett to depart the service of James Caldwell without penalty, "it not being satisfactorily made out to this Court that the said Martha Liggett is legally bound." It was also what made Brigett Cochran, who "hired with" John Walters of Concord Township in October 1773 but departed after two weeks and was later accused of stealing from him, a "singlewoman" in court proceedings, unlike her alleged accomplice, James Hannell, who was his indentured "servant." And it was what saved Mary Broom, brought into court for "disobedience to the orders" of her master Daniel Humphreys, from punishment, she having nothing to answer for, "it not appearing that she was Bound by Indenture."[96]

Whether workers on wages remained liable to the less exacting but still serious sanction of loss of earnings in the event they broke agreements to serve – as observers alleged[97] – cannot so easily be determined from the

---

95 Chester County Common Pleas (*CCCP*), May 1732 (Jonathan Strange agt Humphrey Reynolds). Strange's complaint described Reynolds as a "yeoman." See also *CCCP*, February 1740/1 (Thomas Bissett agt William Morrison); Chester County Quarter Sessions (*CCQS*), February 1740/1 (Petition of John Cartwright). See also *CCCP*, May 1726 (Foster agt Stringer); *CCGQ*, February 1729/30 (Petition of Samuel Chance).

96 *CCGQ*, February 1763 (Petition of Joanna Long); November 1768 (Petition of William Buffington); February 1774 (Examinations of Brigett Cochran, James Hannell); August 1774 (Discharge of Mary Broom).

97 Adolph B. Benson, *Peter Kalm's Travels in North America: The English Version of 1770* (New York, 1937), I, 204. See also Peter Karsten, "'Bottomed on Justice': A Reappraisal of Critical Legal Studies Scholarship Concerning Breaches of Labor Contracts by Quitting or Firing in Britain and the U.S., 1630–1880," *American Journal of Legal History*, 34, 3 (July 1990), 220–1.

Chester court record. Civil suits seeking payment for work invariably alleged prior performance, but supplied few details. The form of wage work transactions suggests the predominance of casual day work in which work debts were either paid immediately at the conclusion of a task or cumulated over time to be presented in periodic mutual accountings in the normal fashion of book debt.[98] Neither pattern is likely to generate disputes over the "entirety" of a contract. Moreover, the amounts in dispute were generally small enough to be settled by a hearing before an individual justice rather than in the county court, and records of hearings before individual justices are very sparse indeed prior to the late eighteenth century.

Nevertheless, the cases that can be traced suggest that wage laborers in breach of employment contracts did *not* face loss of unpaid earnings in colonial Pennsylvania. In July 1767, for example, Eneas Foulk appeared before Richard Riley, JP, of Chichester township to seek payment for work undertaken on behalf of Isaac Pyle. Pyle replied that Foulk had not been paid because he "had not compleated his work according to Bargain." Nevertheless, Riley's decision was for payment for what had been completed – "that the value of the work done & due to the plantiff is but 15/- and no more."[99] Part payment was also judged appropriate some years later by Isaac Hicks, a Bucks County JP, in William Force's suit against James Moon seeking payment "for four months service of the six he hired for." Moon contended that "as the Plff did not stay out the time agreable to contract he owes nothing particularly as he suffered by his going away," but Hicks gave the plaintiff judgment "for the Bal[ance]."[100] Balancing worked

---

[98] See, for example, *The Diary of Benjamin Hawley*, 1769–1782 (transcribed by The Bishop's Mill Historical Institute), Chester County Historical Society.

[99] Richard Riley, "A Record of all My Proceedings Relating to the Office of a Justice of the Peace" (June 1765–February 1776), in 2 vols. (Historical Society of Pennsylvania), entry for 25 July 1767 (Eneas Foulk agt Isaac Pyle). See also Wadsworth, *The Well-Ordered Family*, n.60, this chapter. In Chapter 1, n.89, I noted Winifred Rothenberg's proposition that "an agricultural labor force, unconstrained and free to move, may well be a New England innovation." See her *From Market-Places to a Market Economy: The Transformation of Rural Massachusetts, 1750–1850* (Chicago, 1992), 181. Just as Massachusetts evidence suggests the phenomenon had rather earlier manifestations than Rothenberg allows, Pennsylvania evidence suggests it was not confined to New England. Equally important, as I argued in *Law, Labor, and Ideology*, 272–8, the real "innovation" is the attempt in the early nineteenth century to constrain the mobility of those formerly unconstrained by imposing wage penalties on early departure that had not previously been in evidence.

[100] Isaac Hicks, Docket, 1794–1831, in 2 vols. (Historical Society of Pennsylvania), entry for 26 January 1795 (*William Force v. James Moon*). See also John Graves JP, West Chester Township, Civil Dockets A-Q (1795–1832), Chester County Historical Society, where the following entries all record proportional settlements of disputes over wages or work payments due: 17 October 1805 (*John Bell v. Jesse Mattock*); 5 September 1815 (*John Webber v. Abner Few*); 4 May 1818 (*Joseph Mattock v. Samuel Stark*); 23 April 1821 (parties not recorded); 14 May 1825 (*Daniel Massey v. Daniel Hastead*); 17 July 1828 (*Paul McCloskey v. John Felty*). See also Charles Neimeyer, *America Goes to War: A Social History of the Continental Army* (New York, 1996), 126, for details of agricultural labor agreements from the 1770s specifying part payment for work performed in the event of noncompletion. I am indebted to Peter Karsten for this reference.

both ways. In May 1797, again before Hicks, John Butler demanded payment for thirty days' work, which he had been hired to perform by John Bulgar at 3/9d (three shillings and nine pence) per day. Bulgar contended "that he hired the Plff to assist him in gitting his Indian Corn & Buckwheat for which he agreed to pay him 3/9 and that the gitting lasted but 12 days." He acknowledged that Butler had remained with him for the remainder of the period alleged, but employed only on "trifling matters." Hicks allowed the plaintiff judgment, but at a rate reduced by 40 percent, to 2/3d per day, for the final eighteen days.[101]

In the Delaware Valley as elsewhere, then, the indenture established a crucial line of legal status in the culture of work – a line of demarcation between enforceable and unenforceable obligation. The indenture signified when and when not the assertion of capacity to control or restrain another was legally allowable, of what labor was not "free" and what was. There, as elsewhere, it existed in an environment crosscut by numerous other and intersecting lines of social demarcation – of age and gender, of race – to which the culture of work was also closely related. Occasionally, lines became tangled. In Essex County we encountered juvenile migrants arguing that terms of service could be overridden by the servant's attainment of majority; they claimed a right to disown any obligation to remain with a master once they had reached the age of twenty-one. The same was true in Pennsylvania. In February 1741–2, Joseph Helm, previously bound to Thomas Treese for a term of six years, absented himself from Treese's service, alleging that to stay would mean he would be bound beyond the age of twenty-one, and that the remainder of his term was therefore voided. Instead of treating Helm as a runaway, the court decided he should work at his trade on wages "either with his Master or if the sd Apprentice shall chuse it with some other person by his said Master's Appointment," disposition of the wages to remain subject to the direction of the court "when the Cause receives a full Determination."[102] The matter did not continue, apparently accommodated between Helm and Treese, but in 1737 the court had treated presentation of evidence of the attainment of majority as sufficient to end a term of indentured service, and it did so again some years later, notwithstanding the existence of an indenture for a longer period.[103]

Most often, however, lines of demarcation complemented each other in practice. Collectively, they sustained in the Delaware Valley a substantively differentiated culture of work that, as elsewhere, was more plural than singular, that shared no generic legal regimen of authority and subordination lending people at work a common identity as "servants" and their employers common advantages as "masters," but instead ascribed different

---

[101] Hicks, Docket, 1 May 1797 (*John Butler v. John Bulgar*).
[102] *CCGQ*, February 1741/2 (Complaint of Joseph Helm).
[103] *CCGQ*, August 1737 (Petition of Mathias Lambert); August 1770 (Complaint of Robert Potts). But see also November 1775 (Petition of George Reab).

legal identities according to the different kinds of people – youth or adult, migrant or Creole – involved. As elsewhere, too, that culture of work was itself a hierarchy, one in which the legal freedoms of adult white Creole males stood out against, and were buttressed by, enforceable obligations of service visited more weightily upon others. We have observed the same hierarchy in the Chesapeake and in New England, so to encounter it in the Delaware Valley is no surprise. As in Essex County, however, the subordinations encountered in Chester were essentially temporary and life-cyclical. Not until the widening spread of African enslavement had established race as the cardinal measure of servility does one find a segment of the early American population designated as a permanent underclass of workers. It is in racial slavery, in eighteenth-century America, that one encounters "master and servant" not as a temporary and essentially delimited legal hierarchy, but as an expansive polarity of freedom and its absence.

Conclusion

"None but *negers* are *sarvants*."[104] For working white Americans in the early nineteenth century, this was the transcendent principle of the legal culture of work that they inherited from the eighteenth century. With due allowance for the slow atrophy of early America's statutory categories of temporary youthful and migrant servants, it was also an accurate claim. The workings of the household meant that it was a claim made far more realistically by men than by women, but that per se does not make it exclusively a male claim.[105] Nor was it a claim created in a recent revolutionary departure from an oppressive ancien regime, but one we have seen sedimented over many years of labor importation, during which the legal incidents of servitude on the mainland had become identified with specific categories of European migrant labor and with the absolute servitude of slavery.

[104] Quoted in Charles William Janson, *The Stranger in America* (London, 1807), 88 (emphasis in original).
[105] The particular language in fact is that of a "servant-maid" quoted "word for word" by an English visitor (Janson) to illustrate "the arrogance of domestics in this land of republican liberty and equality." Ibid., 88. The locale is not identified, but in adjoining passages Janson is describing an early phase of his visit, spent in the vicinity of Middletown, Connecticut, en route from Boston to New York. For commentary and additional illustrations, see David R. Roediger, *The Wages of Whiteness: Race and the Making of the American Working Class*, 3rd ed. (London and Brooklyn, N.Y., 2007), 47–50.
On women's work in New England at the time of Janson's visit, see Nancy F. Cott, *The Bonds of Womanhood: "Women's Sphere" in New England, 1780–1835* (New Haven, 1977), 19–62. The late Jeanne M. Boydston's outstanding *Home and Work: Housework, Wages and the Ideology of Labor in the Early Republic* (New York, 1990), 1–55, charts both the gendered division of labor during the seventeenth and eighteenth centuries, and the gathering expression in the culture of the new republic of a loss of status (amounting to a loss of presence) for women engaged in household work resulting from secular transformation in the definition of work in general. This matter is taken up at greater length in Chapter 8.

During the first half of the nineteenth century, the claim began to sound increasingly hollow. The ambit of master and servant law steadily widened until it had absorbed the employment contract as a whole, underwriting "an employer's right and capacity, *simply as an employer contracting for the performance of services*, to exert the magisterial power of management, discipline and control over others."[106] To be sure, this generalization of master and servant doctrine beyond its formerly specific categories into nineteenth-century employment law at large was – at least at first – a generalization of a conceptual structure and language of legitimate authority in work relations, not of specific criminal disciplines. "Free labor" was not a meaningless designation. But the generalization was nevertheless deeply significant, for what distinguished the nineteenth-century version from what had gone before was its all-encompassing quality, finding disciplinary authority to inhere in the contract of employment itself rather than in the particular socio-legal statuses characteristic of particular workers – youthful, indentured, imported, and so forth – by whom duties of obedience were owed. "We understand by the relation of master and servant nothing more or less than that of the *employer* and the *employed*."[107] This had its consequences. In the first half of the nineteenth century, wage labor throughout the Eastern states found itself challenged for the first time by legal strictures that tightened the slacker economic disciplines of the previous century.[108] In the antebellum South, the status of "free labor" remained qualitatively distinct from slave, but white workers found the claims to legal privilege and civic status that they had historically founded on their absolute difference from slaves increasingly vulnerable. Indeed, what crept into their language and behavior were intimations of their willingness to work *as hard as* slaves if that were the price to be paid to keep their share of racial privilege within their grasp.[109]

Ironically, given the intervening Revolution, English influence bulked large in this nineteenth-century restatement of the law of master and servant in America. This was not a matter of specific statutory example; indeed, as the thesis-writer Timothy Walker put it, "what a contrast is here presented to the laws of England, which leave hardly any thing to the discretion of

---

[106] Tomlins, *Law, Labor, and Ideology*, 230–1 (emphasis in original).

[107] Timothy Walker, *Introduction to American Law* (Philadelphia, 1837), 243. "The legal relation of master and servant" wrote Walker, "must exist ... wherever civilization furnishes work to be done." Compare argument in *State v. Higgins*, 1 N.C. [Supreme Court of North Carolina] 36 (1792), 39: "the mechanic to whom we send a job, is not our servant ... There is no authority on one side, no subjection on the other. The mechanic is employed, not directed. His time is his own, not ours. He may postpone our work to make room for another's. The relationship between him and us supposes no superiority on our side, and therefore it is not the relation which exists between master and servant."

[108] Tomlins, *Law, Labor, and Ideology*, 223–92.

[109] Christopher L. Tomlins, "In Nat Turner's Shadow: Reflections on the Norfolk Dry Dock Affair of 1830–31," *Labor History*, 33, 4 (Fall 1992), 511–12, 516–17. For a graphic depiction of the material economy of labor in the early republic, see Seth Rockman, *Scraping By: Wage Labor, Slavery, and Survival in Early Baltimore* (Baltimore, 2009).

the employer and the employed."[110] Rather, it was a matter of the influence of authoritative English common-law reports and treatises – the product of common-law judging and reconceived common-law doctrine – all of which encouraged American legal culture in a rejection of earlier delimited and localized approaches to master and servant in favor of more expansive conceptions. During the seventeenth and eighteenth centuries, I have argued here, English America's colonial legal cultures had severally felt the original influence of English laws but had simultaneously refracted them through dissimilar regional cultures of origin and settlement that, in combination with distinctive local environments and distinct statutory regimes, had produced differentiated legal cultures of work. The impulse of the nineteenth century was different. Legal elites reached beyond that earlier localized history to champion a new legal culture not of provincial differences but of widely applicable principles.[111]

Once upon a time, Horace Wood noted – curtly – in his 1877 *Treatise on the Law of Master and Servant,* "servant" had indeed been a term of discrete legal application and consequence. "Others, as clerks, farm hands, etc. were denominated laborers or workmen, and were in many respects subject to different rules." But "no practical end" would be served by dwelling on the matter. "Those who have any curiosity upon those points can consult nearly any of the old writers upon legal subjects, and have their curiosity fully gratified." What mattered was "how the relation *now* exists" in America. And how did it now exist? Wood's answer was succinct. "All who are in the employ of another, in whatever capacity, are regarded in law as servants."[112] A decade after the Civil War's erasure of slavery, a year after the end of Reconstruction, all of America's working people had been sent out on the lonely sea of industrialization in the same legal-conceptual boat.

[110] Walker, *Introduction,* 250.
[111] On which, see Laura F. Edwards, *The People and their Peace: Legal Culture and the Transformation of Inequality in the Post-Revolutionary South* (Chapel Hill, 2009). Examining North and South Carolina, Edwards finds in the venerable local tradition of "the peace" (a concept with clear early-modern English resonance) the embodiment of a particularized social order, patriarchal and hierarchical in appearance, in which all situated within the compass of the locality enjoyed some quantum of capacity to act, irrespective of whether they could be considered bearers of civic rights (for example, white men) or not (the poor, women, even in some cases the enslaved). Although hierarchical locality persisted deep into the nineteenth century, the workings of the peace were rendered increasingly invisible, and the ambit of its authority increasingly tenuous, as state-wide elites – who conceived themselves members of a national political and legal culture – undertook the creation of a liberal, rights-based, legal order that had the effect of excluding from recognition all those who could not make definitive claims to be bearers of rights. On the strength of localism and elite transcendence see also, generally, Kenneth A. Lockridge, *Settlement and Unsettlement in Early America: The Crisis of Political Legitimacy before the Revolution* (Cambridge and New York, 1981). For a distinct example of the same kind of transition from particularist, non–rights based civic order to universalist rights-based order, see Middleton, *From Privileges to Rights.* See also Chapter 8. For the eventual collision of incompatible universal claims (slavery and freedom), see Chapter 10.
[112] Horace Gay Wood, *Treatise on the Law of Master and Servant* (Albany, 1877), 2, 3, 3–4.

PART III

"What, then, is the American, this new man?"

'Tis with pleasing wonder that we look back upon this country in general, and this town in particular, and compare the present condition and appearance with what they were a century ago, yea but little more than half a century ago. Instead of a desolate uncultivated wilderness – instead of mountains and plains covered with thick untraversed woods – and swamps hideous and impassable, the face of the earth is trimmed, and adorned with a beautiful variety of fields, meadows, orchards and pastures. *The desert blossoms as the rose: the little hills rejoice on every side; the pastures are clothed with flocks, the valleys also are covered over with corn; they shout for joy, they also sing.* Instead of the dreary haunts of savage beasts, and more savage men, wounding the ear and terrifying the heart with their dismal yells, we find now only harmless retreats, *where the fowls of heaven have their habitation which sing among the branches.* Instead of the smoky huts and wigwams of naked swarthy barbarians, we now behold thick settlements of a civilized people and convenient and elegant buildings ... improvements in arts, agriculture and all the elegances of life.

Nathan Fiske, *Remarkable Providences to be Gratefully Recollected,*
Religiously Improved, and Carefully Transmitted to Posterity.
A sermon preached at Brookfield on the last day of the year 1775.

8

Modernizing: Polity, Economy, Patriarchy

Things are come to that pass now, that tho' Masters have the Name of Government indeed, the Servants really govern throughout this Nation, and especially that Part of them who we hire for daily Labour, who if but one crooked Word be spoken to them, will turn their Backs upon you, and upon your Business, and be gone, in spight of Contracts and Bargains and in spight of any Damages you may suffer by it.

Daniel Defoe, *The Great Law of Subordination Consider'd* (1724)

The original political right that God gives to Adam is the right, so to speak, to fill the empty vessel.

Carole Pateman, *The Sexual Contract* (1988)

I doubt not but we shall soon have a very severe Law upon that Subject. *But of this hereafter.*

Daniel Defoe, *The Great Law of Subordination Consider'd* (1724)

At a strategic moment early in his extended study of the culture of eighteenth-century working people, *Customs in Common*, the late E. P. Thompson invokes Daniel Defoe's vexed anatomy of English social relations, *The Great Law of Subordination Consider'd* (1724), to oil the hinge of a fundamental transformation he contends was afoot in eighteenth-century English society. Pointedly, Thompson notes Defoe's observation that an England was coming into being in which, unless decisive measures were taken, "the Poor will be Rulers over the Rich, and the Servants be Governours of their Masters, the Plebeij have almost mobb'd the Patricij ... in a Word, Order is inverted, Subordination ceases, and the World seems to stand with the Bottom upward."[1] In the throes of his anxiety for orderliness, says Thompson, Defoe has correctly foreseen two essential characteristics of the coming century: First, growing social polarization between on the one hand the world of the "patrician" gentry (an "agrarian

---

[1] E. P. Thompson, *Customs in Common: Studies in Traditional Popular Culture* (New York, 1991), 16; Daniel Defoe, *The Great Law of Subordination Consider'd; or, the Insolence and Unsufferable Behavior of SERVANTS in England Duly Enquir'd into. Illustrated with a Great Variety of Examples, Historical Cases, and Remarkable Stories.... As also a Proposal, Containing such Heads or Constitutions, as wou'd Effectually Answer this Great End, and bring Servants of Every Class to a Just (and yet not a Grievous) Regulation* (London, 1724).

bourgeoisie," crowned at its metropolitan apex by a parasitic "banditti," the whole representing "predatory oligarchic power" in operation[2]) and on the other the local, customary, and largely opaque world of "plebeian" culture; but also, second, a simultaneous erosion of the mechanisms upon which patricians had relied in earlier generations to maintain plebeians in place – the "old means of social discipline";[3] more precisely, the forms and institutions of legal subordination.

For Thompson, Defoe's narrative offers concrete examples of the impact of waxing freedom in the petty interactions of daily life.[4] He draws particular attention to Defoe's indignant account of a poor cloth worker's carefully calibrated defiance of a magistrate before whom he has been hauled to answer for neglecting his work. Defoe's story is elaborately scripted:

Justice: Come in Edmund, I have talk'd with your Master.
Edmund: Not *my Master*, and't please your Worship, I hop I am *my own Master*.
Justice: Well, your Employer, Mr E–, the Clothier; will the word Employer do?
Edmund: Yes, yes, and't please your Worship, any thing, but *Master*.

In Thompson's reading, the exchange captures perfectly the lofty arrogance of patrician society's encounters with cowering plebs, but also the ragged notes of uncertainty beginning to be audible in their interactions, the notes that sound the passing of those old legal disciplines. Edmund's refusal to accept the label of routine subservience and his subsequent success in avoiding punishment for his neglect of work, Thompson tells us, "is a large change in the terms of relations: subordination is becoming (although between grossly unequal parties) negotiation."[5]

---

[2] Thompson, *Customs in Common*, 84, 27, 33; and see generally 24–33.

[3] Ibid., 42; and see generally 35–42.

[4] Ibid., 16, 37–8, 43.

[5] Ibid., 38. Defoe sustains his narrative of Edmund the cloth worker over several pages of *The Great Law*, but does not locate it with any specificity. The question arises whether this narrative has any grounding in "historical reality." Thompson assumes it is fictional and thinks of it as a moralistic anecdote – evidence of beliefs held rather than a historical circumstance encountered. Certainly *The Great Law* is composed of many anecdotal narratives, of which this is only one, albeit one of the longest. Its "actuality" might seem beside the point. But it would not do to dismiss the matter, for the question of what it can tell us about historical reality beyond providing evidence of Defoe's beliefs is not unimportant, and in fact may supply its larger significance. In *History and the Early English Novel: Matters of Fact from Bacon to Defoe* (Cambridge, 1997), Robert Mayer argues that Defoe was a pivotal figure in the early eighteenth century's transformative rearrangement of the literary relationship between reality and representation. The rearrangement would call forth novelists like Samuel Richardson and Henry Fielding, whose work was produced intentionally as fiction. But Defoe situated his work prior to the divide. Defoe, says Mayer, "sought to ensure that his most famous narratives would be read not as fiction but as history" (181). In his hands "if a narrative was substantially true, if it was a historical account based on reliable sources, neither a fictional frame, nor a fictionalized narrator, nor even the use of fictional material, altered the narrative's essentially historical character" (170). The result was "works that could be, and at first were, read as histories,

Thompson's interpretation of Defoe's narrative conveys an important claim about the role of law in the century's large change in relations of subordination. Law in the early eighteenth century, he writes elsewhere, was "class-bound and mystifying." But it was also beginning to be possessed of its own "logic, rules and procedures."[6] Although capable of "being devised and employed, directly and instrumentally, in the imposition of class power," law had nevertheless come to exist in its own right, that is "simply *as law*." Because law was possessed of "its own characteristics, its own independent history and logic of evolution," it could display "an independence from gross manipulation" and grant the Edmunds of the world a real measure of justice in the face of power.[7] Both in setting and outcome, this representative plebeian's defiance demonstrated in microcosm that the law was on its way "to a role more prominent than at any other period of our history," that, in the wake of the Glorious Revolution, it had become society's foremost "arbitrating authority," and that, to the extent it remained true to the distinct identity that its forms and rhetoric nourished – transcendent values of equity and of "the rule of law" – it could be accepted on all sides as a "medium within which other social conflicts [might be] fought out" and therefore recognized as "an unqualified human good."[8]

Though by reputation and conviction Thompson was a critic of received liberal history and political theory, the themes he chose to emphasize

that later were read as fictions, and, most paradoxically, that sometimes have been read as both" (154). Below I consider whether we can locate Defoe's narrative of Edmund the cloth worker more precisely, and thereby improve our understanding of it as history.

[6] E. P. Thompson, *Whigs and Hunters: The Origin of the Black Act* (Harmondsworth, UK, 1977), 260. And see *Customs in Common*, 34–5.

[7] Thompson, *Whigs and Hunters*, 260, 262, 263.

[8] Thompson, *Customs in Common*, 34; *Whigs and Hunters*, 265–7. For extended commentaries on Thompson's formulation see, for example, Adrian Merritt, "The Nature and Function of Law: A Criticism of E. P. Thompson's 'Whigs and Hunters'," *British Journal of Law and Society*, 7, 2 (Winter 1980), 194–214; Perry Anderson, *Arguments Within English Marxism* (London, 1980), particularly 199–205. Merritt criticizes Thompson for his reliance on an idealist liberal meta-narrative that spuriously invokes law, equity, and justice as universal essences autonomous of social relations. "Law can never be seen '*simply as law*', '*simply*' in terms of its own logic'. Blind formalism like that belongs only in the sterile environment of traditional law schools" (199). Thompson's invocation of the rule of law as an "unqualified human good," she argues, is no more than a "fetishism" of law (208) that is atheoretical and disarming. More forgiving, Anderson concludes that Thompson's growing legalism is attributable to changes in his politics, reflecting an increasingly libertarian conceptualization of "the rule of law" founded less on bourgeois conceptions of legality than on native English traditions of oppositional radicalism. (Anderson's judgment is confirmed by the tenor of Thompson's final book, *Witness against the Beast: William Blake and the Moral Law* [New York, 1993]). Anderson nevertheless finds Thompson's legalism romantic and simplistic and, like Merritt, ultimately disabling. Thompson's rhetorical counterposition of "traditional freedoms" to "new statism" extols only a negative liberty and a naive faith in the good offices of the householder (205). See in addition Christopher Tomlins, "How Autonomous Is Law?" *Annual Review of Law and Social Science*, 3 (2007), 49–52. For additional evaluations, see Morton J. Horwitz, "The Rule of Law: An Unqualified Human Good?" *Yale Law Journal*, 86, 3 (January 1977), 561–6; Karl Klare, "Law-Making as Praxis," *Telos*, 40 (1979), 133–4.

when it came to eighteenth-century law – its elevation from mere tool to "hypostatized construct,"[9] and the acceleration of freedom and consent in productive relations that accompanied that elevation – have always enjoyed an intimate relationship in liberal history, where they perform as twinned signifiers of "progress," the gathering disengagement of modernity from feudalism and the posited release of individual energies (social and political, intellectual and scientific) by which disengagement is signified.[10] Quintessentially, liberalism defines its difference as a theory of polity and economy precisely in terms of the emergence of changes in polis and society that underscore the primacy of *"meum and tuum,"* of individuated property right, to civic right. Necessarily, labor must become legally free in that large change, else the individual at large would not be empowered at all, but merely those who enjoyed command of what individuals, en masse, produced. Here lies the revolutionary promise of the new property theory of the seventeenth century, the theory that Grotius began and that after him Locke thought the particular promise of the Atlantic world's new commonwealths: human equality in place of natural subjugation; hierarchy and command undone by contract and consent; humanity in thrall to scarcity replaced by "the ease and bounty of a civil, laborious life."[11] And with the possibilities of propertied abundance – the "sufficiencies" of an economy uncontained – would come the prospect of ever greater inclusion in the politics of *vita activa.* Thus, Locke imagined governance not as a visitation of sovereignty upon subjects from above but founded on the consent of those who, by natural right, had acquired private property by individual exertion and who sought its protection through their own civic action in the consensual creation of a body politic.[12] Property begun in an individual's own labor became the basis of the state, its security the state's reason for being. Men would no longer be born slaves to the necessities

---

[9] Anderson, *Arguments Within English Marxism,* 200.

[10] For the latter, see J. Willard Hurst, *Law and the Conditions of Freedom in the Nineteenth-Century United States* (Madison, Wis., 1956). Much of the more recent writing on the history of Anglo-American labor law has undertaken a critical reexamination of this paradigm. See Karen Orren, *Belated Feudalism: Labor, the Law and Liberal Development in the United States* (New York and Cambridge, 1991); Robert J. Steinfeld, *The Invention of Free Labor: The Employment Relation in English and American Law and Culture, 1350–1870* (Chapel Hill, 1991), and *Coercion, Contract and Free Labor in the Nineteenth Century* (New York and Cambridge, 2001); Christopher Tomlins, *Law, Labor, and Ideology in the Early American Republic* (New York and Cambridge, 1993).

[11] Paul Corcoran, "John Locke and the Possession of Land: Native Title vs. the 'Principle' of *Vacuum Domicilium,*" 18. Australasian Political Studies Association Annual Conference, 2007, Monash University, available at http://arts.monash.edu.au/psi/news-and-events/apsa/refereed-papers/#political_theory (accessed 22 August 2009).

[12] John Locke, *Two Treatises of Government: In the Former, the False Principles and Foundation of Sir Robert Filmer, and His Followers, are Detected and Overthrown. The Latter is an Essay Concerning the True Original, Extent, and End of Civil-Government* (London, 1698), 184–202 [§§25–51 "Of Property"], 238–65 [§§95–131 "Of the Beginning of Political Societies," and "Of the Ends of Political Society and Government"]; Barbara Arneil, *John Locke and America: The Defence of English Colonialism* (Oxford, 1996), 43, 155–62.

of subsistence, but free to fabricate and circulate and enjoy as they willed "the sheer unending variety of things" that is modern life.[13] They would no longer be born superiors and subordinates, but co-equal makers of contracts, individual, social, and political. Once accepted, "this foundation leads to a rethinking of all human communities, and the establishment of equality and voluntariness as key elements shaping relations of power within them."[14] Here in full flush was the fleeting glimpse caught by everyman's colonizer, John Smith, in the first moments of England's contacts with "New" England: "euery man ... master and owner of his owne labour and land."[15] Invented in England's encounter with America, propertied independence would become the touchstone of Lockean civic modernity. Here was civility's ultimate gift to the barbarous.[16]

In this telling, the two stories, of civic modernizing and of the legal transformation of labor, necessarily become one. For as, "in social reality labour is becoming, decade by decade, more 'free' of traditional manorial, parochial, corporate and paternal controls, and more distanced from direct client dependence upon the gentry," so the reproduction and eventual worldwide transmission of that fundamental transformation in society's productive relations relies for its permanence upon the law that defines, records, and implements those relations. "Productive relations themselves are, in part, only meaningful in terms of their definitions at law."[17]

Locke wrote to elevate consent as a paradigmatic discourse of human society. He did so to devastate the political theories of Sir Robert Filmer, notably Filmer's patriarchal construction of politics which relied upon the household and its hierarchical order of paternal subjection (the "claim that every person 'is born subject to the power of a Father'"[18]) as a model of proper authority by which to constitute the state, and to establish in its place a distinct trajectory for state formation grounded on individual property right. Locke's success in the matter has been widely celebrated: Can there really be any doubt of Locke's centrality in Anglo-America's dominant

---

[13] Recall Hannah Arendt, *The Human Condition* (Chicago, 1958), 136, 7–9, on the conditions and elements of *vita activa*, cited in the Prologue to this book. For the strategic social and political importance of modernity's sheer variety of "things," see T. H. Breen, *The Marketplace of Revolution: How Consumer Politics Shaped American Independence* (New York, 2004).

[14] William James Booth, *Households: on the Moral Architecture of the Economy* (Ithaca, N.Y., 1993), 101. Of all recent American historians, Joyce Appleby is perhaps the most successful in conveying the sheer exhilaration conveyed in these manifestations of early liberal thought. See her *Capitalism and a New Social Order: The Republican Vision of the 1790s* (New York, 1984), and *Liberalism and Republicanism in the Historical Imagination* (Cambridge, Mass., 1992).

[15] John Smith, *A Description of New England*, in Philip L. Barbour, editor, *The Complete Works of Captain John Smith* (Chapel Hill, 1986), I, 332.

[16] Locke, *Two Treatises of Government*, 184–202 [§§25–51 "Of Property"]; Arneil, *John Locke and America*, 132–67. And see Chapter 4, section I.

[17] Thompson, *Customs in Common*, 9; *Whigs and Hunters*, 267.

[18] Booth, *Households*, 98.

tradition of liberal modernism?[19] Thompson, for one, testifies – involuntarily – to the extent of the ideational shift that Locke helped induce. As a conception of social and political order, Thompson has argued, patriarchy is bounded in time. Patriarchy embodies "a very specific set of theories and institutions where the monarch or the head of the household commanded authority over subjects, wife, children, apprentices, servants, etc."[20] These were not only under challenge by the beginning of the eighteenth century, Thompson's Lockean chronology tells us, they had already begun to decompose, giving way to a different determinative context – of wealth and poverty and the struggles over distribution that are modernity's mark. Bernard de Mandeville helps him mark the transition. "It is impossible," Mandeville wrote in 1723, "that a Society can long subsist, and suffer many of its Members to live in Idleness, and enjoy all the Ease and Pleasure they can invent, without having at the same time great Multitudes of People that to make good this Defect will condescend to be quite the reverse, and by use and patience inure their Bodies to Work for others and themselves besides." These, Thompson tells us, are the "class-bound apologetics" that called a new politics and its symbol, "economic man," into existence.[21] They and their ilk have kept him in being ever since. They are the key to the social relations of Anglo-American industrialization. They are the key to its successor, globalization, for they are "the hidden text of the discourse between North and South."[22] Displacing the patriarchal polis, the politics

---

[19] The returns are debated in Arneil, *John Locke and America*, 11–16; Gordon S. Wood, *The Creation of the American Republic, 1776–1787* (Chapel Hill, 1969), 218–19, 283–9, 601–2; J.G.A. Pocock, *The Machiavellian Moment: Florentine Political Thought and the Atlantic Republican Tradition* (Princeton, 1975), 526–52. For more recent commentary bearing on the matter, see Holly Brewer, *By Birth or Consent: Children, Law, and the Anglo-American Revolution in Authority* (Chapel Hill, 2005); Brian Balogh, *A Government Out of Sight: The Mystery of National Authority in Nineteenth-Century America* (Cambridge and New York, 2009), 41–8.

[20] Thompson, *Customs in Common*, 500. Because of his insistence that "patriarchy" represents a particular form of social and political organization that is specific to a particular historical moment that no longer pertains in the eighteenth century, Thompson argues that it cannot be used as a general description or categorization of social practice. He comments that "feminist theorists, who allocate a central place to patriarchy, are rarely historians," and criticizes their indiscriminate invocation of the practices of patriarchy "to cover every situation and institution of male-domination" (499–500). Time has passed patriarchy by. But as Carol Pateman has, tellingly, written, to abandon patriarchy "would mean that … feminist political theory would then be without the only concept that refers specifically to the subjection of women, that singles out the form of political right that all men exercise by virtue of being men. If the problem has no name, patriarchy can all too easily slide back into obscurity beneath the conventional categories of political analysis." Carol Pateman, *The Sexual Contract* (Cambridge, 1988), 20. See also 21–2.

[21] Thompson, *Customs in Common*, 14–15. The citation to Bernard de Mandeville is to *The Fable of the Bees: Or, Private Vices, Publick Benefits. With an Essay on Charity and Charity-schools. And a Search into the Nature of Society* (London, 1724), 326. We shall see, in fact, that Mandeville distinguishes society's "members" from its "people" in precisely the fashion that the classical household [*oikos*] distinguishes its patriarchal head from its interior supporting cast.

[22] Ibid.

of "economic man" dictate a new and universal trajectory for struggle and its objectives.

These interlocked themes – escape from subsistence, the decomposition of patriarchy, the appearance of discourses of consent in polity and economy, the freeing of labor and the changing contours of exploitation and distribution, the emergence of law as supreme social mediator and the consequent "rethinking of all human communities" in contractarian terms – have been accepted as fundamentals of mainstream Anglo-American history, whether of liberal or, in Thompson's case, radical bent.[23] All crowd into the specific interpretation that Thompson gives to the story of Edmund the cloth worker's encounter with the magistrate.[24] Edmund's avoidance of penalty for his "refusal ... to submit to the work-discipline demanded" shows that "[p]aternalist control over the whole life of the labourer was in fact being eroded"; the refusal itself evidences the "newly-won psychology of the free labourer." And the location of the refusal (before a magistrate) signals conclusively the replacement of the old legal disciplines by the rule of law. "[A] substantial proportion of the labour force actually became *more* free from discipline in their daily work, more free to choose between employers and between work and leisure, less situated in a position of dependence in their whole way of life, than they had been before."[25] As befits "a Man of the Left,"[26] Thompson's telling tale does not have a classic liberal ending: the laborer's new procedural freedoms do not herald substantive autonomy. They are prelude, rather, to the factory discipline that would penetrate and reconstitute the lives of the eighteenth century's "idle and disorderly" plebeians.[27] Still, factory discipline was not a return to old legal burdens only temporarily abated; it was itself a further signifier of modernity. That is, rather than a reversion to the discipline of renewed legal unfreedom, factory discipline meant a transition to a new kind of freedom, one measured in relativities of deprivation (crudely, *need*), one exposed to a new oppressive reality – a structure of command grounded on control of the detail of production. Factory discipline was *modern* discipline – the discipline of the clock, not the dock.[28] In relation to this discipline, law stood as salve, even salvation.[29]

---

[23] For liberal versions, see, for example, Patrick S. Atiyah, *The Rise and Fall of Freedom of Contract* (Oxford, 1979); Gordon S. Wood, *The Radicalism of the American Revolution: How a Revolution Turned a Monarchical Society into a Democratic One unlike any that had Ever Existed* (New York, 1992). For a radical version of the American case, see Morton J. Horwitz, *The Transformation of American Law, 1780–1860* (Cambridge, Mass., 1977).

[24] The interplay between these large themes of social transformation and Defoe's anecdote also exemplify Thompson's methodology, which he describes as the ornamentation of "impressions" and "hunches" with "elegant or apt quotations." *Customs in Common*, 24.

[25] Ibid., 37, 38 (emphasis in original).

[26] Morton Horwitz's phrase, in "The Rule of Law," 566.

[27] Thompson, *Customs in Common*, 38, 39.

[28] Ibid, 352–403. [These pages of *Customs in Common* reprint Thompson's well-known essay, "Time, Work-Discipline and Industrial Capitalism," *Past and Present*, 38 (December 1967).]

[29] Thompson, *Whigs and Hunters*, 262–7. As in *The Making of the English Working Class* and *Customs in Common*, Thompson's setting is England, but the lesson is for the world.

Thompson, however, tells only a fragment of Defoe's tale, and in certain crucial details his rendition is incorrect. Add what's missing, correct what's wrong, and the meaning of the story changes rather dramatically. The alteration makes it a different microcosm, one that does not illustrate the liberal conjuncture's "rise" of free labor at all but in very basic ways calls it in question.

By re-telling Thompson's telling tale, I will show that a condition of "free labor" did not arise in the course of a unidirectional eighteenth-century transformation of Anglo-American polis and society from rule by traditions of patriarchal magistracy to the rule of individuality and consent. In Part II, we have already seen that the question of labor's legal freedom was both situational and relative: some who labored and had once been unfree became freer; others who labored and who had once been free became less so. Many, meanwhile, were enslaved, and were thereby rendered absolutely and irrevocably and perpetually unfree. In this chapter we shall see specifically that patriarchal authority and its social relations of subordination did not decompose. Far from it. Both in the civic realm (the state) and the domestic (the household), it was composed anew.

To investigate the new, extended, contours of patriarchal authority, and – in the following chapter – the rise of slavery in Anglo-America, is to offer new lines of sight, both legal and political, on the development of the new commonwealths that colonizing formed in mainland America and on the entwined fate of labor in that process of development. Investigation establishes as well a further and distinct standpoint from which to examine colonizers' new theory of property, and what has traditionally been accepted as their accompanying desire to rethink "all human communities" in terms of equality and voluntariness, which is to say their commitment to improvement and progress. The objective in Part III of this book, then, is to grapple with the liabilities of modernity.

I.   Re-telling Tales

In the second part of this book, just concluded, I offered an account of the law of labor unfreedom and its subjects in early modern England and in England's mainland American colonies that showed how law's institutional interactions with regional culture in both locales created a legal culture of work in no sense uniformly unfree, but rather shot through with gaping holes through which (particularly in America) plebeian bodies – white bodies, to be sure, and mostly male – can be found constantly slipping. This account, if correct, undermines the temporal and causal trajectory that both liberal and radical historiography have normalized, generally without much question. The history of labor un/freedom, the ordering of its segmentations and imbrications, is simply not one that can be traced to

Liberalism's rule of law (Locke's, Blackstone's) is "a cultural achievement of universal significance" that arms all those who struggle against oppression, economic or imperial (265–6).

or explained by the classic engine of modernization, capitalism, alone. Its secrets lie as much in the processes and demands of colonizing, and their far less linear historical trajectory. Colonizing's incessant demands for labor, the forms in which both the supply of labor and the work performed were organized in response, and the social and ideological practices that resulted, interrupt conventional narratives of Anglo-American modernity and the waxing formal freedoms in relations among law, economy, and society that are their marker. The juxtaposition of the first and second parts of this book prepares the way, I hope, for the altered constellation – the reassemblage of parts – that will make the interruption explicit here, in the third.[30]

Colonizing induces a new constellation because it introduces us to a temporality distinct from modernity's idealization of "progress." It draws to our attention the constancy of differentials and occlusions in the measurement of civic capacity, the ease with which liberal modernity actually coexists with innovations – disciplined service, gendered subalternship, and racialized enslavement – that seem to contradict it. Certain coexistences encountered in the first part of this book have already pointed the way. There I presented English colonizing discourse as a discourse of improvement (a manuring of lands and sometimes, but only incidentally, of the people found wandering upon them) that constructed an armature for itself out of *ius naturale* and *gentium* by conjuring into coexistence with the new commonwealths it desired to create an array of threats to confront and, where necessary, destroy: savages to conquer and brutes to exterminate; marauding enemies to pen behind constantly expanding frontiers. Outside *ius gentium*'s interior gestures of courtesy, owed one European sovereign by the next, lay another realm of action far more characteristic of world historical experience, in which – notwithstanding the protests of scholastic critics – the judgments of nature and of the community of the humane were co-opted as legitimate and sufficient grounds for making war when necessary to civilize and cultivate. Here were the origins of the discourse of sovereign right by conquest and then by use that would sustain European empires for half a millennium as they departed on one civilizing mission after another into the zones of exception they had created for themselves beyond the boundaries of the old medieval map. Colonizing, one may argue, is the normalization of exception.[31] It occurs in the world's

---

[30] See generally Christopher Tomlins, "Afterword: Constellations of Class in Early North America and the Atlantic World," in Simon Middleton and Billy G. Smith, editors, *Class Matters: Early North America and the Atlantic World* (Philadelphia, 2008), 213–33.

[31] On "exception," see Giorgio Agamben, *Homo Sacer: Sovereign Power and Bare Life*, trans. Daniel Heller-Roazen (Stanford, Calif.: Stanford University Press, 1998), 18: "The particular 'force' of law consists in th[e] capacity of law to maintain itself in relation to an exteriority. We shall give the name relation of exception to the extreme form of relation by which something is included solely through its exclusion." Agamben here draws upon the theory of sovereignty developed in the early 1920s by Carl Schmitt, who held that "For a legal order to make sense, a normal situation must exist, and he is sovereign who definitely decides that such a normal situation actually exists," but also and necessarily

barbaric zones as an unending condition of emergency – the unending necessity that order and improvement be visited upon the disordered by the civil, lest they face otherwise, as Robert Cushman wrote, "a vast and emptie *Chaos*."[32] Once they had landed, colonizers strove to familiarize the exceptional, to make it (in everyone's interest) a bit more like home.[33]

But colonizing is as potent a description of the sovereign impulse to create "due regulation and order" in locales of exception *within* the physical boundaries of the homeland as much as in the world beyond. Both are meet for improvement. England's transoceanic colonizing lived cheek by jowl with like initiatives to civilize "the rude parts" of the British archipelago. Indeed, the two overlapped: in the tracts of the Hakluyts and others, the inhabitants of those rude parts are precisely the instrument for their schemes. A disorderly population that threatens social order within the realm can be shipped to an archipelago of plantations overseas to become a tractable labor force that "improves" the wilderness. The experience improves the population. By subtraction, it also improves the realm.[34]

The intimacies of colonizing and the improvement of labor are nowhere more clearly underscored as they bear down on each other during the course of the eighteenth century than in the work of Daniel Defoe. For Defoe's vexed and vexatious *Great Law* itself is best read, like so much of his work, as a colonizing discourse.[35] Like all such discourses it elaborated upon a project of discovery, in this case of an England, a Britain, that in crucial respects remained regionally detached from the dictates of its metropolitan center. The conjectural narratives that illustrated the *Great Law*'s polemic had been accumulated during Defoe's many years of travel "through the whole island of Great Britain," travels eventually summarized

that "sovereign is he who decides on the exception." Carl Schmitt, *Political Theology: Four Chapters on the Concept of Sovereignty* (Chicago, 1985), 13, 5.

[32] Robert Cushman, "Reasons & Considerations Touching the Lawfulnesse of Remouing out of *England* into the parts of *America*," in William Bradford et al., *A Relation or Iournall of the Beginning and Proceedings of the English Plantation Setled at Plimoth in New England, by Certaine English Aduenturers both Merchants and Others* (London, 1622), 69 (emphasis in original).

[33] See generally Christopher L. Tomlins, "The Many Legalities of Colonization: A Manifesto of Destiny for Early American Legal History," in Christopher L. Tomlins and Bruce H. Mann, editors, *The Many Legalities of Early America* (Chapel Hill, 2001), 1–5.

[34] See Jane H. Ohlmeyer, "'Civilizinge of those Rude Partes': Colonization within Britain and Ireland, 1580s–1640s," in Nicholas Canny, editor, *The Origins of Empire: British Overseas Enterprise to the Close of the Seventeenth Century*, volume I of *The Oxford History of the British Empire*, William Roger Louis, general editor (Oxford, 1998), 124–47; Mark Netzloff, *England's Internal Colonies: Class, Capital, and the Literature of Early Modern English Colonialism* (New York, 2003), 91–134, 208–10. See generally Part I of this book.

[35] See J. A. Downie, "Defoe, Imperialism, and the Travel Books Reconsidered," in Roger D. Lund, editor, *Critical Essays on Daniel Defoe* (New York, 1997), 78–96. Downie writes that an "insistence on imperialism runs throughout Defoe's writings on economics, and finds a place in his narratives" (87). See also Maximilian E. Novak, *Economics and the Fiction of Daniel Defoe* (Berkeley and Los Angeles, 1962). "In whatever form, Defoe propagandized for travel, foreign commerce, and colonization" (146). The *Great Law*'s stress on labor discipline complemented those prime directives.

in his *Tour* of the same name, published immediately after the *Great Law*, in 1724–6. In the manner of the narratives that composed the younger Hakluyt's *Principall Navigations*, Defoe's *Tour* was a manufacture of nation, though on this later occasion the direction of composition was from the center outward, the reverse of Hakluyt. Consistently engaging in its capacity to express the island's regional variation, Defoe's chorography also suggested that variation always hung on the frontier of profound alterity to a metropolitan norm. Take, for example, his well-known account of the "Peakrills," the cave-dwelling lead miners of the Derbyshire peak district, whom Defoe described as "subterranean wretches," creatures from "the dark regions below," whose speech required the services of an interpreter before it could be comprehended in "the world of light" that Defoe inhabited. So great was their remove from the villages and country estates of the south which, earlier in the *Tour*, Defoe had described with an easy and delighted familiarity, that the Peakrills seemed a different race of beings, "rude boorish" and "uncouth" in manner, collectively "strange, turbulent, quarrelsome."[36] In a word, foreign. One might even hazard barbaric. Describing his journey onward from the peak district, his descent into the West Riding of Yorkshire from Blackstone Edge in the Pennines, Defoe had resort to a familiar and unmistakable trope that put the Peak's alterity beyond doubt: "We thought now we were come into a Christian country again, and that our difficulties were over."[37]

Unfamiliar legal cultures attracted Defoe's curiosity no less than unfamiliar peoples. Defoe found the Peak District's barmote (mining law) court

[36] Daniel Defoe, *A Tour Throughout the Whole Island of Great Britain*, Introduction by Pat Rogers (London, 1971), 460, 463–7. On the south and east, see 47–336. Peter Earle has commented that Defoe "knew the south and the east of the country best. He wrote his descriptions of these parts first and clearly got bored with the project as he went on." Peter Earle, *The World of Defoe* (London, 1976), 126.

[37] Defoe, *A Tour Throughout the Whole Island*, 490. Defoe's text pointedly contrasts barrenness and plenitude, wilderness and cultivation, arbitrariness and authority. Note, for example, the palpable relief that attended his arrival at the Duke of Devonshire's estate at Chatsworth in Derbyshire, an aristocratic island of civility and social-spatial order amid the deep foreignness and desolation of the Peak. To the northeast of Chatsworth lay "a vast extended moor or waste, which, for fifteen or sixteen miles together due north, presents you with neither hedge, house or tree, but a waste and howling wilderness, over which, when strangers travel, they are obliged to take guides ... Nothing can be more surprising of its kind, than for a stranger ... wandering or labouring to pass this difficult desert country, and seeing no end of it, and almost discouraged and beaten out with the fatigue of it ... on a sudden the guide brings him to this precipice, where he looks down from a frightful height, and a comfortless, barren, and, as he thought, endless moor, into the most delightful valley, with the most pleasant garden, and most beautiful palace in the world." 476–7, and generally 475–7. These discursive tropes of savagery and civility, waste and garden, barbarity and *civitas* are, we saw in Chapter 4 (section I), deeply embedded in English colonizing discourse. They are part and parcel of the cultural negotiations of early modernity. See also generally Christopher Tomlins, "Law's Wilderness: The Discourse of English Colonizing, the Violence of Intrusion and the Failures of American History," in John Smolenski and Thomas J. Humphrey, editors, *New World Orders: Violence, Sanction and Authority in the Colonial Americas* (Philadelphia, 2005), 21–46; Francis Barker, *The Culture of Violence: Essays on Tragedy and History* (Chicago, 1993).

"very remarkable," particularly its jurisdiction over the Peakrills' "subterranean quarrels and disputes."[38] He found the extensive authority that Halifax magistrates exercised over the West Riding's cloth manufacture equally interesting. Indeed, the extent of Defoe's interest strongly suggests that Halifax might well have been the "certain Town of Note" that was the site for the incident recounted in the *Great Law* and picked over by E. P. Thompson.[39] The suggestion must remain speculative for there is no way to corroborate it. What is not speculation, however, is the contrast in the two accounts of difference within the island that the *Tour* and the *Great Law* present. In the *Tour*, Defoe's mien is primarily chorographic narrative. Like the voyaging narratives that Hakluyt assembled in the *Principal Navigations*, he told of what had been found and seen – people, places, flora, fauna, climates, cultures, trades, and commodities. In the *Great Law*, in contrast, Defoe is explicitly normative. The *Great Law* tells tales not to illustrate difference but to instantiate difference's depravity and to demand its overthrow. The book is a polemic against social chaos. It seeks colonization of the internal lands of the island.[40]

The errant cloth worker's full name was Edmund Pratt.[41] He was a "journeyman weaver."[42] He had been hired by a clothier, E–, to fill an order that E– had received from a third party. E– had supplied the materials expeditiously and the whole was to be finished by an agreed date. But after completing about half the job Pratt ground to a halt, preferring the Alehouse to his loom. When E– "entreated" him to finish the job, he answered "*flat* and *plain*" that he had no need of the money. E– then went to the magistrate to swear out a warrant for Pratt's arrest on a charge of neglecting his work. Thompson tells us that the magistrate summonsed the cloth worker to answer to his employer's complaint of neglect, leading to the dialog already recounted.[43] But this is not so. What the magistrate told the clothier was that "the Case did not lie before him" and that no warrant could be granted. He had no jurisdiction over the matter, the magistrate said, because Pratt "was not an Apprentice, or a hir'd Covenant-Servant, bargain'd with for the Year." He advised the clothier that his only option,

---

[38] Defoe, *A Tour Throughout the Whole Island*, 460. And see also Chapter 5, nn.65–70 and accompanying text.

[39] Defoe, *Great Law of Subordination Consider'd*, 91; *A Tour Throughout the Whole Island*, 491–3. Peter Earle notes Defoe's consuming interest in the cloth industry in *The World of Defoe*, 126.

[40] I take this term from Michael Brogden. See his "An Act to Colonise the Internal Lands of the Island: Empire and the Origins of the Professional Police," *International Journal of the Sociology of Law*, 15, 2 (May 1987), 179–208.

[41] The following account, like Thompson's, is based on *The Great Law of Subordination Consider'd*, 91–103. Defoe supplies "Edmund's" full name. Use only of his Christian name reinforced the tale that Thompson wanted to tell, one of an obsequious dependant, a child, hesitantly challenging his subordination for the first time.

[42] Ibid., 91.

[43] Thompson, *Customs in Common*, 37. See also 43 (Edmund was "called before the magistrate to account for default").

if Pratt continued in his refusal to perform, was to sue him for damages for breach of contract. Pratt's refusal to work, then, was not criminally punishable under existing law. "It was not the work of a Justice of the Peace ... he cou'd not make the Fellow work." Only apprentices and yearly servants-in-husbandry could be so compelled. Nor could a civil suit ("*long, chargeable, and uncertain*") produce an award of performance but only damages in lieu – an outcome, according to Defoe, "not worth [the clothier's] while."[44]

Thompson has mistold the tale's most important details. Yet to this point the story might still be judged, if not specifically an illustration of his "rise of free labor" trope, at least not wholly incompatible with it. One might, for example, suppose that the magistrate was reluctant to enforce old laws compelling labor that had fallen into disuse. And indeed, much later in the programmatic climax to his polemic, Defoe includes this charge in his inventory of fault. The laws were not sufficient, and "'tis long since they were made." The laws were ill executed; "Magistrates are degenerated in themselves." The laws in being should be made "more effectual" than they were.[45] This notwithstanding, Defoe's telling tale was not that of a reluctant or degenerate magistrate, but of a magistrate rendered helpless by the law's insufficiencies. The case did not lie, there were no grounds for a criminal complaint, no basis upon which he could proceed. And this is borne out by the reason Defoe gave for telling the story in the first place: his concern was not that appropriate laws were not being enforced, but that appropriate laws did not exist. The *Great Law* was an agitation for a remedy.[46]

Why is this important? First, because according to Defoe the "Deficiency of the Law" rendered the magistrate powerless to act. He could not require Pratt's attendance before him, he could only request it.[47] Second, because

---

[44] Defoe, *Great Law of Subordination Consider'd*, 91–3, 97 (emphasis in original). We have encountered precisely this situation in the mainland colonies discussed in Chapter 7.

[45] Ibid., 286–7. This is Robert Steinfeld's preferred position on the incident. See Steinfeld, *Coercion, Contract and Free Labor in the Nineteenth Century* (Cambridge and New York, 2001), 44 n.20, citing the piece-work clause of the Statute of Artificers as sufficient formal authority for the magistrate to take action. That argument, however, assumes both a uniformity to comprehension of the statute and the existence of a national jurisdiction within which it could be applied that the statute's own composition and history of enforcement comprehensively countervail. See Chapters 5 and 6.

[46] Thus, Defoe's *Preface* to the *Great Law* stated, at ii, "no Men who, in the Course of Business, employ Numbers of the Poor, can depend upon any Contracts they make, or perform any-thing they undertake, having no Law, no Power to enforce their Agreement, or to oblige the Poor to perform honestly what they are hir'd to do, tho' ever so justly paid for doing it." And again, at 92–3, "if the Laws of England are deficient in any thing, it is in this, namely, that they do not empower the Justices to compel labouring People who undertake work, to finish it before they be Employ'd by any other." Magistrates should be enabled to determine such matters "in a summary way," obliging the worker to give bail to perform, "or send him to the House of Correction till he was humble enough to go about it."

[47] Ibid., 93. The magistrate told the clothier, "he cou'd not make the Fellow work unless he would do it willingly ... but *pray go and tell him I would speak with him*," 92 (emphasis in original). This is what Thompson describes as a summons.

Pratt was well aware of the deficiency ("it seems the Fellow knew"), his demeanor before the magistrate ("looking something Confident") takes on a coloration completely at variance with the brow-knuckling ingratiation that Thompson attributes to him. The magistrate was bluffing and Pratt knew it.[48] And third, because Defoe felt all such exhibitions of "insolence" were humiliating, he campaigned for the law to be changed, for magistrates to be furnished with the means to discipline an existing independence.[49] And not only in this case, but all others like it: "A Servant who hires himself to a poor Farmer, to do his business, and runs from him in Harvest, as much as in him lies betrays him [sic], and ruins him; and this very thing is so notoriously practis'd at this time, and is so much a Grievance, that the Parliament, since my writing these Letters, have it under Consideration to oblige Servants to perform their Agreement, and stay out the Year; and to empower the Justices of Peace, and proper Officers, to punish fugitive Servants."[50]

Defoe was confident of Parliament's response. "We shall soon have a very severe Law upon that Subject."[51] And he was right. "More free to choose"? Edmund Pratt had faced the magistrate knowing that a meaningful legal distinction separated his working life from those to which the criminalized disciplines of service applied. The distinction (between *employment* and *service*) kept him from jail, it recognized his mastery of himself, and it acknowledged that his choice to work or not as he pleased was not one to be coerced.

[48] Thompson describes Pratt's behavior as "the calculated obsequiousness" of one who wished "to struggle free from the immediate, daily, humiliations of dependency" but to whom "the larger outlines of power, station in life, political authority, appear to be as inevitable and irreversible as the earth and the sky." *Customs in Common*, 43. He concludes, "Cultural hegemony of this kind induces exactly such a state of mind in which the established structures of authority and modes of exploitation appear to be in the very course of nature" (43). Defoe, in contrast, writes that Pratt's knowledge of the law "made him not only saucy and peremptory to his Employer, but very pert, and almost impudent before the Justice," to whom he spoke "*in as merry a Manner as I could desire*." *Great Law of Subordination Consider'd*, 93, 96 (emphasis in original).

[49] "The unsufferable Behaviour of Servants in this Nation is now (it may be hop'd) come to its Height; their Measure of Insolence, I think, may be said to be quite full." Ibid., i. Insolence is a word often encountered in eighteenth-century Anglo-American discourse applied not only to the behavior, manner, or speech of working people considered by the observer insufficiently deferential, but also to their apparent willingness to work. Thus in 1745, Josiah Tucker, dean of Gloucester, equates the idleness of "the *lower* class of people" with "brutality and insolence." In Thompson, *Customs in Common*, 383. Interestingly for my purposes, the etymology of insolence indicates that the word had also been used to describe unused or neglected land: Thus *Palladius on Husbandry*, 12:57 (c.1420): "Where is lond vnkept & insolent [*regio insolens et incustodita*] Take from the tronke al clene, vntil so hie As beestis may by noon experiment Atteyne; and there let bowis multiplie." See the *Oxford English Dictionary* (entry for "insolent") at http://dictionary.oed.com (accessed 22 August 2009), and Hans Kurath, editor, *Middle English Dictionary* (Ann Arbor, 1952), Part U.2, 207 (entry for "unkept").

[50] *Great Law of Subordination Consider'd*, 282–3.

[51] Ibid., 283.

Justice: Well, but why will you not finish the Piece of Work you began?
Edmund: Does he say, I won't finish it Sir?
Justice: He says you don't finish it.
Edmund: There's much Difference, and 't please you, between don't and won't.

But Parliament annulled the distinction in the Woollen Manufactures Act of 1725. Thereafter the Pratts of the whole island could no longer ignore their employers and instead lie "Drunk and sotting in the Alehouse" whenever they chose. Neglect or abandonment of work by weavers was made a criminal offense, punishable by imprisonment. By a stroke of law, Parliament made Pratt's employer what a year previously he had not been – Pratt's master.[52]

The Woollen Manufactures Act was but one of many similar statutes passed by Parliament in the century following 1720, collectively establishing an ever-widening ambit for criminalized discipline in the employment relationship.[53] In 1765, Blackstone confirmed the emergence of

---

[52] Ibid., 91, 97. See 12 Geo. I, c. 34 (1725), *An Act to Prevent Unlawful Combinations of Workmen Imployed in the Woollen Manufactures, and for Better Payment of their Wages*, at §II: "if any person actually retained or employed as a woolcomber or weaver, or servant in the art or mystery of a woolcomber or weaver shall ... depart from his service before the end of the time or term for which he is or shall be hired or retained, or shall quit or return his work before the same shall be finished, according to agreement, unless it be for some reasonable or sufficient cause ... [he] shall be committed to the house of correction, there to be kept to hard labour for any time not exceeding three months."

[53] The following are the most important: 7 Geo. stat. 1, c. 13 (1720), *An Act for Regulating the Journeymen Taylors within the Weekly Bills of Mortality*; 9 Geo. c. 27 (1722), *An Act ... for Better Regulating* [*Journeymen Shoemakers*]; 13 Geo. II, c. 8 (1740), [journeymen and other persons employed in the leather trades]; 20 Geo. II, c. 19 (1747) *An Act ... for the Better Regulation of [Certain] Servants and of Certain Apprentices* (and extending to "servants in husbandry ... artificers, handicraftsmen, miners, colliers, keelmen, pitmen, glassmen, potters, and other labourers employed for any certain time, or in any other manner," amended in 1758 to apply to hirings in husbandry for less than one year); 22 Geo. II, c.27 (1749), *An Act for the more Effectual Preventing of Frauds and Abuses committed by Persons employed in the Manufacture of Hats, and in the Woollen, Linen, Fustian, Cotton, Iron, Leather, Fur, Hemp, Flax, Mohair and Silk Manufactures* (and extending to "any Person or Persons whatsoever, who should be hired or employed" in any of the stated industries); 6 Geo. III, c. 25 (1766), *An Act for Better Regulating Apprentices and Persons working under Contract* (and extending to "Artificers, Callicoe Printers, Handicraftsmen, Miners, Colliers, Keelmen, Pitmen, Glassmen, Potters, Labourers, and others"); 17 Geo. III, c. 56 (1777), *An Act for Amending and Rendering More Effectual* the Act of 22 Geo. II, c.27. The trend culminated in the Act of 4 Geo. IV, c. 34 (1823), *An Act to Enlarge the Powers of Justices in determining Complaints between Masters and Servants, and between Masters, Apprentices, Artificers and Others.*" For summaries and further details, see Marc Linder, *The Employment Relationship in Anglo-American Law: A Historical Perspective* (Westport, Conn., 1989), 62–4; George White, *The Laws Respecting Masters and Work People* (London, 1824; repr. New York, 1979). In this light it is not at all surprising that when Lord Mansfield and his King's Bench brethren came to consider the meaning of employment halfway through this hundred-year sequence of increasing statutory severity, they determined that employment and service had become legally indistinguishable. Whether working by the day or the piece, in one's own house or elsewhere, to be *employed* by another was, "*quoad hoc*," to be the *servant* of a *master*, subject to all the statutory and common-law disciplines that service entailed.

"master and servant" as a generic legal category applicable to all relations of employment "whereby a man is directed to call in the assistance of others, where his own skill and labour will not be sufficient to answer the cares incumbent upon him."[54] Robert Steinfeld agrees that "these eighteenth- and nineteenth-century statutes represented a genuinely new departure,[55] and no wonder. Throughout the century Parliament responded continuously and increasingly generally to the rapid expansion and extension of English labor and product markets. One can term the process a "uniformalization" of the legal culture of work – the creation of a ubiquitous legal structure for an increasingly uniform economy, grounded on the criminalization of employment contract breach wherever it might occur, every "County, Riding, Division, City, Liberty, Town, or Place."[56] As Defoe put it at the outset, "the Circumstances of things are alter'd in the Nation." All the laws in being between masters and servants, employers and workers, required Parliamentary inspection and "a new Regulation." The "unsufferable Burthen" of insubordination was "a *National Grievance.*" Its resolution lay in law "strictly observ'd" throughout "*Great-Britain.*"[57]

Over the course of the eighteenth century, Mandeville's multitudes would be inured to work by law at least as much as by the relativities of their material deprivation. Indeed, the surplus that supported the leisure of Mandeville's minority, which it was supposedly the lot of the multitude to produce, was far more an artifact of law than of need. Take our

---

Hart v. Aldridge, 1 Cowp. 55, 98 English Reports 964 (1774). See also *Blake v. Lanyon*, 6 T.R. 221, 101 English Reports 521 (1795).

[54] Sir William Blackstone, *Commentaries on the Laws of England* (1st edition Oxford, 1765–69; facsimile edition Chicago, 1979), I, 410.

[55] Steinfeld, *Coercion, Contract and Free Labor,* 42. Steinfeld does refer to the statutes as a "revitalization" of elements of Tudor legislation, but his larger argument presents them as a departure from the "comprehensive" regulation and compulsory labor provisions of the Tudor statutes in favor of penal enforcement of contracts that were ostensibly freely entered, and hence an unmistakably coercive accompaniment of modern "free" labor. I have already had occasion to question the comprehensiveness of the Tudor statutes, but I am certainly at one with Steinfeld in his conclusion that compulsion and modern free wage labor are no contradiction.

[56] This statement of spatial ubiquity is taken from 22 Geo. II, c. 27 (1749). On market extension, see Steinfeld, *Coercion, Contract and Free Labor,* 42–7, particularly 46. On state formation and trends in the responsiveness of local government to national policies, see Joan R. Kent, "The Centre and the Localities: State Formation and Parish Government in England, circa 1640–1740," *The Historical Journal,* 38, 2 (1995), 363–404. Kent argues that "institutional changes and innovations in procedure ... made government in the localities more uniform, more professional, and more accountable," and as well that local elites grew willing "to implement national policies" (363). For the same, expressed as legal effects, see Christopher W. Brooks, "Litigation, Participation, and Agency in Seventeenth- and Eighteenth-Century England," in David Lemmings, editor, *The British and their Laws in the Eighteenth Century* (Rochester, N.Y., 2005), 155–81.

[57] Defoe, *Great Law,* 286, 287, 297 (emphasis in original). On the ideological and cultural formation of Britain during the eighteenth century, see David Armitage, *The Ideological Origins of the British Empire* (Cambridge, 2000), 170–1; Linda Colley, *Britons: Forging the Nation, 1707–1837* (New Haven, 1992).

representative weaver: once his needs were sufficiently met, his choice was to stop producing altogether. He preferred his own leisure to subsidizing that of others:

> Edmund: I work for nothing but Money; and why should I work if I do not want Money? would anybody work if they had Money enough?
>
> Justice: No, not if they had enough, it may be, they would not; but what do you call enough?
>
> Edmund: Why, if in the Morning I have enough to spend for that Day, that's enough to me; for to Morrow I can work for more.[58]

For the minority to get its leisure subsidized, Pratt's exercise of his own leisure-preference – what Defoe was pleased to call his "insolence" – had to be curbed: hence the Woollen Manufactures Act and its progeny. Once bodies had chosen to work, inuring them to that work required that they be prevented from working only as they chose. By the mid-nineteenth century, according to Daphne Simon's venerable estimate, ten thousand criminal prosecutions for breach of employment contracts were occurring every year.[59]

But there was more to it than that. Reminiscent of the younger Hakluyt, Defoe's travel narratives and his writings on economics constantly stressed the intertwined relationship between English domestic prosperity and order, labor mobilization, and transoceanic expansion.[60] Take for example his *Plan of the English Commerce*: "An Encrease of Colonies encreases People, People encrease the Consumption of Manufactures, Manufactures Trade, Trade Navigation, Navigation Seamen, and altogether encrease the Wealth, Strength, and Prosperity of England."[61] In Defoe's schema, the

---

[58] *Great Law of Subordination Consider'd*, 101.

[59] Daphne Simon, "Master and Servant," in John Saville, editor, *Democracy and the Labour Movement: Essays in Honour of Dona Torr* (London, 1954), 160–200; Steinfeld, *Coercion, Contract and Free Labor*, 72–82. See generally Douglas Hay, "England, 1562–1875," in Douglas Hay and Paul Craven, editors, *Masters, Servants and Magistrates in Britain and the Empire, 1562–1955* (Chapel Hill, 2004), 91–116.

[60] The comparison to the younger Hakluyt is far more than a matter of chance. Defoe's works reproduce both the younger Hakluyt's reliance on chorographic narrative and his conception of colonial commerce (shared with his elder cousin) as an intra-imperial monopoly that directly increases the wealth of the metropolis. The temporal gap between Hakluyt and Defoe in writing upon the economics of empire is filled by such as Francis Cradocke, *Wealth Discovered: Or An Essay upon a Late Expedient for Taking Away All Impositions and Raising a Revenue without Taxes* (London, 1661); Thomas Mun, *England's Treasure by Forraign Trade. Or, The Balance of Our Forraign Trade is the Rule of our Treasure* (London, 1664); Josiah Child, *A New Discourse of Trade* (London, 1694); and Charles Davenant, *Discourses on the Publick Revenues and on the Trade of England* (London, 1698). For commentary on Cradocke et al., addressing in particular such of their writings on plantations and colonies as influenced John Locke, see Arneil, *John Locke and America*, 88–117. See also Appleby, *Liberalism and Republicanism in the Historical Imagination*, 34–57, and Istvan Hont, "Free Trade and the Economic Limits to National Politics: neo-Machiavellian Political Economy Reconsidered," in John Dunn, editor, *The Economic Limits to Modern Politics* (Cambridge, 1990), 41–120.

[61] Daniel Defoe, *A Plan of the English Commerce* (London, 1728), 367.

role of working people in both metropolis and colonies was to be industrious and disciplined, work hard, accept their due subordination, and spend their earnings in consuming each other's products, thereby increasing commerce.[62] The "domestic" relationship between colonizing the island and mobilizing labor charted in the *Great Law* and the *Tour*, in other words, was reproduced at a transoceanic level in Defoe's speculations on the relationship between mobilizing labor and empire abroad.[63]

As the eighteenth century progresses, the "massive movement of people and goods" that marks the expansion of English empire becomes, both conceptually and institutionally, more and more sophisticated.[64] At the end of the century, one encounters that sophistication most clearly in Patrick Colquhoun's treatises *On the Police of the Metropolis* (1796), *On the Commerce and Police of the River Thames* (1800), and *On Indigence* (1806), which contemplate the complete and systematic consolidation of the terms of all transactions involving labor power around the money wage through an intensification of work discipline, an assault on leisure-preference, and a persistent criminalization of perquisites, complemented by "a free circulation of labour." In his *Wealth, Power and Resources of the British Empire* (1814), Colquhoun extends his scheme into a full-blown imperial political economy.[65] In the works of the Hakluyts, colonization and labor interacted principally through the *export* of disorderly population in the expectation it might become productive overseas. In Defoe's works, disorderly population is no longer for export. Intensified statutory discipline at home becomes part of the repertoire of improvement – it improves a realm that is simultaneously undergoing improvement by domestic colonizing and by the expansion of opportunities for domestic consumption and wealth accumulation that commodity-producing, manufacture-demanding colonies overseas provide. By the end of the century, Colquhoun's generalization of the wage form improves all the labor of the empire, binding all into one political economy through the extension of free circulation and commensurability throughout the British Empire, safeguarded by further intensifications of legal-contractual discipline.

---

[62] See Downie, "Defoe, Imperialism and the Travel Books," 92–3; Earle, *The World of Daniel Defoe*, 130–1, 161–2, 171–81.

[63] For recent (and distinct) explorations of which, see Hay and Craven, eds., *Masters, Servants, and Magistrates in Britain and the Empire*; and Peter Linebaugh and Marcus Rediker, *The Many-Headed Hydra: Sailors, Slaves, Commoners, and the Hidden History of the Revolutionary Atlantic* (Boston, 2000).

[64] Simon Newman, "Theorizing Class in Glasgow and the Atlantic World," in Middleton and Smith, eds., *Class Matters*, 34.

[65] Patrick Colquhoun, *A Treatise on the Police of the Metropolis* (London, 1796); Colquhoun, *A Treatise on the Commerce and Police of the River Thames* (London, 1800); Colquhoun, *A Treatise on Indigence* (London, 1806); and Colquhoun, *A Treatise on the Wealth, Power, and Resources of the British Empire* (London, 1814). See also Mark Neocleous, "Theoretical Foundations of the 'New Police Science,'" in Markus Dubber and Mariana Valverde, editors, *The New Police Science: The Police Power in Domestic and International Governance* (Stanford, Calif., 2006), 29–34.

In the mainland colonies, Part II showed, the legal culture of work as it affected Europeans was in no intelligible sense pervasively "unfree." Nor would that situation change much during the eighteenth century, except insofar as the spread of African slavery both prompted and permitted the white working population to elaborate upon its sense of its own defining difference.[66] Scholars have often read well-known English manuals that digested law and applicable procedure to advise seventeenth- and eighteenth-century Justices of the Peace as if they were also standard descriptions of the law of labor as it prevailed in early America; but they were not. Manuals published in the colonies for the use of local justices ignored English statutes disciplining labor, making offhand reference to their irrelevance to the mainland colonies' situation.[67] In marked contrast,

[66] See, for example, Simon Middleton, *From Privileges to Rights: Work and Politics in Colonial New York City* (Philadelphia, 2006), 139–46.

[67] See, for example, the *Conductor Generalis; or The Office, Duty and Authority of Justices of the Peace* (title varies) published in numerous editions between 1711 and 1794 in New York, Philadelphia, Woodbridge, N.J., and Albany, N.Y. The *Conductor* was an abridgment of well-known English manuals: Michael Dalton, *The Countrey Justice: Containing the Practice of the Justices of the Peace Out of Their Sessions* (London, 1619; published in numerous editions throughout the following century); Richard Burn, *The Justice of the Peace and Parish Officer* (London, 1743; published in numerous editions throughout the following century); and particularly William Nelson, *The Office and Authority of a Justice of Peace* (London, 1704; published in numerous editions). It was used widely throughout the middle colonies, as the preface to the edition published in Philadelphia 1792 notes. "For a number of years previous to the late revolution, this book has had a general and very extensive circulation, and as there have been several impressions of it since that period, it is manifest, that it is still looked on as a useful and necessary publication." The 1792 preface continued, "when it is considered, that the legislatures of most, if not all, of the United States, have adopted the laws of England as the ground-work of their respective codes, it will necessarily follow, that the republication of what, before that era, was deemed important, cannot, at present, be without its advantages. This, too, may account for what may, at first sight, appear as an absurdity; namely the frequent citing of British acts of parliament, and quoting of precedents and authorities from the most eminent lawyers of that kingdom." It is significant, then, that like its predecessors this 1792 edition was completely bare of English master/servant law. On eighteenth-century American JP manuals in general, see John A. Conley, "Doing it by the Book: Justice of the Peace Manuals and English Law in Eighteenth Century America," *Journal of Legal History*, 6, 3 (December 1985), 257–98. On the eighteenth-century American manuals' indifference to English labor law, see Tomlins, *Law, Labor, and Ideology*, 254–5, 256–7; see generally 239–58. Commentators like Benjamin Franklin insisted categorically that "the Statutes for Labourers ... are not in force in America, nor ever were." Leonard W. Labaree et al., editors, *The Papers of Benjamin Franklin* (New Haven, 1959–), XVII, 352. (It is worth noting that Franklin's statement was a retort to Josiah Tucker, dean of Gloucester, who, like Defoe, was one of the eighteenth century's foremost "propagandists of [labor] discipline." Thompson, *Customs in Common*, 383.)

In each of the main regions of settlement, we have seen, local statutes not English law set the terms and limits of the master-servant regime. Unlike the JP manuals published in the middle colonies and New England, which confined themselves to abridging English manuals, southern manuals attempted a more complete integration of local statutes with such English law as was in local use. Thus see George Webb, *The Office and Authority of a Justice of Peace ... Collected from the Common and Statute Laws of England, and Acts of Assembly, Now in Force; and adapted to the constitution and practice of Virginia* (Williamsburg, 1736),

nineteenth-century American authorities showed themselves well aware of the English statutes and of the common-law discourse of master and servant that supplied their terms of reference.[68] Courts cited the statutes knowledgeably, though opining how in America "public opinion [would

which precisely because it was not simply an abridgment is identified in Charles Warren, *History of the Harvard Law School and of Early Legal Conditions in America* (New York, 1908), I, 127, as the first law book *written* by an American. Webb's manual reproduces Virginia master-servant law and the law of slavery as it stood in the wake of the *Act Concerning Servants and Slaves* (1705) as amended (1726). As seen in Chapters 6 and 7, the statutes and local courts overwhelmingly identify the category "servant" as encompassing indentured migrants. Manuals published after Webb's confirmed this identification. Thus, in his *Office and Authority of a Justice of Peace Explained and Digested, under Proper Titles* (Williamsburg, 1774) – conceived as a revision and update of Webb – Richard Starke prefaced his title "Servants" with the statement "It must be understood that Servants are here distinguished from Slaves, and that they are also different from Hirelings, who engage themselves in the Service of another, without being obliged thereto by Transportation, or Indenture" (318–19). This was the only occurrence of the word "hireling" in the entire manual. In other words, hired labor existed entirely outside Virginia's master-servant regime. The point was underlined twenty years later by William Waller Hening in the first edition of his *The New Virginia Justice, Comprising the Office and Authority of a Justice of the Peace, in the Commonwealth of Virginia* (Richmond, 1795), at 405: "Persons contemplated by the act of the General Assembly, under the denomination of servants, are neither *Slaves, Hirelings*, who are citizens of this commonwealth, or *Convicts*." The same was the case in North Carolina. See James Davis, *The Office and Authority of a Justice of the Peace* (Newbern, N.C., 1774), 310–20; John Haywood, *The Duty and Office of Justices of Peace ... According to the Law of the State of North-Carolina* (Halifax, N.C., 1800), 212. See also *State v. Higgins*, 1 N.C. 36 (1792).

[68] In the early nineteenth century, John Bristed's *America and her Resources* (London, 1818), 460, could still be found denying the very existence of the relation of master and servant in America. By then, however, local abridgements and treatises had begun to chart a general turn to the use of master and servant as a generic common-law category for employment relations. For example, in the second edition of his *New Virginia Justice ... Revised, Corrected, Greatly Enlarged, and Brought Down to the Present Time* (Richmond, 1810), at 393–5, William Waller Hening noted that "the relation of master and servant" had become "of general concern" and added an entirely new section to his manual entitled "Master and Servant," dependent in its entirety on Blackstone's *Commentaries* and other late eighteenth-century English sources, that for the first time brought hireling labor in Virginia within the ambit of the relation. Hening's second edition continued to include the section on local servant law that had appeared in 1795, but it was completely separated from the new "Master and Servant" title, and had been amended to indicate that "Persons contemplated by the act of the general assembly, under the denomination of servants" were "such as were formerly denominated indented servants, concerning whom ... many laws have been enacted, which have now become obsolete" (527–8). See also Hening's third edition (Richmond, 1820), 466–8, 625–6. For comparable developments over the same period in the law in New England and New York, see Zephaniah Swift, *A System of the Laws of the State of Connecticut* (Windham, Conn., 1795), I, 218–24, and II, 59–67; Tapping Reeve, *The Law of Baron and Femme, of Parent and Child, of Guardian and Ward, of Master and Servant, and of the Powers of Courts of Chancery* 2nd ed. (Burlington, Vt., 1846), 339–77 (1st ed. New Haven, 1816); and Chancellor James Kent, *Commentaries on American Law*, in 4 volumes (New York, 1826–30), II, 201–15. In Philadelphia, the clerks keeping the docket of the Mayor's Court begin using "Master and Servant" as a descriptive category in January 1796 and reorganize cases on the docket accordingly. See City of Philadelphia Archives, Mayor's Court Docket. Timothy Walker's *Introduction to American*

not] tolerate a statute to that effect."[69] Throughout the nineteenth century, American courts applied all such powers as they possessed – common law and statutory – to effect a regulation of all such labor indiscipline as they could reach. How could anyone possibly think, said the U.S. Supreme Court in *Robertson v. Baldwin* (1896), that the Thirteenth Amendment's prohibitions against involuntary servitude could protect sailors from arrest and imprisonment for departing their employment? Even after such legalized disciplines were finally relaxed, well into the twentieth century, labor was still not "free" of legal impediment for the employment contract "was deemed to include 'implied' terms which reserved to the employer the full authority and direction of employees."[70]

To pore over the history of Anglo-American labor law from early modernity to the present, then, is to uncover a world that simply does not comply with "the implied Whiggism of standard labor history"[71] or with that of its traditional radical alternatives. It is a world in which, in England, over the course of the eighteenth century, "employees" become "servants,"

Law (Philadelphia, 1837) embraces master and servant as a generic legal category of American law, adverting all the while to its "strangeness" to republican ears. Thirty-six years and a civil war later, James Schouler found master and servant "rather a repulsive title ... fast losing favor in this republican country" and "hostile to the genius of free institutions." See his *Law of the Domestic Relations* (1st ed., Boston, 1870), 8, 599. Thirty years on, the 6th (1905) edition of Schouler's thesis reported (this time, however, in a footnote) that master and servant was still "rather repulsive" and still "fast losing favor" (3–4, n.2). As to its hostility to the genius of free institutions, Schouler had fallen silent. Rather more matter-of-factly, as already noted, Schouler's contemporary Horace Gay Wood held in his *Treatise on the Law of Master and Servant* (Albany, 1877), generally regarded as the first modern American treatise on the subject, that master and servant embraced "all who are in the employ of another, in whatever capacity" (3–4). See the conclusion to Chapter 7.

[69] *Robertson v. Baldwin*, 165 US 275 (1896), 281. The statement was of course quite incorrect, for long before 1896 there were lots of statutes "to that effect." Penal sanctions for the enforcement of labor contracts were used to mediate the abolition of slavery in the North prior to the Civil War, with little evidence of public disapproval. They were also used in the Northwest Territory, in the South following the war, and in colonized territories such as Hawai'i. See Steinfeld, *Coercion, Contract and Free Labor*, 255–89. Amy Stanley has also shown how, after the Civil War, vagrancy laws North and South coerced free workers and freedmen both to enter and remain in binding wage contracts on penalty of imprisonment, again without evidence of disapproval from "opinion leaders." See Amy Stanley, *From Bondage to Contract: Wage Labor, Marriage, and the Market in the Age of Slave Emancipation* (New York, 1998), 98–137.

[70] *Robertson v. Baldwin*, 165 US 275 (1896), 281, 287–8; James B. Atleson, *Values and Assumptions in American Labor Law* (Amherst, 1983), 14, and generally 1–16. See generally David Montgomery, *Citizen Worker: The Experience of Workers in the United States with Democracy and the Free Market during the Nineteenth Century* (New York and Cambridge, 1993), 13–114; Tomlins, *Law, Labor, and Ideology*, 265–92. See also Karen Orren, *Belated Feudalism: Labor, the Law and Liberal Development in the United States* (New York and Cambridge, 1991), 68–159; Lea VanderVelde, "The Gendered Origins of the *Lumley* Doctrine: Binding Men's Consciences and Women's Fidelity," *Yale Law Journal*, 101, 4 (January 1992), 775–852.

[71] William H. Sewell, Jr., "History in the Paranoic Mode?" *International Labor and Working-Class History*, 39 (Spring 1991), 21.

not vice versa. It is a world in which, hard on the heels of the eighteenth-century creation of the English employee-servant, one encounters the nineteenth-century creation of the American equivalent. This is a world in which Edmund Pratt cannot play the role Edward Thompson assigned him, of exemplar of labor's journey along a trajectory from subordination to negotiation, because no such journey occurred: by concentrating upon the loosening of the bonds of explicit servitude – apprenticeship, indentured servitude, and eventually slavery – we have ignored the changes, the tightenings, in the social and legal meaning of employment that began in England during the eighteenth century and continued in America during the nineteenth century. It is a world, finally, in which many of the phenomena over which we pore are consequences of expansion and circulation. It is a world of empire and of empire's unremitting thirst for improvement.[72]

Though Edmund Pratt cannot, therefore, stand for "progress," neither does he stand for a uniform declension, from autonomy to subjection. That would be nothing more than revision by inversion. Rather, he stands at the beginning of the eighteenth century for the possibility that remained in "the human condition of plurality."[73] Of all the social orders of early-modern society, working people "may well have been the least homogenous."[74] Both in early-modern England and in early mainland America, working people were constituted in an extraordinary variety of relationships: they were apprentices – in husbandry and in trades; they were servants – minor and adult, domestic and out-of-doors, in husbandry, under covenant; they were housewives and "helps"; they were outworkers and artisans; they were day-laborers, workmen, yeomen, journeymen, artificers, artisans, hirelings. In England's American colonies, besides all these, they were indentured servants, and slaves as well. Widely varying conditions of autonomy and dependence, profoundly fractured by race, gender, wealth, and age, were represented in a variety of legal categories of labor spread across multiple economic functions and regional cultures ranging from forms of employment whose original distinguishing characteristic was that their denizens claimed immunity from direction from any source,[75] through the relatively

---

[72] I pursue this matter further in "Afterword: Constellations of Class in Early North America and the Atlantic World," 219–33.

[73] Arendt, *The Human Condition*, 7. Recall that for Arendt, "plurality is specifically the condition – not only the *conditio sine qua non*, but the *conditio per quam* – of all political life."

[74] A. Hassell Smith, "Labourers in Late Sixteenth-Century England: A Case Study from North Norfolk [Part 1]," *Continuity and Change*, 4, 1 (1989), 31.

[75] In 1771, for example, the Pennsylvania glass manufacturer Henry William Stiegal offered a reward for apprehension of a craftsman who had quit his employment in a dispute over wages owed as a runaway. The workman offered a public rejoinder in the *Pennsylvania Packet* (11 November 1771), p. 3, col. 1: "As [Mr. Stiegal] has forfeited the covenants on his part, I have a right to leave his employ and to bring an action against him; for, I am not by the laws of nature, to drudge and spend my whole life and strength in performing my part of the articles, and Mr. Stiegal not paying me my wages. I have taken the opinion of an eminent gentleman of the law upon the articles, who declares, no person can be justified in apprehending me, as I am no servant, and that any person so doing will subject himself to an action of false imprisonment."

greater answerability of the hireling, to the variety of degrees and tempo-
ralities of subjection and attachment represented in the household and its
different forms of service, and so on to the total and permanent subjection
of enslavement.[76]

What this suggests is that, prior at least to the early eighteenth century
in England, the early nineteenth in America, work as an activity cannot
be allowed to imply a single conceptualization of labor as a form of social
action, such that *labor* can be understood as an expression of common-
denominator social and legal characteristics reproduced across a diversity
of relationships. To encounter labor in English and American history is to
encounter not a single form of relationship but multiple forms, some of
sanctioned abuse and abasement (those old disciplines), some of temporary and shifting attachment, some of autonomy and self-direction. It is an
encounter not with a uniform subjectivity but with multiple subjectivities.

When, eventually, these multiple forms began to be represented as a single form, the nature of that form was in good part consequential upon the
deployment in English and American law of generic rules implementing
uniform relations of subjection (master and servant) to pertain between
those who worked and those for whom they worked.[77] It is at this point, not
by the action of *need* but by the action of *law*, that one begins to encounter
labor in the uniformalized category, the single subjectivity (crudely, wage-
work) that it has assumed in liberal modernity, to which all the rest – slavery, housewifery, &c. – become "other." Liberal historiography has labeled
this uniformalized category "freedom," and certainly the assertion of their
freedom was a matter of the first importance to its inhabitants, as indeed
it always had been. But the truth of the claim lies in the details, and in the
legal details of the uniformity that prevailed one finds something rather
less than freedom.[78]

Modernity's single subjectivity, "free" labor, does have a history, therefore, just not the history of progress that normalizes it. Earlier chapters have
shown that both in England and its mainland American colonies, many of
those who worked – usually adult, male and white; often (but by no means
always) skilled – could and did engage in work relations that were initiated
in voluntary transactions governed by civil and not criminal law. They have
also shown that early-modern regulatory regimes were highly porous; that

---

[76] Legal descriptions of these different statuses were composed of definitional specificities
rather than generalities. Prior to Blackstone, at least, English law books bespeak a concern with the creation of authoritative orderings of specificities, not with jurispruden-
tial generalizations. Law's claims to discursive generality and universality – Thompson's
"equity" and "justice" – are historical and political specificities, not essences. See generally Peter Goodrich, *Languages of Law: From Logics of Memory to Nomadic Masks* (London,
1990), 1–148.

[77] I use the term "generic" advisedly, for what I am arguing for is precisely the creation
of a general legal category in a place where previously there had existed a series of
particulars.

[78] I have explored some of these ambiguities in *Law, Labor and Ideology*. See also Steinfeld,
Coercion, Contract and Free Labor; Orren, *Belated Feudalism*.

in England particular regional legal cultures could sustain the negotiation of practical freedoms by such workers even when hemmed in by legislation that purported to impose national regulation; and that in any case, even in statutory form "national" regulatory generalities were a composite of regional particularities that responded to a complex array of interests and collective claims of civic right. As the tale of Edmund Pratt suggests, that is, the freedom of work organized transactionally by contracts and agreements was not a modern invention. During the eighteenth century, this chapter has so far argued, that situation had begun to change. By colonizing the island the metropolitan state displaced porous, decentralized, and disparate early-modern regulatory regimes in favor of a regime that was coherent, pervasive, nationally enforced.

Though this new national regime was founded on coercive resort to criminal sanctions, what it criminalized was *contract* breach. No one was compelled to enter upon work, unless without visible means of support. Need and law cooperated to drive people to work and keep them in it, but this was quite compatible with an ideology of "consent."[79] The "new laws" that Defoe had deemed "absolutely necessary to enforce the Obedience of Servants" were to "oblige them to continue in their Places, according to the Time they respectively *agree* for, when they are hir'd."[80]

Neither in England nor its colonies, however, did this emerging social world of covenants and contracts, of free labor exercised and its exercise enforced, encompass the full extent of the world of work. This world of labor sat atop another, defined by distinct structures of socio-legal relations – the world of the household, of production but also of reproduction. Law's manifold contributions to the "inurings of bodies" are clearly on display in the construction of the household too, in the law of man and wife, and of parent and child. Each was a body of doctrine with which the law of master and servant enjoyed growing commonality: by the early nineteenth century the three were intimately intertwined as the law of domestic

---

[79] One should note, of course, that "need" was hardly autonomous of "law." As Defoe has shown us, law's manipulation of "need" was a crucial aspect of the production of disciplined labor in both the English and the American case. Thus, in the course of the manual *Laws Concerning Masters and Servants* (London, 1767), written to instruct English JPs, its author, a "Gentleman of the Inner-Temple," observes that the wage-fixing clauses of the Statute of Artificers remain in effect and urges, Defoe-like, that they be used to drive down the price of labor. "High Wages serve only to debase the Morals of Servants, and make them more idle; a Fellow who earns three Shillings a Day, is not content now a days with keeping *Saint* Monday as it is called, but thinks it early enough to begin the Week on *Thursday* Morning, as he can by *Saturday* Night, get enough to subsist him till *Thursday* again; By which the Master loses one half of his Time, and the Servant gains nothing; but wastes one half of the Week in spending what he has got in the other half" (233). For further exploration of the law-need axis in the English case, see Richard J. Soderlund, "'Intended as a Terror to the Idle and the Profligate': Embezzlement and the Origins of Policing in the Yorkshire Worsted Industry, c.1750–1777," *Journal of Social History*, 31, 3 (Spring 1998), 647–69. For the same in the American case, see Tomlins, *Law, Labor, and Ideology*, 96n.; Stanley, *From Bondage to Contract*, 98–137.

[80] Defoe, *Great Law of Subordination Consider'd*, 301 (emphasis added).

relations, a new composition laboriously constructed over the previous two centuries.[81] But the law of the household had a genealogy distinct from the contractual world of labor, one founded in patriarchy. Nor was the household the sum of patriarchy's prescriptive ambition. Indeed, the development of polity and economy, the new world of economic and civic action, was balanced on patriarchy no less than on the new property (the "*meum* and *tuum*") from which Lockean liberalism constituted and theorized its state and its workers. Patriarchy's presence in the mix was just a little bit less overt, that's all.

II. Household and Polis

Once more, Daniel Defoe supplies a first point of entry. For Defoe, the subordination he thought appropriate to the ordering of the labor process properly began in the household. The chaos of insubordination in service and labor that so vexed him in the *Great Law* was a marker of a more general crisis in the household, one in large part the fault of "the very *Masters* and *Mistresses* of Families themselves" who had improperly "slacken'd the Reins of Family Government." Heads of households were failing in the performance of an essential jurisdictional role – that of "good Governour to his Family," of ensuring "justice" within the household – upon which order in society and economy was founded.[82] "As things are now, Masters, or Heads of Families, are no more Masters; *Subordination* seems to be at a *Crisis*, and the Government is shar'd between the Head and the Tail, the Master and his hir'd Servant; the last receives the Wages indeed, but the work is done when and how the hir'd Gentlemen please to perform; and if they think fit, 'tis often not done at all."[83]

Though Defoe's demand in 1724 that Parliament adopt a "severe law" was addressed to the necessity for social discipline in the emerging national economy that he would shortly describe in the *Tour,* Defoe's conception of the structure of that economy remained in large part familial. Discipline hence meant reinforcing magisterial authority in the household. Defoe wanted measures that made "sufficient Provision ... for preserving the Government of our Families from the Encroachments and Usurpation of our Servants."[84] Household discipline could not exist without the state: it was precisely to the state that Defoe went in his quest for enforcement of household rule. But household discipline could not be created by the state: proper discipline required the reassertion of an original capacity of moral command, "an orderly and vertuous Governing of Families," without

---

[81] On the processes of composition of domestic relations law, see Holly Brewer, "The Transformation of Domestic Law," in Michael Grossberg and Christopher Tomlins, editors, *The Cambridge History of Law in America* (Cambridge and New York, 2008), I, 288–323.

[82] Defoe, *Great Law of Subordination Consider'd,* 286–7, 292, 293.

[83] Ibid., 288–9.

[84] Ibid., 288.

which "no Laws, Acts of Parliament, or publick Regulations, will be effectual to this Purpose."[85]

Scholarly debates over the relationship between household, state, and economy have focused on changes over time in the distribution among different jurisdictional locations of socially authoritative rule over economic activity. Predominantly, change has been given a unidirectional character. Flows of authority have been thought of as one-way movements away from the pre-modern or early-modern autarkic patriarchal household toward social interdependence structured by a politics of individual consent, instancing one of whig history's most enduring clichés: the decomposition of patriarchy in a posited shift "from status to contract."[86]

Patriarchy, however, is not necessarily the embodiment of status; nor is consent patriarchy's nemesis. In early-modern England, status meant the enjoyment of differential legal capacities, and hence the determination of legal outcomes, largely by inherited position within a hierarchical social-political structure ("Aristocracy ... an Assembly of certain persons nominated, or otherwise distinguished from the rest"[87]) in which allegiance flowed upward to elite lordship in exchange for downward flows of protection.[88] Such status relations could certainly be conceptualized as patriarchal in origin, but not necessarily so.[89] Contract, in contrast, posits formal equivalence in legal capacity, hence the determination of outcomes according to individual consent without the necessity of reference to subject position within any social or legal hierarchy. But contract is not

[85] Ibid., 293.

[86] Henry Sumner Maine, *Ancient Law: Its Connection with the Early History of Society, and its Relation to Modern Ideas* (New York, 1864), xl. See generally Steven Mintz and Susan Kellogg, *Domestic Revolutions: A Social History of American Family Life* (New York, 1988). Among labor law historians, Robert Steinfeld has subtly addressed household and market as jurisdictions, but appears generally inclined to go along with the traditional status-to-contract shift. The effect of this is a progressive "silencing" of the household as the "market" (notwithstanding its contradictions, ambiguities, and coercions) takes over, an interpretive schema that imposes a logic of irreversible liberal modernizing. See Steinfeld, *The Invention of Free Labor,* 3–9, 55–60, 147–63, 185–7. On markets, see his "The *Philadelphia Cordwainers'* Case of 1806: Alternative Legal Constructions of a Free Market in Labor," in Christopher L. Tomlins and Andrew J. King, editors, *Labor Law in America: Historical and Critical Essays* (Baltimore, 1992), particularly 20–4. For distinct accounts of the status-contract trajectory in the American case, see Jeanne Boydston, *Home and Work: Housework, Wages, and the Ideology of Labor in the Early Republic* (New York, 1990), and more generally Linda K. Kerber, *Women of the Republic: Intellect and Ideology in Revolutionary America* (Chapel Hill, 1980). I explore Boydston's account further in section IV of this chapter.

[87] Thomas Hobbes, *Leviathan: or the Matter, Forme, & Power of a Common-wealth Ecclesiasticall and Civill* (London, 1651), 98.

[88] Steve Hindle, *The State and Social Change in Early Modern England, 1550–1640* (New York, 2002), 42, 44. See generally Richard Lachmann, *From Manor to Market: Structural Change in England, 1536–1640* (Madison, Wis., 1987); also the discussion in Chapter 2 of relations of ligeance and their exploration in *Calvin's Case* (1608).

[89] Sir Thomas Smith, *De Republica Anglorum: A Discourse on the Commonwealth of England* (written between 1562 and 1565; first published 1583), L. Alston, editor (Cambridge, 1906), 23, 25–6.

incompatible with patriarchy.[90] Though "status to contract" is not a meaningless formulation, historically it obfuscates more than it clarifies. Rather than status to contract, we are better off conceptualizing the birth of liberal modernity in a movement from lordship to consent.[91]

Lordly hierarchies constituted the essence of the state (as seventeenth-century Anglo-American colonizing designs attest). Lordly hierarchies were patriarchal, in that lordship depended for its practical longevity on the maintenance and servicing of lineage – the preservation of concentrations of landed wealth through primogeniture. They were dependent too upon delegation of much of the practice of governance – the discipline, education, and maintenance of dependents, for example – to household heads.[92] But within a decentralized political-governmental structure founded on landed lordship, subordinate household heads' capacity to exercise their own patriarchal authority was at best qualified.[93] In champion England, for example, the character of most land tenures meant ultimate authority rested with manorial landlords, their institutions, and the body of manorial custom and law governing subordinate tenures.[94] Regionally, the extent of household autonomy, and hence of effective jurisdiction, varied inversely with the strength of manorial lordship (and, in incorporated towns, of corporate governance). External scrutiny was "tightest in well-governed corporate towns, close in nucleated villages, [but] comparatively loose in the scattered woodland and upland settlements where family and household enjoyed most autonomy."[95] Patriarchal households were strongest, that is, where manorialism was weakest.

[90] Gordon J. Schochet, *Patriarchalism in Political Thought: The Authoritarian Family and Political Speculation and Attitudes Especially in Seventeenth-Century England* (Oxford, 1975), 7–10.

[91] See generally Holly Brewer, *By Birth or Consent: Children, Law, and the Anglo-American Revolution in Authority* (Chapel Hill, 2005).

[92] Carole Shammas, "Anglo-American Household Government in Historical Perspective," *William and Mary Quarterly*, 3rd Ser., 52, 1 (January 1995), 108. See also generally Carole Shammas, *A History of Household Government in America* (Charlottesville, 2002), 24–52; Markus Dirk Dubber, *The Police Power: Patriarchy and the Foundations of American Government* (New York, 2005), 3–46.

[93] Studies of English family structure and kinship indicate that kinship ties and extended families were strongest among elites and weakest at the bottom. The core of most English households was nuclear, not extended. In other words, insofar as decentralized landed lordship actually left significant room for ordinary household heads to exercise autonomous jurisdictional authority over household subordinates (and here recall the clearly delimited authority of the patriarchal household unit outlined in More's *Utopia*: see Chapter 4, section I), the effective ambit of that authority was not very extensive. See Ralph A. Houlbrooke, *The English Family, 1450–1700* (London and New York, 1984), 14–15, criticizing the views of Lawrence Stone, *The Family, Sex and Marriage in England, 1500–1800* (New York, 1977), e.g., 6–7. See also Brewer, *By Birth or Consent*, 230–87; Dubber, *Police Power*, 36–40.

[94] Brewer, *By Birth or Consent*, 339–40. See also A.W.B. Simpson, *A History of the Land Law* (Oxford, 1986), 155–72.

[95] Houlbrooke, *The English Family*, 23. See also generally Barry Levy, *Quakers and the American Family: British Settlement in the Delaware Valley* (New York, 1988); Margaret R. Somers, "Rights, Relationality and Membership: Rethinking the Making and Meaning

Both legally and politically, the exercise of governance internal to the household by its patriarchal head was compromised by clear jurisdictional boundaries. In the late sixteenth and seventeenth centuries, parents were severely restricted in their capacity to exercise determinative legal control over the legal actions of their children. Children could and did bind themselves to contracts, usually labor contracts, often at very young ages, without parental consent. Nor were parents able to assert a supervening custody right that trumped the claims of others – masters and/or guardians.[96] In matters falling within ecclesiastical court jurisdiction too, such as marriage contracts or wills, children could act legally without any requirement of parental consent. In general, "The head [of household] in early modern England, as in the rest of western Europe, exercised no power over life or limb of his dependents; he could not take as many wives as he pleased, force a son or daughter to marry, or sell his servants. Over time, the medieval monarchies and the Christian church, for their own reasons, had worked to limit such prerogatives of patriarchs."[97]

"Worked to limit" carries the connotation that although monarchy and church made inroads on its expression, patriarchal prerogative had nevertheless provided the original pre-modern default understanding of political authority, and that the household had anciently been its institutional expression and locale. Classical political theory does indeed grant the autarkic patriarchal household major significance in the creation of human societies, polities, and economies, a significance revived in early-modern European political theory. Crucially, however, classical political theory did not depend on familial analogies to produce an account of political obligation, or of institutional structure. Rather, the two were held separate: the autarkic household was conceived to be a crucial condition for the existence of political association, but not itself an instance of political association, nor an institutional model for association. No familial account of the origins of political obligation was attempted before the later sixteenth century.[98] Moreover, when it did appear, principally in English political thought, it did so already intertwined with contractual theories of association. Politically, that is, patriarchal and contractual accounts of association rose together, as two sides of the same argument, not as successive alternate statements in a teleological process of modernization.

Little "genuine" political theorizing occurred in England before the second half of the sixteenth century. According to Gordon Schochet, "prescription appears to have been the most widely accepted basis of legitimacy. Obedience was due to the reigning king simply because he was in

of Citizenship," *Law & Social Inquiry*, 19, 1 (1994), and "Citizenship and the Place of the Public Sphere: Law, Community and Political Culture in the Transition to Democracy," *American Sociological Review*, 58, 5 (October 1993).

[96] Brewer, *By Birth or Consent*, 230–87.

[97] Shammas, "Anglo-American Household Government," 107. See also Peter Laslett, *Family Life and Illicit Love in Earlier Generations: Essays in Historical Sociology* (Cambridge and New York, 1977), 4.

[98] Schochet, *Patriarchalism and Political Thought*, 19, 54.

power."[99] To the extent that the obligation to obey kingly power was theorized, its foundations were located in God's injunction to obey magistrates.
But obedience could be owed without much theorizing of its foundations
because the practical reach of monarchical power, hence the effect of obedience, was delimited. Political authority was not centralized but dispersed
through structures of local and regional lordship.[100] When necessary, dispersed lordly authority could make its opinions known collectively, through
Parliament,[101] but Parliament's relationship to the monarchy was advisory.
As long as the monarch did not seek to enlarge the practical extent of its
own sphere, Parliament had no need to extend or theorize a countervailing claim to its own sovereign authority.

The appearance of contending theories of political obligation and association signifies the growth of pressure upon the sixteenth century's practical accommodation of delimited central monarchical power with regional
lordly authority. Tudor and Stuart ambitions to create a more powerful
metropolitan state – one that possessed ascendancy over both church and
magnates, one with executive authority rather than merely influence in the
regions – meant resistance. Resistance required theorization. Debates over
the origins of political obligation and association, that is, arose not in a
vacuum but coincident with contests over the proper location of legitimate
rule, and the role of particular institutions in exercising rule.

Smith and Hooker

At the outset, patriarchal and contractual accounts were not distinct. The
sudden efflorescence of patriarchalism in English political thought attests
to a growing awareness of the capacities of households and their heads to
take part in the maintenance of a social order undergoing political and economic crisis and experiencing stress and fragmentation in the institutional
hierarchies relied upon to that point; it was a seizure upon the household
as a newly appropriate model of hierarchical obligation.[102] But patriarchalism's early exponents expressed no intimation of any necessary contradiction between patriarchal and contractual modes of thought. Thus, in *De
Republica Anglorum* Sir Thomas Smith (1513–77) found "in the house and
familie ... the first and most naturall (but private) apparance of one of the
best kindes of a common wealth, that is called *Aristocratia*, where a few and
the best doe governe ... not one alwaies." He found in the collectivity of

99 Ibid., 37. For, as it were, "pre-political" theorizing in England, see Ernst H. Kantorowicz,
   The King's Two Bodies: A Study in Mediaeval Political Theology (Princeton, 1957).
100 We have seen (Chapters 5 and 6) that those structures were highly uneven in their
   effectiveness.
101 As Brewer notes, "a Parliament whose members (of both houses) were substantial property owners could be seen, as it was in the late Middle Ages, as a division of lordship
   rather than the representation of those below." *By Birth or Consent*, 46.
102 See, for example, David Underdown "The Taming of the Scold: The Enforcement of
   Patriarchal Authority in Early Modern England," in Anthony Fletcher and John Stevenson,
   editors, *Order and Disorder in Early Modern England* (Cambridge, 1985), 116–36.

houses and families the material that constituted the nation: "so from one to another in space of time, of many howses was made a streete or village, of many streetes and villages joyned together a citie or borough. And when many cities, boroughes and villages were by common and mutuall consent for their conservation ruled by that one and first father of them all, it was called a nation or kingdome."[103] Still, Smith called the household nothing more than a metaphor for *Aristocratia*, for it was "but an house," no more than "a litle sparke resembling as it were that government."[104] And both Smith's households and the nation they spawned had their origins in a distinctly contractual moment – an initial "society or common doing of a multitude of free men collected together and united by common accord and covenauntes among themselves, for the conservation of themselves aswell in peace as in warre." House and family did not precede the moment of covenant but rather grew from it: "if this be a societie, and consisteth onely of freemen, the least part thereof must be two. The naturalest and first conjunction of two toward the making of a *further* societie of continuance is of the husband and of the wife."[105] Husband and wife formed their further, private, society in an association that was highly gendered in its division of labor, yet not overtly patriarchal in its internal order, in that "ech obeyeth and commaundeth other, and they two togeather rule the house."[106] Households coalesced in "cities, boroughes and villages," which, in their turn, created a state that was overtly patriarchal, "ruled by that one and first father of them all," but who did so "by common and mutuall *consent*."[107] Initially a kingdom, on the death of the first patriarch king the political form of the nation became an "*aristocratia*" of male heads of families (the founding king's "brethren", his "sonnes," their "sonnes and nephewes, and such"). Finally, as their numbers increased over time, "it came to passe that the common wealth must turn and alter as before from one to a few, so now from a few to many … bearing office and being magistrates." And so the commonwealth became a patriarchal republic, the prince governing with the advice of a parliament constituted from among all the sorts of men who ruled.[108]

[103] Smith, *De Republica Anglorum*, 23, 24.
[104] Ibid., 23.
[105] Ibid., 20, 22 (emphasis added).
[106] Ibid., 23. "House" meant "the man, the woman, their children, their servauntes, bond and free, their cattell, their household stuffe, and all other things, which are reckoned in their possession, so long as all these remaine togeather in one" (23).
[107] Ibid., 24 (emphasis added). The "consent" referred to here is the consent of the various cities, boroughs, and villages to submit "for their conservation" to a single ruler. How consent is obtained, and from whom, is left unclear. Smith refers to "societie" consisting of "freemen" but it is clear from the text that both husbands and wives are encompassed in the category "freemen." Overall, Smith's formulation is passive – "And when many cities, boroughes and villages were by common and mutuall consent for their conservation ruled by that one and first father of them all, it was called a nation or kingdome" (24).
[108] Ibid., 24, 25, 27.

Aristotle gave Smith's theory of rule its second contractual moment (the common and mutual consent of households coalesced in cities) but not the first. In identifying the covenant of freemen as an original point from which both family and, eventually, the patriarchal state grew, Smith rejected Aristotle's derivation of "the entire social order from the primitive household."[109] But in fact Smith's primary goal was less to explain rule than to describe its appearance in the contemporary English state. The existence of law and governance was not per se problematic, hence theorizing the basis of obligation was unnecessary. Even when "the common wealth is evill governed by an evill ruler and unjust.... Certaine it is that it is alwayes a doubtfull and hasardous matter to meddle with the chaunging of the lawes and government, or to disobey the orders of the rule or government, which a man doth find alreadie established."[110]

Smith's near contemporary, Richard Hooker (1554–1600), followed a course of reasoning in many respects similar. But Hooker was more faithful to Aristotle, more overt in his attempts to theorize rule, and more explicitly patriarchal both in his account of the nature of rule within households and the relationship between rule in the household and in the state.

Like Smith, Hooker began with men in a natural state, "living singly and solely by our selves," who "forasmuch as we are not by our selves sufficient to furnish our selves with competent store of things needful for such a life as our Nature doth desire ... are naturally induc'd to seek Communion and Fellowship with others," voluntarily uniting in "Politick Societies," which "could not be without government, nor government without a distinct kind of Law," through which to address the "defects and imperfections" of their original condition.[111] Unlike Smith, however, Hooker represented family not as a *further* society consequent upon the original formation of society among freemen, but more in Aristotelian vein as an explicitly patriarchal order of being, anterior to political society, itself founded in nature. In their natural state, "to take away ... mutual grievances, injuries and wrongs," men had ordained "some kind of Government publick" and had yielded themselves "subject thereunto." But men had done so already as patriarchs of families. "To fathers within their private Families Nature hath given a supream Power; for which cause we see throughout the World, even from the Foundation thereof, all Men have ever been taken as Lords and lawful Kings in their own Houses." In Hooker's discourse, patriarchy was synonymous not only with nature, but with Creation itself.[112]

A natural order of patriarchy and hierarchy in the family predisposed household heads to accept patriarchal monarchic rule in the state. But familial patriarchy did not furnish an unproblematic theory of rule in the state, for Hooker could discover no natural origin for any obligation of

---

[109] Schochet, *Patriarchalism and Political Thought*, 50.

[110] Smith, *De Republica Anglorum*, 13.

[111] *The Works of that Learned and Judicious Divine, Mr. Richard Hooker, in Eight Books of the Laws of Ecclesiastical Polity, Compleated out of his own Manuscripts* (London, 1705), 85.

[112] Ibid., 86.

household heads to accede to the rule of other men as such: "Howbeit, over a whole grand multitude, having no such dependency upon any one, and consisting of so many Families, as every politick Society in the World doth; impossible it is, that any should have compleat lawful Power but by consent of Men, or immediate appointment of God." Rule in the state had to be by virtue of the consent of male household heads, or divine right, because rulers as such did not possess "the natural superiority of Fathers."[113]

The contributions of Smith and especially Hooker to late sixteenth-century English political thought signify a rapidly emerging awareness, amid the contemporary "crisis of order," of the patriarchal household as a key institution of contemporary social ordering,[114] and at the same time a comparative lack of differentiation between contractual and patriarchal discourse. Each discourse provided key conceptual components of both men's work. As patriarchal and contractual thought became more sophisticated, and as the political and institutional crisis of the English state deepened during the seventeenth century, exponents came to concentrate precisely on the nexus between obligation in household and state. As they did so, their diverging theories of obligation yielded different implications for theories of rule in household and in state. At the end of the century, with contractual theory clearly ascendant in the representation of the basis of rule in the state, patriarchy had become as well secured in the household.

Filmer and Locke

"Crises of legitimation engender questions about the entitlement of those in power to rule, and about the obligation which subjects have to obey them."[115] So it was that, during the course of the seventeenth century, patriarchal and contractual theories of rule became explicitly opposed, each developing in identification with a different side in England's long revolution. Patriarchalism became a key discourse in defense of monarchical ascendancy. On his coronation, according to James VI of Scotland, a king became "by the law of nature ... a naturall Father to all his Lieges."[116] As a father was "bounde to care for the nourishing, education and vertuous gouernment of his children," so was a King "bounde to care for all his subjects."[117] But natural fatherhood was not the basis of kingly rule. Writing five years after Hooker, James VI found that subjects obeyed their

---

[113] Ibid.

[114] Schochet, *Patriarchalism and Political Thought*, 57, 63–4.

[115] Daniela Gobetti, *Private and Public: Individuals, Households and Body Politic in Locke and Hutcheson* (London and New York, 1992), 17.

[116] *The True Lawe of free Monarchies: or, The Reciprock and Mutuall Dutie Betwixt a free King and his naturall Subjectes* (Edinburgh: printed by Robert Waldegrave, 1598), sig. B₅v. And see James's first address to the English Parliament following his coronation (also noted in Chapter 2) which included the statement, "I am the Husband and all the whole Isle is my lawfull Wife; I am the Head and it is my Body." King James VI and I, *Political Writings*, Johann P. Sommerville, editor (Cambridge, 1994), 136.

[117] *True Lawe of free Monarchies*, sig. B₅v.

king not as a father in a great household but as the ruler designated by
God to rule over them. It was God's grace that created legitimate rule,
God's "throane in the earth" upon which kings sat, whose "*minister*" they
were, and on whose behalf they administered justice and judgment to the
people, procured obedience and peace, decided controversies, and sought
prosperity. It was to God (not the people) to whom was owed "the count
of their administration." Politically, the subject of James's discourse, the
"reciprock and mutuall dutie betwixt a free king and his naturall subjects,"
was a creature of the king's accountability to God for the fairness of his rule
over subjects required to submit to it. "*Monarchie*" was "the true paterne of
Diuinitie." Fatherhood carried no comparable determinative or reciprocal
weight. The relationship between king and subject was merely analogous to
the natural order of the household, not founded in it.[118]

It was in Filmer that the two became united (or, as Daniela Gobetti puts
it, "assimilated"[119] – rendered conceptually identical):

> If we compare the Natural Rights of a Father with those of a King, we find
> them all one, without any difference at all, but only in the Latitude or Extent
> of them: as the Father over one Family, so the King as Father over many
> Families extends his care to preserve, feed, cloth, instruct and defend the
> whole Commonwealth. His War, his Peace, his Courts of Justice, and all his
> acts of Sovereignty, tend only to preserve and distribute to every subordinate
> and inferior Father, and to their Children, their Rights and Privileges; so
> that all the Duties of a King are summed up in an Universal Fatherly Care
> of his People.[120]

Like James VI, Filmer grounded the rule of the king not in the consent
of household heads, here labeled "subordinate and inferior," but in a grant
from God. The grant that Filmer stressed, however, was not as conceived by
James, that of God's ministry to his people. Rather, "the ultimate ground
of paternal/kingly power [was] the *proprietorship* over the earth and its creatures which God assigned to Adam in creating him." Here, in Adam, was a
beginning that embodied a threefold assimilation – of household patriarchy, monarchical dominion, and property. In creating this "one adult self-
sufficient male," God chose to make simultaneously the first "monarch of
the world" (the original embodiment of *monarchia universalis*) and the first
patriarchal proprietor of everything in it – *imperium* and *dominium* over all,
by God's grace. "All human beings, starting with Eve, are thus not merely
Adam's dependents, but rather his possessions."[121]

---

[118] Ibid., sigs. B$_3$r, B$_3$v.

[119] Gobetti, *Private and Public*, 44, 46.

[120] Sir Robert Filmer, *Patriarcha: Or the Natural Power of Kings* (London: Printed by Walter Davis, 1680), 24.

[121] Gobetti, *Private and Public*, 49 (emphasis added). It was precisely proprietorial authority over the earth and its creatures, one should note, that had been underlined across the years of English colonizing discourse since the early seventeenth century. See Chapter 4.

Conjoined in Adam, the state and patriarchal proprietorship were one and the same hierarchy, monarch and household head rendered identical.[122] But as Gobetti points out, "if paternal power and political power have the same origin, foundation, nature, and extent, then a problem of conflicting jurisdictions immediately arises."[123] The monarch is a patriarch, but not all patriarchs can be monarchs. Filmer's patriarchal conjunction had obliterated the Aristotelian distinction between the interior hierarchy of the household and the exterior world of politics created by independent and equal heads of household, as well as the contractarian ideal of an original compact of free and equal individuals. "There never was any such thing as an Independent Multitude, who at first had a natural Right to a Community: this is but a Fiction, or Fancy of too many in these days, who please themselves in running after the Opinions of Philosophers and Poets, to find out such an Original of Government, as might promise them some title to Liberty, to the great Scandal of Christianity, and Bringing in of Atheism, since a natural freedom of mankind cannot be supposed without the denial of the Creation of Adam."[124] Assimilation of household and state meant humans were born into an undifferentiated (non-plural) condition "of subjection to their father/monarch ... without any right of redress."[125]

Patriarchal theory had, it appeared, assimilated to itself the logic of early-modern lordship, creating a socio-political structure "in which the distinction between a private and a public sphere is merely rhetorical, and where fathers, dispossessed of their natural authority, will only exercise authority over household dependents as delegates of the sovereign ... In the logic of assimilation, the monarch dispossesses fathers of their power and incorporates their domains into his. Households are no longer the private possessions of adult males who can dispose of them at their discretion, but are merely branches or agencies of a centralized public power."[126] In fact, Filmer stopped short of so complete an assimilation, arguing that households and their heads retained an existence and a jurisdiction distinct from the domain of the monarch. Yet precisely to avoid compromising the greater patriarchal jurisdiction of the monarch, Filmer rendered

---

[122] For Filmer's decisive unification of arguments for monarchic divine right with patriarchal authority, see Schochet, *Patriarchalism and Political Thought*, 139–40.

[123] Gobetti, *Private and Public*, 53.

[124] Sir Robert Filmer, "Observations upon Aristotle's Politics, Touching Forms of Government," in *Observations Concerning the Original and Various Forms of Government* (London: Printed for R.R.C., 1696), Preface. Filmer continued: "And yet this conceit of Original Freedom is the only Ground upon which not only the Heathen Philosophers, but also the Authors of the Principles of the Civil Law; and Grotius, Selden, Hobs, Ashcam, and others raise, and build their Doctrines of Government, and of the several sorts or kinds, as they call them, of Commonwealths. Adam was the Father, King, and Lord over his Family: a Son, a Subject, and a Servant or a Slave, were one and the same thing at first; the Father had power to dispose, or sell, his Children or Servants."

[125] Gobetti, *Private and Public*, 52.

[126] Ibid., 53–4.

the lesser patriarchal jurisdiction of the father dependent where it counted most, in the reproduction of subordination in the household itself:

> though by the Laws of some Nations, Children, when they attain to years of Discretion, have Power and Liberty in many actions; yet this Liberty is granted them by Positive and Humane Laws only, which are made by the Supreme Fatherly Power of Princes, who Regulate, Limit, or Assume the Authority of inferiour Fathers, for the publick Benefit of the Commonwealth: so that naturally the Power of Parents over their Children never ceaseth by any Separation, but only by the permission of the transcendent Fatherly Power of the Supreme Prince, Children may be dispensed with, or priviledged in some cases, from obedience to subordinate Parents.[127]

Filmer, patriarchy's defender, thus chose to subordinate the household head to the state in the interests of maintaining the monarch's supervening paternal authority. Patriarchal intervention by the monarch in the realm of the father expressed the public interest of the commonwealth, distinct from and superior to that of natural fathers, heads of household, and expressed in laws that trumped unalloyed parental power.[128]

If the contradiction in patriarchal reasoning lay precisely in its denial of patriarchal autonomy to household heads in the interests of the greater patriarchy of the state, in contractual reasoning, supposedly patriarchalism's obverse, the contradiction lay in the continuing effusions of patriarchy that it accommodated. In appearing to separate paternal from political power, in creating private and public, contractualists appeared to refute patriarchalism's attempts to derive politics from nature. Political authority was conventional, founded on the consent of plural free and equal persons, not a natural order of subordination founded on the natural ascendancy of fathers over children. Yet contractualists did not deny that patriarchal ascendancies were natural, or that politics could be hierarchical. In fact, their segregation of the household from the polis allowed them to achieve what patriarchal theory could not – the possibility of an autonomous patriarchal household founded in nature. So doing, contractual theory actually tracked the social emergence of the patriarchal household out of its original subordination to lordship and toward the relative autonomy that, amid the fragmentation of other institutions, took shape during England's long seventeenth-century trudge toward modernity. They created the political and philosophical conditions necessary to support what, in the later

---

[127] Filmer, *Observations Concerning the Original and Various Forms of Government*, 226.

[128] Gobetti, *Private and Public*, 54. See also Pateman, *The Sexual Contract*, 84. Pateman too notes the "insoluble problem" of Filmer's identification of paternal and political right – that patriarchal kings and patriarchal fathers contradicted each other. Filmer, we have seen, gave primacy to the patriarchal king. His solution to the problem of the household head – which was no solution philosophically but only practically – was to continue ascribing unlimited power over household dependents to fathers while actually limiting power according to the actualities of state ascendancy. Rather than assimilate all households to the great household of the king, Filmer allowed the distinct existence of private households but in subordination to the state.

eighteenth century, Blackstone would confidently dub "the empire of the father."[129] And at the same time, because they founded politics on contract among formally free and equal individuals whose actual (though hidden) identity as political actors was determined by sex-right, contractualists also ensured that patriarchy would be central to the political public realm as well as the familial private realm that they had succeeded in creating.

The best illustration of these implications of the course of contractualist theory, and also the most logical choice of counterpoint to Filmer (because so much of his theorizing was devoted to a refutation of Filmer's patriarchalism) is to be found in the work of John Locke. Locke made manifest his ambition to undermine patriarchalism's defense of political absolutism in the subtitle of his *Two Treatises of Government* (1689), which promised that the reader would find in the first treatise "The False Principles and Foundation of Sir Robert Filmer, and His Followers are Detected and Overthrown."[130] Locke's, however, was not an assault on hierarchy as such.[131] Rather, it was a forceful and successful attempt to distinguish politics as a sphere of activity from human beings' social or private relations.

Politics and patriarchy, Locke argued, were quite distinct. Political authority and obligation was founded in convention, not nature (or grace). The power of a magistrate over a subject, even in matters of life and death, was founded on the subject's consent that the magistrate wield the power. The powers of "a Father over his Children, a Master over his Servant, a Husband over his Wife, and a Lord over his Slave," in contrast, were different from political powers and not to be appropriated to politics by the magistrate. Alike in the one respect that they were not political, they were dissimilar in others, some founded in nature, others on agreement, others apparently on sheer force. Because their practice often coincided – "All which distinct Powers happening sometimes together in the same Man" – analogical reasoning resulted in confusions. Hence "it may help us to distinguish these Powers one from another, and shew the difference betwixt a Ruler of a Common-wealth, a Father of a Family, and a Captain of a Galley."[132]

Paternal and conjugal authority was founded in nature. "The Law of Nature" obliged all parents "to preserve, nourish, and educate the Children, they had begotten, not as their own Workmanship, but the Workmanship of their own Maker, the Almighty, to whom they were to be accountable for them." The powers that parents enjoyed were consequent upon that duty.[133] Nature, too, was at the root of the submission every wife owed her husband.[134] Entry upon marriage was contractual, but in marriage, just as

---

[129] Blackstone, *Commentaries on the Laws of England*, I, 441.

[130] Locke, *Two Treatises of Government* (for the complete title see earlier in this chapter, n.12).

[131] Ibid., 204 [§54].

[132] Ibid., 166 [§2].

[133] Ibid., 205 [§56]. Schochet notes that the "parental" power of the First Treatise was treated as a synonym for "paternal" power in the Second. See Schochet, *Patriarchalism and Political Thought*, 248–50.

[134] As to the relationship between nature and God, said Locke, God gave no political (magistratical) authority to Adam over Eve, to men over their wives, "but only foretels what

Eve had been made subject to Adam by God, so "every Husband hath [a Conjugal Power] to order the things of private Concernment in his Family, as Proprietor of the Goods and Land there, and to have his Will take place in all things of their common Concernment before that of his Wife."[135]

The submission of servant to master, in contrast, was that of one free man to another, and hence could have no natural foundation. A servant was merely one who sold "for a certain time, the Service he undertakes to do, in exchange for Wages he is to receive."[136] The distribution of power in the relationship purportedly extended no further than was encompassed by the contract itself. Locke was willing to acknowledge that exogenous conditions could make a nonsense of actual bargaining. The bare equality of property in self was easily overwhelmed by the disparities of power inherent in differential proprietorship of things (land, commodities). Nonetheless, in Lockean discourse, exchanges between a "Rich Proprietor" and the "Needy Beggar" who "preferr'd being his Subject to starving" still qualified as consensual and contractual because the contract was not the point of origin of the disparities between them.[137]

Yet in fact the contract was precisely the means to the reproduction of exogenous asymmetries as endogenous conditions of service itself.[138] Hence the separation – and equality – that Locke argued for was not only purely formal, but in fact nonexistent. Considered as a contractual institution, "servitude *structurally requires* an asymmetrical power relation."[139] The service contract both acknowledges the anterior condition of disciplinary asymmetry structurally essential to the operation of the institution and reproduces it in each specific instance of contracting. The servant would discover that entry into the transaction had transferred to the master as a matter of course much more than a right to the services sold: the wage that purchased the value that service added also purchased control over the detail of the servant's performance. "The contract in which the [servant] allegedly sells his labour power is a contract in which, since he cannot be separated from his capacities, he sells command over the use of his body and himself."[140] Historically, this had by no means been true of all

should be the Womans Lot, how by his Providence he would order it so, that she should be subject to her husband, as we see that generally the Laws of Mankind and customs of Nations, have ordered it so; and there is, I grant, a Foundation in Nature for it." Locke, *Two Treatises*, 46 [§47]. See also Pateman, *The Sexual Contract*, 52–3.

[135] Locke, *Two Treatises*, 46 [§48].

[136] Ibid., 228 [§85].

[137] Ibid., 41 [§43].

[138] On exchange asymmetry, see William M. Reddy, *Money and Liberty in Modern Europe: A Critique of Historical Understanding* (New York, 1987), 62–106.

[139] Gobetti, *Private and Public*, 74 (emphasis added). See generally Christopher L. Tomlins, "Law and Power in the Employment Relationship," in Tomlins and King, eds., *Labor Law in America*, 71–98, and "Subordination, Authority, Law: Subjects in Labor History," *International Labor and Working-Class History*, 47 (Spring 1995), 56–90; Steinfeld, *Coercion, Contract and Free Labor*, 10–26.

[140] Pateman, *The Sexual Contract*, 151. Ton Korver puts it thus, writing of the modern employment contract: "To enter a labor contract ... is to accept a non-negotiable status. The regular purposive contract is neutral to status, for it regards it as a datum of the transaction

contracts for the performance of work.[141] It was rather a convention. But in English law during the course of the eighteenth century it would be a convention extended to and inserted in the meaning of employment in general.[142]

Slavery, as we shall see in Chapter 9, required the greatest asymmetry of all – so great, indeed, that for Locke it could not be encompassed by contract. Slavery was at once a permanent alienation to another of property in person, and an exhibition of absolute magistracy – vesting powers of life and death in the master – that comported neither with the lesser asymmetries of the other nonpolitical relations nor with the conventional foundation of politics.[143] Locke set an absolute, but at the same time low, threshold for the difference of slavery: "if once Compact enter ... Slavery ceases."[144] Free men could sell themselves, and command of

at hand. The labor contract, in contrast, first defines the status of employers and employees as those who may issue and enforce orders and those who have to obey. The duty to obey is a personal one. An employee cannot let himself be represented by someone else. However interchangeable and substitutable the job that the employee has to perform may be, the worker himself is contractually bound to an individual, nonsubstitutable responsibility for his indistinguishable task. For the employee there is no intermediate zone between being there in person and quitting." Ton Korver, *The Fictitious Commodity: A Study of the U.S. Labor Market, 1880–1940* (Westport, Conn., 1990), 3. It is apparent from William James Booth's analysis of Lockean thought that this is a sufficient description of individual autonomy and freedom from a Lockean point of view. See Booth, *Households,* 162–76, confirming (at 164) that from a Lockean point of view "even the most severe constraints on available options [work or starve] do not render the labor contract unfree."

[141] In addition to the employment relationships discussed in Chapter 7, see Tomlins, *Law, Labor, and Ideology,* 229n. (discussing *locatio operis,* or the hiring of labor and services according to the law of bailments).

[142] See section I, this chapter. The historical arguments are summarized in Christopher Tomlins, "Early British America, 1585–1830," in Hay and Craven, eds., *Masters, Servants, and Magistrates in Britain and the Empire,* 117–52.

[143] Locke followed law of nations scholars (as we shall see in Chapter 9) in founding slavery on capture. "Freedom from Absolute, Arbitrary Power, is so necessary to, and closely joined with a Man's Preservation, that he cannot part with it, but by what forfeits his Preservation and Life together. For a Man, not having the Power of his own Life, cannot, by Compact, or his own Consent, enslave himself to any one, nor put himself under the Absolute, Arbitrary Power of another, to take away his Life, when he pleases. No body can give more Power than he has himself; and he that cannot take away his own Life, cannot give another power over it. Indeed having, by his fault, forfeited his own Life, by some Act that deserves Death; he, to whom he has forfeited it, may (when he has him in his Power) delay to take it, and make use of him to his own Service, and he does him no injury by it ... This is the perfect condition of Slavery, which is nothing else, but the State of War continued, between a lawful Conquerour, and a Captive." *Two Treatises,* 182–3 [§§23–4]. There is something of a contradiction, however, in Locke's contention that "a Man, not having the Power of his own Life, cannot, by Compact, or his own Consent, enslave himself to any one," given that he also argues that "whenever he finds the hardship of his Slavery out-weigh the value of his Life, 'tis in [the slave's] Power, by resisting the Will of his Master, to draw on himself the Death he desires." By choosing to induce his own death in preference to slavery, the slave does in fact retain power over his own life. In that sense the slave does consent to slavery as long as s/he prefers it to death and Locke's statement that slavery is the absence of compact is therefore incorrect.

[144] Ibid., 183 [§24]. See also 302 [§174].

their bodies, for "a certain time" and remain free. "For, it is evident, the Person sold was not under an Absolute, Arbitrary, Despotical Power. For the Master could not have power to kill him, at any time, whom, at a certain time, he was obliged to let go free out of his Service."[145] Free men could consent that powers of life over themselves be vested in the state for the whole of their lives without being thought slaves to the state's magistracy. The line Locke's formula drew was the line of permanent subjection to an extreme instance of private power ("Absolute, Arbitrary, Despotical Power") – the involuntary alienation of self for life to a private magistracy.[146]

Patriarchy, hierarchy, and coercion to the very lintel of slavery were all thus quite compatible with Locke's account of nonpolitical relations. So, however, were they with his account of the *polis*.

I have argued that, considered as tendencies in English political theory, patriarchalism and contractualism developed more or less simultaneously, rather than sequentially, and that their relationship was more one of interaction than simple opposition. Even during the tumult of the English Revolution, their separation was incomplete: sophisticated royalists, for example, defended the monarch's paternal powers but were willing to derive them not directly from primordial patriarchy but from "the consent of the people," by which they meant an original and irrevocable compact among then-existing household heads to "reduce themselves into a civill unitie, by placing over them one head, and by making his will the will of

---

[145] Ibid., 183 [§24].

[146] Pateman, *The Sexual Contract*, 70. The shallowness of Locke's threshold for the difference compact makes is evident in the extent to which his account of slavery simultaneously reproduces and differs from that of Hobbes. In *Leviathan* (1651), Hobbes too founds slavery on capture, and distinguishes between slavery and servitude by the entry of compact. But the compact of servitude in Hobbes begins in capture, not freedom – it is a permanent condition of parole forced upon captives by the alternative of immediate death; it signifies not freedom but lifetime service. "Dominion acquired by Conquest, or Victory in war, is that which some Writers call DESPOTICALL, from Δεσπότης, which signifieth a *Lord* or *Master*; and is the Dominion of the Master over his Servant. And this Dominion is then acquired to the Victor, when the Vanquished, to avoyd the present stroke of death, covenanteth either in expresse words, or by other sufficient signes of the Will, that so long as his life, and the liberty of his body is allowed him, the Victor shall have the use thereof, at his pleasure. And after such Covenant made, the Vanquished is a SERVANT, and not before: for by the word *Servant* (whether it be derived from *Servire*, to Serve, or from *Servare*, to Save, which I leave to Grammarians to dispute) is not meant a Captive, which is kept in prison, or bonds, till the owner of him that took him, or bought him of one that did, shall consider what to do with him: (for such men (commonly called Slaves,) have no obligation at all; but may break their bonds, or the prison; and kill, or carry away captive their Master, justly:) but one, that being taken, hath corporall liberty allowed him; and upon promise not to run away, nor to do violence to his Master, is trusted by him." G.A.J. Rogers and Karl Schuhmann, editors, *Thomas Hobbes Leviathan: A Critical Edition* (Bristol, UK, 2003), 161. The master/servant compact in Locke is presented ideally as a temporary and partial alienation – a sale of services. Yet the coerced lifetime use of his body at the pleasure of the master agreed by a captive exhibiting "sufficient signes" of will when confronted by imminent death will qualify not only for Hobbes but also for Locke as the entry of compact and hence cessation of slavery.

them all."[147] Contractualists were content to see a politics of consent and mutual compact conditioned by precisely the same original structure of familial patriarchy while arguing that the character of rule established by a compact among original patriarchs was qualitatively different from that which characterized their own households. "This kind of Authority is not to be indured in a State, because it is incompetent with liberty, provided onely for slaves, and such as have no true direct interest in the State."[148]

The Aristotelian distinction between polis and household could thus be detected in both strands of English political thought, so it is unsurprising that it should be found also in Locke. What was original to Locke's political theory was the further claim that legitimate governance was founded on continuing consent, not simply an original compact, for this enabled Locke at once to allow that government could be traced to familial origins and at the same time to deny those origins any value to the explanation of current political obligation. "Allegiance was due to the state because of the trust that it held and only so long as that trust was not violated. Thus, each generation and, in fact, each individual person theoretically retained the right to determine whether or not a government was properly performing its functions. If the answer was no, the base of political authority was liable to be withdrawn."[149] The state was continuously reaffirmed as conventional, and the distinction between polis and household, correspondingly continuously underscored. Consent purported to render familial hierarchy an asymmetry exogenous to politics no less than it purported to render material asymmetries exogenous to employment.

Yet, how credible, in fact, is the distinction? Locke's consenting individuals were all male proprietors.[150] This has been held irrelevant to the actual nature of the polis. Locke's theorizing was descriptive, not normative – "how *some* political societies *may* have *first* been established."[151] The qualifications of consenting individuals are hence not fixed. But if, as Carol Pateman puts it, civil freedom per se "is a masculine attribute and depends upon patriarchal right,"[152] the credibility of the "descriptive" liberal divorce of polis from patriarchy becomes less tenable. One discovers, rather, another instance of structural requirement. And indeed, Pateman's assertion is entirely accurate. Contract theorists challenged paternal right – generational dominion of fathers over sons – as the basis for political society, but not conjugal right, or what Pateman calls sex-right, the procreative precondition of fatherhood and the original political dominion

---

[147] See Schochet, *Patriarchalism and Political Thought*, 103–4, discussing [Dudley Digges], *The Unlawfulnesse of Subjects Taking up Armes against Their Sovereaigne in What Case Soever* (1643).

[148] Ibid., 105, discussing [Henry Parker], *Jus Populi: or, A Discourse Wherein Clear Satisfaction is Given* (London, 1644), 28.

[149] Schochet, *Patriarchalism and Political Thought*, 267.

[150] Pateman, *The Sexual Contract*, 3, 11, 13, and generally 1–18.

[151] Schochet, *Patriarchalism and Political Thought*, 263 (emphasis in original).

[152] Pateman, *The Sexual Contract*, 2.

granted Adam. Locke granted marriage foundational character – "the first Society was between Man and Wife"[153] – and correspondingly attempted to restate that foundational social compact in voluntaristic terms: its genesis was "voluntary Compact between Man and Woman."[154] But voluntary compact reproduced a "natural" subordination. "Locke agrees with Filmer, that there is a natural foundation for a wife's subjection. Thus Locke's first husband, like Adam, must have exercised conjugal right over his wife before he became a father. The 'original' political right or government was, therefore, not paternal but conjugal."[155] Just as the service contract was negotiated subject to conditions precedent that reproduced within the contractual relationship exogenous asymmetries of power, so male conjugal right was a condition precedent to marriage (and thus a condition precedent to all social formation) similarly reproduced as an exogenous asymmetry within the marriage contract.

The individuals that contractualism released from paternal dominion engaged in their acts of political creation on the same foundation of anterior control of procreative activity that patriarchal theory had embraced. Just as Filmer's father "denies any procreative ability to women, appropriates their capacity and transforms it into the masculine ability to give political birth," so Locke's victorious sons transmute "the awesome gift that nature has denied them ... into masculine political creativity."[156] Filmer's appropriation was an affirmation of a politics that assumed an absolutist hierarchy among men and hence severely limited political participation. Locke on the other hand embraced a desirably universal and continuing right of consent, though one contradicted in fact by exclusions. Both, however, appropriated to men alone the capacity for politically generative action.

There was nevertheless a major difference between Filmer and Locke in the theory and strategy of their appropriations. Filmer's paternalism, founded on hierarchical absolutism and the assimilation of family and monarchy, had no need to justify differentiation within the polis or out of it, either between men and women or among men. Political obligation was consequential upon the universal social-political rule of paternal right, of which the monarch's claim was the first and most fundamental instance. Denying that the foundation of political obligation lay in paternal right or familial duty, emphasizing instead that its foundations lay in the consent of autonomous individuals, Locke (unlike Filmer) had to find means

---

[153] Locke, *Two Treatises of Government*, 223 [§77].

[154] Ibid., 223 [§78]. Conjugal society consists chiefly in such "Communion and Right in one anothers Bodies, as is necessary to its chief End, Procreation" [§78]. Husband and wife have but one common concern, yet have different understandings and hence unavoidably sometimes different wills; in which case, "it therefore being necessary, that the last Determination, *i.e.* the Rule, should be placed somewhere; it naturally falls to the Man's share, as the abler and the stronger" 226 [§82]. See also 46 [§47].

[155] Pateman, *The Sexual Contract*, 93.

[156] Ibid., 95, 102.

to justify differentiation – to explain why autonomy, and hence participation in consent, was not universally enjoyed. None of these means could appear unmediated as limits on rights of participation; the very absence of such limits was the essence of contractualism's ascendancy as a theory of the polis. All, however, justified Locke's continuing discriminations in his descriptions of political participation, for all were reincarnated by contractualist theory *socially*, in the household, at a remove from the polis but still the condition of its formative contract. As Aristotle had indicated, as Locke fully accepted, the household remained the condition for the existence of the polis, because it was the locus of production and reproduction of the free individuals whose consent fashioned the polis. And by the eighteenth century, the household had become definitively what before it had not been, a private patriarchal order.[157]

III. Locke's Oikos

The process of producing and reproducing free individuals within the household was deeply conditioned by law. Not, to be sure, by the same law; we have already encountered Locke's "insistence on the specificity" of the subordination produced in each type of interpersonal relation existing within the household.[158] The servant's subordination was conditioned by contract, the child's by age, the slave's by the immanence of death, the wife's (the most stable of all) by nature. But the household stands as the crucial and historically specifiable point of intersection in the genealogy of each of these strands of legal discourse: the law of service and of employment, the law of conjugal and familial relations, the law of slavery. Well into the late nineteenth century, Anglo-American writers treated the interrelationship of these strands, spun together over the previous two centuries,[159] as both obvious and natural, a timeless legal homology – "the domestic relations" – that boxed the compass of normative social life.[160] Hence, the full title of Tapping Reeve's seminal American treatise, published in 1816: *The Law of Baron and Femme, of Parent and Child, Guardian and Ward, Master and Servant.*[161] Kent's *Commentaries on American Law* offered precisely the same

[157] In Locke it is clearly a paternal order, an empire of which the father was the prince, "Ruler in his own Household." *Two Treatises of Government*, 213 [§65], 221–2 [§§74–6], and generally 203–22, [§§52–76].

[158] Gobetti, *Private and Public*, 67.

[159] See generally Brewer, *By Birth or Consent*; Tomlins, *Law, Labor, and Ideology*. For the creation of an Anglo-American law of slavery, see Chapter 9.

[160] For examples of more contemporary scholarship attempting (from rather different perspectives) to bring employment and family law back together, see Mary Ann Glendon, *The New Family and the New Property* (Toronto, 1981); Amy Stanley, "Conjugal Bonds and Wage Labor: Rights of Contract in the Age of Emancipation," *Journal of American History*, 75, 2 (September 1988), 471–500; Stanley, *From Bondage to Contract*; VanderVelde, "Gendered Origins," 775–852.

[161] (New Haven, 1816), with *The Powers of the Courts of Chancery* and *An Essay on the Terms Heir, Heirs, and Heirs of the Body* thrown in for good measure.

set of structural connections.[162] A half century later, James Schouler was still presenting the law of service and employment as a subcategory of the law of domestic relations.[163] So was Irving Browne, although in a manner that hinted at an emerging separation.[164]

The commonalities among the domestic relations were commonalities of legal authority: of masters over apprentices, servants, slaves, employees; of husbands over wives; of parents over children. Categorical commonality did not mean that these were identical relations. Marriage and unenslaved service were distinguished from involuntary relations by the appurtenances of consent they had acquired. But consent applied to entry into a relationship already legally defined, not to entry upon a process of mutual design. Master-slave and parent-child relations were of course distinguished by the complete involuntariness of entry – at least so far as the slave or child was concerned – but otherwise they also came as, so to speak, preexisting conditions. Despite dramatic nineteenth-century reform movements, moreover, the domestic relations the century inherited exhibited substantial staying power, such that, in their essentials, legal structures governing production and reproduction put in position in the early decades of the nineteenth century remained in place at the century's end. Slavery's abolition, for example, did not mean the obliteration of master and servant law. If anything, by liberating master-servant's application to hirelings from the inhibiting impediment of an obvious (and damaging) comparison, it achieved the reverse. Emancipation, whether gradual or cataclysmic, eliminated a peculiarity from American law, not a genus, as one can tell from the renewed relations of restraint into which those emancipated were injected.[165] Contemporaneous changes in the law of coverture in marriage, meanwhile, were held "minor and relatively inconsequential" by disappointed mid-nineteenth century reformers, tinkerings that left the structure of coverture untouched. Even in areas of family law where more substantial reform did take place, as in paternal rights to the custody of children,

---

[162] Kent, *Commentaries*, II, Part 4 (1–253): "Of the Law Concerning the Rights of Persons."

[163] The full title of Schouler's treatise (1st edition Boston, 1870) was *A Treatise on the Law of the Domestic Relations; Embracing Husband and Wife, Parent and Child, Guardian and Ward, Infancy, and Master and Servant.* Schouler in 1870 was still reproducing a classically Lockean discourse of (a) consent's reproduction of exogenous asymmetries, and (b) the specificities of each relation of subordination. For example (at 599): "The relation of master and servant *presupposes* two parties who stand on an unequal footing in their mutual dealings; *yet not naturally so*, as in other domestic relations."

[164] Thus the title of Browne's treatise suggested a different slant than Schouler's: *Elements of the Law of Domestic Relations and of Employer and Employed* (Boston, 1883).

[165] See, e.g., ch. DCCCLXXXI, *An Act for the Gradual Abolition of Slavery* (1 March 1780), in *Statutes at Large of Pennsylvania*, X, 67–73; ch. LXII, *An Act for the Gradual Abolition of Slavery* (29 March 1799), in *Laws of the State of New-York, Passed at the twenty-second session, second meeting, of the Legislature* (Albany, 1798), 721–3, and ch. CXXXVII, *An Act Relative to Slaves and Servants* (31 March 1817), in *Laws of the State of New-York. Passed at the Fortieth Session* (Albany, 1817), 136–44; Stanley, *From Bondage to Contract*, 122–30.

"changed rules and rights overlaid but did not obliterate and replace older visions of marital rights."[166]

To the legal theorists of the early republic, men such as Reeve and Kent, those "older visions" of marital (and familial and employment) relations expressed the essential enduring order of human affairs "derived from the law of nature, and ... familiar to the institutions of every country."[167] As in other incarnations,[168] however, the law of nature furnished not a transhistorical meta-narrative of the human condition but rather an ark of convenience for – in this case – the numerous elements of the laws of sub-ordination that liberal modernity had excepted from its selective assault on patriarchal politics: the very elements, in fact, that sustained produc-tion and reproduction within the walls of the households of the free indi-viduals who formed the liberal polis.

In performing that role, the household appeared Aristotelian in its rela-tionship to politics and the state, "the root of our economy ... an asso-ciation of persons united in a certain purpose and mutuality (*philia*), in relations of domination and subordination, and striving for those ends that composed the good life as they understood it."[169] As William James Booth has put it, the Aristotelian household economy (*oikos*) is to be understood as the principal institution in which "human interchange with nature is conducted, in which that interchange is organized according to what is appropriate for the persons involved and for ends determined within the community of the *oikos*."[170]

As an organic community – that is, viewed from the "outside"– the *oikos* sought a collective freedom from dependencies upon others through autarky. At the same time, it "contained" the effects of the activities neces-sary to achieve that end by construing economic activity according to a standard of sufficiency, the securing of a *sufficient* livelihood, rather than a drive for wealth (*pleonexia*) that would trespass on and consume "that space needed for other and higher human possibilities."[171] The household

[166] Hendrik Hartog, "Mrs. Packard on Dependency," *Yale Journal of Law and the Humanities*, 1, 1 (December 1988), 89, and generally 79–103. See also Hendrik Hartog, *Man and Wife in America: a History* (Cambridge, Mass., 2002), for the argument that "the long nineteenth century of American marriage law" (1790–1950 by Hartog's reckoning) was characterized by "a legal vocabulary continuous with a long patriarchal tradition," albeit one "inflected and transformed ... in the American context, on the American conti-nent, through multiple marital regimes" (39). For compatible arguments in the realm of employment relations, see Tomlins, *Law, Labor, and Ideology*, 223–92; Christopher L. Tomlins, *The State and the Unions: Labor Relations, Law, and the Organized Labor movement in America, 1880–1960* (Cambridge and New York, 1985); Orren, *Belated Feudalism*, 68–159.

[167] Kent, *Commentaries*, II, 33.

[168] See Chapter 3.

[169] Booth, *Households*, 1.

[170] Ibid., 8; see generally 1–93. On the relevance of *oikos* to *œconomy* – that is, the theory and practice of colonial American household order, see Boydston, *Home and Work*, 18–20.

[171] Booth, *Households*, 88. William Manning made the point in 1798. "For the prinsapel hapi-ness of a Man in this world is to eat & drink & injoy the good of his Labour, & to feal that his Life Libberty & property is secure, & not in the abundance he poseses nor in being

economy of the *oikos*, then, gave leisure – release from toil, opportunity to participate in *vita activa* – primacy over accumulation as a value to be cherished. But the leisure that it was the object of the *oikos* to produce was not designed for equal distribution; it was not the role of the *oikos* economy to relieve all within from toil. Rather, its "containment" of economic activity had a dual meaning: the necessities of production were prevented (contained) from consuming the whole life and energies of the household by confining (containing) production within that portion of the household whose unrelieved duty it was to produce. Viewed from the "inside," the *oikos* was a rank-ordered hierarchy: "master, wife, servant, slave." This interior order "determines the source of command and of the purposes to be served by the economy":[172]

> The *oikos* is a community of persons living together, bound by a *philia* and sharing a common purpose, wealth creation within the framework of need-satisfaction and autarky. Giving this community its distinctive form, however, is its order, both human and inanimate: everyone and everything has its proper place ... [T]here is an order of authority and appropriate functions among [the household's persons]. The master oversees the *oikos*' outdoor work and the wife is the guardian of its indoor functions; a good steward manages the work of the household's servants and slaves. The master, the wife, and the servile laborers – these are the elements that compose the *oikos* hierarchy, and rulership is essential to that composition.[173]

The point of the ruled hierarchy of the *oikos*, its reason for being, is to realize the purposes of the *oikos* master. Those purposes – freedom from the necessities and obligations of self-support, allowing virtuous civic participation and a life of "*ta kala*" (noble and free action) – are not ignoble or necessarily self-serving, but their realization requires servile persons

---

the instrument of other mens miseryes." William Manning, *The Key of Libberty: Shewing the Causes Why a Free Government has always Failed, and a Remidy Against It* (Billerica, Mass., 1922), 66. On the ideology of "sufficiency," see generally Daniel Vickers, "Competency and Competition: Economic Culture in Early America," *William and Mary Quarterly*, 3rd Ser., 47, 1 (January 1990), 3–29.

[172] Booth, *Households*, 8. "The subordination of the laborer and the suppression, or containment, of the economy are thus intimately bound one to the other" (32). The contained economy "is understood as one in which compulsion reigns, whether induced by poverty and appearing in the forms of the unceasing necessity to labor or of submission to an employer or, in its most radical guise, caused by the subordination of slave to master. Being 'inside' the contained economy entails, in varying degrees, a constrained and unfree life, one without leisure and so with limited possibilities for the cultivation of excellence and for sharing in the higher *philia* that binds the truly human communities" (91). On the ubiquity of inside-outside distinctions in master-servant law – where the "inside" of the relation is both a rank-ordered hierarchy and an organic union to be protected from interferences from the "outside" – see Karen Orren, "Metaphysics and Reality in Late Nineteenth-Century Labor Adjudication," in Tomlins and King, eds., *Labor Law in America*, 160–79. The parallels to the other domestic relations (for example, the common vocabulary of "seduction" and "enticement") are obvious.

[173] Booth, *Households*, 39–40.

to undertake the "necessitous struggle for livelihood"[174] that sustains the master in their enjoyment.

> If nature were so abundant that there was no scarcity ... the economy could be contained without hierarchy, without transferring its burdens onto the shoulders of the servile. That not being the case, however, a human solution must be found to the scarcity and containment problems: slaves and servants, one's wife and children ... It is thus that the ancient theory of the economy moved from general propositions about scarcity and the neediness of the human condition, from theories of the good life and its relation to the production of human livelihood, to the necessary hierarchy that stands at the very center of their idea of community.[175]

The precise meaning of *oikos* freedom inhered in the containments that sustained it. The "hierarchy, domination and exclusion" central to the *oikos* community were not simply functional disciplinary controls in a common fight against scarcity – requirements of production – but chosen conditions of social existence.[176] The *oikos* was not a creature of survivalist necessity, not an organic disciplined pursuit of material self-sufficiency amid scarcity with a bonus of freedom at least for some. Rather, it was a creature of choice; choice of what constituted "the good life," choice of how to attain it, choice of who should enjoy it, choice of who should be worked to sustain it.[177]

In canvassing the dimensions of choice, it cannot but be immediately noticeable that the pinnacle of command and of benefit in the *oikos* economy is occupied by a male patriarch. Sexual differentiation characterizes the organization of the *oikos* as a whole: each side of the division between free and unfree is characterized by a further gendered division. "There is a vertical division of labor within the household, a division corresponding to the free or servile statuses of the various groups comprising the home's order. In the Homeric world the free plow and reap, but as a sport, a demonstration of prowess ... The servile, on the other hand, labor to produce, and they do so under the compulsion of a master. And within that ordering there is a further status differentiation: that between male and female. Free men and free women have different activities appropriate to their gender, as do their servile counterparts."[178] Yet it is clear that the luxuries of a life of

---

[174] Ibid., 27.

[175] Ibid., 92.

[176] The same is true, of course, of the managed division of labor of the modern world. The joining of authoritative hierarchy (management) to a distribution of functions is no more a requirement of modern technologies of production than of ancient. In both cases the arrangement is chosen. See Dan Clawson, *Bureaucracy and the Labor Process: The Transformation of U.S. Industry, 1860–1920* (New York, 1980); Christopher Tomlins, "'Of The Old Time Entombed': The Resurrection of the American Working Class and the Emerging Critique of American Industrial Relations," *Industrial Relations Law Journal*, 10, 3 (1988), 426–44, at 433–4, 442–3.

[177] This, as we have seen, was the political economy of Mandeville and Defoe.

[178] Booth, *Households*, 25. The principal axis of gender difference in work is location. "Indoor work is the business of the household's females ... The work of men is outdoors" (24).

ta kala, of release from toil, that it is the function of the *oikos* to produce are not distributed to the general advantage of free people as such, but to the advantage of free men. Certainly women exercise command in the *oikos* economy. Mostly they command other women; sometimes they might command men.[179] But their commanding role is functional and intermediate, for this is an economy focused on the interests of the *oikos* master. Though separate strands, the vertical and sexual divisions of labor are part of the same phenomenon, a hierarchical structure of household authority which is male in authorship and ultimate benefit.[180]

Liberal political theory contends that the contractarian assault on patriarchy "dismantle[d] ... the premises of natural subjection within the household community," resulting in an "egalitarian/voluntarist reconstruction" of the household no less sweeping than the reconstruction of the polis.[181] In fact, liberalism's reconstruction of the polis was highly conditional. First, it was founded upon a recomposition of patriarchal sex right in the polis that was in its turn dependent not upon the dismantling of "natural subjection" in the household, but its reassertion. The form of the reassertion did little to disturb the household master's actual position, filling Locke's contractualism with "philosophical embarrassments." Second, it was founded upon a highly formalistic conception of consent, one that saw nothing short of "actual or threatened ... violence" as an impediment.[182]

Finally, liberalism's reconstruction was founded upon a conception of the economic sphere's autonomy – its separation from the polis – that bore little actual relation to reality: "control over economic activities is taken from the household despot ... ends and choices become the rightful property of autonomous individual agents."[183] The economy, then, becomes the "private" to the polis's "public" sphere. Yet, neither liberalism's economy

---

This underlines a further, major, dimension to the dialectic of inside and outside that is integral to households, domestic relations law, and the politics of social spheres.

[179] That is, where male servants or slaves are engaged in indoor work, they are within the sphere of the *oikos* mistress and subordinate to her authority (although even here there is likely to be a steward to act as overseer).

[180] Booth implies that gender and economy offer distinct sites for analysis of the dynamics of the household (*Households*, 2–3). Indeed, the household must be approached as a place of gendered hierarchy no less than of economic hierarchy. Given, however, that Booth's analysis from the site of economy suggests that the *oikos* was organized to subsidize one sex, it seems to me to risk distortion to imply that gender and economy are not related.

[181] Ibid., 97, 100–1. Contrast Pateman, *The Sexual Contract*, 40–1, 52–3, 58–60.

[182] Booth, *Households*, 101, 134. Booth's analysis of the liberal household shows that its voluntarist bets are substantially hedged when it comes to spousal and parental relations. According to Booth, "tensions" occur in Lockean thought "where the contractarian drive of Locke's analysis encounters relations that appear to him as less amenable to egalitarian, voluntaristic redefinition." Booth attempts to turn these "tensions" into exceptions by calling them "embarrassments," but it is difficult to maintain a paradigm of freedom and equality in human relations where these are riddled by subordinations founded in "nature." See Booth, *Households*, 101, 101–6.

[183] Ibid., 152; for a summary of Booth's "disembedded" (uncontained) liberal political economy, see 173–6.

nor its polity can be located outside the civil (public) realm of law and police, the conditions of freedom and coercion.[184] They are the joint creations of the same civil transformation, and rendered interdependent by it. The true antinomy of private and public is rather the opposition of nature to civil jurisdiction that contractualism creates, the private "womanly [and] natural," the public "masculine [and] civil." As Pateman puts it, "what it means to be an 'individual', a maker of contracts and civilly free, is revealed by the subjection of women within the private sphere."[185]

Interlude

One can use these observations on the distribution of subjection and freedom, private and public, to return once more for a moment to Daniel Defoe's story of Edmund Pratt, and cast it in a slightly different light. From the outside, Pratt's household economy was, one might say, successfully "contained." He had earned a sufficiency from his labors – enough, at least, to afford him the modicum of leisure that enabled him to drink rather than to weave E–'s cloth. He was indifferent to accumulation for its own sake.[186] If not exactly a life of *ta kala*, Pratt's was clearly an existence marked by a felt quantum of autonomy, which his own description of his legal standing vis-à-vis E– expressed quite substantively.[187] However much the clothier might have complained about it, his legal relationship with Pratt was not that of master and servant but of customer and supplier. They were in fact two men, respectively heads of their own households, meeting in a proceeding that expressed their jural equality. This perfected transactional encounter – a Lockean moment – was, to Defoe, insolence personified. It was the cause of the clothier's frustration, the object of Defoe's indignation, and the stimulus for Parliament's intervention.

In Defoe's story, Pratt has neither wife nor children. He is an obstinate old man, obdurately set in his ways, the eccentricities of his self-perception underlined by his riddling speech: "I lodge in an Alehouse, so that I am always at Home; he can't keep bad Hours that is at-home in good Season; nor you can't deny me Drinking in my own Chamber, tho' it be on a Sunday."[188] But it is safe to say that, had Pratt been married, the "inside"

[184] See generally Tomlins, "Constellations of Class," 213–33; Dubber, *Police Power*; Steinfeld, *Coercion and Contract*, 1–26; Robert Hale, "Coercion and Distribution in a Supposedly Non-Coercive State," *Political Science Quarterly*, 38, 3 (June 1923), 470–94.

[185] Pateman, *The Sexual Contract*, 11. Pateman continues (12–13), "Most contemporary controversy between liberals and socialists about the private and the public is not about the *patriarchal* division between natural and civil. The private sphere is 'forgotten' so that the 'private' shifts to the civil world and the *class* division between private and public. The division is then made within the 'civil' realm itself, between the private, capitalist economy or private enterprise and the public or political state, and the familiar debates ensue.

[186] "When I have finish'd ten – Yards, I come for my Money, which is ten Shillings, as by Agreement, and then I go ... to the Alehouse, and work hard to spend it, and when it is all spent, then I come to work again." Defoe, *Great Law of Subordination Consider'd*, 99.

[187] Ibid., 93–5.

[188] Ibid., 100.

story of his household would have been that of a typical putting-out weaver's household, organized as a little occupational hierarchy that serviced its male head's production of cloth from his loom.[189]

Seen through the lens of the eighteenth century's expanding law of master and servant, the story of Edmund Pratt signifies a descent from a modest autonomy grounded on his mastery of his own little *oikos* to a legalized subordination within the larger *oikos* of another. The story of a married Pratt's fictional wife and children, seen through the lens of their legal relations with him, would have shown less change. Married or single, the weaver lost the legal capacity to refuse those who would require him to work at their pleasure rather than his own. But that was a capacity his wife and children would not have had to lose.[190] Nor did the artisan's decline from leisure mean that his and theirs had now become a uniform subordination. However mean the working man's "outside" relations might become, inside he was the master of his household.

IV. Locke's Mainland

I have argued that the location of liberalism's birth in a movement from status to contract is deceptive, that liberal modernity was born in the passage from lordship to consent, a passage that underlines the *ascendancy* of patriarchal household government by locating it in relationship to lordship's relative decline rather than simply assumes its "natural" primordial origins. This argument also emphasizes the deep compatibility between an ideology of consent in the civil sphere and the continuation of patriarchy in the private. It denies the claim that the latter was eviscerated by revolution.[191]

In the early American case, one can observe the relationships between lordship and household government, and between patriarchy and consent, exemplified several times over. From the beginnings of English colonizing, households in general assumed a more extensive jurisdictional presence in social life than they had enjoyed in England, due in part to the relative paucity of lordly institutions in early American state forms, in part to the demographic and social instability that had disrupted household formation in early seventeenth-century England.[192] But there was no uniformity; the distribution of lordly institutions varied substantially by place

---

[189] On which see Thompson, *Customs in Common*, 371–81.

[190] While artisans celebrated "Saint Monday" with drink and conviviality, their wives and children worked. Ibid., 374, 376.

[191] Gordon Wood, for example, assumes patriarchal government was "traditional" and "ancient" until finally called into question by liberal political theory and by the American Revolution. See Wood, *The Radicalism of the American Revolution*, 145–7. So also Rhys Isaac, *Landon Carter's Uneasy Kingdom: Revolution and Rebellion on A Virginia Plantation* (New York, 2004), xi, 180–3 (the Revolution's assault on patriarchal monarchy destroyed "the keystone of the cosmic arch of public and private authority").

[192] "The rather undeveloped state of governmental institutions enhanced the authority of the household head." Shammas, "Anglo-American Household Government," 126. See also Mintz and Kellogg, *Domestic Revolutions*, xiv, 1, 7–8.

and design. The proprietary colonies were founded upon the presumption that lordship would be pervasive in their social and political structure, as represented, for example, by the seigneurial authority accorded proprietors, the practice of primogeniture, and the political and legal powers granted to prominent landholders.[193] Notwithstanding the efforts of promoters to plant families, and so "fix the people on the soil,"[194] lordship's ascendancy was complemented by the weak contribution of formed families to the European migration stream entering those areas of settlement. Predominantly youthful male migration patterns and the catastrophic disease environment were formidable obstacles to family formation in the seventeenth-century Chesapeake.[195] Carolina and New York both spun lordly patterns into the design of their polities.[196] In the New England and Delaware Valley colonies, in contrast, complete households played a crucial associational role in the structure of European migration and social life. "English migrants who ventured to New England sought to avoid the disorder of English family life through a structured and disciplined family ... [E]stablishment of a holy commonwealth in New England represented a desperate effort to restore order and discipline to social behavior. And it was the family through which order could most effectively be created."[197] The same was true for each of the major migrant groups to populate the Delaware Valley.[198] We have already seen that patterns of English and mainland variation in the relationship of household and lordly jurisdiction correlated with patterns of English migration to the mainland. Relatively lord-free pastoral regions characterized by high familial solidarity and household-centered socio-political behavior supplied the strategic core of the migration to New England and the Delaware Valley. Low-solidarity arable regions dominated by lordly elites set the tone for the social and political order of the Chesapeake.[199]

Political Economy and Household – "Lockean" New England

How deeply was the jurisdictional imprint of these distinctive household regimes etched into the political economy of English America? Stephen

---

[193] See Chapter 4, section II. On primogeniture, see Holly Brewer, "Entailing Aristocracy in Colonial Virginia: 'Ancient Feudal Restraints' and Revolutionary Reform," *William and Mary Quarterly*, 3rd Ser. 54, 2 (April 1997), 307–46.

[194] Julia Cherry Spruill, *Women's Life and Work in the Southern Colonies* (New York, 1972 [1938]), 9.

[195] See Chapter 1, section IIB.

[196] See Chapter 4, section II.

[197] Mintz and Kellogg, *Domestic Revolutions*, 8. Mary Beth Norton, *Founding Mothers and Fathers, Gendered Power and the Forming of American Society* (New York, 1996), 12–14, usefully contrasts the Chesapeake and New England colonies, but overemphasizes the normality of English household stability.

[198] See generally Barry Levy, *Quakers and the American Family: British Settlement in the Delaware Valley* (New York, 1988); Aaron Fogleman, *Hopeful Journeys: German Immigration, Settlement, and Political Culture in Colonial America, 1717–1775* (Philadelphia, 1996).

[199] See Chapters 1 and 5.

Innes argues that the course of New England's economic development was decisively influenced by the interplay between a "distinctive civic ecology" based on strong families, strong town organizations, and a vibrant public sphere, and a "culture of discipline" that "fostered industrious and 'striving' behavior, communal responsibility, and a high ratio of savings and investment relative to income by its limitations on leisure."[200] Crucial to that civic ecology was the first generation's pre-migration origins in East Anglia, with its relative freedom from lordly tenures and social relations, and from the manors and trade corporations that embodied and implemented them. Crucial to the culture of discipline was New England's shared ascetic Protestantism, which succored ethics of hard work and enterprise and mediated (through denunciation) its dark side, "calculative and secularized rationalism."[201] The result was a Lockean commonwealth that considerably antedated Locke: guarantees of basic political liberties and accountable political authority; guaranteed property rights, a labor theory of property and a will theory of contract; and mobile labor and capital liberated from the restraints of "patrimonial mercantilism" (coercive state or corporate regulation). Puritan New England was a "regime of economic freedom" whose founders "from the very beginning" envisioned a dynamic and diversified "industrializing economy," not the static undifferentiated "household-based agricultural economy" of earlier portrayals.[202]

The claim for the novelty of New England's economic culture is not per se problematic; English migrants indeed established a distinctive political-legal and economic culture in New England from which vast swathes of contemporary English law and political-institutional restraint were absent.[203] The devil is in the details.[204] Innes reads seventeenth-century economic culture according to the bundle of practices, values, and attitudes that characterize those species of activity that only came to be demarcated as distinctively "economic" in the nineteenth century. The activity thus identified for investigation becomes identified precisely by its status as recognizable precursor to the particular genus of economic modernism that only emerges later.[205] Thus, "economic culture" becomes the cultural

200 Stephen B. Innes, *Creating the Commonwealth: The Economic Culture of Puritan New England* (New York, 1995), 9.

201 Ibid., 37.

202 Ibid., 14, 50, 90–1, 98, and generally 1–38, 64–106.

203 Ibid., 175–82, 220–36. Innes's research, for example, provides major resources for critical reconsideration of Richard B. Morris's *Government and Labor in Early America* (Boston, 1981 [1st edition New York, 1946]). See Chapter 6, section II.

204 In a sense I mean this quite literally. For that sense, see Carol F. Karlsen, *The Devil in the Shape of a Woman: Witchcraft in Colonial New England* (New York, 1989), 77–116. Carlson describes how women who "stood in the way" (116) of forms of male economic activity could encounter trouble in the shape of witchcraft accusations. As I try to show here, *Creating the Commonwealth* "bedevils" women in Carlson's sense by casting them "out" of the economy altogether.

205 Innes acknowledges and defends the anachronism. "In economic affairs and the creation of a civil society, the saints' progressive tendencies are unmistakable. There is ample evidence that in their productive activities, exchange ethics, and political economy, the

conditions encouraging the emergence of the modern capitalist-indus-trialist economy, which in turn identifies the early-modern economy with particular specialized locales wholly exterior to households: market spaces where particular forms of exchange occur, industrial spaces where particu-lar kinds of commodities are fabricated. Overwhelmingly in orthodox lib-eral discourse, work – descriptively, conceptually, culturally – is associated with these exterior spaces.[206] Overwhelmingly, these spaces, and the activi-ties and occupations that are undertaken in them, are male. So, hence, is the early modern economy. Households are interior spaces in this account, where families reside, where the civic culture is reproduced and discipline inculcated through education and example but where economic activity is not to be found. Households become support mechanisms, integral to the cultural reproduction of "the economic" but not part of the economy. Here, and only here, is where "the issue of gender" and "women's role" gain attention.[207]

Separation of household from economy, of what women and children do from work, reads liberal modernism's category of "the economic" back into the forms of seventeenth-century behavior that constituted New England's "economy." But this is deceptive. Central to the discourse of European work and life in New England, for example, was the ideal of com-petency, or "comfortable independence."[208] Competency was a "masculine ideal," a yeoman/artisan restatement of the *oikos* philosophy of *ta kala*, on display, for example, in the boisterous sufficiency that satisfied Edmund Pratt. As in the *oikos*, the achievement of comfortable independence was a household project, envisaged by male household heads as the employment of themselves and their families in more or less self-directed household production. Competency subordinated familial dependents (women, chil-dren) to the achievement of a patriarchal ideal,[209] but it hardly separated

Bay Colonists were discernibly and irrevocably capitalists. In their behavior in the mar-ketplace, in their public policies regarding property, law, contract, and (especially) land tenure, as well as in their Weberian virtues of industry, enterprise, and prudence, the New Englanders ... had clearly crossed the threshold that separates a pre-capitalist from a capitalist society." *Creating the Commonwealth*, 39, 45. The issue, however, is not whether the New Englanders Innes examines were capitalists or not, but whether the social and ideological locales which Innes investigates to arrive at that conclusion are the most, or only, appropriate locales upon which to arrive at what is "economic" behavior. That is, do we assess "economic culture" according to these measuring sticks because we have already been directed to these measuring sticks by our modern understanding of what "economy" constitutes? That is an anachronism that Innes does not address. Instead, by the end of *Creating the Commonwealth* (see 308) it has become anachronistic in Innes's book to be anything *other than* capitalist.

[206] Note the trenchant critique offered by Chris Tilly and Charles Tilly, *Work Under Capitalism* (Boulder, Colo., 1998).

[207] Innes, *Creating the Commonwealth*, 31, 149. The maleness of work is particularly evident in Innes's conceptualization of workplaces, work discipline, and calling. See 107–26.

[208] Daniel Vickers, *Farmers and Fishermen: Two Centuries of Work in Essex County, Massachusetts, 1630–1850* (Chapel Hill, 1994), 14.

[209] The conceptualization of "independence," Vickers notes, specifically excluded women. Ibid., 14.

them from "the economic." On the contrary, in the case of farming and farm formation – the primary occupations of rural male New Englanders during the first two centuries of European settlement – "farmers usually worked the lands they occupied in household units, of which nuclear family members constituted the core. The most basic lines of economic power ... were those that linked parents with their children and organized daily work among them."[210]

This household-based agricultural economy was indeed long-lived. "Mixed family farming, the division of labor by gender, and a patriarchal household structure" predominated in the region's rural economy into the late eighteenth century. During the century, growing population and the beginnings of land scarcity created a supply of property-less late-adolescent male labor for hire. The elaboration of exchange networks encouraged some diversification of male productive effort into craft manufacture, and also saw a greater incidence of youthful dependents laboring outside the family. But though extremes of intergenerational interdependence declined, "most householders and their sons spent the majority of their working days on the exploitation and improvement of their own family property." Nor did hirable labor appear as a distinctive "class or ... age cohort." No large-scale turn toward commercial or industrial activity occurred prior to the end of the eighteenth century. And when it did, "it was the traditionally dependent portion of the population – women, children, and younger men – who provided the bulk of that labor." As long as adult men clung to their ideal of competency, it was the age and gender specificities of the New England farm household that constructed the region's emergent workforce. "The practice of working for pay *outside* the family spread first among those with the longest tradition of dependence *inside* the family."[211]

Though men were not the first industrial workforce, the eventual industrialization of the male economy would imprint two entirely misleading identities on the culture of work; that it was masculine and that it was remunerated.[212] Retroactively, women who worked for wages were rendered exceptional to work's gendered identity. Women who worked in any other sense – unremunerated reproductive and household labor – were not "workers" in work's cultural sense at all.[213] One might explain this

[210] Ibid., 35. Innovations that responded to the peculiar demands of new farm formation in an environment of severe capital and labor shortages relative to land tended to bind all family members even more tightly into household production than had been the case in England, and prolonged intergenerational dependencies far beyond the English norm of early adulthood. (51, 76, 252–3).

[211] Ibid., 205, 239, 245, 323. See also Christopher Clark, *The Roots of Rural Capitalism: Western Massachusetts, 1780–1860* (Ithaca, N.Y., 1990); Barbara M. Tucker, *Samuel Slater and the Origins of the American Textile Industry, 1790–1860* (Ithaca, N.Y., 1984), 139–62.

[212] See generally Ava Baron, editor, *Work Engendered: Toward a New History of American Labor* (Ithaca, N.Y., 1991); Tilly and Tilly, *Work Under Capitalism*, 22–3, 128–30.

[213] "In industrial America," Jeanne Boydston observes succinctly, the housewife was "a blank." Boydston, *Home and Work*, xi. As Reva Siegel summarizes the matter: "Census

disappearance of women as a consequence of the impact of industrialization on the household, the creation of distinct disaggregated zones of economic workplace and noneconomic home, except that industrialization
did not constitute a transformative moment in the history of production
and household in America. The foundations "had been laid earlier, in the
fabric and evolution of colonial life itself, and especially in the changing
relations of gender and labor over the course of the preindustrial period."
Change was long-term, not sudden, critically mediated by culture rather
than determined by sudden transformations in material life. "Changing
attitudes toward women's labor contributions ... were not paralleled by
changes in the work itself." The gender division of labor remained stable.
The matter was one of cultural redefinition of the value of what women did.
In the early colonies, women were "openly and repeatedly acknowledged"
as vital economic agents, as workers whose labor in household and community was crucial to the fate of both. But "new cultural understandings of
what constituted 'economic' and what constituted 'non-economic' terrain"
arose from growing population density, commercial expansion and attendant civic effects – heightened concern for property titles, the monetization
of transactions, the erosion of social collectivity, an increased formality in
legal relations in general. These trends "heightened the association of *men*
with the symbols of economic activity and profoundly weakened the ability
of women to lay claim to the status of 'worker'."[214]

Good evidence for the cultural mediation of the meaning of women's
work is the decreasing presence of women in the archives (largely local
court records) from which histories of work have emerged.[215] Histories of

measures of the economy that appeared in the aftermath of the Civil War characterized
[labor within the household] as 'unproductive,' and, consistent with this gendered valuation of family labor, excluded women engaged in income-producing work in the household from the count of those 'gainfully employed.'" Reva Siegel, "Home as Work: The
First Women's Rights Claims Concerning Wives' Household Labor, 1850–1880," *Yale Law
Journal*, 103 (1994), 1092.

[214] Boydston, *Home and Work*, 3–4, 5, 11, 20–1, 27. As commerce placed increasing emphasis
on the household economy's "outside," on markets and cash relations, on credit networks,
on the world of more-or-less contractual meetings that involved mostly men, "economy"
came to be associated with what men in the household's gendered division of labor did.
Clearly the inside functions of the household went on apace. Just as clearly, recognition that this was "economic" activity died and, as Boydston puts it, "a gender *division* of
labor" became "a gendered *definition* of labor" (55, emphasis in original). Throughout
this transformation in the discourse of the economy, households in practice remained
"'mixed economies'– economic systems that functioned on the bases of both paid and
unpaid labor and were dependent on both" (123). What this means is that the process
of socioeconomic transformation celebrated in liberal thought as the "uncontaining" of
the economy – its liberation from household hierarchies by market ideologies of unconstrained participation and individual self-government – was in fact nothing of the sort.
Rather, this was a refiguring of containment, a market-driven ascendancy of commerce
and, eventually, industry (the exterior of the economy) built upon a formidable discursive containment of the economy's interior element, a containment so complete, in fact,
that the interior vanished from view.

[215] Daniel Vickers indicates that the records upon which he relies are not so much silent on
women's work as too sparse to permit observations with statistical significance. *Farmers*

litigation record women's increasing civic invisibility, which suggests that the economic identification of work with men is an artefact of legal culture. Seventeenth-century New England courts "had been occupied by the sorts of community activities to which women were integral: maintaining harmonious neighborly relations, ensuring equitable local trading, and monitoring sexual and moral conduct." During the eighteenth century the courts' prime constituency became "propertied men active in the expanding economy." The volume of their litigation grew astronomically; courts became "adjuncts and facilitators" of the transactional networks into which farmers and tradesmen were increasingly drawn. "Women's economic and social activities did not change markedly," but "in a schematic sense what was happening in court reveals a new set of divergences in men's and women's spheres taking hold gradually throughout the century," foreshadowing the nineteenth century's more explicit reservation of "the public realms of commerce, law, and politics" to men. This was not simply a cultural reflection of a causal sequence occurring at some more basic social level: the occlusion of women's legal presence was in part attributable to shifts occurring from early on in the eighteenth century in the legal system itself; the increasing resort to professional attorneys and "stricter attention paid to common law procedures and rules of evidence" that is associated with the gradual "anglicization" of local colonial legal cultures. In instrumental procedural terms, anglicization "reshaped the county court from an inclusive forum representative of community to a rationalized institution serving the interests of commercially-active men." In its wider cultural resonances, anglicization was a significant element in the appearance of "a more traditional type of patriarchy in Britain's New World colonies."[216]

Such legal-cultural agency is highly significant. Stephen Innes analyzes legal materials for his history of New England's economic culture not simply because they are valuable sources of information about behavior and events but because law per se is a crucially important modality of rule. For Innes (in a fashion reminiscent of E. P. Thompson, with whom I began), "the rule of law" is New England's distinguishing characteristic,

---

and Fishermen, vi–vii, 12. His requirement is continuity of observable data over two centuries – a threshold that, if Boydston is right about women's work's cultural disappearance during the eighteenth century, women's work could not meet. If Boydston is right, however, one should expect to find at least some evidence of women at work in seventeenth-century legal records. And in fact one does. Thus, according to Gloria Main, Essex County court records show seventeenth-century Salem women "engaged in men's work [sic] or working with men" – winnowing corn, carrying grain to be milled, milking cows, branding steers. See Gloria L. Main, "Gender, Work, and Wages in Colonial New England," *William and Mary Quarterly*, 3rd Ser., 51, 1 (January 1994), 54 (citing C. Dallett Hemphill, "Women in Court: Sex-Role Differentiation in Salem, Massachusetts, 1636 to 1683," *William and Mary Quarterly*, 3rd Ser., 39, 1 (January 1982), 166–7.

216 Cornelia Dayton, *Women before the Bar: Gender, Law and Society in Connecticut, 1639–1789* (Chapel Hill, 1995), 8, 9, 10, 11, 13, and generally 69–104. On long-term change in the character of litigation and procedure see also Bruce H. Mann, *Neighbors and Strangers: Law and Community in Early Connecticut* (Chapel Hill, 1987).

the foundation of its economic culture, in that it authorizes, embodies, and implements New England's unique "civic ecology" of property rights and personal liberty. The argument is classically Weberian: "Neither capitalism nor civil society could emerge in the absence of some legal/juridical separation between the political realm and the economic realm ... Only after a law-governed regime was established could private actors begin to behave in a rationally-calculating fashion."[217] One can fully endorse this observation of law's cultural significance, pausing only, in light of the discussion in which this book has been engaged, to propose a refinement. It should be clear by now that law does a great deal more than create facilitative frameworks for rationally calculated action. Law is a technology that shapes action in accordance with its own conditions of formation and existence. In Part II my goal was to show how early American economic culture was legally conditioned by regionalized ideologies of law-formation that expressed variant forms of work relations. Here I have stressed the further salience of patriarchy to understanding those work relations. We have also seen that the gradual anglicization of mainland legal cultures (an expression of the process of metropolitan cultural and political ascendancy in Britain and North America already described in this and earlier chapters) would envelop and redirect the formation of work relations. We have now see how it actually undertook that work on the terrain of gender.

Political Economy and Household – the "Lockean" Chesapeake

Histories of England's mainland colonies have generally relied upon differences in material environments and in settlers' extractive ambitions to explain dissimilarities in economic trajectories and in labor systems established in each region of settlement. The most obvious material contrasts in early mainland colonizing were, of course, those distinguishing export-oriented cash-crop plantation economies of the Chesapeake from the non-staple subsistence agriculture of New England. So understood, the organization of work in the two regions of settlement appears quite distinct. The traditional association of the plantation colonies with legal bondage (originally indentured servitude, later slavery), and of New England with a far greater incidence of free labor and a relative absence of involuntary servitude has seemed to follow clearly from differences in factor endowments.[218]

Refracted through the prism of society and culture, the causality of material differences becomes less clear because the systems seem less distinct. Certain contrasts in local conditions and their effects remain obvious. Population growth in the Chesapeake was not self-sustaining until late in the seventeenth century. Unlike New England, then, the region's

---

[217] Innes, *Creating the Commonwealth*, 193–4.

[218] John J. McCusker and Russell R. Menard, *The Economy of British America, 1607–1789* (Chapel Hill, 1991), 235, 236–57.

economy during the seventeenth century was heavily dependent on the importation of labor. Once at work, however, that labor force's salient characteristics rendered it somewhat less distinct from its counterparts to the north than one might suppose. Like rural labor in New England, imported Chesapeake labor was predominantly youthful and predominantly male. In New England, settlers mostly used their own male children for field work; in the Chesapeake, where proportionately fewer families were formed and fewer children born, settlers imported the children of others. Adult Creole labor was of considerable importance in both regions, and not significantly different in legal status. Second, in the Chesapeake, as in New England, work was organized through households. Not just in the north but everywhere, "the household was the predominant unit of production, and the work was done by family members, often without the assistance of outsiders, bound or free."[219] As in New England, further, distributions of tasks and life-chances within households varied significantly according to gender.

Chesapeake households, however, were substantially less stable than those of New England. Both the region's demographic uncertainties and the overwhelming masculine skew in immigration rendered sustained rates of family formation highly problematic. Though the Virginia Company envisaged the settlement of "'honest' laborers with wives and children"[220] – men of families, whose domestic stability and well-regulated households would render them tractable and tie them to the colony – what they managed to recruit was an overwhelmingly unattached and youthful male population, dogged for more than half a century by the constant instabilities of disease and frontier warfare, the often-oppressive discipline of indentured servitude, and sparse opportunities to form families. The minority of female migrants (15–20 percent of the total in the 1620s and 1630s, 30–40 percent after mid-century) that was supposed to foster the ideal of "good wife" domesticity and household stability by supplying potential marriage partners mostly contradicted the ideal in practice by ending up at work in the tobacco fields.

The instability of the Chesapeake household had legal-political effects, notably the relative weakness of households as jurisdictional entities. For Mary Beth Norton, the primary effect was to push the Chesapeake's seventeenth-century legal culture along a path for which she too seeks the label of "Lockean" before Locke. Norton argues Chesapeake legal culture was an exception to an otherwise ubiquitous Anglo-American "unified theory" of patriarchal power, embracing a conception of governance that founded legitimate political and legal authority not on analogies to primordial household hierarchies but on a consensus of free property-holders whose gathering constituted the "formal" public sphere. Norton contrasts the

[219] Ibid., 246.
[220] Kathleen M. Brown, *Good Wives, Nasty Wenches and Anxious Patriarchs: Gender, Race and Power in Colonial Virginia* (Chapel Hill, for the Institute of Early American History and Culture, 1996), 80.

"Lockean" Chesapeake with "Filmerian" New England, where, she argues, demographic stability and the ideological significance accorded the household sustained patriarchal power and its intimate articulation of household with state roles in governance, and where, correspondingly, "what was public – and thus properly subject to regulation by the community – was difficult to distinguish from what was private – and thus exempt from such supervision."[221]

Norton's categories of analysis (like those used by Innes) are anachronistic.[222] More important, her model is of limited service, not because it is anachronistic but because modes of thought and action that Norton treats as sequential and distinct, "primordial" paternalism and contractarian individualism, are in fact simultaneous and intertwined. Her "Lockean" Chesapeake public sphere of free property-holders is more fruitfully described as Aristotelian, balancing household masters on the tips of modest but nevertheless hierarchically organized *oikoi*. And in the Chesapeake, "public" authority and "private" household authority mingled quite routinely in the police of inside relations.[223] Not until Virginia was launched on its journey to maturing slave society does one encounter the beginnings of state abstention from supervision of the detail of master-subordinate relations and the creation of the household as a "de facto private realm of family life."[224] Certainly contrasts between New England and the Chesapeake sustain the assertion that they were characterized by distinct legal cultures, but "Filmerian" and "Lockean" are poor labels. We have seen that Stephen Innes finds New England's legal-political culture just as open to the "Lockean" label (strong public sphere and divergence of public and private realms) as Norton's Chesapeake.[225] Holly Brewer likewise finds ideologies of government by consent strongest in the dissenter colonies of New England and the Delaware Valley, in marked contrast to the Chesapeake's aristocratic commitments to lordship.[226]

Kathleen Brown's account of the political economy of the Chesapeake household is more consistent than Norton's with the overall Anglo-American trajectory canvassed in this chapter. A gendered "language of power" permeated the normative English social order, expressed in the

[221] Norton, *Founding Mothers and Fathers*, 9, 402. See generally 6–56.

[222] Norton, too, acknowledges the anachronism. Ibid., 5.

[223] For legal oversight of master-servant relations in the Chesapeake see Chapters 6 and 7. On more general policing of morality in seventeenth-century Virginia, see Brown, *Good Wives, Nasty Wenches*, 91.

[224] Norton, *Founding Mothers and Fathers*, 49. See also Anthony S. Parent, Jr. *Foul Means: The Formation of a Slave Society in Virginia, 1660–1740* (Chapel Hill, 2003), 105–34, 197–267.

[225] Treated as ideal types, "Filmerian" and "Lockean" philosophies of rule can facilitate analysis of the configuration and reconfiguration of social relations and household structures, not least those that displaced women as such from recognizably public roles into an "interior" sphere. But one must be careful in granting ideal types historical reality.

[226] Brewer, *By Birth or Consent*, 344–5.

internal order of households, the division of labor, the distribution of property ownership between men and women, and the structure of law and governance.[227] Gendered discourse also comported with the ideology of English overseas expansion, in that its "naturalized" explanations of power and weakness were available to explain and justify other exercises of dominion. Wherever they landed, for example, the English consistently remarked on the "unnatural" division of indigenous labor that had men hunt and fish – a life of ease and leisure in English eyes – while women toiled in raising crops. The distribution of tasks did not comport with English agricultural practice that made fields the preserve of men. It became in English eyes "another distinguishing mark of the savage," another error to be corrected by English civility. "The coming of the English would help Indian men to see their errors," assume their laborious responsibilities, and so become civilized. "Only large-scale settlement, with a full representation of English society, would allow such learning to take place."[228] The discourse of gender fit snugly the manifold resorts to natural law that, as we have seen, rendered "acts of dispossession and imperial appropriation ... comprehensible as part of the natural order."[229]

But though in general seventeenth-century English migrants might treat patriarchal representations of household and community as an expression of the appropriate and natural order of things, gender nevertheless proved unstable as a consistent predictor of their social practice. In Chesapeake practice, as in New England, white women could enjoy considerable influence and authority. We have already seen that regional cultures of origin were themselves characterized by distinct authority relations and household practices. Those brought to the Chesapeake tended to trump patriarchy with lordship. Too, though patriarchy might proffer an idealized form of social relations, gender roles, politics, and governance, its actual expression in the stressed demographic circumstances of seventeenth-century settlement was compromised and erratic. Indentured English women ended up working the fields alongside the men. Not until the eighteenth century does one encounter the turn toward "high" patriarchy and its decisive masculinization of law, politics, and the public sphere.[230]

When it came, the Chesapeake's turn to patriarchal stability would be characterized by the same anglicization of social practice and legal culture already noted elsewhere. In the Chesapeake, that is – as in New England, as in the "rude parts" of the home islands – the eighteenth century meant a mimetic bourgeoisification of manners that created a recognizably Anglo-American social and legal order. Where the Chesapeake would differ was

[227] Brown, *Good Wives, Nasty Wenches*, 6, 7.

[228] Karen Ordahl Kupperman, *Indians and English: Facing Off in Early America* (Ithaca, N.Y., 2000), 149–50.

[229] Brown, *Good Wives, Nasty Wenches*, 17. On gender and colonizing, notably reproductive capacity as a colonizer's resource, see also Joyce E. Chaplin, *Subject Matter: Technology, the Body and Science on the Anglo-American Frontier, 1500–1676* (Cambridge, Mass., 2001), 119.

[230] Brown, *Good Wives, Nasty Wenches*, 75–104 and compare 247–366.

that *its* patriarchal stability was definitively a *white* patriarchal stability, built on and assisted by a successful racialization of toil derived from resort to widespread African slavery.[231]

In Chapter 9 I will argue that slavery's installation of racial power was not fully established in the Chesapeake until the second half of the seventeenth century. Before then, just as some white women might slip through holes in a gendered social order, at least some African men might acquire at least some of the markers that English masculinity associated with civic freedom. The fate of African women, though, underscored how limited the racial easement was even before slavery became ubiquitous. African women were labeled drudges from the outset, "an exploitable new source of agricultural labor," and condemned to the very bottom of the colonial social hierarchy, the "nasty wenches" who worked in the fields.[232] Where white women's field labor upset the normative English division of labor, African women's field labor confirmed their racial place. Simultaneously it became a means to normalize English gender roles by releasing white women from drudgery to participate in household formation and achieve an approximation of "goodwife" domesticity.

The substitution (both actual and symbolic) of African women for white women as field workers began in advance of the Chesapeake's comprehensive late seventeenth-century transition to slavery. It was marked by changes to tax laws that cast all African women (enslaved or free, married or unmarried) as the equivalent of field laborers. The tax laws effectively abstracted gender from the determination of African women's status. They became simply "negroes."[233] Laws institutionalizing matrilineal inheritance of enslavement then made them the means to naturalize slave status for *all* "negroes." Womanhood, meanwhile, became irreducibly white, enshrined in Virginia law as a condition of "domesticity and economic dependence."[234] And as slavery took hold, all white males of whatever estate were joined to the social order "with the promise of future status as voters, citizens, and patriarchs." Solidly founded on the twinned creation of division of white from black laborers and unity among white men, the promise would win Virginia a significant degree of political stability.[235]

[231] See generally Rhys Isaac, *The Transformation of Virginia, 1740–1790* (Chapel Hill, 1982), 20–1, 338–9, 344–9; Isaac, *Landon Carter's Uneasy Kingdom*; Parent, *Foul Means* 197–235.

[232] Brown, *Good Wives, Nasty Wenches*, 116.

[233] Ibid., 116–20, 128. See "Minister's Allowance" Act I (1642/3) in Hening, *Statutes at Large*, I, 243: *"Be it also enacted and confirmed* That there be tenn pounds of tob'o. per poll & a bushell of corne per poll paid to the ministers within the severall parishes of the colony for all tithable persons, that is to say, as well for all youths of sixteen years of age as vpwards, as also for all negro women at the age of sixteen years."

[234] Brown, *Good Wives, Nasty Wenches*, 128, 132–3, 135. See also Chapter 9, section IV.

[235] Ibid., 181, 181–6. See generally Edmund S. Morgan, *American Slavery, American Freedom: The Ordeal of Colonial Virginia* (New York, 1975), 295–387. But see also Parent, *Foul Means*, 190–94.

Conclusion

"I long to hear that you have declared an independency." Thus wrote Abigail Adams at the end of March 1776, to her husband John in distant Philadelphia, where he and other delegates to the Second Continental Congress were joined in anxious debate over the latest depredations of the imperial metropolis. Famously, she immediately appended longings for additional declarations that would incinerate other dependencies, equally tyrannous and closer to home:

> and by the way in the new Code of Laws which I suppose it will be necessary for you to make I desire you would Remember the Ladies, and be more generous and favourable to them than your ancestors. Do not put such unlimited power into the hands of the Husbands. Remember all Men would be tyrants if they could. If perticuliar care and attention is not paid to the Laidies we are determined to foment a Rebelion, and will not hold ourselves bound by any Laws in which we have no voice, or Representation.

That men were "Naturally Tyrannical," Abigail Adams thought, was a truth that could admit no dispute. Some men nevertheless had proven themselves able to abdicate "the harsh title of Master." Why not then take it from all? "Why ... not put it out of the power of the vicious and the Lawless to use us with cruelty and indignity with impunity."

John Adams' reply teased his wife, affectionately no doubt. He could not "but laugh" at her "extraordinary" suggestion. "Depend upon it, We know better than to repeal our Masculine systems." Surely, in any case, Abigail knew full well that men only played the master. "Altho they are in full Force, you know they are little more than Theory. We dare not exert our Power in its full Latitude. We are obliged to go fair, and softly, and in Practice you know We are the subjects." Here was the soft banter of good-humored prevarication, the master adroitly protesting his weakness, his power a name only, his subjection (incredulity aside) the reality. John Adams was acting Defoe's long-suffering "good Governour," patiently soothing the little rebellions of malcontents with pleas for their understanding.

Still, humor always has its edge, and at that edge in John Adams' letter lurked a certain knowledge that in the world of the Philadelphia confrérie "the Ladies" were, like many others, woven into subaltern webs that declarations of independence must leave untouched lest the "Tail" seize government from the "Head," and "Ochlocracy" (mob rule) assume the name and power of master:

> We have been told that our Struggle has loosened the bands of Government every where. That Children and Apprentices were disobedient – that schools and Colledges were grown turbulent – that Indians slighted their Guardians and Negroes grew insolent to their Masters. But your letter was the first Intimation that another Tribe more numerous and powerfull than all the rest were grown discontented.

Abigail Adams' response to her husband's jovial obduracy noted the edge but did not retreat from its challenge. Instead she underlined what was at stake, with a thick edge of her own:

> I can not say that I think you very generous to the Ladies, for whilst you are proclaiming peace and good will to Men, Emancipating all Nations, you insist upon retaining an absolute power over Wives. But you must remember that Arbitrary power is like most other things which are very hard, very liable to be broken.[236]

Eleven years after the Adams' exchange, eight of the brethren of 1776 reassembled in Philadelphia, with forty-seven others, to reconstitute the confederation that their earlier declaration had helped call into existence. Their assembly was singular in the confidence of its assumptions: most spectacularly of its authority to act, for whether it actually had any formal basis to do what it actually did is not entirely clear;[237] but also – for

---

[236] Abigail Adams to John Adams, 31 March 1776 (sent 5 April); John Adams to Abigail Adams, 14 April 1776; Abigail Adams to John Adams 7 May 1776 (sent 9 May 1776); all in *Adams Family Papers: An Electronic Archive,* Correspondence Between John and Abigail Adams, Letters during Continental Congress, 1774–1777 (Massachusetts Historical Society), at http://www.masshist.org/digitaladams/aea/ (accessed 22 August 2009). In parallel correspondence with James Sullivan, Attorney-General of Massachusetts – "moderate Jeffersonian ... classical liberal" and advocate for a widened suffrage – John Adams expressed strong opposition to any alteration to existing suffrage restrictions in terms that clearly reflected his correspondence with his wife but substituted an urgent foreboding for humorous indulgence. "Depend upon it, sir, it is dangerous to open So fruitfull a Source of Controversy and Altercation, as would be opened by attempting to alter the Qualifications of Voters. There will be no End of it. New Claims will arise. Women will demand a Vote. Lads from 12 to 21 will think their Rights not enough attended to, and every Man, who has not a Farthing, will demand an equal Voice with any other in all Acts of State. It tends to confound and destroy all Distinctions, and prostrate all Ranks, to one common level." John Adams to James Sullivan (May 26, 1776), in Philip B. Kurland and Ralph Lerner, editors, *The Founders' Constitution* (Chicago, 1987), available at http://press-pubs.uchicago.edu/founders/documents/v1ch13s10.html (accessed 22 August 2009). On Sullivan, see Linda K. Kerber, *No Constitutional Right to be Ladies: Women and the Obligations of Citizenship* (New York, 1998), 22–4.

[237] Neither the convening of the Philadelphia Convention nor its product had formal constitutional-legal standing according to established process. Fifty-five delegates from all states but Rhode Island assembled in May 1787 in Philadelphia at the invitation of the Confederation Congress to attend a convention called at the instigation of the rump Annapolis Convention of September 1786 for the advertised purpose of revising the Articles of Confederation. The process for amending the Articles of Confederation, however, required action in Congress and agreement thereto, followed by unanimous consent of the states – a vote of approval in each state legislature – not agreement by nine of thirteen ratifying conventions. See *Articles of Confederation,* art. XIII ("Every State shall abide by the determination of the United States in Congress assembled, on all questions which by this confederation are submitted to them. And the Articles of this Confederation shall be inviolably observed by every State, and the Union shall be perpetual; nor shall any alteration at any time hereafter be made in any of them; unless such alteration be agreed to in a Congress of the United States, and be afterwards confirmed by the legislatures of every State.") On receiving the draft Constitution from the Philadelphia Convention, the Confederation Congress did not "agree" to it but resolved simply to refer it to the state legislatures without endorsement or recommendation. The state legislatures were

these were fathers unaccompanied by mothers – of its progenerative capacity. Yet perhaps their assumptions were not so singular.[238] After all, the capacity these fathers assumed to be theirs was founded on their right, as Carole Pateman puts it, "to fill the empty vessel," the original political right, descended to them from the first man, Adam, to whom it had been granted by God.[239]

Theirs was an epochal representation of social formation as contract. In it, however, the ladies were once more forgotten. Perhaps the ladies should have been grateful for the lack of attention given the fate of others not forgotten, for the Philadelphia convention of 1787 did what it could to tighten the bands of government involuntarily shaken loose in the earlier struggle for independence and its aftermath. Most important were the bands reuniting in good government states once united (as colonies) in rebellion, whose excesses and fragmentation since had prompted the convention in the first place. The elevated bands of the Constitution's preamble promised a more perfect union of justice, tranquility, and universal well-being; the less elevated instrumentalities of the text settled instead on the purposeful sedimentation of enslavement, without which these founding fathers knew there would be no unity among the states, no federal republic, at all. Precisely 143 words separate the Constitution's soaring self-justification from its pay dirt, the three-fifths compromise.[240] But other bands needed tightening too. Before the founders exited Article I, they had agreed that justice, tranquility, and universal well-being required a guarantee of twenty uninterrupted years of slave importation.[241] A few clauses later, the founders further agreed that restraint of movement was a required element of the fundamental law of a well-ordered republic; the movement of the fugitive slave, that is, but actually of more besides, of any and every person "held to Service or Labour." Disobedient apprentices were joined with insolent Negroes in the fugitive clause, as they had been in John Adams' imagination eleven years earlier.[242] The texts that secured

themselves instructed that the Constitution was to be submitted to ratifying conventions called "in conformity to the resolves of the Convention made and provided." See Carl Van Doren, *The Great Rehearsal: The Story of the Making and Ratifying of the Constitution of the United States* (New York, 1948), 177–8; Max Farrand, *The Framing of the Constitution of the United States* (New Haven, 1913), 7–12, 61; Jack N. Rakove, "Confederation and Constitution," in Grossberg and Tomlins, eds., *Cambridge History of Law in America*, I, 493–502, 511–12; Bruce Ackerman, *We the People: Transformations* (Cambridge, Mass., 1998), 34–65.

[238] As Rakove puts it in "Confederation and Constitution," at 511, though the Philadelphia convention was, in the strictest sense, an extra-constitutional device, that "was how the Anglo-American tradition ordinarily understood conventions of any kind."

[239] Pateman, *The Sexual Contract*, 87.

[240] See *United States Constitution*, Preamble; Art. I, §2, cl. 3. For a cogent demonstration of the absolute centrality of slavery to the debates of the Philadelphia convention, and their product, see David Waldstreicher, *Slavery's Constitution: From Revolution to Ratification* (New York, 2009), 3–10, 57–105.

[241] *United States Constitution*, Art. I, §9, cl. 1.

[242] *United States Constitution*, Art. IV, §2, cl. 3. Of Indians who slighted their guardians the Constitution had less to say other than to claim the guardianship (Art. I, §8 cl. 3), but in

"Liberty to ourselves and our Posterity" were, to that precise end, riddled through with the necessities of containment to sustain hierarchies both civic and personal.[243] The primal American statement of enlightened autonomy sat atop an enacted political and legal economy of alterity and subjection.

In Part II of this book I began the "inside narrative" of English colonizing, the narrative of what colonizers built for themselves within their enclaves. There I concentrated on certain of the freedoms that segments of the working population came to enjoy as they labored – their origins and expression, their legal reality. In this chapter, I have continued to tell the "inside" story of English colonizing, only here the discussion has turned from freedoms to liabilities – the bounds that accompany freedoms and condition both their existence and extent. In the course of the discussion the exterior and interior narratives of English colonizing have merged to form an interlocked meta-narrative of transformative impositions. Both in England and on the American mainland the English colonized barbarous others and simultaneously the rude parts of themselves. New conceptions of property destroyed collectives and created consenting individuals. Improvement bred independence and new dependencies to secure it. Coercive legalities disciplined contracts, patriarchy underpinned politics. The empire of the father shaped the empire the fathers founded.

John Smith's dream of New England as the acme of opportunity for those of small means willing to pledge "long labour and diligence" properly identifies colonizing as the essence of modernity. Expansion answered the question of how to disengage from ancient constraints; colonizing appropriated space wherein men might build propertied freedom by individual effort. Though it largely ignores modernity's origins in colonizing – or at least colonizing as represented in Part I's exterior narrative of appropriation – American historical orthodoxy has long seized upon the social and political modernity colonizing made possible and has lashed it to an idealized temporality of progress that leaves (as Smith had hoped to leave) the pre-modern in its wake.[244] Witness the desire to render so many different

---

that guardianship the federal judiciary that the Constitution created would find extraordinary powers. See, e.g., *Johnson v. M'Intosh* 21 US 543 (1823). Of insolent wives, the Convention had nothing to say at all, but in the newspapers the delegates read they would have found plenty of "runaway" wives advertised by husbands declaring they would not be responsible for debts their wives incurred. On the law of marriage in the era of the Philadelphia Convention and the early Republic, see Hartog, *Man and Wife in America*, 40–62; Linda K. Kerber, "The Paradox of Women's Citizenship in the Early Republic: The Case of *Martin v. Massachusetts*, 1805," *American Historical Review*, 97, 2 (April 1992), 349–78.

[243] It is little remarked, but worth remarking, that in this most public of documents the fugitive clause grants jurisdiction and makes restoration not to a state whose laws may have been offended by mobility but to a private person, "the Party to whom such Service or Labour may be due." The criminal who flees public justice in the previous clause shall be returned to face public justice (*United States Constitution*, Art. IV, §2, cl. 2); the laborer who flees a master shall be returned to face the master. The clause secures the seigneurial right of the household master.

[244] Wood, *The Radicalism of the American Revolution*, is a convenient example.

parts of the mainland "Lockean."[245] But as I have tried to show in this chapter, an exploration of colonizing compounds its interior and exterior narratives and in so doing introduces us to a temporality for modernity quite distinct from that supplied by John Smith, or by historicism's idealization of his dream – or, for that matter, by J.G.A. Pocock's distinct account of *virtù*'s quarrel with commerce.[246] It introduces us instead to constancy – the constancy of differentials and occlusions of freedom and civic identity, and of the easy coexistence of liberal modernity with gendered subalternship and with an expanding discourse of disciplined service.

The republic created in Philadelphia bore all the marks of that constancy. It was founded as a property-based democracy for and by household masters.[247] Its *oikos* ideal successfully accommodated republicanisms otherwise as varied as elite planter aristocracy and yeoman and artisanal proprietorship.[248] In each case the ideal was given expression in a discourse of adult male agency (political and economic independence) made possible by the "leisure" of freedom from all-consuming toil (the planter elite) or the "sufficiency" at least of moderate toil (the proprietor). As in the *oikos* itself, that discourse of agency expressed the continuation of strategies for preventing too great a trespass of household demands on its master's independence – a continuing displacement of substantial responsibilities

---

[245] See section IV, this chapter. The most sweeping statement of the Lockean claim is Louis Hartz, *The Liberal Tradition in America; An Interpretation of American Political Thought since the Revolution* (New York, 1955).

[246] Pocock, *Machiavellian Moment*, 548–52.

[247] See Robert J. Steinfeld, "Property and Suffrage in the Early American Republic," *Stanford Law Review*, 41, 2 (January 1989), 335–76; Boydston, *Home and Work*, 43–4. On its liberal face, this reinscription of relations of household mastery after the Revolution on what otherwise now professed itself a "free"– that is a contractarian – legal-political culture was a meeting between incompatible tendencies. But those tensions were resolvable along the lines of demarcation between polis and household, public and private, that by the time of the Revolution structured political and social life throughout Anglo-America. The public realm was where economically independent heads of households met, their participation sanctified, democratized, and to a degree equalized by the polity's civic guarantees. Relations within households, in contrast, occurred within a separate domestic realm. These were not relations between heads of household, they were relations between heads and dependents. They were household heads' private business, their hierarchical character protected by private law, more or less impervious to revolutionary discourses of *public* liberty. Linda Kerber provides potent illustration of the resolution in "The Paradox of Women's Citizenship in the Early Republic." In "On Language, Gender, and Working Class History," *International Labor and Working Class History*, 31 (Spring 1987), at 9, Joan W. Scott shows in somewhat similar vein how the English Chartist movement drew on Locke's political philosophy to formulate a theory of universal entitlement to political rights based on a proprietorial claim of property in labor-power that simultaneously stated the theory as a theory of *manhood* suffrage. "The Chartists demand for universal manhood suffrage accepted the idea ... that only men concluded and entered the social contract; indeed, the identity that Chartists claimed with those already represented was that all were male property holders."

[248] On the former, see Waldstreicher, *Slavery's Constitution*; on the latter, Stephanie McCurry, *Masters of Small Worlds: Yeoman Households, Gender Relations, & the Political Culture of the Antebellum South Carolina Low Country* (New York, 1995); Manning, *The Key of Libberty*.

for securing survival onto subordinates, built on the same foundation of "inside" hierarchical social relations that presumed the master's control over the disposition of the household's total product and the activities of its producers.

For the proprietor, the prime expression of constancy was the law of his conjugal relations, of family and domestic service, and of employment and apprenticeship (the relations of man and wife, parent and child, master and servant) that I have traversed in this chapter. For the planter, the prime expression lay in the law of slavery. The separation between these *oikoi* – between the planter's slave relations and the proprietor's domestic relations and their respective forms of legal expression – was very real. Their forms of un/freedom were very distinct.[249] Still, John Adams lumped all the transgressors together, discontented children, apprentices, wives, Negroes; feared insolents, all. Slavery was never a matter for the planter alone, nor ever so confined (how ever we remember it) that its history is one of a region.[250]

To this point this book has been written in the shadow of slavery. But the trail of hints and asides and short, incomplete expositions stretching back to Chapter 1 has established the absolute necessity of its presence and signifies its refusal to be contained. The reason is simple enough: slavery was the single most powerful material force in the modernization of the Anglo-American mainland. To the unfreedom of slavery and its relationship to liberal modernity, American freedom's quintessential liability and always its essential inescapable condition, I now turn.

---

[249] Though not so distinct that it would prevent many antebellum feminists and workingmen from examining their own situations through slavery's lens. See Stanley, *From Bondage to Contract*, x–xiii, 175–86; David Roediger, *The Wages of Whiteness: Race and the Making of the American Working Class*, 3rd ed. (London and Brooklyn, N.Y., 2007), 43–163.

[250] As Nell Irvin Painter writes in her biography *Sojourner Truth, A Life, A Symbol* (New York, 1996), 10, "In the nineteenth century – as in our own times, *mutatis mutandis* – northerners preened themselves in their moral superiority to the slave drivers of the South, as though their own section had remained innocent of involuntary servitude. Such self-righteous censure of the South exempts northerners from their own slave-holding legacy, for when Isabella [Truth] was born a slave, a commonplace national institution bound her."

9

Enslaving: *Facies Hippocratica*

Slavery is all but death.

Alberico Gentili, *De Iure Belli Libri Tres* (1598)

[The slave] can know law only as an enemy.

William Goodell, *The American Slave Code in Theory and Practice* (1853)

Wherefore hear the word of the LORD, ye scornful men, that rule this people which is in Jerusalem. Because ye have said, We have made a covenant with death, and with hell are we at agreement; when the overflowing scourge shall pass through, it shall not come unto us: for we have made lies our refuge, and under falsehood have we hid ourselves: Therefore thus saith the Lord GOD, Behold, I lay in Zion for a foundation a stone, a tried stone, a precious corner stone, a sure foundation: he that believeth shall not make haste. Judgment also will I lay to the line, and righteousness to the plummet; and the hail shall sweep away the refuge of lies, and the waters shall overflow the hiding place. And your covenant with death shall be disannulled, and your agreement with hell shall not stand; when the overflowing scourge shall pass through, then ye shall be trodden down by it.

Isaiah 28: 14–18

At the beginning, the fate of English mainland colonizing had balanced upon twinned conceptual structures. A legal anthropology of civility and barbarity had sustained initial claims of *imperium* and *dominium,* justifying occupation and government of alien lands. A discourse of "commoditie" had spoken simultaneously of the use and improvement of those lands. The labor of transformation that all this envisaged had reinforced English justifications for keeping.

Colonizers' actual capacities to make productive use of mainland resources depended upon the development of markets – markets in products, obviously, but also in land and labor. Initiated in the colonizer's first acts of intrusion, markets widened and deepened over the course of the seventeenth century as the accumulation of voyages, projects, and plans collectively bound the mainland into the transoceanic networks of adventure and return that were creating the English Atlantic world.[1] Even as

---

[1] See generally Bruno Latour, "Drawing Things Together," in Michael Lynch and Steve Woolgar, editors, *Representation in Scientific Practice* (Cambridge, Mass., 1990), 25–6, 60;

seigneurial proprietorship succeeded corporatized commerce in the English model, colonizers' retention and extension of their hold on the mainland remained a function of their capacity to commoditize an ever-wider array of action.

Colonizers' commoditization of American land was a radical extension of processes that, during the sixteenth century, had begun to alter the course of first English then Irish life. Cadastral mapping and survey of land in England and Ireland had "gradually naturalize[d] a perspective on agrarian space which foregrounded its status not as social realm but as marketable commodity."[2] With the transformation of land had come the transformation of social relations on the land. In its mind's eye, Spenser's *View of the Present State of Ireland* (1596) centered on the promise of a "transformative cartography generat[ing] a new spatial order and annihilat[ing] a landscape of custom and use," and on the complete submission of the Irish to that order, "lyke captiues trembling at the victors sight."[3] John Norden's *Surveyor's Dialogue* (1607) acknowledged how, to many Englishmen, the new spatial order constructed by land surveyors supplied "the cords whereby poore men are drawne into seruitude and slauery." As Bernhard Klein notes, the offices of extraction, surveyor (of land) and overseer (of labor), sprang more or less at the same time from the same etymological root.[4]

In the grand scheme of *keeping*, commoditization of labor was no less essential than commoditization of land. Broadly imagined from early on as a spatial order of commodity-producing plantations – an archipelago of order in the wilderness – English mainland settlements required constant infusions of labor, preferably cheap. Norden's "poore men" were indeed drawn into servitude by that demand, making their way throughout the seventeenth century to the new-commoditized lands of the Atlantic seaboard as commoditized migrant labor. So too, Spenser's Irish captives. Still, these migrants were the offspring of Christian European lands, a circumstance that imposed limits of duration and treatment on the character of their servitude in North America.[5] In the legal economy of seventeenth-century colonizing, complete commoditization was to be the fate of others unbound from that circumstance, "exotic peoples, those polluted but

---

Stephen Greenblatt, *Marvelous Possessions: The Wonder of the New World* (Chicago, 1991), 9; Tzvetan Todorov, *The Conquest of America: The Question of the Other* (Norman, Okla., 1999), 251–4.

[2] Bernhard Klein, *Maps and the Writing of Space in Early Modern England and Ireland* (Basingstoke, 2001) 44. See, generally 61–75. On cadastral mapping, see Roger P. Kain and Elizabeth Baigent, *The Cadastral Map in the Service of the State: A History of Property Mapping* (Chicago, 1992).

[3] Klein, *Maps and the Writing of Space*, 67; *Amoretti and Epithalamion*, Written not long since by Edmund Spenser (1595), I.4. And see Rebecca Ann Bach, *Colonial Transformations: The Cultural Production of the New Atlantic World, 1580–1640* (New York, 2000), 48, and generally, 37–65.

[4] Klein, *Maps and the Writing of Space*, 46, 43.

[5] See, e.g., Act XIV (March 1659/60), *An Act for repealing an Act for Irish Servants*, in William Waller Hening, *The Statutes at Large; Being a Collection of all the Laws of Virginia, from the First*

desired, low Others," offspring of the lands of barbarians, thrust, involuntarily, into the migrant stream to feed mainland demand.[6] Barbarians were savages and infidels, brutes and beasts, perpetual enemies of Christians. Barbarians could be wholly transformed, irreversibly commodified, for they were such as Christians might justly enslave.[7]

One such low other makes an early appearance on the English stage in William Shakespeare's *Titus Andronicus* (written c. 1592) in the character of Aron the Moor. Aron is the quintessential exotic barbarian – savage and infidel, polluted and desired. Traditionalists mock Aron, like the play itself, as a young dramatist's clumsy caricature.[8] But Aron's appearances always

Session of the Legislature, in the Year 1619 (New York, 1823), I, 538–9, providing that "no servant comeing into the country without indentures, of what christian nation soever, shall serve longer then those of our own country," i.e., England "of the like age." The act repealed was Act VI (March 1654/55), *Statutes at Large*, I, 411, which specified that Irish servants without indentures were to serve six years if over sixteen years of age, or until age twenty-four if under, "notwithstanding the act for servants without indentures [that is Act XXVI (1642/3), *Statutes at Large*, I, 257, specifying that servants without indentures were to serve four years if over twenty years of age, five years if between twelve and twenty, and seven if under twelve] it being only the benefitt of our own nation." Hening's *Statutes at Large* are available at http://www.vagenweb.org/hening/ (accessed 22 August 2009).

6 Robert Blair St. George, *Conversing by Signs: Poetics of Implication in Colonial New England Culture* (Chapel Hill, 1998), 12. In English portrayals, it is well known, the Irish came close to the requisite barbarity. But as Brian Lockey's analysis of Spenser shows, ambivalence rather than certainty attended English discussion of "the essence of … Irish barbarism." Brian C. Lockey, *Law and Empire in English Renaissance Literature* (Cambridge and New York, 2006), 119, and generally 113–41.

7 Richard Tuck, *The Rights of War and Peace: Political Thought and the International Order From Grotius to Kant* (Oxford, 1999), 40–7. Note generally Sir Edward Coke, in *Calvin's Case* (1608) 77 Eng. Rep. 397: "All infidels are in law *perpetui inimici*, perpetual enemies (for the law presumes not that they will be converted, that being *remota potentia*, a remote possibility) for between them, as with the devils, whose subjects they be, and the Christian, there is perpetual hostility, and can be no peace; for as the Apostle saith, 2 Cor. 6. 15. *Quæ autem conventio Christi ad Belial, aut quæ, pars fideli cum infideli* [And what covenant has Christ with Belial? Or what has a believer to do with an infidel?] and the law saith, *Judæo Christianum nullum serviat mancipium, nefas enim est quem, Christus redemit blasphemum, Christi in servitutis vinculis detinere.* Register 282. [No Christian should be sold in slavery to a Jew, for it is unlawful that one whom Christ has redeemed should be held in the bonds of servitude to someone who blasphemes against Christ]. *Infideles sunt Christi et Christianorum inimici* [Infidels are enemies of Christ and of Christians]." Translations from Latin by Steve Shepherd. See Steve Sheppard, editor, *The Selected Writings and Speeches of Sir Edward Coke* (Indianapolis, 2003), I, 675. See also *Butts against Penny* 83 English Reports 518 (1677).

8 Harold Bloom, self-described "last High Romantic Bardolator," finds Aron "hilarious" and *Titus Andronicus* "indefensible," a "poetic atrocity" with "no intrinsic value," a play so "ghastly bad" that it is explicable only as a "send-up … howler … bloody farce." See his *Shakespeare: The Invention of the Human* (New York, 1998), 78, 79, 80, 83, 86. Bloom's high-end contempt was not shared by Tudor-Stuart audiences: From the day of its first performance in 1594 until the closing of the theaters in 1642, *Titus Andronicus* was an extraordinarily popular play. The impact of performances during the 1590s was "overwhelming," demand for the play in print continuous for thirty years. Ballads were sung of the play's fame, and Ben Jonson paid tribute to it in his own *Bartholomew Fair* (1614): "Hee that will sweare, Ieronimo, or Andronicus are the best playes, yet, shall passe vnexcepted

deceive.[9] He is present on stage throughout the play's first act, when all the principals are introduced, but silent, simply standing and waiting upon the Goth queen Tamora and her sons (Alarbus, Chiron, and Demetrius), whom Titus has brought as spoils of war to Rome. There is no reason for an audience to think him anything but a prop – bit player, mere attendant. Aron speaks for the first time only when the stage finally clears and he is alone. His words exult in the remarkable reversal of Tamora's fortunes that the audience has just witnessed. Entering the first act the helpless captive of the Andronici, she leaves it, to their discomfit, betrothed to the newly elected Emperor Saturninus, hence their future Empress. And all the while, Aron boasts, she is in fact besotted with him, "faster bound to Aron's charming eyes /Than is Prometheus tied to Caucasus." Her good fortune will be his as well. But why is Aron's exultation so fierce? Because he is slave as well as lover, and detects in Tamora's elevation a chance to escape his slavery, to overcome it. "Then, Aron, arm thy heart and fit thy thoughts /To mount aloft with thy imperial mistress ... /Away with slavish weeds and servile thoughts."[10]

Throughout the play, Aron is driven by scalding fury. Usually cloaked in sardonic humor, Aron's fury outs at the end. "Ah, why should wrath be mute, and fury dumb? /I am no baby, I, that with base prayers /I should

at, heere, as a man whose Iudgement shewes it is constant, and hath stood still, these fiue and twentie, or thirtie yeeres." (The reference to Ieronimo is to Thomas Kyd's *The Spanish Tragedy* (c.1587), also immensely popular with Elizabethan audiences.) See Jacques Berthoud, "Introduction," in William Shakespeare, *Titus Andronicus*, Sonia Massai, editor (Harmondsworth, U.K., 2001), 7; the Booke-holder's speech from Ben Jonson, *Bartholomew Fair*, Carroll Storrs Alden, editor (New York, 1904), 8, lines 25–8.

[9] Commonly given as "Aaron" in modern editions, the moor's name is "Aron" in the first quarto and in the folio. Ian Lancashire has established that Aron is the name of a very common English plant, also found in Africa and Egypt. Early Modern English Dictionaries Database entries between 1587 and 1611 describe the plant Aron as "bespotted heere and there with blackish spots" similar to an adder's, and growing "in woods neere vnto ditches vnder hedges, euerie where in shadowie places." The root of the plant made the purest form of starch, "most hurtfull for the hands." In the play, at 2.3.35, Aron likens himself to an adder; at 2.3.74 he is described as "spotted, detested and abominable." And as Lancashire observes, he will indeed prove very hard on the hands, accounting for both of Lavinia's and one of Titus's own. Aron's significance is archly foreshadowed early on when, interring his dead sons brought home from war, Titus remarks of their tomb, at 1.1.157, "Here grow no damnèd drugs." Aron's fate, decreed at the end of the play by Lucius, 5.3.179–83, is to be planted. "Set him breast-deep in earth, and famish him." This strange wild plant that dwells in the shadows is to be "fastened in the earth" to die of starvation. Ian Lancashire, "Understanding Shakespeare's *Titus Andronicus* and the EMEDD [Early Modern English Dictionaries Database]," *Early Modern Literary Studies*, Special Issue 1 (1997), 18–20, available at http://purl.oclc.org/emls/si-01/si-01lancashire.html (accessed 22 August 2009). Note that the EMEDD database has since been renamed the Lexicons of Early Modern English database. It can be accessed at http://leme.library.utoronto.ca/.

[10] William Shakespeare, *Titus Andronicus*, Russ McDonald, editor (New York, 2000), 2.1.1–18. All text references are to this edition unless explicitly stated otherwise. Later, in dialog with Tamora, Titus's daughter Lavinia refers to Aron as "your Moor." *Titus Andronicus*, 2.3.68.

repent the evils I have done; /Ten thousand worse than ever yet I did / Would I perform, if I might have my will. /If one good deed in all my life I did, /I do repent it from my very soul."[11] Commentators have concentrated on his transgressions: Aron is the personification of "evil," a "monstrous" character.[12] But to see nothing but monstrosity is to conspire in the reproduction of Aron as monster. Certainly Aron's infidel atheism and the crimes he commits throughout the play – "forgery, planting evidence, incitement to rape, slander leading to decapitation of the innocent, dismemberment, promise-breaking, and outright murder" – encourage us to see him as the epitome of alien brutishness.[13] Still, the better question is causal. Why is Aron furious?

Aron's crimes are all crimes of vengeance.[14] His vengeance is very much his own; Aron is no cypher obediently pursuing his mistress's wish to see

[11] Ibid., 5.3.184–90. Except in soliloquy, Aron's fury has been more or less hidden until this point in the play, at least in the sense that his hatreds have taken the form in dialog of taunting and humor. Aron only "speaks out" in the final scenes after he has been made a prisoner by the Andronici, who then gag him. See 5.1.87–151.

[12] McDonald, "Introduction," xxxvi, xxxix.

[13] "As a Moor (or blackamoor), Aaron [sic] probably would have served the Elizabethan audience as a magnet for revulsion ... the extreme case of the cultural Other." McDonald, "Introduction," xxxix.

[14] As drama, *Titus Andronicus* conforms broadly to the genre of "revenge tragedy" found in the classical Roman work of Seneca and reestablished in the later 1580s by Kyd's immensely popular *The Spanish Tragedy* (c. 1587). Revenge tragedy is distinguished by a particular plot form: an introductory assertion of a prior foundational injustice, followed by unremitting and often fantastic rage and violence in the service of injustice's resolution. John Nettles writes, "the play usually opens after the commission of a murder, with the victim's loved ones, or the ghost of the victim himself, demanding that the killer or killers be brought to justice; the culprit(s) are shown to be living in some elevated state, having profited from the crime; the agent of vengeance then spends the bulk of the play overcoming obstacles in order to gain the opportunity and fortitude necessary to exact that vengeance, which must be death; revenge is finally achieved, but at the cost of many lives, including the revenger's. These plays tend to be soaked in blood and steeped in madness." John Nettles, "Perverse Justice in Kyd's Spanish Tragedy," at http://parallel. park.uga.edu/~jnettles/kyd.html para 1 (accessed 13 February 2003). *Hamlet* (c. 1600), a more mature exploration of the potential of revenge tragedy than *Titus Andronicus*, conforms more strictly and conservatively to the conventions of the plot form. In contrast, *Titus Andronicus* begins in a confusion of competing foundational injustices and continues to layer them one on the next throughout. Titus returns from war against the barbarian Goths with his captives to find Saturninus and Bassianus, the two sons of the late emperor, on the brink of civil war over the succession. Marcus Andronicus, tribune and Titus's brother, is conspiring to install Titus as emperor "to set a head on headless Rome." Bassianus, the younger son, offers to ally with the Andronici against his brother, but Titus swears loyalty to Saturninus, and Saturninus chooses Titus's daughter, Lavinia, as empress to cement their alliance. With the connivance of Marcus and Titus's sons, Bassianus seizes and abducts Lavinia, claiming she is already betrothed to him. Saturninus denounces the Andronici as traitors and conspirators and Bassianus as traitor and rapist. He announces he will make Tamora (whose firstborn Alarbus has moments before been slaughtered by the Andronici) his empress instead. By the end of the first act, Shakespeare has given every principal in the play an entirely plausible claim to have been wronged and a reason to seek revenge. The stage then clears for Aron who,

the Andronici destroyed. Indeed, while Tamora's attention wanders occasionally from the task at hand, Aron remains completely focused on the destruction of the Andronici. "Vengeance is in my heart, death in my hand, /Blood and revenge are hammering in my head." Why is his fury so much greater than hers? "What signifies my deadly-standing eye, /My silence, and my cloudy melancholy, /My fleece of woolly hair that now uncurls / Even as an adder when she doth unroll /To do some fatal execution?"[15] Can it be that he has been made furious by his enslavement and by the contempt his blackness earns?

Tamora has good reason to hate the Andronici. At the beginning of the first act, Titus decrees her captive firstborn son Alarbus must be sacrificed "T'appease the[ ] groaning shadows that are gone" in the war just concluded. Alarbus is promptly disemboweled, dismembered, and burned before Tamora's eyes.[16] But Aron hates them even more. His deep hatred of the Andronici and their allies is lent a particular edge by their contempt for him. Titus's daughter Lavinia and her betrothed, Bassianus, thoroughly enjoy an exchange of racial banter at Aron's expense: "swart Cimmerian ... Spotted, detested and abominable ... barbarous Moor ... raven-colored love."[17] Titus's last surviving son Lucius later assails him with a similar barrage: "barbarous Moor ... ravenous tiger ... accursèd devil ... inhuman dog! unhallow'd slave!"[18] But actually Aron encounters the same from all sides, and it leaves him with few loyalties, whether to Tamora's sons or even Tamora herself. His child, whom Tamora bears, revolts its nurse: "shame ... disgrace ... a devil ... /A joyless, dismal, black and sorrowful issue ... loathsome as a toad /Amongst the fair-faced breeders of our clime." Fair Tamora wants the child immediately destroyed because its blackness will expose her adultery to the Emperor. She orders Aron to kill it. "The empress sends it thee, thy stamp, thy seal, /And bids thee christen it with thy dagger's point." Aron kills the nurse instead. Demetrius snarls

in soliloquy, begins to reveal *his* reasons to seek revenge. *Titus Andronicus*, 1.1.1–498. On the multiple resonances of revenge tragedy for the moment of English colonizing, see Christopher Tomlins, "Law's Wilderness: The Discourse of English Colonizing, the Violence of Intrusion, and the Failures of American History," in John Smolenski and Thomas J. Humphrey, editors, *New World Orders: Violence, Sanction and Authority in the Colonial Americas* (Philadelphia, 2005), 21–46, and "In a Wilderness of Tigers: Violence, the Discourse of English Colonizing, and the Refusals of American History," *Theoretical Inquiries in Law*, 4, 2 (July 2003), 451–89; David Harris Sacks, "Discourses of Western Planting: Richard Hakluyt and the Making of the Atlantic World," in Peter C. Mancall, editor, *The Atlantic World and Virginia, 1550–1624* (Chapel Hill, 2007), 436–46.

[15] *Titus Andronicus*, 2.3.32–6, 38–9. This entire passage speaks a consuming, deadly, long-suppressed rage.

[16] Ibid., 1.1.129, and generally 1.1.99–148.

[17] Ibid., 2.3.55–87. Within a few minutes of this exchange, Bassianus has been murdered by Chiron and Demetrius at Aron's instigation. Aron persuades Saturninus that the culprits are Titus's sons, Martius and Quintus. They are executed. Meanwhile, Chiron and Demetrius rape and mutilate Lavinia, again at Aron's instigation. 2.1.103–35, 2.3.116–2.4.10.

[18] Ibid., 5.3.4–5, 14.

that Aron is "hellish ... loathèd ... foul," and attempts to skewer the baby for his mother. "I'll broach the tadpole on my rapier's point."[19] Aron spirits the child away but they fall captive to Lucius, who repeats Demetrius's threats. "Too like the sire for ever being good. /First hang the child, that he may see it *sprawl.*"[20]

Whether against Tamora's sons or against Lucius, Aron defends the child fiercely and lovingly – the only unmediated humanity anyone in the play exhibits.[21] Looking at it he sees the only thing like himself in the entire play:[22] "Look how the black slave smiles upon the father, /As who should say 'Old lad, I am thine own' ... thick-lipped slave ... tawny slave ... villain." In Aron's mouth these are terms of endearment. In Lucius's mouth they are racial invective: "Say, wall-eyed slave, whither wouldst thou convey /This growing image of thy fiendlike face?"[23]

Jacques Berthoud argues that Aron is the epitome of self-sufficient autonomy,[24] but in this he is mistaken. Throughout, Aron's métier is deception and trickery, not direct action; he exploits the stupidity of Chiron and Demetrius, he manipulates Saturninus, he so befuddles Titus that Titus entreats him to assist in chopping off his own hand. Each becomes his unwitting accomplice, for Aron manipulates by dissembly, ever the dutiful attendant, willing assistant.[25] Reliance on deceit suggests Aron's opportunities for autonomous action are constrained, particularly when contrasted with the brutal directness that Lucius displays throughout.[26] Aron lets men's cattle stray to their destruction, he burns their barns and haystacks in the night.[27] Berthoud rightly observes, "Every moment of his life represents

---

[19] Ibid., 4.2.52–105. Aron's pride in his blackness is conveyed forcefully in this scene: "ye sanguine, shallow-hearted boys! /Ye white-limed walls! ye alehouse painted signs! /Coal-black is better than another hue /In that it scorns to bear another hue; /For all the water in the ocean /Can never turn the swan's black legs to white, /Although she lave them hourly in the flood." 4.2.97–103.

[20] Ibid., 5.1.50–51 (emphasis added).

[21] Meredith Anne Skura, "Discourse and the Individual: The Case of Colonialism in *The Tempest*," *Shakespeare Quarterly*, 40, 1 (Spring 1989), 65.

[22] "What the child has done is to convert his father's black skin ... into a social bond. Indeed, it has turned him inside out, for the social self, until then buried within him, is now in front of him, smiling back at him." Berthoud, "Introduction," 43. After he is captured by Lucius, Aron effectively sacrifices himself to try to ensure the child's survival by offering Lucius a complete account of all that has happened in exchange for the child's life. *Titus Andronicus*, 5.1.53–150.

[23] *Titus Andronicus*, 4.2.120–1, 4.2.176, 5.1.27, 5.1.29, 5.1.44–5.

[24] Berthoud, "Introduction," 40–1. Berthoud here alludes to the "autarkic selfhood" of the enraged Senecan protagonist. See Sacks, "Discourses of Western Planting," 441.

[25] Indeed throughout the play, until he takes his leave of them, Aron is always careful to address Tamora and her sons respectfully. Tamora is "Madam ... great empress," Chiron and Demetrius "lords ... Young lords." See, e.g., *Titus Andronicus*, 2.1.45, 2.1.69, 2.1.112, 2.3.30, 2.3.52.

[26] Aron's only resource in the play is speech, which he uses to flatter, persuade, cajole and, finally, torment.

[27] *Titus Andronicus*, 5.1.132–3. Aron's recitation of his evils emphasizes indirection and concealment, weapons of the weak: "Few come within the compass of my curse, /Wherein

a nullification of those collaborations that build up and preserve human communities."[28] But what "human community" should a slave expect from slaveholders? Only when alone with the one thing like him in the play, his son, does Aron enjoy any community of his own.

In the figure of Aron, put on stage right at the outset of England's renewed transatlantic adventuring, Shakespeare gives a slave visage and voice. The visage is black, the voice is fury. And at the end of the play, the furious slave, more or less on the loose since the end of the first act, is captured, gagged, and dispatched by lawful decree of his Christian enemy.[29] "Set him breast-deep in earth and famish him. /There let him stand and rave and cry for food. /If anyone relieves or pities him, /For the offense he dies. This is our doom."[30] In a play full of cruel, grotesque, exotic deaths, Aron's public execution (and this by design, for he is a rebellious runaway slave, and as such another of mankind's "common enemies") is the cruelest, the most grotesque, the most exotic of all.

I did not some notorious ill: /As kill a man, or else devise his death; /Ravish a maid, or plot the way to do it; /Accuse some innocent, and forswear myself; /Set deadly enmity between two friends; /Make poor men's cattle break their necks; /Set fire on barns and haystacks in the night" 5.1.126–33, and see also 5.1.134–40.

[28] Berthoud, "Introduction," 41. In *Worlds Apart: The Market and the Theater in Anglo-American Thought* (Cambridge and New York, 1986), Jean-Christophe Agnew addresses the intricate sociology of looming modernity presented by the Tudor-Stuart theater. For Agnew, modernity means a new society of unbounded market exchange, with all its threats to social unity, traditional ways of life, and what one might call face value. His subject is the interrelationship of theater and market as spheres for the performance of social transformation – the disintegration of old ways and organic human relations and the emergence of new unfixed identities. In *Titus Andronicus* Aron is the starkest embodiment of the market, for in person he is the market's ultimate creation and most complete transformation, a human commodity. No wonder, then, that he stands for the nullification of human communities. See also St. George, *Conversing By Signs*, 155–6: "As scorned and debased objects of the Briton's psychic instability and economic zeal, Africans appeared in Elizabethan drama ... as the 'Black-a-Moor,' the erotic rebel, the 'Aetheopian' Satan, the African slave ... the colonized figuration of suppressed desire, and chattel property ... treacherous devils, market ciphers, and transatlantic cargo."

[29] Maurice Hunt points out that the play is set in time in the closing decades of the fourth century C.E., "the time that Christianity passed from being a favored religion of Rome to being the official faith of the Empire." Hunt argues that the introduction of Christian themes in the latter stages of the play to replace the pagan themes of the beginning can be seen as representative of a "profound transition from pagan to Christian religious values," personified most clearly in Lucius, whose ultimate triumph and punishment of evil becomes that of a Christian redeemer. Maurice Hunt, "Exonerating Lucius in *Titus Andronicus*: A Response to Anthony Brian Taylor," *Connotations*, 7.1 (1997–8), 87–93, at 90, available at http://www.uni-tuebingen.de/connotations/ (accessed 22 August 2009).

[30] *Titus Andronicus*, 5.3.179–82. Aron is to die a slow, torturous, closely observed death, enforced by a decree (doom) penalizing on pain of death any expression of the elementary human virtue of empathy (relief, pity). Hunt, interestingly, describes the manner of Aron's execution as routine for a "gracious Christian governor," and argues that it would have been perceived by an Elizabethan audience as perfectly just, even "decorous." See Hunt, "Exonerating Lucius," 92.

I. Histories of Fury

English colonizers' resort to massive race enslavement to sustain and advance their laborious intrusions upon the North American mainland is perhaps the most abrupt and conclusive retort to American history's compulsive narrative of freedom and consent, and as such its most persistent and lasting liability. How, after all, does one reconcile "the brute fact that slavery was an intrinsic part of the American experience" with the enduring exceptionalist trope of America the "source of redemption from the burdens of history," the paradise promising "fulfillment of man's highest aspirations?"[31] One cannot. In Anglo-America, modernity's hopes and slavery's brute facts come wrapped together as one.[32]

Scholars have developed two distinct strategies to sort through the dialectic of American slavery. The first strategy has been championed by Orlando Patterson, who observes that for most of human history, freedom has been intimately related to the existence of slavery – which means that slavery is a necessary condition for the realization of the "most profoundly cherished ideals and beliefs in the Western tradition" rather than a barrier that must be surmounted by them – and by Edmund Morgan, who argues that American slavery is a signal instance of this intimate relationship in action.[33] One may indeed agree, yet simultaneously note that in the Anglo-American canon "freedom" and "slavery" were not philosophical concepts abstracted from particular bearers, each a structural locale inhabitable potentially by anyone, but rather were determined by their bearers. It was not only that (in Aristotelian mien) the elevated freedom of the free depended upon the resources generated by the enslavement of the slave, not only that for freedom to persist for the one the enslavement of the other must be far more complete than the servitude of any of Mandeville's masses, but also that the intended beneficiary was always only white and the unwilling benefactor black.[34] The Anglo-American version

---

[31] David Brion Davis, *The Problem of Slavery in Western Culture* (Ithaca, N.Y., 1966), 10.

[32] Tomlins, "In a Wilderness of Tigers," 464–6; William A. Pettigrew, "Free to Enslave: Politics and the Escalation of Britain's Transatlantic Slave Trade, 1688–1714," *William and Mary Quarterly*, 3rd Ser., 64, 1 (January 2007), 8–9.

[33] Orlando Patterson, *Slavery and Social Death: A Comparative Study* (Cambridge, Mass., 1982) viii–ix; Edmund S. Morgan, *American Slavery, American Freedom: The Ordeal of Colonial Virginia* (New York, 1975), 363–87.

[34] Patterson notes, "the focus of this 'we-they' distinction was at first religious" and only later "racial." *Slavery and Social Death*, 7. In the Anglo-American Atlantic, however, virtually every manifestation of slavery is racialized from the outset. Exceptions will be noted below, where attention will also be given to the terms upon which religious community was held no barrier to enslavement as long as the slave was racially distinct.

In this chapter, I concentrate on African enslavement. This is not intended to minimize instances of enslavement of the indigenous population by the English; it simply acknowledges that mainland slavery was overwhelmingly an enslavement of imported Africans. It is worth noting, however, that slave relations between the English and indigenous populations had a distinct dynamic. As Joyce Chaplin simply but subtly observes, among colonists "African bodies were clearly marked for slavery" whereas "English and Indian bodies were, in this regard, dangerously undifferentiated: either could be enslaved, depending

of the "intimate" relationship was reliant upon the irrevocable, perpetual, *racialized* difference of the protagonists.[35]

Jessamy: I say, Sir, I understand that Colonel Manly has the honour of having you for a servant.

Jonathan: Servant! Sir, do you take me for a neger ... I am a true blue son of liberty ... no man shall master me.[36]

The second strategy has been to blur slavery's edges, first by hiding it among other putatively similar institutions – the commonplace of likeness – then by proclaiming the inevitability of its demise. Gordon Wood has represented slavery as just one more dependency among many during the two centuries of "monarchical society" prior to the American Revolution, one that did not seem to contemporaries "all that different from white servitude and white labor" at least until the sweep of revolutionary egalitarianism abruptly exposed its continuance as an anomalous aberration.[37] Then, although the revolutionaries were unable *completely* to abolish slavery, in the very instance of their Revolution they "suddenly and effectively ended the cultural climate that had allowed black slavery," thus condemning the institution to its inevitable, inexorable extinction.[38]

But the dependencies thought characteristic of early American society, those of European servitude, of work, do not provide the desired camouflage. When one measures the incidence of migrant servitude, when one

on who had the upper hand." Joyce E. Chaplin, *Subject Matter: Technology, the Body, and Science on the Anglo-American Frontier, 1500–1676* (Cambridge, Mass., 2001), 228.

[35] The matter is debated by Philip D. Morgan in *Slave Counterpoint: Black Culture in the Eighteenth Century Chesapeake and Lowcountry* (Chapel Hill, 1998), 8–18. See generally Winthrop D. Jordan, *White Over Black: American Attitudes Toward the Negro, 1550–1812* (Chapel Hill, 1968). See also Aldon T. Vaughan, *Roots of American Racism: Essays on the Colonial Experience* (New York and Oxford, 1995). Barbara Jeanne Fields argues that "racism" as an explanation of slavery awaits the founding of the republic, and that "race" can only do explanatory work in the early history of American slavery if traced as prejudice of color. See her "Slavery, Race and Ideology in the United States of America," *New Left Review*, I/181 (May–June 1990), 101. I argue in this chapter that prejudice of color is on display in Anglo-American discourse from the outset.

[36] Royall Tyler, *The Contrast: A Comedy in Five Acts* (Philadelphia, 1790), 26–7 (Act II Scene 2) 34–5. *The Contrast* was first performed in 1787.

In the republican discourse of the Revolutionary era, slavery connoted political dependence, lack of autonomy. It had been a term of opprobrium used by revolutionary elites to characterize the consequences of the colonies' *political* subordination to Britain. The racial character of American slavery substantially mitigated possible crossover effects between elite republicanism and domestic political culture, for politics and freedom were "white" phenomena, while domestically slavery was black. Race enabled republicans to segregate (contain) slavery culturally, and thus continue to be slaveholders. It also enabled slavery to continue to exist in alliance with republicanism "and to perform the service it had pioneered in colonial times: that of limiting the need for free citizens (which is to say white people) to exploit each other directly." See Fields, "Slavery, Race and Ideology," 108, and generally 101–8. The classic statement of this argument is Morgan's in *American Slavery, American Freedom*.

[37] Gordon S. Wood, *The Radicalism of the American Revolution: How a Revolution Turned a Monarchial Society into a Democratic One unlike any that had Ever Existed.* (New York, 1992), 54, 51–6, 186–7.

[38] Ibid., 186.

examines the law of work and labor, slavery's absolute difference becomes obvious, both in nature and extent. That absolute difference was produced in and reproduced by the Anglo-American law of slavery. And when one comes to the inevitability of slavery's demise, one must note more obstinate facts. Slavery of course expanded, it did not contract, after the American Revolution.[39] Rates of slave population increase prevailing in the quarter-century after the Revolution hardly decreased from those of the quarter-century before. By the early nineteenth century the half million enslaved Africans of 1776 had become a million. By 1860 they were four million, spread over a vastly larger expanse of territory.[40] This is not evidence of a cultural climate hostile to black slavery. The slave populations of most of the northern states were indeed freed, but agonizingly slowly thanks to the dictates of northern gradual abolition laws. Tens of thousands remained enslaved for decades, and those who did gain their freedom under the laws were instantaneously (and once again involuntarily) entrapped in other forms of carefully legislated, elaborately elongated, servitude.[41] And what of the cultural climate of these northern states when it came to the actual work of abolition and its intended beneficiaries? "Contempt more bitter, opposition more active, detraction more relentless, prejudice more stubborn, and apathy more frozen, than among slave-owners themselves."[42] Slavery's penetration of the territories north of the Ohio River was restrained but not prevented by the Northwest Ordinance of 1787.[43] To the south and west expansion was rapid and unconfined.[44] None of this is surprising, for the post-Revolutionary epoch saw the legal-cultural climate that had allowed black slavery not ended but reinforced. Only a few years after the Revolution and the brief burst of emancipations that the political and economic dislocations of the Revolutionary war inspired, the U.S. Constitution embedded protection of slavery and transatlantic slave trading deep in the Republic's fundamental law. Inland, domestic

[39] For a succinct summary, see Ira Berlin, *Many Thousands Gone: The First Two Centuries of Slavery in North America* (Cambridge, Mass., 1998), 223–4.
[40] Calculated from *Historical Statistics of the United States, Earliest Times to the Present: Millennial Edition* (New York, 2006), vol. 2, table Bb1–98 (Black population, by state and slave/free status: 1790–1860); vol. 5, table Eg1–59 (Population, by race and by colony or locality: 1610–1780). Except where noted otherwise, all statements regarding early American populations are derived from this source, hereafter cited as *HSUS*.
[41] Berlin, *Many Thousands Gone*, 228–55. See also the conclusion to this chapter.
[42] William Lloyd Garrison, "To The Public," *The Liberator* (first issue, 1 January 1831). See also generally Mark A. Graber, *Dred Scott and the Problem of Constitutional Evil* (New York, 2006). I discuss Graber's book further in Chapter 10.
[43] In 1800, more than 20% of blacks in the Northwest Territory (135 of 635) were enslaved; in 1810, 12.4% (429 of 3,454); in 1820, 14.4% (1107 of 7691). Slaves remained in the region into the 1840s. Calculated from *HSUS*, vol. 2, table Bb1–98 (figures for the East North Central census region, plus Wisconsin). On slavery in the Northwest Territory, see Lea VanderVelde and Sandhya Subramanian, "Mrs Dred Scott," *Yale Law Journal*, 106, 4 (January 1997), 1047–50. See also Chapter 10, section I.
[44] See *HSUS*, vol. 2, table Bb1–98 (figures for the East South Central and West South Central census regions, plus South Carolina, Georgia, and Florida from the South Atlantic census region).

commerce in slaves was never interrupted.[45] I noted at the end of Chapter 8 that the Republic's commitment to the restraint of labor mobility (Article IV, Section 2, Clause 3) applied not just to slaves but to any person "held to Service or Labour"; that is, it applied to those persons "bound for a Term of Years" acknowledged in Article I.[46] But Article I allowed that the relativities of freedom noted in Article IV might be suspended for civic purposes – that is, for the purpose of defining membership in the polity – by holding persons bound to a term of service to be "free" when it came to enumeration and representation. Hierarchy thereby became polarity. The fugitive clause meant that those bound to service for a term of years had no more freedom of movement than slaves, but like became unlike in Article I to serve the higher purpose of white civic solidarity.[47] We have already seen that popular discourse reproduced constitutional law's racialized

---

[45] The coastwise trade in slaves was regulated, but not outlawed, by a ban on trading in vessels "of less burthen than forty tons" included in 1807's congressional legislation outlawing the international slave trade following the expiration of 1787's twenty-year moratorium. See Don E. Fehrenbacher, *The Slaveholding Republic: An Account of the United States Government's Relations to Slavery*, completed and edited by Ward M. McAfee (New York, 2001), 146–7.

Debating the role of slavery in the making of the U.S. Constitution, Gordon S. Wood insists that "the fact that slavery had been taken for granted for thousands of years prior to the mid-eighteenth century *must* be the starting point in any assessment of its influence on early American politics and nationhood." Gordon S. Wood, "Reading the Founders' Minds," *New York Review of Books*, 54, 11 (28 June 2007), available at http://www.nybooks.com/articles/20342 (accessed 22 August 2009) (emphasis added). Given its ancient pedigree, Wood argues, it is remarkable that post-Revolutionary Americans began questioning slavery. Wood's fact, however, is relevant only if Americans had no cultural foundations in Western Europe, where slavery had *not* been taken for granted for hundreds of years. "Why should you impose upon free people the shameful and intolerable yoke of slavery?" wrote Alberico Gentili in the 1580s (*De Iure Belli Libri Tres, Volume Two – The Translation of the Edition of 1612*, John C. Rolfe, trans. (Oxford 1933), 336.) See also David Northrup, "Free and Unfree Labor Migration, 1600–1900: An Introduction," *Journal of World History*, 14, 1 (June 2003), 127, who notes one should not "lose sight of how unnatural an institution slavery was for seventeenth-century northern Europeans, whose own lands and laws had not known the institution for centuries." (For the short-lived attempt during the reign of Edward VI to reestablish slavery in England in punishment of vagrancy, abandoned after two years on the grounds that "thextremitie of some [of the laws] have byn occasion that they have not ben putt in ure," see C.S.L. Davies, "Slavery and Protector Somerset; the Vagrancy Act of 1547," *Economic History Review*, 2nd Ser., 19, 3 (December, 1966), 533–49.) In this light the relevant fact here is that at the time of their Revolution, Anglo-Americans had been happy for the better part of two centuries to embrace slavery for racial others and continued for the better part of another century to do so.

[46] That is, sailors who had signed articles for a voyage, indentured servants, and apprentices, as well as northern state blacks subject to terms of service under gradual emancipation laws. For evidence of disciplinary and runaway incarcerations stretching well into the nineteenth century, see for example the "Prisoners for Trial" Docket of the Prison for the City and County of Philadelphia, vols. 1–21 (1790–1840), Archives of the City and County of Philadelphia (401 North Broad Street, Philadelphia).

[47] I discuss this matter in Christopher Tomlins, "The Threepenny Constitution (and the Question of Justice)," *Alabama Law Review*, 58, 5 (2007), 984–8.

representation of freedom and otherness in its own earthily simple claim
that none but "negers" were "sarvants."[48]

The antebellum republic prospered no less mightily from slavery than
had the colonies it succeeded. For most of the seventy years between the
creation of the republic and the Civil War, trade in slave-produced agricultural commodity exports, notably cotton, earned the revenues that
financed American economic growth and underpinned the emergence of
powerful regional economies. "While the immigration of people and particularly capital into the United States played an important part in [U.S.]
growth in the thirty years after 1815, it was the growth of the cotton textile industry and the demand for cotton which was decisive." The cotton
trade was the economy's only "major expansive force." Cotton exports were
"strategic ... the major independent variable in the interdependent structure of internal and international trade," the major stimulus to economic
development in the West and Northeast. Relatively speaking, as is usually
the case with primary product exporting regions, the South actually benefited least: "income received from the export of cotton" and other agricultural staple exports "flowed directly out of the regional economy again
in the purchase of goods and services" – manufactures and insurance and
shipping services from the North, foodstuffs from the West.[49] The United
States of the antebellum nineteenth century retained all the vested interest
in the "brute fact" of slavery that had developed in the English America of
the previous two centuries.

Points of Departure

Shakespeare shows us that racialized representations of slavery were well
embedded in English cultural cosmology in the late sixteenth century.[50] In
1619, according to tradition, the first actual African slaves were introduced
to Virginia when in August of that year a Dutch ship in urgent need of

[48] Quoted in Charles William Janson, *The Stranger in America* (London, 1807), 88. And see
the conclusion to Chapter 7. On the Constitution, slavery, and inevitable demise, see
Graber, *Dred Scott*, 105, 93–115; David Waldstreicher, *Slavery's Constitution: From Revolution
to Ratification* (New York, 2009). On the federal government and slavery prior to the Civil
War, see Fehrenbacher, *The Slaveholding Republic*.

[49] Douglas C. North, *The Economic Growth of the United States, 1790–1860* (New York, 1966), 67.
For contemporary analysis and commentary see, for example, John C. Calhoun, "Rough
Draft of What is Called the South Carolina Exposition" (19 December 1828), in Ross M.
Lence, editor, *Union and Liberty: The Political Philosophy of John C. Calhoun* (Indianapolis,
1992), available at http://oll.libertyfund.org (accessed 22 August 2009).

[50] See also Jordan, *White Over Black*, 3–43, 44. Interestingly, Jordan ignores *Titus Andronicus*,
in which, in Aron, race and slavery are comprehensively assimilated, for the rather distinct representations of race in *Othello*, where they are not. Aron does not accord with
Jordan's thesis that Englishmen gathered their initial impressions "of the *Negro* before he
became preeminently the *slave*" (43, emphasis in original), and hence that "at the start of
English settlement no one had in mind to establish the institution of Negro slavery" (the
basis of Jordan's famous observation that Negro slavery was an "unthinking decision")
because "Negro" and "slave" were not conjoined (44).

supplies happened to make landfall at Point Comfort in the Chesapeake and swapped its cargo of "20. and odd Negroes" for provisions.[51] In fact, the Dutch ship was no Dutch ship, and the landing was no happenstance.[52] Indeed, a census taken at "ye begininge of March 1619" may suggest earlier unremarked landings. The census records the presence of thirty-two "non-Christian" Negroes in the James River settlements. If the recording

[51] John Rolfe to Sir Edwin Sandys (January 1619/20), in Susan M. Kingsbury, editor, *The Records of the Virginia Company of London* (Washington, D.C., 1933), III, 241–8, at 243.

[52] Though Rolfe did not have all the facts to hand, read in full, his report to Sandys itself suggests a more purposeful encounter. This has been borne out by recent research. Rolfe wrote, "About the latter end of August, a Dutch man of Warr of the burden of a 160 tuñes arriued at Point-Comfort, the Commando[rs] name Capt Jope, his Pillott for the West Indies one Mr Marmaduke an Englishman. They mett w[th] the Trēr [*Treasurer*] in the West Indyes, and determyned to hold consort shipp hetherward, but in their passage lost one the other. He brought not any thing but 20. and odd Negroes, w[ch] the Governo[r] and Cape Marchant bought for victuall[es] (whereof he was in greate need as he p[r]tended) at the best and easyest rat[es] they could. He hadd a lardge and ample Commyssion from his Excellency [the Duke of Savoy] to range and to take purchase in the West Indyes." The report continues: "Three or 4. daies after the Trēr arriued. At his arriuall he sent word p[r]sently to the Gou[r]no[r] to know his pleasure, who wrote to him, and did request myself Leiften[a]nte Peace and M[r] Ewens to goe downe to him, to desyre him to come vp to James Cytie. But before we gott downe he hadd sett saile and was gone out of the Bay." Ibid., 243.

Research undertaken, principally by Engel Sluiter, "New Light on the '20. and Odd Negroes' Arriving in Virginia, August 1619," *William and Mary Quarterly*, 3rd Ser., 54, 2 (April 1997), 395–8, and John K. Thornton and Linda M. Heywood, *Central Africans, Atlantic Creoles, and the Foundation of the Americas, 1585–1660* (Cambridge and New York, 2007), 5–8, has now established conclusively that the Dutch man of war was an English ship, the *White Lion*, sailing under a Dutch flag in the company of a second English ship, the *Treasurer*, both carrying letters of marque as privateers (the *White Lion* from the port of Vlissigen [Flushing], the *Treasurer* from the Duke of Savoy, both then in conflict with Spain). We should note that Samuel Argall, then Governor of Virginia 1617–19, was an investor in the *Treasurer*'s voyage, which had been organized by Argall's patron and Virginia Company luminary Robert Rich, Earl of Warwick. Off Campeche in the Gulf of Mexico the privateers had stopped the Spanish ship *São João Bautista* bound for Vera Cruz with a cargo of 350 slaves from São Paulo de Luanda (Portuguese Angola). It is unclear how many had survived the middle passage, but after the English appropriations only 147 were left on board, "many sick … many had already died" (in Sluiter, 397). The *White Lion* landed its Africans at James City, the *Treasurer*, arriving four days later off Point Comfort, clearly intended the same, but left before doing so, discovering that the Duke of Savoy was no longer at odds with the Spanish and fearful that the ship would therefore be pursued as a pirate. The *Treasurer* returned several months later to complete the transaction, landing several additional Angolans. The involvement of Warwick's faction of the Virginia Company in the affair strongly suggests that the attempt to land shipments of Angolans in Virginia was no happenstance. On this matter see also Robert McColley, "Slavery in Virginia, 1619–1660: A Reexamination," in Robert H. Abzug and Stephen E. Maizlish, editors, *New Perspectives on Race and Slavery in America: Essays in Honor of Kenneth M. Stampp* (Lexington, Ky., 1986), 16–17; John Thornton, "The African Experience of the '20. and Odd Negroes' Arriving in Virginia in 1619," *William and Mary Quarterly*, 3rd Ser., 55, 3 (July 1998), 421, 434. During the 1620s, other privateers brought cargoes of Angolans seized in the Atlantic slave trade to the Chesapeake. See Alden T. Vaughan, "Blacks in Virginia: Evidence from the First Decade," in Vaughan, *Roots of American Racism*, 128–35.

date is taken to be March 1618/19, this would indicate the presence of a substantial group of blacks already in Virginia six months before the "20. and odd" were landed in August. If the recording date is March 1619/20, or six months after the landing reported by Rolfe, the disparity in numbers suggests the possibility of earlier unremarked landings, or additional landings between August 1619 and March 1619/20. Either way, "it seems the colony first acquired African labor … more deliberately" than the old story of a chance appearance by a Dutch trader suggests.[53] Six years earlier, moreover, George Chapman's *Memorable Maske of the Two Honorable Houses or Innes of Court*, performed before James I at White-Hall in February 1613, had already specifically associated the English New World with Africans and slavery. The masque centered attention upon a procession of indigenous "Virginian Princes," each attended by two Moores "attir'd like *Indian slaues.*" Slaves, it seems, would not be recognized as such, however attired, unless they were black. But Chapman's masque also rendered Virginia's princes swarthy (olive skinned, black haired). And at the masque's climax, all – princes and slaves alike – were required to prostrate themselves before "this our Britan *Phoebus*, whose bright skie /(Enlightened with a Christian piety) /Is neuer subiect to black Errors night, /And hath already offer'd heauens true light, /To your darke Region."[54] Subalterns figured by prejudice of color inhabited England's North American *imaginaire* from the outset. Just as there was never any original English New World moment when the indigenous population was not considered a degraded obstacle to English occupation of American land, nor, one may argue, was there a moment when the presence of enslaved Africans was not embedded in the emerging meaning of England's Virginia.

Long before the establishment of the first English mainland colonies, sixteenth-century European colonizing had made slaves commonplace in the New World. Though the struggling English settlements were remote from the main currents of the intercontinental slave trade during the first half of the seventeenth century, the Atlantic was sufficiently replete with slaves to afford them opportunities for piecemeal acquisitions. More than a century of contact and trade among the European populations of the Western Mediterranean and Africa's Atlantic littoral had generated a population of relatively acculturated Africans – "Atlantic Creoles" in Ira Berlin's formulation – many of whom had been acquired as slaves in the

53 William Thorndale, "The Virginia Census of 1619," *Magazine of Virginia Genealogy*, 33, 3 (Summer 1995), 166, 155–70. Thorndale dates the census to March 1618/19. Martha W. McCartney, "An Early Virginia Census Reprised," *Quarterly Bulletin – Archeological Society of Virginia*, 54 (1999), 178–96, disputes Thorndale's assessment and dates the census to March 1619/20.

54 George Chapman, *The Memorable Maske of the Two Honorable Houses or Inns of Court; the Middle Temple, and Lyncolns Inne. As it was performd before the King, at White-Hall on Shroue Munday at Night; Being the 15 of February, 1613. At the Princely Celebration of the Most Royall Nuptialls of the Palsgraue, and his Thrice Gratious Princesse Elizabeth. &c* (London, 1613), sigs. A₃v., EV.; Bach, *Colonial Transformations*, 175–6. For further analysis of *The Memorable Maske*, see Chapter 10, section IV.

normal course of commodity exchange (or commodity exchange's illegal sector, privateering) and were available for sale onward in opportunistic spot transactions.[55] By mid-century, the expansion of slavery in the English Caribbean had created a further point of "local" origin for mainland slaves. Intercolonial trading networks exchanged mainland produce and Indian captives for Caribbean slaves. Caribbean planters would later migrate to several mainland colonies, taking their slaves with them.[56]

Why belabor the matter? After all, Orlando Patterson has told us, "There is nothing notably peculiar about the institution of slavery," nothing that should lead one to find its presence in the early modern English imagination or its transoceanic adventures startling. Slavery is pervasive in human social organization. "It has existed from before the dawn of human history right down to the twentieth century, in the most primitive of human societies and in the most civilized."[57] Still, to explain the course that the Anglo-American law of slavery followed during the first two centuries of English colonizing requires more than a demonstration that slaves were always present, for the measure is not just the slave's presence but also the means of slavery's sustenance, the instrumentalities by which slavery as an institution is produced and reproduced. At a certain point in the history of each mainland colony, that is, the simple presence of *slaves* turns into the presence of *slavery*. The colony no longer simply acknowledges that slaves have been brought within its precincts and deals with their presence with such resources as it has to hand, it consciously creates a distinct and highly consequential legal condition of being that has no prior existence within its institutional structure, qualitatively distinct from and absolutely subordinate to all other social and legal conditions of existence. It endows that condition with dedicated institutions, practices, and cruelties, considered necessary to ensure its indefinite perpetuation: specialized jurisdictions, elaborated restraints, calibrated corporeal punishments and mutilations, deliberate sanctioned killings. All are peculiar to that one condition of existence, to which no one not of that order of being is subject. And it

---

[55] Berlin, *Many Thousands Gone*, 17–46. For a critique and refinement of Berlin's arguments, see Heywood and Thornton, *Central Africans, Atlantic Creoles*, 49, 236–331.

[56] See, for example, April Lee Hatfield, *Atlantic Virginia, Intercolonial Relations in the Seventeenth Century* (Philadelphia, 2004), 137–68. The intercolonial trade in slaves from roughly the mid-seventeenth century until the early nineteenth century has been explored systematically in Gregory E. O'Malley, "Beyond the Middle Passage: Slave Migration from the Caribbean to North America, 1619–1807," *William and Mary Quarterly*, 3rd Ser., 66, 1 (January 2009), 125–72. We should note O'Malley's point that slaves acquired in the intercolonial trade with the Caribbean were just as likely to be recently arrived Africans as those clearly arriving on the mainland directly out of Africa. "Caribbean planters had little reason to sell seasoned slaves" while "Mainland planters questioned the motives of anyone offering seasoned slaves for sale" (136). O'Malley observes carefully, "Just what proportion of seventeenth-century North American slaves were Atlantic creoles remains contested and unclear, but seasoned West Indian slaves likely contributed little to their number" (137).

[57] Patterson, *Slavery and Social Death*, vii.

defines by preemptive ascriptive characterization the identity of the population that shall thenceforth be confined within that condition.[58] In other words, the colony creates a regime. What is of principal concern here, therefore, are the institutional contours of the mainland's several slavery regimes, together with elaboration of the means designed in each case to ensure slavery's indefinite perpetuation.[59]

---

[58] Here I mean to suggest that the now-familiar distinction between *societies with slaves* and *slave societies* (on which see, for example, Berlin, *Many Thousands Gone,* 7–13; Philip D. Morgan, "British Encounters with Africans and African-Americans circa 1600–1780," in Bernard Bailyn and Philip D. Morgan, editors, *Strangers Within the Realm: Cultural Margins of the First British Empire* (Chapel Hill, 1991), 156–219) might usefully be supplemented by a third characterization, *societies with slavery.* Obviously slaves are present in a *society with slaves* but their presence per se is relatively inconsequential to the society's development unless and until slavery is consciously instantiated as an institution to the perpetuation of which the society is committed. It is that decision that makes it a *society with slavery.* But this does not mean the society has or necessarily ever will become a slave society – not at least in Frank Tannenbaum's classic description of a totalized presence that penetrates every facet of society and culture from which nothing can escape, "nothing, and no-one," that is "white and black, men and women, old and young" (see Frank Tannenbaum, *Slave & Citizen: The Negro in the Americas* (New York, 1946), 117); nor even by Morgan's less totalized but still ubiquitous measure, "central to the economic functioning of that society" (163). In the North American case, virtually every mainland colony became a society with slavery; not all made the further and final move to become slave societies.

[59] As this indicates, my focus in this chapter is on the legal regimes created to institutionalize slavery in the mainland colonies, which I address primarily, though not exclusively, through exegeses upon statute law. Though mindful of Philip Schwarz's critique of "the notion that statutes fully control society," I do not embrace Schwarz's corollary that statute law cannot be "a valid historical guide to past societies," which may be taken to imply – wrongly in my view – that the construction of legal regimes (the designs of legislators) has nothing to tell us about the composition of the social. Statute law cannot be the only guide, but it certainly can be *a* guide – and not only to practice but also (perhaps more important when it comes to the design of institutions) to desire. Schwarz's observations pertaining to slavery in Virginia actually adopt more or less the same position, for they underline the importance of recognizing the "hard realities of the legal system" and the "ultimate domination of slaves through the law – and through the use of force authorized by law" in response to historians who would discount slavery's severe statutory form in favor of reliance upon the quotidian reciprocities of social interaction for information about its realities. As Schwarz says, "the claim of the legal system to supreme power over bondspeople was of a different order than the claim of legal systems over other people ... [T]he *unambiguous* message of the slave codes was domination of African American slaves by whites." See Philip J. Schwarz, *Slave Laws in Virginia* (Athens, Ga., 1996), 9, 10 (emphasis added). See also Philip J. Schwarz, *Twice Condemned: Slaves and the Criminal Laws of Virginia, 1705–1865* (Baton Rouge, La., 1988), 6–34.

We can all agree, I think, that statutes should not be treated as a straightforward index of empirical phenomena except where complementary non-statutory evidence can be brought to bear. For work tending to show a close relationship between statute law and social practice in the case of slavery, see Gwenda Morgan, *The Hegemony of the Law: Richmond County, Virginia, 1692–1776* (New York, 1989), 101–37; Robert Olwell, *Masters, Slaves, and Subjects: The Culture of Power in the South Carolina Low Country, 1740–1790* (Ithaca, N.Y., 1998), 57–101; Anthony S. Parent, Jr., *Foul Means: The Formation of a Slave Society in Virginia, 1660–1740* (Chapel Hill, 2003), 105–34.

Transplants and Timing

By this measure, according to some, Anglo-American slavery indeed presents us with a paradox. Slavery as such had not existed in England for hundreds of years.[60] Though the mainland's mature slave regimes were dense in law, earthy and instrumental, butchers' bills of ends and means dedicated to enslaving people and perpetuating their enslavement, the absence of a specifically English law of enslavement poses "the paradox of a colonial slavery without initial authority or systematic legal rules," an institution conjured *"ex nihilo."*[61]

In fact, Anglo-American slave regimes were not conjured *ex nihilo*. Their sources are quite easily identified: ideas long established in the law of nature and nations that furnished a respectable genealogy for European enslavement of others; familiar English common-law practices and regulatory statutes adapted to serve new purposes; and the experience accumulated by other colonizers confronting the unique demands of local circumstance and spawning their own innovations.

I have argued that as a process, English colonizing was in largest part a deliberate transplantation of peoples and institutions undertaken to "man, plant and keep" mainland territories. To that end, promoters of colonies had resort both to a broad, discursive, extrastructure of ideas that explained and justified their enterprises, and a more detailed, technical, intrastructure of institutions and processes that managed mobility and distributed migrants. The establishment of Anglo-American slave regimes is consistent with the intellectual thrust of English colonizing and conformed to this pattern. Establishment rested initially upon an explanatory extrastructure that rendered enslavement legally familiar – appropriate, reasonable, and legitimate – and a technical intrastructure of processes to manage and oversee an enslaved population. We have seen that the law of nature and nations served precisely to explain and justify the larger colonizing enterprise of which mainland slavery regimes were subsystems. Unsurprisingly, the extrastructure of slavery is to be found there too, for English statute and common law offered no more intellectual resources to establish a legal basis for slavery per se than it did for the initial appropriation of mainland territory. But English law – the common law of property and inheritance, and the established metropolitan state's habit of resort to police legislation to control the mobility of population and contain threats to social order – had proven to be of considerable importance for management of the actual process of colonizing and the internal life of English

---

[60] David Eltis, *The Rise of African Slavery in the Americas* (Cambridge and New York, 2000), 1–2, 5–7, 14–15; Sally E. Hadden, "The Fragmented Laws of Slavery in the Colonial and Revolutionary Eras," in Michael Grossberg and Christopher Tomlins, editors, *The Cambridge History of Law in America* (Cambridge and New York, 2008), I, 257.

[61] Jonathan A. Bush, "Free to Enslave: The Foundations of Colonial American Slave Law," *Yale Journal of Law and the Humanities*, 5 (1993), 418–19, 421. See also Alan Watson, *Slave Law in the Americas* (Athens, Ga., 1989), 63–4.

colonies. And it did the same for slave law's intrastructural management of people.[62] Anglo-American slave law thus began by joining within itself intellectual arguments and justifications from *ius naturale* and *gentium* with the peculiarly protean transactional capacities and policing technologies of English common and statute law.[63] Together these furnished resources of explanation and management easily mobilized, as the occasion demanded, to legitimize English colonizers' transactions, insure their investments and otherwise define the relativities of unfreedom in their settlements to whatever extent they found desirable.

Both extrastructure and intrastructure began as transoceanic transplants, lifted from one context to be embedded in another. Taken together they suggest that Anglo-American slave regimes had plural origins. But these transoceanic transplants did not express anything like the detailed morphology of "social death"[64] characteristic of Anglo-American slave law. As settlements with slaves turned into societies with slavery, local innovations increasingly supplemented transplants, compensating for their deficiencies and limitations. Local innovations themselves then became "second-order" transplants, ideas and techniques that moved from settlement to settlement, regime to regime, filling in much of the regulatory detail that created commonalities within regions of settlement, and also (more interestingly) among regions usually thought quite distinct, repeatedly enumerating all the ways in which summary mutilations and executions defined the slave's life on the edge of death.

To understand the precise course of Anglo-American slavery regimes one must attend also to timing. Though slaves were present on the mainland virtually from the outset of English settlement, for the first half of

---

[62] As Sally Hadden has recently shown, many of the institutions that scholars associate with control of slaves – such as slave patrols, and the requirement that slaves carry passes or tickets when away from their master's plantation – had their origins in a more general police of movement extending to far wider categories of strangers and travelers, intended to forestall unauthorized departures, or simply mobility in general, among those elements of the population held to be dangerous or suspicious: servants without tickets of leave, debtors, Indians. Sally E. Hadden, *Slave Patrols: Law and Violence in Virginia and the Carolinas* (Cambridge, Mass., 2001), 3–4, 6–40. In time, of course, the unsupervised slave so easily identified by racial distinctiveness became the most suspicious and dangerous figure of all, and the object of virtually exclusive attention. But for the time being the suspicious, dangerous slave could be policed in the same manner as the suspicious, dangerous vagrants, rogues, and vagabonds, of early English modernity.

[63] These components are all explored further below. On the common law of property and inheritance, see, for example, Thomas D. Morris, *Southern Slavery and the Law, 1619–1860* (Chapel Hill, 1996), 39–43. On police laws, see, for example, Bradley J. Nicholson, "Legal Borrowing and the Origins of Slave Law in the British Colonies," *American Journal of Legal History*, 38, 1 (1994), 41–9. As to the law of nations, we have seen law of nations justifications for slavery entering English legal discourse in the late 1580s with the publication of the commentaries that became Gentili's *De Iure Belli*. See also the better known and more comprehensive treatise of Hugo Grotius first published in 1625, *De Jure Belli ac Pacis Libri Tres*, Francis W. Kelsey, trans. (Oxford and London, 1925), 255–8, 690–6, 718, 761–9.

[64] Patterson, *Slavery and Social Death*, 5.

the seventeenth century labor supply overwhelmingly took the form of migrant English family groups and single adolescent males. Before the 1660s, the supply of slaves to the English colonies was insignificant and slave populations throughout the English colonies were tiny. Though distinct in appearance and remarkable both for the lack of any end point to their condition of servitude and for their enslavement's heritability,[65] African slaves were not otherwise so dissimilar in the way they were used from others bound to servitude, nor so numerous, to require dedicated legal attention. Small numbers of slaves (in the first Virginia colony, for example, no more than 150 in 1640, out of a total population approaching 10,500)[66] could be accommodated within laws adopted to police European migrant servitude, and were. African slavery did not become institutionally entrenched on the mainland until the second wave of English mainland colonizing began after the Stuart Restoration, when it was aggressively promoted as the key to development of the new proprietary colonies of the southern Atlantic and mid-Atlantic regions – Carolina and New York, and New York's offshoots in the Jerseys and Pennsylvania – at the same time as purposeful expansion began in the Chesapeake.[67] Timing has implications both for the development of the institution and for representations of the motives of those who enslaved.

II. Slavery is All but Death

Slavery was well known to the Christian law of nature and nations that structured sixteenth-century European colonizing. It was a central and accepted component of the law of war, said Francisco de Vitoria, citing Justinian, that whatever was captured in war became the captor's property, extending to people themselves. Vitoria, however, distinguished wars against infidels and heathen, whose enslavement was indubitably lawful, from wars among Christians. It was "a received rule of Christendom that Christians do not become slaves in right of war." Hence, "enslaving is not lawful in a war between Christians."[68]

---

[65] Both characteristics are clear in estate inventories from the 1640s and 1650s. See Morris, *Southern Slavery and the Law*, 40–1 (1640s); Jordan, *White over Black*, 75–7 (1650s). More fragmentary evidence from the 1620s tending to show the same is summarized by Alden Vaughan in "Blacks in Virginia," 128–35. Measures formalizing slavery's heritability begin to appear in the late 1650s. See section IV, this chapter.

[66] See *HSUS*, vol. 5, table Eg14, Eg53 (Virginia total population, black population).

[67] See, e.g., Pettigrew, "Free to Enslave," 3–38; Parent, *Foul Means*, 55–79. On the relationship between proprietorial neo-feudalism and slavery, see Holly Brewer, "Power and Authority in the Colonial South: The English Legacy and its Contradictions," in Joseph P. Ward, editor, *Britain and the American South: From Colonialism to Rock and Roll* (Jackson, Miss., 2003), 27–51; Holly Brewer, "Slavery and 'Inheritable Blood' in the Wake of the Glorious Revolution: The Struggle over Locke's Virginia Plan of 1698" (unpublished paper, presented to the History Department, Yale University, November 2008).

[68] Francisco de Vitoria, *On the Indians Lately Discovered* and *On the Indians or on the Law of War Made by the Spaniards on the Barbarians* (1539), in Francisci de Victoria, *De Indis et De Iure Belli Relectiones*, Ernest Nys, editor, John Pawley Bate, trans. (Washington, D.C., 1917), 155–6, 181.

Vitoria's brief exposition of the legal basis of slavery was taken up in late sixteenth-century England by Alberico Gentili (1552–1608). Gentili followed Vitoria in two respects. First, there could be no "true condition of slavery" among Christians. "The rule has been established by invariable custom that there shall be no slaves."[69] This did not mean that Christians might not hold slaves. "The condition of slavery is a just one. For it is a provision of the law of nations."[70] The rule was in the nature of a prudential exception to an otherwise prevailing truth: Christians should not enslave other Christians, for such would be to the ruin of Christianity.[71]

Second, slavery originated in capture. Capture created a relation of total domination between captive and captor, rendering the captive completely dependent upon the captor's inclination whether or not to withhold death. Thus, in *De Re Militari et Bello* (1563), Pierino Belli observed that "beyond a doubt slaves are so called from being 'spared' (*servari*).[72]

---

[69] Gentili, *De Iure Belli*, 329. See also Sir Thomas Smith, *De Republica Anglorum: A Discourse on the Commonwealth of England* (1583), L. Alston, editor (Cambridge, 1906), 133, referring to the "perswasion ... of Christians not to make nor keepe his brother in Christ, servile, bond and underling for ever unto him, as a beast rather than as a man."

[70] Gentili, *De Iure Belli*, 330. Gentili held that Christians might themselves justly be enslaved (though not as we have just seen by other Christians) for "slavery belongs to the law of nations, and today is common to Christians with all infidels." The justice of Christians' enslavement depended under the law of nations on the circumstances. In the law of nations slavery originated in capture. "Our countrymen who were captured by the Turks are slaves of the Turks, as others have well and truly noted. Some authorities wrongly question this on the ground that the cause of the Turks, who hunt us down and seize our goods, cannot be just. But this has been discussed before and an exception made of pirates; and the same thing has been said of others with whom we have no friendship. Hence, a threefold inquiry may be made about the Turks: when they wage war, when they practice piracy, and when they seize us in other ways than in warfare." 332. On pirates, see Chapter 3, section III.

[71] Vitoria, *On the Indians or on the Law of War*, 181, 183. Vitoria's statement of the "rule" appears to be original; he offers no citation in support. Gentili took it up fifty years later, again without citation, but with a somewhat tentative historical allusion: "It is *generally believed* that in the wars of the Christians there was no slavery." In explanation, Gentili invokes the universality of Christendom and the Roman law of *postliminium* (the right enjoyed by persons and things taken by an enemy to be restored to their former state on escape or liberation, or by negotiation at the conclusion of hostilities) as a basis: "For those wars are more than civil, since all men are brothers in Christ, since we are members of the one body of which Christ is the head, and since it is commonly believed that there is one Church of Christ and a single Christendom. From this it follows that an enemy may not be held captive perpetually." Yet Gentili also acknowledges, as Vitoria did not, that "The Apostle [Paul] allows Christians to be made slaves, and that too by other Christians," citing *Ephesians* Ch. VI and *Philippians*; and he adds that commentators have held "a baptized person may remain the slave of a Jew, and with still more justice, of a Christian." Gentili, *De Iure Belli*, 328, 332.

[72] Pierino Belli (1563), *De Re Militari et Bello Tractatus*, Herbert C. Nutting, trans. (Oxford, 1936), 85–6. Belli adds, "nature herself admonishes us that it is humane to spare a captured enemy and not to kill him." Similarly, Gentili states that "slavery was introduced because through it the killing of captives was prevented." Gentili, *De Iure Belli*, 332. Observations on the relationship between capture, servitude, and slavery in Thomas Hobbes's *Leviathan* (1651) and John Locke's *Two Treatises of Government* (1689) are in accord with these sources. See Chapter 8, nn.143, 146, and this chapter, n.104.

Enslavement transmutes the imminence of physical death into social death. The social death of enslavement is not an alternative to physical death, however, but a variation. Titus Andronicus decreed the death of his captive Alarbus, and Alarbus was duly hacked to pieces. Had Titus decreed Alarbus a slave he would have died too, just not quite in the same manner. For, as Gentili puts it, "one who is made a slave becomes another person and ceases to exist."[73] The socially dead slave continues to live physically but on the constant edge of physical death: the slave embodies physical death *currently* withheld. Slavery was in other words death postponed, permission to continue to live subject to the captor's absolute dominion. "A state of slavery exists when there is no hope of freedom ... [B]y it one is subjected to another's domination and reduced to the condition of a beast. One is deprived of one's nature and becomes a chattel instead of a person. Therefore, those who were slaves were commonly called 'bodies' [Σώματα] by the Greeks. Slavery is all but death."[74] In the Anglo-American law of slavery, death will prove to be the slave's constant companion, always standing ready.

In addition to his amplification of Vitoria, Gentili gave slavery an additional foundation, the Thomistic argument that "liberty is according to nature, but only for good men." Gentili elaborated:

> The objection is made, that natural reason, which is the basis of the law of nations, could not introduce slavery if we are all free by nature; therefore slavery is said to be contrary to nature and to owe its origin to the cruelty of the enemy. But there are many answers to this objection. I agree with Thomas Aquinas that slavery is really in harmony with nature; not indeed according to her first intent, by which we were all created free, but according to a second desire of hers, that sinners should be punished.[75]

Whereas capture in war could ensnare any participant, Gentili here specifically identified a distinct population properly subject to slavery, the sinful and wicked, whom elsewhere he classed among the common and perpetual enemies of mankind: pirates and robbers; thieves and criminals;

Slavery's origin in capture was accorded substantially earlier recognition in English law in Henry of Bratton (Bracton)'s *De Legibus et Consuetudinibus Angliæ* [*On the Laws and Customs of England*] written by multiple authors during the first half of the thirteenth century. Thus, for example, in explaining bondage, *De Legibus* defines servitude as the subjection of one person to the dominion of another derived from "the practice of princes [in ancient times] to sell captives and thus preserve rather than destroy them." And again, "the law says one captured by the enemy is a slave." See *Bracton: On the Laws and Customs of England*, Samuel E. Thorne, trans. (Cambridge, Mass., 1968), II, 30, 34. Bracton, however, is in very large part a reception of Justinian's *Institutes* into England, and the passages cited are attributable to the twelfth-century glossator Azo of Bologna, much of whose work found its way into *De Legibus*. Hence, Bracton attributes servitude and its explanation to the *ius gentium* (at 30). In other words, writers whether in the thirteenth century or the seventeenth are all drawing on the same law of nations sources.

[73] Gentili, *De Iure Belli*, 118.

[74] Ibid., 328.

[75] Ibid., 330.

savages and brutes. The means of their enslavement was not war but judgment by higher authority: "If some earthly city should decide to commit
certain great crimes," Gentili wrote, quoting Augustine, "it would have to
be overthrown by decree of the human race."[76] In 1625, Grotius would
take a similar position. In the law of nations, enslavement after capture in
a public war (a war between states) required no crime in justification: "all
without exception who have been captured" become slaves. But in addition, nature specifically sanctioned wars against barbarians and savages,
criminals and beasts, and the punishment (enslavement) that accompanied such wars. For although "apart from a human act, or in the primitive
condition of nature, no human beings are slaves" and hence "*in this sense* it
is correct to accept what was said by the jurists, that slavery is contrary to
nature," no one by nature had the right "never to enter slavery" (never to
be enslaved). "[*I*]*n that sense* no one is free." Thus Albutius: "No one is born
free, no one a slave; it is after birth that fortune has imposed these distinctions upon individuals." Grotius, in short, detected no necessary conflict
between slavery and nature. It was not at odds with natural justice that
slavery should have its origin in a human act, "should arise from a convention or a crime."[77] Pierino Belli had been the first of the treatise writers
to advert to a wider basis for enslavement in the law of nature and nations
than capture in a just war alone, arguing in 1563 that where strangers
were concerned, simple seizure and enslavement could be justified: "not
only in war does enslavement take place, but also apart from it. For if a
person should go among a people with whom his countrymen had no ties
of hospitality or friendship, or if anyone from such a place should come
amongst us, he would be the slave of the person seizing him. With good
right, therefore, the Spaniards enslaved those Indians of the West, who live
far away from our world ... as allowed by the law just cited; unless one were
to assume that this law refers to a foreigner captured as he goes among
strangers, and not to foreigners captured in a strange land."[78] Belli thus
attempted to justify expeditions to lands "far away from our world" to seize
and enslave their inhabitants by attributing to those inhabitants the character of natural enemies.

Within early modern Christian European tradition, then, it was well
established that enslavement was just under the law of nations, and also
justifiable under, or at least reconcilable with, the law of nature. It was
also clear that enslavement was for others – captives, criminals, savages,
strangers: that is, not one's own kind. Finally, in the work of certain of the
treatise writers – Belli and later Grotius – one can detect a "loosening" of
the bounds of allowable enslavement coincident with European colonizing
and the acceleration of the Atlantic trade in African slaves.

[76] Ibid., 122, 122–4.
[77] Grotius, *De Jure Belli ac Pacis*, 506, 551 (emphasis added), 690 (emphasis added).
[78] Belli, *De Re Militari*, 85.

Though this tradition's influence on Anglo-American slave law has not been much explored,[79] it is noticeable that the first explicit definition of those who might be enslaved advanced by the English on the American mainland embraced slavery more or less precisely in the vein of Christian European law of nature and nations discourse: "lawfull Captives taken in just warres," along with heathen outsiders – "strangers ... sold to us" – and those "judged thereto by Authoritie." The words appear under the title "Liberties of Forreiners and Strangers" in Nathaniel Ward's *Body of Liberties* (1641) married to biblical rules (*Leviticus* 25: 38–46) that underscored slavery as a condition for heathen, in perpetuity.[80] Ward's *Body of Liberties* was formulated for the Massachusetts Bay colony General Court and formally embraced in the colony's *Lawes and Libertyes* (1648).[81] The definition was quietly broadened in 1658.[82] In 1664, the amended definition was

[79] Commentary on Locke's theory of slavery in his *Two Treatises of Government* (1698), for example, either ignores its debts to 150 years of law of nations writing, or goes no further than brief reference to Grotius. See n.104, this chapter. For acknowledgment of the influence of law of nature and nations writing on European colonizers, see Hadden, "Fragmented Laws of Slavery," 257.

[80] See William H. Whitmore, editor, T*he Colonial Laws of Massachusetts ... Together with the Body of Liberties of 1641* (Boston, 1890), 52. For Leviticus 25: 38–46, see n.241, this chapter.

[81] Originally published in manuscript in 1641, first ordered for publication in 1647 and first printed in 1648, supplemented, as *The Book of the General Lawes and Libertyes Concerning the Inhabitants of the Massachusets. Collected out of the Records of the General Court for the Several Years wherin they were Made and Established, and now Revised by the same Court and disposed into an Alphabetical Order*, in John D. Cushing, editor, *The Laws and Liberties of Massachusetts, 1641–91*, 3 vols. (Wilmington, Del., 1976), I, 3–65. See also Chapter 6, nn.69–76 and accompanying text.

[82] Considerable change attended the *Body*'s definition of those appropriately enslaved during the three decades following its initial formulation. When published in 1648 in *The Book of the General Lawes and Libertyes*, the definition appeared not as an element of the "liberties of forreiners and strangers" and thus in effect stated as an exception to them, but baldly under its own title, "bond-slavery" separated from the provisions with which it had been formerly united. See Cushing, ed., *The Laws and Liberties*, I, 10. In 1658, ten years after the 1648 edition of the *General Lawes and Libertyes*, the General Court undertook a revision, ordered published in 1660. In the revised edition the bond-slavery title reads: "It is Ordered by this Court & Authority thereof; That there shall never be any bond slavery villenage or captivity amongst us, unless it be Lawfull captives, taken in just warrs, as willingly sell themselves, or are sold to us, and such shall have the liberties, and christian usuage, which the Law of God established in Israel, concerning such persons, doth morally require, provided this exempts none from servitude, who shall be judged thereto by Authority." See Cushing, ed., *The Laws and Liberties*, I, at 75. This version omitted the words "and such strangers" that in the original had preceded "as willingly sell themselves." The apparent effect was to limit slavery to lawful captives alone. But after examining corrections written into a copy of the 1660 edition by Edward Rawson, first Secretary of the Massachusetts Bay Colony, who was effectively the editor of the revised edition, George H. Moore concluded that the General Court had actually intended greatly to *expand* the scope of slavery allowed under the title by removing the qualifier "strangers" such that the title would allow enslavement of "Lawfull captives, taken in just warrs, [*or such*] as [*shall*] willingly sell themselves, or are sold to us" (Rawson's corrections here inserted in italics) specifically to cover the continued enslavement both of those strangers (heathen) who had converted to Christianity and children born to converted Christian parents. And indeed, when in 1670 the General Court appointed a committee

transplanted to the entire mid-Atlantic region through its adoption as a key element of the founding laws of the Duke of York's proprietary, the eponymous *Duke's Laws*.[83]

To identify Massachusetts in 1641 as the source of essential definitional key words for Anglo-American slavery is at odds with the usual chronology, in which mainland slavery has its beginning in Virginia in 1619. That earlier beginning would prove symptomatic of an occasional coastwise trade that would scatter a few hundred slaves among the mainland settlements during the first half century of English presence. Nevertheless, though slaves were present in Virginia virtually from the beginnings of the colony,[84] colonists took no particular steps to "define" who might be enslaved. In 1640, the Virginia colony had no more than 150 blacks in a population of more than 10,000; in 1660, fewer than 1,000 in 26,000. Rather than a crucial point of origin in the development of an Anglo-American slave regime, during its first forty years Virginia instead accumulated a few slaves by occasional purchase and subjected them to much the same daily disciplines that policed its much larger population of youthful migrant servants.[85] In fact, the Massachusetts Bay colony actually had more need at an early point in its development for a clear legal definition

to examine the laws in force for "literall errors or misplacing of words or sentences therein," one of the committee's reported errors was that in "tit. Bondflauery, read 'or such as shall willingly,' &c." The amendment was duly included in an errata list appended to the 1672 printing of the *Lawes and Liberties* (in Cushing, ed., *The Laws and Liberties*, II, 396). See George H. Moore, *Notes on the History of Slavery in Massachusetts* (New York, 1866), 14–16. Moore commented (at 16–17): "As the circumstances under which all these laws and liberties were originally composed and after long discussion, minute examination, and repeated revisions, finally settled and established, forbid the supposition that slavery came in an unbidden or unwelcome guest – so is it equally impossible to admit that this alteration of the special law of slavery by the omission of so important and significant a word could have been accidental or without motive." He continued: "If under the original law the children of enslaved captives and strangers might possibly have claimed exemption from that servitude to which the recognized common law of nations assigned them from their birth; this amendment, by striking out the word 'strangers,' removed the necessity for alienage or foreign birth as a qualification for slavery, and took off the prohibition against the children of slaves being 'born into legal slavery in Massachusetts.'"

[83] "Noe Christian shall be kept in Bond Slavery, Villenage or Captivity, except Such as shall be judged thereunto by Authority or Such as willingly have sould or shall sell themselves ... This Law shall not extend to sett at liberty Any Negroe or Indian Servant who shall turne Christian after he shall have been bought by Any Person." *Duke's Laws* (1665) in Gail McKnight Beckman, comp., *The Statutes at Large of Pennsylvania*, I: 1680–1700 (New York, 1976), 78. The *Duke's Laws* were compiled from the laws of the existing colonies, particularly Massachusetts Bay, for use in the new proprietorship of New York. (The draft of the *Duke's Laws* reproduced by Beckman is the original draft filed by the Duke of York in 1667, now in the Public Records Office, London. In other drafts the final sentence of the bond slavery clause does not appear.)

[84] Virginia's blacks were overwhelmingly though not exclusively enslaved (owned for life). See Morgan, *Slave Counterpoint*, 8; Morris, *Southern Slavery and the Law*, 39–42; McColley, "Slavery in Virginia, 1619–1660," 18–19.

[85] Morgan, *Slave Counterpoint*, 8–13; Hadden, *Slave Patrols*, 3–4, 6–40; Jonathan A. Bush, "The First Slave (And Why He Matters)," *Cardozo Law Review*, 18, 2 (1996), 603–8.

of enslavement than Virginia, given that only eight years after the arrival of the English and directly in the wake of the Pequot War of 1637, the colony's government had begun shipping Indians taken captive during the war to the Caribbean, where they were exchanged for "salt, cotton, tobacco and Negroes."[86] Ward's "lawfull Captives taken in just warres," and "strangers ... sold to us" clearly fit the bill going in both directions. During the 1640s and 1650s, there were more slaves in New England and the mid-Atlantic region together than in the Chesapeake.

All this notwithstanding, clear outlines of a legal-institutional structure for mainland slavery regimes did not really appear until a flurry of local enactments that began in the 1660s and accelerated between 1680 and 1715. By the 1660s, a majority of the mainland's small black population was to be found in the Chesapeake, and the first enactments occurred there. But by then slavery was expanding and gaining definition everywhere, actively promoted as a source of labor for the vast new proprietary colonies of the mid-Atlantic and Carolina, and on the rise in New England as well. By the end of the century the mainland's slave population had grown tenfold, from nearly 3,000 (4 percent of total population) to nearly 30,000 (more than 11 percent). By 1760, it stood at well over 300,000 (20 percent). In the Chesapeake and the Carolina lowcountry, maturing planter elites engrossed land and sought more and more labor to work it. In the Chesapeake, a black population of 1,700 in 1660 had grown to 20,000 by the early 1700s and 150,000 by 1750. In the area that would become South Carolina, where settlement began in 1670, there were some 1,500 slaves by 1690, nearly 6,000 by the end of the 1700s, and 50,000 (two-thirds of total population) by 1750. The slave population of the mid-Atlantic and Southern New England (divided fairly consistently throughout, approximately one-third in New England, two-thirds in the mid-Atlantic) also grew, from some 1,200 in 1660 to over 5,000 by 1700, 30,000 in 1750, and 50,000 (10 percent of the mainland's black population) by the 1770s.[87]

It was the 1660s, therefore, when slavery's mark on the mainland began to grow indelible. David Brion Davis has argued that "no British founders of North American colonies, except for South Carolina, intended to

---

[86] Lorenzo J. Greene, *The Negro in Colonial New England, 1620–1776* (New York, 1968 [1942]), 16–17. Greene reports, at 60, that in 1645 John Winthrop's brother-in-law Emanuel Downing petitioned Winthrop to engage the Pequots in "juste warre" once more, so that more captives might be acquired to exchange in Barbados for "a stock of slaves sufficient to doe all our business." See also Stephen Innes, *Creating the Commonwealth: The Economic Culture of Puritan New England* (New York, 1995), 105; C. S. Manegold, *Ten Hills Farm: The Forgotten History of Slavery in the North* (Princeton, 2010).

[87] Population figures calculated from *HSUS*, vol. 5, table Eg1–59. New York always had the largest slave population of all the northern colonies. In the mid-Atlantic, the larger part of the remainder was to be found in New Jersey. Slavery was not insignificant in Pennsylvania, but for most of the century after settlement, Pennsylvania's slave population did not exceed 15% of the region's total. In New England, Massachusetts and Connecticut had significant concentrations of slaves, but slaves' incidence in overall population reached mid-Atlantic levels only in Rhode Island.

create slave societies."[88] Although true enough of the original Chesapeake and New England settlements, the course of mainland slavery after 1660 calls the contention into question. All the Restoration proprietors, not merely Carolina's, favored the introduction of slavery; most sought it avidly. The first mid-Atlantic proprietor, James, Duke of York, planned to make New York the principal point of entry on the northern mainland for the Company of Royal Adventurers into Africa, first chartered in 1660, reconstituted in 1663 with slave trading as a stated objective, reconstituted once more in 1671 under the Duke of York's leadership as the Royal African Company. The Duke's representatives worked to encourage the development of markets for slaves throughout his province; hence the significance of the inclusion of Massachusetts' broadened definition of allowable enslavement in the *Duke's Laws*.[89] New York, the Jerseys, and Pennsylvania would all build closely related slavery regimes on the common foundation that the *Duke's Laws* provided.

In the century following 1660, Anglo-American slavery regimes emerged in multiple regional centers experiencing rapid expansion of their slave populations relatively simultaneously. Each center showed a propensity to embrace fundamental laws first formulated elsewhere. Key elements of the legal regimes established in the mid-Atlantic colonies, for example, were transplanted from their Restoration contemporary, South Carolina. In turn, crucial elements of South Carolina's slave law were transplanted from the Caribbean island of Barbados. Overall, mainland slavery regimes followed two relatively distinct paths, one characteristic of the original planta-

---

[88] David Brion Davis, *Inhuman Bondage: The Rise and Fall of Slavery in the New World* (Oxford, 2006), 126.

[89] Leslie M. Harris, *In the Shadow of Slavery: African Americans in New York City, 1626–1863* (Chicago and London, 2003), 26–9. On the creation of "a new pattern" of English colonizing after mid-century, "violent, coercive, and state orchestrated," see Alison Games, *The Web of Empire: English Cosmopolitans in an Age of Expansion, 1560–1660* (New York, 2008), 287, 289–93. On the Royal African Company, the predecessor Royal Adventurers, and the close involvement of numerous members of the Stuart family in both, particularly the Duke of York, see K. G. Davies, *The Royal African Company* (London, 1957), 41–4, 57–74, 103–4, 156. On the significance of Stuart attempts to promote slavery after the Restoration, see Brewer, "Slavery and 'Inheritable Blood'." Others involved in the Royal African Company's affairs included several of the Carolina proprietors, including Sir George Carteret and John, Lord Berkeley, who as Jersey proprietors from 1664 to 1672 would promote slavery in the Jerseys, and Sir Peter Colleton, brother to Sir John Colleton (another of the Carolina proprietors), a Bahamas Company adventurer and close acquaintance of John Locke. Locke himself held £400 of stock in the Company between 1672 and 1675, a period when he also had investments in plantations in the Bahamas and in Caribbean sugar. On Locke as investor, see Barbara Arneil, *John Locke and America: The Defence of English Colonialism* (Oxford, 1996), 68–9, 139, and Brewer, "Slavery and 'Inheritable Blood'." Designating the New York/New Jersey region as a favored point of entry for Royal African Company slaves remained very much in evidence in Crown colonial policy forty years on. See the instructions issued in 1702 by the Queen in Council to Edward Lord Cornbury, governor-designate of the provinces of New York and New Jersey, in section V of this chapter.

tion colonies of the Chesapeake, the other more typical of the Restoration colonies.

Barbados – Seed Crystal

Barbados was the seed crystal for the slavery regimes of the Restoration colonies; it also had some influence on Virginia. Settled in the late 1620s and 1630s by English planters using indentured European labor to produce tobacco and cotton, by the 1650s Barbados was increasingly dependent on the importation of slave labor to work capital-intensive sugar plantations. After 1640, slave importation consistently averaged some 2,000 per annum. By the late 1650s, slaves were approaching half the island's population (20,000 of 42,000); by the 1680s, 70 percent (46,000 of 66,000).[90] Barbados slavery thus entered its phase of rapid growth well in advance of the mainland. In 1661, almost exactly at the moment that the strong Restoration push to establish slavery on the mainland was getting under way, Barbados became the first English colony to legislate extensively on slavery.

Barbados had initially adopted laws to govern slaves piecemeal, more or less in step with the demographic transformation of its labor force. As the comprehensive *Act for the Better Ordering and Governing of Negroes* (1661) noted, "heretofore many good Lawes and ordinances have bin made for the governing regulating and ordering the Negroes Slaves in this Island." When slaves first began appearing on the island in the mid-1630s, for example, the Governor and Council had established a legal basis for enslavement by ordering that "Negroes and Indians, that came here to be sold, should serve for Life, unless a Contract was before made to the contrary." Barbados relied upon adaptations of English police laws disciplining vagrancy and the movement of population when it came to actual enforcement of the regime.[91] But the inexorable increase of the slave population provoked the Assembly to doubt the adequacy of those initial efforts. "Masters of families and other the Inhabitants of this Island" had been lax in living up to their obligations to oversee their slaves; the laws comprehended neither the unique demands of the plantation system's massive concentrations of enslaved alien laborers nor the unique deviance of Negroes, "heathenish [and] brutish ... uncertain and dangerous." Neither had parallel in English experience. Hence the Act of 1661. The "better ordering" it promised "absolute Needful for the publique Safety."[92]

---

[90] Richard Dunn, *Sugar and Slaves: The Rise of the Planter Class in the English West Indies, 1624–1713* (Chapel Hill, 1972), 75–6, 87–9, 230, 312.

[91] See Richard B. Sheridan, *Sugar and Slavery: An Economic History of the British West Indies, 1632–1775* (Kingston, Jamaica, 1994 [1974]), 236; David Barry Gaspar, "With a Rod of Iron: Barbados Slave Laws as a Model for Jamaica, South Carolina and Antigua," in Darlene Clark Hine and Jacqueline McLeod, editors, *Crossing Boundaries: Comparative History of Black People in Diaspora* (Bloomington, Ind., 1999), 344–5.

[92] *An Act for the Better Ordering and Governing of Negroes* (Barbados, 1661), CO 3/2/16–26 (Public Record Office, Kew, London), preamble. (Fragments of the 1661 Act are

The detail of the Barbadian *Better Ordering* statute followed from its two claims of uniqueness, and from the further claim that English law offered "noe track to guide us where to walke nor any rule sett us how to govern such slaves." Cast by necessity upon its own devices, the Assembly chose to "revive whatsoever wee have found necessary and usefull in the former Lawes" and to add such laws of its own devising as might promise "peace and utility." The resulting statute dealt extensively with Barbadian slavery – relations between slaves and the white population as a whole; slaves and their masters; slave discipline; and slave protections. Slaves were merchandise until sold, and property thereafter. In either state it was appropriate to safeguard them against "evil disposed person[s]" as any other species of merchandise or property, goods and chattels. And, "being created Men," albeit heathen, slaves were also deserving of protection "somewhat further."[93] But being the kind of people they were – uncouth and alien, increasingly numerous, increasingly rebellious – slaves were profoundly dangerous. The Assembly's foundational intent was rigorous coercive control: a regime of whipping, dismemberment, and death administered as a completely distinct jurisdiction by special courts of justices and freeholders.[94]

reproduced in Stanley Engerman et al., editors, *Slavery* (Oxford 2001), 105–113.) I am very grateful to David Barry Gaspar for his generosity in providing me with a copy of the original statute in manuscript.)

[93] Ibid., preamble. In *De Iure Belli*, at 333, Gentili wrote, "This kindness we should show even to dumb beasts ... And from these precepts [we] deduce rules for mankind, forbidding one to injure or press with the yoke those whom we can accuse of nothing more serious than that they are of a different race from our own ... Thus our law restrains the cruelty of masters, as well as their shamelessness and ill-treatment of their slaves."

[94] On Barbados's slave law, see generally Hadden, "Fragmented Laws of Slavery," 259–63.

Barbados's slave courts deserve some attention, for they would spread far and wide in the Restoration-era mainland colonies. The courts were a Barbadian innovation. They had no real parallel in English law. Bradley Nicholson has contended that they "followed the example of the Statute of Artificers, which stated that servants would be tried by two Justices of the Peace or a town mayor and 'two other of the discreetest persons' of the town." See Nicholson, "Legal Borrowing," 46; *An Acte towching dyvers Orders for Artificers Laborers Servantes of Husbandrye and Apprentises* (1563) 5 Eliz. c.4 [popularly known as *The Statute of Artificers*, sometimes *The Statute of Apprentices*], in *The Statutes of the Realm*, IV (London, 1819), 414–22. But Nicholson's contention is a little misleading. The Statute of Artificers did not create courts with general and exclusive jurisdiction over "servants." It enacted both summary and administrative procedures to enforce the "dyvers Orders for Artificers Laborers Servantes of Husbandrye and Apprentises" that comprised the substance of the Statute. The procedures distinguished between parish jurisdictions overseen by "twoo Justices of the Peace of the Countye" and municipal jurisdictions, that is corporate town or borough jurisdictions, overseen by corporate officers with judicial powers equivalent to those of County Justices – the "Maio[r] or other Head Officer of the Citie Burghe Town Corporate and twoo Aldermen, or twoo other discrete Burgesses of the same Citie Burghe or Town Corporate yf ther bee no Aldermen" (Clause VI). Aldermen were originally officers of mercantile or craft guilds; as guilds became increasingly identified with municipal corporations, aldermen became members of the ruling municipal body. Aldermen had the powers of magistrates. "Burgesses" could mean simply freemen of a borough, but in this context far more likely carries the more particular meaning of non-Aldermanic officer of a

Barbados became a luxuriant breeding ground for slave law in the English Caribbean and beyond. As the island became more and more the province of large planters, numbers of land-poor Barbadian whites began migrating elsewhere in the Caribbean, settling Jamaica and the Leeward Islands, taking their slaves and slave law with them. Barbadian planters also moved to the mainland. Carolina is their best-known destination, but Barbadian planters also moved to other mainland settlements along lines of passage created by the island's commercial networks. Not a few went to Boston. Others settled in East Jersey. Still others headed for Virginia.[95]

corporate borough or town. In that capacity Burgesses enjoyed authority to preside as magistrates over local courts.

The Statute of Artificers does not make provision for Justices or their municipal equivalents to be joined by non-judicial persons in *any* trial proceeding held under the authority of the statute. It does envisage combining multiple justices with "suche discrete and grave psons of the said Countie ... as they shall thinck meete" in an annual *administrative* proceeding for the setting of wage rates. Municipal judicial officers similarly joined with such "discrete and grave psons ... of the said Citie or Towne Corporate" in wage-setting proceedings (Clause XI). The purpose of including such "discrete and grave psons" in wage-setting was advisory only: the actual wage assessments were compiled by the judicial personnel – county justices outside the towns and municipal judicial officers within them. On this, see Michael F. Roberts, "Wages and Wage-Earners in England: The Evidence of the Wage-Assessments, 1563–1725" (unpublished D.Phil. thesis, Oxford University, 1981), 54–66.

The Statute makes provision for the presence of non-judicial personnel in a non-administrative proceeding in a single and particular respect only: if a "Servaunte Woorckman or Laborer" should "wilfullye or maliciously make any Assaulte or Affray upon his M^r M^{rs} or Dame, or upon any other that shall at the time of such Assaulte or Fraye have the chardge or oversight of any suche [assailant]," and if convicted thereof "before any twoo of the Justices Maio^r or Head Officer aforesaid," the offender was to serve one year's imprisonment. If the offense were slight, however, the penalty might be mitigated "by the discression of twoo Justices of Peace if it bee wthout a Towne Corporate," or if within by the discretion of "the Maio^r or Head Officer of the same Towne Corporate wth two others of the discretest psons of the same Corporaĉon at the least." If on the other hand the assault were sufficiently aggravated as to require additional "open" [that is, public] punishment "so as yt extende not to lief nor lyme," punishment was to be set by the Justices of the County meeting in Open Sessions [that is, at Quarter Sessions] if the offense were outside a corporate town, or if within by "the said Maio^r or Head Officer and syxe or four at the least of the discreetest psons of the same Corporaĉon" (Clause XIV). The sense of the provision is to grant "the discreetest psons of the ... Corporaĉon" an advisory role in determining post-conviction punishment. The provision is clear that they play no role in the trial process.

Though meant as I have indicated, the words of the Statute could have been read (or remembered) a century after in a distinct and more expansive way. South Carolina's 1690/1 *Act for the Better Ordering of Slaves* (7 February 1690/1), in *The Statutes at Large of South Carolina*, ed. David J. McCord (Columbia, S.C., 1840), vol. 7, 343–7, which is modeled on Barbados's 1661 Act, uses the terms "discreet and sufficient" in describing the qualifications of the three freeholders who are to join the two justices in composing that colony's slave courts. (The 1661 Barbados statute uses the terms "able, good, and legall" to describe the freeholders.) It is certainly conceivable, in other words, that in some fashion the general form of the courts was suggested by some acquaintance with or memory of the Statute. And indeed that may be all that is necessary for the purposes of "legal borrowing."

95 See Gaspar, "With a Rod of Iron"; David Barry Gaspar, "'Rigid and Inclement': Origins of the Jamaica Slave Laws of the Seventeenth Century," in Christopher L. Tomlins and

Barbadian transplants influenced the development of slave regimes in each of slavery's three mainland centers – the Chesapeake to some extent, but particularly Carolina and the mid-Atlantic. The timing of slavery's growth in each region explains the timing of the waves of statutes that followed: growth meant both an absolute and a relative increase in the sheer numbers of debased laborers to be overseen. Increasing numbers of slaves were boxed in by increasingly oppressive police regimes. But other factors were in play that dictated the creation of the institution as a condition of absolute difference, elaborated in detail. As increasing demand for slaves outran the spasmodic "Atlantic Creole" supply of the first half century, as new suppliers gained access to mainland markets, planters turned increasingly to slaves directly imported out of Africa.[96] "Outlandish" Africans were physically and culturally distinct from somewhat acculturated Atlantic Creoles. In the 1660s and after, therefore, Anglo-Americans began fashioning slavery both as a culture of work and as a culture of absolute subjugation, the former an expression of greed, the latter of whites' fear of the growing numbers of aliens their greed had introduced into their midst and their deep-rooted impulse to dominate completely those who so unsettled them.

III. Mainland Slavery Regimes: South Carolina

In the wake of post-Restoration colonizing's penetration of the southern mainland and the mid-Atlantic region, and as both wartime interruptions and general stagnation of supply increasingly cut into European servant migration in the later seventeenth century, settler demand for labor turned toward slaves everywhere from the Carolinas to southern New England.[97] The rapid post-Restoration expansion in English resort to slaves and accompanying creation of slavery regimes had two major points of departure, Carolina and the Chesapeake, and a third ultimately less significant (but still important) in the mid-Atlantic. We will get to the mid-Atlantic settlements in due course. For the present let us concentrate on mainland slavery's traditional home, the South Atlantic, and its two most populous centers: first South Carolina, second Virginia.

The histories of slavery in South Carolina and Virginia are quite distinct. Attempts to settle the vast region that would become the Carolina proprietary began in the 1660s. By the end of the century the population

---

Bruce H. Mann, editors, *The Many Legalities of Early America* (Chapel Hill, 2001), 78–96; Nicholson, "Legal Borrowing," 49–53; Hatfield, *Atlantic Virginia*, 137–68.

[96] Early eighteenth-century Chesapeake evidence indicates that trade in slaves gathered momentum after 1680, and particularly after 1698 when the Royal African Company lost its monopoly and new English suppliers entered the business. See n.160, this chapter. On the loss of the Royal African Company's monopoly in 1698 and the development of an aggressive free trade in slaves, see Pettigrew, "Free to Enslave," 7–33.

[97] On the curtailment of European servant migration, see Chapter I, sections IIA and IIB. For trends in black population, see *HSUS*, vol. 5, table Eg41–59.

of that part of the proprietary domain that would become South Carolina had grown to a little over 6,000. By 1780, the population of the lower South's colonies (including Georgia) exceeded 250,000.[98] Initially the settlers' economy was one of trade with the region's indigenous inhabitants for hides and Indian slaves for shipment to Caribbean plantations. By the 1670s, planters migrating with their slaves from Barbados were developing additional commodities for trade back to the West Indies: wood products, cattle, and corn. Lumber, food crops, and ranging cattle all meant increased European demand for land, culminating in the Yamasee War of 1715–17. Expanding cultivation in coastal regions, and the development of new staple crops, notably rice, further stimulated demand for labor, which took the form primarily of massive importation of African slaves. The coastal parishes, where slaveholding was concentrated, dominated the colony's Assembly and its legislative output throughout the period (1690–1740) when its slavery regime was in formation.[99]

Institutionally and culturally, Carolina was fruitful territory for slavery. Carolina was chartered in 1663 as a proprietary enterprise on the palatine model. The proprietors had direct or indirect connections with plantation slavery in Barbados, or with the English slave trade, and the Carolina proprietary courted land-hungry Barbadian planters who had been eyeing other parts of the Caribbean and the mainland. Slavery was not named in the proprietors' initial "Declaration and Proposals" (1663), which offered land to all settlers in exchange for population on the headrights model developed in the Chesapeake. One hundred-acre grants (in "free and common soccage") were promised to every male settler, with additional 50-acre allotments for each accompanying male indentured servant capable of bearing arms, and 30 acres for women-servants. The servants themselves were to receive respectively 10- and 6-acre allotments on the expiration of their indentures. Those granted land were assured of local self-government and liberty of conscience.[100] But there were few takers. A group of

---

[98] Squatters began moving south from Virginia into the Albemarle Sound region in the 1650s. Robert M. Weir, "'Shaftesbury's Darling': British Settlement in the Carolinas at the Close of the Seventeenth Century," in Nicholas Canny, editor, *The Origins of Empire: British Overseas Enterprise to the Close of the Seventeenth Century*, volume I of *The Oxford History of the British Empire*, William Roger Louis, general editor (Oxford, 1998), 381. For population, see *HSUS*, vol. 5, table Eg16–18 (total population of South Carolina, Georgia, Florida).

[99] Weir, "'Shaftesbury's Darling'," 387–9; Morgan, *Slave Counterpoint*, 7, 35–60; Peter Wood, *Black Majority: Negroes in Colonial South Carolina From 1670 through the Stono Rebellion* (New York, 1975), 13–62; Alan Gallay, *The Indian Slave Trade: The Rise of the English Empire in the American South, 1670–1717* (New Haven and London, 2002), 48–50, 330–1, 357; Rachel N. Klein, *Unification of a Slave State: The Rise of the Planter Class in the South Carolina Backcountry, 1760–1808* (Chapel Hill, 1990), 7.

[100] See, "Charter of Carolina – 1663," and "A Declaration and Proposals of the Lord Proprietor of Carolina, Aug. 25–Sept. 4, 1663," both in Francis Newton Thorpe, *The Federal and State Constitutions, Colonial Charters, and other Organic Laws of the States, Territories and Colonies Now or Heretofore Forming The United States of America* (Washington, D.C., 1909), V, 2743–53, 2753–5; L. H. Roper, *Conceiving Carolina: Proprietors, Planters and Plots, 1662–1729* (New York, 2004), 15–18; Wood, *Black Majority*, 13–15.

Barbadian adventurers proposed to adapt the terms of land distribution by establishing for every member of the group a flat rate head right of 100 acres payable for each person "white or black, young or old" whose passage they underwrote. To assist recruitment, they also sought enlargement of the allotments reserved to servants payable on expiration of their indentures. And they sought an additional head right for each slave they transported.[101] In 1665, the proprietors improved upon their original proposals in certain "Concessions and Agreements" entered into with "adventurers of the Island of Barbados and their associates" by allowing them 80 acres for each transported European male servant capable of bearing arms, 40 for each European woman and child, and 40 for each slave older than fourteen. Allotments for freed servants were raised to 40 acres, and might be varied beyond that level by Act of Assembly. Efforts to settle followed, but were unsuccessful until 1669/70, when a mixed expedition of English and Barbadian adventurers established continuous settlement at Albemarle Point, subsequently Charles Town, under the sponsorship of proprietor Anthony Lord Ashley (Anthony Ashley Cooper, later the Earl of Shaftesbury).[102]

Ashley had prepared the way by persuading his fellow proprietors once more to enlarge the head right to a flat 150 acres to the importer of any servant. Whether this extended to importers of slaves was left ambiguous by the proprietors, but not by the Barbadians who predicated their continued participation on the availability of the head right to importers of "negroes as well as Christians."[103] Ashley had also prepared the way by drafting – with the assistance of his secretary, John Locke – the "Fundamental Constitutions of Carolina," which took the metropolitan language of palatine jurisdiction and manorial organization typical of English colonial charters since the early 1620s to its most elaborated level in the course of creating perhaps the most over-determined political-legal order (certainly the most complex) anywhere on the Atlantic coast. Land holding and local government was framed in a meticulously detailed spatial structure of seigneuries, baronies, colonies, and manors. The objective was the foundation in landed property of an elaborately hierarchical culture of governance that invested authoritative oversight in a local hereditary nobility fused institutionally with the proprietors. Of most immediate importance, however, the Fundamental Constitutions acknowledged – in the course of guaranteeing religious toleration – both that the practice of holding slaves would extend to Carolina and that Carolina slaveholders would enjoy the same absolute power over their slaves that Barbados had established in its 1661 "Better Ordering" statute. "Since charity obliges us to wish well to the souls of all men ... it shall be lawful for slaves, as well

---

[101] Wood, *Black Majority,* 14–17.
[102] Ibid., 17–20; Roper, *Conceiving Carolina,* 18–20, 41–9; "Concessions and Agreements of the Lords Proprietors of the Province of Carolina, 1665," and "Charter of Carolina – 1665," both in Thorpe, *Federal and State Constitutions,* V, 2756–61, 2761–71.
[103] Wood, *Black Majority,* 19–20.

as others, to enter themselves, and be of what church or profession any of them shall think best, and, therefore, be as fully members as any freeman." Yet, since "religion ought to alter nothing in any man's civil estate or right … no slave shall hereby be exempted from that civil dominion his master hath over him, but be in all things in the same state and condition he was in before." Thus, on the one hand, "No person whatsover shall disturb, molest, or persecute another for his speculative opinions in religion, or his way of worship"; on the other, "Every freeman of Carolina shall have absolute power and authority over his negro slaves, of what opinion or religion soever."[104] The prudential concerns of early modernity that Christians not

---

[104] "The Fundamental Constitutions of Carolina – 1669," in Thorpe, *Federal and State Constitutions*, V, 2772–86, particularly 2785 (§§107, 109, 110).

Like his ownership of shares in the Royal African Company (see n.89 this chapter), John Locke's role in the preparation of the *Fundamental Constitutions* has been taken to signify his endorsement of Anglo-American racial slavery. See, e.g., M. Seliger, "Locke, Liberalism and Nationalism," in John W. Yolton, editor, *John Locke: Problems and Perspectives* (Cambridge, 1969), 28–9. See also David Armitage, "John Locke, Carolina, and the Two Treatises of Government," *Political Theory*, 32, 5 (2004), 619–20. For a distinct analysis, see James Farr, "'So Vile and Miserable an Estate': The Problem of Slavery in Locke's Political Thought," *Political Theory*, 14, 2 (May 1986), refined and restated in his "Locke, Natural Law, and New World Slavery," *Political Theory*, 36, 4 (August 2008). For an examination of the conjunction of Locke's political theory with his detailed knowledge of racial slavery and his activities as secretary of the Board of Trade (1696–1700) that stresses Locke's opposition to Anglo-American slavery, see Brewer, "Slavery and 'Inheritable Blood'."

Locke's most extended commentary on slavery occurs in his *Two Treatises of Government*, the opening statement of which – entirely consonant with Locke's intent to shred Filmer's patriarchal construction of politics and its endorsement of "absolute, arbitrary power" – describes slavery as "so vile and miserable an Estate of Man, and so directly opposite to the generous Temper and Courage of our Nation, that 'tis hardly to be conceived, that an Englishman, much less a Gentleman, should plead for't." *Patriarcha*, said Locke, seemed intended to "perswade all Men that they are Slaves, and ought to be so." John Locke, *Two Treatises of Government: In the Former, the False Principles and Foundation of Sir Robert Filmer, and His Followers, are Detected and Overthrown. The Latter is an Essay Concerning the True Original, Extent, and End of Civil-Government* (London, 1698), 1. The *Two Treatises* thus treat "slavery" as a statement in Anglo-American political theory signifying the negation of the founding of polities in compact and personal relations in consent. Slavery had been current in this sense in the political rhetoric of the English Civil War, again in the Glorious Revolution, and would be again in the political rhetoric of the American Revolution (provoking Samuel Johnson's famous question, "How is it we hear the loudest yelps for liberty among the drivers of negroes?" for which see Charles Grosvenor Osgood, editor, *Boswell's Life of Johnson* (New York, 1917), 353).

Locke's political writings do not explicitly address Anglo-American racial slavery, with the details of which he was familiar, although his theorization of slavery as a condition of absolute subjection is consonant with the relevant clauses of the *Fundamental Constitutions*. The theory of slavery presented in the *Two Treatises* is unoriginal except in its orientation to Anglo-American political theory. Locke reproduces as abstract theorizing the account of slavery as a human institution founded upon capture in just wars long since developed in the historical-empirical accounts of the sixteenth- and early seventeenth-century law of nations writers with whom we are already well acquainted – notably Vitoria, Gentili, and Grotius. Thus, Locke writes, "the perfect condition of Slavery … is nothing else, but the State of War continued, between a lawful Conquerour and a Captive" (183 [§24]). As for Gentili so also for Locke, that perfect condition was one of death interrupted (in

hold Christians in slavery held no sway in the face of racial differentiation. Indeed, the Constitutions' mingling of racial slavery with religion is no oddity but actually fundamental to the terms of mainland slavery's post-1660 expansion: everywhere, expansion was predicated on discarding the early modern injunction against enslavement of co-religionists, a decisive modernization in Anglo-American slave law.[105]

Carolina's utopian spatial and religious order thus came accompanied by acceptance of a social regime that locked the slave down. Yet Carolina's was not at this point a fully institutionalized slavery. The Fundamental Constitutions conceded slaveholding but not to the extent of instantiating it in dedicated institutions. Affirmation of the "absolute dominion" of the master was in effect recognition of a domestic dominion that would not be contested. Its affirmative legalization (institutionalized reproduction and perpetuation) would not begin until the 1680s.

Gentili's words "all but death"). In enslaving the captive, the captor simply delayed death so that he might "make use of him to his own service." *Two Treatises of Government*, 183 [§23]. Locke's analysis of conqueror's rights hedged the extension of enslavement beyond the relationship of lawful captor and captive that was slavery's "perfect condition." The lawful conqueror's power encompassed only those – the guilty – who had actively fought, assisted, or agreed in the war against him; it did not extend to the innocent. The lives of the guilty were forfeit at the conqueror's pleasure, and thus they might be enslaved; but their estates were not forfeit, beyond just compensation to the conqueror for the costs of war and the wrongs done him, and might pass to their (innocent) wives and children over whom the conqueror enjoyed no despotical power. "The short of the Case in Conquest, is this, The Conqueror, if he have a just Cause, has a Despotical Right over the Persons of all that actually aided and concurred in the War against him, and a Right to make up his Damage and Cost out of their Labour and Estates, so he injure not the Right of any other. Over the rest of the People, if there were any that consented not to the War, and over the Children of the Captives themselves, or the Possessions of either he has no Power, and so can have by Virtue of Conquest no lawful Title himself to Dominion over them." *Two Treatises of Government*, 318 [§196] and generally 303–18 [§§175–96]. But although comprehensive, Locke's statement of limitations of conqueror's right is not novel – the same can be found in the law of nations treatises. See, for example, Vitoria's discussion of the conqueror's rights over the guilty and whether the conqueror may despoil and enslave the innocent in *On the Indians or on the Law of War*, 171–3, 178–87. See also Gentili, *De Iure Belli* – "property may be taken from the enemy, provided that in so doing justice and equity are observed. The victor will not make everything his own which force and his victory make it possible to seize." (305). Gentili also raised doubts about slavery in perpetuity (328), the capture and enslavement of women and children (251–60, 208–11) and of the (non-culpable) vanquished population in general (336–9) – and discussed at length the extent to which victors might assume the property of those they had conquered (291–335). Not until Grotius does one encounter categorical claims for the conqueror's right to enslave not only all who have been captured in war (making no distinction between guilty and innocent) but also their descendants in perpetuity, and also the right to assume the entirety of their possessions. *De Jure Belli ac Pacis*, 690–1. These are the expansive claims that Locke attempts to counter. Locke also attempts to counter Grotius's representation of enslavement as founded on consent, as in the case of "persons … who surrender themselves, or promise to become slaves" (690), though with imperfect success (see Chapter 8, n.143). It is for these counters to Grotius that Locke's account of slavery is chiefly important.

[105] See this chapter, nn.180–87 and 192, and accompanying text for a fuller discussion of the enslavement of Christians in English America.

South Carolina did not begin to experience a major influx of slave labor until around the turn of the century. Migrating Barbadian planters had brought their slaves with them. Others became available in the small lots marginal to the greater Atlantic slave trade typical of the mainland colonies for most of the seventeenth century. In all, these sources resulted in a slave population in the region of some 1,500 by 1690, approaching 40 percent of total population.[106] Thereafter the influx began to accelerate, essentially doubling each decade; perhaps in the region of 1,000 in the 1690s, a more reliable 3,000 in the first decade of the new century, 6,000 in the second, nearly 12,000 in the third, more than 20,000 in the fourth. These volumes indicate that entering slaves were no longer the Barbadian Creoles or small lots on the margin of the Atlantic slave trade of Carolina's first quarter-century but almost entirely directly out of Africa. Already by 1700 blacks and whites were approximately equal in number in the South Carolina population; by 1710, blacks were in the majority.[107] By 1740, Africans outnumbered Europeans more than two to one (39,000 to 15,000).[108] Slave importation fell off almost completely in the 1740s in the wake of the Stono revolt of 1739 and the part played in that revolt by newly arrived Africans.[109] But arrivals surged again in the 1750s, peaking at nearly 22,000 in the 1760s. Over the period from 1750 through 1790, slave arrivals averaged nearly 17,000 per decade.[110]

Overall population figures show that natural increase did not contribute consistently to black population growth. Throughout the first half of the century, slave importation accounted for virtually all the increase in South Carolina's black population. Between 1700 and 1730, annualized rates of natural increase averaged slightly in excess of 1 percent; between 1730 and 1750, rates turned slightly negative. Between 1750 and 1775 rates were positive again, in the range of 1–1.5 percent per annum, but the years after 1775 until 1790 saw a return to negative natural increase. The colony's dependence on slave importation for labor also meant that for most of the century the white population of South Carolina formed a much smaller proportion of total population than in the Chesapeake. Rapid growth in importation saw the enslaved component of population grow from some 30 percent of population at the colony's inception to 48 percent in 1700, 65 percent by 1720, and 72 percent by 1740, before

---

[106] *HSUS*, vol. 5, tables Eg16, Eg55 (South Carolina total population, black population).

[107] Ibid. Robert V. Wells, *The Population of the British Colonies in America before 1776: A Survey of Census Data* (Princeton, 1975), 167, reports a slight plurality of blacks by 1708 (4100 of 9580) outnumbering Europeans (4,080) and Indians (1,400). For slave import volumes, see Morgan, *Slave Counterpoint*, 59 (table 9); O'Malley, "Beyond the Middle Passage," 140, 142 (table 2).

[108] *HSUS*, vol. 5, tables Eg16, Eg55 (South Carolina total population, black population).

[109] Morgan, *Slave Counterpoint*, 59 (table 9), 455–6. In April 1740, seven months after the Stono Rebellion, the South Carolina Assembly imposed a prohibitive tariff on slave imports. The tariff was repealed in 1752. Olwell, *Masters, Slaves, and Subjects*, 28.

[110] Morgan, *Slave Counterpoint*, 59 (table 9).

leveling off and then steadily declining back toward 50 percent over the next forty years.[111]

The development of a detailed law of slavery to complement the constitutive concessions of the Fundamental Constitutions awaited the moment that slave numbers began to increase late in the seventeenth century, and particularly when those directly out of Africa became a significant proportion of the slave population. As in Barbados in the 1640s and 1650s, initial moves to a law of slavery took the form of piecemeal legislation policing mobility of both servants and slaves (1683) and apparently ineffectual attempts to curtail trading with servants and slaves (passed repeatedly throughout the 1680s and '90s).[112] Adoption of more general statutes for the "better ordering" of Negroes and slaves began in February 1690/1, at which point the enslaved population of the colony approached 1,500 in a total of 3,900, and continued through 1740, comprising in all seven iterations and elaborations of better ordering.[113] As important, by 1700 imported Africans already comprised half of South Carolina's slave population. A decade later they were two-thirds, a proportion maintained with some variation until the 1740s, when the curtailment of slave importation and a modest upturn in natural increase lowered the African proportion of the slave population to 40 percent by 1750. It continued slowly to decline thereafter.[114]

The first general statute, *An Act for the Better Ordering of Slaves* (February 1690/1), concentrated on the control of slave mobility. It elaborated a structure of regulation based on tickets-of-leave that strictly constrained the movement of slaves outside home plantations and enlisted the entire population of plantation masters in policing observance and punishing slaves discovered at large without permission.[115] It also established detailed

---

[111] Rates of natural increase taken from Morgan, *Slave Counterpoint*, 84 (Table 20); Population proportions calculated from *HSUS*, vol. 5, tables Eg16, Eg36, Eg55 (South Carolina total population, white population, black population).

[112] See, e.g., *An Act to Prevent Runaways* (7 November 1683, reenacted 23 November 1685, title only); *An Act Inhibiting the Trading with Servants or Slaves* (25 September 1682 [*quaere* 1683], title only, the same title enacted 28 February 1686, 25 March 1691, 15 October 1692, 16 March 1695/6), all in *The Statutes at Large of South Carolina*, ed. Thomas Cooper (Columbia, S.C., 1837), vol. 2, v, 13–14, 22–3, 52–4, 73, 118.

[113] Although such general and comprehensive slave law statutes have commonly been referred to as "codes," they are not codes in the sense of the classic definition of code as "a complete written formulation of a body of law" systematically developed and organized. Here, consequently, I have preferred to avoid use of the term.

[114] Morgan, *Slave Counterpoint*, 61 (table 10).

[115] Tickets of leave for slaves moving beyond the confines of their master's or mistress's house, land, or plantation at any time day or night were mandated in 1686; anyone encountering a slave who could not produce a ticket was granted authority to apprehend, chastise, and correct the slave and have him, her, or them returned whence they came. *An Act Inhibiting the Trading with Servants or Slaves* (28 February 1686), in *The Statutes at Large of South Carolina*, vol. 2, 22–3, at 23. An act of this title was first adopted in 1682, but the text is missing. Without the text of that act, it is impossible to know when the ticket system was first put in place.

runaway and enticement regulation, again enlisting the white population as a whole in enforcement. It established a graduated schedule of
punishments for slaves who "offered any violence ... to any white person"
(whipping on the first offense; nose-slitting and burning on the second;
death on the third), mandated frequent searches for weapons and stolen
goods, adopted summary procedures and penalties peculiar to slaves to
be employed in all cases of slave crime – whether theft, assault, murder,
or insurrection, whether capital or non-capital – and created dedicated
juryless courts of two justices and three "discreet and sufficient" freeholders to administer them. It required that slaves have "convenient clothes"
once a year, rendered the killing of slaves by whites punishable if purely
wanton or bloody-minded, but not otherwise, affirmed that profession of
Christianity would not free slaves, and declared them freehold property
except insofar as necessary for the payment of debts, in which case they
were to be accounted chattel. The Act's single most important provision was
its adoption (Clause VIII) of the summary *in banc* slave courts of justices
and freeholders employing a distinct and expedited criminal process and
with full jurisdiction over all defined slave "crime," non-capital and capital,
as created in Barbados in 1661.[116] Overall, in the specifics of its provisions
and language this first Carolina "better ordering" statute was a highly con-
densed, somewhat indifferently drafted, version of the Barbadian statute.
(A second iteration of the Barbadian Act, *An Act for the Governing of Negroes*,
was adopted in August 1688 and has been considered by some the most
likely source for the Carolina statute,[117] but the order of clauses and repli-
cations in language show the Act of 1661 was the Carolina statute's point
of origin.) Unlike the Barbadian statute, however, Carolina's included no
explanatory preamble or general statement of policy. A strictly instrumental measure, its framers – thirty years after the Barbados Act – appear to
have felt no need to explain the necessities of their invention. They made
only incidental mention of its subjects, "negro or Indian slave[s]," seeing
no necessity for elaboration. The Act was adopted during the short-lived
administration of the renegade proprietor and self-proclaimed governor
Seth Sothell, and like all laws passed during Sothell's governorship, it was
disallowed by the proprietors after his demise.[118] But it was reenacted in
September 1693 in slightly revised form, and renewed in July 1695 for
twelve months.[119] Its provisions can be found at the core of every subsequent attempt at comprehensive control of the colony's slave population.

[116] *An Act for the Better Ordering of Slaves* (7 February 1690/1), in *The Statutes at Large of South
Carolina*, ed. David J. McCord (Columbia, S.C., 1840), vol. 7, 343–7.

[117] See, e.g., Wood, *Black Majority*, 51–2.

[118] M. Eugene Sirmans, "The Legal Status of the Slave in South Carolina, 1670–1740,"
Journal of Southern History, 28, 4 (November 1962), 465.

[119] *An Act for the Better Ordering of Slaves* (11 September 1693), title only, "The original Act not
now to be found," and *An Act to Revive the several Acts within mentioned* (16 July 1695), title
only, "The original Act not now to be found," both in *Statutes at Large of South Carolina*,
vol. 2, 78, 96.

In 1696, as slave numbers continued to grow at rates that by that point were clearly outpacing European population growth, and particularly as directly imported Africans approached 50 percent of all slaves,[120] Carolina adopted the first of several revised and expanded iterations of statutory slave law "to Prevent the mischeifs which (as the number of slaves shall Increase) Too much Liberty may occasion." Again entitled *An Act for the Better Ordering of Slaves*, the 1696 statute elaborated upon the procedures to be followed by Carolina's new slave courts; created a graduated schedule of punishments for runaways that included bodily mutilation of repeat offenders (males above sixteen years old to be castrated, women to have one ear sliced off or be transported); rewarded those, including other slaves, who assisted in runaway recaptures; rendered enticement to depart a felony; required white supervision of all outlying locations (every "Plantation or Cow Pen") where slaves were present; and required masters of families to police slave access to firearms and other weapons.[121] The 1696 statute did not depart the form of its predecessor except in one important respect, adding a preliminary statement that declared who were slaves in the colony. This was the first explicitly constitutive statement of the ambit of slavery in Carolina and thus, however inadequately, the first legal foundation for slavery as an institution in the colony. It was not subtle.

> Bee it Enacted ... That all Negroes Mollatoes and Indians which at any time heretofore have been bought and sold or now are held and taken to be or hereafter shall be Bought and sold for slaves are hereby made and declared they and their children slaves to all Intents and Purposes; except all such Indians Negroes Mollatoes and Mustees which heretofore have been or hereafter shall be for some particular Merritt made free by their Respective masters and owners, And except all such Negroes Mollattoes Mustees and Indians which can prove they ought not to be sold for slaves.

The definition was tautologous; slaves were they who had hitherto been recognized as such or would be thereafter. And slavery was what it was ("to all intents and purposes"[122]). These were definitions by way of prevailing

---

[120] Between 1690 and 1700, South Carolina's white population increased by 50%, 2,400 to 3,600; the black population increased by 100%, 1,500 to 3,000. *HSUS*, vol. 5, tables Eg36, Eg55 (South Carolina white population, black population); Morgan, *Slave Counterpoint*, 61 (table 10).

[121] *An Act for the Better Ordering of Slaves* (Carolina, 1696), Records of the General Assembly: Acts, Bills and Joint Resolutions – Acts of the General Assembly, March 2–16, 1696 (Governor John Archdale), 60–6. South Carolina Department of Archives and History (Columbia, S.C.). In "The Legal Status of the Slave in South Carolina," Eugene Sirmans confuses the 1712 *Better Ordering* Act (see below) with that of 1696.

[122] The phrase "to all intents and purposes" originates in sixteenth-century English statutory and legal discourse. It first appears in 25 Henry VIII c.22 (1534), *An Acte for the Establishment of the Kynges Succession*, in *The Statutes of the Realm*, III (London 1817), 471–4, at 472, and frequently thereafter. The Crown adopted the formulation "to all Entents, Constructions, and Purposes" in the Commission of Royal Assent to c.20 and 21 of 33 Hen. VIII (1542), *An Acte for due Pces to be had in Highe Treason in Cases of Lunacye or Madnes* and *The Bill of Atteynder of Mestres Katherin Hawarde late Queene of England*, in *Statutes of the Realm*, III, 855–7, 857–60. For the text of the Commission, see *The Statutes of the Realm*, I

practice. But the statement underlined that slavery was racial – Negroes and Indians; that it extended to the product of European union with either – that is to mulattos and mestizos ("mustees"); that it was in perpetuity ("they and their children"); and that it included any and all who appeared to fall within the Act's definition, requiring those who sought exception to prove the negative.

The 1696 Act was renewed in 1698.[123] It was revised and further extended in 1701. The revisions imposed additional mutilations on serial runaways – one emasculated for a second offense was to have his Achilles tendon slashed through for a third ("the cord of one of his legs to be cut off above the heel"); they imposed further controls upon slaves' access to firearms ("no Negro or slave shall carry out the limits of his master's fenced ground any sort of gun, or firearm without a certificate"); to alleviate the costs of compliance they compensated owners £20 for "every Negro or slave that shall be killed or suffer death in pursuance of the directions of authority of this act"; and for the first time they introduced detailed restrictions on slaves' access to Charlestown, and prohibitions on all unsupervised work. For that owners of slaves had allowed their slaves "to do what and go whither they list, & to work where they please" in exchange for an agreed return to the owner, a practice that had resulted in slaves "looking for opportunity to steal & stealing goods to raise money to pay their masters as well as to maintain themselves & other slaves their companions in drunkenness and other more mischievous devices & consultations," the 1701 revisions specifically prohibited any such agreements and fined owners 10/- "for every day he, she, or they shall suffer any slave to as aforesaid." And for that "great number of slaves which do not dwell in Charlestown do on Sundays resort thither to drink, quarrel, curse, swear & profane the Sabbath, besides the contriving of other dangerous plots & designs which may in time tend to the harm of the inhabitants of this colony," all slaves so found in Charlestown without a ticket from their master specifically stating their reason to be there at that time were to be taken up by the constables and "publicly and severely whipped" and the master fined £ 5/-.[124]

(London, 1810), lxxiv. In modern usage the phrase has come to signify "as far as practicable," but its original signification in statutory construction is far more universal, meaning coverage of any and every eventuality, a signification reinforced by the frequent addition of an accompanying phrase, immediately following (precise wording varies) "any licence dispensacion or any other acte or actes goinge afore or insuyng the same or to the contrary thereof in any wyse not withstondyng" (this example taken from the *Acte for the Establishment of the Kynges Succession*, 472).

[123] *An Act for the Better Ordering of Slaves* (8 October 1698), title only, in *Statutes at Large of South Carolina*, vol. 2, 156.

[124] A transcription of a manuscript copy of the *Act for the Better Ordering of Slaves* (28 August 1701), formerly thought lost, recently discovered in the Bodleian Library, Oxford (Rawlinson MSS C155, fols. 273r–77r) can be found at pages 408–18 of L. H. Roper, "The 1701 'Act for the better ordering of Slaves': Reconsidering the History of Slavery in Proprietary South Carolina," *William and Mary Quarterly*, 3rd Ser., 64, 2 (April 2007), 395–418.

The "better ordering" legislation of 1701 remained unamended for more than ten years. By the end of that period the slave population had grown to exceed the white, while the proportion of directly imported Africans had grown to two-thirds of all slaves. Europeans might not have been aware that they had become a numerical minority in the colony, but the influx of 3,000 Africans, near doubling the size of the slave population in 1700, could not have gone unnoticed, whether in the sheer numbers of slaves or the continuing transformation of the population's character, from familiar Creole to outlandish African. When in 1712 the legislature turned once again to "better ordering," better than every other person in the surrounding region was a slave, two-thirds of whom had arrived within the last decade on a slave ship from (if later trends applied) Angola.[125] How were these demographic facts acknowledged?

The most striking changes introduced in 1712 lie not in the substance of the legislation but in its presentation. The statute cleaves to the template embraced by each successive iteration of "better ordering" adopted since 1690. It displays the same core concerns. The passage of successive statutes does not signify reform or rejection of previous legislation. Each is rather a refinement of what has gone before. Additions accumulate from year to year as the legislature attempts greater and greater comprehensiveness, embraces ever deeper institutional and procedural density, and displays a burgeoning regulatory sophistication born of experience, as well as a certain fastidiousness in drafting and design that revises the order in which clauses appear. The legislature is of course free to make such substantive adjustments to the materials that lie before it as seem appropriate, and it does so: in the case of runaways, for example, clause XIX of the 1712 Act once more carefully recalibrates the mutilation schedule. The runaway shall be whipped severely but precisely, "not exceeding forty lashes," for the first departure; branded on the check for the second; the third departure shall merit another severe whipping and the loss of an ear; emasculation shall be reserved for the four-time runaway, if male, while if female her other ear shall be cut off and her other cheek branded. The five-timer who has managed to survive mutilation the last time around and once more has departed shall be crippled. Similar piecemeal adjustments occur throughout.[126]

But the substantive adjustments of 1712 are really background to the most important change, the addition of a self-justificatory preamble in which, for the first time, Carolina planters explain themselves. Disappointingly, theirs is not an original self-explanation. Instead, like the substance of the original 1690/1 template, it has been copied from Barbados, though this time the source is not the original Barbados "better ordering" statute of

---

[125] *HSUS*, vol. 5, tables Eg36, Eg55 (South Carolina white population, black population); Morgan, *Slave Counterpoint*, 60, 61 (table 10), 63 (table 11).

[126] *An Act for the Better Ordering and Governing of Negroes and Slaves* (7 June 1712), in *Statutes at Large of South Carolina*, vol. 7, 352–65.

1661 but the revised Barbados statute of 1688, which in 1712 finally comes into its own as a clear influence upon the Assembly's revision of its predecessors' work. That influence is noticeable right from the beginning, announced in the title of the statute itself. Until 1712 the act had always been *An Act for the Better Ordering of Slaves* (1690/1, 1693, 1695, 1696, 1698, 1701). In 1712, the Carolina Assembly appropriates the Barbadian title of 1688 – *An Act for the Governing of Negroes* – renaming its handiwork *An Act for the Better Ordering and Governing of Negroes and Slaves.* Immediately below the title appears the copied preamble, which adopts verbatim (except in one crucial regard) the language of the revised Barbados statute's preamble as the foundational statement of the legalities of slavery in Carolina:

> WHEREAS, the plantations and estates of this Province cannot be well and sufficiently managed and brought into use, without the labor and service of negroes and other slaves; and forasmuch as the said negroes and other slaves brought unto the people of this Province for such purpose, are of barbarous, wild, savage natures, and such as renders them wholly unqualified to be governed by the laws, customs and practices of this Province; but that it is absolutely necessary, that such other constitutions, laws and orders, should in this Province be made and enacted, for the good regulating and ordering of them, as may restrain the disorders, rapines and inhumanity, to which they are naturally prone and inclined; and may also tend to the safety and security of the people of this Province and their estates; to which purpose [&c][127]

What the Carolina preamble excluded was the Barbadian preamble's spare statement of provision and protection ("such encouragements and allowances as are fit and needful to their support; that ... the Negroes and other Slaves be well provided for, and guarded from the cruelties and insolences of themselves, or other ill-tempered People or Owners"), an exclusion replicated in the substance of the Carolina legislation, which ignored the Barbadian statute's censure of "Masters and Owners ... who do not make sufficient conscience of providing what is necessary for their Negroes and

---

[127] Compare the Preamble of the 1688 Barbados statute, *An Act for the Governing of Negroes* (8 August 1688), in Richard Hall, comp., *Acts, Passed in the Island of Barbados. From 1643, to 1762, Inclusive* (London, 1764), 112–21, at 112–13 (it is worth noting that neither preamble labels "negroes and other slaves" inhuman, but rather "prone and inclined" to acts of inhumanity):

> WHEREAS the Plantations and Estates of this Island, cannot be fully managed and brought into use, without the labour and service of great number of Negroes and other Slaves: And forasmuch as the said Negroes and other Slaves brought unto the People of this Island for that purpose, are of barbarous, wild and savage nature, and such as renders them wholly unqualified to be governed by the Laws, Customs and Practices of our Nation: It therefore becoming absolutely necessary, that such other Constitutions, Laws and Orders, should be in this Island framed and enacted for the good regulating or ordering of them, as may both restrain the disorders, rapines and inhumanities to which they are naturally prone and inclined, with such encouragements and allowances as are fit and needful to their support; that from both, this Island through the blessing of God thereon, may be preserved, His Majesty's Subjects in their lives and fortunes secured, and the Negroes and other Slaves be well provided for, and guarded from the cruelties and insolences of themselves, or other ill-tempered People or Owners: To which purpose [&c].

other Slaves, or allowing them time to plant or provide for themselves."[128]
These Barbadian provisions were extremely modest, no more than the
expression of sentiment, but their excision from the Carolina statute signifies a thinking decision to make the latter unrelievedly and exclusively a
police measure directed to detailed and coercive control of slave mobility
and general behavior.

The 1712 statute's substantive concentration on controlling the slave
was of course completely consistent with every preceding Carolina "better
ordering" statute since 1691. So too, the statute reproduced its predecessors' definition (first adopted 1696) of those within the statute's ambit.
No such definitional language appears in the Barbadian statute, which
assumes, as it were, that the identification of "Negroes and other slaves"
required no more precise statement than that they were those "brought
unto the People of this Island" for the purpose of labor and service on
their plantations and were of such a "barbarous, wild and savage nature" as
to disqualify them from government by "the Laws, Customs and Practices
of our Nation"; that is, not only were they from outside "our nation"
(strangers) but also so alien in their barbarity as to be unassimilable in any
respect to the island's laws, customs, and practices.[129] The Carolina definition remains tautologous: slaves are they who theretofore have been or
thereafter will be sold as slaves.[130] The only innovation introduced in 1712
is procedural: all claims to exception were to be heard by the Governor
and council. As to the condition of slavery, that also remained tautologous: the condition of slavery was in definition what it was in practice – the
experience of those enslaved, without limit, "to all intents and purposes."
What the intents and purposes of slavery were (in statutory construction) lay wholly in the realm of the masters and owners of slaves. What
that meant, insofar as the condition was described in the "better ordering" statutes, was indeed "no hope of freedom ... subject[ion] to another's
domination ... reduc[tion] to the condition of a beast"[131] – a qualitatively
distinct status appropriate to those of "barbarous, wild, savage natures,"[132]

[128] Ibid., 113, 119.
[129] For an earlier and more explicit statement of slaves' otherness that closely recalls early
modern humanism's law of nations doctrine, see the preamble to Barbados's 1661 *Act
for the Better Ordering and Governing of Negroes* (discussed further below) describing slaves
(Negroes) as "an heathenish brutish and an uncertain dangerous kinde of people."
Eugene Sirmans writes, "Throughout the history of Negro servitude in Barbados, the
colonists there disliked specific legal definitions of slavery and preferred the institution
to be defined by custom rather than by law. Consequently, their slave laws dealt with the
control of slaves instead of their legal status." Sirmans, "The Legal Status of the Slave in
South Carolina," 462.
[130] The first part of Clause I of the 1712 Act reads "That all negroes, mulatoes, mustizoes or
Indians, which at any time heretofore have been sold, or now are held or taken to be, or
hereafter shall be bought and sold for slaves, are hereby declared slaves; and they, and
their children, are hereby made and declared slaves, to all intents and purposes." *An Act
for the Better Ordering and Governing of Negroes and Slaves* (S.C., 1712), 352.
[131] Gentili, *De Iure Belli*, 328.
[132] *An Act for the Better Ordering and Governing of Negroes and Slaves*, 352.

brutes,[133] whose brutality required they be sealed within specialized regimes of control – "other" laws, customs procedures, and practices that were themselves wholly set off, quarantined, from "ours."

During the following decade, South Carolina formally separated from North Carolina (1712), fought the transformative Yamasee War (1715), and shed (directly as a consequence) proprietary for royal governance (1719).[134] Throughout, the slave population grew apace. By 1720 there were nearly two slaves for every white person. Africans alone, virtually all of them recently arrived, numerically outnumbered Europeans. Supplementary statutes adopted during the decade registered whites' increasing concern, which became alarm, at this state of affairs: "the number of negroes do extremely increase in this Province," the Assembly observed in 1714, "and through the afflicting providence of God, the white persons do not proportion-ably multiply," greatly endangering the province's safety.[135] The Assembly imposed a £2 head tax payable on disembarked Africans. Simultaneously it expressed misgivings about the efficiency of the slave courts, the key insti-tutions in the administration of white security and slave control; "justice hath been obstructed and delayed." The composition of the slave courts did not change; as when they were first created, each consisted of a bench of two justices and three freeholders exercising summary jurisdiction with no jury. But the 1714 statute allowed that the courts might exercise full jurisdiction by majority of three rather than require the full bench reach agreement. It also established three as a quorum for all court busi-ness. In capital cases the majority of three had to include both justices; in non-capital cases it need not. Other procedural refinements embraced in 1714 attempted to enhance the certainty of conviction and punishment of slaves accused of assaulting whites. At the same time, the Assembly noted that certain of the province's control mechanisms were proving costly; the compensation paid to owners for slaves executed for capital crimes was exhausting the treasury. In consequence it varied capital crime penalties to allow transportation as an alternative to execution for slaves convicted of capital crimes other than murder, their sale in other colonies to set off at least in part the cost of compensating owners for their loss.[136]

---

[133] *An Act for the governing of Negroes* (Barbados, 1688), 116.

[134] Weir, "'*Shaftesbury's Darling*': British Settlement in the Carolinas," 386. The law of slavery in North Carolina was largely transplanted from Virginia. See *An Act Concerning Servants and Slaves* (N.C., 1741), in *A Collection of All the Public Acts of Assembly, of the Province of North Carolina: Now in Force and Use* (Newbern, N.C., 1751), ch. 24.

[135] *An Additional Act to an Act Entitled 'An Act for the Better Ordering and Governing Negroes and all other Slaves* (18 December 1714), in *Statutes at Large of South Carolina*, vol. 7, 365–8, at 367. On population, see *HSUS*, vol. 5, tables Eg36, Eg55 (South Carolina white population, black population); Morgan, *Slave Counterpoint*, 61 (table 10).

[136] *An Additional Act* (S.C., 1714), 365, 365–6, 367. Any slave or slaves accused of assaulting a white person might be convicted and condemned simply on oath of the victim without more ado; punishment was left to the discretion of the judges. Assault by a slave on a white person, unless in defense of another white person, was punishable by the familiar graduated menu of severe whippings on the first occasion followed, on the second, by whippings, mutilations, and burnings, and on the third by death or other appropriate

The transportation experiment did not last long. Three years later, contemplating the devastation of the Yamasee War, fearing that brutish Africans might make common alien cause with savage Indians and tip the balance against the white minority,[137] the Assembly abruptly attempted to halt "the great importation of negroes" by increasing the head tax payable on disembarked Africans from £2 to £40. As to those already in the colony, experience had proven that transportation had no deterrent effect on their crimes at all; if anything transportation was "an encouragement to pursue their villanies." Death was fully reinstated. The treasury's crisis was instead to be solved by shifting the burden of compensation to an assessment payable in equal parts by the slaveholders of the parish wherein the capital crime had taken place. The 1717 statute did nothing to revoke the changes in slave court procedure, however, confirming their incorporation within the body of "better ordering" law.[138]

Further restatements of "better ordering" were adopted in 1722 and 1735: after the turn of the century, in other words, and in addition to specific interventions as in 1714 and 1717, the comprehensive statute was revisited, refined, and reenacted roughly once every ten years. The 1722 restatement is most notable, perhaps, for the steady drumbeat of "death" that sounds throughout. As in 1712, punishment schedules are once more meticulously recalibrated among the usual array of options – whippings, burnings, mutilations, hangings – but as penalties for repeat offenders are adjusted, recidivists are turned off earlier in the schedule, with greater acceleration and lessened judicial discretion. Penalties become more severe: any injurious assault on a European by a slave means death. Weapons are to be searched out relentlessly; slave patrols are granted greater access to plantations – in the name of security, that is, the absolute sphere of the plantation master becomes subject to routine "outside" intervention. Simultaneously, small changes in the working of the statute's preamble remind us that because South Carolina has become a royal colony, both the point of comparison for judging the barbarity of slaves, and the implications of that barbarity, have changed. No longer are slaves for their wild and savage natures "unqualified to be governed by the laws, customs and practices *of this Province*"; that is, the local law of the proprietary colony of South Carolina. Now, rather, it is the laws, customs, and practice of *England* from which their brutishness expels them. It becomes England's responsibility – more particularly the Crown's – to do as a sovereign should, to "tend to the safety and security of

penalty as the court might decide. See the *Better Ordering* Act of 1712 (repeating with insignificant adjustment provisions of previous *Better Ordering* statutes). The 1714 statute also prohibited owners from allowing slaves to keep gardens or raise stock for their own use.

[137] Gallay, *The Indian Slave Trade*, 345.

[138] *A Further Additional Act to an Act Entitled 'An Act for the Better Ordering and Governing Negroes and all other Slaves; and to an Additional Act to an Act Entitled 'An Act for the Better Ordering and Governing Negroes and all other Slaves* (11 December 1717), in *Statutes at Large of South Carolina*, vol. 7, 370, and generally 368–70.

the people of this Province" in return for enjoyment of their allegiance, by acknowledging that slaves' savage difference renders them prone to acts of inhumanity and hence meet for subjection (as they had been since 1690/1, rendered explicit in the 1712 Act's preamble) to an entirely distinct order of government. Yet, for that slaves were not incapable of rationality, "any two justices of the peace of the county ... shall and may inquire, by the best means they can, whether slaves, throughout the several plantations, are sufficiently provided with corn or other provisions," the want of "a sufficient allowance" of which might provoke them to run away.[139]

Little changed in the 1735 restatement, by which time slaves outnumbered Europeans approximately three to one, and there were two Africans for every white. At some point the numerical disparities become so deeply established as to be irrevocable; one exhausts the repertoire of coercions; one looks to express stability and control in more ways than simply whipping, burning, mutilating, and killing dissenters. And indeed, such provisions as were added in 1735 suggest that since 1722 South Carolina had become somewhat more used to itself as a stable slave society: what particularly exercised the Assembly in 1735's revisitation and reenactment of the "better ordering" statute was that slaves were undermining slavery not by cunning rebellions and savage assaults but by dressing too well – wearing clothes "much above the condition of slaves" – and by opening small businesses, "houses of entertainment or trade," not just in their masters' names but in their own. Here, amid the painstaking calibrations of death and disablement, the elaborated pornography of punishments, the minutely detailed regulations for the taking up of runaways, all dictating who could go where, all intended to keep the slave cowed and physically immobilized, one discovers the Assembly's newest preoccupation was with slaves whose modest displays of initiative suggested they had not so much *left* their place as were in danger of *forgetting* it.[140]

Five years later the Assembly returned yet again to South Carolina's "better ordering" laws, adopting a revised *Act for the Better Ordering and Governing of Negroes and other Slaves in this Province* in May 1740. We have become familiar with, perhaps wearied by, these serial revisions and reenactments: 1740's was the tenth return to the basic law of slavery since 1690/1. Each comprehensive statute reiterated and built upon, refined and deepened, the body of regulations, procedural and coercive, that had accumulated to create the colony's slavery regime in all its public and legal aspects. What had begun as the fifteen crudely drafted clauses of 1690/1 had become forty by 1735: set in type, four pages had become more than twelve. Only five years later the Assembly required fifty-eight dense clauses to complete its work: the twelve pages of 1735 leaped to twenty in 1740. But although it retained much of the substance and the institutional framework

---

[139] *An Act for the Better Ordering and Governing of Negroes and other Slaves* (23 February 1722), in *Statutes at Large of South Carolina*, vol. 7, 371–84, at 371, 378 and generally.
[140] *An Act for the Better Ordering and Governing of Negroes and other Slaves* (29 March 1735), in *Statutes at Large of South Carolina*, vol. 7, 385–97, at 396.

of its predecessors – it was clearly of the same family – the 1740 statute was more remarkable as a reconceptualization of the institution of slavery, at least as it had been expressed in South Carolina's law over the previous half century, than simply one more elaboration. One clear indicator that the innovations of 1740 were something other than the latest fine-tuning in a regular series is how long thereafter they endured. After 1740, regular return to the "better ordering" statute ceased. The statute as readopted that year in all essentials defined South Carolina's slavery regime for the next 125 years.

One might imagine that the precipitant of reconceptualization was the Stono Rebellion, which had erupted eight months earlier, in September 1739. On learning of the outbreak of war between England and Spain, a group of some twenty slaves gathered at the Stono River west of Charlestown and resolved to head for Florida, about 150 miles to the south. That first day they traveled about ten miles, killing, plundering, and burning (with some discrimination) as they went; and their numbers grew to upward of one hundred. Late in the day they were confronted by mounted militia at the Edisto River. Nearly half were killed and the rest scattered. A large group later reformed and over the next few days continued southward about thirty miles before it was attacked once more by pursuing militia and wiped out.[141]

The mark of Stono is certainly evident on the 1740 Act. Before business was closed, the Assembly noted that "the exigence and danger the inhabitants at that time were in and exposed to, would not admit of the formality of a legal trial of such rebellious negroes, but for their own security, the said inhabitants were obliged to put such negroes to immediate death." The Act's last substantive clause (LVI) granted a blanket immunity to all those who had taken part in suppressing the revolt, no matter that what had been done did not comport with the requirements of legislation then in force:

> All and every act, matter and thing, had, done, committed and executed, in and about the suppressing and putting all and every the said negro and negroes to death, is and are hereby declared lawful, to all intents and purposes whatsoever, as fully and amply as if such rebellious negroes had undergone a formal trial and condemnation, notwithstanding any want of form or omission whatever in the trial of such negroes; and any law, usage or custom to the contrary thereof in any wise notwithstanding.[142]

It is significant that Stono's clearest impress upon the Act appears as the felt necessity for retroactive immunization of those who suppressed the revolt. This was not of course an immunization against actions brought by the victims or their kin; no such possibility existed. Rather, it immunized some whites from actions brought by other whites; it protected those who

---

[141] Olwell, *Masters, Slaves, and Subjects*, 21–4.

[142] *An Act for the Better Ordering and Governing Negroes and other Slaves in this Province* (10 May 1740), in *Statutes at Large of South Carolina*, vol. 7, 397–417, at 416–17.

had wounded, mutilated, or killed slaves in the course of suppressing the revolt from the possibility of suits or criminal prosecutions pressed by slave owners seeking compensation and damages for the loss of their slaves and penalization of the perpetrator.[143] Still, even though the woundings and killings had arisen in the course of suppressing one of the most feared events in a slave society – a slave revolt – the immunization clause seems still to express a certain embarrassment that statutory procedure had broken down, that chaos had overwhelmed law. In its very grant of immunity, the clause necessarily declares the absence of a legal process, the necessitous resort to an immediate violence, a matter for regret.

In this, Clause LVI is of a piece with the 1740 Act as a whole; for throughout, what the Assembly does is dress the slavery regime instantiated in the Act's predecessors in new clothes, of a fashion one might best describe as balanced, polite, and above all sedulously respectful of the proprieties of English law.[144]

This re-presentation begins in the statute's very first words. Gone is the old preamble adopted from Barbados in 1712 and repeated ever since that pleaded both the special necessity of slavery and simultaneously cited the exceptional nature of slave laborers – their "barbarous, wild and savage natures" – as justification for the creation of a distinct apparatus of "constitutions, laws and orders ... for the good regulating and ordering of them" alongside that which governed Europeans but separate from it, anomalous but essential. Instead, slavery is taken for granted and the colony's law of slavery is confidently assimilated to the colony's law as such, no longer exceptional, a sequestration, but instead just one more legal categorization of a form of social action. Like other categorizations, slave law requires its own particular conventions and practices because like other species of social action slavery has its own quirks and specialized needs. But again like other particularized legal categories, slave law is part of law "as such"; it can be comfortably accommodated within a common discourse and logic of procedures and ideals:

> WHEREAS, in his Majesty's plantations in America, slavery has been introduced and allowed, and the people commonly called negroes, Indians, mulattoes and mustizoes, have been deemed absolute slaves, and the subjects of property in the hands of particular persons, the extent of whose power over such slaves ought to be settled and limited by positive laws, so that the slave may be kept in due subjection and obedience, and the owners and other persons having the care and government of slaves may be restrained from exercising too great rigour and cruelty over them, and that the public peace and order of this Province may be preserved: [&c][145]

---

[143] Clause LVI is intended to "prevent ... any person or persons being questioned for any matter or thing done in the suppression or execution of the said rebellious negroes, as also any litigious suit, action or prosecution that may be brought, sued or prosecuted or commenced against such person or persons for or concerning the same." Ibid., 416.

[144] Olwell, *Masters, Slaves, and Subjects*, 66–7.

[145] *Act for the Better Ordering and Governing Negroes and other Slaves in this Province* (SC 1740), 397.

The theme of slavery's legal normality, its balance of subjugation and obligation, extends throughout. First, the 1740 Act is densely procedural; it represents slaves as properly beneficiaries of appropriate procedural protections, for "natural justice forbids that any person, of what condition soever, should be condemned unheard, and the order of civil government requires that for the due and equal administration of justice, some convenient method and form of trial should be established."[146] Second, protections extend to the enumeration of penalties for the mistreatment of slaves, not only by strangers but by their owners, and extending beyond the squalid beatings, maimings, and other cruelties that comprise the physical mechanics of domination to the requirement that masters furnish sufficient "cloathing, covering [shelter] or food." For "cruelty is not only highly unbecoming those who profess themselves christians, but is odious in the eyes of all men who have any sense of virtue or humanity."[147] Slaves were not to be overworked; they were to be allowed certain highly restricted forms of autonomy – to work from home, to trade, to move about – though always within the ubiquitous system of ticketed permissions.[148] Third, the Act's discussions of penalties, heavy as always on capital punishment and intent on maintaining the wide ambit of death in cases of "crimes and offences of an enormous nature ... which being peculiar to the condition of this Province, could not fall within the laws of England," nevertheless eschews the lascivious exactitude with which prior "better ordering" statutes had enumerated graduated penalties for repeat offenders (whippings, burnings, slittings, hacking off body parts), preferring the more decorous formulation of "corporal punishment, not extending to the taking away life or member" left in its exact measure to the discretion of the court.[149]

The Act's show of respect for legality and humanity was, one may suppose, real enough; it was part and parcel of the discourse of English-trained lawyers whose influence was demonstrated in the Act's procedural density and high-flown rhetoric.[150] But it was also somewhat deceptive. For, while employing the new, polite language of legality and humanity, the Assembly simultaneously reenacted all the familiar features of South Carolina's slavery regime: the definition of who were to be slaves, the means of dealing with runaways, the ever-adaptable multi-faceted ticket system, the multiplicitous schedules of offenses, the thicket of regulations and restrictions afflicting all matters of mobility and appearance, of property and behavior – the places slaves could not go, the clothes they could not wear, the stock they could not raise, the houses, rooms, stores and grounds they could not rent, the things they could not own, the liquor they could not drink, the knowledge they could not have, all eminently punishable in the breach; and especially the key to the regime itself, those courts of justices

---

[146] Ibid., 400 (Clause IX).
[147] Ibid., 410, 410–12 (Clauses XXXVII–XXXIX).
[148] Ibid., 408, 410, 413 (Clauses XXXIII, XXXIV (provisos), XXXV, XXXVI, XLIV.
[149] Ibid., 401, 402, 405 (Clause X, XVI, XXIV).
[150] Olwell, *Masters, Slaves, and Subjects,* 66–7.

and freeholders, copied from Barbados, completely intact after a half century of operation, with their novel composition, summary *in banc* processes, and summary jurisdiction over all slave matters. The one innovation in fifty years had been the adoption in 1714 of majority verdicts (three of five) when the full bench was sitting, and designation thenceforth of three members of the five – at least one to be a justice (two in capital trials) – as a sufficient quorum for all business. Under the majority rule, quorum verdicts had to be unanimous. In 1740, the Assembly slipped in a new provision endorsing majority verdicts within the quorum in all non-capital trials, which meant conviction could be had by agreement of no more than two of the formally required five members, as long as one of the two was a justice. In capital cases unanimity within the quorum was maintained, but the Act no longer required that both justices be present.[151]

In an imaginative analysis of the 1740 Act, Robert Olwell has drawn attention to the Assembly's turn away from the exceptionalism of earlier "better ordering" statutes in favor of an attempt to "anglicize" South Carolina's slavery law by "graft[ing] slavery onto the existing English criminal statutes."[152] Indeed, it is indisputable that in drafting the Act's preamble, the explanation and justification of why there should be an Act in the first place, the Assembly quite clearly restated the relationship between slave law and English law. What had formerly been presented as "stranger" became a close relative. But in the substance of its behavioral coercions and punishments, slave law had always been grafted onto existing English criminal statutes, drawing from its inception on police statutes disciplining the movement of population and forcing vagrants to work. Nor was it remarkable in doing so. Starting with Barbados, every colony attempting to create a comprehensive law of slavery had begun by feeding off English police laws and criminal law; these continued throughout to furnish much of the disciplinary substance of English America's slave law.

What was notable about the efforts to create a comprehensive law of slavery in the various British American Caribbean and mainland colonies was that even though the available English laws were highly coercive, they were always found insufficient to the task of institutionalizing slavery and securing a slave society. The Barbados Council and Assembly had made this crystal clear as they moved to enact the very first *Act for the Better Ordering and Governing of Negroes*, the first comprehensive slave statute of British America, in 1661. Here was the point of origin of the language of innovation in the face of absolute necessity, of exceptional laws required by the dangerous alien difference of their subjects, that was picked up in the Carolina statutes in 1712 and repeated again and again – 1722, 1735 – until 1740.

> Whereas heretofore many good laws and ordinances have been made for the governing and regulating and ordering the Negroes Slaves in this Isle

---

[151] *Act for the Better Ordering and Governing Negroes and other Slaves in this Province* (S.C., 1740), 401 (Clause XI).

[152] Olwell, *Masters, Slaves, and Subjects*, 71.

& sundry punishments appointed to many their misdemeanours Crimes and offences which yett not mett the effect hath been desired and might have been reasonably expected ... And those former Laws being in many Clauses imperfect and not fully comprehending the true constitution of this Government in relation of their Slaves their negroes an heathenish brutish and an uncertain dangerous kinde of people to whom if surely in anything wee may extend the legislative power given us of punishionary laws for the benefit and good of this plantation not being contradictory to the Laws of England there being in all the body of that Lawe noe track to guide us where to walke nor any rule sett us how to govern such slaves ... wee have therefore upon mature and serious Consideration of the premises thought good to renewe and revive whatsoever wee have found necessary and usefull in the former Lawes of this Isle concerning the ordering and governing of Negroes and to add thereunto such further Lawes and ordinances as at this time wee think absolute needful for the publique safety and may prove to the future behoofefull to the peace and utility of this Isle by this Act repealing and dissolving all other former Lawes made concerning the said Negroes and for the time to come.[153]

Given this statutory genealogy, the newness of the 1740 Act lies not in its disciplinary substance – which, overwhelmingly, was not new at all – but in those elements that embodied the garb of legality and humanity in which the Assembly desired to dress its slavery regime. "In the dark soil and peculiar climate of the low country" (that is, South Carolina's plantation-intensive coastal plain), Olwell writes of the 1740 Act, "those limbs of 'Albion's Fatal Tree' that were unequal and brutal flourished, while other branches that stressed due process and equality before the law withered."[154] But this is a little misleading. Of course the unequal and the brutal flourished and would continue to do so, but there was nothing very new in that; the Assembly's designs for the colony's slavery regime had always been a flourishing compound of subjugation and brutality. What made the 1740 statute different was that for the first time the Assembly turned precisely to sentiments of due process and, though certainly not equality, of solicitude and protection, so as to press its claim of English cousinage. The appearance of these sentiments should not be taken as an indicator of "enlightenment" for the benefit and advancement of slaves. It signifies, rather, the maturation of their masters' grasp of how the discourse of legality served both slavery and their own self-esteem. A half century after the crude list of threats and tortures that was Carolina's first attempt at a comprehensive law of slavery, the Act of 1740 took care to underline that here were men versed in the rule of law and obedient to the dictates of natural justice; men of virtue and humanity, civilized men. Recalling the tinge of embarrassment at the slaughter of the Stono rebels that attended Clause LVI, one may be confident that when in the summer of 1740, just a few weeks after the Act was formally adopted, upwards of seventy slaves were brought to trial in St. John Berkeley Parish north of Charles Town for engaging in a

---

[153] *Act for the Better Ordering and Governing of Negroes* (Barbados, 1661), preamble.
[154] Olwell, *Masters, Slaves, and Subjects,* 71.

purported slave conspiracy and a third of them executed,[155] everything was done with impeccable if self-serving attention to legal propriety.[156]

IV. Mainland Slavery Regimes: Virginia

Carolina's direct links with Barbados made the island's slave laws an obvious point of reference for Carolina planters. South Carolina statutes would in turn inform those of neighboring Georgia.[157] But Barbados's influence spread far wider. In the case of Virginia, Barbadian trading links created channels of communication that introduced migrating planters and elements of Barbadian slave law into the Chesapeake.[158] Barbados indeed was a principal source of the Caribbean slaves who likely constituted the larger element in the mainland's initial slave populations.[159] Virginia's acting Governor Edmund Jennings informed the Board of Trade in 1708 that before 1680, "what negros were brought to Virginia were imported generally from Barbados for it was very rare to have a Negro ship come to this Country directly from Africa."[160] Barbadian slavery intersects with slavery in the Chesapeake on both sides of the sill.

Though slaves had accompanied the European intrusion into Virginia virtually from the beginning, persistence rates were low (there is no reason to believe that black mortality was lower than white): Virginia had

---

[155] Ibid., 26.

[156] Gallay writes, "If the Carolinians ... were a law-abiding people, they obeyed only those laws that suited them and then used the law to secure their place in power and the subjection of their social inferiors. If they were a civil people, it was a civility of convenience." *The Indian Slave Trade,* 357.

[157] Jordan, *White Over Black,* 104. See *An Act for the Better Ordering and Governing Negroes and other Slaves in this Province,* in *Colonial Records of the State of Georgia, Volume 18: Statutes Enacted by the Royal Legislature of Georgia from its First Session in 1754 to 1768* (Atlanta, 1910), 102–44, enacting with minor and formal modifications South Carolina's *Act for the Better Ordering and Governing Negroes and other Slaves in this Province* (S.C., 1740).

[158] Hatfield, *Atlantic Virginia,* 154–67. (Hatfield seems to me correct in her assertion of Virginia awareness of Barbadian slave law, but certain of her examples of specific influence are unsourced. Treated as legal regimes, of the three major mainland regime types – lower South [South Carolina and Georgia], Chesapeake [Virginia and Maryland], and mid-Atlantic [New York, New Jersey and Pennsylvania] – the Chesapeake slavery regime is least like the Barbadian.)

[159] O'Malley, "Beyond the Middle Passage," 138–40; Parent, *Foul Means,* 66–9.

[160] Jennings added that after 1680, "the Trade of Negros" had gathered momentum, particularly after 1698 (when the Royal African Company lost its English monopoly on the trade). The Governor of Maryland had dispatched a more detailed report ten days earlier, adding Jamaica to Barbados as early sources of supply, citing in addition a sloop-born coastal trade with New England, usually in small lots (7–10 slaves per shipment), "and sometimes, tho very seldom, whole ship Loads of Slaves ... brought here directly from Affrica by Interlopers." See Edmund Jennings to the Board of Trade (27 November 1708) and Governor John Seymour to the Board of Trade (18 November 1708), both in Elizabeth Donnan, *Documents Illustrative of the History of the Slave Trade to America* (Buffalo, N.Y., 2002 [Washington, D.C., 1935]), 4, 88–90 at 89, and 21–3 at 22. See also Hatfield, *Atlantic Virginia,* 147.

fewer than one hundred blacks in its population before the 1630s. Spot importations and natural increase among survivors had produced a black population of 950 by1660.[161] Not all Virginia's blacks were slaves, of course, but overwhelmingly the colony's "negroes" *were* enslaved and subject to distinctive treatment as such from the beginning.[162] And during the 1660s their numbers began to grow substantially. Between 1660 and 1680, the black population grew by 2000; it increased much more rapidly thereafter. Between 1680 and 1710, the black population grew by more than 16,000, more than matching white population growth numerically, far outstripping it in rate of growth. Indeed, much of this early rapid growth in black population was concentrated in the two decades after 1680, a period when white population hardly increased at all. In 1680 there were more than thirteen whites for every black in Virginia; by 1700, fewer than three.[163]

As in Carolina, the transition to rapid growth in the black population was a creature of mass importation of slaves either directly from Africa or transshipped via Caribbean entrepôts: some 4,000 during the first half of the growth spurt after 1680 (that is, through 1695); more than twice as many during the second (1695–1710).[164] These imports far outstripped the circulation of slaves between Virginia and the Caribbean that had brought Virginia much of its earlier black population. And again as in Carolina (and, before Carolina, in Barbados), rapid growth in the African component of the colony's slave population would prove the greatest spur to the creation of a comprehensive law of slavery.

An examination of the development of Virginia's slavery regime reveals a familiar sequence: initial reliance on the common law of property and inheritance for transactional purposes and, for the ordering and government of slaves, on laws created piecemeal largely on an English template of population controls, followed by the development of a distinctive slavery regime more or less in step with the demographic transformation of its labor force. Virginia of course had an extensive and detailed regime of statutory policing of labor mobility to draw upon, developed to control its population of indentured servants long before slaves were more than a tiny minority of the working population.[165] And so, unlike Carolina, Virginia's comprehensive law of slavery would grow up in large part within the shell of

[161] *HSUS*, vol. 5, table Eg53 (Virginia black population). Blacks appear in Maryland in the 1630s and by 1660 the black population was some 760. Growth thereafter was steady but at rates substantially lower than Virginia. See *HSUS*, vol. 5, table Eg52 (Maryland black population).

[162] For the history of Virginia's unenslaved blacks in the seventeenth century, see T. H. Breen and Stephen Innes, *"Myne Owne Ground": Race and Freedom on Virginia's Eastern Shore, 1640–1676* (New York, 1980). But see also Morgan, *Slave Counterpoint*, 16; Kathleen M. Brown, *Good Wives, Nasty Wenches and Anxious Patriarchs: Gender, Race and Power in Colonial Virginia* (Chapel Hill, 1996), 113.

[163] *HSUS*, vol. 5, tables Eg34, Eg53 (Virginia white population, black population).

[164] Morgan, *Slave Counterpoint*, 58–61 (including tables 9 and 10); O'Malley, "Beyond the Middle Passage," 138–40, 141 (table 1).

[165] See Chapter 6, section II.

existing laws governing migrant servants. But distinctions that came to be embedded within that body of law made clear the difference between temporary migrant servitude and the permanence and perpetuity of enslavement. And alongside Virginia's seventeenth-century servant statutes there emerged a further body of law specific to blacks that both constructed and underscored the terms of their difference.

The earliest acknowledgments of the presence of slaves as such and of their difference – both as a category of property and in racial status – come not from legislation but from local practice. Two wills from 1627, of John Throgmorton and of Governor George Yeardley, place "negars" in a distinct category from "servants." The same can be seen in estate inventories dating from the 1640s, which place time-to-serve values on white indentured servants but lifetime values on blacks and their children; clearly the latter are slaves.[166] Simultaneously, public punishments inflicted upon whites for miscegeny enforced a degraded and inferior social status upon blacks.[167] The first reference to "negroes" as such in Virginia legislation (Act X of 1639/40) formally prescribed blacks' social and civic inferiority by requiring that "All persons *except* negroes be provided with arms and ammunition" on pain of fine.[168] At this point the black population was still well under two hundred, amid ten thousand whites.

References to "slaves" as such did not appear in Virginia legislation until the later 1650s, by which time the black population was approaching nine hundred. The first such reference, in Act I of 1655/6, was not to blacks, but Indians, granting a conditional exception from enslavement to Indian children voluntarily surrendered as hostages. Then Act XVI of 1659/60 granted 80 percent discounts on imposts payable by foreign merchants on tobacco exports (2/- per hogshead instead of 10/-) when the tobacco in question had been acquired in exchange for imported "negro slaves" (an inducement to traders to bring slaves to Virginia). Act XXII of 1660/1 required that English servants running away "in company with any negroes who are incapable of makeing satisfaction by addition of time" – that is, slaves – serve their companions' lost time as well as their own.[169]

---

[166] Vaughan, "Blacks in Virginia," 133–4, and see generally 128–35. See also Alden T. Vaughan, "The Origins Debate: Slavery and Racism in Seventeenth-Century Virginia," in Vaughan, *Roots of American Racism*, 136–74. For disputes arising out of transactions and estate inventories showing blacks were enslaved, see Morris, *Southern Slavery and the Law*, 40–41.

[167] Morris, *Southern Slavery and the Law*, 23, 40 (cases from 1630 and 1640). See also Jordan, *White Over Black*, 78–80. The earliest recorded proceedings differentiating between white and black servants in assessing runaway penalties (whites to serve additional time after their indentured time of service has expired, blacks to serve for life), also date from 1640. See Complaint of Hugh Gwyn (9 July 1640), and Complaint of Cap.t Wm Pierce (22 July 1640), Minutes of the Council and General Court of Virginia, in Willie Lee Rose, *A Documentary History of Slavery in North America* (Athens, Ga., 1999), 22–3.

[168] Act X (January 1639/40), in Hening, *Statutes at Large*, I, 226 (emphasis added). See also Act I (March 1642/3), in Hening, *Statutes at Large*, I, 240–4, at 242, identifying "all negro women at the age of sixteen years" as tithable laborers; Brown, *Good Wives, Nasty Wenches*, 116–20; Parent, *Foul Means*, 107–110.

[169] *An Induction to the Acts concerning Indians*, Act I (March 1655/6); *An Act for the Dutch and all other Strangers for Tradeing to this Place*, Act XVI (March 1659/60); *English Running Away*

Before 1660, then, the Assembly had acknowledged the presence of slaves in the colony and advertised an interest in acquiring more, but it had given little indication of interest in developing a law of slavery as such. Matters changed during the 1660s as the number of slaves in the colony doubled. Enactments were piecemeal; though slave importation rates were accelerating, actual numbers were still low. But rates of white population growth were lagging. By the end of the decade, at more than 5 percent of total population, blacks had become a more visible presence in the colony.

Assembly activity in the 1660s added materially to the as yet scant body of law touching upon slavery circulating in the English mainland colonies. Three utterly fundamental enactments bore decisively upon who should be accounted a slave and what degree of power should be exercised over them. In Act XII of December 1662, considering whether children "got by any Englishman upon a negro woman should be slave or ffree," the Assembly provided that "all children borne in this country shalbe held bond or free only according to the condition of the mother."[170] The statute's genealogy is unclear; no such legal rule was then in place in any British colony, island, or mainland.[171] Six years earlier the Assembly had endorsed conventional

---

with Negroes, Act XXII (March 1660/61), all in Hening, *Statutes at Large,* I, 393–6 at 396, 540; II, 26. Note the language of Act I of March 1655/6: not an exemption of Indians from slavery but rather a conditional exception offered in a statute intended as a general inducement to Indians to accept English settlement rather than fight it: "If the Indians shall bring in any children as gages of their good and quiet intentions to vs and amity with vs, then the parents of such children shall choose the persons to whom the care of such children shall be intrusted and the countrey by vs their representatives do engage that wee will not vse them as slaves, but do their best to bring them vp in Christianity, civillity and the knowledge of necessary trades."

[170] *Negro Womens Children to Serve According to the Condition of the Mother,* Act XII (December 1662), in Hening, *Statutes at Large,* II, 170. See, generally, Parent, *Foul Means,* 115–17.

[171] April Lee Hatfield argues that in adopting Act XII, Virginia was following Barbados (*Atlantic Virginia,* 157) but offers no specific evidence of a Barbadian rule of matrilineal determination of status in the case of mixed unions prevailing at that time. Hilary Beckles, *Natural Rebels: A Social History of Enslaved Black Women in Barbados* (New Brunswick, N.J., 1989), 133, holds matrilineal heritability of slave status was "consistently" institutionalized in Barbadian slave codes, but no such rule appears in either the 1661 or 1688 *Better Ordering* acts. In *Laboring Women: Reproduction and Gender in New World Slavery* (Philadelphia, 2004), 79–85, Jennifer L. Morgan offers examples of Barbadian planter estate inventories of the 1650s that show planters associated "increase" (children), whether actual or potential, with enslaved women, not enslaved men, in making bequests, and evidence exists of the same practice at the same time in Virginia. In 1652, "a planter in Virginia sold a ten-year-old black girl 'with her Issue and produce duringe her (or either of them) for their Life tyme' and 'their Successors forever'." Stephen Botein, *Early American Law and Society: Essay and Documents* (American Bar Association, 1980), 17. In *Good Wives, Nasty Wenches,* 132, Kathleen Brown argues that in the 1650s Virginia courts "were already inclined to view the children of enslaved women as slaves." But though certainly suggestive of a practice of matrilineality, none of the evidence available speaks clearly to the question of matrilineal determination of status in mixed (slave/non-slave) unions. In his *True and Exact History of the Island of Barbados* (London, 1657), 54–5, Richard Ligon tells the story of a child born of a union between a Christian servant and an Indian woman slave, but says nothing of its fate.

common-law patrilineality in considering a petition for freedom from one Elizabeth Key, daughter of the union of a white man, Thomas Key, with "his Negro woman," when it had held that "by the Comon Law the Child of a Woman slave begot by a freeman ought to be free."[172] Clearly, says Thomas Morris, "there was uncertainty about the status of persons born of miscegeneous relationships" in mid-seventeenth century Virginia.[173] Act XII resolved the uncertainty in favor of marshaling female slaves' reproductive labor for the expansion of slavery. But given that English common law assumed patrilineality, what was Act XII's point of reference? The question had been discussed in the later medieval reception of Roman law and subsequently taken up in early modern law of nations doctrine. Consistently, matrilineality had always been the clear rule in the case of slavery.[174] Hence, the likeliest source of the rule adopted by Act

---

Not only does seventeenth-century Barbadian statute law contain no reference to matrilineal heritability, neither does that of South Carolina, which as we have seen closely followed the substance of Barbadian slave law. In South Carolina the rule was "all Negroes Mollatoes and Indians which at any time heretofore have been bought and sold or now are held and taken to be or hereafter shall be Bought and sold for slaves are hereby made & declared *they and their children* slaves for all Intents and purposes." *An Act for the Better Ordering of Slaves* (Carolina, 1696), clause 1 (emphasis added). That is, slavery lay in store for *any* child born of *any* enslaved parent whether male or female. (This was also the case in Antigua after 1672 – children born of any mixed union were to be enslaved for life. Before 1672, the rule in Antigua had been that such children were to be enslaved until age 18 or 21, then freed. Dunn, *Sugar and Slaves*, 228 note 8.) It is likely that Carolina's 1696 statute reproduced what was already the case in Barbados. See Ligon, *True and Exact History*, 43. South Carolina did not clearly adopt matrilineal heritability until 1740. See *An Act for the Better Ordering and Governing Negroes and other Slaves in this Province*, 397 (Clause I), in which the phrase "and shall follow the condition of the mother" was simply tacked on to the end of the latest version of Clause I as it had developed over previous iterations of the *Better Ordering* Statute. All "negroes and Indians, (free Indians in amity with government, and negroes, mulattoes and mustizoes, who are now free, excepted) mulattoes or mustizoes who now are, or shall hereafter be, in this Province, and all their issue and offspring, born or to be born, shall be, and they are hereby declared to be, and remain forever hereafter, absolute slaves, and shall follow the condition of the mother."

[172] Morris, *Southern Slavery and the Law*, 44.

[173] Ibid.

[174] Take for example the *Summa Theologica* of St. Thomas Aquinas, in particular the *Tertiae Partis Supplementum* [Supplement to the Third Part] completed after Aquinas's death in 1274 and attributed to his confederate Fra Rainaldo di Piperno. Thus, in the *Supplement*'s discussion of Matrimony, "*Questio LII* on "The Impediment of the Condition of Slavery," Article IV of the *Questio* asks "Whether children should follow the condition of their father?" The *Supplement* answers first with analogies from nature – "If a man sows on another's land, the produce belongs to the owner of the land. Now the woman's womb in relation to the seed of man is like the land in relation to the sower;" and, "in animals born from different species the offspring follows the mother rather than the father, wherefore mules born of a mare and an ass are more like mares than those born of a she-ass and a horse" – and then by citing civil law (*XIX, ff. De statu hom. vii, cap. De rei vendit.*) "the offspring follows the womb [*partus sequitur ventrem*]," which "is reasonable since the offspring derives its formal complement from the father, but the substance of the body from the mother." Indeed, the *Supplement* considered *partus sequitur ventrem* peculiarly appropriate to the case of slavery, for "slavery is a condition of the body, since a slave is

XII is the civil law maxim *partus sequitur ventrem* (literally "the offspring follows the womb").[175] Had the rule been derived from English common

to the master a kind of instrument in working." In other conditions of life, although the mother provided the substance of the body, "in matters pertaining to dignity as proceeding from a thing's form, they follow the father, for instance in honors, franchise, inheritance and so forth. The canons are in agreement with this (*cap. Liberi, 32, qu. iv, in gloss.: cap. Inducens, De natis ex libero ventre*) as also the law of Moses (Exodus 21)." Hence "in the genealogies of Scripture, and according to common custom, children are named after their father rather than from their mother. But in matters relating to slavery they follow the mother by preference." See *The Summa Theologica of St. Thomas Aquinas,* Literally translated by Fathers of the English Dominican Province, Second and Revised edition (1920), *Supplementum Tertiae Partis* Question 52, Article 4, available at http://www.newadvent.org/summa/ (accessed 22 August 2009); and Divi Thomae Aquinatis, *Summa Theologica* [Editio Altera Romana] Volumen Quintum, *Tertiae Partis Supplementum* (Romae, 1894), 270–1.

Why dwell on Aquinas? Because, as argued earlier in this book, to widely recognized authorities in sixteenth- and seventeenth-century law of nature and nations (which we have already seen was of considerable influence in the English conceptualization of colonizing), Aquinas was of fundamental importance. That importance extends to matters of legal detail. Thus, in Book II of *De Jure Belli ac Pacis* (first published 1625), Hugo Grotius offers quite specific opinions on matrilineal heritability in the precise circumstance of slavery, drawing inter alia on the *Supplement.* Discussing "what according to the law of nature should be decided concerning those who are born of slaves," Grotius answered that "By the Roman law and by the universal customary law relating to captives ... in the case of persons of servile rank, as in the case of animals, the offspring follows the mother" (256). Grotius specifically noted that the Roman rule diverged from the law of nature to the extent that the latter tended to favor the father (as in English law) where "the father can be recognized with sufficient certainty" (the bastardy exception). Grotius concluded, tepidly, that in such cases "the children would not be less likely to follow the condition of the father than that of the mother" (256–7). He also took note of legal practices alternative to both Roman and natural law that held the status of a child of mixed-status heritage was to be determined by following whichever parent was of the lower status (257). Nevertheless, in Book III's chapter on captives and their enslavement in the law of nations, Grotius held that the descendants of slaves remained slaves in perpetuity, "that is to say those who are born of a slave mother after her enslavement" (691). Grotius noted, "it has been acceptable to the nations that children should follow the status of the mother," adding that, in the case of bastardy, the father being "indicated by no adequate presumption," it was "'a law of nature, that he who is born outside of lawful matrimony follows the status of his mother.'" In other words, the law holding that in the case of slavery the child followed the condition of the mother "represents a general custom which has grown up from a natural reason" (692).

[175] See Warren Billings, "The Cases of Fernando and Elizabeth Key: A Note on the Status of Blacks in Seventeenth-Century Virginia," *William and Mary Quarterly,* 3rd Ser., 30, 3 (July 1973), 467–74. Thomas Morris rejects this conclusion, noting that the specific source Billings chooses to illustrate the possibility of civil law influence, Henry Swinburne's *A Briefe Treatise of Testaments and Last Willes* (London, 1590) – known to have circulated widely in Virginia – does not support matrilineal heritability in the case of slavery. But this is not so. What, in fact, did Swinburne write? "Of all Men which be destitute of libertie or freedome, the slaue is in greatest subiectiŏ, for a slaue is that person which is in seruitude or bondage to an other, euen against nature. Neither hath he any thing of his owne, but whatsoeuer he possesseth, all is his Lordes ... even his children also are infected with the Leprosie of his fathers bondage." The civil law was otherwise. "And although by the ciuill lawe the wife being a free woman, the children are likewise free, *Quia partus sequitur ventrem;* in so much that if the mother be free, either at the conception or at the birth of the

law[176] one might expect it would have been widely adopted in English colonies. But Virginia embraced matrilineal heritability in isolation. Maryland's 1664 *Act Concerning Negroes & other Slaves* specifically endorsed common-

child, or in the meane time, by the same ciuill lawe, that child shall be free, notwithstandinge the bondage of the father: Yet it is otherwise by the lawes of the realme, for the child dooth follow the state & condition of the father, and therefore in England the father being a bondman, the child shal be in bondage, without distinction whether the mother be bond or free." The only exception to patrilineal heritability in English law was in the case of children born bastards: "the law dooth not acknowledge any father in this case, for by the lawe a bastard is sometimes called, *filius nullius*, the sonne of no man." Such a child would not be infected by the father's bondage. But Swinburne then acknowledged that civil law matrilineal heritability did not protect children from slavery any more than common-law patrilineal heritability: "the ciuill lawe and the laws of this realme differ in this, whether the bondage of the father or of the mother, doo make the child bonde." See *A Briefe Treatise of Testaments and Last Willes*, 43–4. The difference was not that fathers made slaves and mothers made free people. The difference was which parent was determinative in the case of mixed-status unions, which in turn depended on whether or not the parents were married. In English law, the general rule was patrilineal heritability except in the case of bastardy. In civil law, the principle was matrilineal heritability; hence in the case of mixed-status unions the status of the mother was determinative, married or not. The latter was precisely what Act XII enacted. [Note that Swinburne cites Bracton as authority for the distinctions he draws between patrilineal and matrilineal heritability. But Bracton added one further source of distinction: "he who is begotten of a free father who has connexion with a neif [female villein] established in a villain tenement [is born unfree], whether they are married or not." To this extent Bracton made English patrilineality an exception to a more general (Roman law) rule of matrilineality, as befits the great debts of *De Legibus* to Roman law. See *Bracton: On the Laws and Customs of England* II, 30, 31. By the time of *Coke upon Littleton* (1628) that distinction had disappeared and the statement of the English rule was straightforward: "if a Villeine taketh a freewoman to wife, and haue issue betweene them, the issues shall be Villeines. But if a Niefe taketh a freeman to her husband, their issue shall be free. This is contrarie to the Ciuill law; for there it is said, *Partus sequitur ventrem*." Sir Edward Coke, *The First Part of the Institutes of the Lawes of England. Or, A Commentarie vpon Littleton, not the Name of a Lawyer onely, but of the Law it selfe.* (London, 1628), §§187, 188 (123).]

[176] Morris's preferred position is that English law "provided ample doctrines to explain the law of 1662." These were the law of bastardy, which "would hold that the child followed the mother," and the law of chattel property, which held that the increase of chattel property belongs to the owner of the property. For proof Morris turns not to any source potentially knowable by contemporaries but to Blackstone's 1769 *Commentaries*. On the first matter Blackstone (citing *Coke upon Littleton*, §§187, 188) is entirely consistent with Swinburne, holding that English law was patrilineal as opposed to civil law matrilineality except in the case of bastards: "In case of a marriage between a freeman and a neife [female villein], or a villain and a freewoman, the issue followed the condition of the father, being free if he was free, and villein if he was villein; contrary to the maxim of the civil law, that *partus sequitur ventrem*. But no bastard could be born a villein, because by another maxim of our law he is *nullius filius*; and as he can gain nothing by inheritance, it were hard that he should lose his natural freedom by it." (One should note, this is less a statement of matrilineal heritability in the case of bastards than a *denial* of patrilineality in that case.) On the latter he is entirely consistent with the *Summa Theologica*, "Of all tame and domestic animals, the brood belongs to the owner of the dam or mother; the English law agreeing with the civil that '*partus sequitur ventrem*' in the brute creation, though for the most part in the human species it disallows that maxim." In Blackstone, in other words, one simply encounters civil law once again. William Blackstone, *Commentaries on*

law patrilineality.[177] Maryland revisited the matter in 1681, but the 1664 rule remained intact.[178] New York in 1706 was the only other colony clearly to endorse matrilineal heritability as a legal rule before the mid-eighteenth century.[179]

the Laws of England (Chicago, 1979), II, 94, 390. Morris, *Southern Slavery and the Law*, 45 and generally 43–7.

[177] "All Children born of any Negro or other slaue shall be Slaues *as their ffathers were* for the terme of their liues. And forasmuch as diver freeborne English women forgettfull of their free Condicōn and to the disgrace of our Nation doe intermarry with Negro Slaues by which also diuers suites may arise touching the Issue of such woemen and a great damage doth befall the Masters of such Negroes for preuention whereof for deterring such free-borne women from such shamefull Matches Bee itt further Enacted … That whatsoever free borne woman shall inter marry with any slaue from and after the Last day of this present Assembly shall Serue the master of such slaue dureing the life of her husband. And that *all the issue of such freeborne woemen soe marryed shall be Slaues as their fathers were.* And Bee itt further Enacted that all the Issues of English or other freeborne woemen that haue already marryed Negroes shall serve the Masters of their Parents till they be Thirty years of age and no longer." *Archives of Maryland, Volume 1: Proceedings and Acts of the General Assembly of Maryland, January 1637/8–September 1664* (Baltimore, 1883), 533–4 (emphasis added).

[178] In 1681, Maryland reenacted the 1664 statute in amended form that granted white women servants coerced by their masters to "Intermarry with Negroes and Slaues" their immediate freedom together with that of any children produced by the marriage. Otherwise "Children already borne or heereafter to bee borne of any Negroes or other Slaues within this Province shall bee Slaues to all intents & purposes as theire fathers were for the Terme of theire naturall Liues." Patrilineality was, however, qualified in the case of mulatto children of freeborn white women, who were forced into service for up to thirty-one years rather than enslaved. In 1681, Maryland in effect moved to the position taken in Antigua prior to 1672.

In 1692, Maryland further amended the Act so that "Children born already or here-after to be born of any Negroes or other Slaves with[n] this Province shall be Slaves to all intents and purposes as their *parents* were for the terme of their naturall lives." Freeborn white women voluntarily intermarrying with "negros or other Slaves" were, if free, forced into service for seven years and their children bound out until age twenty-one; if already servants, the women were in addition to serve their masters additional time at the discre-tion of the court for the damage done to forfeit their freedom; if their relationship was out-of-wedlock they were to serve seven years and the child until age thirty-one. None, however, was to be enslaved as in 1664; and as in the 1681 Act coerced relationships brought instant freedom to mother and child. Maryland's omnibus *Act Relating to Serv[ts] and Slaves* (1715) repeated the 1692 provisions as to women and children. As to who should be slaves, the relevant clause now omitted any mention of parentage and stated simply that "all Negroes and other Slaves Already Imported or hereafter to be Imported in this province and all Children now born or hereafter to be born of such Negroes and Slaves shall be Slaves dureing their naturall lives." *Archives of Maryland, Volume 7, Proceedings and Acts of the General Assembly, October 1678–November 1683* (Baltimore, 1889), 203–5; *Volume 13, Proceedings and Acts of the General Assembly, April 1684–June 1692* (Baltimore, 1894), 546–9 (emphasis added); *Volume 30, Proceedings and Acts of the General Assembly, April 26, 1715–August 10, 1716* (Baltimore, 1910), 283–92, at 289–90.

[179] See Section V, this chapter. On New York prior to the English conquest (1664) see Harris, *In the Shadow of Slavery*, 22–6. South Carolina (see n.171, this chapter) eventually adopted the rule, but not until 1740. Georgia followed South Carolina in 1754 in the course of adopting wholesale South Carolina's *Act for the Better Ordering and Governing Negroes and other Slaves in this Province* for its own purposes. None of the New England settlements

In 1667, a second and equally important measure declared Christian baptism would not free a slave. We have seen that exponents of *ius naturale* and *gentium* had long held it to be a convention among Christians that Christians should not enslave other Christians. In Barbados, contemporary understanding at mid-century was that the laws of England forbade enslavement of Christians;[180] among the Dutch in New Netherland, baptism of slaves had ceased in the 1650s because of unresolved doubts both as a matter of religion and civil law.[181] In the English mainland colonies the

adopted the rule, though in *The Negro in Colonial New England*, 126, Lorenzo Greene claims that "custom and tradition achieved the same end." William H. Williams makes the same argument for Pennsylvania and Delaware in *Slavery and Freedom in Delaware, 1639–1865* (Wilmington, Del., 1996), 19.

One might note that in *Titus Andronicus*, where I began this chapter, Shakespeare's portrayal of slavery assumed patrilineal heritability, faithful to English law. Aron himself addresses his child as "black slave ... thick-lipped slave" notwithstanding the child was born of a free white woman. And when Aron attempts to protect the child from Lucius by invoking the mother and her "royal blood," Lucius, addressing Aron as "wall-eyed slave," calls the child his "fruit of bastardy" who is "too like the sire for ever being good." *Titus Andronicus*, 4.2.120, 4.2.176, 5.1.45, 5.1.48–50.

[180] In his *True & Exact History*, at 49–50, Richard Ligon tells of an encounter in Barbados with a slave who desired to become a Christian: "I promised to do my best endeavor; and when I came home, spoke to the Master of the Plantation, and told him, that poor *Sambo* desired much to be a Christian. But his answer was, That the people of that Iland were governed by the Lawes of *England*, and by those Lawes we could not make a Christian a Slave. I told him, my request was far different from that, for I desired him to make a Slave a Christian. His answer was, That it was true, there was a great difference in that: But, being once a Christian, he could no more account him a Slave and so lose the hold they had of them as Slaves, by making them Christians; and by that means should open such a gap, as all the Planters in the Iland would curse him. So I was struck mute, and poor *Sambo* kept out of the Church; as ingenious as honest, and as good a natur'd poor soul, as ever wore black, or eat green" (50). Subsequently, the Barbados Assembly took steps actively to discourage proselytizing of slaves. See *An Act to prevent the People called Quakers, from bringing Negroes to their Meetings* (21 April 1676), altered and enlarged (17 April 1678), revived and made perpetual (8 June 1681), all in Hall, comp., *Acts, Passed in the Island of Barbados*, 97–8, 102–3, 104. Two months prior to the revival and continuation of the act against the Quakers, the Barbados Assembly declared that "as to making the negroes Christians, their Savage Brutishness renders them wholly uncapable." In 1696, in contrast, Jamaica's *Act for the better Order and Government of Slaves* called for the instruction of slaves in Christianity, but at the same time reassured masters that slaves would not be freed by any profession of Christianity. See Dunn, *Sugar and Slaves*, 249–50, 250 n.44; Jordan, *White Over Black*, 185.

[181] In the Netherlands, critics of slavery "did not question the right to enslave heathens but ... encouraged the catechization of slaves and suggested they be set free soon after they were converted." In New Netherland, some Dutch Reformed ministers also took the view that no Christians could be slaves – and chose to abstain from instruction and baptism of slaves. One minister wrote to the Classis of Amsterdam in June 1664 that parents wanting "nothing else than to deliver their children from bodily slavery" saw Christian conversion simply as a means to that end and did not genuinely "striv[e] for piety and Christian virtues." But belief that conversion mandated emancipation was a minority position both in the Netherlands and New Netherland, and Christianized blacks were kept in slavery in the colony. After the English takeover in 1664, doubts (as in Barbados) about the effect of English law encouraged slave owners' hostility to proselytizing until 1706, when the New York legislature passed its "Negro Baptism" Act. See Gerald Francis De Jong,

tide turned in the late 1650s when slave Christianity was addressed somewhat elliptically in Massachusetts, then directly six years later in the *Duke's Laws*.[182] Virginia's was the first statutory declaration on the matter. Act III of September 1667 noted that "doubts have risen whether children that are slaves by birth, and by the charity and piety of their owners made pertakers of the blessed sacrament of baptisme, should by vertue of their baptisme be made ffree." To resolve those doubts, so that masters might "more carefully endeavour the propagation of christianity," Act III declared "that the conferring of baptisme doth not alter the condition of the person as to his bondage or ffreedome." This was the first unambiguous statutory declaration in Anglo-American slave law that profession of Christianity would not free a slave, hence that Christians might hold Christians as slaves.[183] Carolina's *Fundamental Constitutions* (1669) took the same position.[184] In 1639, the Maryland Assembly had appeared to countenance the possibility that Christians might be held as slaves in the colony, but briefly, indirectly, and ambiguously.[185] In 1671, Maryland ended local doubts by enacting a

---

"The Dutch Reformed Church and Negro Slavery in Colonial America," *Church History*, 40, 4 (December 1971), 423–36, at 424, 430–2; Harris, *In the Shadow of Slavery*, 17–18, 22–3; Joyce D. Goodfriend, "The Souls of African American Children: New Amsterdam," *Common-Place*, 3, 4 (July 2003), www.common-place.org (accessed 22 August 2009).

[182] See nn.82–3, this chapter. A. Leon Higginbotham, *In the Matter of Color: Race and the American Legal Process, the Colonial Period* (New York, 1978), at 270, argues that in fact the first edition of the *Duke's Laws* (1665) should count as the first statutory endorsement of the principle that profession of Christianity would not free a slave. Certainly that is what the relevant provision stated, but it is a bit difficult to accept Higginbotham's description of the *Duke's Laws* as a statute. Rather, they were the proprietor's seigneurial proclamation of laws for his province.

[183] *An Act Declaring that Baptisme of Slaves doth not Exempt them from Bondage*, Act III (September 1667) in Hening, *Statutes at Large*, II, 260. For examples of Virginia slaves freed on account of their profession of Christianity prior to 1667, see Parent, *Foul Means*, 110–13. Parent discusses the significance of slave baptism "as a method of social control" at 236–64. Clearly, Act III makes no exception for children of *Christianized* slaves (that is, children born to Christians), perhaps on the grounds that they were born into slavery and that no one could be called a Christian until baptized whether as an infant or as an adult. (At the end of the century it was reported that "the negroes born in this country ... are generally baptized and brought up in the Christian religion." Minutes of Council (2 June 1699) *Board of Trade, Virginia* vol. lii, in Philip A. Bruce, *Institutional History of Virginia in the Seventeenth Century* 2 v. (New York, 1910), I, 9.) Act III was complemented by Act V of October 1670, which prohibited non-European Christians from purchasing Christian servants but allowed them to own slaves "of their owne nation." See Hening, *Statutes at Large*, II, 280–1: "WHEREAS it hath beene questioned whither Indians or negroes manumitted, or otherwise free, could be capable of purchasing christian servants. It is enacted that noe negroe or Indian though baptised and enjoyned their owne ffreedome shall be capable of any such purchase of christians, but yet not debarred from buying any of their owne nation." For further Virginia legislation on the matter, see Act I (November 1682), in Hening, *Statutes at Large*, 490–1 (quoted at length in n.192, this chapter).

[184] See section III, this chapter.

[185] See *An Act for the Liberties of the People* (February–March 1638/9) in *Archives of Maryland, Volume 1*, at 41: "Be it Enacted ... that all the Inhabitants of this Province being Christians (Slaves excepted) Shall have and enjoy all such rights liberties immunities priviledges and free customs within this Province as any naturall born subject of England hath or

clear statutory declaration following and elaborating upon Virginia's example.[186] Subsequently the Carolinas (1690/1), New Jersey (1704), and New
York (1706) all adopted statutes following through on their basic laws.[187]

ought to have or enjoy in the Realm of England by force or vertue of the common law
or Statute Law of England (saveing in such Cases as the same are or may be altered or
changed by the Laws and ordinances of this Province)."

[186] *An Act for the Encourageing the Importacon of Negros and Slaues into this Province* (March–April
1671), in *Archives of Maryland, Volume 2, Proceedings and Acts of the General Assembly, April
1666–June 1676* (Baltimore, 1883), 272 (emphasis added): "Whereas Severall of the good
people of this Prouince haue been discouraged to import into or purchase within this
Prouince any Negroes or other Slaues and such as haue Imported or purchased any
such Negroes or Slaues haue to the great displeasure of Almighty God and the prejudice of the Soules of those poore people Neglected to instruct them in the Christian
faith or to Endure or permitt them to Receive the holy Sacrament of Baptisme for the
Remission of their Sinns upon a mistake and vngrounded apprehension that by becomeing Christians they and the Issues of their bodies are actually manumited and made
free and discharged from their Servitude and bondage be itt declared and Enacted ...
That where any Negro or Negroes Slave or Slaues being in Servitude or bondage is are
or shall become Christian or Christians and hath or have Received or shall att any time
Receive the Holy Sacrament of Babtizme *before or after* his her or their Importacon into
this Prouince the same is not nor shall or ought the same be denyed adjudged Construed
or taken to be or to amount vnto a manumicon or freeing Inlarging or discharging any
such Negroe or Negroes Slaue or Slaues *or any his or their Issue or Issues* from his her their
or any of their Servitude or Servitudes Bondage or bondages Butt that Notwithstanding
any such Act or thing Acts or things And Notwithstanding any such becomeing Christian
or Christians or Receiveing the Sacrament of Babtizme Every such Negroe and Negroes
slaue and slaues and all and every the Issue and Issues of every such Negroe and Negroes
Slaue and Slaues Is are and be and shall att all tymes hereafter be adjudged Reputed
deemed and taken to be and Remayne in Servitude and Bondage and subject to the same
Servitude and Bondage to all intents and purposes as if hee shee they every or any of
them was or were in and Subject vnto before such his her or their Becomeing Christian
or Christians or Receiveing of the Sacrament of Baptizme any opinion or other matter
or thing to the Contrary in any wise Notwithstanding." As the text indicates, Maryland's
statute was extremely thorough. It addressed not only slaves who became Christian after
their importation but also slaves who were Christian prior to their importation, and also
the progeny of Christian slaves (that is, those *born* to Christians).

[187] For the Carolinas, see *An Act for the Better Ordering of Slaves* (7 February 1690/1), in *The
Statutes at Large of South Carolina*, vol. 7, 343. (The Carolina statute was as terse on the
matter as Maryland's was elaborate: "no, slave shall be free by becoming a christian." The
principle had, of course, long since been acknowledged in the Fundamental Constitutions
(1669). See section III, this chapter.) For New Jersey, see *An Act for Regulating Negro,
Indian and Mallatto Slaves within this Province of New-Jersey* (1704), in Bernard Bush, com-
piler, *New Jersey Archives, Vol. 2, Laws of the Royal Colony of New Jersey, 1703–1745* (Trenton,
1977), 28–30, at 30. For New York, see *An Act to Incourage the Baptizing of Negro, Indian and
Mulatto Slaves* (21 October 1706), in *The Colonial Laws of New York, from the Year 1664 to the
Revolution* (Albany, 1894), I, 597–8. No such laws were passed in New England; Puritan
divines contended none were needed. In *The Negro Christianized* (Boston, 1706), 26–7,
Cotton Mather held that, were there any grounds to fears that baptism would give slaves
legal title to their freedom, masters might simply retain their services by negotiating "suf-
ficent *Indentures*." But there were no grounds: "it is all a Mistake. There is no such thing.
What *Law* is it, that Sets the *Baptised Slave* at *Liberty?* Not the *Law of Christianity*: that allows
of *Slavery*; Only it wonderfully Dulcifies, and Mollifies, and Moderates the Circumstances
of it. *Christianity* directs a *Slave*, upon his embracing the *Law of the Redeemer*, to satisfy
himself, *That he is the Lords Free-man*, tho' he continues a *Slave*. It supposes, That there

Virginia's refusal to allow a common Christianity to stand in the way of enslavement decisively modernized the institution, overriding *ius gentium* conventions with the priorities of forced labor that attended slavery's mainland growth. Virginia's final major slave statute of the 1660s, Act I of October 1669, was entirely congruent. In it the Assembly followed Barbados in granting slaveholders and those acting for them an absolute immunity against prosecution for the death of slaves under punishment. For that "the obstinacy of many [negroes cannot be] by other than violent meanes supprest, *Be it enacted and declared* ... if any slave resist his master (or other by his masters order correcting him) and by the extremity of the correction should chance to die, that his death shall not be accompted ffelony, but the master (or that other person appointed by the master to punish him) be acquit from molestation."[188] By the end of the decade committed to unrestrained enslavement, Virginia had also committed itself to the quantum of terror that sustaining the institution required.

Severally, the measures adopted in the 1660s elaborated upon the qualitative distinctions that differentiated between the two components of Virginia's imported bound labor force, black slaves (at the end of the decade about one-third of the bound labor force, up from roughly a quarter in 1660) and migrant indentured servants (about two-thirds, down from three-quarters). Slavery was for life and in perpetuity – children born to a slave were simultaneously born to enslavement; Christians might be slaves; and slaves might be beaten to death with impunity. Still, though the slave population was growing in the 1660s, the decisive turn to slavery in Virginia's labor force was not fully under way. For purposes of day-to-day police it was sufficient that slaves remain a distinct and exceptional class

are *Bond* as well as *Free*, among those that have been *Renewed in the Knowledge and Image of Jesus Christ.*" [Here Mather cited Colossians 3:11, where Paul writes that for those who have accepted Christ "there is neither Greek nor Jew, circumcision nor uncircumcision, Barbarian, Scythian, bond nor free: but Christ is all, and in all" (AV). Paul argues not that Christianity abolishes distinction, but rather that Christianity transcends distinction.] "Will the Canon-law do it? No; The *Canons* of Numberless *Councils,* mention the *Slaves* of *Christians,* without any contradiction. Will the *Civil Law* do it? No: Tell, if you can, any part of *Christendom,* wherein *Slaves* are not frequently to be met withal. But is not *Freedom* to be claim'd for a *Baptised Slave,* by the *English* Constitution? The English *Laws,* about *Villians,* or, *Slaves,* will not say so; for by those *Laws,* they may be granted *for Life,* like a *Lease,* and passed over with a *Mannor,* like other *Goods or Chattels.* And by those *Laws,* the Lords may sieze the Bodies of their *Slaves* even while a Writt, *De libertate probanda,* is depending. These English *Laws* were made when the *Lords* & the *Slaves,* were both of them *Christians;* and they stand still unrepealed. If there are not now such *Slaves* in *England* as formerly, it is from the *Lords,* more than from the *Laws.* The *Baptised* then are not thereby entitled unto their *Liberty.*"

[188] *An act about the casuall killing of slaves,* Act I (October 1669) in Hening, *Statutes at Large,* II, 270. Compare the *Act for the Better Ordering and Governing of Negroes* (Barbados, 1661), Clause 20 (in part): And it is further Enacted and ordeyned by the authoritie aforesaid that if any Negro under punishment of his Master or his Overseer for running away or any other Crimes or misdemeanors towards his said Master shall suffer in life or in Member noe person whatsoever shall be accomptable to any Law therefore."

within the ambit of the established general law of servitude. Thus in 1670, Act I amending established regulations for the taking up and punishment of runaways declared its application to "every servant of what quality soever," to which it added parenthetically that slaves "(are also comprehended in this act)."[189] In the same session, when the Assembly attempted its first general definition of who were to be slaves in order to resolve a dispute whether Indian captives taken by other nations might be bought by the English as "servants for life" (Act XII), it adopted a formulation that continued to trade on the early-modern distinction between Christian and non-Christian origins *overseas* to identify those who might be enslaved. Slaves were "all servants not being christians imported into this colony by shipping." Such persons, brought from overseas, "shalbe slaves for their lives." However, such as "shall come by land" (that is, Indians) "shall serve, if boyes or girles, until thirty yeares of age, if men or women twelve years and no longer."[190]

Act XII had indicated that race was not the sole determinant of legal enslavement. Notwithstanding its racial markers, Act XII still turned on the contrast of "Negro" with "Christian" rather than "White," assimilating race to the terms of European colonizers' established anthropology, as expressed in the law of nations, deeply embedded in the discourses of English colonizing and justifiable enslavement, that distinguished inhabitants of Christian and non-Christian ("savage," or "barbarous") lands. But Bacon's Rebellion ended the exemption of Indians,[191] and in Act I of 1682, *An Act to Repeale a Former Law Makeing Indians and Others Ffree*, the Assembly pulled the piecemeal allusions of the previous twenty years together in a comprehensive statement defining who should be slaves that merged race completely into that older law of nations anthropology. Slaves, said the Assembly, had come to Virginia in two varieties – heathen, and captives in war; or in other words "negroes, moores, mollatoes and others borne of and in heathenish, idollatrous, pagan and mahometan parentage and country [who] have heretofore, and hereafter may be purchased, procured, or otherwise obteigned as slaves of, from or out of such their heathenish country by some well disposed christian," and "Indians that are taken in warre or otherwise by our neighbouring Indians, confederates or tributaries to his majestie, and this his plantation of Virginia are slaves to the said neighbouring Indians that soe take them, and by them are likewise sold

---

[189] *An Act Concerning Runaways*, Act I (October 1670), in Hening, *Statutes at Large*, II, 277.

[190] *What Tyme Indians to Serve*, Act XII (October 1970), in Hening, *Statutes at Large*, II, 283.

[191] Bacon's Laws (June 1676) reversed Act XII's prohibition on the enslavement of Indian captives, providing in its place "that all Indians taken in warr be held and accounted slaves dureing life." Act I (June 1676, Laws of Virginia – Bacon's Laws) in Hening, *Statutes at Large*, II, 346. Although Bacon's Laws were repealed in their entirety the following February, the Assembly continued the substance of this law by order adopted at the same time, and adopted it anew in virtually the same language in 1679. See Act IV (February 1676–7), and unnumbered Assembly order, same session, in Hening, *Statutes at Large*, II, 380–1, 404; Act I (April 1679), in Hening, *Statutes at Large*, II, 433–40, at 440.

to his majesties subjects here as slaves." From this evidence the Assembly developed a general definition that presaged the recreation of slavery as a self-contained, racially distinct jurisdiction: "all servants except Turkes and Moores, whilest in amity with his majesty which from and after publication of this act shall be brought or imported into this country, either by sea or land, whether Negroes, Moors, Mollattoes or Indians, who and whose parentage and native country are not christian at the time of their first purchase of such servant by some christian, although afterwards, and before such their importation and bringing into this country, they shall be converted to the christian faith; and all Indians which shall hereafter be sold by our neighbouring Indians, or any other trafiqueing with us as for slaves are hereby adjudged, deemed and taken, and shall be adjudged, deemed and taken to be slaves to all intents and purposes, any law, usage or custome to the contrary notwithstanding."[192]

Definitions aside, as rates of importation accelerated the Virginia legislature began to assemble, component by component, a panoply of mechanisms and punishments similar in broad outline to that established in Barbados twenty years earlier. As in Barbados, some elements invoked familiar English police laws: Act VII of 1672, for example, reminded justices of the peace of the "severall wholesome lawes and statutes" of England made for "the suppression of vagrants and idle persons" and enjoined their strict execution against all vagabonds and dissolute persons.[193] Others

[192] Act I (November 1682), in Hening, *Statutes at Large*, II, 490–1. Act I's definition also addressed what the Assembly evidently had reason to believe was an unintended effect of its declaration of September 1667 (Act III) that conversion of an enslaved heathen to Christianity after his importation did nothing to alter the slave's condition of bondage. The question was whether a slave "obteigned ... by some well disposed christian" who "after such their obteining and purchaseing such negroe, moor, or molatto as their slave out of a pious zeale, have wrought the conversion of such slave to the christian faith, which by the laws of this country doth not manumitt them or make them free" might subsequently *sell* "such negroe, moor, or molatto" as a slave even though at the time of sale the slave was indubitably a Christian. "It hath and may often happen that such master or owner of such slave being by some reason inforced to bring or send such slave into this country to sell or dispose of for his necessity or advantage, he the said master or owner of such servant which notwithstanding his conversion is really his slave, or his factor or agent must be constrained either to carry back or export again the said slave to some other place where they may sell him for a slave, or else depart from their just right and tytle to such slave and sell him here for noe longer time then the English or other christians are to serve, to the great losse and damage of such master or owner, and to the great discouragement of bringing in such slaves for the future and to noe advantage at all to the planter or buyer." Hence the language holding heathen background at the moment of first purchase fully determinative of eligibility for sale as a slave on any and all future occasions. Once enslaved one remained a slave, intervening conversions notwithstanding. Only those originally Christian might not be enslaved. The Assembly's language covered both slaves sold onward by their original Virginia owners, and also slaves become Christians who had been imported from elsewhere and subsequently sold. The latter situation was most likely to arise among slaves in intercolonial trade imported from the Caribbean or accompanying migrating planters.
[193] *An Act for Suppressing of Vagabonds and Disposeing of Poore Children to Trades*, Act VII (September 1672), in Hening, *Statutes at Large*, 298.

anticipated the likely effect of an increasing incidence of barbarous and alien slaves in Virginia. Thus, immediately after enacting Act VII the Assembly passed Act VIII, *for the apprehension and suppression of runawayes, negroes and slaves*, which, perceiving in slave runaways a spirit of "rebellion," legalized the killing of any "negroe, molatto, Indian slave, or servant for life" who resisted being taken up.[194]

Act X of 1680, adopted after another decade of growth saw the black population of Virginia closing in on 7 percent of the total population and, more immediately, in the wake of an alleged "Negro Plott" uncovered in the Northern Neck,[195] improved upon the language of rebellion by raising for the first time the specter of organized "Negroes Insurrections" arising from "negroe slaves" gathering "under pretence of feasts and burialls," and in consequence prohibited "any negroe or other slave" from bearing arms – "any club, staffe, gunn, sword or any other weapon of defence or offence." Act X added three other clear echoes of Barbados's comprehensive slave law, thereby becoming Virginia's first general disciplinary statute specific to slaves. To the weapons ban Act X added a ticket system for the detailed control of movement; henceforth no slave was to depart "his masters ground" without written certificate of permission from master, mistress, or overseer; nor might permission be granted "but upon perticuler and necessary occasions." Any "negroe or slave" caught abroad without a certificate was to be whipped by the nearest constable and returned to his master.[196] Act X also provided that upon sworn testimony of an injured party, "any negroe or other slave [that] shall presume to lift up his hand in opposition against any christian" was to be whipped; and finally, that any "negroe or other slave" runaway who lay "hid and lurking in obscure places, committing injuries to the inhabitants" and resisted apprehension might lawfully be killed.[197]

[194] *An Act for the Apprehension and Suppression of Runawayes, Negroes and Slaves*, Act VIII (September 1672), in Hening, *Statutes at Large*, 299–300. Resort to the language of *rebellion* to describe slaves who were runaway reproduced the style of Barbados. It also, of course, rendered the slave far more than the equivalent of an absconding servant; it placed the slave in a position of defiance of lawful state authority, rebellion being by definition an act of disobedience to lawful rule or authority punishable as insurrection or treason. As such its use recalls the use of language of disloyalty and treason against local Indians in 1622 and the licensing of their pursuit and slaughter in succeeding colony charters. See Chapter 4, section II.

[195] Morgan, *Slave Counterpoint*, 21.

[196] Act X, *An Act for Preventing Negroes Insurrections* (June 1680), in Hening, *Statutes at Large*, 481. Note that migrant indentured servants were not required to carry tickets of leave to enjoy ordinary mobility; rather, on completion of their terms of service they were required to obtain certification that their term of indenture had expired so that they might work on their own account for hire or upon shares. See, e.g., Act XV, *Concerning Hiring of Servants* (March 1657/8), in Hening, *Statutes at Large*, I, 439–40.

[197] Act X (1680), 480–1. This provision was revised and updated in 1691 by the first clause of Act XVI, *An Act for Suppressing Outlying Slaves* (April 1691), in Hening, *Statutes at Large*, III, 86–8, which closely reproduces Clauses 18 and 19 of the *Act for the Better Ordering and Governing of Negroes* (Barbados, 1661) amended and reenacted in Clause 18 of the *Act for the Governing of Negroes* (Barbados, 1688). See generally Parent, *Foul Means*, 148–51.

Noticeably, Act X appeared to include free blacks within the disciplines of the ticket system. Punishment was due "any negroe or slave" caught going abroad without a certificate of permission. One might speculate this is a copyist's error: in all other instances the phrase defining the ambit of the Act's application is "negroe or *other* slave." But the language "negroe or slave" was repeated in Act III of 1682, which amended Act X, both in the Act's title, "for the further better preventing such insurrections by negroes or slaves," and in its substance. Act III provided that no master or overseer of a plantation was to permit any "negroe or slave" not of that place to remain there more than four hours, on penalty of two hundred pounds of tobacco and cask. The Assembly stated its goal was to clarify the intent of Act X, which in light of Act III emerges not only as the suppression of gatherings of slaves but also the prevention of interactions between free blacks and slaves.[198] Always few in number, Virginia's free black population became an object of ever greater suspicion the more the colony's enslaved black population expanded.[199] That suspicion climaxed ten years later, after a decade of particularly rapid growth in slave importation, when the Assembly passed yet another anti-insurrection act, *An Act for Suppressing Outlying Slaves* (Act XVI, 1691), to which were annexed two ostensibly unrelated provisions clearly intended completely to isolate such free blacks as remained in the colony, one punishing all significant interaction between whites and blacks in the colony outside the parameters of the master-slave relationship, the other prescribing the effective suppression altogether of the colony's free black population. The Act's insurrection clause, which closely resembled Clauses 18 and 19 of Barbados's 1661 Act (as amended in 1688), provided for a heightened repression of runaways who secreted themselves "in obscure places" from which they committed injuries and other depredations upon the inhabitants of the colony: they were to be systematically sought out and captured or killed, and their owners compensated for the loss by the public. To this was added a clause "for prevention of that abominable mixture and spurious issue which hereafter may encrease in this dominion ... by negroes, mulattoes, and Indians intermarrying with English, or other white women" that ordered the expulsion from the colony of any English or other white man or woman intermarrying with any "negroe, mulatto, or Indian man or woman bond or free."[200] As to those "unlawfull[y] accompanying" one another, any free English woman bearing the bastard child of any Negro or mulatto was to be fined

[198] Act III, *An Additional Act for the Better Preventing Insurrections by Negroes* (November 1682), in Hening, *Statutes at Large*, 492–3. One finds in Virginia, as elsewhere at this time, a tendency to use "negro" and "slave" as synonyms. Here, however, it would have been redundant to use both, absent the usual qualifier "other." Given the title of the statute and its terms, its intent seems precisely to encompass all "negroes" as well as all "slaves."

[199] Morgan, *Slave Counterpoint*, 16, 489–90. It is unlikely that in 1680 free blacks in Virginia numbered more than 30–60 (1–2% of the black population).

[200] Act XVI (1691), 86–7. This is the first appearance in the language of a Virginia statute of "white" as a synonym for English or European heritage.

£15 or sold into service for five years (or if already a servant to serve five years after her time by indenture had expired) and the child bound to service for thirty years. Finally, reflecting upon the "great inconveniences" attending the existence of a freed black population "by their either entertaining negro slaves from their masters service, or receiveing stolen goods, or being grown old bringing a charge upon the country," the Act required the transportation out of the colony of all freed slaves within six months of their manumission.[201] The following year, in further familiar signs of a tightening slavery regime, the Virginia Assembly created special courts operating under commissions of oyer and terminer, "without the sollemnitie of jury," and with exclusive jurisdiction over capital crimes committed by slaves; it annexed to the statute in question unrelated clauses appropriating all livestock then in possession of slaves to the possession and use of their owners.[202]

Act XVI of 1691 underscores how, by the late seventeenth century, Virginia's black population had been completely assimilated to slavery, whether in fact, by actual enslavement, or virtually, by the unrelieved civic degradation, isolation, or expulsion of those formally free. It confirmed that a free black population was an anomaly, and simultaneously left little room for a white population that consorted in any manner with blacks of any status outside the strictly delimited ambit of slave relations. There followed in 1705, and then roughly at twenty-year intervals corresponding with important demographic turning points, the enactment of comprehensive statutes that gathered the laws enacted piecemeal into consolidated statutes that filled out the colony's slave regime in full substantive detail.

The first of these came in 1705, *An Act Concerning Servants and Slaves*,[203] omnibus legislation that underscored the radical re-formation of the colony's bound labor force that had been under way during the previous quarter-century. In the 1670s, the Chesapeake's migrant indentured servant population had topped out at approximately 5,500, about 10 percent of the white population and 16 percent of the total labor force. The black population stood at somewhat over four thousand. Ten years later there were three slaves for every servant; by 1705, six. By then the region's servant population was well below four thousand, while the black population had risen to more than twenty thousand, 40 percent of labor force and approaching 25 percent of total population.[204] At this point, slaves directly

---

[201] Ibid., 87–8.

[202] Act III, *An Act for the More Speedy Prosecution of Slaves Committing Capitall Crimes* (April, 1692), in Hening, *Statutes at Large*, III, 102–3, amended by Act XI, *An Act for the Speedy and Easy Prosecution of Slaves, Committing Capitall Crimes* (October 1705), in Hening, *Statutes at Large*, III, 269–70, and again by ch. IV, *An Act Directing the Trial of Slaves, Committing Capital Crimes; and for the more Effectual Punishing Conspiracies and Insurrections of them; and for the Better Government of Negros, Mulattos, and Indians, Bond or Free* (May 1723), in Hening, *Statutes at Large*, IV, 126–34. For the record of the oyer and terminer courts during the eighteenth century, see Schwarz, *Twice Condemned*, 73–91, 114–36.

[203] Ch. XLIX (October 1705), in Hening, *Statutes at Large*, III, 447–62.

[204] Calculated from *HSUS*, vol. 5, tables Eg14, Eg34, Eg53 (Virginia total population, white population, black population). See also Morgan *Slave Counterpoint*, 61 (table 10).

imported from Africa – disparaged and feared for "the gross bestiality and rudeness of their manners, the variety and strangeness of their languages, and the weakness and shallowness of their minds"[205] – accounted for 50 percent of all slaves in the Virginia colony, and approximately 12.5 percent of its entire population (one person in eight). Virginia's 1682 and 1705 statutes thus bracket both a profound transition in the composition of the bound segment of the labor force from youthful white migrants to imported African slaves, and a major intensification of dependence on bound labor. By 1705, both in size and in economic importance, Virginia's slave population had far outstripped the size of the white servant population at any point during the seventeenth century. This was the point of completion of Virginia's transition to a slave society.

Simple demography is a key marker of Virginia's transition. But so is law. The two are intimately related. Though the timing of the 1705 statute can be explained by the particularly rapid increase in resort to African slave imports in the face of the renewed shut-down of the European servant trade after 1701,[206] its precise purpose was to amalgamate the substance of the prevailing seventeenth-century law of servitude with the slave laws that had grown up in its shadow, and to reorganize the whole around slavery as the norm of bondage.

The 1705 statute elaborated the substantive implications of the series of distinctions already established in Virginia law between those servants who were slaves and those who were not. Beginning from the familiar position that "servant" meant "imported servant," the statute repeated 1682's established reliance upon a non-Christian point of origin to distinguish between servants who would be accounted slaves, liable to be bought and sold as such, and those who would not, while refining the range of exceptions beyond "Turks and Moors in amity" with the Crown to include any other non-Christians who could "make due proof of their being free" in England, or other Christian Country, prior to arrival in Virginia. (As to those professing Christianity, post-enslavement conversion, as established in 1667, counted for nothing.) The remainder of the Act similarly amalgamated Virginia's long-standing servant statutes with the slave statutes of the previous half century: Act XII of 1662 (children to follow the condition of the mother); Act III of 1667 (baptism no exemption from bondage); Act I of 1669 (immunity for the death of a slave during punishment); and the multi-clause insurrection statutes of 1680 (Act X), 1682 (Act III), and 1691 (Act XVI). Minor adjustments appear in certain clauses: The clause

---

As reported in Chapter 1, n.16, there is some inconsistency between black population numbers reported for the first decade of the eighteenth century by John J. McCusker in *Historical Statistics* and by Morgan in *Slave Counterpoint*. Inconsistencies can also be found later in the series. Importantly, the trends reported do not diverge; variation exists solely in relative assessments of how rapidly the population is growing at particular intervals.

[205] Minutes of Council (2 June 1699), in Bruce, *Institutional History of Virginia*, I, 9.

[206] Farley Grubb and Tony Stitt, "The Liverpool Emigrant Servant Trade and the Transition to Slave Labor in the Chesapeake, 1697–1707: Market Adjustments to War," *Explorations in Economic History*, 31, 3 (July, 1994), 376–405.

in Act III (1682) restraining "negroes or slaves" from tarrying on foreign plantations was redrawn to apply only to slaves; free whites intermarrying with Negroes or mulattos were no longer liable to be transported out of the colony but instead jailed for six months and fined £10. The killing of obstinate runaways licensed by Act X and Act XVI was supplemented by a provision allowing a county court, "upon the application of the owner of the said slave ... to order such punishment to the said slave, either by dismembring [castrating], or any other way, not touching his life, as they in their discretion shall think fit, for the reclaiming any such incorrigible slave, and terrifying others from the like practices."[207] Otherwise the two bodies of statutes remained intact, though now joined in one. Powers and duties common to all relations of servitude were specified, that is, but discriminations in treatment and in the availability of redress were prominent. For example, masters were forbidden to "whip a christian white servant naked" but could brutalize or kill a slave without fear of retribution. Servants, but not slaves, could complain to a Justice of a master's neglect of duty, or mistreatment, or nonpayment of wages. Servants were also held entitled to maintenance if sick during their term of service, to freedom dues at the end of it, and to the protection of the courts in renegotiating indentures. All were required to obey their masters' just and lawful commands, neither servants nor slaves were allowed to trade without permission, and procedures for the taking-up of runaways were specified without distinction between servants and slaves, except insofar as slaves who could not speak English were concerned.[208] Servants, however, were expected to make redress by additional service or by offer of compensation, provisions meaningless in the case of a slave. Generally, the legally conditioned freedoms of the dwindling band of European servants contrasted clearly with the established racial categorizations and miscegenation penalties of enslavement, representing "servitude" not as a common condition but a rigidly policed racial hierarchy.[209]

[207] Here one may detect the influence of Carolina, which had adopted castration as a punishment for incorrigible runaways in 1696. See section III, this chapter.

[208] Ch. XLIX (1705) provides, at clause xxiv, that "when any negro, or other runaway, that doth not speak English, and cannot, or through obstinacy will not declare the name of his or her master or owner, that then it shall be sufficient for the said justice to certify the same ... and the county of his or her residence and distance of miles, as aforesaid; and in such case, shall by his warrant, order the said runaway to be conveyed to the public gaol, of this country, there to be continued prisoner until the master or owner shall be known."

[209] During the same session but in a separate statute, the Virginia Assembly followed the practice of Barbados in declaring slaves real estate for certain purposes, namely inheritance, but chattels for certain other purposes, namely the settlement of debts. See ch. XXIII (October 1705), *An Act Declaring the Negro, Mulatto, and Indian Slaves within this Dominion, to be Real Estate*, in Hening *Statutes at Large*, III, 333–5. Both in its main clauses and in its listed exceptions the Virginia statute was in every essential a copy of Barbados Act 42 (29 April 1668), *An Act Declaring the Negro-Slaves of this Island, to be Real Estates*, as amended by Barbados Act 60 (29 January 1672), *A Declarative Act upon the Act making Negroes Real Estate*, both in Hall, comp., *Acts, Passed in the Island of Barbados*, 64–5, 93–4. In

The demographic transformation of Virginia's labor force from the mid-seventeenth century's mix of independent planter-producer households, migrant European indentured servants, free local hirelings, and a scattering of free blacks, Indian servants, and "Atlantic Creole" slaves to the eighteenth century's heavy and ever-growing reliance on racial slavery was confirmed after the turn of the century by twenty years of constantly accelerating importation. By the 1720s, Virginia's slave population exceeded thirty thousand, approaching one-third of total population.[210] Though upwards of 25,000 Africans had been imported since the turn of the century, by the 1720s the incidence of recently arrived Africans in the slave population had decreased slightly, to 45 percent.[211] It is unlikely this small decrease in the incidence of Africans among slaves was noticeable in daily life. As a proportion of total population Africans remained approximately one person in seven, much as they had been twenty years earlier.

Virginia greeted the continuing rapid expansion of slavery with revised legislation "for the more effectual punishing conspiracies and insurrections" among slaves, and generally "for the better government of Negros, Mulattos, and Indians, bond or free." Holding that "laws now in force, for the better ordering and governing of slaves, and for the speedy trial of such of them as commit capital crimes," were "insufficient to restrain their tumultuous and unlawful meetings, or to punish the secret plots and conspiracies carried on amongst them," the Assembly addressed the deficiencies within the framework of a revision of the procedures for slave trials first established in 1692.[212] The Act

Atlantic Virginia, at 156, April Hatfield argues that the Virginia Assembly took the same step shortly after, in 1671. See Act IV (September 1671), *An Act Providing How Negroes Belonging to Orphants of Intestates shall be Disposed of,* in Hening, *Statutes at Large,* II, 288. But this is not so. In 1671, the Assembly simply deferred to the county courts "who are hereby authorized and impowred either to cause such negroes to be duly apprized, sold at an outcry, or preserved in kind, as they then find it most expedient for preservation, improvement or advancement of the estate and interest of such orphants." Act IV (1671), at 288. Barbados in contrast legislated on the matter precisely to take jurisdiction away from the courts and their conflicting rulings "sometimes ... for the one, and at other times for the other" and to provide a clear rule. Act 42 (1668), at 64. Virginia's 1705 Act bred considerable litigation leading to amendments in 1727 that limited the definition of slaves as real estate. The definition was finally repealed altogether in 1748, making slaves chattel for all purposes. Although the repeal statute was one of nine disallowed by royal proclamation in 1751, it is plain from the Assembly's response that local practice had always resisted 1705's definition of slaves as real estate, and that the definition had long since ceased to have any practical effect. See ch. XI (February 1727), *An Act to Explain and Amend the Act, For Declaring the Negro, Mulatto, and Indian Slaves, within this Dominion, to be Real Estate ...,* in Hening, *Statutes at Large,* and ch. II (October 1748), *An Act Declaring Slaves to be Personal Estate, and for Other Purposes Therein Mentioned* in Hening, *Statutes at Large,* V, 432–43. For the Assembly's response to the 1748 Act's disallowance, see the note added by Hening to ch. II, beginning 432, at 440–2.

210 Calculated from *HSUS,* vol. 5, tables Eg14, Eg53 (Virginia total population, black population). Compare Morgan *Slave Counterpoint,* 61 (table 10).

211 Morgan, *Slave Counterpoint,* 59 (table 9), 61 (table 10).

212 Ch. IV (May, 1723), *An Act Directing the Trial of Slaves, Committing Capital Crimes; and for the more Effectual Punishing Conspiracies and Insurrections of them; and for the Better Government*

made conspiracy a capital crime, imposed very strict controls on slave movement, and prohibited gatherings of more than five slaves from different plantations. It comprehensively revised the procedure of the slave courts operating under commissions of oyer and terminer created in 1692: evidentiary requirements were eased; the taking of evidence from "Negroes, Mulattos, or Indians, bond or free" was encouraged. Inter alia the Act made manumission a virtual impossibility and further degraded any remaining free blacks in the colony by depriving them of the suffrage "at the election of burgesses, or any other election whatsoever."[213] Though Virginia colony legislation had not to this point been quite as explicit or precise as Carolina in its cataloguing of punishments, the 1723 Act is notable for the steady drumbeat of death and dismemberment that echoes throughout.

Three years later, amendments to the Act of 1705 placed particular emphasis on the effects of the immense influx of Africans over the past two decades by enacting in great detail (16 clauses of 24 in the Act as a whole) a series of regulations intended to deal specifically with non–English speaking runaways, and to improve the capacities (and willingness) of local officers to abide by prescribed procedures. Throughout, the slave runaway clauses used "negro" as a synonym for slave. A second group of amendments focused on prevention of clandestine escapes by sea, and a final group added various penalties punishing white laborers for various forms of deceit: runaway white servants who disguised themselves and changed their names; tradesmen and workmen "on wages" who misrepresented their skills or refused or neglected work. This final group of clauses was explicitly confined in scope to migrants (at this point craftsmen were about the only category of English labor still coming into Virginia under indenture) and did not reach the white Creole population. The effect of the 1726 statute was therefore to strengthen further the association of whiteness and freedom from restraint in matters of work discipline, while treating imported white labor as a partial (and temporary) exception that was nevertheless – like all whites – wholly distinguishable from slave labor, particularly the Africans at whom most of the 1726 amendments were directed.[214]

A further restatement of Virginia's omnibus *Act concerning Servants, and Slaves* came in 1748, coinciding with the moment of peak incidence of slaves in total population. At mid-century, the colony had well in excess of 100,000 slaves, comprising some 45 percent of a total population of

---

of Negros, Mulattos, and Indians, *Bond or Free* (May 1723), in Hening, *Statutes at Large,* IV, 126–34, at 126. For the Act of 1692, see n.202, this chapter, and accompanying text.

[213] Ch. IV (1723), clause xxiii. See, generally, Parent, *Foul Means,* 155–8.

[214] Ch. IV (May 1726), *An Act for Amending the Act concerning Servants and Slaves; and for the Further Preventing the Clandestine Transportation of Persons out of this Colony,* in Hening, *Statutes at Large,* IV, 168–75. In his *Office and Authority of a Justice of Peace* (Williamsburg, 1736), at 281–7, George Webb reproduces the law of servant as well as slave runaways, but all his form examples assume the subject will be slaves.

236,000.[215] Once more the Assembly reaffirmed that origin in non-Christian lands was the key signifier of enslavement, repeating word for word the provisos and exceptions of the 1705 statute. But in one detail the Assembly altered its definition of who would be slaves under Virginia law: the distinction drawn in the 1748 statute was no longer one within the general category "servant," as it had been since 1670, but between two different categories of people. In the 1748 statute, "slaves" ceased to be that subcategory of "servants" imported into the colony whose origins were non-Christian; instead, they became all "persons" so originating. The substance of the Act differed in virtually no respect from the 1705 Act, as amended in 1726, but the formalization in law of the distinction between white migrant servants imported under indenture and black slaves imported for sale (such that there was now no overlap at all between servant and slave) meant that the substantive provisions fell, quite neatly and quite explicitly, into two separate halves. Once more, throughout the Act the Assembly emphasized that so far as white labor was concerned, the ambit of statutory regulation was limited to migrants bound (or if underage to be bound) by indenture. Once more the effect of the Act's strictures left virtually no room in Virginia, even theoretically, for "Negroes, Moors, mulattoes" other than as slaves.[216] This was underlined in the same session of the Assembly by passage of an amended version of the colony's 1723 "conspiracies and insurrections" Act that addressed fear of "negroes [who] under pretence of practising physic, have prepared and exhibited poisonous medicines, by which many persons have been murdered," and prohibited "any negroe, or other slave" from preparing or administering "any medicine whatsoever" on pain of death. The title and preamble of the Act underlined the assimilation of all "negroes, mulattoes, and Indians, bond or free" to one alien and dangerous category, finding it "absolutely necessary, that effectual provision should be made for the better ordering and governing of slaves, free negroes, mulattoes, and Indians, and detecting and punishing their secret plots, and dangerous combinations, and for the speedy trial of such of them as commit capital crimes."[217] Reenacting the

---

[215] Calculated from *HSUS*, vol. 5, tables Eg14, Eg53 (Virginia total population, black population). Compare Morgan, *Slave Counterpoint*, 61 (table 10). See also Morgan, Slave Counterpoint, 59 (table 9).

[216] Ch. XIV (October 1748), *An Act Concerning Servants and Slaves*, in Hening, *Statutes at Large*, V, 547–58, clause i and ii. This Act was among those disallowed in 1751 for procedural reasons by royal proclamation; it was reenacted in 1753, as *An Act for the Better Government of Servants and Slaves*, ch. VII (November 1753), in Hening, *Statutes at Large*, VI, 356–69.

[217] Ch. XXXVIII (October 1748), *An Act Directing the Trial of Slaves Committing Capital Crimes; and for the more effectual punishing Conspiracies and Insurrections of them; and for the better Government of Negroes, Mulattoes, and Indians, Bond or Free*, in Hening, *Statutes at Large*, VI, 104–12, at 104 (clause i, preamble). On poisoning, see Schwarz, *Twice Condemned*, 92–113. The 1748 Act was in turn amended by ch. XXVI (October 1765), *An Act for Amending the Act Entitled An Act Directing the Trial of Slaves Committing Capital Crimes*, in Hening, *Statutes at Large*, VIII, 137–8, to grant all justices prospective commissions of oyer and terminer generally empowering them to try slaves on capital charges, rather than require application for a commission specific to each slave held for trial, so that trials might proceed immediately as cases arose.

1723 Act in all essentials, the Assembly added provisions that completed the degradation of free blacks in the colony by denying them admission to any court of record, or appearance before any magistrate in any cause whatsoever, except as they were required to give evidence in the trial of a slave for a capital offense; and by holding them liable to be punished as a slave would be for lifting a hand in opposition to any Christian "not being a negroe, mulattoe, or Indian." So offending, he or she "shall for every such offence, proved by the oath of the party, before a justice of peace, of the county where such offence shall be committed, receive thirty lashes, on his, or her bare back, well laid on."[218]

Virginia's final return to its comprehensive slave law before the Revolution came in 1769, when the Assembly amended its general "servants and slaves" Act one last time. Always the mainland colony with by far the largest number of slaves, at the end of the 1760s Virginia's slave population approached 190,000. As a proportion of total population, however, this represented a decline from the late 1740s peak when it must have seemed that the colony's rapidly increasing population of slaves (then 45 percent of total population up from 33 percent ten years earlier) would soon outnumber its whites. After mid-century, though continuing to grow in round numbers, the slave population settled into a constant range of 41–42 percent of total population, where it would remain for the next fifty years. African importation continued, but the main surge (the thirty years from 1720 to 1750) was over. More and more, slave population growth was attributable to natural increase.[219] By this point a slave society for a good seventy years, Virginia had become a mature and demographically stable slave society.

The 1769 amendments hint at that maturity and stability. Most of the Act is taken up with fiddling adjustments to the detail of long-established procedures for taking up slave runaways. The Assembly had never tired of periodically tweaking and tuning these provisions, in place for nearly a century, presumably in the hope that the right combination of fees payable and other inducements might actually persuade local officers to implement the laws in a manner that realized their intended purpose while avoiding squabbles and litigation over payments for services rendered.[220] The very ordinariness of their tinkering in 1769 conveys a certain complacency, even boredom, on the part of the burgesses. Slavery had long since become a routine. But in one respect at least, the 1769 statute did more than simply fiddle with the administration of slavery's routines. Though rather less elaborately than South Carolina in 1740, it gestured toward

[218] Ibid., 110 (clause xx).

[219] Calculated from *HSUS*, vol. 5, tables Eg14, Eg34, Eg53 (Virginia total population, white population, black population), vol. 1, table Aa602 (Virginia total population 1790–1840), vol. 2, table Bb49 (Virginia slave population 1790–1860). Compare Morgan, *Slave Counterpoint*, 61 (table 10), and see also 81 (table 19: Black Population Growth in Virginia).

[220] Ch. XIX (November 1769), *An Act to Amend the Act Intituled an Act to Amend the Act for the Better Government of Servants and Slaves*, in Hening, *Statutes at Large*, VIII, 359–61, clauses iii–vii. See, generally, Schwarz, *Slave Laws in Virginia*, 123–5.

the master class's desire to conduct its regime with a certain delicacy, to declare its own humanity and respectability by tempering regrettably necessary brutalities with displays of wise discretion. The message is visible in faint outline in the Act's initial clause, which reads as follows:

> WHEREAS by an act of the General Assembly made in the twenty-second year of his late majesty George the second, intituled An Act directing the trial of slaves committing capital crimes, and for the more effectual punishing conspiracies and insurrections of them, and for the better government of negroes, mulattoes, and Indians, bond or free, the county courts within this dominion are impowered to punish outlying slaves who cannot be reclaimed, by dismembering such slaves, which punishment is often disproportioned to the offence, and contrary to the principles of humanity: Be it therefore enacted, by the Governor, Council, and Burgesses, of this present General Assembly, and it is hereby enacted by the authority of the same, That it shall not be lawful for any county court to order and direct castration of any slave, except such slave shall be convicted of an attempt to ravish a white woman, in which case they may inflict such punishment; any thing in the said recited act, to the contrary, notwithstanding.[221]

One could be forgiven for finding little of significance in the sentiments expressed. What had the Assembly done but refocus one of the master class's more grotesque practices on deterring trespasses upon its patriarchal and sexual property rather than on punishing (evidently ineffectively) incorrigibles' sabotage of its economic interests through their obstinate refusals to cooperate in their own subjugation? On the other hand, in a century of slavery legislation whose chief characteristic was a consistent display of no consciousness other than brutality, this was the first occasion upon which the burgesses had allowed themselves to indulge in a display of "principles of humanity," of concern for "proportion." The burgesses were not making concessions to the humanity of their slaves. As in South Carolina, it was their own humanity that they desired should be recognized. Nor should one allow their new-found delicacy to camouflage the brute practicalities upon which their rule daily depended. Rather, as in South Carolina, their sentiments signified the maturation of their grasp of how discourses of legality served both their regime and their self-esteem. "From the beginning of the legally supported institution in the 1660s," Philip Schwarz remarks, Virginian slaveholders "insisted that slavery must be based on the law."[222] Were not the legitimacy of their institutions and their own pretensions to civility advanced, then, by such displays of their own humanity in their treatment of underlings, of their wise recognition of the proprieties, the necessities, of proportionate correction? Was this not their habit in daily life?[223] Should it not be registered in their law? So slavery matured in Virginia.

---

[221] Ibid., clause i.

[222] Schwarz, *Twice Condemned*, 13.

[223] See, for example, Rhys Isaac, *Landon Carter's Uneasy Kingdom: Revolution and Rebellion on a Virginia Plantation* (New York, 2004), 17–34. See also Schwarz, *Twice Condemned*, 23–4.

V. Mainland Slavery Regimes: New England and the Mid-Atlantic

For much of the first half century of continuous English mainland settlement, the black population of all the seaboard settlements together could be counted in the hundreds. Though most were slaves they inhabited a range of statuses from slavery, through forms of servitude known among European migrants, all the way to occasional outcroppings of freedom. Before 1660, as it grew, this tiny black population became less rather than more concentrated: from the mid-1630s until the later 1650s, more blacks were to be found outside the borders of the Chesapeake colonies, in New England and the mid-Atlantic settlements, than within them.[224]

We know this dispersion did not last. By 1660, when the total black population on the mainland stood just below three thousand, 60 percent of it was to be found in the South Atlantic settlements. The South Atlantic share had become 80 percent by 1690 (some 13,400 of 16,700), a level at which it held relatively constant for the next thirty years before resuming its climb, topping out in the 1780s at 90 percent.[225]

The black population concentrated in the South Atlantic colonies was virtually wholly enslaved. Unenslaved blacks were present in both Virginia and South Carolina throughout the eighteenth century, but theirs was a status progressively degraded to a level little different from the slaves surrounding them. Unenslaved blacks were in any case so few in number – no more than 1 percent of the black population of Virginia and South Carolina – that for purposes of measuring population, scholars of slavery treat "black" or "negro" and "slave" as synonymous. Different colonies in fact exhibit some variation. In Maryland in 1755, where 45,312 mulattos and blacks constituted 30 percent of the total population, some 4 percent (1817) were free. This actually represented one of the "freest" black populations anywhere in the South Atlantic colonies, matched nowhere else and approached, possibly, only in North Carolina.[226] As in North Carolina, Maryland's free black population was almost entirely mulatto, probably originating in marriages between free or servant black males and free or servant white females: 40 percent of the 1755 mulatto population was free (1,460 of 3,608), compared with 0.8 percent of blacks (357 of 41,704), all of whom were likely manumitted slaves.[227] But overall it is highly unlikely that prior to the 1780s the unenslaved black population of all the South Atlantic settlements together ever exceeded at most 1.75 percent of the total black population. This in turn means that over the same period, the enslaved black population of the South Atlantic region always accounted

---

[224] See *HSUS*, vol. 5, table Eg41–59 (all colonies and localities, black population).

[225] Ibid.

[226] For population numbers, see ibid. and also table Eg169–181 (Population of Maryland by Age, Sex, Race, Slave or Servant Status and Taxable Status, 1704–82). On Virginia and South Carolina, see Morgan, *Slave Counterpoint*, 489–91. On North Carolina, see John Hope Franklin, *The Free Negro in North Carolina, 1790–1860* (Chapel Hill, 1943), 10, 35–6, 59, 105.

[227] Calculated from *HSUS*, vol. 5, table Eg169–181.

for 80 percent or more of *all* mainland blacks, whether free or slave.[228] In other words, during the century following the turn of the English mainland colonies to slavery, never fewer than 80 percent of the entire mainland black population lived under the South Atlantic slave regimes so far described. By mid-century, with those regimes well settled into maturity, upwards of 90 percent of mainland blacks were subject to them.

Obviously, then, the black populations of the mid-Atlantic and New England colonies were much smaller than of the South Atlantic plantation settlements. They were not distinctively freer. First, it is clear that in broadly chronological terms the trajectory of enslavement was not significantly different in the mid-Atlantic and North Atlantic settlements than in the South: everywhere, the mid-seventeenth century's hints at some variety of status for blacks had been snuffed out in favor of the uniformities of enslavement by the early eighteenth.[229] Restrictive police legislation focused on free blacks, both colonial and municipal, confirms that, as in the South Atlantic settlements, free black populations continued to exist throughout the eighteenth century; scholars have acknowledged data that suggest fragmentary estimates.[230] But generally, as in the South, black or "negro" is taken to mean enslaved; the numbers that the data fragments hint at are thought sufficiently small to require no allowance for free blacks in population estimates before the late eighteenth century. One may hypothesize, accordingly, that for most of the eighteenth century the free black populations of the middle and northern colonies were not significantly larger, proportionate to the black population as a whole, than in the South.[231]

In the northern settlement regions, enslaved blacks numbered some five thousand at the turn of the eighteenth century and over fifty thousand by the 1770s.[232] As between the two northern settlement regions, New England and the mid-Atlantic, the numbers divide fairly consistently, averaging a little less than one-third in New England and a little over two-thirds in the mid-Atlantic. New England's slaves were concentrated in the colonies of

---

[228] Calculated from ibid., table Eg41–59. Between 1690 and 1730, this proportion hardly varied. Between 1730 and 1760, it rose to the region of 86%, and thence to 88% in 1780.

[229] In New York, for example, a free black population numbering some 20% of the total black population (and 4% of total population) in the 1660s had shrunk to a tiny fraction of that number by the early eighteenth. See Harris, *In the Shadow of Slavery*, 22; Berlin, *Many Thousands Gone*, 187.

[230] Harris, *In the Shadow of Slavery*, 33, 39; Berlin, *Many Thousands Gone*, 187. Berlin estimates a free black population in the 1770s of no more than "several hundred" in all mid-Atlantic and New England settlements combined (228).

[231] Using the same crude deflator of 1.75% for the mid-Atlantic and New England colonies as for the South Atlantic colonies produces a total free black northern population slowly rising to slightly in excess of 900 in the 1770s – a figure that accords well with Ira Berlin's "several hundred." Calculated from *HSUS*, vol. 5, table Eg42–50.

[232] Calculated from ibid., table Eg41–50. Thereafter, emancipation slowly reduced slavery's numbers in the "free" New England and mid-Atlantic states to 36,000 by 1800 and 18,000 by 1820. See *HSUS*, vol. 2, table Bb1–18 (black population, by state and slave/free status, 1790–1860).

Massachusetts, Connecticut, and Rhode Island, with a much smaller number in New Hampshire. In the mid-Atlantic region, New York – until quite late in the seventeenth century the only colony in the region with slaves – accounted for the majority of the region's slaves, most of the time close to 60 percent. The larger part of the remainder was to be found in New Jersey. Slaveholding was by no means insignificant in Pennsylvania, but for most of the century after first settlement Pennsylvania's slave population did not account for more than some 15 percent of the region's total.[233]

The incidence of slaves in population was uniformly far lower in northern settlements than in the South. Incidence was always highest in New York, consistently 12–13 percent between the mid-seventeenth and early eighteenth century, peaking at 15 percent in 1720 and then leveling off at 14 percent until the 1760s before declining to 10 percent by 1780 (overall average, 12.1 percent). New Jersey was consistently at 6–8 percent for the entire century following 1670 and Pennsylvania 2.5 percent, with the exception of a sudden jump to 6.5 percent in the first two decades of the eighteenth century[234] (coincident with New York's peak) and an equally sudden regression to its mean thereafter. In New England, Connecticut's incidence of slaves in total population varied from 0.3 percent to 3 percent and averaged 1.7 percent. In Massachusetts, the rate varied from 0.5 percent to 2.5 percent and averaged closer to 1.6 percent. In New England, only Rhode Island approached the rates of the mid-Atlantic settlements, varying between 3 percent and 10 percent and averaging 5.8 percent.[235]

Northern slavery was as varied an institution in occupational structure as it was in distribution. The northern economies lacked staple agriculture as such; by the eighteenth century they were far more diversified than the classic plantation economies of the South Atlantic. They had significant hinterland sectors characterized by the production of vendible surpluses in a variety of agricultural and resource commodities (wheat, livestock, and fish); they had urban areas specializing in artisan manufacturing to consume hinterland products, a seaport-based commercial sector to market them, and an intercolonial carrying trade to transport them. Slavery did not alter the organizational structure or comparative advantages of the northern economies but was rather absorbed into them, a significant labor force component that would prove adaptable to most forms and structures of economic activity: urban and rural; artisanal and agricultural; landed and maritime; household and proto-industrial.[236]

---

[233] Calculated from *HSUS*, vol. 5, table Eg41–50.

[234] Explicable by the interruption of European migration and consequent crisis in labor supply.

[235] Calculated from *HSUS*, vol. 5, tables Eg1–11, Eg21–31, Eg41–50.

[236] For occupational diversity among the northern economies, see, e.g., Harris, *In the Shadow of Slavery*, 30–1; Daniel Vickers, "The Northern Colonies: Economy and Society, 1600–1775," in Stanley L. Engerman and Robert E. Gallman, *The Cambridge Economic History of the United States*, volume 1, *The Colonial Era* (Cambridge and New York, 1996), 209–48. On the northern economies generally, see John J. McCusker and Russell R. Menard, *The Economy of British America, 1607–1789* (Chapel Hill, 1991), 91–116, 189–208 (note that

Slavery was never irreplaceable in the northern settlements; these were never "slave societies" in the South Atlantic sense. But in each of the colonies where slaveh&lding attained significance (Massachusetts, Connecticut, and Rhode Island in New England; New York, New Jersey, and Pennsylvania in the mid-Atlantic), dedicated controls were adopted to guarantee its disciplines. These were, that is, much more than "societies with slaves"; they were societies with slavery. Each had the legal regime to prove it.

The legal character of slavery in the northern settlements varied as much as its occupational structure and distribution. The slavery regimes of the New England settlements largely developed piecemeal through local and provincial enactment of police regulations. The size and significance of the slave population was such that slave law did not progress much beyond the essential menu of means to control a subordinated population; it did not construct an institution in detail. In the mid-Atlantic, in contrast, the slave population was much more densely regulated, each colony passing comprehensive enabling legislation that to an important degree created an institutionalized regime of slavery.

New England

Slaves appear in New England in the later 1630s, a moment in the colonization of the mainland when the mainland black population – amounting in all to some six hundred people – was fairly evenly distributed across the three main regions of settlement. In 1640, some two hundred blacks were scattered across New England settlements, most (150) in Massachusetts Bay, the remainder in New Hampshire and Connecticut.[237] In 1641, the General Court accepted Nathaniel Ward's *Body of Liberties* as established authority (though not fundamental law) for the colony, which meant that it accepted the *Body*'s list of permissible modes of enslavement: "lawfull Captives taken in just warres ... strangers as willingly selle themselves or are sold to us."[238] The *Body* also included a prohibition on "man-stealing" (a capital crime) that was tested in 1646 in an indictment of two local merchants for their part in an African slave-raiding expedition.[239] No action occurred beyond an order for the return of those taken who had been

McCusker and Menard include Delaware among the "Middle Colonies," whereas I follow a census regions approach and include Delaware in the South Atlantic region).

[237] See *HSUS*, vol. 5, tables Eg43, Eg45, Eg47 (New Hampshire, Massachusetts, Connecticut: black population). O'Malley, "Beyond the Middle Passage," 157, emphasizes Caribbean sources for seventeenth-century New England slaves brought in "a slow but steady trade" often (as we have already seen) in exchange for Indian captives. Greene, *The Negro in Colonial New England*, 15–16 reports that slaves had actually been brought into the region in the 1620s by Samuel Maverick, who was the first permanent English settler in the Shawmut region (Winnisimmet), then within the territory claimed by the (failed) colony of Wessagusset, later to be dominated by Boston. See also Edgar J. McManus, *Black Bondage in the North* (Syracuse, N.Y., 1973), 6.

[238] Discussed in section II of this chapter.

[239] Jordan, *White Over Black*, 69–70.

imported into the colony; during the second half of the century, Boston merchants began to engage in slave-trading, though not at this point on the scale of their eighteenth-century counterparts.

The forms of servitude and enslavement endorsed by the *Body of Liberties* extended to enslavement as punishment: "those Judged thereto by Authoritie." It is clear from piecemeal case records that for a brief period beginning in 1638, Massachusetts' magistrates were quite willing to condemn whites to slavery. But punitive slavery was certainly not life-time slavery; nor was it heritable. It was used more as a form of short-term indeterminate sentencing.[240] The *Body* further provided that whatever the basis (captivity, sale, or punishment), those enslaved "shall have all the liberties and Christian usages which the law of God established in Israell concerning such persons doth morally require." This would remain a dis-tinguishing feature of Massachusetts slavery in that no separate structure of extraordinary or summary jurisdiction devoted exclusively to slave crime and discipline was ever established in the colony, unlike that initiated in Barbados and copied elsewhere on the mainland.[241]

Massachusetts slavery at mid-century was not unlike slavery of the same period further to the south: low in incidence, not fully differenti-ated from unenslaved servitude, and although overwhelmingly racialized in identity not yet the only identity for blacks. As numbers grew from the late seventeenth century onward, differentiation became much more

---

[240] William Androws, sentenced to slavery in October 1638, was released from slavery in July 1639; Thomas Dickinson was sentenced to slavery in October 1639 and discharged in July 1640; Thomas Savory was convicted of housebreaking in April 1640 and sold for a slave "vntil hee have made double restitution"; in July 1640, Jonathan Hatch was commit-ted as a slave "for the pʳsent"; in January 1641/2, Elizabeth Sedgwicke, a serial thief, was condemned to slavery "till shee have recompenced double for all hir thefts" (118). *Records of the Court of Assistants of the Colony of the Massachusetts Bay, 1630–92* (Boston, 1904), II, 78–9, 86, 90, 94, 97, 118. And see *Jordan, White Over Black*, 68.

[241] McManus, *Black Bondage in the North*, 68. At the same time, this reference in the title on bond-slavery seems clearly intended to invoke Leviticus 25: 38–46 (AV), thus contem-plating that slavery shall be a condition of heathen and in perpetuity: "[38] I am the LORD your God, which brought you forth out of the land of Egypt, to give you the land of Canaan, and to be your God. [39] And if thy brother that dwelleth by thee be waxen poor, and be sold unto thee; thou shalt not compel him to serve as a bondservant: [40] But as an hired servant, and as a sojourner, he shall be with thee, and shall serve thee unto the year of jubile. [41] And then shall he depart from thee, both he and his children with him, and shall return unto his own family, and unto the possession of his fathers shall he return. [42] For they are my servants, which I brought forth out of the land of Egypt: they shall not be sold as bondmen. [43] Thou shalt not rule over him with rigour; but shalt fear thy God. [44] Both thy bondmen, and thy bondmaids, which thou shalt have, shall be of the heathen that are round about you; of them shall ye buy bondmen and bondmaids. [45] Moreover of the children of the strangers that do sojourn among you, of them shall ye buy, and of their families that are with you, which they begat in your land: and they shall be your possession. [46] And ye shall take them as an inheritance for your children after you, to inherit them for a possession; they shall be your bondmen for ever: but over your brethren the children of Israel, ye shall not rule one over another with rigour."

pronounced: ambiguities lessened, distinctions and identities sharpened, and disciplinary controls became more ubiquitous. The trajectory of definition and increasing severity, in other words, was the same as elsewhere. But the overall incidence of slavery did not change and slavery per se had no transformative impact on Massachusetts society and economy akin to the plantation colonies or even New York. In the rural economy, slaves to some degree substituted for the indentured servants Massachusetts never could recruit in any significant number, filling life-cyclic gaps in a rural labor force overwhelmingly dependent on deployable family members. But the household farm economy turned far more often to task-swapping and hired help than to slaves to cover life-cycle gaps. Slaves had more presence in urban areas where their labor was of importance to artisanal and proto-industrial production (filling gaping American holes in the traditional tripartite master-journeyman-apprentice structure of the trades), in maritime trades and in household service.[242] This seems particularly true of Boston, where, during the first half of the eighteenth century, the incidence of slaves in city population more than doubled, from approximately 4 percent of population to over 8 percent. By the early 1740s, 45 percent of Massachusetts' black population was concentrated in Boston, up from approximately 25 percent in 1710.[243]

The eighteenth century's combination of rising overall numbers of slaves and the growing visibility of urban slaves with a low and essentially unchanging incidence of slavery in the province as a whole resulted in laws that largely confined regulatory activity to reinforcement of blacks' confinement within slavery, along with a particularized police of their mobility and public behavior in Boston. That is, rising numbers particularly in urban areas resulted in a more clearly defined institution and heightened controls, but low overall incidence meant the development of Massachusetts' slave law never progressed beyond the stage of piecemeal disciplinary regulation from which the South Atlantic settlements had departed by the early 1690s (following Barbados's earlier example) in their creation of comprehensive slave regimes. Thus, in 1693, in the first enactment of its kind, the General Court amended liquor licensing laws to require licensed innholders and

---

[242] Joanne Pope Melish, *Disowning Slavery: Gradual Emancipation and "Race" in New England, 1780–1860* (Ithaca, N.Y., 1998), 16–23; Daniel Vickers, *Farmers and Fishermen, Two Centuries of Work in Essex County, Massachusetts, 1630–1850* (Chapel Hill, 1994), 59, 230–1. On urban slavery, see Berlin, *Many Thousands Gone,* 179; Gary B. Nash and Jean Soderlund, *Freedom By Degrees: Emancipation in Pennsylvania and its Aftermath* (New York and Oxford, 1991), 14–26; Harris, *In the Shadow of Slavery,* 30–1. On the truncated structure of the artisan trades in eighteenth-century British America, notably the scarcity of journeymen, see Christopher L. Tomlins, *Law, Labor, and Ideology in the Early American Republic* (Cambridge and New York, 1993), 111–12.

[243] Calculated from *HSUS,* vol. 5, table Eg45 (Massachusetts black population), and Gary B. Nash, *The Urban Crucible: Social Change, Political Consciousness and the Origins of the American Revolution* (Cambridge, Mass., 1979), 107, 409. Nash reports approximately 350 blacks in a Boston population of approximately 8,000 in 1710, compared to 1,374 in a total city population of approximately 16,000 in 1742.

common victuallers to refuse service to "any apprentice, servant, or negro" except by special order or allowance of their masters. In 1703, the General Court locked blacks deeper into enslavement by adopting legislation to discourage manumission: slave owners desirous of manumitting a slave were required to post £50 bonds to cover the costs to towns of the slave's potential future indigence. Slaves had no settlement.[244] The same year, "Whereas great disorders, insolencies and burglaries are ofttimes raised and committed in the night time by Indian, negro and molatto servants and slaves," the General Court banned all movement of such servants and slaves after 9 P.M. unless on a specific errand for a master or owner. It empowered not only local officers – justices, constable, tythingmen, and watchmen – but all householders to apprehend offenders, who were to be taken before a justice of the peace and ordered to the nearest house of correction "to receive the discipline of the house and then be dismiss'd" or, in lieu, "openly whip'd by the constable."[245] Over the following years, Boston selectmen passed numerous police ordinances to control the movement and activities of slaves, stressing the importance of enforcing the curfew, proscribing gatherings for funerals after dark, banning the carrying of sticks or canes that might be used as weapons, and prohibiting loitering.[246] A province law of 1753 sought to suppress "riotous, tumultuous and disorderly assemblies" in Boston and other towns in which "men, children and negroes" displayed pageants and shows, abused and insulted inhabitants, demanded money with menaces and generally engaged in "horrid profaneness, impiety and other gross immoralities," cultivating "a mobbish temper" and "opposition to all government and order," by enacting a ban on all assemblies of more than three people armed or disguised or costumed, on penalty of fine or imprisonment or, if Negroes, a whipping. The Act included separate and further bans on such assemblies at night, and on lighting bonfires, with the same penalties. The ubiquity of whipping penalties for black offenders suggests both a desire to differentiate them from whites and to humiliate them with public corporal punishment. Whipping was also recognition that imprisonment of a slave punished the slave's master with a loss of time that could never be made up.[247]

[244] Ch. 20 (November 1693), *An Act of Supplement and Addition to Several Acts and Laws of this Province*, in *The Acts and Resolves, Public and Private, of the Province of the Massachusetts Bay*, volume 1 (Boston 1869), 154–5; ch. 1 (28 July 1703), *An Act Relating to Molato and Negro Slaves*, in *Acts and Resolves*, vol. 1, 519. On the question of manumission as a consequence of conversion in Massachusetts, see n.187, this chapter.

[245] Ch. 11 (1 December 1703), *An Act to Prevent Disorders in the Night*, in *Acts and Resolves*, vol. 1, 535–6. Two years later, the General Court enacted Massachusetts' first anti-miscegenation statute, ch. 10 (5 December 1705), *An Act for the Better Preventing of a Spurious and Mixt Issue*, in *Acts and Resolves*, vol. 1, 578–9.

[246] McManus, *Black Bondage in the North*, 81, 82.

[247] Ch. 18 (5 January 1753), *An Act for Further Preventing all Rioutous, Tumultuous and Disorderly Assemblies or Companies of Persons, and for Preventing Bonfires in any of the Streets or Lanes within any of the Towns of this Province*, in *Acts and Resolves*, vol. III, 647–8, renewed by ch. 14 (15 October 1756), vol. III, 997–8.

The particular target of the 1753 statute appears to be African-inflected black festivals, notably Negro Election Day, then on the rise in New England and characterized by costumed parades, role reversals, and race mixing. Their appearance signifies the increased importance of Africans in the Massachusetts slave population.[248] Although New England's benign disease environment favored natural increase in the black population no less than the white, rising black population numbers were also an indicator of the incidence of newly arrived Africans in an enslaved population hitherto largely obtained through mercantile coastal and Caribbean connections.[249] As elsewhere, Africanization attracted anxious attention in the association of blacks with disorder, insolence, a ubiquitous "strangeness" of manner. One of the first provincial laws directly addressing slavery (1705) suggests a desire to limit the influx by imposing duties of £4 per head on imported blacks. Accompanying acts in 1709 and 1712 attempted first to limit and then to ban the importation of Indian slaves in the same way, while simultaneously offering bounties for those ever elusive white servants.[250]

Slavery in Massachusetts was hardly mild; among the northern settlements, however, it remained comparatively stunted. This indeed was the case throughout New England. In Connecticut, where slavery's numeric profile was broadly similar to Massachusetts, slave law took essentially the same form and followed the same chronological trajectory: police laws and restraints of increasing severity but no comprehensive institutionalization.[251]

[248] Berlin, *Many Thousands Gone,* 191–2. In the mid-Atlantic, the equivalent festival was Pinkster (derived from the Dutch word *Pinksteren* for Pentecost).

[249] O'Malley, "Beyond the Middle Passage," 159, 162, 164–5, 166 (table 11), reports a steady influx of slaves transshipped from Caribbean entrepôts into the New England colonies during the first half of the eighteenth century, increasingly supplemented by direct importation of small consignments of Africans by New England merchants active in the transatlantic trade to the plantation colonies. From 1740 direct importation predominated, resulting in a 72%–28% split in total slave imports in favor of direct importation from Africa.

[250] The £4 impost was annexed to the December 1705 anti-miscegenation statute (n. 245). The impost was to be remitted on any slave reexported within twelve of months upon production of proof that the slave in question had been sold out of the province. For attempts to discourage importation of Indian slaves and encourage importation of white servants, see ch. 11 (26 February 1708/9), *An Act to Encourage the Importation of White Servants,* in *Acts and Resolves,* vol. 1, 634. This statute was reiterated and revised in ch. 3 (23 August 1712), *An Act Prohibiting the Importation or Bringing into this Province Any Indian Servants or Slaves,* in *Acts and Resolves,* vol. 1, 698, its language signifying considerable apprehension at the importation not only of Indian but indeed any slaves. The Act's preamble complained of "divers conspiracies, outrages, barbarities, murders, burglaries, thefts, and other notorious crimes and enormities, at sundry times and especially of late ... perpetrated and committed by Indians and other slaves within several of her majestie's plantations in America." It complained that Indians and other slaves manifested a "malicious, surley and revengeful spirit," and that they were "rude and insolent in their behaviour, and very ungovernable." It warned that "the over-great number and increase [of Indian and other slaves] within this province is likely to prove of pernicious and fatal consequences to her majestie's subjects and interests here, unless speedily remedied, and is a discouragement to the importation of white Christian servants."

[251] McManus, *Black Bondage in the North,* 73, 75.

Even in Rhode Island, where the incidence of slaves in overall population was triple that of the colony's neighboring settlements to the north and west (and at its peak in the mid-eighteenth century peak was exceeded only in New York), no slave "code" as such was ever adopted.[252] Rhode Island's police laws were, however, harsh. As elsewhere, elements of the laws extended to the generality of the black population.[253] As elsewhere, too, manumission was strongly discouraged.[254] In 1714, additionally, "whereas several Negro and Mollatto Slaves, have Ran-away from their Masters and Mistresses, under pretence of being Employed in their Service," the General Assembly adopted legislation requiring that any such "slave or slaves" seeking passage out of the colony or travelling at large produce on demand a certificate of permission (ticket of leave) to be abroad from their masters or from "some person in Commission for the Peace." Ferrymen transporting slaves without certificates were subject to fines of 20/- and liable too for the potentially much greater costs to masters of recovery (or loss) of any slave transported who actually ran off. The statute also required not only township justices but "all other [His Majesties] Subjects in this Colony" to take up, examine, and secure any slave or slaves travelling through their township without a certificate.[255] This of course meant a colony-wide white police of all black mobility. Finally, and significantly, in 1718 Rhode Island became the only New England settlement to create

[252] Incidence of slavery in Rhode Island calculated from *HSUS*, vol. 5, tables Eg7, Eg46 (Rhode Island, total population, black population). Initially, Rhode Island resisted the encroachments of slavery. "Whereas, there is a common course practised amongst English men to buy negers, to that end they may have them for service or slaves forever; for the preventinge such practices among us, let it be ordered that no blacke mankind or white being forced by covenant bond, or otherwise, to serve any man or his assighnes longer than ten years, or until they come to bee twentie four years of age, if they bee taken in under fourteen, from the time of their cominge within the liberties of this collonie." In John Russell Bartlett, editor, *Acts and Orders Made at the Generall Court of Election held at Warwick this 18th of May, anno. 1652*, in *Records of the Colony of Rhode Island and Providence Plantations, in New England* (Providence, 1856–65), I, 243. The order was enforced by £40 fines. Edgar McManus calls the Act a legalization of slavery akin to the Massachusetts *Body of Liberties'* title on bond slavery, but this seems unsustainable on its face. See *Black Bondage in the North*, 59. It is obvious, however, that the attempt to discourage slavery failed. During the course of the eighteenth century, indeed, not only did the colony become the New England settlement with the highest incidence of slavery, but Newport displaced Boston to become the single most important mainland node in the Atlantic slave trade.

[253] On Rhode Island's police laws, see McManus, *Black Bondage in the North*, 73, 75, 77–8, 80, 83. As elsewhere, slave regimes were not constructed simply out of provincial law. Localities (the townships in Rhode Island) passed their own municipal regulatory ordinances as well.

[254] *An Act Relating to Freeing Mulatto and Negro Slaves* (February 1728/9), in *Records of the Colony of Rhode Island*, vol. 4, 415–16: masters required to post bond of £100 "to secure and indemnify" townships from the cost of supporting indigent freed slaves.

[255] *An Act to Prevent Slaves from Running Away from their Masters &c* (27 October 1714), in John D. Cushing, editor, *The Earliest Acts and Laws of the Colony of Rhode Island and Providence Plantations, 1647–1719* (Wilmington, Del., 1977), 206–7. See also *Records of the Colony of Rhode Island*, vol. 4, 179–80.

slave courts with summary jurisdiction.[256] In embracing this particular departure from regional practices that elsewhere did not segregate slaves in a separate court system, Rhode Island advanced furthest among the New England colonies to an elaborately institutionalized slavery regime.

The Mid-Atlantic Settlements

Both geographically and in character, slavery in Rhode Island sat, as it were, "between" New England and the mid-Atlantic settlements to the south. In both northern regions, slaves were to be found in household farm agriculture and in urban trades and domestic service. Unlike Connecticut and Massachusetts, however, Rhode Island developed a form of large-scale commercial agriculture, particularly in the stock-rearing and dairying Narragansett country. Here, slave incidence in general population rose far above the colony-wide eighteenth-century average of 7 percent, approaching 30–35 percent.[257] In this aspect Rhode Island was much more like the mid-Atlantic settlements. "Throughout the grain-producing areas of Pennsylvania, northern New Jersey, the Hudson Valley, and Long Island – the North's breadbasket – slavery spread swiftly during the eighteenth century."[258] In New Jersey, arable agriculture in the five east central counties bordering Raritan Bay remained predominantly small-unit in organization (50–400 acres) but had been reliant on slave labor from

[256] *An Act for the More Speedy Tryal of Such Negro and Indian Slaves as shall be found Purloining and Stealing, &c.* (1718), in Cushing, ed., *Earliest Acts and Laws of the Colony of Rhode Island*, 235–6. The courts' jurisdiction was township-based and extended to "all Negro and Indian Slaves that shall be found Purloining, Stealing or Thieving" within the town in question. Trial, adjudication and sentencing all obtained before a bench of the town's Assistants, Justices of the Peace, and Town Wardens, and required a quorum of two. The courts' jurisdiction did not extend to capital trials: they had authority to inflict only non-capital punishments ("Whipping, Banishing &c"). Though summary, jurisdiction was not final. Appeal might be had to the General Court of Trials by a convicted slave's master on posting bond.

[257] Incidence in population calculated from *HSUS*, vol. 5, tables Eg7, Eg46 (Rhode Island total population, black population). The colony-wide peak was reached in 1750 at 10.1%. The average incidence for 1650–1700 is 4.9%. On the Narragansett region, see Berlin, *Many Thousands Gone*, 55–6, 181. Berlin suggests that in northern regions like the Narragansett, country slaves might have constituted between one-third and one-half of the labor force. But Berlin offers no definition of "labor force," which (as we have seen) is a problematic concept in application to early America (see chapter 1, section IIA, and also n.263, this chapter). Douglas Harper, "Slavery in Rhode Island," states that in the mid-eighteenth century one-third of the Narragansett population was black. See http://www.slavenorth.com/rhodeisland.htm (accessed 22 August 2009). See also Greene, *The Negro in Colonial New England*, 104–8.

[258] Berlin, *Many Thousands Gone*, 180. O'Malley, "Beyond the Middle Passage," 159, 164–5, 166 (table 11) emphasizes Caribbean transshipment as the main source of slave imports to Pennsylvania and New Jersey, resulting in a 36%–64% split in total slave imports in favor of Caribbean sources. New York also imported slaves from Caribbean entrepôts, but overall its pattern of importation was quite distinct from its neighboring colonies, a 67.5%–22.5% split in total imports in favor of direct importation from Africa.

the inception of settlement.[259] That reliance grew with the extension of markets for farm produce. In Monmouth County, for example, the incidence of slavery increased from 9 percent to 12.5 percent over the course of the eighteenth century compared with a colony-wide average of 7 percent. Monmouth consistently accounted for about 16 percent of New Jersey's black population. The vast majority of New Jersey slaves were to be found in this core group of five counties, joined by Hunterdon County to their west.[260] In Pennsylvania, Ira Berlin reports a mid-eighteenth century shift in the principal locale of slavery from Philadelphia to its hinterland, notably Chester County, and to the more westerly and more distant Maryland border county of Lancaster, corresponding with labor shortages and growing demand for agricultural produce. (In both counties, both unit size and mode of husbandry were comparable to Monmouth.)[261] Certainly, between 1720 and 1775, Philadelphia's share of the colony's black population dropped from 70 percent to 20 percent. Still, one can be confident that Philadelphia remained throughout the single largest concentration of blacks in the colony. Philadelphia's slave population did not show a lot of variation between 1740 and the mid-1750s, then underwent a decade of quite rapid if uneven growth before falling again back toward 1740s levels. In the same period (1756–63) that Berlin reports Chester's slave population more than doubling, from under 300 to over 600, Philadelphia's slave population also doubled, from 1,214 to 2,366. In other words, Philadelphia's slave population was consistently about four times as large as that of Chester County. Even though the city's slave population decreased quite rapidly thereafter, it is likely that at least into the early 1770s there were still as many slaves in Philadelphia as in Chester and Lancaster Counties combined.[262] It seems incorrect, therefore, to hold that "on the eve of the American Revolution, slavery in Pennsylvania would be *fully* identified with the countryside," let alone that slaves were by then "the

---

[259] Graham Hodges, *Slavery and Freedom in the Rural North: African Americans in Monmouth County, New Jersey, 1665–1865* (Madison, Wis., 1997), 4–12.

[260] Calculated from *HSUS*, vol. 5, tables Eg10, Eg49 (New Jersey total population, black population), and from county census data reproduced as an appendix to McManus, *Black Bondage in the North*, 212–14.

[261] Berlin, *Many Thousands Gone*, 181. On small farm slavery in Monmouth County, see Hodges, *Slavery and Freedom*, 43–90.

[262] Berlin, *Many Thousands Gone*, 181. Nash and Soderlund estimate that Chester's slave population in 1765 was 552. See *Freedom by Degrees*, table 1-8. Lancaster County's slave population expanded more rapidly, but the expansion began later than in Chester and from a much lower initial base, and continued longer. According to Nash and Soderlund, Lancaster County's slave population grew "eightfold" between 1759 and 1780. 838 slaves were reported in 1780, suggesting a slave population in 1759 of approximately 100. Chester's at that point was still below 300 (293 in 1760). Philadelphia's was more than three times the size of the Chester and Lancaster slave populations combined. *Freedom by Degrees*, 32, 36, 38. For the Philadelphia slave population, see Sharon Salinger, *"To Serve Well and Faithfully": Labor and Indentured Servants in Pennsylvania, 1682–1800* (Cambridge and New York, 1987), table A.3. For the colony-wide black population, see *HSUS*, vol. 5, table Eg50.

largest element in the rural labor force."[263] That said, there is no doubt that slavery in Pennsylvania became much more dispersed during the second half of the eighteenth century than it had been during the first half, that urban slavery was relatively less important in the 1770s than it had been fifty years before, and that Pennsylvania slaves were increasingly engaged in rural pursuits.

In New York, one encounters a similar pattern of dispersion, somewhat more gradual in gradient and occurring over a longer period, but also on a much larger scale. Mid-Atlantic slavery originated in 1626 in the Dutch settlement of New Netherland, under the auspices of the Dutch West India Company. Effectively a company monopoly for the first fifteen years, slaveholding extended to individual settlers after 1640 and quickly spread to New Amsterdam's agricultural hinterland and into the Hudson Valley. Neither the Dutch nor their English successors had any more success recruiting migrant indentured servants than the New England settlements: throughout the colonial period, slaves were always the largest component of the bound labor force, urban and rural.[264] At the time of the English conquest, forty years after the first introduction of slaves, New Netherland had a total population of approximately 5,250, 12 percent of which (635) was black. New Amsterdam's population was about 1,875, 20 percent black (375). I have already noted that at this point some 20 percent (75) of New Amsterdam's blacks were free – a proportion that would not be reached again until the 1780s. Overall 60 percent of the colony's black population was concentrated in New Amsterdam, compared with one-third of its white population.[265]

---

[263] Berlin, *Many Thousands Gone,* 181 (emphasis added). On any reasonable definition of "labor force" (see Chapter 1 for discussion of this problematic concept), the second statement does not stand up. Consider that in 1775 the total population of Pennsylvania was approximately 283,681; the black population was approximately 6,808 (both calculated from *HSUS,* vol. 5, tables Eg11, Eg50, assuming a constant rate of growth 1770–80). The Philadelphia total population was 20,300; the Philadelphia slave population was 1,112 (taken from Salinger, *"To Serve Well and Faithfully,"* table A.3). Hence the total rural population of Pennsylvania was 263,381 and the total black rural population was 5,696. Chapter 1's discussion of labor force cited (n.47) Carole Shammas's labor force estimates, which for the mid-Atlantic in 1774 were 51.8–54.5% of total population (a lower-bound estimate and a likely estimate). On these figures, if the *entire* black rural population were participating in the rural labor force in 1775 it would constitute no more than 4.0–4.2% of that labor force. (An alternative upper-bound estimate using Nash and Soderlund's higher Philadelphia total population estimate of 33,290 for 1775 and their lower Philadelphia black population estimate of 842, both in *Freedom by Degrees,* 18 (table 1-4) and holding other figures and assumptions constant, adjusts the range of black incidence in rural labor force upward by less than half a percentage point, to 4.4–4.6%.)

[264] Harris, *In the Shadow of Slavery,* 15, 16, 32; Samuel McKee, Jr., *Labor in Colonial New York, 1664–1776* (New York, 1935), 90–7, 114–69; Simon Middleton, *From Privileges to Rights: Work and Politics in Colonial New York City* (Philadelphia, 2006), 21–2, 131–62. Joyce D. Goodfriend, "Burghers and Blacks: The Evolution of a Slave Society at New Amsterdam," *New York History,* 59, 2 (April 1978), 125–44.

[265] See *HSUS,* vol. 5, tables Eg9, Eg48 (New York total population, black population); Harris, *In the Shadow of Slavery,* 22. In 1790, free blacks were one-third of the city's black

During the first half century of English rule, New York's black population grew at much the same rate as its white population, averaging a constant 12 percent (in a range of 11.5–13 percent) of total population throughout. During the same half century, however, the black population became more widely distributed in rural areas. By 1700, the proportion of the colony's black population concentrated in the city had fallen from 60 percent to 30 percent; the proportion of the city population that was black had also fallen from 20 percent to below 15 percent.[266] By 1720, the proportion of colony blacks concentrated in the city had declined again, to a little over 20 percent, where it would remain until the 1750s before declining again to about 12 percent by 1780. Over the same period, the rate of growth of the black population of both colony and city equaled, even somewhat outstripped, that of the whites: black incidence in total population rose from an average 12 percent during the first half century of English rule to an average 14 percent over the second; as a proportion of city population it trended back from below 15 percent at the beginning of the century to 18 percent in the 1750s, before beginning a fairly steady decline to 11 percent of city population by 1780.[267] Slavery did not leave the city; throughout the century, New York City had the largest urban black population in the northern colonies; for the first half of the century (until overtaken by Charleston) the largest anywhere on the mainland. The city's whites, particularly artisans, "invested heavily in slave labor, and hardly any trade failed to utilize them."[268] Still, faster rates of black population growth in the city's hinterland and in the Hudson Valley signify even heavier investment there: in other words, even as the city's reliance on slave labor intensified during the eighteenth century, in the colony as a whole reliance on slavery grew faster. As a result, slave labor in New York, as in Pennsylvania, became relatively more agricultural in occupational orientation.[269]

Mid-Atlantic slavery formed a distinctive pattern; numerically significant in particular concentrations and highly diversified, with strong links to both urban proto-industry and commercial agriculture. To what extent

---

population. See Shane White, *Somewhat More Independent: The End of Slavery in New York City, 1770–1810* (Athens, Ga., 1991), 26.

[266] Calculated from *HSUS*, vol. 5, tables Eg9, Eg48; Harris, *In the Shadow of Slavery,* 22; McManus, *Black Bondage in the North,* Appendix (County Level Population Data, 1698–1800), 208–11. (I have produced New York City white and black population estimates from McManus's discontinuous county data by extrapolating rates of increase/decrease from neighboring years and/or using the same ratios as present in immediately contiguous years. These estimates should be considered no more than rough approximations.) See also Nash, *Urban Crucible,* table 13. The proportion of the colony's white population concentrated in the city also declined but rather less, from about a third to about a quarter.

[267] Calculated from *HSUS*, vol. 5, tables Eg9, Eg48; McManus, *Black Bondage in the North,* 209–11. See also Harris, *In the Shadow of Slavery,* 27, 46–7.

[268] Berlin, *Many Thousands Gone,* 180; Middleton, *From Privileges to Rights,* 133; Nell Irvin Painter, *Sojourner Truth, A Life, A Symbol* (New York, 1996), 9.

[269] Painter, *Sojourner Truth,* 6–7, notes the wide dispersion of the black population in rural New York counties at the end of the eighteenth century.

were these shared characteristics manifest in a common regional slavery regime?

Along with Carolina, the English mid-Atlantic settlements all originated as proprietary colonies established after the Restoration – New York and the Jerseys in 1664, Pennsylvania some fifteen years later. This was precisely the moment at which mainland slavery became inevitable, when mainland demand for slaves began to increase and supply to flow directly out of Africa. The Restoration proprietaries were crucial in this development. All their founders (not merely Carolina's) pursued the introduction of slaves and slavery more eagerly than had any previous founders of mainland colonies. One might argue that in the mid-Atlantic this represented acquiescence in facts already on the ground – non-indigenous slavery had been present in the region since the first Dutch settlements were founded in the 1620s – except that the English embrace of slavery was particularly aggressive, and the English understanding of what slavery entailed more severe than anything the Dutch had introduced.[270] The founding statement of local law for the Duke of York's proprietary, the *Duke's Laws* (1665), included a broad definition of who might be enslaved, taken from Massachusetts, that was stated in terms of exceptions, that is, who might *not* be enslaved: "No Christian shall be kept in Bondslavery, villenage or Captivity, Except such as shall be judged thereunto by Authority, or such as willingly have sould, or shall sell themselves," in which case a record of their servitude was to be entered in the local sessions court; nor was anything in the law as stated to be construed "to the prejudice of Master or Dame who shall by any Indenture or Covenant take Apprentices for Terme of Years, or other Servants for Term of years or Life."[271] New York proceeded over the following half-century to develop a slavery regime that extended well beyond the *Duke's Laws,* simultaneously making few efforts to establish European migrant servitude with anything like the rigor of the Chesapeake or Delaware Valley regions. In this, New York law complemented proprietorial and Crown desire to see the settlement become the strategic point of entry on the northern mainland for the Royal African Company.[272] That desire remained very much in evidence forty years later,

---

[270] Harris, *In the Shadow of Slavery,* 16–27; Higginbotham, *In the Matter of Color,* 100–38; Middleton, *From Privileges to Rights,* 21, 46. But see also Goodfriend, "Burghers and Blacks," 125–44.

[271] For the *Duke's Laws,* see section II, this chapter. (As indicated there, in the original draft the *Laws'* exception of Christians from slavery did not extend to "Any Negroe or Indian Servant who shall turne Christian after he shall have been bought by Any Person," but this wording does not appear in all drafts of the Laws.) The *Duke's Laws* were intended to have effect throughout the Duke's proprietary, thus extending ab initio to the territories that would become the Jerseys and Pennsylvania.

[272] Like its original slave laws, New York's master/servant law drew substantially on the *Lawes and Libertyes* of Massachusetts which, we have seen, sketched master-servant relationships substantially freer of detailed statutory discipline than those outlined in contemporary British law, or in the statute law of migrant servitude developed in the Chesapeake colonies, or that would appear in neighboring Pennsylvania. See Chapters 6 and 7. Proprietorial policy was to encourage the development of markets for slaves in the Duke's

as recorded in the instructions issued in 1702 by the Queen in Council to Edward Lord Cornbury, governor-designate of the provinces of New York and New Jersey:

> You are to give all due Encouragement and invitation to Merchants and others who shall bring Trade unto Our said Province, or any way contribute to the Advantage thereof, and in particular the Royal African Company of England.
>
> And whereas we are willing to recommend unto the said Company that the said Province may have a Constant and Sufficient Supply of Merchantable Negroes at moderate Rates in mony or Commodities, so you are to take especial care that Payment be duly made, and within a competent time according to their agreements.
>
> And You are to take care that there be no Trading from Our said Province to any place in Africa within the Charter of the Royal African Company, otherwise than prescribed by an Act of Parliament, Intituled *An Act to Settle the Trade to Africa.*
>
> And You are yearly to give unto Us and Our Commissioners for Trade and Plantations an Account of what number of Negroes our said Province is yearly supplied with, and at what Rates.[273]

The *Duke's Laws* and their endorsement of slavery extended to the Jerseys (formerly part of New Netherland). Originally included in the Duke of York's patent, the territory was quickly granted by the Duke to distinct proprietors, Sir George Carteret and Lord Berkeley of Stratton. They demonstrated their own interest in encouraging slavery within their new patent, "that the planting of the said Province may be the more speedily promoted," by including provisions for head rights in land for those importing slaves into the area of the proprietorship in their *Concessions and Agreement* of February 1664/5. Their guarantees induced migration of numbers of Barbadian slaveholders, amongst others, who settled around Raritan Bay, creating what would become New Jersey's principal region of slave-serviced commercial farming.[274] The division of the Jerseys in 1676 brought the

province. New York hence made few attempts to attract migrant servants. See Harris, *In the Shadow of Slavery*, 27–9, 32–3; McKee, *Labor in Colonial New York*, 90–103. As a result, the law of master-servant relations and of migrant servitude in New York remained undeveloped, confined to little more than reiteration of provisions already in the *Duke's Laws*. See *A Bill Against Fugitive Servants and the Entayners of Them* (22 October 1684) and *A Bill Concerning Masters, servants, Slaves, Labourers and Apprentices* (24 October 1684), both in *Colonial Laws of New York*, I, 147–8, 157–9.

[273] *Instructions for our Right Trusty and Well beloved Edward Lord Cornbury Our Captain General and Governor in Chief in and over Our Province of Nova Caesarea or New-Jersey in America. Given at Our Court at St. James's the 16th day of November, 1702, in the first year of Our Reign*, in Julian P. Boyd, editor, *Fundamental Laws and Constitutions of New Jersey, 1664–1964* (Princeton, 1964), 127–54, at 148–9.

[274] See *The Concessions and Agreement of the Lords Proprietors of the Province of New-Jersey* (10 February 1664/5), in Boyd, ed., *Fundamental Laws and Constitutions*, 51–66, at 61–3. On Barbadian migration to New Jersey, see Berlin, *Many Thousands Gone*, 55. For county-level data illustrating the long-term concentration of New Jersey slavery around Raritan Bay, see McManus, *Black Bondage in the North*, 212–14 (Appendix).

relationship between slavery and East Jersey into sharp relief, for after the separation (and after the finalization of a succeeding East Jersey patent to twenty-four Quaker proprietors in 1682) it was the East Jersey Assembly that began to enact statutes formalizing and institutionalizing slavery. None appear in West Jersey.[275] East Jersey began adopting slave laws as soon as the new Assembly was called into session in March 1682, amending elements of the *Duke's Laws* that protected servants so that they applied to "white servants" alone; requiring of owners of Negro slaves simply "sufficient Accommodation of Victuals and Clothing"; restricting slave mobility, and penalizing the harboring or entertainment of runaways. In 1683, the Assembly prohibited trading with Negro slaves. In 1694, East Jersey gathered its piecemeal enactments together in its first general statute, "An Act Concerning Slaves &c," which restated what had been enacted to that point and added restrictions on slaves' access to weapons. In February 1695/6, East Jersey adopted summary procedures for the trial of slave crimes that provided for convictions by two justices of the peace (one of the quorum) in non-capital crimes but required three justices to preside and a jury to convict in capital crimes.[276]

After the Jerseys were reunited in 1702 as one royal colony, the East Jersey general statute of 1694 and the 1695/6 trial procedure statute supplied the core provisions for a new colony-wide *Act for Regulating Negro, Indian and Mallatto Slaves.* Trading prohibitions, mobility, and harboring restraints and summary trial procedures all followed the 1694–95/6 model, with certain additions. Noticeable among the additions was a greater severity of punishment, reminiscent of Carolina legislation of the same era: summary conviction for theft of anything with a value over sixpence merited forty lashes; if over 5/-, forty lashes and also branding – with obscene precision – "on the most visible part of the left Cheek near the Nose." In the same Carolina tradition the Act also added castration to its repertoire, here to punish any slave convicted of any attempt "by force or perswasion to Ravish or have carnal knowledge of any White Woman, Maid or Child." The castration clause required conviction by a jury before it could be applied; this notwithstanding, the Act would eventually (1709) be disallowed in England because of it.[277] The 1704 Act also confirmed that no

[275] In fact, ch. 23 of *The Concessions and Agreements of the Proprietors, Freeholders and Inhabitants of the Province of West Jersey* (3 March 1676/7) provided "that all and every person and persons Inhabiting the said Province shall as farr as in us lies be free from oppression and slavery." Boyd, ed., *Fundamental Laws and Constitutions*, 71–104, at 89.

[276] Ch.. VIII, *A Bill for the General Laws of the Province of East Jersey* (March 1682), ch. IX, *A Bill against Fugitive Servants, and Entertainers of them* (March 1682), ch. IV, *An Act against Trading with Negro Slaves* (March, 1682/3), ch. II, *An Act Concerning Slaves &c* (October 1694), ch. III, *An Act Concerning Negroes* (February 1695/6), all in Aaron Leaming and Jacob Spicer, comp., *The Grants, Concessions and Original Constitutions of the Province of New Jersey [and] the Acts Passed during the Proprietary Governments, and other material Transactions before the Surrender thereof to Queen Anne* (Somerville, N.J., 1881; first edition Philadelphia, 1751), 233–9 (at 236–7), 239, 254–5, 340–2, 356–7.

[277] One might note that the Instructions of the Queen-in-Council to Lord Cornbury (1702) had included the requirement that he ensure "no Mans life, Member, Freehold or Goods

more than elsewhere would New Jersey recognize baptism as a basis upon which slaves might procure their liberty. Such was "a groundless Opinion, and prejudicial to the Inhabitants of this Province." Nor was there any place in the province for those who might be freed. Neither manumitted slaves nor their children nor any of their posterity were permitted to own, bequeath, or inherit land in the province.[278]

Several years after the Crown vacated the 1704 Act, the legislature debated and passed a new general regulatory statute, *An Act for Regulating of Slaves*, in March 1713/14.[279] This statute became the core enactment of the New Jersey slave regime. The region had been alarmed by a slave uprising in New York two years earlier; this apart, the 1713/14 Act did not respond to any qualitative change in the nature of New Jersey slaveholding. At the time of its passage, New Jersey accounted for approximately 24 percent of all mid-Atlantic slaves, up from 14 percent in 1680; the colony's "share" would continue to increase slowly through mid-century before leveling off. But demographically, New Jersey was undergoing no rapid transformation as a consequence: the incidence of slavery in New Jersey population as a whole remained constant at 7–8 percent. Densities were highest in the east-central counties, but not startlingly higher, for those counties were also where increases in white settlement were concentrated. Like the 1704 Act, then, the new statute remained within the pattern of the previous thirty years. Its core provisions were traceable to the 1694 and 1695/6 acts.

At the same time, like the 1704 Act, the new statute once more tightened and deepened New Jersey's slavery regime. Manumission was made extraordinarily difficult: free blacks being notoriously "an Idle Sloathful People" and a charge on the places where they might sojourn, masters were required to give security in the amount of £200 (with two sureties) that they would pay any manumitted slave an allowance of £20 per annum for life. The same was required of the executors of wills in which slaves were freed. If either master or executor failed to comply, the manumission was

be taken away or harmed in Our said Province, otherwise than by established and known Laws, not repugnant to, but as much as may be agreeable to the Laws of England." In Boyd, *Fundamental Laws and Constitutions*, 141.

[278] *An Act for Regulating Negro, Indian and Mallatto Slaves within this Province of New Jersey* (1704), in *New Jersey Archives*, Vol. 2, 28–30. For details of the disallowance of this statute, see *Documents Relative to the Colonial History of the State of New York*, John R. Brodhead et al., comp., 15v. (Albany, 1853–87), V, 157. The Crown did not make a habit of disallowing statutes that included castration as a punishment (see, for example, the successive South Carolina *Better Ordering* statutes detailed in section III, this chapter. Here disallowance may be explained by the absence of castration from punishment for rape in English criminal law. Where there was no English point of comparison, as in South Carolina's use of castration to restrain recidivist slave runaways, no intervention occurred.

[279] *An Act for Regulating of Slaves* (11 March 1713/14), in *New Jersey Archives*, Vol. 2, 136–40. Slave population figures calculated from *HSUS*, vol. 5, tables Eg10, Eg48–50 (New Jersey total population, mid-Atlantic settlements [New York, New Jersey, Pennsylvania] black population). For county population data, see McManus, *Black Bondage in the North*, 212–14 (appendix).

rendered void.[280] Simultaneously, the statute rendered it impossible for free blacks to live any kind of self-sufficient life by extending the list of property they were forbidden to own to include inherited property of any kind, any house or houses, and any lands or tenements. These additions apart, the Act's main innovations came in the realm of criminal punishment and procedure. In matters of punishment, explicit mention of the extremes of bodily mutilation (castration, branding) that had resulted in Crown repudiation of the 1704 Act was not repeated. Punishment for attempted ravishment was instead left to the discretion of the two justices presiding over the trial who were authorized "to Inflict such Corporal Punishment (not extending to Life or Limb) ... as to the said Justices shall seem meet." For the first time the 1713/14 Act singled out assaults on any free person "professing *Christianity*" for the same severe treatment.[281] Otherwise all noncapital crimes were punished by whipping in various gradations of severity. In matters of procedure, all non-capital trials of slaves were made summary *in banc* processes before two justices. All juries were eliminated. In its most interesting revision, the Act extended non-jury trials to capital crimes, embracing the special slave court of justices and freeholders pioneered in Barbados and adopted in Carolina. New Jersey required attendance of three justices (one of the Quorum) and five "Principal" freeholders, and seven votes for conviction: otherwise, New Jersey's new court was a faithful replica of Carolina's.[282] Too, New Jersey granted owners of slaves executed for capital crimes public compensation for the loss by district levy.

In the same session, the legislature also adopted a £10 duty on imported slaves, apparently with some desire to moderate the flow of slaves into the colony,[283] although it carefully exempted settlers importing slaves for their own use rather than for sale. The duty had a seven-year limit and seems not to have been renewed; in 1762, when a new £6 duty was imposed, the legislature complained that the absence of a duty on slave imports in New Jersey disadvantaged the colony in competing with its neighbors for European migrants.[284] Whether duties had any impact on slave importation or white

---

[280] *An Act for Regulating of Slaves*, 140. This clause was copied from New York's *Act for Preventing Suppressing and Punishing the Conspiracy and Insurrection of Negroes and other Slaves* (10 December 1712), for which see this chapter, nn.318–19 and accompanying text.

[281] *An Act for Regulating of Slaves*, 139. This provision, too, was copied from New York's 1712 statute.

[282] *An Act for Regulating of Slaves*, 137. New Jersey slave trial procedure was amended in 1768 to eliminate the special courts, found to be "inconvenient," and instead commit slaves for trial in the Supreme Court, Court of Oyer and Terminer and General Goal Delivery, or Court of General Quarter Sessions of the Peace of the County in question, each granted summary juryless jurisdiction in all trials, capital and non-capital. The amending statute made no mention of jury trials. See *An Act to Regulate the Trial of Slaves for Murder and other Crimes, and to Repeal so much of an Act, Entitled, An Act to Regulate Slaves, as Relates to their Trial for Murder, and other Capital Offences* (1768), in *New Jersey Archives*, Vol. 4, 480–1.

[283] See *An Act for Regulating of White Servants, and taking up Souldiers and Sea-men Deserting Her Majesties Service and Coming into this Colony*, in *New Jersey Archives*, Vol. 2, 140–2.

[284] *An Act for Laying a Duty upon Negroes and Mulatto Slaves, imported into this Province* (1762), and see also two acts "*Laying a Duty on the Purchasers of Slaves Imported into this Colony* (1767, 1769), all in *New Jersey Archives*, Vol. 4, 171–5, 435–6, 510–12.

migration propensities is unclear: the black population grew throughout the century but so did the white at similar rates, so that the incidence of slavery in New Jersey population remained remarkably constant. Nor did densities change much from patterns established early in the century that concentrated on the east central counties, with a slow spread westward. This "steady state" slavery called forth little additional colony-level legislation. In 1751, the legislature grouped in one statute three police prohibitions directed specifically at slaves, imposing bans on the sale of liquor to slaves and on gatherings of more than five at any one time, and establishing a nighttime curfew of nine P.M.[285] Otherwise the legislature contented itself by supplementing general police legislation (on matters such as deer hunting, trapping, and liquor licensing) with provisions – additional restraints, punishments and the like – specific to slaves.

Of the three mid-Atlantic encounters with slavery, New Jersey's might be thought the median experience. Demographically, New York was the regional leader, with 50–60 percent of the mid-Atlantic's rapidly expanding black population throughout the eighteenth century, a colony-wide incidence of blacks rising from 12 percent at the time of the English takeover toward 15 percent over the following century, higher in New York City where the colony's black population tended to concentrate. Pennsylvania in contrast was the regional laggard (though clearly not attributable to any personal lack of enthusiasm on the part of its proprietor[286]), its black population growing at a substantially slower rate than its neighbors for much of the eighteenth century.

Still, Pennsylvania was no laggard when it came to the construction of a slave regime. In fact, it was in important ways a leader, borrowing, adapting, and improving upon legislation already adopted elsewhere in the region, influencing its neighbors in turn. The East Jersey enactments of 1694 and 1695/6 provided elements for the Pennsylvania model: like them, Pennsylvania's *Act for the Better Regulation of Servants in this Province and Territories* (1700) underscored the distinction between white servants and black, punishing the former for various offenses (running away, clandestine trading, or embezzlement) by requiring additional service after the expiration of their indentured time, specifying that the latter, whose time of course never expired, were to be severely whipped.[287] The *Act for the Trial of Negroes*, passed the same day, also created a specialized

---

[285] See *An Act to Restrain Tavern-Keepers and others from Selling Strong Liquors to Servants, Negroes and Molatto Slaves, and to Prevent Negroes and Molatto slaves, from Meeting in Large Companies, from Running About at Nights, and from Hunting or Carrying a Gun on the Lord's Day* (1751), in *New Jersey Archives*, Vol. 3, 180–1.

[286] Gary Nash and Jean Soderlund report that Penn owned at least twelve slaves and favored slave labor over indentured servitude because slaves could be held for life. See their *Freedom by Degrees*, 12.

[287] Ch. XLIX, *An Act for the Better Regulation of Servants in this Province and Territories* (27 November 1700), in *The Statutes at Large of Pennsylvania, from 1682 to 1801*, II (1700–12), 54–6.

summary jurisdiction for slave crimes, as East Jersey had.[288] But the Trials Act improved upon East Jersey by introducing into the mid-Atlantic the familiar Barbados-invented special slave courts of justices and freeholders (in Pennsylvania's case, two justices and six freeholders) that all the Restoration settlements adopted seriatim: Carolina (1691), Pennsylvania (1700), New York (1712), New Jersey (1714).[289] The title of the Pennsylvania statute is deceptive, for it extended beyond trials to the police of weapons and assemblies: "any negro" convicted before a magistrate for carrying weapons without his master's license was to be whipped; any Negroes who met "in great companies or numbers" (defined as more than four) "and upon no lawful business of their masters or owners" were to be severely whipped.[290] Pennsylvania's Trials Act was also the point of origin for the region's poenal experiment with castration of slaves for attempts to rape, ravish or seek carnal knowledge of white women. But the slave courts were the Act's centerpiece. Their jurisdiction extended to "high and heinous enormities and capital offenses."[291] Their purpose was "speedy trial and condign punishment." Their process was summary and juryless, their powers absolute. As elsewhere, their creation stands as the key instantiation of slavery institutionalized as a distinct legal regime.

The castration clause got the slave trials statute disallowed five years later (though not before New Jersey had followed the example). The legislature promptly reenacted the statute in its entirety save only the offending clause, which it replaced with a poenal cocktail; the offender was to be severely whipped, branded, and sold out of the province, never to return on pain of death.[292] The revised Trials Act was perfectly acceptable to the

---

[288] Ch. LXI, *An Act for the Trial of Negroes* (27 November 1700), in *The Statutes at Large of Pennsylvania*, II, 77–9. A very similar statute appears among the "Laws Enacted May 22 1697," but the record does not include formal indicia of Assembly passage and Governor/Council assent. *Statutes at Large of Pennsylvania*, I, 225.

[289] Pennsylvania's Trials Act (1700) was also adopted in Delaware in 1726. See Williams, *Slavery and Freedom in Delaware*, 21.

[290] The language of the statute made it clear that all the "negroes" in question were slaves, for none is mentioned without the hovering "master or owner." Note also that the Act's ban on assembly in groups larger than four was put in effect at a time when the colony's black population was little over 400, amid 17,500 whites. The same ban had been enacted in New York some years earlier. See McManus, *Black Bondage in the North*, 73. In 1702, New York reduced the allowable crowd to three, in line with city regulations adopted two years earlier. See New York's *An Act for Regulateing of Slaves* (27 November 1702), in *Colonial Laws of New York*, I, 519–21, discussed at nn.318–19, this chapter.

[291] "Murder, manslaughter, buggery, burglary, rapes, attempts of rapes, and other high and heinous enormities and capital offenses." Lesser slave offenses (e.g., carrying weapons) were tried summarily before a magistrate. The specifications of process made no mention of juries. *An Act for the Trial of Negroes*, 77, 79. Rape was a capital crime in Pennsylvania only for slaves; white rapists were whipped and imprisoned. Castration for attempted rape was a punishment only for slaves (the penalty had first appeared in the 1697 draft law). White rapist repeat offenders were liable to castration but not for attempts. See ch. IV, *An Act Against Rape or Ravishment* (27 November 1700), in *The Statutes at Large of Pennsylvania*, II, 7.

[292] Ch. CXLIII, *An Act for the Trial of Negroes* (12 January 1705/6), in *The Statutes at Large of Pennsylvania*, II, 233–6. The legislature also took the opportunity to confirm that theft

Crown: Pennsylvania's slave courts would remain in place until the adoption of the 1780 gradual emancipation statute.

With the core of Pennsylvania's slavery regime in place, over the next several years, as the colony's black population increased fivefold, legislative attention turned to the control of slave importation. After the New York scare of 1712 focused attention on "divers plots and insurrections ... not only in the islands but also on the mainland of America, by negroes," the legislature imposed a prohibitive import duty of £20 per capita, but this was overruled by the Crown. So was a subsequent £5 duty that the legislature had limited to three years' operation.[293] But by then the legislature had taken to adopting and readopting the £5 duty through successive continuing acts, writing each statute to expire before it could undergo Crown review.[294] The legislature did not revisit general slavery legislation until 1726, when it enacted a hybrid statute *For the Better Regulating of Negroes in this Province.* The legislature resorted to a multitude of borrowings to supplement the colony's existing slavery regime, and in the same statute explicitly addressed itself to the colony's free black population, grown sufficiently numerous, it would appear, to attract attention in the form of its own police laws.[295] Supplements to the existing slave laws were brief: Clause I provided public compensation for owners of slaves executed under authority of the Trials Act; Clause II added a surcharge of £5 in import duties payable on any slave imported who had been convicted elsewhere of any crime or misdemeanor and sentenced to transportation, and created a reporting mechanism to acquire the necessary information.[296] The

---

of goods was within the slave courts' jurisdiction: thefts of £5 were treated as high and heinous crimes to be punished in the same manner as an attempted rape (the brand to read "T" instead of "R"); under £5 the penalty was – inevitably – whipping, at the discretion of the court, not to exceed the "severe" level of 39 lashes.

[293] Ch. CXCII, *An Act to Prevent the Importation of Negroes and Indians into this Province* (7 June 1712; disallowed 20 February 1713/14), in *The Statutes at Large of Pennsylvania,* II, 433–6; ch. CCXVIII, *An Act for Laying a Duty on Negroes Imported into this Province* (28 May 1715, disallowed 21 July 1719), in *The Statutes at Large of Pennsylvania,* III, 117–21.

[294] See, e.g., ch. CCXXVII, *An Act for Continuing a Duty on Negroes Brought into this* Province (22 February 1717/18, apparently never submitted to the Crown for consideration), in *The Statutes at Large of Pennsylvania,* III, 159–64; ch. CCXL, *An Act for Continuing Several Acts Therein Mentioned, Laying a Duty on Wine, Rum, Brandy, Spirits, Cider, Hops, Flax, Negroes and Vessels, until the Fourteenth Day of May, in the Year One Thousand Seven Hundred and Twenty Two* (24 February 1720/1, apparently never submitted to the Crown for consideration), in *The Statutes at Large of Pennsylvania,* III, 238–40; ch. CCXC, *An Act for Laying a Duty on Negroes Imported into this Province* (5 March 1725/6, expired before being considered by the Crown), in *The Statutes at Large of Pennsylvania,* IV, 52–6; ch. CCCIV, *An Act for Laying a Duty on Negroes Imported into this Province* (10 May 1729, apparently never considered by the Crown), in *The Statutes at Large of Pennsylvania,* IV, 123–8.

[295] Ch. CCXCII, *An Act for the Better Regulating of Negroes in this Province* (5 March 1725/6), in *The Statutes at Large of Pennsylvania,* IV, 59–64.

[296] This provision extended to slaves the earlier ch. CCXLVIII, *An Act for Imposing a Duty on Persons Convicted of Heinous Crimes and Imported into this Province as Servants or Otherwise* (5 May 1722), in *The Statutes at Large of Pennsylvania,* III, 264–8.

next six clauses of the statute were all addressed specifically to free blacks. Adopting the common regional language of condemnation of free blacks as "an idle, slothful people,"[297] the legislature enacted the same inhibitions on manumission as Massachusetts had in 1703, requiring bonds from owners or their executors to indemnify localities from the costs of supporting indigent manumittees. Other clauses provided that vagrant free blacks, adult or minor, were to be bound into service; that they might not trade with slaves, nor harbor or entertain them. Intermarriage was banned completely, and miscegenation of any kind punished. In its final five clauses, the statute embraced near verbatim two clauses from New Jersey's 1714 statute, addressing respectively slave mobility and harboring,[298] Massachusetts' 1693 ban on tippling and its 1703 nine P.M. curfew,[299] and finally for good measure South Carolina's frequently repeated attempt to bar slave owners from allowing their slaves to seek their own employment in exchange for remittance of wages.[300]

The 1726 statute rounded out Pennsylvania's slave law regime. Certain general police laws enacted thereafter contained provisions specific to slave offenders, almost invariably specifying that they should be whipped. Municipal ordinances added further layers of policing.[301] But none of these enactments nor ordinances appreciably amended the direction of slave law in the colony. By 1726, then, the regime was essentially complete.

By now it will be clear that the slave regimes of the mid-Atlantic were constructed as it were out of interchangeable parts.[302] Many of the parts were local, borrowings within the region, as suggested by the statutes' overlapping titles; some, however, carried the resonance of slave regimes that one might think quite unrelated to those of the mid-Atlantic, notably the mainland's premier "slave society" of Carolina/South Carolina and its Caribbean inspiration, Barbados. Patterns of intercolonial commerce, it has been suggested, help explain the transit of ideas.[303] So do patterns of intercolonial migration. As migration into New Jersey shows, Carolina

---

[297] See New Jersey's *Act for Regulating of Slaves* (1714), at 140, copied from New York's *Act for Preventing Suppressing and Punishing the Conspiracy and Insurrection of Negroes and other Slaves* (1712), in *Colonial Laws of New York,* I, 761–7, discussed further at nn.318–19, this chapter.

[298] See New Jersey's *Act for Regulating of Slaves* (1714), at 139–40. New Jersey's harboring clause had in turn been closely modeled on New York's *Act for Regulateing of Slaves* (1702), in *Colonial Laws of New York,* I, 519–21, discussed further at nn.310–11, this chapter.

[299] See *An Act of Supplement and Addition* (Massachusetts, 1693), and *An Act to Prevent Disorders in the Night* (Massachusetts, 1703).

[300] See, for example, the *Act for the Better Ordering of Slaves* (Carolina, 1701).

[301] McManus, *Black Bondage in the North,* 79, 96.

[302] To a degree the origins of slave law in the region thus replicate the origins of law in the region in general, in that the *Duke's Laws,* which provided the region with its jumping-off point, were themselves constructed out of interchangeable parts borrowed from elsewhere.

[303] See generally Hatfield, *Atlantic Virginia,* 1–7.

was hardly the only mainland Restoration proprietary to host migrating Barbadian planters and their slaves. To intercolonial mobility one can add spatial and temporal proximity. Spatial proximity helps explain the local interchanges among the mid-Atlantic settlements; temporal proximity helps explain the similarities between their slave regimes and the Carolinas. All the Restoration proprietaries encountered slavery on the cusp of its mainland expansion; none thought it novel; all encouraged its expansion to one degree or another; all made use of it. Though demographically and economically less significant – in the long run[304] – than in the plantation settlements to the south, slave regimes became well entrenched in the mid-Atlantic settlements. Mid-Atlantic slavery would resist eradication long into the nineteenth century.

These impressions of mid-Atlantic slavery can be solidified by examining the slave law regime of New York, the point of origin for and epitome of slavery in the region.

We have seen that New York fell to the English with slavery attached. As in what would become New Jersey, Delaware (here treated as part of the South Atlantic settlements), and to some degree Pennsylvania, Dutch and before them Swedish settlers had farmed with slaves. The *Duke's Laws* confirmed the entrenchment of a more severe genus of slavery throughout the territory ceded to the English in 1664, and the laws devolved with that territory as it was split into various smaller proprietary units until local legislatures framed detailed slavery regimes.

In New York, that legislative process began in the early 1680s. Promoted as a slave trading center after the English takeover, New York attracted relatively few transatlantic migrants. In the twenty-odd years between 1664 and the moment when English migration into the Delaware Valley got under way in the early 1680s, New York's white population doubled from some 4,500 to approximately 9,000. At that point Pennsylvania had fewer than 1,000 scattered inhabitants, mostly Swedish and Dutch remnants. Within a decade Pennsylvania's white population had grown by 10,000, to 11,000, while New York's grew by only 3,000 to 12,000. By the early eighteenth century, unsurprisingly, Pennsylvania had become the most populous of the mid-Atlantic settlements.[305] Significant migrant inflows and rapid growth rates throughout the century ensured that Pennsylvania's introduced population remained overwhelmingly European. New York, in contrast, lacked migrants. In 1699, Governor Bellomont told the Lords of Trade that those who sought labor in the colony had no choice but slaves: there were "no other servants in this country but Negroes."[306] Though not literally true,

---

[304] For most of the eighteenth century, New York represented the fifth largest concentration of slaves in the English mainland colonies (behind Virginia, South Carolina, Maryland, and North Carolina. Indeed, North Carolina did not exceed New York in numbers until the 1730s. In 1780 there were as many slaves in New York as in Georgia. See *HSUS*, vol. 5, table Eg41–59 (all colonies or localities, black population).

[305] Ibid., table Eg9–11 (mid-Atlantic colonies, total population).

[306] In Edgar J. McManus, *A History of Negro Slavery in New York* (Syracuse, N.Y., 1966), 41–2.

Bellomont's report was an accurate summary of New York's comparative disadvantage in attracting European migrants vis-à-vis the Delaware Valley settlements, and the consequences when it came to meeting local demands for labor. The colony had a black population of 1,200 in 1680 and well over 2,000 by 1700. By the early 1770s, New York's black population had increased tenfold, to more than 20,000 – nearly four times larger than Pennsylvania's. Its white population in contrast was roughly 150,000, not much more than half Pennsylvania's.[307]

Initially, rather like East Jersey in 1682 and 1683 (and Virginia somewhat earlier), New York at the provincial level constructed its slave law regime piecemeal, amending the *Duke's Laws* to bring slaves within the *Laws'* police of servants and of master-servant relations. New York's amendments were highly abbreviated: they simply inserted "slaves" into the same body of law that governed European servants wherever it seemed appropriate to do so. Thus, the Act of 1684 *Concerning Masters servants Slaves Labourers and Apprentices* simply reenacted the *Masters Servants and Labourers* title of the *Duke's Laws* (itself adopted virtually intact from the same title of the *Laws and Liberties* of Massachusetts) with additions dealing with slaves and apprentices. The *Duke's Laws* had prohibited servants from trading goods on pain of corporal punishment inflicted at the discretion of two justices, so the 1684 Act simply added slaves to the clause. It also added them to the *Duke's Laws'* runaway provisions. It did *not* add them to the clause that listed protections of servants against abuse and their means of redress. The Act's most extensive amendments to the *Duke's Laws* did not concern slaves at all, in fact, but focused on policing competition for apprentice labor in the artisan trades, enacting three new and substantial clauses intended to protect master tradesmen from those who would entice their apprentices away, or entertain them, or attempt to use them to embezzle or steal from their masters.[308]

Province law, however, was not the sum of slave law in New York. At the time the 1684 Act was passed, about 35 percent of the colony's black population (then around 1,400) was concentrated in New York City. Over the next quarter century the city's black population nearly doubled, to some 900. Over the same period, much of the detail of New York's slave regime was produced by the city's Common Council. As Leslie Harris notes, between 1681 and 1683 the Common Council adopted a series of local police laws controlling slave mobility and social life. "Laws prohibited slaves from leaving their masters' houses without permission, possessing weapons of any kind, and gathering in groups of four or more." Additional laws "forbade whites and free blacks from entertaining slaves in their homes, selling them liquor, or taking goods or money from them." In 1692, more

---

[307] *HSUS*, vol. 5, tables Eg9, Eg11, Eg29, Eg31, Eg48, Eg50 (New York and Pennsylvania, total population white population, black population).

[308] *A Bill Concerning Masters servants Slaves Labourers and Apprentices* (1684), in *Colonial Laws of New York*, I, 157–9.

laws proscribed slaves from making loud noises, profaning the Sabbath by
playing in the street on Sundays, or tippling. In 1700, yet more municipal
laws limited slave gatherings to no more than three persons and enjoined
masters to follow the Sabbath laws.[309]

New York took a decisive step toward constructing a provincial slave
regime in 1702, when the colony's first comprehensive slave law, *An Act for
Regulateing of Slaves*, was enacted. Pennsylvania had already taken the same
step in 1700; New Jersey (1704) would soon follow. The proximity of the
three suggests common awareness that the mid-Atlantic settlements were
experiencing a rising rate of slave importation, and in certain respects the
three acts reproduce the same agenda. Still, comparing the three, New
York's Act was the least similar. It confirmed familiar restraints already in
place in province or city law, such as bans on trading with or entertaining slaves. Explicit in its sensitivity to urban slavery, the Act extended the
New York Common Council's prohibitions on assembly to the province as
a whole, reduced the number of slaves permitted to gather to three, and
prescribed severe whipping for violators. It also prescribed severe penalties – imprisonment and corporal punishment "(not extending to life or
limb)" at the discretion of any two justices – for assaults upon "any ffree-
man or Woman professing Christianity,"[310] though it did not (unlike New
Jersey) adopt Pennsylvania's rape/ravish/carnal knowledge clause. As elsewhere, the Act plainly embraced a public colony-wide punitive regime for
non-capital slave crimes based on whipping, for it required that every city
and town within the province "have and appoint a Common Whipper for
their slaves"; that is, that they establish "whipper" as a public paid office.
Simultaneously, however, the Act created a devolved and private punitive
regime by endorsing the punitive authority of slave owners. "Hereafter it
shall and may be lawful for any Master or Mistress of slaves to punish their
slaves for their Crimes and offences att their Discretion, not extending to
life or Member." Slave owners, that is, were confirmed to possess a power to
punish slaves' "crimes" virtually as they saw fit without pretence of trial. As
another clause of the Act put it: "slaves are the property of Christians, and
cannot without great loss or detriment to their Masters or Mistresses, be
subjected in all Cases criminal, to the strict Rules of the Laws of England,"
a sentiment commonly uttered in the restoration colonies but normally
accompanied by the creation of slave courts enjoying a specialized summary jurisdiction. In 1702 at least New York seemed willing to eschew summary trial procedure, preferring summary private punishment.[311]

Subsequent New York provincial laws indicate a piecemeal development
of forms of summary jurisdiction amid a slave regime characterized by a
deep and at the same time somewhat casual cruelty. For example, the *Act*

---

[309] Harris, *In the Shadow of Slavery*, 33. See also McKee, *Labor in Colonial New York*, 142–4;
Middleton, *From Privileges to Rights*, 143–4.

[310] This provision would be copied virtually word-for-word in New Jersey's *Act for Regulating
of Slaves* (1713/14), in *New Jersey Archives*, Vol. 2, 136–40.

[311] *Act for Regulateing of Slaves* (1702), in *Colonial Laws of New York*, I, 519–21.

to prevent the running away of Negro Slaves out of the Citty and County of Albany to the French at Canada (1705) required only "the Oaths of Two or More Credible Witnesses before ye Court of Sessions of the Peace" for summary conviction. The process was casual – particularly in light of the cruelty of the penalty. All convicted runaways were executed.[312] The excuse was wartime fear that runaway slaves would give the colony's enemies vital information. The Act would expire after the war was over. Indeed the Act did expire. It was then renewed, being judged "of great Use."[313] In a different vein but evincing a like cruelty, the *Act for Suppressing of Immorality* (1708) required that slaves found by a justice to have talked "impudently" to any "Christian" be severely whipped.[314] More conventionally, the *Act for preventing the Conspiracy of Slaves* (1708) placed any slave accused of murder or attempted murder or killing ("unles by Misadventure or in Execution of Justice") or conspiracy to kill or to attempt to kill "his her or their Master or Mistress or any other of her Majesties Leige People not being Negroes Mulattos or Slaves" on trial before three justices, who were authorized "to hear and determine the same and put their Judgments in Execution." The procedure was summary, the penalty of course was death, and "in such manner and with such Circumstances as the aggrevation and Enormity of the[ ] Crime ... shall merrit and require."[315] In other developments, the legislature had earlier passed New York's "Negro Baptism" Act (1706) denying that Christian conversion could free a slave and adding the "condition of the mother" clause that – as in Virginia – protected white miscegenators while ensuring black slavery's heritability.[316]

[312] *An Act to Prevent the Running Away of Negro Slaves out of the Citty and County of Albany to the French at Canada* (4 August 1705), in *Colonial Laws of New York*, I, 582–4.

[313] *An Act for Reviving and Continuing an Act, Entituled, An Act to Prevent the Running Away of Negro Slaves out of the City and County of Albany to the French at Canada* (21 July 1715), in *Colonial Laws of New York*, I, 880–1.

[314] *An Act for Suppressing of Immorality* (18 September 1708), in *Colonial Laws of New York*, I, 617–18.

[315] *An Act for preventing the Conspiracy of Slaves* (30 October 1708), in *Colonial Laws of New York*, I, 631.

[316] *An Act to Incourage the Baptizing of Negro, Indian and Mulatto Slaves* (21 October 1706), in *Colonial Laws of New York*, I, 597–8. This matter is generally discussed at nn.180–87, this chapter. In the particular case of the mid-Atlantic, we have already noted the inconsistency in different copies of the *Duke's Laws* on the question whether the original draft's denial that freedom could be had by conversion to Christianity had been put in effect throughout the Duke of York's proprietary. In New York's case, however, it is worth noting the proviso to *An Act for Naturalizing all those of Foreign Nations at Present Inhabiting within this Province and Professing Christianity, and for Encouragement of others to Come and Settle within the Same* (1 November 1683) adopted by the first New York General Assembly, in *Colonial Laws of New York*, I, 123–4. The Act stated that "Severall persons of diverse forreigne nations professing Christianity, now are and for diverse years past have been actuall and settled dwellers and inhabitants within this Province under the allegiance of his Majestye of Great Brittaine ... and soe desire to continue and remaine and be naturalized and become as his Majesties naturall borne Subjects." It established means whereby naturalization might take place both for those already inhabiting and those ("professing Christianity") who might arrive at any time thenceforth. It specified that

Following the New York City slave insurrection of 1712, the provincial legislature revisited the colony's slave law regime, notably 1702's *Act for Regulateing of Slaves*. At this point, the rate of black population growth in both province and city was accelerating, and in both cases (but particularly in the city) had exceeded white rates of growth. Through the late 1690s the city's white population had grown more rapidly than the black; black incidence had fallen to slightly over 14 percent. In the colony overall it stood below 12 percent. About one-third of the colony's black population was concentrated in New York City. During much of the following decade all growth rates slowed, but by 1712 they had picked up again, and over the next ten years black incidence in city population would approach 19 percent, in the province, 16 percent. The distribution of the black population continued to shift away from the city; by 1720 fewer than 25 percent of New York blacks were in the city. But white population growth in the city was slower, explaining the rising incidence of blacks in the urban population. These demographic trends – rising rates of African slave importation, increasing incidence in both city and country populations – furnished the environment for the "scare" of 1712 resulting in the legislature's revision of province law.[317]

Somewhat surprisingly, given the fear the insurrection had excited, the 1702 Act was reenacted largely as it stood; the same bans, penalties, and allowances. Perhaps the Conspiracy Act of 1708 had already supplied the answer to extremity. However, two important new sections were added. The first completed the lockdown of blacks in slavery by enacting the extreme discouragements to manumission (manumitting masters to provide security in the amount of £200 that they would pay manumitted slaves £20 annual upkeep for life) copied word for word two years later by New Jersey.[318] The second completed the slavery regime's complex of specialized institutions by embracing the special slave court of justices and freeholders

upon naturalization all such would become "naturall borne subjects and shall have and Enjoy all Such privileges freedoms and imunityes, within this province as others his Majesties subjects doe have or Enjoy." And it provided that "nothing Conteined in this act, is to be Construed to discharge or Sett at Liberty any servant bond man or slave but only to have relacon to such persons as are ffree at the Making hereof" (123).

[317] These population trends are calculated from *HSUS*, vol. 5, tables Eg9, Eg29, Eg48 (New York total population, white population, black population) and from the city population data reported in McManus, *Black Bondage in the North*, 208–11 (appendix). For comments on the latter see n.266, this chapter.

[318] *An Act for Preventing Suppressing and Punishing the Conspiracy and Insurrection of Negroes and Other Slaves* (10 December 1712), in *Colonial Laws of New York*, I, 761–67, at 764–5. The discouragement was so extreme that in 1717 the legislature decided it would actually provoke slaves to run off or otherwise avoid "serveing their Masters or Mistresses truely and faithfully, as they ought to doe," and substituted instead the more common requirement that masters manumitting slaves (or their executors) post bonds with sureties to cover the cost of any former slave's subsequent indigence. See *An Act for Explaining and Rendring More Effectual an Act of the Generall Assembly of this Colony, Entituled, An Act for Preventing Suppressing and Punishing the Conspiracy and Insurrection of Negroes, and Other Slaves* (2 November 1717), in *Colonial Laws of New York*, I, 922–3.

exercising summary jurisdiction in capital cases already so familiar from examinations of other Restoration colonies – Carolina, Pennsylvania, and New Jersey. In New York the court was composed of three justices (one of the quorum) and five freeholders; convictions required the agreement of any seven of the eight; death sentences came with add-ons at the discretion of the court, as in the 1708 Conspiracy Act: "in such manner and with such circumstances as the aggravation and enormity of the[ ] Crime ... shall merit and require."[319] Pennsylvania had been the first of the mid-Atlantic settlements to adopt the Restoration model, then New York, then New Jersey in a copy of the New York clause.

The 1712 Act completed the assemblage of New York's provincial slavery regime. It was not quite the last word. The Act was revisited in 1730, its penalties adjusted and its provisions minimally amended (for example, the possession and use of guns and pistols banned in 1712 was widened to include swords, clubs, and "any other Kind of Weapon whatsoever"). Passage of the 1730 Act formally repealed the prior iterations of 1702 and 1712. Also repealed were hitherto distinct statutes – the Conspiracy Act of 1708 and the Manumission Act of 1717 – the provisions of which were incorporated in the 1730 revision so as to create a final, single, fully comprehensive statute.[320]

Noticeably, unlike the culminating Carolina *Better Ordering* Act of 1740, or Virginia's 1769 amendments, there is nothing in New York's final, single, fully comprehensive 1730 statute that even hints at a desire on the part of the master class to proclaim its own humanity, respectability, and wisdom in the conduct of its slavery regime. Nor would any such language be adopted in the years to come. New York seems to have preferred displays of brutality unmoderated by pretensions to gentility. That preference was well on display in the aftermath of the 1741 conspiracy scare (to which New York elites responded with a savagery qualified by none of South Carolina's acknowledgment of abnormality),[321] again in 1745 (reconfirmation of the summary execution of slaves convicted of running away to French Canada),[322] and again in 1755 (in times of "Alarm or Invasion"

---

[319] *An Act for Preventing Suppressing and Punishing the Conspiracy and Insurrection of Negroes and Other Slaves* (1712), 765–6. Note that although slaves were ordinarily to be tried summarily and *in banc*, a slave's master might request the slave be given a jury trial. No peremptory challenges to jury members were permitted.

[320] *An Act for the more Effectual Preventing and Punishing the Conspiracy and Insurrection of Negro and other Slaves; for the Better Regulating them and for Repealing the Acts herein Mentioned Relating Thereto* (29 October 1730), in *Colonial Laws of New York*, II, 679–88. For the weapons ban, see 687.

[321] The most recent account of the 1741 New York slave conspiracy is Jill Lepore, *New York Burning: Liberty, Slavery, and Conspiracy in Eighteenth-Century Manhattan* (New York, 2005). See also Thomas J. Davis, *A Rumor of Revolt: The "Great Negro Plot" in Colonial New York* (New York, 1985). For South Carolina, see section III, this chapter.

[322] *An Act to Prevent the Runing Away of Slaves out of the City and County of Albany to the French at Cannada* (14 May 1745), in *Colonial Laws of New York*, III, 448–9. In substance, the 1745 Act differed little from its predecessors of 1705 and 1715. In procedure, it conformed to the special slave court process created in 1712.

slaves taken up by any person more than a mile from their owners' habitation without written permission might be summarily killed by their discoverer without liability).[323] For signs of elites' maturation as governors of subjects, one searches the legislation institutionalizing the mid-Atlantic slave regimes in vain.

Conclusion

Those who celebrate the American Revolution and its aftermath as the beginning of American slavery's end do history no favors. At the outset I noted the centrality of slavery to the political economy of the Republic's great leap forward during the first half of the nineteenth century. Nationwide, the numbers of the enslaved did their own leap at the same time – this is hardly surprising – from somewhat under 600,000 in 1780 to nearly 4 million in 1860.

The temporary anxieties of wartime aside, emancipation left little lasting mark on the post-Revolutionary South Atlantic. There, slavery never stopped growing. By the end of the 1780s, fueled by the Founders' reinvigorated slave trade, it was growing rapidly. "Far more black people lived in slavery at the end of the revolutionary age than at the beginning."[324]

What of the "free" states? All of the mid-Atlantic states retained sizeable slave populations well into the nineteenth century. Pennsylvania's gradual abolition statute (1780) was – beneath its rather smug grandiloquence – so gradual that for nearly thirty years it freed no one from slavery or the involuntary indentured servitude that replaced slavery for newborns.[325] Pennsylvania had slaves into the 1840s. The state did not definitively abolish slavery until 1847.[326] In 1785, New York relaxed somewhat

---

[323] *An Act for Regulating the Militia of the Colony of New York* (19 February 1755), in *Colonial Laws of New York*, III, 1051–71, at 1061.

[324] Berlin, *Many Thousands Gone*, 223.

[325] Ch. DCCCLXXXI, *An Act for the Gradual Abolition of Slavery* (1 March 1780), in *Statutes at Large of Pennsylvania*, X, 67–73. The legislature esteemed it "a peculiar blessing granted to us, that we are enabled this day to add one more step to universal civilization by removing as much as possible the sorrows of those who have lived in undeserved bondage." But "as much as possible" was not very much at all – none of those living at the time in undeserved bondage had their sorrows removed, and their children yet to be born remained yoked by indenture until age 28. The statute abolished Pennsylvania's slave courts, but provided that slaves might not bear witness against freemen. Domestic slaves accompanying sojourners, temporary residents, and members of Congress from other states remained outside the Act's provisions. In October 1781 the legislature adopted ch. CMLIII, *An Act to Give Relief to Certain Persons Taking Refuge in this State with Respect to their Slaves* (1 October 1781), in *Statutes at Large of Pennsylvania*, X, 367–8, providing exemption from the gradual abolition Act of all slaves brought into Pennsylvania by refugees from the English – "virtuous citizens of America and inhabitants of states that have been invaded [who] are obliged, by the power of the enemy, to take refuge in this state" – for the duration of hostilities and for six months thereafter.

[326] For slaves in Pennsylvania through the 1840s, see *HSUS*, vol. 2, table Bb17 (Pennsylvania, slave population). On the gradual abolition process, see generally Nash and Soderlund, *Freedom by Degrees*, 99–204. The 1847 abolition statute was *An Act to Prevent Kidnapping*,

its discouragement of manumission and gave slaves "the privilege" of juries in capital cases, but failed to pass an emancipation statute. Rather, in 1788 New York prepared itself for the coming of the new republic by adopting a new revised comprehensive slave law that guaranteed slavery's maintenance and perpetuation.[327] New York City's slave population actually grew by 22 percent in the 1790s. The state legislature did not broach the subject of emancipation again until 1799, when it adopted a brusque version of Pennsylvania's 1780 statute replacing slavery with twenty-five (female) or twenty-eight (male) years of servitude for all children born of slaves after July 4 of that year. In 1817, those born before July 4, 1799 were declared free as of July 4, 1827. Ten thousand blacks remained enslaved in the state as of 1820, and even after 1827, state law permitted temporary and part-time residents to keep slaves in the state for up to nine months at a time.[328] New Jersey did not begin gradual emancipation until 1804, and like Pennsylvania and New York forced blacks born free into extended servitude. In 1846, New Jersey enacted an abolition statute that allowed all slaves then remaining in the state to be retained in "apprenticeship for life." Slavery continued in the state in this form into the 1860s.[329] In northern New England where slavery – outside Massachusetts – was sparse, declines were more rapid.[330] In Massachusetts, Chief Justice William

Preserve the Public Peace, Prohibit the Exercise of Certain Powers Heretofore Exercised by Judges, Justices of the Peace, Aldermen, and Jailors in this Commonwealth, and to Repeal Certain Slave Laws (3 March 1847), in *Laws of the General Assembly of the Commonwealth of Pennsylvania, Passed at the Session of 1847* (Harrisburg, 1847), 206–8. Among other matters the Act repealed 1780's provision that slaves could not bear witness against freemen.

[327] Ch. 68, *An Act Granting a Bounty on Hemp to be Raised within this State, and Imposing an Additional Duty on Sundry Articles of Merchandise, and for Other Purposes therein Mentioned* (12 April 1785), and *An Act Concerning Slaves* (22 February 1788), both in *Laws of the State of New York Passed at the Sessions of the Legislature held in the years 1785–1788* (Albany, 1886), II, 120–2, 675–9; McManus, *Black Bondage in the North*, 171–2.

[328] For New York City's slave population, see White, *Somewhat More Independent*, 27–55. (White shows that the late eighteenth-century increase in the free black population of New York City was not due to any decline of slavery, which continued to increase in numbers through 1800, but to migration to the city of unenslaved blacks and to natural increase.) For the state, see *HSUS*, vol. 2, table Bb13 (New York, slave population). New York's gradual manumission statute was ch. LXII, *An Act for the Gradual Abolition of Slavery* (29 March 1799), in *Laws of the State of New-York, Passed at the twenty-second session, second meeting, of the Legislature* (Albany, 1798), 721–3. For the 1817 delayed abolition statute see ch. CXXXVII, *An Act Relative to Slaves and Servants* (31 March 1817), in *Laws of the State of New-York. Passed at the Fortieth Session* (Albany, 1817), 136–44. The statute continued those then enslaved in a condition of slavery for a further ten years, absent individual manumission. The condition of slavery described in the Act was somewhat ameliorated compared with the 1788 slave law, but was still hedged about with restrictive police regulations. Children born to slaves prior to July 4, 1827 remained subject to the terms of the 1799 gradual abolition Act. Some would thus find themselves bound into involuntary indentured servitude into the 1850s. The delayed abolition statute permitted long-term residents (ten years) departing permanently to take their slaves with them and allowed slaveholding sojourners to keep their slaves in the state for up to nine months.

[329] Berlin, *Many Thousands Gone*, 234. *HSUS*, vol. 2, table Bb15 (New Jersey, slave population).

[330] Ibid., table Bb1–Bb12 (New England census region, Black population by state and slave/free status).

Cushing held slavery incompatible with the 1780 state constitution's declaration of rights, but the actual effect of this apparent termination of legal protection for the institution in the state was uncertain: in Massachusetts, and also in New Hampshire, "ambiguous judicial decisions and constitutional interpretations discouraged slaveholding without clearly outlawing it."[331] Connecticut and Rhode Island, meanwhile, both followed the mid-Atlantic's miserly emancipation model with its required servitude and embedded race controls. Each adopted the requisite statute in 1784. Rhode Island did not formally abolish slavery until 1843, nor Connecticut until 1848.[332] Overall, 27,000 blacks remained enslaved in the "free" states of New England and the mid-Atlantic in 1810, 18,000 in 1820, nearly 3,000 in 1830. Considering the United States as a whole, in 1800, 89 percent of blacks were enslaved. In 1860, 89 percent.[333]

Elsewhere in this book I have written of law as a technology of colonizing – a means by which designs, structures, institutions might be imagined, created, implemented, and implanted. One can think of the statute law of slavery precisely as an exercise in the employment of law as a technology of and for colonizing. Jurisdiction after jurisdiction drew upon an ever-expanding bank of resources to create a series of regimes amounting collectively to an Anglo-American law of slavery. The law of nature and nations supplied foundational ideas and general principles; the Tudor-Stuart police of population supplied instruments; local innovations made up for English law's insufficiencies and spread through developing channels of migration and commerce; a later transatlantic commerce brought self-edifying trinkets of legality and humanity, imported like London fashions by maturing provincial slave societies desirous of imagining themselves civilized. Dipping again and again into this box of treasures, legislators constructed bodies of laws where none such had previously existed (there being no common law *of* slavery, only adaptations of common-law concepts *to* slavery), bodies individually congruent to the specifics of time and place and purpose and population, collectively amounting to an overlapping sequence of regimes dedicated to the forced extraction of labor under

---

[331] Melish, *Disowning Slavery*, 1, 64–6. Massachusetts never enacted any final abolition legislation, New Hampshire not until 1857. For Cushing's decision, see *Commonwealth v. Jennison* (1783, unreported), the third in a series of cases known collectively as *Quock Walker Cases*. On the case and its ramifications, see Higginbotham, *In the Matter of Color*, 91–9; Emily Blanck, "Seventeen Eighty-Three: The Turning Point in the Law of Slavery and Freedom in Massachusetts," *New England Quarterly*, 75, 1 (March 2002), 24–51.

[332] Melish, *Disowning Slavery*, 66–74, 76; Berlin, *Many Thousands Gone*, 234; McManus, *Black Bondage in the North*, 168, 181. Slaves were still to be found in both Connecticut and Rhode Island into the 1840s. See *HSUS*, vol. 2, tables Bb9, Bb11 (Rhode Island slave population, Connecticut slave population).

[333] Calculated from *HSUS*, vol. 2, table Bb1–98 (Black population by state and slave/free status, 1790–1860: all census regions). On slavery as an effectively national institution throughout the antebellum period, see Steven Hahn, "'Slaves At Large': The Emancipation Process and the Terrain of African American Politics," in *The Political Worlds of Slavery and Freedom* (Cambridge, Mass., 2009), 1–53.

extreme duress from a population specifically imported en masse, then held in perpetuity, for that purpose. In some places the regime created lay heavily on the land, in others more lightly; in some it became mature in its brutalities, in others not. I have attempted both to describe the variation in regimes created but also to underline their essential common purpose through a genealogy of the statute law in which early American slavery was defined and institutionalized.

One can look at this genealogy of statutes and observe a specifically Anglo-American variation on "social death" under construction. One can also observe in each statute the bared desires of civility. For above all else statute law reveals the *imaginaire* of its authors, and in the statute law of slavery one encounters not simply the means to the social death of the slave but also the self-representation of the dominating master, he who stands over, whips, burns, dismembers, and destroys (if he so wishes) the enslaved body that is the object of his attention. In this regard, Anglo-American slave law stands very much in the tradition of Anglo-American colonizing as I have explored it here. Both master and slave are products of colonizing's "civilizing process," its declaration of war on brutes.

I have had little to say here of Anglo-American slavery as a social system, other than to describe its institutionalization as manifested in a series of legal regimes. As a social system, historians have judged, Anglo-American slavery was marked by "continuous, if unequal, dialogue, between rulers and ruled, dominators and dominated."[334] Scholarly commitments to human agency and to the "complexity" of all human phenomena virtually require that oppression breed resistance, that exploitation be met by fight-back that compels the oppressor to acknowledge the humanity of the oppressed. "Even a brutal regime could not crush the slaves' unquenchable human spirit."[335] No doubt. Still, as Patterson argued some years ago, denying slaves their humanity was never the purpose of slavery regimes per se. Not one of the regimes examined here relied upon defining the enslaved as non-human in order to keep them enslaved; nor did any of these regimes create slavery as a condition of existence that denied slaves' humanity.[336] Rather, slavery being "on offer" as an alternative to death, a conditional permission to continue to live granted the slave by the enslaver, at the enslaver's pleasure, the purpose of the regime was to construct the terms of that permitted conditional existence, the terms that defined what life on the cusp of death actually meant. The essence of those terms was as absolute a degree of control as (humanly) possible, expressed in some regimes systematically and comprehensively, in others haltingly and

---

[334] Olwell, *Masters, Slaves, and Subjects,* 6.

[335] Morgan, *Slave Counterpoint,* xxiv. For a description of slave resistance and revolt in Virginia, see Parent, *Foul Means,* 135–72.

[336] Patterson, *Slavery and Social Death,* 22–3. And see Walter Johnson, "On Agency," *Journal of Social History,* 37, 1 (2003), 113–24, and "Inconsistency, Contradiction, and Complete Confusion: The Everyday Life of the Law of Slavery," *Law and Social Inquiry,* 22, 2 (April 1997), 413–15.

piecemeal, but always control. Control of entry, control of life within, control of exit, whether by manumission or death. Slavery regimes established the means by which that category of humans named as slaves might be placed uniquely and absolutely at the disposition of that category named masters (or mistresses or owners).

Statute law expresses the desire of the legislator. Law placed on the books is never law one can assume is law in action. Both capacity and resistance mediate implementation. But desire has teeth, nowhere more so than in the Anglo-American slave regimes encountered in this chapter. Those unwilling to go along were to be tortured until they did. Those who continued unwilling would be killed. In English America, such regimes began to be put in place shortly after the middle of the seventeenth century. At that time their cords bound three thousand people into slavery. Two hundred years later they remained in place. At that time they bound four million.

10

Ending: "Strange Order of Things!"

Jurisprudence is the knowledge of things divine and human,
The science of the just and unjust.
>	Bracton, *De Legibus et Consuetudinibus Angliae* (c. 1240)

It is the first of its kind;
it is an astonisher in legal history. [Laughter.]
It is a new wonder of the world. [Laughter and applause.]
>	Abraham Lincoln, Speech in Chicago, (1858)

Amazement is not the beginning of knowledge,
unless it is the knowledge
that the view of history which gives rise to it
is untenable.
>	Walter Benjamin, "Theses on the Philosophy
>	of History" (c. 1940)

In March 1857, a half century after Benjamin Henry Latrobe's extension to
the original building had finally made room for the House of Representatives,
the U.S. Capitol was again undergoing enlargement, this time to accommodate the gathering swarm of legislators that for years had been arriving in
Washington from the states carved out of the new territories of the trans-
Mississippi west. On the sixth of the month, fresh from Buchanan's inaugural on the East portico two days earlier, a crowd gathered deep in the belly
of the building to hear the justices of the United States' Supreme Court
pronounce judgment in a case addressing precisely the terms upon which
westward movement would continue – *Dred Scott v. Sandford*.[1]

Chief Justice Roger Taney led off and spoke for more than two hours.
Though the din of construction should have been muffled in the ground
floor courtroom, it seems it was hard to hear him; but perhaps that is not
altogether surprising, for Taney was elderly and in poor health. Ten days
shy of his eightieth birthday, Taney was a decade older than the republic
for which he spoke, literally a child of the Revolution, born nine months
(less two weeks) after the English colonies had declared their independence. Taney had already been old, relatively speaking, when he became

---

[1] *Dred Scott, Plaintiff in Error, v. John F. A. Sandford*, 60 U.S. 393 (1857); Don E. Fehrenbacher,
The Dred Scott Case: Its Significance in American Law and Politics (New York, 1978), 1.

the Court's fifth chief justice in 1836; a close ally of Jackson's, handpicked by the president, he was the oldest chief justice ever appointed. It would remain his distinction well into the twentieth century. Twenty years on, his body was decrepit, but not his mind, nor, despite infirmities, his stamina. Only John McLean had been on the Court longer, and Taney would outlive him by more than three years, remaining stubbornly in place until he died in October 1864 in the waning months of the Civil War. Since the beginning of the century only one other man – Taney's immediate predecessor, John Marshall – had been chief justice. None but Marshall would preside longer.[2]

The *Dred Scott* decision stands at the convulsive climax and endpoint to the constellation of colonizing, work, and civic identity with which this book has been concerned. The decision itself did not fashion the constellation's end. Far from it. What *Dred Scott* offered was recurrence – the indefinite continuation of what had been. The decision stands as my endpoint because its recommended resolution of the bitter sectional dispute over slavery's rights to grow with the republic was rejected; and because what followed, as a necessary consequence of rejection, was not more of the same at all, but a jagged interruption – the Civil War.

Out of the war's maelstrom, a new constellation would appear. The republic would not stop growing. Expansion – so immanent a condition of American history – was too manifest a destiny to be stayed. But the shape of things after the war would be quite different from that which had prevailed before, for the war's destructive energies threw open "the most fundamental questions of economy, society and polity."[3] On that open terrain, a new *polis*, national in scope and nationalist in ambition, would encounter and in due course meld with new going concerns, industrial and agricultural. Conjoined, they would imagine, construct, and eventually consolidate a new economy. New migrations would be set in motion, new social and legal configurations appear. New zones of exception, foreign and domestic, would be discovered and pried open. New passions would be aroused, new ambitions fulfilled, new enemies encountered, new fears inspired.[4]

---

[2] Fehrenbacher, *The Dred Scott Case*, 1–2; Sean Wilentz, *The Rise of American Democracy: Jefferson to Lincoln* (New York, 2005), 363, 454; Christopher Tomlins, editor, *The United States Supreme Court: The Pursuit of Justice* (Boston, 2005), 520–21.

[3] Eric Foner, *Nothing But Freedom: Emancipation and its Legacy* (Baton Rouge, 1983), 1; Wilentz, *Rise of American Democracy*, 794–5.

[4] The developments alluded to in this paragraph have generated an immense historical literature. For a tiny sample, recent and not so recent, see Sven Beckert, *The Monied Metropolis: New York City and the Consolidation of the American Bourgeoisie, 1850–1896* (Cambridge and New York, 2001); Richard Franklin Bensel, *Yankee Leviathan: The Origins of Central State Authority in America, 1859–1877* (New York and Cambridge, 1990); John R. Commons, *Legal Foundations of Capitalism* (New York, 1924); Christina Duffy Burnett and Burke Marshall, editors, *Foreign in a Domestic Sense: Puerto Rico, American Expansion, and the Constitution* (Durham, N.C., 2001); Sarah H. Cleveland, "Powers Inherent in Sovereignty: Indians, Aliens, Territories, and the Nineteenth Century Origin of Plenary Powers over Foreign Affairs," *Texas Law Review*, 81, 1 (November 2002), 1–284; George

Three years after the war began – seven after *Dred Scott* – a public meeting took place in New York to commemorate the thirty-first anniversary of the founding of the American Anti-Slavery Society. It was May 1864, nine months since the slaughter at Gettysburg and the chaos of the draft riots. Totalized warfare was at hand. Grant's armies were pressing relentlessly upon Northern Virginia; the campaign in which Sheridan would eventually destroy the Shenandoah Valley was getting under way; Sherman was preparing for the siege and sack of Atlanta and his ruthless march onward to the sea. Perhaps the crowd that had gathered at the Church of the Puritans (George Cheever's church) in Union Square thought it would hear exultant proclamations of victory at last at hand. If so, it was in for disappointment. The words of the first speaker, Wendell Phillips, were of his deep unease – not about the course of the war but what would follow. "The vessel of state" had been overtaken by a "fearful storm"; none knew where shelter might be found, or when. Phillips spoke ritually of republican institutions, but not of their fortitude under fire, or their renewal in the time to come. Something different – a new and rougher beast – was in the corner of his eye. "The youngest of us are never again to see the republic in which we were born."5

M. Frederickson, *The Inner Civil War: Northern Intellectuals and the Crisis of the Union* (New York, 1965), particularly 183–238; Morton J. Horwitz, *The Transformation of American Law, 1870–1960: The Crisis of Legal Orthodoxy* (New York, 1992); Roger L. Ransom and Richard Sutch, *One Kind of Freedom: The Economic Consequences of Emancipation* (Cambridge and New York, 1977); Julie Saville, *The Work of Reconstruction: From Slave to Wage Laborer in South Carolina, 1860–1870* (Cambridge and New York, 1994); Martin J. Sklar, *The Corporate Reconstruction of American Capitalism, 1890–1916: The Market, the Law, and Politics* (Cambridge and New York, 1988); Amy Dru Stanley, *From Bondage to Contract: Wage Labor, Marriage, and the Market in the Age of Slave Emancipation* (Cambridge and New York, 1998); Christopher Tomlins, "The Supreme Sovereignty of the State: A Genealogy of Police in American Constitutional Law, from the Founding Era to *Lochner*," in Markus D. Dubber and Mariana Valverde, editors, *Police and the Liberal State* (Stanford, Ca., 2008), 33–53; Barbara Young Welke, *Recasting American Liberty: Gender, Race, Law, and the Railroad Revolution, 1865–1920* (Cambridge and New York, 2001) and *Law and the Borders of Belonging in the Long Nineteenth Century United States* (Cambridge and New York, 2010); Michael Willrich, *City of Courts: Socializing Justice in Progressive Era Chicago* (Cambridge and New York, 2003).

5 *The Liberator*, vol. 34, no. 21 (Boston, 20 May 1864), page 1, col. 3; William Butler Yeats, "The Second Coming," *The Dial* (Chicago), November 1920. Phillips warned of "A million of men" returning to civilian life "half unfitted for citizenship by the habits of a camp," of "idolized officers – the only available candidates for office for a century to come," of "military ambition biased toward military occupation – the grave of all free governments," and of the crushing burden of war debt, a "mortgage" on "the labor of the next half-century" that would "[rob] the laboring masses of the Northern states ... of just the surplusage which constituted its nucleus of intellectual and moral progress." He warned as well of the venality of fund-holders – "in the history of all free States the source of corruption and the grave of independence" – of a government become habituated "to the exercise of despotic power," and of its indifference both to the hatreds it had nurtured in the South and to the material and political needs of the people it had freed.

I. The Facts of the Matter

The dispute that ended up in Taney's courtroom had begun quietly
enough eleven years earlier, in April 1846, when petitions were filed in the
Circuit Court of St. Louis County, Missouri by two slaves, Dred Scott and
his wife, Harriet Scott. Each alleged that periods of residence on free soil
had rendered the petitioner a free person. Each sought leave to file suit *in
forma pauperis* against Irene Emerson, then the Scotts' owner of record, for
unlawfully detaining the petitioner in slavery.[6]

Dred Scott had been born in 1799, in Southampton County, Virginia to
slaves owned by the family of Peter Blow. Blow subsequently migrated from
Virginia to Huntsville, Alabama and thence, in 1830, to Missouri. Late in
1833, after Blow's death, Scott was sold to Dr. John Emerson, a military
surgeon from Pennsylvania, who would use him as a valet. Soon after the
sale, Scott left St. Louis with Emerson for Fort Armstrong, Illinois, where
they remained two years (1834–6). Early in 1836, Emerson was posted to
Fort Snelling, located on the west bank of the upper Mississippi River in
what was at that time the Wisconsin Territory, later (after 1838) the Iowa
Territory. Scott and Emerson arrived at Fort Snelling in May.[7] Harriet
Robinson (born c. 1820) was already in residence at Fort Snelling at the
time of their arrival. She has been identified as one of several slaves who in
1835 accompanied Major Lawrence Taliaferro, U.S. Indian Agent for the
Upper Mississippi River region, and his wife from their home in Bedford,
Pennsylvania to St. Peter's Indian Agency in the vicinity of Fort Snelling.[8]
Some time between May 1836 and September 1837, at Fort Snelling, Harriet
Robinson, then seventeen years old, married Dred Scott. The ceremony
was performed by Taliaferro, in his capacity as a justice of the peace.[9]

In April 1838, the Scotts left Fort Snelling for Fort Jessup, Louisiana,
where Dr. Emerson had been posted six months earlier, and where, in
February, he had married Irene Sanford. The Emersons and the Scotts
returned to Fort Snelling in October 1838 and remained there until May
1840, when Dr. Emerson was ordered to Florida. The Scotts and Mrs.
Emerson took up residence in St. Louis and Dr. Emerson traveled alone

---

[6] Fehrenbacher, *The Dred Scott Case*, 250–1. The larger dispute by which the Scotts' suits
  would be enveloped also began more or less at the same time, in the sense that the
  final, accelerating erosion of the antebellum constitutional order can be dated to the
  introduction on August 8, 1846, of the Wilmot Proviso in the House of Representatives
  by Congressman David Wilmot (D-Pa). The Wilmot Proviso was a rider added to a bill
  appropriating funds to underwrite the last stages of negotiations settling the Mexican-
  American War the effect of which was to prohibit the introduction of slavery into any territory acquired by the United States from Mexico. See generally Wilentz, *Rise of American
  Democracy*, 596–601.

[7] Fehrenbacher, *The Dred Scott Case*, 239–44.

[8] Lea VanderVelde, *Mrs. Dred Scott* (New York, 2009), 13–14. See also Lea VanderVelde
  and Sandhya Subramanian, "Mrs. Dred Scott," *Yale Law Journal*, 106, 4 (January 1997),
  1044–6.

[9] On the significance of the Scotts' marriage ceremony, see VanderVelde and Subramanian,
  "Mrs. Dred Scott," 1050–6; VanderVelde, *Mrs. Dred Scott*, 115–18.

to his posting in Florida, where he remained for approximately a year. Emerson then quit the army and returned briefly to St. Louis before moving with his pregnant wife to Davenport in the Iowa territory to establish a civilian medical practice. Emerson died in Davenport in December 1843. His will named his wife's brother, John Sanford, an executor. Her father, Alexander Sanford, was made administrator. Though uncomplicated, the estate was not finally settled for several years.[10]

When the Emersons left for Davenport, the Scotts, and their daughter Eliza – born in 1838 on a Mississippi steamboat north of the Missouri state line – remained in St. Louis on loan to Irene Emerson's brother-in-law, Captain Henry Bainbridge. A second daughter, Lizzie, was born at the Jefferson barracks in St. Louis, probably in 1845. (In the interim two sons had died in infancy.) Dred Scott likely remained in Bainbridge's service through early 1846, accompanying him on military service to Fort Jessup, Louisiana, and to Corpus Christi, Texas. He was definitely back in St. Louis by March of that year, however, because that month Irene Emerson's father, Alexander Sanford, hired both Scotts to the wife of one Samuel Russell. The Scotts filed their freedom petitions the next month.

The Scotts' suits came to trial in June 1847. Trial testimony failed to establish conclusively that the defendant, Irene Emerson, was their owner of record, and the jury found against the Scotts.[11] After extended procedural delay a new state circuit court trial of the original suits took place in January 1850, and resulted in a jury verdict in the Scotts' favor.

The outcome of the second circuit court trial was appealed to the Missouri Supreme Court, at which point Harriet Scott's suit was merged with Dred's by stipulation of counsel.[12] In March 1852, the Missouri Supreme Court upheld the appeal, effectively dismissing earlier slave state decisions supportive of freedom under like circumstances, notably its own *Rachael v. Walker* (1836).[13] In November 1853, a new suit was filed on Dred Scott's behalf in the U.S. Circuit Court for the district of Missouri, alleging that John Emerson's executor, John Sanford, now residing in New York, had become Dred Scott's owner of record (Sanford did not deny ownership) and that Sanford was wrongfully detaining Scott, a free citizen of Missouri, and his wife and daughters in slavery. In May 1854, issue was joined in the U.S. Circuit Court solely on the question whether, on facts agreed by counsel for both sides, Scott was indeed free. The court instructed the

---

[10] VanderVelde and Subramanian, "Mrs. Dred Scott," 1058–9; Fehrenbacher, *The Dred Scott Case*, 245–9.

[11] Fehrenbacher, *The Dred Scott Case*, 249. On the Scotts' reasons for filing suit, see VanderVelde and Subramanian, "Mrs. Dred Scott," 1060–83; VanderVelde, *Mrs. Dred Scott*, 229–32.

[12] On the significance of the merger of suits to the eventual outcome, see VanderVelde and Subramanian, "Mrs. Dred Scott," 1083–1120.

[13] *Scott, a man of color, defendant in error, v. Emerson, plaintiff in error*, 15 Mo. 576 (1852). See *Rachael, a woman of color, v. Walker*, 4 Mo. 350 (1836); Fehrenbacher, *The Dred Scott Case*, 250–65.

jury that the law was with the defendant, in effect replicating the decision of the Missouri Supreme Court, and a verdict was returned against Dred Scott. Scott's counsel filed exceptions, establishing grounds to appeal to the U.S. Supreme Court on a writ of error.[14] Three years later, a majority of the U.S. Supreme Court found (7–2) that the plaintiff in error (Scott) had no standing to sue. Inter alia it declared unconstitutional any limitation on the westward extension of slavery.

Begun in obscurity, Dred Scott's case would end in notoriety. During the eleven years the case was before this court or that, in one suit or another, it took on the appearance of a cork tossed on an ever rougher sea. The final verdict became the rod which, throughout the northern states, Abraham Lincoln used to belabor Stephen A. Douglas, their struggle for Douglas's Senate seat in 1858 the prelude to the larger unraveling of the republic itself.[15]

The first clear statement of what was at stake came with the Missouri Supreme Court's refusal, in March 1852, to uphold "the forfeiture of emancipation" visited upon Irene Emerson in the second state circuit court trial of the Scotts' petitions. Notwithstanding objections from the court's president that the question before it had been settled, conclusively, in "repeated adjudications," the court held that it was not bound to recognize in Dred Scott's years of residence at Fort Armstrong and Fort Snelling either an implied emancipation by John Emerson "from the fact of having voluntarily taken his slave to a place where the relation of master and slave did not exist," or as an emancipation effected by "the constitution and laws of other States and territories" to which the courts of Missouri were obliged to concede. "Every State has the right of determining how far, in a spirit of comity, it will respect the laws of other States. Those laws have no intrinsic right to be enforced beyond the limits of the State for which they were enacted. The respect allowed them will depend altogether on their conformity to the policy of our institutions." In this matter no respect was due: conformity to Missouri institutions was so far lacking in the laws of other jurisdictions that surrender to their application would require that the state's courts effect a confiscation of the lawfully held property of the state's own citizens. To yield before "the command of a foreign law" would mean humiliation. Here and throughout, the court stressed its sovereign duty to protect Missouri's citizens from menaces arising beyond the state's borders. Missouri was "surrounded by free soil" on three sides, bounded on the east by the free state of Illinois, on the west and to the north by territory subject to the prohibitions on slavery included in the so-called Missouri Compromise of 1820. "Considering the numberless instances in which those living along an extreme frontier would have occasion to occupy their slaves beyond our boundary, how hard would it be if our courts should liberate all the slaves who should thus be employed! How unreasonable to ask

---

[14] Fehrenbacher, *The Dred Scott Case*, 267–83.
[15] Wilentz, *Rise of American Democracy*, 734–44.

it!" Admitting that prior decisions in like circumstances had favored the slave's emancipation, the court held them nothing more than the exercise of discretion. Discretion was properly a creature of circumstance. "Times now are not as they were when the former decisions on this subject were made. Since then not only individuals, but States, have been possessed with a dark and fell spirit in relation to slavery, whose gratification is sought in the pursuit of measures, whose inevitable consequence must be the overthrow and destruction of our government." Such being the times "it does not behoove the State of Missouri to show the least countenance to any measure which might gratify this spirit." Nor in any case, the court added, should detention in slavery be considered a burden upon those detained. "[T]he consequences of slavery … are much more hurtful to the master than the slave." Slavery had civilized the "cruel" and "miserable" African. When at some moment yet to be "our slaves" might be returned "to the country from which they have been torn," they would as a result of their enslavement bear with them "the blessings of civilized life." It would then be clear beyond doubt that "the introduction of slavery amongst us was, in the providences of God, who makes the evil passions of men subservient to his own glory, a means of placing that unhappy race within the pale of civilized nations."[16]

By the time Dred Scott's case reached Taney's courtroom five years later, the spirit of the times had become only more ominous, the conflict between slave states and free only more intense. Taney acknowledged the stakes. The question brought before the Court, brought there for the first time, was "very serious." But the question had been brought "by those who have a right to bring it," and it was the Court's duty to meet the question "and decide it." In meeting and deciding, he would add a few moments later, the province of the Court was not "justice or injustice." The only province of the Court was the law.[17]

What was the question before the Court? Empirically the question stemmed from the Scotts' mobility; legally it had been brought by Dred Scott's counsel, on his behalf. But it was not Scott's standing ("right to bring") that Taney so readily recognized: his judgment would explain at length why, in fact, Scott had no right to be there as plaintiff in error, no effective presence, legal or physical, at all. The underlying question – the question really brought "by those who have a right to bring it" – was not the question whether a slave might challenge a master, but the question of the rights of the slaveholder vis-à-vis the constitutional order of which slavery itself was the long-established pre-existing condition. The reason the question was now before the Supreme Court was that, such being the nature of the constitutional order, it could be decided with conviction nowhere else.

---

[16] *Scott v. Emerson*, 582–7, 589.
[17] *Scott v. Sandford*, 403, 405. John Sanford's name was misspelled on the Supreme Court docket.

In one respect, however, the Scotts and the question the Court chose to address did have something in common, for like them the question was there because of movement – the ceaseless flow of population migrating into the immense tranches of land over which, successively, the settler republic created in 1787 claimed an inherited sovereignty, and from the changes that the movement of population had wrought in the sectional balance of power within the republic. Throughout the seventy years of the republic's existence, every westward colonizing thrust, every extension of settler sovereignty, had sparked debate over the place of slaves and slavery in the land area over which jurisdiction was claimed.

An initial and quite durable consensus acknowledged slavery in those regions where it already existed and excluded it, at least formally, from those where it had made no substantial appearance. Thus, the Northwest Ordinance agreed by the Confederation Congress in 1787 purported to exclude slavery from the 260,000 square miles of sparsely settled land lying north of the Ohio River and east of the Mississippi claimed severally by the successor states of Massachusetts, Connecticut, New York, and Virginia on the basis of their colonial charters, and ceded by them during the 1780s for the common benefit of all those former colonies that had united as states by subscribing to the Articles of Confederation. Three years later, the new United States Congress passed the kindred Southwest Ordinance (1790), organizing the less extensive claims to land (some 40,000 square miles) lying south of the Ohio River and east of the Mississippi ceded to the U.S. government by North Carolina. The terms of the Southwest Ordinance were identical to the Northwest Ordinance, save only that it lacked any prohibition on slavery. Settlement and slavery were already well established immediately to the north of the Southwest Territory in the Kentucky region of Virginia, admitted to the Union as a separate state in 1792. The Southwest Territory, like Kentucky thickly settled and with slavery well-established, was itself admitted to the Union in 1796 as the state of Tennessee. Remaining lands south of Tennessee and east of the Mississippi lying within the ambit of claims made by the former colony of Georgia would be organized as the slaveholding Mississippi Territory in 1798. The states of Mississippi and Alabama formed from the Mississippi Territory would be admitted in 1817 and 1819, roughly in sequence with the states of Indiana (1816) and Illinois (1818) formed from the Northwest Territory. All told, the southwestern territories east of the Mississippi claimed by former English colonies and organized under slaveholding regimes after the creation of the first republic amounted in extent to some 180,000 square miles. A further 65,000 square miles of former Spanish Florida became the Florida Territory in 1822, eventually admitted to the Union as the slave state of Florida in 1845.

Thomas Jefferson's purchase of the French territory of Louisiane in 1803 doubled the continental land area claimed by the United States. The purchase added roughly 830,000 square miles, from the mouth of the Mississippi to an indeterminate line above the 49th parallel and from the

Mississippi River to the Continental Divide, to the land area claimed by the original thirteen states over which the United States already asserted an overall jurisdiction. Jefferson was in doubt of the constitutionality of an acquisition of territory beyond the bounds of the territories claimed by the original thirteen states. His doubts were shared in New England. In debate some years later over the admission of Louisiana, the Massachusetts Federalist Josiah Quincy would inform the House of Representatives that "The proportion of the political weight of each sovereign State, constituting this Union, depends upon the number of the States which have a voice under the compact. This number the Constitution permits us to multiply at pleasure, within the limits of the original United States; observing only the expressed limitations in the Constitution. But when in order to increase your power of augmenting this number you pass the old limits, you are guilty of a violation of the Constitution." It was "a fundamental principle, that the proportion of political power, subject only to the internal modifications permitted by the Constitution, is an inalienable, essential, intangible right. When it is touched, the fabric is annihilated."[18] But Southern sentiment, then nationalist and expansive, was fully in favor. African slavery had already been established in the southern region of the purchase under antecedent Spanish and French colonial regimes; the terms of purchase ensured its continuation by guaranteeing existing inhabitants "free enjoyment" of their property. Jefferson helpfully proffered a model slave code. By the time of the purchase, writes Fehrenbacher, "it had already become the accepted rule that slavery was legal in any federal territory from which it had *not* been excluded by federal law."[19] Organization of the purchase into two territories – a southern Orleans Territory approximating the land area of the state of Louisiana, the vast remainder (780,000 square miles) renamed the Louisiana Territory – proceeded without significant or lasting restraint on the spread of slavery, and slaveholders migrated with settlement northward up the west bank of the Mississippi as far as St. Louis. On admission of Louisiana as a slave state in 1812, the Louisiana Territory was reorganized as the Missouri Territory, again without any mention of slavery exclusion. In 1819, however, proposals to admit Missouri as a slaveholding state and to organize the Arkansas territory without imposition of limits on slavery excited opposition, leading eventually to the trade-off admission of Maine (1820) and Missouri (1821), and the exclusion of slavery from the remainder of the Louisiana Purchase north of the Arkansas Territory's border at 36°30' (the new state of Missouri excepted). The whole network of bargains comprised the famous Missouri Compromise.

---

[18] Annals of Congress, House of Representatives, 11th Cong. 3rd Sess. (January 1811) 535, 537, and see generally 526–37; Mark A. Graber, *Dred Scott and the Problem of Constitutional Evil* (Cambridge and New York, 2006), 118–19.

[19] Don E. Fehrenbacher, *The Slaveholding Republic: An Account of the United States Government's Relations to Slavery*, completed and edited by Ward M. McAfee (New York, 2001), 260 (emphasis added).

The Missouri Compromise effectively governed the disposition of U.S. territory for the next three decades. Throughout, population continued to press westward, but relative to the republic's first three decades, settlement densities shifted substantially from the southwest to the northwest. After a fifteen-year hiatus, admission of states beginning with Arkansas in 1836 balanced southern against northern sectional interests, as indeed had been the case, less formally, since the admission of Louisiana in 1812. Thus, Arkansas (1836) was followed by Michigan (1837); Florida and Texas (1845) by Iowa and Wisconsin (1846, 1848). Trade-offs notwithstanding, sustained rapid northern population growth meant growing economic and political ascendancy for northern interests. Throughout, northern state and territorial populations became increasingly antagonistic to the expansion of slavery, though popular antipathy was mostly racial in motivation, directed at blacks whether enslaved or free.[20]

The year 1846 brought a new expansion crisis, grounded on the territorial bounties of the Mexican-American War, in the shape of the Wilmot Proviso, the attempt by northern Democrats in Congress to exclude slavery from any and all lands acquired by the United States by treaty from the Republic of Mexico. From this moment on, slavery would remain securely lodged in the throat of national politics. New sectional trade-offs steered by the increasingly influential Senator Stephen A. Douglas (D-Illinois) addressed the question of slavery within the limits of the lands (another 500,000 square miles) ceded by Mexico in the 1848 Treaty of Guadalupe-Hidalgo by admitting California as a free state (1850) and organizing the New Mexico and Utah Territories without mention of slavery exclusion, leaving the matter to be decided (Douglas's particular innovation) by popular vote. Simultaneously, the domestic slave trade in the District of Columbia was ended and a strict federal fugitive slave law was passed. Though the Utah Territory was of course north of 36°30′ (as indeed was the Oregon Territory, organized in 1848), it was not within the limits of the Louisiana Purchase. In 1854, however, Douglas's Kansas-Nebraska Act organized territory within the Louisiana Purchase west and north of Missouri without regard for the terms of the Missouri Compromise of 1820, leaving the question of slavery exclusion there for decision by "popular sovereignty" on the Utah/New Mexico model. Popular sovereignty might produce majorities in either direction, of course, but it was entirely clear that the Kansas-Nebraska Act had rendered the Missouri Compromise's prohibition on slavery within the Louisiana Purchase north of 36°30′ null and void.

An unremitting thirst for new land and the contradictions attending its settlement, then, were the backdrop to the "dark and fell spirit" by which the Missouri Supreme Court felt threatened in 1852.[21] In the gathering

---

[20] Ibid., 266. On the significance of shifting settlement densities, see Graber, *Dred Scott*, 114.

[21] In 1838, John Quincy Adams had compared "the rapacity with which the members of all the new states fly at the public lands" to "the thirst of a tiger for blood." See Henry Adams, *The Degradation of the Democratic Dogma* (New York, 1919), 31.

storm of sectional discord, the essential question had become, precisely, who could go where. The judgment that Taney read to the crowd in his basement courtroom was intended to exorcise the spirit, to remind his audience of the historical and legal foundations upon which their fore-bears had agreed to pursue a mutual interest in loco-motion, and to secure their continuance. A judicial resolution of the republic's crisis had been promised for some years.[22] Crafting it required that the Scotts remain slaves. Indeed, it required a declaration that the opportunity to enslave was free to grow unconfined. Though this might strike some in the audience as unfortunate, it was surely a matter of far less import than the survival of the republic that the European settlers from whom they were all descended had worked so hard to create. It was, after all, an essential premise of the Chief Justice's argument, one he had good reason to believe was widely enough shared in popular opinion to be relatively uncontroversial, that in the republic the settlers had created the Scotts and their kind had always been held "so far inferior that they had no rights which the white man was bound to respect."[23]

In *Dred Scott v. Sandford*, Roger Taney's opinion for the Court found that Scott had no standing to sue for his freedom in federal courts because he was "a negro, whose ancestors were imported into this country, and sold as slaves," and that as such he was socially and civically dead, not "a member of the political community formed and brought into existence by the Constitution of the United States," hence not entitled to "the rights and privileges and immunities, guarantied by that instrument to the citizen."[24] Two of the eight associate justices disagreed. John McLean thought the matter of Scott's civic standing rather one of "taste" than of law. "On the question of citizenship ... we have not been very fastidious. Under the late treaty with Mexico, we have made citizens of all grades, combinations and colors."[25] Benjamin Curtis told the Court that at the time the Articles of Confederation were ratified, "free native-born inhabitants of the States of New Hampshire, Massachusetts, New York, New Jersey, and North Carolina, though descended from African slaves," had been citizens of those states, and that nothing had transpired in the formation and ratification of the federal constitution to except those inhabitants from enjoyment of the privileges and immunities of United States citizenship.[26] The other six associate justices either agreed with Taney or did not voice disagreement. One, Justice Peter Daniel, marveled at the "magic" by which one previously a slave might allegedly, by mere emancipation, without positive act of law – without "co-operation or warrant of the Government" – become a citizen "perhaps in opposition to its policy or its guaranties."[27]

[22] Fehrenbacher, *The Slaveholding Republic*, 280.
[23] *Scott v. Sandford*, 393, 407.
[24] Ibid., 403.
[25] Ibid., 533. As we shall see, McLean was mistaken.
[26] Ibid., 572–3.
[27] Ibid., 477.

Second, Taney found that the institution of slavery, perfectly lawful throughout much of the United States, might not lawfully be excluded from any of the territories that the United States acquired on the behalf and for the use of all its citizens. The exclusion of slavery from the Northwest Territory had been the work of the Confederation Congress. "The new Government took the territory as it found it, and in the condition in which it was transferred, and did not attempt to undo anything that had been done."[28] Nor had the new government power to do anything else: constitutional empowerment of Congress "to dispose of and make all needful Rules and Regulations respecting the Territory or other Property ... belonging to the United States"[29] was not such a power as extended to such fundamental sovereign acts as control of citizens' egress and access to territory with their property. Nor could territorial governments exercise a greater power in making needful rules and regulations than their federal creator. Nor in any case did that power extend beyond the original limits of the United States. Congressional power in general – such as the power "to acquire territory outside of the original limits of the United States, and what powers it may exercise therein over the person or property of a citizen of the United States, while it remains a Territory" – was exercised "by the General Government as the representative and trustee of the people of the United States ... for their common and equal benefit"[30] and subject to the strict limitations of the Constitution itself, notably in this case the Fifth Amendment's prohibitions of any deprivation of life, liberty, or property without due process of law.

Here too, six of the associate justices agreed with the Chief Justice in all essentials while McLean and Curtis dissented. Both stressed that though the Northwest Ordinance had been passed by the Confederation Congress it had been implemented and administered by the U.S. Congress, which they took to be good evidence that the territories clause empowered Congress to make laws, rules, and regulations tending to prohibit slavery. Both also insisted that the acquisition of new territories beyond the limits of the United States as they were in 1787 had been anticipated by the framers who had therefore intended the territories clause to convey broad powers to make and administer new acquisitions as well as existing territories. Nor, added Curtis, could any substantive protection of property be found in the Fifth Amendment, but only a due process right. "A citizen of the United States owns slaves in Cuba, and brings them to the United States, where they are set free by the legislation of Congress. Does this legislation deprive him of his property without due process of law? If so, what becomes of the laws prohibiting the slave trade? If not, how can a similar regulation respecting a Territory violate the fifth amendment of the Constitution?"[31]

---

[28] Ibid., 438.
[29] U.S. Constitution, art. IV, §3, cl. 2.
[30] *Scott v. Sandford*, 393, 446, 447–8, 450.
[31] Ibid., 627.

Reaction to the decision reproduced the deadlock that Taney had intended to cut through. Democratic Party sources defended the Court; Republican sources vilified it. Alluding to the decision in his First Inaugural address, four years later, Abraham Lincoln vacated it. "I do not forget the position, assumed by some, that constitutional questions are to be decided by the Supreme Court; nor do I deny that such decisions must be binding, in any case, upon the parties to a suit, as to the object of that suit, while they are also entitled to very high respect and consideration in all parallel cases by all other departments of the government ... At the same time, the candid citizen must confess that if the policy of the government, upon vital questions affecting the whole people, is to be irrevocably fixed by decisions of the Supreme Court, the instant they are made, in ordinary litigation between parties in personal actions, the people will have ceased to be their own rulers, having to that extent practically resigned their government into the hands of that eminent tribunal."[32] Taney had characterized his opinion as a statement of the Court's duty to act within the province of the law, to apply the Constitution as framed, "to administer it as we find it." Lincoln's response was to declare the law's insufficiency and confine the Court's import by turning for comprehension of the Constitution to popular majorities. "Shall fugitives from labor be surrendered by national or by State authority? The Constitution does not expressly say. *May* Congress prohibit slavery in the Territories? The Constitution does not expressly say. *Must* Congress protect slavery in the Territories? The Constitution does not expressly say. From questions of this class spring all our constitutional controversies, and we divide upon them into majorities and minorities. If the minority will not acquiesce, the majority must, or the government must cease. There is no other alternative; for continuing the Government is acquiescence on one side or the other."[33] As far as Lincoln was concerned, the 1860 election had established who was in the majority. Well before his inauguration Lincoln had already made it clear the majority would not acquiesce.[34]

The *Dred Scott* decision, indelibly associated with Roger Taney, has been vilified by generations of American constitutional lawyers and historians as "the most infamous decision in American constitutional history."[35] In Cass Sunstein's view, for example, it was "an abomination."[36] Don

---

[32] Abraham Lincoln, "First Inaugural Address" (March 4, 1861), in Marion Mills Miller, editor, *Life and Works of Abraham Lincoln* (New York, 1907), V, 142–3.

[33] *Scott v. Sandford*, 405; Lincoln, "First Inaugural Address," 141.

[34] Wilentz, *Rise of American Democracy*, 779–88. On the role of the *Dred Scott* decision in the final crisis of 1860–1, see Louise Weinberg, "*Dred Scott* and the Crisis of 1860," *Chicago-Kent Law Review*, 82, 1 (2007), 97–140.

[35] Paul Finkelman, "The Taney Court, 1836–64: The Jurisprudence of Slavery and the Crisis of the Union," in Tomlins, ed., *The United States Supreme Court*, 98.

[36] Cass R. Sunstein, "Dred Scott and its Legacy," in Robert P. George, editor, *Great Cases in Constitutional Law* (Princeton, 2000), 86, 87. Sunstein adds that the decision was "reckless and wrong" (75), "a blunder and an abuse" (78), an exercise in judicial casuistry (79) that failed to decide what it "should" have decided: "freed slaves should have qualified as citizens" (86).

Fehrenbacher's comparatively more restrained assessment is that Taney's opinion was "weak in its law, logic, history, and factual accuracy."[37] This is but a tiny sampling of a large volume of opinion.

It is worth noting, therefore, a dissenting voice, raised some 150 years after the event, that speaks against the consensus and in defense of the Court's decision. In *Dred Scott and the Problem of Constitutional Evil* (2006), Mark Graber has observed that the majority's substantive conclusion – "that slavery could not be banned in the territories and that former slaves could not be American citizens" – had at least as much legal, logical, historical, and factual support as the position taken by the minority. More important, the views of the court majority were faithful to the dominant traditions of antebellum constitutionalism, restated by Graber with admirable clarity as a single cold equation. "In order to form 'a more perfect union' with slaveholders, citizens in the late eighteenth century fashioned a constitution that plainly compelled some injustices and was silent or ambiguous on other questions of fundamental rights. The constitutional relationships thus forged could survive only as long as a bisectional consensus was required to resolve all constitutional questions not settled in 1787." The republic's foundational commitment to bisectionalism, Graber continues, "meant that crucial (not all) political elites in both the free and slave states had to approve all constitutional settlements on slavery issues. Human bondage under these conditions could be eradicated quickly only by civil war, not by judicial decree or the election of an antislavery coalition."[38]

As Graber states it, the problem posed by *Dred Scott* is one of "bleak alternatives": whether compromise with evil in order to preserve a given constitutional order is appropriate given the consequences of a collapse of that order; "whether antislavery Northerners should have provided more accommodations for slavery than were constitutionally strictly necessary or risked the enormous destruction of life and property that preceded Lincoln's 'new birth of freedom'." The *Dred Scott* majority's position in Graber's estimation was faithful to constitutional bisectionalism. The devastation wreaked by the war that followed rejection of the continuation of bisectional compromise on offer in *Dred Scott* demonstrates the cogency of the majority's position. But Lincoln chose justice over law; that is, he chose to reject continued constitutional accommodation of slavery. "*Dred Scott* was wrong and Lincoln right only if insufficient reasons existed in 1861 for antislavery Americans to maintain a constitutional relationship with slaveholders," which means ultimately "only if John Brown was correct when he insisted that slavery was sufficiently evil to warrant political actions that 'purge[d] this land in blood'."[39]

---

[37] Fehrenbacher, *The Dred Scott Case*, 384.

[38] Graber, *Dred Scott*, 3–4. For a distinct historical analysis of *Dred Scott* that also yields a dissenting conclusion, see Austin Allen, *Origins of the Dred Scott Case: Jacksonian Jurisprudence and the Supreme Court, 1837–1857* (Athens, Ga., 2006).

[39] Graber, *Dred Scott*, 4, 8.

For my purposes, in drawing this long book to a close, it is sufficient to state that I think Mark Graber quite correct in proposing that the American Civil War was avoidable on the terms offered by the majority in *Dred Scott*, namely the preservation of slavery through rededication of the United States to constitutional bisectionalism, or as Graber puts it, to a "willingness to abide by clear constitutional rules protecting evil that were laid down in the past and a willingness to make additional concessions to evil when resolving constitutional ambiguities and silences in the present."[40] Graber also argues, normatively, that the terms should have been accepted, slavery accommodated, Lincoln discarded, and the war thereby presumably avoided. I will leave this normative question to the very end. Here, accepting that Graber is entirely correct in his assessment of the terms on offer in *Dred Scott*, the question I want to consider is the proper historical characterization of their rejection.

Lincoln's refusal to abide by the terms of constitutional bisectionalism was necessarily a repudiation of the constitutional order brought into being in 1787.[41] The repudiation was announced as such in the First Inaugural's majoritarian condemnation of law's insufficiencies. It was implemented subsequently by what would prove to be overwhelming force, sufficient to amount to the destruction of the antebellum republic. In his Second Inaugural, Lincoln made the war's destructive effect entirely clear:

> One-eighth of the whole population were colored slaves, not distributed generally over the Union, but localized in the Southern part of it. These slaves constituted a peculiar and powerful interest. All knew that this interest was, somehow, the cause of the war. To strengthen, perpetuate, and extend this interest was the object for which the insurgents would rend the Union, even by war.

[40] Ibid., 3. See also Walter Johnson, "Inconsistency, Contradiction, and Complete Confusion: The Everyday Life of the Law of Slavery," *Law and Social Inquiry*, 22, 2 (April 1997), 406–8. Assessing the implications of Thomas D. Morris's *Southern Slavery and the Law, 1619–1860* (Chapel Hill, 1996), Johnson argues that the Civil War was the consequence of a constitutional crisis, not of any uncontainable "underlying contradictions" in slavery itself. "The progress of racism, liberal capitalism, Enlightenment humanitarianism, evangelical Christianity, and the self-protecting policy of the existing social order ... were transforming the law of slavery – fitfully, inconsistently, and ultimately incompletely – but never in a way that indicated any underlying or unresolvable contradiction" (406).

[41] Graber, *Dred Scott*, 91–114, 189–91. On the constitutional order created in 1787, see David Waldstreicher, *Slavery's Constitution: From Revolution to Ratification* (New York, 2009); Paul Finkelman, *Slavery and the Founders: Race and Liberty in the Age of Jefferson* (2d ed., Armonk, N.Y., 2001), 3–36, 81–104. For additional arguments holding the *Dred Scott* decision consistent with mid-nineteenth-century constitutionalism and with the intent of the Philadelphia Convention, see Paul Finkelman, "*Scott v. Sandford*: The Court's Most Dreadful Case and how it Changed History," Jack M. Balkin and Sanford Levinson, "Thirteen Ways of Looking at *Dred Scott*," and Austin Allen, "Rethinking *Dred Scott*: New Context for an Old Case," all in *Chicago-Kent Law Review*, 82, 1 (2007), at 4–5, 76–81, and 144–68, respectively. An extensive literature is ably summarized in Gerald Leonard, "Law and Politics Reconsidered: A New Constitutional History of *Dred Scott*," *Law & Social Inquiry*, 34, 3 (Summer 2009), 747–85.

...

The Almighty has his own purposes. "Woe unto the world because of offenses! for it must needs be that offenses come; but woe to that man by whom the offense cometh." If we shall suppose that American slavery is one of those offenses which, in the providence of God, must needs come, but which, having continued through His appointed time, He now wills to remove, and that He gives to both North and South this terrible war, as the woe due to those by whom the offense came, shall we discern therein any departure from those divine attributes which the believers in a living God always ascribe to Him? Fondly do we hope – fervently do we pray – that this mighty scourge of war may speedily pass away. Yet, if God wills that it continue until all the wealth piled by the bondsman's two hundred and fifty years of unrequited toil shall be sunk, and until every drop of blood drawn with the lash shall be paid by another drawn with the sword, as was said three thousand years ago, so still it must be said, "The judgments of the Lord are true and righteous altogether."[42]

In declaring the purpose of the Civil War to be the creation of a new Union cleansed of slavery and of the bisectional constitutional order that had enabled it, Lincoln's Second Inaugural declared the demise of the historical constellation that has been the subject of this book. That is, it declared an end to the particular conjunction of un/freedom that the law and work of colonizing had brought into being in the 250 years that followed the beginning of continuous English settlement. That conjunction had manned, planted, and secured the mainland for its settler colonists, first against its existing inhabitants, later against the metropolitan imperial state. Originating as a succession of new commonwealths, distinct jurisdictions instantiated as separate bundles of territorial claims, the English mainland colonies had grown by the later eighteenth century from a coterie of vulnerable beachhead settlements into a loose, largely autonomous coalition of expansive settler societies possessed of a common language, a common interest in commercial and territorial extension, divergent but complementary regional economies, and relatively distinct political-legal cultures. When the occasion required it of them, these societies were able to create a sufficiently homogenous national elite and sufficiently cohesive aggregate institutions to survive a profound crisis of rupture with the transoceanic metropolis, to fight a war against the metropolitan imperial state, to expel a loyalist minority that identified with that state rather than with its local successors, and to emerge from the strains of war and expulsion intact. The constituent elements of the confederation of states that appeared in the wake of rupture with the metropolis were in all essentials a continuation of what had preceded them, the individual states successors

---

[42] Abraham Lincoln, "Second Inaugural Address" (March 4, 1865), in Miller, ed., *Life and Works*, V, 224–5. See also Balkin and Levinson, "Thirteen Ways," 94–5; Lucas E. Morel, "Lincoln, God and Freedom: A Promise Fulfilled," in Harold Holzer and Sara Vaughn Gabbard, editors, *Lincoln and Freedom: Slavery, Emancipation and the Thirteenth Amendment* (Carbondale, Ill., 2008), 55.

of the preceding colonies. In the tighter federation they would eventually create, central government would "tread lightly in domestic policy," working largely in conjunction with state and local governments rather than in its own bureaucratic right. That government would largely interpret its own sovereignty as "contingent on the consent of the individual states.["](43)

The Civil War destroyed the first decentralized, bisectional republic, snapping the political sinews that had held together its loose national elite, shattering the institutions that elite had created. What took their place, at first, was a politically majoritarian "new Union state" – the "almost complete fusion of [Republican] party and state" perfected in the North to fight the war and vigorously applied to the remainder of the country, particularly the South, after the war.[44] But the fusionist war-fighting state was unstable. That instability initiated, in its turn, the "great transformation of American statecraft and public law" that took hold during the half century that followed the end of Reconstruction and created the twentieth century's American nation-state. For the sake of convenience the transformation can be summarized under three heads: a "reconfiguration of sovereignty around a more positivist notion of a modern state"; a "redefinition and expansion of the legislative and regulatory authority of that state"; and "a realignment in the relationship of the rule of law and administration.["](45)

The precise nature of the transformed political-legal order that emerged after the Civil War can be, and is, hotly debated. No one would suggest that the formative conjunction of law and colonizing I have explored in this book simply ceased to be as a result of the Civil War.[46] What is clear, however, is that the conjunction was fundamentally reconfigured, and that the form of the state that continued to pursue it after the war was quite distinct from that which had preceded the war. Continuities were severed, an "epistemological break" in state form and function occurred. "Other

---

[43] Brian Balogh, *A Government Out of Sight: The Mystery of National Authority in Nineteenth Century America* (Cambridge and New York, 2009), 57, and see 68, 217, 219–20; Bensel, *Yankee Leviathan*, ix; Waldstreicher, *Slavery's Constitution*, 88–105. See also Jack P. Greene, *Peripheries and Center: Constitutional Development in the Extended Polities of the British Empire and the United States, 1607–1788* (New York, 1990), 212–17. On the continuity of postcolonial with colonial America, see Jack P. Greene, "Colonial History and National History: Reflections on a Continuing Problem," *William and Mary Quarterly*, 3rd Ser., 64, 2 (April 2007), 240–9.

[44] Bensel, *Yankee Leviathan*, ix, x.

[45] William J. Novak, "Police Power and the Hidden Transformation of the American State," in Dubber and Valverde, eds., *Police and the Liberal State*, 56–7. For a somewhat more restrained view of state transformation that gives greater emphasis to the pivotal role of juridical institutions and ideology, see William E. Forbath, "Politics, State-Building and the Courts, 1870–1920," in Michael Grossberg and Christopher Tomlins, editors, *The Cambridge History of Law in America* (Cambridge and New York, 2008), II, 643–96.

[46] Anyone who *would* suggest that is urged to read the *Insular Cases* alongside *Dred Scott*. See for example *De Lima v. Bidwell*, 182 U.S. 1 (1901); *Downes v. Bidwell*, 182 U.S. 244 (1901). See also James G. Wilson, *The Imperial Republic: A Structural History of American Constitutionalism from the Colonial Era to the Beginning of the Twentieth Century* (Aldershot, U.K. and Burlington, Vt., 2002), 161–2, 219–21, 247–51.

than ... pleas for a return to 'the Constitution as it was,' the modern state's inheritance from the antebellum period was nil." To that considerable, secular, extent, the American Civil War was indeed a profound endpoint to what had preceded it.[47]

But fully to understand the war as an *end*, one must also loosen one's purchase on the secular, enter somewhat into the profoundly eschatological mentalité – which one might also term "stir to the mind," or *energia*[48] – that framed how the war came to be understood, and prosecuted, and its ends finally defined. From this standpoint the American Civil War becomes an instantiation of sacred violence prosecuted in religious time; in a moment of time "out of joint."[49] From this standpoint, that is, the war was a messianic and revolutionary war undertaken for a messianic, revolutionary purpose.[50] So understood, the American Civil War most profoundly brought a final and climactic end to what had been.

II.   American Histories

What would come after the war does not belong in this book. *Dred Scott* does belong, however, because the decision itself was grounded upon an

---

[47] Bensel, *Yankee Leviathan*, ix. For the concept of epistemological break, see Louis Althusser, *For Marx* (London, 1969), 13, 39. Althusser uses the concept to describe a "discontinuity ... within the continuity of a historical process" (39). Here I wish to use it to connote a radical break with a preceding state structure and discourse, brought about in this case by massive, eventually total, warfare. On the war as agent of revolutionary change, see James McPherson, *Abraham Lincoln and the Second American Revolution* (New York, 1991), 3–22. On the war as agent of constitutional transformation, see Bruce Ackerman, *We the People: Transformations* (Cambridge, Mass., 1998), 160–63.

[48] See Stephen Greenblatt, *Shakespearean Negotiations: The Circulation of Social Energy in Renaissance England* (Berkeley and Los Angeles, 1988), 5–6.

[49] Such a time is "spectral ... a moment that no longer belongs to time," a moment, for Derrida, invoking Shakespeare, when "the time is out of joint" (*Hamlet*, 1.5), "a moment that no ethics, no politics, whether revolutionary or not, seems possible and thinkable and *just* that does not recognize in its principle the respect for those others who are no longer or for those others who are not yet *there*." See Jacques Derrida, *Specters of Marx: The State of the Debt, the Work of Mourning, and the New International*, Peggy Kamuf, trans. (New York, 1994), xix, xx. Or, as Robert A. Ferguson has it, it is time "*beyond* the convenient artifice of men." See Ferguson, *Law and Letters in American Culture* (Cambridge, Mass., 1984), 311 (emphasis in original), and see generally 272–304, and 305–17.

[50] For this, one need do no more than return to Lincoln's Second Inaugural and pay particular attention to its points of biblical reference, notably Matthew 18:7 (AV) and Psalms 19:9 (AV), but also the clear echoes of Revelation 16:7 (AV) and Revelation 16 generally. On the profoundly evangelical, revivalist, and above all Biblicist character of antebellum American religious culture in general and Lincoln's own quickening wartime providentialism in particular, see Mark Noll, "American Religion, 1809–1865," in Joseph R. Fornieri and Sara Vaughn Gabbard, editors, *Lincoln's America, 1809–1865* (Carbondale, Ill., 2008), 72–93. See also Fehrenbacher, *The Slaveholding Republic*, 319–22, and generally 295–338. For Lincoln as revolutionary, see McPherson, *Abraham Lincoln and the Second American Revolution*, 23–42; Gary Wills, *Lincoln at Gettysburg: The Words that Remade America* (New York, 1992), 37–9, 145–7. For the Gettysburg Address as prolegomenon to the Second Inaugural, see Wills, *Lincoln at Gettysburg*, 177–89.

explicit invocation of the law/colonizing conjunction with which this book has been concerned. Considered as a complete text, the decision also contains within itself elements of the fissure that would shortly bring to an end what had begun 250 years before. Considered dialectically, that is, the decision exhibits elements of what would come after. But the sublative (expressing the destination or outcome) capacities of the dialectic of majority and minority were limited; necessarily so, because on neither side of the argument was *Dred Scott* actually intended to achieve anything other than a continuation of what had been. Though majority and minority apprehended current reality distinctly, neither couched its representation in terms that aspired to any fundamental departure from what was.[51] Rather, the decision yielded two distinct but overlapping statements of the historical conditions for a continued constitutionalized existence for slavery. Each side argued the same history with different emphases, inserting into it along the way the details of Dred Scott's case as if into an established template from which each could extract an outcome without any fundamental alteration to the template's design.[52]

Taney rested his opinion for the Court on a history of the legalities of civic membership (citizenship), of territory, and of property on the American mainland. The three components were complementary. However, their historical appearance and legitimacy was grounded on and determined by a distinct history of the spatial and social relations pertaining among three races: the "dominant" white race, the "uncivilized" yet "free" Indian race, and "negroes of the African race," variously held "degraded" and "unhappy." Taney's history, one of racial fortune and destiny, focused turn by turn on the relationship between the white race and each of the other races. His terms were bilateral and exclusive. No relationship existed between the Indian race and the African race in Taney's narrative, underlining their complete difference in "situation."[53]

Though primarily a narrative of the mainland since Independence, Taney's account actually encompassed the mainland's history from an identified moment of origin, "from the time of the first emigration to the English colonies," until "the present day."[54] As such it essayed completion; it allowed no moment to exist outside itself which it did not include, no moment, therefore, from which its account might be falsified. It is also noticeable that in the formulation Taney uses to establish the temporal seal on his own authority – "from the time of the first emigration to the English colonies to the present day" – the "English colonies" actually precede "the first emigration." For purposes of origination, and hence priority, the English colonies are established in sovereign metropolitan time,

[51] Graber, *Dred Scott*, 76–83.
[52] Ibid., 46–76.
[53] *Scott v. Sandford*, 403, 404, 405, 409, 412. VanderVelde also notes the significance of the triracial thematic in Taney's opinion in *Mrs. Dred Scott*, 309–17.
[54] *Scott v. Sandford*, 404.

before any actual arrival of migrants. This is entirely consistent with, and indeed central to Taney's history of the mainland, in which there is no moment in which "the white race" is not sovereign and dominant. In this regard the opinion replicates the jurisdictional discourse of English claims of *imperium* and *dominium*.

Of the Indian race Taney had rather less to say in *Dred Scott* than he had already said elsewhere, but what he did say was of considerable importance in establishing the terms of his history. Taney's history of relations between Indians and whites was spatial. The Indian race had formed no part of "the colonial communities." It had "never amalgamated with them in social connections or in government." Indians, though uncivilized, had their own civic identity. They were free and independent and self-governing. Though "many of the[ir] political communities were situated in territories to which the white race claimed the ultimate right of dominion," the claim was made "subject to the right of the Indians to occupy it as long as they thought proper." Neither the English nor the colonial governments had sought dominion over Indian governments, but had regarded and treated them as foreign governments. Though "the course of events" had brought Indian tribes within the limits of the United States "under subjection to the white race" and into a state of pupilage, their members continued to be "foreign." Taney allowed that an individual Indian who exchanged spatial for social relations – who left his nation or tribe and took up residence among white people – might expect to enjoy "all the rights and privileges which would belong to an emigrant from any other foreign people" extending to the opportunity, like any subject of any foreign government, to be naturalized and made a citizen of the United States. But while they remained in their "untutored and savage state" no one would actually think of admitting Indians "as citizens in a civilized community," or even anticipate that they might ask for or be capable of enjoying the privileges of an American citizen.[55]

Taney's history of relations between the white race and the African race on the mainland contrasted in important respects. Unlike the "situation" of Indians vis-à-vis whites, the situation of Africans could not credibly be represented as spatially differentiated, except in the one crucial respect of point of origin. Nor did Taney's history of African-white relations have any spatial element outside point of origin. Rather, it stressed sociality and the differentia of authority that structured it: white domination, black subalternship. First, however, came the differentia of origin. Negroes of the African race had been imported "into this country" by the white race and sold as slaves. The single point of spatial reference established white racial priority in the country into which Africans were imported. The terminology of "importation" of course emphatically underlined priority in relations of power, and from it flowed the main stream of Taney's social narrative. Africans were "a subordinate and inferior class of beings, who had been

[55] Ibid., 403–4, 420.

subjugated by the dominant race, and, whether emancipated or not, yet remained subject to their authority, and had no rights or privileges but such as those who held the power and Government might choose to grant them." At the moment that the white race – elsewhere denominated as "the citizen race, who formed and held the Government" – had separated their thirteen colonies from Great Britain and had formed new sovereignties that had taken their places "in the family of independent nations," Negroes of the African race "had for more than a century before been regarded as beings of an inferior order, and altogether unfit to associate with the white race, either in social or political relations; and so far inferior, that they had no rights which the white man was bound to respect," and liable to be reduced to slavery "justly and lawfully" for their own benefit.[56]

In this tripartite history, Taney's account of the Indian race was, for Taney, comparatively benign. Taney could afford to be benign in *Dred Scott*, for the Indian race was not the main subject. Indeed, a comparatively benign description of the Indian race doubled down upon the degradation of the "unfortunate" African race.[57] When, ten years earlier, in *United States v. Rogers*, the Indian race had been the main subject, its history had been told quite differently. Then the Indian race had been "the unfortunate race." Then "the native tribes who were found on this continent at the time of its discovery" had "*never* been acknowledged or treated as independent nations by the European governments, nor regarded as the owners of the territories they respectively occupied." On the contrary, "the whole continent was divided and parcelled out, and granted by the governments of Europe as if it had been vacant and unoccupied land, and the Indians continually held to be, and treated as, subject to their dominion and control." And though "from the very moment the general government came into existence to this time" (again one should note the historicist seal of temporal exclusivity) "it has exercised its power over this unfortunate race in the spirit of humanity and justice," there could be no doubt that as the sovereign successor on the continent to the governments of Europe, the general government had "maintained the doctrines upon this subject which had been previously established by other nations, and insisted upon the same powers and dominion within their territory." Notable also in *Rogers* was the refined inflection Taney gave to the history of citizenship, foreignness, and race. In *Dred Scott* it appeared that with enough of the soap of white association, Indians might wash away their difference and become citizens. In *Rogers*, however, "a white man who at mature age is adopted in an Indian tribe" could not thereby become an Indian. Only those "who by the usages and customs of the Indians are regarded as belonging to their race" could

---

[56] Ibid., 403, 404–5, 407, 420.

[57] Taney has no substantive reason to introduce the Indian race into his opinion. Indians are there for rhetorical purposes. First, inclusion underscores that the account is *complete*; second, inclusion allows Taney to underscore the *difference* of Africans.

be Indians. Indians could cease to be Indians, but no such abdication of race membership could ever extend to "a white man, of the white race."[58]

As this brief excursus indicates, each of Taney's three races is rendered entirely homogenous in its external aspect by the precision of its location vis-à-vis the others. The Indian race, spatially separated from the others, is the "untutored and savage" race. Indians may be claimable for civility to the extent they individually separate from the group and learn whiteness, but the lesson is long and hard and the hatch works only in one direction: not even the meanest white could lose his whiteness, no matter how hard he might try.[59] Africans are the "enslaved" race. The situation of "the unhappy black race" was "altogether unlike that of the Indian race" because Africans had always lived in close proximity to whites. But individual Africans could never erase the "indelible marks" of slavery – the ancestral degradation that separated them as a race from whites and denied them civic identity. Taney acknowledged that internal distinctions among free Negroes, mulattos, and slaves might exist, but thrust them aside for an overweening and uniform racial character. Taney also acknowledged that "negroes of the African race" might have rights, and (hypothetically) that those, unlike the native born, who were citizens of foreign governments, might be eligible for naturalization. Like foreign Indians, the foreign African could be examined for the extent to which he had learned whiteness. But naturalization for the foreign-born, like rights for the native-born, was a matter of policy and choice, and matters of policy and choice were matters wholly within the sphere of the white race – the citizen race that formed and held the government. Hence it was that no Negroes of the African race had "rights which the white man was *bound* to respect."[60]

Finally, the white race. Whites, in effect, were the positive counterpart to the negative of degraded blacks, characterized by an entirely homogenous "public opinion" and an absence of significant intra-group difference. Though Taney makes some allowance for different conditions of white men,[61] their dominance as the "citizen" race effaces distinction whether of class or condition, particularly in matters of interracial relations. "[M]en in every grade and position in society" shared the same opinion of blacks' degraded and inferior condition, and acted upon it "daily

---

[58] *United State v. William S. Rogers*, 45 U.S. 567, 572 (emphasis added), 573 (1846). Taney's exclusivist history of course is somewhat undermined by the somewhat distinct and somewhat more nuanced histories of "the Indian race" told by Marshall in *Johnson v. M'Intosh*, 21 U.S. 543 (1823), *Cherokee Nation v. Georgia*, 30 U.S. 1 (1831), and *Worcester v. Georgia*, 31 U.S. 515 (1832), although in practice they amounted to the same outcome; that the views of the "Courts of the conqueror" (*Johnson*, 588) were decisive in disposing of the conquered.

[59] It is noticeable that Indians in Taney's discourse are prompted to be invisible, in that they are either spatially distant or, at least potentially, assimilated.

[60] *Scott v. Sandford*, 403, 404–5, 407, 408, 409, 410, 413, 414, 420, 421, 422. See generally Graber, *Dred Scott*, 47–57.

[61] In *U.S. v. Rogers*, for example, at 573, Taney disparages "men of that class who are most likely to become Indians by adoption."

and habitually ... without doubting for a moment the correctness of this opinion." Though distinctions among whites of gender, age, and wealth might be of significance in particular circumstances among themselves, as in the matter of their eligibility for full political participation, "yet they are [all] citizens." It is worth stressing, indeed, that a necessary and powerful attribute of Taney's racialized history of the mainland was that its account of the interior relations of each race constantly emphasized the relative absence of meaningful distinction, which in the case of the citizen race implied internal relations of comparative civic equality.[62]

It is easy to see how Taney's intensively racialized history negated any possibility that Dred Scott could successfully claim the status of a United States citizen for the purposes of suing for his freedom. Once one also acknowledges the Indian aspect of that racialized history, referenced in *Dred Scott*, more completely displayed in *Rogers*, one can see how Taney's account of territory and property in *Dred Scott* relies upon the same discourse of racial ascendancy that has already disposed of Scott's civic claims, for what that discourse produces in its spatial aspect is the impossibility of restraining the white race from going anywhere it wishes, in whatever form it desires.

We have seen that Taney's historical account of territory in *Rogers* is the same narration of racial fortune and destiny told in *Dred Scott*, this time focused upon degraded Indians as "the unfortunate race," this time emphasizing that the inherited historical purpose of "the general government" is to divide, parcel out, and grant all the territory within its claimed dominion "as if it had been vacant and unoccupied land" without regard for counterclaims never treated as consequential by predecessor European colonizers. Such was, in *Rogers* – as it would be in *Dred Scott* – "the law as we find it."[63] Given a history the premise of which is that for 250 years white racial destiny has been realized by unrestrained expansion and unhindered access to mainland territory acquired in one fashion or another first by European colonizers and more recently by action of the successor "general government" without regard – other than common humanity – for "the unfortunate race" of Indians, the possibility that the citizen race's mobility could actually be restrained could be admitted only if an intent to restrain the mobility of citizens within the territories of the United States were clear and explicit in the laws framing the power and capacities of the general government. No such intent to restrain was to be found in the Constitution, or corresponding capacity among the powers granted the general government. As to the mobility of citizens specifically accompanied by their African slaves, Taney's racialized history had already conclusively established that "negroes of the African race" had been imported "into this country" by the white citizen race and sold as slaves, nor did anyone deny that slaves were property. Within the context of a racialized history it was hardly problematic to conclude that the Fifth Amendment's

---

[62] *Scott v. Sandford*, 407, 422.
[63] *United States v. Rogers*, 572.

prohibition on deprivations of property must necessarily extend to slaves and therefore encompassed laws that attempted to prevent citizens accompanied by slaves from gaining access to U.S. territory on the same basis as citizens not accompanied by slaves.

Once its historical premises are excavated, Taney's legal logic on both fronts, citizenship and territory, becomes unimpeachable.[64] Those premises were, moreover, very widely shared. As Graber notes, "The Taney Court ruling on citizenship captured the dominant 'herrenvolk egalitarianism' of the middle nineteenth century."[65] Nor was Taney's account of territory – his expansionist history of white racial destiny – in any sense exceptional to the same "herrenvolk" ideology.

Neither of the Court's dissenters offered a history that decisively contradicted Taney's. Each, rather, varied particular elements.

Justice McLean's account of citizenship was brief. McLean simply claimed that the citizen race was not as "fastidious" as Taney represented, pointing in particular to the intake "of all grades, combinations and colors" in the aftermath of the Treaty of Guadalupe-Hidalgo's transfer (1848) of 500,000 square miles of Mexico to the United States. In this matter, in fact, McLean was mistaken. The citizen race had been remarkably fastidious, as the Treaty of Guadalupe-Hidalgo itself makes clear. Articles 8 and 9 read, where relevant, as follows:

> [Article 8 §1] Mexicans now established in territories previously belonging to Mexico, and which remain for the future within the limits of the United States, as defined by the present treaty, shall be free to continue where they now reside, or to remove at any time to the Mexican Republic, retaining the property which they possess in the said territories, or disposing thereof, and removing the proceeds wherever they please.
>
> ...
>
> [Article 8 §2] Those who shall prefer to remain in the said territories may either retain the title and rights of Mexican citizens, or acquire those of citizens of the United States. But, they shall be under the obligation to make their election within one year from the date of the exchange of ratifications of this treaty; and those who shall remain in the said territories after the expiration of that year, without having declared their intention to retain

---

[64] For a strong defense of Taney's legal craftsmanship in *Dred Scott*, see Leonard, "Law and Politics Reconsidered," 770–82.

[65] Graber, *Dred Scott*, 31. According to Austin Allen, Taney Court justices "considered their institution a facilitator of popular will," which is to say they evinced a Jacksonian commitment "to allow 'the people' – an undifferentiated mass of white males generally lacking individual influence – opportunity to rule themselves." Allen, *Origins of the Dred Scott Case*, 15. See also Fehrenbacher, *The Slaveholding Republic*, 266. The essential premises of "herrenvolk" ideology in the American case are excavated by David R. Roediger, *The Wages of Whiteness: Race and the Making of the American Working Class* (3rd ed., London and Brooklyn, N.Y., 2007), and Alexander Saxton, *The Rise and Fall of the White Republic: Class Politics and Mass Culture in Nineteenth-Century America* (rev. ed., London and New York, 2003).

the character of Mexicans, shall be considered to have elected to become citizens of the United States.

...

[Article 9] The Mexicans who, in the territories aforesaid shall not preserve the character of citizens of the Mexican Republic ... shall be incorporated into the Union of the United States and be admitted, at the proper time (to be judged by the Congress of the United States) to the enjoyment of all the rights of citizens of the United States, according to the principles of the Constitution; and in the mean time shall be maintained in the free enjoyment of their liberty and property, and secured in the free exercise of their religion without restriction..[66]

Annexed Mexicans who elected U.S. citizenship, whether avidly or silently, gained only the possibility of admission at such time as Congress determined was "the proper time." Such Mexicans, further, were warned by the treaty's language that they were forbidden from maintaining – "shall not preserve" – the character of citizens of the Mexican Republic, or, as Article 8 §2 put it more simply, "the character of Mexicans." As David Kazanjian has observed, "The Mexican citizen must negate itself and then present that negated self before the U.S. citizen's representative for judgment."[67] And judgment of what? The character that the erstwhile Mexican citizen had to put off, in order to put on the character of an American citizen, was not character inflected by liberty, property, or religion, all of which were guaranteed those who maintained the character of Mexicans, including indeed Mexicans residing within the (new) borders of Mexico. "In the said territories, property of every kind, now belonging to Mexicans not established there, shall be inviolably respected. The present owners, the heirs of these, and all Mexicans who may hereafter acquire said property by contract, shall enjoy with respect to it guarantees equally ample as if the same belonged to citizens of the United States."[68] Judgment of suitability for citizenship must therefore inhere in something other than these conventional and measurable instantiations of character. McLean notwithstanding, the judgment Article 9 required of Congress was judgment how successfully annexed Mexicans had put off their own race to assimilate to the racial

---

[66] Treaty of Peace, Friendship, Limits, and Settlement between the United States of America and the United Mexican States concluded at Guadalupe Hidalgo, February 2, 1848 [Article 8, Article 9] as amended and ratified by the U.S. Senate, March 10, 1848. Text available at http://avalon.law.yale.edu/19th_century/guadhida.asp (accessed 22 August 2009). The U.S. Senate substituted "at the proper time (to be judged by the Congress of the United States)" for the negotiated language of the original text, which specified "as soon as possible." Compare the original text available at http://www.loc.gov/rr/hispanic/ghtreaty/ (accessed 22 August 2009).

[67] David Kazanjian, *The Colonizing Trick: National Culture and Imperial Citizenship in Colonial America* (Minneapolis, 2003), 207, and generally 206–9.

[68] Treaty of ... Guadalupe Hidalgo, February 2, 1848, Article 8 §3, text available at http://avalon.law.yale.edu/19th_century/guadhida.asp (accessed 22 August 2009).

character of the citizen race. In this respect they were no different than Taney's individual Indians.

Still, what matters is not whether McLean was correct, but whether he thought he was correct. In believing that United States citizenship was in fact already open to "all grades, combinations and colors," McLean was advertising his willingness to allow the homogenous citizenship described by Taney to be fractured and remade along differentiated lines of class, caste, and capacity. Precisely what the implications of this might be for the substance of citizenship, McLean did not indicate. However, his co-dissenter Benjamin Curtis, also willing to entertain Scott's claim to citizenship, addressed that matter in some detail. In the process of awarding citizenship to Scott, Curtis carefully emptied the concept of citizenship of virtually all substantive content:

> One [state] may confine the right of suffrage to white male citizens; another may extend it to colored persons and females; one may allow all persons above a prescribed age to convey property and transact business; another may exclude married women. But whether native-born women, or persons under age, or under guardianship because insane or spendthrifts, be excluded from voting or holding office, or allowed to do so, I apprehend no one will deny that they are citizens of the United States. Besides, this clause of the Constitution does not confer on the citizens of one State, in all other States, specific and enumerated privileges and immunities. They are entitled to such as belong to citizenship, but not to such as belong to particular citizens attended by other qualifications. Privileges and immunities which belong to certain citizens of a State, by reason of the operation of causes other than mere citizenship, are not conferred. Thus, if the laws of a State require, in addition to citizenship of the State, some qualification for office, or the exercise of the elective franchise, citizens of all other States, coming thither to reside, and not possessing those qualifications, cannot enjoy those privileges, not because they are not to be deemed entitled to the privileges of citizens of the State in which they reside, but because they, in common with the native-born citizens of that State, must have the qualifications prescribed by law for the enjoyment of such privileges, under its Constitution and laws. It rests with the States themselves so to frame their Constitutions and laws as not to attach a particular privilege or immunity to mere naked citizenship.[69]

Mere naked citizenship (bare civic life) might, therefore, grant Dred Scott standing to sue for his freedom from a master's restraint in federal court. Further than that it would not go, not for Scott, not for anyone else. Citizenship had not the content, for example, to prevent Illinois or Indiana – or Curtis's own Massachusetts – from invoking "the power to determine what persons from abroad shall be admitted to, or excluded from, the territorial limits of the state" and, in the name of "preservation, and the advancement of the welfare of its own citizens," bar from entry those whom it chose.[70] No citizen of the United States was entitled on

---

[69] *Scott v. Sandford*, 583–4.

[70] Benjamin R. Curtis, "Speech in Faneuil Hall" (26 November 1850), in George Ticknor Curtis, *A Memoir of Benjamin Robbins Curtis, with some of his Professional and Miscellaneous Writings* (Boston, 1879), I, 129, 130–1.

account of that bare citizenship to all the privileges of any citizen.[71] Thus might a state say of a citizen – colored or pauper, vagabond or fugitive[72] – "Are not these persons foreigners to us ... what right have they to come here at all, against the will of the legislative power of the State?"

> Whatever natural rights they have, and I admit those natural rights to their fullest extent, *this* is not the *soil* on which to vindicate them. This is *our* soil, sacred to *our* peace, on which we intend to perform *our* promises, and work out, for the benefit of ourselves and our posterity and the world, the destiny which our Creator has assigned to *us*.[73]

The McClain-Curtis narrative of citizenship, then, was not of a non-racialized U.S. citizenship but of a citizenship of which race became not the sole determinant but instead one of a plethora of "grades, combinations and colors," none of which could furnish sufficient grounds for exclusion *from* citizenship, all of which, however, might be treated as perfectly legal and appropriate axes of discrimination *among* citizens.[74] Where Taney embraced a citizenship filled with substantive content protected by racial exclusivity, McLean and Curtis were ready to distribute citizenship more widely while simultaneously depriving it of content. In their view, citizenship was mostly an empty vessel that could be filled with all manner of discrimination: of race and gender, of age and ability, of class and caste and nativity.[75] Thus, for McLean, Scott's citizenship claim was open-and-shut. Being born within the United States and subject to its laws, Scott was a citizen of the United States and had standing to sue in its courts.

[71] *Scott v. Sandford*, 583.

[72] Ibid., 583–4.

[73] Curtis, "Speech in Faneuil Hall," 133, 136 (emphasis in original). In Curtis's Massachusetts, Black "foreignness" was not simply a figure of speech. See generally Kunal M. Parker, "Making Blacks Foreigners: The Legal Construction of Former Slaves in Post-Revolutionary Massachusetts," *Utah Law Review*, 2001, 1 (2001), 75–124. On the reconstruction of the freed slave as alien presence and desired absence, see Joanne Pope Melish, *Disowning Slavery: Gradual Emancipation and 'Race' in New England* (Ithaca, N.Y., 1998). As Melish writes, at 2, "the promise implicit in antislavery rhetoric [was] that abolition, by ending 'the problem' – the sin of slavery and the troublesome presence of slaves – would result in the eventual absence of people of color themselves. In other words, whites anticipated that free people of color, would, by some undefined moment (always imminent) have disappeared."

[74] Compare William J. Novak, "The Legal Transformation of Citizenship in Nineteenth Century America," in Meg Jacobs et al., editors, *The Democratic Experiment: New Directions in American Political History* (Princeton, 2003), 94–5: "The integrated legal status of the rights-bearing citizen was not born free in America as the natural outgrowth of Lockean-liberal political philosophy and the original founding of a constitutional nation-state in 1787." Rights and duties "were not determined by abstract reflection on the state of nature but through the elaboration of a great hierarchy of very specific and highly differentiated legal statuses."

[75] *Scott v. Sandford*, 583–4. In embracing a substantive conception of citizenship, in other words, Taney was the innovator. Because Taney's conception of citizenship had content it became precious, hence a privilege of "the citizen race" to be protected. Because McLean and Curtis denied citizenship intrinsic content it became simply a category of procedural convenience that could be distributed widely. It granted the holder standing, a not inconsiderable advantage, but no substantive right. Compare Linda K. Kerber, "The Meanings

"In the argument, it was said that a colored citizen would not be an agreeable member of society," but that was "more a matter of taste than of law." Nothing substantive followed, however, from mere standing. For example, "If Congress should deem ... free colored persons injurious to the population of a free Territory, as conducing to lessen the value of the public lands, or on any other ground connected with the public interest, they have the power to prohibit them from becoming settlers in it. This can be sustained on the ground of a sound national policy."[76] So, presumably, could virtually any other discriminatory practice or ban.

The McClain-Curtis account of territory was in most respects similar to their account of citizenship – an emendation of Taney's history that produced a distinct outcome, rather than an alternative account that produced a new outcome. Both grounded their understanding of territory on the same historical narrative of predestined settler expansion that Taney supplied, but substituted for Taney's overtly racialized gloss one that stressed an overweening *national* destiny. McLean celebrated "a country more than five times greater in extent than the original thirteen states," a country of "flourishing states" formed "from the sources of the Ohio to the Gulf of Mexico, extending to the Lakes on the north and the Pacific Ocean on the west, and from the lines of Georgia to Texas," a story of "public lands ... sold," of "wildernesses reduced to cultivation."[77] Curtis too stressed the grandeur and inevitability of continent-wide expansion. Expansion, he argued, was built into the fabric of the Constitution. It could not for a moment be doubted that the framers had intended to express in the Constitution the actuality of their expectation that "the United States might be, what they have now become, a great and powerful nation, possessing the power to make war and to conclude treaties, and thus to acquire territory."[78] So obvious had the destiny of the United States been to the framers, Curtis held, that they had implanted in the Constitution all the authority necessary to acquire whatever territory the United States would ever acquire and to "to dispose of and make all needful regulations" for that territory. "No reason has been suggested why any reluctance should have been felt, by the framers of the Constitution, to apply this provision to all the territory which might belong to the United States." A history of extraordinary foresight became the basis for Curtis's equally extraordinary post hoc reconstruction of the territories clause: "I construe this clause, therefore, as if it had read, Congress shall have power to make all needful rules and regulations respecting those tracts of country, out of the limits of the several States, which the United States have acquired, or may hereafter acquire, by cessions, as well of the jurisdiction as of the soil, so far as

of Citizenship," *Journal of American History*, 84, 3 (December 1997), 833–54; James H. Kettner, *The Development of American Citizenship, 1608–1870* (Chapel Hill, 1978), 287–333. See generally Welke, *Law and the Borders of Belonging*.

[76] *Scott v. Sandford*, 60 U.S. 393, 543.
[77] Ibid., 545–6.
[78] Ibid., 611.

the soil may be the property of the party making the cession, at the time of making it."[79]

The *Dred Scott* minority's preference for a nationalist account of territorial expansion did not undermine Taney's explicitly racialized history of American destiny so much as muffle it in the interests of establishing "nation" as an alternate embodiment of consensual destiny, and hence as a platform from which to criticize the antebellum constitutional practices embraced by the majority which had managed expansion through sectional compromise. The minority's representation of citizenship, similarly, did not establish a history for citizenship distinct from Taney's valorization of racial exclusivity so much as adjust the account to render race one unexceptional discriminatory hierarchy among many, all of which might be accommodated alongside wholesale distribution of citizenship as a minimalist signifier of national membership – "mere naked citizenship" – a lowest common denominator, empty of any substantive content that might interfere with wholesome discriminations, whether racial or otherwise. Each minority position tended thus to substitute nation for race as the decisive term in determination of the dispute's outcomes, simultaneously offering assurances that racial interests and discriminations would be maintained. As such, each minority position recognizably, if fragmentarily, portended the legal-political settlement – the new constellation of colonizing and law, of territory and citizenship – that would congeal after the Civil War's revolutionary moment of interruption.[80]

III. Eternal Return

Analysis of the *Dred Scott* decision allows us to see that majority and minority embraced the same determinative history of European mainland settlement as, from its beginnings to the moment of the decision itself, the fateful realization of an expansionist destiny. The different conclusions majority and minority reached in determining how that history should be read in the conjuncture of bisectional crisis are accounted for by the distinct values they respectively assigned to the terms "race" and "nation" in working out Mark Graber's cold constitutional equation. The decision's "future echo" of the eventual postwar settlement prefigures the resumption of that history clothed in the new nationalist garb embraced by the minority, a reconfigured constitutional discourse that would fill the place of the sectional pluralism destroyed in the revolutionary passions of the Civil War with a new white nation.

---

[79] Ibid., 611, 613–14.

[80] Foreshadowed in the conclusion to Chapter 7. See also Laura F. Edwards, *The People and their Peace: Legal Culture and the Transformation of Inequality in the Post-Revolutionary South* (Chapel Hill, 2009), 286–98; Dorothy Ross, "Lincoln and the Ethics of Emancipation: Universalism, Nationalism, Exceptionalism," *Journal of American History*, 96, 2 (September 2009), 379–99.

The history shared by majority and minority was so tenacious in large part because it was grounded upon the actuality of 250 years of European settlement and expansion dating, as Taney had put it, "from the time of the first emigration to the English colonies." Throughout that history – and the resonance is clear on both sides of *Dred Scott* – the idealized settler-colonist, the bearer of expansion, is figured as John Smith's man of small means, willing to pledge "long labour and diligence," seeking opportunity for unrestrained realization and exercise of his capacities in territory that is a place of plenty, open to occupation, redeemable through hard work. In *Dred Scott* he is Taney's Jacksonian citizen, the undifferentiated substance of whose citizenship Taney guarded by invocation of its racial exclusivity, whose entry anywhere upon the territory of his citizenship wearing the civic badge of his property could not be restrained. He is, equally, the minority's free laborer on free soil, pioneer spearhead of national destiny, whom they would protect by empowering him to exclude those threatening others, whether themselves citizens or not, that the corruptions of slavery or skin color, or other characteristic flaw or condition of dependency, had rendered in some way "foreign."

The mythopoeic settler-colonist is a constant in Europeans' history of the mainland. Twenty years before *Dred Scott* he can be found in "the scarce-born village of Pike Creek" in the southeastern corner of Wisconsin, then still the free soil Michigan Territory, where, in February 1836, his name was Jason Lothrop – "Baptist minister, schoolteacher, boardinghouse proprietor and civic leader," and founder of the Pike River Claimants' Union "for the attainment and security of titles to claims on Government lands." Some time in the late 1940s, Willard Hurst, the founding father of modern American legal history, discovered Lothrop and made him emblematic of "the release of individual creative energy" amid widely shared opportunity that Hurst held to be the singular mark of American law.[81] Hurst's transfiguring meta-narrative built American legal modernity on the *nomos* of freedom – opportunity to release creative human energy, liberty to exercise choice – uniquely embodied in the United States where "unclaimed natural abundance" and "technical command of nature" combined to create "conditions of freedom" for all. Pike Creek in 1836 stands as the moment of origin of *American* law. In the constitution of Lothrop's Claimants Union glistened "a pattern of attitudes and values which explains much about nineteenth-century law in the United States." The moment is sublime. Here, in this obscure corner of the American Midwest, "we" articulated ideas of "special significance for the future of mankind."[82]

---

[81] James Willard Hurst, *Law and the Conditions of Freedom in the Nineteenth Century United States* (Madison, Wis., 1956), 3, 6.

[82] Hurst, *Law and the Conditions of Freedom*, 4, 6. And see Christopher Tomlins, "Law's Wilderness: The Discourse of English Colonizing, the Violence of Intrusion, and the Failures of American History," in John Smolenski and Thomas J. Humphrey, editors, *New World Orders: Violence, Sanction and Authority in the Colonial Americas* (Philadelphia, 2005), 42–4. *Law and the Conditions of Freedom* is famous for its invocation of "we." Hurst, in Paul

The documents in which Hurst found Lothrop and his Claimants Union show he was one of a group of settlers who had originally joined together in a "Western Emigration Company" to remove from Oswego County in New York to what they described as "a new country." Their effort of removal itself entitled them to reward, they said, because it was a transforming journey, conducted on behalf of civilization, into a void where human sociability did not exist. "We have left our friends, deprived ourselves of the many blessings and privileges of society, have borne the expenses, and encountered the hardships of a perilous journey, advancing into a space beyond the bounds of civilization." Their civilizing mission was to transform that space, through their improving labor, from open prairie hunted by Indians to enclosed agricultural smallholdings. Their claim to possession would be signified by the erection of "a house body, or frame of sufficient dimensions for a family to dwell in, or half an acre ploughed, or a piece enclosed with at least 100 rails." Lothrop and his companions considered their place of settlement fruitful, but perilous, "a state of nature," prone to "anarchy" and "confusion," to "bitter quarrels, even bloodshed." In advance of government instrumentalities their "protective union" was constituted to resolve disputes among themselves and to guard their claims against threats from others: from other migrants, described variously as "malignant ... unprincipled and avaricious men," or the "mob"; from the "unfeeling speculator"; and in particular from the indigenous population, whose very presence challenged their possession "as the country had not yet been surveyed," whose competing practices were threatening physically – they "fired the prairies ... for hunting purposes" which endangered the settlers' farms – and whose brutishness was manifest in thieving habits and a "constant desire for whiskey" that was both morally repugnant and a continuing source of disturbance.[83]

It will be clear from the settlers' own account that theirs was a story of work and law in every respect utterly continuous with the primal motive force – colonizing, unceasing expansion – of American history.[84] Their

Kahn's words, invokes law "as the experience of a unitary actor of which each citizen is a part." But "There is not first a transhistorical, communal subject who decides to maintain a common past. There is only the experience of law's rule that shows itself 'as if' it were the extended temporal experience of a single subject." See Paul Kahn, *The Cultural Study of Law: Reconstructing Legal Scholarship* (Chicago, 1999), 45. On the construction of "we" as an icon of American culture and history, see also Rebecca Ann Bach, *Colonial Transformations: The Cultural Production of the New Atlantic World* (New York, 2000), 230–1.

[83] Reverend Jason Lothrop, "A Sketch of the Early History of Kenosha County, Wisconsin, and of the Western Emigration Company," *Wisconsin Assembly Journal*, II (1856), appendix 14, 450–79, particularly 461–3, 472–5. I am grateful to Arthur McEvoy for making this material available to me.

[84] "Occasionally," writes Patricia Nelson Limerick, "continuities in American history almost bowl one over." See her *The Legacy of Conquest: The Unbroken Past of the American West* (New York, 1987), 48, and generally 41–8, 55–96. For a wide-angle perspective on continuities in Anglophone settlement in general, see Peter Karsten, *Between Law and Custom: "High" and "Low" Legal Cultures in the Lands of the British Diaspora – The United States, Canada, Australia and New Zealand, 1600–1900* (Cambridge and New York, 2002), 23–118, 534–6.

resort to law to frame their migration, create jurisdiction, gain access, begin property, and undo others' restraints, potential and actual, could not better illustrate the enabling conjunctions of law and colonizing, of work and civic identity, with which we have become familiar. They had told the story themselves. Hurst, however, did not see it quite that way. His settlers were not colonists. True, they were trespassers, "ahead of official survey, without color of title." But their intrusion was on lands already taken into U.S. possession, declared "public." Hurst admired their impatient determination to meet "the challenge of the unexploited continent." He credited their resort to law as resort to an instrumentality to be put to work in that service; and this was the sum of the release he interrogated. That law, for example, would remove the Indian was not a story that Hurst told at all. In what could have been a brilliant observation, Hurst wrote of contract's "capture of the land" as its "first and most dramatic victory." He was ready, it seems, to acknowledge that law was capable of waging war. It would have been a telling insight had he remarked on whom its war was waged. Instead, Hurst rested his meaning entirely on the land's capture by one intra-European principle, market exchange, from another, a "feudal type of tenure."[85]

What was the nature of the space that Willard Hurst chose to stage the opening scene of his epic of American law? Pike Creek is dug deep in the rich sod of the Upper Mississippi Valley, pastoral and pristine. It is empty yeoman space, safely divorced from the coastal colonies and their compromised histories, which Hurst always avoided, far from the pitiless warfare and removals of the South's western frontier, part of the old northwest territory, soil so fresh it was supposed to have made Dred Scott free. Unfortunately for Dred and Harriet, and Eliza, and Lizzie, it did not. We know from their story that slavery was alive and well in free territory, taken there by the soldiers and government agents sent to police the line of European settlement. We know how intimately the legal economies of colonizing and slavery were related – so much so it would require a war to pry them apart. But like Lothrop's Indian neighbors, slavery had no place in Hurst's meta-history of how American law came to be.[86] Why such elisions and occlusions in a narrative? "If the land is a place of fulsomeness and abundance, it is at the same moment one of ideal emptiness, a depopulated landscape … [F]rom the point of view of those for whom there is space and validity, emptiness … may even be a definition of the ideal."[87] For Hurst, America was "a relatively clean slate"[88] that could be appropriated and organized by a few squatters.

[85] Hurst, *Law and the Conditions of Freedom*, 5, 10, 12–13.
[86] *Law and the Conditions of Freedom* is not devoid of mention of either (see, e.g., 25, 29, 35, 37), but both are incidental to Hurst's thesis, as indeed is *Dred Scott*, which Hurst described as an attempt by the Supreme Court "to affect the political environment in the interest of an already outdated balance of power" (116 n.11).
[87] Francis Barker, *The Culture of Violence: Essays on Tragedy and History* (Chicago, 1993), 3–4.
[88] Hurst, *Law and the Conditions of Freedom*, 35.

If we backtrack Jason Lothrop and his companions to the New York from which they had departed on their expedition west, what meta-history do we find *there*? The same; a narrative, once more, of beginnings in a fruitful and abundant landscape, a landscape that might cultivate and transform even the most wretched of those who fetched up on its shores, a landscape, above all, in which men were nurtured by law. "Men are like plants," wrote Hector St. John Crèvecoeur from his comfortable farm in Orange County, New York, some sixty years before Lothrop set off for Wisconsin. "The goodness and flavour of the fruit proceeds from the peculiar soil and exposition in which they grow."[89] America had regenerated the poor of Europe with "new laws, a new mode of living, a new social system." In Europe "they were as so many useless plants, wanting vegitative mould, and refreshing showers; they withered, and were mowed down by want, hunger, and war." In America, "by the power of transplantation, like all other plants they have taken root and flourished!"

> By what invisible power has this surprising metamorphosis been performed? By that of the laws and that of their industry. The laws, the indulgent laws, protect them as they arrive, stamping on them the symbol of adoption; they receive ample rewards for their labours; these accumulated rewards procure them lands; those lands confer on them the title of freemen, and to that title every benefit is affixed which men can possibly require. This is the great operation daily performed by our laws.[90]

Like John Smith, Crèvecoeur in lyric prose rendered colonizer and law and colonized landscape continuous – indistinguishable. "Let us follow one of these colonists in his progress towards the wilderness; he may well serve as an epitome by which we may judge of the rest." The colonizer's labor was transformative. He and his kind would "clear these rough forests ... enrich the soil with cattle, meadows, and buildings ... make every vale to smile under their feet." And their constant companion will be "the law ... and its plain meaning ... the only forcible standards which strike and guide their senses and become their rule of action." Law was "to them an armour serving as well for attack as for defence; 'tis all that seems useful and pervading."[91] It had made citizens of those "not numbered in any civil lists of their country, except in those of the poor." It had recreated them

---

[89] J. Hector St. John de Crèvecoeur, "What is an American," in *Letters from an American Farmer* (New York, 1904), 56. On Crèvecoeur, see generally Norman S. Grabo, Crèvecoeur's America: Beginning the World Anew," *William and Mary Quarterly*, 3rd Ser., 48, 2 (April 1991), 159–72. On the creation of an America pastoral idiom in the late colonies and early republic, see Thomas Hallock, *From the Fallen Tree: Frontier Narratives, Environmental Politics, and the Roots of a National Pastoral, 1749–1826* (Chapel Hill, 2003), 1–7, 18–25, 77–89.

[90] Crèvecoeur, "What is an American," 52–3.

[91] J. Hector St. John de Crèvecoeur, "Reflections on the Manners of the Americans," in Henry L. Bourdin et al., editors, *Sketches of Eighteenth Century America: More "Letters from an American Farmer" by St. John de Crèvecoeur* (New Haven, 1925), 62, 64, 77.

"a people of cultivators ... unfettered and unrestrained."[92] It had recreated the very land under their feet.

> The instant I enter on my own land, the bright idea of property, of exclusive right, of independence exalt my mind. Precious soil, I say to myself, by what singular custom of law is it that thou wast made to constitute the riches of the freeholder? What should we American farmers be without the distinct possession of that soil? It feeds, it clothes us, from it we draw even a great exuberancy, our best meat, our richest drink, the very honey of our bees comes from this privileged spot. No wonder we should thus cherish its possession, no wonder that so many Europeans who have never been able to say that such portion of land was theirs, cross the Atlantic to realize that happiness. This formerly rude soil has been converted by my father into a pleasant farm, and in return it has established all our rights; on it is founded our rank, our freedom, our power as citizens, our importance as inhabitants of such a district.[93]

One can proceed ever earlier, through serial new beginnings in new American places, serial encounters between a plentiful landscape and a colonizer's impulse to plant, serial invocations of the ordered possession that results from the colonizer's work and of the law that waters the endeavor. They are tales of industrious and wondrous transformations, often against the odds. "Tis with pleasing wonder that we look back upon this country in general, and this town in particular, and compare the present condition and appearance with what they were a century ago," Nathan Fiske told his Brookfield congregation in 1775. "Instead of a desolate uncultivated wilderness ... the face of the earth is trimmed, and adorned with a beautiful variety of fields, meadows, orchards and pastures." The landscape had been given new voice. No more "dismal yells" of "savage men, wounding the ear and terrifying the heart." The valleys *"shout for joy, they also sing."*[94] Perhaps Fiske had in mind William Bradford's extraordinary and moving description of the first landfall in America of those who would settle Plymouth Plantation, eighty miles to the east of Brookfield, 150 years before. "Being thus passed ye vast ocean, and a sea of trouble before in their preparation," Bradford had written of the founders of the Pilgrim commonwealth, "they had now no freinds to wellcome them, nor inns to entertaine or refresh their weatherbeaten bodys, no houses or much less townes to repaire too, to seeke for succoure." All about them lay "a hidious & desolate wildernes, full of wild beasts and willd men," the whole untamed, "woods and thickets ... wild & savage," standing far distant "from all ye civill parts of ye world."[95]

[92] Crèvecoeur, "What is an American," 49–50, 53.

[93] J. Hector St. John de Crèvecoeur, "On the Situation, Feelings, and Pleasures, of an American Farmer," in *Letters from an American Farmer*, 27.

[94] Nathan Fiske, *Remarkable Providences to be Gratefully Recollected, Religiously Improved, and Carefully Transmitted to Posterity. A sermon preached at Brookfield on the last day of the year 1775* (Boston, 1776), 25–6. On the pastoral idiom in Virginia, see Anthony S. Parent, Jr., *Foul Means: The formation of a Slave Society in Virginia, 1660–1740* (Chapel Hill, 2003), 200–01.

[95] William Bradford, *Bradford's History "Of Plimoth Plantation": From the Original Manuscript* (Boston, 1898), 94–5.

Yet was this not the same land that, forty years before the *Mayflower* stood into shore, "with arme aduaunced" had "stretche[d] out it selfe towards England onelie ... praying our ayde and helpe"?[96] Fiske could reflect with satisfaction that "Culture and husbandrie" had not only brought the land to yield up all such things as were "necessary for mans lyfe," but had taught it to vocalize its thanks.[97]

American history is an eternal succession of beginnings – each a primal enactment of foundation in a moment of purity and human invention that fills the void beyond civility with legality. In Plymouth's case the void was filled by those "whose names are underwriten," who had voyaged "to plant ye first colonie in ye Northerne parts of Virginia" and now did "covenant and combine our selves togeather into a civill body politick, for our better ordering & preservation & furtherance of ye ends aforesaid"; by virtue whereof they empowered themselves "to enacte, constitute, and frame such just and equall lawes, ordinances, acts, constitutions, & offices, from time to time, as shall be thought most meete and convenient for ye generall good of ye Colonie."[98] English colonizing was replete with texts that employed the same tropes to create conjectural legal histories of invention and foundation, then used those histories to establish its claim to inhabit the spaces it had penetrated and transformed. "You have your *Commission*, your *Patents*, your *Charters*," John Donne had reminded those traveling to Virginia in 1622, "your *Seales* from *him*, upon whose acts, any private Subject, in civill matters, may safely rely."[99] Had not God and His Majesty together bestowed upon those of small means such blessings of freedom from others' restraints, asked John Smith at the outset, as would render every one of them "*here* ... master and owner of his owne labour and land"? Had not the very same "Heaven and earth" framed that place for men "of *our* constitutions"?[100]

96　Sir George Peckham, *A True Reporte, Of the late discoueries, and possession, taken in the right of the Crowne of Englande, of the New-found Landes: By that valiant and worthye Gentleman, Sir Humfrey Gilbert Knight* (London, 1583), sig. B₄r. And see Chapter 4, section I.

97　Ibid., sig. F₃r. Note David Kazanjian's penetrating analysis of Charles Brockden Brown's *Memoirs of Carwin, the Biloquist* which turns on Carwin's mastery of "the shrill tones of a Mohock Savage" and their transformation into a modernized European vocalization. "By attending to this inaugural scene," Kazanjian argues, "we can read Carwin's tale as an allegory for late eighteenth- and early nineteenth-century efforts by the U.S. government to 'civilize' or assimilate Iroquois communities through land expropriation and forced education. That such an allegory should take the form of a colonial distinction between inarticulate, savage tones and an articulate, civilized voice shows how the figure of articulation indexes the emergence of imperial citizenship in early America." Kazanjian, *The Colonizing Trick*, 13, 139–72. For a fascinating analysis of colonizers' conquest of mainland America's "aural landscape," see Sarah Keyes, "'Like a Roaring Lion: The Overland Trail as a Sonic Conquest," *Journal of American History*, 96, 1 (June 2009), 19–43.

98　Bradford, *Bradford's History*, 110.

99　*A Sermon Preached to the Honourable Company of the Virginian Plantation. 13° November 1622. By Iohn Donne, Deane of St. Pauls, London,"* (London, 1622), 11, available at http://www.lib.byu.edu/dlib/donne/ (accessed 22 August 2009). See Chapter 4, section II.

100　John Smith, *A Description of New England*, and *A Map of Virginia*, both in Philip L. Barbour, editor, *The Complete Works of Captain John Smith* (Chapel Hill, 1986), I, 144, 332 (emphases added).

IV. Phantasmagoria

If each of these beginnings invokes the particular conjunction of the colonizing impulse and law for which *Dred Scott* sought continuance, to which
Lincoln's answering inaugurals signified a halt, can one identify that discursive end's originary twin – the discursive onset of the 250-year conjunction that the Civil War brought to a close? When and where, that is, did the
conjunction of law and colonizing that has occupied this book commence?
And what does that beginning signify?

On the 14th of February, 1613, in London, Princess Elizabeth, the
seventeen-year-old daughter of James I and Anne of Denmark, married
Frederick V, Prince-Elector of the Rhenish Palatinate (Rheinland-Pfalz).
After the marriage, Elizabeth would leave England for Frederick's court in
Heidelberg, never to return.

Princess Elizabeth's marriage forged a dynastic alliance that would eventually prove of consequence to the course of Anglo-American history. She
would bear her husband eight children, the youngest of whom (born in
1630) was Sophia, Countess Palatine of Simmern. In 1658, Sophia married
Ernst August, Duke of Brunswick-Lüneburg. In 1692, Ernst August would
become the first Elector of Hanover. Sophia's marriage in 1658 established
the basis for the Hanoverian succession to the English throne confirmed
in the Act of Settlement of 1701. On the death of Queen Anne, daughter
of James II and Sophia's first cousin once removed, Sophia's son, George
Louis, who in 1698 had succeeded his father as Elector of Hanover and
Duke of Brunswick-Lüneburg, became George I of England. Sixty years
later George's grandson, Sophia's great-grandson, Princess Elizabeth's
great-great-grandson, would become infamous among the Sons of Liberty
as "the Royal Brute of Britain,"[101] George III.

Securing the Stuart line's claim to the English throne by the imaginative expedient of diverting it through a German princeling was not what
James I had in mind when arranging his daughter's marriage. A canny
monarch will always seek insurance for his dynasty, for unexpected death
was an ever-present accompanist even to royal life in the early seventeenth
century. James's eldest son and heir, Prince Henry, provided sad but incon-
trovertible proof by dying suddenly and inconveniently of typhoid fever
shortly after his intended brother-in-law's arrival in England, causing a
postponement of his sister's wedding ceremony. But James still had his
younger son, Charles, to follow him. Elizabeth's match was supposed to
shore up the English state in a different manner, by securing strategic protestant allies within a Europe ever more polarized by the threat of religious
warfare.

At the time of his marriage to Princess Elizabeth, Frederick V was the
Calvinist leader of the League of the Evangelical Union, an association
of Protestant princes within the Holy Roman Empire. The Evangelical
Union, also known as the Union of Auhausen, was a military alliance that

---

[101] Thomas Paine, *Common Sense* (Edinburgh, 1776), 54.

had been established in May 1608 by Frederick's father, Frederick IV, to arm the Protestant German princely states against the resurgence of Catholicism within the Habsburg Holy Roman Empire. Elizabeth's marriage to Frederick V strengthened ties between the Protestant English Crown and Northern European Protestant rulers to whom James already had somewhat less direct dynastic connections through his father-in-law, Frederick II, King of Denmark and Norway, whose own line was thickly intermarried with the rulers of the German princely states. Elizabeth's marriage was thus an important move in James I's policy to secure England vis-à-vis continental powers on both sides of the religious divide, a policy that would later see him attempt (unsuccessfully) to marry his son Charles to the Catholic Spanish infanta, Maria Anna.

Unfortunately for her father's careful strategizing, fate had its own plans for Elizabeth and her young husband. Frederick's Evangelical Union had limited resources with which to offset the forces that confronted protestant rulers within the Habsburg Empire. The Union did not extend to the powerful Protestant Electorate of Saxony; it was dogged by disputes between its Lutheran and Calvinist princes; and its formation quickly generated the creation in 1609 of a counter-alliance, the Catholic League, led by Duke Maximilian I of Bavaria. In 1619, when the Protestant estates of Bohemia rebelled against the Holy Roman Emperor and offered the crown of Bohemia to Frederick V, his rash acceptance (against his father-in-law's advice) triggered disaster. Overborne by superior Catholic League forces, the Evangelical Union signed the Treaty of Ulm in July 1620 and retreated into neutrality. Without allies, Frederick's undermanned army was defeated at the Battle of White Mountain, near Prague (November 1620), and Frederick – who became known derisively as the Winter King – was removed from the Bohemian throne. The Holy Roman Emperor deposed Frederick from his Electorate as well, installing Duke Maximilian in his place. Frederick and Elizabeth became exiles in The Hague, and the Evangelical Union was forced to disband. As the threat to Protestantism in Germany grew, Denmark was drawn into the fray. The Thirty Years War began in earnest.

Dynastic maneuver and alliance, treachery and warfare, sudden death or exile were all staples of early modern European monarchic life, so although the future course of Princess Elizabeth's life was obviously unknowable to anyone celebrating her marriage, its twists and turns, had they been somehow available for inspection, would likely not have seemed all that far-fetched. Both of Elizabeth's paternal grandparents (Mary, Queen of Scots and Henry Stuart, Lord Darnley) had married young and died violently; her own father had only narrowly escaped Catholic assassins a few years before; she herself, unknowing, had been the conspirators' intended nine-year-old replacement. Still, she was a young woman, known to be saddened by the prospect of imminent departure for a new life in a strange German city, distant from her parents. No doubt the festivities attending her marriage on a gloomy mid-February day (always the worst month of an English winter) were a welcome distraction.

"In the old Europe," Frances Yates writes, "a royal wedding was a dip-lomatic event of the first importance, and royal wedding festivities were a statement of policy."[102] On the evening of February 15th, immediately fol-lowing the wedding ceremony on the 14th, festivities were dominated by a "Memorable Maske," a "noble and magnificent performance" mounted in honor of James I and his daughter by two of the Inns of Court, the Middle Temple and Lincoln's Inn.[103] Masque was an elaborate form of court enter-tainment particularly popular in Tudor-Stuart England that combined music, dance, song, and acting with elaborate costume and staging. James I was a known aficionado. Like Carnival and Pageant, Masque was primar-ily allegorical in narrative structure. Hugely expensive, its object was to flatter its patron with displays of conspicuous consumption that conveyed "the richness and importance of a court that would be demeaned by any-thing less than elaborate and costly show." Customarily a fully elaborated masque contained a subversive "anti-masque" counter-theme intended to create a contrast to the masque's main narrative that would be resolved in a concluding spectacle of order and magnificence, usually centering on the presence of the monarch, that was the masque's fulfillment. The "ideal prescription" for masque was to lead spectators "to fuller understanding through their contemplation of an image which impresses itself upon them by the power music, dance and word have to imitate the deeper harmonies of the universe."[104]

The Memorable Maske was written by the playwright George Chapman and staged by Inigo Jones. Its theme was Virginia. The masque began with a torch-lit parade of several hundred masque participants and attendants from the Inns of Court to the royal palace at White-Hall. The torch bear-ers were "of the *Indian* garb," the chief masquers likewise richly attired "in Indian habits" and "altogether estrangfull, and *Indian* like ... Their vizerds

[102] Frances Yates, *The Rosicrucian Enlightenment* (London, 1972), 1.
[103] George Chapman, *The Memorable Maske of the Two Honorable Houses or Inns of Court; the Middle Temple, and Lyncolns Inne. As it was performd before the King, at White-Hall on Shroue Munday at Night; Being the 15 of February, 1613. At the Princely Celebration of the Most Royall Nuptialls of the Palsgraue, and his Thrice Gratious Princesse Elizabeth. &c* (London, 1613). Yates reports that the masque performed on the evening of the 15th February was in fact a rival production commissioned by the Inner Temple and Gray's Inn and written by Francis Beaumont. This is incorrect. The published account of the Beaumont Masque indicates it was due for performance on Shrove Tuesday, the 16th and begun that day but then postponed until the 20th February. It appears that James I disfavored the Beaumont Masque. See Francis Beaumont, *The Masque of the Inner Temple and Grayes Inne, Presented before His Maiestie, the Queenes Maiestie, the Prince, Count Palatine and the Lady Elizabeth their Highnesses, in the Banquetting House at White-hall on Saturday the Twentieth day of Februarie, 1612 [1613]* (London, 1613). Yates, *Rosicrucian Enlightenment*, 6. A third masque, commis-sioned by the King himself and written by Thomas Campion, had taken pride of place on February 14th, the night of the wedding itself.
[104] David Lindley, "Music, Masque and Meaning in *The Tempest*," in Peter Hulme and William H. Sherman, editors, *William Shakespeare*, The Tempest: *Sources and Contexts, Criticism, Rewritings and Appropriations* (New York, 2004), 193, 194. See generally David Bevington and Peter Holbrook, editors, *The Politics of the Stuart Court Masque* (Cambridge, 1998).

of oliue collour; but pleasingly visag'd: their hayre, blacke and lardge, wauing downe to their shoulders," each attended by "two Moores, attir'd like *Indian* slaues," the whole company escorting "two Carrs Triumphall" bearing "Virginean Priests, by whom the Sun is there ador'd; and therefore called the Phœbades." Arriving at White hall, the masquers presented themselves as Indian princes come to England to honor the marriage of Princess Elizabeth.[105]

On its performative surface the masque simply displayed Virginian obeisance to the English crown. But the narrative of obeisance Chapman wrote was rather more complex. The story the masque told was of "a troupe of the noblest Virginians" borne to Britain by the effect of the motions of the earth on their island, a huge golden rock, "one of the most remote parts of the world [brought] to touch at this all-exceeding Iland" (Britain), which though itself an island did not move but was "diuided from the world (*diuisus ab orbe Britannus*)" so that "though the whole World besides moues; yet this Ile stands fixt on her own feete, and defies the Worlds mutability." The Virginian princes had "attended hether the God of Riches," Pluto, "all triumphantly shyning in a Mine of gould. For hearing of the most royal solemnity, of these sacred Nuptialls; they crost the Ocean in their honor, and are here arriu'd."[106] Upon their arrival, the Goddess Honour appears from her British temple, attended by her priestess Eunomia, "the sacred power of Lawe."[107] She addresses Pluto:

> Plutus? The Princes of the Virgine land,
> Whom I made crosse the Britan Ocean
> To this most famed Ile, of all the world,
> To do due homage to the sacred Nuptials
> Of *Lawe*, and *Vertue*, celebrated here,
> By this Howre of the holy Eeuen I know,
> Are ready to perform the rites they owe
> To setting *Phœbus*; which (for greater State
> To their apparance) their first act advances.[108]

The Phœbades ("Priests of the Sunne") appear, and as the Virginian mine opens to reveal its riches they begin to sing three hymns of worship to the setting sun. But as they sing the second hymn, Honour speaks again, not in counterpoint but interruption:

> This superstitious Hymne, sung to the Sunne,
> Let us encounter with fit duties done
> To our cleere Phœbus; whose true piety,
> Enjoyes from heauen an earthly deity

[105] Chapman, *The Memorable Maske*, sigs. Ar-A$_4$r.

[106] Ibid., sigs. B$_3$r, B$_4$v.

[107] In the Greek pantheon, Eunomia is goddess of good order and lawful conduct. Eunomia is associated with the internal stability of a state, the enactment of good laws, and the maintenance of civil order. See http://www.theoi.com/Ouranios/HoraEunomia.html (accessed 22 August 2009).

[108] Chapman, *The Memorable Maske*, sig. D$_2$r.

and a distinct, competing chorus intervenes, directed not toward the setting sun but toward the person of the King:

> Rise, rise O Phœbus, ever rise,
> descend not to th'inconstant streame,
> But grace with endless light, our skyes,
> to thee that Sun is but a beame
> …
> O may our Sun not set before,
> he sees his endless seed arise:
> And deck his triple crowned shore,
> with springs of humane Deities[109]

As the new voices sing, so the Phœbades continue their hymns to the setting sun. The two choruses vie in discordant aural competition. Finally the Phœbades complete their refrain ["Set Set (great Sun) our rising loue /shall euer celebrate thy grace"] and fall silent, whereupon Honour directs the second chorus to "conclude this Song, /To him, to whom all Phœbus beames belong." The voices respond:

> Rise stil (cleere Sun) and neuer set,
> but be to Earth her only light:
> All other Kings in thy beames met,
> are cloudes and darke effects of night.
> As when the Rosie Morne doth rise,
> Like Mists, all giue thy wisedome waie;
> A learned King, is, as in skies,
> To poore dimme stars, the flaming day.[110]

As the celebratory chorus dies away, Eunomia (law) addresses the Virginians:

> Virginian Princes, ye must now renounce
> Your superstitious worship of these Sunnes,
> Subiect to cloudy darknings and descents,
> And of your sweet deuotions, turne the euents
> To this our Britan *Phœbus*, whose bright skie
> (Enlightned with a Christian Piety)
> Is neuer subiect to black Errors night,
> And hath already offer'd heauens true light,
> To your darke Region, which acknowledge now;
> Descend, and to him all your homage vow.[111]

All then join in harmony to celebrate the nuptials. "Bright Panthæa borne to Pan, /Of the Noblest Race of Man, /Her white hand to Eros giuing, /With a kisse, ioin'd Heaven to Earth /And begot so faire a birth, /As yet neuer grac't the liuing."[112]

---

[109] Ibid., sig. D₄v.
[110] Ibid., sigs. D₄r, Ev.
[111] Ibid., sig. Ev.
[112] Ibid., sig. E₂v.

At this high moment of state, a major celebration of dynastic order, *The Memorable Maske* enacts sovereign possession of Virginia by "this our Britan *Phœbus*," that is, James I, as the overthrow of magic and superstition and the beginning of law. The masque represents Virginia as an island of riches that has floated across the Atlantic – "the Britan Ocean" – and fetched up against unmoving Britain. This in itself can be read as an allusion to the Roman law of alluvion (Chapman was a classical scholar, after all, writing a masque for lawyers) in that, in determining the ownership of land affected by the action of rivers, the *Digest* held that "if the force of the river should detach part of your land and bring it down to mine, it obviously remains yours," but added, "Of course, if it adheres to my land, over a period of time, and trees on it thrust their roots into my land, it is deemed from that time to have become part of my land."[113] More telling, however, is the masque's interior conflict and how it is resolved – the conflict, that is, between the Phœbades' hymns of worship to the setting sun and the counter-chorus that directs its praises to the ever-rising sun of King James. Honour sees to the ascendancy of the counter-chorus, but final, emphatic resolution of the conflict, and hence emergence of the masque's intended meaning, awaits the intervention of Eunomia (law) who commands the silent Virginians to turn away from the Sun and henceforth direct their "sweet deuotions" toward James.

The Memorable Maske was not the only entertainment presented during Princess Elizabeth's marriage festivities to bring myth, magic, spectacle, and arch allusion to the new world of Virginia to the dank darkness of an English winter. All of this and much more besides (youthful love and betrothal, dynastic succession, murderous intrigue, violence, the wonder of illusion) is to be found in William Shakespeare's *The Tempest*, one of a number of plays performed at court during the weeks of wedding festivities.[114]

Though Shakespeare and Chapman were, in some fashion, rivals, *The Tempest* was hardly the same kind of event as *The Memorable Maske*. For one thing it had not been written to mark the Princess Elizabeth's marriage, but some years earlier (probably c.1610/11).[115] Nor had it been designed as an extravagant display of homage but as theatrical, though perhaps epideictic, entertainment.[116] Still, in certain respects the two performances

---

[113] See *The Digest of Justinian*, Latin text edited by Theodore Mommsen with the aid of Paul Krueger, English translation edited by Alan Watson, in 4 vols. (Philadelphia, 1985), IV, 41.1.7.2. The same was in Bracton: "where the violence of a stream has swept away a parcel of your land and attached it to that of your neighbour; it is clear that it remains yours. If it is attached to your neighbour's land for a long time and the trees it carried with it strike root there, from that time they are deemed to be part and parcel of his property. See *Bracton: On the Laws and Customs of England (De Legibus Et Consuetudinibus Angliæ)*, Samuel E. Thorne, trans. (Cambridge, Mass., 1968), II, 44.

[114] Others by Shakespeare that were performed included *Much Ado About Nothing, Othello, The Winter's Tale, Julius Caesar* and possibly *The Merry Wives of Windsor*. See E. K. Chambers, *William Shakespeare: A Study of Facts and Problems* (Oxford, 1930), II, 343.

[115] Virginia Mason Vaughan and Alden T. Vaughan, editors, *The Tempest* (London, 1999), 1.

[116] Edward Berry, *Shakespeare and the Hunt: A Cultural and Social Study* (Cambridge, 2001), 206.

were not entirely distinct. *The Tempest* clearly lent itself to spectacle – it is, in all senses, the most phantasmagoric of Shakespeare's plays: the most aural and visual, the most musical, the most varied in the modalities of theatricality employed, even including (on a more modest scale than *The Memorable Maske*) its own masque sequence. As is the case in Shakespeare in general, *The Tempest* was also highly topical. The play is replete with sly allusion to New World colonizing that reference both key Virginia sources[117] and wider current debates.[118]

In referencing Virginia *The Tempest* was no different from other contemporary theater. The colony's depressingly frequent early disasters were a matter of common knowledge on the London street, and theater companies needled the Virginia Company's failures and pretensions mercilessly. Company nerves were raw. William Crashaw had no kind words for "Plaiers" when he preached his sermon in February 1609/10 before Lord De La Warre, Lord Governor and Captain General of Virginia, then about to depart with another fleet of supply to shore up the tottering colony. On the company's enemies list, "plaiers" ranked with papists and the devil:

> As for *Plaiers*: (pardon me right Honourable and beloued, for wronging this place and your patience with so base a subiect,) they play with *Princes* and *Potentates*, *Magistrates* and *Ministers*, nay with *God* and *Religion*, and all *holy things*: nothing that is good, excellent or holy can escape them: how then can this *action?* But this may suffice, that they are *Players*: they abuse *Virginea*, but they are but *Players*: they disgrace it: true, but they are but *Players*, and they haue *played* with better things, and such as for which, if they speedily repent not, I dare say, vengeance waites for them. But let them *play* on: they make men laugh on earth, but *hee that sits in heauen laughes them to scorne;* because like the flie they so long play with the candle, till first it singe their wings, and at last burnes the~ altogether. But why are the *Players* enemies to this Plantation and doe abuse it? I will tell you the causes: First, for that they are so multiplied here, that one cannot liue by another, and they see that wee send of all trades to *Virginea*, but will send no *Players*, which if wee would doe, they that remaine would gaine the more at home. Secondly, as the *diuell* hates vs, because wee purpose not to suffer *Heathens*, and the *Pope* because

---

[117] For example, William Strachey, *A True Reportory of the Wracke, and Redemption of Sir Thomas Gates, Knight; Upon and From the Ilands of the Bermudas: His Coming to Virginia, and the Estate of that Colonie then, and after, under the Government of the Lord La Warre, July 15, 1610.* First published in *Purchas his Pilgrimes* (London, 1625), IV, 1734–58. In Vaughan and Vaughan, editors, *The Tempest*, appendix 1, 288–302. But see Roger Stritmatter and Lyne Kositsky, "Shakespeare and the Voyagers Revisited," *Review of English Studies*, 58, 236 (2007), 447–72, and "'O Brave New World': *The Tempest* and Peter Martyr's *De Orbe Novo*," *Critical Survey*, 21, 2 (Summer 2009), 7–42.

[118] For which, see, for example, John Gillies, "Shakespeare's Virginia Masque," *ELH* (*English Literary History*), 53, 4 (Winter 1986), 673–707. For discussion of themes common to *The Memorable Maske* and *The Tempest* (reproduction and education) distinct from those emphasized here, see Joan Pong Linton, *The Romance of the New World: Gender and the Literary Formations of English Colonialism* (Cambridge, 1998), 155–84. See also Jeffrey Knapp, *An Empire Nowhere: England, America, and Literature from* Utopia *to* The Tempest (Berkeley, 1992), 220–42.

we haue vowed to tolerate no *Papists*: so doe the *Players*, because wee resolue to suffer no *Idle persons in Virginea*, which course if it were taken in *England*, they know they might turne to new occupations.[119]

Robert Johnson's *New Life of Virginea*, published two years later, renewed Crashaw's attack, targeting "the licentious vaine [vanity] of stage poets" who had helped the "malitious and looser sort" to "whet their tongues" with "scornful taunts against the action itselfe, in so much as there is no common speech nor publike name of anything this day, (except it be the name of God) which is more vildly depraued, traduced and derided by such unhallowed lips, then the name of Virginea."[120]

One cannot know who in particular Crashaw and Johnson had in mind. It is highly unlikely it was Shakespeare, who when Crashaw preached his sermon had still to turn to *The Tempest*. Crashaw was probably thinking of Ben Johnson and George Chapman's *Eastward Ho!* Perhaps Crashaw's fury might help account for Chapman's groveling depiction of Virginia suppli-cant in *The Memorable Maske* – a belated attempt to atone for *Eastward Ho!*, which had landed him in prison. Perhaps it even accounts for the care with which Chapman depicted "the lawfulnesse of that Action," which had been "the first and fundamentall" question Crashaw's sermon had attempted to answer. Johnson wrote somewhat later, and after *The Tempest*'s first per-formance, but may simply have been following Crashaw's lead. *The Tempest* took no obvious position in the contemporary politics of the Virginia enterprise, nor in any case did its Virginia references so outrun others as to mark it unambiguously as Shakespeare's "American" play. It was, like all his plays, capacious in the wholesale range of meanings it canvassed.[121]

---

[119] William Crashaw, *A Sermon Preached In London before the right honorable the Lord Lawarre, Lord Gouernour and Captaine Generall of Virginea, and others of his Maiesties Counsell for that Kingdome, and the rest of the Aduenturers in that Plantation. At the said Lord Generall his leaue tak-ing of England his Natiue Countrey, and departure for Virginea, Febr. 21. 1609 ... Wherein both the lawfulnesse of that Action is maintained, and the necessity thereof is also demonstrated, not so much out of the grounds of Policie, as of Humanity, Equity, and Christianity* (London, 1610), sig. H$_4$v-r.

[120] Robert Johnson, "Epistle Dedicatorie" to *The New Life of Virginea: Declaring the Former Successe and Present estate of that plantation, being the second part of Nova Britannia* (London, 1612). See also Crashaw's brief renewal of his complaints in his own "Epistle Dedicatorie" to *Good Newes from Virginia. Sent to the Covnsell and Company of Virginia, resident in England. From Alexander Whitaker, the Minister of Henrico in Virginia* (London, 1613).

[121] Leo Salingar, "The New World in 'The Tempest'," in Jean-Pierre Maquerlot and Michèle Willems, *Travel and Drama in Shakespeare's Time* (Cambridge and New York, 1996), 209–12. See also Meredith Anne Skura, "Discourse and the Individual: The Case of Colonialism in 'The Tempest'," *Shakespeare Quarterly*, 40, 1 (Spring 1989), 42–69. The sheer variety of critical attention to *The Tempest* and discussion of its meanings over time is well con-veyed in Virginia Mason Vaughan and Alden T. Vaughan, "Introduction," in Vaughan and Vaughan, editors, *The Tempest*, 1–138. See also, in particular, Hulme and Sherman, *The Tempest*, 85–350; Peter Hulme and William H. Sherman, editors, *The Tempest and Its Travels* (Philadelphia, 2000). It is worth noting that the critical commentary adduced by Hulme and Sherman in *The Tempest and Its Travels* comfortably accommodates the play to Alison Games's narrative of "the Mediterranean origins of the British Empire." See Alison Games, *The Web of Empire: English Cosmopolitans in an Age of Expansion, 1560–1660* (New York, 2008), 47–79.

But though not obviously "about" Virginia as such, *The Tempest* addressed the nature of power in a setting, both descriptive and textual, that one can certainly call colonial.[122] Moreover, it explored, subtly, the theme addressed in an explicitly Virginian setting in *The Memorable Maske*, that of the conjunction of magic and law; or, more precisely, the displacement of magic by law.

As a theatrical event *The Tempest* proceeds on two levels.[123] The play's minimally sketched outer shell depicts a fateful return encounter between Prospero, sometime Duke of Milan, and Alonso, the reigning King of Naples, who twelve years before had conspired with Prospero's younger brother Antonio to usurp Prospero's dukedom and dispose of the incumbent prince and his infant heir Miranda by setting them adrift in the Mediterranean many leagues from land aboard "a rotten carcass of a butt, not rigged, /Nor tackle, sail, nor mast."[124] By intercession of "providence divine,"[125] the butt had fetched up on the shores of a mysterious and exotic island on which Alonso, homeward bound with his courtiers and his son Ferdinand from the wedding of his "fair daughter"[126] Claribel to the King of Tunis, has in turn been wrecked in the fearful storm that opens the play. The dramatic trajectory of the outer play depicts the comeuppance of Alonso and Antonio at the hands of Prospero. The action is interspersed with moments of apparent parody that lampoon plotting courtiers, besotted lovers, and buffoonish servants. By the close, Prospero has won back his dukedom from his usurping brother and has reconciled with Alonso over the betrothal of their heirs, Miranda and Ferdinand. With proper order in both princely houses restored, all leave the island for home.

Within this comedic proscenium occurs an inner play staged by Prospero with the assistance of his servant, the "airy spirit" Ariel, in which, empowered by his "art," Prospero methodically inflicts upon every other participant in turn such precisely calculated degrees of psychological coercion as to cause them to act in ways that completely serve his ends – the restoration of his dukedom – while simultaneously satisfying his craving for revenge.[127] Prospero's "art" has a human aspect: it is the fruit of years of study conveyed to the island in his head and in books from his ducal library with which the noble Neopolitan courtier, Gonzalo, helpfully equipped the boat in which

---

[122] Aviam Soifer, "Assaying Communities: Notes from *The Tempest*," *Connecticut Law Review*, 21, 4 (Summer 1989), 871–97; Francis Barker and Peter Hulme, "Nymphs and Reapers Heavily Vanish: The Discursive Con-texts of *The Tempest*," in John Drakakis, editor, *Alternative Shakespeares* (London, 1985), 191–205; Stritmatter and Kositsky, "'O Brave New World'," 7–42.

[123] Peter Hulme, "Prospero and Caliban," in Hulme and Sherman, editors, *The Tempest*, 233–49.

[124] *The Tempest*, 1.2.146–7.

[125] Ibid., 1.2.159.

[126] Ibid., 2.1.72.

[127] "Prospero's chief magical activity throughout *The Tempest* is to harrow the other characters with fear and wonder and then to reveal that their anxiety is his to create and allay." Greenblatt, *Shakespearean Negotiations*, 142.

Prospero was originally set adrift.[128] But it is in equal part an aspect of the island itself, to which Prospero has gained access through his mastery of Ariel.[129] Magic enables Prospero to summon the opening storm, to dispose of all the principals – not least his own adolescent daughter – precisely to his liking in their relations to each other, to determine their comings and goings, to set them asleep or wake them up, to manipulate their appetites, torture them with lust or grief, conjure illusions to amaze and torment them, and even, when necessary, take complete physical control of them. In the inner play Prospero behaves as puppet master, all-knowing, all-(for) seeing, who plots and obtains the outcomes that are the key components in his strategic design for his own restoration and dynastic immortality (the bonding of Ferdinand and Miranda, the consent of Alonso to their match, the disgrace of Antonio) like so many moves on a board. The inner play is tense, obsessively controlled and controlling, and deadly serious. It is an elaborate drama of manipulation that occurs in terse sequential haste, virtually in real time,[130] a second layered meaning for "tempest."[131]

The audience is made privy to *The Tempest*'s duality – its outer/inner distinction – virtually from the outset when, at the beginning of the second scene of the first act, immediately after the storm, we learn that the shipwreck we have just observed has in fact been conjured by Prospero. In

---

[128] *The Tempest*, 1.2.73–7, 109–10, 160–8. One should recognize that Prospero's art is not simply magic, but the Machiavellian "art," or policy, of a prince. Prospero gives us to understand that as duke he was a naïf in such matters, a dreaming scholar easily duped by his younger brother: "being so reputed /In dignity, and for the liberal arts /Without a parallel; those being all my study, /The government I cast upon my brother /And to my state grew stranger, being transported /And rapt in secret studies. Thy false uncle ... / Being once perfected how to grant suits, /How to deny them, who t'advance and who / To trash for overtopping, new created /The creatures that were mine, I say, or changed 'em, /Or else new form'd 'em; having both the key /Of officer and office, set all hearts i'th'state /To what tune pleased his ear, that now he was /The ivy which had hid my princely trunk, /And sucked my verdure out on't." And so on. In all, Prospero keeps his lament going for more than 60 lines – 1.2.66–132 – stupefying Miranda with his self-pity ("Your tale, sir, would cure deafness" 1.2.106), so much so one must suspect it is as much an exercise in deceit as all the other aspects of Prospero's account of their beginnings in the island, on which see Barker and Hulme, "Nymphs and Reapers," 199. In fact we know from observation of Prospero's behavior that he is a master of manipulation.

[129] Prospero's magic appears ineffective beyond the island and its immediate environment, else he could long since have used it to depart and reclaim his dukedom. Prospero tells us that he used his art to free Ariel from the pine tree within which Ariel had been confined by his erstwhile mistress, the witch Sycorax, Caliban's mother, the first comer to the island, long dead (1.2.257–93). But it is also clear that Ariel has his own magical powers that greatly amplify Prospero's, or to put it differently, that Prospero is actually dependent upon Ariel to exercise most of the magical powers that he demonstrates in the course of the play.

[130] The obsessiveness of the inner play is exhibited in its recurrent counting (the number three and its multiples recur incessantly), and its constant attention to the passage of time. The elapsed time of the action of the inner play from opening storm to finale is, according to Alonso, exactly three hours. *Tempest*, 5.1.136.

[131] See *Oxford English Dictionary* tempest, †4, "a time; a period, an occasion. *Obs.*" (From the latin *tempestate*).

this long scene (by far the longest in the play) we learn everything that we will need to understand all the moves that Prospero will make throughout the remainder of the play. We are educated in Prospero's grievances and powers, and made aware of his agent, Ariel. We are introduced to those – Miranda and Ferdinand – who are to be the principal means to Prospero's ends. And we are introduced to the play's shadow, Caliban.[132] From the second scene onward, we thus observe all Prospero's manipulations with inside knowledge from the same elevated perspective "above" the action that Prospero himself assumes. We know what he knows. In case we should forget the structural duality that grants us our position of privilege, as it were "alongside" Prospero, the inner play constantly reminds us of it by insistently calling attention to itself both in word and action.

The action of *The Tempest*, then, is highly structured and highly self-conscious. Its manipulations, oiled by Prospero's "art," proceed almost like a clockwork mechanism, virtually without suspense. All the more noteworthy, then, are two crucial and related moments of uncertainty in which this is palpably not the case. The first of these is sprung upon the audience as a moment of exquisite confusion: Prospero's sudden flustered realization that an element of the action of which he has been informed by Ariel, but which he has apparently let slip – "[*aside*] I had forgot that foul conspiracy /Of the beast Caliban and his confederates /Against my life" – is about to reach its climax. "The minute of their plot /Is almost come."[133] The second moment is the play's end, when in effect the inner play continues on beyond the limits of the outer proscenium in an epilogue in which Prospero directly addresses the audience that has been his silent companion throughout in a speech that part entreats, part enjoins the audience to implicate itself in what it has observed by signifying its approval and consent.[134]

The first moment of uncertainty occurs at a highly strategic point in Prospero's inner play, as a masque-like illusion – "Some vanity of mine art"[135] – that Prospero stages to mark the betrothal of Ferdinand and Miranda and to instruct them in the virtues of temperance reaches its climax. It is conveyed in a very precise stage direction that announces the climax of the masque and then its abrupt collapse as Prospero suddenly recalls Caliban's conspiracy: *Enter certain Reapers, properly habited. They join with the Nymphs in a graceful dance, toward the end whereof Prospero starts suddenly and speaks; after which, to a strange hollow and confused noise, they heavily vanish.*[136] There follows an exchange between a startled Ferdinand and Miranda that comments on Prospero's extraordinary perturbation: "[*Fer.*] This is strange. Your father's in some passion /That works him strongly. [*Mir.*] *Never till this day* /Saw I him touched with anger so distempered."[137]

[132] Described in the Folio's "Names of the Actors" as "a salvage and deformed slave."
[133] *The Tempest*, 4.1.139–42.
[134] Ibid., Epilogue, 1–20.
[135] Ibid., 4.1.41.
[136] Ibid., immediately following 4.1.138.
[137] Ibid., 4.1.143–45 (emphasis added).

Prospero struggles to show he remains master – of himself, of events. "You do look, my son, in a moved sort, /As if you were dismayed," he says to Ferdinand.[138] Nothing untoward has occurred. "Our revels now are ended. These our actors, /As I foretold you, were all spirits and /Are melted into air, into thin air."[139] Still, Prospero remains "vexed ... troubled ... A turn or two I'll walk /To still my beating mind."[140] Still calculating, he bids Ferdinand and Miranda "retire into my cell," where he will later reveal them to Alonso, then sets out with Ariel to confront Caliban.[141]

The masque sequence is itself a virtuoso display both of composition and of dramatic versatility. As John Gillies has shown, some of *Tempest*'s most pointed allusions to England's Virginia and its problems are on display in these lines.[142] And, by fashioning an enactment of instructive entertainment before an audience on stage (Ferdinand and Miranda), Shakespeare adds a third ring of play within play that will remind *The Tempest*'s audience of its own position vis-à-vis the instructive entertainment unfolding before *its* eyes, prepare it for its own role as participant in the epilogue, invite it to reflect on the didactic role of court masques, and at the same time distract it – with "graceful dance" – so that the sudden moment of confusion that will disrupt every level of *The Tempest* will indeed be one of real, deep uncertainty. The position of the masque sequence within the inner play is also of great strategic consequence for it occurs precisely between the two moments essential to the fulfillment of Prospero's ambitions: first, the moment already past, at which it has become certain that his manipulation of Ferdinand and Miranda has borne fruit, that they are willingly betrothed;[143] second, the moment to come, already telegraphed, when Prospero will confront Alonso and his usurping brother, and simultaneously reunite Alonso with "Young Ferdinand (whom they suppose is drowned) /And his, and mine, loved darling."[144] This, the crowning moment of *anagnorisis* – the "most high miracle!"[145] that the entire inner play is working to bring about – is Prospero's final and most important manipulation. It will wring from a dazed and wondering Alonso consent

---

[138] Ibid., 4.1.146–7. As Hulme notes, Prospero's comment is a clever tu quoque that attempts to throw the appearance of agitation onto Ferdinand. Hulme, "Prospero and Caliban," 236. Note also the terms of address, "my son."

[139] *The Tempest*, 4.1.148–50.

[140] Ibid., 4.1.158–9, 162–3.

[141] Ibid., 4.1.161, 166. One can read Prospero's lines contemplating Caliban's rebellion at 4.1.188–92 – "A devil, a born devil, on whose nature /Nurture can never stick; on whom my pains /Humanely taken – all, all lost, quite lost! /And, as with age his body uglier grows, /So his mind cankers" – as another, but clumsier, attempt at a tu quoque, in that Prospero sententiously proclaims his own good offices in his relations with Caliban and then puts the effects of ageing, specifically a cankered mind, on Caliban, only a few lines after he has excused his own "weakness," troubled "old brain" and "infirmity" in conversation with Ferdinand and Miranda at 4.1.159–60.

[142] Gillies, Shakespeare's Virginia Masque," 686–702.

[143] *The Tempest*, 3.1.15–96. Hence the "my son" at 4.1.146.

[144] Ibid., 3.3.90–93.

[145] Ibid., immediately following 5.1.171; 5.1.177.

to the match between his son and heir to Prospero's daughter and heir, the match that will ensure Prospero's restoration to his principality and substitute enduring dynastic alliance with the royal house of Naples for his usurping brother's nefarious partnership-in-crime.

The uncertainty wrought by Caliban's conspiracy, then, erupts at a moment that is both freighted with meaning and of great strategic significance in the structure of the play as Prospero's plan ticks its way toward realization. The moment is the pivot on which Prospero's plan turns. What does the conspiracy signify?

Caliban is the one character in *The Tempest* who is beyond Prospero's psychological manipulations. His is an immunity learned of hard experience, for once it had been otherwise. Caliban had already been on the island, a motherless child, when Prospero and Miranda washed up. "When thou cam'st first /Thou strok'st me and made much of me; wouldst give me /Water with berries in't, and teach me how /To name the bigger light, and how the less /That burn by day and night. And then I loved thee / And showed thee all the qualities o'th' isle: /The fresh springs, brine-pits, barren place and fertile. /Cursed be I that did so!" For Prospero had laid Caliban low, displacing and enslaving him. "I am all the subjects that you have, /Which first was mine own king; and here you sty me /In this hard rock, whiles you do keep from me /The rest o'th' island."[146]

Strikingly, in their encounters, it is Caliban who possesses an extraordinary eloquence – "You taught me language and my profit on't /Is I know how to curse"[147] – and Prospero and Miranda, ordinarily articulate, naught but bawling invective and beatings: "Thou most lying slave, /Whom stripes may move, not kindness … /Filth as thou art" says the father.[148] "Abhorred slave, /Which any print of goodness wilt not take, /Being capable of all ill" says the daughter.[149] Before Caliban even appears, they have already colored him in. He is a "freckled whelp, hag-born," says Prospero, a "Dull thing … my slave."[150] He is "a villain … I do not love to look on" says Miranda.[151] Still, says Prospero, "We cannot miss him; he does make our fire, /Fetch in our wood, and serves in offices /That profit us."[152] All others follow Prospero's "art" to do his bidding. Caliban will not be moved but by threats and lashings: "Fetch us in fuel; and be quick – thou'rt best – /To answer other business. Shrug'st thou, malice? /If thou neglect'st, or dost unwillingly /What I command, I'll rack thee with old cramps, /Fill all thy bones with aches, make thee roar, /That beasts shall tremble at thy din."[153]

[146] Ibid., 1.2.333–45.
[147] Ibid., 1.2.364–5.
[148] Ibid., 1.2.345–7.
[149] Ibid., 1.2.352–4.
[150] Ibid., 1.2.283, 285, 308.
[151] Ibid., 1.2.310–11.
[152] Ibid., 1.2.312–14.
[153] Ibid., 1.2.367–72.

Unlike every other event that occurs during *The Tempest*'s three hours, Caliban's conspiracy is not Prospero's invention.[154] It is Caliban's own doing, hatched with Trinculo and Stephano in a parody of Prospero's own plotting that – Caliban knows full well – sorely lacks Prospero's resources. "Remember /First to possess his books, for without them /He's but a sot, as I am, nor hath not /One spirit to command."[155] Prospero's art commands. Caliban must flatter, wheedle, importune the loutish Neopolitan drunkards in a wild frenzy of hope that he can somehow entice them to become the agents of his desperation to be rid of the "tyrant," the "sorcerer," who "Cheated me of the island."[156] The agony of Caliban's need is great, his self-abasement in its service is cruel. His plans are shattered by his co-conspirators' wretched stupidity. "Let it alone, thou fool, it is but trash," he screams as Trinculo crows over the "trumpery," Prospero's "glistering apparel," scattered to catch their eye. "What do you mean to dote thus on such luggage? Let't alone /And do the murder."[157]

Espied by Ariel, who betrays their conspiracy to Prospero, who's so absorbed in his own high plots he forgets about it until just before the moment of fruition, the conspirators are dispersed with such violent ease that it all looks like Prospero's premeditated farce. But where's the farce in Caliban's hatred? Can it be teased with such aloof near-fatal forgetfulness? "I'll yield him thee asleep, /Where thou mayst knock a nail into his head … or with a log /Batter his skull, or paunch him with a stake, /Or cut his wezand with thy knife."[158] Nor, it seems, is hatred Caliban's alone – "They all do hate him /As rootedly as I."[159] Caliban means the island's other shadows, other spirits like Ariel, all there before Prospero appeared,[160] whom Prospero now commands as cattle to serve "My present fancies."[161] Maybe he means Ariel too. "Go bring the rabble /(O'er whom I give thee power) here to this place" Prospero tells Ariel. "Incite them to quick motion" for "I must use you /In … another trick."[162] Unctuous Ariel, whose own deep desire to be rid of Prospero has its own design throughout, promises "Each one tripping on his toe, /Will be here with mop and mow," then like any trusty with a shiv up his sleeve adds a fawning menace – "Do you love me,

[154] Here I differ from Peter Hulme, who argues that nothing can happen in *The Tempest* that is not controlled by Prospero: "The conspiracy is no surprise to him and, even if he has been monitoring its progress offstage (suggested by 4.1.171) [170], the fact that he has not bothered to immobilize the conspirators indicates that he desires the conspiracy to run its course. Clearly it is an essential element in his play." Hulme, "Prospero and Caliban," 234.

[155] *The Tempest*, 3.2.91–4.

[156] Ibid., 3.2.40–2.

[157] Ibid., 4.1.225, 232–3.

[158] Ibid., 3.2.58–9, 89–91.

[159] Ibid., 3.2.94–5.

[160] Prospero calls them Ariel's "meaner fellows." Ibid., 4.1.35.

[161] Ibid., 4.1.122.

[162] Ibid., 4.1.36–9.

master? No?"[163] The enchanted island world is full of the unexpected after all, as Caliban keeps telling us, "full of noises" – if you listen.[164]

Yet for all that, "Prospero *remembers*."[165] And it appears he did hear at least something of Ariel's original report. "Say *again*, where didst thou leave these varlets?"[166]

His surprise is genuine, nonetheless. The conspiracy, though overpowered, exposes Prospero's throat and the limitations of his art, not least to those underlings who may keep their hatreds hooded but know well their master's vulnerabilities. It is surely worth remarking that Prospero's first semi-measured response to the conspiracy, while his mind is still "beating," is not to look to his defenses, but to begin to doubt his own power, to pick, famously, at the "baseless fabric" of the illusions he creates, at the glistering apparel of his imagination, at himself: "The cloud-capped towers, the gorgeous palaces, /The solemn temples, the great globe itself, / Yea, all which it inherit, shall dissolve, /And, like this insubstantial pageant faded, /Leave not a rack behind. We are such stuff /As dreams are made on, and our little life /Is rounded with a sleep."[167] This, the first of twinned reflections on what his "rough magic"[168] can and cannot do, born in the turbulence of Caliban's revolt, points straight to the second, Prospero's equally famous abjuration that follows but a few minutes after. Prospero's art has brought him to the threshold of the final planned moment of his play, but it can no more deliver the actuality of restoration that he desires than it could relieve him of Caliban's hatred. And so "I'll break my staff, / Bury it certain fathoms in the earth, /And deeper than did ever plummet sound /I'll drown my book."[169] Prospero resumes a former fabric, an old attire, and steps into, breaking, the charmed circle: "Behold, sir King, / The *wronged* Duke of Milan."[170]

In stepping out of, stopping, magic – the whole world of *The Tempest* to this point – Prospero steps into, begins, awakens, law. The restoration Prospero seeks – needs – is restoration to a world of authority by right. It must occur by the volitional rules of that world. And it does. Straight away a different clockwork starts its tick. Unbidden, Alonso acts as rule requires: "Thy dukedom I resign and do entreat /Thou pardon me my wrongs."[171] Prospero takes the king's chit to his brother "and require /My

---

[163] Ibid., 4.1.46–8. ("mop and mow" means grotesque and derisive grimaces.)

[164] Ibid., 3.2.135.

[165] Hulme, "Prospero and Caliban," 234 (emphasis in original).

[166] *The Tempest*, 4.1.170. Ariel tells us at 3.2.115 that he will inform Prospero of Caliban's conspiracy, but no information passes between them on stage and at 4.1.168 we learn that Ariel passed up at least one opportunity to tell Prospero of the conspiracy. 4.1.170 is the only indication that a report was ever made.

[167] Ibid., 4.1.151–8.

[168] Ibid., 5.1.50.

[169] Ibid., 5.1.54–7.

[170] Ibid., 5.1.85–6, 106–7 (emphasis added).

[171] Ibid., 5.1.118–19.

dukedom of thee, which perforce I know /Thou *must* restore."[172] Language,
behavior, time all change.[173] Then comes the tableau of *anagnorisis*, staged
as a further signifier of restoration and *worldly* rule – "Ferdinand and
Miranda, *playing at chess*"[174] – with childish banter over the rules of the
game, and Alonso's consent to the children's match, and Prospero's dry
response to Miranda's delighted exclamation at discovering the real world,
"[*Mir.*] O brave new world" – "[*Pro.*] 'Tis new to thee." Assuredly, this law-
bound world is not new to him at all, but a known and predicable world to
which he is returning.[175]

Adding to this welter of restorations underpinned by dynastic legalities and worldly rule come Stephano and Trinculo, restored to place and
remastered, and Caliban – a new development – acknowledged "mine" by
Prospero.[176] The colonizer in the moment of his leave taking lays claim
once more to the island on which he washed up, but in a new legal language
of responsible possession to which Caliban, freed from the old regime of
magic only moments before, is newly required to comply. "Go, sirrah, to
my cell ... As you look /To have my pardon, trim it handsomely." And in
complying, Caliban for the first time in the play yields voluntarily: "Ay, that
I will; and I'll be wise hereafter /And seek for grace."[177] Powerful indeed,
the secular language of persuasive coercion Prospero has recovered.
Caliban's objective position has not changed one whit. Yet in place of the
rebel Prospero will leave behind a compliant servant, one who has indeed
become (as Captain John Smith would notice soon enough) what, formerly,
he had only seemed to be – "a plain fish and no doubt marketable."[178]

[172] Ibid., 5.1.132–4 (emphasis added).

[173] Following 5.1.106, Prospero's language and behavior change from command to suasion,
from a constant hyper-awareness to relaxation, to a demonstrated familiarity with a world
of rule in which all know their place. The time and order of magic that consumes the
play through 5.1.105 is distinctive: Magic requires Prospero's constant and active engagement – without magic all will be chaos in his world for magic is all that keeps others at
bay. Caliban's hatred of him is explicit, Ariel's though hooded is clear to the observer,
we know that the island people also hate Prospero, and we know that the courtiers could
easily overwhelm him were he without magical powers over them (powers demonstrated
when Ferdinand draws on him at 1.2.467–74). As Caliban says of Prospero, without his
magic he's but "a sot" (3.2.93). The beginning of law in the play is a reinstantiation of a
known and rhythmic order. Prospero – "the wronged Duke of Milan" – can once more
slide smoothly up and down predictable hierarchies; the temporality of law, in contrast to
the fevered temporality of magic, is calm and contemplative: "Every third thought shall
be my grave" (5.1.312).

[174] Ibid., immediately following 5.1.171 (emphasis added). On the significance of chess in the
tableau and to the play, see Bryan Loughrey and Neil Taylor, "Ferdinand and Miranda at
Chess," in Stanley Wells, editor, *Shakespeare Survey: An Annual Survey of Shakespearian Study
and Production*, 35 (Cambridge, 1982), 113–18.

[175] *The Tempest*, 5.1.183–4, and generally 5.1.172–215.

[176] Ibid., 5.1.256–76.

[177] Ibid., 5.1.292–6.

[178] Ibid., 5.1.266 (and see 2.2.24–36). For Smith and *his* fish, see the Prologue to this book.
On Caliban's concluding compliance, see Andrew Gurr, "Industrious Ariel and Idle
Caliban," in Maquerlot and Willems, *Travel and Drama in Shakespeare's Time*, 204.

A final reduction completes, and relativizes, the metaphysical transformation that ends *The Tempest*. All depart except the elderly ex-sorcerer, whose play of manipulation continues on beyond the proscenium. It seems its terms are entirely altered, for Prospero's charms are "all o'erthrown," his only strength "mine own, /Which is most faint."[179] Prospero's last words importune the audience to join him in the renunciation of magic for law. The audience is asked to follow Prospero's lead by releasing him from *its* spell. But his protestations of a new powerlessness notwithstanding, Prospero does not implore, rather he coerces the audience's compliance, just as moments before he demanded Caliban's. Prospero declares in *The Tempest*'s very last words the presence of a new and violent power come to rule in place of the magic of the old regime, the violent power of law: "As you from crimes would pardoned be, /Let your indulgence set me free."[180] By joining actor directly to audience in a final moment of uncertainty, the epilogue breaks the last charmed circle in the play, that of the proscenium itself. But this time the uncertainty is anticlimactic. The audience is well aware what penalties unpardoned crimes incur. Prospero knows, in short, that the audience, like Caliban, will bow to the threat, that his new order of law will be secured by the audience's compliant applause.

In *The Memorable Maske* and *The Tempest*, then, one encounters twinned textual figurations that at the outset of English colonizing conjoin the enterprise with the end of myth, the beginning of law. In *The Memorable Masque*, law overcomes myth on the colonizer's behalf; in *The Tempest*, law succeeds myth in securing the colonizer's regime to a world order of like regimes, a *societas gentium*. In *The Memorable Masque*, law is imperious, in *The Tempest*, law is primarily suasive. Both however figure their climactic action as lawful and law as order. In both, law's violence is sheathed but easily glimpsed.

To postulate a shared meaning for these texts as figurations of a "beginning" for the conjunction of law and colonizing that, 250 years later, Lincoln's repudiation of *Dred Scott* "ends" is necessarily to entrust this book's final meaning to allegory, a hazardous undertaking in so determinedly positivist a philosophy of history as American. Still, allegory is no stranger in American history,[181] even if usually acknowledged only in the guise of its weak cousin, metaphor. Here the allegorical form to which I shall have resort is that brilliantly embraced by Walter Benjamin in his 1921 essay "Critique of Violence," which addresses law precisely in its relationship to myth.[182]

[179] *The Tempest*, Epilogue, 1–3.

[180] Ibid., 19–20.

[181] See, e.g., Herman Melville, *Moby-Dick, or, The whale* (New York, 1851); Herman Melville, *The Confidence Man: His Masquerade* (New York, 1857); Michael Paul Rogin, *Subversive Genealogy: The Politics and Art of Herman Melville* (New York, 1983); John Samson, *White Lies: Melville's Narratives of Facts* (Ithaca, N.Y., 1989).

[182] Walter Benjamin, "Critique of Violence," [*Kritik Zur Gewalt*] in Marcus Bullock and Michael W. Jennings, editors, *Walter Benjamin: Selected Writings* (Cambridge, Mass., 1996),

In largest part, *Critique* animadverts the claim that law's violence serves justice – that legal theory has successfully demarcated a right to coerce in order to create, preserve, or restore justice. "Law's concern with justice is only apparent ... in truth the law is concerned with self-preservation." Law is made by violence and preserved by violence. "[L]awmaking pursues as its end, with violence as the means, *what* is to be established as law, but at the moment of instatement does not dismiss violence; rather, at this very moment of lawmaking, it specifically establishes as law not an end unalloyed by violence, but one necessarily and intimately bound to it, under the title of power."[183] Violence begins law and completes it. As a modality of rule, of well ordering, law is extortion. It demands with menaces.

But no remedy for human problems, no "deliverance from the confines of all the world-historical conditions of existence obtaining hitherto," is possible "if violence is totally excluded in principle."[184] In what form, under what circumstances, can violence be morally acceptable? Is there a "pure" violence? The violence "envisaged by legal theory" had been exposed as devoted solely to the making and preserving of law. "Among all the forms of violence permitted by both natural law and positive law, not one is free of the gravely problematic nature ... of all legal violence."[185] What then of alternatives? What of the prehistoric, the mythic violence that the gods visited upon humanity – the violence of the *Erinyes* (Furies) against Orestes, of Apollo and Artemis against Niobe's children? Was this "a purer sphere"?

The archetype of mythic violence, Benjamin argued, was "a mere manifestation of the gods"; neither a means to their ends, nor even a display of their will, but simply a sign of their existence. The gods are prior to law. They punish a fated guilt, a guilt foreseen; their violence *begins* the law that decrees the punishment of that guilt. "Niobe's arrogance calls down fate upon her not because her arrogance offends against the law but because it challenges fate – to a fight in which fate must triumph and can bring to light a law only in its triumph."[186]

I, 236–52. See also Walter Benjamin, "The Right to Use Force," in the same, at 231–4, and "Theological-Political Fragment," in *Walter Benjamin: Selected Writings*, III, 305–6. On the origins of the relationship between myth and law in Benjamin's thought, see Gershom Scholem, *Walter Benjamin: The Story of a Friendship* (New York, 2003), 40. I develop my own thoughts on the myth/law relationship in Benjamin's work in Christopher Tomlins, "Toward a Materialist Jurisprudence," in Daniel W. Hamilton and Alfred J. Brophy, editors, *Transformations in American Legal History, II: Law, Ideology, and Methods – Essays In Honor of Morton J. Horwitz* (Cambridge, Mass., 2010). On "Critique of Violence" see also Christopher Tomlins, "To Improve the State and Condition of Man: The Power to Police and the History of American Governance," *Buffalo Law Review*, 53, 4 (Fall 2005), 1215–71.

[183] Benjamin, "The Right to Use Force," 232; "Critique of Violence," 248.

[184] Benjamin, "Critique of Violence," 247.

[185] Ibid., 247.

[186] Ibid., 248. At a festival in Thebes to honor the goddess Leto [Latona, *Lat.*], mother of Apollo and Artemis, the Anatolian princess Niobe addresses the throng: "What folly ... is this! – to prefer beings whom you never saw to those who stand before your eyes! Why should Latona be honored with worship and none be paid to me? My father was Tantalus,

We find ourselves suddenly and precisely in the midst of Prospero's play. As sorcerer, Prospero is prior to law.[187] He takes the island from Caliban by force. He enslaves Caliban by force. When Caliban and his allies rebel they challenge fate to a fight they cannot win. Their punishment – *dogs and hounds, hunting them about, Prospero and Ariel setting them on*[188] – is for the guilt of a rebellion foreseen. Caliban hates Prospero, one may propose, precisely because he has broken no law. There is none to break. Rather, law comes after, established by its signifiers, Prospero's power and Caliban's punishment. It is that establishment of law to which Caliban consents at the end of the play: to the "pardon" that it offers, to the rightness of his subjection that it signifies, to the priority it bestows upon the master he willingly acknowledges for the first time. Prospero can renounce magic because his mythic violence (his play) has established the conditions for law's new/resumed existence. Law is the continuation of his play, but by other means. "Since this cause has devolved on me, I will ... establish a tribunal, a tribunal to endure for all time," says Athena in *Eumenides* of the court created to render a judgment on Orestes rather than leave him to his fated destruction by the Furies. It is "the first trial," she tells the jury, "ever held for bloodshed." Aeschylus, David Luban argues, means this "to stand for the beginning of the system of justice."[189] But justice has no system. Justice is not what tribunals have in mind; Roger Taney has told his audience this very clearly indeed. What Athena's tribunal stands for is the beginning of law. This is the beginning to which Caliban consents, to which Prospero in the epilogue requires *The Tempest*'s audience to consent as well.

"Far from inaugurating a purer sphere, the mythic manifestation of immediate violence shows itself fundamentally identical with all legal

who was received as a guest at the table of the gods; my mother was a goddess. My husband [Amphion] built and rules this city, Thebes; and Phrygia is my paternal inheritance. Wherever I turn my eyes I survey the elements of my power; nor is my form and presence unworthy of a goddess. To all this let me add I have seven sons and seven daughters [known as the Niobids], and look for sons-in-law and daughters-in-law of pretensions worthy of my alliance. Have I not cause for pride? Will you prefer to me this Latona, the Titan's daughter, with her two children? I have seven times as many. Fortunate indeed am I, and fortunate I shall remain! Will any one deny this? My abundance is my security. I feel myself too strong for Fortune to subdue. She may take from me much; I shall still have much left. Were I to lose some of my children, I should hardly be left as poor as Latona with her two only." Leto is angered and her children, Apollo and Artemis, kill Niobe's children "from above" with poisoned darts, first the sons, then the daughters. "Speech only delays punishment," says Apollo. In her grief Niobe turns to stone. See Thomas Bulfinch, *Mythology: The Age of Fable* (New York, 1913), 112–14.

[187] Note Donna Hamilton's observation that Prospero "speaks with the flat, impenetrable voice of the gods." Donna B. Hamilton, *Virgil and* The Tempest: *The Politics of Imitation* (Columbus, Ohio, 1990), 110.

[188] *The Tempest*, stage direction at 4.1.254.

[189] David Luban, *Legal Modernism* (Ann Arbor, 1994), 300–1. See also David Harris Sacks, "Discourses of Western Planting: Richard Hakluyt and the Making of the Atlantic World," in Peter C. Mancall, editor, *The Atlantic World and Virginia, 1550–1624* (Chapel Hill, 2007), 436–46.

violence, and turns suspicion concerning the latter into certainty of the perniciousness of its historical function, the destruction of which becomes obligatory. This very task of destruction poses again, ultimately, the question of a pure immediate violence that might be able to call a halt to mythic violence."[190] Only the destructive violence of God is pure and immediate. "Just as in all spheres God opposes myth, mythic violence is confronted by the divine. And the latter constitutes its antithesis in all respects."[191] This, precisely, was Lincoln's final retort to Taney's law in his Second Inaugural, the retort that proves him the revolutionary he had of necessity to become to end an evil rather than compromise with it.[192] Divine violence strikes "without warning, without threat, and does not stop short of annihilation. But in annihilating it also expiates." Mythic violence was "bloody power over mere life for its own sake," divine violence "pure power over all life for the sake of the living." Mythic violence "demands sacrifice"; divine violence "accepts it."[193]

V. Beginning and End

We know about the violence of the beginning. It was violence on law's behalf, in furtherance of its ends, in vindication of "the lawfulnesse of that Action," a relieved violence that demanded sacrifice. "Our hands which before were tied with gentlenesse and faire vsage, are now set at liberty," Edward Waterhouse rejoiced in 1622, after the Jamestown Massacre.

> So that we, who hitherto haue had possession of no more ground then their waste, and our purchase at a valuable consideration to their owne contentment, gained; may now by right of Warre, and law of Nations, inuade the Country, and destroy them who sought to destroy vs: whereby wee shall enioy their cultiuated places, turning the laborious Mattocke into the victorious Sword (wherein there is more both ease, benefit, and glory) and possessing the fruits of others labours.[194]

[190] Benjamin, "Critique of Violence," 249.
[191] Ibid.
[192] Graber, *Dred Scott*, 237–54. "'The Judgments of the Lord are true and righteous altogether'." Abraham Lincoln, "Second Inaugural Address," 225. Lincoln's antipathy for slavery is as clear from the course of his political career as his reluctance to see American "nationality" sundered in order to uproot it. See for example Ross, "Lincoln and the Ethics of Emancipation." It is not the antipathy but the necessitous overcoming of the reluctance that makes Lincoln a revolutionary. One must recognize that he who at the outset embraces "reverence for the laws" as his (political) religion is a different person from he who at the very end will overthrow laws in the name of divine judgment. "Justice ... is destructive in opposing the constructive ambiguities of law." Walter Benjamin, "Karl Kraus," in *Walter Benjamin: Selected Writings*, II.2, 433–58, at 456.
[193] Benjamin, "Critique of Violence," 249–50. Consider the form of words Lincoln chose for his Second Inaugural. "Both parties deprecated war; but one of them would make war rather than let the nation survive; and the other would accept war rather than let it perish. And the war came." Abraham Lincoln, "Second Inaugural Address," 224.
[194] Edward Waterhouse, *A Declaration of the State of the Colony and Affaires in Virginia. With a Relation of the Barbarous Massacre in the time of Peace and League, Treacherously Executed by the Natiue Infidels vpon the English, the 22 of March last* (London, 1622), 22–3.

Forty years after the elder Hakluyt had warned that "conquest is not easie," it seemed, after all, to Waterhouse, that it *was*:

> victorie of them may bee gained many waies; by force, by surprize, by fam-
> ine in burning their Corne, by destroying and burning their Boats, Canoes,
> and Houses, by breaking their fishing Weares, by assailing them in their
> huntings, whereby they get the greatest part of their sustenance in Winter,
> by pursuing and chasing them with our horses, and blood-Hounds to draw
> after them, and Mastiues to teare them, which take this naked, tanned,
> deformed Sauages, for no other then wild beasts, and are so fierce and fell
> vpon them, that they feare them worse then their old Deuill which they
> worship, supposing them to be a new and worse kinde of Deuils then their
> owne.[195]

But time passed, and with it the terrible harshness of the beginning. The "dreary haunts of savage beasts, and more savage men" were softened by improvement. "We are a race of cultivators, our cultivation is unrestrained, and therefore every thing is prosperous and flourishing."[196] The cultivator's laborious hand would lay the mainland's ghosts. "We find now only harmless retreats, *where the fowls of heaven have their habitation which sing among the branches.*"[197] No one conveys better the dream of a conciliated landscape at the heart of the lyric legalism of the colonies' maturity, than Crèvecoeur:

> Often when I plough my low ground, I place my little boy on a chair which
> screws to the beam of the plough – its motion and that of the horses please
> him, he is perfectly happy and begins to chat ... the odoriferous furrow
> exhilarates his spirits, and seems to do the child a great deal of good, for he
> looks more blooming since I have adopted that practice; can more pleasure,
> more dignity be added to that primary occupation? The father thus plough-
> ing with his child, and to feed his family...

"I never see my trees drop their leaves and their fruit in the autumn, and bud again in the spring," he writes a few lines later, "without wonder."[198]

Within Crèvecoeur's writing, however, there accumulate simultaneously, almost imperceptibly, tiny acidic drips that etch an undertone of menace into his reverie of recurrence.[199] At first they trickle in from outside. Their presence is faintly disturbing, but it also assures the American of his difference. "In Italy all the objects of contemplation, all the reveries of the

---

[195] Ibid., 24. It appears Waterhouse thought better of having mastiffs "teare" the Indians, and amended the word to "seaze" in errata.

[196] Crèvecoeur, "Introduction," in *Letters from an American Farmer*, 9.

[197] Fiske, *Remarkable Providences*, 26.

[198] Crèvecoeur, "On the Situation, Feelings, and Pleasures, of an American Farmer," in *Letters from an American Farmer*, 28, 29; Hallock, *From the Fallen Tree*, 21; Parent, *Foul Means*, 200–01.

[199] One such is present even in Crèvecoeur's blissful account of ploughing with his son. The analogy, as Norman Grabo observes, is to Odysseus ploughing with his son Telemachus, feigning madness to avoid the war against Troy, and to the trick by which Palamedes exposes Odysseus' ruse. See Grabo, "Crèvecoeur's America," 168.

traveler, must have a reference to ancient generations, and to very distant periods, clouded with the mist of ages. Here, on the contrary, every thing is modern, peaceful, and benign. Here we have had no war to desolate our fields: our religion does not oppress the cultivators: we are strangers to those feudal institutions which have enslaved so many. Here nature opens her broad lap."[200] But when Crèvecoeur looks more closely at nature's broad lap he finds it is neither peaceful nor benign. It is a buffeting turmoil, "one species of evil is balanced by another ... one element is repressed by the power of another," the whole a fragile "equipoise," an "economy of evil" at the heart of which men struggle to survive, not modern at all but primitive.[201] And then, while traveling in South Carolina, Crèvecoeur discovers that the evil that has begun to haunt him is not in the primal natural world in which men must somehow live, it is in men themselves. The legalized harmonies of his Orange County farm are replaced by a nightmarish landscape polluted by law, by "the mazes of the law" that the "principal classes of inhabitants ... lawyers, planters, and merchants" have wielded against the rest to seize their patrimony. "[N]othing can exceed their wealth, their power, and their influence ... no plantation is secured, no title is good, no will is valid, but what they dictate, regulate, and approve."[202] Their corruption spreads beyond the land; it defiles human life. It is manifest in the "misery and wretchedness," the "cracks of the whip" that "the chosen race" inflicts upon the lives of others. "Day after day they drudge on without any prospect of ever reaping for themselves; they are obliged to devote their lives, their limbs, their will, and every vital exertion to swell the wealth of masters; who look not upon them with half the kindness and affection with which they consider their dogs and horses."[203] On his way to dine at a plantation, Crèvecoeur comes suddenly – "strange order of things!"[204] – face to face with the unspeakable consequence, a grotesque "living spectre" of death:

> I perceived at about six rods distance something resembling a cage, suspended to the limbs of a tree; all the branches of which appeared covered with large birds of prey ... I perceived a negro, suspended in the cage, and left there to expire ... the birds had already picked out his eyes, his cheek bones were bare; his arms had been attacked in several places, and his body seemed covered with a multitude of wounds. From the edges of the hollow

---

[200] Crèvecoeur, "Introduction," 7.

[201] J. Hector St. John de Crèvecoeur, "Thoughts of an American Farmer on Various Rural Subjects," in Bourdin et al., eds., *Sketches of Eighteenth Century America*, 122; Grabo, "Crèvecoeur's America," 162.

[202] J. Hector St. John de Crèvecoeur, "Description of Charles-Town; Thoughts on Slavery; On Physical Evil; A Melancholy Scene," in *Letters from an American Farmer*, 224–5. "The nature of our laws, and the spirit of freedom, which often tends to make us litigious, must necessarily throw the greatest part of the property of the colonies into the hands of these gentlemen." (225).

[203] Ibid., 226, 227.

[204] Ibid., 227.

sockets and from the lacerations with which he was disfigured, the blood slowly dropped, and tinged the ground beneath.[205]

Crèvecoeur gives the dying slave water. His hosts tell him what he has seen is punishment for killing an overseer. "They told me that the laws of self-preservation rendered such executions necessary." He has no answer.[206]

Later, after he has returned to his New York farm, Crèvecoeur finds himself caught in the trails of the War for Independence. He writes again of existential evil – "dreadful scenes to which I have been a witness," death and calamity, flight and abandonment, the fears and hatreds that overwhelm men and women, the nightmares of children. "Though these evils have been gradual, yet they do not become habitual like other incidental evils. The nearer I view the end of this catastrophe, the more I shudder." He writes as everyman's colonist, torn between loyalty to England – "ancient principles ... that nation which I held once so respectable" – and home. Again, he has no answer. "I resemble, methinks, one of the stones of a ruined arch, still retaining that pristine form that anciently fitted the place I occupied, but the centre is tumbled down; I can be nothing until I am replaced."[207] But the laws that had, so to speak, shaped the stone – that created the landscape in which migrants were planted and grew anew, that formed new men and new property, that meant modernity – those laws that had seemed so nurturing had turned instead "voluminous" and oppressive, "galling the very necks, of those whom they protect." And so Crèvecoeur decides to "revert into a state approaching nearer to that of nature," to seek out a place far from "the accursed neighbourhood of Europeans," a place "without temples, without priests, without kings, and without laws" among "the inhabitants of the woods." Flight becomes his only answer to the horror he has encountered – the condemned slave ravening in his cage, the "brutality and bloodshed" of war.[208] Crèvecoeur will escape law's violence by disappearing into the woods. He will seek out a mythic primordial state of being prior to law, where law is not to be found.

Crèvecoeur's fantasy of flight, from law into nature, has a parallel of sorts in Shakespeare's *Titus Andronicus*, a play saturated in law,[209] which in so many respects – not least that it was the work of a youthful Shakespeare – is itself a beginning to *The Tempest*'s end.[210] In *Titus*, the slave Aron, Caliban's

[205] Ibid., 243.

[206] Ibid., 245. And see Robert Olwell, *Masters, Slaves, and Subjects: The Culture of Power in the South Carolina Low Country, 1740–1790* (Ithaca, N.Y., 1998), 70–71.

[207] J. Hector St. John de Crèvecoeur, "Distresses of a Frontier Man," in *Letters from an American Farmer*, 282, 286, 289, 300.

[208] Ibid., 289, 300, 301, 307, 308.

[209] Tomlins, "Law's Wilderness," 22–4; Paul Raffield, "'*Terras Astraea reliquit*': Titus Andronicus and the Loss of Justice," in Paul Raffield and Gary Watt, editors, *Shakespeare and the Law* (Oxford and Portland, Ore., 2008), 203–20, at 204.

[210] *Titus Andronicus* (c. 1592) is one of Shakespeare's first plays, *The Tempest* (c. 1610/11) is one of his last. The elderly wizard conducting his own inside drama is often interpreted as a device that Shakespeare chose as a means to reflect knowingly on his own "art" as dramatist.

forebear,[211] attempts a purposeful escape from the consequences of his many transgressions. With him Aron takes his infant son, born of the Empress Tamora, whom (we saw at the beginning of Chapter 9) Aron has been ordered to kill. Aron intends not the death of the child but its rescue; his flight is rebellion. "Come on, you thick-lipped slave," he says to the child, "I'll bear you hence, /For it is you that puts us to our shifts."

> I'll make you feed on berries and on roots,
> And fat on curds and whey, and suck the goat,
> And cabin in a cave, and bring you up
> To be a warrior and command a camp.[212]

But Aron is captured by his enemies and condemned to die "breast-deep in earth, and famish[ed]," another slave in another cage, his "doom" (sentence) intended "to order well the state."[213]

Aron resembles Caliban in the want of autonomy that is the sign of the subaltern – neither can act except through the favors he curries, each depends upon the success with which he can manipulate wretchedly inadequate others.[214] Both, however, are eloquent in their fury while their adversaries have only the incoherence of invective and the power to order enemies silenced (Prospero with his magic, Lucius with a gag). Aron, like Caliban, knows well how to curse.[215] Caliban's words, high and clear and beautiful, hauntingly echo Aron's:

> I prithee, let me bring thee where crabs grow,
> And I with my long nails will dig thee pignuts,
> Show thee a jay's nest, and instruct thee how
> To snare the nimble marmoset. I'll bring thee
> To clust'ring filberts, and sometimes I'll get thee
> Young scamels from the rock. Wilt thou go with me?[216]

Both, finally, hate – fiercely, unremittingly. Both have good reason.

There the resemblance ends. The atrophy of the rebel from Aron to Caliban is striking. Aron is a titanic and turbulent force of disruption in

---

[211] They are similar in appearance: Prospero describes Caliban as "freckled," Miranda calls him "brutish" and of a "vile race" (1.2.283, 358, 359). Aron is called a "swart Cimmerian ... spotted, detested, and abominable" (2.3.74). See also Skura, "Discourse and the Individual," 65–6, who notes parallels between *The Tempest* and *Titus Andronicus*, and identifies Caliban with Aron's child.

[212] *Titus Andronicus*, 4.2.176–81. As this suggests, one way to conceive of Aron is as a Maroon. For suggestive analysis, see Kathleen Wilson, "The Performance of Freedom: Maroons and the Colonial Order in Eighteenth Century Jamaica and the Atlantic Sound," *William and Mary Quarterly*, 3rd Ser., 66, 1 (January 2009), 45–86; Steven Hahn, "Did We Miss the Greatest Slave Rebellion in History?" in *The Political Worlds of Slavery and Freedom* (Cambridge, Mass., 2009), 55–114.

[213] *Titus Andronicus*, 5.3.179, 203.

[214] See Chapter 9, nn.24–27 and accompanying text.

[215] "If there be devils, would I were a devil, /To live and burn in everlasting fire, /So I might have your company in hell /But to torment you with my bitter tongue." *Titus Andronicus*, 5.1.147–50.

[216] *The Tempest*, 2.2.164–9. Skura, "Discourse and the Individual," 65.

Titus Andronicus. "[I]f you brave the Moor, /The chafèd boar, the mountain lioness, /The ocean swells not so as Aaron storms."[217] Channeled through others or not, Aron's murderous energies are only barely contained by the play. Caliban yearns for affection; his aching loneliness – "in dreaming, / The clouds, methought, would open and show riches /Ready to drop upon me, that when I waked /I cried to dream again" – is deeply marked upon him.[218] Compare, too, *The Tempest*'s baroque structure and obsessive control with the wild anarchy of *Titus Andronicus.* Aron scythes through the Andronici and their cohorts like the grimmest of reapers: he contrives the murder of Bassianus, the rape and mutilation of Lavinia, the beheading of Martius and Quintus, and Titus's eager assent to the amputation of his own hand. Caliban enjoys only the barest glimpse of clownish rebellion before he is crushed. Contrast, finally, the end that awaits each of them: Sentenced to be buried alive and left to starve and rave, Aron spits contempt. "Ah, why should wrath be mute and fury dumb? /I am no baby, I..."[219] Caliban's end is not contempt but compliance.[220]

Over the full course of *Titus Andronicus*, the Roman state that Aron's execution will supposedly "order well" is shown over and over to be rotted through to its core. Those who seize power in the final scene, brutal Lucius and scheming Marcus, the last of the Andronici, can only succeed because their coup is backed by the state's bitterest enemies, "the princes of the Goths," with whom they have cynically allied. We know – because Aron has told us – that among these new allies are secreted friends of the Empress Tamora, the Andronici's mortal enemy.[221] Who will discard whom first? In this "wilderness of tigers" the skills Aron promises to teach his son – to "cabin in a cave," to be "a warrior," to "command a camp" – are those of armed survival. "Perhaps we are to understand that in a collapsing state," Jack D'Amico speculates, "only such a man as Aaron" has the capacity to found a new order. "In his role as patriarch-father Aaron ... takes us back to the lost *virtù* necessary for a state's founding."[222] There is none other in the offing in the corrupt Rome of *Titus Andronicus.* But in *The Tempest* the offing is emptier yet: There is no *virtù* at all in the debased and scheming Neapolitan court, nor in Prospero, who has devoted his own life – and will happily give away his daughter's – to the sole objective of rejoining the world the court inhabits. The only figure of honorable appearance, Gonzalo, is old and foolish, a dreamer easily overmatched in wit, and not a little hypocritical besides.[223] As for Caliban, he is allowed not a tenth of

---

[217] *Titus Andronicus*, 4.2.137–9.

[218] *The Tempest*, 3.2.140–3.

[219] *Titus Andronicus*, 5.3.184–5. At the end of the play, the fate of Aron's child is left entirely unclear.

[220] Compare the "trimming" of Lavinia that Aron gleefully recalls, *Titus Andronicus* 5.1.93–6, with the trimming Caliban is sent to perform on his last exit from *The Tempest*, 5.1.294.

[221] *Titus Andronicus* 4.2.175, 5.1.34–6, 5.1.156.

[222] Jack D'Amico, *The Moor in English Renaissance Drama* (Tampa, Fla., 1991), 140.

[223] See, e.g., *The Tempest*, 2.1.1–184.

Aron's ferocious capacity. His defiance of Prospero's magic is striking, his rebellion against it brave, his defeat complete. At the end of *The Tempest* he has been rendered submissive. The court party can sail for home, ranks augmented, order restored, sway secured by new-instated law. Prospero's seductive epilogue as clearly assures Caliban's continued subalternship as Taney's bisectional constitutionalism would guarantee the slaveholder's indefinite veto.

The difference between these proffered continuances is that Prospero's audience will always accept. His astonishing virtuosity will always gain the seal of applause, even though what our applause signifies is consent to the perpetuation of Caliban's unfreedom. That is the audacity and the cunning of the epilogue. Taney was less lucky in his audience, or perhaps less cunning, or simply fell foul of real life, with only one chance to get the words out right. Some were not astonished at his virtuosity, and did not applaud. Lincoln's repudiation of *Dred Scott* teaches us that there are always alternatives to complicity, howsoever they disturb the customs and conventions that "order well the state."

Perhaps Mark Graber is right – that it always makes more sense to compromise, because the cost of doing otherwise can be so great. Perhaps doing otherwise is in any case foolish: a tilt against a windmill. Perhaps, nevertheless, one should risk the tilt, "cabin in a cave," become a warrior, command a camp. The consequences of our choices when they're made are rarely clear. When, after 250 years on the mainland, the conjunction that had prevailed "from the time of the first emigration to the English colonies" flashed up in an instant at which it could be recognized for what it was, eyes might have averted. But instead it *was* recognized. And the instant was recognized, too, in all its gaunt and brilliant clarity, as a time for choice. And the choice was made. And so the war came. In that moment, if only for a moment, freedom was unbound.

Appendices to Chapter 1

European Migration to English Mainland America, 1600–1780, and the Incidence of Indentured Servitude: Estimates and Sources

Current estimates indicate a total European migration to the English mainland colonies, through 1780, of between 472,600 and 512,900. Of these, some 54,500 were involuntary migrants (convicts or prisoners), the vast majority of whom entered North America during the eighteenth century. Of the 418,100–458,400 voluntary migrants, I estimate 48–50 percent were committed to an initial period of servitude by indenture or other arrangement. This status was substantially more common during the seventeenth century, when it described 59–64 percent of all voluntary migrants, than the eighteenth, when it described 40–42 percent. In what follows here I disaggregate these crude totals by century, region, and component.

The Seventeenth Century: Numbers and Sources

My estimates indicate a total seventeenth-century European migration to the Chesapeake of 108,000 people of whom 80 percent (86,400) were servants, to New England of 24,000 of whom 16.5 percent (4000) were servants, to the Delaware Valley of 15,000, of whom 35 percent (5250) were servants, to the Lower South of 8,000, of whom 40 percent (3,200) were servants, and to New Netherlands of 6,000, of whom 3,300 (55 percent) were servants. On these figures, servants comprised 63.5 percent of all seventeenth century European migrants (102,150 of 161,000). These estimates and proportions are constructed from the following sources:

(1) *The century as a whole*: Henry Gemery, "Emigration from the British Isles to the New World, 1630–1700: Inferences from Colonial Populations," *Research in Economic History: A Research Annual*, V (1980), 179–231, and "Markets for Migrants: English Indentured Servitude and Emigration in the Seventeenth and Eighteenth Centuries," in P. C. Emmer, editor, *Colonialism and Migration: Indentured Labour Before and After Slavery* (Dordrecht, 1986), 33–54, at 40 (table II).

(2) *The Chesapeake*: Russell R. Menard, "British Migration to the Chesapeake Colonies in the Seventeenth Century," in Lois Green Carr et al., editors, *Colonial Chesapeake Society* (Chapel Hill, 1988), 99–132, at 102 for 1600–1630, and at 104–5 (tables 2 and 3) for 1630–1700; James Horn, *Adapting to a New World: English Society in the Seventeenth-Century Chesapeake* (Chapel Hill, 1994), 25. (Horn sets

the incidence of servants at 70–85 percent of total migrants; he proposes that overall migration was approximately 120,000, a figure within the range that Menard considers plausible).

(3) *New England*: Gemery, "Emigration from the British Isles," and sources cited at Chapter 1 nn.7 and 32.

(4) *The Delaware Valley*: David Hackett Fischer, *Albion's Seed: Four British Folkways in America* (New York, 1989), 421; Gary B. Nash, *Quakers and Politics: Pennsylvania, 1681–1726* (Princeton, 1968), 50.

(5) *The Lower South*: John J. McCusker and Russell R. Menard, *The Economy of British America, 1607–1789* (Chapel Hill, 1985), 171–2; David W. Galenson, *White Servitude in Colonial America: An Economic Analysis* (Cambridge and New York, 1981), 54–5, 217; Warren B. Smith, *White Servitude in Colonial South Carolina* (Columbia, 1961).

(6) *New Netherlands*: Ernst van den Boogaart, "The Servant Migration to New Netherland, 1624–1664," in Emmer, editor, *Colonialism and Migration*, 55–81.

The Seventeenth Century: Discussion

Gemery proposes a total British migration during 1630–1700 of 155,000, of which 116,000 is to the Chesapeake and Lower South, and 39,000 to the Middle Colonies and New England. For New England I use the common 21,000 estimate for the 1631–40 period, plus a nominal 500 per decade for the remainder of the century. Servant numbers, at 16.5 percent, are based on the preponderance of the estimated percentages reported in Chapter 1, nn.7 and 32. For the Delaware Valley I use Fischer's estimate of 15,000 for migration to the Delaware Valley and Nash's "at least one third" (which I have converted to 35 percent) for the proportion of servants in that migration. Together, these figures fit Gemery's overall estimate very well. For the Chesapeake I use Menard's decadal migration figures for 1630–1700, supplemented by adjustments he makes to cover the period from 1607 to 1630. It should be noted that this figure is lower than Menard's "best guess" of approximately 123,000 for the entire seventeenth century, but that figure is simply the middle of the range of possibilities (99,000–146,000) that he offers and does not fit well with other estimates of overall seventeenth-century migration. Nor does it fit with the total produced by his decadal series. Disaggregated decadal figures are far more useful to analysis of trends over time than a lump number, so I have chosen to stick with the overall figures they produce. I have deliberately set my estimate of the incidence of servants in Chesapeake migration (80 percent) near the top of the range of conjectural estimates offered by specialists. See, for example, Horn, *Adapting*, 25 (70–85 percent and "nearer the upper bound" than the lower); Alison Games, *Migration and the Origins of the English Atlantic World* (Cambridge, Mass., 1999), 74 (a more precise 77 percent, based on her analysis of the 1635 cohort). For the Lower South I can offer no more than a guess, based in part on the residual of round numbers left from the more reliable estimates for other regions. The figure is clearly an upper bound. To the extent that it is inflated, the Chesapeake numbers could be raised by 4,000–5,000.

These seventeenth-century totals are highly compatible with those offered by Aaron Fogleman, whose estimates are based on ethnicities rather than regions of reception. Fogleman proposes a slightly larger total European migration of 165,200 (compared with my 161,000) but suggests a somewhat lower percentage (59 percent, compared with my 64 percent) of migrants committed to an initial term of servitude. Fogleman's figures include 2,300 involuntary European (mostly Scottish) migrants in the category "convicts and prisoners," as well as some 1,500 miscellaneous (mostly Swedish and German) migrants. It is unlikely that these are counted in the sources I have used. If they are not, then our overall migrant numbers – arrived at by different methods of tabulation – match almost exactly. See Aaron S. Fogleman, "From Slaves, Convicts and Servants to Free Passengers: The Transformation of Immigration in the Era of the American Revolution," *Journal of American History*, 85, 1 (June 1998), 68.

The Eighteenth Century: Numbers and Sources

For the eighteenth century (through 1780), the range of numbers on offer in the literature is substantially wider. An additional hazard for the "regions" approach used here is that the ethnic diversification of European migration to the English mainland colonies during the eighteenth century – on which see Marilyn C. Baseler, *"Asylum for Mankind": America, 1607–1800* (Ithaca, N.Y., 1998) – has encouraged scholars to differentiate migrant numbers and population characteristics by ethnicity rather than region of reception. Aaron Fogleman's research has synthesized much of the existing literature, however, producing a set of estimates greeted as the best currently available for overall eighteenth-century transatlantic migration. See his "Slaves, Convicts, and Servants." For a complete explanation of his estimates, see Aaron Fogleman, "Migrations to the Thirteen British North American Colonies, 1700–1775: New Estimates," *Journal of Interdisciplinary History*, 22, 4 (Spring 1992), 691–709. For comments on Fogleman's figures, see John M. Murrin, "In the Land of the Free and the Home of the Slave, Maybe there was Room even for Deference," *Journal of American History*, 85, 1 (June 1998), 86; Georg Fertig, "Transatlantic Migration from the German-Speaking Parts of Central Europe, 1600–1800: Proportions, Structures, and Explanations," in Nicholas Canny, editor, *Europeans on the Move: Studies on European Migration, 1500–1800* (Oxford, 1994), 199, 201; James Horn, "British Diaspora: Emigration from Britain, 1680–1815," in P. J. Marshall, editor, *The Oxford History of the British Empire*, volume II, *The Eighteenth Century* (Oxford, 1998), 31–2.

Calculating eighteenth-century migration according to ethnic group and time period, Fogleman arrives at a total of 307,400 European migrants, voluntary and involuntary (convict) as shown in Table A1.

Table A1. *Eighteenth-Century Migration to the Thirteen Mainland Colonies, by European Ethnic Group (in thousands)*

Decade Ending	German	Northern Irish	Southern Irish	Scots	English	Welsh	Other	Total
1709	0.1	0.6	0.8	0.2	0.4	0.3	0.1	2.5
1719	3.7	1.2	1.7	0.5	1.3	0.9	0.2	9.5
1729	2.3	2.1	3.0	0.8	2.2	1.5	0.2	12.1
1739	13.0	4.4	7.4	2.0	4.9	3.2	0.8	35.7
1749	16.6	9.2	9.1	3.1	7.5	4.9	1.1	51.5
1759	29.1	14.2	8.1	3.7	8.8	5.8	1.2	70.9
1769	14.5	21.2	8.5	10.0	11.9	7.8	1.6	75.5
1779	5.2	13.2	3.9	15.0	7.1	4.6	0.7	49.7
Tot.	84.5	66.1	42.5	35.3	44.1	29.0	5.9	307.4

Fogleman's total is low (although not unacceptably so) when compared with global estimates in the range of 340,000–370,000 offered by several scholars for this period. See Jim Potter, "Demographic Development and Family Structure," in Jack P. Greene and J. R. Pole, editors, *Colonial British America: Essays in the New History of the Early Modern Era* (Baltimore, 1984), 135–6 (summarizing work of Henry Gemery, David Galenson, and Potter himself); Henry Gemery, "Disarray in the Historical Record: Estimates of Immigration to the United States, 1700–1860," *Proceedings of the American Philosophical Society*, 133, 2 (1989), 123–7, and "European Emigration to North America, 1700–1820: Numbers and Quasi-Numbers," *Perspectives in American History*, new ser., 1 (1984), 283–342.

The Eighteenth Century: Discussion

Fogleman's disaggregated ethnic group figures tend in most cases to inhabit the low end of ranges indicated in the work of other scholars. In the German case, for example, other scholars propose a range of 90,000–120,000. See Marianne Wokeck, "German and Irish Immigration to Colonial Philadelphia," *Proceedings of the American Philosophical Society*, 133, 2 (1989), 128–43, at 128–33, and "The Flow and the Composition of German Immigration to Philadelphia, 1727–1775," *Pennsylvania Magazine of History and Biography*, 105, 3 (July 1981), 249–78, at 260–1. Wokeck has refined and restated her estimates in *Trade in Strangers: The Beginnings of Mass Migration to North America* (University Park, Pa., 1999), 45–53, where she proposes an overall German migration to all of North America of 111,000 and to Philadelphia alone of 80,000. The literature on German migration (excluding Wokeck's most recent work) is discussed in Fertig, "Transatlantic Migration." See also Farley Grubb, "Immigration and Servitude in the Colony and Commonwealth of Pennsylvania: A Quantitative and Economic

Analysis" (Ph.D. dissertation, University of Chicago, 1984), 15–16, 175, and "German Immigration to Pennsylvania, 1709 to 1820," *Journal of Interdisciplinary History*, 20, 3 (Winter 1990), 417–36; A. G. Roeber, *Palatines, Liberty and Property: German Lutherans in Colonial British America* (Baltimore, 1993), ix; Günter Moltmann, "The Migration of German Redemptioners to North America, 1720–1820," in Emmer, ed., *Colonialism and Migration*, 105–22, at 115; Bernard Bailyn, *Voyagers to the West: A Passage in the Peopling of America on the Eve of the Revolution* (New York, 1986), 25–6. Wokeck's refined figure of 111,000 clearly establishes the upper bound in a range of 84,500–111,000, and should be treated as authoritative.

In the Irish case the range of estimates is substantially wider, tending from 65,000 to more than 200,000. The upper bound is supplied largely by Bailyn's claim of 100,000–150,000 "Scotch-Irish" for 1720–60, which may, however, include other Celtic migrants, and by William J. Smyth's proposed average of 5,000 per annum "to colonial America" between 1700 and 1776. Patrick Griffin follows Bailyn, arguing for "more than 100,000." Based on projections of migrant numbers from a surname-sensitive analysis of their descendants (the U.S. population in 1790), Thomas Purvis proposes 114,000 Ulster migrants before 1775. James Horn states that the number for all Irish migrants is "at least 115,000." Marianne Wokeck's systematic study of German and Irish immigration to Philadelphia finds that at the peak (1763–73) of Irish entries to Philadelphia, in excess of two-thirds of all Irish entering the Delaware Valley were from Ulster ports, which, if a constant, would suggest (on Bailyn and Purvis's figures) an all-Ireland total of 150,000–250,000. But Wokeck's counts of actual arrivals at Philadelphia provide much lower overall totals, and have been accepted as the more accurate by L. M. Cullen, who suggests that the Delaware Valley total should be inflated by 50 percent to allow for aggregate Irish migration to all North American ports. Wokeck's recent restatement of her research on Irish immigration in *Trade in Strangers*, 172–3, gives further support to the lower figure, arguing for a total Irish immigration to the Delaware Valley of 51,676. Invoking Cullen's multiplier produces an aggregate of 77,500. Wokeck's restatement also reaffirms the two-thirds preponderance of Northern Irish emigrants and dates the beginnings of that preponderance from the mid-1740s. For Irish migration, see Wokeck, "German and Irish Immigration," 135–43, revised and refined in *Trade in Strangers*, 172–3; William J. Smith, "Irish Emigration, 1700–1920," in P. C. Emmer and M. Mörner, *European Expansion and Migration: Essays on the Intercontinental Migration from Africa, Asia, and Europe* (New York, 1992), 49–78; Bailyn, *Voyagers to the West*, 25–6; Patrick Griffin, *The People with No Name: Ireland's Ulster Scots, America's Scots Irish and the Creation of a British Atlantic World, 1689–1764* (Princeton, 2001), 1, 67; Thomas L. Purvis, "The European Ancestry of the United States Population, 1790," *William and Mary Quarterly*, 3rd Ser., 41, 1 (January 1984), 95–6; Horn, "British Diaspora," 31. L. M. Cullen, "The Irish Diaspora of the Seventeenth and Eighteenth Centuries," in Canny, ed., *Europeans on the Move*, 113–49, particularly 115–16. Fogleman's aggregate Irish migration,

Northern and Southern, of 108,600 [including involuntary migrants, who, A. Roger Ekirch advises, "were often disguised by merchants as indentured servants," *Bound for America: The Transportation of British Convicts to the Colonies, 1718–1775* (Oxford, 1987), 114] is extrapolated from Wokeck's earlier calculations and from research on shipping destinations, the effect of which is to suggest that Cullen's multiplier should be doubled. In light of Wokeck's and Cullen's work, Fogleman's aggregate might best be seen as a well-documented upper bound, establishing the range for Irish immigration at 77,500–108,600.

The German and Irish cases are the best documented in current scholarship on eighteenth-century migration to the mainland. Estimates for other ethnicities are more conjectural. Take Scottish migration. Fogleman's figure for Scottish migration, 35,300, is lower for the whole period through 1775 than Bailyn's estimate of 40,000 for the period 1760–75 alone. The total is also substantially lower than that of 62,500 suggested by Purvis, a figure concurred in by Smout, Landsman, and Devine. See Bailyn, *Voyagers to the West*, 25–6, 170–1, 175, 243; Purvis, "European Ancestry," 95–6; T. C. Smout, N. C. Landsman, and T. M. Devine, "Scottish Emigration in the Seventeenth and Eighteenth Centuries," in Canny, ed., *Europeans on the Move*, 97, 98, 104. Hence the notional range can be set at 35,000–62,500.

Fogleman's figures for English and Welsh migration are also (as he notes himself) somewhat conjectural. As in the Scottish case, reliable data are sparse. Fischer suggests that 7,500 migrants (mostly from northern England and the Welsh border) arrived in the Delaware Valley in the first two decades of the eighteenth century. Bailyn proposes "over 30,000" English migrants for the period after 1760. Galenson offers evidence of but a modest rate of influx for the intervening period. For English migration, see Fischer, *Albion's Seed*, 421; Bailyn, *Voyagers to the West*, 25–26, 170–1, 175, 243; Galenson, *White Servitude*, 51–6, 93. Given the numbers cited and the lack of evidence of any extensive English migration between 1720 and the 1760s, Fogleman's suggested overall figure of 44,100 for the English component of the English/Welsh aggregate (which, if Fischer and Bailyn are correct would imply an average English migration of only 1,600 persons per decade between 1718 and 1760) is not on the face of it unreasonable. Galenson, however, did not take involuntary (convict) migration into account in finding modest rates of English migration in the period between the end of early eighteenth-century Delaware valley migration and the post-1760 revival. On Ekirch's figures, between 1718 and 1775 some 36,000 convicts could be included in the category of English/Welsh migrants entering the thirteen colonies (overwhelmingly the Chesapeake, and particularly Maryland). See *Bound for America*, 114–16, 116. Allowing for these in the overall total requires that one assume a higher average migration rate for English/Welsh migrants (voluntary and involuntary) for the 1718–60 period. Horn's suggestion of 80,000 English/Welsh migrants, 1701–80, reinforces the case for this adjustment. It is likely that, as in the Irish case, convict migrants may have become compounded with the voluntary migrant category because the processes of their transportation did not readily render them an administratively distinct migrant stream (*Bound for America*, 111–19). Hence some convicts probably figure in Galenson's and Bailyn's estimates of post-1718 migration rates. But it is highly unlikely that all do. Thus, a substantial proportion of convict migrants should be considered additional to the figures already mentioned, increasing the estimated English/Welsh totals. Discussing English migration alone, Canny suggests that a figure of 50,000, including convicts, is appropriate for the period 1700–75. See Nicholas Canny, "English Migration into and across the Atlantic during the Seventeenth and Eighteenth Centuries," in Canny, ed., *Europeans on the Move*, 58. As an additional consideration, Fogleman's figure of 29,000 for the Welsh component of the English/Welsh amalgam is based on Purvis, but the ratio of migrants to descendant population suggested by Purvis's other estimates (that is, suggested by his analyses of the relationships between Ulster and Scottish migration and Ulster and Scottish-descended population segments) would argue for a larger estimate, one in the order of 45,000. It is necessary, of course, to adjust any addition to the Welsh component to try to avoid double-counting convict importations. A notional range in the English/Welsh case is thus established as 73,000–95,000.

The overall effect of recognizing the recent research of Marianne Wokeck in the German and Irish cases and of allowing some upward flexibility in the areas of least-reliable data (that is, Scottish, English, and Welsh migration) is to push Fogleman's total modestly upward, to 350,500 (this total accepts Fogleman's figure of 6,000 "other European"). This sits comfortably in the range of scholarship discussed by Potter (see previous discussion). Treating Fogleman's original grand total as an aggregate lower bound, the appropriate range for European migration to the mainland, 1700–80, can be set at 307,400–351,900.

The Eighteenth Century: Incidence of Indentured Servitude

In estimating the incidence of migrant servants in eighteenth-century migration, all scholars note considerable fluctuation in the proportion of servants to total numbers of migrants, varying primarily according to (a) ethnic origin and (b) chronology of migration. In the German case, Moltmann suggests a range of 50–66 percent servants in total migration. Grubb offers "roughly half" as an approximation of incidence over the whole period 1709–1820. His much more detailed studies of redemptioner migration to Philadelphia produce a more exact proportion of 58 percent for the period 1771–3, which also has the virtue of occurring at the midpoint of Moltmann's range. Relying on Wokeck, however, Fogleman arrives at a substantially lower 35 percent overall (this comprises a tripartite periodization of none before 1720, about one-third, 1720–60; and about one-half, 1760–75. See his "Slaves, Convicts and Servants," 72). Wokeck herself puts the incidence of servants in total migration at "at least half" after the

1750s, implying a lower rate than this for the preceding period of heaviest German migration through 1760 (see *Trade in Strangers*, 233). Collectively, the available evidence and opinion suggests that Moltmann's range is set too high, except for the years after 1760, where it is best represented by the 58 percent midpoint that Grubb calculated for Philadelphia, but that Fogleman's overall 35 percent is too low in light of the rise in incidence over 50 percent suggested by Wokeck and Grubb for the 1760s. For purposes of arriving at a very rough estimate of the incidence of servitude in German migration for the entire period, one might choose to accept Fogleman's 35 percent as reasonable for the earlier period and Grubb's 58 percent as reasonable for the later period, arriving at 46 percent. Given that the bulk of German migration occurred prior to 1760 (that is, during the "low-incidence" period), 46 percent can be considered a generous estimate.

In the Irish case, Wokeck, "German and Irish Immigration," estimates the incidence of servants at the peak of entries to Philadelphia at 20–25 percent among Ulster migrants and 50–66 percent among Southern Irish migrants. Applying these proportions to the overall Irish migrant stream, and adjusting to reflect the relative contribution of Southern and Northern Irish migrants, one arrives at an overall figure of approximately 36 percent. This agrees with Fogleman's figure based on the same sources: the addition of convicts to the calculation elevates the proportion of bound Irish migrants (whether voluntary or involuntary) to a bare majority of 51 percent. Once Wokeck's revised and refined figures (*Trade in Strangers*, 172–3) for Irish Delaware Valley migration are fully absorbed into the calculation, however, it seems inevitable that the incidence of servitude in Irish migration will fall, for, as already indicated, Wokeck's figures suggest that the preponderance of Northern Irish in overall Irish migration, clear in the 1760s, was actually well established by the mid-1740s.

In the Scottish case, Bailyn finds that fewer than one in five migrants arriving during 1774–6 were indentured. Can one, however, assume the constancy of the 1770s rate (which reflects the high proportion of family migrants in total movement)? Fogleman applies a rate of 50 percent for the period through 1760, producing an overall proportion of servants in total migration of 21 percent. Including convicts and prisoners, the incidence of bound (voluntarily and involuntarily) migrants on his figures increases to 27 percent of all Scottish migrants.

In the English/Welsh case the incidence of indentured servants among the early eighteenth-century Delaware Valley migrants is likely to have continued at approximately 35 percent (the rate of the late seventeenth century to that area). We know, however, that earlier seventeenth-century English rates were much higher, and Bailyn shows that by the 1770s the rate had returned to better than two-thirds voluntarily bound among all voluntary migrants. Fogleman assumes the two-thirds rate holds for all voluntary English/Welsh migrants during the eighteenth century. Most of the

Table A2. *Eighteenth-Century Migration to the Thirteen Mainland Colonies, by European Ethnic Group and Status (in thousands)*

	(a) Results derived from Fogleman				
	All Migrants	Involuntary	Voluntary	# Servant	% Servant
Irish	108.6	17.5	91.1	39.0	42.8
English/ Welsh	73.1	32.5	40.6	27.2	67.0
Scottish	35.3	2.2	33.1	7.4	22.3
German	84.5		84.5	30.0	35.5
Other	5.9		5.9		
Totals	307.4	52.2	255.2	103.6	40.6

	(b) Results based on sources discussed in this appendix and Chapter 1				
	All Migrants	Involuntary	Voluntary	# Servant	% Servant
Irish	77.5	17.5	60.0	21.6	36.0
English/ Welsh	95.0	32.5	62.5	41.9	67.0
Scottish	62.5	2.2	60.3	12.7	21.0
German	111.0		111.0	51.1	46.0
Other	5.9		5.9		
Totals	351.9	52.2	299.7	127.3	42.4

century's transported convicts and prisoners also came from these sources, which results in a total bound English/Welsh migration (voluntary and involuntary) on his figures approaching 80 percent.

To arrive at an overall proportion of indentured servants in voluntary migrants, the ranges of migrant numbers must be adjusted to allow for involuntary convict migrants. Fogleman suggests that of 52,500 convicts transported, 32,500 (62 percent) were English/Welsh, 17,500 (33.5 percent) Irish, and 2,200 (4.2 percent) Scottish. There is some departure here from Ekirch's figures, unexplained in the English/Welsh case, but for the sake of consistency I will adopt Fogleman's numbers. Applied to the range of 307,400–351,900 voluntary migrants the results are expressed in Table A2. In section (a) I restate Fogleman's results, in section (b) I offer my own variation.

Although calculated differently, the two outcomes are very close. In each scenario, just over 40 percent of all voluntary migrants 1700–75 appear committed to an initial period of servitude. Re-inclusion of all transported convicts as similarly committed to an initial period of servitude (Ekirch's work would actually caution *against* doing this; see *Bound for America,*

119–20), raises the percentage of migrants committed to an initial period of servitude, 1700–75, to slightly in excess of 50 percent.

Finally, treating the entire seventeenth- and eighteenth-century period (through 1775) as a whole, the result is that on Fogleman's figures some 48 percent of all voluntary migrants into mainland English America were committed to an initial period of servitude; including all convicts as above, the percentage rises to 54 percent. On my adjusted figures, the result is 50 percent and 55 percent respectively. Thus, in each case, notwithstanding the adjustments in proportions and in particular ethnic contributions that I have proposed, the overall totals my estimates indicate agree very closely with Fogleman's.

APPENDIX II

Seasoning and General Mortality in the Chesapeake Region: Estimates and Sources

The seasoning and general mortality estimates used in the text to refine estimates of servant persistence in the seventeenth-century Chesapeake population are derived from the following sources: Horn, *Adapting to a New World*, 138; Canny, "English Migration," 48; Lorena Walsh, "Servitude and Opportunity in Charles County, Maryland, 1658–1705," in Aubrey C. Land et al., editors, *Law, Society and Politics in Early Maryland* (Baltimore, 1974), 111–33, at 115–17; Lorena Walsh and Russell R. Menard, "Death in the Chesapeake: Two Life Tables for Men in Early Colonial Maryland," *Maryland Historical Magazine*, 69, 2 (Summer 1974), 211–27; Lois Green Carr and Russell R. Menard, "Immigration and Opportunity: The Freedman in Early Colonial Maryland," in Thad W. Tate and David L. Ammerman, editors, *The Chesapeake in the Seventeenth Century: Essays on Anglo-American Society* (New York, 1979), 206–42; Carr, "Emigration and the Standard of Living," 274–5; Morgan, *American Slavery, American Freedom*, 175–6, 297–8; Darrett B. Rutman and Anita H. Rutman, "Of Agues and Fevers: Malaria in the Early Chesapeake," *William and Mary Quarterly*, 3rd. Ser., 33, 1 (January 1976), 31–60; Darrett B. Rutman and Anita H. Rutman, *A Place in Time: Middlesex County, Virginia, 1650–1750* (New York, 1984), 258 nn.15 and 16; Terry L. Anderson and Robert P. Thomas, "The Growth of Population and Labor Force in the 17th-Century Chesapeake," *Explorations in Economic History*, 15 (1978), 298–9; Kevin P. Kelly, "A Demographic Description of Seventeenth-Century York County, Virginia," Unpublished Research Paper, Department of Historical Research, Colonial Williamsburg Foundation.

It is generally agreed that "seasoning" (high rates of mortality among landed immigrants, attributable to the debilitating effects of mosquito-born disease and dysentery on the entering population), was extreme in the Chesapeake, and that general mortality rates were also severe. Horn proposes an early mortality rate of up to 40 percent over the first two years; Walsh finds a rate of 40 percent over three years not unreasonable. (Alison Games, *Migration and the Origins of the English Atlantic World*, 101, has suggested that early mortality in the Chesapeake could have been as high as 50 percent in the first year, but this figure is not supported in other sources.) Along with Morgan and the Rutmans, Walsh proposes that seasoning and general mortality would account for 45–50 percent of entering servant migrants before the end of their terms. Carr and Menard suggest that mortality averaged 10 percent per annum and that no more than 60 percent of immigrant servants survived their terms. Anderson and Thomas propose an average early mortality rate of 35 percent after surveying seventeenth-century sources ranging from a high of 60 percent to a low of 25 percent. As to general mortality, Kelly finds average death rates in York County, Virginia ranging from 39 to 68 per 1,000 during the second half of the seventeenth century, depending upon parish. An average of Kelly's averages produces a rate of 54/1,000.

Table 1.2 in Chapter 1 assumes an average contract term of five years (that is, 10 percent longer than the average of 4.5 years for contracts concluded in England prior to departure) and a survival rate over a five-year term of 60 percent of entrants. In the context of the literature on the seventeenth-century Chesapeake discussed above, both assumptions are generous and thus will tend if anything to inflate servant incidence in population. Because in the text I have drawn attention to the possibility that children judged to serve by custom of country may have formed a significant proportion of the indentured servant workforce, I have calculated supplementary estimates which test the effect of longer average contract terms – seven years and nine years respectively – and inflated migrant numbers. See Appendix III. (Both nine-year estimates are intended as outliers. It is virtually impossible that the number of custom of country children serving longer than negotiated terms could be sufficient to have the effect of doubling the average contract length of the entire migrant servant population.)

Appendix Figure A1 applies an attrition rate of 32.8 percent to the hypothetical annual servant entry cohort, calculated to reflect an initial early mortality of 25 percent, and a subsequent constant death rate of 54/1000 (5.4 percent) per annum to the survivors. Thus, where N^1 is the size of the entry cohort, the percent of survivors (N^2) is calculated as $[(N^1 - 25 \text{ percent})(-5.4 \text{ percent})(-5.4 \text{ percent})(-5.4 \text{ percent})(-5.4 \text{ percent})]$. This produces the consensus 60 percent survival rate over a five-year term while adjusting the outcome by a constant discount to allow the equation to reflect the differential annual survival rates of each of the hypothetical entry cohorts that contribute to overall servant population in any given year (i.e., assuming a five-year contract, although each cohort individually experiences a 60 percent survival rate over the five-year term, in any given year the servant population is composed of the sum of five different cohorts of entrants each at a different stage in its rate of decay.) The discount has been calculated on the basis of the following matrix, which is based on a hypothetical annual entry cohort of 100. As the matrix illustrates, the average annual population for each decade will be the sum of $C_1–C_5$ in Y_5 for a five-year term, $C_1–C_7$ in Y_7 for a seven-year term and $C_1–C_9$ in Y_9 for a nine-year term. In the seven-year and nine-year cases the attrition rate necessarily rises because (as the matrix shows) the 54/1,000 death rate must be presumed to apply during the additional two and four years of service.

	C1[b]	C2	C3	C4	C5	C6	C7	C8	C9	Total, & avg. rate
Y1[a]	N-25%= N^1 [75]									
Y2	N^1-5.4%= N^2 [70.95]	N-25%= N^1 [75]								
Y3	N^2-5.4%= N^3 [67.12]	N^1-5.4%= N^2 [70.95]	N-25%= N^1 [75]							
Y4	N^3-5.4%= N^4 [63.49]	N^2-5.4%= N^3 [67.12]	N^1-5.4%= N^2 [70.95]	N-25%= N^1 [75]						
Y5	N^4-5.4%= N^5 [60.06]	N^3-5.4%= N^4 [63.49]	N^2-5.4%= N^3 [67.12]	N^1-5.4%= N^2 [70.95]	N-25%= N^1 [75]					[336]-500 = 32.8%
Y6	N^5-5.4%= N^6 [56.81]	N^4-5.4%= N^5 [60.06]	N^3-5.4%= N^4 [63.49]	N^2-5.4%= N^3 [67.12]	N^1-5.4%= N^2 [70.95]	N-25%= N^1 [75]				
Y7	N^6-5.4%= N^7 [53.74]	N^5-5.4%= N^6 [56.81]	N^4-5.4%= N^5 [60.06]	N^3-5.4%= N^4 [63.49]	N^2-5.4%= N^3 [67.12]	N^1-5.4%= N^2 [70.95]	N-25%= N^1 [75]			[447]-700 = 36.1%
Y8	N^7-5.4%= N^8 [50.84]	N^6-5.4%= N^7 [53.74]	N^5-5.4%= N^6 [56.81]	N^4-5.4%= N^5 [60.06]	N^3-5.4%= N^4 [63.49]	N^2-5.4%= N^3 [67.12]	N^1-5.4%= N^2 [70.95]	N-25%= N^1 [75]		
Y9	N^8-5.4%= N^9 [48.1]	N^7-5.4%= N^8 [50.84]	N^6-5.4%= N^7 [53.74]	N^5-5.4%= N^6 [56.81]	N^4-5.4%= N^5 [60.06]	N^3-5.4%= N^4 [63.49]	N^2-5.4%= N^3 [67.12]	N^1-5.4%= N^2 [70.95]	N-25%= N^1 [75]	[545]-900 = 39.5%

Appendix Figure A1: Computation of Attrition Rates, Seventeenth-Century Chesapeake

[a] Y1 = Year One

[b] C1 = Notional Entry Cohort [N=100]

Supplementary Estimates

Table A3. *European Servant Migration and Persistence in Population, Maryland and Virginia, 1600–1700: Alternate Estimates*

Decade Ending	White Population at End of Decade	% Servant Estimate A[b]	% Servant Alternate B[c]	% Servant Alternate C[d]	% Servant Alternate D[e]	% Servant Alternate E[f]
1610[a]	0.35	**	**	**	**	**
1620[a]	2.18	37.2	47.3	49.2	50.6	67.4
1630[a]	2.45	44.1	57.0	58.4	61.2	81.4
1640	10.85	22.0	28.5	29.3	30.5	40.6
1650	22.53	9.3	11.9	12.4	12.8	17.0
1660	33.74	12.9	16.6	17.2	17.8	23.6
1670	45.35	11.1	14.3	14.8	15.3	20.4
1680	56.89	9.7	12.5	12.9	13.4	17.8
1690	65.56	5.5	7.0	7.3	7.5	10.0
1700	68.55	5.5	7.0	7.3	7.5	10.0

[a] **Approximation**

[b] **Estimate A** reproduces the results from Chapter 1, Table 1.2. It assumes an average 5-year term of service (based on the hypothesis that 80% of total estimated servant migrants had concluded indentures prior to embarkation with terms averaging 4.5 years in length and 20% were serving by custom of country with terms averaging 7 years in length) and 60% survival. Total attrition was calculated at 32.8% (5 cohorts of entrants). This rate builds in the impact of seasoning mortality and general mortality on the servant population over 5 years. (For the computation of attrition rates over different periods, see Appendix II.)

[c] **Alternate estimate B** attempts a more complex scenario. It inflates the total number of migrants to the Chesapeake to 123,200, the midpoint of Menard's range for the century as a whole. (See Menard, "British Migration to the Chesapeake Colonies," table 1.) Alternate B distributes this total by decade according to the breakdown offered by Menard in table 3 of "British Migration" supplemented by the approximations for 1610–20 and 1620–30 used in Chapter 1, Table 1.1. It assumes that 80% of migrants were servants. It divides the migrant servant population into two groups, two-thirds serving 5-year terms and subject to the 32.8% attrition rate, one-third serving 7-year terms and subject to the 36.1% attrition rate. This estimate attempts to capture more fully than A both the substantial population of young servants serving by custom of country, and the total migrant population estimate preferred by some specialists. It is likely that the range between estimates A and B is the best approximation of "reality" available through the techniques used here.

Table A3. *Continued*

_d **Alternate estimate C** employs the same population assumptions as estimate A, but assumes an average 7-year term (or 55% longer than the average 4.5-year contract term concluded in England). An average 7-year term is credible only if one assumes that fewer than half (c.45%) of total estimated servant migrants had concluded indentures prior to embarkation with terms averaging 4.5 years in length and that the remainder were all serving by custom of country with terms averaging 9 years in length. There is no empirical basis for this assumption. Total attrition was calculated at 36.1% (7 cohorts of entrants).

_e **Alternate estimate D** returns to the 5-year term that is the basis of Table 1.2 but inflates the overall number of migrants to the Chesapeake to 146,700, which is Menard's absolute upper bound figure for the century. See Menard, "British Migration to the Chesapeake Colonies," table 1, and 2–3. Menard himself discounts this figure, nor is it supported in any other source I have consulted. Alternate D distributes this inflated migration in the same fashion as Alternate C. It assumes that 82% were servants. Total attrition was calculated at the 32.8% rate.

_f **Alternate estimate E** applies the 7-year term that is the basis of Alternate C to the greatly inflated figure of 146,700 for all migrants to the Chesapeake used in Alternate D. It assumes that 80% were servants. Total attrition was calculated at the 36.1% rate.

Table A4. *Servant Persistence in the Maryland Population, 1640–1760*

Decade Ending	Servant Migration to Maryland	Servant Population[b]	White Population	% Servant
1640	560	188	563	33.4
1650	1440	484	4204	11.5
1660	3680	1236	7668	16.1
1670	9760	3279	12036	27.2
1680	9920	3333	16293	20.5
1690	3975[a]	1336	21862	6.1
1700	4200[a]	1411	26377	5.3
1707 census[c]		3003	36836	8.1
1755 census[d]		8841	108193	8.2

Source: Chapter 1, Table 1.1, supplemented by Abbot Emerson Smith, *Colonists in Bondage: White Servitude and Convict Labor in America, 1607–1776* (Chapel Hill, 1947), 324; *Historical Statistics of the United States*, vol. 5, tables Eg169, Eg172 (Maryland Population, 1704, 1755).

[a] estimates

[b] 1640–1700 adjusted as in Chapter 1, Table 1.2

[c] Total population reported was 41,193: number of slaves 4,657; number of "souls" 33,833; number of servants 3,003. Maryland white population in 1700 was 26,377 and in 1710, 34,796. In 1704, the white population was 30,437. In 1707, servants and slaves together thus constituted 18.6% of total population. The increase in the size of the servant population in the early 1700s, as compared with the population estimates for the previous two decades, accords with the argument advanced by Farley Grubb and Tony Stitt for the major effects of European war in the 1680s and 1690s in interrupting servant migration to the Chesapeake, followed by temporary alleviation of the interruption during the period of peace lasting 1697–1702. See Farley Grubb and Tony Stitt, "The Liverpool Emigrant Servant Trade and the Transition to Slave Labor in the Chesapeake, 1697–1707: Market Adjustments to War," *Explorations in Economic History*, 31, 3 (July 1994), 376–405.

[d] Total population reported was 153,505; total whites 108,193: total free whites 99,352; total servants 8,841; convicts 1,981. Servants were thus 5.8% of total population and 8.2% of the white population. The African-American population was 45,312: number of mulattoes 3,608; number of Negroes 41,704; number of slaves – black and mulatto together – 43,495. The sum of the servant, slave, and convict populations comprises 35% of total population.

Table A5. *Servant Incidence in the Virginia Population, York County, 1660–1700*

Year	Population[a]	% White	% Black	% Tithable	% Unfree	% Slave[b]	% Servant[b]	% Slave[c]	% Servant[c]
63	2257	86.0	14.0	48.8	19.9	10.2	9.7	6.6	13.3
68	1905	85.6	14.4	46.5	21.5	12.2	9.3	7.2	14.3
73	2153	84.6	15.4	44.6	19.8	12.0	7.8	9.5	10.3
78	2167	82.1	17.9	43.3	25.0	12.2	12.9	12.0	13.1
83	2481	84.6	15.4	41.6	21.9	11.3	10.6	12.9	8.9
88	2458	76.9	23.1	40.5	20.5	18.1	2.4	12.1	8.4
93	2631	68.7	31.3	39.5	21.6	21.1	0.4	20.8	0.8
98	2820	69.0	31.0	38.8	20.8	20.4	0.4	20.0	0.7

Source: Kevin P. Kelly, "A Demographic Description of Seventeenth-Century York County, Virginia," Unpublished Research Paper, Department of Historical Research, Colonial Williamsburg Foundation. Kevin Kelly's York County research enables us to refine estimates of the incidence of indentured servitude in overall population, and also to track the reorientation of planters in that area toward heavy dependence upon slavery, a development that occurred earlier in York County than elsewhere in the tidewater region. Table A5 shows Kelly's estimate of county population during the last four decades of the seventeenth century, the proportion of tithables in that population, the proportion of unfree tithes, and the distribution of the unfree between categories of indentured servant and slave. Kelly's detailed results are consistent with my more general estimates for the Chesapeake region (see Table 1.2 in Chapter 1).

[a] This is Kelly's "Preferred Estimate" of three undertaken.
[b] This is Kelly's first attempt at a distribution of unfree tithes.
[c] This is Kelly's second distribution, based on the proportion slaves:servants in York County inventories, by decade.

1638–59 inventories show a ratio of 0.41 (71% servant)
1660–9 inventories show a ratio of 0.48 (67% servant)
1670–9 inventories show a ratio of 0.92 (52% servant)
1680–9 inventories show a ratio of 1.44 (41% servant)
1690–9 inventories show a ratio of 24.9 (3.8% servant)

Table A6. *Servant Incidence in the Philadelphia Population and Workforce, 1720–1775 (Adapted from Salinger Estimates)*

Decade Ending	Servant Population	Philadelphia Population[a]	% Servants in Population	Philadelphia Workforce[b]	% Servants in Workforce
1730	285	7075	4.0	3870	7.4
1740	575	10117	5.7	5362	10.7
1750	635	13926	4.6	6490	9.8
1760	903	18598	4.9	8688	10.4
1770	238	26789	0.9	10972	2.2
(1775)	457	32073	1.4	12914	3.5

[a] Population figures taken from Susan Klepp, "Demography in Early Philadelphia, 1690–1860," *Proceedings of the American Philosophical Society*, 133, 2 (1989), 103–5, table 2.
[b] Work force estimates are derived from Salinger but adjusted to Klepp's population figures.

Table A7. *Slave Incidence in the Philadelphia Population and Workforce, 1720–1775 (Adapted from Salinger Estimates)*

Decade Ending	Slave Population	Philadelphia Population[a]	% Slaves in Population	Slave Workforce	Philadelphia Workforce[b]	% Slaves in Workforce
1730	880	7075	12.4	616	3870	15.9
1740	1209	10117	11.9	882	5362	16.5
1750	1131	13926	8.1	792	6490	12.2
1760	1136	18598	6.1	795	8688	9.2
1770	1682	26789	6.3	1139	10972	10.4
(1775)	1394	32073	4.3	655	12914	5.1

[a] Population figures taken from Susan Klepp, "Demography in Early Philadelphia, 1690–1860," *Proceedings of the American Philosophical Society*, 133, 2 (1989), 103–5, table 2.
[b] Workforce estimates are derived from Salinger but adjusted to Klepp's population figures.

Table A8. *Servants and Slaves in the Philadelphia Population (Adapted from Salinger Estimates)*

Decade Ending	Servant Population	Slave Population	Servant: Slave Ratio	Philadelphia Population[a]	% Servants in Population	% Slaves in Population
1730	285	880	1:3	7075	4.0	12.4
1740	575	1209	1:2	10117	5.7	11.9
1750	635	1131	1:2	13926	4.6	8.1
1760	903	1136	1:1	18598	4.9	6.1
1770	238	1682	1:7	26789	0.9	6.3
(1775)	457	1394	1:3	32073	1.4	4.3

[a] Population figures taken from Susan Klepp, "Demography in Early Philadelphia, 1690–1860," *Proceedings of the American Philosophical Society*, 133, 2 (1989), 103–5, table 2.

Table A9. *Servants and Slaves in the Philadelphia Population and Workforce (Adapted from Salinger Estimates)*

Decade Ending	Combined Servant/Slave Population	Philadelphia Population[a]	% Servant/Slave in Population	Combined Servant/Slave work force	Philadelphia Workforce	% Servant/ Slave in Workforce
1730	1165	7075	16.5	901	3870	23.3
1740	1784	10117	17.6	1457	5362	27.2
1750	1766	13926	12.7	1427	6490	22.0
1760	2039	18598	11.0	1698	8688	19.5
1770	1920	26789	7.2	1377	10972	12.6
(1775)	1851	32073	5.8	1112	12914	8.6

[a] Population figures taken from Susan Klepp, "Demography in Early Philadelphia, 1690–1860," *Proceedings of the American Philosophical Society*, 133, 2 (1989), 103–5, table 2.

APPENDIX IV

Servants' Ages

My own survey of the county court records for York County, Virginia for the years 1646–1700 discloses 430 instances in which servants entering without indenture were brought before the court to have their ages determined. Of these instances, 73% (313 of 430) were recorded in the twenty years beginning 1660. In these cases the mean age determined was 14.3 years (median 15.0). In the case of boys (N=364) the mean age determined was 14.6 years (median 15.0). The youngest recorded was 5. In the case of girls (N=58) the mean age determined was 12.3 (median 14.0). The youngest was 3. In the eight remaining cases, the gender of the child was not clear from the record. See also Russell R. Menard, "From Servants to Slaves: The Transformation of the Chesapeake Labor System," *Southern Studies*, 16 (Winter 1977), 363–5.

In his path-breaking study of more than half a century ago, Abbot Emerson Smith observed that "during the seventeenth century there were certainly a great many servants brought to the colonies without indenture who were under age." Smith found 134 such cases recorded in Northumberland County, Virginia 1668–74; "about the same" in Lancaster County, Virginia during the 1670s and another 64 during the three years 1697–9; and 128 in Talbot County, Maryland, 1662–74. Smith reports that "most" were 13–18 years old, the youngest 9. See Abbot Emerson Smith, *Colonists in Bondage: White Servitude and Convict Labor in America, 1607–1776* (Chapel Hill, 1947), 231. For other narrative accounts of the transportation of unaccompanied children as servants, see Robert C. Johnson, "The Transportation of Vagrant Children from London to Virginia, 1618–1622," in Howard S. Reinmuth, Jr., *Early Stuart Studies: Essays in Honor of David Harris Wilson* (Minneapolis, 1970), 137–51; Peter Coldham, "The 'Spiriting' of London Children to Virginia," *Virginia Magazine of History and Biography*, 83, 3 (July 1975), 280–7. Other scholars have added a degree of precision to the subject. Thus, Edmund Morgan finds that in Lancaster County, Virginia, 1662–80, of 296 servants without indenture brought into court for determination of term of service, 264 were adjudged younger than 19, and 133 younger than 16 (mean age was 16.0); in Norfolk County, Virginia, 1662–80, of 72 servants without indenture, 71 were adjudged younger than 19 (median 15.5). Edmund S. Morgan, *American Slavery, American Freedom: The Ordeal of Colonial Virginia* (New York, 1975), 216. Douglas Deal finds that in Accomack County, Virginia, 1663–97, of 270 servants without indenture, 266 were adjudged younger than 19 (median age 14.0); in Northampton County, Virginia, 1663–97, the median age of 88 servants without indenture adjudged in county court was 13.0. See Douglas Deal, *Race and Class in Colonial Virginia: Indians, Englishmen, and Africans on the Eastern Shore During the Seventeenth Century* (New York, 1993), 129. Were one to estimate the average number of "custom of country" hearings across these six counties alone for a representative period, say 1660–80, the result would suggest some 650 individual hearings per decade, a figure equivalent to roughly 10 percent of the estimated total number of migrants into all of Virginia during the same period (and certainly in excess of 10 percent of estimated servant migration). "Custom of country" servants were also likely to make up a larger proportion of the actual servant population than their numbers would suggest for, being younger, they generally served longer. James Horn observes generally that of Lancaster County's servants in the 1650s, "a large proportion were in their midteens or younger." *Adapting to a New World*, 184. Lorena Walsh finds that in Charles County, Maryland, 1658–81, nearly 50 percent of servants served according to custom of country. In the case of male servants, the mean age determined was 16.47, decreasing to 15.82 during the subsequent two decades. In the case of female servants, the mean age was 18.19 decreasing to 17.44. See Lorena S. Walsh, "Servitude and Opportunity in Charles County, Maryland," in Aubrey C. Land et al., editors, *Law, Society and Politics in Early Maryland* (Baltimore, 1974), 111–33, at 112–13. Gloria L. Main concludes that an actual majority of the servants imported into Maryland after 1680 came without prior indentures and served by custom of country. See Gloria L. Main, *Tobacco Colony: Life in Early Maryland, 1650–1720* (Princeton, 1982), 99.

Evidence from the Delaware Valley and from New England indicates that importation of servants in their early teens was a general, not merely a Chesapeake, phenomenon. On the Delaware Valley, see Chapter 1, nn.114–15 (ages of servants brought before courts in the late seventeenth-century Chester County settlements). In New England, servant importation was minimal after 1640 and there were no requirements for the recording of youthful migrant servants' ages. Nevertheless, to the extent that details of migrant servants crop up in local court records they are overwhelmingly in their early- to mid-teens. See, e.g., *Richard Coye v. Mr William Hubbard, sr.* (March 1655), *Records and Files of the Quarterly Court of Essex County*, I, 381–2.

Russell Menard has hypothesized that the proportion of youthful servants increased markedly over the course of the seventeenth century, from 5 percent below age 16 in the 1630s to perhaps 15 percent in the 1680s and 40 percent in the 1690s. The figures suggested above (10%+ for the period 1660–80) are clearly in line with this trend. Menard associates the decline in age at entry with a decline in the social status of the emigrant servant population, arguing that migrant servants were increasingly from the margins of English society, and in particular that "servants by custom had perhaps usually been life-cycle servants in England," implying that servants with pre-negotiated indentures were not. See his "British Migration to the Chesapeake Colonies," 127, 128. It may indeed be the case that servants were becoming younger, but this may have as much to do with record keeping as anything else. (In Virginia, for example, there was no requirement that unindentured servants have their ages recorded in court before March 1657/8. See 9 Commonwealth Act 18, in William Waller Hening, *The Statutes at Large; Being a Collection of all the Laws of Virginia* (New York, 1823), I, 441–2.) Certainly it would be wrong to assume that the importation of young unindentured servants had not excited attention from early on. As Warren Billings has noted, the importation of servants without indenture was an issue virtually from the beginning of the Virginia settlement, leading to passage of the first "custom of country" legislation in 1643 (18 Car. I Act 26). See Warren M. Billings, "The Law of Servants and Slaves in Seventeenth Century Virginia," *Virginia Magazine of History and Biography*, 99, 1 (January 1991), 45–62, at 48–9. See also Holly Brewer, *By Birth or Consent: Children, Law, and the Anglo-American Revolution in Authority* (Chapel Hill, 2005), 270–80. That many of these migrants were in their early teens, as they were later in the century, is suggested by the 1643 Act's provision of statutory terms of service for children under age 12 (7 years) as well as those aged 12–20 (5 years), but also – and with greater emphasis on the significance of this age cohort – by 1 Commonwealth Act II (October 1649), Assembly legislation dealing with the listing of tithable persons: "Whereas it appeareth to severall Grand Assemblies that the lists of tithable persons are very imperfect, and that notwithstandinge the yearly importation of people into the collonie, the number of tithables in the said lists is rather diminished then *[sic]* augmented, which is in great part conceived, by this Assembly, to happen, in that all under the age of sixteen yeares are exempted from the lists, and that once passing under that age they are seldom or never acknowledged to exceed the same ... Bee it therefore enacted ... That all male servants imported herafter into the collony of what age soever they be, shall be brought into the lists...." In *Statutes at Large*, I, 361.

Menard's division of the indentured population into life-cycle servants and others according to whether or not they were in their early teens and had not negotiated indentures prior to embarking is also open to debate. Life-cycle service in England could begin any time after age 10, with increasing incidence of entry at ages 12–15. Peak incidence of service was in mid- to late-teens, with movement out of service beginning by age 20–21 and accelerating after age 24. In other words, the age-profile of those entering and occupied by life-cycle service in England and indentured service in early America coincides quite precisely. It is clear that indentured servitude became a means for substantial numbers of farmers, adult laborers, and tradesmen to finance emigration – some 20 percent of those embarking under indenture were, we have seen, 25 or older, and amongst those in the range 20–24 would be numbers of laborers and tradesmen who had recently exited periods of service or apprenticeship. But both servants embarking without indenture and those with indentures are more likely than not to have been recruited from among the youthful male population either entering or already part of the life-cycle servant labor force of seventeenth-century England. (The same, Fertig argues, was true of their German counterparts in the eighteenth-century middle colonies. See his "Eighteenth-Century Transatlantic Migration," 278, 282.) Servants imported without indenture were most likely drawn from among those entering service for the first time at the beginning of the life cycle, without any experience of negotiating yearly service contracts and, therefore, without the knowledge to negotiate indentures. Those embarking under indenture are likely to have been drawn in good part from the population of youthful servant labor somewhat further along in the cycle, with some skills to offer (in the case of those coming from the artisan trades) and with some experience in reaching bargains. Certainly, as Galenson among others has shown, indenture terms do vary with increasing age in favor of the servant, indicating a premium on age and acquired skill in the negotiating process. See Galenson, *White Servitude in Colonial America,* 28–30, 103–9. On the age profile of life-cycle service in England, see Ann Kussmaul, *Servants in Husbandry in Early Modern England* (New York and Cambridge, 1981), 70–85; Graham Mayhew, "Life-Cycle Service and the Family Unit in Early Modern Rye," *Continuity and Change,* 6, 2 (1991), 201–26. See also Paul Griffiths, *Youth and Authority: Formative Experiences in England, 1560–1640* (Oxford, 1996), 290–389.

It should be noted that multiyear indentured servitude was institutionally and legally a distinct institution from life-cycle service. It was, however, known in English law where, as I show in Chapter 2, it was an institution reserved for the poorest and youngest of the rural population.

For emphasis on the youthfulness of Chesapeake indentured servants similar to mine, see Jacqueline Jones, *American Work: Four Centuries of Black and White Labor* (New York, 1998), 60–2. On the social background of those indentured prior to embarkation, see Mildred Campbell, "Social Origins of Some Early Americans," in James M. Smith, editor, *Seventeenth-Century America: Essays in Colonial History* (Chapel Hill, 1959), 63–89; David Galenson, "'Middling People' or 'Common Sort'? The Social Origins of Some Early Americans Reexamined," *William and Mary Quarterly,* 3rd Ser., 35, 3 (1978), 499–524; Horn, *Adapting to a New World,* 31–8.

At bottom the issue here is really the reliability of the conclusions that historians have drawn regarding the characteristics of the migrant servant population as a whole reached on the basis of records of indentures agreed prior to embarkation, given that the latter tend to bias the age range and skills of the migrant servant population upward, and the term of service downward. See Gemery, "Markets for Migrants," 36. As Gemery notes, once it is recognized that a substantial number of migrant servants were being indentured by custom of country after disembarkation throughout the century, and that this group was overwhelmingly younger and less skilled than those traveling under indenture, the age, skill, and term length profile of migrant servants as a whole must be adjusted. We must also look on the legal-institutional context of indentured servitude in a new light, as a policing of adolescence as much as of work discipline. On this see also Games, *Origins of the English Atlantic World*, 74.

Index

Absconding and runaways
  Massachusetts, in, 308
  Pennsylvania, in, 323, 356
  slaves, 454, 463, 470
  Virginia, in, 268, 270–1, 298–301
Acquisition, colonization and, 113–16
Act Concerning Masters Servants Slaves
    Labourers and Apprentices (New York
    1684), 499
Act Concerning Negroes & other Slaves
    (Maryland 1664), 458–9
Act for preventing the Conspiracy of Slaves
    (New York 1708), 501, 502–3
Act for the Better Ordering and Governing
    of Negroes (Barbados), 428, 438,
    450–1, 467
Act for the Better Regulation of Negroes in
    this Province (Pennsylvania 1726), 496
Act for the Better Regulation of Servants
    in this Province and Territories
    (Pennsylvania 1700), 494
Act for the Trial of Negroes (Pennsylvania
    1700), 494–6
Act of 1381, 72
Act of Settlement of 1701, 544
Act to prevent the running away of Negro
    Slaves out of the Citty and County of
    Albany to the French at Canada (New
    York 1705), 500–1
An Act Concerning Servants and Slaves
    (Virginia 1705), 468–70
An Act Concerning Servants and Slaves
    (Virginia 1748), 472–4
An Act for Regulateing of Slaves (New York
    1702), 500
Act for Suppressing of Immorality (New
    York 1708), 501
An Act for Suppressing Outlying Slaves
    (Virginia 1691), 467–8
An Act for the Better Ordering and Governing
    of Negroes (South Carolina 1712), 441–4
An Act for the Better Ordering and
    Governing of Negroes and other Slaves

in this Province (South Carolina 1740),
  446–52
An Act for the Better Ordering of Slaves
    (South Carolina 1690/91),
    437–8
An Act for the Better Ordering of Slaves
    (South Carolina 1696), 439–40
An Act for the Better Ordering of Slaves
    (South Carolina 1698), 440
An Act for the Better Ordering of Slaves
    (South Carolina 1701), 440
An Act to Repeale a Former Law Makeing
    Indians and Others Ffree (Virginia
    1682), 464–5
Adams, Abigail, 395–6
Adams, John, 395–6, 397, 400
Adams, Jonathan, 308
Aeschylus, 562
Agricultural transition in England
  enclosure, 200–2
  engrossment, 202
  generally, 199–202
Albion's Seed (Fischer), 215–16
Alcohol, 254
Alexander, William, 168, 175
Alexander VI (Pope), 102–3, 105
Alfonso V (Portugal), 101
Algonquians, 24, 27
Allen, David Grayson, 221, 222
American Anti-Slavery Society, 511
American Civil War, 523–6
American Revolution
  patriarchy, effect on, 399
  slavery, effect on, 504–6
Anderson, Terry, 39
Andrews, Charles M., 159
Anghie, Anthony, 122, 128
Anne (Denmark), 544
Anne (England), 544
Apprenticeship
  husbandry, in, 79, 80
  Massachusetts, in, 255–7
  Statute of Artificers, under

Apprenticeship (*cont.*)
   children, 242–3
   crafts, 240–1
   husbandry, 79, 241–2
Archer, Henry, 315
Archer, James, 300–1
Arendt, Hannah, 15
Argall, Samuel, 261–2
Aristocratia, 363–5
Aristotle, 365, 376
Aron. *See Titus Andronicus* (Shakespeare)
Articles of Confederation, 396–7, 516
Artisans, 294
"Autoptic imagination," 95
Avalon, 158, 170, 171–2, 176

Babb, John, 303
Bacon, Francis, 90, 91
Bacon's Rebellion, 269–71, 275, 276, 464
Bailyn, Bernard, 51, 52, 53
Bainbridge, Henry, 513
Bale, Richard, 318
Ballard, Thomas Jr., 303
Banner, Stuart, 153
Barbados
  Act for the Better Ordering and Governing
    of Negroes, 428, 438, 450–1, 467
  slavery in
    generally, 428–31
    slave trade from, 432, 433, 436,
      452, 497
"Barbarians," 135–8, 402–3, 422–3
Bastardy, 301–3
Beames, John, 72–3
Belli, Pierino, 421, 423
Bellomont, Richard Coote, 498–9
Belvin, William, 303
Benjamin, Walter, 560
Berkeley, Lord, 490
Berlin, Ira, 415–16, 486
Bermuda Company, 164, 165
Berthoud, Jacques, 407
Bilder, Mary, 81
Bindoff, Stanley, 238
Black Death, 195, 233–5
Blackstone, William, 70–1, 74–5, 349–50,
   369–70
The Body of Liberties (Ward), 252, 253–4,
   424, 479–80
Book of Orders, 212
Booth, William James, 378
Bound labor. *See* Indentured servitude;
  Slavery
Bradford, William, 154, 157, 542
Brandon, George, 324–5

Brass, Tom, 10
Bray, Robert, 318
Breach or nonperformance of contract
  criminal law involving, 358
    Massachusetts, in, 314–15
    Pennsylvania, in, 323–5
    Virginia, in, 303–6, 314–15
Brewer, Holly, 392
Brooke, Nicholas, 299
Broom, Mary, 326
Brown, John, 522
Brown, Kathleen, 392–3
Browne, Irving, 377
Bulgar, John, 328
Butler, John, 328

Cabot, John, 93–4, 95
Caldwell, James, 326
Caliban. *See The Tempest* (Shakespeare)
Calvert, Cecilius, 169, 172, 176–7
Calvert, George, 158, 170, 171–2
Calvin, Robert, 83–4
Calvin's Case, 82–9, 90, 91, 92
Carolina Charter of 1663, 74, 159–60,
   178, 432
Carolina Charter of 1665, 74, 178
Carolinas. *See* North Carolina; South
   Carolina
Carteret, George, 490
Cartography, 185–6
Castration of slaves, 439–40, 474–5, 494–6
Chapman, George, 415, 546–7, 551
Charles I (England), 169, 544, 545
Charles II (England), 278
Charter colonies, 157–66. *See also*
   specific colony
Chesapeake region. *See* Maryland; Virginia
Cheseley, William, 301
Chew, John, 299
Children
  apprenticeship
    generally, 80–1
    Massachusetts, in, 255–7
    Statute of Artificers, under, 242–3
  indentured servitude and
    age estimates, 593–7
    generally, 42, 80–1
    Massachusetts, in, 255–7, 309–12
    Pennsylvania, in, 290–1
    Virginia, in, 275–6
Christianity. *See also specific branch*
  evangelism as purpose of colonization
    English colonization, in, 109–13
    generally, 99
    Spanish colonization, in, 100–4

Hakluyt the elder and, 109, 110–13
Hakluyt the younger and, 109
slavery and, 271–4, 420–1, 425, 460–3, 465
Vitoria and, 108–9
Cities, centrality to colonization, 140–2
Citizenship in *Dred Scott* decision
dissenting opinions, 532–6
Taney opinion, 527–32, 538
Civil War, American, 523–6
Civil War, English, 203, 213–14
Cochran, Brigett, 326
Cogswell, Thomas, 311–12
Coke, Edward
Calvin's Case and, 84, 85–6, 87, 88–9, 90
colonization, on, 156
legal system and, 211
Cole, Samuel, 320
Colonization. *See also specific colony*
acquisition as purpose of, 113–16
charter colonies, 157–66
cities, centrality of, 140–2
Coke on, 156
commoditization of labor in, 402–3
commoditization of land in, 401–2
conquest and, 128, 131–2
corporate colonies, 160–6
Crown colonies, 166, 444
Dutch colonization, 180–1, 277
evangelism as purpose of
English colonization, in, 109–13
generally, 99
Spanish colonization, in, 100–4
freedom of labor and
effect on, 342–4, 351–2
ideal of, 3–5
generally, 133–4
Gentili on, 23, 138, 143, 144, 145, 155
Grotius on, 24, 144, 145, 146–8, 155–6
Hakluyt the elder, on, 5, 67, 76–7, 113, 121, 165, 344
Hakluyt the younger on, 76–7, 113, 121, 344
historical background, 93–4
humanism and, 139–40
"just war" and
English colonization, in, 128–9, 130–1
Spanish colonization, 105–6, 123–8
land, importance of, 134–8, 142–55
law and
limitations of, 186–8
role of, 5–7, 185
legal justifications generally, 97–9
migration, relationship with, 67–70
mobility, importance of, 70–8

natural law and, 99–100
Netherlands, by, 180–1, 277
Papal authority, rejection of, 107–9
philosophical justifications, 94–7, 104–6
pluralism and, 188–9
possession and, 95–9, 113–20, 184
property rights (*See* Property rights)
proprietary colonies
early colonies, 166–77
Restoration colonies, 178–83
royal colonies, 166, 444
settlement and improvement, 142
slavery, relationship with, 418–19
Smith (John) on, 1–5, 12, 293, 538, 541
sovereignty and, 95–9, 113–20, 155–6, 184
Spain, by
evangelism as purpose of, 100–4
"just war" and, 105–6, 123–8
philosophical justifications, 104–6
structures of, 156–60
success of, 183–4
terra nullius and, 116–20, 143
trade as purpose of, 110–13, 165
unoccupied lands, of, 116–20
Vitoria on, 104, 107–9, 138, 155–6
Winthrop on, 293
Colquhoun, Patrick, 352
Columbus, Christopher, 93–4, 101–4
Comaroff, Jean, 186–7
Comaroff, John, 186–7
Commentaries on American Law (Kent), 376–7
On the Commerce and Police of the River Thames (Colquhoun), 352
Commoditization of labor, 402–3
Commoditization of land, 401–2
Compensatory service, 308
Condon, David, 300–1
Connecticut
colony, slavery in, 477–8, 479, 483
state, slavery in, 506
Conquest
colonization and, 128, 131–2
slavery and, 421–2
Constitution
household model of labor relations, in context of, 396–400
master and servant law, in context of, 396–400
Native Americans under, 397–8
patriarchy, in context of, 396–400
slavery under, 398, 411–13
women under, 397–8
Constitutional Convention of 1787, 396–7
Constitutions of Clarendon, 71–3

Contract, breach or nonperformance of.
  See Breach or nonperformance of
  contract
Convict servitude, 36, 291
Cooper, Anthony Ashley, 141–2, 178–9, 433
Corn, cultivation of, 290
Cornbury, Edward, 489–90
Corporate colonies, 160–6. *See also*
  specific colony
Cotton, John, 149–51, 252
Council for New England, 73–4, 166–7,
  173, 174
Coy, Richard, 309–10
Craft apprenticeship, 240–1
Crane, Richard, 300
Crashaw, William, 152–3, 550–1
Crèvecoeur, Hector St. John, 541–2, 564–6
Criminal law
  breach or nonperformance of
    contract, involving, 358
  convict servitude, 36, 291
  labor generally, 350, 355
  slavery, involving
    generally, 494–6
    New York, in, 499–504
    South Carolina, in, 444
    Virginia, in, 471–2
Critique of Violence (Benjamin), 560
Crown colonies, 166, 444. *See also*
  specific colony
Curtis, Benjamin, 519, 520, 534–7
Curtis, Thomas, 299
Cushing, William, 505–6
Cushman, Robert, 343–4
Customs in Common (Thompson), 335

D'Amico, Jack, 568
Daniel, Peter, 519
Davis, David Brion, 426–7
The Decades of the New Worlde or West India
  (Eden), 106
Dee, John, 94, 95–6, 107, 109, 113, 121
Deeds of indenture, 32
Defoe, Daniel
  generally, 111–12
  The Great Law of Subordination Consider'd,
    335–6, 344–9, 359, 382–3
  Hakluyt the younger compared, 345,
    351, 352
  regulation of labor, on, 350, 351–2, 358,
    359–60
De Iure Belli (Gentili), 24, 116–17, 122–5,
  128, 134–5
De Jure Belli ac Pacis (Grotius), 24, 145
Delaware, slavery in, 498

Delaware Valley. *See* New Jersey;
  Pennsylvania
De La Warre, Lord, 550
Demography of England
  agricultural transition and
    enclosure, 200–2
  engrossment, 202
  generally, 199–202
  disease, effect of, 195–6
  famine, effect of, 195–6
  Fischer on, 215–17
  geographic factors, 197–8
  manorialism and (*See* Manorialism)
  population changes, 195–6
  population redistribution, 197–8
De Re Militari et Bello (Belli), 421
De Republica Anglorum (Smith), 363
Dickeson, Arthur, 303
Digest (Justinian), 116, 118–19, 120, 145–7
Discourse on the Western Discoueries
  (Peckham), 122–5, 135–8
Disease
  England, in, 195–6
  Native Americans, effect on, 23
  Virginia, in, 25
Diversity
  manorialism, in
    arable *versus* pastoral societies, 213–14,
      227–8
    East Anglia, 206
    geographic diversity, 213–14, 227–8
    institutional diversity, 207–9, 210–12,
      214–15
    southwestern England, 207
  migration, in
    generally, 193–5
    interactive nature of, 228
Dodge, William, 309
Dominium. See Possession *(dominium)*
Donne, John, 144–5, 156–7
Dorchester Company, 174
Douglas, Stephen A., 514, 518
Downing, William, 310
Dred Scott and the Problem of Constitutional
  Evil (Graber), 522
Dred Scott v. Sandford
  citizenship and
    dissenting opinions, 532–6
    Taney opinion, 527–32, 538
  constitutional order of slavery, as
    challenge to, 515
  dissenting opinions, 532–7
  factual background, 512–16
  generally, 16, 509–11
  historical background, 516–18

Lincoln and, 16, 521, 522–5, 544, 560,
569
migration, and right of, 516, 537–43
Native Americans and, 528, 529–30,
531–2
possession and, 528
race and
dissenting opinions, 532–6
Taney opinion, 527–32, 538
reaction to, 521–2
sovereignty and, 528
standing of slaves to sue for freedom, 519
territories and
dissenting opinions, 536–7
legality of slavery in, 520, 522
Taney opinion, 527–32
"Dual migration," 51–4
Duke of York, 180–1, 277, 424–5, 427, 490
Duke's Laws
New Jersey, in, 490, 491
New York, in, 499
Pennsylvania, in, 277–8, 286, 288
slavery and, 424–5, 427, 460–1, 489, 498
Duncombe, John, 299
Dunn, Richard S., 34
Duration of indentured servitude, 44, 265,
266
Dutch. *See* Netherlands
Dutch, Hezekiah, 318
Dutch, Samuell, 318

Ea quae (Papal bull), 102
Earl of Desmond, 171
East Anglia
manorialism in, 206
migration from
generally, 203–4
Massachusetts, to, 217–18, 225–6
Eastward Ho! (Chapman), 551
Economic culture
Massachusetts, of, 384–90
Virginia, of, 390–4
The Economy of British America, 1607–1789
(McCusker/Menard) 22
Eden, Richard, 106
Edward I (England), 72
Edward III (England), 233
Eirenarcha (Lambarde), 211–12
Elites
family and, 361
migration, role in, 215–21
Elizabeth, Princess (England), 544–5, 549
Elizabeth I (England), 76–7, 95, 96
Ellesmere, Lord Chancellor, 91
Elliott, J.H., 29

Eltis, David, 11
Emerson, Irene, 512, 513, 514
Emerson, John, 512–13, 514
Emory, Georg, 315
Employment contracts, 371–2
Enclosure, 200–2
Endecott, Zarubbabell, 315
Endicot, John, 308
Engerman, Stanley, 10
England. *See under specific topic*
English Civil War, 203, 213–14
Engrossment, 202
Ernst August (Hanover), 544
"Eutopolis," 140–1
Evangelical Union, 544–5
Evangelism, colonization and
English colonization, in, 109–13
generally, 99
Spanish colonization, in, 100–4
Everitt, Alan, 227
Exception, 343–4

Family. *See also* Household model of labor
relations; Patriarchy
elites and, 361
indentured servitude, relationship with,
290–1
Famine in England, 195–6
Fehrenbacher, Don, 521–2
Ferdinand (Aragon), 102–4
Fifth Amendment, 520
Filmer, Robert, 339, 367–70, 375
Fischer, David Hackett, 53, 188–9, 215–17,
223, 227, 283
Fisher, Frederick, 238
Fishing industry, 315–20
Fisk, William, 315
Fiske, Nathan, 542–3
Fitzmaurice, Andrew, 139, 142
Fleta, 72
Fornication, 301–3
Foulk, Eneas, 327
Frame of the Government (Penn), 280, 283,
284–5
Franklin, Benjamin, 75, 90
Frederick II (Denmark and Norway), 545
Frederick IV (Rheinland-Pfalz), 544
Frederick V (Rheinland-Pfalz), 544, 545
Free denizens, rights of, 82–9
Freedom of labor
colonization and
effect of, 342–4
ideal of, 3–5
Defoe on, 344–9
diversity of labor, relevance of, 356–7

Freedom of labor (*cont.*)
  generally, 335–42
  historical background, 357–8
  indentured servitude, coexistence with,
    7–11
  leisure preference and, 350–1
  Marxist theory and, 9–10
  slavery, coexistence with, 7–11
  statutory discipline and, 352–5
Freedom of movement
  colonization, importance to, 70–8
  indentured servitude, control through,
    78–82, 89–92
  manorialism and, 207–9
  migration, importance to, 70–8, 89–92
Free Society of Traders, 287, 289–90
Frobisher, Martin, 94, 95
Froude, J.A., 193
Fullar, John, 315
Fundamental Constitutions of Carolina,
  142, 178–80, 433–5, 437, 461

Galenson, David, 29
Gedney, Bartholomew, 320
Gell, Richard, 309
*General and Rare Memorials Pertayning to the
  Perfect Art of Navigation* (Dee), 95
Gentili, Alberico
  colonization, on, 23, 138, 143, 144, 145,
    155
  "just war," on, 24, 116–17, 128–9, 130–1,
    134–5, 176
  property rights, on, 117
  slavery, on, 421–3
  vacant lands, on, 120–1
George I (England), 544
George III (England), 544
Georgia
  Georgia Charter of 1732, 74
  migration to, 26–7
Germany, migration from, 27–8, 43, 52–3,
  61, 63, 217
Gilbert, Humphrey, 82, 95, 96, 113, 131, 157
Gill, James, 324
Gillies, John, 555
Glascock, George, 301
Glorious Revolution, 337
Gobetti, Daniela, 367, 368
Godfrey, John, 314
Gorges, Fernando, 173, 176–7
Government and Labor in Early America
  (Morris), 228–9, 231–2
Graber, Mark, 522–3, 532, 537, 563, 569
Grant, Ulysses S., 511
Gray, Robert, 143–4, 145, 148, 154

The Great Law of Subordination Consider'd
  (Defoe), 335–6, 344–9, 359, 382–3
Greene, Jack, 183–4
Grotius, Hugo
  colonization, on, 24, 144, 145, 146–8,
    155–6
  property rights, on, 338
  slavery, on, 423
  sovereignty, on, 145–6

Hakluyt, Richard (elder)
  Christianity and, 109, 110–13
  colonization, on, 5, 67, 76–7, 113, 121,
    165, 344
  conquest, on, 131, 564
  "Eutopolis" and, 140
  generally, 94
  "keeping," 92, 97, 134
  "manning," 11–12, 21, 65–6
  migration, on, 352
  "planting," 70
  possession, on, 5
  sovereignty, on, 5
Hakluyt, Richard (younger)
  Christianity and, 109
  colonization, on, 76–7, 113, 121, 344
  Defoe compared, 345, 351, 352
  generally, 94
  "Poly-Olbion" and, 193, 194, 346
  property rights, on, 95–6, 97, 107–9, 110
Hale, Mathew, 91–2
Hall, Richard, 326
Hallyard, Benjamin, 299
Hammon, Benjamin, 309
Hannell, James, 326
Harris, Leslie, 499
Heath, Robert, 169, 171–2, 176–7, 178
Heathens, 480
Heiford, Samuel, 315
Helm, Joseph, 328
Henry, Prince (England), 544
Henry II (England), 86, 88
Henry the Navigator (Portugal), 101
Henry VII (England), 93
Henry VIII (England), 87, 109
Hewson, Thomas, 319–20
Hicks, Isaac, 327–8
Hinderson, Peter, 318
Hobbes, Thomas, 373
Holland. *See* Netherlands
Hooker, Richard, 365–6
Horn, James, 223–4
Household labor, 54
Household model of labor relations
  colonial America generally, 383–4

Constitution in context of, 396–400
contractualism distinguished, 371–2,
    373–4, 381
Defoe on, 359–60
Filmer on, 367–70
generally, 358–9, 376–8
Hooker on, 365–6
Massachusetts, in, 384–90
master and servant law compared, 82,
    382–3
monarchy and, 362–3
oikos and, 378–81
patriarchy and, 360–2
political authority distinguished, 370,
    373–6
Smith on, 359–60, 366
Virginia, in, 390–4
Hubbard, William, 309–10
Hulsebosch, Daniel, 85
Humanism, colonization and, 139–40
Humphreys, Daniel, 326
Hunt, William, 205
Hurst, Willard, 538–40
Husbandry, apprenticeship in
generally, 79, 80
Statute of Artificers, under, 79, 241–2
Hyde, Robert, 304–6

Imperium. See Sovereignty *(imperium)*
Indentured servitude
absconding and runaways
    Massachusetts, in, 308
    Pennsylvania, in, 323, 356
    Virginia, in, 268, 270–1, 298–301
children and
    age estimates, 593–7
    generally, 42, 80–1
    Massachusetts, in, 255–7, 309–12
    Pennsylvania, in, 290–1
    Virginia, in, 275–6
convict servitude, 36, 291
deeds of indenture, 32
"dual migration," effect of, 51–4
duration of, 44, 265, 266
England, gender distribution in, 58
family, relationship with, 290–1
free labor, coexistence with, 7–11
generally, 29–31
Maryland, in
    numerical estimates of, 35–42
    places of origin, 224
    slavery, effect of, 40–2
    tables, 37–8, 587–8
Massachusetts, in, 56
    absconding and runaways, 308

children, 255–7, 309–12
    limited impact of, 258
    numerical estimates of, 33–4
    outsiders, 254–5, 257
migration, relationship with
    control of mobility through, 78–82
    Massachusetts, in, 56
    Pennsylvania, in, 42–3, 64
    Virginia, in, 60–1
mobility, control of, 78–82, 89–92
New York, in, 322
numerical estimates of
    downward revision, argument for,
        31–5, 64–6
    Eighteenth Century, 579–82
    Maryland, in, 35–42
    Massachusetts, in, 33–4
    Pennsylvania, in, 42–51
    Virginia, in, 35–42
Penn on, 288–9
Pennsylvania, in, 64
    absconding and runaways, 323, 356
    breach or nonperformance of contract,
        323–5
    children, 290–1
    demand for, 289–90
    family, relationship with, 290–1
    freedom dues, 323–5
    historical background, 286
    law, centrality of, 288–9
    migration to, relationship with, 42–3
    numerical estimates of, 42–51
    Penn and, 286–7
    petitions and, 323–5
    rise of, 287–8
    rural areas, 291–2
    slavery, effect of, 47–51
    tables, 37–8, 590, 591–2
    urban areas, 292–3
policing of, 81–2
slavery and
    compared, 271–4, 276
    effect of, 40–2
    effect on, 40–2
Virginia, in
    absconding and runaways, 268, 270–1,
        298–301
    Bacon's Rebellion, effect of, 269–70
    bastardy and, 301–3
    breach or nonperformance of contract
        and, 303–6
    children, 275–6
    duration of, 265, 266
    fornication and, 301–3
    harshness of, 265–9

Indentured servitude (*cont.*)
  migration, relationship with, 60–1
  numerical estimates of, 35–42
  petitions and, 269
  places of origin, 224
  rise of, 263–5
  slavery, effect of, 40–2
  slavery compared, 271–4, 276
  statutes governing, 271–5
  tables, 37–8, 587, 589
  women and
    England, gender distribution in, 58
    generally, 329
Independence
  patriarchy, effect on, 399
  slavery, effect on, 504–6
Indians. *See* Native Americans
On Indigence (Colquhoun), 352
Indigenous peoples. *See* Native Americans
Infidels, 402–3
Inflation, 234
Innes, Stephen, 247–8, 307, 384–5, 389–90, 392
Institutionalization of slavery, 416–17, 419–20
Inter caetera (Papal bull), 102–4, 105, 107, 114
The Invention of Free Labor (Steinfeld), 231–2, 233
Involuntary servitude, 355
Ireland
  Calvin's Case and, 82–9
  migration from, 27–8, 43, 52–3, 61, 63, 217, 283
Iroquois, 27
Isabella (Castile), 102–4
Isin, Engin, 140

Jackson, Andrew, 509–10
Jacob, Richard, 314
James I (England)
  accession of, 72, 82–3, 84, 86–7
  authority of, 366–7
  charters granted by, 158, 160, 170
  letters patent granted by, 164, 166–7
  The Memorable Maske of the Two Honorable Houses or Innes of Court (Chapman), depiction in, 546–9
  proprietorships granted by, 168
  succession and, 544, 545, 546
James II (England), 544. *See also* Duke of York
Jamestown, 260–1
Jamestown Massacre, 24, 262
James VI (Scotland). *See* James I (England)
Jarmin, William, 316–17

Jefferson, Thomas, 516–17
Jeggles, Thomas, 318
Jenkins, David, 300–1
Jenkins, Henry, 300
Jennings, Edmund, 452
John (England), 86–7, 88
John, David, 325
Johnson, Ben, 551
Johnson, Robert, 551
Jones, Diana, 302
Jones, Inigo, 546
Jones, Jacqueline, 29
Jurisdiction. *See* Possession (*dominium*)
Justinian, 116
"Just war"
  colonization and
    English colonization, 128–9, 130–1
    Spanish colonization, 105–6, 123–8
  Gentili on, 116–17, 128–9, 130–1
  Grotius on, 24
  Vitoria on, 123–8

Kansas-Nebraska Act, 518
Kazanjian, David, 533
Keaton, William, 298
Kent, James, 376–7, 378
Key, Elizabeth, 455–6
Key, Thomas, 455–6
Kirke, David, 173
Klein, Bernard, 402
Knott, Richard, 316–17, 319
Knowlton, Thomas, 314
Knowlton, William, 314
Kussmaul, Ann, 227

Labor. *See under specific topic*
Lambarde, William, 211–12
Land. *See also* Property rights
  commoditization of, 401–2
  importance to colonization, 134–8, 142–55
  possession (*See* Possession (*dominium*))
  seizure of, 153–4
  sovereignty (*See* Sovereignty (*imperium*))
  terra nullius, 116–20, 143, 151
  unoccupied lands, colonization of, 116–20
Larkum, Mordecai, 314
Las Casas, Bartolomé de, 104
Latrobe, Henry, 509
Law. *See under specific topic*
Lawes and Libertyes (Massachusetts), 247, 250, 253–5, 286, 424
Lawes Divine, Morall, and Martiall (Virginia), 261
Laws Agreed Upon in England (Pennsylvania), 286–7
Legal culture of work, 263, 350, 391

Legal system in England, 211
Legitimacy of property. *See* Property rights
Leisure preference, 350–1
Lemon, James T., 323
Letters patent, 82, 114, 116, 157, 160, 164, 166–7. *See also specific colony*
Leviathan (Hobbes), 373
Levy, Barry, 226, 283–4
Leyenda Negra Hispanoamericana (Montesinos/Casas), 104
Ligeance, 84
Liggett, Martha, 326
Limits of the British Empire (Dee), 95
Lincoln, Abraham
  Douglas and, 514
  Dred Scott decision and, 16, 521, 522–5, 544, 560, 569
  second inaugural, 563
Line, Moses, 324
Local labor practices
  generally, 296–7
  Massachusetts, in, 307–22
  Pennsylvania, in, 322–9
  Virginia, in, 297–307
Locke, John
  Fundamental Constitutions of Carolina and, 178–9, 433
  master and servant law, on, 371–2
  patriarchy, on
    contractualism distinguished, 371–2, 373–4, 381
    generally, 370
    master and servant law and, 371–2
    natural law and, 370–1
    political authority distinguished, 370, 373–6
    political society and, 338, 339–40
    slavery, on, 372–3, 434–5
London, migration from, 203, 283–4
London and Bristol Company, 164, 165
Long, Joanna, 326
Lothrop, Jason, 538–40
Louisiana Purchase, 516–17
Lower South. *See* Georgia; North Carolina; South Carolina
Luban, David, 562
Lucassen, Jan, 10

MacMillan, Ken, 114
Maine, 74, 173, 176–7
Mandeville, Bernard de, 340, 350–1, 409
Manorialism, 204–15
  diversity in
    arable *versus* pastoral societies, 213–14, 227–8
    East Anglia, 206

geographic diversity, 213–14, 227–8
  institutional diversity, 207–9, 210–12, 214–15
  southwestern England, 207
  historical background, 204–6
  law and, 212–13
  Maryland, in, 259
  miners and, 209–10
  mobility and, 207–9
  Pennsylvania, in, 280–1, 287
Manumission Act of 1717 (New York), 503
Manumission of slaves, 482, 484, 492–3, 497, 502, 504–5
Maria Anna (Spain), 545
Maritime industry, 315–20
Marshall, John, 510
Martire, Pietro, 106
Marxist theory, 9–10
Maryland
  Act Concerning Negroes & other Slaves (1664), 458–9
  Assembly, 461
  indentured servitude in
    numerical estimates of, 35–42
    places of origin, 224
    slavery, effect of, 40–2
    tables, 37–8, 587–8
  manorialism in, 259
  Maryland Charter of 1632, 74, 172–3
  migration to
    places of origin, 215
    socioeconomic makeup of, 218–19, 222–5
    tables, 37–8, 587
  mortality estimates for, 583–5
  seasoning estimates for, 583–5
  slavery in, 476
    indentured servitude, effect on, 40–2
    tables, 37–8
Mason, John, 173
Massachusetts
  apprenticeship in, 255–7
  bound labor in, 312
  breach or nonperformance of contract in, 314–15
  economic culture of, 384–90
  Essex County, local labor practices in, 307–22
  fishing industry in, 315–20
  hired labor in, 312–15
  household model of labor relations in, 384–90
  indentured servitude in, 56
    absconding and runaways, 308
    children, 255–7, 309–12
    limited impact of, 258

Massachusetts (*cont.*)
    numerical estimates of, 33–4
    outsiders, 254–5, 257
    Lawes and Libertyes, 247, 250, 253–5, 286, 424
    local labor practices in, 307–22
    maritime industry in, 315–20
    Massachusetts Bay Charter, 89, 250
    migration to, 23–4
        demographics, 54–5
        families and, 55–6
        indentured servitude, relationship with, 56
        places of origin, 54, 215, 217–18, 225–6
        socioeconomic makeup of, 217–18, 220–2
    Native Americans in, 23–4
    patriarchy in, 384–90
    quantum meruit in, 313
    slavery in, 476–85
        colony, 477–8, 479–83
        state, 505–6
    statutory regulation of labor in
        mobility of labor, 246, 248
        political context, 250–2
        price controls, 247
        sumptuary controls, 248–50
        wage controls, 246–7, 248–50
    wages, actions for, 309–10, 313
    women, subjugation of in patriarchy, 384–90
Massachusetts Bay Company, 174, 175
Master and servant law
    Blackstone on, 349–50
    children and, 56
    Constitution in context of, 396–400
    contractualism and, 371–2
    evolution of, 353–6, 357
    generally, 329–31
    household model compared, 376–8, 382–3
    slavery compared, 82
    Statute of Artificers, under, 245–6
Matrilineage, 455–6, 457–9
Maximilian I (Bavaria), 545
Mayflower Compact, 218
McCusker, John, 22
McKee, Samuel, 294
McLean, John, 510, 519, 520, 532–7
Meager, John, 318
The Memorable Maske of the Two Honorable Houses or Innes of Court (Chapman), 415, 546–9, 560
Menard, Russell, 22, 35
Mercantilism, 229, 239

Mexican-American War, 518
Mid-Atlantic region. *See* New Jersey; New York; Pennsylvania
Migration
    colonization, relationship with, 67–70
    diversity in
        generally, 193–5
        interactive nature of, 228
    Dred Scott decision and right of, 516, 537–43
    "dual migration," 51–4
    Dutch migration, 27–8, 277, 286
    East Anglia, from, 203–4, 217–18, 225–6
    elites, role of, 215–21
    Fischer on, 215–17
    free denizens, rights of, 82–9
    generally, 21–2
    Germany, from, 27–8, 43, 52–3, 61, 63, 217
    Hakluyt the elder on, 352
    indentured servitude, relationship with
        control of mobility through, 78–82
        Massachusetts, in, 56
        Pennsylvania, in, 42–3, 64
        Virginia, in, 60–1
    Ireland, from, 27–8, 43, 52–3, 61, 63, 217, 283
    law, role of, 220
    London, from, 203, 283–4
    manorialism and (*See* Manorialism)
    Maryland, to
        places of origin, 215
        socioeconomic makeup of, 218–19, 222–5
        tables, 37–8, 587
    Massachusetts, to, 23–4
        demographics, 54–5
        families and, 55–6
        indentured servitude, relationship with, 56
        places of origin, 54, 215, 217–18, 225–6
        socioeconomic makeup of, 217–18, 220–2
    mobility, importance of, 70–8, 89–92
    natural subjects, rights of, 82–9
    Netherlands, from, 27–8, 277, 286
    New Jersey, to, 27–9
    New York, to, 27–9
    North Carolina, to, 26–7
    numerical estimates of
        Eighteenth Century, 575–9
        Seventeenth Century, 573–5
    Penn and, 142, 286–7
    Pennsylvania, to
        families and, 62–4

generally, 27–9
indentured servitude, relationship
 with, 42–3, 64
places of origin, 61, 215, 225–6,
 283–4, 286
socioeconomic makeup of,
 219, 225–7
tables, 37–8
places of origin generally, 203
pluralism, role in, 189–90
poverty and, 59
Scotland, from, 27–8, 52–3, 61
slavery and, 516, 537–43
South Carolina, to, 26–7
Southwest England, from, 204, 215
statutory regulation of labor, relationship
 with, 228–30
Sweden, from, 27–8, 277, 286
tables, 576–81
Virginia, to
 demographics, 58
 families and, 58–60
 generally, 24–6
 indentured servitude, relationship
  with, 60–1
 places of origin, 57, 215
 socioeconomic makeup of, 218–19,
  222–5
 tables, 37–8, 587
 Virginia Company and, 24, 80–1, 261,
  264
Wales, from, 27–8, 43, 283
Miners, 209–10
Minors. *See* Children
Missouri Compromise of 1820, 514, 518
Mobility
 colonization, importance to, 70–8
 indentured servitude, control through,
  78–82, 89–92
 manorialism and, 207–9
 migration, importance to, 70–8, 89–92
Modernization of labor law, 335–42
Moffett, Margaret, 324
Monarchy, authority of, 362–3, 366–7
Montesinos, Antonio de, 104
Moon, James, 327–8
More, Thomas, 97, 138–40, 143, 144
Morgan, Edmund, 307, 409
Morgan, Philip, 34
Morris, James, 304–6
Morris, Richard, 228–9, 230, 231–2, 248
Morris, Thomas, 456
Moses, his Judicialls (Cotton), 252
Mullins, Elizabeth, 302
Mythic violence, 560–3

Native Americans
 Constitution, under, 397–8
 disease, effect of, 23
 Dred Scott decision and, 528, 529–30,
  531–2
 generally, 22
 Gentili on, 120–1
 legal status of, 163
 New Jersey, in, 27
 New York, in, 27
 Pennsylvania, in, 27
 possession by, 120–31
 property rights, 151–2
 slavery and, 409, 454–5, 464
 sovereignty of, 120–31
 Spanish war on, philosophical
  justification for, 104–6
 Virginia, in, 24–5
 Vitoria on, 110, 128, 132
Natural law
 colonization and, 99–100
 patriarchy and, 370–1
 slavery and, 422–3
Natural subjects, rights of, 82–9
Ne exeat Regnum, 71
Netherlands
 colonization by, 180–1, 277
 migration from, 27–8, 277, 286
 slavery and, 413–14
New England. *See* Connecticut;
 Massachusetts; New Hampshire; Rhode
 Island
New England Charter, 73–4, 78, 82, 89, 157,
 159, 175
New England Company, 174
Newfoundland, 164
New Hampshire
 colony, slavery in, 477–8, 479
 state, slavery in, 505–6
New Jersey
 migration to, 27–9
 Native Americans in, 27
 slavery in
  colony, 478, 479, 485–6, 490–4, 498
  generally, 476–9
  historical background, 488–90
  state, 505
Newport, Christopher, 154–5
New Scotland, 168–9, 175
New York
 Act Concerning Masters Servants Slaves
  Labourers and Apprentices (1684),
  499
 Act for preventing the Conspiracy of
  Slaves (1708), 501, 502–3

New York (*cont.*)
   An Act for Regulateing of Slaves (1702), 500
   Act for Suppressing of Immorality (1708), 501
   Act to prevent the running away of Negro Slaves out of the Citty and County of Albany to the French at Canada (1705), 500–1
   indentured servitude in, 322
   Manumission Act of 1717, 503
   migration to, 27–9
   Native Americans in, 27
   slave insurrection of 1712, 502
   slavery in
      colony, 498–504
      criminal law involving, 499–504
      demographics, 494
      generally, 476–9
      historical background, 487–90
      inheritance and, 459
   1712 act re, 502–3
   1730 act re, 503–4
   state, 504–5
   statistics, 498–9
Nicholas V (Pope), 101
Nicolls, Richard, 277
Nies, John Jacob, 325
Nonperformance of contract. *See* Breach or nonperformance of contract
Norden, John, 402
Norman, John, 314–15
North Carolina
   Carolina Charter of 1663, 74, 159–60, 178, 432
   Carolina Charter of 1665, 74, 178
   Fundamental Constitutions of Carolina, 142, 433–5, 437, 461
   migration to, 26–7
   separation of South Carolina from, 444
Northern England, migration from, 215, 225–6, 283–4, 286
Northwest Ordinance of 1787, 411, 516, 520
Norton, John, 315
Norton, Mary Beth, 391–2
Nowel, Increase, 252

Oikos, 378–81
Olwell, Robert, 450, 451
Ordinance of Labourers (1349), 78–9, 233–6
Overview of book, 11–17
Oviedo, Gonzalo Fernández de, 106

Papal bulls. *See specific bull*
Park, Daniel, 303

Pateman, Carole, 374–5, 382, 397
Patriarchy
   American Revolution, effect of, 399
   colonial America generally, 383–4
   Constitution in context of, 396–400
   Filmer on, 367–70
   Hooker on, 365–6
   Locke on
      contractualism distinguished, 371–2, 373–4, 381
      generally, 370
      master and servant law and, 371–2
      natural law and, 370–1
      political authority distinguished, 370, 373–6
   Massachusetts, in, 384–90
   model of labor relations, as, 360–2
   possession and, 367
   Revolution, effect of, 399
   Smith on, 359–60, 366
   sovereignty and, 367
   Thompson on, 340
   Virginia, in, 390–4
   women, subjugation of in
      generally, 381–2, 395–6
      Massachusetts, in, 384–90
      Virginia, in, 390–4
Patterson, Orlando, 409, 416, 507
"The peace," 331
Peckham, George, 97, 132, 135–8, 140, 144, 157
Penn, William
   charter of, 181–3, 278
   Frame of the Government, 280, 283, 284–5
   indentured servitude, on, 288–9
   migration and, 142, 286–7
   plans for government, 282
   settlement and, 142, 286–7
   socio-religious society, on, 278–81
Pennsylvania
   Act for the Better Regulation of Negroes in this Province (1726), 496
   Act for the Better Regulation of Servants in this Province and Territories (1700), 494
   Act for the Trial of Negroes (1700), 494–6
   anti-proprietary sentiment in, 284–6
   Charter of 1681, 74, 181–3
   Chester County, local labor practices in, 322–9
   corn cultivation in, 290
   Duke's Laws, 277–8
   early proposals for government, 281–2
   "first purchasers," 279–81, 283–4
   Fundamental Constitutions, 282–3

hired labor in, 326
indentured servitude in, 64
  absconding and runaways, 323, 356
  breach or nonperformance of contract, 323–5
  children, 290–1
  demand for, 289–90
  family, relationship with, 290–1
  freedom dues, 323–5
  historical background, 286
  law, centrality of, 288–9
  migration to, relationship with, 42–3
  numerical estimates of, 42–51
  Penn and, 286–7
  petitions and, 323–5
  rise of, 287–8
  rural areas, 291–2
  slavery, effect of, 47–51
  tables, 37–8, 590, 591–2
  urban areas, 292–3
Laws Agreed Upon in England, 286–7
local labor practices in, 322–9
manorialism in, 280–1, 287
migration to
  families and, 62–4
  generally, 27–9
  indentured servitude, relationship with, 42–3, 64
  places of origin, 61, 215, 225–6, 283–4, 286
  socioeconomic makeup of, 219, 225–7
  tables, 37–8
Native Americans in, 27
pass laws, 323
Quaker factionalism in, 284–6
slavery in
  colony, 478, 479, 486–7, 494–7, 498
  generally, 476–9
  historical background, 488–90
  indentured servitude, effect on, 47–51
  state, 504
  tables, 37–8, 590–2
statutory regulation of labor in
  generally, 276–7, 286, 293
  historical background, 277–8
  socio-religious order and, 278–9
  wages, actions for, 326–8
  wheat cultivation in, 290
Pequots, 24
Pequot War, 425–6
Perambulation of Kent (Lambarde), 211–12
Philadelphia Convention of 1787, 396–7
Phillips, Wendell, 511
Philosophical justifications for colonization, 94–7, 104–6
Pike River Claimants' Union, 538

Pirates, 129–30
Places of origin. *See* Migration
Plan of the English Commerce (Defoe), 351–2
Plantations, 56–7, 60–1, 264, 292, 306–7.
  See also Slavery
Pluralism
  colonization and, 188–9
  migration, role of, 189–90
Plymouth Plantation, 154, 157, 173, 542
Pocock, J.G.A., 399
On the Police of the Metropolis (Colquhoun), 352
Policing
  indentured servitude, of, 81–2
  slavery, of, 419
"Poly-Olbion," 193–5
Poole, William, 308
Poor laws in England, 76
Population of England. *See* Demography of England
Possession *(dominium)*
  Calvin's Case and, 90
  colonization and, 95–9, 113–20, 184
  Dred Scott decision and, 528
  Hakluyt the elder on, 5
  law and, 220, 401
  Native Americans and, 120–31
  patriarchy and, 367
Poverty and migration, 59
Pratt, Edmund. *See The Great Law of Subordination Consider'd* (Defoe)
The Principall Nauigations, Voiages, and Discoveries (Hakluyt the younger), 193, 345
Privy Council, 212
Property rights. *See also* Land
  generally, 149–51
  Gentili on, 117
  Grotius on, 338
  Hakluyt the younger on, 95–6, 97, 107–9, 110
  Native Americans and, 151–2
  possession (*See* Possession *(dominium)*)
  seizure of land, 153–4
  sovereignty (*See* Sovereignty *(imperium)*)
  Vitoria on, 115–16, 118, 123
  Winthrop on, 149
Proprietary colonies. *See also specific colony*
  early colonies, 166–77
  Restoration colonies, 178–83
Prospero. *See The Tempest* (Shakespeare)
Puritanism, 174–5, 217–19, 248–9, 250–1, 293, 307, 511

Quakerism, 62, 225, 226–7, 277, 284–5
Quantum meruit, 313

"Queen Betty's Law." *See* Statute of
Artificers (1563)
Quincy, Josiah, 517

Race
Dred Scott decision, in
dissenting opinions, 532–6
Taney opinion, 527–32, 538
slavery and, 270, 410
Rachael v. Walker, 513
Raleigh, Walter, 96, 109, 113, 131, 157
Rawlens, James, 247
Reeve, Tapping, 376, 378
Regulation of labor. *See* Statutory
regulation of labor
Relectiones (Vitoria), 122–5, 132
Requerimiento (Spain), 104
Revolution, American
patriarchy, effect on, 399
slavery, effect on, 504–6
Revolution, Glorious, 337
Reynolds, Humphrey, 325–6
Rhode Island
colony, slavery in, 477–8, 479, 484–5
state, slavery in, 506
Rice, cultivation of, 26
Rich, Robert, 174
Richard II (England), 72–3
Richards, Edward, 324–5
Riley, Richard, 327
Roanoke, 259–60
Robbarts, Michaell, 300–1
Robertson v. Baldwin, 355
Rogers; United States v., 529–30, 531–2
Romanus pontifex (Papal bull), 101
Royal colonies, 166, 444. *See also specific
colony*
Rumerye, Thomas, 314–15
Runaways. *See* Absconding and runaways
Russell, Samuel, 513
Russell, William, 318

Salinger, Sharon, 44–6, 47, 292
Sanford, Alexander, 513
Sanford, Irene, 512
Sanford, John, 513
"Savages," 135–8, 402–3, 422–3
Schochet, Gordon, 362–3
Schouler, James, 377
Schwarz, Philip, 475
Schweitzer, Mary, 47
Schweitzer, Mary M., 291–2
Scotland
Calvin's Case and, 82–9
migration from, 27–8, 52–3, 61

Scott, Dred, 512–16, 540
Scott, Eliza, 513
Scott, Harriet, 512–16, 540
Scott, Lizzie, 513
Servants. *See* Indentured servitude; Master
and servant law
Settlement. *See* Migration
Shakespeare, William, 403–8, 413, 549–50,
555, 566
Sherman, William T., 511
Sidney, Algernon, 282
Simon, Daphne, 351
Slave courts, 444
Slavery
absconding and runaways, 454, 463, 470
American Revolution, effect of, 504–6
Barbados, in
generally, 428–31
slave trade from, 432, 433, 436, 452,
497
"barbarians" and, 422–3
castration of slaves, 439–40, 474–5,
494–6
Christianity and, 271–4, 420–1, 425,
460–3, 465
colonization, relationship with, 418–19
commoditization of labor and, 402–3
Connecticut, in
colony, 477–8, 479, 483
state, 506
conquest, relationship with, 421–2
Constitution, under, 398, 411–13
contradictory nature of, 409
criminal law involving
generally, 494–6
New York, in, 499–504
South Carolina, in, 444
Virginia, in, 471–2
Delaware, in, 498
Dred Scott decision (*See Dred Scott v.
Sandford*)
Duke's Laws and, 424–5, 427, 460–1, 489,
498
Dutch and, 413–14
freedom, as condition of, 409–10
free labor, coexistence with, 7–11
Gentili on, 421–3
Grotius on, 423
heathens and, 480
indentured servitude and
compared, 271–4, 276
effect on, 40–2
independence, effect of, 504–6
inevitability of demise, arguments
against, 410–13

institutionalization of, 416–17, 419–20
law, role of, 506–8
Locke on, 372–3, 434–5
manumission, 482, 484, 492–3, 497, 502, 504–5
Maryland, in, 476
  indentured servitude, effect on, 40–2
  tables, 37–8
Massachusetts, in, 476–85
  colony, 477–8, 479–83
  state, 505–6
master and servant law compared, 82
matrilineage in, 455–6, 457–9
migration, and right of, 516, 537–43
Native Americans and, 409, 454–5, 464
natural law, under, 422–3
Netherlands and, 413–14
New Hampshire, in
  colony, 477–8, 479
  state, 505–6
New Jersey, in
  colony, 478, 479, 485–6, 490–4, 498
  generally, 476–9
  historical background, 488–90
  state, 505
New York, in
  colony, 498–504
  criminal law involving, 499–504
  demographics, 494
  generally, 476–9
  historical background, 487–8
  inheritance and, 459
  1712 act re, 502–3
  1730 act re, 503–4
  slave insurrection of 1712, 502
  state, 504–5
  statistics, 498–9
numerical estimates, 28
origins of, 413–16
Pennsylvania, in
  colony, 478, 479, 486–7, 494–7, 498
  generally, 476–9
  historical background, 488–90
  indentured servitude, effect on, 47–51
  state, 504
  tables, 37–8, 590–2
policing of, 419
race and, 270, 410
Revolution, effect of, 504–6
Rhode Island, in
  colony, 477–8, 479, 484–5
  state, 506
rise of, 424–8
South Carolina, in, 431–52
  assimilation into legal normalcy, 448–52

criminal law involving, 444
historical background, 431–7
procedural laws re, 448–52
rise of, 26–7
1714 act re, 444
1717 act re, 445
1722 act re, 445–6
1735 act re, 446
statistics, 436–7
taxation of, 444, 445
transportation, 444–5
standing to sue for freedom, 519
taxation of slaves, 444, 445, 483
territories, legality in, 520, 522
tickets of leave, 437, 466
Titus Andronicus (Shakespeare), depiction in, 403–8
Virginia, in, 452–75
  Christianity and, 271–4, 460–2
  criminal law involving, 471–2
  historical background, 452–3
  indentured servitude, effect on, 40–2
  indentured servitude compared, 271–4, 276
  local practices, 454
  race and, 270
  rise of, 25–6, 270–1
  1769 act re, 474–5
  statistics, 471
  statutes governing, 271–5, 453–4
  tables, 37–8
  Vitoria on, 420
  women and, 459
Slave societies, 417
Sloper, Thomas, 303–4
Smith, Abbot Emerson, 7
Smith, Edmund, 299
Smith, John
  ambitions for America, 1–5, 15–16, 398, 399
  colonization, on, 1–5, 12, 293, 538, 541
  freedom of labor, on, 7, 339
Smith, Robert, 324
Smith, Rogers, 14
Smith, Thomas, 259–60, 363–5, 366
Socage, 161
Somers, Margaret, 78–9, 214–15, 223
Sophia (Simmern), 544
South Carolina
  An Act for the Better Ordering and Governing of Negroes (1712), 441–4
  An Act for the Better Ordering and Governing of Negroes and other Slaves in this Province (1740), 446–52

South Carolina (*cont.*)
  An Act for the Better Ordering of Slaves
      (1690/91), 437–8
  An Act for the Better Ordering of Slaves
      (1696), 439–40
  An Act for the Better Ordering of Slaves
      (1698), 440
  An Act for the Better Ordering of Slaves
      (1701), 440
  Carolina Charter of 1663, 74, 159–60,
      178, 432
  Carolina Charter of 1665, 74, 178
  Fundamental Constitutions of Carolina,
      142, 433–5, 437, 461
  migration to, 26–7
  rice cultivation in, 26
  separation from North Carolina, 444
  slave courts, 444
  slavery in, 431–52
    assimilation into legal normalcy,
        448–52
    criminal law involving, 444
    historical background, 431–7
    procedural laws re, 448–52
    rise of, 26–7
  1714 act re, 444
  1717 act re, 445
  1722 act re, 445–6
  1735 act re, 446
  statistics, 436–7
  taxation of, 444, 445
  transportation, 444–5
  Stono Rebellion, 447–8
Southwest England
  manorialism in, 207
  migration from, 283–4
    generally, 204
    Maryland, to, 215
    Virginia, to, 215
Southwest Ordinance of 1790, 516
Sovereignty (*imperium*)
  Calvin's Case and, 90
  colonization and, 95–9, 113–20, 155–6,
      184
  Dred Scott decision and, 528
  Grotius on, 145–6
  Hakluyt the elder on, 5
  law and, 220, 401
  Native Americans, of, 120–31
  patriarchy and, 367
Spain
  colonization
    evangenlism and, 100–4
    "just war" and, 105–6, 123–8

    philosophical justification for, 104–6
  Requerimiento, 104
Spenser, Edmund, 140–1, 402
Spring, Robert, 303–4
Standing of slaves to sue for freedom, 519
Statute of Artificers (1563), 236–45
  apprenticeship under
    children, focus on, 242–3
    crafts, 240–1
    husbandry, 79, 241–2
  colonial America, incorporation in
      generally, 245–6
  conscious economic policy, lack of, 229
  courts, 429–30
  generally, 229, 239, 244–5
  historical background, 236–9
  institutional diversity and, 244
  mercantilism and, 239
  purposes of, 79
  wages under, 237–8, 239–40
Statute of Labourers (1351), 78–9, 233–6
Statutory regulation of labor. *See also specific*
    statute
  generally, 231–3, 293–5
  Massachusetts, in
    mobility of labor, 246, 248
    political context, 250–2
    price controls, 247
    sumptuary controls, 248–50
    wage controls, 246–7, 248–50
  migration, relationship with, 228–30
  Ordinance of Labourers, 233–6
  Pennsylvania, in
    generally, 276–7, 286, 293
    historical background, 277–8
    socio-religious order and, 278–9
  Statute of Labourers, 233–6
  Virginia, in
    easing of restrictions, 261–2
    generally, 258–9
    historical background, 259–62
Steinfeld, Robert, 10, 231–2, 233, 350
Stono Rebellion, 447–8
Strachey, William, 144
Strange, Robert, 325–6
Sunstein, Cass, 521
Surveyor's Dialogue (Norden), 402
Sweden, migration from, 27–8, 277, 286
Symonds, Samuel, 310
Symonds, William, 143

Taliaferro, Lawrence, 512
Taney, Roger
  Dred Scott decision

citizenship and, 527–32, 538
generally, 509–10, 515, 518–22
race and, 527–32, 538
territories and, 527–32
tragedy of, 569
Taxation of slaves, 444, 445, 483
The Law of Baron and Femme, of Parent and Child, Guardian and Ward, Master and Servant (Reeve), 376
The Tempest (Shakespeare), 549–60, 562, 566–9
Terra nullius, 116–20, 143, 151
Territories in *Dred Scott* decision
dissenting opinions, 536–7
legality of slavery in, 520, 522
Taney opinion, 527–32
Thirsk, Joan, 198, 205, 227
Thirteenth Amendment, 355
Thirty Years War, 545
Thomas, Robert, 39
Thomas Aquinas, 104, 456–7
Thompson, E.P., 209, 335–42, 346, 347, 356, 389
Throgmorton, John, 452
Tickets of leave, 437, 466
Title to property. *See* Property rights
Titus Andronicus (Shakespeare), 403–8, 566–9
Tobacco, cultivation of, 25
Tookey, Job, 317
A Tour Throughout the Whole Island (Defoe), 344–5, 346, 352
Trade, colonization and, 110–13, 165
A Treatise of the Newe India (Eden), 106
Treatise on the Law of Master and Servant (Wood), 331
Treaty of Guadalupe-Hidalgo, 518, 532–4
Treaty of Tordesillas, 96, 102
Treaty of Ulm, 545
True Reporte (Peckham), 122–5, 135–8
Tuck, Richard, 144, 147
Two Treatises of Government (Locke), 370

Underdown, David, 213–14
Union of Auhausen, 544–5
Unoccupied lands, colonization of, 116–20
Urselton, Francis, 314
Utopia (More), 97, 138–40

Vespucci, Amerigo, 94, 106
Vickers, Daniel, 307, 310
View of the Present State of Ireland (Spenser), 402
Violence and myth, 560–3

Virginia
An Act Concerning Servants and Slaves (1705), 468–70
An Act Concerning Servants and Slaves (1748), 472–4
An Act for Suppressing Outlying Slaves (1691), 467–8
Act III of 1667, 460–2
Act III of 1682, 467
Act I of 1655/56, 454
Act I of 1669, 463
Act I of 1670, 464
Act I of 1682, 464–5
An Act to Repeale a Former Law Making Indians and Others Ffree (1682), 464–5
Act VIII of 1672, 466
Act VII of 1672, 465–6
Act XII of 1662, 455–9
Act X of 1680, 466–7
Act XVI of 1659/60, 454
Act XVI of 1691, 467–8
Act XXII of 1660/61, 454
Act XXVIII of 1632, 265
Act XXX of 1631/32, 265
Assembly, 263–7, 268–71, 455
disease, effect of, 25
economic culture of, 390–4
First Charter of Virginia (1606), 73, 77–8, 82, 89, 157, 160, 167, 175
household model of labor relations in, 390–4
indentured servitude in
absconding and runaways, 268, 270–1, 298–301
Bacon's Rebellion, effect of, 269–70
bastardy and, 301–3
breach or nonperformance of contract and, 301–3
children, 275–6
duration of, 265, 266
fornication and, 301–3
harshness of, 265–9
migration, relationship with, 60–1
numerical estimates of, 35–42
petitions and, 269
places of origin, 224
rise of, 263–5
slavery, effect of, 40–2
slavery compared, 271–4, 276
statutes governing, 271–5
tables, 37–8, 587, 589
Lawes Divine, Morall, and Martiall, 261
local labor practices in, 297–307

Virginia (*cont.*)
  The Memorable Maske of the Two Honorable
    Houses or Innes of Court (Chapman),
    depiction in, 546–9
  migration to
    demographics, 58
    families and, 58–60
    generally, 24–6
    indentured servitude, relationship
      with, 60–1
    places of origin, 57, 215
    socioeconomic makeup of, 218–19,
      222–5
    tables, 37–8, 587
  mortality estimates for, 583–5
  Native Americans in, 24–5
  patriarchy in, 390–4
  seasoning estimates for, 583–5
  Second Charter of Virginia (1609), 73,
    82, 89, 163
  slavery in, 452–75
    Christianity and, 271–4, 460–2
    criminal law involving, 471–2
    historical background, 452–3
    indentured servitude, effect on, 40–2
    indentured servitude compared,
      271–4, 276
    local practices, 454
    race and, 270
    rise of, 25–6, 270–1
  1769 act re, 474–5
  statistics, 471
  statutes governing, 271–5, 453–4
  tables, 37–8
  statutory regulation of labor in
    easing of restrictions, 261–2
    generally, 258–9
    historical background, 259–62
  The Tempest (Shakespeare), depiction in,
    549–60
  Third Charter of Virginia (1612), 73, 77–8,
    89, 163–4
  tobacco cultivation in, 25
  women, subjugation of in patriarchy, 390–4
  York County, local labor practices in,
    297–307
Virginia Company
  assumption of Crown rule from, 165, 166
  Council for New England compared, 167
  legal culture of work and, 263, 391
  migration and, 80–1, 264
  plantations and, 264
  settlement and, 24, 261
Vitoria, Francisco de
  Christianity and, 108–9

  colonization, on, 104, 107–9, 138, 155–6
  conquest, on, 106
  "just war," on, 105–6, 114–15, 122–5,
    126–8, 130, 135–7
  Native Americans, on, 110, 128, 132
  property rights, on, 115–16, 118, 123
  slavery, on, 420

Wages
  actions for
    Massachusetts, in, 309–10, 313
    Pennsylvania, in, 326–8
  compensatory service, 308
  controls on, 246–7, 248–50
  Statute of Artificers, under, 237–8, 239–40
  Winthrop on, 249–50
Wahunsonacock, 154–5
Waler, Mathew, 315
Wales, migration from, 27–8, 43, 283
Walker, Timothy, 330–1
Walters, John, 326
Walzer, Michael, 307
War. *See also specific war*
  "just war" (*See* "Just war")
Ward, Nathaniel, 252, 424, 426, 479
Waterhouse, Edward, 563–4
Wealth, Power and Resources of the British
  Empire (Colquhoun), 352
Welch, Phillip, 310
Western Emigration Company, 539
Wheat, cultivation of, 290
Wheat, Jane, 308
Williams, Robert, 99
Williams, Roger, 149–51
Wilmot Proviso, 518
Wing, Jeremiah, 303
Winthrop, John
  "City upon a hill," 141, 175
  colonization, on, 293
  freedom of labor, on, 248, 254
  legal system and, 248–9, 252
  property rights, on, 149
  socioeconomic background of, 217–18
  wage controls, on, 249–50
Women
  Constitution, under, 397–8
  indentured servitude and
    England, gender distribution in, 58
    generally, 329
  slavery and, 459
  subjugation of in patriarchy
    generally, 381–2, 395–6
    Massachusetts, in, 384–90
    Virginia, in, 390–4
Wood, Andy, 209

Wood, Gordon, 410
Wood, Horace, 331
Wood, Rachel, 302–3
Woodward, Donald, 238
Woollen Manufacturers Act of 1725, 349, 351
Workforce
  defined, 40

household labor, 54
  tables, 39
Wrightson, Keith, 208–9

Yamasee War, 26, 432, 444, 445
Yates, Frances, 546
Yeardley, George, 452
Youth. *See* Children